GUIDE TO THE BIBLE

GUIDE TO THE BIBLE

AN INTRODUCTION
TO THE STUDY OF HOLY SCRIPTURE

PUBLISHED UNDER THE DIRECTION OF

A. ROBERT (†) AND A. TRICOT

Professors of Sacred Scripture at the Catholic Institute of Paris

SECOND EDITION
Revised and enlarged

Translated from the recast and enlarged Third French Edition by

EDWARD P. ARBEZ, S. S.,

Professor Emeritus of Semitic Languages and Literature

and MARTIN R. P. McGUIRE,

Professor of Greek and Latin at the Catholic University of America.

VOLUME I

DESCLÉE COMPANY

PARIS — TOURNAI — ROME — NEW YORK

1960

NIHIL OBSTAT
PATRICK W. SKEHAN
Censor Deputatus

IMPRIMATUR   January 21, 1960
✠ PATRICK A. O' BOYLE
Archbishop of Washington

The nihil obstat and imprimatur are official declarations that a book of pamphlet is free of doctrinal or moral error. No implication is contained therein that those who have granted the nihil obstat and the imprimatur agree with the contents, opinions or statements expressed.

Library of Congress Catalog Card Number : 52-4101

Printed and bound in Belgium by Desclée & Cie., S. A., Tournai

COLLABORATORS

His Eminence, Cardinal E. TISSE-RANT, President of the Pontifical Biblical Commission, Member of the French Institute at Rome.

† F. M. ABEL, o. p., Ecole Biblique Française, Jerusalem.

† G. BARDY, Dijon.

P. BENOIT, o, p., Ecole Biblique Française, Jerusalem.

J. BONSIRVEN, s. j., Pontifical Biblical Institute, Rome.

L. BOUYER, p. o., Institut Catholique, Paris.

G. BRILLET, p. o., Paris.

H. CAZELLES, s. s., Institut Catholique, Paris.

† J. CHAINE, Facultés Catholiques, Lyon.

† L. DELAPORTE, Institut Catholique, Paris.

† L. DENNEFELD, University of Strasbourg.

E. DRIOTON, Institut Catholique, Paris.

A. GELIN, s. s., Facultés Catholiques, Lyon.

PAUL HENRY, s. j., Institut Catholique, Paris.

† J. HUBY, s. j., Paris.

C. F. JEAN, c. m., Ecole de Louvre, Paris.

† M. J. LAGRANGE, o. p., Ecole Biblique Française, Jerusalem.

A. F. DE LAPPARENT, s. s., Institut Catholique, Paris.

J. LEBRETON, s. j., Institut Catholique, Paris.

P. LEMAIRE, o. f. m., Institut Biblique Franciscain, Jerusalem.

M. LOBIGNAC, s. j., Pontifical Biblical Institute, Jerusalem.

Th. MAERTENS, o. s. b., Abbaye de St. André-lez-Bruges.

E. OSTY, s. s., Institut Catholique, Paris.

† A. ROBERT, s. s., Institut Catholique, Paris.

A. TRICOT, Institut Catholique, Paris.

L. VAGANAY, Facultés Catholiques, Lyon.

R. DE VAUX, o. p., Ecole Biblique Française, Jerusalem.

† L. VENARD, Vienne (Isère).

A. VINCENT, University of Strasbourg.

L. H. VINCENT, o. p., Ecole Biblique Française, Jerusalem.

M. VLOBERG, Paris.

TRANSLATORS' NOTE ON
THE FIRST ENGLISH EDITION

To emphasize the excellent qualities of Robert-Tricot, Initiation
Biblique, *is hardly necessary. The first edition, which appeared
in 1939, was received very favorably everywhere, and the new
revised and enlarged edition of 1948 deserves even greater praise.
We are confident that in English translation the work will receive
an equally cordial welcome throughout the English-speaking world,
and that it will immediately take its place as an indispensable
help and guide not only for seminarians but also for the teachers
of religion in our secondary schools and colleges, for college and
university students, and for the educated Catholic laity in general.*

*We have tried to make our rendering as accurate as possible,
but we hope that at the same time it is sufficiently smooth and
readable. Some additions have been made in bibliography and
in the notes, and the section on translations of the Bible into French
has been replaced by a corresponding section on translations of
the Bible into English. All changes from the original text, however
small, are indicated by the use of square brackets.*

*For quotations from the Book of Genesis, we have used the new
translation,* The Book of Genesis *(Saint Anthony Guild Press,
1948), made by members of the Catholic Biblical Association
of America and sponsored by the Episcopal Committee of the
Confraternity of Christian Doctrine. All other quotations from
the Old Testament are from Challoner's revision of the Douai
version. All quotations from the New Testament are from the
Confraternity of Christian Doctrine Revision (Saint Anthony
Guild Press, 1941).*

*We wish to express here our deep gratitude to the following
colleagues, former students, and friends, who, upon invitation,
were kind enough to make preliminary translations of the greater
portion of the* Initiation Biblique : *Mr. Noel D. Moulton,
Department of Romance Languages, The Catholic University of
America; Sister Thomas Aquinas Carroll, R. S. M., Mt. Mercy*

College, Pittsburgh, Pa.; Sister Jerome, O. S. B., Sister Elizabeth Ann, O. S. B., and Sister Jane Frances, O. S. B., of Mount Saint Scholastica College, Atchison, Kas.; Sister Aileen, O. S. B., Villa Madonna Academy, Covington, Ky.; Sister Alberta Savoy, Marymount College, Salina, Kansas; Sister Mary Sarah Muldowney, Saint Joseph's College, West Hartford, Conn.; and Mr. William Barron, Department of History, The Catholic University of America.   We assume full responsibility for the translation in its final form, and for any errors or stylistic blemishes which it may contain.

TRANSLATORS' NOTE ON
THE NEW ENGLISH EDITION OF VOLUME I

The third French edition of Initiation Biblique was published in 1954.   As indicated in the Editors' " Note on the Third Edition" (see infra), it differs very much from the preceding editions.   In the case of the matter covered in the first half of the work, e.g., the old chapter on Inspiration by L. Pirot has been replaced by a new one by P. Benoit, the old sections on the Prophetical and Sapiential Books by J. Chaine have been replaced by new treatments written by A. Gelin and A. Robert, respectively, and the sections on Languages and Systems of Writing, on the Historical Books of the Old Testament, and the chapter on Literary Genres have all been recast and enlarged.   In fact, the editors have been too modest in their statement of changes!   The first half of Initiation Biblique, in particular, has been subjected to a fundamental recasting and revision, and the new edition is quite superior in every way to the second.

Volume I of the English translation, based on the second French edition of Initiation Biblique of 1948, was published in 1951 and enjoyed a very favorable reception in the English-speaking world.   The publishers stock of Volume I was exhausted by the end of 1957.   The Translators, accordingly, were very pleased to accept the invitation of Desclée and Co. to prepare a second edition of Guide to the Bible, Volume I, based on the third French edition of 1954.

The translation of the new chapters and sections has been done jointly by Father Arbez and Dr. McGuire.   The old translation *has been reexamined throughout. A few awkward expressions have been recast and misprints — surprisingly few, considering the nature of the work — have been removed. Monsignor P. W. Skehan has made some minor revisions in his excellent section on Translations into the Vernacular, which replaced the corresponding section by G. Bardy in the French original. Furthermore, in the chapter on the Transmission of the Text he has added new and important material on the Torgums ascribed te Onkelos and Jonathan.*

Special attention is called to the important additions made by Father Arbez to the new English edition. These include appendices to the chapter on Inspiration which cover inspiration in Protestantism and Islam, detailed and very helpful analyses of the contents of the individual books of the Pentateuch, and an extended treatment of the Dead Sea Scrolls. The Translators have added much new bibliography in the footnotes and at the ends of chapters. In this connection it is a pleasure to note that so many pertinent articles could be cited — and deserved to be cited for their scholarly value — from the Catholic Biblical Quarterly *and* Theological Studies. *Since the new edition of Volume I has so much new material and a different pagination from the first edition,* Indices *have been specially prepared for it by Dr. McGuire. The rich content of the work will thus be much more accessible for reference and consultation.*

The Translators again wish to thank the Reverend Professor A. Tricot who, following the death of his distinguished colleague, Father A. Robert, has become the sole Editor and Director of Initiation Biblique, *for granting permission to make additions to the text and bibliography. These additions and bibliography have made the translation all the more useful for the English-speaking world. A grateful word of acknowledgement is due to Miss Mary Anderson for the care and accuracy with which she deciphered the handwritten translations and bibliographical notes of the Translators and prepared a good typed manuscript. Finally, they wish again to express their warm appreciation to Desclée and Co., and in particular, to M. Gustave Pairoux of the New York Branch, for their willingness to make changes even in page proof and for the high standard of the typesetting.*

PREFATORY LETTER

of His Eminence CARDINAL A. LIÉNART,
BISHOP OF LILLE,

to the Reverend A. ROBERT and A. TRICOT,
Professors at the Catholic Institute of Paris.

Reverend and dear Fathers :

I congratulate you sincerely for having undertaken the publication of a Guide to the Bible.

The word of God contained in Holy Scripture ought not remain a dead letter. It was given to be read, meditated upon, and understood by priests and by the faithful. Yet, in order that the contemporary intellect find less obscurity and more light in Scripture, it must be prepared to make contact with a literature which is so different from our own. If we recall that the oldest parts of the Bible go back to a period more than thirty centuries ago and that the most recent already have nearly nineteen hundred years behind them, the difficulties involved are self-evident. Furthermore, the minute and continuous criticism to which the sacred texts have been subjected has contributed to the creation of such a state of confusion that a good guide has become necessary.

This Guide *which you are now presenting to the public deserves full confidence, for it is the common work of a pleiad of specialists equally distinguished for the soundness of their doctrine and for the breadth of their learning. True Biblical science has not succumbed to the assault which has been made upon it, and the enormous work accomplished by exegetes of all schools does not show on its final balance sheet the demolition of the principles of the Church respecting Sacred Scripture. These principles not only continue in force, but, through controversy, they have even acquired a greater and more delicate precision. Working patiently, the Catholic Church has been able to separate truth from error. You have been right in thinking that the time had come for putting at the disposal of all the results acquired by this scholarly labor.*

The reader will be grateful to you for offering him such a methodical and such a complete exposition of all that it is necessary for him to know in order to obtain a full understanding of the Bible. In place of being a sealed book, it will become for him an open book, and he will take delight, moreover, in tracing through its pages the magnificent history of Divine Revelation and of our Redemption.

I send, then, with my congratulations, my very best wishes for the success of your work. I am,

Very faithfully yours in Christ,

✝ ACHILLE CARDINAL LIÉNART.

Lille, July 18, 1938.

FOREWORD

The Bible holds a unique place in the moral and religious life of mankind. It enjoys this privilege primarily because, in the eyes of believers, it is the word of God Himself. Under the compelling influence of a mystery which is so deep and so fruitful in consequences of all kinds, innumerable souls, longing for light and comfort, come to the Holy Book as to an ever flowing fountain of spiritual life. In our time, as in past centuries, there are many who study and meditate upon the Scriptures in order to understand or to defend better the truths proposed to their faith. Moreover, through her heads and most authoritative representatives, the Church never ceases to remind her children that, whatever their condition in life or their degree of culture, they must endeavor to know the history of Revelation and Revelation itself.

On the other hand, even among those who refuse to accept any dogma and do not believe in the divine origin of the Bible, there are many who read or study this book because of the problems which are inherent in its subject matter and with respect to which every thinking man must sooner or later take a stand.

In Biblical studies, furthermore, history in the strict sense necessarily occupies an important place, a fact which is welcomed by our contemporaries, especially since the history of the ancient Orient is involved, and a knowledge of this is indispensable for a precise understanding of the part which the early civilizations of the Near East, the Nile Valley, and the eastern Mediterranean basin have played in the development of mankind.

Finally, on the aesthetic side, the Bible has a strong attraction for many because of the nobility, the number, and the splendor of its images, the magnificence of its descriptions, the variety of its literary genres, the depth of its lyrical power, and so many other qualities which have been the source or the occasion of the happiest inspirations for artists of all ages.

For all these reasons, the Bible continues to have a current appeal. This unquestionable fact, however, would seem to be somewhat forgotten or ignored. Doubtless we have never ceased to be nourished by the Bible, at least indirectly; but too many Catholics appear, if not to be unaware of, yet to neglect the treasure from which so much wealth can so easily be obtained. The faithful ought to remember that the Bible belongs to all, and that the Church herself recommends it to them to be read and studied.

But in order really to be profitable spiritually as well as intellectually, the reading, and *a fortiori*, the study of the Bible demand serious and methodical preparation. By its origin, its nature, its contents, and its purpose, the Bible is a book apart. That is why the Church, knowing the handicaps and dangers which may arise in this field from studies made without proper knowledge and judgment, warns the faithful of the difficulties which they may encounter. In his Encyclical, *Providentissimus Deus*, Pope Leo XIII has said :

" In addition to the usual reasons which make ancient writings more or less difficult to understand, there are some which are peculiar to the Bible. For the language of the Bible is employed to express, under the inspiration of the Holy Ghost, many things which are beyond the power and scope of the reason of man — that is to say, divine mysteries and all that is related to them. There is sometimes in such passages a fullness and a hidden depth of meaning which the letter hardly expresses and which the laws of interpretation hardly warrant. Moreover, the literal sense itself frequently admits other senses, adapted to illustrate dogma or to confirm morality. Wherefore it must be recognized that the sacred writings are wrapt in a certain religious obscurity, and that no one can enter into their interior without a guide ".

To these theological and spiritual considerations, we may add a purely scientific one. In order to understand the Bible, and especially in order to interpret it accurately, one must have an adequate knowledge of ancient Oriental history, of the institutions, customs, and traditions, religious ideas and practices, and also of the literary productions of the various peoples with whom Israel was in immediate contact, and who in one way or another and in different degrees exercised an influence upon her. The "Biblical environment", taken in its broadest meaning, is a natural setting, and a knowledge of this setting is indispensable for the understanding of the Sacred Books. In their course from the mountains to the sea the waters of a river reflect many landscapes without undergoing any change themselves; in the same way, many different forms of civilization, beliefs, and political and social conditions are reflected in the Bible without its being changed in any of its essential elements. But in order to distinguish what is transitory from what is eternal, in order to bring out the transcendental nature of revealed religion, and in order to follow the history of this religion as it progressed from the beginnings until Gospel times, one must know how to make use of all the resources offered by modern science, and yet must always keep in mind the guiding principles of the Church. For the Church received the Old Testament from the Synagogue, presided over the formation of the New Testament corpus, and is alone the *authorized* interpreter of Scripture.

On the occasion of the fiftieth anniversary of the publication of the Encyclical, *Providentissimus Deus*, Pope Pius XII, in his own Encyclical, *Divino afflante spiritu*, of September 30, 1943 [1], again dealt with the subject treated by Pope Leo XIII, namely, Biblical studies. After recalling the work accomplished by his predecessors in promoting these studies and in assuring their progress, the Pope indicates and defines in the clearest fashion the objectives, rules, and methods of Catholic exegesis of Scripture. This exegesis ought to be at once traditional and modern : traditional in its concern for safeguarding and emphasizing the truths set forth in the Bible, the book of Divine Revelation, and modern through its care in employing for the study and understanding of the sacred text all the help furnished

---

[1] For the text of the Encyclical, see *Acta Apostolicae Sedis*, XXXV (1943), 297-326. The English translation provided by the Vatican was published by the National Catholic Welfare Conference, Washington, D. C., 1943. It is also available in *Rome and Study of Scripture. A Collection of Papal Enactments on the Study of Holy Scripture together with Decisions of the Biblical Commission.* (5th ed., revised and enlarged, St. Meinrad, Indiana, 1953; a Grail Publication), 79-107. See also L. Cerfaux, *Encyclique sur les Études Bibliques* (Brussels, 1945) On the various official documents of the *Magisterium* of the Church and the directives issued concerning the subject of exegesis, see G. Courtade, " Lettres Encycliques ", *DBV, Suppl.* V (1952), 375-387.

by History and Criticism in this field.   No commentary can serve as a substitute for reading and meditation upon the Encyclical, *Divino afflante spiritu*.   Everyone who desires to undertake or make further progress in the study of the Bible must first steep himself in the teaching contained in its pages.

It is evident, therefore, that the study of the Bible offers, besides its great attraction, some very real difficulties, and these difficulties are more or less consciously felt by those persons, especially numerous in our age, who experience the need of renewing their contacts with the sources of Catholic doctrine and spiritual life in a direct and personal manner. Unfortunately, it sometimes happens that such people wander aimlessly or grope about, either for lack of a guide, or also because they are troubled by the assertions of certain authors imbued with rationalistic prejudices.

Therefore, it seemed to us that there was now need for a book which should be a *Guide to the Bible*.   This work is not a text-book, since its treatment is neither didactic nor academic; neither is it an encyclopedia, since it is impossible to cover all matters pertaining to the Bible in one volume.   We have intended simply to describe the chief problems in a brief synthesis, to outline the present state of the science of exegesis, to sketch the results acquired, and to emphasize the direction and to indicate the orientation of researches in progress.   In a word, we wished to instruct, or rather to stimulate reflection and to awaken in the reader the desire to go to the texts and draw from the fountain itself the doctrine of life.   We have hoped, above all, that this work will be regarded as a collective effort inspired by the love of truth and the desire to help those who seek.

* * *

The book which is offered to the public is the fruit of collaboration.   In such a vast and complex subject matter, it would have been difficult for a single author to speak on all subjects with authority.   We turned, therefore, to scholars qualified by their knowledge and their publications, and asked each specialist to give us an objective and documented exposition which should contain, together with the received teaching of the Catholic Church, the results of his own personnal research. Some, perhaps, will be surprised to find so many pages without notes. We ask such readers to put aside their misgivings and to have full confidence in the scholarship of our collaborators. Scholarly documentation underlies each contribution.

We thank all those who were kind enough to join in this collective effort in spite of all kinds of restrictions which were imposed on them. Each and all have made valuable contributions, and we are grateful to them for having answered our appeal so wholeheartedly.

A work written in collaboration is necessarily less homogeneous in its different parts than a book which comes from a single pen. Hence the reader will notice, here and there, slight differences of opinion, especially in matters of chronology, on which it is not always possible to get absolute agreement. On the other hand, everyone will agree that a work of this kind is all the richer precisely because of the diversity of opinions and viewpoints which it contains.

A. ROBERT and A. TRICOT

NOTE ON THE THIRD EDITION

The present edition of the *Guide to the Bible* has not only been revised and enlarged, but has in large part been *recast*. It will be appropriate therefore to indicate the more significant changes which have been made.

The following chapters (or sections of chapters) are new : Ch. I, Inspiration (P. Benoit); Ch. V, The Books : *Prophetic Books* (A. Gelin), *Sapiential* Books (A. Robert); Ch. XXII, The Apostolic Age (A. Tricot); Ch. XXX, The Bible and Theology (Paul Henry); Ch. XXXI, the Pastoral Function of the Bible (Th. Maertens); Ch. XXXII, the Bible and the Liturgy (L. Bouyer).

The treatments of the following subjects have been recast to a greater or less degree : *Languages* (Hebrew, by H. Cazelles), in Ch. III; *Systems of Writing* (by Cardinal Tisserant), in Ch. IV; *The Books of the Bible* (*The Law* and the *Historical Books of the Old Testament*, by A. Robert), in Ch. V; *The Literary Genres* (by A. Robert and A. Tricot), in Ch. VI; the *Political Geography of Palestine* (by L. H. Vincent), in Ch. XII; *Biblical Archaeology*, (by P. Lemaire), in Ch. XIV; *The Religions of Western Asia* (by H. Cazelles and A. Vincent), in Ch. XXIV; *Islam* (by A. Vincent), in Ch. XXIX.

Other changes of less significance — corrections, retouches, and minor additions — have been made in the body of the work.

The epoch-making discoveries made since 1947 in the Desert of Juda in Palestine have been put to good use in the treatment of the *Apocrypha of the Old Testament* (Ch. II), of *Writing* (Ch. IV), of the *Transmission of the Text* (Ch. VII), and of the *Essenes*.

In the chapter devoted to *Literary Genres* (Ch. VI), much more space has been given to the exposition of the principles and the applications of the theory of "literary forms" (*Formgeschichliche Methode* or *Form Criticism*).

R. and T.

TABLE OF ABBREVIATIONS

1. Books of the Old and New Testament.

Abd.	(Abdias)	Jud.	(Judith)
Acts	(Acts)	3, 4 Kgs.	(3, 4 Kings; 1, 2 Kings in the Hebrew)
Ag.	(Aggeus)		
Am.	(Amos)	Lam.	(Lamentations)
Apoc.	(Apocalypse)	Lev.	(Leviticus)
Bar.	(Baruch)	Lk.	(Luke)
C. C.	(Canticle of Canticles)	1, 2 Mach.	(1, 2 Machabees)
1, 2 Chr.	(1, 2 Chronicles or 1, 2 Paralipomenon)	Mal.	(Malachias)
		Mk.	(Mark)
Col.	(Colossians)	Mt.	(Matthew)
1, 2 Cor.	(1, 2 Corinthians)	Mich.	(Micheas)
Dan.	(Daniel)	Nah.	(Nahum)
Deut.	(Deuteronomy)	Neh.	(Nehemias, or 2 Esdras in the Vulgate)
Eccles.	(Ecclesiastes)		
Ecclus.	(Ecclesiasticus)	Num.	(Numbers)
Eph.	(Ephesians)	Os.	(Osee)
1, 2 Esd.	(1, 2 Esdras)	1, 2 Par.	(1, 2 Paralipomenon; 1, 2 Chronicles in the Hebrew)
Est.	(Esther)		
Ex.	(Exodus)		
Ez.	(Ezechiel)	1, 2 Pet.	(1, 2 Peter)
Gal.	(Galatians)	Philem.	(Philemon)
Gen.	(Genesis)	Phil.	(Philippians)
Hab.	(Habacuc)	Prov.	(Proverbs)
Heb.	(Hebrews)	Ps.	(Psalms)
Isa.	(Isaias)	Rom.	(Romans)
Jas.	(James)	Ruth	(Ruth)
Jer.	(Jeremias)	1, 2 Sam.	(1, 2 Samuel; 1, 2 Kings in the Vulgate)
Job	(Job)		
Joel	(Joel)	Soph.	(Sophonias)
Jn.	(John)	1,2 Thess.	(1, 2 Thessalonians)
1,2,3 Jn.	(1, 2, 3 John)	1, 2 Tim.	(1, 2 Timothy)
Jon.	(Jonas)	Tit.	(Titus)
Jos.	(Josue)	Tob.	(Tobias)
Jdgs.	(Judges)	Wis.	(Wisdom)
Jude	(Jude)	Zach.	(Zacharias)

2. Manuscripts.

At the beginning of all modern editions of the original texts, there are lists or tables of the manuscripts accompanied by an indication of the abbreviations or *sigla* employed to designate the Greek uncial and minuscule manuscripts and the manuscripts of the ancient versions. It will suffice here to observe that there are several systems of designation in use, associated respectively with the names of Tischendorf, Gregory, von Dobschütz, and von Soden.

3. Dictionaries, Periodicals, etc.

AAS = *Acta Apostolicæ sedis*, (Vatican City)

BA = *The Biblical Archeologist*, New Haven.

BASOR = *Bulletin of the American Schools of Oriental Research*, New Haven.

BIBL = *Biblica*, Rome.

CBQ = *Catholic Biblical Quarterly*, Washington.

DACL = *Dictionnaire d'Archéologie chrétienne et de liturgie* (Cabrol-Leclercq).

DAFC = *Dictionnaire apologétique de la Foi catholique* (A. d'Alès).

DBV = *Dictionnaire de la Bible* (Vigouroux) and *Supplément* (Pirot-Robert-Cazelles).

DTC = *Dictionnaire de théologie catholique* (Vacant-Mangenot-Amann).

DZ = *Enchiridion Symbolorum et Definitionum* (Denzinger-Bannwart).

EB = *Encyclopaedia Biblica* (Cheyne-Black).

Ench. B = *Enchiridion Biblicum*, Rome.

EThL = *Ephemerides Theologicae Lovanienses.*

HDB = *Dictionary of the Bible* (Hastings).

JTS = *Journal of Theological Studies*

LTK = *Lexikon für Theologie und Kirche* (Buchberger).

NRTh = *Nouvelle Revue Théologique.*

NTA = *New Testament Abstracts.*

PG = *Patrologia Graeca* (Migne)

PL = *Patrologia Latina* (Migne).

RB = *Revue Biblique.*

RGG = *Die Religion in Geschichte und Gegenwart* (Gunkel-Zscharnack).

RSR = *Recherches de Science Religieuse.*

RSPT = *Revue des Sciences Phil. et Théol.* (Paris).

ThS = *Theological Studies.*

ThW = *Theologisches Wörterbuch zum Neuen Testament* (Kittel).

TABLE OF CONTENTS

TABLE OF CONTENTS

VOLUME I

GUIDE TO THE BIBLE

INTRODUCTORY OBSERVATIONS

by A. ROBERT.

INTRODUCTORY OBSERVATIONS

I. — The Names for the Bible.

The collection of books whose divine character is proclaimed by both Jews and Christians has been called by different names. The following appellations are found most frequently : the Scriptures, or Holy Scripture, or simply Scripture; the Sacred Books; the Bible; Testament. These last two names require explanation.

The word Bible is a transliteration of the Greek τὰ βιβλία, " the books ". In Late Latin the Greek word was taken to be in the feminine singular : *Biblia, Bibliæ*, the *Bible*. In speaking thus, as in using the expression *Scripture*, Christians affirm implicitly that they are referring to *the Book* par excellence, the Book which, because of its origin, contents, and purpose takes precedence over all others. They also affirm that, for the same reason, this book, in spite of the different elements of which it is composed, realizes the unity of its parts in a higher synthesis.

The word Testament is an approximate translation of the Greek διαθήκη and refers to a fundamental idea of Revelation, that of covenant. In the deep consciousness which it had of its predestination, the people of Israel never ceased to affirm that several times in its history, and especially on Mount Sinai, God pledged Himself to procure the welfare of the chosen nation, if it would agree, however, to certain religious and moral conditions solemnly proclaimed. We have here a covenant (in Hebrew, *berith;* in Greek, properly συνθήκη, as Aquila, Symmachus, and Theodotion understood). But since God makes known His will to men, and promises them temporal and spiritual benefits " as an inheritance ", the notion of a covenant becomes that of an inheritance, usually translated by διαθήκη. This word acquires an even more precise meaning when, alluding to the sacrifice on Calvary, the Epistle to the

Hebrews (9 : 15-22) teaches that the death of the testator secures to the children of God their right to the eternal inheritance.

Finally, the Biblical writings are called a Testament because they relate the origin, the development, and the fulfillment of God's promises, and state authoritatively the conditions which must be met in order to share in them. We recognize two Testaments, the Old and the New, according to the Divine Economy before and after our Lord and according to the books which deal with it.

2. — The Number, Designation, and Classification of the Biblical Writings.

I.   *The Old Testament.*

The Jews accept only 39 books, and, originally, they even reduced this number in an artificial manner to 24 or 22, on the basis of the number of letters in the Hebrew alphabet. Protestants follow the Jewish tradition of 39 books. Catholics, in accordance with the computation of the Council of Trent (Sess. IV, *Decret. de canon. Script.*), recognize 45 books. The list follows [1] : Gen., Ex., Lev., Num., Deut. (these five books as a whole are called the Pentateuch), Jos., Jdgs., Ruth, 1-4 Kgs. (1 and 2 Kings are also called 1 and 2 Samuel), 1 and 2 Paralipomenon (or Chronicles), 1 and 2 Esd. (or Esdras and Nehemias), *Tob.*, *Jud.*, Est., Job, Ps., Eccles., C. C., *Wis.*, *Ecclus.*, Isa., Jer. (the Decree of the Council of Trent considers Lamentations as belonging to the Book of Jeremias), *Bar.*, Ez., Dan., the 12 Minor Prophets (Os., Joel, Am., Abd., Jon., Mich., Nah., Hab., Soph., Ag., Zach., Mal.), 1 and 2 *Mach.*

These books were divided by the Jews into three groups : 1° the Torah, i. e., the Law, which consists of the Pentateuch; 2° the Prophets, both the Former (Jos., Juds., Sam., Kings), and the Latter (three Major Prophets — Isa., Jer., Ez., and the Twelve — our Minor Prophets); 3° " the Writings " [2].

---

[1] The books questioned by Jews and Protestants are in italics. For further details, see Chapter II, THE CANON OF THE SCRIPTURES, pp. 70-71.

Translator's note. — [2 Called also *Hagiographa* (the Greek term), i. e. " Sacred Writings ". The order of the books of the Latter Prophets and in the Writings shows notable variations in the various Jewish authorities. E. P. A.]

Since the thirteenth century, Catholics have been accustomed to make this division : 1º the Historical Books (the Pentateuch and the books mentioned above which follow the Pentateuch as far as Est. inclusive, and then Mach.); 2º the Didactic Books (from Job to Ecclus.); 3º the Prophets (four Major Prophets, including Dan., and twelve Minor Prophets).

2. *The New Testament.*

Protestants are practically in agreement with Catholics in counting 27 books in the New Testament. Like those of the Old Testament, they are arranged in three groups : 1º the Historical Books, which contain the Four Gospels (Mt., Mk., Lk., Jn.) and Acts; 2º the Didactic Books, namely, the fourteen Epistles of Saint Paul (Rom., 1 and 2 Cor., Gal., Eph., Phil., Col., 1 and 2 Thess., 1 and 2 Tim., Tit., Philem., Heb.), and the seven " Catholic " Epistles (1 and 2 Pet., 1, 2, and 3 Jn., Jas., Jude); 3º one prophetic book, Apoc.

3. — The Division of the Books into Chapters and Verses.

The division by chapters of approximately equal length dates only from the beginning of the thirteenth century. It is due to Stephen Langton († 1228), who was a professor at the University of Paris, and subsequently became Archbishop of Canterbury and a cardinal. It was introduced into the so-called Parisian Bible, about 1226, and then was employed in all later editions of the Bible, including the printed Hebrew Bible [1]. The modern chapter division does not differ appreciably from that of Stephen Langton.

The division by verses is more recent. It received its final form from the celebrated printer Robert Estienne (Stephanus) in 1551 [2]. In spite of its inconsistencies, it has been consecrated by usage, and is employed in all editions of the Bible [3].

Translator's note. — [1 So already in the *Biblia Rabbinica* of Felix Pratensis, Venice, 1516-1517].

Translator's note. — [2 New Testament, 1551; Old and New Testaments, 1555].

Translator's note. — [3 Including the printed Hebrew text, Antwerp, 1571. E. P. A.].

GUIDE TO THE BIBLE

BIBLIOGRAPHY.

J. Massie, " Testament ", *HDB*, Vol. IV. — H. Lesêtre, " Nouveau Testament ", *DBV*, Vol. IV. — L. G. da Fonseca, " Διαθήκη, fœdus an Testamentum ", *Biblica* (1927), 31 ff., 161 ff., 290 ff., 418 ff., *ibid.* (1928), 26 ff., 143 ff. — H. B. Swete, *Introduction to the Old Testament in Greek*, Cambridge, 1914, pp. 342-358. — E. Mangenot, " Chapitres de la Bible ", *DBV*, Vol. II; *id.*, " Versets de la Bible ", *DBV*, Vol. V. — E. Jacquier, *Le texte du Nouveau Testament*, Paris, 1913. — J. Balestri, *Biblicae Introductionis Generalis Elementa*, Rome, 1937, pp. 63-67, 75 ff., 118 ff. — J. Behm, " Διαθήκη ", in Kittel, *Th. W.*, II (1935), p. 127-130, and pp. 133-135.

PART I

GOD'S BOOK

CHAPTER I

INSPIRATION

by P. Benoit

I. — THE EXISTENCE OF INSPIRED BOOKS.

II. — THE NATURE OF THE CHARISM OF INSPIRATION.

III. — THE TOTAL AND ANALOGICAL EXTENSION OF INSPIRATION.

IV. — GOD THE AUTHOR OF SCRIPTURE. THE CRITERION OF INSPIRATION.

V. — INERRANCY.

[Appendix I. Biblical Inspiration in Protestantism.

Appendix II. Inspiration in the Qoran and in the Bible.

by E. P. Arbez].

CHAPTER I

INSPIRATION

I. — THE EXISTENCE OF INSPIRED BOOKS

From the beginning, the Church has held that the " Sacred Books " which make up her " Holy Writ " are writings containing the " Word of God ", and that the collection of these writings constitutes by that very fact a " Canon " with normative authority for her faith and life. This legacy came to her from the Synagogue, but she enlarged it at an early date with her own writings inherited from the Apostolic Age. The progressive formation of that Canon, of the Old and then the New Testament, will be set forth in a subsequent chapter. It will suffice here to recall the evolution of the formulas which express and justify that faith in the divine origin of the Sacred Scripture.

The Jews found therein God's word written at his command. God had told Moses to write down his words (Ex. **17** : 14; **34** : 27), so that the whole " Law, " i.e., in fact the whole Pentateuch, was received as a book which God had caused to be written through Moses (cf. Deut. **31** : 24). So also in the case of the " Prophets : " they had spoken at God's command, under the impulse of the Spirit, to describe the " visions " received from him, to utter his " oracles " and even to write them in order that their memory might be preserved (Isa. **30** : 8; Jer. **30** : 2; **36** : 2; Hab. **2** : 2). Although the " Hagiographers " did not express so clearly their divine commission, yet the conviction had become firmly established that they, too, had written in the name of God to explain to the Chosen People the divine meaning of its history, and to give it practical rules for its worship and life. All this ensemble made up the " Holy Books " (1 Mach. **12** : 9; 2 Mach. **8** : 23), the " divine oracles " (Philo), in a word, " Scripture, " which the Rabbis quoted as decisive authority by means of such expressions as : " He has said, " " as it has been said, " " as it is written. " [1]

We find the same expressions used by Jesus and the Apostles and with the same import : " the Scripture " (Mk. **12** : 10;

---

[1] Cf. J. B. FREY, " La Révélation d'après les conceptions juives au temps de Jésus-Christ ", *RB* (1916), pp. 472-510; especially pp. 480-495.

Lk. **4** : 2I; Jn. **2** : 22; **7** : 38; Acts **8** : 32; Rom. **4** : 3, etc.);
" the Scriptures " (Mt. **22** : 29; Mk. **12** : 24; Lk. **24** : 27; Jn. **5** : 39;
Acts **17** : 11; I Cor. **15** : 3, etc.). — That is, the Law of Moses,
the Prophets, and the Psalms (Lk. **24** : 24) " must be fulfilled "
(Mt. **26** : 54; Mk. **15** : 28; Lk. **24** : 44; Jn. **13** : 18; Acts **1** : 16;
Jas. **2** : 23, etc.) and " cannot be broken " (Jn. **10** : 35;
cf. Mt. **5** : 17 ff; Lk. **16** : 17; Jas. **4** : 5), for they contain " the
oracles of God " (Rom. **3** : 2; cf. Heb. **5** : 12), the " word of
God " (Jn. **10** : 35; cf. Mt. **15** : 6) which cannot fail (Rom. **9** : 6).
It is God who spoke to " Moses " (Mk. **12** : 26; Jn. **9** : 29;
Acts **1** : 44; Rom. **9** : 15). It is God who promised or announced
beforehand by the mouth of the prophets (Lk. **1** : 70; Acts **3** : 18;
Rom. **1** : 2; Heb. **1** : 1). It is the Holy Spirit who declared
by the mouth of David (cf. Acts **1** : 16; **4** : 25; Mt. **22** : 43)
or of Isaias (Acts **28** : 25). So the absolute authority of Scripture
continues to be invoked with the traditional formulas of
Judaism : " It is written " (Mt. **4** : 4; Mk. **11** : 17; Lk. **7** : 27;
Jn. **2** : 17; Acts **2** : 35; Rom. **1** : 17; Pet. **1** : 16, etc.); " God
says " (2 Cor. **6** : 16); " Scripture says " (Rom. **9** : 17); or
simply : " He (it) says " (2 Cor. **6** : 2, etc.).

The conviction of the divine origin of Scripture was so
firmly established that at first no one thought of proving or
defining it. Yet two texts of the New Testament sum it up very
well. According to 2 Pet. **1** : 21 the prophets spoke, not of their
own initiative, but " as they were moved by the Holy Spirit. "
And this impulse of the Holy Spirit is expressed still more
clearly in 2 Tim. **3** : 15-17, which, in speaking of the Sacred
Writings, declares that " all Scripture is inspired by God. "
The term θεόπνευστος used here for the divine breath has an
almost technical meaning, from which has come our word
" inspiration. " It is not found elsewhere in the Bible, but
we have its equivalents in the Jewish authors who wrote in
Greek. *Josephus* (*Against Apion* 1. 7. 37) speaks of the ἐπίπνοια
which enabled the prophets to know old and hidden things.
Philo uses frequently similar terms (ἐπιπνεῖν, καταπνεῖν) to
describe the manner in which the Spirit moved his " interpreters. "

On the strength of that faith held from the beginning, the
Church has never ceased to repeat by the mouth of her Doctors

as well as by the pronouncements of her Magisterium her conviction that in the Scriptures she has God's own Word.

If we analyse the statements of the Fathers, we can draw from them several mutually complementary formulas : Sacred Scripture has been "inspired" or "dictated" *by the Holy Spirit;* therefore God is its *author,* and the human writer is only God's instrument — referred to in figurative speech as a plectrum, a zither, a calamus, etc.), so that in short it contains *the Word of God.*

These expressions are found also in the pronouncements of the Church's Magisterium, in which they appear according to a progression which finds its explanation in the errors to be opposed. — 1. Until the fifth century the Church is engaged primarily in defining and defending the precise contents of her Canon; she enumerates the books which she receives as sacred and as the bases of her faith (*Enchiridion Biblicum*[1], 8-27; [cf. S. Muñoz Iglesias, *Doctrina Pontificia I. Documentos Biblicos,* Madrid 1955, pp. 1-13, and pp. 153-165]) [2]. 2. From the sixth to the thirteenth century, she states that those books are canonical because God is their author; and more precisely, in answer to the heresies which belittled or even rejected the Old Testament Revelation, she affirms that God is *the one and same Author of the Old and the New Testament (Ench. B.* 28-39; [Muñoz Iglesias p. 7 ff., and 164 ff.]). 3. At the Council of Florence (1441) a reason is given which is not really new : the one and the same God is the author of the Old and New Testament because the saints of both Testaments have spoken *under the inspiration of the same Holy Spirit. (Ench. B.* 40-49; [Muñoz Iglesias p. 173 ff.]).   The substance of that

---

[1] *Enchiridion Biblicum,* Rome, 1935 (2nd edition 1954).

Translator's note. — [2 The work of *S. Muñoz Iglesias* contains the documents in the original Greek and Latin languages with a Spanish translation and brief Spanish introduction to each document.   Before the "Documents" there is a full historical Introduction (pp. 3-150) dealing with the Biblical controversies which have occasioned the interventions of ecclesiastical authority.   Three appendices (pp. 613-679) give the texts condemning a number of publications, or commending others, or dealing with the Holy Places in Palestine.

It is natural that the doctrine of Inspiration did not develop in a vacuum. The development took place in the midst and under the influence of historical circumstances with which we must be acquainted in order to understand correctly the definitions and the pronouncements of the Church.   *Muñoz Iglesias* has rendered a real service by gathering together in his Introduction the material on the historical background of the doctrine of Inspiration].

statement is repeated by the Councils of Trent (1546; *Ench. B.* 57; [Muñoz Iglesias pp. 179-181 ff.]) and of the Vatican (1870; *Ench. B.* 77; [Muñoz Iglesias p. 194]).   4. The Vatican Council, however, states in negative terms what inspiration is not, but later Leo XIII in the Encyclical *Providentissimus* (1893) gives a positive description (*Ench. B.* 125; [Muñoz Iglesias pp. 235-236]) which is taken up and developed by Benedict XV in the Encyclical *Spiritus Paraclitus* (1920; *Ench. B.* 448; [Muñoz Iglesias pp. 409-410]) and by Pius XII in the Encyclical *Divino Afflante* (1943; A.A.S. XXXV, p. 314 and *passim;* [Muñoz Iglesias pp. 518-560. *Divino Afflante Spiritu* is edited also in English by the National Catholic Welfare Conference, Washington, D.C.]).

The problem has shifted in the last centuries and it has become imperative to make a more searching analysis of the respective parts of God and of man in the composition of Sacred Scripture.   We must clearly realize the nature of the problem, understand its genesis, and offer the solution which has been found acceptable at the present time.

II. — THE NATURE OF THE CHARISM OF INSPIRATION.

At the very outset, a distinction must be made between Prophetic inspiration and Scriptural inspiration.   Failure to perceive this distinction has resulted in misunderstanding the statements of the ancient writers and easily led to insoluble difficulties.   For these writers were interested especially in the case of the prophet proper and expressed themselves in terms suitable to him.   Now it is clear, in that extreme case, that God's influence manifested itself to a maximum degree, in a sovereign manner which left but little room for human initiative.   God's word is so peremptory that its interpreter can only receive and transmit the message.   Scripture is full of texts which illustrate that irresistible hold of the Spirit on the prophet.   The spirit " comes upon " him (1 Sam. **10** : 6, 10); it " is upon " him (Num. **24** : 2; 1 Sam. **19** : 20; 23); it " puts him on " (1 Chr. **12** : 18 (19); 2 Chr. **24** : 20), so that the inspired man can say nothing but what Yahweh says to him (Num. **23** : 12; **24** : 13).   The Spirit enters into him and speaks to him (Ez. **2** : 2; **3** : 24); he puts his words in his mouth (Num. **22** : 38;

Jer. **1** : 9; Isa. **59** : 21; cf. Ex. **4** : 15), or on his tongue (2 Sam. **23** : 2). He opens his eyes (Num. **24** : 4, 16), and his ears (1 Sam. **9** : 15; 2 Sam. **7** : 27; Isa. **22** : 14); he " reveals " (1 Sam. **3** : 21; Dan. **10** : 1) to him " secrets " (Am. **3** : 7; cf. Deut. **29** : 28) which he could not know of himself. Without God's commission, the words of the (false) prophet are falsehood (Jer. **14** : 14; **23** : 16). When his commission is there, it is compelling, owing to God's initiative (Am. **7** : 14-16); it over-comes all resistance of the one whom God appoints (Am. **3** : 8; Jer. **1** : 5-7; **20** : 7-9; Jonas, *passim*). In short, what is required of such a prophet is that he be only a docile and faithful instrument. He is an agent who speaks, not on his own account, but in the name of Him who moves him, as is well summed up in 2 Pet. **1** : 21. His words are the very words .of God. And when he is commanded not only to utter them, but also to write them, the shade of difference in the material execution of the command does not alter the substance of his charism : it remains a case of " prophetic inspiration. "

The case of " Scriptural inspiration " is altogether different. This involves not only the expression or the writing down of words received from above, but the composition of a book, with all that this implies of human initiative and work. Now this case occurs also in Sacred Scripture, where it is even the most frequent one, and it is remarkable that here there is no mention of a " revelation " which makes known to man in an inescapable way truths which he had only to transcribe just as he received them directly from God. On the contrary, we see writers composing historical books or sapiential collections; they mention their sources (1 Kgs. **11** : 41; **14** : 19, 29; Prov. **31** : 1, etc.) and make no secret of the hard work which this cost them (Ecclus. : Prologue; 2 Mach. **2** : 24, 32). The action of the Holy Spirit which moved and led them in their task is not even mentioned. We know from the faith of the Synagogue, and then of the Church, that the action of the Spirit was at work; but obviously it must have been exerted in a rather different way from that noted above in the case of prophetic inspiration.

Now it is clear that the ancient Christian writers spoke of the inspiration of the Scriptures chiefly in terms drawn from the special description of the prophet proper. Any inspired author is received by them after the fashion of an instrument which

has to transmit God's word; the author's own personality is
hardly noticed. True, they did not go so far — as Philo did
practically [1] — as to put on the same footing the heralds of
Biblical revelation and the ecstatic "mediums" of pagan
oracles, such as the Pythia or the Sibyl, deprived of consciousness
and intelligence by the irruption of the divine spirit
(ἐνθουσιασμός).

They were aware of the differences, and these were fundamental : the religious and moral significance of the message,
the supreme, not induced, influence of the Spirit, lastly and
chiefly the enlightening of the mind which heightens, but does
not destroy, the personality of the inspired man [2].

Their expressions may have been influenced at times by the
beliefs of their surroundings. Those resemblances in terminology
must not blind us to the divergence of the fundamental
concepts [3].

Nevertheless, the early writers had in mind primarily the
typical case of the "prophet" and applied the special mode
of his charism to the inspiration of all the Scripture. Therefore
they emphasized less than we do the person or the role of the
human writer. As we shall note soon, the reasons which
helped to focus the attention on the human element were not
yet an important factor. There was no preoccupation at that
time with religious psychology, or with the evolution of language
and doctrine, or with possible conflicts between the profane
sciences and the Bible. They heard God speaking in the Sacred
Book, even in the least significant words of the Sacred Book, with
all the absoluteness of truth and all the fulness of meaning
which such an origin implies. A proof of this may be seen in
the manner in which Jews and Christians, the Rabbis and

---

[1] Cf. J. B. FREY, op. cit., pp. 495-498. [On "ἔκστασις" see Oepke in Kittel
Th.W, II, pp. 448-451. The seer, the prophet, even the poet were supposed
to be put out of themselves, while a god or some supernatural agency came
into them and spoke through them; a god was in the man : ἔνθεος, hence
enthusiasm].

[2] We are referring here to the genuine prophets of the Old and the New
Testament, not to certain "nabis", or to cases of "glossolalia" (speaking
in tongues), where a charism of lower grade is to be recognized. (Cf. 1 Sam.
19 : 20-24; 1 Cor. 14 : 2-33).

[3] Cf. H. BACHT, "Wahres und falsches Prophetentum. Ein kritischer
Beitrag zur religionsgeschichtlichen Behandlung des frühen Christentums",
Biblica 32 (1951), pp. 237-252.

St. Paul use Scripture, arguing from a sentence, even from one word, without considering the context which would help to interpret it according to the intention of the writer [1].

The Fathers speak of the inspired man as a plectrum on which the Spirit plays, as a pen moved by the Spirit. Clearly those figures must not be taken strictly, and it seems certain that the word " dictation " did not imply for the ancients the same amount of passivity as for us [2]. Nevertheless the Fathers had no difficulty in seeing the absoluteness of God's thought in each word of Scripture. And if any passage seemed to offer too material a sense, they had recourse to allegorical interpretation, for instance, in order to find, under the letter that kills, the spirit that gives life (cf. 2 Cor. 3 : 6).

This calm conviction lasted undisturbed until the dawn of modern times. The Scholastic theologians also, as St. Thomas, studied the phenomenon of Inspiration especially under its " prophetic " aspect. Yet St. Thomas' genius, as we shall see, allowed its share to the psychology of the human messenger, and even considered the case where the influx received from above is limited to making him think, speak, and write on matters known to him naturally. Thus were laid the foundations for developments which were to prove very fruitful. However, the possibilities of these conditions and limitations of the inspiring impulse were not examined seriously, because scholars were not as yet sufficiently aware of the human factors entering into the composition of the Bible. Hence, until the eighteenth century, both Catholics and Protestants considered inspiration primarily as a " dictation ", in which one listens to God who speaks and pays but little attention to the human instrument He is using.

The situation was to change with the rise of modern philology, philosophy, history, and scientific discoveries. On the one hand,

---

Translator's note. — [1 Cf. Jos. BONSIRVEN, L'Evangile de Paul (Paris, 1946), p. 15f. and his : Exégèse rabbinique et exégèse Paulinienne (Paris, 1938); David DAUBE, The New Testament and Rabbinic Judaism (London, 1956); Israel FRANKEL, Peshat in Talmudic and Midrashic Literature (Toronto, 1956); Jos. KEULERS, De Boeken van het Nieuwe Testament, Vol. 5, Roermond, 1953), pp. 12-14; BÜCHSEL, s. v. ἀλληγορέω : in Kittel, ThW, I, pp. 260-264.
[2] Cf. J. M. VOSTÉ, De Divina Inspiratione et Veritate Sacrae Scripturae, (2nd ed., Rome, 1932), p. 81 f., and note, pp. 98-100; A. BEA, s. J., De Scripturae Sacrae Inspiratione (2nd ed., Rome, 1933), p. 28; [id., De Inspiratione et Innerrantia Sacrae Scripturae (new impress., Rome, 1954), pp. 8-13].

the new interest in religious psychology and the newly developed sense of historical evolution led scholars to observe more closely the ideas peculiar to each sacred writer and their place in the development of Revelation.   The great strides made by philology confirmed that attitude by paying closer attention to the language of each writer, with its peculiarities of time, place, and literary dependence.   On the other hand, the revolution which took place in our knowledge of the structure of the universe and of the history of ancient times compelled men to recognize in the Bible, especially in respect to profane matters, ideas or beliefs which belonged to another age and could no longer be accepted as they stand.   The Holy Book lost that halo of absolute and undisputed truth in all matters which its isolation secured for it formerly.   It was no longer the only source of information, and as a consequence it came to have a more relative value.

The rediscovery of the human aspect of the Bible occasioned varied reactions.   Some adopted radical negative views; they gave up belief in the divine origin of the Bible and made inspiration — when they still spoke of it —, a natural gift, analogous to what any poet can claim.   Others, wishing to preserve the traditional faith, upheld the reality of a truly supernatural inspiration, but limited it as much as possible : it was only a " negative assistance " which preserved the human author from error; or else it was only a " subsequent approval " whereby the Holy Spirit took over as His own, after the event, a work composed originally as any other human work; or again, inspiration was a positive influx which accompanied the composition of the work, but it was limited to a part of that work, that in which matters of faith and morals were involved. By these different expedients, it was thought possible to do more justice to the human element present in the Bible, and to admit the existence of errors which would not be imputable to the Holy Spirit.   But these new ideas went too far in their concessions, and the authority of the Church rejected them. The Vatican Council (*Ench. B.* 77) [Muñoz Iglesias p. 194] declared them insufficient : " The Church holds [the Books] to be sacred and canonical, not because having been written by sole human industry, they were aftewards approved by her authority; nor only because they contain revelation without error ". And in its turn the Encyclical *Providentissimus* (*Ench. B.* 124 [Muñoz Iglesias pp. 234-235]) rejected the idea of inspiration restricted to matters of faith and morals : " The system of those who, to rid themselves of these difficulties, do not hesitate to concede that divine inspiration regards the things of faith and morals, and nothing beyond, cannot be tolerated. " The Encyclical gives a definition of inspiration according to which inspiration is a positive supernatural influx which moves the human author to write and which guides him throughout his work to its final completion, in such a way that the result, i. e., the whole Scripture, properly conceived and willed and carried through under the impulse of the Holy Spirit, can truly claim God as its author. " For, by supernatural power, He so moved and impelled them to write, He so assisted them when writing, that the things which He ordered, and those only, they first, rightly understood, then willed faithfully to write down, and finally expressed them in apt words and with infallible truth. Otherwise, He would not be the Author of the entire Scripture. " (*Ench. B.* 124; [Muñoz Iglesias p. 236]).

Yet the Church did not claim to give a full account of the phenomenon of inspiration; it left to the free inquiry of theologians the care of a closer analysis of its nature. The theologians undertook the task bravely. One of them, a man of great authority, Cardinal Franzelin, S. J., already in 1870 proposed a solution which in a way served as the starting point of the discussion, for, though indeed his statements influenced those used by the Vatican Council and the Encyclical *Providentissimus*, his system in detail was not adopted in full, officially [1].

In fact, a number of theologians judged it questionable. In short it represented a kind of compromise between the old and the new systems : the *dictation* was kept for the *thoughts* but given up for the words. The thoughts were all from God, who otherwise would not be truly the " author " of the book; therefore He had infused them all in His human interpreter, either by " a revelation " of new ideas or at least by means of " a suggestion " of the ideas which the inspired man had before, but which God recalled to his mind in order to have them

---

[1] Cf. G. *Courtade*, " J. B. Franzelin, Les formules que le Magistère de l'Eglise lui a empruntées ", in *RSR* 40 (1952) : *Mélanges Jules Lebreton*, II, pp. 317-325, esp. pp. 318-323.

included in the Book. In either case, the Holy Spirit accepted
responsibility for the whole contents of the book, acting as the
principal cause, while the man was only his very passive
instrument. But the question of the literary form of the book
was an altogether different matter. This was left to the initiative
of the writer who acted here as the principal cause; he chose
freely the verbal clothing of the thoughts received from God
and was assisted in this task only to prevent error on his part.
In short, the charism of inspiration took a twofold form :
it was understood in the old full sense of a " revelation " in all
that was connected with the thought; as regards the wording,
it was only " the negative assistance " advocated by some
moderns. Both God and man indeed were " authors ", but in
different ways : one was the author of the substance, the other
of the form.

Confronted by this ingenious solution, a number of theologians, while recognizing its merits, felt themselves in the
presence of an unsatisfactory compromise. They could not
understand this coordinated rather than subordinated cooperation of the two causalities, divine and human, which belonged
in fact to a special school of theology. They could not conceive
the possibility of thoughts communicated to a human mind
without at the same time involving their literary expression.
They doubted that that division of responsibilities between
God and man was able to solve the problems arising from the
Bible. For, after all, the thoughts rather than the wording
were in question. Their human limitations, their contingent
character, even their possiblity of error, caused difficulty and
this was the point to account for. Nothing was achieved so
long as a " revelation " or a direct " suggestion " from God
maintained that character of absolute divine truth which modern
discoveries seemed to be breaking down.

Hence a reaction began to take shape, which, while availing
itself of Franzelin's praiseworthy attempt, looked for a better
solution in a fuller recourse to the teaching of St. Thomas.
Among the many scholars who took a distinguished part,
Fr. Lagrange, O.P., deserves special mention. Thanks to their
steady and continuous efforts during the last fifty years,
Catholic theologians have in our time come to a solution to
which apparently most scholars give their adherence, if not in all

details, at least as regards its main lines. In the presentation of this solution, some of its leading characteristic features will be emphasized in the interest of greater clarity.

1. — *THE SACRED WRITER " AN INSTRUMENT " OF GOD.*

This is, as we have seen, a traditional idea, received from the Fathers and adopted by the teaching authority of the Church. (Encyclical *Providentissimus, Ench. B.* 125 : " The Holy Spirit used men as instruments to write; cf. Encycl. *Spiritus Paraclitus, ibid.* 448; Encycl. *Divino afflante Spiritu,* AAS XXXV [1943] p. 314 [Muñoz Iglesias, p. 544; NCWC ed. 1933 : " The Sacred writer in composing the sacred book is the " organon " or instrument of the Holy Spirit, that is, a living and rational instrument "]). This idea, if understood properly, sheds much light on the problem. It is fundamentally correct, but it may become false if taken in too narrow a sense. It is correct to the extent that it illustrates well the simul-taneous concurrence of the divine and human activities. As a principal cause uses an instrumental cause by making the latter's peculiar efficiency subservient to its own higher effi-ciency, so that the resulting work is at the same time and fully the effect of both causes, of both together and of each according to its rank, so God by his sovereign activity influences the activity of the inspired writer so thoroughly that the resulting work will be entirely His work and entirely the work of that man, and simultaneously, though in different degrees. This is not the parallel working of juxtaposed causes, each acting within its domain to produce two distinct effects, but the close compenetration of two superimposed causes, which work in harmony to produce a single common effect.

But the whole problem consists in understanding rightly how God moves the man. For there are different kinds of instruments. One thing is the instrumentality of the regene-rating baptismal water or of the wonderworker; another, that of a man who thinks or acts under the influence of his Creator. In the first instance, which is that of instrumental causality proper, the instrument does not have within itself the principle of the action it produces, so that the effect produced is not truly proportionate to it : the gift of sanctifying grace is infinitely above the virtue proper to the material element, i. e. water, and the disproportion is just as great between the miraculous healing and the action — gesture or word — of the wonder worker who performs it. If the charism of inspiration were to be understood in this way, the human author would be really nothing but a scribe without initiative, little more than a copyist, as irresponsible for his message as the Delphic Pythia sputtering Apollo's oracles. Now all we know of Scripture is against such a view. The Biblical prophet, controlled as he may be by the Spirit, remains conscious of and responsible for the divine oracle which he understands before transmitting it [1], and which he transmits in the full integrity of his own personality, clothing it with his usual devices and language. With even greater justification, the " hagiographer ", historian, sage or poet, who composes a book under God's guidance, giving to his task all his labor, often even without being conscious of the divine impulse which guides him, deserves to be regarded as a true author of the work which bears so definitely the imprint of his genius. Yet we may still use in this connection the word " instrument ", provided we take it in a broad sense which it quite readily admits. St. Thomas, in fact, says that our soul in its natural operations acts as an instrument in the hands of the principal cause, that is, God [2].

Indeed it would be going too far to make the inspired man an instrument in such a broad sense, for his peculiar case implies a closer dependence on the divine agent, which is marked by two characteristic features of any true instrument : on the one hand, in so far as he is inspired, he does not act on his own initiative as he does in his natural activity, but he thinks, speaks, or writes only when the Spirit moves him; and on the

---

[1] It may happen that the inspired man does not understand the message entrusted to him, either because he receives the message in a material way without grasping it (a classic case is that of Pharaoh, Gen. 41 : 8, or Caiaphas, Jn. 11 : 51), or because, understanding the obvious sense, he does not perceive the other meanings included by God. In such cases and as regards the other meanings unknown to him, he is truly " an instrument " in the strict sense. It is to be noted that it is only in connection with such cases that St. Thomas uses the term *instrumentum*. (Cf. *Somme Théologique*, ed. Revue des Jeunes, *La Prophétie*, [Paris, 1947], p. 291 f.). But we are considering above all the normal case where the inspired man understands the message entrusted to him by God. (Cf. *infra :* III, 5).

[2] *Contra Gentiles* III 149, " Our soul works under God as an instrumental agent under a principal agent ".

other, he does not receive the full knowledge, " through principles ", of the supernatural message given to him, but he remains rather in the dependent attitude of the disciple whose words rest, consciously or not, on the higher knowledge of his master. These are two manifest features in Scripture with regard to a " prophet ", affirmed by faith and theology about anyone inspired, which suffice fully to justify the traditional appellation of " instrument " given to him. But we must not go further and, taking the term too strictly, exaggerate the dependence of the human interpreter so as to rob him of his personality and his initiative.

In short, the designation of the inspired man as an instrument brings into play an " analogous " notion which must be applied with discrimination, according to the higher exigencies of philosophy and theology. Now philosophy teaches us that man, to remain man, must think, speak, and write freely and personally; and theology teaches us that God, in the mysterious power of His sovereign causality, is able to move that man from within, according to his peculiar state of a free being, in a way which determines him without destroying his personality, but rather raises it higher. This is what happens in the charism of inspiration. Under the supremely efficacious impulse of the Spirit, the inspired man is led ineluctably to think, say, and write what God wills and as God wills; in that sense he is truly an instrument more strictly than when he acts of himself according to the natural order of things. But on the other hand, the power that moves him is so delicate in exercising its mastery that not only is the man not diminished, but rather he is raised higher, he thinks better, he wills more strongly, in short he carries out his work with a freedom so respected and so complete that he may not be conscious of being guided by an almighty hand. In this sense, he is an instrument of a very special kind, proper to his nature as a thinking man [1], quite different from the material pen held

---

[1] Encycl. *Divino afflante Spiritu, Ench. B*. 556 [Muñoz IGLESIAS, p. 544]; NCWC, ed. 1933 : " For having begun by expounding minutely the principle that the inspired writer, in composing the sacred book, is the Holy Spirit's " organon " or instrument, a living and rational instrument, [Catholic theologians] rightly observe that, impelled by the divine motion, he so uses his faculties and powers, that from the book due to his work all may easily infer " the special character of each one, and, as it were his personal traits ". Cf. Encycl. *Spiritus Paraclitus, Ench. B*. 448 [Muñoz IGLESIAS 409 f.].

by the writer. This true autonomy of the inspired man working under God's influence will appear more clearly still if we analyze more closely the processes of his thought.

2. — REVELATION AND INSPIRATION.
IDEAS AND JUDGMENT.

On this point especially St. Thomas' treatise on " Prophecy " (*Summa Theologica* II^a II^{ae}, qu. 171-174) has shed welcome light. Going back to the distinction which is fundamental in psychology, between the " representations ", ideas, images or sensations which supply its matter to thought, and " the judgment " which the intellect passes on them by illuminating them with its " light ", and which is itself the formal element of knowledge, St. Thomas distinguishes clearly the divers modalities which the divine charism may assume according as it affects the one or the other of those two elements. Three main cases are possible. Sometimes, he says, the divine Spirit enlightens his interpreter on both grounds at the same time; he gives him new, supernatural " representations " [1] and he grants him at the same time the necessary supernatural light that he may pass judgment on them according to His intentions. This is the case of true prophecy in its fullest sense, such as Isaias or Jeremias exhibit in transmitting to the people the " vision " or the " oracle " which they have just received. Sometimes God grants man only " representations ", without " light " to enable him to pass judgment. There is then no true knowledge, and we may speak of prophecy only in a very improper sense, as in the case of Pharaoh receiving from God dreams which Joseph must interpret for him. Sometimes, finally, God grants him the " light " alone, without new " representations ", that is to say, He causes him to reflect upon his ordinary notions, such as he may have acquired through the normal exercise of his natural faculties and his work. This intermediate case is not as specific as the first; hence

---

[1] This may happen in several ways which St. Thomas analyzes in detail, according as the representations supplied thus are intellectual, imaginative or sensible, or else as they are entirely new to the prophet's mind, or on the contrary proceed only from a new arrangement by God of his earlier representations. (Cf. *La Prophétie*, p. 243 f.). It is not necessary here to go into the detail of these analyses, interesting as they may be, in order to account for the various kinds of visions reported in the Bible.

St. Thomas here speaks of " hagiographer " rather than of " prophet ", but it stands much higher than the second and belongs still in a certain way to the genus " prophecy ", for it implies actually a supernatural illumination of " judgment ", which after all constitutes the main element of knowledge.

Obviously this last case is the one to which moderns have given special attention, for it was the problem which was exercising their minds especially, the problem of so many sacred writers who composed sacred books, though they were not real " prophets " and did not receive from heaven " visions " or " oracles ", and worked only on the conceptual or imaginative material they found in their minds or in the milieu in which they lived. St. Thomas, who dealt explicitly with " prophecy ", paid only passing attention to this case. For the moderns, on the contrary, who were wrestling with a new kind of problem, this was a matter of supreme importance, lower perhaps in dignity than that of the real " prophet ", but far more frequent in the Bible and therefore most worthy of attention. Adopting a terminology which was not fully worked out, but at least prepared in St. Thomas [1], they applied to this case the term " inspiration " and reserved that of " revelation " for the first case, where the Spirit not only enlightens His interpreter's judgment, but also " reveals " to him concepts which he could not acquire through his own efforts.

Thanks to this capital distinction, it became possible to move ahead. It relieved the scholar from the necessity of looking in each concept of the sacred writer for a notion " revealed " or at least " suggested " to him directly by God, with all the absoluteness which such an origin normally implies. It allowed him to recognize a thought of human origin, with all the limitations, and with all the circumstances of time and place, of culture and mentality, which are its necessary consequences. The definite assurance that there was an " inspiration ", a divine " light " illuminating this human datum, sufficed to justify the sacred authority of the book produced by the hagiographer, and its character of " Scripture " acknowledged by the faith of the Church, without taking from it the deeply human features which are so evident.

---

[1] Cf. *La Prophétie*, pp. 277-288.

Yet this did not solve all the difficulties. The human writer indeed got back his title to his " representations ", which God graciously received as they were with all their imperfections. But was much more accomplished thereby than when he got back his title to the " words ", which Franzelin tried to secure for him? From the moment that the " judgment " remained under the control of the divine light, did not the judgment itself, which is " the formal element of knowledge ", retain the prerogatives of God's absolute truth? Did not the difficulty raised by modern discoveries remain entire? Were we required to recognize in each and every affirmation of the sacred writer a judgment uttered in God's name, with all the absoluteness of the divine thought, although the evidence compelled us to recognize in it, as much as and more than in the " representations " used by him, limitations, imperfections, and even — according to some — errors? It was therefore necessary to scrutinize that judgment in itself and to see whether, though God shed His inspiring light on it, He had really meant to attach to it all the absoluteness of His thought and truth? The theologians have tried their skill, and though they have not yet obtained on this point results as unanimously accepted as on the foregoing ones, yet this is the problem on which all their effort should now be concentrated.

3. — *PROPHETIC INSPIRATION AND SCRIPTURAL INSPI-*
   RATION.   SPECULATIVE JUDGMENT AND PRACTICAL
   JUDGMENT [1].

When St. Thomas speaks of the prophet's judgment illuminated by the light received from above, he thinks essentially of the speculative judgment, which alone is important in the question before him; the prophet, as he studies him, is commissioned to unfold to men God's secrets and to transmit to them in His name a teaching of truth; his mission therefore rests primarily on the plane of knowledge. The role of the charism which illumines his judgment is to guarantee it with the " certitude of divine truth ". What is involved therefore is a judgment of the speculative order, the object of which is to know and to utter truth. Now this is a way of considering

---

[1] This subject has been developed in *La Prophétie*, pp. 313-328.

things which, while perfectly justified in the case of a prophet giving out a revelation, is perhaps not so clearly justified, if one tries to apply it in the same manner to the Biblical writers in general. In short, it is based on a questionable methodology, which formerly was prevalent and is still so for some, viz, that of regarding the whole Sacred Book as a collection of doctrines, as a " Denzinger " before its time, each sentence of which can be taken as a dogmatic statement.

As we have seen, the discoveries of modern times have made us aware of another way of formulating the problem and of approaching the Sacred Book. By forcing us to disclaim in many Biblical statements affirmations of divine truths, which would be contradicted by the established acquisitions of reason, they have compelled us to read Scripture in a different way and to understand that its intention is often to do something else than reveal doctrines of faith. It has become better understood that, all important as the purpose of doctrinal teaching is, it is not the only one which Scripture seeks to achieve. Beside the " prophet ", whose single role is to communicate to men the knowledge of a divine revelation, we have come to perceive better the significant role of the sacred writer whose mission is quite different, and who speaks of many things in a human way, without any purpose of formal teaching, and solely to the extent that they are of use to him in achieving the end for which he is writing his book. This is what we outlined above in distinguishing " scriptural inspiration " from " prophetic inspiration "; and this is what we can explain on the psychological level by distinguishing the exercise of the " practical judgment " beside " the speculative judgment ".

Contrary to the latter, which has truth as its object, the former proposes a good to itself. Through it, practical reason guiding the will disposes the means with a view to reaching an end which may be something very different from the attainment of some matter of knowledge. In the case before us of an author writing a book, it is natural for us to consider, beside the speculative judgment which is exercised in respect of the store of knowledge he means to communicate, the exercise of the practical judgment striving to ensure that very communication. Now this second mode of his mental activity is no less important than the first; it is often even more important.

The speculative activity, of course, may possibly be first and control the whole work; the author has begun by seizing upon a certain truth and in writing is exclusively concerned with making it known. In this case, his speculative judgment certainly holds the first place in his mind, and the practical judgment comes into play only as an humble servant, to ensure as faithfully as possible the transmission of the truth possessed. But it is quite possible also that the practical judgment may be first and control the exercise of the speculative judgment; the author writes his book to produce a certain effect, to move his readers to adopt a certain attitude to life, political, social, or religious, even simply to act on their hearts to calm them, comfort them, or entertain them. And the thought content of his work is organized solely with this concrete end in view. It may even be that his work does not involve any affirmation of a truth; he may deliberately choose a fictional, unreal genre, or else, when relating some beliefs or opinions, he may refuse to guarantee them himself and may be satisfied with stating them simply to produce the impression which is his sole concern. Most frequently, however, if his purpose involves the seriousness and loftiness of a spiritual message — as is the case in the Bible —, he will bring into play a certain amount of knowledge of objective truth, but he will do so only to the degree that such knowledge is useful for his purpose. In other words, his practical judgment will command and regulate the exercise of his speculative judgment; he will not pronounce on all things in absolute fashion as they are in themselves, but only to the extent that they matter to his purpose. His point of view, the extent of his affirmation, his manner of exposition, all this will be determined by the concrete end he assigns to his work. This evaluation of the respective roles and purposes of the speculative and practical judgments is essential, and we shall see its decisive importance in the question of inerrancy. For the time being, it will suffice to see its consequences for the nature of the inspiring charism.

That charism indeed will vary according to the activity which it stimulates in the mind of the inspired man. If it arouses him primarily to contemplate a divine truth, it will be the " light " which is the object of St. Thomas' special study, which raises his intelligence and enables him to know with divine certitude. This is what we call " prophetic inspiration ". But if it stimulates him to undertake the practical task of composing a book, it will be first an impulse to the will, a direction of the practical reason, which will enable the inspired man to will effectively and to carry out his undertaking under the best conditions. This is " Scriptural inspiration " proper. Lastly — and this is the normal case — if that concrete work is concerned with the teaching of truth, the inspiring influx will address itself both to the practical reason and to the speculative reason with every possible shade of variation according to the extent that the teaching of truth is involved.

This last mode, a varying combination of prophetic inspiration and Scriptural inspiration, is very important. Again, we say, it is the most frequent case. Some theologians, (E. Levesque), reacting quite naturally to an idea of inspiration conceived in an entirely speculative fashion and understood in effect as a " revelation ", went too far in the opposite direction by regarding it exclusively as an impulse to the will. Of itself, it is claimed, it has no direct influence on the knowledge of the inspired man, the acquisition of that knowledge being attributed to an earlier stage of his work. Whether he acquired his knowledge through supernatural revelation or through the natural exercise of his intelligence, he is already provided with this knowledge when divine inspiration seizes him and moves him to write. The serious difficulty raised by such a view is that it withdraws from the influence of inspiration the properly intellectual activity of the author and, where the stock of knowledge is not revealed, it makes his knowledge purely human in origin. The later impulse and will to write what he knows indeed may give authority to his knowledge, though indirectly, but does not secure for it the advantage of a direct illumination which raises and strengthens it. Now this seems to be really required both by traditional Faith and by the theology of St. Thomas. Hence we hold that we must maintain that purely " scriptural " inspiration, if the impulse to write is not concerned with the activity of knowing — an unfrequent case —, is necessarily combined with " prophetic " inspiration (without always implying an accompanying " revelation ") to the full extent that the composition of the book includes a teaching of truth. But this extent varies considerably as we have said, and we shall come back to it; to such a degree, in fact, that the combinations of the two aspects — the " prophetic " and the " scriptural " — of inspiration take on in practice very different forms, which make it a fundamentally " analogical " reality. Were one to treat inspiration " univocally ", without taking into account the actual psychology of the inspired man, it would be exposed to the dangers of inflexibility and distortion.

This " analogical " character of inspiration will become clearer to us if we try to pursue it in all the domains which it covers.

III. — THE TOTAL AND ANALOGICAL EXTENSION OF INSPIRATION.

1. — *INSPIRATION EXTENDS ANALOGICALLY TO ALL THE FACULTIES OF THE SACRED WRITER.*

We have just seen that the divine charism is diffused throughout the whole mind of the inspired person, through his intellect as well as his will, through both his speculative and practical reason, to the extent that inspiration causes them to play a greater or lesser role in the interests of the work to be produced. We must go further and recognize that inspiration extends likewise to the lower faculties, memory, imagination, and sensation, i.e., to the physical faculties most active in the execution of the work, since they also contribute to the final result — the book which is to be written. The thought and the will would be ineffective if words were not produced which would transmit the message to men's ears and eyes. Thus we come to that " verbal " inspiration which certain exegetes have found so shocking. But it shocked them only because they conceived inspiration univocally, as a revelation. They rightly thought it inadmissible that God's " dictation " should extend to the very words, so that the human writer had left to himself only a secondary and subordinate role — that of a mere typewriter. What we have said above fortunately rids us of such a material view. For we have restored to the sacred writer his whole personality as a free being, thinking and acting on his own, though moved by God : the wording chosen by him is truly his wording, reflecting his mind and his culture, and expressing his thought. But the words are at the same time the words of God, for the charism given from above penetrates him so thoroughly that it leads him on to the final stage of his work; far from paralyzing him, it exalts him to a better, more appropriate use of his vocabulary, so that the literary form of expression which he adopts is the one which answers best God's intentions respecting his work. The breath of inspiration reaches his words, as it reaches his thoughts and volitions, but in different ways, proportionate to the role of each of those components, with that flexibility at once discreet and all-powerful, which excites his whole activity and guides it throughout until it terminates in the book which is its fruit.

2. — INSPIRATION EXTENDS ANALOGICALLY TO THE WHOLE CONTENT OF THE SACRED BOOK.

On this point also, some timid souls have wished to withdraw from the influence of the charism of inspiration certain parts of Scripture, namely, those of no significance for faith or morals. Again, this was because they conceived inspiration after the manner of revelation. It seemed to them, and correctly, that many details of the Sacred Book contain no teaching of truth even if they do not seem tainted with error. The Church is opposed to such a restriction, she has maintained that Scripture in its entirety and in all its parts, however small, enjoys the charism of inspiration. But that does not mean that Scripture enjoys this charism always in the same degree, and the more flexible conception of this charism which we have proposed does full justice to the Church's claim by allowing us to understand it correctly.

Indeed the least part of the text belongs to the whole and plays a useful role in it. Not without reason did the sacred writer add this or that picturesque detail or insert in passing this or that minor item of information. He did so as a writer familiar with his art, who judged such a detail or such information appropriate to the general effect he wished to produce. As an integral part of the whole, the detail enjoys naturally the influx of inspiration which commanded the work in its totality; it is truly inspired, but in its proper place, and according to its role, which in both cases may well be quite subordinate. Though he regarded it as suitable, the human writer probably gave it only little importance and little attention. So also, consequently, the Spirit of God, whose sovereign action is so completely one with that of the writer, undoubtedly did not shed his light nor commit his authority on this point to the same extent as on some other matter of incomparably greater importance. In the richly varied diffusion of the charism of inspiration, such a detail probably received only little light, and little weight, and so we ought to take it, if we do not wish to distort the real intentions of the human writer, and through him, of God. In the letter of the sacred text as in the mind of the writer, inspiration extends to everything, but in an analogical way proportionate to the relative significance of each element.

3. — INSPIRATION EXTENDS ANALOGICALLY TO ALL THE AUTHORS OF THE SACRED BOOK.

So far we have been speaking of the human author, the sacred writer, as if he were a single known person, responsible for the book that bears his name. This is a convenient simplification, and from the point of view of the ancients it corresponded pretty well to reality. But the advances of the Biblical sciences have compelled us to adopt on this point much more complex views. The Pentateuch has ceased to be in our eyes entirely the work of Moses alone. The Book of Isaias has gradually been divided into a number of different collections, not all of them belonging to the prophet Isaias. And what should we say of the Sapiential Books, to which so many anonymous writers have contributed? Even the writings that are most homogeneous in origin have been retouched, adapted, and enriched with glosses at different times. In short, the Sacred Book appears to us more and more as a complex collection on which many successive generations have worked, a building erected by the labor of many hands. It is a collective work, the work of a whole people which has deposited in it through the centuries the treasure of its tradition. And what is true of the Old Testament holds also, due proportion being observed, for the New.

Apart from the indisputable writings of some better known personages, we find in it in a way the testimony of the whole apostolic generation. In the case of the Gospels, for example, the first and the fourth reached their final stage only after a rather long period of growth in which several hands may have collaborated.

This complex genesis of the sacred books, however, does not change anything in their sacred character, for it is its final result, the Book in its last state, which the Church has received as Canonical Scripture, and it is that which is inspired. It is therefore necessary to admit that all those who contributed to produce it enjoyed inspiration. This exigency may seem difficult to satisfy if inspiration is conceived as a revelation of divine truths, for, after all, many of the modifications made in the Bible do not possess that character; but it becomes easy with the flexible and analogical notion we are advocating. The influx of inspiration was imparted in varying modes and intensity to all those who collaborated in God's book. He moved one to compose its substance, another to work it over by adding glosses [1].

Clearly the latter is not inspired in the same way as the former; each one partakes of the charism to the extent, great or small, that he collaborates in the book, and that extent is liable to the widest variation. In the different authors, as in the different parts of the Book and in the different faculties of the writer, we find that analogical diffusion of the charism of inspiration which alone does full justice to the concrete reality of Scripture [2].

---

[1] We are referring obviously only to the glosses embodied in the work before its reception into the Canon of the Synagogue or of the Church. For those introduced later cannot claim to belong to the inspired text. The distinction, easy in theory, is often rather difficult in practice. Biblical scholarship may try to determine the ancient or recent character of the modifications of the text; the Church alone has authority to decide whether such or such a gloss, such or such a reading, belongs to the text received by her as " canonical ". She does so very rarely, and the exegete must usually speak *ex hypothesi*, supposing that the text he is dealing with is that of Tradition, *salvo iudicio Ecclesiae*.

Translator's note. — [2 On the subject of the preceding paragraph, see R. A. F. MACKENZIE, " Some Problems in the Field of Inspiration " *CBQ* XX 1958 1-8, espec. pp. 2-5. The question is treated more fully by Dom Célestin CHARLIER, *La lecture chrétienne de la Bible* (3rd ed., Maredsous, 1950); Ch. IV, " The Birth of the Bible ", Ch. V, " The Book of Mankind "; Ch. VII, " The Work of the Spirit "].

4. — *DOES INSPIRATION EXTEND*
TO THE TRANSLATIONS OF THE BIBLE?

If inspiration extends to the anonymous corrector, subordinate as his work may have been, must it not be extended also to the translator? The problem must be approached from a twofold point of view : the character of the translation, and the use of the Church. As a rule, if the translation is only the materially correct transposition into another language, it does not seem necessary that it should enjoy the charism of inspiration. The translator's natural talent alone may suffice to give to the original inspired text a faithful expression with authentic value, without being for that reason itself inspired. But the case is different if the translator makes a personal contribution and transforms, modifies, or glosses the text he is rendering, for his intervention affects the very substance of the text, the sense of which it changes, and the modifications introduced can possess authority only if they are guaranteed by the same Spirit of God who inspired the original. With all that, the changes must possess authority, and it is here that the second factor intervenes, namely, the usage of the Church. If she did not receive such a version as her canonical text — which is, as we shall see, our sole criterion for the fact of inspiration — there is no question of recognizing an inspired character in that version. This reason alone excludes all the versions which appeared after the Scriptures were received in the Church. Now this is true of most of them, and the Church does not regard them as inspired. The changes in the sense of the original consciously made in them have only the human authority of their translators. Even the Vulgate, recognized by the Roman Church as her official version, received thereby only a guarantee of substantial authenticity and doctrinal authority; it did not for that reason become " inspired " in its text itself. But the problem is more delicate in the case of the versions made before the Canon was settled, namely, the Greek Versions, for they are the ones which the Church received from the very beginning. Did she regard them as mere versions? Or actually as her canonical text, endowed with divine authority? The second alternative is not doubtful for the books whose Semitic original was lost : Ecclesiasticus, for instance, or, again, the

Greek Gospel of St. Matthew, considered *ex hypothesi* as the translation of an Aramaic work. But what should we think of the Greek translations, the Hebrew or Aramaic original of which was preserved, i.e., practically the whole Septuagint?

It may be said that all the ancient Fathers before St. Jerome and even after him received that version as inspired, as the Church's text. True, they based their conviction on a rather childish legend about the miraculous way the Septuagint was produced [1]. Hence modern scholars, rightly rejecting that legend, rejected also the conviction that the version was inspired which, according to them, was based on the legend. However, it could be that in criticizing the naïveté of the Fathers they may themselves have become guilty of another naïveté, namely, that of considering the Septuagint merely as a more or less successful translation. Now the latest works of contemporary exegesis allow us to see more and more clearly that it is in reality something quite different : a consciously free interpretation which appreciably modifies the sense of the Hebrew original by toning down certain archaic concepts and by introducing some new doctrines. This work of Hellenistic Judaism gathers in the attainments of a whole age in the history of the Chosen People and thus represents a new stage in the progress of Biblical revelation. Though not familiar with critical methods as technical as ours, the Fathers were perfectly aware of that progress; they regarded as providential the modifications made by the Greek in the Hebrew and they believed that the Holy Spirit had guided that transposition of the sacred text which he was preparing for the Church. This was a singularly profound perception which was not necessarily bound up with their belief in the legend of the Seventy Elders. It should rather give us grounds for reflection, because it still has significance. Already before them, the writers of the New Testament, without concern about the legend or learned comparisons between the Hebrew and the Greek texts, acted practically as if the Septuagint was for them God's inspired word. They quoted it as it was,

---

Translator's note. — [1 On the authority of the Septuagint, see Irenaeus, *Adv. Haereses* 3. 21. 1-3; ed. by F. SAGNARD O. P., in *Sources Chrétiennes* (Paris-Lyon 1952) with the editor's notes and references, pp. 351-355, and p. 432 f.].

and they built their arguments of faith upon its text, even where it departed from the Hebrew [1].

In short, they treated it not as an acceptable translation, but as the very text of God's word. These facts are suggestive, and in order to do them justice, it was proposed lately to come back to the belief in the inspiration of the Septuagint [2].

The Church certainly professed that belief in the first centuries. She never afterwards rejected it explicitly, though she left it dormant; ultimately it belongs to her alone to decide on it. While awaiting her decision and to prepare it, exegetes and theologians may at least show that that belief is both fitting and possible. That it is fitting, we have just seen. That it is possible, we believe that we have made it such by the arguments presented above on the nature of inspiration. It was difficult to admit that the Seventy Elders of the legend had enjoyed a " revelation " which dictated the words of their translation; but it is easy to conceive that the many anonymous writers who cooperated in the production of the Septuagint could have been moved by the Holy Spirit to mark this new stage in the progress of the Sacred Text [3].

5. — DOES INSPIRATION EXTEND
TO ALL THE SENSES OF SCRIPTURE?

Scripture has several " senses ". Though God deigns in a way to come down to the level of the man whom He uses, and for whose thoughts, words, and resulting book He accepts responsibility, yet God is infinitely above the instrument He

---

[1] We are quite aware that the " Septuagint " is not a perfectly defined entity and that its origin is still obscure. This Greek version may have circulated in different forms. But such critical incertitude is of no interest for our theological inquiry, which envisages the Septuagint as a whole, as the text received *ex hypothesi* by the Church.

[2] P. BENOIT, " La Septante est-elle inspirée? ", in *Vom Wort des Lebens* (Festschrift Max Meinertz) (Münster i. W., 1951), pp. 41-49; P. AUVRAY, " Comment se pose le problème de l'inspiration des Septante? ", *RB* (1952), pp. 321-335. [*Transl.'s note.* Cf. above p. — n. —. On BENOIT's article, see *Theol. Revue* (1952), p. 146. The reviewer, Jos. REUSS, thinks that this distinguished essay calls attention to a problem that deserves careful examination. Father MACKENZIE (above p. 31) examines the point briefly, *op. cit.*, p. 6-7 : " So far the arguments are to me unconvincing ". Cf. also the reference to Gelin in *CBQ* XX (1958), p. 88].

Translator's note. — [3 The Septuagint was the first Bible of the Church for several centuries, even in the West. When in the West a Latin text was used, it was translated from the Septuagint. St. Jerome's translation from

is using, and the transcendence of His sovereign action must necessarily make itself felt in the work which is produced. While God causes the writer to think and write words, the primary sense of which is what the writer conceived and willed, He Himself, the Author of the whole Scripture, could prepare for those words applications and wider senses of which the writer was not conscious. He could lead him to choose such or such terms or to relate such or such events to which He intended to give new meanings under the pen of other authors at later stages of His revelation. The chapter on Hermeneutics will examine more precisely the nature of these different senses. They are mentioned here only to state to what extent, analogically, they may or may not claim the authority of inspiration.

Indeed it would be a shortsighted view if one were to acknowledge as inspired only the primary, literal sense, for this would be a restriction of the effect of inspiration to the conscious psychology of the human author, when in fact it extends to the text itself which leaves his hand. This is, in short, the text received by the Church, the one which takes its place within the framework of the Sacred Book, where it brings to the other books the contribution of its own message and receives from them in turn its full significance. In the light of the other texts which take up its words again in connexion with higher realities, some of its terms come to bear a *sensus plenior*. Confronted with the Messianic fulfilments, some persons or events of which it speaks take on the value of " types, " giving a " typical " sense to the texts which mention such persons or events. Such senses are truly " Scriptural, " because they are deposited objectively in Scripture, which, in explaining itself, enables us to see them

---

the Hebrew displaced it later, but only gradually. In the East, the Septuagint continued to be used — or translations from it were used — excepting, e. g., the Syriac, which was (for the most part) translated from Hebrew. This shows that the Septuagint never ceased to be recognized. Indeed the Fathers of Trent asked the Holy See to publish an edition of the Septuagint. This was done by Sixtus V *(Vetus Testamentum juxta Septuaginta ex auctoritate Sixti V. Pont. Max. editum :* [Rome 1587] — the so-called *Vaticana Sixtina*. An " Apostolic Letter " (1585) pointed out the value of the Septuagint to the Church *(ap.* BALESTRI, *Biblicae Introd. Generalis Elementa* [Vatican Press, 1932] p. 145.). All this shows that the Septuagint continued to be looked upon with respect, but it does not give the precise answer to the problem envisaged by Fr. BENOIT.]

in germ in older texts by the light of more recent texts. They must be called " inspired ", for indeed it is through the charism of inspiration that God prepared them beforehand in the text. The fact that the human author did not perceive them does not matter at all, for God used him, as an instrument in the strict sense of the term (see above p. 20, n. 1), to compose the book in which He deposited those hidden treasures. Only to the " consequent " and " accommodated " senses can we deny the right to be considered " Scriptural " and " inspired, " because they do not result from Scripture alone, but they are added to it through human reasoning. However, the secondary senses — *plenior* and typical — are not inspired in the same way as the primary sense; they are, as it were, extensions of it, exhibiting the benefit of a subtler light which may have penetrated the mind of the human author without enlightening him. In this connection also the diffusion of the charism of inspiration may be said to have taken place analogically. [1]

Translator's note. — [1 On the senses of Scripture, see *Guide to the Bible* I, p. 749 ff. and the Bibliography, pp. 779-780. See also BALESTRI (cited above, pp. 34-35, n. 3) pp. 457-534; P. GRELOT, in : ROBERT-FEUILLET, *Introduction à la Bible* I (Tournai, 1957), pp. 168-212, especially p. 202 ff., on the Scriptural senses, viz. literal, *plenior*, typological, consequent, accommodated. It will be seen that Catholic Scholars do not agree among themselves. Thus the " *consequent* " sense in which P. BENOIT refuses to see a scriptural sense proper is regarded by J. COPPENS as a true scriptural sense, and GRELOT inclines strongly to include the " consequent " sense in the *sensus plenior* (p. 209). Looking over the discussions of the senses of Scripture in recent times, we get the impression of some confusion. Further discussion no doubt will help to clarify the point of controversy and bring about a better understanding of agreements and differences. On the problem of the *sensus plenior*, much discussed in these last few years, the reader may see the following studies (besides numerous articles which will be found registered in theological and scriptural reviews, especially *CBQ*, which has been giving excellent bibliographies these last years) : J. COPPENS, in *NRTh.* (1932), pp. 674-693; (1948), pp. 794-810; (1949), pp. 3-38, pp. 337-366, pp. 477-496; J. GRIBOMONT, " Le lien des deux Testaments selon la théologie de S. Thomas : Notes sur le sens spirituel et implicite des Saintes Écritures ", in : *ETh. L* (1946), pp. 70-89; L. CERFAUX, J. COPPENS, J. GRIBOMONT, *Problèmes et méthode d'exégèse théologique* (*Anal. Lovan. Bibl. et Orient.*, Series II, (1950, on this, cf. WEISENGOFF in *CBQ* XIV [1952], 83-85); J. COPPENS, " Nouvelles réflexions sur les divers des Saintes Ecritures ", *NRTh* (1952), pp. 3-20; *id.*, *Les harmonies des deux Testaments* (new enlarged ed., Tournai-Paris 1949), especially pp. 31-58 on the plenary sense. See the account of this study by : DUBARLE, O. P., in : *Bibliotheca Orientalis* [1950], pp. 113-114, and DE VAUX, O. P., in *RB* [1950], pp. 280-281); R. C. FULLER, " The Interpretation of Holy Scripture ", 38-39, in *A Catholic Commentary on Holy Scripture* (London, 1953). There is a fine and careful study of the plenary sense by R. E. BROWN, ss, *The Sensus Plenior of Sacred Scripture* (Baltimore [1955]. See, among others, on this work,

The tenor of this statement should be carefully noted. It is not claimed that the charism of inspiration extends to the mind of the reader. He may need an assistance of the Holy Spirit to understand Scripture properly, but this does not mean that for that reason he is " inspired. "

What we wish to say here is that, when God inspired a book, He did not destine it for all readers of all ages equally and univocally. Some are disposed to think so, and, on opening the Bible, persuade themselves that God speaks to them just as He spoke to the contemporaries of Moses, of the prophet, or the chronicler. This may be a pious view, but it is not entirely right. It misjudges again the human circumstances of God's word and goes straight to its absolute origin, forgetting the limitations of time and place to which God's word condescended to subject itself. By choosing to express itself through such a man of such a people and such a time, God spoke first to that man's contemporaries, to the people whom that man knew and for whom he was writing. True, He did not consent to be restricted by the limited horizon of His instrument; He who was preparing universal and eternal salvation was speaking also beforehand to the men of future generations. But He spoke to them through those of that present generation, as well as to those who would succeed them in the progressive and continuous advance of the religious history of the world. Here also there is, in the historical transmission of God's word, an analogical diffusion which it is important to take into account. The best way of understanding it satisfactorily is not to overlook all the links between us and the concrete time and environment in which it was manifested, but rather to recapture it in its source, just as it was first made known. Thus we shall be able to distinguish in it what was contingent, as it no longer has any significance for us except as a matter of information and memory, and its enduring elements which, enriched by all the development of the later Revelation, have become the great stream that waters our faith.

F. L. MORIARTY S. J., *Theol. Studies* [1955] p. 398 f.). Earlier material connected with this subject will be found also in the following : TAYMANS, S. J., in *NRTh* (1952), pp. 234-239; VACCARI, S. J., La " theoria " nella scuola esegetica di Antiochia ", *Bibl.* (1920), pp. 1-36; LEVIE, S. J., " La crise de l'Ancien Testament ", *NRTh* (1929), pp. 818-839; *id.*, Exégèse catholique et exégèse protestante ", *ibid.* (1949), pp. 1009-1029].

IV. — GOD THE AUTHOR OF SCRIPTURE.
THE CRITERION OF INSPIRATION.

We have postponed purposely the study of these two subjects to the end of our theological inquiry into the nature of inspiration. For it seems to us that, to be treated properly, they must profit from that whole investigation and discussion.

Some prefer, it is true, to start from the traditional notion of God " the Author of Scripture " and to conclude therefrom the manner in which He inspired His human instrument. Their method, however, is less reliable, for the notion of " author " which seems so clear to them cannot in fact be applied so simply in the singular and unique case of God. God cannot be an author after the manner of a man. Attributing to Him " thoughts " which He communicates to a secretary, leaving it to the latter to find a literary form of expression, is an anthropomorphism which can only mislead research. Instead of adopting such a weak starting point, it is better to face resolutely the absolutely original case of a transcendent being who makes a mind think, by an impulse given from within, in a way which compels it without violating in any manner its free mode of action but rather raises it in the process. This is what God does, what He alone can do. In short, this is a theological problem which is a part of the more general problem of the way in which God moves His creature. It is in this way that we have wished to approach the problem and it is enough for us that at the conclusion of our inquiry it seems justified to call God the Author of the Book [1].

God is the Author because the book was really produced under His total influence and contains only the thoughts

---

[1] This presentation of the argument finds support in the formulas used by the Magisterium of the Church where the notion of God " the Author of Scripture " appears as the *consequence* from the fact of Inspiration. Thus the Council of Florence (1441) states : [The Church] professes that the one same God is the author of the Old and New Testament — because the Saints of both Testaments spoke under the inspiration of the same Holy Spirit ". (*Ench. B.* 47 [Muñoz IGLESIAS, p. 173 f.]). The Vatican Council declares : " Those [books] the Church holds as sacred and canonical — because, having been written under the inspiration of the Holy Spirit, they have God as their author. " (*Ench. B.* 77 [Muñoz IGLESIAS, p. 194]). The *Encyclical Providentissimus*, after defining the action of the influx of inspiration, concludes : " Otherwise, He (the Holy Spirit) would not be the Author of the entire Sacred Scripture ". (*Ench. B.* 125; [M. IGLESIAS, p. 235; *Rome and the Study of Scripture* [St. Meinrad, Ind., 1953], p. 24]).

and the words which He wanted to be there; but He is the author in a peculiar sense, proper to His unique case, which can be true of no other human book. In short, the notion of author can be applied to God only in an "analogical" and "eminent" way, as is the case with all human notions which theology transfers to Him. As God is the author of Scripture, He alone finally knows what book He has caused to be written. This is a strictly supernatural fact which He alone can make known by revealing it, and this brings us to the criterion of inspiration. This criterion can only be the word of the Church, which proposes that divine revelation to the faith of her children.

We need not dwell on false or insufficient criteria which have been proposed at times. The internal taste of the reader, advocated by some Protestants, is clearly too subjective and liable to fail; the affirmation of the inspired man himself can only result in a vicious circle, not to mention the fact that often, most often perhaps, the inspired man was not conscious of the charism that guided him.

Another criterion has been advanced, which seems to be more objective : that of the mission of the inspired man, "a prophet" or an "apostle." But this also soon turns out to be defective. First, it does not escape the danger of the vicious circle, for indeed how can the prophet be recognized otherwise than by his own word, and how can he be distinguished with certainty from a false prophet? Further, it is not homogeneous in relation to the fact which it claims to prove, for "prophetic" or "apostolic" inspiration is one thing, and "Scriptural" inspiration is another; many of the Biblical books were written neither by a prophet nor by an apostle. Lastly and chiefly, it is hardly in harmony with the actual historical formation of the Sacred Books. We sketched above the complexity of that formation (III, 3) and it was most appropriate to discuss it before taking up the present problem. If any one believes that he can ascribe each of the sacred books to some definite personage, there can he question of seeking the guarantee of his divine charism in the qualifications of that personage; but if one gives up the idea of such an over-simple solution, such a criterion vanishes. Did each one of the many anonymous collaborators in the Old or

New Testament enjoy an official mandate from the Synagogue or from the Church?

In short, only one criterion is valid : the affirmation of the Church, which maintains that it has received that Writing from the hand of God and that it finds in it its rule of faith. This is an affirmation of the supernatural and revealed order, alone homogeneous to the supernatural fact of inspiration, and which for that reason is alone capable of supporting it efficaciously. This affirmation is not proposed by the Church as a conclusion of historical science, which it could submit to the judgment of the faithful, but as a truth of faith which it asks them to believe. Indeed the Church has been able to derive help from historical arguments to support its certitude. If we study the inquiries made of old by the Fathers and in various episcopal sees to determine definitely the proper limits of its Canon, we see that it had recourse largely to the criterion of Apostolicity; but this historical criterion could not of itself establish its decision of supernatural faith, and it was not decisive. In any event, this criterion could not be used in the case of the Old Testament. What the Church declares to be inspired, is not this or that author, but the text itself as she considers that she has received it from the beginning. And she makes this declaration by virtue of her tradition and of the authority she has from God. This is what is decisive for the faith of her children. They may themselves examine the historical origin of the sacred books and discuss critically the genuineness of some of them [1]. But in order to know if such a text or such a form of the text belongs to inspired Scripture, they can only rely submissively upon the sovereign judgment of the Church.

V. — INERRANCY.

God can neither deceive nor be deceived. His word is always truthful. If, then, He moves a man to write in His name, He cannot allow him to teach error. The charism of inspiration

---

[1] The problem of the authenticity [or genuineness] of a sacred book therefore is quite distinct from that of its canonicity. This does not mean that it becomes indifferent and may be easily solved negatively. The historical guarantee of a Gospel, e.g., depends largely on its Apostolic origin, immediate or mediate ; and, the belief that New Testament revelation came to an end with the Apostolic generation makes it difficult to include in the Canon a book which would not have some connection with the one or other of the Apostles.

necessarily accompanies the privilege of inerrancy. This is a dogma of faith which the Church has always professed [1].

Nevertheless inerrancy is not the purpose nor the sole consequence of inspiration. It would be so if God had caused the sacred books to be written only to teach truth, which is not the case. To think this would be to confuse the role of the " prophet " proper, whose mission indeed is the transmission of a " revealed " message, and that of the sacred writer or " hagiographer ", who undertakes to write a book. We noted above how greatly this latter task differs from the former and how its purpose is much more complex. An author does not necessarily write to " teach " the mind of his reader; he may rather wish to reach his heart, to rouse him, to comfort him, to charm him; and even when he wishes to convey knowledge to his intelligence, he can use varied means to present his teaching in an accessible and pleasant form. The sacred writers did not proceed otherwise, as the least familiarity with the Bible will easily convince the reader [2]. The divine charism which guided them has endowed their work with perfections which answer these varied ends, holiness, beauty, charm, persuasive force, among which truth certainly holds a choice place, but not a unique one, nor even is it always present. He could not allow the presence of a formal erroneous teaching, but neither did He bring it about that the formal teaching of some truth should always be included. Inerrancy is guaranteed by inspiration when truth is at stake, but inerrancy is not always involved, because truth is not always at stake.

---

[1] The statements of the Magisterium always connect closely inerrancy and inspiration, which shows clearly the strict correlation which exists between these two notions. Encycl. *Providentissimus :* " So far it is from being possible that any error can coexist with inspiration, that inspiration not only is essentially incompatible with error, but excludes and rejects it as absolutely and necessarily as it is impossible that God Himself, the Supreme Truth, can utter that which is not true ". (*Ench. B.*, 124; [Muñoz IGLESIAS, p. 235; *Rome and the St. of Script.*, p. 24]). Encycl. *Spiritus Paraclitus :* " Jerome teaches that immunity and freedom from all error and falsehood is necessarily bound up with the divine inspiration of the Sacred Books and their supreme authority ". (*Ench. B.*, 450; [M. IGLESIAS, p. 411, ff.]) : Decree of the Bibl. Commission on the Parousia : " Keeping before one's eyes... the Catholic dogma regarding the inspiration and inerrancy of the Scriptures ". (*Ench. B.*, 420; [Muñoz IGLESIAS, p. 389; *Guide to the Bible* I, p. 770]).

[2] Cf. 2 Tim. 3 : 16-17 : " All Scripture is inspired by God and useful for teaching, for reproving, for correcting, for instructing in justice, that the man of God may be perfect, equipped for every good work. " This text suggests many different practical ends which vary and accompany " teaching. "

These considerations may seem to be matters of ordinary common sense. But it is because they were neglected that discussions ended in impasses. The whole Bible had come to be regarded as a collection of " revelations; " and from the moment that the advances of modern science seemed to make questionable the truth which one was wont to find in everyone of its thoughts, confusion ensued. Some gave up the whole idea of inerrancy. As was done before in the case of inspiration, others had recourse to expedients which meant sacrificing the parts that were considered the most compromised in order to save the rest. Thus arose the systems of " implicit quotations " or of " apparent history ", and even the restriction of inerrancy to matters of faith and morals [1].

These expedients actually rested on correct principles. What was wrong was that these principles were not brought out with sufficient clarity, and hence could be misapplied with dangerous consequences. Hence the Church had to warn against their rash application.

We must therefore come back to these principles themselves to find in them the key to the necessary distinctions. While doing so, we shall evaluate in the light of these principles the various proposed solutions. In short, the problem is to see clearly the limitations and qualifications which the teaching of truth may admit; or, to take up again the psychological analysis begun above, the question is to analyze the qualifications which may be imposed on the speculative judgment of the writer by the actual purpose he is pursuing in the light of his practical judgment. We shall examine the matter under three main headings.

1. The first concerns the *formal object* of the judgment, i.e., stated more simply, the manner in which the author envisages the matter of which he is speaking. None of us deals with everything as a whole, according to its very essence; usually we choose in it the special aspect which alone is of interest to us and we ignore the rest. The structure of the universe, for instance, the nature and the paths of the heavenly

---

Translator's note. — [1 For details about these points, see LEMONNYER, " Apparences historiques ", in *DVB, Suppl.* I, 588-595; and " Citations Implicites ", *ibid.* II, 51-55. For the texts of the Biblical Commission bearing on the questions, see *Ench. B.* 160-161; Muñoz IGLESIAS, pp. 264-266].

bodies, are not envisaged in the same way by the scientist who is inquiring into their mechanical laws, by the poet who appreciates their beauty, by the religious thinker who sees in them a striking manifestation of the Creator's power. The poet and the religious thinker are not mistaken and do not lead into error when they speak of such matters from their point of view, without troubling their heads about the laws of the scientist, or even when they follow the mistaken views of ordinary people; for their " truth " keeps solely and deliberately to their own ground, namely, that of poetry or of religious contemplation. This example, chosen designedly, finds an easy application in the Bible. The sacred writers did not speak of the structure of the universe with scientific accuracy, for the essentially religious purpose assigned to them by the Holy Spirit did not in any way include the teaching of such profane truth [1]. They could speak of these things according to the views held in their days; they themselves shared such views but they did not make them the object of their teaching, and thus they do not lead us astray. For — and therein lies precisely their privilege of inerrancy — under inspiration they touched on such natural phenomena only in order to offer thereby a religious teaching which itself was true.

In his Encyclical *Providentissimus* (*Ench. B.* 121), Leo XIII had referred in this connexion to a language based on " what seems apparent to the senses ", and suggested that that criterion should be applied to other forms of profane knowledge, such as history especially (*Ench. B.* 123; [M. Iglesias, p. 234; *Rome and the St. of Script.*, p. 23]). Some concluded therefrom that the sacred writers only wrote according to " apparent history ", following people's inaccurate reports, without concerning themselves about the reality of the facts they were relating. In the Encyclical *Spiritus Paraclitus* (*Ench. B.* 455-450; [M. Iglesias, pp. 417-420]), Benedict XV sharply disapproved of such an interpretation of the mind of his predecessor, and it is easy to understand the opportuneness of his warning. History is

---

[1] The Encycl. *Providentissimus* (*Ench. B.* 121, [Muñoz IGLESIAS, p. 232; *Rome and the St. of Script.*, p. 22) makes its own the following statement of St. Augustine : " The Spirit of God... did not intend to teach men these things, that is to say, the essential nature of the visible universe, things in no way profitable to salvation. "

connected with the very nature of the Biblical message far more closely than are the physical sciences; the Biblical message is essentially historical. While we separate outright divine revelation and the scientific knowledge of the universe, we may not regard revelation as unconnected with and indifferent to history, in which, on the contrary, it traces the development of God's plan of salvation.

Yet this repudiation of a method generalized in too material a manner does not forbid us to apply to the realm of history the principle which is being examined here. For it is one thing to withdraw historical facts altogether from Biblical teaching, and another to recognize that they concern the sacred writer and are the object of his teaching only from a certain point of view, as bearers of a higher truth. Just as the scientific fact, the historical fact may be looked at in many different ways. Only the professional historian, especially such as our modern age has produced, tries to find the fact in its objective reality, known as fully and as accurately as possible. The poet, the man of letters, and novelist will use the fact differently and keep of it only what matters to their purpose. The religious historian especially, such as we find him in the Bible, is concerned with knowing and relating the fact only to the extent that it belongs to the spiritual content which alone is of value to him. The Holy Spirit which guides him will bring him to speak of the fact only to that end and He will guarantee its truth only from that particular point of view which alone is the object of its teaching. It would be going against God's intention if Scripture were taken as a work of scientific history and if one were to seek in it for the truth peculiar to such a genre. The charism of inspiration shed its light upon the historical facts only from the angle which mattered to the purpose of the Sacred Book, and it could very well leave all the rest in the background, in a state of imperfect, even inaccurate, knowledge.

2. The judgement is qualified not only by the formal aspect which it considers in its object but also by the *degree of affirmation* it adopts. Here again many different shades are possible : there is the definite affirmation, there is also the statement of a probability, or of a possibility, even of a mere conjecture or of a doubt. According to these different shades of affirmation,

one commits oneself more or less; one may even not commit
oneself at all, when one reports an opinion for which one accepts
no responsibility. Now these various shades of affirmation occur
in the thought of the sacred writer as in any other writer,
and the Holy Spirit who makes him think commits Himself
only within the limitations of greater or lesser certitude with
which He wishes to guarantee the statement. This is definitely
stated in a decree of the Biblical Commission : " All that the
sacred writer asserts, enunciates, suggests must be held to be
asserted, enunciated, suggested by the Holy Spirit " (June 18,
1915, on the Parousia. *Ench. B* 420; [Muñoz Iglesias, p. 389;
Guide to the Bible I, p. 770]). Any one can see that an " enun-
ciation " is less than an " assertion, " and that a " suggestion "
means a lesser degree of affirmation. Hence it is supremely
important to appreciate in each case to what extent the sacred
writer, and God through him, commits himself. If one were
to take each one of his statements, consisting of subject, verb
and predicate, as an absolute affirmation, this would be
a delusion and an injustice. One speaks the truth or is mistaken
only to the precise extent that one decides to express one's
mind.

This principle finds a privileged application in the case
of quotations. An author may reproduce the view of another
without adopting it as his own or in accepting it only with
more or less clearly stated reservation. This is true even
when he does not say explicity that he is quoting another man's
thought, but relates it without warning, as the ancients were
used to do. It is this contingency that the system of " implicit
quotations " has thrown into relief; in the case of a manifest
error in the Sacred Book, it proposes to see in it an opinion
which the writer reproduces without endorsing it. The system
is quite correct in principle, but requires a delicate touch in
handling it. It is valid if it can be shown that the author is
quoting without approving. This point is just what is difficult
to establish and, in the absence of proof, there is a risk of trans-
forming a correct distinction into a handy, but dangerous
device, dangerous because lacking all objective basis. This
the Church noted quite rightly in a decision of the Biblical
Commission (Feb. 13, 1905, *Ench. B.* 160; [Muñoz Iglesias,
p. 254; *Guide to the Bible* I, p. 755]); it recalls the conditions

set forth above, and approves the principle of this solution but warns against its misuse.

3. A third element is also required in order that the writer's judgment may be regarded as containing or not containing a teaching of truth, namely, its *proposal to the assent of the reader.* This may look self-evident, and yet many useful distinctions may still be suggested under this head. It must not be thought, indeed, that everything that an author writes, even by way of affirmation, constitutes by that very fact a truth about which he means to be believed : not all of his thoughts belong in the same way to the purpose of his work. Some are close to his heart and represent the essential element of his teaching : he writes in order to teach them. Others are of less significance in his eyes. In his own mind he may perhaps be quite convinced of their truth, but they do not matter directly to that work and he introduces them only as a means of conveying his central thought. On secondary points he will not insist on being accepted so long as the major teachings which he means to give are accepted.

This distinction between the private person of a writer and his public personality as an " author " is of peculiar importance in the case of the sacred writer. It is only in the latter capacity that he is " inspired, " not in the former. The charism of inspiration does not enlighten all his thought and does not correct all errors to the point of conferring omniscience; it enlightens him to make him write this or that book, intended for this or that actual purpose, and guarantees his knowledge only to the extent that this matters directly to his purpose. Hence he will continue to entertain on many points the erroneous notions of his natural knowledge, and it may well be, it will even happen necessarily, that such errors will show through in many a passage of his book; yet they will not damage his teaching of truth because such errors do not belong to his formal teaching, but constitute its material accompaniment about which he does not commit himself as an author and about which God likewise does not pledge his authority. There may be in the Sacred Book many true affirmations which do not fall under the privilege of inerrancy because they are not taught. They are inspired because they play their part in the work as a whole which God causes to be written; but they are not inerrant, because that part is subordinate and is not necessarily bound up with the essential message which is the proper object of the teaching of the book. It would be useless to deny that the sacred writer affirms that the sun turns around the earth, or that Baltasar " son of Nabuchodonosor " was defeated by " Darius the Mede " (Dan. 5 : 2; 6 : 1), and it would be just as naïve to claim that he was not convinced of these two points. He certainly did believe them as he presents them, and accordingly he affirms them. But he does not teach them as an inspired writer, because they are not of importance to the purpose for which he is writing and about which only he commits the truth of God [1].

But does not this explanation really amount to the same thing as the theory of inerrancy restricted to matters of faith and morals condemned by the Church? (Encyc. *Spiritus Paraclitus; Ench. B.* 454; [Muñoz Iglesias, p. 415 f.]). Not at all! For such a restriction is wrong in advocating a material criterion and deciding a priori that God could " teach " only religious truths. Such a decision cannot be justified rightly and is also contradicted by the facts. God could teach any kind of truth, historical or even physical, if it mattered directly to the object of his revelation, and the Bible shows us that He has done so. The creation of the world and the Exodus are truths of a kind which in themselves do not belong to faith or morals, but which, nevertheless, the Bible teaches formally because they concern essentially the history of salvation. Again, to a too material solution, and one of dangerous application, we must prefer the principle which inspires it and which is correct. We cannot decree a priori what God should teach, but we can and must discern carefully when

---

Translator's note. — [1 Regarding the complicated problems of the names and chronology in Daniel, it will suffice to refer to the commentaries : — e.g., Fr. De Menasce's edition in the *Bible de Jérusalem*, p. 17 f. Baltasar, whose name appears in Babylonian records, is the son of Nabonidus, not of Nabuchodonosor. No Mede named Darius is known from historical sources. According to a Dead Sea Scroll fragment, reproducing a prayer of Nabonidus, it was Nabonidus, not Nabuchodonosor (cf. Dan. 4) who was sick and far from men for seven years. See D. N. FREEDMAN in BASOR 145 [Feb. 1957], p. 31 f.; for a fuller presentation, Fr. J. T. Milik's article, " Prière de Nabonide " *RB* (1956), pp. 405-411, and 415; cp. also M. J. GRUENTHANER, " The Last King of Babylon ", *CBQ* (1949), pp. 406-427].

He teaches, for then only does He pledge His truth. God's teaching cannot be limited to objectively religious and supernatural truths, for it can as well concern natural and profane truths. But it envisages the latter only because of their religious and supernatural significance, and it is only for that reason that they enjoy inerrancy.

Another method has been advocated, which has been regarded with greater favor by the Church and was even directly recommended by the Encyclical *Divino Afflante Spiritu* (*Ench. B.* 558-560; [Muñoz Iglesias, pp. 545-548; NCWC ed., pp. 18-20]), namely that of " Literary Genres " [cf. Chapter VI below]. In contrast to the systems mentioned above, which too often looked like expedients, this has in its favor the fact that it considers in their ensemble and applies with discrimination all the formal principles we have just stated. For indeed a " literary genre " is nothing else but a certain form of expression which an author chooses deliberately to present his thought and by which he indicates by the very form of his work how he wishes to be understood. Whether he chooses to speak in verse or in prose, in a literal or figurative form of expression, in the form of a scientific account, or in the form of a polemic discussion or of an apologetic pleading, etc., in each case he uses the procedures proper to the " genre " adopted by him and thus enables the reader to understand correctly his real intention. Indeed, according to each case, he considers this or that aspect of the things of which he is speaking, he gives to his affirmations various shades of positiveness, qualifies the manner in which he presents his thought to his reader, in a word he brings into play the several methods analyzed above by enabling the reader to recognize them by means of the literary form he has adopted. In short, the method of " literary genres " is only the scientific and objective application of the principles which we have recognized as alone valid, and this is what gives it its value.

This is also what determines the proper use which is to be made of the method. The distinctions we have insisted upon will be legitimate only if they rest on objective criteria. The formal object of a writer, the shades of his affirmation, his intention to teach, must not be settled a priori to get around some difficulties, but must be recognized from the observation of actual evidence supplied by the author himself. This means that his " literary genre " cannot be settled by abstract considerations : it must represent something that can be controlled. For this reason the Encyclical urges a searching study of the literary genres used in the Ancient Orient. The sacred writers used the styles of composition current in their time and surroundings, and by making ourselves familiar with those forms of writing we shall be entitled to draw conclusions regarding their intentions [1].

May we believe that they availed themselves of all the genres current among their contemporaries? Did they exclude some as " unworthy " of God? Such a question cannot be settled a priori, but only after an actual observation of the Bible. Now, from such an observation it appears that God did go very far in His gracious condescension to speak in " the language of men. " Not only did He make abundant use of their figures, of their approximations, even of their paradoxes, but He even inspired genres which are rather careless of " scientific " truth as we understand it now. As regards history in particular — that field where we are so sensitive — He inspired in His interpreters religious or apologetic presentations which deliberately freed them from the necessity for material correctness in the detail of facts in order that they might concentrate on the great spiritual lessons which come out of them as a whole. One need only recall here the narratives of Exodus, Josue and Judges, or those of Kings and Chronicles. There are even sacred books, as Jonas, Tobias, Judith, Esther, where good commentators concur more and more in the view that they are not historical, but rather edifying narratives. These are facts imposed by a sound interpretation. It is important to familiarize ourselves with them and draw the necessary consequences, instead of denying them and attributing to God intentions which He did not have [2].

[1] Encycl. *Divino Afflante Spiritu :* " What those [forms of expression] were, the commentator cannot determine as it were in advance but only after a careful examination of the Ancient Oriental literatures. " (*Ench. B.* 558 [Muñoz IGLESIAS, p. 545; NCWC ed., 35]).

[2] While admitting the presence of approximations and material inaccuracies in the Bible, yet it must be recognized that all in all we have in it a book of history definitely superior in quality to many similar writings of the Ancient Orient. See Encycl. *Divino Afflante Spiritu :* " This same investigation [carried out during the past forty or fifty years; cf. the preceding sentence] has also clearly shown the special preeminence of the people of Israel among all the

In fact, we forget too often that God chose as His interpreters men of the Ancient Near East. This is a stumbling block to us moderns of the West. We judge their writings according to the norms of our historical science which we naively set up as a standard, and we wonder when we find them falling short of our ideal. We are the ones who are in the wrong.

Steeped as we are in Greco-Latin culture, we conceive " truth " as something abstract and speculative, which was not their concept. Certainly, truth in itself is one and absolute. Nevertheless, it is equally certain that our human mind attains truth in many different ways. The Semitic mind conceives it more concretely, more personally, as a truth of life. " To know " for the Semite means, not to grasp an abstract, " idea, " but to meet " a person "; it is not an operation of the intelligence divested as completely as possible of sensible attachments, but a movement of our whole being which involves the heart and the body as well as the mind. For him God is not an abstract Essence, a pure idea which can be reached at the end of an act of " contemplation. " He is Creator, Judge, a Father whom one approaches through love, by obedience to His will, by " walking with Him. " Underlying all this there are, as it were, two philosophies : on the one hand, an Essentialism proceding from a Dualism which dissociates mind from matter, the concept from its origin in sense perception; on the other hand, an Existentialism based on a Monism which grasps in vital unity the Creator and His creature, mind and matter, knowledge and love. We may debate the respective merits of these views; our Greek inheritance predisposes us unconsciously in favor of the former, but it is the latter that God chose when speaking to us through Semites. To receive His word properly, there is need of more than a moral conversion, there is need of a mental conversion [1].

If we look in the Bible for statements of speculative " truths, " a collection of " doctrines ", we approach it as Greco-Latins.

---

other ancient nations of the East in their mode of writing history well, both by reason of its antiquity and by reason of the faithful record of the events; and this may well be attributed to the charism of divine inspiration and to the peculiar religious purpose of biblical history. " (*Ench., B.*, 558-559; [Muñoz IGLESIAS, pp. 545-546; NCWC ed., 36]).

[1] Encycl. *Divino Afflante Spiritu :* " The interpreter must as it were go back wholly in mind to those remote centuries of the Orient. " (*Ench. B.* 558; [Muñoz IGLESIAS, p. 545; NCWC ed., 35]).

But it is as Semites that we should open that book to meet there God as He presents Himself to us : a God who acts, enters our history, speaks to our hearts, who indeed " reveals " Himself to our knowledge, but through a vital approach which demands in return a knowledge consisting of love, obedience, and total surrender. There is there a whole program which differs from our Occidental education; it is absolutely necessary for us to become thoroughly familiar with it if we wish to read the Sacred Book as it should be read; not to look in it for what it does not offer us and be scandalized, but rather to look in it for what it does offer us and to live by it.

Moreover, we are not only Westerners, but Moderns, who have gone through the crisis of Rationalism and remain imbued with its scientific positivism. In spite of ourselves, rational truth has come to take precedence with us over religious truth. Hence the itch for material accuracy, the mania for the detail of the event, so that we forget its significance as a sign, which alone counts in the end. " We strain out the gnat but swallow the camel " (Mt. 23 : 24). Such critical exigency is useful, but in its subordinate role; it must not be a shortsightedness which prevents us from seeing the horizon. " These things you ought to have done, while not leaving the others undone " (Mt. 23 : 23). The ancient sacred writers, who saw in everything the problem of God, reached better than we the essential truth of history, even if they did not keep so close to accuracy of the details. And the Fathers of the Church, Greek and Latin as they were, still had that religious sense which made them go straight to the substance, without becoming entangled in minor defects. It is that sense of faith that we must recover if we also wish to hear what the Bible wants to say to us. Then many false problems will disappear. We shall find in the Bible the full truth, because we shall look for it there solely where God has placed it.

May not these last considerations be regarded as a digression from our problem of inspiration? I do not think so. I think rather that these reflections reach the deepest roots of the question. Inspiration and inerrancy of Scripture, to be understood rightly, claim our entire mental effort. For this reason the foregoing essay has deliberately considered the problem from the standpoint of principles. It is said at times that stating

principles is easy, but that their application is difficult. This is
only partially correct. Certainly all has not been said when
it is understood, however clearly, how God spoke, and within
what limits He wished to confine His teaching of the truth.
There still remains to determine in that light the meaning
of each actual text, and this is a matter for an exegesis which
requires considerable tact. But it is just as certain that,
to be effective, that exegesis must be guided by a very clear
perception of the principles which underlie the composition
of the sacred book. Such a clear view of the principles is the
essential foundation of a sound exegesis — which will not
cause scandal by its errors — and also of a truly fruitful Biblical
theology.

APPENDIX I

BIBLICAL INSPIRATION IN PROTESTANTISM.

Though the Reformers rejected the traditional criteria of
inspiration, they kept the belief in inspiration. This was
quite natural since they raised the Bible to a place of absolute
supremacy as the sole norm of faith. Scripture is *fons* and *judex*
in all matters of faith and doctrine, *and exclusively so;* Scripture
is the queen *(regina)*, as God's word which cannot deceive.
Whatever expressions Luther may use, his fundamental
conviction remains that the Bible " is the Holy Ghost's own,
peculiar book, writing and word ". Calvin holds that " Scripture
is from God ", the " instrument of the Spirit ", " the word
is the means *(organum)* whereby the Lord grants to the faithful
the illumination of His Spirit ". (H. J. Kraus [see Bibliography],
pp. 4-8). Indeed, Luther and Calvin, the former especially,
express some " critical " views about the authorship of the
Pentateuch; and Karlstadt does so more definitely in his
De canonicis scripturis libellus (1520), but they do not mean
to question their fundamental thesis of the inspiration and
supreme authority of Scripture (H. J. Kraus, *op. cit.*, pp. 13-15;
25-27). The later orthodox theologians of the Reformation
even hardened the concept of inspiration. Thus, Johann Gerhard
(1582-1637), a leading authority much consulted in his day,
teaches that : " Divine inspiration is an action by which God

communicated to the intelligence of the writer not only the concepts of all the things to be written in conformity with the objects [= realities], but the very words and everything [else] by which those concepts were to be expressed, and He moved their will to the act of writing ". The human authors of the Bible are " God's *Handlanger* " [unskilled laborers, such as hodmen], " the hand of Christ ", " secretaries of the Holy Ghost ". (H. J. Kraus, p. 30). An even stronger statement by Johann Andreas Quenstedt (1517-1588), the " bookkeeper " of old Lutheran dogmatics (W. Koch, in *LTK* 8, 584) is quoted by H. H. Farmer (*The Interpreter's Bible*, I [New York and Nashville, 1952], p. 16). According to him, there is no room for any kind of error or mistake in any form whatsoever in the " *amanuenses* [secretaries] of the Holy Spirit ". In the question of the vowel points of the traditional Hebrew text, a matter to which the early Reformers were rather indifferent, the later theologians held that the vowel points were a genuine part of the sacred text. Else, according to Gerhard, it would mean that God had not handed Scripture through the prophets in its very wording, " since the words cannot be at all without the vowel points ". (H. J. Kraus, p. 31). However, such a rigid doctrine could not be maintained indefinitely. In time, critical notions — of which something appears in Karlstadt (mentioned above) — adopted by scholars under humanistic influence, were to shake the orthodox view to its foundation.

Catholic scholars were among the first to apply the new learning to Scriptural problems and other scholars —as we shall see — followed.

Among Catholics, the following may be mentioned. The Belgian Andreas Masius (Maes) 1515-1573, a distinguished Orientalist whom R. Simon described as one of the most learned and judicious interpreters of Scripture in these last centuries " (*Histoire Critique*, p. 31), in his *Josuae imperatoris historia illustrata atque explicata* " (Antwerp, 1574), an edition with commentary of the Hebrew-Greek text of Josue (cf. F. Stummer, *Die Bedeutung R. Simons für die Pentateuchkritik* [Münster i.W., 1912], p. 17 f.); the Spanish Jesuit, Benedict Pererius (Pereyra), 1535-1610, author of a commentary on Daniel (1587), and especially on Genesis (4 vols., Rome, 1591-1599), and the Belgian Jesuit, Jacques Bonfrère (1573-1642), with his commentary on the Pentateuch (Antwerp, 1631), a work closely studied by Protestant theologians (H. J. Kraus 41) — both Jesuits admitvarious additions and modifications in the Pentateuch; Bonfrère rejects the well worn expedient that Moses, being a prophet, could speak of things after his time —; the French Oratorian, Johannes Morinus (Jean Morin) 1591-1659 — a convert from Calvinism — who specialized in textual criticism, who attacks the value of the traditional Hebrew text and supports the authority of the Samaritan and Greek; the French critic Richard Simon (1638-1712), an Oratorian from 1662 to 1678, the "father of modern critical study of the Old Testament", of whose *Histoire critique de l'Ancien Testament* (denounced bitterly by his opponents), Johann Salomo Semler (see below) had a German translation published in 1776, so that the views of the French scholar became known in Germany (cf. H. J. Kraus, 59; F. Stummer, *op. cit.*); Jean Astruc (1684-1766), whose "conjectures" about the sources of Genesis (Brussels, 1753; in German, Frankfurt a. M, 1783) led to the problem of the sources of the Pentateuch, much beyond what had been foreseen by the author.

Among non-Catholics we may mention : the Dutch scholar, Hugo Grotius (de Groot) 1583-1645; the English Deists, such as Lord Herbert of Cherbury 1581-1648; Thomas Hobbes 1588-1679; the Jewish Dutch philosopher, Baruch de Spinoza (d'Espinosa) 1632-1677 (*Œuvres Complètes*, in Bibliothèque de la Pléiade, Paris, 1954, edited by Roland Caillois, Madeleine Francès, and Robert Misrahi), his views on Scripture, especially in the *Tractatus theologico-politicus* (1670), pp. 655-964, esp. chaps. I-XII). All these, in various ways and different degrees, contributed to undermine the traditional belief in inspiration; they denied or questioned the current theories of authorship and dates of the Biblical writings, often especially of the Pentateuch; they suggested difficulties against the integrity of the text, or against the orthodox Protestant view of verbal inspiration and the notion of inerrancy so intimately bound up with the doctrine of inspiration.

The conflict between the two tendencies — the ancient belief and the new learning — comes to a head in the XVIIIth century. Johann David Michaelis (1717-1791) tries to reconcile orthodoxy and criticism; Johann Salomo Semler (1725-1791) advocates

the new views which win the day. Michaelis placed his great
knowledge in the service of tradition but the result is an
uncertain equilibrium (H. J. Kraus, pp. 87-93). Semler, after
a painful struggle of conscience frees himself from all " dogmatic
traditions ", and rejects the views of the Reformers altogether.
R. Simon's influence seems to be paramount in that spiritual
revolution (cf. H. J. Kraus, pp. 96-97). Semler examines the
problem of the Canon (*Abhandlung von freier Untersuchung
der Canons*, 1771) as a question of purely profane historical
criticism, without paying any attention to inspiration : " Divine
is what makes us morally better ". (H. J. Kraus, p. 99). The
Old Testament Canon comes out as a collection of gross Jewish
prejudices, only a small portion of which has any value for
Christians. Thus there appears a tendency to loosen what
is kept of Christianity from connection with the Old Testament
— an attitude which was to gain considerable ground in the
XIXth and the XXth centuries, especially through the influence
of the radical views of Schleiermacher and Hegel in his earlier
period (cf. H. J. Kraus, pp. 175-179). Friedrich Delitzsch
(1850-1922) in his *Die grosse Täuschung* will deny to the Old
Testament any place in the Church (Kraus, pp. 274-283).
Adolf von Harnack (1851-1930), the leader of liberal Protestantism, influential teacher of so many candidates for the ministry,
whose idea of a personal God became progressively vague
(cf. *LTK* 4, 829), proposes in his work on Marcion (*Das Evangelium vom fremden Gott* (2nd ed., 1924) to reject the Old
Testament : it was a mistake to reject the Old Testament
in the IInd century; to keep it in the XVIth century was
a fate which the Reformation could not escape; but to keep
it in Protestantism since the XIXth century is the result of
a religious-ecclesiastical paralysis. (Cited in Kraus, p. 351).
However there continued to be notable scholars who ably
maintained the conservative view in the XIXth and XXth
centuries. Thus, Franz Delitzsch (1813-1890), Hermann L.
Strack (1848-1922), S. R. Driver (1845-1914), Eduard König
(1846-1936).

But, all in all, it was the radical view that prevailed more and
more. J. Wellhausen (1844-1918) carried on to its final form
the theory of the origin of the Pentateuch (fundamental in
biblical criticism) after the earlier work of E. Reuss (1804-1891),

K. H. Graf (1815-1869), and A. Kuenen (1828-1891). The
radical theory helped largely to ruin the belief in the inspiration
of the Bible. Wellhausen felt deeply the consequences which
his teaching had on his students. A letter of Wellhausen
(quoted by Kraus, p. 236 f.) to the Minister of Worship and
Education of Prussia (Apr. 5, 1882) reveals his state of mind :
" Your Excellency perhaps will recall that at Easter 1880
I presented a request to be transferred, if possible, to the Faculty
of Philosophy, and I tried to state my reasons for that request.
I became a theologian, because the scientific study of the Bible
interested me. It has gradually become clear to me that
a professor of theology has also the practical duty to prepare
the students for service in the Evangelical Church, and that
I do not come up to that practical duty; rather in spite of all
reserve on my part I make my hearers unfit for their task.
Since then, my professorship of theology has been a heavy
burden on my conscience ".

In fact, the question of inspiration which once played such
an important role is practically ignored in liberal Old Testament
scholarship, especially perhaps in Germany. It seems to be
regarded as a theological problem or, better perhaps, as
a question dealing with the " supernatural " which has little
appeal for men out of touch with the " supernatural ". If we
look at modern Protestant introductions, we shall find rather
full studies of the Canon, but nothing on inspiration, though
this should not of itself be construed as necessarily implying
a denial of inspiration. But in any case, it is easy to find
authors who definitely reject all idea of inspiration proper.
Thus Balzer, reviewing Niebergall's *Praktische Auslegung* in
Theologische Rundschau no. 8 [1908], p. 200) says : " What
interests us primarily is the way in which Niebergall explains
the effect on Scripture on the men of our day ". Niebergall,
he explains, " rejects naturally the former [view] "; " he does
not want any part of inspiration or any toned down idea of
[inspiration] ". The Bible is due to religious men who wanted
to influence others religiously. Hence from " the Bible, the
classic book of religion ", there go forth religious influences.
" Scripture is the word of God in the sense that it calls forth
in us thoughts of God which mean in our time the same as the
several layers [of writings it contains] meant in their time ".

Similar ideas are defended by L. Kessler, whose work is reviewed by Nikel in the *Theologische Revue* 9/10, 1907. Criticism has done away with the idea of inspiration as well as with that of revelation. However, the notion of inspiration is not to be given up altogether; it is to be understood as " the expression of the experience which the believing community (makes through Scripture) ". We may say that the reader will find the edification he is looking for.

We have treatments on inspiration in English in several works — commentaries of popular character — on the Bible. The most important is that by Herbert H. Farmer, " The Bible : Its Significance and Authority ", in the elaborate *Interpreter's Bible I* (New York and Nashville, 1952), pp. 3-31. He rejects the idea of " a completely inerrant record ". This could only have been produced by God suspending " the normal processes " of composition, by supposing the writers to be in God's hand, not as " cooperating persons ", but " passive instruments like a pen " (p. 16A). There has been some " divine guidance and inspiration " but " without impairing [the] full dignity " of the writers, and " without setting up supernatural infallibilities " among men. (Cf. pp. 16B; 26; 29). In fact there is no real " infallibility of the Scripture "; the Christian reader is to be " guided in the last resort by his own conviction of truth ". Hence, the right " to set to one side some of the biblical content " (cf. p. 25). The author tries indeed to set up some principles of discrimination (p. 26 ff.) to prevent excesses. A number of the cautions and explanations developed by him are of course perfectly acceptable, as can be seen by referring to Father Benoit's study on inspiration, but in his context they seem insufficient and unsatisfactory. Particularly unsatisfactory are the author's views of the relation between God and the writer. Had he been acquainted at firsthand with Catholic studies on inspiration, he might at least have understood that there can be cooperation between God and man without damage to the integrity and dignity of the human writer. But the fact is that the author, who does not mention a single Catholic scholar in his selected bibliography (p. 31), shows a surprising lack of understanding of the Catholic Church and of her real teaching (cf. p. 13-14). The reader will find our subject treated also in such one-volume commentaries as

Peake's Commentary on the Bible (London, 1920), by Principal
E. Griffith-Jones (pp. 1-17, " Meaning and Aim of the Bible ");
also in *A New Commentary on Holy Scripture Including the
Apocrypha* (New York, 1928), where Bishop Charles Gore writes
on " The Bible in the Church " (pp. 1-18); or in the *Abingdon
Bible Commentary* (Abingdon-Cokesbury Press, 1929), where
Wilbur F. Tillett examines briefly " The Divine Element in
the Bible " (pp. 26-31). In all these as, in H. H. Farmer, there
is the praiseworthy wish to maintain a certain religious authority
for the Bible, though with many differences in views. But there
is no inspiration in any traditional sense, nor any inerrancy
proper. To put it bluntly, there is a lack of logical coherence
in all these explanations; there is something subjective and
emotional, but no real theology of inspiration.

    Since about 1920 there has begun, especially in Germany,
a reaction against the negative criticism of the Old Testament.
There is a movement in favor of a recognition of the theological
value of the Old Testament. The unity of the Old and New
Testament is emphasized again, and and special attention is
paid to the Christological teaching of the Old Testament.
All this is done without rejecting or neglecting the proper
scientific study of the Bible. See, e.g., W. Eichrodt's *Theologie
des Alten Testaments* (1933); W. Vischer's, *Das Christuszeugnis
des Alten Testaments* (1936 f.); Edmond Jacob's, *Théologie de
l'Ancien Testament* (1954); Th. C. Vriezen's, *Hoofdlijnen der
Theologie van het Oude Testament* (2nd ed., 1954) — not to
mention many articles on the subject in journals. All this
means a return to more traditional views. It may help to
appreciate better the inspiration of the Bible, without which
the Bible is not the Bible, but a collection of religious writings
not essentially different from the Qoran and other similar
works.

                        BIBLIOGRAPHY.

    For fuller details on the history of the criticism of the Old Testament
see the excellent work of J. COPPENS, *The Old Testament and the Critics*
(Engl. translation by E. A. RYAN, S. J., and E. W. TRIBBE, S. J., Paterson,
N. J. 1942). See also especially the work referred to several times, Hans
Joachim KRAUS, *Geschichte der historisch-kritischen Erforschung des
Alten Testaments von der Reformation bis zur Gegenwart* (Neukirchen,

1956). Many references to works — especially in English — dealing with modern developments (unity of the Bible, authority of Scripture, etc.) will be found in Vriezen's HOOFDLIJNEN (see above), especially in the bibliographies to the five chapters of his Introduction (pp. 11-137). This work is available in English and German translations.

APPENDIX II.

INSPIRATION IN THE QORAN AND IN THE BIBLE.

by E. P. Arbez

The Qoran deals with a multitude of subjects : God in countless places, His incomparable greatness, His absolute power, His wisdom, omniscience, goodness, and justice; stories of prophets of old, as *Hūd* (26, 123 ff.), *Salih* (26, 141 ff.), *Shuʾayb* (11, 85 /84 ff.; 26, 176 ff.; 29, 35 /36); narratives about personages of the Old and New Testament, as, e.g., *Adam* (2, 28/30 ff.; 15, 26 ff.), *Abraham* (14, 38/35 ff.; 19, 42/41 ff.), *Moses and Pharaoh* (7, 101/103 ff.; 11, 99/96 ff.; 14, 5 ff.; 18, 59/60 ff.; 23, 47/45 ff.; 28, 2/3 ff.), *Joseph* (ch. 12), *Zacharias* (19, 2/3 ff.), *Mary and Jesus* (3, 30/33 ff. 37/42 ff.; 5, 109/110 ff.; 19, 16 ff.); stories like that of *the Seven Sleepers* (18, 9/8 ff.); dietary laws (6, 144/143 ff.); regulations about the treatment of orphans (4, 2 ff.); inheritance (4, 7/8 ff.); marriage (4, 23/19 ff.; 33, 48/49 ff.); denunciations of unbelievers, with numerous references to the Jews and their attitude to the Prophet, etc.. Throughout, God (Allah) is the speaker, as is clear from the many texts marked by the use of the first person plural *(We)*, or else God speaks through the intermediary — Spirit or angel (Gabriel) — of His revelation. Only three places are an exception, viz., the opening sura *(al-Fātiha)*, ch. 1, and the two concluding suras, chs. 113 and 114, known as the *Muʾawwidatāni* (from : *ʾawwada*, to invoke God's protection) : the two invocations for protection. These three suras differ in tone from the rest of the Qoran. Sura 1 is a prayer of Mohammed — the Our Father of Islam — possibly a liturgical addition. Suras 113 and 114 are rather " charms ", formulas to avert evil. These three texts were absent from the codex of *Ibn Masʾūd* (33 Hegira = 653/54 A. D.) and they may be additions, but nevertheless are regarded as genuine compositions of the Prophet. (A. Jeffery, *Materials for the History of the Text of the Qur'an* [Leiden, 1937], p. 21); F. M. Pareja, *Islamologia* [Rome, 1951], p. 381 f.; R. Blachère, *Introduction au Coran* [Paris, 1947], p. 188-190; R. Bell, *Introduction to the Qur'an* (Edinburgh, 1953), p. 52; M. A. Draz [Prof. at the Cairo Univ., al-Azhar], *Initiation au Koran* [Paris, 1951], p. 22 and 32).

Everywhere else, outside the three passages just mentioned, God is addressing the Prophet, that is to say, we find in the Qoran revelations of God, which the Prophet merely receives without taking any active personal part in it, whenever God chooses to reveal something to him. On this matter of revelation, there is abundant material in the Bible which may be compared with the Qoran. It may be said at once that there is a striking difference between the Bible and the Qoran in this respect. In the Bible, the one favored with a revelation is not purely passive. He reacts to God's word in various personal ways. *Abraham* receives promises from God, but he points out the difficulties in the way of their fulfilment (Gen. **15**). *Moses* is chosen to lead Israel out of Egypt, but he pleads and insists on his unfitness (Ex. **3** : 11; **4** : 1). *Isaias* in the presence of the divine Majesty is deeply conscious of his unworthiness, but he offers himself spontaneously to become God's envoy (**6** : 5, 8). *Jeremias* pleads his inability to speak (**1** : 6 ff.) and describes in moving terms what a painful burden his mission is (**20** : 7 ff.). *Ezechiel* objects to a feature of God's command which he finds particularly repulsive (**4** : 12, 15). Thus the man to whom God gives a mission is far from being a purely passive instrument; he keeps his individuality and personality, and reacts as a normal man. In the Qoran — and it should be noted that we are considering the *text* of the Qoran, not the *Tradition* which gives the historical background, therefore, strictly the data of the text of the Bible and of the Qoran — the revelation is recorded without any mention of the Prophet's reaction. Thus in 96, 1-5, which is commonly regarded as the call of the Prophet to his mission : " Proclaim in the name of thy Lord "... " Proclaim : thy Lord is the most generous ". The text records the command of God; the Prophet can only comply; nothing is said of his attitude. (Most translators render : " Read ". The original meaning of the verb is " to say aloud ", " call "; cf. Ed. Montet, *Le Coran* [Paris, 1929], p. 850, n. 2; R. Blachère, *Le Coran* [Paris, 1949, text], p. 9, and reff. On the circumstances of this revelation : cf. Blachère, *op. cit.*, p. 2 and 3; Tor Andrae, *Mohammed : The Man and His Faith* (New York, 1936], p. 55 ff.; R. Blachère, *Le Problème de Mahomet* [Paris, 1952], p. 38 ff.; A. Guillaume, *The Life of Muhammad* [London, 1955], 104 ff.; Gaudefroy-Demombynes, *Mahomet* [Paris, 1957], 67 ff.; W. M. Watt, *Muhammad at Mecca* [Oxford, 1953], 39 ff.).

God gives his revelation and He himself guarantees to Mohammed's hearers, through the Qoran, the truth of that revelation. Thus 53, 2-5 and 10-11 : " Your companion (Moham.) has not gone astray nor is he deceived. He does not speak out of (his own) inclination (= not of his personal initiative). It is a revelation which is revealed, which one strong in power has taught him — He revealed to his servant (Moham.) what he revealed (= what he pleased to reveal). The heart did not lie about what he (Moham.) saw " (= he was not deluded by his imagination) ". The word *revealing* here = the Arabic root *waha*. Cf. 81, 22 : " Your companion is not possessed " (or, mad); also 26, 192-195 : " Verily it is a revelation of the Lord of the Worlds which the Faithful Spirit (= the Archangel) has brought down upon thy heart — in clear Arabic speech ". Revelation, " to bring down ", = Arabic root *nazala*.

The Prophet experienced difficulties in keeping peace in his harem. The text itself says nothing of his troubles; we hear only that Allah intervenes through revelation to remind Mohammad's wives of their duties (33, 28 ff.), or to justify Zaynab's divorce from Zayd, Mohammed's adopted son, so that the Prophet could marry her as he wished (33, 36 ff.; see the edifying comment of Draz, *Initiation*, p. 123); but from the text itself, we would not suspect the psychological imbroglio in which the Prophet had become involved. " No believer, man or woman, when Allah and His Apostle have decided an affair, has any choice (= right to say anything) in this affair; and whoever disobeys Allah and His Apostle, does go astray manifestly " (vs. 36). Then (vs. 37) Allah explains that at first the Prophet told Zayd to keep his wife, while he concealed within himself " what Allah was to bring to light ". — the

Prophet was " afraid of men " (= public opinion) " while Allah had a better right to be feared ". And so after the proper formalties, " We gave her to you as a wife ". And this becomes a rule for the Believers : they may marry without sin the wives of their adopted sons ". The command of Allah must be fulfilled ". So, here again, as the text stands, all the Prophet has to do is to obey — and there is no further problem.

From various other revelations (e.g., 73, 8 ff.; 93; 94), we may gather that the Prophet experienced difficulties : he was accused of forging revelations, of magic, of borrowing from Jewish and Christian sources, etc. We find all this in the form of more or less definite allusions in the text — so that in fact the Qoran can become as an autobiography of the Prophet to one who can read between the lines (cf. Pareja, *Islamologia*, p. 378) — but only as allusions. We do not see the Prophet pouring out his soul's troubles before God, like the prophets of Israel. For then the Qoran would cease to be the word of God exclusively. Allah being truly the sole speaker in the Qoran, the Qoran is from beginning to end the word of Allah to his Prophet in a succession of revelations; the Prophet's role is to receive them and to reproduce them in the Qoran. Viewed in that light, the Qoran is not properly speaking the work of Mohammed. Moslems see in Mohammed merely the transmitter of the word of God, and they are careful in quoting from the text to use formulas which safeguard its divine origin — without reference to Mohammed as the author.

Non-Moslems start from the completely different view that Mohammed is the author. Hence a number of problems which can have no sense for Moslems, such as the question of the sources of the Qoran, e.g., indebtedness to Judaism or Christianity through oral tradition, since there were no written Jewish-Christian sources accessible to him in Arabic at that time, and the Prophet was not acquainted with foreign languages. (Cf. Pareja, *op. cit.*, 378). Cp. 29, 47/58 : " Thou wast not reciting any Scripture before this, nor wast thou tracing it with thy right hand. Then those who seek vanity would be in doubt ". The last sentence is somewhat uncertain. On the question of the " sources ", see, from the non-Moslem standpoint : Abr. I. Katsh, *Judaism in Islam : Biblical and Talmudic Backgrounds of the Koran and its Commentaries :*

Suras II and III. (New York, 1954); R. Bell, *The Origin of Islam in Its Christian Environment* (London, 1926); Tor Andrae, *Mohammed: The Man and His Faith* (New York, 1936; see Index s. v. Christianity, and Judaism); from the Moslem standpoint : M. A. Draz, *Initiation...,* p. 99-133.

The Bible and the Qoran can be compared only as records of revelation. In the Bible, the integrity of the man used by God is not impaired. In the Qoran, Mohammed is nothing but God's instrument, " only the mouth-piece of Allah " (A. Jeffery, *The Qur'an as Scripture* [New York, 1952], p. 4). And this is no caricature. According to Draz, this circumstance becomes — strangely enough to non-Moslems — an argument for the supernatural origin of the Qoran (*Initiation...,* p. 99). Now is it possible not to attribute the language and thoughts of the Qoran to the person who utters them, neither as the expression of his own thought nor as reproducing what he has learned naturally from his surroundings? How can we make him a mere receptacle which has everything from an external superhuman being? This is most disconcerting. But this is the explanation we shall have to admit once it has been shown that, in this case, there is no valid natural explanation. (Not quoted literally). He then goes on to show the inanity of a search for " sources " (pp. 100-133), after arguing in the preceding chapter (p. 85 ff.) that there is in the Qoran perfect literary beauty, and a perfect order which reveals the guidance of an intelligent higher Being who had before him the plan from the very beginning. This is a point on which Moslem apologists insist, because Western critics usually take exception to the order of the Qoran. (Cf. also, Maulvi Mohammad Ali, *The Holy Qur'an: Arabic and English with Commentary* [Lahore, 1920], p. xxviii f.). Thus, to mention only a few recent authors, R. Bell, *Introduction* (p. 72 ff.; 85 ff.), speaks of the " disjointedness " of the Qoran; A. Jeffery, *The Qur'an as Scripture* (p. 5 refers to " the uncouthness and dreary monotony of the Qoran ". Nor is the unequalled-unsurpassable beauty of the Qoran, a thesis founded on the Qoran itself, an acceptable argument from the Western point of view. Of the several texts of the Qoran (**2**, 21/23; **11**, 16/13; **17**, 90/88; **29**, 49/50 and 50/51), it will suffice to quote the last passage. " They (the Unbelievers) say : If only signs were sent down upon him

(Mohammed) from his Lord! Say : The signs are only with Allah (= He has reserved to Himself the power of working miracles). I am only a clear warner. Is it not enough for them that We have sent down upon thee the Scripture which is recited to them? .Indeed, there is in this a mercy (grace) and a reminder for a people who believe ". (For an unfavorable view of the thesis of unsurpassable character of the Qoran, see A. Jeffery, *The Qur'an as Scripture*, p. 4-5), and full details in Abdoul Masih al Ghawiry, *Les Miracles de Mahomet* [Harissa (Liban) - Alger, 1937, p. 163-284, a very sharp criticism of the Qoran as literature, etc.].

In conclusion we can say that in the Qoran there is nothing that can be compared with what we are wont to consider as inspiration. We might expect to find in place of inspiration something like revelation — the Qoran in fact is a record of revelations. However, on closer study, revelation in the Qoran bears but little resemblance to Biblical revelation. Indeed following the view defended by Draz of the origin of the Qoran, instead of the Qoran being a miracle, we have something like a mediumistic composition which we are asked to receive as divine on the strength of its own affirmation.

BIBLIOGRAPHY ON INSPIRATION.

There is a copious literature on the subject. A selection will be given here of the more important and more recent works.

J. B. FRANZELIN, *Tractatus de Divina Traditione et Scriptura*, Rome 1870; 4th ed., 1896. — E. LEVESQUE, *Essai sur la nature de l'inspiration des Livres Saints*, in *Revue des Facultés catholiques de l'Ouest*, 1895. — TH. M. PÈGUES, " Une pensée de saint Thomas sur l'inspiration scripturaire ", *Revue Thomiste* (1895), pp. 95-112; *id.*, " A propos de l'inspiration des Livres Saints ", *RB* (1897), pp. 75-82. — M. J. LAGRANGE, " Une pensée de saint Thomas sur l'inspiration scripturaire ", *ibid.* (1895), pp. 563-571; *id.*, " L'inspiration des Livres Saints ", *ibid.* (1896), pp. 199-220; *id.*, " L'inspiration et les exigences de la critique ", *ibid.* (1896), pp. 496-518; *id.*, review of Nisius, *ibid.* (1900), pp. 135-142, and of Pesch, *ibid.* (1906), 303-314; *id.*, *La méthode historique*, Paris, 1903. — D. ZANECCHIA, *Divina inspiratio Sacrarum Scripturarum ad mentem sancti Thomae*, Rome, 1898; *id.*, *Scriptor sacer sub divina inspiratione iuxta sententiam Cardinalis Franzelin*, Rome, 1903. — TH. CALMES, *Qu'est-ce que l'Écriture Sainte? Les Livres inspirés dans l'Antiquité chrétienne. Théorie de l'inspiration*, Paris, 8th ed. 1907. — F. PRAT, " Les historiens inspirés et leurs sources ", *Études* (1901), pp. 474-500; *id.*, *La Bible et l'histoire*, 5th ed., Paris, 1908. — E. MANGENOT, " Inspiration ", *DBV*, III (1903), cols. 887-911; *id.*, " Inspiration de l'Écriture ", *DTC*, VII (1923), cols. 2068-2266. — L. BILLOT, *De Inspiratione Sacrae Scripturae*, 4th ed., Rome, 1928. — CHR. PESCH, *De Inspiratione Sacrae Scripturae*, Freiburg im Br., 1906; *id.*, *Supplementum*, *ibid.*, 1926. — E. HUGON, *La causalité instrumentale en théologie*, Paris, 2nd ed., 1924, esp. Chap. II, " La causalité instrumentale dans l'inspiration scripturaire ". — A. DURAND, " Inspiration de la Bible ", *DAFC*, II (1911), cols. 894-917; *id.*, " Inerrance biblique ", *ibid.*, cols. 752-787; *id.*, " Critique biblique ", *ibid.*, I (1911), cols. 760-819. — E. MERKELBACH, *L'inspiration des divines écritures*, 2nd ed., Liège, 1913. — J. M. VOSTÉ, *De natura et extensione inspirationis biblicae secundum principia Angelici Doctoris*, Rome, 1924; *id.*, *De Scripturarum veritate iuxta recentiora Ecclesiae documenta*, *ibid.*, 1924; *id.*, *De divina inspiratione et veritate Sacrae Scripturae*, 2nd ed. *ibid.*, 1932. — M. VAN DEN OUDERIJN, *De Prophetiae charismate in populo israelitico*, *ibid.*, 1926. — A. LEMONNYER, " Apparences historiques ", *DBV*, *Suppl.* I (1928), cols. 588-596; *id.*, " Citations implicites ", *ibid.*, II (1934), cols. 51-55. — H. LUSSEAU, *Essai sur la nature de l'inspiration scripturaire*, 2nd ed., Rome, 1935. — A. BEA, *De Scripturae Sacrae inspiratione quaestiones historicae et dogmaticae*, 2nd ed., Rome, 1935. — H. HOEPFL, " Critique biblique ", *DBV*, *Suppl.*, II (1934), cols. 175-240. — G. COURTADE, " Inspiration et inerrance ", *DBV*, *Suppl.*, IV (1949), cols. 482-559. — G. CASTELLINO, *L'inerranza della Scrittura*, Turin, 1949. — H. HOEPFL and B. GUT, *De inspiratione Sacrae Scripturae*, 5th ed., Rome, 1950. — E. FLORIT, *Ispirazione biblica*, 2nd ed., Turin, 1951; *id.*, *La verità nella S. Scrittura*, 2nd ed., Rome, 1951. — S. TROMP, *De Sacrae Scripturae inspiratione*, 5th ed., Rome, 1953.

In addition to these special works, one should consult the Manuals of General Introduction to Holy Scripture, especially the following : CORNELY, *Introductionis in S. Scripturae libros compendium*, 12th ed. by A. Merk, Paris, 1940. — Pontifical Biblical Institute, *Institutiones biblicae scholis accommodatae*. Vol. I, *De S. Scriptura in universum*, 5th ed., Rome, 1937. — J. RENIÉ, *Manuel d'Écriture Sainte*. Vol. I, *Introduction générale*, 6th ed., Lyons, 1949. — H. SIMON and J. PRADO, *Praelectiones biblicae. Propaedeutica biblica sive Introductio in universam Scripturam*, 6th ed., Turin, 1950. — J. BALESTRI, *Biblicae introductionis generalis elementa*, Rome, 1932. — H. LUSSEAU and M. COLLOMB, *Manuel d'Études bibliques.* Vol. I, Paris, 1936. — G. M. PERRELLA, *Introduzione generale alla Sacra Bibbia*, Turin, 1948 [2nd ed., 1952].

[J. COPPENS, Note on Father Benoit's chapter on Inspiration, *EThL* (1955), pp. 571-573. P. BENOIT, " Note complémentaire sur l'Inspiration ", *RB* (1956), pp. 416-422 (a reply to Coppens). See also further notes and an article by Coppens on the same subject in *EThL* (1956), p. 715 ff., and *ibid.* (1957), pp. 35-57. J. T. FORESTELL, C.S.B., " The Limitation of Inerrancy ", *CBQ* (1958), pp. 9-18. R. A. F. MACKENZIE, S. J., " Some Problems in the Field of Inspiration ", *ibid.*, pp. 1-8. J. L. McKENZIE, S. J., *The Two-Edged Sword*, Milwaukee, 1956, Chaps. I and II.]

CHAPTER II

THE CANON OF THE SCRIPTURES
by A. TRICOT.

APPENDIX

THE APOCRYPHA
OF THE OLD AND NEW TESTAMENTS.

[Including a special Section, *The Dead Sea Scrolls*, by E. P. Arbez].

CHAPTER II

THE CANON OF THE SCRIPTURE [1]

INTRODUCTORY OBSERVATIONS.

1° The word " canon " and its derivatives.

Canon. — The Greek word κανών, which was probably borrowed from the Semitic languages, and in any case is closely related to the Hebrew word *qaneh* (a reed used for measuring; cf. Ez. **40** : 3, 5), was simply transcribed into Latin under the form *canon*. It meant originally an object used as a measure, a rule, or a model; then, in its derived meaning, a thing measured or ruled. The grammarians of Alexandria gave the name κανών to the collection of classical works worthy of being offered as models because of the purity of their language, and Cicero, in a letter to Tiro, wrote : Tu, qui κανών esse soles meorum scriptorum (*Ep. ad famil.*, lib. XVI, ep. 17). According to Pliny, the body of rules and measures to be followed in sculpture was called the canon of Polycleitus. Epictetus called the man who could serve as a model to others because of the rectitude of his life a κανών.

The word κανών occurs four times in the New Testament, and exclusively in the Pauline Epistles : three times with the meaning of something measured (the field which God assigns the Apostle for his apostolate, 2 Cor. **10** : 13, 15, 16), and once with the meaning of a rule of life (Gal. **6** : 16).

The early ecclesiastical writers used the word in the transferred sense to designate the rule of tradition (ὁ κανών τῆς παραδόσεως, in Saint Clement of Rome), the rule of faith or of truth (ὁ κανὼν τῆς πίστεως, τῆς ἀληθείας in Polycrates of Ephesus, Saint Irenaeus, Clement of Alexandria, Saint Hippolytus), the rule of Christian life or ecclesiastical discipline (ὁ κανών τῆς ἐκκλησίας, ὁ ἐκκλησιαστικὸς κανών in Clement of Alexandria and Origen).

Translator's note. — [1 For a complete recent treatment of the canon of the Old and New Testament, see G. M. PERRELLA, *Introduzione generale alla sacra Bibbia* (2nd ed., Turin, 1952), pp. 109-180.]

From the early fourth century, the established regulations or the decrees promulgated by ecclesiastical authority are currently called κανόνες, e.g., at the Council of Antioch in 341.

Among Latin writers, expressions which had exactly the same meaning *(regula fidei, regula veritatis)* were used in the third century by Tertullian and by Novatian.

From the very beginnings of the Church, Scripture was regarded as containing a rule of faith and of life, and its authority was considered equal to that of the ecclesiastical magisterium. Consequently it was natural to speak of the canon of the Scriptures to designate that written rule, and the name canon was given to the collection of inspired books. The use of the word canon in the sense of the collection of authoritative writings is attested as early as the third century in the East as well as in the West. Origen (Latin translation) says of certain books that they are not *in canone* (*Hom. in Josue*, 2 : 1; **15** : 6; *Comm. in Cant.*, prologue), and the author of the so-called monarchian prologue of the Gospel of Saint John speaks of the canon which begins with Genesis *(in principio canonis)*. In the following century, *ca.* 350, Saint Athanasius says of the Shepherd of Hermas that " it is not part of the canon " (*De decr. synod. Nicaen.*, 18), and in his XXXIXth Paschal Letter, composed in 367, he gives a list of the writings which are in the canon (τὰ κανονιζόμενα). At about the same time, in Asia Minor, the Council of Laodicea decided that only the canonical books (τά κανονικά) of the Old and the New Testaments ought to be read (canon 59). The canonical books *(canonici)* are enumerated in the African list first published by Mommsen (1886), and the Syrian translator of the Ecclesiastical History of Eusebius of Cesarea translates the words γραφάς οὐκ ἐνδιαθήκους by " books not placed in the canon ". It is quite clear that after the middle of the fourth century the use of the word canon becomes current among Greek and Latin authors. Saint Amphilochius, Saint Gregory Nazianzen, Priscillian, Rufinus, Saint Jerome, Saint Augustine, etc., offer ample proof of this fact.

Thus we see in what manner and with what meanning the word canon was given to the collection of Scriptures. Contrary to the views held by some writers, it has never had the meaning of a list, index, or catalogue. The two ideas of a rule and of a thing regulated, of authoritative books and of a definite and limited collection, were closely associated in the minds of the Fathers when they spoke of the canon of the Scriptures. In the course of time the second meaning became the accepted one. Ordinarily, by the canon of the Old and New Testaments we mean the collection of divinely inspired books which contain revelation or the infallible rule of faith and morals. It is in this sense that the Council of Trent has given a definition of the canon of the Scripture, specifying the books which the Church recognizes as canonical and inspired *(Decretum de canonicis Scripturis)*.

Canonical. — The adjective κανονικός (in Latin, *canonicus*) is derived from the noun κανών. Origen was the first to use this adjective to describe the books which were the rule of faith, or regulative, and which formed a collection fixed by authority in respect to its extent, and therefore regulated (cf. *Comm. in Cant.*, prologue). The adjective *regularis* applied to the Sacred Books in *In Matth.*, *Comm. series*, 117, must translate κανονικός. From the beginning of the fourth century the adjective " canonical " passes into general use.

To Canonize. — The verb κανονίζειν (to receive into the canon), also a derivative of κανών, was used by Origen *(libri canonizati)*, by Saint Athanasius (τὰ κανονιζόμενα), by Theodoret (οἱ πατέρες κανονίσαντες), etc. Actually, the coinage of this word was not a happy one, since it appears to signify that a book becomes canonical through incorporation by the Church into the collection of Scripture, whereas a work is canonical because of divine inspiration, which alone can confer on it the character of an infallible rule. As a matter of fact, this word was not kept by the Latin authors, who preferred the expression *libri canonici* to the phrase *libri canonizati*.

Canonicity. — In order that a book may be called canonical, its inspired character must have been officially recognized by the Church. It is to be emphasized that this declaration made by the ecclesiastical magisterium adds nothing to the internal value of the work which is proclaimed to be canonical, since inspiration is the very condition of canonicity, but it invests the book with an absolute authority from the point of view of faith, and at the same time it becomes the sign of inspiration. Such is the teaching of the Vatican Council (Session III, Apr. 24,

1870, " Const. de fide cath. ", cap. 2) : *Eos (libros) Ecclesia pro sacris et canonicis habet, non ideo, quod sola humana industria concinnati, sua deinde auctoritate sint approbati ; nec ideo dum-taxat, quod revelationem sine errore contineant ; sed propterea, quod Spiritu sancto inspirante conscripti Deum habent auctorem atque ut tales ipsi Ecclesiae traditi sunt.* The same teaching is found in the Encyclical *Providentissimus Deus* of Leo XIII (Nov. 18, 1893), and in the Encyclical *Divino afflante Spiritu* of Pius XI (Sept. 30, 1943).

Protocanonical and deuterocanonical books. — Sixtus of Sienna (*Bibliotheca sancta*, Venice, 1566, lib. 1, sect. 1) was the first to make use of the words *protocanonical* and *deuteroca-nonical* to distinguish two classes of writings in the Old and New Testaments : " The first class consists of those books which one may call protocanonical and about which there has never been any doubt or discussion in the Catholic Church; the second contains the books which were once designated by the term ecclesiastical, but which are now called deutero-canonical ".

The following books of the Old Testament are deutero-canonical : Tob., Jud., Wis., Ecclus., Bar., 1 and 2 Mach., as well as the last seven chapters of Esther (**10** : 4-16 : 24 in the Vulgate) and three passages in Daniel (**3** : 24-90; **13**; **14**); in the New Testament : Heb., Jas., 2 Pet., 2 and 3 Jn., Jude, and Apoc. It is customary to add to this list the following fragments of the Gospels : Mk. **16** : 9-20; Lk. **22** : 43-44; Jn. **5** : 3-4; **7** : 53-8 : 11. But it is wrong to do so, because the problems connected with these passages belong to the history of the text and to textual criticism.

This distinction between protocanonical and deuterocanonical books, which evokes memories of controversies or of doubts concerning the canonicity of certain books, is legitimate from the point of view of history. But we do not have the right to conclude from this that the deuterocanonical books do not possess the same normative value as the protocanonical ones, or that they are inferior to these in content.

Protestants and Jews give the name *Apocrypha* to those books and parts of books in the Old Testament which they do not consider inspired and canonical. [This is a regrettable practice,

because such a use of the word apocrypha for the deuterocanonical books is not justified by the ancient historical use
of the term. E. P. A.].

2⁰ Division and Object of this Study.

The first ecclesiastical writers knew only one collection of
the Scriptures. For them the Old and the New Testaments
constituted a single collection of holy books containing two
closely connected parts. But it soon became customary to
give different names to these two parts, since certain writings
deal with the Old Covenant and others with the New [1]. The
distinction seemed all the more natural, inasmuch as the Church
had received the books of the first group from the Synagogue,
but had herself watched over the formation of the second.
The distinction was justified, furthermore, by the fact that the
writings of the Old Testament contain God's revelation to
Israel through Moses, the prophets, and other inspired men,
while those of the New Testament contain God's revelation
to mankind through Christ and the Apostles. It is usual,
therefore, to study the history of each group separately.

The history of the canon of the Old Testament aims to
determine the manner in which the collection of books which
the Synagogue considered sacred was formed among the Jews,
and the conditions under which these books were received by
the Church as being guaranteed by the authority of God Himself.
In the case of the New Testament, the historian must try to
discover precisely in what way the collection of twenty-seven
writings which the Church has retained as " Scripture ", and
which she has added to those which she received from the
Synagogue, was gradually formed, and the circumstances under
which this formation took place. In both instances, our problem
is to reconstruct a history which is quite clear in its result or
final stage, but which has many elements in its earlier phases

---

[1] The Greek word διαθήκη (covenant) which, in the Septuagint, corresponded to the Hebrew word berîth (pact), was translated in Latin by
testamentum. But the Latin word is ambiguous and does not correspond
exactly either to the Hebrew or to the Greek. The same is true of the English
word " Testament ". [For the etymology of Hebrew berîth, see Biblica (1955),
169 ff., and 565 ff. Cf. G. E. MENDENHALL, " Covenant Forms in Israelite
Tradition ", BA (1954), pp. 50-76; BEHM in Kittel's Th.W, II, cols. pp. 105-137;
ARNDT-GINGRICH, Greek-English Lexicon of the New Testament (Chicago, 1957),
p. 182.]

that we do not know or are controversial. A few points only
can be established with complete certainty. For the rest, in
the absence of facts and documents, we can only resort to
hypotheses.

I. — HISTORY OF THE CANON OF THE OLD TESTAMENT.

1. — *THE JEWISH CANON AT THE BEGINNING OF THE CHRISTIAN ERA.*

In the first century of our era the Jews possessed a collection
of holy books which they held to be inspired by the Spirit of
God, and in which they saw the expression of the divine will,
i.e., a rule which defined what they were required to believe
and practice. On this historical point the testimony of Josephus,
of the Fourth Book of Esdras, and of the Talmud, leave no
room for doubt.

In his treatise *Against Apion*, composed in 97-98, Josephus
speaks thus of the sacred books of the Jews : " We do not have
an infinite number of books which disagree or contradict each
other [as do the Greeks], but only twenty-two, which contain
the annals of all times, and enjoy deserved credit. First, we
have the books of Moses, of which there are five... The prophets
who came after Moses wrote the history of their times in thirteen
books. The last four [books] contain hymns to God and moral
precepts for mankind. All that took place from the time of
Artaxerxes until our own day has been related; but these
writings do not enjoy as much credit as the preceding ones,
because there was no longer a continuous succession of prophets.
The facts give proof with what respect we approach our own
books " (**1**, 8, 38-42).

In the apocalypse which is known under the name of the
Fourth Book of Esdras and which was composed about the end
of the first century of our era, Esdras is represented as dictating
in forty days to five secretaries the text of ninety-four books,
of which twenty-four " are to be published in order to be read
by the worthy and the unworthy ", and seventy " are to be
withheld and entrusted only to the wise " (**14**, 45-46) [1]. Thus

---

[1] The Latin text of chapter **14**, as the text of the whole book for that matter,
must be corrected by means of the Oriental versions. [For the full text, see
R. H. CHARLES. *The Apocrypha and Pseudepigraphica of the Old Testament*,
(Oxford, 1913), Vol. II, p. 624].

Pseudo-Esdras recognizes the existence of an official collection of twenty-four books, while he places his apocalypse among the seventy secret books which must remain in the hands of the wise. The narrative is obviously legendary, but what the author says about the number of sacred books must reflect the opinion of his day.

In the Babylonian Talmud (*Baba Bathra*, fol. 14ª and 15ª) a *baraitha* [1], attributed to Juda the Holy (136-217), gives the list of the twenty-four books which the Synagogue considered sacred, and presents this list as one handed down by the Fathers.

All the evidence leads us to believe that in these texts we have the echo of the same tradition, and a tradition which was already old when Josephus and Pseudo-Esdras were writing, therefore much earlier than the Jewish synod of Jamnia or Jabneh (*ca.* 90-100) which seems to have fixed and closed officially the Jewish canon of the Scriptures. Hence officially it may be concluded that at the beginning of the Christian era the sacred books of the Jews numbered twenty-four. Josephus, it is true, counts only twenty-two, a number which corresponded to the number of letters in the Hebrew alphabet and which Origen and Saint Jerome will retain. But in this computation, Ruth was joined to Judges, and Lamentations to Jeremias, in accordance with the arrangement of the Greek Bible.

These books were the following : the five books of Moses (Gen., Ex., Lev., Num., Deut.); the Prophets, arranged in two series : that of the Former Prophets (Jos., Jdgs., Sam., Kgs.) and that of the Latter Prophets (Jer., Ez., Isa., and the Twelve Minor Prophets); the Writings, or Hagiographa of the Christian writers (Ruth, Ps., Job, Prov., Eccles., C. C., Lam., Dan., Est., Esd.-Neh., Chron.) [2].

The existence of this sacred collection in the first century of our era is also established by the New Testament. The

---

Translator's note. — [1] An Aramaic term, meaning literally, " external ", " outside ", denoting the traditions of the Tannaim, i.e. authorities on the Oral Law from the time of the schools of Hillel and of Shammai to that of Judah ha-Nasi (*ca.* 50 B.C. — 200 A.D.) — not included in the Mishna of Juda ha-Nasi, but gathered in a separate collection. E. P. A.].

[2] These books are enumerated according to a manner which, if it is not the most ancient, is at least the one which is in closest conformity with Talmudic tradition. As regards the order of books within the group of Latter Prophets and the group of Writings, there are discrepancies between the Talmud, certain Hebrew manuscripts, and the Bibles printed according to the Massora.

New Testament writers cite Scripture only in general terms (γραφή or γραφαί). But the New Testament contains either direct quotations, allusions, or reminiscences from nineteen of the Old Testament books mentioned above [1]. The only books to which there are no references are Ruth, Eccles., C. C., Est., Esd.-Neh., all belonging to the Writings. This omission is easy to explain, since these books offered few points of contact with the ordinary teaching of Christ and the Apostles. In the case of the Minor Prophets, there are similarly no references to Abdias and Nahum, but we know through other sources that they were certainly counted among the " Twelve " (cf. Ecclus. **49** : 10). It should also be noted that the text of Saint Matthew (**23** : 35), where mention is made of the murder of Abel (cf. Gen. **4** : 8) and of Zacharias (cf. 2 Chron. **24** : 20-21), refers to two books, of which one was the first and the other the last in the Jewish collection of the Scriptures.

The threefold division (Law, Prophets, Writings), assumed by Josephus and indicated by the Talmud, is confirmed by the New Testament, where we find the expressions " Moses and the Prophets " (Lk. **24** : 27), " Moses, the Prophets and the Psalms " (Lk. **24** : 44). This division of the Sacred Books into three groups was already old, for it is attested as early as 130 B. C. by the prologue to the Greek version of Ecclesiasticus, where the grandson of Jesus Ben Sirach enumerates on three different occasions the three classes of " books handed down from the fathers " : the Law, the Prophets, and the (other) Writings.

2. — FORMATION AND FIXATION OF THE JEWISH CANON [2].

How, by virtue of what principle, by what authority and at what period was the selection of writings which composed this sacred library made, and was the selection made once and for all? These questions have occupied both the theologians and historians of Judaism, and their answers do not always agree. Since the group of Mosaic books (the Torah or the

---

[1] Cf. W. DITTMAR, *Vetus Testamentum in Novo* (Göttingen, 1903).

Translator's note. — [2] For the views of modern Jewish scholars, see Ez. KAUFMAN, " Toldot ha-emunah ha-yisre'elit ", 8 (Tel Aviv, 1956), pp. 409-418; M. S. SEGAL, *Mebō' ha-Miqrā* (Jerusalem, 1950), pp. 809-884)].

Pentateuch) was recognized in the first place as possessing an absolute normative authority, and since the other books were subsequently associated with those of Moses — and all scholars are in agreement on this point — it seems obvious that we should examine, at the outset, under what conditions and at what date in the history of Israel the Law was proclaimed to be " Scripture " because of its divine origin and treated as such.

The Law. — It does not appear that before the period of Josias (640-608) appeal was habitually made in Israel to the authority of any written text whatsoever which would have had the recognized character of an official sacred code. The religious life of the nation, in its beliefs, institutions, and customs, rested especially on a living tradition which went back to Moses and was perpetuated after him through the prophets, priests, and kings, who were viewed as the representatives of God and the authorized interpreters of His will. Without doubt the religious history of Israel, from beginning to end, is dominated by the memory of Moses and of his work, of the revelation on Mount Sinai, of the alliance that was then made between Yahweh and His chosen people, etc. Without doubt also the ancient writings which were entrusted to the safekeeping of the priests were carefully preserved (cf. Deut. **31** : 24-26; Jos. **24** : 26; I Sam. **10** : 25) very much like the official annals in the royal archives (2 Sam. **20** : 24; I Kgs. **11** : 41). But there is no reason to believe that the Mosaic Code enjoyed " canonical " authority before the reign of Josias. In fact, Biblical history itself shows that, before the reform made by that prince, many practices connected with worship and with the liturgy of the Temple did not conform to the prescriptions of Leviticus, and that on many points civil legislation did not agree with the laws found in the Pentateuch. It is to be noted, furthermore, that when the most ancient of the prophets who wrote spoke of " the law " they were not thinking of a written code, but of the teaching given in the name of God by inspired men or by the priests (cf. Os. **4** : 6; **8** : 1; Am. **2** : 4; Isa. **1** : 10; Mich. **4** : 2). Similarly, in the Psalms written before the Exile, the word " law " does not refer to the Book of the Law, but to the whole body of precepts which deal with moral life and piety.

From the reign of Josias the situation is quite different. In 621, the High Priest, Helcias, " found the book of the Law in the house of Yahweh ", and gave it to the king. The circumstances of this discovery and the reforms which followed are related in 2 Kgs. 22–23, and 2 Chron. 34–35. Whether we identify the roll which was discovered with the whole Pentateuch or see here a reference to Deuteronomy only, it is certain that from this time forward the " Book of the Law " was considered the collection of laws established by God for Israel. The prophecies and the work of Jeremias bear witness to this effect, and the first formal citations of " the Law of Moses " are found in the Books of Kings, which were written less than fifty years after the death of Josias (cf. 1 Kgs. 2 : 3, and Deut. 29 : 8; 2 Kgs. 14 : 6, and Deut. 24 : 16).

During the Exile, the prestige and the authority of the Torah did not cease to grow, since the exiles loved to gather around the priests to hear them read the Sacred Books. About this same time the first scribes or " men of the book " made their appearance. Then, when national and religious life had been restored through the work of Nehemias the governor and by that of Esdras, who was both priest and scribe, the Jewish community received and recognized officially the collection of the Mosaic books as a sacred code (cf. Esd. 7 : 11-26; Neh. 8). This solemn promulgation was the termination of a long process.

From the end of the fifth century B. C., " the Law of Moses " is read in the synagogues of Palestine and of the Diaspora, is studied and commented upon by scribes, and occupies a unique place in the hearts and minds of pious Jews. When the Samaritans, on being excluded from the Jewish community and from participation in the worship of the Temple, began their schism in 408, they took with them, as a sacred code, the Books of Moses. References to the Torah become more numerous in the literature which comes after Esdras. There are sixty references in Chronicles in comparison with two in the Books of Samuel and seven in the Books of Kings. All these facts or signs show that the Law was officially recognized as a " canonical " book.

The Prophets. — Under this general heading the Jews placed two series of writings, each belonging to a different genre. The first series comprises the *Former Prophets* (Josue, Judges, Samuel, and Kings), who are primarily historians. The second series, the *Latter Prophets* (Isaias, Jeremias, Ezechiel, and the Twelve Minor Prophets), represents the prophets in the strict sense.

In the Jewish canon the series of Former Prophets comes immediately after the books of the Law. These writings, in which the story of Israel from Josue to the time of the Captivity was related, appeared as a natural sequel to the Torah, which contained the history of the patriarchs and of great ancestors until the death of Moses. This was in itself a primary reason for their being treated with reverence. Moreover, as they were so thoroughly permeated with the theocratic spirit, and reflected the most authentic prophetic doctrine, their authority was all the greater. The Jewish doctors placed these books in the same section as the works of the prophets, either because they thought that they had been written by prophets (cf. Josephus, *Contra Apion.* 1 : 8, 40), or because they read therein the history of several prophets (for example, Samuel, Nathan, Elias, Eliseus, and Isaias). As far as their incorporation in the canon is concerned, the fortune of these books is linked with that of the Latter Prophets.

As champions of Yahwism, inspired preachers, avengers of outraged justice, and judges of kings, the prophets were the representatives of God in the midst of the Jewish nation. The oracles of the prophets who lived before the Exile had generally been collected by their disciples and remained in their possession. They acquired even greater prestige and honor when events confirmed the prophecies made to the people and to their rulers. After the return from the Captivity, the heirs to the prophetic tradition gathered these writings together. But the collection of the Latter Prophets must not have been definitely closed until some time after the death of Malachias, who is the last in time of the Twelve Minor Prophets, because it seems unlikely that the prophecies of a contemporary of Nehemias should have been put at once on the same level with those of Isaias or of Jeremias.

In one of the letters which are inserted at the beginning of the Second Book of Machabees (2 : 13), Nehemias is said to have collected " the books concerning the kings and the prophets ". This must refer to the collection of both the Former and the Latter Prophets, but it does not follow that this collection was then complete and finally closed. A passage in Daniel (9 : 2) seems to imply that at the time when that book was written the prophetic writings were gathered together in one collection, for Jeremias is mentioned as being one of the " books ", that is to say, one of the holy books. Yet too much cannot be made of this passage, since opinions concerning the date of the composition of Daniel differ. On the other hand, a *terminus ad quem* is indirectly indicated by the author of Ecclesiasticus. The hymn in which Jesus Ben Sira (*ca.* 180 B. C.) celebrates the ancestors of Israel, and in which he follows fairly closely the order of the Biblical writings, proves that he knew all the books contained in the section that was called " Prophets " (Jos. : 46 : 1 ff.; Jdgs. : 46 : 11; Sam. : 46 : 13; Kgs. : 47 : 12–49 : 7; Isa. : 48 : 22 ff. [1]; Jer. : 49 : 6 ff.; Ez. 49 : 8; the Twelve Minor Prophets : 49 : 10).

On the basis of all these data we are justified in concluding that the group of writings comprised under the term " Prophets " had been defined in the first half of the century, and that, from that time forward, its authority or normative value was considered as being equal to that of the Books of Moses. In that period, when the voice of the prophets was no longer making itself heard in Israel (cf. 1 Mach. 9 : 27), Judaism was conscious of the dangers to which the national religion was exposed through the impact of Greek civilization following upon the conquests of Alexander the Great, and it sought in its history and in its traditions for help against the menace of encircling paganism.

It should be observed that this section comprising the Prophets did not contain the book of Ruth, nor the triad, Chronicles, Esdras, Nehemias (all three the work of one author), nor Lamentations, nor the Book of Daniel, either because these writings were not recognized as " Scripture " at the time that the collection was made, or because they had not yet been made public. Furthermore, according to the most ancient Jewish tradition, the Book of Isaias was placed after those of Jeremias and of Ezechiel, doubtless because this was the order

---

[1] It is interesting to note in the case of Isaias that Jesus Ben Sira read Chs. 40-66, which are often called Deutero-Isaias, following Chs. 1-39.

in which the prophecies of each of these prophets had been put in book form.

The Writings or the Hagiographa. — This third group (see the list above, p. 73) presents a composite appearance, and this explains why the name " Writings " was given to it by the Scribes and has been retained in the Rabbinic tradition.

It seems that this section was built around the book of Psalms, which, considered as a whole, is made up of collections which antedate the Exile. This book enjoyed great prestige, both because of David and because of immemorial liturgical usage. According to 2 Mach. **2** : 13, " the writings of David " — this term surely refers to the Psalms — were among the books collected by Nehemias in the " library " which he founded. The author of Ecclesiasticus alludes to several of the Hagiographa : Prov. : **47** : 14 ff.; Job : **49** : 9 (in the Hebrew); Neh. : **49** : 11 ff. His grandson cites the " Writings " as one of the three groups of books which the Jews considered sacred, and which, in his day, were read in Egypt in the Greek translation (cf. Ecclus., Prologue).

Five books, called the five *Megilloth* (rolls) by the Rabbis, were used for official readings at the following feasts : Passover (C. C.), Pentecost (Ruth), the anniversary of the destruction of Jerusalem in 586 (Lam.), Tabernacles (Eccles.), and Purim (Est.). But we cannot say exactly when this usage was adopted.

Judging by the place it occupies in the division called " Writings ", the Book of Daniel was one of the last to be included. And the large work which originally contained Chronicles, Esdras, and Nehemias, did not enter the collection of the Hagiographa in its original form nor at one time. In the Jewish canon these three books are in last place, and their order does not correspond to the chronology of events, since Esdras and Nehemias are found before Chronicles.

In short, the Hagiographa were grouped progressively through the care of the Scribes during the period which extends from the fourth century to the end of the second, and especially after the persecution of Antiochus Ephiphanes, when Judas Macchabeus ordered the sacred rolls which had escaped destruction to be sought out and collected (1 Mach. **1** : 59-60;

2 Mach. 3 : 14). The limits of the collections were not yet clearly defined around 130, the date of the Greek translation of Ecclesiasticus, since the author of the Prologue seems to have considered the work of his grandfather on a par with the books which figured among the Writings.

Such seem to have been the successive steps in the formation of the Jewish canon of the Scriptures. Obviously none of the three collections, the history of which we have just sketched in its main features, was established by virtue of an official decision. The same observation must be made regarding the recognition of the sacred character of each particular book. The Jews never had any rules established by a religious authority which would allow a decision to be made in the matter of canonicity. Furthermore, it does not appear that an assembly of doctors ever participated in the establishment of the canon. According to the Talmud, the men of the " Great Synagogue " are supposed to have written the most recent of the sacred books, and to have definitely fixed the content of the sacred collection. But the " Great Synagogue " is only an invention of the Scribes, who were eager to link the institutions and practices of Judaism with the legislation of Moses and with the prophetic tradition. As for the role played by Esdras, it was not that imagined by certain Fathers, who were misled by the marvelous account contained in the apocryphal composition which circulated under the name of the ancestor of the Scribes (4 Esdr. 14). Esdras may have played an important role in the official promulgation of the Law — and history bears witness to it, but the formation of the canon was not his work.

On the other hand, it is not necessary to think that, because the Sacred Books were included in the collection of the Scriptures, the text of these books was fixed *ne varietur*. The idea of a text which must not be touched because it is sacred was adopted by the doctors only when Judaism ceased to be a religion of the Spirit to become a religion of a Book. A comparison of the Septuagint version with the Hebrew Massoretic text is especially instructive in this respect, for it proves that at least in the case of several of the writings recognized as " Scripture " the work of recension continued almost until the Christian era. For examples, cf. Ex. 35–40; Jos. 7–8; Jer., Job, etc. It would be a mistake to imagine that ancient Judaism was like Pharisaic Judaism; the former had much more vitality and plasticity than is generally suspected.

So far as we can judge, the Law, which is the foundation of the Scriptures, was recognized and declared sacred by both priests and prophets and by common accord. Later, the other writings were added to the Law, because they were, as it were, an extension of the Law, because they seemed apt to insure its practice, and especially because they contained the teaching of men inspired by the Spirit. The liturgy of the synagogue, which from the time of Esdras included the reading of a passage of Scripture, certainly helped to form a strong tradition concerning the canon of the Sacred Books. In the last century B. C., this tradition became stronger under the influence of the Scribes. The sacred collection was thenceforth regarded as a perfect whole, the content of which could not be changed. Certain doctors, it is true, in the following centuries discussed the authority of this or that work (Ez., Prov., C. C., Eccles., Est.), but these were only academic disputes. After the destruction of Jerusalem, the Pharisaic scribes tried to preserve what remained of the past, and above all the Scriptures. The synod of Jamnia (Jabneh), *ca.* 90-100, confirmed the canon as it had been established for two centuries. From that time, the great aim was to preserve the text exactly, and doctors, copyists, and even translators devoted themselves to this task with scrupulous care.

There is one more question to discuss regarding the Jewish canon, namely, whether it was the same in the Diaspora as in Palestine, at Alexandria as at Jerusalem. We know that the Hellenistic Jews, whose main center was Alexandria, read the Scriptures in the Greek version which had been made for them. Now the Septuagint Bible contained, besides the books of the Jewish canon, all those which are called deuterocanonical, and two of these at least (Wis. and 2 Mach.) were written in Greek. Various hypotheses have been advanced to explain this difference of content between the Hebrew Bible and the Greek Bible. Some scholars have imagined that, towards the end of the first century of our era, the Palestinian doctors removed from the canon several books which up to that time had belonged to it, but there is no positive proof for this

supposition. Others have maintained that the Jews of
Alexandria and of the entire Diaspora had a scriptural canon
which was larger and richer than that of the Jews of Palestine.
To support this thesis, they cite the following facts : 1º In the
Alexandrine collection the so-called deuterocanonical books
did not form an appendix, but were interspersed among those
which had been translated from the Hebrew Bible. 2º These
books were highly esteemed by the Hellenistic Jewish doctors,
who used them in their teaching exactly as they employed
those which the Palestinian scribes considered canonical.
3º They came to the Christian Church through the Greek Bible
which was in use in Hellenistic circles.

All these facts are true, but there are others which, when
considered as a whole, furnish certain proof that the canon
of Scripture was the same in Egypt as in Palestine : 1º History
has preserved no trace of a controversy between the two halves
of the Jewish world concerning the matter of the canon.
2º Philo, who made extensive use of scriptural texts, never
cites any of the so-called deuterocanonical books. 3º The New
Testament writers who have quoted from these books never,
in such cases, employed the technical term γραφή (Scripture).
4º Josephus, who made use of the Greek Bible and used all its
books without distinction, knew only one Jewish canon. 5º The
Greek versions of Aquila, Symmachus, and Theodotion, who
were Hellenistic Jews, bear similar testimony. 6º The same is
true of the ancient Christian writers, and among them Origen and
Saint Jerome, who were particularly well informed on the
subject.

No doubt, therefore, is possible; but it remains true nevertheless that, in practice, the Alexandrines added to the books
of the official canon certain writings which the doctors of
Jerusalem refused to admit in their sacred collection. This
divergence is explained by the fact that the two groups did
not have exactly the same ideas on questions of revelation
and inspiration. In Palestine eyes were fixed on the past and
the extraordinary manifestations of God's Spirit were limited
to a definite period in Israel's history, while at Alexandria men
believed that divine Wisdom continued to communicate Itself
to the just and could instruct them in all things as It had
formerly taught the prophets (cf. Wis. 7 and 8; and also Philo,

especially in *Quis rerum div. heres, De migr. Abrahae, De vit. Mos.*, in the passages indicated by Leisegang in his *Indices* to the Cohn-Wendland edition of Philo's works).

Under these conditions it is easy to understand that the concept of an hermetically sealed collection of Scripture was not as strong in the Hellenistic circles of the Diaspora as in the Palestinian world in which the views of the Pharisaic doctors were dominant.

3. — *THE CHRISTIAN CANON OF THE OLD TESTAMENT.*

The Christian canon of the Old Testament contains all the books in the Greek Bible which was in use at Alexandria and in the Diaspora, including the books or portions of books called deuterocanonical, namely, Tob., Jud., Wis., Ecclus., Bar. and the Letter of Jeremias, 1 and 2 Mach., Est. (**10** : 4–**16** : 24), Dan. (**3** : 24-90; **13–14**). It is generally agreed that Christ and, after Him, the Apostles gave their sanction to the authority and the normative value of the books of the Jewish canon, for in their teaching they frequently invoked the testimony of the Scriptures, which were regarded as " the word of God " (Mk. **7** : **13**; Rom. **3** : 2). But have we the right to maintain that they also guaranteed the canonicity of the other writings which the Hellenistic Jews admitted in their Bible, i. e., the deuterocanonical books or parts of books?

The answer to this question can only be furnished by an examination of the books of apostolic origin and by tradition, since neither the Savior nor the Apostles have given any formal pronouncement on the precise content of the Christian canon of the Old Testament. In the New Testament, we find manifest borrowings from several of the deuterocanonical books [1], especially from Ecclus., Wis., and 2 Mach. It is obvious that, in practice, the Apostles and New Testament writers employed the Greek Bible without making any distinction between the books of the Jewish canon and the deuterocanonical books, except that they did not cite the latter as " Scripture ". This procedure corresponded to that current among the Jews of

---

[1] For details, see W. DITTMAR, *op. cit.* The number of citations from the Old Testament in the New (from 270 to 350) cannot be determined exactly, because it is difficult in certain cases to distinguish between formal citations and mere allusions.

Alexandria. It resulted in giving sanction to the authority of the deuterocanonical books, which were thus kept in the scriptural collection of the early Church.

Saint Clement (end of the first century) [1], Hermas (140-154), and Saint Hippolytus († 235) at Rome, Saint Irenaeus († ca. 189) in Gaul, Tertullian († after 225) and Saint Cyprian († 258) in Africa, Clement of Alexandria († 215), Saint Gregory Thaumaturgus († 270), and Saint Methodius († 312) in the Orient, used all the books of the Old Testament as they read them in the Greek Bible or in the Old Latin Version made from the Greek [2]. Several of these authors, it is true, relied on apocryphal works and even quoted them as " Scripture ", but this mistake in no wise diminishes the value of their testimony concerning the deuterocanonical books.

In the East, however, it was never forgotten that there were differences between the list of sacred books received from the Jews of Palestine and that received from the Jews of Alexandria, and that these differences had arisen before the Christian period. This was a fact, furthermore, which had to be taken into consideration in discussions with Jews. Saint Justin († ca. 165), in disputing with Trypho, wishes to draw his arguments exclusively from the Jewish canon of the Scriptures. Saint Melito, bishop of Sardis, ca. 170, made a catalogue of the books of the Old Testament " which were generally recognized as inspired ". and included only those of the Jewish canon (except Esther). Origen († 254) reproduces the same canon, adding only the Epistle of Jeremias. Eusebius of Caesarea († 340) is in the same tradition; and likewise Saint Athanasius († 373), who counts Baruch and the Epistle of Jeremias among the canonical writings, but rejects Esther as " un-canonical ". Saint Cyril of Jerusalem († 386), Saint Epiphanius († 403), Saint Gregory Nazianzen († 390) and his disciple Saint Amphilochius († after 394), Rufinus († 410), and Saint Jerome († 420) all remain faithful to the Jewish canon when they list the books which are received in the Church, Baruch being most frequently

---

[1] For references to patristic texts, see the works mentioned in the *Bibliography* (1. Documents).

[1] If the catalogue found in the *Codex Claromontanus* dates from about the year 300 and comes from Egypt in its original form, which was Greek, as Harnack thought, it bears witness to the same practice as regards the use of the deuterocanonical books.

included and Esther most frequently rejected. The other books, i.e., the deuterocanonical, are useful for the instruction of catechumens (Saint Athanasius), or ought to be set apart and given second rank (Saint Cyril of Jerusalem), or cannot be cited to confirm the authority of the Faith (Rufinus), or are to be read for the edification of the people, but should not be employed as proof in dogmatic expositions, since they are not inspired, *non sunt in canone* (Saint Jerome).

That this unfavorable attitude towards the canonicity of the deuterocanonical books was general throughout the East is clear from the *confirmatur* contained in canons 59 and 60 of the Council of Laodicea in Phrygia (the date commonly assigned is 363, but, according to Hefele-Leclercq, it took place sometime between 343 and 381). Canon 59 prescribes that the canonical books only shall be read, and Canon 60 lists for the Old Testament only the books of the Hebrew Bible [1].

Such was the principle generally in force in the East, and to reject it would be to reject the evidence. But it must be observed that there was a kind of counterpart to this position. These same Fathers actually professed the highest esteem for the deuterocanonical books, they joined them with the other books for liturgical use, and several among them, including Saint Jerome, sometimes in citing them employed the same expressions as in citing the protocanonical books : " It is written ", " God says in Scripture ".

The attitude of the Western Churches towards the so-called deuterocanonical books in this period was quite different, no distinction being made among the writings contained in the sacred collection. Saint Hilary († 367) reproduces Origen's canon, yet considers the deuterocanonical books as inspired and cites them as " Scripture ". In Spain, Priscillian († 385) does not seem to suspect that the canonicity of these books is open to discussion. Mommsen's Catalogue or the Catalogue of Cheltenham, which is of African origin and to be dated around 360, includes all the deuterocanonical books. With Saint Augustine, the Councils of Hippo (393) and of Carthage (397 and 419) declare these books to be canonical, and Pope

---

[1] The authenticity of Canon 60 has been challenged by Westcott. But whether it is authentic or not, this list of the Scriptures is a very early witness to the practice of the Churches of Asia Minor.

Innocent I does the same in his letter to Exuperius of Toulouse (405).

We can say that from Saint Augustine's time the canon was fixed or closed such as the Church was to define it officially at the Council of Trent. The Greeks gradually came to agree with the views held in the West. In 692, the Council in Trullo adopted for the Churches of the Byzantine Empire the scriptural canon of the Latin Church in the form in which it had been promulgated in 419 by the Fourth Council of Carthage. Later, some Greek ecclesiastical writers appeared as partisans of the canon of the Hebrew Bible, as, e.g., Saint John Damascene († 754), but an ever growing majority conformed to the prescriptions contained in the decree passed by the Council in Trullo. In the West, certain doctors, influenced by the pronouncements of Saint Jerome regarding the deuterocanonical books, refused to consider these books as equal to the others on the score of canonicity, but they employed them in teaching and in the liturgy. The Church itself, while giving complete freedom to those who maintained their stand on the authority of Saint Jerome [1], remained faithful to the ideas of Saint Augustine and did not question the inspiration of the deuterocanonical books. The general belief on this point was confirmed officially by Pope Eugene IV in the *Decretum pro Jacobitis*, promulgated at the Council of Florence (Monophysites of Alexandria and Jerusalem; the Bull *Cantate Domino* of Feb. 4, 1441) [2].

We know how the Council of Trent, in 1546, answered the negations of the Reformers respecting the deuterocanonical books, and also their doctrine on the criterion of canonicity. Basing itself upon the tradition which guaranteed the divine authority of the books received in the Church from time immemorial, it defined the canon in the decree *De canonicis Scripturis* and proclaimed that the inspiration of all the canonical writings was a truth of Catholic Faith : " That there can be no doubt possible respecting the Sacred Books which the Council itself holds to be such, the list of these books is established as follows. For the Old Testament : five books of Moses

---

Translator's note. — [1 Cf. H. H. HOWARTH, " The Influence of Saint Jerome on the Canon of the Western Church ", *Journal of Theological Studies*, X (1909), 481-496; XI (1910), 321-347; XII (1911), 1-18].

Translator's note. — [2 See A. FRIES, C. S. S. R., " Der Schriftkanon bei Albert dem Grossen ", *Divus Thomas* (1951), 345-368, and 402-428].

(Genesis, Exodus, Leviticus, Numbers, Deuteronomy); Josua, Judges, Ruth, and four books of Kings; two books of Paralipomenon; the First Book of Esdras, and the Second, which is called Nehemias; Tobias, Judith, Esther, and Job; the Davidic Psalter of one hundred fifty Psalms; Proverbs, Ecclesiastes, Canticle of Canticles, Wisdom, Ecclesiasticus; Isaias, Jeremias with Baruch, Ezechiel, and Daniel; the Twelve Minor Prophets (Osee, Joel, Amos, Abdias, Jonas, Micheas, Nahum, Habacuc, Sophonias, Aggeus, Zacharias, and Malachias); two books of Machabees, the First and the Second ". The definition of the Council of Trent was renewed by the Vatican Council in 1870.

II. — History of the canon of the New Testament.

The books or writings which the Council of Trent, in conformity with the ancient tradition, received as " sacred and canonical " are twenty-seven in number : the four Gospels, the Acts of the Apostles, fourteen Epistles of Saint Paul, two of Saint Peter, three of Saint John, one of Saint James, one of Saint Jude, and the Apocalypse of Saint John *(Decretum de canonicis Scripturis)*. Among these writings, seven are called deuterocanonical, because they were not always universally recognized as canonical, namely, Heb., Jas., 2 Pet., 2 and 3 Jn., Jude, and Apoc.

Just as in the case of the Old Testament, the New Testament collection was only gradually established. The Apostles did not bequeath their writings to their successors under the form of a sharply and specifically defined collection. Christ Himself had not written : He had taught. His immediate disciples taught before they wrote, and in their minds writing was never anything more than auxiliary to the spoken word. The New Testament writings are for the most part of an occasional character, composed to meet particular situations or needs, and their authors had neither the intention nor the thought of collaborating in a common work. The Churches which possessed these various documents exchanged them with one another on a mutual basis, and a collection was gradually formed. There is thus a history of the canon of the New Testament.

1. — *FORMATION OF THE COLLECTION.*

In the beginnings of the Church, the rule of Faith was contained exclusively in the teaching given by those who had received from Christ the command to preach the Gospel. But gradually as communities and missionaries multiplied, as those who had been " eyewitnesses and ministers of the Word " (Lk. 1 : 2) went elsewhere or died, as the expectation of the Second Coming became less intense and the new cult was being organized, the usefulness of a written Gospel appeared more and more evident. Since the Apostolic catechesis had been committed to writing under the form of the three recensions which we call the Synoptic Gospels, these texts, naturally, were held in special esteem, for they contained the teaching of the Master together with a history of His life. The communities of Syria had the Gospel according to Matthew, those of Greece, the Gospel according to Luke, and that of Rome, the Gospel according to Mark. As these Churches maintained constant relations with one another — and we have concrete and precise evidence on this point, there is strong probability for believing that they had made an exchange of their written catecheses before the end of the first century. The contrary would be all the more surprising, inasmuch as several of Saint Paul's letters had been communicated under these conditions before the year 100, as we shall see shortly in connection with Saint Clement. The Fourth Gospel bears witness to this diffusion of the synoptic narratives, for two of these at least, namely the Gospels of Mark and Luke, were known by the author, and by the Christians of the province of Asia for whom John's book was intended. In the case of the Second Gospel, this is confirmed by the accounts of the Elders collected by Papias (cf. Eusebius, *H. E.*, III, **39**, 15).

The writings of the Apostolic Fathers [1] furnish definite proof that, from the first decades of the second century, the great

---

[1] For the exact references, see the *Index* to K. BIHLMEYER's edition, *Die apostolischen Väter* [a revision of FUNK's edition] (Tübingen, 1920). [See also J. A. KLEIST, S. J., *The Epistles of Saint Clement of Rome and Saint Ignatius of Antioch*, Westminster, Maryland, 1946, and *the Didache, the Epistle of Barnabas, the Epistles and Martyrdom of Polycarp, the Fragments of Papias, the Epistle to Diognetus*, 1948 (Ancient Christian Writers. The Works of the Fathers in Translation. Edited by J. QUASTEN and J. C. PLUMPE, Nº 1 and 6)].

Churches were in possession of a book, or of a group of books, to which the name " Gospel " was currently given and to which reference was made as to a document having authority and universally known. The earliest example of the use of the word εὐαγγέλιον to designate the *written* Gospel is found about 100-110 in the *Didache* and in Saint Ignatius of Antioch. When the Apostolic Fathers refer to the Gospel, they never mention any author's name, but content themselves with a reference to the word of the Lord (ὁ Κύριος) [1]. Moreover, they employ the Gospel according to Matthew more than the others [2].

These same writers were acquainted with several letters of Saint Paul : Rom., 1 Cor., Eph., Heb. (Saint Clement of Rome); 1 Cor., Eph. (Saint Ignatius); Rom., 1 and 2 Cor., Gal., Phil., 1 and 2 Tim (Saint Polycarp), etc. There is every reason to believe that their correspondents also had copies of these epistles. While the Apostle himself was still alive, the Churches of Achaea, Macedonia, and Asia, must have exchanged among them the letters which they had received from their founder. The Second Letter of Saint Peter undoubtedly alludes to the collection which was formed in this way (3 : 15-16). That Luke and Timothy themselves actively engaged in bringing together the writings of their master, seems most probable when we know that the letters of Saint Ignatius were already collected before his death (cf. Saint Polycarp, *Phil.* 13, 2).

About 125 A. D., therefore, there were two groups of writings which enjoyed an Apostolic guarantee and whose authority was recognized by all the communities possessing them. The heads of the Churches, however, had made no official pronouncements on the character of the books employed for instruction and in the liturgy. The collection varied from one Church to another not only in respect to the number of received books but also in respect to their nature, some writings which ought never to have been recognized as canonical (Saint Clement's Letter to the Corinthians, the *Didache*, the Letters of Saint Ignatius) enjoying, in certain places, an authority comparable to that accorded to the Epistles of Saint Paul.

---

[1] Cf. *The New Testament in the Apostolic Fathers*, by a Committee of the Oxford Society of Historical Theology (Oxford, 1905).

Translator's note. — [2 See A. Wikenhauser, *Einl. in das N. T.* (2nd ed., 1956), p. 145].

From this period on we have positive proof of the belief in
the sacred character and in the normative value of the writings
which constituted the nucleus, as it were, of the collection which
was in the process of becoming the Canon of the New Testament.
Saint Ignatius puts the Gospel on the same level with the
ancient Scriptures (*Ad Smyrn.* **5**, **1**; **7**, 2). The author of the
Epistle of Barnabas (*ca.* 120), in citing a statement of our Savior
recorded in Mt. **22** : 14, uses the formula of introduction
employed for the Old Testament : ὡς γέγραπται. The homily
known as the Second Letter of Saint Clement (between 120
and 150) contains a reference to the Gospel (Mt. **9** : 13) in
these terms : " Another Scripture says " (**2** : 4). In another
passage of the same document (**14** : 2) the (written) teaching
of the " Apostles " and that of the " books " (of the Old
Covenant) are presented as having one and the same authority.
As regards the Epistles of Saint Paul, two texts list them among
the Scriptures : 2 Pet. **3** : 15-16, and the Letter of Polycarp
to the Philippians, **12** : 1 (with citations from Ps. **4** : 5 and
Eph. **4** : 26). These are the only instances in which, before 140,
any New Testament writings are called " Scripture ". The
number, certainly, is very small, but the force of usage, which
reserved this title for the books of the Old Testament, must
be taken into account. This usage went back to the first
preachers of Christianity and was to exercise its influence still
on Saint Justin and Saint Hippolytus.

From 140 to 220, Christianity makes more and more contact
with the pagan world, and the conquest of the latter has begun.
During this period, the pastors of the Church are on the watch
to preserve in its purity the Apostolic teaching which is menaced
by heretics, while its learned men make themselves apologists
of a religion to which the imperial power has avowed its hostility.
The testimonies on the New Testament collection become more
numerous and more precise.

About 140, Papias, bishop of Hierapolis in Phrygia, knows
among other Apostolic writings, the Gospels of Mark and
Matthew — he is the first to cite these names, — 1 Jn., 1 Pet.,
and Apoc., and he says that the last was " inspired by God ".
In the same period, in Roman circles, the author of the Shepherd
of Hermas appears familiar with the Synoptic Gospels, with
the Gospel of Saint John, and with the Apocalypse. Marcion,

on his side, is a witness to the existence of a New Testament collection through the expurgated canon which he draws up. Of the Gospels, he retains only that of Saint Luke, corrected in accordance with his own personal ideas, and of the Epistles of Saint Paul he keeps only ten, arranged in the following order (according to Tertullian and Saint Epiphanius) : Gal., 1 and 2 Cor., Rom., 1 and 2 Thess., Laodiceans (Eph.), Col., Phil., and Philem.

Some years later, about 150-155, Saint Justin speaks of the " Memoirs of the Apostles " or " Gospels " which are read " with the writings of the Prophets " in the meetings devoted to worship (1 *Apol.* **67**, 3 ff.; cf. **66**, 3, and *Dial.* **103**, 8). In addition to the four Gospels, he is acquainted with Acts, Rom., 1 Cor., Gal., Eph., Col., 2 Thess., Heb., 1 Pet., and he cites the Apocalypse, which he knows was written by John the Apostle (*Dial.* **81**, 4). His disciple Tatian utilized the four Gospels at Rome to construct a harmony of the Gospels, which was given the title *Diatessaron* [1]. This work was translated from Greek into Syriac about 172 and was adopted as an official text by the Churches in the region of Edessa. At this date, therefore, the Church of Rome and the Syrian Churches of Osrhoëne employed our four Gospels, and these four exclusively, for catechetical and liturgical purposes.

Saint Irenaeus (*ca.* 180-190) is a witness to the same usage in respect to the Gospels. Furthermore, he cites all the books of the New Testament, except Hebrews, which he does not regard as Pauline, and Phil., Jude, 2 Pet., and 3 Jn. For his citations from the New Testament he uses the same introductory formula as in citing from the Old, and he stresses the unity of the Scriptures (he uses the plural), which have the Word of God, Jesus Christ, as their author. The testimony of Saint Irenaeus is all the more important since the bishop of Lyons was familiar with the practices of the Churches of Asia Minor, Rome, and Gaul [2].

Saint Hippolytus, like Saint Irenaeus, regards the New Testament as a collection which is sacred and closed, and in which no other writings except those of the Apostles should

---

[1] A fragment of the Diatessaron in the original Greek was found at Dura-Europos in 1933 and is to be dated from *ca.* 220 A.D.

[2] J. Hoн, *Die Lehre des hl. Irenäus über das N. T.* (Münster i. W., 1919).

have a place. He cites all books with the exception of Phil., Jude, 2 and 3 Jn. He too does not accept a Pauline authorship for Hebrews.

The *Muratorianum* [1] or the Canon of Muratori gives us even more exact information on the books which were accepted by the Church of Rome *ca.* 180-190. This document, of which only 85 lines are preserved, was discovered by Muratori at Milan in 1740. Zahn and Lagrange attribute the work to Saint Hippolytus. The Ms., dating from the VIIIth century, is written in a barbarous Latin, through which the original language, Greek, is recognizable. Strictly speaking, this catalogue — the oldest which we possess for the New Testament — does not have the character of an official document, but it betrays the hand or manner of a person in high office. According to the text — taken *prout sonat*, without any other changes except orthographical corrections — the writings of the Apostles (l. 80), composed for the whole Church (ll. 55-59), are received for public reading (ll. 73 and 77). The Gospels are mentioned first [2]. Then come the Acts of the Apostles and the Epistles of Saint Paul in the following order : 1 and 2 Cor., Eph., Ph., Col., Gal., 1 and 2 Thess., Rom., Philem., Tit., 1 and 2 Tim., Jude, 1 and 2 Jn., Apoc. The Apocalypse of Peter is said to be received by some, while others " do not wish that it be read in the assembly ". The Shepherd of Hermas, which " has been written recently ", should not be counted " among the Apostolic writings ", and it ought not to be read in public. Finally, to be rejected are : a letter to the Laodiceans and one to the Alexandrians, " attributed falsely to Paul in order to support the heresy of Marcion ", as well as all the books of the Gnostics. No mention is made of Heb., of 1 and 2 Pet., nor of 3 Jn. On the other hand, the Wisdom of Solomon appears among the books received.

In North Africa, Tertullian († after 225) utilizes the New Testament writings as normative texts in matters of Faith and morals. He presents the Gospels as irrefutable proofs in

---

[1] For the text, see the works of ZAHN, PREUSCHEN, LAGRANGE, listed in the *Bibliography* (p. 126) and in the *Institutiones Biblicæ*, published by the Pontifical Biblical Institute (5th ed., Rome 1937), Vol. I, pp. 210-212.

[2] The first two Gospels certainly were at the head of the list, for line 1 refers to the Gospel of Mark.

arguments and discussions (cf. his use of the word *instrumentum*, which is borrowed from juridical terminology, *Adv. Marc.* **4**, 2). Only Jas. and 2 Pet. are not cited in his works. Tertullian attributes Hebrews to Barnabas and excludes it from the body of Scripture.

If we base our judgment on Clement of Alexandria, the New Testament collection, towards the end of the second century, did not have as sharply defined limits in the Church of Egypt as in the Churches of the West. Clement recognized as " Scripture " all the books which subsequently remained in the official collection, but in his doctrinal and apologetic treatises he employed also Christian apocryphal works and the writings of the ancient philosophers, quotations from these last being intermingled with those from the Sacred Books. Eusebius tells us (*H. E.* VI, **14**, 1) that he considered as " Scripture " the Epistle of Barnabas and the Apocalypse of Peter. Further, the First Letter of Clement, the *Didache*, the Shepherd of Hermas, the *Kerygma Petri* or Preaching of Peter were, in his eyes, inspired books. As a catechist, Clement adhered to the rule of Faith (χανών) furnished by Scripture and Tradition; but, as an apologist, he used all the writings which presented themselves to him under the aegis of a great name, whether the name was that of a philosopher or that of an Apostle. In this he was only following the example already given by Alexandrian Judaism. The list in the *Codex Claromontanus* [1], which contains, along with all the Catholic Epistles, the Epistle of Barnabas, the Shepherd, the Acts of Paul, and the Apocalypse of Peter, bears witness to views as broad as those of Clement in respect to the question of canonicity.

From what has been said, it is evident that the New Testament collection, towards the end of the second century, was nearly the same in the great Churches of both East and West. Our four Gospels, which were sharply distinguished from the apocryphal gospels, formed its base and at the same time its first section. The " canon of the Gospels " possibly became fixed *ca.* 150-160, when Polycarp of Smyrna went to Rome to confer with bishop Anicetus. This is only an hypothesis, but it has its justification in the circumstance that the canonicity

[1] See p. 84, n. 1.

of the four Gospels is established *de facto* from this period. The second section comprised thirteen epistles of Saint Paul, 1 Pet., 1 Jn., Jude, Acts, and Apoc. It is probable that 2 and 3 Jn. formed one unit with 1 Jn., as Philem. with Col. All these writings enjoyed the same authority as the books of the Old Testament. As regards Heb., Jas., and 2 Pet., certain Churches only received them as " Scripture ".

In the Chester Beatty Papyri (**P**45, 46, 47), we now possess an almost complete New Testament collection. The Catholic Epistles alone are wanting. U. Wilcken, one of the most distinguished papyrologists, assigns **P**45 (Gospels and Acts) and **P**46 (Pauline Epistles) to the beginning of the third century, but believes that **P**47 (Apocalypse) is some twenty years later. Heb. is in the *Corpus Paulinum*, but not the Pastoral Epistles.

Without question, the writings recognized as normative for the Faith owed their first title of authority to their Apostolic origin. Two of the Gospels had even been written, it is true, by disciples, Saint Mark and Saint Luke; but they reproduced the Apostolic catechesis and could be considered as approved by the Apostles themselves. Liturgical use gave the second title; early and general use was equivalent to an official consecration. The third title was orthodoxy in doctrine; the teaching contained in the work had to be in accord with the ever living Apostolic tradition, as in shown by the example of Serapion, bishop of Antioch from 190 to 212. On being questioned about the Gospel of Peter, Serapion, who did not know the book, authorized its reading. Then, after examining the work, he changed his mind and condemned the book as tainted with heresy (Cf. Eusebius, *H. E.*, VI, 12, 3 ff.).

These titles were lacking in the case of the apocryphal books as also in the case of some ecclesiastical writings which enjoyed the honor of being read publicly in certain Churches. The apocryphal literature offered, for the edification of the faithful, other gospels and other acts which were put under the aegis of Apostles' names; but the source of these productions was generally known, several among them having a pronounced heretical flavor. Zahn has noted in the Apostolic Fathers four citations which he considers were taken from apocryphal gospels (2 Clem. 5, 2-4; 8, 5; 12, 2-6; Saint Ignatius, *Ad Smyrn.* 3, 2). It is possible that the words cited come from non-canonical writings, although another source, namely oral tradition, is not to be completely excluded (cf. the *Sayings of Oxyrhynchus*). But in any case, the extremely small number of citations of this kind is a witness to the credit already enjoyed in this period by the canonical Gospels. Ecclesiastical writings such as the First Epistle of Clement, the Didache, the Epistle of Barnabas, the Shepherd of Hermas, remained on the fringes of the collection without being incorporated into it, because it was known that they did not come from the Apostles. Three of these works, it is true, were occasionally cited as " Scripture " (Didache and Barn., by Clement of Alexandria; Hermas, by Saint Irenaeus, Tertullian, and Clement), but it would not be proper, in this case, to speak of any general use [2].

Among the influences which helped to hasten the formation and delimitation of the collection must be mentioned, in the first place, the reaction produced in the Church by the invasion of Gnostic writings, the pretentions of Marcion [1], and the Montanist doctrines. Without doubt, even before these dangers, pastors were anxious to define more precisely the distinctive characteristics of the books which were to be regarded as authoritative. Furthermore, the Edict of Diocletian (303), which ordered the Sacred Books to be sought out and burned, surely had the indirect result of leading certain Churches to differentiate more sharply between what was " Scripture " and what was not. A bishop was actually considered to be a *traditor* only when the books surrendered to the Roman authorities were sacred books.

2. — *THE FIXATION OF THE CANON.*

I. — **Among the Greeks.**

Origen († 254), Clement's successor as head of the Catechetical School at Alexandria, had visited the Churches of Rome, Palestine, Syria, Achaea, Cappadocia, and Arabia. He knew, therefore, what books were received in these places as authoritative or canonical. Yet we do not see that any change was

---

Translator's note. — [[1] Cf. J. RUWET, S. J., " Les *agrapha* dans les œuvres de Clément d'Alexandrie,", *Biblica* (1949), 133-160].

Translator's note. — [[2] On Marcion, see J. QUASTEN, *Patrology.* I Utrecht-Brussels, 1950, pp. 268-271, and the literature there cited.]

made under his influence in the Alexandrian collection of the New Testament, and this fact may be considered a proof that the scriptural collections in his time were nearly identical in the great Churches. According to Eusebius *H. E.* VI. 25), Origen had distinguished two classes of writings in the New Testament : those which were recognized by all (ὁμολογούμενα) and those which were questioned (ἀμφιβαλλόμενα). In actual fact, he considered that even the books in the second group were inspired, and he was not led to hesitate by the doubts which had been cast on Heb., 2 Pet., 2 and 3 Jn. He believed that the First Letter of Clement, the Epistle of Barnabas, the Shepherd of Hermas, the Gospel according to the Hebrews, and the Acts of Paul were also inspired writings, but he did not put them among the authoritative books.

Origen was no longer in Egypt, when, in connection with millenarism, a violent attack developed there against the Johannine authorship of the Apocalypse. The authority of the book, however, rested on the best tradition (cf. Saint Justin, Saint Irenaeus, Tertullian, Saint Hippolytus, Clement of Alexandria), and Origen had never doubted that its author was the Apostle John. Without daring to reject it, Dionysius of Alexandria († 264) denied its Apostolic origin, a denial which had serious consequences.

When Eusebius of Caesarea († 340) was drawing up, in the manner of an historian, a catalogue of the writings which had more or less sound titles to be included in the New Testament (*H. E.* III. 25), he let himself be influenced by the opinions which were current in the Greek world and did not give sufficient consideration to the practice of the Churches in the West. He indicates as books " received by all " (ὁμολογούμενα) : the four Gospels, Acts, fourteen Epistles of Saint Paul (including Heb.), 1 Jn., 1 Pet., and, " if one wishes ", Apoc.; as books " questioned, but generally received " (ἀντιλεγόμενα, γνώριμα ὅμως τοῖς πολλοῖς) : Jas., Jude, 2 Pet., 2 and 3 Jn.; as books " questioned, and spurious " (νόθα) : the Acts of Paul, the Shepherd, the Apocalypse of Peter, the Epistle of Barnabas, the Didache, the Apocalypse of John, " if one wishes ", and the Gospel according to the Hebrews; as books " entirely absurd and impious " (ἄτοπα πάντη καὶ δυσσεβῆ) : the heretical Gospels and Acts. It may be admitted that the list was not drawn up according to very rigid principles and that its character was such as to cause hesitation or to produce confusion. Eusebius does not commit himself on the Apocalypse; further, he designates as "questioned" certain books whose authority was accepted almost everywhere; and finally, he does not formally exclude the writings which he calls "spurious". The fact remains, nevertheless, that his catalogue comprises our twenty-seven (or without the Apocalypse, twenty-six) canonical books.

In the second half of the fourth century, Saint Cyril of Jerusalem, the Council of Laodicea, Saint Gregory Nazianzen, and Saint Amphilochius have the same canon, without the Apocalypse; likewise Saint Basil, Saint Gregory of Nyssa, and Saint Epiphanius, but with the Apocalypse. Saint Athanasius in 367, in his XXXIXth Pascal Letter, lists the twenty-seven books, and he declares that all are Apostolic and canonical, without making the slightest distinction among them. He adds that the Didache and the Shepherd of Hermas, although "not canonized", are to be employed in the instruction of catechumens on the same rank with Wis., Ecclus., Est., and Jud.

We may say that the canon is fixed among the Greeks from this period. The canonicity of the Apocalypse will still be discussed from the fifth to the seventh century by some theologians, but in the end it will be accepted by all, in part under the influence of the Churches of the West which had never had any doubts on the subject. Mss. ℵ (4th cent.) and A (5th cent.), both probably Egyptian in origin, contain the New Testament complete, and, in addition, Barn. and the Shepherd (in ℵ), and 1 and 2 Clem. (in A).

2. — Among the Latins.

The Churches of the West, in general, exhibited great fidelity in retaining the books which had been transmitted to them as coming from the Apostles, but they raised objections against accepting as canonical those which they had not recognized from the beginning.

Saint Cyprian († 258) cited all the writings of the New Testament, except Philem., Heb., Jas., 2 Pet., Jude, and 2 and

3 Jn. No inference can be drawn from his silence in respect to Philem., Jude, and 2 and 3 Jn., for the brevity of these epistles is a sufficient explanation, and we know, furthermore, that a bishop introduced a passage from 2 Jn. at the Council of Carthage in 256. Heb., Jas., and 2 Pet., then, remain as books not included in the collection of the African Church about the middle of the third century. This corresponds to the practice attested by Tertullian. There is every reason to believe that the collection was the same at this date in the Churches of Rome, Dalmatia, Gaul, and Spain, i.e., in the Christian world of the Latin tongue.

A century later, Heb., Jas., and 2 Pet. are known from Saint Hilary († 367), who, during his exile in the East, made contact with the Greeks. On the other hand, Heb., Jas., and Jude are not in the African catalogue (*ca.* 360) published by Mommsen. The author of Ambrosiaster (*ca.* 370) considers Heb. canonical, but he does not believe that this epistle was written by Saint Paul. Saint Ambrose († 397), on the contrary, cites it as Pauline, and, besides, he is acquainted with Jude and 2 Pet. Priscillian († 385), who constantly relies upon the authority of the canonical books, had a collection of the whole New Testament. The same is true of Jerome when he undertook the revision of the Old Latin Version in 382 (cf. his letter to Paulinus, *Epist.* 53, *ca.* 394). Saint Filastrius of Brescia, in his *Diversarum Hereseon liber* (*ca.* 383), gives a list which contains the seven Catholic Epistles; he omits Hebr. here, but speaks elsewhere of this work as having been written by Saint Paul (**60**, 4; **61**, 1-2).

These different testimonies show that the authority of the Epistle to the Hebrews and of the Catholic Epistles was recognized progressively in the West during the second half of the fourth century, i.e., during the same period in which the Apocalypse was an object of discussion in the Churches of the Greek East. This enrichment of the Latin canon was recorded and confirmed officially in Africa by the Councils of Hippo (393) and Carthage (397 and 419), and in Italy [1] and

---

[1] It is to be noted that three of the Mss. containing this letter, and among them the best Ms. of all, read *Apostoli Pauli epistulæ XIII.* The others have XIV.

Gaul by the letter of Innocent I to Exuperius of Toulouse (405) [1]. The canon of the New Testament approved by the councils of 393 and 397 comprises twenty-seven writings, and among these are *Epistulæ Pauli apostoli XIII, eiusdem ad Hebræos una*. As we see, Heb. is in last place and is supernumerary, the custom persisting of always counting only thirteen Epistles of Saint Paul. There is even justification for thinking that, in the case of Heb., the conciliar formula indicates a recent addition. But Saint Augustine, from 397 (*De doctr. Christ.* II, 8, 13), Rufinus of Aquileia, before 410 (*Comm. in symb. apost.*, 37), and the Council of Carthage held in 419 all mention fourteen letters, listing Heb. in the *Corpus Paulinum*, as had been done by the Council of Laodicea in 363 and by Saint Athanasius in 367, in accordance with the usage followed in the Greek Churches (cf. P[46] — Chester Beatty Papyri — where Heb. comes immediately after Rom.).

But this does not mean that all doubts relative to the authenticity of Heb., Jas., Jude, 2 Pet., 2 and 3 Jn., had completely disappeared. In respect to Heb., Saint Jerome declares that it matters little to whom this epistle should be assigned, since it was written by an ecclesiastical author and is read daily in the Churches (*Epist.* 129 *ad Dardanum*, 3; cf. *De viris*, 59; *Epist.* 53, etc.), while Saint Augustine reveals himself as hesitant from 406, preferring to rely in this matter on " the authority of the Churches of the East " (*De pecc. mer. et remiss.* 1, 50), and in his last writings cites this epistle as an anonymous work. On Jas., Saint Jerome observes : " It is claimed that this Letter was written by another under his name (the Apostle's), although, little by little, it has gained authority "; on Jude : " This Epistle is rejected by the largest number, yet it is deserving of authority because of age and usage, and it is included in the Sacred Scriptures "; on 2 Pet. : " The majority deny that this Letter is his (Peter's), in view of the differences in its style in relation to his first Letter "; on 2 and 3 Jn. : " The two Letters are attributed to John the Presbyter " (*De viris*, 1, 2, 4, 9).

---

[1] Not much weight can be given here to the *Decretum Gelasianum*, or Pseudo-Gelasius, even if a distinction is made between the various documents which constitute this work, for none of these goes back to the time of Pope Damasus (366-384).

While making these reserves or merely reporting them for the sake of information, the two Doctors employed these same epistles as inspired and canonical texts, in accordance with general practice and the decisions of African councils approved by Rome (cf. canon 39 of the Council of Carthage, 397, *in fine*). Saint Jerome and Saint Augustine, then, held that all the books of the New Testament were of Apostolic origin, or that those books which had not been written by Apostles were at least guaranteed by Apostolic authority. This belief rested on ancient tradition, which, in spite of some hesitation and fluctuation, was marked by definite and certain continuity. It was confirmed, furthermore, by ecclesiastical usage.

Thus there was agreement in the Latin Church with respect to the writings of the New Testament which all were to consider canonical. Two centuries later, Saint Isidore of Seville evoked the doubts raised by some at an earlier date respecting the Apostolic origin of several works in the New Testament (Heb., Jas., 2 Pet., and 2 and 3 Jn.), but he regarded these books unquestionably as inspired and canonical. In the Middle Ages, we still encounter some discussions regarding Heb. But Saint Thomas Aquinas († 1274) and Nicolas of Lyra († 1340) maintained that this epistle was Pauline and thus put to rest all remaining doubts. It is a curious fact that during this same period the apocryphal letter of Saint Paul to the Laodiceans (Col. 4 : 16) enjoyed great authority in the Latin Church, without, however, being held to be canonical. We find it in more than a hundred Latin Mss, and especially in the *Codex Fuldensis* of the Vulgate. Similarly, the *Shepherd of Hermas* and the *Third Letter of Paul to the Corinthians* (apocryphal) figure in the same Latin Mss of the Middle Ages, although none in this period considered these texts as canonical.

When the Humanists entered upon the scene at the beginning of the XVIth century, they did not fail to recall and to take pleasure in emphasizing the divergent views found in ecclesiastical tradition regarding the origin and canonicity of certain books of the Bible. Erasmus († 1536) was censured by the theologians of the Sorbonne for having evoked — without refutation — the doubts expressed by some of the ancient Fathers in respect to the Apostolic origin of Heb., Jas., 2 Pet., 2 and 3 Jn., and Apoc. However, he accepted these books as canonical, and, about the same time, Cardinal Cajetan († 1534) professed opinions quite analogous to those of the learned humanist. Martin Luther († 1546) had already adopted a radical position in his *New Testament*, printed in 1522. According to him, the names and qualifications of the authors of the Sacred Books mean little; the value and authority of these writings are to be judged on the basis of their teaching respecting the work of Christ and justification. There is no other criterion for the canonicity of a book than that.

When the Council of Trent took up the question of the canon of Scripture, it reacted strongly against the assertions of Luther and it defined its position in most explicit terms. We have seen above (pp. 86-87) the Decree promulgated on April 8, 1546. This document of the ecclesiastical Magisterium fixed definitely the catalogue or canon of the Sacred Books for both the Old and New Testaments.

As we know, the Fathers gathered at Trent had planned, from the beginning of their deliberations, to determine precisely upon what authorities they might base their definitions in the dogmatic and in the moral order. Hence they were led to declare what were the Sacred Books received and recognized in the Church as a base for the rule of Faith, with Tradition being regarded as another base. They abstained deliberately from examining the proofs for the canonicity of certain writings discussed in the past and decided to proclaim as canonical — without any restriction — all the books " that were traditionally read in the Catholic Church and contained in the ancient Latin Vulgate ". The question of canonicity was settled, but the problems relating to the authenticity of the Sacred Books, however, was not, since the council had no intention of solving them. This observation is important. Actually in the official list of canonical books, Heb. appears among " the fourteen letters of Saint Paul, a letter bears the name of " the Apostle James ", and another that of " the Apostle Jude ". However, it is the feeling of theologians and exegetes that this does not imply that Paul himself wrote Heb., or that James is the Apostle James the Less, or that Jude is the Apostle Jude Thaddeus.

3. — Among the Syrians.

In the first centuries of Christianity, there were two Syrias :
one was Hellenized, spoke Greek, and had Antioch as its capital,
while the other remained Semitic, employed an Eastern
Aramaean dialect called Syriac, and had as its principal centers
Edessa and Nisibis. The Churches of Mediterranean Syria,
especially that of Antioch, were in continuous relations with
the Churches of Rome and Alexandria. The same was not
true, however, of the Christian communities in the region of
Edessa, which constitued a national Church from the time
that Christianity became a state religion under Abgar IX
(*ca.* 200). Since each half of the Syrian world went its own
way, it will be convenient to examine first the history of the
canon among the Greek-speaking Syrians, and secondly the
history of the canon among the Syrians using Syriac.

We have seen earlier (p. 89) that, already in the lifetime
of Saint Ignatius, Christian Antioch possessed various New
Testament writings (Gospels and Pauline Letters). In the
time of Saint Theophilus and Serapion, about 180-210, the
collection appears to have comprised all the books of the New
Testament, with the exception of the four shorter Catholic
Epistles. A century later, Lucian of Samosata, who was trained
at Edessa, rejected the Apocalypse under the influence of the
Eastern Syrians, and this explains why Saint John Chrysostom
(† 407), Theodore of Mopsuestia († 428), and Theodoret († 457)
never cite this book. The canon of Antioch in the fifth century,
therefore, did not contain 2 Pet., 2 and 3 Jn., and Apocalypse,
and, under the influence of Antioch, Constantinople did not
accept these writings either. Furthermore, since the three
longer Catholic Epistles (Jas., 1 Pet., 1 Jn.) did not appear in
the collection of Edessa, Theodore of Mopsuestia declared them
to be non-canonical. Cosmas Indicopleustes (*ca.* 550), although
well acquainted with the traditions of the Syrians, recognized
as authentic Jas., 1 Pet., and 1 Jn., but doubted the canonicity
of the shorter Epistles. In the same period, a favorable reaction
towards the Apocalypse took place in Antiochene circles, and
this book was again accepted by the Churches of Antioch and
Constantinople (cf. Leontius of Byzantium, *ca.* 530, and Andreas
of Caesarea, *ca.* 600). Eventually, the shorter Epistles were

incorporated into the official collection, and we know that Saint John Damascene († 754) had the complete canon of twenty-seven books.

Tatian, as was stated earlier (p. 91), during his sojourn in Rome had composed a harmony of the four Gospels. When he returned to his native country, Adiabene, he translated his Diatessaron into Syriac about the year 172. This translation became the official Gospel of the Syrians of Mesopotamia and remained such to the fifth century, i.e., until the adoption of the Peshitto as a canonical text (see pp. 607-609). A Syriac version of the " Separate " Gospels *(Da-Mepharreshe)*, made about 200, could not supplant the Diatessaron, as is evident from the Gospel quotations in Aphraates and Saint Ephraim (middle of the fourth cent.). These two writers had at their disposal the Book of Acts and the Epistles of Saint Paul, but we do not know when the Syriac translation of these works was made. Curiously enough, Philem. was not then in the Syrian *Corpus Paulinum*, although this *Corpus*, on the other hand, contained a Third Epistle to the Corinthians (apocryphal). The Syriac Catalogue of Sinai, which dates from about 400, lists the fourteen Epistles of Saint Paul, but mentions neither the Catholic Epistles nor the Apocalypse. At the beginning of the fifth century, the Peshitto was adopted as the official text of the Scriptures, and Jas., 1 Pet., and 1 Jn. entered the Syriac canon. The four shorter Catholic Epistles and the Apocalypse were still missing when the Syrian Church split into two heretical sects after the Councils of Ephesus (431) and Chalcedon (451). The Nestorians remained faithful to the incomplete canon of the Peshitto, while the Monophysites admitted 2 Pet., Jude, 2 and 3 Jn., and Apoc. into this canon fifty years after they had separated from the Catholic Church.

APPENDIX

THE APOCRYPHA OF THE OLD AND NEW TESTAMENT.

1ᵉ The Word " Apocryphal " and Its History.

In Classical Greek the word ἀπόκρυφος was employed to indicate something hidden or secret. The Septuagint translators used the word in this sense (Isa. **45** : 3), and also Saint Paul

(Col. 2 : 3). The ecclesiastical writers of the first centuries of our era used the term to designate *pseudepigrapha*, or works of unknown origin whose content was open to suspicion, or which had not been admitted into the Churches for public reading, or which, consequently, did not figure in the canons or official lists. In practice the adjective was taken in a pejorative sense and, finally, in ecclesiastical circles, it became the equivalent of " suspect " or " heretical ".

Following Saint Jerome, Protestants label as *apocryphal* all the books of the Old Testament which were not in the Hebrew Bible, namely, the books or parts of books, which the Catholic Church calls *deuterocanonical* (See above, p. 70). Protestants likewise deisgnate as *apocryphal*, the *Prayer of Manasses*, *Books III and IV Esdras*, and *Books III and IV Machabees*. The books of the Old Testament which the Catholic Church designates as apocryphal are very commonly called *pseudepigraphical* by Protestants.

Apart from the question of origin or authorship, the word *apocryphal*, from the Catholic point of view, has its full and proper meaning only in relation to the canon of the Scriptures. Any writing is *apocryphal* which, although it presents itself more or less avowedly as inspired Scripture, is not in the official canon of the Sacred Books. This is, basically, a very old idea in the Church, for we already find its germ in Saint Irenaeus and Origen.

2ᵉ Classification, Literary Genre, Influence.

The Apocrypha fall into two series (the Apocrypha of the Old Testament and the Apocrypha of the New Testament), depending on their Jewish or Christian origin, and whether the subject treated is connected with the Old Testament or the New. Ordinarily, the title of the work in itself gives a sufficiently clear indication.

The Jewish Apocrypha are divided into two groups : the first containing works of Palestinian origin, and the other, works produced by the Jews of the Diaspora. But in practice, they are usually arranged according to the genre to which they belong (pseudo-historical, prophetic or apocalyptic, haggadic [1]

---

[1] The term *haggada* was used to designate the rabbinical teaching on questions of practical morality (see p. 685).

or paraenetic). The Apocrypha of the New Testament are classified according to the subject treated, but especially according to literary genre, under one of the following titles : gospels, acts, epistles, apocalypses.

The Apocrypha of the Old Testament are products of Judaism, while those of the New owe their inspiration to Christianity. The former reflect the religious and moral ideas of the Jewish world around the beginnings of the Christian era, while the latter reflect the beliefs, doctrines, and traditions which were current in certain circles, orthodox as well as heretical, in the first centuries of the Church.

The Apocrypha constitute a strange literature, and the first impression experienced by the reader in dealing with this material is a little like that of a traveller who ventures into a jungle. In order to offer greater satisfaction to that instinctive need which is felt by every believing soul in its attempts to give reality to its beliefs, to penetrate the mysteries of the present life and especially of the life to come, to enter into contact with the world of God and of spirits, the anonymous authors of these writings make use of all the means suited to strike the imagination of the reader, to satisfy his curiosity, and to win his assent.

To give greater success to their inventions and their dreams, this very special class of " sacred writers " resorted most frequently to literary fiction, and, in doing so, they hid themselves behind the names and personalities of the great men of the remote past who had been the friends and intimates of God. They show at times that they are well informed on the history of the Jewish nation, on the legislative work of Moses, on the lives and deeds of the patriarchs and prophets, on Messianic ideas and outlooks, on the Gospel history, and on the lives of the Blessed Virgin and the Apostles. For the sake of creating a stronger impression on the mind of the reader, they make free use of pretended revelations, appeal to their own divine inspiration, and claim for themselves a knowledge of things or traditions not yet disclosed.

All literary genres are represented in these productions, which were inspired by religious sentiment, born of the imagination, and conceived and utilized as a means of instruction or propaganda.

Some of the Jewish Apocrypha have the appearance of being commentaries on the Mosaic Law and, in such cases, reveal a marked paraenetic character. Others add pseudo-historical materials and details to Biblical narratives, and fall under the genre of " fictional history " or " pious fiction ". Others, finally, and these are definitely apocalypses, describe the events which are to indicate the liberation of the Jewish people and the end of this present world. In all these writings there is affirmed the faith of a people that suffers and protests, a people that waits and hopes tirelessly — an indomitable faith in the justice and fidelity of the God of Israel. Naturally, Messianic ideas have an important place in the Jewish apocrypha. However, in most cases, the strictly spiritual element is missing from the tableaux devoted to the person and work of the Messias. The divine Messenger is almost always represented as a glorious and victorious king whose first task will be to restore national independence and to guarantee to his faithful the joys of temporal revenge.

In the rich crop of New Testament Apocrypha, the gospels form the largest group. The Prologue to Saint Luke's Gospel (1 : 1-4) proves by itself alone that writings of the gospel type had multiplied in the lifetime of the Apostles themselves, both to satisfy the curiosity of believers and to give support to missionary propaganda. The Church, as we know, has retained as authoritative only the four accounts of the history of Jesus which are found in the canon.

The canonical Book of Acts was concerned almost entirely with Peter and Paul. Hence, apocryphal acts made up for the silence of Saint Luke on the activities of the other Apostles, especially in respect to the evangelization of the countries of the East. Some imaginary letters were composed on the model of the writings of Saint Paul, who in his own lifetime had complained of such forgeries. The Apocalypse of Saint John was also imitated in works of this genre which circulated under the names of the Apostles Peter and Paul.

The apocryphal books which were composed on the fringes of the Old Testament, especially the apocalypses, enjoyed a great success in the Jewish world, both in Palestine and in the various centers of the Diaspora. The reader found in these works supplementary information on the history of Israel, proof of the divine mercy towards the chosen people, and, above all, a source for reviving and cherishing old dreams of national revenge and liberation. The Christians themselves were interested in some of these productions, especially those which were closely related to recognized Biblical writings. The *Third Book of Esdras*, which had been admitted into the Septuagint, where it is 1 Esdras, is found in numerous Mss. of the Old Latin Version. The *Book of Henoch* figures in the Ethiopic Bible. The *Prayer of Manasses*, and III and IV (chs. 3-14) *Esdras* have been kept in the Clementine edition of the Vulgate, where they follow the canonical books in the form of an appendix. Finally, the Roman liturgy has retained and utilized a number of texts borrowed from the Apocrypha of the Old Testament. Thus, among other examples, the offertory of the Mass *Pro eligendo Summo Pontifice* is borrowed from *III Esdras*, and in the *Dies irae* the testimony of David is brought in to confirm that of the *Jewish Sibyl* (... *teste David cum Sibylla*).

The apocryphal literature of the New Testament exercised an enormous influence on Christian belief and thought of the first centuries. At a very early date, the responsible religious authorities had been able to put the faithful on their guard against the questionable character of these writings, many of which were clearly heretical, but their vehement remonstrances and their severe condemnations did not succeed in eliminating them completely. Down to the end of the Middle Ages, and even into the Renaissance period, popular piety, poetry, and the plastic arts were to draw freely from these books, in which legend took the shape of history, imagery was so picturesque and so touching, and what were called " the ancient traditions " were so easy to understand.

3. The Principal Apocryphal Books.

1. Apocrypha of the Old Testament.

Pseudo-historical genre.

1. *The Book of Jubilees* (or *Little Genesis*). Original text in Hebrew. Author : a Palestinian Jew, of Pharisee background and training; perhaps an Essene. The history of the world

is related in jubilee periods of 49 years each. The narratives of Genesis are glossed and enriched with traditions and legends current in the Jewish milieux of the time. It exhibits a marked reaction against the attempts of Hellenization. Date: *ca.* 100 B.C.

2. *The Third Book of Esdras* (or *I Esdras* in the Greek Bible). A conglomeration of pieces borrowed from three canonical books (2 Chr., Esd., Neh.), with the addition of a legend relating to Zorobabel. It was composed in Greek in the Alexandrian milieu to serve apologetic ends. Date: *ca.* 100 B.C.

3. *The Third Book of Machabees.* An account of a persecution againt the Jews of Alexandria in the time of Ptolemy IV (221-204 B.C.), falling under the genre of the edifying novel. It is the work of an Alexandrian Jew. Date: the beginning of the Christian era.

4. *The Ascension of Isaias.* A work of Palestinian origin. A mosaic of texts (the vision and martyrdom of Isaias, and the testament of Ezechias). It is a book composed in the first century A.D. by a Christian who made use of Jewish traditions as found in diverse writings. The text is preserved complete in an Ethiopic version.

5. *The Life of Adam and Eve* (or *The Apocalypse of Moses*). A strange work of very marked haggadic character building on the narrative of Genesis, giving an account of the origins of the Israelites and describing the coming of the Messias. Of Palestinian origin and written first in Hebrew. Date: *ca.* the end of last century B.C.

6. *The Letter of Aristeas.* A work of propaganda emanating from Alexandrian Judaism and composed *ca.* 100 B.C. It is the marvelous story of the Greek translation of the Hebrew Bible made in seventy two days at the demand of Ptolemy II Philadelphus (285-247). The author stresses the superiority of Jewish wisdom over pagan philosophy, the glory of Jerusalem and the Temple, and the excellence of the Mosaic Law.

Prophetic or apocalyptic genre.

1. *The Book of Henoch* (or the *Ethiopic Henoch*). A collection, in six sections, of exhortations, prophecies, and other writings

attributed to the patriarch Henoch. A composite work produced in the Palestinian milieu and written originally in Hebrew or Aramaic. Basically, it is an exposition of Jewish religious and moral beliefs of Messianic and eschatological character in the period shortly before the beginning of the Christian era. Date : between 150 and 50 B.C. The Ethiopic version was made in the fourth century A.D. from a Greek translation. This apocryphal work exercised considerable influence in Christian circles in the first centuries of our era.

2. *The Book of the Secrets of Henoch* (or the *Slavonic Henoch*). A typically apocalyptic work. Henoch relates the visions which he had when he visited the seven heavens. He describes the creation of the world and he unveils the secrets which were revealed to him regarding the future. Author : a Palestinian Jew who wrote in Greek. Only a version in Old Slavonic is extant. Date : the beginning of our era.

3. *The Assumption of Moses.* A tableau sketched by Moses of the destinies of Israel from the entrance of the Hebrews into the Promised Land down to the days of King Herod. It is the work of a rigid Pharisee, very strict regarding the observation of the Law and hostile to the Sadducees. Date : the first years of the Christian era.

4. *The Fourth Book of Esdras* (or *Apocalypse of Esdras*). A work from the end of the first century A.D. (certainly after 70) composed in Hebrew or in Aramaic by a Palestinian Jew who — perhaps — had contacts with Christianity. It is a book in which the sorrow and scandal felt by a Jew at the spectacle of the fall of Jerusalem and destruction of the Temple are described in emotional tones and language. It comprises seven visions which are conversations with God and which are concerned with the miserable lot of Israel, the last times, and the future glory of Jerusalem. None of the Jewish Apocrypha enjoyed such a wide and prolonged popularity in the Christian world as this work.

5. *The Apocalypse of Baruch* (or *Second Book of Baruch*). A work of Palestinian origin, written in Hebrew or Aramaic and preserved in a Syriac version. It was composed at the beginning of the second century A.D., after the *Apocalypse*

of Esdras. It contains Messianic and eschatological ideas current in the Jewish world following the catastrophe of the year 70.

6. *The Third Book of Baruch* (or the *Greek Baruch*). Date : middle of the second century A.D. A work of Jewish origin, but recast later by a Christian. Baruch describes what he was permitted to see in his journey to the five heavens.

7. *The Jewish Sibyl* (or *the Sibylline Books*). Already in the fifth century B.C. oracles attributed to the Sibyls and presented as divinely inspired circulated throughout Greece and Asia. The Alexandrian Jews made use of this means of religious propaganda, and, from the second century B.C., they put in circulation Sibylline oracles of their own composition in order to defend or spread the beliefs of Israel. Thus a Jewish Sibyl appeared beside the pagan Sibyls. The Christians were later to make use of the same device. The collection of Sibylline oracles comprises fourteen books, of which Book III is definitely Jewish. It is a collection of heterogeneous pieces dating from the second century B.C. The principal themes are the defense of monotheism, criticism of idolatry, the coming of the Messias, and eschatalogy. Book IV, composed at the end of the first century A.D., is likewise of Jewish stamp or inspiration, but it has been retouched by a Christian hand.

Haggadic and paraenetic genre.

1. *The Prayer of Manasses.* A short work belonging to the genre of penitential psalms. Based on 2 Chr. 33 : 11-13, it was written to exhort men to repentance and to encourage them to put trust in God. It is the work of a Hellenized Jew who wrote at the beginning of our era.

2. *The Testaments of the Twelve Patriarchs.* The twelve sons of Jacob appear in turn to make recommendations to their descendants. Each discourse is divided into three parts — biographic, paraenetic, and prophetic. Jewish moral teaching is presented here in its loftiest form. The original work was composed in Hebrew by a Pharisee of the same training and spirit as the author of the *Book of Jubilees*. Date : *ca.* 100 B.C.

3. *The Fourth Book of Machabees.* A product of Hellenistic Jewish philosophy. The author wishes to prove that Reason governed by Piety can control the passions. In support of his

thesis, he recalls the heroic courage of Eleazar and the seven brothers, whose martyrdom is related in 2 Machabees. Date : the first century A.D. (before the year 70).

4. *The Psalms of Solomon.* A collection distinct from the *Odes of Solomon*, which are Christian canticles of Syrian origin written between 100 and 150 A.D. The *Psalms of Solomon* comprise eighteen hymns very closely related to those in the Davidic Psalter. They were composed in Hebrew by a Palestinian Jew, a Pharisee (or by several), *ca.* the middle of the last century B.C. These prayers, in which the sentiments of the traditional hope and faith of Israel are expressed in a very simple but noble form, are cries from the soul and the heart to God in the face of oppression by impious pagans and of the infidelity of the official priesthood.

The texts mentioned below, and in particular, those found among the Dead Sea Scrolls, emanate from the same dissident religious group, the Community of the New Covenant. All reflect the same spirit of strict fidelity to the Law and of unfailing attachment to the Sadokite sacerdotal line.

5. *The Damascus Document* (or *Sadokite Document*). This work, discovered at Cairo in 1897 and published in 1910, sheds new light on the internal movements which agitated the Jewish world in the religious sphere and in its national life. The group or sect of the New Covenant had as its founder, in the days of Antiochus Epiphanes, a " Teacher of justice ", whose name is unknown. The first nucleus had been established by a sacerdotal elite, the sons of Sadoc, " the guardians of the Covenant ". Around them there was formed a community whose members supported the Machabees in the struggle against Hellenism. Later, this association separated itself from the Hasmonean high priests and opposed them. Since the group thus aroused the active hostility of the high priesthood, all members of the group — or at least a good part of it — took refuge in Damascus to devote themselves " to seeking God through a return to the Law ". The *Sadokite Document*, written in Hebrew *ca.* 100 B.C., has all the appearance of being the rule and plan of life of the adherents of the New Covenant.

6. *The Commentary on Habacuc.* This Hebrew text found at Qumran [see *Appendix* below] in 1947, was written *ca.* 50 B.C.

by a member of the New Covenant, either at Damascus or in the sister-community established at Qumran. It is inspired by the same ideas and reflects the same judgments as the *Sadokite Document*.

7. *The Hymns of Thanksgiving*. These poetical compositions — five in number — found at Qumran have the same origin and belong to the same period as the *Commentary on Habacuc*. These hymns easily bear comparison with the psalms of the Davidic Psalter.

8. *The Rule of the Community* [or *Manual of Discipline*]. This Hebrew text found at Qumran is closely related to the *Sadokite Document*, exhibiting the same principles, the same religious ideal, and the same cult of the Law. The doctrine of divine election and of predestination is presented as the basis for the moral and spiritual life of the members of the Community, " the sons of light and children of divine grace ". Obviously, a rule that is so precise in details and so imperative in its precepts was made for a group of a monastic type, whose members lived under the tutelage and control of Sadokite priests. All evidence would seem to confirm the belief that it was the rule of the Essene community established at Qumran itself a century before our era.

9. *The War of the Children of Light against the Children of Darkness* [revised title : *The Rule of War;* see *Appendix* below]. This Hebrew Ms from Qumran reflects and exhibits the vocabulary, principles, and spirit of the New Covenant. The sons of light are the sons of Levi, Juda, and Benjamin, camped in the Desert of Juda under the command of the Sadokite priests. Their adversaries are the sons of darkness, the disciples of Belial. The document is a kind of soldier's handbook, with a song of victory and a canticle of thanksgiving. Probable date : the last century B.C.

APPENDIX

THE DEAD SEA SCROLLS
by E. P. Arbez

Because of the extraordinary and continued interest aroused by the Dead Sea Scrolls, especially in the English-speaking world, a much fuller treatment of these documents than that given in *Initiation Biblique* is desirable, if not necessary, in the *Guide to the Bible*.

The region where the discoveries were made lies on the N. W. shore of the Dead Sea, about 8 miles S. of Jericho, 15 miles E. of Jerusalem, and a little over one mile from the Dead Sea. In the northern part of this section we have Khirbet Qumran, *ca.* 2 miles N. of Ain Feshka, frequently mentioned in the first reports to help locate the site. In the southern part are the caves of the Wady el Murabbaat, *ca.* 12 miles S. of Khirbet Qumran and *ca.* 3 miles W. of the Dead Sea. The Khirbet Mird is roughly between these two points, *ca.* 9 miles S. E. of Jerusalem, a short distance N. of the monastery of Mar Saba. (See e.g., *Rand McNally Bible Atlas*, by E. G. Kraeling : [New York, 1956] p. 15 ff.; J. T. Milik, *Dix Ans de Découvertes dans le Désert de Juda* [Paris, 1957], maps in front of book and p. 16; for details of the whole region : *Map of Western Palestine*, C. R. Conder and H. H. Kitchener).

The story of the accidental discovery of the first cave of Qumran in the early spring of 1947 by a shepherd, Muhammad ed-Dib (" the Wolf ") has been told repeatedly and need not be told again. (See early reports by J. C. Trever, *BA* [Sept., 1948], pp. 46-51, by Mar A. Y. Samuel, *ibid* [May, 1949], pp. 26-31, and by R. de Vaux, O. P., *RB* [1949], pp. 234-337). The account which in this country contributed most to arouse the interest of the general public is probably that of E. Wilson in the *New Yorker* (May 14, 1955), " A Reporter at Large : The Scrolls from the Dead Sea ". This is an excellent lively account where the author limits himself to reporting the facts; but unreliable where he ventures beyond his depth into historico-religious interpretation of the evidence. Other good accounts may be found in M. Burrows, *The Dead Sea Scrolls*, Part, (New York, 1955); G. Vermès, *Discovery in the Judean Desert*

(New York, 1956); J. M. Allegro, *The Dead Sea Scrolls* (Penguin Books, 1956), pp. 15-40; Milik, *op. cit.*, pp. 13-22. Yigael Yadin, son of Dr. E. L. Sukenik of the Hebrew University, Jerusalem, also gives a full account in his : *Ha-megillot ha-genuzot mi-midbar Yehudah* (Jerusalem-Tel Aviv, 1957), which is of special importance because of the part played by Dr. Sukenik in the early stages of the discovery. Sukenik, fully convinced of the genuineness of the discovery and of the antiquity of the Mss, which he connected with the Essenes, wanted to secure for Israel all the first Mss discovered, a project which his son Yadin finally succeeded in carrying out in 1954 (see Yadin, *op. cit.*, pp. 43-57).

The first Mss were bought partly by Mar A. Y. Samuel, head of the Syrian Orthodox Convent of St. Mark in Jerusalem, and by E. L. Sukenik of the Hebrew University. Those acquired by Mar Samuel comprised a complete text of *Isaias*, a text of *Habakuk* (chs. 1-2) with a *pesher* (explanation) applying the words of the prophet to the historical circumstances of the writer, and the *Rule* of the Community *(Serek hayahad)*, a " sectarian " document as it was defined at first by some as belonging to a Jewish sect, or *Manual of Discipline*. The latest study of the *Rule* is that just published by P. Wernberg Moller, *The Manual of Discipline. Translated and Annotated, with an Introduction* (Leiden, 1957), the first volume in the series of studies on the texts of the Desert of Judah edited by J. Van der Ploeg, O. P. Some fragments purchased by the Palestinian Museum in Jerusalem in 1950, probably belonging to the original find of 1947, are reproduced in *Discoveries in the Judaean Desert:* Vol. I *(Qumran Cave I)*, by D. Barthélemy, O.P. and J. T. Milik (Oxford, 1955), pp. 107-118. (Cf. also Menahem Zahary's article in *Ha-Do'ar* [Feb. 17, 1956, p. 304; in Hebrew]). With this document we should mention the Hebrew *Damascus Document* (known also as the *Damascus Covenant* or the *Zadokite Document*) which was found originally in a mediaeval copy in 1895 by Sol. Schechter among the Mss of the Genizah of the Synagogue in Old Cairo. It was edited as *Fragments of a Zadokite work* by Schechter in 1910. (Cf. R. H. Charles in *Apocrypha and Pseudipigrapha of the Old Testament*, II [1913], pp. 785-834). Critics differed considerably about the date of the composition, placing it from some time B.C. to the Middle

Ages. It was soon realized that the work was related to some Qumran documents in language and thought. In fact, some fragments of the work have been identified among the Dead Sea Mss, so that the Zadokite fragments must be studied with the new Mss. (Cf. H. H. Rowley, *The Zadokite Fragments and the Dead Sea Scrolls* [Oxford, 1952]; Chaim Rabin, *The Zadokite Documents* [Oxford, 1954]; Y. Yadin, *Megillot Genuzot...*, pp. 127-154; Baillet, *RB* [1956], pp. 513-523; S. Zeitlin, *The Zadokite Fragments* [a very good facsimile edition of the Cairo Mss (*Jewish Quarterly Review*, Monograph Series 1, 1952)]. In the lot of Mss bought by Mar Samuel was a scroll which could not be unrolled. It was supposed by some to be the apocryphal book of Lamech, only the title of which was known (cf. *CBQ* [1950], p. 231 f.). It turned out later to be an Aramaic apocryphon of Genesis (cf. Rershay, *Ha-Do'ar* [Feb. 24, 1956], p. 320; in Hebrew). *Isaias*, the *Rule*, and *Habakuk* were published in a photographic edition, with transcription in square writing, under the title : *The Dead Sea Scrolls of S. Mark's Monastery*, by M. Burrows with the assistance of J. C. Trever and W. H. Brownlee (Amer. Schools of Oriental Research, New Haven, 1950 and 1951).

The other Mss had been bought by Dr. E. L. Sukenik. They comprised a) an incomplete text of Isaias, b) a collection of *Hymns of Thanksgiving (Hodayot)*, and c), the *Rule of War* (*Serek ha-milhamah*, called first, *War of the Children of Light and the Children of Darkness*). Sukenik published two preliminary studies of the Mss, *Megillot Genuzot* [Jerusalem, 1948 and 1950], followed in 1954 by a posthumous edition of the three texts *(Osar hamegillot shebidey ha-universita ha-ibrit)* as well as an English edition, *The Dead Sea Scrolls of the Hebrew University* (Jerusalem, 1955). It may be said here that E. L. Sukenik fully accepted the genuineness of the discovery and the antiquity of the texts, which he connected with the Essenes. Of these texts, *The Scroll of the War* was published (in Hebrew) by Y. Yadin with an elaborate introduction and commentary (over 400 pages) in 1955 (Jerusalem, Bialik Foundation), and again by Father Jean Carmignac as *La Règle de la Guerre* (Paris, 1958; Hebrew text with French transl. and full commentary). Cf. also A. M. Haberman in *Ha-Do'ar* (Feb. 24, 1956), p. 320 (in Heb.). The *Hymns* are studied

thoroughly by Jacob Licht in his *Megillot ha-hodayot* (Jerusalem,
1957, Bialik Foundation) in a splendid Hebrew edition, with
introduction, text, and commentary. Finally, after Mr. J. Bi-
berkraut had succeeded in opening the so-called Book of Lamech,
N. Avigad and Y. Yadin were able to publish the scroll as
A Genesis Apocryphon (Jerusalem, 1956). This edition, both
English and Hebrew-Aramaic, is only preliminary, comprising
only the parts of the text which could be read. It will take
some time before other parts can be deciphered. This work
is the oldest Aramaic apocryphon that has reached us, and this
alone would make it especially valuable. The detailed
description of Sarah's beauty was featured in the daily press.

Thus all the scrolls of the discovery have become available
and a considerable number of books and articles have been
published about them. While there are considerable differences
in the interpretation of the texts, especially of the historical
allusions in them, there is general agreement on the authenticity
of the finds and the age of the texts, which naturally varies
according to the texts, roughly between 100 B.C. and 70 A.D.,
with the possibility that some texts found later may be older.
Thus F. M. Cross proposes to date one fragment about the end
of the second century B.C. : " A Ms of Samuel in an Archaic
Jewish Bookhand from Qumran ", *Journal of Biblical
Literature* (1955), pp. 165-172. The connection of the
Mss with the Essenes is also pretty commonly admitted.
However, as was to be expected, there has been some dissent.
Thus, in a most radical form, Dr. S. Zeitlin of Dropsie College
has consistently and stubbornly rejected the conclusions of
other scholars as completely wrong and unscientific. He has
even referred to the whole matter as a " hoax ". His radicalism
does not seem to have made much of an impression (cf. Y. Yadin,
Ha-megillot ha-genuzot mi-midbar Yehudah (Jerusalem-Tel Aviv,
1957), p. 181. For a more sympathetic view, see Dr. Yehudah
Rosental, " The Riddle of the Hidden Scrolls ", *Jubilee Volume
of Ha-Do'ar* (1957), pp. 53-63 (in Hebrew). Another most
unconventional view, hardly likely to be adopted by many
scholars, is that of H. E. Del Medico, *L'énigme des manuscrits
de la Mer Morte* (Paris, 1957), who sees in the Mss a collection
of writings of more or less heretical character condemned by
the Rabbis to burial in a Genizah. Some of the texts are

Christian or have been revised by a Christian. The Essenes had nothing to do with them, since, according to Del Medico, they did not exist. Other writers who go their own way are P. Kahle, *Die Hebräischen Handschriften aus der Höhle* (Stuttgart, 1951), who holds that the Mss, of different dates, were concealed *ca.* the third century A. D., and G. R. Driver, who in his *Hebrew Scrolls from the Neighborhood of Jericho and the Dead Sea* (Oxford, 1951) opposes a pre-Christian and early date of the Mss, rejecting the archaeological evidence and the arguments from palaeography as inconclusive, and sets a date *ca.* 500 A.D.

Now to go back to the account of the discovery. The first cave, identified, at the end of Jan., 1949, by a Belgian officer, Phil. Lippens, on U.N. service in Transjordan, who communicated the news to Mr. L. Harding of the Service of Antiquities and to Father de Vaux, O.P., in Jerusalem, was visited by them Feb. 15 — March 5, 1949. This was the first official scientific visit. Before this, plans had been made, and sometimes carried out, to visit it — E. L. Sukenik, in Nov. 1947 and Jan. 1948, Father Yusuf of the Syrian Monastery, in Aug. 1947, not to speak of earlier clandestine visitors. But other caves with Mss were found, mostly by Ta'amireh Bedouins, who have made a good business of it, in the Qumran region. Other caves were discovered in the *Murabba'at* region (1951-1952) which yielded texts mostly from the time of Bar Kokheba and the second Jewish revolt, 132-135 A.D. (Cf. de Vaux, *RB* [1953], pp. 268-275; Milik, *RB* [1953], pp. 276-294), and Khirbet Mird (1952), with material from the library of an ancient monastery (fifth and sixth cent. A.D.) : texts in Christian Aramaic of Palestine (cf. Milik, *RB* [1953], pp. 526-530), in Greek, and in Arabic. From unidentified caves the Ta'amireh got (1952?) Nabataean papyri (see Starky, *RB* [1954], pp. 161-184), fragments of a Greek version of the Minor Prophets (see Barthélemy, O. P., *RB* [1953], pp. 18-29), Hebrew and Aramaic texts, the dates varying from the end of the first century A.D. to Bar Kokheba.

The texts found in the Qumran region, especially in Cave 4, represent all the Protocanonical Books, except Esther. These allow us to form an idea of the Hebrew text of these books. In all essentials, their text is that of our Hebrew Bible. But in a number of instances, there are differences; the Hebrew text will agree with the LXX, which thus appears to follow a recension of the Hebrew different from the traditional Hebrew. This happens in the books of Samuel. See F. M. Cross, " A New Qumran Biblical Fragment Related to the Original Hebrew Underlying the Septuagint ", *BASOR* (Dec., 1953), pp. 15-26; also the recent Hebrew commentary on Samuel *(Sifrey Shemuel)* by M. S. Segal (Jerusalem, 1956), pp. 48-52 of the Introduction, and pp. 11-12, etc., of the Commentary.   Several Mss of Daniel represent the traditional text (cf. Barthèlemy, *Discoveries in the Judaean Desert*, I, pp. 150-152) — thus without any new material which could help to solve its problems.   But Qumran Cave 4 has yielded a non-Biblical Aramaic text which has a bearing on the book of Daniel, viz., *The Prayer of Nabonidus.* The prayer is introduced by a remark about the king's sickness — a malignant inflammation — and his stay in Teima which, according to the prayer, lasted seven years.   The prayer refers to the intervention of a Jew, one of the exiles of Babylon. This text reminds us of Daniel 4 and 5, which speak of Nabuchodonosor (605-502 B.C.) and his son Baltasar, while the prayer mentions — more correctly from the historical standpoint — Nabonidus (555-539 B.C.), who was the last king of Babylon and had a son Baltasar (Belsharusur). (Cf. Milik, *RB* [1956], pp. 407-411 and p. 415).   Some books are represented by fragments in archaic characters; so Exodus (cf. P. W. Skehan, *Journal of Biblical Literature* [1955], pp. 182-187), Job (cf. Milik, *Dix ans...*, p. 26).   On the Biblical texts, see Barthélemy-Milik, *Discoveries...*, I, pp. 49-72).

Among the Deuterocanonical Books we have Tobias, found in three Aramaic fragments and one in Hebrew.   These represent the long recension of the book which we read in the *Codex Sinaiticus* and in the Old Latin.   A fragment in Hebrew of Ecclesiasticus agrees with the Hebrew text of that book discovered in 1895 ff.   There are also fragments in Greek of the Epistle of Jeremias which in the Greek Bible forms a separate book after the book of Baruch, and in the Vulgate is chap. 6 of Baruch.

The *Apocrypha* are represented rather generously among the texts of Qumran Cave 4.   Thus for the *Book of Jubilees* there are parts of ten Mss of the original text postulated by the Ethiopic version (cf. Barthélemy-Milik, *Discoveries...*, I, pp. 82-84); for the *Book of Henoch*, five Aramaic fragments corresponding to Henoch's journey into the other world (chaps. 1-36) and to his visions of the history of the world to the time of the author (chaps. 83-90 and 106-107), and four Aramaic fragments corresponding to chaps. 72-82 which deal with astronomical matters, and finally an Aramaic text corresponding to the beginning of the section 91-108, " the Apocalypse of Weeks ", a section preserved in Greek under the title of *Letter of Henoch* in a Chester Beatty Papyrus. (On the composite origin of the *Book of Henoch*, see Milik (*Dix Ans...*, p. 31). See also the articles of P. Grelot, *RB* [1958], pp. 33-69, and Milik, *ibid.*, 70-77, and Barthélemy-Milik, *Discoveries...*, I, pp. 84-87. Of the Testaments of the Twelve Patriarchs we have fragments from Qumran Caves 1 and 4, viz., the Testament of Levi in Aramaic, as well as Aramaic fragments found before in the Cairo Genizah; these texts agree with a Greek text of Mt. Athos (copied in the tenth cent. A.D.) (cf. Milik, *RB* [1955], pp. 398-406, and *Discoveries...*, I, pp. 87-91).

As indicated earlier, we have also an apocryphal *Genesis* in Aramaic, with some of the text corresponding to Gen. **5** (the miraculous birth of Noe; a parallel also in *Book of Henoch* 106); then a passage corresponding to Gen. **6** f. (the Flood : a parallel in *Jubilees* 5 f.), and a long section corresponding to Gen. **12-15**. On this see also Y. M. Grintz, *Ha-Do'ar* (Feb. 7, 1958), pp. 272-273 (in Hebrew). Other apocrypha found are connected with the name of Jeremias or of Josue (Milik, *Dix Ans...*, p. 33). The latter text is used by J. L. Teicher in support of his far-fetched hypothesis of an Apocryphal Gospel — a Christian work. (See the [London] *Times Literary Supplement* [March 21, 1958] p. 160. For an appreciation of Teicher's views, see Y. Yadin, *Megillot genuzot...*, p. 214 f.). There is also an Aramaic vision of Amran, Moses' father, and a number of Hebrew fragments called tentatively *Sayings of Moses*, a work modeled on Deuteronomy, which contains among other things an elaborate description of the holy days of the Pentateuch (Barthélemy-Milik, *Discoveries...*, I, pp. 91-97; cf. Menahem Zahary's article in *Ha-Do'ar* [Sept. 30, 1955], p. 758). On further apocryphal literature in the Qumran texts, see Milik, *Discoveries...*, I, pp. 82-107. Among the texts not yet referred to may be mentioned a number of " *pesher* " 's (explanations) of Micheas (Milik, *RB* [1952], pp. 412-418), Nahum, Sophonias, Isaias, the Psalms (cf. *Discoveries*..., I, pp. 77-82; also A. M. Haberman, for the *Pesher* on the Psalms, *Ha-Do'ar* [April, 1955], p. 414). There is also a group of texts, " Mishmarot " (Hebrew), meaning literally, " watches ", i.e., divisions for the service of the Temple (cf. Luke 1, 5, who mentions the τάξις τῆς ἐφημερίας, " the order of the division ", for Temple service). This shows the interest taken by our group in Temple matters, even if they were unable to take part in its service under the prevailing circumstances. Contrary to an opposing view held by many, that the *Qumran* community rejected sacrifices altogether, several texts rather show that they believed in the sacrifices prescribed in the Law (J. Carmignac, *RB* [1956], pp. 524-526). From Cave 3 comes (1952), finally, the *Copper Scroll*, the discovery of which gave rise to many hypotheses. It was opened at last at the Manchester College of Technology in 1955 and deciphered by J. M. Allegro. It is a list in Hebrew (Mishnaic Hebrew) of treasures of gold and silver, precious vessels containing incense and perfumes, said to have been hidden in different parts of Palestine. No scholar takes this seriously, and no treasure hunt has been started (cf. Milik, *Dix Ans*..., pp. 38-39; J. M. Allegro, *The Dead Sea Scrolls*, pp. 36, 92, 181-184; Y. Yadin, *Ha-megillot ha-genuzot*..., pp. 176-180).

At Khirbet Qumran, there is an extensive installation which evidently served a community : buildings with rooms identified as a community hall with seats along the wall; a kitchen; industrial quarters; laundry; a scriptorium, etc. To supply the necessary water, there are, according to the plan, a number of cisterns of varying size, six altogether, some of them quite large. An aqueduct brought the water from the outside and conduits distributed it to the various parts of the installation (for a fine, large size plan, see *RB* [1956, October]; a smaller one, but very clear, in Milik, *Dix Ans*..., p. 48; Y. Yadin, *Megillot genuzot*..., pp. 66-78). Next to the building is the cemetery with over a thousand tombs, the bodies laid North-South (on this, see Milik, *RB* [1958], pp. 70-77; Y. Yadin, *op. cit.*, pp. 79-80; A. Parrot, " Les Mss de la Mer Morte : le point de vue archéologique ", in *La Bible et l'Orient* [Paris, 1955], pp. 61-65 and pp. 65-67).

What community occupied the site? The texts of Philo (*ca.* 20 B.C.-50 A.D.), Josephus (37-97 A.D.) and Pliny (23-79 A.D.) allow us to identify the group as Essenes — never mentioned in the New Testament, which refers, however, to the other Jewish sects. For the arguments, see e.g., Milik, *Dix Ans...*, chaps. 3 and 4; M. Burrows, *Dead Sea Scrolls*, pp. 227-298 (cf. *EThL* [1951], pp. 508-509; A. M. Haberman, " The Sect of the Desert of Judah ", *Ha-Do'ar* [June 8, 1956], p. 580 f.; Shne'ur Zalman Zeitlin, *Ha-Do'ar : Jubilee Vol.* [1957], pp. 48-52. This identification is widely accepted now, and seems to be the best at present. If so, we have in the Qumran texts a most valuable source of information about a remarkable group of men for the period immediately before and after the beginning of the Christian Era. They were men of intense spiritual life, devoted to a high religious ideal, searching the Scriptures to know the will of God, looking forward to the time when God's purpose would be fulfilled. We find there a most welcome light on Judaism in a period about which our information was limited. It was only natural for scholars to look for possible connections between the Essenes and Christianity, and there cannot be any doubt that there are resemblances. Some authors, going far beyond the evidence, would make Christianity a sort of re-edition of Essenism — somewhat like Renan's view of Islam as a Beduin edition of Judaism. Thus, for instance, E. Wilson, depending on an arbitrary interpretation of some texts by Dupont-Sommer (*Aperçus préliminaires sur les Mss de la Mer Morte* [Paris, 1950], pp. 38, 55, 110, 120-122; *id., The Jewish Sect of Qumran and the Essenes* [Engl. transl. New York], pp. 147-166), has popularized a view which enjoys a kind of " succès de scandale ". Cf. also the unscientific publications, like that of A. Powell Davies, *The Meaning of the Dead Sea Scrolls* [Washington, 1956] (and in expanded form under the same title, as a Signet Key Book [1956]).

We may admit as a hypothesis that John the Baptist spent his youth as a disciple of the Qumran Community until he received a personal call from God which took him away from the community to begin his mission of Forerunner (cf. Jean Steinmann, *S. Jean-Baptiste et la spiritualité du désert* [Paris, 1955]). There are points of contact between the new texts and the language and thought of the Fourth Gospel, and this confirms the view of its Jewish origin; also resemblances between the life of the Qumran Community and the Early Church as described in Acts. (For details, see K. Stendahl ed., *The Scrolls and the New Testament* (New York, 1957), which contains contributions by several Catholic writers (R. E. Brown S. S., J. A. Fitzmyer, S.J., K. Schubert, E. Vogt, S.J.); R. E. Murphy, O. Carm., in *CBQ* (1956), pp. 263-272; M. Burrows, *op. cit.*, pp. 326-345; G. Graystone, S. M., *The Dead Sea Scrolls and the Originality of Christ* (New York, 1956); J. Daniélou, S. J., *Les Manuscrits de la Mer Morte et les origines du Christianisme* (Paris, 1957); *id.*, " La Communauté de Qumran et l'organisation de l'Eglise Ancienne ", in *La Bible et l'Orient* (Paris, 1955), pp. 104-116; L. W. La Sor, *Amazing Dead Sea Scrolls and the Christian Faith* (Chicago, 1956). But all the resemblances do not compromise the originality of Christinanity. See W. F. Albright, *The Archaeology of Palestine* (1954; a Pelican Book), pp. 148-149; and also the Jewish scholar Th. Gaster, who declares that, in spite of the points of resemblance, it must be stated emphatically, particularly in view of recent exaggerated claims, that the men of Qumran were in no sense Christians and held none of the fundamental theological doctrines of the Christian faith (*The Dead Sea Scriptures* [New York, 1956; an Anchor Book], pp. 12-20).

As regards the Old Testament, the new evidence confirms the antiquity and reliability of the traditional Hebrew text — and even in some instances (as the Psalms) an older date of composition than supposed by critics (Cf. W. F. Albright, *L'Archéologie de la Palestine* [Paris, 1955], p. 258). At the same time the new evidence furnishes materials for the history of the Hebrew text at an older period — e.g., for a recension corresponding to the Hebrew text from which the LXX was translated. We learn much about Hebrew when it was still a living language, at least in some circles. The *Copper Scroll* gives us the oldest text in the form of Hebrew which is used in the Mishnah. From the spelling of the Mss, even from the mistakes in them, we can learn much about the pronunciation of Hebrew at that time. (See the recent work in [Hebrew] of Z. Ben-Hayim, *The Literary and Oral Tradition of Hebrew and Aramaic amongst the Samaritans* [2 vols., Jerusalem, 1957; in progress], according to whom the Samaritan tradition at a former date was shared by Jews, and our new texts confirm this; also, id., (" Traditions in the Hebrew Language with Special Reference to the Dead Sea Scholls, " in : *Scripta Hierosolymitana* : Vol. IV [1958], p. 200-214). The Aramaic texts of Qumran teach us something about the language of Christ. The inventory and the identification of the texts discovered in the Dead Sea region, their editing and their interpretation, will keep scholars busy for many years.

BIBLIOGRAPHY.

Articles and books on the subject are being published constantly, so that Christ. BURCHARD, *Bibliographie zu den Handschriften vom Toten Meer* (Berlin, 1957) will soon need a supplement. References will be found, eg., in *RB*, *Biblica*, CBQ, and N T Abstracts. There is an excellent bibliography (to 1952) in H. H. ROWLEY, *Zadokite Fragments;* see also *Haberman, 'Edah we-Edut* (Jerusalem, 1952; especially valuable for the Hebrew [Israeli] bibliography). Millar BURROWS, *The Dead Sea Scrolls*. A. G. LAMADRID, *Los discubrimientos de Qumran* (Madrid, 1956). J. T. MILIK, *Dix ans de découvertes....* J. VAN DER PLOEG, O. P., *Vondsten in de Woestijn van Juda* (Utrecht and Antwerp, 1957). Géza VERMÈS, *Discovery in the Judaean Desert* (New York, 1956; French original, *Les Mss du désert de Juda* [1953]). H. J. SCHONFIELD, *Secrets of the Dead Sea Scrolls* (New York, 1957; cf. *CBQ* [1958], 266-268). The *Revue Biblique* has been publishing articles ever since the discovery and reports on the work done at the various caves. Van der Ploeg (as noted above) has begun a series of publications on the Scrolls. The Librairie Letouzey et Ané (Paris) has started a series " Autour de la Bible " with the volume by J. CARMIGNAC, *Règle de la Guerre*. It will also publish the *Revue de Qumran*, dedicated entirely to Qumran, which will help to centralize the work done on the subject. *Discoveries in the Judaean Desert : Qumran Cave* 1, by D. BARTHÉLEMY, O. P., and J. T. MILIK (Oxford, 1955) will be followed by a series of volumes on the finds in the different caves.

2. Apocrypha of the New Testament [1]

GOSPELS

1. *The Gospel according to the Hebrews* (or *of the Nasoraeans*). The most important of the Apocryphal Gospels. Basically, it is closely related to the canonical Gospel of Saint Matthew. It is written in Aramaic and was in use among the Judeo-

Translators note [[1] See J. DORESSE, *Les livres secrets des Gnostiques d'Egypte* [Paris, 1958], pp. 237-263, and 277.]

Christians. Date : end of the first century. A few fragments only are extant.

2. *The Gospel of the Ebionites* (or *of the Twelve Apostles*). Of Judeo-Christian origin. It was composed probably in Greek and before the middle of the second century. Only a few short fragments are preserved.

3. *The Gospel according to the Egyptians.* A work of Gnostic tendencies, employed in certain churches of Egypt. It was composed in Greek about the midle of the second century. Only some fragments are extant.

4. *The Gospel of Peter.* This work, represented by a single fragment (the end of the Passion and the account of the Resurrection), was written in Egypt and exhibits Docetic tendencies. Date : second half of the second century.

5. *The Gospels of Matthias, Philip, Thomas, Andrew, Bartholomew, and Barnabas.* All these writings are known only through brief allusions in ancient ecclesiastical authors. Composed in the third century to serve propaganda purposes, they did not attach themselves to the authentic Gospel tradition, but narrated episodes featuring the marvelous — often in a puerile manner, after the manner of popular tales. They were closely related to apocalyptic. Being suspected of Gnosticism, they were suppressed by ecclesiastical authority.

6. *The Protoevangelium of James.* An edifying, but typically legendary narrative, of the infancy of the Blessed Virgin Mary and of her life down to the Massacre of the Innocents and the flight into Egypt. It was composed in Greek by an Alexandrian about the middle of the second century. This work exercised a great influence on Christian art.

ACTS.

1. *The Acts of John.* A legendary account of the life of the Apostle John, composed in Asia Minor, *ca.* 150-180. Two-thirds of the text is preserved.

2. *The Acts of Paul and Thecla.* A narrative of the missionary journeys of Paul, which supplements the canonical Book of Acts. A work composed by a priest belonging to the Province of Asia *ca.* 160-170.

3. *The Acts of Peter.* A fictional narrative of popular character, from the end of the second century. Produced in Asia Minor, as were the preceding works, and inspired by them. The extant text is very fragmentary.

4. *The Acts of Thomas.* A narrative of Syrian origin that is typically legendary, being filled with marvelous adventures. Date : third or fourth century.

EPISTLES.

1. *The Third Epistle to the Corinthians.* This letter forms a part of the *Acts of Paul.* It is an exposition — under the name of Paul — of the orthodox doctrine on the Incarnation and Resurrection of Jesus.

2. *The Epistle to the Laodiceans.* A little mosaic of texts borrowed from the canonical Pauline Epistles. Of Western origin, and composed at the end of the second century [1].

3. *The Letter of the Apostles.* A polemic against the teachings of Simon Magus and the Corinthians. Written in Asia or Alexandria. Date : *ca.* 180.

4. *The Correspondence between Seneca and Saint Paul.* A kind of literary exercise represented by fourteen letters which have no historical or doctrinal value. Of Western origin. Date : fourth century.

APOCALYPSES.

1. *The Apocalypse of Peter.* An Alexandrian composition from the middle of the second century. It deals with the end of the world, with the torments reserved for the damned, and with the joys in store for the just. This short work exercised a great influence in Christian circles.

2. *The Apocalypse of Paul.* A description of paradise and of the life of the elect with God, and of hell and the punishments inflicted on the wicked. Of Palestinian origin, and written in 380.

Translators note — [1 The Latin text is reproduced by E. NESTLE, *Novum Testamentum Græce et Latine,* 10 th. ed., p. XII.]

3. *The Christian Sibyl.* This title corresponds to Books I-II, VI-VIII, and XI-XIV, of the *Sibylline Oracles.* These books are a chaotic collection made up of elements of varied character reflecting popular beliefs and also certain theological teachings. The oldest parts belong to the third century.

BIBLIOGRAPHY.

I. Documents. — E. PREUSCHEN, *Analecta.* 2. *Zur Kanonsgeschichte,* 2nd ed., Tübingen, 1910. — A. CAMERLYNCK, *Compendium introd. gener. in S. Script., pars I^a,* Bruges, 1911. — Th. ZAHN : the works cited below. [C. H. TURNER, *Latin Lists of the Canonical Books, JTS,* I (1899), 554 ff.; II (1900), 236 ff. and 577 ff.; IV (1902), 426 ff.; XIII (1911), 511 ff.].

II. Comprehensive studies. — Dictionary articles, especially those in *DBV, DTC, DAFC,* and *HDB.* Chapters in Manuals or Introductions to the Bible, among which may be mentioned : J. RUWET, *De canone,* in *Institutiones biblicæ scholis accommodatæ.* I. *De S. Scriptura in universum,* 5th ed., Rome, 1937. — S. ZARB, *De historia canonis utriusque Testamenti,* 2nd ed., Rome, 1934. — A. BARUCQ and H. CAZELLES, " Le Canon des livres inspirés ", in Robert-Cazelles, *Introduction à la Bible,* I, Tournai, 1957, pp. 31-68. [For the Canon among Protestants, see H. H. HOWORTH, " The Anglican Canon, Its Origin and Authority ", *JTS,* VIII (1906). 1 ff.; Luther and Karlstadt, *ibid.,* 321 ff.; Luther, Zwingli, Lefèvre, Calvin, IX (1907), 188 ff.; and X, 183 ff. See also *id.,* " The Roman Canon and the Book of Esdras A, " *JTS,* VII (1905), 343 ff., with the rejoinder by H. Pope, O. P., *ibid.,* VIII (1906), 218 ff.].

III. On the canon of the Alexandrians, see the articles by J. Ruwet in *Biblica,* 1942, 1948, and 1952.

IV. The Canon of the Old Testament. — J. GOETTSBERGER, *Einleitung in das A. T.,* Freiburg im Br., 1928, pp. 351-388. — L. DENNEFELD, *Histoire des livres de l'A. T.,* Paris, 1929. — J. P. VAN KASTEREN, *Le canon juif vers le commencement de notre ère, RB* (1896),pp. 408-415, and 575-594; *id., L'Ancien Testament d'Origène, RB* (1901), pp. 413-423. — J. B. FREY, *La révélation d'après les conceptions juives au temps de J. C., RB* (1916), pp. 480-493. Non-Catholic works : H. E. RYLE, *The Canon of the Old Testament,* 3rd ed., London, 1904; *id., Philo and Holy Scripture,* London, 1895. — G. WILDEBOER, *De la formation du canon de l'Ancient Testament,* 4th ed., Lausanne, 1908 (translation of the Dutch original which was first published at Groningen, 1889 ff.). [English translation of Wildeboer by B. W. BACON, *The Origin of the Canon of the Old Testament,* London, 1895]. — O. EISSFELDT, *Einleitung in das Alte Testament,* Tübingen, 1934, pp. 614-630. — G. ÖSTBORN, *Cult and Canon : A Study of the Canonization of the Old Testament,* Uppsala, 1950 (see also the review by Nötscher in *Theologische Revue* [1953], pp. 53-55). — A. BENTZEN, *Inledning til det Gamle Testamente,* Copenhagen, 1941, pp. 353-365. — A. LODS, *Histoire de la littérature hébraïque et juive,* ed. A. Parrot, Paris, 1950, pp. 1006-1023. — M. GOGUEL, P. LESTRINGANT, E. JACOB, and Others, *Le problème biblique dans le protestantisme,* Paris, 1955, especially pp. 14 ff., 45 ff., and 71 ff. — R. H. PFEIFFER, *Introduction to the Old Testament,* New York, 1941, pp. 50-70, and 856 ff. — STRACK und BILLERBECK, *Kommentar zum N. T. aus Talmud und Midrash,* 4 vols. (Munich, 1922-1928), Vol. IV, pp. 415-451 (on Jewish views on the canon and on inspiration). For further Jewish views, see S. ZEITLIN, *A Historical Study of the Canonization of the Hebrew Scriptures,* Philadelphia, 1933. For the Canon of the Old Testament in the Orthodox Church, see M. JUGIE, *Histoire du canon de l'A. T. dans l'Eglise Grecque Russe,* 1909, and also his articles in *Echos d'Orient,* 1907, 193 ff., and 344 ff.].

V. The Canon of the New Testament. — E. JACQUIER, *Le N. T. dans l'Eglise chrétienne,* vol. I, Paris, 1911. — M. J. LAGRANGE, *Histoire ancienne du canon du N. T.,* Paris, 1933. — W. S. REILLY, " Le canon du N. T. et le critère de canonicité ", *RB* (1921), pp. 195-205. — A. WIKENHAUSER, *Einleitung in das N. T.,* Freiburg i. Br., 1956, pp. 14-45. — Non-Catholic works : B. F. WESTCOTT, *A General Survey of the History of the Canon of the New Testament during the First Four Centuries,* 7th ed., London, 1896. — TH. ZAHN, *Geschichte des Ntl. Kanons,* 2 vols., Leipzig, 1888-1892; id., *Forschungen zur Geschichte des Ntl. Kanons und der altkirchlichen Literatur,* Leipzig, 1881-1907; id., *Grundriss der Geschichte des Ntl. Kanons,* 2nd ed., Leipzig, 1904. — J. LEIPOLDT, *Geschichte des Ntl. Kanons,* 2 vols., Leipzig, 1907-1908. — A. HARNACK, *Das N. T. um das Jahr 200,* Freiburg i. B., 1889; id., *Die Entstehung des N. T. und die wichtigsten Folgen der neuen Schöpfung,* Leipzig, 1914. — M. ALBERTZ, *Die Botschaft des N. T. I,* 1 : *Die Entstehung des apostolischen Schriftenkanons,* Zollicon-Zurich, 1952.

VI. The Apocrypha of the Old and New Testaments. — See the two following comprehensive articles. — J. B. FREY, *Apocryphes de l'Ancien Testament,* and E. AMANN, *Apocryphes du Nouveau Testament DBV, Supplément,* Vol. I, Paris, 1926, cols. 354-533. — [S. ZEITLIN, " The Apocrypha ", *Jewish Quarterly Review* (1947), pp. 219-248. — C. C. TORREY, *The Apocryphal Literature,* New Haven, 1945. — P. RIESSLER, *Altjüdisches Schriftum ausserhalb der Bibel,* Augsburg, 1942 (most complete collection). For a good bibliography on the Apocrypha and Pseudepigrapha of the Old Testament, see R. H. PFEIFFER, *Introduction to the Old Testament,* New-York, 1941, pp. 875-884]. For texts see R. H. CHARLES, *The Apocrypha and Pseudepigrapha of the Old Testament in English,* Oxford, 1913. — E. HENNECKE, *Neutestamentliche Apocryphen,* 2nd ed., Tübingen, 1920. — M. R. JAMES, *The Apocryphal New Testament,* Oxford, 1924. [B. PICK, *The Apocryphal Acts,* (Paul, Peter, John, Thomas), Chicago, 1909. — M. D. GIBSON, *Apocrypha Sinaïtica,* London, 1896 (Studia Sinaïtica, V); id., *Apocrypha Arabica,* London, 1901 (Studia Sinaïtica, VIII). — A. S. LEWIS, *The Mythological Acts of the Apostles,* London, 1904 (Horae Semiticae, IV). — J. R. HARRIS, *The Odes and Psalms of Solomon,* Oxford, 1911. The following English editions with brief introductions and notes are published by the Society for the Promotion of Christian Knowledge

(SPCK), London : Box, *The Apocalypse of Ezra* (II Esdras, 2-14), 1917;
Charles-Oesterley, *The Book of Enoch*, 1917; *id.*, *The Testaments of the
XII Patriarchs*, 1925; BOX-LANDSMAN, *The Apocalypse of Abraham*, 1918;
E. W. BARNES, *Joseph and Osenatti*, 1918. — C. W. EMMET, *IIIrd and
IVth Books of Machabees*, 1918. — H. W. BATES, *Sibylline Oracles :
Bks.* 3-5, 1918; BOX-GASELEE, *The Testament of Abraham*, 1927;
H. St. J. THACKERAY, *The Letter of Aristeas*, 1917]. Texts translated into
French with introductions : F. MARTIN, *Le livre d'Hénoch*, Paris, 1906. —
E. TISSERANT, *L'Ascension d'Isaïe*, Paris, 1908. — J. VITEAU, *Les Psaumes
de Salomon*, Paris, 1911. — L. GRY, *Les dires prophétiques d'Esdras*, Paris,
1938. — C. MICHEL and P. PEETERS, *Les Evangiles apocryphes*, Paris,
vol. I, 1911; vol. II, 1914. — E. AMANN, *Le Protévangile de Jacques*,
Paris, 1910. — L. VOUAUX, *Les actes de Paul et ses lettres apocryphes*, Paris
1913; *id.*, *Les actes de Pierre*, Paris, 1922. — F. AMIOT, *Evangiles apocryphes*,
and J. BONSIRVEN, *En marge de l'Ancient Testament*, 2 vols. in the *La Bible
apocryphe*, Paris, 1952-1953. — A. DE SANTOS BOLERO, *Los Evangelios
apocrifos* (edición critica y bilingüe), Madrid, 1956 (a good edition with
Greek and Latin texts accompanied by a Spanish translation). — G. GRAF,
Geschichte der christlichen arabischen Literatur. I, Vatican City, 1944,
pp. 198-224. — E. SJÖBERG, *Der Menschensohn im äthiopischen Henochbuch*,
Lund, 1946. — A. KAHANA, ed., *Hasefarim ha-hisonim*, 3 vols., Tel Aviv,
1936-1937 (Hebrew translation of the Apocrypha of the O. T. with introduction and commentary). — R. PHEIFFER, *History of N. T. Times, with
an Introduction to the Apocrypha*, New York, 1949, pp. 233-522, and
Bibliography, pp. 534-541. — S. ZEITLIN of Dropsie College has begun,
with other Jewish scholars, the publication of " Jewish Apocryphal
Literature ". To date [1958] have appeared *I and II Mach.*, 2 vols.,
New York, 1950 and 1954; the *Letter of Aristeas*, 1951; *III and IV Mach.*,
1953; *Wisdom*, 1957; *Tobias*, 1958. Each contains an introduction, the
Greek text, and an English translation and a commentary. On the Dead
Sea Scrolls, see G. VERMÈS, *Les manuscrits du désert de Juda*, 2nd ed.,
Paris, 1954, with its select Bibliography, and also the references given
above by Father Arbez in his special section on these documents.

PART II
BIBLICAL LITERATURE

CHAPTER III

LANGUAGES [1]

by H. Cazelles and E. Osty.

The Bible was written in three languages : Hebrew, Aramaic, and Greek. Hebrew and Aramaic are closely related and belong to the Semitic group. Greek is a very different language which belongs to the Indo-European family.

HEBREW [2]

by H. Cazelles.

Most of the Old Testament by far is written in Hebrew. The name " Hebrew " as a designation of the language of

---

Translator's note. — [1 On the Semitic languages in general, see : J. NOU-GAYROL and H. CAZELLES, " Langues et Écritures Sémitiques ", *DBV, Suppl.* V (1957), 299-334 (with excellent bibliography). G. RINALDI, *Le lingue semitiche : Introduzione generale e bibliografica*, Turin, 1954. A. M. HONEYMAN, " Semitic Epigraphy and Hebrew Philology ", in H. H. ROWLEY, Ed., *Old Testament and Modern Study*, Oxford, 1951, pp. 264-282. I. WOLFSON, *Ta'rīh al lugāt al sāmiya*, Cairo, 1939. J. H. KRAMERS, *De semitische Talen*, Leiden, 1941. G. BERGSTRÄSSER, *Einführung in die semitischen Sprachen*, Munich, 1928. A. UNGNAD, *Das Wesen des Ursemitischen*, Leipzig, 1925. H. FLEISCH, *Introduction à l'étude des langues sémitiques*, Paris, 1947. C. SARAUW, *Über Akzent und Silbendildung in den älteren semitischen Sprachen*, Copenhagen, 1939. M. COHEN, *Le système verbal sémitique et l'expression du temps*, Paris, 1924. The basic work of reference is C. BROCKELMANN, *Grundriss der vergleichenden Grammatik der semitischen Sprachen*, Berlin 1908-1913. See also J. FRIEDRICH, *Extinct Languages*, New York, 1957 (a good survey on the decipherment of languages and important for students of the Bible).]

Translator's note. — [2 In addition to the works listed in the Bibliography of the Old Testament see : W. F. ALBRIGHT, " The Language of the Old Testament ", in *Introduction to the Revised Standard Version*, New York, 1952, pp. 32-41. Z. CHOMSKY's articles (in Hebrew) in *Ha-Do'ar* (1956), 518 ff.; (1957), 328 ff. and 348 ff. W. CHOMSKY, *David Kimḥi's Hebrew Grammar (Mikhlol)*, New York, 1952; id., *Hebrew the Eternal Language*, Philadelphia, 1957. *Yehudah Ibn Kuraish : Iggeret*, ed. M. Katz in a Hebrew translation from the Arabic, Tel Aviv, 1950. (This treatise by a scholar of the 8th-9th century A.D. on the language of the Bible compared with Aramaic, Mishnaic Hebrew, and Arabic is the first work on comparative Semitic philology and exercised a great influence on subsequent Hebrew grammarians. (See BAUER-LEANDER, *Historische Grammatik der hebräischen Sprache* I, Halle/Salle [1918], pp. 36-40). D. YELLIN, *Diqduq ha-lashon ha-'ibrit (Hebrew Grammar)* I, Jerusalem, 1942. M. S. SEGAL, *Yesodey ha-fonetika ha-'ibrit (Elements of Hebrew Phonetics)*, *ibid.*, 1928. Chayim ROZEN, *Ha-'ibrit Shelanu*, Tel Aviv, 1957 (a scientific study of Hebrew based on the principles of De Saussure, etc.). Z. BEN-HAYYIM, *The Literary and Oral Tradition of Hebrew and Aramaic among the Samaritans*, 2 vols., *ibid.*, 1957 (in Hebrew; a third vol. to follow).]

Israel appears only in the 2nd century B.C.   In the 5th century B.C. Nehemias (Neh = 2 Esd. 13 : 24), concerned about the growing disuse of the national language, calls it " Judaean ", *Yehudit* [1]. In the classical period, *Isaias* (19 : 18) in the 8th century B.C., apparently calls the national language " the language of Canaan ", which he contrasts with Egyptian.

Indeed, when the tribes of Israel settled in Canaan reached the stage of composing literary works, they adopted the language of their predecessors, which was in fact very closely related to their own.   We can form an idea of Canaanite from the glosses in the Tell el Amarna Letters written by the princes of Canaan to the Pharaoh, their overlord, in the 14th century B.C., and we can supplement these indications by a prudent use of the " Amorrhean " peculiarities of the Mari Letters (18th century) and of some cuneiform letters found in Palestine, by the Proto-Phoenician texts of Ras-Shamra (Ugarit) 14th century, and by some inscriptions (Phoenician, Aramaic, Moabite, Israelite) belonging to the end of the second millennium and the beginning of the first.   More enigmatic, the Proto-Sinaitic (15th century) and the pseudo-hieroglyphic (Byblos 15th century?) inscriptions might also shed some light [2].

All these languages form the West-Semitic branch, in which morphology and roots are very closely related.   Hebrew is only a subdivision of this branch.   It was written in Phoenician characters which had preserved only part of the phonemes of primitive Semitic — which had more laryngeals especially — and it may be that this script gives a false impression of the form of the spoken language.   Moreover, we should not imagine

---

Translator's note. — [1] The *Douay, A.V., Jewish V.* (Philadelphia), *American V.* (Chicago), and the *Basic Bible,* all read, " the Jew's language "; *Moffatt* has " Jewish "; the *R.S.V.* reads, " the language of Judah ".   Cf. also 2 (4) Kgs. 18 : 26, which also mentions *Yehudit* as the language of the people, i.e., Hebrew.]

Translator's note. — [2] On these inscriptions see : Joh. FRIEDRICH, *op. cit.,* pp. 159-162, and pp. 131-136.   J. G. FÉVRIER, *Histoire de l'écriture,* Paris, 1948, pp. 178-182, and pp. 182-186.   G. R. DRIVER, *Semitic Writing,* London, 1948, *passim.   Jaarbericht van het Vooraziatisch-egyptische Genootschap Ex Oriente Lux* Leiden (1948), pp. 399-405.   Cf. *Comptes Rendus Académie Inscript. et Belles-Lettres* (1946), pp. 360-365 and pp. 472-479.   Dhorme in *Syria* (1946/ 1948) : pp. 1-35.   D. DIRINGER, *The Alphabet,* New York 1948, pp. 158-165, 205 f.   Albright, *BASOR,* N° 116, Dec., 1949), 12 ff.
On Ras. Shamra, see M. D. CASSUTO, art. " Ugarit ", in *Entzyk. Miqra'it,* vol. I, 79-89 (with good bibliography and Plates).]

that Hebrew was a unified tongue. The Bible itself refers to dialectal differences. Thus the Ephraimites pronounced *sibboleth*, while the Judaeans and Transjordanians pronounced *shibboleth*. The language of the North has some peculiarities which clash with the Judaean dialect, immortalized by the " Yahwist " of the Pentateuch, that is used as a rule in the Bible. Besides, Hebrew changed in course of time. The late documents (priestly documents, chronicles) have a syntax of their own which cannot be harmonized with that of Isaias. Nor should we forget the progressive influence of Aramaic, the language of the Persian empire, and later the introduction of Grecisms.

Hebrew is not limited to the Bible. The discoveries of the Mss of the Desert of Juda show that Hebrew had a second spring shortly before the Christian era. It was a written language rather than a spoken language, evolving into the Hebrew of the Mishnah compiled towards the end of the 2nd century A.D. There are traces of Mishnaic Hebrew in both Talmuds. But the Rabbinic Hebrew of the Middle Ages stands in the same relation to Biblical Hebrew as Scholastic Latin to Classical Latin. Thanks to the efforts of Ben Yehudah, Hebrew has become again in our time a living language and the vehicle of a literature in the Jewish homeland and then in the State of Israel. The vocabulary, naturally, has been enriched considerably, and the structure of the verb has changed in some respects. We must distinguish Modern Hebrew sharply from Yiddish, which is a High German dialect written in Hebrew characters [1].

Translator's note. — [1 The commonly accepted view is that Hebrew gradually ceased to be spoken in Palestine after the return from the Babylonian Exile and was displaced in daily life by Aramaic. The change was completed some time B.C., so that Aramaic was the common language of the Jews in the days of Christ. In favor of this view may be adduced : 1) the names of persons mentioned in the New Testament, for example the names beginning with *Bar* (son of) as Bar-Abbas, Bar-Jesus, Bar-Jona, Bar-Nabas, Bar-Sabas, Bar-Talmai (Bartholomew), Bar-Timai (Bartimaeus); or names of persons like Kepha (Cephas), Martha, Mattai : (Matthaeus), Zakkai (Zachaeus), Taddai (Thaddeus), Lebbai (Lebbaeus), etc.; 2) such Greek forms as *Ioudaios*, *Galilaios*, *Pharisaios*, Saddoukaios, (Sadducee), Nazaraios ("of Nazareth", Jn. **18**: 5), etc., all derived from Aramaic; 3) topographical designations even connected with Jerusalem and its vicinity, as Bethesda (Bethzatha, Jn. **5** : 2), Gabbatha, Golgotha (Golgotta), Hakeldama; 4) some words or phrases reproduced in the New Testament : *Abba* (" Father ", Mk. **14** : 36), *Talitha Koumi* (Mk. **5** : 41), *Eli, Eli, lema sabactani* (*shebaqtani*, Mt. **27** : 46), *Maran atha* (*Maran tha*, 1 Cor. **16** : 22).

However, a number of scholars hold that Hebrew, though largely influenced by encroaching Aramaic in vocabulary and grammar, continued to be the

For a long time Hebrew used only the consonants of the Phoenician alphabet. Under the influence of Aramaic, a first attempt at expressing the vowels was made by means of the *matres lectionis* (" mothers " = " guides to reading "), i.e. by using some consonants — such as *h* and *w* — as vowels. However, this system, used very extensively in the manuscripts of the Desert of Judah, was not sufficiently complete nor accurate. The subsequent vowel systems (Babylonian, Palestinian, and finally that of Tiberias) [1] are very precise, but late : they give us only an approximate idea of the Classical Hebrew vowels, and we must control their data by means of the Greek and cuneiform transcriptions. Hence our uncertainty regarding the correct phonemes of Classical Hebrew. The 22 signs of Phoenician are used to render 29 different consonants (*s* corresponds to two different sounds and *b*, *g*, *d*, *k*, *p*, *t* also

spoken language of the people in the southern part of the land and did not die out before the third century A.D. Some of the arguments at least that are employed to support this view are inconclusive. Thus, the national language mentioned in the account of the seven brothers and their mother (2 Mach. **7** : 8, 21, 27) does not necessarily mean Hebrew. Commentators state that it was Hebrew or Aramaic, according to the view held by them on the language spoken in Palestine at that time. Again, when Josephus (*Bell. Iud.* I. 1 [3]) refers to the earlier account composed by him in his native language, some take this as meaning Aramaic (so H. St. J. Thackeray), while others take it as meaning Hebrew (so in the " Introduction " [in Hebrew] to Ben Yehudah's *Dictionary* [see Bibliography at the end of this chapter]). The strongest argument in favor of the continuity of Hebrew as a vernacular is the language itself of the Mishnah, which gives the impression of being an independent living Hebrew, drawing a good part of its vocabulary from the popular speech of every class, and not only from the language of scholarly books. For earlier discussions of the subject, see the references given by K. ALBRECHT, *Neuhebräische Grammatik...*, (Munich, 1913), pp. 4-5. As supporters of Mishnaic Hebrew as a living language, see : MAYER-LAMBERT, *Traité de grammaire hébraïque*, (Paris, 1931-1938), p. 5 f.; M. H. SEGAL, *A Grammar of Mishnaic Hebrew*, (Oxford, 1927), pp. 1-20; W. CHOMSKY, *Hebrew the Eternal Language*, (Philadelphia, 1957), pp. 206-227; id., in *Jewish Quarterly Review*, 41 (1951), p. 337. J. T. MILIK, on the basis of many points of contact between Mishnaic Hebrew and Punic, thinks that Mishnaic Hebrew might be regarded as a kind of *koine* developed in Judaea, from the beginning of the Persian period, out of the Hebrew spoken in Judaea and the Phoenician spoken along the coasts of Palestine. See his *Dix ans de découvertes dans le Désert de Juda* (Paris, 1957), p. 89. On Eliezer Ben Yehudah's outstanding contribution to the revival of Hebrew, so that it has become the national language of Israel, see the articles (in Hebrew) by D. PERSKY in *Ha-Do'ar*, Jan. 10 (1958), pp. 192-194, Jan. 17, pp. 208-210, Jan. 24, pp. 228-230, Jan. 31, p. 245 f. See also *Sefarad* 14 (1945), p. 430, and W. CHOMSKY, *op. cit.*, p. 232 ff.] Ch. RABIN, " The Historical Background of Qumran Hebrew, " *Scripta Hierosolymitana IV* (1958), 145 f., 151].

Translator's note. — [1 See especially, P. KAHLE, in Bauer-Leander, *Historische Grammatik*, I, pp. 91-114].

are pronounced *v, gh, dh, kh, ph, th* after a vowel); the 9 vowel
signs (10, if we include silent *e*), on the other hand, are too
numerous. The fundamental sounds were *a, i, u* (with their
Latin value).

Hebrew — like Hamito-Semitic — is a language with radical
consonants which are clearly evident. In the great majority
of cases, there are *three* radical consonants, hence the feature
of *triliteralism*, characteristic of these languages. Exceptionally,
there are *two* radical consonants : hence the name *biliteralism*.
The attempt has been mode by several scholars — so far
unsuccessfully — to reduce *triliteralism* to *biliteralism* [1].

The root is primarily verbal, denoting a concrete action.
But alongside of the verbs of action, there are verbs expressing
a state with peculiarities of conjugation. According as the
action is taking place or is not taking place any longer, Hebrew
uses two forms of the root — improperly called " tenses " :
one form with a presformative, viz., *y q t l* (from root *q t l*) for
the action which is taking place; and a form *qtl* without prefor-
mative for the action which is no longer taking place, but is
completed or unreal. These two " tenses " are conjugated by
means of remnants of pronouns, added especially as endings,
to denote the several persons. Through internal modifications
of the root (doubling a consonant, adding or lengthening of
a vowel) moods are formed which express the various modalities
of the action (intensive, passive, reflexive). The infinitives
and the participles are verbal substantives; in general, substantives are formed on the root according to a rather large number
of themes. Some very simple substantives (denoting kinship,

Translator's note. — [1 The term Hamito-Semitic signifies that the Hamitic
languages (Lybico-Berber, Ancient Egyptian or Cushite) and the Semitic
languages are related and have a common ancestry. See M. COHEN, in Meillet-
Cohen, *Les langues du monde*, 2nd ed., Paris, 1952, pp. 81-181, especially
pp. 81-98. " L'unità linguistica semito-camitica ", *Reale Accademia d'Italia*
(Estratto degli Atti dell' VIII. Conv., Oct. 4-11, 1938). The thesis of a primitive
Semitic-Hamitic unity has been making progress, but there are special difficulties
in that we lack ancient documents in the Hamitic languages. A related question
is that of the original home of the primitive group : Africa or Asia? See
H. FLEISCH, *Introduction à l'étude des langues sémitiques* (Paris 1947), p. 13 f.
and pp. 22-30. On the triliteral characteristic (especially in the Semitic languages), see *id.*, *L'Arabe classique : Esquisse d'une structure linguistique*
(Beyrouth, 1956), pp. 21-26, and 136-137. He gives illustrations of the innate
tendency towards triliteralism in popular Arabic. Thus, French *marquer*
has given rise to the Arabic root *MRK* in the verb *marrak*].

parts of the body), and the pronouns cannot be explained on the basis of triliteral roots [1]. Wes hould note, finally, the existence of an imperative for the second person.

The substantive is not clearly distinguished from the adjective. Hebrew is not a precise language. It has lost the case endings of primitive Semitic. A poor language, more synthetic than analytic, it has few conjunctions and prepositions (both of which in fact belong to the same category). The conjunction " and " (Hebrew w) is used, not only to co-ordinate sentences, but also to express various kinds of subordination : anteriority, finality, etc. Classical Hebrew had no punctuation sign, apart from a dot separating the words (and even this not always), and in exceptional cases, a line separating the clauses.

Hebrew therefore was a simple language, and this is one of the difficulties of exegesis. The significance of the word depended especially on the tone or the situation in which it was used; it is the exegete's task to find again the particular, concrete circumstance to which the language adapted itself fully. The limited number of roots used in the Bible, a text made for the people (excepting the Sapiential Books), should not deceive us. The wealth of the vocabulary in the Book of Job shows that the men of letters in Israel had at their disposal ample means of expression.

II. — ARAMAIC [2]

by E. Osty.

Even before Israel's settlement in Canaan, Assyrian documents mention the existence of sedentary or nomadic tribes of Aramaeans. As they were energetic and restless, they contin-

---

Translator's note. — [1 They are biliteral roots, very limited in number, inherited from a very early stage of the language. Hence there is question of a primitive biliteral stage of development. Cf. H. FLEISCH, *L'Arabe classique*, p. 22].

Translator's note. — [2 See G. GARBINI, " L'Aramaico antico ", in *Atti della Accad. Nazionale dei Lincei* (Science Morali... Memorie, VII, Ser. 8a, [1950]), 236-284. J. BRIGHT, " A New Letter in Aramaic Written to a Pharaoh of Egypt, " *BA* 12 (1949), 46-52. In the Arab review *Al-Kitab* (Feb., 1952), pp. 247-248, there is a summary of a lecture by Murad Kāmil on Aramaic letters discovered recently in Egypt. One of the letters, important for legal history, has the phrase, " and afterward, " at the beginning of each new development. M. KĀMIL is reported to be engaged in bringing out an edition of all the new Aramaic texts mentioned.]

ually gave trouble to their neighbors, and founded a number of more or less ephemeral kingdoms. They never achieved the political unity of a great empire. And yet their language, endowed with a wonderful power of expansion, spread over the whole Near and Middle East from the Mediterranean coast to Iran, and from the sources of the Tigris and the Euphrates to the Persian Gulf. In all these regions, the indigenous languages disappeared before Aramaic, or at least had to admit it as the language of business and diplomacy.

Israel did not escape this irresistible linguistic movement. At the end of the eighth century (2 Kgs. **18** : 26), only the ruling class understood Aramaic; the common people knew only Hebrew. This situation lasted a few more centuries. But after the return from the Exile, the efforts of Esdras to insure the linguistic unity of the Jews prove that Hebrew was having its troubles. The infiltration of Aramaic proceeded silently. For many years the two languages existed side by side, and there was thus a bilingual period. Hebrew had the advantage of being the ancestral language, the language of the Law and of the liturgy, while Aramaic enjoyed the advantage of being a " universal " language which was flexible and steadily gaining. From the second century B. C., at a time when a whole apocalyptic literature written in Hebrew was flourishing, the people, in order to understand the reading from Scripture which was given in the synagogue, needed a translation into their current spoken language, namely, Aramaic. This is the origin of the Targums or interpretations. After having been long improvised orally, they were subsequently given a permanent written form.

The fortune of Aramaic was of long duration. It was spoken and written in Palestine, Syria, Babylonia, in the district of Edessa and the neighboring mountainous regions, in Egypt by the Jewish colony of Elephantine, etc., giving way only to the invasion of Arabic. Of Western Aramaic, as of Eastern Aramaic, there survive only a few insignificant linguistic islands [1].

---

[1] [Cf. A. DUPONT-SOMMER, *Les Araméens* (L'Orient Ancien Illustré, Paris, 1949), pp. 73-103].

Table of the Different Aramaic Dialects.

Aramaic
- Eastern
  - Region of Edessa — Syriac
  - Babylonia — Mandaean, Babylonian Talmud
- Western
  - Galilaean — Christian Palestinian, Samaritan, Talmud of Jerusalem
  - Judaean — Biblical (Chaldaic of St. Jerome), Targums of Onkelos and Jonathan

In comparison with Hebrew, Aramaic is a much more developed language. On the one hand, we notice signs of long usage and wear: weakening of the vocalic and consonantal system; complete disappearance of declensions, of which traces remain in Hebrew; the death throes of the passive and the jussive; absence of the article, which is replaced by the " emphatic state ". On the other hand, the language becomes more flexible, more capable than Hebrew of expressing the different aspects of narrative and the connections of thought. The vocabulary is richer, and the particles are more numerous. The " periphrastic conjugation " develops. The order of words in the nominal sentence is less strictly fixed than in Hebrew. Finally subordination is more frequently employed.

As a Biblical language, Aramaic has a twofold interest. Some texts of the Old Testament are written in Aramaic, which is for this reason called " Biblical ". They are: Esd. 4: 8–6: 18; 7: 12-26; Dan. 2: 4a–7; Jer. 10: 11; Gen. 31: 47. This " Biblical " Aramaic can receive clarification from inscriptions and especially from the letters discovered in Elephantine, which date from the 5th century B. C., but unfortunately are not vocalized. It is closer to the Aramaic of Esdras than to that of Daniel (e.g., in the form of the pronouns), and this is a valuable element for dating [1]. Furthermore, Aramaic, and more accurately the Galilean dialect, is the maternal language of Jesus, of His first disciples, and of the first catechesis, and a language which was not only spoken, but almost certainly written as well. Hence its importance, either for understanding accurately and minutely the meaning of the Master's words, or for interpreting correctly the Gospel accounts and many other parts of the New Testament.

Unfortunately contemporary documents from the time of Our Lord are very scarce. One of the scrolls from the Desert of Judah, written in Aramaic, has been unrolled recently, but deciphered only in part. It has been published by N. Avigad and Y. Yadin under the title, *A Genesis Apocryphon,* Jerusalem, 1956 (the Aramaic text with Hebrew and English translation, an analysis of the scroll, facsimiles and introduction [2]). There are also other fragments which will help in restoring the missing link between the Aramaic of Elephantine and Christian Palestinian Aramaic, which is undoubtedly more ancient than that of the Targum of Onkelos.

III. — GREEK
by E. Osty.

The Book of Wisdom, the Second Book of Machabees, and the whole New Testament were written in Greek. But this Greek is very different from that of Xenophon, Demosthenes, and Isocrates. It was long considered by reputable scholars to be a mysterious and irreducible " quantity ", as original and unique as the religious ideas which it expressed. The progress of grammatical science, the methodical study of official and private inscriptions, especially the discovery in Egypt of a quantity of non-literary texts written on papyrus

Translator's note. — [1 See G. R. DRIVER, *Aramaic Documents of the Fifth Century B. C.* (Oxford, 1957). E. G. KRAELING, *The Brooklyn Museum Papyri. New Documents of the Fifth Century B.C. from the Jewish Colony at Elephantine* (New Haven, 1952].

Translator's note. — [2 See B. Y. KUTSCHER, " The Language of the *Genesis Apocryphon* ", *Scripta Hiersolym.* IV (1958), pp. 1-35].

in the language of daily life, have thrown much light on this problem. The essential points may be summarized as follows.

1. Biblical Greek is the Greek of the Κοινή. This is the conventional name for the Greek language, which, from the time of Alexander, prevailed over local idioms or dialects (Attic, Ionic, Doric, Aeolic) and became the universal language of business and social intercourse throughout the Eastern Mediterranean area. It is basically Attic, but came under considerable Ionic influence, both in morphology and in vocabulary. The principal changes, however, resulted from the process of diffusion itself. Since it was a language spoken by all, and was required to express everything conveniently, simplicity became a necessity. Hence a number of innovations were introduced : a tendency to replace difficult words and forms by more common and regular ones : οἷς, ναῦς, ὕς gave place to πρόβατον, πλοῖον, χοῖρος; the reduction of irregularities in declension or conjugation; the almost complete disappearance of the " Attic declension "; encroachment of the first aorist upon the second, hence the forms εἶπα, εἶπας, εἶπαν; an important decrease of the verbs in μι, which are assimilated to the verbal type in ω : δεικνύω beside δείκνυμι; the plural of οἶδα is formed from the singular thus : οἴδαμεν, οἴδατε, οἴδασιν; the plural of ἔθηκα follows a similar pattern : ἐθήκαμεν, ἐθήκατε, ἔθηκαν; the forms of the middle voice are gradually absorbed by those of the passive; decay of forms which are seldom used or are difficult to use, such as the dual and the optative, the reciprocal and reflexive pronouns, correlatives; in syntax, a striving for simplicity, impoverishment in the particles, decline of the " optative of courtesy ", a tendency to prefer analytical constructions (prepositions followed by a case, and conjunctions followed by a finite mood) to synthetic constructions (the case alone or the infinitive alone). The most curious example is the history of ἵνα.

In short, the language is simple, more within the reach of all, and freed from its burden of morphological difficulties, but it is also less subtle and less flexible. We must mention in addition a tendency to renovate vocabulary — old words disappear in favor of young competitors. There is a strong liking for diminutives and sonorous forms : ὑπάρχω for εἰμι;

παιδάριον for παῖς; ὠτάριον for οὖς, etc. A few Latinisms remind us that Rome holds political power: κεντυρίων, λεγιών, etc.

Such is the language that we find in the writings of the New Testament.

2. Biblical Greek is for the most part *Greek of the popular* κοινή. On the whole, the authors of the New Testament do not belong to educated circles. The writer of the Epistle to the Hebrews has certainly a strong feeling for form, and for oratorical " cadence " particularly. He even dislikes hiatus. But such refinements of style are exceptional. When Saint Luke wishes, he can write the Greek of the " better class " people of his time. But nearly all the pages of the New Testament are written in the language of daily conversation which the papyri have revealed to us. There are no long periodic sentences. Most clauses are independent, and are joined together by the simplest of conjunctions: καί. The " historical " present and the " descriptive " imperfect are often used. Tenses are often mixed — Mk. 9: 17-17; Jn. 6: 14-21. " Indirect discourse ", or similar learned and abstract presentations of thought, are rarely found. A great number of words which are forbidden by the " Atticists " occur almost everywhere, but especially in Mark. Sometimes there are mistakes in agreement, especially in the Apocalypse. This last book and the Gospel of Mark are perfect examples of popular Greek, unaffected and spontaneous, and for these very reasons admirably adapted for impressing memory and vision.

3. Biblical Greek was strongly influenced by the Semitic genius and by the languages through which this genius expressed itself in Palestine: Hebrew and Aramaic. This influence was inevitable. Aramaic was the mother tongue of all the authors of the New Testament, except Luke[1]; Jesus preached in Aramaic, and it was in this tongue that the Apostles began to announce the message of the Gospel and also to commit it to writing. Hebrew, it is true, was almost a dead language — all efforts which have been made to prove the existence of a gospel written

---

Translator's note [[1] Luke himself may very well have been a Semite. Cf. JOÜON, *L'Evangile de N. S. Jésus-Christ* (Paris, 1930) 505 f; MOULTON-HOWARD, *Gramm of N. T. Greek*, I, p. 15; II, p. 481; W. F. ALBRIGHT, *Archaeology of Palestine* (1954), p. 199].

in " Hebrew " have failed — but Hebrew survived in the Septuagint Version, which followed the original so closely that in many places it was scarcely anything more than a transcription. The Septuagint was pre-eminently the religious book of all the Jews of the Diaspora. Constant reading of and meditation on the Holy Book influenced to a unique degree not only their thought, but also their language. When the authors of the New Testament started to write, the words and constructions of the Greek Bible came spontaneously to their pens. But sometimes they looked for them deliberately. It is not necessary to suppose that, when Luke was writing the first two chapters of his Gospel, he used written Aramaic sources, for they contain no characteristic Aramaisms. It is more likely that he wanted to write " in the manner " of the Septuagint, and, as a great artist, he succeeded admirably. [1]

It is as easy to affirm in a general way the influence of Palestinian speech on Biblical Greek as it is difficult to arrive at exact details and to distinguish accurately Aramaisms and Hebraisms. The wisest course is to adopt the following position :

1º In a great number of cases, popular Greek and the dialects of Palestine coincide : they have the same liking for parataxis and " direct style ", pleonastic repetition of pronouns, disregard of nuances, etc. Therefore it is useless to resort to Semitic influence as an explanation for a grammatical phenomenon which is normal in Greek.

2º Sometimes a construction or an expression which is very rare in popular Greek occurs frequently in Biblical Greek, where it is derived from Hebrew. We should not hesitate to see here an influence of Hebrew through the medium of the Septuagint. This is true of many expressions in which ἐνώπιον is used.

3º We may attribute with certainty to the influence of the Septuagint, and consequently to Hebrew, the following facts : the use of Καὶ ἐγένετο at the beginning of a sentence; the explanatory λέγων following εἶπεν, and equivalent to a colon (Lk. 7 : 39–13 : 27–14 : 3-7); the un-Greek use of οὐ πᾶς with the

---

Translator's note [1 See R. LAURENTIN; *Structure et Théologie de Luc*, I-II (Paris 1957), pp. 12-13, and his copious bibliography].

meaning of " no ", " no one " (Mt. 24 : 22; Lk. 1 : 37); certain
irregular constructions : ποιεῖν ἔλεος μετά τινος (Lk. 10 : 37),
ἀρέσκειν ἐνώπιόν τινος (Act. 6 : 5), etc.; the meaning given to
certain words and expressions : σπλαγχνίζεσθαι : " to be moved
with pity "; ἀποκρίνομαι " to begin to speak "; ἀναστάς, to
indicate the beginning of an action or departure; γινώσκω in the
meaning of Lk. 1 : 34; a large number of expressions in which
υἱός is an element, and also κάρπος; λαμβάνειν πρόσωπον, " to be
partial "; πορεύεσθαι ἐν πάσαις ταῖς ἐντολαῖς (Lk. 1 : 6) : to
observe all the commandments) "; σὰρξ καὶ αἷμα " human
nature ", etc.

It is almost impossible to determine with accuracy the
linguistic influence which was specifically Aramaic. With
many reservations and with much hesitancy we may mention,
however : asyndeton, the periphrastic construction, the impersonal plural, the frequent use of the aorist ἤρξατο, etc.

We must also note the influence of Christian thought on
vocabulary. A large number of words acquired a meaning in
conformity with the ideas which the authors wanted to express,
such as ἀγάπη, ἀπολύτρωσις, χάρις, παρουσία, παλιγγενεσία, etc.

Finally, the diversity of origin and education among the
authors, and the very different conditions under which their
writings were composed, have occasioned a great deal of variety
in Biblical Greek. There are profound differences between
Matthew, John, Paul, and Luke. Even the same writer also —
and this is not one of the least of the original features in the
New Testament — offers examples of strikingly different styles.
One should compare, with this in mind, Lk. 1 : 1-4; Lk. 1 : 5–3 :
22; Lk. 11 : 5-13.

BIBLIOGRAPHY

1. Hebrew : GESENIUS-BERGSTRÄSSER, Hebräische Grammatik, 29th ed.,
Leipzig, 1918-1929. [There is an English translation of the 28th ed.,
(Leipzig, 1909) by A. E. COWLEY, Oxford, 1910]. — J. TOUZARD, Grammaire
hebraïque abrégée, 2nd ed., Paris, 1905; new ed. by A. Robert, 1949. —
P. JOÜON, Grammaire de l'hébreu biblique, Rome, 1923. — M. LAMBERT,
Traité de grammaire hébraïque, Paris, 1931-1938. [H. BAUER and
P. LEANDER, Historische Grammatik der hebr. Sprache des A. T., 1 (all
published), Halle/Saale, 1918. — G. R. DRIVER, Problems of the Hebrew
Verbal System, Edinburgh, 1936 (with copious bibliography). — D. YELLIN,

History of the Development of Hebrew Grammar, Jérusalem, 1945 (in Hebrew). — J. WEINGREEN, *A Practical Grammar of Classical Hebrew*, Oxford, 1939. — BROWN, DRIVER, and BRIGGS, *A Hebrew and English Lexicon*, Oxford, 1906]. — GESENIUS-BUHL, *Hebräisches und Aramäisches Handwörterbuch* 17th ed., Leipzig, 1921. — [F. ZORELL, *Lexicon Hebraicum et Aramaicum Veteris Testamenti*, Rome, 1946 ff. (in Latin. — L. KOEHLER, *Lexicon in Veteris Testamenti Libros*, Leiden, 1953, with *Supplementum*, 1958 (in German and English). *Yehudah Gur* (Grazowski), *Hebrew Dictionary*, Tel Aviv, 1946 (in Hebrew). Eliezer Ben Yehuda, *Complete Dictionary of Ancient and Modern Hebrew*, Jerusalem, (16 vols. 1940-1959 (in Hebrew). — L. ROST and G. LISOWSKY, *Konkordanz zum Hebräischen Alten Testament*, Stuttgart, 1955 ff. (9 of 12 fascicles published at end of 1957). — Z. S. HARRIS, *A Grammar of the Phoenician Language*, New Haven, Conn., 1936; *id.*, *Development of the Canaanite Dialects*, *ibid.*, 1939. — R. DE LANGHE, *Les Textes de Ras-Shamra-Ugarit et leurs rapports avec le milieu Biblique de l'A. T.*, 2 vols., Paris, 1945 (with complete bibliography). — C. H. GORDON, *Ugaritic Handbook*, in *Analecta Orientalia*, Rome, 1947. — K. ALBRECHT, *Neuhebräische Grammatik auf Grund der Mischnah*, Munich, 1913. — M. S. SEGAL, *A Grammar of Mishnaic Hebrew*, Oxford, 1927. — E. PORATH, *Mishnaic Hebrew*, Jerusalem, 1938 (in Hebrew)].

II.   Aramaic. — L. STRACK, *Grammatik des Biblisch-Aramäischen*, 6th ed., Munich, 1921. — G. DALMAN, *Grammatik des Jüdisch-palästinischen Aramäisch*, 2nd ed., Leipzig, 1905; *Aramäisch-Neuhebräisches Wörterbuch*, Frankfort, 1897-1901. — STEVENSON, *Grammar of Palestinian Jewish Aramaic*, Oxford, 1924. [H. H. ROWLEY, *The Aramaic of the Old Testament*, Oxford, 1929. — H. BAUER and P. LEANDER, *Grammatik des Biblisch-Aramäischen*, Halle/Saale, 1927. — L. PALACIOS, O. S. B., *Grammatica Aramaico-Biblica*, 2nd ed., Rome, 1957. — M. L. MARGOLIS, *A Manual of the Aramaic Language of the Babylonian Talmud*, Munich, 1910. — J. T. MARSHALL, *Manual of the Aramaic Language of the Palestinian Talmud*, Leiden, 1929. — G. LEVIAS, *A Grammar of Babylonian Aramaic*, New-York, 1930 (in Hebrew). — A. COWLEY, *Aramaic Papyri of the Fifth Century B. C.*, Oxford, 1923. — F. SCHULTHESS, *Grammatik des christlich-palästinischen Aramäisch* (edited by E. LITTMANN), Tübingen, 1924. — F. SCHWALLY, *Idioticon des christlich-palästinischen Aramäisch*, Giessen, 1893]. — Stanley A. COOK, *A Glossary of the Aramaic Inscriptions*, Cambridge, 1898. — J. CANTINEAU, *Le Nabatéen*, 2 vols., Paris, 1930-1932. — F. ROSENTHAL, *Die Sprache der Palmyrenischen Inschriften u. ihre Stellung innerhalb des Aramäischen*, Leipzig, 1936. — *id.*, *Die aramäistische Forschung seit Th. Nöldeke's Veröffentlichungen*, Leiden, 1939].

III.   Greek. — BLASS-DEBRUNNER, *Grammatik des neutestamentlichen Griechisch*, 6th ed., GÖTTINGEN, 1931, 8th ed., 1949. — J. H. MOULTON, *Grammar of New Testament Greek*, Edinburgh, 1919-1929. — F. M. ABEL, *Grammaire du grec biblique*, Paris, 1927. — DOM B. BOTTE, *Grammaire grecque du Nouveau Testament*, Paris, 1933. — A. T. ROBERTSON, *A Grammar of the Greek New Testament in the Light of Historical Research*,

London, 1919. — [J. VERGOTE, *Grec Biblique, DBV, Suppl.*, vol. III, cols. 1320-1369]. — W. BAUER, *Griechisch-Deutsches Wörterbuch*, 4th ed. Berlin, 1952; 5th ed., 1957 ff.; — W. F. ARNDT and F. W. GINGRICH, *A Greek-English Lexicon of the New Testament and Other Early Christian Literature*, Chicago, 1957; a translation and adaptation of the 4th ed. of Bauer's work]. — F. ZORELL, *Lexicon graecum Novi Testamenti*, 2nd ed., Paris, 1931. — MOULTON-MILLIGAN, *The Vocabulary of the Greek Testament*, London, 1914-1929. [G. KITTEL, *Theologisches Wörterbuch zum Neuen Testament*, Stuttgart, 1932 ff. vols. I-VI, a-Π in 1958, in course of publication. — On the Semitic substratum of the Gospels : see : P. JOÜON, S. J., *L'évangile de N. S. Jésus- Christ*, Paris, 1930; Verbum Salutis, 5. — C. C. TORREY, *The Four Gospels :A New Translation* (N. Y. 1933; reprinted, 1947; *id.*, *Our Translated Gospels* (N. Y. 1936) *id.*, *Documents of the Primitive Church*, N. Y., 1941. — W. C. ALLEN, *The Gospel According to Saint Mark*, London, 1915. — C. F. BURNEY, *The Poetry of Our Lord*, Oxford, 1925. — E. C. COLWELL, *The Greke of the Fourth Gospel*, Chicago, 1931. — M. BLACK, *An Aramaic Approach to the Gospels and Acts*, Oxford, 1946. Cf. P. BENOIT, O. P., in *RB* (1947), pp. 440-443. — Dom H. CONNOLLY in *Downside Review* (1947), pp. 25-37. — J. BONSIRVEN, S. J., in *Biblica* (1949), pp. 456-459. — DEBRUNNER, *Theol. Zts.* (1947), pp. 377-381. — J. BONSIRVEN, S. J., " Les Aramaïsmes de Saint Jean l'Évangéliste, " *Biblica* (1949), pp. 405-431. — J. DE ZWAAN, " John Wrote in Aramaic, " *JBL* (1938), pp. 156-171. — E. LITTMANN in *ZNTW* (1935), pp. 20-34 (on Torrey). — Also the following articles : A. T. OLMSTEAD in *JNES* (1941), pp. 41-75, (1943), pp. 1-34. — E. J. GOODSPEED, *ibid.* (1942), pp. 315-340. — S. I. FEIGIN, *ibid.* (1943), pp. 187-197. — H. F. D. SPARKS, *The Semitisms of Saint Luke's Gospel, JTS* 44 (1943), pp. 129-138. — J. BONSIRVEN, S. J., *Biblica* (1948), pp. 205-219].

CHAPTER IV

SYSTEMS OF WRITING
by His Eminence Cardinal E. TISSERANT.

I.   — Hebrew writing.

II.   — Greek writing.

III. — Writing materials.

CHAPTER IV

SYSTEMS OF WRITING

I. — HEBREW WRITING.

The characters in which the oldest of our Sacred Books were written were certainly not the ones which we know through the manuscripts of the Hebrew Bible. Origen and Saint Jerome were aware of this fact, for they had learned it from their Jewish masters. They knew also that the archaic writing resembled that of the Samaritans of their times. Through they lacked manuscripts written in the ancient character, they could see in their primitive form at least the four letters of the ineffable name (YHWH). These were preserved in copies of the Greek version of Aquila, similar to the copy whose fragments were discovered in the genizah of Cairo in 1897, or of the Minor Prophets found in one of the caves (*RB* [1953], p. 1).

When did the archaic system of Hebraic-Samaritan writing originate? Several scholars in the 18th century, whose view was repeated by Voltaire, held that the Jews learned writing only in the time of the Judges. This was taught by Gesenius in 1815, who concluded that Moses could not be the author of the Pentateuch. Renan, in his *History of the People of Israel*, still maintained that " writing in Israel was later than Moses and Josue by some three or four hundred years ". As the discovery of cuneiform tablets in Egypt and Palestine showed that the petty princes of Canaan were using the Assyro-Babylonian system of writing in the first half of the 14th century B. C., Winckler and Naville (beginning of the 20th century) had good ground for advancing the hypothesis that Moses could have written in cuneiform characters.

But the thorough exploration of Serabit el Khadim (since 1904) and the excavations at Byblos and at Ras Shamra (1921 ff., 1929) have revealed the simultaneous existence of three alphabets which could be known to the Hebrews at the time of the Exodus.

The first one, which could be called South-Palestinian because of the find of an ostracon in Gezer (1929), is known especially from the Proto-Sinaitic inscriptions. These belong very likely to the time of the XIIth Egyptian Dynasty (*ca.* 2160-1781), while the Gezer ostracon was in a Middle Bronze stratum — i.e. in the first half of the second millenium in both cases. (See col. 2 of " Table of Hebrew Writing ") [1].

The second system was used in the city of Ugarit, on the Syrian shore, at Ras Shamra, a little to the north of Latakia (Arabic Ladiqiya, Greek Laodicea). Ugarit was for several centuries an important commercial center. There were found in its ruins Sumerian, Akkadian, and Hittite documents, and also tablets with cuneiform alphabetic characters, an alphabet of 29 signs. The language of these tablets is very close to Phoenician and Hebrew. The Ugarit finds show that in the 15th century B. C. there was an alphabet which lent itself to writing Hebrew. Of that system we know only texts written on clay tablets. It may have been used, with the necessary adaptations, in writing on papyrus or on leather. The climatic conditions of Ras Shamra would not allow the preservation of perishable materials such as leather and parchment. This is all the more regrettable as we know that the Phoenicians imported from Egypt large quantities of papyrus prepared for writing [2].

The Phoenician alphabet properly so-called became known at first from inscriptions on stone (Mesha Stone, Siloam inscription, stamps on earthenware jars and seals). Several important inscriptions were found later in Northern Syria and in Byblos. The dates of these inscriptions are not all certain : thus that of Ahiram's sarcophagus (probably *ca.* 1100 B. C.), for which dates between the 13th and the 10th centuries have been proposed [3].

Translator's note. — [1 On the early alphabetic inscriptions from Sinai, see especially W. F. ALBRIGHT, *BASOR*, N⁰ 110 (April, 1948), pp. 6-22, and the references there given].

Translator's note. — [2 On Ugaritic writing, see the work of R. DE LANGHE listed in the Bibliography to Chapter III, and W. F. ALBRIGHT, *BASOR*, N⁰ 118 (1950), pp. 12-24, and N⁰ 119, pp. 23-24].

Translator's note. — [3 On the Ahiram inscription and the Gezer Calendar, both now dated *ca.* 1000 B.C., see R. DE VAUX, O. P., in *RB* (1946), p. 462 ff.; W. F. ALBRIGHT, *Journal of the American Oriental Society* (1947), pp. 132-160; id., *Archaeology of Palestine* (Harmondsworth, 1954), pp. 190-194. For the inscriptions of Mesha and Siloam, see, e.g., G. A. COOKE, *A Textbook of North Semitic Inscriptions* (Oxford, 1903), pp. 1-17; M. LIDZBARSKI, *Altsemitische Texte.* I (Giessen, 1907), pp. 5-10; R. DUSSAUD, *Les monuments palestiniens et judaïques* (Paris, 1912, with an excellent plate of the Mesha inscription].

We have now material which enables us better than the inscriptions on the monuments to follow the development of the Hebrew alphabet and to visualize the forms of the characters used in the transmission of the Biblical text since the time of the Kings : the ostraca found in Palestine itself, in Samaria, contemporary with Achab (*ca.* 869-850) and Jehu (*ca.* 842-815), and at Tell Duweir (Biblical Lakish [Lachis]) contemporary with Jeremias (6th century B. C.); the papyri found in Egypt (5th century B. C.) at Elephantine [Syene, Arabic Aswan] and in the Fayyum district; and lastly, among the Dead Sea Mss., some fragments of Exodus and Leviticus in archaic writing [1].

Thanks to the documents mentioned above we can follow pretty accurately the development of Hebrew writing, which is really Phoenician writing. But another system became prevalent in Israel, the " square writing " which, according to Rabbinical tradition, was brought from Mesopotamia by Esdras and is, for that reason, called " Aššurit " (Assyrian). This name may seem strange, since the Aramaic notes on cuneiform tablets until the Seleucid period (312 B. C.) are written in the archaic (Phoenician) alphabet. However, we have no positive evidence contradicting the statment about the date of the introduction of the square writing in Palestine. It will be enough to note that the archaic writing did not disappear suddenly : it was still used on the coins of the Hasmonaeans (2nd century B. C.) and of Bar Kochba (2nd century A. D.).

The forms of the square writing used on the monuments appear only toward the beginning of the Christian Era in

Translator's note. — [1 On the Lakish ostraca (587 B.C.), see H. TORCZYNER, L. HARDING, A. LEWIS, and J. L. STARKEY, *The Lachish Letters* (Oxford, 1939); H. TORCZYNER, *Te'udot Lakish* (Jerusalem, 1940; in Hebrew). Z. ZOLLI, " La tavoletta di Gezer, " *Biblica* (1946), pp. 129-131. D. DIRINGER, " Early Hebrew Writing, " *BA* (1950), 74-95; *id.*, " The Royal Jar Handle Stamps, " *ibid.* (1949), pp. 70-86. E. O'DOHERTY, " The Date of the Ostraca of Samaria, " *CBQ* 15 (1953), pp. 24-29. R. E. MURPHY, O. CARM, " A Fragment of an Early Moabite Inscription from Dibon, " *BASOR*, Nº. 125,) (Feb., 1952), 20-23. E. G. KRAELING, *The Brooklyn Museum Aramaic Papyri from...* *Elephantine* (New Haven, 1953, with plates at end). J. C. TREVER, " A Palaeographical Study of the Jerusalem Scrolls, " *BASOR*, Nº. 113 (1949), pp. 6-23. A. BIRNBAUM, " The Date of the Isaiah Scroll, " *ibid.*, pp. 33-35; *id.*, *The Hebrew Scripts* (London, 1954)] N. AVIGAD; " The Palaeography of the Dead Sea Scrolls and Related Documents ", *Scripta Hierosolym.* IV (1958), pp. 56-81 (with good reproductions of the alphabets of all the documents).]

inscriptions of synagogues in Galilee and in epitaphs near Jerusalem and in Judaea. Until 1947 only one manuscript fragment from the period about the beginning of our era was known, the Nash Papyrus, which was dated variously between 50 B. C. and 100 A. D. Next came the fragments from the genizot of Chufut-Kale (Crimea) and Cairo. The oldest of these fragments might go back to the 6th century A. D.; the oldest dated Mss belong to the end of the 9th and 10th century.

Since 1947 abundant material has been found hidden in the caves of Qumran and Murabba'at. Their publication will make available a large quantity of specimens older than 70 A. D. for Qumran and 130 A. D. for Murabba'at. Since the Qumran finds provide us also with fragments of archaic Mss, it may be hoped that the study of all these texts will yield important data regarding the evolution of square writing from its beginnings. Father Vaccari (*Biblica*, 34 [1953], p. 397 ff.) notes that from the graphic point of view the large Isaias - Scroll fits very well into the 2nd century B. C., halfway between the Elephantine papyri and the inscriptions or graffiti of the first century A. D.

The period between the two wars (70-130 A. D.) seems to have been decisive for the settling of the graphic forms. The Murabba'at Mss have regularly the final letters, which are unknown or used sporadically before 70 A. D. These mss also often have *apices* at the left top of certain letters, a usage that is common in mediaeval mss.

II. — GREEK WRITING.

When the Pentateuch was translated into Greek under the Ptolemies, Greek writing had already been in existence for five or six centuries. The Septuagint was written in the characters used in Egypt for copying literary texts on papyrus. These characters became somewhat modified with the introduction of parchment, which from the fourth century A. D. gradually supplanted papyrus. The small uncial of the famous manuscrits of the fourth and fifth centuries, the *Vaticanus*, *Sinaïticus*, and *Alexandrinus*, resembles, to some extent, the letter forms in the inscriptions of the age of Pericles. In the sixth

HEBREW WRITING

1	2	3	4	5	6	7	8	9	10	11
'										א
b										ב
g										ג
d										ד
h										ה
w										ו
z										ז
ḥ										ח
ṭ										ט
y										י
k										דכ
l										ל
m										םמ
n										ןנ
s										ס
ʿ										ע
p										ףפ
ṣ										ץצ
q										ק
r										ר
šś										ש
t										ת

1. Transcription. — 2. Sinaitic writing of Serabit al-Knadim. 3. — Sarcophagus of Ahiram (13 th century B. C.) [end of 11 th century B. C.]. — 4. Inscription of Mesa, king of Moab (9th century B. C.) — 5. Ostraka of Samaria. — 6. Petition of the Jews of Elephantine on papyrus (408-7 B. C.). — 7. Funeral inscriptions in Palestine (1ts century B. C.). — 8. Nash Papyrus. — 9. Codex Petropolitanus Prophetarum, 916 A. D. — 10. Roll of the Law (13th century A. D.). — 11. Printed alphabet.

THE DEAD SEA SCROLLS

1	2	3	4	5	6	7	8	9	10	11
ʾ	א	א	א	א	א	א	א	א	א	א
b	ב	ב	ב	ב	ב	ב	ב	ב	ב	ב
g	ג	ג	ג	ג	ג	ג		ג	ג	ג
d	ד	ד	ד	ד	ד	ד	ד	ד	ד	ד
h	ה	ה	ה	ה	ה	ה	ה	ה	ה	ה
w	ו	ו	ו	ו	ו	ו	ו	ו	ו	ו
z	ז	ז	ז	ז	ז	ז		ז	ז	ז
ḥ	ח	ח	ח	ח	ח	ח	ח	ח	ח	ח
ṭ	ט	ט	ט	ט	ט			ט		ט
y	י	י	י	י	י	י	י	י	י	י
k	כ	כ	כ	כ	כ	כ	כ	כ	כ	כ
l	ל	ל	ל	ל	ל	ל	ל	ל	ל	ל
m	מ	מ	מ	מ	מ	מ	מ	מ	מ	מ
n	נ	נ	נ	נ	נ	נ	נ	נ	נ	נ
s	ס	ס	ס	ס	ס	ס	ס	ס	ס	ס
ʿ	ע	ע	ע	ע	ע	ע	ע	ע	ע	ע
p	פ	פ	פ	פ	פ	פ	פ		פ	פ
ṣ	צ	צ	צ	צ	צ	צ	צ	צ	צ	צ
q	ק	ק	ק	ק	ק	ק	ק	ק		ק
r	ר	ר	ר	ר	ר	ר	ר	ר	ר	ר
š/ś	ש	ש	ש	ש	ש	ש	ש	ש	ש	ש
t	ת	ת	ת	ת	ת	ת	ת	ת	ת	ת

1. Transcription. — 2. The Large Isaias Scroll (1 Q Isa), *ca.* 100 B. C. — 3. The Rule (Manual of Discipline) (1 Q S), 1st cent. B. C. — 4. The Second Isaias Scroll (1 Q sb), end of the 1st cent. B. C. or beginning of 1st cent. A. D. — 5. The Commentary on Habacuc (1 Qq Hab), 1st cent. A. D. — 6. The War of the Children of Light (1 Q M), 1st cent. A. D. — 7. The Hymns of Thanksgiving (1 Q H), 1st cent. A. D. — 8. The Fragment of Exodus from Murabba'at, *ca.* 100 A. D. — 9. The Beth Mashko Document (Mur.), between 132 and 135 A. D. — 10. A Letter of Simeon Bar Kochba (Mur.), between 132 and 135 A. D. — 11. The printed Hebrew alphabet.

N.B. The documents on which cols. 8-10 are based do not contain all the letters of the Hebrew alphabet. For fuller information and bibliography, see G. Vermès, *Discovery in the Judean Desert* (New York, 1956), who drew up this table.

SYSTEMS OF WRITING

GREEK WRITING

1	2	3	4	5	6	7	8	9	10	11

1. 4th century B. C.: Papyrus of Timotheus of Miletus (Berlin Museum). — 2. 1st century A. D.: Papyrus of the Odyssey (British Museum, Pap. CCLXXI). — 3. 4th century A. D.: Codex Vaticanus B (Vat. Gr. 1209): straight (upright) uncial. — 4. 4th century: Freer manuscript of the Gospels (Washington): slanted uncial. — 5. 5th-6th centuries: Greek-Coptic manuscript of the Gospel of Saint John (Borg. Copt. 109): straight uncial. — 6. 8th-9th centuries: Almagest of Ptolemy (Paris Gr. 2839): slanted uncial. — 7. 9th century: Chain on Job (Vat. Gr. 749): straight uncial. — 8. 8th-9th centuries: *Doctrina Patrum* (Vat. Gr. 2200): cursive. — 9. 879 A. D.: Commentary of Hesychius on the Psalms (Pal. Gr. 44): straight minuscule. — 10. 1073 A. D.: Homilies of Saint Basil on the Psalms (Reg. Gr. 13): slanted minuscule. — 11. Printed alphabet.

century the uncial became larger and thicker. Slanted writing, of which several ancient specimens have recently been found, became frequent from the seventh century, and at the same time the straight uncial became contracted in certain letters and was decorated with *apices* which spoiled its simplicity. From the ninth century we meet the minuscule derived from cursive forms, which, though rarely found in literary manuscripts, had had a development of their own in private documents.

Abbreviations, limited at first to *nomina sacra*, became more common in the twelfth century because of the mixture of numerous shorthand signs with the regular letters.

III. — WRITING MATERIALS.

The excavations of Judea and Galilee are extraordinarily poor in written documents. The Jews, therefore, must have habitually written on perishable materials. They probably used specially prepared skins, wooden tablets, and papyrus. None of the archeological sites explored in Jewish lands presents soil dry enough for these materials to be preserved. But how is the lack of inscriptions on stone to be accounted for? Would it be because the Jews were loath to imitate the Tables of the Law, on which the Decalogue had been inscribed by the hand of God? It is an extraordinary fact, at all events, that in this East where men wrote so much, only a single monumental inscription has survived from the pre-Hellenistic period, and one which was not intended to be seen, namely the inscription in the tunnel of Siloam.

The Jews wrote on clay, as we know from an allusion in Ezechiel **4** : **1** and from the actual evidence furnished by ostraca from Samaria and Lakish. Isaias **40** : **8** and Habacuc **2** : **2** refer to documents written on wood. The scribes used pointed reeds (Ps. **44** : **2**) and, during the whole Biblical period, ink was prepared from lampblack mixed in a solution of gum arabic.

The Bible does not say explicitly of what materials books were made, but the Hebrew word for book, *sefer*, comes from a root meaning " to scrape ". It is therefore natural to think that Jewish books were made of skins prepared in the manner most customary in the East (Diodorus **2** : **32**; Herodotus **5** : **58**).

The Letter of Aristeas says expressly that the copy of the Law sent to Ptolemy was on rolls of leather, and Rabbinical tradition prescribes that copies of the Torah intended for public reading must be written on skins which have not been slit, or *gewil*. This usage is still in force.

The Jews, at least in Egypt, used papyrus for secular writings, and perhaps also for copies of the Bible intended for private use (cf. the Nash Papyrus). Papyrus seems to have been the material used by the Christians for copies of their sacred books, although Saint Paul does speak of his parchments (μεμβράναι). It was probably the length of the sacred books which caused parchment to be preferred. The *Vaticanus* and the *Sinaïticus*, e.g., contains the whole inspired text in a single volume, while thirty or forty papyrus rolls would have been required for this same amount of text.

Paper, which is of Chinese origin, was made almost everywhere in the Arab world after the fall of Samarcand (704), but did not become a serious competitor of parchment, at least so far as the sacred books are concerned. For these a solid and durable, and, therefore, more noble material was preferred. Only printing succeeded in dethroning parchment : the first printed edition of the Bible already contained a number of copies on paper.

[Bibliography on Writing. — B. L. ULLMAN, *Ancient Writing and its Influence* (New-York, 1932); D. DIRINGER, *The Alphabet* (New-York, 1948); J. W. FLIGHT, " History of Writing in the Near East ", in *The Hoverford Symposium on Archaeology and the Bible* (New Haven, Conn., 1938), pp. 110-135; G. R. DRIVER, *Semitic Writing* (London, 1948); S. YEIVIN, *History of Hebrew Writing* (Jerusalem, 1938, in Hebrew); W. F. ALBRIGHT, *The Archaeology of Palestine* (revised ed., 1954; a Pelican Book), pp. 177-203. — W. SCHUBART, *Griechische Paläographie* (Munich, 1925); R. MARICHAL, L'écriture latine et l'écriture grecque du Ier au VIe siècle, *L'Antiquité Classique*, 19 (1950), 113-144. — N. H. TUR SINAI (Torczyner), s. v. " Alphabet ", in *Entzyklo. Miqra'it* I (Jerusalem, 1950), pp. 372-415 (in Hebrew). — F. M. CROSS, " Evolution of the Proto-Sinaitic Alphabet ", *BASOR*, No. 134, (Apr., 1954), pp. 15-24. — E. A. SPEISER, " A Note on Alphabetic Origins ", *ibid.*, No. 121, (Feb., 1951), pp. 17-21. See especially the excellent comprehensive survey, by J. NOUGAYROL, J. J. FÉVRIER, and G. RYCKMANS in the article, " Langues et Écritures Sémitiques, " *DBV*, *Suppl.* 5 (1957), cols. 268-284, 299-317, and 330-334 (with valuable bibliography)].

CHAPTER V

THE BOOKS

by J. CHAINE, A. GELIN, J. HUBY, and A. ROBERT.

I. — THE BOOKS OF THE OLD TESTAMENT.

1. — *THE LAW OR THE PENTATEUCH* [A. ROBERT].

[Analysis of the Books of the Pentateuch by E. P. ARBEZ].

2. — *THE HISTORICAL BOOKS* [A. ROBERT].

3. — *THE PROPHETICAL BOOKS* [A. GELIN].

4. — *THE SAPIENTIAL BOOKS* [J. CHAINE and A. ROBERT].

II. — THE BOOKS OF THE NEW TESTAMENT [J. HUBY].

1. — *THE GOSPELS AND THE ACTS OF THE APOSTLES.*

2. — *THE EPISTLES.*

3. — *THE APOCALYPSE.*

CHAPTER V

THE BOOKS

I. — THE BOOKS OF THE OLD TESTAMENT.

1. — *THE LAW (PENTATEUCH)*
[A. Robert]

Name and content.

The Jews called the first five books of the Bible *Torah*, or *Law*. They spoke also of " the five fifths of the Law ". This expression gave rise to the Greek name, ἡ πεντάτευχος (Βίβλος), and from the Greek has come our term, Pentateuch.

Each of the five books was provided by the Greeks with a name suited to its content : Genesis, the book of origins; Exodus, which tells of the going forth from Egypt; Leviticus, a collection of ritual prescriptions, which, therefore, concerns the tribe of Levi; Numbers, which begins with the account of a census; Deuteronomy, or Second Law, according to a faulty interpretation of Deut. **17** : 18, which happens, however, to correspond very well to the nature of the book.

The Pentateuch is peculiar in that it consists of a series of legislative texts embodied in the framework of an historical narrative. The general theme which unifies such diverse elements may be expressed in the following proposition, which has the force of a thesis : There exists a divine, immutable plan which is progressively realized despite all obstacles, and its objective is the formation of the people of Israel as a theocratic nation with Palestine as its country and the Mosaic Law as its charter.

Origin and historical value.

I. **The traditional position.**

a) The Pentateuch bears neither title nor signature. Except in Deuteronomy, Moses does not speak in the first person. The literary activity of the founder of the religion of Israel is noted, in passing, in reference to certain facts (Ex. **17** : 14; Num. **33** : 2) or to certain prescriptions (Ex. **24** : 4; **34** : 27). Deuteronomy claims Moses as the author of the code (Deut. **4** : 44, 45; **31** : 9; cf. **27** : 2-8; Jos. **8** : 32), and of the final canticle (Deut. **31** : 22). Josue refers to a law of Moses (**1** : 7-8; **8** : 30-31), capable of receiving additions (**24** : 26).

b) The prophets before the Exile often speak of the Torah of Yahweh, thus referring certainly to a traditional body of teaching of Mosaic origin of which they are, with the priests (Jer. **2** : 8; **18** : 18; **26** : 4-5), the guardians and interpreters. Moreover, unlike the priests in this respect, they are concerned only with the moral prescriptions (cf. Jer. **7** : 21-23). In 622 there occurred the important event related in 2 Kgs. **22** and 2 Chron. **34**, namely, the discovery of the *Book of the Law* in the Temple of Jerusalem. Various expressions in the narrative, as well as the nature of the reform which was soon brought about by Josias, show that reference is made to Deuteronomy. Moses speaks there in the first person, both in the speeches and in the Code, and the word *Torah* takes on the meaning of a body of doctrine at once exhortatory and legislative : it is the Word *par excellence*, Revelation in its full sense, priestly and prophetic, if not sapiential.

c) Although he is very ritualistic, Ezechiel understands the word *Torah* in the same sense as his pre-exilic predecessors. Proverbs takes a marked universalist attitude, but includes a number of veiled references to parts of the Pentateuch, and chiefly to Deuteronomy. Under these conditions, the word *Torah* can have only a very much broadened signification. The same holds true in the case of the postexilic Psalms, even though in appearance they are narrowly legalistic, like Ps. **119**. The author of Chronicles often refers to our five books, as to a written text which possesses authority : e.g., 2 Chron. **23** : 18; **25** : 4. Ritualistic prescriptions are recalled in Esdras (**3** : 2-4; **6** : 18) and Nehemias (**1** : 7-9; **8** : 13-18; **10** : 29-39), which belong to all the Codes. Moreover, it is important to note that the account of Esdras (Esd. **9** : 11) employs, under cover of the authority of the prophets, expressions taken verbatim from the Pentateuch (Deut. **7** : 1; Lev. **18** : 24, 25; Deut. **7** : 3; **23** : 7), and cites as written in the Law an injunction which is not found there in those terms (Neh. **10** : 35; cf. Lev. **6** : 1-6). On his part, the author of Chronicles has a dynamic notion of the work of Moses, for he sees it completed by the prophets, e.g., 2 Chron. **29** : 25, and especially by David, e.g., 2 Chron. **8** : 13-14. Thus even in these legalistic writings the notions of the Torah and of Mosaic authorship retain an undeniable elasticity.

Daniel (**9** : 10, 11) also cites the prophets side by side with Moses. Ecclesiasticus (**24** : 23 [32-33]) sees in the Torah of Moses the consummate expression of wisdom; but, following the example of Proverbs, he does not attach any less importance to the teaching ot the prophets and the sapiential writers, and his book is filled with their precepts. He is therefore convinced that the teachings coming from both sources share legitimately in the notion of the Torah and should be considered as an expansion and explanation of the Mosaic work. Finally Baruch (**2** : 2, 3, 28-35) refers to Moses, and in **3** : 9-14, **3** : 37-4 : 4, he manifests the same attitude as Ecclesiasticus [1].

d) Our Lord and the Apostles invoke the authority of Moses. Sometimes they refer in merely general terms to the law of Moses (Lk. **2** : 22, etc.), or speak of the book of Moses (Mk. **12** : 26, etc.) as different from the other parts of the Jewish canon (Lk. **24** : 27, 44; Acts **28** : 23). Again, they mention facts reported in the Pentateuch (Mk. **12** : 26, Heb. **9** : 19), and especially laws (Mt. **8** : 4; Mk. **1** : 44; Lk. **5** : 14; Mk. **7** : 10-**20** : 35; Jn. **7** : 22-8 : 5; Rom. **10** : 5; 1 Cor. **9** : 9; Heb. **7** : 14). There is also question of the Messianic prophecies (Jn. **1** : 45). Twice only (Acts **3** : 22 and Rom. **10** : 19) are specific passages quoted (Deut. **18** : 15-19, and **32** : 31). In Jn. **5** : 45-47, Moses is referred to in a connection outside the book which is attributed to him.

e) The Jews of the Christian era received from their ancestors their belief in the Mosaic authorship of the Pentateuch. None before Spinoza in the seventeenth century cast doubt

---

[1] On the notion of the Law in Proverbs, Psalm **119**, Chronicles, and Ecclesiasticus, see A. ROBERT, " Les attaches littéraires bibliques de Prov. I-IX ", *RB* (1934), 42-68; 112-204; 374-384; (1935), 344-365; 502-525; *id.*, " Le sens du mot Loi dans le Ps. CXIX ", *ibid.* (1937), pp. 182-206; *ibid.* (1939), pp. 5-20; *Le Yahwisme de* Prov. X, 1-XXII, 16; XXV-XXIX, in *Mémorial* LAGRANGE, (1940), pp. 163-182.

upon it. They accepted it indeed in so absolute a fashion that,
according to some, Moses composed in advance the account
of his own death (see e.g., Josephus, *Ant. Jud.* IV, **8**, 48).
The same unanimity reigns among the Fathers of the Church,
and clearly echoes the testimony of Scripture and Jewish
tradition. If they seek confirmation for their belief, they do
so, not through reasoning upon the literary characteristics of
the Mosaic work, but through stressing its doctrinal profundity,
its authority, and its antiquity : it could have had no other
author save the first and greatest of the prophets. See the
texts in the article, " Pentateuque ", by E. MANGENOT, *DBV*,
V (1912), cols. 73-75.

In short, the various organs of tradition concur in this general
statement : *Moses wrote.* Such universal testimony is a fact
that, with all due deference to certain radical critics, cannot
be set aside *a priori*, but requires an adequate explanation.
Tradition, however, does not say explicitly anywhere that Moses
composed the entire Pentateuch. His work is usually spoken
of only in general terms; rarely are individual passages
mentioned. Moreover, even in the postexilic period of Judaism,
which was wrongly believed to have been dominated by the
most rigid legalistic principles, the inspired writers do not
establish a very clear line of demarcation between the personal
literary activity of the first of the prophets and that of his
successors. This lack of precision, far from hindering critical
investigation, rather invites it. At the same time, it imposes
limits which must not be ignored.

2. Observations on certain literary characteristics of the Pentateuch.

In spite of its unity of plan, spirit, and doctrine, the
Pentateuch gives evidence of being definitely complex.
" Though not easily discernible in Saint Jerome's Vulgate or in
the Septuagint, this difference of redaction is very apparent even
in a good translation based on the Hebrew; it is strikingly
clear to specialists in the original tongue " (E. AMANN,
" Pentateuque ", *DTC*, XII, col. 1181). The observations
which may be made in this regard concern the subject matter
and form, and can be grouped under the four following
headings :

a) Respecting the subject matter, there is a lack of continuity and order both in the narrative sections and in the laws. Thus, there is no sequence between the narrative in Gen. **4** : 26 and **5** : 1, or in Gen. **19** : 38 and **20** : 1. Gen. **2** : 4^b–**4** : 26 is a block of material which breaks the thread of the account of **2** : 4^a–**5** : 1 ff. The laws of Ex. **25–40**, Lev., and Num. **1** ff. are not fitted into any concrete and precise historical context. In the body of the Codes also no logical sequence is discernible.

b) Respecting the form, there are surprising differences in the vocabulary, syntax, and especially — a fact which is more striking and less open to challenge — in the style and general procedures of composition. This is clearly brought out, e.g., by a comparison of Leviticus and Deuteronomy.

c) The variable use of the divine names Yahweh and Elohim is a singular phenomenon. If we can accept the calculations of J. Battersby-Harford (*Since Wellhausen* [1926], p. 12), the Masoretic text contains from Gen. **1** : 1 to Ex. **3** : 15 (52½ chapters) 178 examples of Elohim and 146 of Yahweh, while, from Exodus **3** : 16 to the end of this same book (37½ chapters), the name Elohim occurs 44 times as against 393 examples of Yahweh. The proportions are less marked in the Septuagint, but not to the point of removing the problem. Now this problem can be stated thus : If it is true that the names for God often change without apparent reason, how does it happen that in a great many other cases they vary according to the theological conceptions and literary characteristics of the various sections? Thus stated, the problem of the names of God is only a particular, though singularly striking, aspect of *a* and *b*, and it suggests the same principles of solution.

d) Lastly, if we admit the reality of the problems mentioned, we must admit also the existence of double narratives. See, for example, Gen. **1** : 1–**2** : 4^a and **2** : 4^b–**2** : 25; Ex. **3** : 1–**4** : 31 and **6** : 2-13; **7** : 1-7; Lev. **11** : 1-47 and Deut. **14** :3-21; Ex. **21** : 1-11 and Lev. **25** : 39-55; Deut. **15** : 12-18. It must be understood that we are concerned here, not with the simple repetition of identical material, but with the repetition of the same basic subject matter with certain more or less marked divergences. Thus defined, the existence of these double narratives does not constitute, in relation to the preceding evidence, a new problem. It is simply a crucial instance which reveals clearly the convergence of all the observations made above on subject matter and form. Consequently the problem of the double narratives cannot be solved except in the way that we believe should be adopted in dealing with *a*, *b*, and *c*.

3. The critical hypothesis [1].

Since the seventeenth century a critical hypothesis has progressively developed, and we may say that, on the whole, the two phases of its evolution have coincided with the two logical aspects of the problem : analysis and synthesis of source material, or, in other words, identification and chronology of sources.

a) The analysis of the sources.

The literary peculiarities considered above (cf. 2) have gradually been noted and defined. From the beginning they were regarded as evidence for a multiplicity of sources. The whole task of literary criticism, accordingly, was to determine their extent and their characteristics. The pioneers were Richard Simon (1678) and Jean Astruc (1753). On the basis of their observations, theories succeeded theories. Eichhorn (1780-1783) and Ilgen (1798) distinguished in Genesis several primitive narratives which were parallel and were then brought together by one or by several editors. This is the *First Documentary Hypothesis*. Geddes (1792, 1800), Vater (1802-1805), and De Wette (1805), extending their investigation to cover all the legislative texts and the entire Pentateuch, found in them nothing more than a collection of materials devoid of parallelisms. This is the *Fragment Hypothesis*. De Wette later agreed with the views of Ewald (1831), which were adopted and developed by Bleek (1836) and Fr. Delitzsch (1852), namely, that excerpts from other sources had probably been incorporated into one basis document. This is the *Development or Supplement Hypothesis*. Ewald returned (1843-55) to the documentary hypothesis and fused it with that of supple-

---

Translator's note. — [1 For an excellent historical sketch of the Pentateuch problem and its present status, see J. COPPENS, *The Old Testament and the Critics*. English translation by E. A. RYAN ad E. W. TRIBBE (Paterson, N. J., 1942)].

ments. He was followed by Knobel (1857, 1861) and Schrader (1869). With Hupfeld (1853) and Riehm (1854), the documentary hypothesis again appeared. As a result of the studies of Dillmann (1875 f.) and of Fr. Delitzsch (1880), this conception developed into the *New Documentary Theory*, which claims in our day the majority of advocates. It maintains that the Pentateuch is the product of the combination of four sources, composite in themselves, yet each forming a coherent whole both as to style and doctrine. They are called : P, the Priestly Code (in German *Priesterkodex*); E. the Elohist; J, the Yahwist (Jahvist); and D, the Deuteronomist.

b) The synthesis of the sources.

If the existence of four documents is admitted, it remains to determine their relative and absolute chronology as well as the date of the final redactions. The theory which is still most commonly held was elaborated by Reuss (1833), Graf (1866), and Kuenen (1869). Wellhausen (1878 f.) gave it its final form. In order to fix the chronology of the sources, he compares a certain number of laws with one another, and then brings these into relation with events described in the historical and prophetical books. He considers that there were four legislative sequences. They are concerned respectively with : unity of the place of worship, the distinction between priests and levites, sacred titles, and feasts. Let us consider, e.g., the question of the single place of sacrifice. JE permits plurality of altars : Ex. **20** : 22; cf. **22** : 29, 30 and **22** : 8. This is the primitive practive, while, on the other hand, Deut. **12** suppresses local places of worship. Finally P, in Lev. **17** : 3-9, etc., supposes the unity of worship to have been established in an irrevocable manner and as existing from the time of the wandering in the wilderness. P is therefore considered to belong to a late period in which the liberties permitted in JE were forgotten, and when the polemics of D no longer had any justification. Thus is established the chronological sequence, JE, D, P. History seems to confirm this conclusion, because, until the Deuteronomic reform of Josias in 621, kings and prophets tolerated the high places and even sacrificed in them without scruple : Jdgs. **6** : 24; **13** : 19; **18** : 30-31; I Sam. **7** : 17; **9** : 13, 14; **10** : 8; **14** : 35 ;**16** : 2-5; **20** : 6-9; 2 Sam. **28** : 18; I Kings

15 : 14; **18**; **22** : 43, 44; 2 Kings **12** : 2, 3; **14** : 3, 4; **15** : 3, 4, 34, 35; Os. **4** : 15; Am. **4** : 4.   The law of worship in one place is not, therefore, of Mosaic institution, but developed by gradual evolution.   The examination of other series of laws leads to similar results.

The literary conclusions of this study are as follows.   J was written in the South towards the middle of the ninth century; E, in the North in the course of the eighth.   J and E were combined when D was composed shortly before 622 B. C. Then D was joined to JE either during or after the Exile. P originated between 540 and 500 out of the legalistic movement of which Ezechiel was the center, and before 455 it was joined to the other three.

If such was the progressive formation of the Pentateuch, critics add, it follows that its accounts do not deserve our confidence.   JE incorporated ancient etiological legends; D and P superimposed their theological point of view.   Furthermore, since the books posterior to the Pentateuch underwent its influence, the entire history of Israel must be reconstructed according to critical methods.

The theory of Wellhausen rapidly became classic among non-Catholic exegetes.   His position, it is true, has encountered some adversaries who have attacked it both in its general thesis and in certain details, as, for example, Klostermann (1893-1907), Dahse (1903), Eerdmans (1908-1912), Wiener (1912), Löhr (1924), Volz (1933), Rudolph (1933-1938), Cassuto (1934).   Several scholars modify the chronology of the sources, as E. König (1893), Hölscher (1922), Horst (1923), Welch (1924), Oestreicher (1924, 1925), and Kennett (1933).   In general, however, critics take the basic positions of the master as their point of departure and seek to push their analysis further.   Thus, they have come to distinguish, within the major documentary sources, independent entities or successive layers.

However, while this work of literary criticism was going on, another school had its birth. [1]   Without necessarily questioning the essentials in the conclusions of Wellhausen, it approached the problem from another angle or by another route.   Gunkel

---

[1] See Ch. VI below.

(1888-1913) was the founder of the new school. Its principal object is to relocate the Biblical texts in both form and content in the large context of the literatures of the Ancient Near East. These literatures cannot be thought of except in terms of their milieux; they are bound up with the events which transpire in the life of peoples and in their institutions, especially their religious institutions. This is what Gunkel calls their *Sitz im Leben*. When this vital foundation of the literary forms has been uncovered, their structure, purpose, meaning, and development become evident. Hence, Gunkel and his followers constitute what is called the *Formgeschichteschule* or the *Gattungsgeschichteschule* (" the School Concerned with the History of Literary Forms ", or " The School Concerned with the History of Literary Genres ").

But it must be understood that the history to be reconstituted is not that of the large literary entities. Rather for each of the existing types, one tries to separate or isolate the smallest units in its content, to discover their physiognomy and their *Sitz im Leben*, and to trace their development before they were written down. The task is easy enough in the case of the legal texts, but, on the other hand, the narratives present a complex problem. Beginning with the documents distinguished by Classical Biblical Criticism, especially J and E, scholars concentrate on identifying and separating the " motifs " or themes of myths, tales, sagas, and legends. It is understood from the outset that the objective elements of genuine history are not to be sought here, but, at most, the reflection of certain situations or institutions, and, especially, the expression of the popular soul, a more interesting phenomenon than the facts of history. The " motifs " develop in a parallel manner, chiefly around sanctuaries. In the course of time they make contact and intermingle. They were collected with care and respect, without too much effort being made to remove the divergencies they exhibited. Finally, the redactor of each document integrated them into a whole which he was able to organize and imbue with his teaching.

The thought of Gunkel dominates contemporary exegesis. In various shades, it is found in Gressmann (1910 ff.), Hempel (1930), Eissfeldt (1932), Von Rad (1938 ff.), Noth (1943), and Weiser (1949). Like their master, they give primary place to the idea of tradition, without contesting, however, the existence of the four chief documents of Wellhausen.

The point of view of the so-called Uppsala School is quite different. Already in 1931 ff., Pedersen made a sharp attack on the classical theory, and for the literary conception of the Old Testament he substituted a sociological approach, stressing the importance of cult and its forms. From 1945 ff., Engnell has investigated the Old Testament in thorough fashion from this point of view and has proposed an absolutely new solution for the Pentateuch Question. According to him, a cycle of traditions, which he considers to be sacerdotal, is represented by the first four books and was given its written form by an editor in the age of Esdras and Nehemias. Deuteronomy and the books that follow, from Josue to Kings, are regarded as the final stage and outcome of the traditions connected with the history of Deuteronomy, which was committed to writing after 562 B. C.

Thus, in whatever manner it is envisaged, the problem of the Pentateuch appears as an extremely complex one. However, it would seem that the various attempts at its solution, when considered in perspective and with full allowance being made for exaggerations, tend toward a point of equilibrium under the sign of *Gattungsforschung* and within the framework of a modified and more flexible Wellhausen approach.

4. Some reflexions on the critical hypotheses.

The literary phenomena examined above are factual data, and the method employed to separate and distinguish them is legitimate in itself, despite errors in application to which it has too often succumbed. This will be admitted without difficulty, if one has a proper idea of the certitude which obtains in respect to literary material (see PINARD DE LA BOULLAYE, " Essai sur la convergence des probabilités ", *Revue néoscholastique* [1914-1919], pp. 394-418, and *ibid.* [1920], pp. 5-36; reprinted in his *Étude comparée des Religions*, Vol. II (3rd ed., Paris, 1929], pp. 509-554), and if one has a good understanding of the respective value of the four characteristic features mentioned in 2 (pp. 160-162). Accordingly, it is no longer possible to maintain unity of redaction for the Pentateuch. We must even recognize that, through the action of constants and convergences, the indices in question suggest the existence of several parallel lines which may be called, according to the point of view, documents or traditions. In every way, one will see in them the expression of beliefs, of preoccupations, and of language, not only on the part of a definite author, but also reflecting a milieu or a school, and not only belonging to the time of redaction but also to the past. It is in this sense the majority of exegetes speak today of JEDP.

The question of the relative or absolute chronology of redactions can no longer have, in such a perspective, the importance which it had for Graf-Wellhausen. It cannot, however, be ignored, for, whatever may be in it of the past, a definite redaction reveals the present state of the mind or minds that made it, and it constitutes a genre which can correspond to a literary and theological stage of development. It is precisely with the great religious stages of Israel that the classical critics connected the composition of the documents of the Pentateuch, and we cannot truly say that they were wrong, even if their synthesis cannot be accepted without reservations and corrections. Thus, to take up the first case presented by Wellhausen. It seems certain that beside the temporary altars authorized by Ex. **20** : 22-26, under certain conditions, for meeting the needs of private worship, there existed a principal sanctuary where legal disputes were judged as in a court of last resort (Ex. **22** : 8), and at which one cele- brated pilgrim feasts annually (Ex. **23**; 14-19; **34** : 23-36). In Ex. **23** : 19 and **34** : 26 there is even mention of the " house of God ", an expression which in the Bible always designates a sanctuary : Jdgs. **19** : 18 (cf. **18** : 31); 1 Sam. **1** : 7; 2 Sam. **12** : 20 (cf. 6); 1 Kgs. **7** : 12, etc. The need of a single national sanctuary is, in fact, postulated by Yahwist orthodoxy. Deut **12** and Lev. **17** only emphasize this need more strongly, in keeping with new situations.

But it is especially the content of documents, even to the least details, which now occupies the attention of exegetes. In order to understand them better, to ferret out their origins, and to trace their earliest developments, these basic units are compared with similar compositions of the Near East. Such a method is legitimate, for it extends the field of investi- gation in space and time, it is postulated by the progress of

sociology, and it imposes itself upon us irresistibly as a consequence of the enormous development in Near Eastern
archaeology during the past decades.

Archaeology has brought texts to light, established the
antiquity of systems of writing, and has succeeded in deciphering
them; it has furnished precise chronological and topographical
data, and it has given us the elements of the general or special
history of numerous sites. The very life of antiquity, with its
literatures, laws and law codes, institutions, and religions,
is presented to us under a tangible form. All this information
makes it possible for us to clarify many passages in Scripture,
to complete fragmentary knowledge, and often to correct our
mistakes in perspective. But, especially, it demonstrates that
Israel was a late comer in world history, that in every way she
was a part of her milieu, and that she was profoundly influenced
by it. As a result of the establishment of these facts, the
a priori scepticism of the Old Critical School *respecting historical
matters* is eliminated by calling attention to the fixity and
antiquity of traditions. On the other hand, the a priori
scepticism *respecting religious matters* can obtain support, owing
to the exaggerations and misuse of the comparative method,
which results in a failure or refusal to recognize the transcendence
of Revealed Religion.

Exegetes have not escaped this danger, and here the radical
rationalism of Gunkel joins that of Wellhausen. No purpose
is served by saying that facts are facts, and that in such cases
it is not the business of philosophy to intervene. For the facts
must be judged and classified especially when they concern
a Religion which presents itself as revealed and which, consequently, relates miracles and transmits divine communications.
But the principles of Hegelian philosophy guide the methodology
and outlook of the leading German exegetes. From this source
has come the idea of a social evolution, which, under the impulse
of an internal determinism, consists in a series of forward
movements, each of which resolves its contrary in a higher
unity. Accordingly, monotheism could only have arisen in
the great prophetic period, and perhaps even in its later phase,
as a result of purely immanent causes. Before that time
there could only be question of animism and polytheism, i.e., of

a religion characterized by the predominance of ritualistic practices, a religion imported from Babylon.

Such presuppositions clearly authorize an unlimited application of the comparative method and give the illusion that the mystery of Yahwism finds its full explanation in its general milieu. But it is equally clear that the deliberate elimination of the idea of transcendence is in conflict with the testimony of the whole Bible and leads to the twisting of texts. It is forgotten that transcendence does not signify perfection in all respects, nor immediately (see PINARD DE LA BOULLAYE, *Étude comparée des Religions*, Vol. II, pp. 73-83, and pp. 195-242; also M. J. LAGRANGE, *Études sur les Religions sémitiques* [2nd ed., Paris, 1905], pp. 5-27). The monotheism of Israel remains inexplicable, unless it was communicated by the Most High, but it required centuries for the people to grasp its profundities and to conform to its demands. Accordingly, the believing exegete can move about freely in the comparative field. He should remember only that the Religion of Israel, in its essence, cannot be reduced to its milieu, and that, after the manner of a living organism, it developed according to its own law even when it was deriving nourishment from outside sources.

This attitude of religious respect and scientific probity is particularly appropriate in the study of the narratives in Genesis. The ancient traditions which relate the origins of mankind show numerous contacts with Babylonian literature. Those which deal with the age of the Patriarchs have, undoubtedly, a solid historical framework and have received precious confirmation from archaeological data (see R. DE VAUX, " Les patriarches hébreux et les découvertes modernes ", *RB* [1946], pp. 321-328; *ibid.* [1948], pp. 321-347; *ibid.* [1949], pp. 5-36). This does not prevent them from having all the characteristics of popular accounts. Whether there is question of the first or second set of traditions just mentioned, it would be a mistake in method, entailing serious consequences, to try to impose upon them our Western conception of literary genres and of truth (cf. A. BEA, *De Sacrae Scripturae Inspiratione* [2nd ed., Rome, 1935], Nos. 89-90). But it would be equally unreasonable to deny them any historical value whatever on the pretext that they exhibit mythical or legendary traits, that they are inspired by a rudimentary philosophy of nature, and that they are merely preoccupied with explaining certain characteristic facts of human psychology : the origins of a people, a sanctuary, or an institution, and the names of persons and places (cf. W. F. ALBRIGHT, *From the Stone Age to Christianity* [2nd edition, with a New Introduction, New York, 1957; an Anchor Book], pp. 64-76).

The preceding reflexions show in what light the problem of the Pentateuch presents itself today and also the direction that may be taken towards its solution. Fifty years ago, after great controversies, the road to be followed by Catholic opinion was indicated in two decrees of the Pontifical Biblical Commission : one on Mosaic authorship of the Pentateuch (June 27, 1906), and the other on the historical character of the three first chapters of Genesis (June 30, 1909). From that time, exegetes have not ceased to work upon the question, and new tendencies are in evidence. Taking into account results acquired, and recalling also its decree of June 23, 1905 respecting narratives having the appearance of being historical, the Biblical Commission issued a number of precise and important directives in its letter of Jan. 16, 1948, to Cardinal Suhard of Paris (see *Guide to the Bible*, I, pp. 773-775). This letter mentions as established facts the existence of sources and the progressive additions of legislative and historical matter to the Mosaic inheritance. It urges scholars to study, without prejudice, current hypotheses and to interpret critically and carefully the literary genre and historical value of Gen. I-II. Father A. Bea furnished an authorized commentary on these directives in an article in *Civiltà cattolica*, for April 17, 1948. (There is a French translation in *Documentation catholique*, No. 1018 [June 6, 1948], cols. 717-726). The Encyclical *Humani Generis* warns readers of this letter against the dangers of its possible misuse [1].

_____

Translator's note. — [1 On the Pentateuch Question and related matters, see the following recent, or fairly recent, studies : C. R. NORTH, in H. H. ROWLEY, ed., *The Old Testament and Modern Study* (Oxford, 1951), pp. 48-83; N. ROTH, *Ueberlieferungsgeschichte des Pentateuch* (Stuttgart, 1948; cf. *Theologische Revue* [1950], pp. 191-193); H. H. ROWLEY, ed., *Eleven Years of Biblical Bibliography* (Indian Hills, Col., 1957), pp. 23-24, pp. 260-264, etc.; G. VERMÈS, " Notes sur la formation de la Tradition juive ", *Cahiers Sioniens* (Dec., 1953), pp. 320-342; EZ. KAUFMAN, *Toldot ha-Emunah ha-yisre'elit*; vol. I (Jerusalem, 1937); W. M. VALK, " Moses and the Pentateuch ", *Scripture* (July, 1952), pp. 60-67; L. JOHNSON, " Reflections on Some Recent Views of Deuteronomy ", *Scripture*

ANALYSIS OF THE PENTATEUCH

by E. P. Arbez

1. The Book of Genesis

Genesis is analyzed more fully on account of its special importance. The traditions (sources) contained in Genesis are marked by the following symbols : J (Jahwist), E (Elohist), P (Priestly Code). The treatment is brief but sufficient to help the reader who wishes to have a general idea of the current literary analysis of the book. We have followed as models, e.g., G. RYCKMANS, *Het Boek Genesis* (Bruges, 1926), and other Catholic writers. See especially A. VAN HOONACKER, *De compositione litteraria... Hexateuchi*, edited with a most valuable and interesting introduction (in Flemish) by J. Coppens (Brussels, 1949).

Genesis is divided into two very unequal parts, **1-11**, covering the beginnings and the early history of mankind as a whole; and **12-50**, the history of the Patriarchs of Israel.

A. Gen. **1-11**.

Two accounts of Creation : **1** : **1-2** : 4ᵃ (P), and **2** : 4ᵇ-25 (J). The *first account*, characterized by orderliness, repetition of refrain-like formulas, and the absence of anthropomorphisms, distributes the different works over a period of six days followed by a day of rest. God merely speaks and things spring into being. The author insists that creation was good (**1** : 3, 10, 12, 18, 21, 25), even very good (31), i.e., fully answering God's

---

(Jan., 1952), pp. 12-20; C. A. SIMPSON, " The Growth of the Hexateuch ", in *The Interpreter's Bible*, I (1952), pp. 185-199; E. AUERBACH, " Die grosse Ueberarbeitung der biblischen Bücher ", *Vetus Testamentum, Suppl.* I (Leiden, 1953), pp. 1-10; R. DE VAUX, " A propos du second centenaire d'Astruc : Réflexions sur l'état actuel de la critique du Pentateuque ", *ibid.*, pp. 182-198; A. PARROT, " Autels et installations cultuelles à Mari ", *ibid.*, pp. 112-119; B. GEMSER, " The Influence of the Motive Clause in Old Testament Law ", *ibid.*, pp. 50-66; J. BRIGHT, *Early Israel in Recent History Writing* (Chicago, 1956); R. C. DENTAN, ed., *The Idea of History in the Ancient Near East* (New Haven, 1955); C. R. NORTH, *The Old Testament Interpretation of History* (London, 1946); E. JACOB, *La tradition historique en Israël* (Montpellier, 1946); H. H. ROWLEY, *From Joseph to Joshua. Biblical Traditions in the Light of Archaeology* (Oxford, 1950; cf. *Theologische Revue* [1952], pp. 52-54).

purpose. The same view of the original goodness of creation runs through the second account also, which details the great care taken of man by God (2 :8-9, 18-25).

The *second account*, marked by anthropomorphisms, is devoted especially to the creation of man and his wife (Eve, *Hawwāh* : 3 : 20), and like the first account (1 : 26-31), though in a very different way, it brings out the dignity of man (2 : 7-18 ff.). God, called Yahweh Elohim in 2 : 4b-3 : 24 (Elohim in 1) places man in a garden in Eden (2 : 8), a region which cannot be identified in spite of the geographical note in 2 : 10-14. Under penalty of death, man is forbidden to eat of the tree of the knowledge of good and evil (2 : 17). Man's disobedience (3 : J) destroys the goodness — harmony — of creation. The temptation, described with remarkable insight, at the instigation of the serpent, is followed by God's sentence on the actors of the drama : the original harmony is destroyed by man's sin. However, there is left to man the hope of final victory.

The consequences of sin manifest themselves in the narrative of Cain and Abel (4 : 1-16 [J]) and in that of Cain's descendants (4 : 17-24 [J]) : Man who has rebelled against God becomes an enemy to his fellowman. The background of the narrative supposes agriculture, domestication of animals, some organization of worship and the spread of mankind, thus, conditions of life that only developed long after the first generation. At the end of the chapter (4 : 25-26), there is mention of Seth and Enos, who find their place again in P's list ot the Patriarchs before the Flood : a total of ten. — Adam to Noe (5). The same formulas are repeated in each case, with a noteworthy variation in the case of Henoch who is taken by God (5 : 21-24). A characteristic of the list is the extraordinary longevity attributed to the Patriarchs. There are also differences between the numbers in the Hebrew and those in the LXX and in the Samaritan recension. These numbers follow a pattern and are not to be interpreted as referring to the actual ages of the individuals concerned. *The account of the Flood* (6, 1–9 :17) is a composite text (J and P) as may be seen (Richard Simon already pointed this out in the 17th century) from differences in style, vocabulary, statements of time, etc. The Flood comes as a punishment for the corruption of mankind (6 : 5-8). The strange opening paragraph (**6** : 1-4) about the sons of God and the daughters of men cannot be related easily to the narrative of the Flood, though in its present context it seems meant to serve as an illustration of the corruption of the world. Thanks to his upright life, Noe and his immediate family find favor and he is told to prepare the ark in view of the coming judgment (**6** : 9–**7** : 16). The water rises over the earth (**7** : 17-24), then gradually goes down until at last Noe can leave the ark and offer a sacrifice to God (**8** : 1-22). This is, as it were, a new beginning : God makes a covenant with Noe (**9** : 1-17); man is confirmed in his dignity of lord of creation, and is allowed to eat the flesh of animals, though not their blood (**9** : 2-4; cf. **1** : 28-30).

After J's account of the three sons of Noe, whose descendants people the earth (including the episode of Noe's drunkenness and the attitude of his sons, which leads to the curse on Chanaan, the son of Cham, and the blessing of Sem and Japhet (**9** : 18-27), comes the *Table of Nations* (**9** : 28–**10** : 32 [mostly P]) which reflects the geographical and historical relationships of the peoples as known in the time of the author. The narrative of the *Tower of Babel* (**11** : 1-9) is J's account of the spread of men through the earth and of the differences of their languages. This is a punishment. But P sees in the spreading of the descendants of Noe's sons according to their families and their languages (**10** : 5, 20, 31) the fulfilment of God's will (**9** : 17; cf. **1** : 26, 28). The narrative now (**11** : 20-26 [P]) limits itself to the line of Sem, which leads to Abraham from whom the ancestors of the Chosen People descend. Beginning with Sem and ending with Abraham's father, Thare, we have nine names. The numbers become more manageable and even, towards the end, closer to normal. The last paragraph (**11**: 27-32 [J and P]) about Thare's family forms the transition to the second part of Genesis.

The Church has steadfastly upheld the principle of " historicity " in Biblical narratives in general (*Ench. B.* no. 161, June 23, 1905) and applied the principle to Gen. **1**–**3** in particular (*ibid.*, nos. 336-342, June 30, 1909) as well as to the whole section, Gen. **1**–**11** (*ibid.*, nos. 577-581, Letter to Cardinal Suhard of January 16, 1948; and no. 618, *Humani Generis*, August 12, 1950). At the same time, however, we are reminded that the

Old Testament, being an Ancient Near Eastern work, must be understood in the light of its background and due attention must be given to the literary forms of expression used in the Ancient Near East (*Divino Afflante Spiritu*, September 30, 1943; *Ench. B.* nos. 558-560). The problem is especially delicate in the case of Gen. 1–11. We cannot speak here of history in the usual sense of the word. It is impossible to imagine a historical tradition reaching back across an untold number of centuries which would have preserved the original facts faithfully; even in the ancestry and family of Abraham polytheism extended its corrupting influence (Jos. 24 : 2; cf. Gen. 31 : 53 and 19-30; **35** : 2). Nor may we postulate a revelation of the facts in the proper sense of the word; nothing in the text supposes or demands this. What may be supposed rather — especially in the case of 1–3, which are particularly important theologically — is reflection, meditation on the facts of sin and evil in its different aspects in the world of man, meditation under *divine guidance*, which enlightened the mind of the author and helped it to reach true conclusions. The original goodness of creation as the world left the hands of the all-wise and all-good God was destroyed by the sin of the first man which extended its influence to his descendants. The expression of the truth thus reached under divine guidance was naturally conditioned by the literary traditions of the Ancient Near East, by the psychology of its people and their very notion of historical truth. It is along some such lines that the Letter to Cardinal Suhard invites us to look for the solution of the problems posed by these chapters, even if we cannot find the full answer to all the questions now (cf. *Ench. B.* no. 581, especially).

BIBLIOGRAPHY.

L. F. HARTMAN, C. SS. R., " Sin in Paradise ", *CBQ* (1958), pp. 26-40 (with good bibliography of important studies published in the last decade). A. M. DUBARLE, O. P., " La condition humaine dans l'Ancien Testament ", *RB* (1956), pp. 321-345; *id.*, " Le péché originel dans la Genèse ", *RB* (1957), pp. 1-34 (an excellent summary of the latter article in *Theology Digest*, VI [1958] 2, pp. 95-99). Y. LAURENT, " Le caractère historique de Genèse II-III dans l'exégèse française au tournant du XIXe siècle ", *EThL* (1947), pp. 36-69. E. ARBEZ and J. WEISENGOFF, " Exegetical Notes on *Genesis* 1 : 1-2 ", *CBQ* (1948), pp. 140-150. N. H. RIDDERBOS,

"Genesis 1 : 1-2", *Oudtest. Studien*, XII (1958), pp. 214-261; B. GEMSER, "God in Genesis", *Oudtest. Studien*, ibid., pp. 1-21. W. F. ALBRIGHT, "The Refrain : ' and God saw ' : *Ri tob* in Gen.", *Mélanges Robert*, Paris, 1957, pp. 22-26. H. JUNKER, "Die theologische Behandlung der Chaosvorstellung in der Biblischen Schöpfungsgeschichte", *ibid.*, pp. 27-37. A. GAUDEL, "Péché Originel", in *DTC* 12¹ (1933), cols. 275-287. A. KOLPING, "Inhalt und Form in dem Bericht über Urstand und Erbsünde", *Altestamentliche Studien Nötscher*, Bonn, 1950, pp. 137-151. J. DE FRAINE, "Jeux de mots dans le récit de la Chute", *Mélanges Robert*, pp. 47-59. CH. HAURET, *Origines : Genèse* 1-3, Paris, 1953. P. F. CEUP-PENS, O. P., *Quaestiones selectae ex historia primaeva*, 3rd ed., Turin, 1953 (see also *EThL* [1957], pp. 586-589). On Gen. 2-3 and the Sumerian myth of Enki, etc., see M. Lambert and J. Tournay, *Rev. Assyr.* (1949), pp. 105-136. CHAS. VIROLLEAUD, *Légendes de Babylone et de Canaan*, Paris, 1949. E. DHORME, "L'Arbre de Vie et l'Arbre de Vérité", *RB* (1907); reprinted in *Recueil E. Dhorme*, Paris, 1951, pp. 557-560. J. DE FRAINE, "De conceptu vitae aeternae in epopaea Gilgamis", *Verbum Domini*, 2 (1949), pp. 102-111. M. J. GRUENTHANER, "The Serpent of Genesis 3", *American Ecclesiastical Review* (1945), pp. 149-152. M. M. LABOURDETTE, O.P., *Le Péché originel et les origines de l'homme*, Paris, 1953. TH. C. VRIEZEN, *Onderzoek naar de Paradijsvoorstelling bij de oude semietische Volken*, Wageningen, 1957. A. DE GUGLIELMO, "Mary in the Protoevan-gelium", *CBQ* (1952), pp. 104-115. J. FISCHER, "Deutung und literarische Art von Gen. 6 : 1-4", *Alttestamentliche Studien Nötscher*, Bonn, 1950, pp. 74-85. J. HEUSCHEN, "Le Déluge biblique", *Revue Ecclés.* (Liège, 1952), pp. 129-145; *id.*, "De babylonisch-assyr. Zondvloedtraditie", *ibid.*, pp. 164-169. R. LARGEMENT, "Le thème de l'Arche dans les traditions suméro-sémitiques", *Mélanges Robert*, Paris, 1957, pp. 60-65. E. DHORME, "Le Déluge babylonien", *RB* (1930); reprinted in *Recueil E. Dhorme*, pp. 561-584. A. R. HULST, "Kol basar in der priesterlichen Erzählung", *Oudtest. Studien*, XII (1958), pp. 28-68. A. HEIDEL, *The Gilgamesh Epic and Old Testament Parallels*, 2nd ed., Chicago, 1949. R. LABAT, *Le Poème Babylonien de la Création*, Paris, 1935. O. E. RAVN, "Der Turm zu Babel", *Zeitschrift der Deutschen Morgenlandgesellschaft* (1937), pp. 352-372. J. CHAINE, "La tour de Babel", *Mélanges Podechard*, Lyon, 1945, pp. 17-26 (see also his Commentary on Genesis). A. PARROT, *Ziggurats et tour de Babel*, Paris, 1949. J. SIMONS, "The Table of Nations (Gen. 10) : Its General Structure and Meaning", *Oudtest. Studien*, X (1954), pp. 155-184. E. DHORME, "Les peuples issus de Japhet d'après le chap. 10 de la Gen.", *Syria* (1932); reprinted in *Recueil E. Dhorme*, pp. 167-184. B. BALDI, O. F. M., in G. Rinaldi, ed., *Secoli sul Mondo*, 2nd ed., Turin, pp. 117-132, and 576-578 (on the Indo-Europeans, Hamites, and Semites). On the Semites—Arabs—in Gen. 10 : 21 ff., cf. F. X. KORTLEITNER, *De antiquis Arabiae incolis eorumque cum religione Mosaica rationibus*, Innsbruck, 1930. There is abundant material in JAWAD 'ALI, *History of the Arabs before Islam* (in Arabic) I, Bagdad, 1951, but the Arab "traditions" about personages and tribes mentioned in the Bible hardly have any independent value (cf. *Guide to the Bible*, Vol. II, pp. 486-487, note 1). D. BUZY, " Le concordisme préhistorique ou la fin du concordisme? ", *Mélanges Podechard*, pp. 17-26. E. P. ARBEZ, " Gen. I-XI and Prehistory ", *American Ecclesiastical Review* (Aug., Sept., Oct., 1950; part of last article missing). H. JUNKER, *Die biblische Urgeschichte*, Bonn, 1932. Claus SCHEDL, *Geschichte des Alttestament. I, Urgeschichte und Alter Orient*, Innsbruck, 1956 (very good). E. R. GALBIATI (on Gen. **1-11**) in G. Rinaldi, ed., *Secoli sul Mondo*, 2nd ed., Turin, 1957, pp. 91-113 and pp. 575-576. FRIED. SCHMIDTKE, " Urgeschichte der Welt im sumerischen Mythus ", *Alttestamentliche Studien Nötscher*, Bonn, 1950, pp. 205-223. E. DHORME, " L'aurore de l'histoire babylonienne ", *RB* (1924 and 1926); reprinted in *Recueil E. Dhorme*, pp. 3-79. M. CASSUTO, *From Adam to Noah*, Jerusalem, 1944 (in Hebrew); *id., Abraham, ibid.*, 1949. W. F. ALBRIGHT, *From the Stone Age to Christianity* revised ed., New York, 1957 (an Anchor Book). H. CAZELLES, " Le Mythe et l'Ancien Testament ", in *DBV, Suppl.*, VI (1957), p. 246 ff.

B. *History of the Patriarchs of Israel :* Gen. **12–50.**

The Hebrew Patriarchs themselves are not mentioned by name in any of the ancient records (but cf. N. SCHNEIDER, " Patriarchennamen in zeitgenossischer Keilschrifturkunde ", *Biblica* [1952], pp. 516-522; C. F. JEAN, " Les noms de personnes dans les lettres de Mari et dans les plus anciens textes du Pentateuque ", in : *La Bible et l'Orient* [Paris, 1955], pp. 121-128). But archaeological discoveries have restored to us the historical background into which these narratives of Genesis fit (cf. *Guide to the Bible*, II, p. 49). Archaeology confirms the general historical character of our narratives, which thus appear to reflect conditions quite different from those of the much later composition of the book. (Cf. E. DHORME, " Abraham dans le cadre de l'histoire ", *RB* [1928 and 1931], reprinted in *Recueil E. Dhorme*, pp. 191-272; N. GLUECK, " In the Footsteps of Abraham our Father ", *Ha-Do'ar Jubilee Vol.* [1957], pp. 44-45 [in Hebrew]; R. DE VAUX, " Les Patriarches Hébreux et les découvertes modernes ", *RB* [1956], pp. 321-368; [1948], pp. 321-347; [1949], pp. 5-36; W. F. ALBRIGHT, " The Old Testament and the Archaeology of the Ancient Near East ", in : *Old Testament and Modern Criticism*, ed. H. H. ROWLEY [Oxford, 1951], pp. 27-47; *id., The Archaeology of Palestine* [1954], pp. 204-208; H. H. ROWLEY, " Recent Discoveries and the Patriarchal Age ", *Bulletin of the John Rylands Library*, [Sept. 1949], pp. 44-79. C. SCHEDL, *Geschichte des Alten Testaments*, 2 [Innsbruck 1956], pp. 3-110).

Abraham: **12** : **1**–**25** : 18.

The Abraham narratives are made up from different traditions. His date is *ca.* 1850 B.C. The clan to which Abraham (originally Abram : **17** : 4-5) belonged left Ur of the Chaldees in Lower Mesopotamia (L. Woolley, *Ur : The First Phases* [1946; a Penguin Book]; *id.*, *Ur of the Chaldees* [1952; a Pelican Book] for Haran, in the northwestern part of Mesopotamia (**11** : 31). Abram himself leaves Haran for Canaan at God's command (**12** : 1-9 [J]; on **12** : 6, see *CBQ* [1952], p. 249). Famine drives him to Egypt where Sarai, his wife, later called Sarah (**17** : 15) is kidnapped for Pharaoh's harem (**12** : 10-20 [J]; a duplicate version by E in Gen. **20**; cf. also **26** : 1-11 [J]). Lot, Abram's nephew, settles in the region of Sodom (**13** [J]). Abram rescues Lot from a raid by four kings of the East (**14** [a special source]). Amraphel was commonly identified with Hammurabi, but no longer; the identification of the names is at best difficult philologically. Hammurabi's date, formerly 19th century B.C., is put now in the 18th-17th century, *ca.* 1728-1686. The name Thidal (Thadal) is a Hittite name (Tudkhalias) borne by several Hittite Kings, e.g. Tudkhalias I *ca.* 1730. In fact, we have as yet no historical evidence bearing on our narrative of Gen. **14**. Abram meets Melchisedec the priest king of Salem (identified by Jewish tradition with Jerusalem). God promises a son to Abram who shall inherit the land and He makes a covenant with Abram. The long delayed fulfilment of the promise is a test of Abram's faith (**15** [J]). Agar indeed bears a son to Abram but he is not the son of the promise (**16** [J]). This is followed by P's account of the covenant and of the institution of circumcision as the sign of the covenant (**17**). In a mysterious apparition at Mamre, Abram receives the promise of the birth of Isaac within a year (**18** : 1-15 [J]). He pleads with God for the wicked cities of the plain which God intends to destroy (**18** : 16-35 [J]). God's judgment is executed on Sodom and Gomorra (**19** : 1-29 [J]). The incestuous origin of Moab and Ammon, closely related to the Hebrews, is related in **19** : 30-38 (J). The account of Abram's sojourn in Gerara, again involving Sarah (**20**), is E's parallel to **12** : 10 ff. The birth of Isaac at last fulfills the promise (**21** : 1-8 [J and P]) and leads to the expulsion of Agar and her son

Ismael (**21** : 9-21 [E]).   Abram and Abimelech make an
agreement at Bersabee concerning a well (**21** : 22-32 [E]) the
name of which is explained as " Well of the Seven " (28-30)
and " Well of the Oath " (31).   Abram's faith is put to the
severest test in the account of **22** : 1-19 (E) where God asks
him to sacrifice his son Isaac.   A brief section (**22** : 20-24 [J])
gives a list of the descendants of Nahor-Aramaean tribes.   On
the occasion of Sarah's death (**23** [P]) Abram buys a burial
place, the cave of Macphela near Hebron, from Hittite inhabitants of the region.   In a narrative — exceptionally fine from
the literary standpoint (**24**), J relates the marriage of Isaac
with Rebecca (Ribqāh, perhaps a metathesis of Biqrāh, " cow ",
a name which would go very well with those of Lia and Rachel,
" cow " and " ewe ").   In **25** : 1-18, three appendices close
the Abraham section : a list of sons of Abraham and Cetura —
North Arabian tribes (**25** : 1-4 and 5-6 [J]); Abraham's death
(**25** : 1-11 [P]); and Ismael's descendants (**25** : 12-18 [P]).
On Abraham, see : R. DE VAUX, O.R., and Others, " Abraham
Père des Croyants ", in *Cahiers Sioniens, 2* (1951) : contributions
by different writers on several aspects of Abraham. TH. BÖHL,
" Das Zeitalter Abrahams ", *Der Alte Orient*, 29 1 (1930),
12-24.   L. WOOLLEY, *Abraham : Recent Discoveries and Hebrew
Origins*, London, 1936.   Cassuto's article " Abraham " in
Entzykl. Miqra'it I, Jerusalem, 1950, pp. 61-67.   HEINISCH-
HEIDT, *History of the Old Testament*, Collegeville, Minn., 1952,
pp. 52 ff., and 442 ff.

Isaac and Jacob **25** : 19–37-1.

Isaac is dwarfed by the great figure of his father Abraham
and his scheming son Jacob.   He plays a personal part only
in **26** (J) which relates his sojourn in Gerara (1-14, cf. **12** :
10-20 and **20**), his disputes over wells (15-22; cf. **21** : 25-34),
and his settling in Bersabee (23-33, cf. **21** : 22-34).   In **21**
and **26** mention is made of the Philistines who settled in Palestine
about 1200 B.C., thus at a much later date (Cf. W. F. ALBRIGHT,
Archaeology of Palestine [1954], 112 ff.).   Before this we have
in **25** : 19-34 (mostly J) the birth of Esau and Jacob, and
Esau's selling his birthright.   At Rebecca's suggestion, Jacob
secures Isaac's blessing (**27** : 1-40 [mostly J]) and he flees to
Paddan Aram, to the home of Laban (his uncle), to escape

Esau's wrath (**27** : 41-45 [J]). P's parallel account of the journey (**27** : 46-**28** : 5) features as its motive marriage with a wife of his clan (cf. **24** : 3 ff.). For this reason, Esau marries a daughter of Ismael (**28** : 6-9 [P]), but too late to remedy the situation (cf. **26** : 34-35). From Jacob's journey, we have the account of a dream at Bethel : Jacob is assured of God's protection. The narrative also explains Bethel's fame as a holy place (**28** : 10-22 [J and E]). Near Haran, Jacob meets Rachel, Laban's daughter (**29** : 1-14 [J]); he marries first Lia — thanks to a trick of Laban — and then Rachel, who was his real choice (**29** : 15-30 [E²]. On those marriages, see : *RB* [1917], 272 ff.; A. VAN PRAAG, *Droit matrimonial assyro-babylonien* [Amsterdam, 1945], p. 195; R. DE VAUX, *Les institutions de l'Ancien Testament*, I [Paris, 1958], 45 ff.). The birth of the twelve sons of Jacob, and the rivalry of the mothers are related by J and E in **29** : 31–**30** : 24. Jacob outwits Laban and becomes wealthy (**30** : 25-43 [J and E]). He finally leaves Haran stealthily, but is overtaken by Laban (**31** : 1-42 [E]). After recriminations and explanations, both make a compact settling the boundary between them and an agreement about the rights of Laban's daughters (**31** : 43–**32** : 3 [J and E]). To prepare his meeting with Esau, Jacob sends a humble message to his brother (**32** : 4-14 [J]; 14-22 [E]. During the night Jacob has a mysterious encounter with God, and the new name Israel he receives for his victory (**32** : 29; cf. **35** : 9-10) presages his success over men (**32** : 23-32 [J]; on v. 28, cf. *CBQ* [1952], 250). The meeting with Esau takes place without untoward incident and Jacob then settles in Sichem (**33** : 1-20 [J]). Simeon and Levi treacherously avenge the honor of their sister Dina (**34** [J]; on v. 7, see *CBQ* [1952], 251). Various events from Jacob's return journey are grouped in **35** (E and P) : in Bethel Jacob cleanses his people of all idolatry; he worships God, who renews His promises (1-15; the name Bethel [6-7, 15], cf. **28** : 19; on the memorial pillar [14], cf. **28** : 18; on the name Israel [10], cf. **32** : 29). Then are mentioned the birth of Benjamin and the death of Rachel near Ephratha — Bethlehem (16-20); Reuben's incest (21-22); the list of Jacob's twelve sons (23-26); the death of Isaac in Hebron (27-29), which the sequence of the narratives suggests had taken place long before, and Isaac is on his death bed in

27 : 1-2, **7**.   Chapter **36** (P) deals with the history of Esau.
It brings together a number of notices — at times divergent —
without any attempt at harmonizing them (on **36** : 6-8 and
37 : 1 and **36** : 31, cf. *CBQ* [1952], 251) : Esau's wives (**36** : 1-5;
cf. **36** : 34-35 and **28** : 6-9); his moving to the land of Seir
(**36** : 6-8; the separation of the two brothers is depicted as
taking place amicably, as in the case of Abraham and Lot;
cf. **36** : 7 and **13** : 6); the descendants of Esau in Seir-Edom
(**36** : 9-14); the chiefs of Edom (**36** : 15-19 and 40-43); the
Horite (Hurrite) aborigines of the country (**36** : 20-30), and the
kings of Edom before the conquest of Edom by Israel (**36** :
31-39; cf. Voltaire's view *apud* A. LODS, *Histoire de la littérature
hébraïque et juive* [Paris, 1950], p. 92; *CBQ* [1952], 251;
N. GLUECK in *BA* 10 [1947], 80).

The History of Joseph : **37** : 2–**50** : 26.

The history of Joseph takes place some time after 1700 B.C.
in Egypt (from **37** : 25 on) apparently under the rule of foreign
conquerors (among whom Semitic elements figured also), known
as the Hyksos, *ca.* 1700-1580 B.C.   These are reckoned as
the XVth and XVIth Dynasties.   (On the Hyksos, Shepherd
Kings as they are called often, cf. the popular account —
in Greek — by the Egyptian priest Manetho [3rd cent. B.C.]
quoted by Josephus, *Against Apion* **1** : 75 ff. [Loeb Classical
Library ed. of Josephus, I, p. 193 ff.]; also in *Manetho*, ed.
W. G. WADDELL [*LCL* 1948, p. 76 ff.]); P. MONTET, *Le drame
d'Avaris : Essai sur la pénétration des Sémites en Egypte*
[Paris, 1940]).

Joseph is the central personage throughout except in **38**,
which is J's account of the mixed origin of the tribe of Juda
and in **49** — of unknown origin, apart from 29-33 (the death
of Jacob), attributed to P — which contains the oracles of
Jacob concerning the destinies of the Twelve Tribes.   (On **49**,
cf. E. BURROWS, *The Oracles of Jacob and Balaam* [London,
1939]; J. COPPENS, *EThL* [1939], 509-510).   Though the
name Joseph appears in Egyptian texts in the form Jashupi'ira
= Josef-el (cf. Haag, *Bibellexikon* [Einsiedeln, 1955], col. 854),
Joseph himself is not found in Egyptian records.   However,
the background of the Genesis narratives agrees with what
we know of Egypt (Cf. L. SPELEERS, " Egypte ", *DBV, Suppl.*,

Vol. II (1934), 756-919, and B. VAN DE WALLE, " Inscriptions
Egyptiennes ", *ibid.*, Vol. IV (1949), 417-482, especially 467-469).
The Biblical narrative is a masterpiece of Hebrew literary
composition, far superior to the moralizing story in the Qoran
(XII, " Joseph "). The dreams of Joseph — rather premonitions,
not precisely manifestations of God as in the case of the earlier
Patriarchs — add to the resentment of his brothers. They
think of killing him (37 : 18-20), but finally they sell him to
a caravan of Ismaelites (37 : 25, 27, 28b — the " *they* " are
Joseph's brothers; also 39 : 1 [E]). In 37 : 28a, it is Madianites
who find Joseph in the cistern where he has been placed (37 : 22)
and take him to Egypt where he is sold as a slave (37 : 36 [J]).
Chapter 37 is a combination of J and E. Another point of
difference : in 21-22, Reuben is the one who wants to prevent
the murder, but in 26 and 27 Juda is against killing Joseph.
Several writers have called attention to resemblances between
the Joseph narrative and the cuneiform autobiographical
document (15th century B.C.) of King Idrimi of Alalakh (= Tell
Aksharra, about 15 miles N.E. of Antioch. Cf. S. SMITH,
" The Statue of Idrimi ", *British Institute of Archaeology in
Ankara* [1949]; cf. *RB* [1950], 174-176; *BASOR*, no 118 [1950],
14-20; *CBQ* [1951], 105f; L. WOOLLEY, *A Forgotten Kingdom*
[1953; a Pelican Book], pp. 117-126, 141, 160, 164, 186).

In 39, J carries on the narrative of Joseph's life in Egypt
begun in 37. Putiphar (the name is the same as that of the
personage mentioned in 41 : 45, 50; 46 : 20, viz. Putiphera
[" he whom Ra gave ", " the gift of Ra "]), commander of
Pharaoh's bodyguard, places all his confidence in Joseph
(39 : 1-6). Putiphar's wife tries in vain to seduce Joseph
(39 : 7-12) and the scorned woman avenges herself by a false
accusation. Hence Joseph is cast into prison (39 : 13-20).
But even there Joseph wins the warden's favor (39 : 21-23;
cf. 4-6). The next section (40 : 1–41 : 32 [E]) shows Joseph
interpreting the dreams of the royal butler and the chief baker,
who had fallen into disfavor. Joseph, forgotten by the chief
butler, who had been restored to favor, is asked, after the
failure of the specialists, to interpret Pharaoh's dreams. The
dreams presage years of plenty to be followed by a severe
famine (41 : 1-32). Joseph, recognized as one having " the
spirit of God " (41 : 37 ff.), is appointed viceroy to prepare

Egypt for the coming years. He marries Asenath, the daughter of Putiphera, the high priest of On (Heliopolis — great center of sun-worship — and thus comes into the highest nobility of the land (**41** : 33-57 [E]). V. 45b, questioned by the Confraternity Edition, may be kept if we understand or correct (with Ibn Ezra, † 1167, Ehrlich, Riessler, American Version) and read : " and Joseph's name (fame) spread through the land of Egypt ". The Egyptian words and names in this section should be noted, as well as the Egyptian coloring of the account : the investiture of the new viceroy (**41** : 37); the exclamation, Abrek (**41** : 43, " Bow down "? ; cf. *Entzklop. Miqra'it*, I, 67-68); Sofnath-pa'ansah and Asenath (**41** : 45; cf. *ibid.*, I, 481 f).

The famine brings Joseph's brothers to Egypt to buy food. The account of their first visit (**42**) is attributed to E, but has traces of another tradition (J) in **42** : 27-28 (cf. **43** : 21). The money is found in the mouth of the sack on the brothers' way home; in **42** : 35 they find it at home when they empty their sacks. On their second visit (**43-44** [J]; **45** [J and E]), Joseph puts his brothers to the test to ascertain their feelings towards one another. He finds out their attitude towards Benjamin, the youngest son. There is no longer any trace of jealousy. In **44** : 16 ff. Juda makes an impassioned appeal for Benjamin, and offers himself to bear the consequences of the crime supposedly committed by Benjamin (cf. **43** : 8-9 [J]; according to another tradition, Reuben offers himself for Benjamin [**42** : 37 f.; cf. **37** : 22-23]). On Juda's speech in **44**, see D. G. MAESO's fine analysis in *Sefarad* (1946), 3-19 (in Spanish). Joseph makes himself known to his brothers and sends a message to his father, with an invitation of Pharaoh to come to Egypt (**45**) and settle in the eastern part of the Delta (Goshen; cf. v. 10; **46** : 28; **47** : 1 ff.; cf. also A. MALLON, *Les Hébreux en Egypte* [Rome, 1921], p. 93 ff.). Jacob then leaves for Egypt (**46** : 1-7 [J and E] from Bersabee (v. 5 [E], — from Hebron (**37** : 14 [J], and **35** : 27 [P]). The list of Jacob's family [**46** : 8-27] which interrupts the narrative, belongs to P.

The clan of Israel thus settles in Egypt (**46** : 28-34; **47** : 1-12; Chapter **46** : 34 may contain an anachronistic remark true of the time after the expulsion of the Hyksos (On **47** : 11, see B. COUROYER, O. P., " La résistance Ramesside du Delta et la Ramsès biblique ", *RB* [1946], 75-98). The next section

(**47** : 13-26 [J]) explains how Joseph's policy led to the
enslavement of the people, whose lands became the property
of the state. As Jacob's death draws near, he asks Joseph
to have his body buried in the family sepulcher (**47** : 27-31
[J]). Jacob adopts and blesses the sons of Joseph (**48** : 1-2
and 7-22 [J and E]; 3-6 [P.]). Thus, the fact is explained
that Manasse and Ephraim are tribes in Israel just like the
other tribes. Jacob, mourned by Egypt, is buried in Canaan
according to his requests (**50** : 1-14 [J and E]; 12-13 [P]).
Joseph reassures his brothers and points out the religious
lesson of his destiny : the evil intended against him by his
brothers has been turned to good by God (20 [J]; 15-21 [E]).
Joseph dies at the age of 110 years — the ideal length of a
blessed life (H. DUESBERG, *Les scribes inspirés*, vol. I, Paris,
1938, p. 761), after asking to be taken to Canaan when God
takes Israel back to the Promised Land (**50** : 22-26 [J and E]).

2. — Book of Exodus.

The narratives of the Patriarchs in Genesis are a popular
account of small clans of semi-nomads moving about with
their flocks, but favoring sacred places : Bethel, Sichem by the
oak of Moreh (**12** : 6; cf. *CBQ* [1952], 249), Bersabee in the
Negeb, Mamre by Hebron. They tend to become sedentary;
they stay in some places long enough to engage in agriculture
(**26** : 12-14; cf. **27** : 28; **37** : 7). Their wealth consists, above
all, of flocks of sheep and goats, and cattle (**12** : 16; **13** : 2, 5, 7 f.;
20 : 14; **26** : 14; **32** : 6, 15 f.; **34** : 28; **37** : 12 ff.; **38** : 12; **46** :
32 ff.; **47** : 8 f.; **50** : 8). For transport they use asses (**12** : 16;
23 : 3, 5; **24** : 35; **32** : 16; **34** : 28), even for longer journeys
between Canaan and Egypt (**42** : 26 f.; **43** : 24; **44** : 13), just
like the caravan of Semites represented in a tomb at Beni
Hasan (Upper Egypt) at a much earlier date (1st half of 19th
cent.; see the fine reproduction in L. H. GROLLENBERG, *Atlas of the
Bible* [London-New-York, 1956], p. 38). So also in the Mari
cuneiform texts (Mari = Tell Hariri near Abu Kemal, E. Syria)
discovered in 1933, the ass appears commonly as the means
of transport. True, in several places in Gen., the camel also
is mentioned (**12** : 16; **24**, throughout; **32** : 16; Ex. **9** : 3). Several
authors question the use of the camel in the time of the

Patriarchs. Thus, W. F. ALBRIGHT (*Archaeology of Palestine*, p. 206 f.; cf. GROLLENBERG, *op. cit.*, p. 49), referring to the representation of a camel, notes that this cannot be used as an illustration of Genesis, for, most probably, the camel began to be used in that region only *ca.* 1100 B.C. There is also the circumstance that the Mari texts (as far as I know) make no mention of the camel (cf. J. BOTTÉRO, *Archives Royales de Mari*, VII : *Textes économiques et administratifs* [Paris, 1957], pp. 245-261). It may be noted also that Egyptian writing does not use the camel as a sign, though it employs a considerable number of animals. Other authors, however (R. DE VAUX, *RB* [1949], 5 ff.; R. DUSSAUD, *La pénétration des Arabes en Syrie avant l'Islam* [Paris, 1955], p. 207), admit that the camel may have invaded some texts unduly but are unwilling to sacrifice all the camels of the Patriarchs. They appeal to some archaeological evidence which, they hold, supposes a much more ancient use of the camel. (Cf. on the question : A. POHL, *Orientalia* [1950], 251 f.; Isserlin, *Palestine Exploration Quarterly* [1952], 50 f.; *Entzyklop. Miqra'it* 2, pp. 520-524; and, especially, R. J. FORBES, " The Coming of the Camel ", *Studies in Ancient Technology*, vol. II [Leiden, 1955], pp. 187-208).

The Patriarchal clans maintain their connections with their Mesopotamian cousins. They speak the language of Canaan — an older form of Hebrew than that found in the Bible — and apparently they continue to use it during their sojourn in Egypt. (Cf. E. DHORME, " La langue de Canaan ", *RB* [1913-1914], *Recueil...*, pp. 405-487, and 501-505). With Joseph holding power in Egypt, Jacob and his clan move to Egypt where they are to grow into a great people (Gen. **46** : 3; **50** : 20). This development takes place during the long period — several centuries — between the time of Joseph and the Exodus, somewhere around 1250 B.C., under the XIXth *Dynasty* (cf. Haag, *Bibellexikon*, cols. 33-35; CL. SCHEDL, *Geschichte des Alten Testament*, vol. II [1956], pp. 133-137), though another view dates the Exodus in the 15th century B.C. under the XVIIIth Dynasty. Of that long period, the Bible relates nothing, but passes directly from Joseph to the sufferings of the Hebrews. (Cf. H. H. ROWLEY, *From Joseph to Joshua : Biblical Tradition in the Light of Archaeology* [London, 1950]; see a good summary with bibliography in R. NORTH, S. J., *Geographia exegetica*

[Rome, 1956], p. 15 ff.; also the Commentaries on Exodus by TH. BÖHL [1928, in Dutch], S. R. DRIVER [1929], HEINISCH [1934, in German], M. D. CASSUTO [1954, in Hebrew], PIROT [1956, in French]; see also CL. SCHEDL, *op. cit.*, vol. II, pp. 113-233. On the question of the relationship of Hebrews and Habiru or Hapiru, Apiru, cf. *Guide to the Bible*, II, pp. 23 and 193, and the bibliography cited; CASSUTO'S, *Commentary*, p. 5, and p. 184 f.; R. DUSSAUD, *op. cit.*, p. 179 f.; J. BOTTÉRO, *Problème des Habiru* [Paris, 1954]; M. GREENBERG, *The Hab-piru* [New-York, 1955]; on these two works, cf. R. DE VAUX, *RB* [1956], 261-267; W. F. ALBRIGHT, *BASOR*, no. 149 [Feb., 1958], 37-38; E. DHORME, " Les Habiru et les Hébreux ", *Revue d'Assyriologie,*[1954], 256-264).

We may divide Exodus into six parts as follows :

A. *Israel in Egypt :* 1 : 1–13 : 16
B. *The Journey to Sinai :* 13 : 17–18 : 27
C. *The Covenant at Mt. Sinai :* 19 : 1–24 : 18
D. *Laws about the Sanctuary and Its Ministers :* 25 : 1–31 : 18
E. *The Golden Calf; Renewal of the Covenant :* 32 : 1–34 : 35
F. *The Execution of the Prescriptions regarding the Sanctuary and Its Ministers :* 35 : 1–40 : 38.

A. 1 : 1–13 : 16.

The dominant figure through Exodus and the other books of the Pentateuch is Moses. He is — as it has been remarked — as essential to the understanding of the origin of Israel as the person of Mohammed is to the understanding of the origin of Islam. On the many different aspects and problems of Moses see especially, *Moïse, l'homme de l'Alliance* (Tournai and Paris, 1955; published originally in *Cahiers Sioniens* [Paris, 1954] nos. 2-4, as a collection of essays by several Catholic authors); also, Haag, *Bibellexikon*, cols. 1160-1169 (by Cazelles-Van den Born); H. Cazelles, " Moïse ", in *DBV, Suppl.*, vol. V (1957), col. 1331 ff.

After the list of names 1 : 1-5 (P) comes the account of the oppression by a " new king who knew nothing of Joseph " (1 : 8) in 1 : 6-22 (J and E). Pharaoh uses Hebrew slave labor for his building undertakings, quite in the tradition of the

Ancient Orient, and tries to prevent the increase of the Hebrew population by ordering the death of the newborn male children. Moses is saved from this fate in an extraordinary manner, for he is even rescued by the daughter of Pharaoh himself (2 : 1-11 [J and E]). His name, most probably of Egyptian origin, receives a popular explanation from Hebrew in 2 : 10 (cf. e.g., Koehler, *Lex. V. T.*, p. 572; Haag, *Bibellexikon*, col. 1160). With the narrative of Moses' exposure in a papyrus basket and rescue may be compared the legend of Sargon of Akkad in the 23rd century B.C. (cf. Cl. Schedl, *op. cit.*, vol. II, p. 118; *Recueil E. Dhorme...*, p. 62 f.). Moses is obliged to flee for his life to Madian (S. of Edom, E. of the Gulf of Aqaba) where he marries Sepphora, one of the daughters of " the priest " of Madian, Raguel (2 : 18; Jethro, in 3 : 1; 4 : 18; cp. Num. 10 : 29; in Hebrew, the name Re'u'el appears in the same form in Gen. 36 : 4, 10, 13, 17; the Vulgate in Gen. 36 spells it Rahuel; the LXX has *Ragouēl* in Gen. and Ex.).

The oppressed Hebrews appeal to God (2 : 23-25 [P]; the incompleteness of the sentence at the end of 25 is to be noted). God appoints Moses to deliver Israel (3 [J and E]). The scene is Horeb, the mountain of God, where God manifests Himself in the burning bush. He gives him a " sign " (3 : 12) which is understood variously : the future coming to the mountain shall be the sign (LXX, Vulg., A. V., R.S.V., Dhorme, etc.); according to others, the sign has been omitted in our text *(Bible du Centenaire,* Am. V., *Bible de Jérusalem).* God reveals His name (vss. 13-15) : " I am who am " — i.e., the one who is truly active — in opposition to the other gods who have no reality. (So the usual view; cf. A. VAN HOONACKER, *De compositione litteraria et de origine mosaica Hexateuchi...,* edited with a valuable Introduction [in Flemish] by J. COPPENS, [Brussels, 1949]; according to another view : " I am who I am ", or : " I am what I am ", i.e., God does not reveal a name which would express his real being. In any case, the phrase is the basis of the name Yahweh. (Cf. Haag, *Bibellexikon*, pp. 767-768; E. P. ARBEZ, *CBQ* [1955], 481-484). Moses then receives instructions regarding his mission (3 : 16-20). His brother Aaron shall be his mouthpiece (4 : 10-17). Moses receives the power to work miracles (4 : 1-9; 17-21). Israel shall not leave Egypt empty-handed (3 : 21-22). Moses returns to Egypt

(4 : 18-31. On the mysterious episode of vss. 24-26, cf. J. Coppens : *EThL* [1941], 68 ff.; H. Junker, " Der Blutbräutigam ",
in *Alltestamentliche Studien Nötscher* [Bonn, 1950], pp. 120-128;
Joh. De Groot, " The Story of the Bloody Husband... ",
Oudtestamentische Studien, II [1943], 10-17. Ch. 4 is based on
J and E). The first interview with Pharaoh only aggravates
the condition of the Hebrews (5 : 1-18); hence the complaint
against Moses' intervention (5 : 19–6 : 1; 5, J mostly. On
the use of straw in making bricks, cf. E. Power, S. J., *Verbum
Domini* [1925], 187-190; A. Lucas, *Ancient Egyptian Materials*
[3rd ed., London, 1948], pp. 62-64; Nims, *BA* [1950], 22-28).

6 : 2–7 : 7 is regarded as P's account of Moses' call (parallel
to 3-4). God reveals Himself as Yahweh, under which name
He did not manifest Himself before. For to the Patriarchs
he was known as El Shaddai (Gen. **17** : 1; **28** : 3; **35** : 11; **43** : 14;
48 : 3; **49** : 25), i.e. Mountain God = lofty, exalted (?), or God
Almighty (LXX; Vulg., etc.). God will fulfill his promises
to the Fathers and orders Moses to go to Pharaoh (6 : 2-13).
Moses will have Aaron as his assistant in his difficult task
(6 : 28–7 : 7). Just before this latter paragraph, there is inserted
a genealogy of Moses and Aaron — primarily a genealogy of
the Tribe of Levi to which they belong.

The Ten Plagues, which will force Pharaoh after long resistance
to release the Hebrews, are described in **7** : 8–**12** : 36. In these
accounts the critics distinguish three main strands of tradition,
but they recognize that E is hard to isolate. P closely associates
Moses and Aaron in the struggle with the magicians who try
to match Moses and Aaron's prodigies (e.g., **7** : 8-13; 14-25;
27–8 : 3; **9** : 8-12). J represents Moses as meeting Pharaoh
alone when he tries to obtain leave for the Hebrews to go
to the desert; God Himself intervenes directly to bring on
or to stop the plagues (e.g., **8** : 16-20; **9** : 1-7; **9** : 13 ff.). To
E they attribute the passages where Moses' hand — with
or without his staff — is the instrument of the plagues (e.g.,
7 : 14 ff.; **9** : 22 ff.; **10** : 12 ff.). The three traditions do not
contain accounts of all the plagues, but only of some of them.
All of them are represented, more or less fully, in the account
of the death of the firstborn (**11**) (cf. **12** : 1-13, 29 ff.). With
the narratives of Exodus should be compared the poetic accounts
in Ps. **78 (77)** : 43-50; **105 (104)** : 26-38; Wis. **16-18**. The data

of the tradition are treated freely by each author according
to his purpose. It has long been noted that the plagues are
related to various natural phenomena in Egypt, but it is clear
that Exodus intends more than these natural occurrences.
The plagues reveal the superiority of Yahweh over all the
gods and magic of idolatrous Egypt.

The section concludes with the institution of the Passover
(**12** : 1-14; cf. 21-28) with which is connected the feast of the
Unleavened Bread *(Mazzot)* (**12** : 15-20). These two feasts,
perhaps originally distinct (cf. Haag, *Bibellexikon*, col. 1097,
s.v. " Mazzoth ", and 1265, *s.v.* " Paschafest ") are merged
together in a commemoration of the historical event of the
Exodus, an event of decisive importance for the creation of
the people of Israel. The texts are assigned to J (**12** : 21-39),
P (**12** : 1-20 and 43-50), and D (**13** : 1-16) (a prescription about
the firstborn male of man and beast as belonging to God;
cf. Ex. **22** : 28-29; **34** : 19-28. This is connected with the
Tenth Plague; cf. **12** : 29 ff.). Among important texts dealing
with the Passover, see Lev. **23** : 4-8; Num. **28** : 16-25; Deut. **16** :
1-8. The original meaning of the feast (Hebrew, *Pesaḥ;* Greek,
πάσχα) is disputed. Ex. **12** : 13, 23 connects it with " skipping ",
" passing over " the dwellings marked with the blood of the
lamb. Ex. **11** : 1[b] is difficult, as will be seen from the different
views taken by translators and commentators. In fact, the
several parts of the text hardly agree among themselves.
Possibly part of the verse is a gloss inspired by such texts
as **3** : 21-22; **11** : 2-3; **12** : 35-36 : " The Hebrews shall leave
showered with gifts by the Egyptians ". We might render
11 : 1[b] : " After that he will send you away, as a bride is sent
away ". The following sentence is quite different : " He will
certainly drive you away from here ". Cf. J. COPPENS, in
EThL (1947), 178-179; J. MORGENSTERN, *Journal of Biblical
Literature* (1949), 1-28.

B. **13** : 17–**18** : 27.

The departure from Egypt was mentioned in **12** : 37-42
(J and P) and the account continues in **13** : 17-22 (the three
traditions). It is pretty generally agreed that the number
in **12** : 36; **38** : 26; Num. **1** : 46; **2** : 32; **11** : 21; **26** : 51 — about
600.000, not including women, children, and Levites — is

utterly impossible. This would suppose a Hebrew population of about three million! Not to speak of the impact of the sudden departure of such a number of people on the life of Egypt, such a huge number could not live in Sinai. The number may be regarded as the result of some artificial reckoning quite independent of mathematics. The actual total may have been *ca.* 6000, perhaps a little more (cf. Haag, *Bibellexikon*, cols. 136-137; SCHEDL, *op. cit.*, vol. II, p. 130; cf. also *Westminster Historical Atlas of the Bible* [1945], pp. 37-38). The description of Israel in **13** : **18** moving out of Egypt " in battle array ", " well-equipped " (so most translations) is questionable. More probably the text is to be read that they took with them their possessions (EHRLICH, RIESSLER, SCHLÖGL) or went as free men (E. POWER, S. J.). According to **13** : **17** the Hebrews did not take the normal direct road to Palestine along the Mediterranean. The actual course of their journey is uncertain. Some names of encampment indeed are mentioned, but their identification is doubtful. They reached the Red Sea (rather, according to the Hebrew, more probably, the Sea of Reeds or Rushes), possibly in its southern part, N. of Suez, and crossed it under circumstances which made the deepest impression on the people thus delivered from imminent destruction, while their Egyptian pursuers were annihilated (**14**; the three traditions. On the itinerary of the Exodus, cf. Haag, *op. cit.*, cols. 137-138; SCHEDL, *op. cit.*, vol. II, pp. 130-134; E. G. KRAELING, *Bible Atlas* [Chicago, 1956], pp. 102-107 and Map, p. 232; Grollenberg, *Atlas*, pp. 45-51; Z. VILNAY, *Ha-ares bā-miqrā* [Jerusalem, 1954], pp. 4-9, in Hebrew; *Westminster Historical Atlas of the Bible* [1945], pp. 38-39). The great event of the Crossing is celebrated in the Canticle of **15** : **1-21** (a special tradition). The hymn of victory includes not only the miraculous crossing (1-12), but also the great deeds which Yahweh will accomplish for his people : the conquest of Canaan, the building of the Temple, Yahweh's dwelling place (13-18). (Cf. M. J. LAGRANGE, *RB* [1899], pp. 532-541; on v. 2, E. P. ARBEZ, *CBQ* [1945], p. 65 f).

Some episodes from the journey to Sinai are recorded in **15** : **22–18** : **27**. The people complain of the bitter water at Marah — the first of the many occasions when Israel rebels (**15** : **22-26** [J]). In the desert of Sin (**16** [P]) they obtain as food manna, described as miraculous, though it finds partial analogy in a substance produced by a plant in Sinai, and the quails which cross Sinai in the spring and in the fall (here in the spring, as also in Num. **11** : 31-34 [J]). At Raphidim Moses relieves the lack of water by striking the rock (**17** : 1-7 [J and E]); the place is called Massa and Meribāh because of their trying the Lord and quarrelling. (Cf. the narrative of P and E on the stay in Cades, Num. **20** : 1-13). Here also takes place the battle with Amalec **17** : 8-16 (E), a bitter enemy of Israel (Deut. **25** : 17-19; 1 Sam. 15), living in the southern region (Gen. **14** : 7; Num. **13** : 29; Judgs. **1** : 16; cf. also Num. **14** : 39-45). On **17** : 16, cf. L. Delaporte in *Biblische Zeitschrift* (1915, no. 2). The content (**17** : 1 and **19** : 2) suggests the placing of Jethro's visit (**18** : 1-2 [E]) at Raphidim, but **18** : 5 clearly says that the place was " near the mountain of God " (Horeb, **3** : 1). In fact, the sequel — the appointment of judges — in **18** : 13 ff., compared with Deut. **1** : 9 ff., rather inclines us to see in Horeb (Sinai) the place of the event. Jethro appears here (**18** : 12) as a worshipper of Yahweh. (On **18**, see Brekelmans in *Oudtestamentische Studiën*, X [1954], 215-224).

C. **19** : 1–**24** : 18.

The Covenant at Mt. Sinai. Here begins the legislative section of the book — and legislation will occupy a considerable part of the following books of the Pentateuch. There is now abundant legal material from the Ancient Middle East with which the laws of the Pentateuch may and should be compared. (See the English translations in J. B. Pritchard, ed., *Ancient Near-Eastern Texts Relating to the Old Testament* [Princeton, 1950, a new edition in 1955, on which see *RB*, 1957, 306-308] 159-198, with bibliography; see also Schedl, *op. cit.*, vol. II, pp. 162, 164-165; H. CAZELLES, *s.v.* " Loi Israélite ", *DBV*, *Suppl.*, V [1957], pp. 497-530; R. PFEIFFER, *Introduction to the Old Testament*. [New York], 1941), pp. 211 ff.; G. R. DRIVER and J. C. MILES, *The Babylonian Laws*, vol. I, *Legal Commentary* [Oxford, 1952], and vol. II [1955], *Transliteration, Philological Notes and Glossary*. The work contains, beside the Code of Hammurabi, the other Babylonian Laws found on clay tablets). The scene is Mt. Sinai (see above on **13** : 17). Sinai is the mountain of God, Horeb, as it is called in other places. It is in the southern part of the peninsula, and is identified commonly with the *Jebel Musa* (Mt. of Moses), over 6,000 feet high. The precise date is not given in the text (**19** : 1 = " on that day "). God is about to make a special covenant with Israel. The people must prepare themselves (**19** : 3-15 [J and E]). God manifests himself in awe-inspiring greatness and majesty in the great theophany (**19** : 16-25 [J and E]. On **19** : 25, cf. A. CONDAMIN, in *RSR* [1912], 122; E. P. ARBEZ, *CBQ*, [1955], pp. 459-466-478, and reff.).

The Ten Commandments (**20** : 1-17 P) are found in a slightly different version also in Deut. **5** : 6-21. Both texts may embody some developments or explanations. The original form may have been that preserved in 13 ff. (Cf. A. VAN HOONACKER, *De compositione...*, pp. 67-68; R. H. PFEIFFER, *Introduction...*, pp. 228-232). This section stands unconnected, while **20** : 18-21 (E) seems to connect more naturally with the theophany in **19**, across **20** : 1-7.

The Book of the Covenant (cf. **24** : 7 for the name) contained in **20** : 22–23 : 19 (E) belongs to the oldest Mosaic tradition, though its present form supposes some adaptation to different conditions of life — a population settling down to agriculture (see below on **34** : 10 ff.). On this section, see H. CAZELLES, *Etudes sur le Code de l'Alliance* (Paris, 1946). On the different formulations of the laws, and for a comparison with ancient Oriental laws from the literary point of view, cf. AAGE BENTZEN, *Inledning til det Gamle Testamente* (Copenhagen, 1941), p. 313 ff.; also IVAN ENGNELL, *Gamle Testamentet : En traditionshistorisk Inledning*, vol. I (Stockholm, 1945), pp. 88-95. Its prescriptions concern :

a) the religious life : **20** : 22-26. This supposes the possibility of altars in different places. It is an important text in Pentateuch criticism, and should be compared with the regulations of Lev. **17** and Deut. **12**. (Beside the Commentaries, see JOH. GOETTSBERGER, *Einleitung in das A. T.*, [Freiburg i. B., 1928], pp. 93-102; A. VAN HOONACKER, *De compositione...*, pp. 33-37; 68-69; *Theol. Revue* [1903], 110; [1924], 387; E. ROBERTSON, *Journ. of Jewish Studies* [1948], 12-21). **22**, 28-30 : law of first fruit and firstborn; **23** : 10-19 : Sabbath and Festivals (cf. Ex. **34** : 18-23 [J]; Deut. **16** : 1-6 [D]; Lev. **23** [P], and the developments in Num. **28** and **29**). A careful comparison shows three chief feasts : Passover *(Pesach)* and Unleavened Breads, Feast of Weeks *(Shabu'ot)*, 50 days after Passover, and Feast of Tabernacles in the fall, called *Sukkot*. (See A. VAN HOONACKER, *De compositione...*, pp. 37-39). We can observe the growth of the ritual. In the course of time, several other feasts were added : **23**, 19$^{\rm b}$; cf. **34**, 26; Deut. **14**, 19. (See *Theologie und Glaube* [1909], pp. 379-381; *Biblische Zeitschrift* [1911], 322-323; *RB* [1912], 148; Skoss' edition of 'ALI ben SULEIMAN'S *Genesis*, p. 38 f.; C. H. GORDON, *Ugaritic Handbook*, [Rome, 1947], no. 52, 14; CASSUTO, *Commentary*, pp. 212-213; Lefebvre, *Romans... égyptiens* [Paris, 1949], pp. 11-12);

b) the moral-social life : **22** : 15-27; **23** : 1-9 (on **22**, **24** cf. S. Bernfeld, *Introduction to the AT* (= *Mabo;* in Hebrew) 4 : I, p. 11);

c) civil law : **21** : 1–**22** : 14 : slaves; personal injuries; property damage; trusts and loans (On **21** : 8 : S. BERNFELD, *op. cit.*, 4 : I, p. 11; on **21** : 10 : LEVY, *Famille Israélite*, p. 168; MERX, *Chrestomathia Targumica*, pp. 251-252; on **21** : 37 : *Theol. Quartaslschrift* [1910], 163-170; on **22** : 1-3 : *Theologie und Glaube* [1910], pp. 485-487).

The Book of the Covenant is followed (**23** : 20-32 [E]) by promises of God for fidelity of the people, and in **24** by the account of the ratification of the Covenant (1-11 [J and E]) and of Moses' return to the Mountain, where he remains forty days and forty nights (12-18 [E and P]).

D. **25**–**31**.

(P) God gives to Moses detailed instructions concerning the Sanctuary (Tabernacle), its furnishings and its ministers. (Cf. JOH. GOETTSBERGER, *Einleitung*, pp. 102-109, on the ministers of the Sanctuary, and p. 110 f. on the sacrifices). This section embodies old material which goes back to the very beginning of the organization of divine worship together with later developments of the original institutions. (Cf. A. VAN HOONACKER, *De compositione...*, pp. 39-41, and pp. 43-44). The main items are : collecting the contributions (**25** : 1-9), the Ark (**25** : 10-22), the table of the shewbread (**25** : 23-30), the lampstand (**25** : 31-40), the tent and its cloth furnishings (**26** : 31-37), the altar of holocausts (**27** : 1-8), the court around the tent (**27** : 9-19), the oil for the lamp of the Sanctuary (**27** : 20-21), the priestly vestments (**28** : 1-5, and 31-43), the Ephod and the breastplate (**28** : 6-30), the consecration of the priests (**29** : 1-9), ordination sacrifices (**29** : 10-35), consecration of the altar of holocausts and the daily holocausts (**29** : 36-46), the altar of incense (**30** : 1-10), the census tax (**30** : 11-16. Cf. E. A. SPEISER, on census and ritual expiation in Mari and Israel, *BASOR*, no. 149 [1958], 17-25), the laver (**30** : 17-21), the anointing oil (**30** : 22-33), incense (**30** : 34-38), the choice of those who are to do work on the Sanctuary — Beseleel and Oholiab are to direct the work (**31** : 1-11), Sabbath regulations (**31** . 12-17), the two tablets of the testimony (commandments) (**31** : 18; cf. **24** : 12).

E. 35–40.

This long section relates the execution of the commands given to Moses in **25–31**. The wording is practically identical, except that, naturally, we have here the narrative form. In the Hebrew, there are some changes in the order of the items. The Greek (LXX) follows a different order in the parts corresponding to the Hebrew **36** : 8–**39** : 43, and supposes a large number of textual variants in the Hebrew from which it is derived.

F. 32 : 1–34 : 35.

(J and E). In the text of Exodus, this section comes before E. It describes Israel's fall into idolatry by the worship of the Golden Calf (**32** : 1-6) — more correctly a young bull, a common symbol of the divinity in the ancient Near East. In **32** : 4 the Confraternity Version, following the common view, says that the gold offered by the people was fashioned with a graving tool, but this is somewhat difficult to harmonize with the context supposing a statue (v. 4, end; vv. 8 and 24). The difficulty is avoided by correcting — or understanding differently — the text, viz., that the gold was poured into a mould and thus a statue of a calf was made (A. EHRLICH [1908]; RIESSLER [1924]; American Version [1927]; N. SCHLÖGL [1922]; same sense also in Jesuits' Beyrout *Arabic Translation*

[1897]; cf. also the Vulgate and Syriac). Moses intercedes for the people as he has done before and will do again often (**32** : 7-24). The zealous Levites punish the idolaters (**32** : 25-29). Moses makes atonement (**32** : 30-35). The order to move from Sinai (Horeb) is given (**33** : 1-6). The next vv. (**33** : 7-11), which suppose the tent of meeting — not built at this point — where Moses used to come before God, are out of context. Moses prays (**33** : 12-17) to understand God's ways, even to see God as He is — a most extraordinary favor which cannot be granted fully (**33** : 18-23). The Covenant is renewed (**34** [J, mostly]; cf. **19** : 1–20 : 21). New tablets are made (vv. 1-9), and prescriptions of largely ritual character are the basis of the Covenant (vv. 10-26). Some critics regard this section as a ritual " Decalogue " (cf. R. H. PFEIFFER, *Introduction*, pp. 221-226; A. Weiser, *Einleitung...* [1949], p. 84; O. EISSFELDT, *Einleitung* [1934], pp. 240-251). Moses remains forty days and forty nights on Mt. Sinai (cf. **24** : 18); he writes on the tablets prepared by him (**34** : 4) the words of the Covenant, the Decalogue (cf. **20** : 1 ff.). From his prolonged stay in the presence of God, his face had become radiant, and he puts a veil over it (**34** : 27-33 [P]). The last vv. (**34** : 34-35) extend the remark about the radiance of Moses' face and the veil worn on his visits to the tent whenever he went in to converse with the Lord.

3. — The Book of Leviticus.

Known also among the Jews as *Torat Kohanim*, " the Law of Priests ". (Cf. Segal, *Mabō'*, I, p. 7-8; also *Entzyklop. Miqra'it*, II, 878. This name, which corresponds exactly to the name used in the LXX, Syriac Peshitto, and Vulgate, is ancient). It is the ritual book of the Old Testament. Attributed by the critics to P, it contains very ancient material. (For a good survey of the critical hypotheses about the "Sources" of Leviticus, see Cassuto, *Entzyk. Miq.*, II, 878-881). (For illustrative material, see *Montserrat Biblia Illustrada*, XXIV, 2 [1934], pp. 270-295). Two fragments of Lev. in archaic writing have been found among the Dead Sea MSS (cf. *RB* [1949], 597 ff.).

A. 1–7.

Sacrifices. The subject is treated in two parallel sections, viz., a) 1–5, concerned primarily with the matter of the sacrifices, and b) 6–7, which describe the functions of the ministers at the different kinds of sacrifices.

a) 1–5.

1. The holocaust *('ōlāh)*. Chap. 1. This kind of sacrifice in which the victim was completely burnt on the altar is a very ancient institution. It is apparently supposed in Abel's sacrifice (Gen. 4 : 1 ff.), and quite definitely in Noe 's offering (Gen. 8 : 20 ff.) or in Gedeon's case (Jdgs. 6 : 19 ff.) or in the narrative of Manoe (Jdgs. 13 : 19 ff.), not to mention the story of Jephte (Jdgs. 11 : 31). The sacrificial victim is taken from the herd or from the flock (3-13) or is a turtle dove or pigeon (abundant in Palestine) (14-17); thus, in short, clean domestic animals (as the ass) and clean wild animals (as the gazelle). The blood — the seat of life — belongs to the Lord (5); this will be repeated often in the book. In 1 : 9 we have the first occurrence in Lev. of characteristic expressions often used in this book (and in *Num.*). One is the word rendered : " oblation " in our new Catholic edition, which other translators render " offering made by fire ", on the supposition that it is connected with the Hebrew word " fire ". The other is the phrase " sweet-smelling " (so our new version, with the Greek and the Vulgate, and most modern versions). Some recent authors, quite in keeping with the etymology of the word translated " sweet ", prefer " appeasement " or the like; hence " a soothing smell " *(American Version*, Moffatt, *Bible de Jérusalem*, Dhorme).

2. Cereal offerings. Chap. 2 (*Minḥāh*, properly, " present ". On the word, cf. N. SNAITH, *Interpreter's Bible*, vol. I, p. 224). This sacrifice, which supposes agricultural life, is commonly associated with some other kind of sacrifice. It must be unleavened (2 : 4-11), and seasoned with salt (2 : 13), which has a purifying quality.

3. Peace offerings. Chap. 3 *(Shelamim)*. Here the choice parts belong to the Lord, the rest is consumed by those who offer the sacrifice, which is thus a sacred meal of communion with God. This was a very common form of sacrifice.

4. Sin offerings. Chap. 4 *(Hattāt)*. They are offered to remove " sin ", i.e., a state of uncleanness due to some inadvertence, not necessarily a moral offence. It may be offered for the High Priest (3-12) or the community (13-21) — with the same ritual — or for a " prince " — head of a tribe or part of a tribe (sheikh) (22-26) or for ordinary private persons (27-33) — with the same ritual in these last two cases. The subject is continued in 5 : 7-13, which examines the question of substitute offerings when the man cannot afford those envisaged in 4 : 27 ff. Four special cases are studied in 5 : 1-6 : When is a sin-offering required? The guilty party must confess his sin publicly (5 : 5).

5. Guilt offerings (5 : 14-26, Hebrew; Vulgate and English versions, 5 : 14-19 and 6 : 1-7). Not always clearly distinguishable from trespass offerings *(āshām)*, above.

However, here the " guilt " is connected with some damage or wrong done to God or man which can be repaired by paying an estimated amount, plus a fine of one fifth of the value (5 : 16; and 5 : 24 = Vulg. 6 : 5).

b) 6 : 1–7 : 38 (Hebr. 6 : 1-23 = Vulg. 6 : 8-30; 7 is identical in Heb. and Vulg., but different in Greek). This is a kind of supplement regarding the different kinds of sacrifices and the priests.

1. The holocaust, 6 : 1-6 (= Vulgate 6 : 8-13); cf. above 1 : 3-9. In 6 : 2b for : " the holocaust is to remain, etc. ", the Hebrew reads literally : " This is the holocaust on the hearth of the altar until the [following] morning and the fire of the altar is kept burning on it ". This refers to a holocaust offered in the late afternoon, and implies, of course, one offered in the morning; thus, the practice prescribed in Ex. 29 : 38 ff., and (Num. 28 : 3 ff., but different from 2 (4) Kgs. 16 : 15) which refers only to the holocaust *('ōlāh)* of the morning and the oblation *(minhah)* of the evening; cf. also Ez. 46 : 13-15. Here 6 : 2b, implying an evening holocaust left burning through the night, may be a gloss meant to harmonize Lev. with Ex. and Num. which reflect a later usage. (Cf. the Commentaries). In any case, the Hebrew is to be corrected in some way. In 6 : 3, " clothed in his linen robe ", should be rather " in a linen

robe ". For the Hebrew word, see M. LAMBERT, *Grammaire Hébraïque*, p. 142, n. 1 and, p. 157.

2. The cereal offering : **6** : 7-16 (Vulg. **6** : 14-23) ; cf. a) 2 above. No leaven is allowed, contrary to Canaanite ritual, where this symbolized the ebullience of the forces of nature.

3. Sin offerings : **6** : 17-23 = Vulg. **6** : 24-30; cf. a) 4 above under what conditions it may be consumed by the priests; cf. also **6** : 9, for the partaking of the cereal offering.

4. Guilt offerings : **7** : 1-6 (cf. above **5** : 14 ff.) ; on the rights of the priests, and **7** : 7-10 and **7** : 28-34, which state their rights in the several cases mentioned before.

5. Peace offerings : **7** : 11-21 : cf. above, Chap. **3**. The text distinguishes two kinds : offered in thanksgiving *(tōdāh)* (vv. 12-15) to be consumed on the same day or in fulfilment of a vow *(neder)* as a free will offering *(nedābāh)* (16-17), to be consumed no later than the next day. Some regulations follow : (**7** : 17-21), viz., who may partake of that sacrifice (20-21) or how the remains are to be treated (18-19), and furthermore, a prohibition against fat and blood (**7** : 22-27) (cf. **3** : 17). The penalty threatened in vv. 21, 25, 27 (to be cut off from one's people) is practically a death sentence : in the desert, one thus cast out is doomed to die. (Cf. Ex. **30** : 33-38; **31** : 14).

In **7** : 35-38, the conclusion of this first part, the shares allotted to the ministers of the altar are provisions made by God forever in return for this service. The scene is Mt. Sinai (v. 38) : cf. **1** : 1.

B. **8–10**.

The ordination of Aaron and his sons (cf. JOH. GOETTSBERGER, *Einleitung*, pp. 102-109). Cf. Ex. **29**, which contains God's prescriptions regarding this matter. Here (Lev. **8**) they are carried out by Moses.

a) **8**. The ordination. Aaron and his sons receive their sacred vestments (1-13); the altar is consecrated by a sin-offering (14-17), then the holocaust is offered (18-21), and the ordination ceremony takes place (22-36). The ordination is called in **8** : 22, 28-33, as in Ex. **29** : 22, 26 f., 31, 34, and Lev. **7** : 37, *millū'îm*, lit. " fillings ", from the verb *millē'*,

" to fill " (the hands) (Ex. **28** : 41, etc.), viz. with the parts
of the sacrificial victim, as a symbol of the priestly investiture.
Cf. the Akkadian : *mallū gāt-*, " to fill the hand of " = to
entrust, to invest one with power, etc.

b) **9.** Aaron and his sons, on the octave (v. 1; cf. **8** : 33-35)
enter upon their functions by offering the different sacrifices
(holocaust, etc.). The Glory of the Lord, often mentioned
in the P Tradition, manifests itself in a bright fire or light —
within a protecting cloud. It is a sign of God's dwelling in
His Chosen People, especially in the Tabernacle, and, later,
the Temple (cf. Ex. **16** : 10; **24** : 16; **29** : 43; **40** : 34; Lev. **9** :
4-23 f.; Num. **14** : 10, etc. See B. STEIN, *Der Begriff Kebod
Jahweh und seine Bedeutung für die Alttestamentliche Gotteser-
kenntnis* [Emsdetten i. W. 1939]; Haag, *Bibellexikon*, 699-703).

c) **10** : 1-5. The case of Aaron's two sons (Nadab and Abiu),
who used profane fire and are punished with death, shows
that the liturgical prescriptions must be observed scrupulously
Their bodies are taken outside the camp just as they are,
without ceremonies. This is the occasion for special rules
of mourning for priests; for them, the usual forms of mourning
are forbidden (6-7). So also is the use of wine forbidden while
they are exercising their functions (8-11). Vv. 12-15 regulate
the eating of the portions of the sacrifices assigned to the
priests (cf. **7** : 7-10 and **28** : 24). An error of Eleazar and
Ithamar — sons of Aaron — in a sin offering upsets Moses.
Aaron excuses himself and his sons by referring to their special
circumstances: they did not feel able to carry out the prescription
(16-20. The episode is not clear, and the explanations of
Commentators are involved).

C. **11–16.**

Clean and Unclean; the Day of Atonement (see J. DÖLLER,
Die Reinheits- u. Speisegesetze des AT [Münster i. W.,
1917]; W. H. GISPEN, The " Distinction between Clean and
Unclean ", *Oudtest. Studien*, V [1948], pp. 190-196).

a) **11.** Clean and unclean land and water animals (2ᵇ-8;
9-12); birds (13-19) and insects (20-23). Cf. the list in *Deut.* **14.**
The rule is that an animal is clean and edible if it is cloven-footed

and chews the cud (3). If it fulfills only one of those requirements, it is unclean. Hence are excluded, e.g., the camel
(4), the hare or rabbit (6) which chew the cud but are not
cloven-footed, and the, pig which is cloven-footed but does
not chew the cud. In the famous case of the hare, we do not
have a scientific judgment from the standpoint of natural
sciences, but a view based on the current popular estimation
of the time which the legislator follows. (Cf. H. JUNKER,
Die biblische Urgeschichte ([Bonn, 1932], 16-17; A. SCHULZ,
Biblische Zeitschrift [1911], pp. 12-17). The rule for creatures
which live in the water is that they must have both fins and
scales (9). No example is given, but the eel would be excluded.
For the birds no rule is given, but only an enumeration of
those regarded as unclean. Their identification (13-19) as
also that of the insects (20-23) is doubtful in many cases.
(See e.g., under the Latin names of the Vulgate, Hagen, *Realia
Biblica* [Paris, 1914], pp. 381-460, or more fully, the relevant
articles by L. FONCK in Hagen, *Lexicon Biblicum* [3 vols.,
Paris, 1905-1911]; also the Bible Dictionaries [in English,
under the names used in A.V. and the Hebrew Dictionaries
under the names of the Hebrew Bible]). Vv. 29-30 add some
animals which live on or in the ground (mole, rat, etc.; skunk
in v. 30 [of the Confraternity Version] is only a misprint for
skink). Vv. 24-28 and 31-43 give rules concerning uncleanness
resulting from contact with the various unclean animals.
Vv. 44-47 state that all uncleanness from such animals must
be avoided : the people are consecrated to the Holy God.

In all these chapters, the Law may be regarded as a codification of customs inherited from a distant past. How the
various animals in **11** and the other items in the next chapters
came to be regarded as unclean — or clean — cannot be said
for certain. Natural repugnance on account of the habits
of some of the animals (e.g., feeding on cadavers), reasons of
hygiene, the circumstance that some animals were consecrated
to false gods, may explain some cases. As regards various
states of man, birth and death, etc., there may have been at
work some ancient notions, as fear of mysterious forces. The
regulations serve to inculcate ritual cleanliness as the basis
of holiness befitting a people consecrated to God.

b) **12.** Childbirth is a source of uncleanness, more serious in the case of a girl than of a boy (7 days + 33 days for a boy; 14 days + 66 in the case of a girl). The mother must undergo purification.

c) **13-14.** Leprosy. The various forms of true leprosy known in the Ancient Orient must have occurred among the Hebrews also. However, here its characteristic signs (the body slowly eaten by the disease, hideous mutilations, etc.) are not referred to. Besides, **14** : 1-32, the ceremonies for the cleansing of a " leper ", imply evidently that the name leprosy applies also to various kinds of skin troubles different from true leprosy which were regarded as " unclean " and barred the victim from associating with his fellow men. The priest is the judge in all these cases.

1. Leprosy in human beings. Various symptoms on the skin of the body (2-17) are examined at different times to ascertain whether they are superficial or go deeper before passing on the case; 18-23 refer to the case of a boil or inflammatory tumor; 24-28, a burn on the skin; 29-37, a sore on the head or the chin (in the hair); 38-39, white blotches on the skin (tetter, eczema, etc.?) : 40-44, loss of hair, which may be simply baldness (40-41), but also may be due to some trouble which makes the man leprous — unclean. Conclusion, 45-46 : the leper must keep away from other people while he remains in that condition.

2. Leprosy in clothing articles : **13** : 47-59; cases of fungus growth which may or may not be corrected.

3. Leprosy in buildings : **14** : 33-57. Similar symptoms may appear in houses where the evil can be remedied; a sin offering is to be made (49-53) — apparently a survival and adaptation of an old custom. Else the house is to be destroyed (43-45).

15. Matters connected with sex. The legislation does not treat the matter from the moral point of view, but only from the ritual standpoint. It considers only certain physical conditions which are not necessarily connected with morality but may entail some ritual disabilities. The moral aspects are treated in the Decalogue and in some special sections (adultery, incest, etc. Cf. J. Döller, *op. cit.*, pp. 11-76, and 231-282).

1. In man : 2-18. This includes gonorrhoea, a contagious disease (2 ff.), and other accidental conditions (16 ff.).

2. In woman : 19-30. Ordinary menstrual flow (19 ff.) and unusual flow of blood are dealt with (25 ff.; cf. Mk. 5 : 25 ff., and parallels).

16. The Day of Atonement (*Yom Kippūr;* in the Prayer-Book : *Yom (ha)* — *kippurim;* cf. Lev. **23** : 27-28, **25** : 9; Num. **29** : 11. The verb *kipper* is used throughout Lev. **16.** Cf. S. LANDERSDORFER, *Studien zum biblischen Versöhnungstag* [Münster i. W., 1924]; *id.*, " Keilinschriftliche Parallelen zum biblischen Sündenbock ", *Biblische Zeitschrift*, [1931], 2-38). On this holy day, cf. also Lev. **23** : 26-32; Num. **29** : 7-11. In the Talmud, the treatise *Yoma* (the Day) treats the subject. The yearly Day of Expiation — a day of fasting (29 and 31 : " to mortify oneself " = to fast) — for all the uncleannesses falls on the 10th of the seventh month (Tishri, = Sept.-Oct. The date varies in our calendar. In 1956, it was September 15; in 1957, October 5; in 1958, September 24). It became most important in Jewish life, so that later it came to be known as " the Great Day ", or, in the Talmud, " The Day ". The High Priest, who alone functions on that day, wears simple vestments (3-4; 32-33). Two male goats are chosen, and a ram (5). Lots are cast to determine which goat is for Yahweh, and which for Azazel (8-10). Then come the rites for the bullock (11-14), and for the goat which is the sin-offering of the people (15-19). The scapegoat — which bears the transgression of Israel — is driven into the desert (20-22) : the sins inspired by the devil are thus sent back symbolically to the devil who dwells in the desert (cf. Mt. **12** : 43; Luke **11** : 24). The scapegoat is " for Azazel " and " sent off to Azazel " (**8** : 10, 26). Azazel (etymology doubtful) is apparently the name of a demon living in the desert — another inheritance from some ancient popular tradition adopted and adapted by the legislator. Note that the goat is not offered in sacrifice to Azazel. Azazel plays an important part in later Jewish tradition (the *Book of Henoch* mentions him often).

D. **17–26** : 46.

The Law of Holiness. (Cf. S. R. DRIVER, *Introduction to the Literature of the Old Testament* [2nd ed., 1897, reprinted 1956], pp. 47-59; Haag, *Bibellexikon*, p. 682 f.; R. H. PFEIFFER : *Introduction...*, pp. 239-250; a good outline by H. CAZELLES, *Lévitique* [Bible de Jérusalem, 1951], 15 f.). This section was first distinguished as a separate code belonging to P by A. KLOSTERMANN in 1877. It is characterized by a number of phrases (embodying the idea of holiness) from which its name is derived. Thus : " I am Yahweh " (**18** : 5, 6, 21; **19** : 12, 14, 16, 18, 28, 30, 32, 37; **21** : 12; **22** : 2, 3, 8, 30, 31, 33; **26** : 2, 45), expanded in places by such phrases as " I am Yahweh who make him (you, them) holy " (**20** : 8; **22** : 32; **21** : 15-23; **22** : 9-16). Note also : " You shall be holy because I Yahweh your God am holy " (**20** : 7; **21** : 6). Its language has a number of peculiarities. The holiness of God means that he is far above and away from all things. A person or thing consecrated to him is set apart from the rest of the people or things. Hence he or it must be free from anything that makes him or it unsightly before God : in a state of ritual cleanness. But holiness in our texts becomes also a moral notion : merely ritual cleanness does not suffice. The Holy God demands moral cleanliness. From repetitions of the contents it may be gathered that the Code of Holiness is not a perfect literary unit.

a) **17**. Sacrifices and blood. The slaughtering of an animal for food must take place at the Sanctuary, where the priests will dispose of the blood in the proper way (3-9). Cf. the more lenient regulation in Deut. **12** : **15** f. Note the sanction of the law here (4) and in the following vv. (9, 10, 14, 29) : The transgressor " shall be cut off from among his people ". The reason for the law is the danger of idolatry to which the people succumbed in the past (7). Blood is absolutely forbidden as food : it is reserved to God. The prescription applies to all, including aliens in Israel (10-12). Vv. 13-14 : this prescription applies to clean animals caught in hunt; the blood is to be poured out. A dead animal *(nebēlah)* or one killed by another animal *(terefah)* may not be eaten (15-16).

b) **18–20**. Moral prescriptions. **18**. Marriage (cf. LÉVY, *La famille Israélite*, p. 180 ff.). Prohibited degrees (3-18).

The phrase (in our translation) : " to have sexual intercourse "
= in Hebrew, " to uncover the nakedness of ". On v. 8,
cf. A. VAN PRAAG, *Droit matrimonial assyro-babylonien*
(Amsterdam, 1945), p. 170, and on v. 16, p. 114 (note). V. 18
is taken correctly as prohibiting marriage with two sisters.
A few propose to render : " You shall not take a wife to another ",
i.e. a prohibition of polygamy. (So A. V. [margin]; also
S. BERNFELD, *Introduction to the O. T.*, I, p. 5 [in Hebrew],
beginning of 2nd paragraph). Vv. 19-20, 22-23, condemn
various forms of immorality. Note in **19** the inclusion of
a case of uncleanness mentioned before several times (**12** : 2;
15 : 19 ff., 25 ff., 33), though this is not a moral question. V. 21
(Cf. **20** : 3 ff.; Deut. **18** : 10), prohibition of human sacrifices;
literally " you shall not give any of your offspring to let go
through [the fire] to Moloch ". The practice is referred to
several times in the Old Testament : Jer. **7** : 31; **19** : 5-6; **32** :
35; Ez. **16** : 21; **20** : 31; 2 (4) Kgs. **16** : 3; **17** : 17; **21** : 6; **23** : 10.
The hypothesis has been advanced lately that " *molek* " here
means " votive offering ". (Cf. H. CAZELLES, s.v. " Molok ",
in *DBV, Suppl.;* *BASOR*, no. 139, [Oct., 1955], pp. 21-22;
E. JACOB, *Théologie de l'A. T.*, [Neuchâtel-Paris, 1955], p. 48,
n. 1; P. VAN IMSCHOOT, *Théologie de l'A. T.* [Tournai, 1954],
p. 23, n. 7; E. DHORME, *La religion des Hébreux nomades*,
[1937], p. 214 f.; id., *Revue de l'Histoire des Religions*, [1936],
I, 276 ff.; W. KORNFELD in Haag, *Bibellexikon*, 1152-1154).
It must be said that it is difficult to exorcise the person of
Moloch everywhere. Vv. 24-30 : an exhortation not to fall
into any of those abominations.

19. Rules of moral conduct and worship. Vv. 2-4; 11-12,
recall the Decalogue. Vv. 9-10; 13-18; 32-36 : charity and
justice in dealing with one's neighbor. V. 16b : Our Version,
with several others, agrees with the Jewish view of the verse;
others understand it as referring to plotting to bring about
a sentence of death against a man by a false accusation. V. 18b :
the great commandment, " You shall love your neighbor as
yourself ". V. 19 : strange mixtures used in magic; pagan
practices are condemned, (cf. also vv. 26-28). V. 29 : religious
prostitution condemned.

20. Vv. 2-7, and 27 (which belongs after v. 6) : Penalties
for certain offenses against religion. Vv. 8-21 : Penalties for

offenses against the family. In some cases, the guilty parties are " cut off from their people " (5, 6, 18) or they are put to death (10-13; 15-16); in one case, by fire (v. 14) — so also a priest's daughter **21** : 9; in v. 17, by a public execution. There follows an exhortation (cf. **18** : 24 ff.) to keep all the commandments, to abstain from all uncleanness (22-25) as befitting a people which belongs to Yahweh the Holy One (26).

c) **21–22.**   Priests and sacrifices.

1.   Special rules for the priests concerning mourning (**21** : 1-6), marriage (7-8), and family honor (9; cf. **20** : 14); and for the chief priest (10-15).

2.   Physical irregularities preventing exercise of priesthood (16-24).

3.   **22** : 1-16 : Rules concerning partaking of sacrificial meals : for the priests (1-9), for lay persons (10-16). Vv. 17-30 : The sacrificial victims must be without blemish.   Vv. 31-33 : Concluding exhortation.

d) **23.**   The liturgical year.

1.   The Sabbath (1; Ex. **20** : 8-11).

2.   Passover and Unleavened Bread (5-8) (Ex. **12** : 1-20; Deut. **16** : 1-8).   Lev. distinguishes the Passover (first month, fourteenth day) and Unleavened Bread (on the fifteenth and following days).   In Deut. the celebration takes place at the one Sacred Place.

3.   The Feast of Weeks.   *(Shabu'ot,* Pentecost; Tob. **2** : 1; Ex. **34** : 22; Deut. **16** : 10 ff.).

4.   The New Moon of the seventh month *(Tishri) :* = *Rosh hā-shanāh* in the modern calendar (23-24; Num. **28** : 11-15). At an earlier date every new moon was a holy day (1 Sam. **20** : 5-24; Amos **8** : 3; Isa. **1** : 13) as with the Canaanites.   (Cf. the *Musāf :* Additional prayer for the New Moon when it falls on a Sabbath, in Singer-Adler, *Authorized Daily Prayer Book* [London, 1912], p. 161 f., 225 f., and clxiv f.; clxxxviii f.; Chief Rabbi J. H. HERTZ, *Authorized Daily Prayer Book* [New York, 1948], p. 774 ff.; D. DA SOLA-POOL, *Book of Prayer* [Sefardic usage, New York, 1954], p. 343 ff.).

THE BOOKS205

5. Vv. 26-32 : The Day of Atonement *(Yom Kippūr)* : cf. **16**.

6. Vv. 33-36 : The Booths (Tabernacles; *Sukkot*) or Harvest (Ex. **23** : 14 ff.; on the fifteenth of the seventh month). A supplement (39-44) on the same subject, coming after the conclusion (37-38), dwells on the joyful character of the festival (cf. Deut. **16** : 13-15).

e) **24**. Additional Laws.

1. Vv. 1-4 : The everlasting sanctuary light (Ex. **27** : 20 f.; **25** : 31-35; **37** : 17-20).

2. Vv. 5-9 : The showbread (Ex. **25** : 23-30).

3. Vv. 10-23 : A case of blasphemy; the law of blasphemy and the penalties for murder, injuries, etc. The matter is unrelated to the context. According to vv. 14, 16 blasphemy is punished by stoning (cf. **20** : 27). V. 20 states the *lex talionis* (Ex. **21** : 23-25; Deut. **19** : 21; cf. also Code of Hammurabi nos. 195-214 (J. B. PRITCHARD, ed., *Ancient Near Eastern Tests*, p. 175), and the Assyrian Laws no. 50 ff., (*ibid.*, p. 184). The *lex talionis* should not be judged as breathing a spirit of merciless revenge or heartless justice; it is rather meant to check unbridled ferocious passion such as is expressed in the old song of Lamech (Gen. **4** : 23-24).

f) **25**. The holy years.

1. The sabbatical year, 2-7. The seventh year is a year of rest for the land (cf. Ex. **23** : 10-11). No fear of want should be felt. The people thus are, as it were, made to return to the conditions of pastoral life. The same matter is treated in Deut. **15** : 1-11, which adds for that year the relaxation — or remitting — of debts in favor of fellow-Israelites (Deut. **15** : 3) (the *Shemittāh*). There was to be also a freeing of the Hebrew slave in the seventh year of his service (which did not necessarily coincide with the sabbatical year) : Ex. **21** : 2; Deut. **15** : 12-18. This latter law was not observed strictly (Jer. **34** : 8-22). The other law of the sabbatical year could occasion practical difficulties under the conditions of life in a settled society. (Cf. 1 Mach. **6** : 49 ff., which refers to a shortage of food in such a year).

2. The jubilee year, 8-55 (from *yobel,* the ram's horn blown at the beginning of that year (9), on the tenth day of the seventh month). It prescribes the rest of the land (11) — but the people must have no fear of want (18 ff.) — the freeing of Hebrew slaves (40 f.) (47-55), but non-Hebrew slaves have a different status (44-46); redemption of the land — which really belongs exclusively to Yahweh (23 ff.) — and of houses (29 ff.), with differences according as they are in a walled town or in villages.

g) **26.** Hortatory conclusion. The fundamental requirement is fidelity to Yahweh, which excludes all pagan symbol (1-2). God will reward obedience generously (3-13), but disobedience shall be chastised most severely (14-39). But in the depth of their misery, they will turn back to God, and God in his mercy will remember his covenant with Israel (40-45).

The Code of Hammurabi also ends with a long epilogue in which the law is presented as embodying justice, able to secure firm guidance and good government, and their rights to the oppressed. The king after Hammurabi is urged to follow that law and thus to maintain peace and security in the land (col. 25, 60 ff.). The curses take up more space — as also above in Chap. **26** — (cols. 26-28). They are curses on a king who would alter or disregard the laws and statues, and the divinity is called upon to chastise him and his people with the direst punishments. But the spirit of the epilogue is quite different from that of the conclusion of the Code of Holiness : the author of the Law of Holiness is intensely religious and looks forward, beyond sin and its punishment, to conversion, and God's mercy keeping its promise to Israel.

There are numerous points of contact between the Law of Holiness (H) and Ezechiel. Hence the problem of the relationship between H and the prophet : Does Ez. depend on H, which then would be pre-exilic, or does H depend on Ez., so that H would belong somewhere around the middle of the 6th century or later? Most critics favor this second view, while admitting that H embodies materials of much older date. Others hold that H belongs to the period before the Exile, e.g., to the last period of the monarchy, and contains materials of higher antiquity. It is evidently impossible to attempt a solution here. To understand the problem properly, we should study the data of Ez. closely — and Ez. has not yet yielded all his secrets. (See the Commentaries on Ez., especially the careful suggestive statements of Dr. A. VAN DEN BORN in his recent Commentary in *De Boeken van het Oude Testament*, XI, 1, [Roermond-Maaseik, 1954], pp. 8-9; also his fuller treatment in *Studia Biblica* 28 [1953-1954], 94-104).

E. **27.** An Appendix which defines more precisely matters left out in the preceding section.

a) The redemption of vows (2-25). 1. Vows by which a person is vowed (2-8) — as, e. g., in the case of Jephte (Jdgs. **11** : 30 ff.), Manoe (*ibid.* **13** : 3 ff.), Samuel (1 Sam. **1** : 11). 2. Vows the object of which is an animal (9-13). 3. Vows concerning a house (14-15). 4. Vows concerning a field (16-25).

The legislator takes into account the means of the person who made the vow (8). The appraisal is made by the priest (8, 11-12, 14, 18, 23) according to the standard of the sanctuary shekel of 20 geras ("grains"; Babylonion, *girū*) to the shekel (27; cf. 3). On this special shekel, cf. Ex. **30** : 30, 24; **38** : 24-26; Lev. **5** : 15; Num. **3** : 47. (The precise value of the Hebrew measures of weight are not certain; they are calculated according to the Babylonian system. Cf. *Guide to the Bible*, II, p. 99 f.; G. A. BARROIS, in *Interpreter's Bible* I, p. 156 f.; TRINQUET, "Métrologie Biblique", in *DBV, Suppl.*, V (1957), cols. 1212-1250).

b) Vows which cannot be redeemed (26-33). 1. A first-born clean animal belongs to God by right and therefore cannot be the object of a vow; an unclean animal may be redeemed (26-27). 2. *Herem* (anathema) — whatever is made "sacred" by ban (28-29; cf. Jos. **6** : 17 ff.; **7** : 11; 1 Sam. **15** : 3). 3. Tithes (30-33).

Conclusion (34; cf. **26** : 46).

4. — The Book of Numbers.

Name. Like the other books of the Pentateuch, this fourth book of the Law, is called in the Jewish tradition by one of the first words of its text : *Be-midbar* ("in the desert", from the fifth word of **1 : 1**). Another name, attested by Saint Jerome and used long after him, is *Wayyedabbēr* (" and he spoke ", the opening word). However, the Jewish tradition knows also titles for the books of the Pentateuch derived from their contents, which therefore correspond to those of the Greek-Latin Bible. Thus, in the present case, *Piqqūdim* (" enrollment ") = ἀριθμοί, *Numeri* (" numbers ").

Contents and divisions. The book contains an account of the period between the first of the second month of the second year of the Exodus (**1 : 1**) and the arrival on the Plains of Moab (**33 : 48** ff.), some time after Aaron's death on the first of the fifth month of the fortieth year of the Exodus (**33 : 38**). The book may be divided naturally into 3 main parts : A, In the Desert of Sinai : preparation for leaving Sinai : **1 : 1–10 : 10**; B, Journey from Sinai to the Plains of Moab : **10 : 11–22 : 1**; C, On the Plains of Moab : **22 : 2–36 : 13**. The book contains, beside narratives, a considerable amount of legal material scattered through the different parts. According to the critical view, the greater part of the book belongs to P whose manner is recognizable in the genealogies, enumerations with repeated phrases, chronological and similar material. There are also large sections from the JE traditions, whose individual contributions cannot always be separated. (For a good brief statement of the critical analysis, see A. S. HARTOM in : *Entzyklop. Miqra'it*, 2 (1954), 140; cf. B. D. EERDMANS, " The Composition of Numbers ", *Oudtest. Studiën*, 6 [1949], 101-216).

A. 1 : 1–10 : 10. *In the Desert of Sinai.*

a) The census **1–4** (P); cf. Num. **26**; 2 Sam. **24**; Ex. **30 : 11-16**. (See especially E. A. SPEISER, " Census and Ritual Expiation in Mari and Israel ", *BASOR*, no. 149 [1958], pp. 17-25; J. BOTTÉRO and A. FINET, *Archives Royales de Mari*, XV : = *Répertoire Analytique des Tomes I-V* [Paris, 1954], p. 329 : s.v. " Recensement ", etc.). It is to be a census of the whole community by clans and ancestral homes, registering each male individually (**1 : 2**). The census is to be taken with the assistance of twelve men (**1 : 4-15**); it does not include the Levites (**1 : 48-54; 4–5**). Note that none of the names here or in **13 : 4-15** contains the name of Yahweh — all are pre-

Yahwistic names. The list may be presumed to reproduce
an ancient source (A. Edelkoort: p. 18; in Dutch. Hommel maintains that the proper names of P, especially in Numbers, are
very ancient [Moses' time] and cannot be explained from
the Persian period as claimed by Wellhausen. Cf. C. JEAN,
in *DBV, Suppl.*, IV [1949], s.v. " HOMMEL ", col. 121). The
result of the census is recorded, 1 : 20-46. Note the repetition
of the formulas and the high numbers for each tribe, comprising
the males of twenty and more fit for military service. Next
(2) comes the arrangement of the tribes " around the meeting
tent, at some distance from it " (2 : 1-2) in perfect order.
(Cf. with this Ez. 48 which likewise groups the tribes around
the central sanctuary in the future ideal state). Here again,
we find identity of formulas, repetition of the high numbers
of 1 : 20-46; cf. the phrase 2 : 34, " and the Israelites did just
as Yahweh had commanded Moses " (cf. 1 : 54; Gen. 6 : 22;
7 : 5; Ex. 39 : 32). The grouping of the tribes cannot be
explained as due to the imagination of a late writer, for then
we should expect the grouping to correspond to the situation
after the entry into Palestine. This is not the case. Hence
we may suppose the use of an old source (A. EDELKOORT,
in *Tekst en Uitleg* series [Groningen, 1930], p. 18). The total
is 603,550 (1 : 46 and 2 : 32; also Ex. 38 : 26). The number
of the Levites (Num. 3 : 39) is 22,000 males a month old or
more. As remarked before, such high figures supposing a
population of some three million Israelites cannot be taken
as mathematical quantities. If they were correct, it is estimated
that the Hebrews in Egypt would have formed *ca.* one third
or more of the total population of the country ! (Cf. the Commentaries. For an attempt to save as much as possible, see
CEUPPENS, O. P., *Het Boek Exodus* [Brugge, 1932], p. 50, and
VALVEKENS, O. PRAEM., *Het Boek Numeri* [*ibid.*, 1932], p. 12.
The latter states : " Such a large number seems to many,
Catholics included, improbable, even impossible; various solutions have been proposed which are not fully satisfactory ".
Edelkoort (p. 91) remarks that Sinai could not support such
a huge population — and, in addition to the human population,
we would have to think of the needs of their flocks and herds.
esven in Canaan later such a large population is hardly possible,
Epecially with the Canaanites still there. Add also the diffi-

culty — not to say the impossibility — of moving efficiently such a huge multitude encumbered by baggage and animals.

The special status of the Tribe of Levi is defined in 3 and 4. There are : (1) the priests descendants of Aaron (3 : 1-5), and (2) the Levites, ministers of lower rank who assist the priests and are connected especially with the care of the tent (1 : 48-53 and 3 : 5-10). The duties of their several clans are defined further in 4 : 1-20 (the Caathites, sons of Qohat), 21-48 (the Gersonites, sons of Gershon) and 29-33 (the Merarites, sons of Merari). Their service lasts twenty years, between the ages of thirty and fifty (4 : 3, 23, 30). Their total is 22,000 (3 : 14-39). The Tribe of Levi take the place of the firstborn in Israel (3 : 11-13; cf. Ex. 13 : 11); as a special census of the firstborn of the tribes gives a total of 22,273, the extra number of 273 firstborn must be redeemed by paying a special tax (3 : 40-51). In 4, v. 32^b should be translated : " And you shall record by name the articles which they are responsible for carrying " (cf. SPEISER, art. cit., p. 23). The law about the census in Ex. 30 : 11-16 provides for an " expiation ", " so that no plague may come upon them for being enrolled ". We find the same preoccupation among other peoples of the Ancient Orient. According to Exodus, each one that is enrolled shall give Yahweh a ransom *(kofer)* or ransom money *(kesef ha kippurim)* for his life (30 : 12), a half shekel, the same amount for all, rich or poor, to pay the ransom *(le-kappēr,* vv. 15-16). This goes back to an old idea, which we find in ancient Babylonian literature and of which we find echoes in the Mishnah and in some ancient Jewish prayers, that on certain occasions the divinity made lists of those who were to live or to die. " The ancient Near Easterner " must have " shrunk from the thought of having his name recorded in lists that might be put to unpredictable uses "…. " It would be natural to propitiate the unknown powers or seek expiation as a general precaution ". In the Bible, we have only an echo of the old idea in the " ransom " which has become a contribution to Yahweh, for the service of the tent (4 : 13^b, 15-16; cf. SPEISER, art. cit., p. 24 f.).

b) Laws (5–6 [P]) not included in the preceding regulations about clean and unclean in Lev. 11-16. They concern : (1) Expulsion of the unclean due to leprosy, discharge or contact with a corpse (5 : 1-4). This corresponds only to conditions found in the desert. (2) Unjust possession (5 : 5-10); in the case of the decease of the injured party without heirs, the amount restored goes to the priest. (3) The ordeal for a suspected adulteress (5 : 11-31). The ordeal — judgment of God — was resorted to in cases where proper evidence was lacking : the suspected person was cleared or proved guilty by being subjected to some dangerous physical test (plunging hand in hot water, carrying a red hot iron, etc.). It is used in the Code of Hammurabi for a charge of sorcery (2) or of adultery (132). (Cf. A. VAN PRAAG, *Droit matrimonial assyro-babylonien* [Amsterdam 194], pp. 30 and 40; E. NEUFELD, *The Hittite Laws* [London, 1951], pp. 98-99). Here the woman goes through a special ritual, culminating in the drinking of bitter water : if nothing happens, she is innocent. (See R. DE VAUX, O. P., " Institutions familiales ", in his *Institutions de l'Ancien Testament*, I [Paris, 1958]; cf. BASSET, *1001 contes, récits et légendes Arabes* [Paris, 1924-1926], II, 3 ff. The ordeal of the suspected adulteress is a survival of a very ancient practice found in the Orient. In the Mishnah there is a special treatise (*Soṭāh*) on the subject. (4) Law concerning the Nazirite (6: 1-21), " one vowed to God ", who during the time of his vow allows his hair to grow, abstains from fermented drinks and does not come near a dead person, even his closest relatives (1-8); a special ritual marks the end of the vow (13 ff.). Cf. Am. 2 : 11-12; Acts 18 : 18; 21 : 23-26; Jdgs. 13 : 4 ff.; 16, 17; 1 Sam. 1 : 11; Lk. 1 : 15. On this also the Mishnah has a special treatise : *Nazir*. (5) The priestly blessing (6 : 22-27). Its place in the text has been a subject of debate : various suggestions have been made of a supposed better context, but the arguments are not convincing. It is an ancient formula of peculiar pattern. It consists of 15 words altogether : first line (v. 24), 3 words; second line (25), 5 words; third line (26), 7 words : thus there is an increase of 2 words with each line. (Cf. J. H. HERTZ, *Pentateuch and Haftorōt*, [London, 1938], p. 594 f.; A. EDEL-KOORT, in *Texkst en Uitleg* series [Groningen, 1930], p. 106 f., CASSUTO in *Entzyklop. Miq.*, 2, pp. 358-359).

c) Offerings of the princes of Israel and " purification of the Levites ", (7 : 1–8 : 26 [P]). (1) Vv. 1-9 connect with the

consecration of the tent (Ex. **40** : 17 ff.). The princes who
had supervised the census (**1** : 4 ff.) offer six baggage wagons
and twelve oxen. These are assigned to the Levites sons
of Gerson and of Merari according to their duties, not to the
sons of Caath (Qehat) who carry their charge on their shoulders.
(2) Vv. 10-83 : For twelve days each one of the princes in
turn — but not in the order of the enumeration in **1** : 4 ff. —
brings his offerings for the dedication of the altar. (Among
these gifts there is a gold cup filled with incense. The Hebrew
enploys the word, *Kaf*, " palm of the hand ". RSV renders
by " dish "; cf. the *Introduction to the RSV of the Old Testament*
[New York, 1952], p. 50). Notice here also the identity of
the account in each case — a characteristic noted before :
1 : 20-47; **2** : 1-34; **3** : 14-33; **4** : 34-45. But this is a feature
which should not surprise in official documents built on a
definite, traditional, pattern. (3) Vv. 84-89; the conclusion
sums up and repeats the offerings. The voice addresses Moses
in the tent : God held converse with Moses (cf. Ex. **25** : 22).
(4) **8** : 1-4 : the setting up of the seven lamps of the lampstand
(cf. Ex. **25** : 31-39; **37** : 17-24; **40** : 4-22). (5) **8** : 5-26 : the
" purification " of the Levites; a lower degree of ordination,
if we may say so, than the " consecration " of the priests.
The Levites are as an offering of Israel and a substitute for
Israel (9-11), purified and set apart (12-15), given to the Lord
instead of the firstborn of the people (16-19) — " given "
(16-19) (cf. **3** : 9), and Yahweh gives them (19) to Aaron for
the service of the tent. The last vv. (23-26) define the age
limits for Levitical service : from 25 to 50, after which the
Levite retires from full activity. Elsewhere, the lower limit
is 30 years (**4** : 3, 23, 35, 43, 47); the LXX harmonizes by
reading 25 in **4**. The Rabbinic interpretation harmonizes
by supposing that from 25 to 30 was a training period
(Cf. EDELKOORT, p. 112). In 1 Chron. **23** : 24, 27, 2 Chron.
31 : 17, and also 1 Esdras **3** : 8, the lower age limit is 20.

d) The Passover, the fiery cloud; the silver trumpets (**9** :
1–10 : 10 [P]). (1) **9** : 1-5 : The Passover — the second since
the Exodus, marking the beginning of the second year in the
desert (**9** : 1) — is celebrated in the desert of Sinai at the regular
time (**9** : 5) : fourteenth of the first month (= *Abib;* Ex. **13** : 4;

later, *Nisan*); cf. Ex. **12** : 2 ff.; Lev. **23** : 5. This does not agree with the dating of **1** : **1** which transports us to the first of the second month (*Jyyār* = April-May; later *Ziv*, 1 Kgs. **6** : 1) of the second year of the Exodus : Num. **1** begins at a point later than Num. **9**. But the dating of Num. **9** : **1** agrees with that supposed in Num. **7**, viz., Dedication of the Tent which took place on the first of the first month *(Abib-Nisan)* of the second year according to Ex. **40** : 2 and 17 (cf. EDELKOORT on **7** : 1, *op. cit.*, p. 108). (2) **9** : 6-14 : A special case is the occasion of a regulation. (Cf. similar instances in Lev. **24** : 10-16; Num. **27** : 1-11; **36** : 1-12). Those unable to celebrate the Passover at the regular date will celebrate it one month later. The wording supposes a situation which would be rather unlikely in the desert : a man prevented from taking part in the regular Passover because he is on a journey far away (10 and 13). This supposes a later situation — an Israelite living outside Palestine. It presupposes also aliens settled in Israel who have embraced Judaism (14; cf. Ex. **12** : 48). (3) **9** : 15-23 : The fiery cloud — a dark cloud by day, a fire at night — appears on the tent (cf. Ex. **13** : 21 f.; **40** : 36-38). The section explains the phenomenon which regulated the movements of the people in the desert. The date in v. 15 — the day when the tent was erected — is the first of the first month of the second year; thus the dating agrees with **7** : 1 and **9** : 1. (4) **10** : 1-10 : The two silver trumpets are blown by the priests (8) to give various signals, viz., to summon the princes to a meeting (4) or to warn to break camp (2), and to mark the stages of breaking camp (5-7). The trumpets will be used after the settlement in Palestine to summon the people against an enemy and for religious feasts (8-10) (Lev. **23**; Num. **28–29**). **10** : 5-6 of the Masoretic Text — followed by *A.V.*, *R.V.*, *S.R.V.*, *American Version*, etc. — is clearly incomplete : it begins an enumeration of signals for the different camps, but in fact gives only those for the camps on the E. side (**10** : 5 = 2 : 3 ff.) and for those on the S. side (**10** : 6 = 2 : 10 ff.). The signals for the other camps on the W. side (2 : 18 ff.) and on the N. side (2 : 25 ff.) are preserved in the Samaritan recension and in LXX; cf. the new Catholic (Confraternity) Version. In favor of this, see, e.g., HOUBIGANT, *Biblia Hebraica* (Paris, 1753) I, p. 458 (his corrected text), and p. 461

(his note). The Vulgate and Moffatt adopt a compromise solution by reading in 6ᵇ " and so do with the others, a blow is to be blown whenever they are to move on ". This reading of the Vulgate and Moffatt is hardly in the style of P, which is not afraid of repeating items in full.

B. **10 : 11–22 : 1.** *The Journey from Sinai to the Plains of Moab.*

a) **10 : 11-28 (P).** The departure from Sinai in the Samaritan recension and Hexapla Syriac is prefaced by a text which is almost word for word that of Deut. **1 : 6-8**; it is not accepted as part of the true text, and in fact not necessary (cf. Hou-BIGANT, *op. cit.,* 1, pp. 459 and 461). Everything is now ready for Israel to resume its march. The departure is dated precisely : the twentieth of the second month (*Jyyar :* Apr.-May) of year 2 of the Exodus; they had been at Sinai almost a full year (cf. Ex. **19 : 1**). They break camp and move on to the Desert of Pharan (**10 : 11-12**), exactly according to **9 : 17.** The journey resembles a religious procession with all the details carefully arranged (**10 : 14** ff.; cf. **10 : 14** with **1 : 7,** 2, 3; **7, 12; 10 : 15,** with **1 : 8, 2 : 5, 7 : 24,** and so on.

b) **10 : 29-32 (J E).** Moses begs Hobab to act as their guide on account of his familiarity with the desert (**31 : "** Serve as eyes for us ". Cf. Arabic *'ayn* (" eye ") which means also " spy ", " lookout ", " vanguard ", etc. Moses promises him a share in the blessings of Israel (**10 : 32**). Hobab probably consented — after much coaxing — for later we find the Qenites, to whom he belongs (Num. **24 : 21**), settled in the Negeb (Jdgs.**1 : 16**). In **10 : 29,** the Masoretic Text reads : " ... said to Hobab, son of Re'u'el (Raguel) the Madianite, the father-in-law of Moses ". Cf. Ex. **3 : 1; 4 : 18; 18 : 1,** 8, 15, where Moses' father-in-law is Jethro the priest of Madian. According to Ex. **2 : 16** the priest of Madian, one of whose daughters he marries (Ex. **2 : 21**) is called Re'u'el (Raguel) (Ex. **2 : 18**). The question of the relationship is further complicated according as we read in Jdgs. **1 : 16 : "** the sons of Jethor (Jether) the Cinite (Qenite) brother-in-law of Moses " (so LXX, Ms *B*) or the sons of Hobab, the Cinite, father-in-law of Moses (so Ms *A*); but in Jdgs. **4 : 11** both Mss *(A* and *B)* make Hobab the brother-in-law of Moses, while the Masoretic Text makes

Hobab the father-in-law (in Hebrew "father-in-law" and "son-in-law" differ only in the vowels : *hōtēn* and *hātān* respectively. The true reading can be settled only after settling the complicated question of the correct reading and interpretation of the other texts.

c) **10** : 33-35 (JE) : A three days' journey " from the mountain of Yahweh " (cf. Ex. **3** : 1; **4** : 27; **18** : 5 " mountain of God ") brings the people to a resting place. These are poetic lines with which Moses used to greet the setting out and the resting of the Ark (cf. Ps. **77**).

d) **11-12** (JE) : Various incidents from the journey. (1) **11** : 1-3 : murmuring of the people at Tabera. They are punished by the fire of Yahweh — lightning — which consumes the outskirts of the camp. Hence the name Tabera (pasture ground?) which here is connected with a similar root meaning " to burn " (cf. Deut. **9** : 22). (2) **11** : 4-35 : murmuring of the people at the instigation of some elements who had joined Israel at the Exodus (**11** : 4; cf. Ex. **12** : 38); they miss the good food of Egypt and are tired of the manna (**11** : 6-9; with 7-8, cf. Ex. **16** : 31. On the manna, cf. YEHUDA FELIKS, *Plant World of the Bible* [Tel Aviv, 1957, in Hebrew], p. 180 f.). Moses takes his trouble to God in prayer (**11** : 10-15). At God's command, Moses summons seventy of the Elders upon whom He will bestow some of the spirit of God to assist him. Moses promises the people flesh to eat till it will become loathsome to them (16-20). Yahweh is powerful enough to work such a wonder (21-23). The Elders, seized by the Spirit, prophesy (24-25) — i.e., speak " in enraptured enthusiasm " — even two men, Eldad and Medad, whose names were on the list but who had not come to the meeting, are themselves also seized by the Spirit (26-27). Moses refuses to stop the manifestation (28-30). Note the intervention of Josue, son of Nun (28), Moses' aide (cf. Ex. **24** : 13, and Ex. **17** : 9 ff.; **33** : 11). The episode of the quails (31-35) becomes an occasion of gluttony, which is followed by the death of many. Hence the name : *Qibrot ha-ta'awah* (34ᵃ, " the graves of greed " — a play on words; according to some perhaps originally the name of a burial place of a Bedouin tribe. The place is identified with Erweys el Ebeirig, N.E. of Sinai; cf. GROLLENBERG, Map 9,

p. 44; E. G. KRAELING, Map 5, pp. 232-233; Vilnay, *Ha-Aretz ba-Miqrā'*, p. 6. This episode of the quails should be compared with Ex. **16** : 8 and 13. (3) **12** : 1-16 (attributed to E. For a proposed re-arrangement of the text of **12–21**, see H. WIENER, *Posthumous Essays* [1932], p. 37 ff.). V. 35^b : in Haserot — identified by some with the Oasis 'Ayn Hodra, the resemblance being clearer in the Hebrew and Arabic alphabets — on the way from Erweys el Ebeirig to the Gulf of Aqaba. Vv. 1-3 relate a scene of jealousy on the part of Aaron and Miriam — jealousy on account of Moses' exceptional rank (6-8), but 1 mentions the Chusite (Kushite) woman Moses had married. Commentators see here a reference to Sephora the Madianitess (Ex. **2** : 21) but they do not explain, naturally, why she should be called a Kushite (Ethiopian) here. Besides, Moses had been married to Sephora a good many years before (cf. Ex. **2** : 23; Moses is eighty when he stands before Pharaoh after his return from Madian (Ex. **7** : 7) — a complaint about Sephora would come rather late. But also it might be rather late for Moses to marry again (cf., e.g., HOUBIGANT, on this passage). Note the praise of Moses (3) — hardly expected under his pen — and rather unconnected with the context. Miriam, apparently the leader (she is mentioned first in 1), is stricken with white leprosy (10) (cf. Ex. **4** : 6) but is restored after seven days (vv. 13-16) (cf. Lev. **13** : 4-6). In **12** : 1-2, our Version and others render the same expression first : " to speak against ", and then : " to speak through ". G. R. DRIVER (*JTS*, 43 [1942], 155 f.) proposes to see here two different verbs : " Miriam and Aaron *turned away from* Moses... Is it with *Moses* alone that Yahweh *speaks*? Does He not *speak with us* also "? For the text of **12** : 6^a, cf. M. LAMBERT, *Grammaire Hébr.*, p. 142, n. 1, and cf. BROCKELMANN, *Hebräische Syntax*, 80^d, and *Vergleichende Gram.*, II, 182^b (p. 263).

e) **13–14** : The twelve spies (P and JE. For details of the analysis, cf. S. R. DRIVER, *Introduction*, pp. 62-63).

(1) **13** : 1-24 (1-16= P). Twelve spies, one from each tribe are sent from an unspecified point in the Desert of Pharan, W. of the Arabah Valley which runs from the Dead Sea to the Gulf of Aqaba to reconnoiter Palestine. However, in **13** : 26 they find their people at Cades (Qadesh) (cf. Num. **20** : 1).

Cades, also Cades Barnea (Num. **32** : 8; Dt. **1** : 19), is recognized in the modern 'Ayn Qedeis (Cf. Grollenberg, *Atlas*, p. 56; E. G. KRAELING, *Atlas*, pp. 116-118; Vilnay, *Ha-Aretz...*, p. 7; *Westminster Atlas* [1945], pp. 63-64; SAVIGNAC, O. P., *RB* [1902], pp. 55-61; Barrois, " Cades ", in *DBV, Suppl.*, I [1928], 993-997).

Vv. 17-24 (JE) : The spies carry out their instructions. There is some confusion in the account of their exploration : v. 21, from Sin (with the letter Sade : Ex. **16** : 1; **17** : 1) — a desert between Cades (Gen. **16** : 14) and the S. of the Dead Sea — to Rohob (Jdgs. **18** : 28) in N. Palestine near the sources of the Jordan. But in v. 22, it is S. Palestine, the region of Hebron where the Anakim live (Jos. **15** : 14; Jg. **1** : 10), about whom strange stories were circulated (Deut. **1** : 28; **2** : 10 ff., etc.). The scouts — with some imagination — describe them as giants, alongside of whom they felt like mere grasshoppers (**13** : 28, 32^b-33). (On **13** : 22, cf. *Verbum Domini* [1932], p. 243). From that district they bring back samples. (On the Negeb, v. 22, and often before, cf. Z. VILNAY, *Madrik Eretz Yisra'el*, III, [Tel Aviv, 1945], pp. 376-423. In " Les Guides Bleus " : *Israel*, by E. J. FINBERT [Paris, 1955], p. 422 ff.). Here also notice the form of the names which do not contain the element Yahweh : Osee (**13** : 8; *Hoshe'a*, in Hebrew) is significantly changed by Moses to Josue (**13** : 6 : Yehoshū'a), the oldest name with " Yahweh " (the etymology of Jochebed (Yokebed), Moses' mother [Ex. **6** : 20], regarded by many as containing Yahweh, is uncertain). The new name is a program for the man who is to carry on Moses' work (cf. EDELKOORT, p. 131). (2) **13** : 25-33 (JE) : The spies bring back a pessimistic report (28-29, 31-33) in which Caleb and Josue (14 : 16) do not concur (30). (3) **14** : 1-9 (JEP throughout **14**). The pessimistic report alarms the people (1-4) in spite of the appeals of Josue and Caleb (5-9). V. 9 : " Their defense has left them; Hebrew : " Their (protecting) shade " = " their gods ". Cf. the places where God's protection is described as His shade : Osee **14** : 8; Ps. **90** (91) : 1; Ps. **120** (121) : 5; " the shade of His hand": Isa. **49** : 2; **51** : 16, etc. (4) **14**: 10-19: Moses pleads with God for the rebellious people who were ready to stone Josue and Caleb (10^a). (5) **14** : 20-38 : God forgives, but the present generation shall not enter the promised land, but only their children and the faithful Josue and Caleb (22-24 and 29-31). Note here the two parallel traditions : 11-25 and 26-35, the latter attributed to P. The concluding verses (36-38) report the punishment of the scouts whose report was responsible for the disturbance (**13** : 22). Naturally Josue and Caleb are excepted. We have here only an allusion to an undefined punishment which must have followed promptly upon their report, and to be interpreted as an act of God. For the Hebrew phrase in 37ª (had given out the bad report about the land (cf. Gen. **37**: 2), see C. BROCKELMANN: *Vergleich-ende Gram.* 2, p. 353, and reff.; and *Hebräische Syntax* 103ª).

(6) **14** : 39-45 (JE). Reacting violently from despair to presumption, the people, against Moses' entreaty, undertake unsuccessfully to invade S. Palestine. Horma (anathema) v. 45 : for the origin of the name see Num. **21** : 1-3; Jdgs. **1** : 17. The place in the Negeb (S. Palestine) is identified with Tell Meshash, between Tell Arad and Bersabee (cf. GROLLENBERG, *Atlas*, Map 9).

f) **15–19.** A group of religious prescriptions attributed to P for the most part : laws in **15**, **18–19** and the account of the rebellion of Core, etc., in **16-17** to show the divine appointment of priests and Levites.

I. **15.** (1) **15** : 1-16 : a law about sacrifices supplementing those of Lev. **1–3** : bread, wine and oil as a cereal offering (*minhah*) accompanying animal offerings (with 2, cf. Ex. **29** : 18; Lev. **8** : 21; **23** : 13, etc.). This is presented as intended for the conditions after the conquest (v. 2). (2) **15** : 17-21 supposes the same conditions (18ᵇ) : sacred contributions from the wheat (bread) of the land. (3) **15** : 22-31 : sin-offerings for unwitting guilt on the part of the community (22-26) or of one individual (27-29). Deliberate sin entails being " cut off from among the people " (30-31). Notice in v. 30, literally, " with an uplifted hand " = " deliberately ", " defiantly " (so only here to describe a man's action). The matter is treated more fully in Lev. **4.** Thus even unintentional failure to observe a commandment involves some kind of disorder which must be expiated. (4) **15** : 32-36 : A man breaks the Sabbath by gathering wood. How such a case is to be handled is settled by a revelation to Moses : the penalty is death by stoning (cf. Lev. **20** : 2, 27; **24** : 14, 16, 23). Here, as Lev. **24** : 10 ff. and Num. **9** : 6 ff., a particular case serves as the occasion of a general rule. (5) **15** : 37-41 : Tassels are to be worn on the cloak as a reminder of the commandments; cf. Mt. **9** : 20 f.; **23** : 5; Lev. **19** : 36; **22** : 33; **25** : 38.

II. **16-17**. Cf. S. R. DRIVER, *Introduction*, pp. 63-65; A. CONDAMIN, S. J., in *RSR* (1912), 123 ff. H. SCHNEIDER, *Nummer*, in *Echter Bibel* [1954], p. 43 ff.) does not mention the different traditions in this section, but his interpretation — that there were two rebellions of different character — agrees with the usual literary analysis. N. Schlögl's translation (cf. E. P. ARBEZ, *CBQ* [1954], 343-345) gives a separate translation of each episode, which agrees with the common literary analysis (pp. 214-217). P. P. SAYDON (in *Catholic Commentary on Holy Scripture* [1951], p. 252 f.) says that " the narrative shows signs of being composite... ". " It is not improbable that two stories relating similar incidents have been amalgamated into one narrative". HARTOM (*Entzyklop. Miq. 2*, 141-142) shows quite well the difficulties of the text if one takes it as a straight account of one single happening. Cf. also his Commentary, and that of J. H. HERTZ, *Pentateuch and Haftorot*, p. 634 f. The note in the new Catholic Version (on **16** : 1 ff.) explains very well that there were " two distinct rebellions ". So also a brief note on **16** in Nácar-Colunga's *Sagrada Biblia* (Madrid, 1949; cf. E. P. ARBEZ, *CBQ* (1954), pp. 452-453) says that it could well be that we have here two distinct episodes. We have in these chapters a composite narrative which combines into one two distinct events, viz., a) a political rebellion of Dathan and Abiram which challenges Moses' civil authority, and b) a religious rebellion of Core and his band against Aaron and Moses as religious leaders.

(1) **16** : 1ᵃ-2ᵇ, 12-15, 25-34 : J and E's account of the rebellion of laymen from the tribe of Ruben, headed by Dathan and Abiram, against Moses' civil authority. Their complaints are inspired by the failure to carry out the promised conquest (14) and by resentment of Moses' civil rule (13ᵇ-15ᵇ). Their punishment — being swallowed up alive by the earth together with their families and possessions (30-33) — is God's judgment against Dathan and Abiram.

(2) **16** : 1ᵃ, 2ᵇ — 11, 16-24, 35; **17** : 1-15 (Hebrew; in the
Vulgate and older English versions [A. V., R. V., S. R. V.] it
= **16** : 36-50. The Confraternity Version follows the Hebrew;
its 35ᵃ is 27ᵃ, which has been transposed by the editors.   To
avoid confusion, a note should have called attention to the
fact that its 27 = 27ᵇ, and 35 = 27ᵃ and 35).   This is P's
account of the rebellion of Core, a Levite of the clan of Caath,
as the leader of a group of 250 prominent men of the community
(**16** : 2ᵃ, 17, 35; cf. **16** : 6, 19, 21; **17** : 5 = Vulg. **16** : 40).   Those
followers of Core are not all of them Levites; cf. **27** : 3 where
the daughters of a man of the tribe of Manasse state that their
father did not die in Core's rebellion — a needless point if all
of Core's followers had been Levites.   The rebellion is religious :
they resent the reservation of priestly rights to the tribe of
Levi (**16** : 3-4, 8-10).   Moses challenges them to a trial : let
them attempt to exercise priestly functions (**16** : 6-7, 16-18).
God will decide, and He does decide (**16** : 35) by sending a fire
which consumes the rebels (**17** : 5 = Vulg. **16** : 40).   Moses
has the censers of Core and his followers rescued to make
a covering for the altar (**17** : 1-5 = **16** : 36-40).   The people
murmur again.   God is ready to destroy them, but Aaron
intervenes and makes atonement.   However, before the scourge
was checked, 14,700 persons had died (**17** : 6-15 = **16** : 41-50).

Thus, according to the analysis of the text, there are two
different events : one connected with Dathan and Abiram,
the other with Core.   The character of the rebellion is different
in both cases, and also the place and the nature of the punishment of the guilty parties.   In the present text, some glosses
have brought together the three names Core, Dathan, and
Abiram, with the result that there seems at first to have been
only one movement headed by these three personages.   Thus,
16 : 24 and 35 (cf. note above on 35).   But here, the word
Dwelling (rightly spelled here with a capital) is the word
Mishkan, a term used most frequently in Ex., Lev., Num.,
of the Tent or Tabernacle, Yahweh's abode (cf. **16** : 19; **17** : 28).
The tents of the rebels are denoted by the usual word (*Ohel*,
26, 27ᵇ).   Hence the presumption that in **16** : 24 and 35ᵃ
(= 27ᵃ), the reference is to Yahweh's Dwelling, and thus the
three names are an intrusion (so also P. P. Saydon, *op. cit.*,
p. 253, on v. 24, for the meaning of *Mishkan*).   Besides, there

was not one single place which could be described sa the dwelling place of their three men : they and their families each had their tents in different parts of the camp. Further, the place where the trial takes place is the space before the Tabernacle in the case of Core and his group (**16** : 16 Heb.) and there God's judgment takes place (**16** : 21-24 and 35 = 27ᵃ and 35). In the case of Dathan and Abiram, God's judgment manifests itself where their tents stand (**16** : 25-26, and 27ᵇ-34). Thus there is no reason for bringing together the three names in question and for connecting them with the Dwelling (of Yahweh). It is clear, then, that here in **16** : 32, " and all of Core's men ", is a gloss. Finally, further references in the Bible keep the case of Core and that of Dathan-Abiram distinct : Num. **26** : 9-11 and **27** : 3 = Core; Deut. **11** : 6 = the Rubenites Dathan-Abiram; so also in Ps. **105** (106) : 17 = Dathan and Abiram swallowed up by the earth. As regards **16** : 1 f., it should be noted that the text is doubtful grammatically, and needs some correcting on any view. The literal translation of the Hebrew (MT) will make this clear : 1. " And there took (verb in sing.) Core son of J., son of C., son of L, and Dathan and Abiram sons of Eliab, and On son of Peleth, sons of Ruben (= Rubenites) ", 2. " And they stood before Moses, and men of the Israelites 250, princes of the community, called of (= to) the council, men of note ". Certainly, this text is obscure and confused : 1 is clearly incomplete, and 2 definitely unsatisfactory. One need only compare the various versions to see that they try, unsuccessfully, to get something out of the Masoretic Text. The new Catholic Version tries to remedy the situation (in part) by the use of brackets. Note that the verb " took " has no object, and possibly should be changed. On, son of Peleth, plays no part whatsoever in the rest of the narrative; to say that he withdrew from the movement at once is a gratuitous hypothesis. In 2, the 250 men are introduced awkwardly : Hebrew grammar requires another construction.

We may therefore suspect the present form of vv. 1-2 and try to correct the text — though the positive solution of the difficulty is uncertain. Some points however are sufficiently clear : On should be dropped, and is dropped quite generally (e.g., Mezzacasa, in *La Sacra Bibbia* [Pontif. Bibl. Inst.] I, p. 352, cf. p. 519. Cf. E. P. ARBEZ, *CBQ* [1954], pp. 455-457;

Cantera, in *Sagrada Bibbia* I, pp. 254 and 287, notes;
cf. E. P. ARBEZ, *ibid.*, 454 f.; also *Leidsche Vertaling;*
cf. E. P. ARBEZ, *ibid.*, 202; Messel [Norwegian Bible],
cf. E. P. ARBEZ, *ibid.*, 205-207), etc. The 250 men go with
Core : they are evidently his band (cf. **16** : 5, 6, 17, 19, 21,
32, 35). Hence possibly : (1) : " Core son of Ishar, son of
Caath, son of Levi, took (?) (2ᵃ) 250 men of the Israelites ... men
of note "; then 1ᵇ " Dathan and Abiram, sons of Eliab son of
Peleth (= Phallu; Num. **26** : 5, 8, 9), son of Ruben (cf. LXX
Sam.; Hebr. Mss), (2) stood before Moses ". Thus, we have
the introduction to two rebellious movements, both incomplete
but especially so in the case of Dathan and Abiram. The
present text obscures the point by throwing all the names
together in an ungrammatical sentence. (For brevity's sake,
we omit the discussion of possible additions in the Core-narrative
expressing different points of view. On this, see, e.g.,
S. R. Driver's, *Introduction*, pp. 64-65 or Messel's note in
op. cit., p. 287).

(3) **17** : 16-26 = Vulg. **17** : 1-11 (P) : Aaron's staff. The
miraculous sprouting of Aaron's staff alone among those of
the twelve Tribes deposited in the Sanctuary shows that God
has chosen the Tribe of Levi. The miraculous staff preserved
in the Sanctuary shall be a lasting " warning to the
rebellious " (25).

(4) **17** : 27-28 = Vulg. **17** : 12-13. It is conjectured that
these verses belong after **16** : 35 (so e.g., EDELKOORT, *op. cit.*,
153; *Bible du Centenaire*, *Bible de Jérusalem*, Confraternity
Version), or after **17** : 15 = Vulg. **16** : 50 (so Messel). In their
present place, they form a transition to the following section :
a law concerning the Tribe of Levi to which is reserved the
awful privilege of approaching Yahweh's Dwelling *(Leidsche
Vertaling; Bible du Centenaire)*.

III. **18** (P). On the clergy. (Cf. NÖTSCHER, *Biblische
Altertumskunde* [Bonn, 1940], pp. 305-320; Haag, *Bibellexikon*,
cols. 1361-1364). The Tribe of Levi is chosen by God for his
service in the Sanctuary. There are four sections : three of
them addressed to Aaron (**18** : 1, 8, 20) (cf. Lev. **10** : 8, where
also Aaron is addressed alone) and one to Moses (**18** : 25).

(1) **18** : 1-7 : Only Aaron and his descendants are the priests responsible for the service of the Sanctuary and the Altar (1ᵇ, 5ᵇ, 7); the other members of the Tribe of Levi, their kinsmen — the Levites — are to be their assistants (2ᵃ, 3, 4, 6). No " stranger " (*zār* : " layman ", in new Catholic Version), i.e., unauthorized person, may presume to fulfill functions reserved to priests or Levites (4b, 7b). Note the play on words : the verb rendered " to be associated with " (*lāwāh*) 2 and 4 and the name Levi (*Lēwi*) are connected by popular etymology (cf. Ancient S. Arabic *lwi* = " priest "). To be responsible, etc., in Hebrew is " to bear the guilt " = " responsibility ", " to be liable for "; v. 6, " dedicated to "; literally, " given " (as in Num. **3** : 9; **8** : 16, 19).

(2) **18** : 8-19 : The priests' revenue is defined from the various offerings and sacrifices, and what members of their families may partake of them (**8** ff.; **11** ff.). This paragraph sums up and gathers together in a convenient form what has been stated in other places. There are similar tariffs of priests' income from the Ancient Orient : a list from Sippar (in Babylonia) in the 9th century B.C.; lists from the Punic world (viz., that found in Marseilles in 1845 from about 300 B.C., one found in Carthage in 1858, and another found there in 1872). Nothing of course demands a late date for the table in 8-19, which is more complete than the other texts (cf. EDELKOORT, *op. cit.*, p. 154).

(3) **18** : 20-24 : revenues of the Levites. Instead of a territory to be assigned in the allotment of the land (24) — cf. Deut. **10** : 9, Jos. **13** : 14; Num. **35** : 6 — the Levites receive all tithes in Israel. Compare this with the regulation of the tithes in Deut. **14** : 28-29, and **26** : 12 which assigns to the Levites the tithes of every third year to be shared with the alien, the orphan, and the widow, and Num. **35** : 1-8, where the Levites receive in different parts of Palestine a certain number of cities with some land around them. These groups of tents naturally correspond to different developments in the economic status of the Levites. (Cf. the Mishnah treatises, *Ma'aserot, Ma'aser sheni*, and *Pe'āh* on the tithes, e.g., in H. DANBY, *The Mishnah* [Eng. transl., Oxford, 1933], pp. 66 ff., 73 ff., and 10 ff.).

(4) **18** : 25-32 : The tithe of the tithes (25; Neh. **10** : 39) is to be paid by the Levites to the priests.

IV. **19** (P). (1) **19** : 1-10 : the ashes of the red heifer. The directions are addressed to Moses (the name of Aaron in 1 is an addition; in 2, " tell " and " to you " = 2nd sing. in Hebr.), to be relayed to Eleazar, who carries out the ceremonies outside the camp (For the hyssop, cf. Y. FELIKS, *Plant World of the Bible* [Tel Aviv, 1957, in Hebr.], pp. 177-179; for cedar, *ibid.*, pp. 76-78; *Entzyklo. Miq.* I, pp. 185-186 (" *Ezob* ") and pp. 553-555 (" *Erez* "); for crimson red dye, Corswant, *Diction. d'Archéol. Biblique*, p. 97). The use of the lustral water is described (11 ff.; cf. Num. **31** : 9 for a mention of the lustral water). This ritual finds analogies in the magical rites of many other peoples, who also regarded contact with a corpse as unclean. We have here as in Lev. **14** : 2 ff. (purification after leprosy), Num. **5** : 10 ff. (suspected adulteress), Deut. **21** : 1 ff. (expiation of untraced death) survival of ancient customs — ultimately out of a magic background — taken over and adapted by the Mosaic Religion. Note the predominance of red : red heifer, blood, cedar wood, red dye (or yarn). In Babylonia, cedar wood played a part in the ritual of cleansing (" holy water ") (cf. EDELKOORT, *op. cit.*, p. 157; Corswant, *op. cit.*, p. 306). The Mishnah has a treatise, *Parāh* (" Heifer ") [DANBY, *op. cit.*, p. 697 ff.] on the subject. (2) **19** : 11-22 : a supplement to Lev. 11-16. Serious uncleanness results from contact with a corpse or anything connected with death (11-13). Purification from such uncleanness (14-22).

V. **20–22** (JE, and P) : The journey from Cades to Moab.

(1) **20** : 1 : Miriam dies and is buried at Cades. The indications of time and place are somewhat vague : " in the first month ". It is surmised that this refers to the third year (Cf. the last preceding date : the second month of the second year [**10** : 11] when the people left Sinai; then they come to the Desert of Pharan [**12** : 16; **13** : 3] and settle in Cades [**13** : 26]). In that case, almost a year has passed since leaving Sinai. The region of Cades — where Israel spent so much time — is referred to here (cf. **13** : 21; **27** : 14; **33** : 36) as the Desert of Sin (Tsin), elsewhere as Pharan.

(2) **20** : 2-5 : Lack of water causes complaints (cf. **11** : 1 ff.; **14** : 1 ff.).

(3) **20** : 6-13 : At God's command, Moses strikes the rock with the staff " from its place before the Lord " (9). Cf. **17** : 23, thus, of Aaron's staff. But this may be a gloss to identify the staff referred to in more general terms in 8. Water gushes forth in abundance (7-11). Moses and Aaron are told that as a punishment for their sin they shall not be allowed to enter the Promised Land (12; Deut. **32** : 49-52). The present context does not explain really the precise nature of their sin (cf. **20** : 24). Commentators try to find it in the words of Moses (10) and in the fact that he struck the rock twice (11), but this does not appear clearly in the text. Hence some look for another original context of 12. (Cf. *Bible de Jérusalem*). V. 13 explains the name Meriba (" contention ") from the " contending " of the people against Yahweh (cf. Ex. **17** : 7; Deut. **33** : 8).

(4) **20** : 14-21 : negotiations with Edom (related to Israel; cf. Gen. **25** : 25; **32** : 4; **36**. On this section, cf. N. GLUECK, *BA* [1947], p. 80 f.; Haag, *Bibellexikon*, pp. 352-355; A. ROBERT, " Idumée ", *DBV*, *Suppl.*, IV, 195-198; and especially the article in *Entzykl. Miq.* 1, pp. 91-103, by N. Glueck and Loewenstamm). The Semites (Edom) dispossessed the earlier population (Horrite, or Hurrian; cf. CONTENAU, *DBV*, *Suppl.*, IV, pp. 128-138; *Entzykl. Miq.* 3 [1958], pp. 57-63), and founded a kingdom around the 13th century B.C. Edom was a strong, prosperous kingdom. Its strong natural borders were protected by powerful fortresses. To force a passage through the territory would have meant a war with great losses for Israel. The situation is that in the 13th century, which confirms a late date for the Exodus. When their request for passage through the land is refused, Israel avoids Edomite territory.

(5) **20** : 22-29 : Aaron's death at Mt. Hor, which is to be sought in the region of Cades (cf. Num. **33** : 30-31; Deut. **10** : 6; cf. A. ROBERT, *DBV*, *Suppl.*, IV, 196), but definitely not at Petra in the heart of Edom, as Josephus has it (*Ant.* **4** : 4, 7 = **4** : 82-83; cf. the note in Vol. II, p. 79, 52, of Shalit's Hebrew transl. of the *Antiquities*). His son Eleazar is invested in his place (cf. **17** : 1 ff.). A month's mourning marks Aaron's

death. All at once, with this narrative we are at the end
of the forty years wandering (Num. 33 : 38; Aaron's death
is dated the first of the fifth month of the year 40 of the Exodus;
cf. Num. 14 : 33; Deut. 1 : 3; 2 : 7; 8 : 2; 29 : 4). The Israelites
had left Sinai on the 20th of the second month of year 2 of the
Exodus (10 : 11); they are in the Desert of Pharan at Cades
(13 : 26) when the scouts return from their exploring. Of the
long period in Cades — 38 years? — we know practically
nothing.

VI. 21 : Incidents after leaving Cades.

(1) 21 : 1-3 (JE) : Victory over the Canaanites at Arad —
Tell Arad about twenty miles S. of Hebron. The name Horma
(" doom ", " destruction ") is explained from the verb *haram*,
" to doom ", and the fulfilment of the vow in case of victory.
Horma was between Tell Arad and Bersabee in the Negeb.
The name recalls the episode of 14 : 39-45, where Israel suffered
a defeat at the hand of the Canaanites. H. Wiener (see above
on Chap. 12) proposes to place this paragraph somewhere
before 14 : 39 ff. : Israel had won a victory (21 : 1-3), but was
afterwards defeated (14 : 39 ff.). Another hypothesis is that
the event is the same as that in Jdgs. 1 : 16 f., though in this
latter context the attack comes from the N., and in Num.
from the S. The fact is that, though 21 : 1-3 clearly breaks
the sequence between 20 : 22-29 (the scene is Mt Hor) and
21 : 4 ff. (they leave from Mt. Hor), we cannot fit 21 : 1-3 into
a satisfactory context. Is this a part of a narrative of an
attempted invasion from the S? Whether it is so or not, it
is not explained why the success was not followed up. In 21 : 1
Israel comes by " the way of Atharim " (otherwise unknown) :
so the Masoretic Text and LXX. All the ancient versions
and the interpretation of the ancient Rabbis and Jewish
commentators of the Middle Ages suppose *ha-tarim :* " the
explorers ", " scouts ".

(2) 21 : 4-9 (JE) : the brazen serpent. Israel resumes
its march through the difficulties of the desert; hence new
murmurings. They advance in a S. direction, to by-pass
Edom, towards the Eastern Red Sea, the Gulf of Aqaba. Against
the plague of the saraph serpents (burning serpents), Moses
sets up on a pole a bronze serpent the sight of which will save

those bitten by a serpent. Cf. 2 Kgs. **18** : 4 : the bronze saraph preserved in the Temple where it had become an object of worship, known as the Nahestan (Nehushtan) from *nahash* " serpent " (Num. **21** : 6, 7, 9) and *nehoshet*, " bronze ", Num. **21** : 9. See Jn. **3** : 14; 1 Cor. **10** : 9; cf. WIS, **16** : 5-7. In **21** : 5 and 7, " complained ", is literally " spoke against ". Here G. R. Driver translates, " turned against " (cf. on **12** : 1-2).

(3) **21** : 10-20 (JE) : journey to Moab. (Cf. E. G. KRAELING, *Bible Atlas*, pp. 118-125, and map, p. 233; GROLLENBERG, Plates, pp. 52-55, Text, pp. 56-57, and map, p. 44; VILNAY, *Ha aretz ba-miqrā'*, with notes on the names, pp. 4-11). The text is fragmentary, only some places of encampment being mentioned. Their identification is doubtful. Obot (10) = el Weibe, W of the Araba, about thirty miles S. of the Dead Sea (Num. **33** : 43). Ijeabarim (Jyye ha-Abarim = ruins of A. (?) " in the desert fronting Moab on the East ". Abarim is apparently the mountain range of the Abarim; cf. **27** : 12; **33** : 47-48; Deut. **32** : 49. In this case it would be the range with Mt. Nebo in Moab opposite Jericho; thus a jump from Obot W. of the Araba to Transjordania in the E. (but cf. Kraeling, *op. cit.*, p. 122 f.). The Wadi Zared (12) is generally taken to be the Wadi el Hasa or el Qurāhī which flows into the Dead Sea from the S.E. N. of the Zared we are in Moab. This brings us considerably S. of the preceding point. Thence they advanced to the other or north side of the Arnon (13), the Wady el Mojib, which enters the Dead Sea about the middle of its E. shore. The Arnon is the boundary between Moab and the Amorites N. of Moab. The Amorites had driven the Moabites to the S. of the Arnon. Then they moved on to Beer (= Well) (16) = Beer Elim (Isa. **15** : 8), somewhere around the beginning of El-Wale, a N. affluent of the Arnon (?). From Beer (18b) they went to Mattanah (18), thence to Nahaliel (19), then to Bamoth (19-20); = Bamot Baal (Num. **22** : 41; Jos. **13** : 17) and the cleft in the plateau of Moab near Phasga (Pisga) = Rās siyagha near Mt. Nebo (20) (cf. KRAELING, *op. cit.*, pp. 125-128), which overlooks the desert (Jesimon). (Cf. GROLLENBERG, Map, p. 44, and p. 59). This is the end of the journey : Israel is ready to cross the Jordan. Some lines of ancient poetry are quoted — as is done often in Arabic narratives, interrupting even if enlivening the story. One

is a quotation from the "Book of the Wars of Yahweh ",
a lost work which apparently sang the " *Gesta Dei per Israel* "
(vv. 14-15). The other lines (vv. 17-18) are from the " Song
of the Well " *(Beer)* which possibly also belonged to the " Book
of the Wars ". The analysis of **21** : 10-20 shows gaps in the
list of the encampments and some difficulties in the geographical
sequence, in so far as the names can be identified. Before
conclusions may be drawn, we should take into account the
lists of Num. and Deut.

(4) **21** : **21–22** : **1** : Kings Sehon and Og.

a) 21-31 (cf. KRAELING, *Atlas*, 122 ff.). Sehon (Sihon) had
defeated the former king of Moab and conquered the land
from the Arnon (S.) to the Jabboc (Nahr ez-Zerqā) (N.), an
E. affluent of the Jordan about twenty-five miles N. of the
Dead Sea (24-26). His capital was Hesebon (Heshbōn, modern
Hesbān) about ten miles from Mt. Nebo (26). Sehon refuses
Israel's request (for peaceful passage S. to N.) and engages
Israel in battle near Jahas (Yahas) a famous city mentioned
several times in the Bible (Jos. **13** : 18; Jdgs. **11** : 20; Isa **15** : 4;
Jer. **48** : 21, 34), and in the 9th century inscription of King
Mesa (Mesha‹) of Moab (2 Kgs. **3** : 4). The territory later
was allotted to the Tribe of Ruben (24-25, 31; Jos. **13** : 15 ff.).
An Amorite poem celebrating their conquest of Moab is quoted
(vv. 27-30; cf. Lagrange, *RB* [1899], pp. 541-552). In 28,
" cities of Moab " is a conjecture for, *Ar Moab* of the Masoretic
Text which = Ar of **15**; the high places of the Arnon = Bamot
(vv. 19-20). In 29, Chamos = Kemōsh, the national god of
Moab, known from the Mesa Inscription and Babylonian
texts; cf. 1 Kgs. **11** : 7, 33 f.; 2 Kgs. **23** : 13; Jer. **48** : 7, 13, 46.
The translation of 30 is conjectured; the passage in the MT
gives no satisfactory sense.

b) 32–22 : 1 : Moses sends men to reconnoiter the land
to Jazer (Ya‹zer) = Khirbet Jizzir (?), about twelve miles
N. of Hesebon. As Israel turns E. to the land of Basan (Bashan),
King Og gives battle at Edrai (Der'a) much further N., about
sixty miles S. of Damascus. His defeat leaves the territory
in the hands of Israel. Thus in two blitz campaigns — as they
are related here — Israel becomes master of Eastern Palestine
(modern Transjordania), the land from the Arnon (S.) to the

S. end of the Sea of Genesaret, to be occupied by (S. to N.) Ruben, Gad, and Manasse. (On this part of E. Palestine, see : *Westminster Atlas* [1945], Map, 20ᵇ; GROLLENBERG, Map, 14; KRAELING, *op. cit.*, p. 122; N. GLUECK, *Explorations in Eastern Palestine* [ASOR, 1951], pp. 238-404; *id.*, *Eastern Transjordan* [Jerusalem, 1945; in Hebr.]). The section concludes with the notice (22 : 1) that after this Israel encamped in the plains of Moab, " on the other side of the Jordan, opposite Jericho ". The geographical standpoint of the writer, as remarked often, is that of one who is W. of the Jordan, in W. Palestine, looking E. across the Jordan. (On this geographical standpoint, cf. GOETTSBERGER, *Einleitung*, p. 60; E. F. SUTCLIFFE, S. J., in *Catholic Commentary on Holy Scripture*, [1953], p. 171, par. 134 a; cf. M. S. SEGAL, Mebō' ha-Miqrā [Jerusalem, 1945; in Hebr.], I, p. 134).

C. **22 : 2–36 : 13.**   On the Plains of Moab.

I. Balaam : **22 : 2–24 : 25.**   According to most critics this section represents JE, though it is admitted that the distribution of the elements is uncertain. According to A. Haldar these are very ancient traditions which cannot be attributed to any of the supposed sources, JE. (*Svenskt Bibliskt Uppslagsverk*, I, p. 280). He believes the oracles of Balaam are of high antiquity, *ca.* 1200 B.C.; so also does Albright. But cf. MOWINCKEL (*Han som Kommer* [Copenhagen, 1951], p. 19 f., and p. 295, n. 11), who questions that date. The text is admittedly difficult. Hence all kinds of corrections have been proposed. Albright has the merit of making few radical changes, so that his text remains close to the traditional form. (Cf. also HARTOM (below), p. 144; JUNKER, *Prophet und Seher im Alten Israel*, p. 79 ff.; E. BURROWS, S. J., *The Oracles of Jacob and Balaam* [Bellarmine Series, London, 1939]; E. SUTCLIFFE, S. J., *Biblica* [1926], pp. 9-18; 31-39; [1937], 439 ff.; W. F. ALBRIGHT, *Journal of Biblical Literature*, [Sept., 1944]; HARTOM in *Entzyklop. Miqr.* 2, pp. 142-144 [p. 143, for the views of the critics]). In NT, cf. 2 Pet. **2** : 15; Jude 11; Apocal. **2** : 14.

Though the Jewish tradition attributes the whole Pentateuch to Moses, it notes in a special way that this section is also itself his work; probably because Moses' name does not appear anywhere here (cf. HARTOM, *Comment.*, p. 87 [in Hebr.]; SEGAL, *Mebō ha-Miqrā*, I, p. 99). Balaam is an enigmatic figure. He is a famous soothsayer or seer in Pethor (= Pitru) on the Euphrates in the land of 'Amaw (Amau) (**22** : 5). He seems to be a worshipper of Yahweh (**22** : 8, 18); he receives revelations from God (**22** : 9 ff., 20), and professes to be able to act only as God directs him (**22** : 12-13, 18-20, 34-35, 38; **23** : 26; **24** : 13). He lives as it were in a supernatural world : divine communications do not surprise him (**22** : 12; **23** : 4-16); the conduct of the talking ass does not appear strange to him (**22** : 28-30). He is regarded as one whose word is powerful (**22** : 6-11). Hence the king summons him to curse Israel, as this will bring about the defeat of Israel. This is a procedure before war (cf. BENTZEN, *Innledning*, p. 253 f.; CASSUTO, s.v. " Berākāh u. Qelālāh, *Entzyklop. Miq.* 2, pp. 356-358). We find examples of this kind of poetry — comminatory utterances regarded as having magical power — in Ancient Arab poetry (e.g., GIBB : *Arabic Literature* [London, 1926], p. 14; R. NICHOLSON, *A Literary History of the Arabs* [London, 1923], p. 72 ff.).

(1) **22** : 1-14 : Balac king of Moab, alarmed at the advance of Israel, asks Balaam to come and curse Israel. Warned by God, Balaam refuses to accompany Balac's envoys. Phathur (5 = Petor) has long been identified with Pitru of the cuneiform texts, on the Euphrates, in the region of Carchemish, some 400 miles from Moab. (Cf. A. L. OPPENHEIM, in Pritchard, *ANET*, p. 278ᵇ; Luckenbill, *Records of Assyria and Babylonia* [Chicago, 1926-27], I, 646 and 647). Strictly speaking, Pitru — a name given by the Hittites — is on the other side of the Euphrates, on the Sagur (modern Sājūr). (Cf. the Monolith-Inscription of Salmanasar III (858-824) in Pritchard, *ANET*, p. 278ᵇ). The difficulty comes from the next words : " in the land of the sons of his people " (MT). An error was suspected, but the conjectures to remedy the error only complicated matters (See the different views in Loewenstamm, *Entzykl. Miq.* 2, pp. 133-134). In fact, without any change in the Hebrew word, " his people ", we should read the proper name " *Amaw* "; hence the land of the sons of Amaw = the Amawites. This is one of the districts of the kingdom of Alalakh mentioned by prince Idrimi (*ca.* 1450 B.C.), son of the king. This was recognized by W. F. ALBRIGHT, *BASOR*, no. 118, [1950],

14-20. Hence the translation of the new Catholic Version, *RSV*, *Bible de Jérusalem*, (so also Mazar [Maisler] in *Entzykl. Miq.* 2, 178, s.v. " Beney 'Ammo "). Cf. *CBQ* (1951), p. 104 f. On the statue of Idrimi, see S. SMITH, *The Statue of Idrimi* (London, 1949; cf. *RB* [1950], pp. 474-476); Sir L. WOOLLEY, *Alalakh : An Account of the Excavations at Tell Atchana in the Hatay* (London, 1955); *id.*, *A Forgotten Kingdom* [1953; a Penguin Book], pp. 117-126, 160, 164). On Balaam's knowledge of Yahweh, see H. CAZELLES in *Bible de Jérusalem*, I, p. 107.

(2) **22** : 15-21 : Again Balac sends envoys to Balaam with a promise of a handsome reward. Balaam's answer again is that he cannot do anything contrary to the will of Yahweh. During the night, the seer is directed to go with the men, but he must do exactly as God tells him. He leaves the next morning with the princes of Moab. Cf. **22** : 18, 35, 38; **23** : 12, 26; **24** : 13, for his rule of conduct.

(3) **22** : 23-35 : the journey to Balac. This clashes violently with the preceding section where God has granted His permission. Nothing in the text allows us to suspect that God's wrath is due to Balaam's secret intention to curse Israel for the promised reward. When he realizes the cause of the ass's strange conduct — the Angel of Yahweh blocking the way (31) — he is ready to give up the journey (32-34), but he is given permission to proceed (35). All we may gather from the text is that — in this section — Balaam undertook the journey of himself without consulting God. This then represents a different tradition. In the end, however, here also Balaam is allowed to go with the warning that he must say only what God tells him. We may only surmise from this narrative that the journey originally was not approved by God : Balaam excuses himself by pleading that he did not know (34), without any mention of any previous permission given by God (20).

This account (**22** : 22-35) is not of a piece with the preceding parts. It is rather a fragment of another tradition about Balaam. It may be explained as a satire in a dramatic form. A renowned seer-magician undertakes a long journey at the invitation of Balac, an enemy of Israel, to curse God's people. The great seer, credited with the knowledge of things supernatural, does not see the angel who bars his way, but the ass sees him. In his blindness, Balaam gives vent to his anger and beats the poor beast. When he finally sees, it is to hear the angel telling him that he was ready to strike him down, but to spare the animal. Surely a ridiculous situation for such a famous seer to find himself in. The situation is dramatized by the story teller, who for this uses the resources of popular art. This does not mean that the writer is a " primitive ", for the popular form can be used to convey a great lesson : God is the sovereign Lord who makes men pliable instruments in his hand and is able to thwart their evil purposes against His people. There is also implicit a spiritual truth : when one deliberately goes against God's will and follows his own mind, one loses the faculty of discerning spiritual values and falls lower than an animal. (Cf. this exposition of the problem with that given by Saydon [*Catholic Commentary on Holy Scripture*, p. 256] and Nácar [*Sagrada Biblia*, p. 209]. There is no intention of making them responsible for the views expressed here).

(4) **22** : 36-40 : meeting of Balac and Balaam. For Ir Moab (36) several prefer Ar Moab mentioned before (**21** : 15, 28). Here apparently the reference is to a city; Ar Moab may also be the Moabite territory, according to Grollenberg, *op. cit.*, p. 143, s.v. The scene of the meeting, however, is not identified definitively, nor is the other place Cariat Husoth (39) (Qiryat Husot), for which LXX has Qiryat Haserōt. (Cf. KRAELING, *Atlas*, p. 125 f.). Balaam reminds Balac of his obligation and limitation (38[b]).

(5) **22** : 41–**23** : 12 : the first oracle. The next morning, from Bamoth Baal (**21** : 19-20), whence he sees a small part of the encampment (See LOEWENSTAMM, *Entzykl. Miq.* 2, 153 for the possible identification). Balaam prepares for the oracle by offering sacrifices on seven altars (seven is a sacred number) and God puts an utterance in his mouth. Note the better logical sequence if one reads the verses in the following order : 2, 4[b], 3, 4[a] (so the New Catholic Version, with Kittel-Kahle after Mowinckel). The oracle (7-10) is a praise of Israel whom God has blessed : a people set apart as the Chosen People, an immense multitude (10[a]; cf. Gen. **13** : 16; **28** : 14).

(6) **23 : 13-26 :** the second oracle. Balac takes Balaam to the top of Phasga (**21 : 20**). There again seven altars are built for sacrifices, as on the first occasion. Balaam meets God and comes back with his oracle (13-24). Again it is a blessing, uttered by God who does not change his mind and fulfills his promise. Balaam can only repeat God's blessing — no prophecy of evil for Israel who is under God's protection, against whom no sorcery has any power, whose strength is irresistible. The interpretation of some verses is uncertain. Thus 23 is understood by many to say that there is no divination in Israel; there is no need for it: God will make his will known through his prophets.

(7) **23 : 27–24 : 13 :** the third oracle. Balac takes Balaam to another place, to the top of Phogor (Pe'or) overlooking the Desert *(ha-yeshimon)* (cf. LOEWENSTAMM, *Entzykl. Miq.*, 2, pp. 289-290). The same preparations are made as on the previous occasions, but this time Balaam does not go to meet God. When he beholds the encampment of Israel, the spirit of God comes upon him and he delivers his oracle (3-9). The opening lines (3·4) — cf. 15^b-16, after which they are corrected — present Balaam as a true prophet inspired by God. Vv. 5-7 describe the splendor and the greatness of Israel. The Hebrew in 6^b compares the camp to " aloe trees planted by Yahweh ". The difficulty is that the stately, longlived aloe tree, an Indian tree, is unknown to Palestine. Hence various suggestions (Cf. YEH. FELIKS, *World of Plants in the Scripture* [in Hebrew], p. 255; M. ZAHARI, *Entzykl. Miq.* 1, pp. 128-129). V. 7 is still more doubtful, especially in its first part. The second part refers to the greatness of Israel's future king. The Greek is quite different; hence the translation of the *Bible de Jérusalem* which sees here a prophecy of " royal messianism ". Vv. 8-9^a (cf. 23, 22, 24) refer to the terrible might of Israel. Balac becomes violently angry on hearing for the third time such blessings on Israel, when he expected curses. But Balaam reminds him that he had warned him : he can say only what Yahweh says (13). Dismissed by the king, Balaam does not leave before delivering his fourth and last oracle.

(8) **24 : 14-25 :** the fourth oracle foretelling the destiny of Moab and its neighbors. This time the oracle comes without

any preparation. a) **24** : 14-19 : opening lines (15-16; cf. **24** : 3-4). The prophecy regards the future (17ᵃ). A mighty king of Israel smites Moab, the Suthites, and Edom (17ᵇ-19). The king is figured in 17ᵇ by a star and a staff or scepter, figure of a ruler. (Several take " staff " as being also a celestial body — a comet (e.g., BUXTORF-FISCHER, 1147ᵇ; EHRLICH, *Chicago Version*, RIESSLER, MOWINCKEL [*Norwegian Bible;* cf. E. P. ARBEZ, *CBQ*, 1954, pp. 205-207, I, 313; also *id.*, *Han som Kommer*, Copenhagen, 1951, p. 19, and p. 295, n. 11]. Comets were taken as omen stars announcing a great ruler). There are points of contact between Balaam's oracles and that of Jacob about Juda (Gen. **49** : 1-10). The resemblance in form supposes that the texts are related from the literary point of view (cf. Gen. **49** : 9 and Num. **23** : 24; **24** : 9 and 17. Note also the name " oracle " (*ne'ūm*) given to Balaam's words (**24** : 3, 4, 15, 16) and to David's last words (2 Sam. **23** : 1). Further, both Jacob (Gen. **49** : 1) and Balaam (**24** : 14, 17) are concerned with a distant future, viz., in Num., directly, the subjugation of Moab and Edom by an Israelite ruler, the dynasty of David (2 Sam. **8** : 2, 13 f.). On the Messianic implications, see P. P. SAYDON, *Catholic Commentary on Holy Scripture*, p. 257. On the Suthites, tribes of Bedouin known from Egyptian and Assyrian texts, cf. PRITCHARD, *ANET*, p. 397ᵃ (Shutu), p. 293ᵇ (Suti), p. 490ᵃ (Sutu); Sir L. WOOLLEY, *A Forgotten Kingdom*, pp. 124 and 129. The text of 18-19 is doubtful.

b) **24** : 20 : Amalec, an ancient people, is to perish forever.

c) **24** : 21-22 : the Cinites (= Qenites). There is a play on the words : " smith " = *qayin;* " nest " = *qēn:* Qenite — all sounding alike. Their home is set in the rocks like an eagle's nest; nevertheless it shall be destroyed. V. 22ᵇ is very doubtful. According to some it means that Ashur shall take the Qenites away as captives; according to others, this is not Assyria, but an Arabian tribe (HOMMEL; GUNKEL; MOWINCKEL; *Entzykl. Miq.* 1, 760; Koehler, *Lexicon*, 93a.

d) **24** : 23-25 : We should expect here the same introduction as in the preceding oracles : " and he saw... " (20, 21).

The Greek has it ("And he saw Gog" — corrected to Og; MOWINCKEL, *Bible de Jérusalem*). The text is uncertain and reconstructed in many different ways. The general idea apparently is that of an enemy attack resulting in the defeat of Assur (22) and Heber (Gen. **10** : 21, 24 f.), but the invader himself is doomed (end of **24**; cf. **20**). According to the conclusion (25), Balaam goes back to his place, i.e., Pitru in N. Syria. This can hardly be explained as meaning, he intended to return home but somehow was prevented. Cf. **31** : 8, which seems to belong to a different tradition.

II. **25** (P, except 1-5 attributed to JE).

(1) 1-5 : Israel, seduced by Moabite women, falls into idolatry. The people are encamped at the Sattim (*Shittim*, "acacias"; Jos. **2** : 1; **3** : 1), N. E. of the Dead Sea, opposite Jericho (modern Tell Kefrin). They are led astray by Moabite women (we should rather expect Madianite on account of the context) and they take part in the licentious rites of Baal Phogor (Pe῾or). Yahweh orders the impalement of the guilty ones.

(2) 6-15 : A leading man of Israel brings in a distinguished Madianite woman (14-15). Without any regard for the social rank of the offenders, Phinees, son of the high priest, slays them and thus checks a plague which had claimed already 24,000 victims (6-9). His zeal earns him the promise of an everlasting priesthood (10-13; cf. Ecclus. **45** : 23-28; 1 Mach. **2** : 26).

(3) 16-18 : Israel takes vengeance on the Madianites on account of the Phogor affair. The narrative is continued in **31** : 1 ff.

III. **26–30** (P) : a group of unconnected ordinances.

1) **26** : the second census (cf. 1 f.) of the men of twenty and more fit for military service (4ᵇ-51) — these total 601, 730 (51). Vv. 8-11 contain glosses based on Num. **16** recalling the rebellion of Core (9ᵇ and 10ᵇ-11), though Core is out of place in the census of Ruben. Vv. 52-56 embody directions about the allotment of the land. The lot shall determine the location, but the size of the tribes is to be considered in determining

the extent of their territory. The Levites have the special census (57-62); their total (from one month old) is 23,000. The conclusion (63-65) notes that those registered on this occasion belong to the new generation; the older generation, with the exception Caleb and Josue, had been doomed to die in the desert (cf. **14** : 29-30).

2) **27** : 1-11 : The case of the daughters of Salphahad (Selophhad) claiming the right to inherit their father's property is the occasion of a law concerning heiresses : it guarantees their right and settles other connected points to secure inheritance within the clan.   V. **13** : Their father " died for his own sin " : he belonged to the generation that was to die in the desert (**14** : 22 ff., 29).   See **36** for a supplement to the present ordinance.

3) **27** : 12-33 : Moses goes up to the Abarim range (**33** : 47; Deut. **32** : 49) to which Mt. Nebo belongs (slightly over ten miles N. of the mouth of the Jordan in the Dead Sea); thence he will view the Promised Land. Before his death, he is to invest Josue as his successor. Josue, who will not enjoy personal revelations, will be guided by means of the directions of the Urim and Thummim. (Cf. **21**; Ex. **28** : 30; Lev. **8** : 8; Deut. **33** : 8; 1 Sam. **28** : 6).

4) **28–29** : These chapters take up again and systematize the ordinances of Ex. and Lev. regarding the sacrifices and the liturgical calendar. a) **28** : 3-8 : the daily morning and evening holocaust = Ex. **29** : 38-42.   b) The rest mostly supplements the religious calendar of Lev. **23**. Num. **28** : 9-10 = the weekly sacrifices on the Sabbath; Num. **28** : 11-15 = the New Moon : not mentioned in Lev.; Num. **28** : 16 ff. = Passover; Lev. **23** : 4 ff.; Num. **28** : 17 : Unleavened Bread (Mazzot); Num. **28** : 28 ff. : Pentecost = Lev. **23** : 15 ff. (in Num. here the feast is called Day of First Fruits; Num. **29** : 1 ff. = New Year's Day = Lev. **23** : 23 ff.; Num. **29** : 7 ff. : Day of Atonement = Lev. **23** : 26 ff.; Num. **29** : 12 ff. : Feast of Booths = Lev. **23** : 33 ff.

5) **30** : Vows. A man's vow is binding (2-3); a woman's vow may or may not be binding according to circumstances (4-17).

IV. **31-36** : Miscellaneous — narrative and legal — material.

1) **31** (P) : a war of extermination against the Madianites to take vengeance on them for the Phogor affair (1-12; cf. **25** : 16-18). The concrete circumstances of the expedition are left out, and only the outcome is described. Israel kills all the men, including the five kings of Madian, and Balaam also, who somehow is with Madian (cf. **24** : 25) and is represented as responsible for the sin of Israel at Phogor (8 and 16). These references to Balaam which present him in a very different light from his role in **22-24** suppose a tradition not otherwise preserved in our text (cf. LOEWENSTAMM, *Entzyklop. Miq.* 2, 134; cf. above **22** : 22-35). It is these vss. (**31** : 8 and 16) and the episode in **22** : 22 ff. that most probably helped create the unfavorable view of Balaam. The Old Testament thus supplies the elements for his severe condemnation by the Jewish tradition (Josephus, *Targum Yerushalmi*) and the New Testament. The Israelites had spared the women and male children (13-16), but they are ordered to slay them all, sparing only the virgins (17-18). (Cf. ancient customs of warfare as in Mesha's Inscription, lines 16-17, " [I took Nebo] and I slew all 7000 men, boys, women, girls, and maid-servants; for I had devoted them [the verb, *haram*] to ʿAshtar-Kemōsh "). Before being allowed back into camp, the warriors with their captives and their booty must undergo purification for a week (19-24). Directions follow about the division of the booty (25-31). The items of the booty are detailed in **32** : 47, 50-52. The amount captured in this raid by 12,000 men (5), not one of whom was lost (49), is enormous beyond probability — the articles of gold alone (52) would weigh well over 500 pounds. The officers make an offering (48-54) as an expiation.

2) **32** (mostly JE). The Tribes of Ruben and Gad (1ᵇ, 25, 29, 31, 33ª) ask leave to settle in the region E. of the Jordan — known now as the ʿAjlūn from the Yarmuk, S. of the Sea of Gennesaret to Hesebon — divided into two parts by the Jabboc, with good pasture land in the part S. of the Jabboc. Of the names of the cities in 13 and (34-38), several appear in Mesha's Inscription. Moses fears that these tribes later might not cooperate with the others in the conquest of W. Palestine (6-15, on the Greek of **32** : 12, cf. H. J. SCHOEPS, *Biblica* [1945],

pp. 307-309), but they assure Moses that they will give their help (16-19). Their request therefore is approved (20-38). In 33 a gloss introduces " the Half Tribe of Manasse son of Joseph " and " the kingdom of Og king of Basan ". However, in the rest of the chapter, only the Rubenites and the Gadites are mentioned in the discussion with Moses. The difficulty was felt by the Samaritan Recension, which introduces the Half Tribe of Manasse throughout the narrative (1, 6, 25, 29, 31). The gloss in 33 about the Half Tribe of Manasse taking over the kingdom of Og was introduced in view of 39-42, which refer to the occupation of Galaad — here (39) (cf. 1) denotes the region between the Jabboc (S.) and the Yarmuk (N.) — by clans of Manasse. (Cf. *Leidsche Vertaling*, 1, 380 and 382; EDELKOORT, *op. cit.;* Confraternity Version). Clearly the narrative (34 ff.) anticipates the actual historical development : the cities were not rebuilt immediately after Moses gave his consent. Likewise, though Half Manasse is mentioned in several places (Deut. **3** : 12 ff.; **4** : 43; **29** : 7, etc.), as in Transjordan — with Ruben and Gad —, their settlement is regarded by several as belonging to a later period, after they had settled first W. of the Jordan (cf. *Leid. Vertal.* 1, 380 f.; EDELKOORT, *op. cit.*, 199; Haag, *Bibellexikon*, 1068-1069). We may find a reflection of later circumstances in the fact that, except in 1ᵃ, the first place is given regularly to Gad (6, 25, 29, 31, 33), as well as in the notices about these two tribes (34 and 37), where Gad comes first. This may well reflect the later relationship of the Transjordanian tribes : Gad became the leading tribe, while Ruben was pushed into the background and was absorbed by Gad and by Moab (cf. Deut. **33** : 20 f., on Gad, and Deut. **33** : 6 f., on Ruben; in Gen. **49** : 3-4, Ruben is " degraded "). Mesha's Inscription (line 10) mentions only Gad : " The men of Gad had dwelt in the land of Atarot from of old ", and line 11 : " I fought against the city and I took it and I slew all the people ".

3) **33** : 1-49 (P) : the stages on the journey from Egypt to the Plains of Moab. (Cf. Ex. **12** : 37 ff.; **13** : 17 ff.; **14** : 1 ff.; **15** : 22 ff.; **16** : 1 f.; **17** : 1 ff.; **19** : 1 ff.; Num. **10** : 11; **11** : 35; **12** : 1-16; **13** : 25 f.; **20** : 14 f., 22 ff.; **21** : 1, 4, 10 ff., 21-35; **22** : 1; Deut. **1** : 1–**3** : 22). See LAGRANGE, " Le Sinaï Biblique ",

RB (1899), 369 ff.; *id.*, " Itinéraire des Israélites ", *RB* [1900], 63 ff., 273 ff., 443 ff.; H. CAZELLES, " Données géographiques sur l'Exode ", *La Bible et l'Orient* [Paris, 1955], pp. 51-60; J. PRADO, " Las primeras etapas del Exodo- al mar Rojo ", *Sefarad* (1957), pp. 151-168 (on H. Cazelles' view). As noted in the new Catholic Version, 1, 404, as well as, e.g., in the *Leidsche Vertaling*, 1, p. 383, *Bible du Centenaire*, etc., this list of Ch. 33 has forty names. The number — not always a definite mathematical quantity in the Bible — may be artificial (one stage to each of the years of the wandering?). This, however, does not allow us to regard the list as unhistorical, for it may have been cut down. It contains twenty-two names not mentioned elsewhere; hence it may not be accounted for as a compilation made from Ex., Num., and Deut. Further- more, some glosses have been introduced. Thus, 33 : 38-40 (death of Aaron, King of Arad; see the note on v. 40 in the new Cath. Version); also in 33 : 3-4 (possibly a quotation from some ancient poem on the Exodus; so the new Cath. Version). Finally, the proper sequence of the names seems to have been disturbed in several places, as noted also by the Confrat. Version. Thus, 36ᵇ-41ᵃ stood originally between 30ᵃ and 30ᵇ (so also Edelkoort, *op. cit.*, p. 201; cf. LAGRANGE, *RB* [1899], 378; [1900], 273 f.). Again, 41ᵇ-49 should be read immediately after 36ᵇ. (On 42, cf. LAGRANGE, *RB* [1898], 112-115; Clermont- Ganneau, *ibid.*, [1906], 412-432 [esp. 427-428]; on 35, Asion Gaber [Esion Geber], cf. N. GLUECK, *Eastern Transjordan*, pp. 86-118 [in Hebr.]).

4) **33 : 50–34 : 29** (P). *a)* **35 : 50-56** : instructions about the conquest of Canaan (W. Palestine). Israel must drive out all the natives and destroy all signs of their idolatry (50-52); else they will suffer harm (55-56). The conquered land is to be apportioned by lot (53-54).

b) **34 : 1-15** : The boundaries of the Promised Land are defined. (Cf. ABEL, O. P., *Géographie de la Palestine*, I [Paris, 1933], 298-310; *Encyclopaedia Hebraica* [in Hebr.], Vol. VI [Jerusalem — Tel Aviv, 1957; the whole volume of 1172 cols. is devoted to " Eretz Yisrael "], cols. 28-36. All the geographies of the Holy Land discuss the boundaries of Palestine, real or theoretical).

c) **34** : 16-29 : The men who are to supervise the allotment of the land are appointed : they will serve under Eleazar and Josue. (Cf. Jos. **13** ff.).

5) **35** (P).

a) 1-8 : Forty eight cities are appointed for the residence of the Levites with pasture lands (cf. Jos. **21**). See above on **18** : 20 ff.

b) **35** : 9-34 : cities of asylum and their use : six cities — three of them in Transjordan and three in W. Palestine — are to be set aside where one may find refuge, in the case of unintentional homicide, before trial (9-15). The purpose is to protect the unintentional homicide from the avenger of blood (*goel [ha-dam]*) (12, 19, 21, 24, 25, 27), the nearest relative who is bound to avenge the death. For examples of blood revenge, cf. e.g., Joab and Abner, 2 Sam. **3** : 22-29; cf. 2 Sam. **2** : 17-32; and cf. the use of the custom in the parable of the wise woman, 2 Sam. **14** : 1-20. The custom of private blood revenge is still current among the Arabs (cf. R. A. NICHOLSON, *A Literary History of the Arabs* [London, 1923], pp. 97 ff.). Vv. 16-29, murder and unintentional homicide : when may the avenger of blood take action? The law acknowledges the custom, but there must be evidence, and from more than one witness (30). Cf. Ex. **21** : 12 f.; Lev. **24** : 17. The provisions of the law for the distinction of intentional and unintentional homicide reflect a rather primitive stage of legal development — behind that of Babylonia, where private blood revenge is abolished and the administration of justice belongs to the government. V. 30 may be regarded as a check to private blood vengeance, even if imperfect. There cannot be any indemnity in the case of murder (31-34 : the murderer's blood must be shed for the blood he has shed. Cf. Hittite law, which does not recognize the death penalty for murder, but only compensation, which includes the funeral expenses. (Cf. PRIT-CHARD, *ANET*, p. 189, 1 ff.; E. NEUFELD, *The Hittite Laws* [London, 1951], p. 1 ff. and 129 ff. Bedouin custom recognizes the *diya* (from the verb, *wāday*), i.e., the price of blood paid by the murderer to the victim's family.

6) **36** : 1-13 (P) : the marriage of heiresses. The five daughters of Salaphahad whose request had been the occasion

of a decision in favor of their right of inheritance (**27** : 5-11) again are the occasion for a decision regarding the conditions of the marriage of heiresses. They are to marry within their own tribe (6-9). This will prevent the land of one tribe from passing into the possession of another tribe (cf. 3 f.). In the present instance, since they married relatives on their father's side, their inheritance was secured completely for their tribe (11-12). V. 13 is the conclusion of the collection of ordinances in **28–30** and **33** : 50–**36** : 12.

5. — Deuteronomy [1].

Name.

In the Hebrew Bible, the title is *Elleh ha-debarim*, or more briefly, *Debarim :* (" These are the) words ", from the opening sentence of the book. An ancient Jewish tradition knows also the name *Mishneh Torah* taken from Dt. **17** : 18 (cf. Jos. **8** : 32) " duplicate of the Law ", translated *Deuteronomion* in LXX; hence the Latin *Deuteronomium* (Deuteronomy) — " Second Law " — and the equivalent title in the Syriac. (Cf. M. S. SEGAL : *Mebō'ha-Miqrā'* I (Jerusalem 1945), 10-12, pp. 6-8; Cassuto, 608). This name Deuteronomy means that the book contains a repetition, a rehearsal, of the Law contained in the preceding books (Ex. — Num.).

General characteristics and divisions.

This book consists essentially of a series of addresses by Moses shortly before his death. In general, the laws are those promulgated before, but they are presented here in a new form

Translator's note. — [1 Cf. A. DILLMANN, *Kurzgefasstes exegetisches Handbuch zum A.T.* (Leipzig, 1886). S. R. DRIVER, in the *International Critical Commentary* (1902). E. KÖNIG, *Kommentar* (Leipzig, 1917). H. JUNKER, in the *Echter Bibel* (Würzburg, 1954). R. A. F. MACKENZIE, S. J., in *A Catholic Commentary on Holy Scripture* (London, 1952). A. TONY, in *Bible de Centenaire.* A. LODS, *Introduction* (Paris, 1936 and 1941). S. MOWINCKEL, in *Det Gamle Testamente,* I (Oslo, 1929). H. CAZELLES, SS., in *La Sainte Bible (Bible de Jérusalem,* Paris, 1950). E. DHORME, *La Bible,* I : *L'Ancien Testament* (Paris, 1956). DOM B. UBACH, *Els Nombres.* — *El Deuteronomi* (Montserrat Bible, 1928, with volume of illustrations, 1954). E. KAUFMAN, *Toledot ha Emunah...* I, pp. 81-112 (and other sections of this work). G. VON RAD, *Studies in Deuteronomy* (London, 1953). U. CASSUTO, article on Deut. in *Entzykl. Mig.* 2, pp. 608-619 (with good bibliography). R. TOURNAY, O. P., " Le Psaume et les Bénédictions de Moïse " [Deut. 33], *RB* (1958), pp. 181-213].

in keeping with the historical circumstances. Moses has carried out the task laid upon him by God; he knows that his days are numbered (e.g., 1 : 37 f.; 31 : 2 f., 14 ff.). He understands the character of his people, their moods and their weaknesses (cf., e.g., 1 : 22 ff.; 1 : 41 ff.; 4 : 9; 8 : 11 ff.). Now, in his last will and testament, as it were, he makes a solemn effort to ensure their lasting fidelity to God's Law. He does not merely recall the terms of God's will, but with his whole heart, reminding them of what God has done for them, of the love God has shown them, appealing to their sense of gratitude, to the love they owe to God in return for his favors, he urges upon them the necessity of faithful obedience to the Law as the essential condition of their happiness and prosperity (cf., e.g., 4 : 37; 6 : 5; 11 : 1-13). Hence the peculiar character of these addresses : they are sermons, homilies, speaking to the heart of the hearers, the appeals of a father concerned for the welfare of his own, trying to convince them that their fidelity will bring them peace and happiness. Hence in this book the style varies considerably from that of the other books, a clearly recognizable mode of expression with its vocabulary and phraseology (some examples will be given further on).

We may recognize the following main divisions :

A. 1 : 1–4 : 43.

A first discourse which recalls the events of the journey from Mt. Horeb — the usual name of Sinai in this book (cf. Ex. 3 : 1; 17 : 8; 33 : 6) — to Baal-Phogor. There is a special historical introduction to this section (1 : 1-5). Several historical notices — which are not part of the discourse — occur : 2 : 10-12, 20-23; 3 : 9-11b; 4 : 41-43.

B. 4 : 44–11 : 32.

A second discourse, with its special historical introduction (4 : 44-49) and its special conclusion (11 : 26-32). This discourse, quite independent from the first discourse, is a partial exposition of the Law. We may note here also some historical notices in 10 : 6-7 and 11 : 30 introduced into the text of the discourse by a reviser.

C. **12** : **1–26** : **19**.

A third (?) discourse with a brief introduction (**12** : **1**), a mere heading which occurs in several other places, so that this part is not marked off as distinctly as the others. It has its own conclusion (**26** : 16-19). In any case, this is regarded as the main part of the Deuteronomic Law.

D. **27** : **1–28** : **69**.

This section may be regarded as a fourth (?) discourse with a brief introduction associating Moses and the Elders of Israel (**27** : **1**) and a conclusion (**28** : **69**) promising blessings for obedience, and curses for disobedience.

E. **29** : **1–30** : **20**.

A fifth (?) discourse, which has its introduction (**29** : **1**) marking it off from the preceding section. The opening words of the following chapter (**31** : **1**) distinguish these two chapters as a separate group.

F. **31** : **1–34** : **12**.

The conclusion of the book consists of the last instructions of Moses (the commission of Josue, the reading of the Law, the placing of the Law in the Ark (**31** : **1**-29) and of the account of his death and burial (**32** : 44-52; **34** : 1-12). Between these prose sections, we have the Song of Moses (**31** : 30–**31** : 43) and the Blessings upon the Tribes (**33** : 1-29).

Some peculiarities of the style of Deuteronomy.

I. In a number of places we meet with a strange mixture of singular and plural forms (2nd pers. sg. and pl.) within the same sentence. This feature does not appear in the new Catholic Version, since it uses *you* for one or several persons. Thus in **4** : 9-14, in vv. 9-10 the 2nd person sing. is used, but in 11-14 the 2nd pl.; in **4** : 23, the first part of the verse is in the pl., the last words in the sing. : " an idol, an image of anything which the Lord *thy* God has forbidden thee "; in **5** : 25-31, in 25 : " When *thou hast* children... and *you* have grown old " (then the 2nd pl. continues), but at the end : " in the sight of the Lord *thy* God to provoke him ". Vv. 26-28 use the 2nd pl., but v. 29 reads : " Yet you shall seek the Lord *thy*

God and *thou* shalt find when *thou* searchest him with *thy* whole heart and *thy* whole soul ". The 2nd sing. then continues through vv. 30-31. Again in **6** : 1-3, v. 1 has the 2nd pl.; v. 2 has the 2nd sing.; v. 3 begins with the 2nd sing. (as far as " that *thou mayest* prosper "), and then 2nd pl. and 2nd sing. : " and that *you* may grow, as the Lord the God of *thy* fathers promised *thee*... ". In **7** : 8, the first part uses 2nd pl., but ends with the sing. : " ...brought *you* out..., and he ransomed *thee* ". In **11** : 8-9, we have : Keep (2nd pl.) which I enjoin on *thee*, then 2nd pl. In **11** : 10-12 we read : " the land into which *thou art* crossing is not like the land of Egypt out of which *you* have come — *thou* sowest *thy* seed and water*est* with *thy* feet "; v. 11 uses 2nd pl., while v. 12 has " the Lord *thy* God " (twice). Other instances which the reader can examine in translations that use *thou* and *you* will be found in the following places : **11** : 18-21; **12** : 1, 5, 9, 13-15; **13** : 1, 4, 6; **14** : 1-2; **18** : 15; **24** : 8-9; **27** : 2 ff.; **28** : 62-63; **29** : 4; **29** : 9-13; **31** : 6.

This mixture of singular and plural has not been explained satisfactorily. It can not be used as a basis for a distinction of different elements which would have been combined into the present book : no analysis can be carried through on that basis. (Cf. A. WEISER, *Einleitung in das A. T.* (Göttingen, 1949, p. 102).

II. There are many words and phrases which recur frequently in this book and give it a special character. The careful reader of the text can not fail to notice them. Some examples will illustrate the point. The phrases, " the statutes and decrees ", "the statutes and commandments", and the like often accompanied by " which I enjoin upon you (to-day) ", occur repeatedly : **4** : 1, 2, 5, 8, 14, 40, 45; **5** : 1, 28; **6** : 1, 2, 6; **7** : 11; **8** : 1, 11; **10** : 13; **11** : 1, 8, 13, 22, 27, 28; **12** : 14, 28; **13** : 1; **15** : 15; **19** : 9; **24** : 18, 22; **27** : 10; **28** : 1, 13, 15; **30** : 2, 8, 11, 16. The idea of absolute fidelity to the Lord and His word is expressed by the verb " to cling to " Him, " to observe carefully " (literally : " to observe and to do ", or " to observe in doing ") : **4** : 6; **5** : 1, 29; **6** : 3, 25; **7** : 12; **8** : 1; **11** : 32; **12** : 1; **13** : 1; **26** : 16; **28** : 1, 13, 15, 58; **31** : 12; **32** : 46; also **4** : 4; **10** : 20; **11** : 22; **13** : 5; **30** : 20. The same idea of total devotion to the

Lord is conveyed by the phrase " with your whole heart and your whole soul ", e.g. : 4 : 29; 6 : 5; 10 : 12; 11 : 13; 13 : 4; 26 : 16; 30 : 2, 6, 10. Palestine is described as " the good land " which God swore to give to the Fathers, which he is giving as a heritage, etc. : 1 : 35; 3 : 25; 4 : 21; 6 : 18; 8 : 7, 10; 9 : 6; 11 : 17.

Idolatry is described as going after or serving other gods : 5 : 7; 6 : 14; 7 : 4; 8 : 19; 13 : 3, 7, 14; 17 : 3; 18 : 20; 28 : 14, 36, 64; 29 : 25; 30 : 17; 31 : 18-20. The deliverance from Egypt, " the house of slavery " (6 : 12; 7 : 8; 8 : 14; 13 : 6, 11), was effected by the Lord's " strong hand and outstretched arm " (4 : 34; 5 : 15; 7 : 19; 11 : 2; 26 : 8); sometimes only " by his strong hand " (3 : 24 [Confraternity Version, " might "], 6 : 21; 7 : 8; 9 : 26; 34 : 12). The Sanctuary which is to be the center of the religious life of Israel is referred to frequently as the place which the Lord chooses as the dwelling place for his name : 12 : 5, 11, 21; 14 : 23-24; 16 : 2, 6, 7, 11, 15, 16; 17 : 8, 10; 18 : 6; 31 : 11. (For a fuller list of such phrases, see S. R. DRIVER, *Introduction to the Old Testament*, pp. 99-102). The style is " solemn, emphatic, repetitious, even tautological " (R. A. F. MACKENZIE, S. J., *A Catholic Commentary on Holy Scripture*, p. 261). The sentences tend to be long, but they are usually clear. The work is a remarkable oratorical composition and supposes practice in the art of public oratory.

ANALYSIS OF THE BOOK.

A. 1 : 1–4 : 43. *The First Discourse.*

a) 1: 1-5 : the introduction proper stating the time and place of the discourse is contained in vv. 3-5 : " in the fortieth year of the wandering, on the first of the eleventh month " (cf. Num. 14 : 33; 33 : 38; Deut. 29 : 4), after the conquest of the East Jordan land (Num. 21 : 21 ff.; 32 : 33; 36 : 13), in the region N. of the Dead Sea opposite Jericho (cf. Num. 22 : 1; Deut. 2 : 26 ff.), thus east of the Jordan. Vv. 1-2 contain a number of place names which, insofar as they are identifiable, take us to the Sinai Peninsula, thus west of the region referred to in vv. 3-5. The first introduction (vv. 1-2), hardly suitable in this place, may be a note intended to serve as a transition from Num. to Deut., a conclusion to Num.

b) **1 :–3** : 29 : this is an historical section which reviews the events since the departure from Horeb (the name in Deut. for Sinai : Deut. **1** : 2, 19; **4** : 10, 15; **5** : 2; **9** : 8; **18** : 16; **28** : 69; Sinai appears only in **33** : 2).

1) Yahweh ordered the earlier generation to conquer Palestine from the south, but their disobedience and lack of faith caused the plan to miscarry (**1** : 6-8; 19-46; cf. Num. **13–14**). Ch. **1** : 7 mentions the different sections of Palestine, the land promised to the Fathers. The conclusion of v. 7 includes Lebanon, as far as the Euphrates, i.e. Syria. This is questioned by some who regard the Euphrates here as a gloss; the river intended originally would be the Leontes or Liba (the modern Nahr Litanī) which flows into the Mediterranean a short distance N. of Tyre. This would reduce Palestine to its historical boundaries. However, the same ideal boundary of Palestine appears in some other texts, and we have no decisive reason for taking the Euphrates here as a gloss. (Cf. L. SZEZEPANSKI, S. J., *Quaestiones Geographico-Topographicae*, I [Rome, 1912], pp. 52-53; F. M. ABEL, O. P., *Géographie de la Palestine*, I [Paris, 1933], p. 299). The appointment of Elders (vv. 9-18) (cf. Ex. **18** : 13-26) who are in charge of the administration of justice, to carry out the provisions of the Law impartially, is mentioned here because their office is connected with the Law taught by Moses. For this purpose, Moses used a military organization (v. 15) found in ancient tribal life. (Cf. H. JUNKER's *Commentary*).

2) **2** : 1-15. This relates the advance of Israel to the conquest of Palestine from the east (cf. Num. **20** : 14-21). Israel was instructed to respect the territories of Seir (Edom) and of Moab. Vv. 10-12 are an archaeological note giving popular traditions of the pre-Israelite inhabitants of Palestine around 4000-3000 B.C. (Cf. W. F. ALBRIGHT, *The Archaeology of Palestine* [1954], pp. 65-79, " The Chaleolithic and Early Bronze Age "). On these early populations which in popular legend were giants : Emim, Enacim, Raphaim, see, e.g., Haag, *Bibellexikon*, 1425 f. On the Horrites (v. 12) see below, v. 22.

3) **2** : 16-23. Israel is told to respect the land of Ammon; the peoples like Moab (vv. 9-19) and Edom (v. 4) are related to Israel. In vv. 20-23 we have another archaeological note

of the same type as that in vv. 10-12; the Zomzommin *(Zamzummim)* are supposed to be called thus as " not able to speak intelligibly " (= *Barbaroi*); the Avvim (Awwim, Jos. **13** : 3) are by some related to the Amu of the Egyptian texts, i.e., Palestinian-Syrian Beduin; the Caphtorim are the Philistines (Caphtor is perhaps to be identified with the island of Crete, the center of an empire about 1600 B.C.), known as Keftiu in Egyptian texts and Kaptaru in the Mari texts (H. Junker, Comm'.), who invaded Palestine in the 13th cent. B.C. (Cf. W. F. ALBRIGHT, *Archaeology of Palestine*, p. 113 ff.). The Horrites, v. 22, (cf. Gen. **14** : 6; **36** : 20 f., 29 f.; also in Gen. **34** : 2; **36** : 2, instead of Hevite according to some) appear in Ugaritic, Akkadian, and Egyptian texts as an ancient non-Semitic population from the 3rd millenium on (Cf. Haag, *Bibellexikon*, pp. 738-739; Contenau in *DBV, Suppl.*, IV, pp. 128-138; *Entzykl. Miq.* 3, pp. 57-63).

4) **2** : 24-37. Sihon, King of Hesebon, comes out to attack Israel and is defeated (cf. Num. **21** : 21-32). V. 34 refers to the " anathema " — *Herem* — the total destruction mentioned in many other places.

5) **3** : 1-7. The victory of Israel over Og, the King of Basan, is related in Num. **21** : 33-35.

6) **3** : 8-11. This is a summary of the campaign against the two kings which leaves the Israelites in possession of the land east of the Jordan. A name calls attention to the different names of Mt. Hermon (v. 9), 9166 ft. high above the Mediterranean (the *Jebel esh-sheikh* according to its Arabic name) which dominates the whole region. Another archaeological note in v. 11 records a popular tradition about the bed of iron of the giant king which was preserved in Rabba the capital of Ammon. The legend was derived probably from the extraordinary dimensions of a basalt sarcophagus nine cubits long and four wide (a cubit = 17.72 inches. The basalt of East Jordan which contains up to 20% iron may be called iron).

7) **3** : 12-22. These verses describe the allotment of the territory conquest on the east side of the Jordan — related also in Num. **32**. Here again in v. 13ᵇ is a historico-geographical note of later date; also, in v. 14, a tradition of the settlement of the Manasseite clan, Jair, which belongs to a later period

(cf. Num. **32** : 41; Jos. **13** : 30; 1 (3) Kgs. **4** : 13; 1 Chron. **2** : 21-23). V. **15** : Machir is also a clan of Manasses (cf. Gen. **50** : 23; Num. **26** : 29; **32** : 39-40). Machir — Manasses, here supposed to be in the land east of the Jordan, is mentioned in Jdgs. **5** : 14 among the West Jordan tribes.

8) **3** : 23-29. Moses prays that Yahweh may grant the favor to enter " the good land " west of the Jordan, but Yahweh rejects that prayer, which is not recorded elsewhere, but maintains his earlier decision against Moses (cf. **1** : 34-38; **4** : 21; Num. **20** : 12; **27** : 12-14; Deut. **32** : 48-52). Moses will only be allowed to view the land from a distance, from the top of Phasga. Leading the people across the Jordan will be the task of his successor Josue. V. 29 : Beth-Phogor means the sanctuary of Baal of Phogor (Beth Baal Phogor); cf. Num. **25** : 3, 5. (Cf. *Entzykl. Miq.* 3, 98 f.). V. 27 : Phasga (cf. v. 17) is one of the summits of the Abarim Mountains (Num. **21** : 11) looking down on the Jordan plain, opposite Jericho; in Deut. **32** : 49 Mt. Nebo is mentioned as an equivalent.

c) **4** : 1-40. The first homiletic section proper exhorts Israel to the faithful keeping of the Law. We observe here several of the characteristics mentioned before : mixture of 2nd sg. and pl., and a number of the phrases peculiar to the book.

1) **4** : 1-9. The Law is to be kept without alteration (v. 2). Unfaithfulness will be punished by destruction (v. 3); obedience will make the greatness of the people, and the nations will admire Israel as a people that has received such a wonderful Law (v. 5 ff.). Therefore always remember the Law revealed under extraordinary circumstances and teach it to the future generations (v. 9).

2) **4** : 9-14. In a great theophany at Horeb, Israel received the Ten Commandments, the Ten Words (*'aseret ha-debarim* [**4** : 13]; *'aseret ha-dibrot*, in the Jewish tradition), the substance of the covenant, the terms of which are developed in the Law. (Cf. Ex. **20** : 1-21; Deut. **5**; cf. *Entzykl. Miq.* 2, pp. 590-596 with bibl.). Moses in v. 12 calls attention to a circumstance which is used against any representations of the Divinity in the following section (v. 15 f.) : in the manifestation at Horeb, the people only heard a voice, but they saw no material form of God which they could be tempted to reproduce (v. 12).

3) **4** : 15-24. Hence the absolute prohibition of any representation of Yahweh, a fundamental requirement of the religion of Israel (vv. 15-18). This is further developed by the prohibition of the worship of the heavenly bodies, which played such a prominent part in the religion of the ancient Semitic peoples (v. 19). Israel, God's very own people by a special choice, called to the knowledge of the one true God, cannot follow the other nations whose lot it is to worship these false divinities (v. 20). The other nations, not chosen, but left to their own devices, have fallen into idolatry. According to a form of expression used frequently in Scripture, no distinction is made between what God wills and what he permits (cf., e.g., Deut. **2** : 30; Jdgs. **9** : 23; 1 Sam. **16** : 14; **18** : 10; **19** : 9; **26** : 19, etc.). V. 22 is a sort of parenthetic remark suggested by the lot of Moses' hearers privileged to " enter the good land " (v. 21) while he himself remains excluded.

4) **4** : 25-31 : The infidelity of the people disregarding the fundamental command of worship of the one God will result in their ruin, though God's mercy will restore them after repentance. This section, which looks forward to the exile of the nation and recalls the prophets' promise of restoration after expiation, may be regarded as a later expansion. (Cf. H. JUNKER, *op. cit.*, p. 21).

5) **4** : 32-40 : The conclusion of the first discourse. God has done wonders for Israel whom he has chosen out of all nations. Let Israel then understand that Yahweh is the only God (v. 39) and see that their fidelity will be the guarantee of their happiness in the land He is giving them (v. 40).

6) **4** : 41-43 : appointment of three cities of refuge. (Cf. Num. **35** : 9-16 and Deut. **19** : 1-13; also Jos. **20** : 7-8). Here three cities are chosen east of the Jordan : Bosor (Beser) mentioned in the stele of Mesa, possibly near Umm el-Amad N.E. of Madaba; Ramoth (Jos. **20** : 8; **21** : 38; 1 (3) Kings **22** : 3; 2 (4) Kgs. **8** : 28; **9** : 1), possibly er-Ramta S.W. of Edrai (Deut. **1** : 4; **3** : 1-10); Golan, whence the name Jolān (Gaulanites) of the Lake of Genesaret. The writer of this notice betrays his position W. of the Jordan by describing these places as being " beyond " (on the other side of) the Jordan, towards the rising of the sun.

B. 4 : 44–11 : 32.   *The Second Discourse of Moses.*

1) 4 : 44-49 : introduction.   This is independent from that
in 1 : 1-5.   In a continuous context, there would be no need
to repeat all these indications of time and place, and the sketch
of the account of the conquest of the East Jordan land.   On
Beth-Phogor, v. 46, cf. 3 : 29.   In v. 48 there is a new name
(Si'on) of Mt. Hermon besides those in 3 : 9, quite distinct
in Hebrew from Sion (Jerusalem).   But probably this new
name is due only to a misspelling of the name Sirion (Sarion)
of 3 : 9.

2) 5 : 1-5 : Moses recalls the new covenant made by God
with Israel, different from that made with the Patriarchs
(Abraham, Isaac, and Jacob).   This covenant at Horeb defined
the new way of life imposed by God.

3) 5 : 6-22.   First of all, the Ten Commandments (cf. above
4 : 9-14) are given to the people under circumstances of exceptional solemnity which emphasize their importance (v. 22).
Cf. 4 : 12.   The two redactions of them in Ex. 20 and
Deut. 5 should be compared.   The original form was
probably very brief (cf. 5 : 17 ff.), but it has been expanded
in different ways.   Let us consider the precept of the Sabbath.
In Ex. 20 : 9-11 the seventh day is to be kept holy because
God rested on it.   In Deut. 5 : 15 the rest on the Sabbath
commemorates God's freeing of Israel from their bondage
in Egypt (cf. 4 : 20, 34; 6 : 21; 7 : 8, etc., for similar references
to the deliverance from Egypt which establishes Yahweh's
sovereign lordship over Israel).   Thus we have two different
reasons for the Sabbath rest representing two different developments of tradition.   Notice also, for instance, the differences
in the precept against coveting in Ex. 20 : 17 and Deut. 5 : 21.
Ex. brackets together under coveting the neighbor's house,
the wife, slaves, ox or ass of the neighbor; the wife is one of
the items of the neighbor's property.   Deut. mentions the
wife by herself, and distinguishes her from the house and other
items of property.   It is tempting to see in Deut. a higher
appreciation of woman.   However Deut. in other places regards
the wife as the man's property, but here Deut. rather regards
coveting another man's wife as lust, a sinful sexual appetite,

and coveting his house, etc., as greed, and therefore Deut.
could make two distinct commandments. (Cf. H. JUNKER,
op. cit., 24 f.).

4) **5** : 23-33 : Moses as mediator. The manifestation of
God has shaken and terrified the people to such a degree that
they ask that Moses may act as the intermediary between
the Divinity and themselves. God grants their request. May
the people always remember the event so that they will remain
forever faithful to the will of God revealed through Moses.
Their reward will be a long life and prosperity in the Promised
Land (v. 33; v. 30 in the Hebrew). Here, as in so many places
of the Old Testament, " life " — as explained here in the second
part of the text — is " long life "; literally : " that you may
prolong (your) days ". For the meaning of death in the Old
Testament, see M. FÉRET, O. P., " La mort dans la tradition
biblique ", in *Le mystère de la mort et sa célébration* (Paris,
1956), pp. 15-133.

5) **6** : 1-3. This forms the introduction and transition to
the commandments, statutes, and decrees revealed by Moses
in God's name. Vv. 2-3 look like two variants of the same
idea. For the land flowing with milk and honey, cf. Ex. **3**: 8, **17**;
13 : 5; **33** : 5, etc.

6) **6** : 4-9. The great commandment is absolute, undivided
loyalty to and love of Yahweh. V. 1 is rendered variously :
" Hear Israel, Yahweh is our God, Yahweh alone "; so, e.g.,
the Confraternity Version, H. JUNKER, *RSV* (margin), *American
Version* (Chicago), A. EHRLICH, *Bible du Centenaire*. Another
possibility is : " Yahweh our God is the one Yahweh ", cf. LXX,
Vulg., *Bible de Jérusalem*, DHORME, *RSV* (text), MOWINCKEL
(Norwegian Bible), NACAR (Spanish Bible), etc.; or : " Yahweh
our God, Yahweh is one ". The last is the Jewish traditional
rendering; cf. *J. V.*, *Bible du Rabbinat* (Paris), ISAAC LEESER,
Het Oude Testament (Kuenen, etc.), Segal-Hartom (in their
edition of the Hebrew Bible with notes), Cantera (Spanish
Bible), Ubach *(Biblia Montserrat)*, etc. The Jewish tradition
has taken this as a declaration of monotheism in the prayer
known as *Shema* (= " Hear ") which consists of Deut. **6** : 4-8;
11 : 13-21; Num. **15** : 37-42 : the pillars of the Jewish Faith
(unity of God, loyalty to God's commandments, Divine Justice,

deliverance from Egypt, and election of Israel). Cf. Chief
Rabbi J. H. HERTZ, *Authorized Daily Prayer Book* (New York,
1948), 108-129; Adler-Singer, *Authorized Daily Prayer Book*
(London, 1912), pp. i-liv. The word of God is to be remembered
at all times and under all circumstances (vv. 7-9). The
expression is figurative and can be paralled from the Amarna
texts (Cf. Ex. **13** : 9, 16; Prov. **3** : 3; **7** : 3). H. JUNKER, *op. cit.*,
26 f. On the basis of these verses arose the phylacteries —
small boxes containing Ex. **13** : 1-6 and Deut. **11** : 18 — bound
on forehead and arm during prayer (cf. Mt. **23** : 5), and the
Mezuzah, a small tube containing Deut. **6** : 4-9 and **11** : 13-21 —
affixed to the doorjamb — which the pious Jew touches with
his finger when coming home. (Cf. ARNDT-GINGRICH, *Greek-
English Lex. of the N. T.* [Chicago, 1957], 876).

7) **6** : 10-15 : In the prosperity of the Holy Land, Israel
must not forget the Lord nor allow itself to be seduced to the
service of the gods of the nations.

8) **6** : 16-19. Do not tempt Yahweh by disobedience to his
commandments, as did your fathers at Massa (Ex. **17** : 1-7),
in spite of all that God had done for them.

9) **6** : 20-25. To ensure the memory of the Law given by
God to Israel when he freed them from Egyptian slavery,
teach it to each generation. The Law marked the beginning
of their freedom and must remain the pledge of their freedom.

10) **7** : 1-11. Israel has been chosen by Yahweh out of all
the nations and is a people sacred to him (v. 6 ff.). It is a free
choice, due to God's love and His fidelity to His gracious
promises to the Fathers. Hence Israel can have nothing
to do with the religion of the nations delivered up to them
by God. No compromise is possible : the destruction of the
people and of their worship must be total — anathema or
herem — as otherwise there would be danger to the faith of
Israel (vv. 1-5; cf. **6** : 10-15). Cf. also **7** : 16; **13** : 9; **19** : 13, 21;
25 : 12. The code of war to be applied to the enemy here is
what we find among the neighbors of Israel (Moabites, Hittites)
and many other ancient peoples (Greeks, Romans, Celts, and
Germans). Cf. H. JUNKER, *op. cit.*, p. 59. Cf. Num. **21** : 2 f.;
21 : 35; Deut. **2** : 34; **3** : 16. The seven nations — elsewhere
six — in Palestine before Israel are enumerated according

to stereotyped formulae (Gen. **15** : 20; Ex. **3** : 8, 17; **13** : 5; **23** : 23; **33** : 2; **34** : 11; Deut. **20** : 17; Jos. **3** : 10; **9** : 1; **11** : 3; **12** : 8; **24** : 11, etc.).

11) **7** : 12-16.   God will reward generously the fidelity of Israel with all kinds of material blessings, as in **28** : 4, 11, 18, 53.   He will free them especially from the special diseases of Egypt (v. 15) (cf. **28** : 60), such as elephantiasis — similar to leprosy — and various eye troubles, still common in Egypt.

12) **7** : 17-26.   Through Yahweh's help Israel will be able to conquer the nations now in the land; what He did in Egypt is a guarantee of what He will do in Palestine.   However, the conquest will be gradual (v. 22) : a sudden total destruction of the occupants would result in the land being overrun by wild beasts.   Nevertheless, the destruction of the enemy is to be total (v. 24), and especially that of the images of their gods (v. 25 f.).   Those consisting of carved wood covered with gold or silver leaves must be destroyed by fire, for the precious metal is desecrated by idolatrous use; it could prove a snare to people who might regard it as possessing special power. (Cf. H. JUNKER, *op. cit.*, p. 30).   On the progress of the conquest, which according to some texts was to be rapid (cf. Deut. **9** : 3, and the account of Jos. **10–11**), see Jdgs., which describes it as more slow (2 : 6–3 : 6) and suggests various reasons for it.

13) **8** : 1-20.   Throughout their sojourn in the desert, Yahweh took most loving care of His people; He helped them even when it looked as if nothing could be done to help.   He was to them a father who is kind, yet strict in order to train His children properly (vv. 1-5).   Now Israel will find itself in the Promised Land, the advantages of which are described in a hyperbolic form inspired by the contrast with the desert with its lack of resources (vv. 7-9; v. 15).   Prosperity may become a temptation to forget that they owe all good things to God (v. 17).   Therefore take care to remember that Yahweh alone, not " the other gods " of the nations, is the giver of the good gifts; their gratitude should go always to Him.   The stones of the land contain iron (v. 9; cf. **3** : 11) and the hills copper.   Traces of mines and smelting works have been found in various locations in Palestine and near the head of the Gulf of Elath (Akalah).   (Cf. W. F. ALBRIGHT, *Archaeol. of Pal.*,

pp. 127-128; Haag, *Bibellexikon*, 1136-1137). V. 15 : " saraph serpents "; cf. Num. **21** : 6 f.   Their name is variously explained : burning, on account of their powerful venom, or fire-spitting; popular imagination worked on the subject — hence, flying serpents (cf. Haag, *Bibellexikon*, 1506 f.).

14) **9** : 1-6. This begins like a new discourse, though, in the present context, it is given only as a subdivision of a larger discourse.   (Cf. **4** : 1; **5** : 2; **6** : 4).   Israel's success is due to God alone, not to any merit of their own (v. 3 ff.).   Only through fidelity to Yahweh may they hope for His protection.

15) **9** : 7-24.   The people's lapse into idolatry at Horeb illustrates vividly their readiness to rebel against Yahweh's commandments (9-12).   Only through a second period of severe fasting did Moses obtain forgiveness for the people (cf. vv. 12-14; 18-19).   V. 21 : cf. Ex. **32** : 20.   Vv. 22-24 sum up other instances of infidelity (Num. **11** : 1 ff.; Ex. **17** : 7).

16) **9** : 25–**10** : 11.   This section consists of a series of supplementary notices loosely connected with the discourse. (Cf. H. JUNKER, *op. cit.*, pp. 33-35).   **9** : 25-29 : goes back to v. 18 f., which it develops; cf. Ex. **32** : 11 ff.   **10** : 1-5 : is inserted here probably as a proof that Yahweh had really forgiven His people since He gave them new tablets of the Commandments; cf. Ex. **34** : 1 ff., 27 ff.   **10** : 6-7 is an historical notice, clearly no part of the original discourse, but introduced on account of the reference to Aaron's death (v. 6) as a punishment of his part at Horeb (**9** : 20).   Ch. **10** : 8-9 is suggested by the mention of the ark in **10** : 5 : the Tribe of Levi is instituted to serve the Ark.   **10** : 10-11 is the conclusion to the series of preceding notices.

17) **10** : 12-22.   Fear and love of God sum up the attitude of Israel towards the Lord and find their expression in perfect obedience to His Law (vv. 12-13).   The sovereign Lord of creation chose their Fathers and their descendants out of pure love (vv. 14-15, 17).   Hence they must open their hearts to his guidance (v. 16; cf. Jer. **4** : 4 and **6** : 10), and treat justly the weak and destitute who are under God's special care : the orphan, the widow, and the alien or stranger (v. 18 f.; cf. Ex. **22** : 20 f.).

18) **11** : 1-32. Yahweh punished severely the rebellious.
This is a warning against disobedience (vv. 1-9). With v. 4,
cf. Ex. **14** : 26 ff.; **15** : 19. On Dathan and Abiram (v. 6),
cf. Num. **16**, but in v. 6 there is no mention of Core. On the
reference to long life (v. 9) cf. **4** : 26, 40; **5** : 33. Continued
enjoyment of the blessings of Palestine will be the reward
of fidelity (vv. 10-25). In v. 10 f. notice the contrast with
Egypt, where the land is watered by hand (in Hebrew, literally,
"with your foot "). The water there was raised from the
channels or irrigation ditches by means of treadmills. In
Palestine, on the contrary, everything depends on the rain,
which is a gift of God. The early rain is that of the fall (October-
November), while the late rain comes in the spring (April)
(v. 14). Vv. 18-20; cf. **6** : 6-9. V. 24 mentions the ideal boundaries of Palestine (cf. **3** : 25). Vv. 29-30; cf. **27** : 2 ff.; Jos. **8** :
32-35. These verses may be regarded with several others as
a later addition, as they suppose knowledge of the region of
Sichem (Neapolis : Nablūs). The Samaritans at a later period
built their temple on Mt. Garizim (cf. Jn. **4** : 20). The Araba
(v. 30) is the deep depression on both sides of the Jordan, the
Dead Sea, and the continuation of the depression to the Gulf
of Aqaba (**3** : 17; **4** : 49). Galgal : the modern Jiljilieh between
the Jordan and Jericho (cf. Jos. **4** : 19 ff.). The oak or terebinth
of Moreb : cf. Gen. **12** : 6; apparently a sacred tree (tree of
the oracle).

C. **12** : 1–**26** : 19.

This part is considered by some as another discourse —
the third — of Moses. Others regard it rather as the continuation of the second discourse. The preceding section,
Chapters **5–11**, in substance develops the first commandment
of the Decalogue : the doctrine of the one God. This section,
which contains special laws concerning a number of different
matters of conduct, is in fact the Deuteronomic Code, a most
important part of the book.

1) **12** : 1-14 : the law of the Sanctuary. It is introduced
by a formula (v. 1) which has been met with a number of times
in the preceding chapters (e.g., **4** : 1; **5** : 1; **6** : 1; **8** : 1), and
thus does not seem to be a definite sign of a new discourse,

but may mark off sections within the same discourse. The
worship of Yahweh will have nothing in common with the
other divinities of Canaan : the sacred places of Canaan may
not be used for Yahweh, but must be destroyed altogether
(vv. 2-3). V. 3 : The sacred poles are symbols of the goddess
(Asherah — hence their Hebrew name), mentioned as Ashratu
or Ashirtu in cuneiform texts and as Ashirat of the Tyrians
in Ugaritic texts. In Ugarit, she was the wife of El, and goddess
of the sea; in other places, the goddess of abundance. The
name of this goddess is to be distinguished carefully from that
of Astarte 1 (3) Kgs. 11 : 5, 23 (etc.), the goddess of Sidon
and of Ugarit, of Moab, and of South Arabia, who was also
a goddess of fertility (cf. KÖHLER, *Lexikon in V. T. Libros*,
p. 745; also, A. JAMME, in Brillant-Aigrain, *Histoire des religions*,
4 [Paris, 1956], 264 ff.). By destroying all the sanctuaries
and symbols of the divinities of Canaan, Israel will break the
hold of the false gods, and Yahweh will remain the sole God
and Master of the land. Instead of worshipping Yahweh at
numerous sanctuaries as the Canaanites do in the case of their
gods, Israel is to worship Yahweh at one sanctuary, " the
place which Yahweh your God will choose out of all your
tribes to place His name there to dwell there " (v. 5). The
Hebrew phrase recalls the Akkadian expression in the Amarna
Letters; the king (Pharaoh) has placed his name *(shakan
shumishu)* on Jerusalem forever, i.e., has made the land his
forever (cf. H. WINCKLER, *Keilinschriftliches Textbuch zum
A. T.* [3rd ed., Leipzig, 1903], p. 8; Pritchard, *ANET*, p. 488[b];
cf. the phrase in Deut. 12 : 11; 14 : 23; 16 : 2, 6, 11; 26 : 2).
The place is to be chosen by Yahweh; this is stated repeatedly
(12 : 5, 11, 14, 18, 21, 26; 14 : 23-25; 16 : 2, 6, 7, 11, 15, 16;
17 : 8, 10; 18 : 6; 26 : 2; 31 : 11), naturally without mentioning
the name of the place. The regular worship of Yahweh is to
be carried on at this place alone : the offering of sacrifices,
the paying of tithes, etc. (vv. 5-7, 10-14). This law (one place
of worship) is given for the future, when the people shall be
settled in Palestine, for circumstances are expected to be
different from those prevailing now (vv. 8-10). During the
time before the settlement in the Promised Land, there was
one place of worship, the sanctuary where the Ark was kept,
but no permanent place; the sanctuary and the Ark moved

from place to place, as the people moved about in their wanderings in the Desert. On the question of the unity of the Sanctuary, see the Commentaries; also the view of Cassuto in *Entzyklop. Miqra'it 2*, pp. 614-615, and, especially, H. JUNKER, *op. cit.*, pp. 3-7. Junker argues that the principle of the unity of the Sanctuary is an ancient tradition which goes back to Moses.

2) **12** : 15-19. This makes a distinction between slaughtering of animals for ordinary meals of which any one may partake and slaughtering for religious purposes. The former is allowed anywhere, provided the prohibition of blood is observed. The latter, being a sacrifice, must take place at the Sanctuary as well as the other offerings which are part of the religious prescriptions connected with the Sanctuary (cf. Lev. **17** : 1 ff.).

3) **12** : 20-28. This is in reality a variant form of the preceding section.

4) **12** : 29-31 : a transition to the fuller development in **13** on idolatry. Beware of all pagan rites, and do not combine with the worship of Yahweh the religious practices of the Canaanites, especially the sacrifices of children (cf. Lev. **18** : 21; **20** : 1 ff.; 2 (4) Kgs. **16** : 3; **17** : 17-31; **21** : 6; Jer. **32** : 35).

5) **13** : 1-6. The principle is (v. 1) : Observe most scrupulously, without any compromise, the law that Yahweh is the sole God. Nothing whatsoever can authorize a departure from that rule : even signs or wonders performed by prophets have no value against the fundamental doctrine of the sole worship of Yahweh. The prophet can be only a false prophet who deserves death. The case is clearly hypothetical; the purpose is evidently to inculcate in the most emphatic manner the duty of fidelity to Yahweh exclusively under all circumstances.

6) **13** : 7-12. The same idea is presented in another striking form : Do not allow yourself to be lured to the worship of other gods by those nearest and dearest to you. On stoning of the guilty party, cf. Ex. **17** : 4; **19** : 13; **21** : 28.

7) **13** : 13-19. This is another hypothetical case meant to stress the point taught in the preceding section : Israel may

not allow a part of the people to fall away from Yahweh. Should this happen, the apostate community should be destroyed without mercy — a case of *Herem* (Num. **18** : 14; **21** : 1-3; Deut. **2** : 34; **3** : 6; **7** : 2; **20** : 17. Cf. *Entzykl. Miq.* 3, pp. 290-292; Haag, *Bibellexikon*, 153 f.). V. 14 : " scoundrels "; Hebrew *beney beliya·al,* " sons of worthlessness " (?) (cf. KÖHLER, *Lex. in V. T. Libros,* p. 130). The word *Beli ya·al* came to be regarded as a proper name of the devil (cf. Vulgate at 1 Sam. **1** : 16, etc.; 2 Cor. **6** : 15; so also in some Apocrypha; cf. Haag, *Bibellexikon,* 177). The word is used as a proper name quite frequently in the Qumran texts (see HABERMAN : *·Edah we-Edut* [Jerusalem, 1952], p. 129; Y. YADIN, *Migillat Milhemet...* [Jerusalem, 1955], pp. 230-231; J. CARMIGNAC, *Règle de la Guerre...* [Paris, 1958], pp. 2-3).

V. 16 : On the Hebrew expression rendered " put to the sword ", see JOÜON, *Orientalia,* 3 (1932), pp. 281-284; Th. J. MEEK, *BASOR,* no. 122 (Apr., 1951), 31-33. V. 17 : " a heap of ruins forever " *(tel ōlām).* This corresponds to the Akkadian *tillu,* Arabic *tell,* a mound of ruins marking the site of a destroyed city. The name appears quite frequently on maps of modern Palestine.

8) **14** : 1-21. Various items are condemned as incompatible with Yahweh worship.

a) Vv. 1-2. The true reason of the condemnation escapes us, except that we find similar practices in pagan nations as well as in Israel, where they were apparently ancient customs that were kept up in spite of the prohibition (cf. Lev. **21** : 5; Jer. **16** : 6; **41** : 5; **47** : 5; **48** : 37; Isa. **3** : 24; **22** : 12; Am. **8** : 10; Mich. **1** : 16, etc.). See also Jer. **9** : 28, who mentions Arabs as those with temples shaved; cf. Herod. **3**, **8**, 3, who says that they cut their hair all around in a circle, with the temples shaved as a sign that they belong to Orotalt *(Ilu-ta·alā,* " God most high " (?) and Alilat (" the goddess ", fem. of *al-Ilah).* On ritual self-inflicted wounds, cf. Osee **7** : 14 (according to the reading of some mss of the Hebrew, LXX, and Syriac), and 1 (3) Kgs. **18** : 28.

b) Vv. 3-21. The list of clean and unclean animals is found also in a fuller form in Lev. **11**. Thus there are two traditions, of which that in Deut. is perhaps more primitive. (For details, cf. the Commentaries on Lev. and Deut.). V. 21ª : cf. Ex. **21** : 33 ff.; **22** : 30. The reason for the prohibition is probably that the blood had not been drained completely. However, Lev. **11** : 40 and **17** : 15 may be taken to imply that this was disregarded at times. On the end of v. 21, see Ex. **23** : 19; **34** : 26.

9) **14** : 22-29. The question of the tithes is treated in Lev. **27** : 30-33 and Num. **18** : 20-22. There are differences between these texts, due most likely to differences in dates : they represent changes in circumstances. But in any case, the practice of tithing is ancient (cf. Gen. **14** : 20; **28** : 22). It reminded the people that they owed their good things to God's blessing (cf. v. 24, end) and must acknowledge God as the master and owner. (Cf. H. JUNKER, *op. cit.*, p. 45). Vv. 24-27 are meant to make the fulfillment of the obligation easier, and thus represent a later interpretation of vv. 22-23. Vv. 28-29 make provision for the Levites and the people without means by leaving for them the tithes of every third year in community stores. The prescription of vv. 22-23 that the tithes were to be brought to the central shrine naturally resulted in depriving the Levites and the destitute who lived at a distance from the shrine.

10) *a)* **15** : 1-6. Every seven years there is " remission " or " relaxation " of debts in addition to the " resting of the land " (Ex. **23** : 10-11; Lev. **25** : 2-7), " in honor of Yahweh " (v. 2). The creditor may not press his claim on an Israelite debtor, though he may do so on a non-Israelite debtor (vv. 2-3). The debt probably consisted in articles of food (wheat, etc.) — in any case not in interest on money, as interest was forbidden (**23** : 20; Ex. **20** : 24). The reason for not claiming the debt in that year was that the seventh year was a sabbatical year when the land rested, and thus did not produce any regular harvest. According to the Jewish view, there was a complete remission of the debt (cf. Neh. **10** : 32), a cancellation. Modern writers hold that this was rather a suspension of payment. This legal provision (vv. 1-3) concludes with an oratorical development assuring the faithful man that God will not let him suffer want for strict obedience to it (vv. 4-6).

b) Vv. 7-11. This is a similar development urging generosity towards the poor, for, as noted in v. 11, in spite of the
rhetorical exaggeration in v. 4 that no one should suffer want
in the land, there will always be poor in the land to whom
charity can be shown (cf. Jn. 12 : 8).

c) Vv. 12-18. In some cases, a man did not succeed in
freeing himself from debt, but rather sank into more serious
indebtedness; the only way to save himself was to sell himself
as a slave to his creditor (v. 12), but he becomes free in the
seventh year (v. 12; cf. Ex. 21 : 2-6). If the slave does not
wish to leave his master, he will go through a ceremony
signifying that he remains bound to his master's house
(vv. 16-17; cf. Ex. 21 : 6). A development in vv. 13-15 and 18
— quite in keeping with the general thought of Deuteronomy —
urges kindness to the slave who is freed.

d) Vv. 19-23. The firstlings belong to the Lord; cf. Ex. 13 :
1-2; 22 : 28-29; Num. 3 : 11-30, 40-45; 18 : 15-18. Notice the
change : the offering of the firstling — which must be without
blemish — is postponed to the time of the yearly visit at the
central shrine.

11) *The liturgical calendar :* 16 : 1-17.

a) 16 : 1-8 : the Passover and Unleavened Bread (cf. Ex. 12;
13 : 3-10; Lev. 23 : 5-8; Num. 9 : 2-14). The feast is held in
the month of Abib, later called Nisan (March-April) when the
ears of wheat begin to form in Palestine. It is the first month
of the year. Deut. does not describe the ritual of the Passover,
which is supposed known. For this, we have to go to Ex.
A point of difference is that in Ex. the Passover is a home
and family festival; in Deut. its place is the central shrine,
where the slaughtering of the sacrificial victim is to be done
(vv. 2, 5-6). In Ex., only small animals (lambs and kids)
are envisaged; this is natural, as one such animal would be
enough for a family. Deut. supposes the possibility of a larger
animal (v. 2, " or from the herd "); at the central shrine, the
large crowds of pilgrims would entail a larger number of people
at the Passover meal.

b) 16 : 9-12 : the Feast of Weeks, i.e., seven weeks after
Passover, Pentecost, the fiftieth day (Ex. 23 : 16; 34 : 22;
Lev. 23 : 15-21; Num. 28 : 16). It was a feast of the harvest.

c) **16** . 13-15 : the Feast of Booths (Tabernacles; Lev. **23** : 34-36, 42-43; Ex. **23** : 16ᵇ; **34** : 22ᵇ). It is a feast of fruit harvest; called " Booths " here in memory of the life in the desert. These three feasts consecrate the three seasons : spring, summer, autumn.

d) **16** : 16-17 : conclusion on the three great feastdays — holy days — of the year.

12) **16** : **18–19** : 21 : regulations about justice.

a) **16** : 18-20. Judges must be appointed throughout the land to insure the proper administration of justice everywhere.

b) **16** : 21-22. This paragraph about forbidden religious symbols looks somewhat out of context. It would form a more coherent section with **17** : 2-7, which deals with a severe offence against religion and the procedure to be followed in convicting and executing the culprit. On the section, cf. H. JUNKER, *op. cit.*, pp. 51-52.

c) **17** : 1. The sacrificial victim must be without blemish (Lev. **22** : 17-25; Mal. **1** : 3).

d) **17** : 8-13. Difficult cases are to be referred to the higher court consisting of the priests of the Tribe of Levi and the judge, who together study and decide the case. The practical details are not stated, namely the precise cooperation of priests and judge. To disobey the verdict based on the law of God is a sin of arrogance towards God and is punishable with death.

e) **17** : 14-20 : the king. Beginning here we have a series of regulations concerning the life of the nation : king (vv. 14-20), priesthood (**18** : 1-8), and prophecy (**18** : 9-22). When settled in their land, Israel may wish to have a king like their neighbors. The king must be one of their own people (v. 15); he must not try to have a great number of horses — chariotry for war — which he would import from Egypt. Such an ambition " might make Israel a vassal of Egypt " (Confraternity Version) or lead him to sell his subjects as slaves in exchange for such military aid (H. JUNKER, *op. cit.*, p. 53). He must not have a large harem, for pagan princesses and women slaves would endanger his attachment to the faith of Israel (v. 17); rather he must rule according to the Law of Yahweh, and, to this end, have a copy of this law constantly with him (vv. 18-20). Most exegetes hold that Moses did not make such a definite provision for the institution of the monarchy. In 1 Sam. **8** : 4 ff. (cf. Jdgs. **8** : 22 f.), the monarchy is judged to be incompatible with the rule of Yahweh. V. 17 especially seems inspired by the case of Solomon 1 (3) Kgs. **11** : 1 ff.). Hence, at least in its present form, the section may be taken as having been influenced by later circumstances. The copy of this law (v. 18) can hardly be supposed to consist only of this paragraph; it is rather a copy of the Law, i.e. of Deuteronomy, in an older form. Possibly the constitution of the monarchy deposited in the Sanctuary by Samuel was incorporated in a book of laws of Mosaic tradition, as suggested by von Hummelauer, S. J.; JUNKER, *op. cit.*, p. 54. (Cf. the discussion of the date of Deut. by CASSUTO, *Entzykl. Miq.* 2, 609-615; S. R. DRIVER, *Introduction*, p. 87 f., and 92 f.).

f) **18** : 1-8 : the priests. The Tribe of Levi, to which the priests belong, has no territory of its own like the other tribes. The Lord is their heritage, and gives them their sustenance (vv. 1-2; cf. **10** : 9; **12** : 12; **14** : 27-29; Num. **18** : 20). The revenues of the priests defined in vv. 3-5 differ in details from those defined elsewhere (Ex. **29** : 27-28; Lev. **7** : 28 ff.; **10** : 12 ff.; Num. **6** : 20; **18** : 18). Note also the practice mentioned in 1 Sam. **2** : 12 ff. Hence it may be concluded that Deut. here is describing a different practice. Vv. 6-8 state that all Levites are entitled to perform their ministry at the central shrine and enjoy the same rights as those settled there already. When a Levite from any community where he resides " goes with all the desire of his soul " (= moved by a strong desire, because such is his desire) comes to the Sanctuary, he shall have the same privileges as those who are there in the service of the Sanctuary, " apart from (= without taking into account) his sales on his patrimony " (?). (The texts are doubtful; cf. the Commentaries).

g) **18** : 9-22 : prophecy. All forms of pagan superstition are forbidden strictly : sacrifices of children, which were regarded as very effective in time of danger (a magical practice), augury, black magic, necromancy (vv. 10-11). Such practices of the pagans are abominations to the Lord. God himself will provide for the guidance of His people by means of prophecy, by sending prophets who will speak in His name (v. 15), and therefore must be obeyed as God Himself (v. 19). The true prophet will be accredited by God as His envoy (v. 21 f.). A false prophet is to be put to death (vv. 20-22). The same thought is developed in another form in vv. 16-18 (cf. 5 : 23 ff.). God appointed Moses to be His prophet, making known God's will in God's name, so in the future God will raise up a prophet to speak in His name. The text and content clearly refer here to the institution of prophecy; this is the primary literal sense. But in course of time, in the Old Testament itself as in the New Testament, the text took on a fuller meaning, as announcing the Messias, the greatest of all the prophets who prepared His coming.

13) **19** : 1-13 : cities of refuge. The preceding section was in the form of words of Yahweh (**18** : 17 ff.). Here the text continues as the discourse of Moses, with the opening words (v. 1) as in **12** : 29. Three cities of refuge have been designated for East Jordan (**4** : 41-43). Here three other such cities are to be designated in Western Palestine (cf. Num. **35** : 10 ff. and Jos. **20**). The purpose of this institution is to protect the innocent from hasty exercise of the right of avenging blood. The institution is ancient, but the formulation of the law may represent different stages of adaptation to the actual circumstances of the post-Mosaic age (cf. Junker, *op. cit.*, p. 57).

14) **19** : 14. Landmarks showing the limits of private property should not be changed (cf. **27** : 17; Osee **5** : 10; Prov. **22** : 28; **23** : 10; Job **24** : 2).

15) **19** : 15-21 : witnesses. One witness does not suffice to convict a man (v. 15; cf. **17** : 6; Num. **35** : 30). A false witness shall suffer the penalty he wished to have inflicted on the innocent party accused by him (vv. 16 ff.; cf. Ex. **21** : 23-25; Lev. **24** : 18-20). We find similar regulations in the Code of Hammurabi (Pritchard, *ANET*, p. 166[a], nos. 1-4).

16) **20** : 1-20 : rules of war.

a) 1-9. After an exhortation — hardly a legal text — to put all their trust in God (vv. 1-4), comes a statement of exemption from war service (vv. 5-9). The exemption in

v. 7 is destined to secure the continuation of the family. The reasons for those in vv. 5-6 are not so clear. That in v. 8 is rather an appeal to self-respect; one could hardly avail himself of it without disgrace. (Cf. 1 Mach. 3 : 56).

b) 10-15. If the enemy submits without battle, he shall be spared, though he will be subjected to forced labor (10-11). Resistance will mean death to the male population; the women and children shall become slaves, and their possessions shall be the victor's booty (vv. 12-15). The law represents the rule of warfare of the Ancient Orient.

c) 16-18 : In dealing with the Canaanites, *herem* is to be enforced strictly — total destruction, to avoid religious perversion. A similar rule was followed by Israel's neighbors (Moab), and many other ancient nations (e.g., Hittites, Greeks, Celts, Romans, Germans).

d) 19-20. Needless wholesale destruction is to be avoided, as exemplified by the example of the trees.

17) **21** : 1-9 : expiation of an untraced murder. Human life is precious before God : the blood of a slain man cries out to God (Gen. 4 : 9 f.). In the present instance, the author of the deed is unknown, so that justice cannot follow its regular course. Hence expiation must be made by the elders of the city nearest to the corpse, because it is its land that has been desecrated. The ceremony is performed by the elders, the representatives of the city (vv. 3-4, 6-8) under the supervision of the priests (v. 5). Though this is a religious ceremony, it is not a sacrifice (cf. the similar cases of the red heifer [Num. **19** : 2 ff.] and the scapegoat [Lev. **16** : 20 ff.].

18) **21** : 10-14. A female captive may be taken as wife after a period of mourning (v. 13). After she has become the man's wife, she cannot be sold as a slave. Thus the law protects the woman and respects her natural feelings. Vv. 12-13 are understood in several ways. Often, her shaving of her head, her paring of her nails, her wearing of an old dress are explained as signs of mourning. However, there are no real parallels to these manifestations, especially on the part of women. Modern Bedouin women of Moab may cut off some of their hair, which they lay on the tomb in sign of mourning, but

there is no shaving of hair. (Cf. on this, *Bible du Centenaire,*
l.c.). According to Junker, *op. cit.*, p. 62, these actions are
symbols of the change in woman's status : she parts as it were
with her old life to enter into the life of a married woman.
Cf. also : *Sacra Bibbia* (Pontif. Inst.) *l.c.* But the shaving
of her head is something rather radical and might be viewed
with great disfavor by the man who had seen her a comely
woman (v. 11). Possibly, with some modern writers, we should
read, instead of *gellehah* of the Masoretic Text (" to shave ",)
the verb *gilletah*, " she will unveil her head " (so, e.g., Ehrlich;
N. Schlögl, *Die hl. Schriften...* I, p. 293; Pirot-Clamer, *La Sainte*
Bible; the *American Version*, Riessler). " To pare her nails "
is hardly a sign of mourning. The Hebrew verb is " to make "
= " to fix ", " to arrange " (cf. French, *se faire les ongles*). I.e.,
the woman is giving up her mourning, and prepares herself
to become a bride.

19) **21** : 15-17. The rights of the first-born son must be
respected by the father even if he cares less for that son's
mother than for his other wife and her son. The law changes
the practice supposed in Genesis where the father is free to
do as he chooses.

20) **21** : 18-21. An incorrigible son who stubbornly refuses
to obey his parents or squanders the family resources may be
brought before the court and sentenced to death. This law
subordinates the authority of the parents, which was once
absolute, to organized justice.

21) **21** : 22-23. The corpse of a criminal executed for a capital
offense is, according to an ancient custom (cf. Num. **25** : 4
[see the Commentaries on this text]; Jos. **8** : 29; **10** : 26; 1 Sam.
31 : 10; 2 Sam. **4** : 12), hung on a tree to add to his disgrace,
but it is buried at sundown. During the night wild animals
might defile the land by dragging parts of the corpse to various
places.

22) **22** : 1-12 : various items.   *a*) Vv. 1-4. Care for lost
property of one's neighbor implies care for his lost animals
even if it involves some trouble for the finder. Cf. Ex. **23** :
4-5. *b*) V. 5. The allusion is perhaps to some pagan practices
connected with immorality. *c*) Vv. 6-7 : respect for lowly
creatures. Man must not abuse his right over the things God

has placed at his disposal. *d*) V. 8. A parapet around the flat roof where people gather will prevent accidents. *e*) Vv. 9-11. God has created each kind of things separately, and this order must be respected. In v. 10, it is pointed out that the weaker animal working with a stronger animal would suffer. *f*) V. 12 (cf. Num. **15** : 38-40). The reason for the precept is not known, though various symbolic explanations are proposed.

23) **22** : 13–23 : 1 : various precepts connected with marriage and chastity.

a) **22** : 13-21. The young woman has been married as a virgin. If the husband takes a dislike to her, to get rid of her he may claim that she was not a virgin when he married her. The false accusation may be refuted by producing the cloth with the stains of blood of the first night, which the young woman left with her parents as evidence of her virginity. The lying husband shall be fined heavily and he cannot divorce her any time afterwards (vv. 13-19). The custom referred to here is not limited to Israel. Cf. *DBV*, s.v. " Virginité ", 2439; M. Molho, *Usos y costumbres de los Sefardies de Salonica* (Madrid-Barcelona, 1950), p. 34 f.; R. DE VAUX, O. P., *Institutions de l'A. T.*, I (Paris, 1958), p. 60; various narratives in the Arabian Nights (Cairo ed. in Arabic, 1279 = 1862), I, pp. 166, 206; II, p. 28. But if the charge is true, the woman is stoned to death at the entrance of her father's house (vv. 20-21).

b) **22** : 22. Adultery is punished by the death of both parties. So also in ancient Oriental law, which, however, allowed the husband to forgive his wife, and thus also her partner in the offense. (Cf. A. VAN PRAAG, *Droit matrimonial assyro-babylonien* [Amsterdam, 1945], p. 219, s.v. " Adultère ").

c) **22** : 23-27 : offenses against a young woman who is betrothed, and therefore treated as if she were married. Vv. 23-24. If such an offense takes place within the city where it is presumed that she could alert people, both parties are dealt with as adulterers. Vv. 25-27. If it happens in the country, when the woman presumably cannot call for help, the man alone is put to death.

d) **22** : 28-29. If the woman is not betrothed, the man must pay the price of the virginity (Ex. **22** : 15-16) and marry the woman without possibility of divorce.

e) **23** : 1. Incest is prohibited (Lev. **18** : 8; **20** : 11; Deut. **27** : 20).

24) **23** : 2–**26** : 19. These chapters contain a number of disconnected prescriptions about various matters. For convenience, the analysis follows the sequence of the chapters, although a number of items could be grouped together under common headings.

a) **23** : 2-9. Various disabilities and historical reasons exclude some people from membership in the community. Thus, mutilations of the sexual members which contradict the order established by God (Gen. **1** : 22-28) (v. 2); the *mamzer* (v. 3) i.e., one of mixed origin, born of a forbidden marriage, thus illegitimate (cf. Zach. **9** : 6; Neh. **13** : 23 ff.); the Ammonite or Moabite (vv. 4-7) this is rather surprising in view of **2** : 9-13 and 16-19 where Israel is enjoined to respect the lands of their kinsmen. The reason given in vv. 5-6, based on the traditions of Num. **22**–**24**, is hardly the original reason. More recent facts from history will explain the bitterness of the attitude (cf. Jdgs. **3** : 12 ff.; **10** : 7 ff.; 2 (4) Kgs. **3** : 4 ff.). Edom, on the contrary, is mentioned favorably (v. 8); in 2 (4) Kgs. **3** : 9. Edom appears as an ally of Israel. Later, however, Edom shook off the authority of Juda (2 (4) Kgs. **8** : 20-22), though Juda tried to restore its authority (2 (4) Kgs. **14** : 7-22; cf. 2 (4) Kgs. **16** : 6). After the destruction of Jerusalem, Edom extended its power northward into Juda's territory (cf. Abd. 6 ff.; Ez. **25** : 12 ff.; **35**; Ps. **137**, etc.). Hence our text probably took its present form before the Exile. No less surprising is the favorable reference to Egypt (v. 8). If only a short time had passed since the days of the Egyptian bondage we should expect bitterness. But probably, by the time this was written many years had passed since the Exodus, and even since the plundering of Jerusalem by Sesac (Sheshonk I) 945-924 B.C. (1 Kgs. **14** : 25 f.).

b) **23** : 10-15. Yahweh is present in the camp in the Ark (v. 15). There must be no uncleanliness (cf. Lev. **15** : 2 ff.; Num. **5** : 1 ff.; 1 Sam. **21** : 5).

c) **23 : 16 17.** The reference is probably to slaves who have escaped from foreign countries.

d) **23 : 18-19.** No sacred prostitution (*kedēshāh* and *kādēsh:* lit. " consecrated woman or man ") is allowed in Israel. The " dog " in v. 19 is the name of the pagan priest in Phoenician texts (see note in Confraternity Version). Cf. 1 Kgs. **14** : 24; **15** : 12; **22** : 47; 2 Kgs. **23** : 7.

e) **23 : 20-21.** Interest on loans to fellow-Israelites is forbidden, though it may be demanded from a foreigner (cf. Lev. **25** : 35-37; Ex. **22** : 24); hence interest is not forbidden absolutely. The practice developed in the Ancient Orient. The rate of interest on money was usually 20% and on grain 35%.

f) **23 : 22-24.** Vows must be fulfilled. Cf. Num. **30** : 3 ff.; Eccles. **5** : 3 f.

g) **23 : 25-26.** It is allowed to pick grapes or ears of corn in passing, but not to come with a basket or sickle as for harvesting. The regulation is probably meant to apply to the poor.

h) **24 : 1-4.** Divorce is taken for granted, but it is restricted in some way since the husband may not take back his divorced wife who has remarried after receiving her bill of divorce. The precise meaning of the expression " something indecent " (v. 1) (cf. **23** : 15) was a matter of dispute in N. T. times (cf. Mt. **19** : 3). According to the Koran, on the contrary, the husband may take back his divorced wife only if she has married another man after the divorce (2, 230). Cf. WENSINCK-KRAMERS, *Handwörterbuch des Islam* (Leiden, 1941) s.v. " Talak ", 719-726.

i) **24 : 5.** A new bridegroom is exempted from military and other service for a year (cf. **20** : 7).

j) **24 : 6.** The bread was prepared at home every day; hence taking the hand mill or part of it as a pledge works an intolerable hardship.

k) **24 : 7.** Kidnapping a fellow Israelite for slavery is a crime deserving of death.

l) **24 : 8-9.** This prescription regarding leprosy refers to the collection of directions given to the priests of the Tribe of Levi (Lev. **13–14**; Num. **12** : 10-15). This is interesting as showing that there existed a special collection entrusted to the priests, besides one like that of Deut. of a more general character (Junker, *op. cit.*, p. 71).

m) **24** : 10-15 and 17-18. These regulations have this in common that they demand consideration for the poor (cf. **24** : 17; **24** : 6; Ex. **22** : 25 f.; Amos **2** : 8). The poor working man needs his day's wages, and can not wait (vv. 14-15). Harshness in demanding a pledge is condemned (vv. 10-13); the debtor has the right to select the pledge (Confraternity Version) and the creditor has no right to keep the mantle in which the poor man sleeps. The same idea underlies the rule of vv. 17-18 (cf. Ex. **22** : 20 ff. and Lev. **19** : 33 f.).

n) **24** : 16. This condemns the old view of collective responsibility : everyone is responsible for his own deeds. For the old practice, see Jos. **7** : 24 ff.; 2 Sam. **21** : 1 ff. For individual responsibility, cf. 2 (4) Kgs. **14** : 5-6; Jer. **31** : 29 f.; Ez. **18** : 1 ff.

o) **24** : 19-22. The old custom to leave something of the harvest in the field or orchard, found in various peoples as a tribute to the spirits of the land, becomes here an act of charity towards the poor.

p) **25** : 1-3. The Law limits the old custom of corporal punishment, so that the flogging may not disable the man (see EHRLICH, p. 322; N. SCHLÖGL, *op. cit.*, I, 301; RIESSLER'S Translation; Amer. Version; JUNKER, *op. cit.*). The number of blows has little to do with the man's disgrace; he is disgraced by the mere fact that he is condemned by the tribunal. Rather, some physical result is meant — Ehrlich. Hence the translation : " be cut to pieces ", reading root NQL, interpreted from Arabic as " needing to be mended ", " to shatter a bone by a blow ". (Cf. 2 Cor. **11** : 24).

q) **25** : 4. Cf. 1 Cor. **9** : 9 (Confraternity Version and note). One must not begrudge to the animal the few ears of grain it may snatch.

r) **25** : 5-10. Levirate marriage (cf. notes in Confrat. V.). There are analogies to this custom in some ancient Oriental codes (cf. A. VAN PRAAG, *Droit matrimonial*, p. 220 s.v. " Lévirat "; Pritchard, *ANET*, p. 182, no. 33). The obligation exists when the man's brother has died without male heir to continue his family, and when the brothers have lived together working the family property together. It is a disgrace for the man not to live up to his obligation.

s) **25** : II-I2. The woman's action is punished severely because it implies shamelessness, and it may disable the man's virility (cf. **23** : 2).

t) **25** . 13-16. Deceit in business is an abomination to Yahweh. The denunciation of the dishonest practice is not accompanied by a sanction; hence it is not a law in the proper sense, but it answers the educative character of the law. (Junker, *op. cit.*, p. 74).

u) **25** : 17-19. Amalec is condemned to total extermination for an attack not related elsewhere (cf. Ex. **17** : 8 ff.). Balaam announced their ruin (Num. **24** : 20). Saul carried out Samuel's command to destroy them (cf. I Sam. **15** : 2 f. and I Par. **4** : 42 f.). This text must be very ancient; it would mean nothing at a later date.

v) **26** : I-II : thanksgiving for the harvest. The time of the ceremony is probably the Feast of Weeks (Pentecost). The ritual consists of the offering of some first fruits of the various products of the land in a basket in undetermined quantity accompanied by the reciting of two formulas (vv. 3— 5-10). The wording of the prayers which mentions so insistently the deliverance from Egypt and the entrance into the Holy Land by God's power may be taken to imply the vivid recollection of the events and thus an early date (Junker, *op. cit.*, p. 75). In v. 5 the wandering Aramaean is Jacob the ancestor of Israel (Gen. **24** : 10; **25** : 20; **28** : 5; **29** : I ff.; **31** : 20-24). The ancestors of the Hebrews were Aramaeans who adopted the language of Canaan (Hebrew) in Palestine. V. 6 : " a nation great ", etc.; for the phrase, cf. **4** : 38; **7** : 1; **9** : 1-14; **11** : 23. V. 8 : cf. **4** : 34; **6** : 22; **7** : 19. V. 9 : cf. **6** : 3; **11** : 9.

w) **26** : 12-15 : the tithes in the third year, known therefore as the year of the tithes (cf. **14** : 28-29). The action commanded benefited the Levites and the needy. It did not take place in the Sanctuary, but the person made his declaration before God, on his word, that nothing had made the tithes unclean.

V. 14. The mourner, from contact with the dead, was unclean (Num. 21 : 14; cf. Ag. 2 : 13; Lev. 22 : 3 ff., offering to the dead (cf. Ecclus. 30 : 18). Others understand this of food sent to the house of the mourner (Tob. 4 : 17; Jer. 16 : 7).

y) **26 :** 16-19 : the conclusion. The covenant has been renewed by Moses speaking in God's name; the terms have been recalled and the people have accepted them. V. 16 : cf. 4 : 5, 8, 14; 11 : 32; 12 : 1; 4 : 29; 6 : 5; 10 : 12; 11 : 13; 13 : 4. V. 17 : cf. 8 : 6; 10 : 12; 11 : 22; 19 : 9.

D. 27 : 1–28 : 69.

This section is not a fully satisfactory literary unit. It consists of several elements combined more or less perfectly (cf. DRIVER, *Introduction*, p. 94 f.; JUNKER, *op. cit.*, p. 77 f.).

I. 27 : 1-26.

a) **27 :** 1—9-10. These verses go together as the transition from 26 : 16-19 to 28 : 1 ff. All these verses are regarded as originally part of an account of covenant renewal by Moses.

b) **27 :** 2-8—11-14. These verses do not form a really coherent unit. Moses orders the people to set up large stones coated with plaster on which to write the text of the law. This is to be done inmediately after crossing the Jordan in order to secure success in getting possession of the land (vv. 2-3). But v. 5 prescribes the building of an altar of rough stones on Mount Ebal. Sacrifices shall be offered on that altar (vv. 6 ff.). This supposes an interval of time between the crossing of the Jordan and reaching Central Palestine. The text of vv. 5-7 continues in vv. 11-14 which outline the ritual of the prescribed ceremony of the renewal of the covenant on Ebal-Garizim. Vv. 4-8 combine the two ceremonies (vv. 2-3 and 5-7—11-14) into one and smooth over the differences between the two groups of vv. Vv. 11-14 announce as part of the ceremony the pronouncing of blessings and curses (vv. 12-13). Mt. Garizim is the place from which the blessings are to be uttered, and Mt. Ebal that from which the curses are to be spoken. The text of the blessings is not preserved here, but only that of the curses (vv. 14-26). The curses are uttered by the Levites (v. 14) from Mount Garizim, which is the mount of the blessings. Here again, then, there is some incoherence, due to some omission and to use of materials of different origin.

Further observations. According to vv. 2-3 and 4ᵇ, the surface of the stones is coated with chalk so that the letters in black paint come out very clearly (v. 8), against the white background. What is supposed written is not only the blessings and the curses, but the Law, i.e. Deuteronomy. V. 4. According to the traditional Masoretic Text, the stones are set up on Mt. Ebal; according to the Samaritan Hebrew, the stones are set up on Mt. Garizim, so that Garizim becomes the place of the altar (v. 5). V. 5 : on the altar; cf. Ex. **20** : 25; Jos. **8** : 30-31.

Vv. 12-13. On these mountains, cf., e.g., Haag, *Bibellexikon*, 347-556, and p. 1509 for map. Garizim is the modern *Jebel et-Tor*, S. of ancient Sichem; Ebal opposite it is the *Jebel islamiyeh* or *esh-shemali* (" the Northern Mt. "). The Samaritan temple was destroyed by the Jews in 128 B.C., but remains and is still the Samaritan place of worship (cf. Jn. **4** : 20). Between these two mountains is (E. to W.) a narrow valley.

Vv. 14-26. There are twelve curses in concise and precise form on sins condemned in different places : 15 : cf. **4** : 16-25; **5** : 8; 16 : cf. Ex. **21** : 17; 17 : cf. **19** : 14; 18 : cf. Lev. **19** : 14; 19 : cf. **24** : 17, 19, 21; 20 : cf. **23** : 1; 21 : cf. Ex. **22** : 18; Lev. **18** : 23; 22 : cf. Lev. **18** : 9; **20** : 17; 23 : cf. Lev. **18** : 17; 24 : cf. Ex. **20** : 13; **21** : 12; Num. **35** : 20f.; 25 : cf. Deut. **16** : 19; Ex. **23** : 8; 26 : a general curse raising the number to twelve. Amen is repeated after each curse.

II. **28** : 1-26. It would be tempting to take this chapter as containing the blessings and curses announced in chap. **27,** but on closer inspection it can be seen that chap. **28** represents a composite, revised text in its present form. We find the expected terse form of expression in the blessings (vv. 3-6) and in the curses (vv. 16-19). But there have been added long developments of a homiletic character, inspired in part by later historical events; thus, we detect allusions to the Assyrian captivity (Fall of Samaria) and the Babylonian Captivity (Fall of Jerusalem) in vv. 36, 37, 41, 49 (cf. also Jer. **48** : 40; **49** : 22). In vv. 54 ff.,which describe the horrors to which the people are driven by famine, we may have a general trait due to common stories about besieged cities (cf. 2 (4) Kgs.

6 : 28 f.; Jer. **19** : 9; Ez. **5** : 10; Lam. **2** : 20; **4** : 10). We find such traits outside the O.T. V. 68 apparently alludes to the Phoenicians who transported slaves by ship to Egypt, a great center of the slave trade.

E. **29** : 1–30 : 20.

In the Hebrew, **28** : 69 is the conclusion of the preceding discourse (which may be taken as beginning in chap. **5**). In the LXX and in the Vulgate, the verse is the introduction to a new discourse of Moses. It declares that the covenant of Deut., the Moab Covenant, is not different from that of Horeb (Sinai).

This section is introduced by the remark (**29** : 1) that " Moses summoned all Israel and said to them ". This makes it very clear that we have here the beginning of a new, independent discourse, not the continuation of the preceding discourse ending in chapter **28**. It may be regarded rather as a parallel — considerably abridged — report of the preceding discourse. Chap. **29** : 1-7 is a summary of the first discourse, **1** : 6–**3** : 29. Chap. **29** : 8-14 recalls briefly the renewal of the covenant to which not only those present now pledge themselves but also their descendants (v. 14). Chap. **29** : 15-20 warns that the curses on unfaithfulness to the covenant will single out the unfaithful individual. In this summary statement, the curses are not enumerated, but they are supposed known. Chap. **29** : 21-28 represents a different point of view. The curses punishing infidelity will come upon the whole people and serve as a warning to future generations and other nations as well. In fact, this part reveals itself as a later addition by the reference to the exile in a strange land (v. 27) : " as is now the case ". The allusion could be to the Babylonian Captivity, but it can be as well to the destruction of the Northern Kingdom in the 8th century (cf. 2 (4) Kgs. **17** : 6-23).

30 : 1-10 goes on from the same standpoint as **29** : 21-28. The exile will not mean the final destruction of the nation. God's mercy awaits the repentant and repentance will bring all the blessings of God.

30 : 11-14 : It is not difficult for the people to find their way back to God : they have God's law, stated clearly, to guide them.

30 : 15-20 : Israel has the choice between life and death, God's blessings and curses.

Notes. Chap. **29** : 3 is one of the many texts in the Old Testament bearing on man's sin and God's action; man's sin is traced back to God. Yet it is clear from countless texts that man is treated as responsible for his decision in favor of good or of evil, and therefore his reward or his punishment is just (cf. **30** : 11-20 : man can know God's will, and he has the choice between obedience and disobedience). But the Old Testament does not explain or even try to explain how man's free will and God's sovereign action do work together. Chap. **29** : 4-5. In the desert for 40 years God provided for His people. From this constant care for them, they should learn that He is what His name implies : the one " who is ", ever present to help His faithful ones in their need. Chap. **29** : 16-17. On the loathsome idols, cf. Lev. **26** : 30; Deut. **4** : 28; **28** : 36, 64. The example of the pagan nations could prove a powerful incentive to idolatry, and so it was repeatedly in the life of Israel. The Hebrew words for poison (v. 17) and head are spelled in the same way *(rosh)*. According to Dhorme *rosh* (head) took on the meaning poison, from the head of the serpent which distills venom. Chap. **29** : 18. The true interpretation of the vs. is doubtful. The insincere man thinks that he can in some way avert the effects of the curse from himself. The end of the verse may refer to a punishment which involves the good and the wicked together (cf. note in Confraternity Version), though the point of view is different here (cf. above on vv. 15-28); viz., the curse will single out the unfaithful without fail. Chap. **29** : 22. As pointed out by JUNKER (*op. cit.*, p. 86), this is clearly a rhetorical description, not one based on actual fact. The catastrophe that overwhelmed the wicked cities is the type of God's judgment (Gen. **19** : 24 ff.; Am. **4** : 11; Isa. **1** : 7; **13** : 19; Jer. **49** : 10; **50** : 40). Chap. **29** : 23-27. The breaking of a solemn covenant was regarded as one of the worst offenses; it brought on necessarily the intervention of the divinities whose names had been invoked in the making of the agreement. Cf. Assurbanipal's (608-633) account of his Arabian campaign (PRITCHARD, *ANET*, pp. 299ᵇ-300ᵃ) : " Irra, the Warrior [i.e. pestilence] struck down Uate " and his army, who had not kept the oaths sworn to me... Famine broke out among them and they ate the flesh of their children against their hunger [cf. **28** : 54 ff.]. Ashur, Sin, Shamash... [gods of Assyria] inflicted quickly upon them the curses written in their sworn agreements... Whenever the inhabitants of Arabia asked each other, " Why have these calamities befallen Arabia "? " Because we did not keep the solemn oaths by Ashur, because we have offended the friendliness of Ashur-banipal, the King beloved by Ellil "! Chap. **29** : 28. This is a note or a gloss on the text (cf. Confraternity Version). The reference is to the curses bound to befall unfaithfulness. " What is still hidden is with Yahweh our God "; the future is with God, who will fulfill in his own time what has not yet been fulfilled; " but what has been revealed " (i.e., what has found its fulfilment in the destruction of the Northern Kingdom) " is for us and our children forever, that we may do all the words of this Law " (i.e., is a warning to us and our children to incite us to faithful observance of the Law). Chap. **30** : 1-3 : cf. Jer. **3** : 11-25; **31** : 15-22. Jeremias, considering the catastrophe of the destruction of the Northern Kingdom in 721 B.C., holds that the repentance of the people can lead to God's forgiveness and the people's restoration. Hence, we must not necessarily conclude that Deut. here has in mind the fall of Jerusalem and the Babylonian Exile of 587. Chap. **30** : 15 : lit., " life and good, death and evil "; the terms must be taken in as broad a sense as possible, and not in a purely spiritual sense. They are chiefly happiness and misfortune in this life.

F. **31** : 1–**34** : 12.

The last dispositions of Moses. This section contains a number of historical notices : the appointment of Josue as Moses' successor who will lead the people in God's name (**31** : 1-8; cf. **31** : 14-15—23); the handing of the Law to the priests who will still take care of it (**31** : 9-13 and **31** : 24-29); the announcement of Moses' impending death, and Moses' compo-sition of his Song as a testimony against the future unfaith-fulness of the people (**31** : 16-22); the Song of Moses (**32** : 1-44); a final appeal of Moses to the people (**32** : 45-47). Moses goes up on Mount Nebo to view Palestine at a distance (**32** : 48-52);

his blessing upon the tribes (33 : 1-29); the death and burial of Moses (34 : 1-12).

a) appointment of Josue. Josue had been designated by God before (Num. 27 : 12-23). His call is now confirmed by Moses, who in the presence of all Israel announces that Josue is to be their leader (31 : 7-8) and by God himself at the Meeting Tent (31 : 14-15 and 23; cf. note on 31 : 14 f. in the Confraternity Version).

b) The Law is left in the care of the priests and of the Elders. Modern criticism of Deut. has come around to a more conservative view, and allows that this section echoes an ancient tradition; the commandments of God were recited on the occasion of the renewal of the Covenant, and Moses can very well be regarded as the one who established the practice (cf. JUNKER, *op. cit.*, p. 89). Some critics propose to read in v. 24 " the words of the song " (a conjecture for which there is some little evidence; cf. *Biblia Heb.* edd. Kittel-Kahle) and also in v. 26, " this scroll of the song " (a conjecture; so EHRLICH, p. 340; MOFFATT, *La Sainte Bible* [ed. A. Clamer]). For this conjecture they reason that the text intended in v. 24 ff. is to serve as a witness against the people's future unfaithfulness — just what is said in v. 21 of " this song " which will bear witness against them. Cf. also v. 30. In favor of the traditional text it may be said that the author intended to say in 31 : 24 ff. that the Song (ch. 32) was the conclusion of the book of Deut. (the words or book of the Law) and the book with the Song was deposited alongside the Ark. Thus the sacred character of the Law was marked very clearly (cf. *Bible du Centenaire*).

c) 31 : 16-22. Moses is to die soon; the future unfaithfulness of the people is revealed to him. The Song of Moses which develops the theme of Israel's unfaithfulness will serve as a witness against them : they were forewarned, and yet became unfaithful : therefore they fully deserve their chastisement. V. 17 : " I will hide my face from them " : cf. 32 : 20; Isa. 8 : 17; 54 : 8; 57 : 17; 59 : 2; 64 : 6; often in the Pss., i.e., I will ignore them, take no interest in them. V. 20 : cf. 6 : 3; 11 : 9; 26 : 15; 27 : 3.

d) **32.** Besides the references given at the beginning of this analysis of Deut., see the following : M. LAMBERT, *Revue des Et. Juives* (1898), pp. 47-52; N. SCHLÖGL, *Bibl. Zeitschrift* [1904], pp. 1-14; P. RIESSLER, *ibid.* (1913), pp. 119-27; J. LINDER, *Zeitschrift f. kath. Theol.* (1924), pp. 374-406; ZORELL, *Verbum Domini* (1927), pp. 197-203. P. W. SKEHAN, *CBQ* (1957), pp. 153-163 (" The Structure of the Song of Moses "); *id., BASOR,* no. 136 (1954), pp. 12-15 (" A Fragment of the Song of Moses (Deut. 32) from Qumran "). Cf. the note in the Confraternity Version for a general analysis of the contents of the Song. The Song is a work of art (cf. DHORME, *L'Ancien Testament* I, p. LIV : " Le très beau cantique de Moïse ") which reflects the influence of later works. Its precise date cannot be defined. Many critics would make it an exilic composition; others regard it as belonging to the age of Jeremias and Ezechiel, or even as early as the 9th cent. B.C. (cf. S. R. DRIVER, *Introduction,* pp. 95-97). The fact is that the Song, " a prophetic meditation on the lessons to be deduced from Israel's national history " (DRIVER, *op. cit.,* p. 97), does not contain allusions to definite facts which could settle the date quite clearly.

Notes. V. 4 : " the Rock ", one of the author's favorite expressions (vv. 15, 18, 30, 31, 37), which appears frequently in the Psalms. V. 5 : The verse is difficult as will be seen from a comparison of the various versions and commentaries (cf. BEN JEHUDAH, *Thesaurus* VI, 2846, note 1). Hence many corrections have been proposed (cf. Kittel-Kahle), but none is fully satisfactory. Vv. 8-9 : There is some uncertainty about the text. The MT (end of 8) has : " after the number of the sons of Israel ". The LXX, which represents a variant form supported by Qumran evidence (see P. W. SKEHAN, *art. cit.*), reads : " after the number of the sons of God ". The precise sense is doubtful. A number of critics understand the text as meaning that each of the gods (sons of gods) received his people, and Yahweh's portion was Israel (v. 9). This can be rejected safely, especially from the point of view of the critics who suppose the Song to be a recent composition. After the preaching of the Prophets, no Hebrew writer would recognize any reality to the gods of the nations and therefore their claim

to any nation such as Yahweh had to Israel. More probably
the reference is to the guardian angels of the nations (cf. Confraternity Version, note); (*La Biblia de Montserrat*, etc.). V. 11 :
cf. H. N. RICHARDSON, *JBL* (1947), pp. 321-324 (on line 8
of the letter from Ugarit). V. 17 : "demons"; the Hebrew
word is found again only in Ps. 106 : 37. Vv. 26-27 : If God
allowed free rein to his wrath and destroyed the unfaithful
people altogether, their enemies, whom He uses to punish
Israel, would attribute their success to themselves. Vv. 28 ff.
refer to the pagan nations, as suggested by the context (v. 27) :
The pagan nations, reflecting on the fate of Israel, should not
fail to see that God is punishing them, and that Israel's God
is different from their own divinities. The God of Israel punishes
His people because of their corruption (v. 32 f.). V. 34 : The
document on which the crimes of the people are noted is kept
in God's treasury. Vv. 37-39 : Yahweh asks ironically where
are the gods on which they relied : gods without any reality,
helpless and powerless — over against Him who is the sole God.
V. 39 : Cf. M. LAMBERT, *Grammaire hébraïque*, nos. 1280-1281 :
" See that I, I am " cf. Isa. 43 : 10 (cf. *La Biblia de Montserrat*),
or, " that I am I "; cf. DHORME, " moi qui suis moi ", i.e., " qui
suis Dieu ", for Yahweh is He " who is " Himself, here speaking
in the first person. In any case, it is an emphatic declaration
equivalent to " that I am Yahweh ", the God who is. V. 43 :
to be read as in Confraternity Version (with correction from
LXX; see Skehan, *art. cit.*). This does away with the difficulty
that the pagan nations (destroyed according to vv. 40 f.)
would be called upon to praise Yahweh's people.

e) 32 : 45-52. Moses makes a final appeal for absolute
obedience to the Law; this is the essential condition on which
depends the people's remaining in possession of the land
(vv. 45-47). Moses in then invited to go up on Mount Nebo
(cf. Arabic *nabawa*, height) a little over ten miles east of the
mouth of the Jordan, in the Abarim range in the northwestern
part of Moab. There he will die after viewing the Promised
Land at a distance (vv. 48-52). (V. 49 f. : cf. Num. 27 : 12-14;
33 : 47-48).

f) 33 : 1-29. Moses' Blessing should be compared with that
of Jacob (Gen. 49). Both poems present " a general similarity

in character and structure ", yet Deut. 33 is original
(S. R. DRIVER, *Introduction*, p. 97). The order followed in
the enumeration of the tribes is different. Simeon is not
mentioned in Deut. 33; it had been absorbed by the Tribe
of Juda (cf. Jos. 19 : 1 ff.). There are considerable differences
of view regarding the date, due to the fact that the allusions
are vague. However it may be said safely that a late date
has no probability. Most authors date the Blessing from the
reign of Jeroboam II, king of Israel (783 B.C. ff.), who restored
the greatness of the Northern Kingdom. Others propose
an earlier date under David, for instance, or still earlier, in
the time of the Judges (see, S. R. DRIVER, *op. cit.*, p. 98; JUNKER,
op. cit., pp. 97-98; CASSUTO, *Entzyk. Miq.* 2, 617-618; cf. MO-
WINCKEL, *Norwegian Bible*, I, 421 ff.). Several propose to
distinguish : *a)* a framework, vv. 2-5 and 26-29; i.e., a psalm
in praise of Yahweh, the Lord and Creator of Israel, who gave
Palestine to His people; and *b)*, the Blessings proper, vv. 6-25,
where each blessing (except that of Ruben, v. 6; cf. Confraternity Version) is introduced by the formula : " of X he said "
(cf. JUNKER, CASSUTO, MOWINCKEL, *ll. cc.*).

Notes. V. 2 is difficult and interpreted variously. V. 3 :
MT is hardly intelligible (Mowinckel); for correction, see Confraternity Version. V. 4 : MT. Cassuto *(l. c.)* calls attention to
the difficulty of this reference to Moses in MT " Moses gave
us a law ". Hence, either this line is omitted (e.g., Mowinckel)
or at least the name of Moses (Confraternity Version); hence in
v. 5 it is Yahweh (not Moses) who is called " king ". In any
case, the verse does not refer to the institution of the monarchy.
V. 6b : some understand this as a wish of a large number (with
the Greek), since it is a blessing (Dhorme; Montserrat Bible);
the other view, however, is more usual. V. 7 : Juda is isolated
from the other tribes and fights for its territory singlehanded.
This fits the period of the Judges (JUNKER; Confraternity
Version). Levi (vv. 8-11) and Joseph (vv. 13-17) received
special attention. Levi the priestly tribe has charge of the
Urim and Thummim (Ex. 28 : 30; Lev. 8 : 8; Num. 27 : 21),
the means of ascertaining God's will in certain cases (cf. 1 Sam.
14 : 41, in the LXX). In critical circumstances, they sided
with Moses (cf. Ex. 32 : 26 ff.). They are also entrusted with

the teaching of the Law and offering sacrifices. On v. 11, see W. F. Albright in *CBQ* (1945), 23 f. V. 12 : obscure; if understood of the Temple, the date should be lowered; according to others, the reference may be to Bethel (JUNKER, *op. cit.*, p. 100). Under Joseph are meant the two largest tribes of North Israel, Ephraim and Manasse, as explained in v. 17. With this blessing cf. that in Gen. **49** : 22 ff., where similar phrases appear. The prominence given to Joseph had led many to suppose a Northern origin for the Blessing. (Cf. JUNKER and CASSUTO, *ll. cc.*). Vv. 18-19 : Zabulon is on the sea coast near Carmel; its ships go out to sea for trade or fishing (?); Issachar's territory lies between Zabulon and Nephthali, its people tending their flocks (?). V. 19 : obscure. Vv. 20-21 : Gad received its territory on the east of the Jordan. V. 20 seems to allude to some deed of valor by Gad; cf. 1 Chron. **5** : 18 ff.; **12** : 8 ff. The Rabbis understand MT in 21 as referring to Moses' burial place; this view is reflected apparently in the Vulgate : " in his portion the teacher was laid up ". This first part of v. 21 needs correcting (Confraternity Version). The latter part of the verse means that Gad faithfully kept up its religious bond with the other tribes west of the Jordan. V. 23. MT has a verb in the imperative : " Take possession of the lake and the land south of it ". This would imply that the territory was still held by the Canaanites. The emendation in the Confraternity Version, on the contrary, means that the tribe already holds the land. This agrees better with the rest of the Blessing, which describes the present condition of the tribes but does not prophecy their future lot (cf. CASSUTO, *l. c.*). Vv. 26 ff. continue the psalm begun in vv. 2-5 (JUNKER, *op. cit.*). V. 26 MT : " There is none like God, o Yeshurun ". For corrections of MT, see Confraternity Version. On v. 26, cf. CASSUTO, *La questione della Genesi* (1934), p. 64, n. 3; H. L. GINSBERG, *BASOR*, no. 110 (1948), 26; CROSS AND FREEDMAN, *BASOR*, no. 108 (1948), 6-7; R. MARCUS, *JBL* (1949), 29-34.

g) 34 : 1-12 : Death and Burial of Moses.

The narrative of vv. 1-8 connects naturally with **32** : 52. On Phasga cf. **3** : 17, 27; **4** : 49; apparently meant as one of the sections of the Abarim range. From the top of Jebel Neba most of Palestine can be viewed. Moses has fulfilled his task, and he has been allowed to view the Promised Land. So he dies " as the Lord had said " (v. 5). The Hebrew literally says : " according to (on) the mouth (= the word) of the Lord ". Out of " on the mouth of the Lord " the Rabbis have developed the view of Moses dying in a kiss of Yahweh welcoming his faithful servant (cf. Renée BLOCH in : *Moïse, l'homme de l'Alliance* (Paris, 1955), p. 137 f.). On Moses' burial, cf., in N. T., Jude v. 9. On v. 7, cf. W. F. ALBRIGHT in *BASOR*, 94 (1944), 32-35; E. P. ARBEZ, *CBQ* (1945), 63-64. On the age of Moses, cf. E. NESTLE, *ZDMG*, 28 (1953), 489 f.; 33, 509 f. V. 10 : Moses' role as a prophet has not been developed in the tradition; see R. BLOCH, *op. cit.*, 138. The origin of this chapter is disputed among the ancient Rabbis. Cf. also B. SPINOZA, *Tractatus theologico-politicus*, in Spinoza, *Œuvres complètes* (La Pléiade, Paris, 1954), pp. 794-795. On Moses' end, cf. Martin BUBER, *Moses : The Revelation and the Covenant* (New York, 1958), pp. 196-201; E. AUERBACH, *Moses* (Amsterdam, 1953), pp. 191-193.

CONCLUDING REMARKS.

The purpose of this rather full analysis of the Pentateuch was twofold. In the first place, it should furnish the reader with information regarding the " Sources ", " Documents ", or " Traditions " admitted by modern critics, and thus make it easier for him to follow the discussion of the problem of the Pentateuch in this work or elsewhere. It was enough for this to give an analysis which limits itself to the outlines, without taking into account the various subdivisions of the " Sources " favored by some authors. To go into more details about such subdivisions would rather complicate the problem. There is also the danger of reducing the Pentateuch to mere fragments, and of losing the sense of the unity which is really present in it.

Second, the analysis has been made with a view to helping the reader to understand the Biblical text better. It is naturally presupposed that the text of the Bible is read and studied together with the analysis. To help the reader, each section is provided with references to literature which may be consulted to clarify obscure points. In the case of some of the less familiar

passages, some notes have been added to remove some difficulties, without however aiming at giving a commentary.
In mentioning the " Sources ", we have used the usual
symbols J, E, P, D. Whatever one may think of the origin
of the Pentateuch, one is by no means rash in admitting sources
of some kind. There is nothing in Catholic teaching opposed
to such a view. Recent pronouncements of the competent
authority suppose the reality of such sources, even if they
leave many points (number, characteristics, dates, etc.) indefinite. This much at least the reader will gather : there are
a number of sections in the Pentateuch which naturally combine
into larger units on account of their peculiarities of style and
vocabulary, religious point of view, etc. As an example of
the study of sources, the reader may be referred to the excellent
article of J. ROTH C.SS.R., " Thèmes majeurs de la Tradition
sacerdotale dans le Pentateuque ", Nouvelle Revue Théologique
(1958), pp. 696-721. The reader will see that the question
can be handled in a constructive manner; criticism is not
necessarily negative and destructive.

2. — THE HISTORICAL BOOKS [1].

[A. Robert]

1. — The Book of Josue.

Content.

Josue continues the sacred history, taking it up at the point
where Deuteronomy has left it. In the first part, the book
recounts the passage over the Jordan and the entrance into
Western Palestine (1 : 1–5 : 12); it describes the capture of
Jericho and the occupation of the country following three
expeditions sent out to the Center, the South, and the North
(5 : 13–11 : 23); and finally, it gives a list of the conquered

Translator's note. — [1 H. H. ROWLEY, ed., From Joseph to Joshua : Biblical
Traditions in the Light of Archaeology (Oxford, 1950). ELISUR, " Strategic
Lines in Josue ", in Kitbey ha-Hebra..., I (1955), pp. 55-57. B. J. ALFRINK,
Het " Stil Staan " van Zon en Maan in Jos. 10 : 12-14 (Nijmegen, 1949).
E. KAUFMAN, The Biblical Account of the Conquest of Palestine (Jerusalem, 1955;
on the English translation, cf. CBQ [1955], pp. 95-97). The art., " Book of
Josue ", in Entzyklop. Miqr. 3, pp. 543-564 (with good bibliography).
J. SIMONS, " Topographical and Archaeological Elements in the Story of
Abimelech ", Oudtest. Studiën (1943), pp. 35-78. E. O'DOHERTY, " The
Literary Problem of Judges, 1 :1-3 : 6 ", CBQ (1956), pp. 1-7].

kings to the east and to the west of the Jordan (12). The second part shows, with great precision, how the territory was divided among the tribes (13 : 1–21 : 43). The third part relates, in the manner of appendices, various events : the affair of the altar in Transjordan (22 : 1-34); Josue's last counsels (23 : 1–24 : 28); the death and burial of Josue and of the priest Eleazar (24 : 29-31, 33); the burial of Joseph's bones (24 : 32).

Origin.

The Old Critical School regarded Josue as a continuation of the Pentateuch, not only from the viewpoint of content but also from that of sources. Whence the name Hexateuch, commonly given by them to the first six books as a whole. They recognize a predominance of P in chapters 13–22; but opinions differ when there is a question of determining the proportion of J, E, D in the other chapters. According to their views, some passages of a deuteronomic nature were added at different periods; the final redaction was made after the Exile; the separation from the Pentateuch took place, however, before the Samaritan schism, probably under Esdras.

Contemporary critics, as their predecessors, recognize the existence in Josue of deuteronomic and sacerdotal elements, but they concentrate their attention especially on the old traditions incorporated into the book. While they admit of division into two parallel series, they are complex and difficult to identify. They differ in their purposes (the events of the conquest and the explanation of topographical details, etc., respectively), and they differ likewise in their respective places of origin (North and South; the sanctuaries of Gilgal and Silo...).

" If the structure of the Book of Josue does not appear to be of high antiquity, it makes use of elements which easily go back to nearly a millenium B. C. " (F. M. ABEL, Le livre de Josué [Paris, 1950], p. 9). This is a guarantee in favor of their veracity. In interpreting these elements, the exegete here, too, should guard himself against an a priori scepticism, yet should understand all that such a history can imply as regards imaginative amplifications and schematization. But, especially, he should not lose sight of the religious purpose of the work, which is to show how the divine promises have been wonderfully realized.

2. — The Book of Judges.

Content.

As its name indicates, this book recounts the story of the Judges, i.e., of the heroes, who, while invested with temporary authority, repelled, in one place or another, the enemies of Israel during the difficult period which extends from Josue to Samuel. It is composed of three parts. The first is a double introduction, which shows, on the one hand, the very relative results of the efforts made by the tribes to establish themselves, each in its own domain (1 : 1–2 : 5); and on the other, the religious motives behind this state of affairs (2 : 6–3 : 6). The second part (3 : 7–16 : 31) is only a series of sketches of the twelve Judges. Six of these receive only a very short notice, and for this reason are named *the Lesser Judges.* These are Samgar (3 : 31), Thola (10 : 1-2), Jair (10 : 3-5), Abesan (12 : 8-10), Ahialon (12 : 11-12), and Abdon (12 : 13-15). The others are *the Greater Judges:* Othoniel (3 : 7-11), Aod (3 : 12-30), Barac (4 : 1-5 : 32), Gedeon (6 : 1–8 : 35), Jephte (10 : 6–12 : 7) and Samson (13–16). The third part is a double appendix, containing episodes which are concerned with the history of the tribes of Dan and of Benjamin : the foundation of the sanctuary of Lais Dan (17 : 1–18 : 31), and the crime of Gabaa (19 : 1–21 : 24).

Literary characteristics.

The book attains unity through the philosophical-religious viewpoint which is expressed with particular clearness in 2 : 11-19. Through serving idols Israel is unfaithful to God, and as a punishment it is delivered into the hands of its enemies. Then, after its repentance, God takes pity on it and raises up a Judge who delivers it. Thereupon the series of events begins again. Such is the cycle which has been called pragmatism in four terms. The stereotyped formulas expressing it are found both in the introduction and the conclusion of the history of the Greater Judges (3 : 7-11; 3 : 12, 14, 15, 30; 4 : 1-3, 23, 24; 5 : 32; 6 : 1, 7; 8 : 28, 33, 34; 10 : 6, 7, 10; 12 : 7; 13 : 1; 15 : 20; 16 : 31). The chronological data which these formulas contain should be noted and likewise the manner in which they give prominence to the unity of the twelve tribes.

The pragmatic point of view is, as it were, an external bond which conceals a number of documents. In fact, there are two introductions, the first of which recounts several events already recorded in Josue (cf. Jdgs. 1 : 27-8, and Jos. 17 : 11-13; Jdgs. 1 : 29 and Jos. 16 : 10; Jdgs. 1 : 30 and Jos. 19 : 15-16; Jdgs. 1 : 31-32 and Jos. 19 : 24-31; Jdgs. 1 : 33 and Jos. 19 : 35-39; Jdgs. 1 : 34 and Jos. 19 : 47). There are two appendices, the main concern of which is different from that of the body of the book. Nor do the story of Abimelech (Jdgs. 9) and the short notices concerning the Lesser Judges fit any better into the framework. Lack of unity can also be suspected in the story of Gedeon (cf. Jdgs. 6 : 11-24, 34-35; 7 : 2-21, 22-27ª; 8 : 4-21; and 6 : 25-32; 6 : 36–7 : 1, 22; 7 : 23–8 : 3, 29; 9 : 1 ff.) and in chapters 19 to 21 (cf. the differences of style and spirit between 19 and 21 : 15-23, and 20 : 1–21 : 14).

Origin.

The Critical School, since Budde, connects the sources of the book with Documents J and E of the Pentateuch. A first editor combined them; a second, as a member of the deuteronomist school, completed them and fitted them into the pragmatic frame; a third, influenced by P, reintroduced a number of passages discarded by his predecessor. Burney [1] thinks that the principal redactor was not a deuteronomist but belonged rather to a prophetic school dominated by the thought of Osee. He worked about 650.

A number of exegetes have given up trying to find the sources of the Pentateuch in Judges. The best qualified representatives of the *Formgeschichte* School, naturally, have not even tried to look for them there. In this case, as in others, they attack and reject the method of literary criticism as being inadequate, and endeavor to uncover the physiognomy of the traditions preserved in the work. In their opinion, these are aetiological legends and sagas in which the high deeds of the tribes or heroes of Israel are glorified.

These ancient traditions, which arose in the early days of permanent settlement, are surely closer to history than

---

[1] *The Book of Judges* (2nd ed., 1920), pp. XLI-I. [See also M. G. GRUEN-THANER, S. J., " Two Sun-Miracles of the Old Testament " *CBQ* (1948), pp. 212-281].

these scholarly analyses wish to grant, and it is not conceivable that men would not be busy, even before the Exile, in collecting these precious memories and determining their meaning in accordance with the theology of the covenant. This was undoubtedly done in two stages, and the second was not necessarily deuteronomic. The deuteronomic impress, however, is evident in later additions, and the sacerdotal supplements are even more easily discernible (H. CAZELLES, " Juges (Le livre de) ", *DBV, Suppl.*, Vol. IV [1949], cols. 1410-1412).

3. — The Book of Ruth.

Content and authenticity.

The author relates, in four chapters, the story of Ruth the Moabite. As a childless widow, she follows her mother-in-law, Naomi, who is also a widow, to Bethlehem. There she is wed by Booz in conformity with the law of levirate (cf. Gen. **38** : 8-11; Deut. **25** : 5-10). From this marriage is born Obed, who will be the grandfather of David.

The authenticity of the passages which concern David has been contested, namely, **4** : 18-22, and even **4** : 17. However, no conjecture can eliminate the evidence of Ruth **4** : 12 (cf. 1 Chron. **2** : 4-15, and 1 Sam. **22** : 3-4).

Character and purpose.

Ruth is remarkable for its picturesqueness, its freshness, and its delicacy. The extreme simplicity of the story shows that the author makes no pretense of advancing a thesis. He does intend, however, to edify by exalting fidelity to family love and obligations. Moreover his story conveys discreetly the knowledge that the God of Israel accepted the service of a foreign woman, though a Moabite, as a recompense for her virtues, even to the extent of allowing her to enter into the line of David's ancestors.

Origin.

The author looks back from afar at the period of the Judges (**1** : 1). He lived after the period of David, and the ancient custom which occasioned Booz's marriage to Ruth had long since gone out of use (**4** : 7). He is concerned with the spirit of the law of levirate rather than the letter, and regards it as suggestive rather than obligatory in its nature [1]. Moreover his style contains neologisms and Aramaic elements, although their number is small [2]. These indications suggest a postexilic origin. This hypothesis is confirmed by the place of the book in the Hebrew canon (it forms a part of *Megilloth*), by the universalist sense of its narrative, and above all by its " Davidical " import. It cannot be maintained, as a number of critics insist, that Ruth may be a protest against the measures spoken of in Esdr. **9–10** and Neh. **13**. The book bears no trace of a polemic intention of this kind, either in its general tenor, or in its different episodes. It is not enough to cite as proof the fact that Ruth is called " the stranger " (**2** : 20) and " the Moabite " (**1** : 22; **2** : 2, 6, 21; **4** : 5, 10). It is more likely that these words, through Isaias **56** : 1-7, allude to Deut. **23** : 4 (3). They emphasize the universalist import of the story and consequently place it in the literary cycle which preceded Malachias. The author wrote, accordingly, before 450.

4. — The Books of Samuel [4].

Title and Content.

The two Books of Samuel formed originally a single work, which was divided for greater convenience [5]. The Hebrew Bible calls them " Books of Samuel " because of the important

---

Translator's note. — [1] J. M. MYERS, *The Linguistic and Literary Form of the Book of Ruth* (Leiden, 1955).]

[2] See P. JOÜON, S. J., *Ruth. Commentaire philologique et exégétique* (Rome, 1924), pp. 8-10. [See also H. H. ROWLEY, " The Marriage of Ruth ", *Harvard Theological Review*, XL (1947), pp. 77-99].

[3] JOÜON, *op. cit.*, p. 11.

Translator's note. .. [4] M. S. SEGAL, *Sifrey Shemu'el* (Jerusalem, 1956; in Hebrew), the most recent detailed commentary on 1 and 2 Sam. It makes use of the evidence furnished by the Dead Sea Mss. P. A. H. DE BOER, "Research into the Text of 1 Sam. **18-31** ", *Oudtest. Studien* (1949), pp. 1-100. S. YEIVIN, " David ", in *Entzyklop. Miqra'it*, 2, pp. 629-643, and " House of David ", *ibid.*, pp. 643-645. VAN DEN BUSSCHE, *Le texte de la prophétie de Nathan sur la dynastie davidique* (Gembloux, 1948). M. NA'OR, " 1 Sam. **7** : 1-12 in the Light of Topography ", in *Kitbey ha-Hebra...*, I (1955), pp. 67-74. RABBAN, " Samuel and Saul's Choice ", *ibid.*, pp. 75-83. B. Z. LURIA, " Saul's Itinerary in His Search for the Lost Asses ", *Yerushalayim* (= *Review for Palestinian Research*), Vol. 2-5, 20-27. I. Press, " The Institution of Kingship in Israel and the Administrative Division of Solomon's Kingdom ", *ibid.*, pp. 28-34].

[5] As were also 1 and 2 Kgs.; 1 and 2 Chron,, and Esdr, and Neh.

role that the prophet of that name played in the significant
events of his age. The Septuagint calls them the First and
Second Books of Reigns (βασιλειῶν). Saint Jerome states [1]
that he prefers the title, " Books of Kings ", and this is the
designation which has prevailed in the Latin tradition.

The two Books of Samuel are concerned with the history
of three persons whose destinies are closely connected with
one another : Samuel, Saul, and David. The first part treats
of the judgeship of Samuel and the foundation of the kingship
(1 Sam. 1-12). The salient facts are Samuel's prophetic call
at Silo, the overwhelming victory of the Philistines which
entailed the capture of the ark of the covenant and the death
of the high priest Heli with his sons, and the election and
anointing of Saul as first king of Israel. The second part relates
the events of Saul's reign with emphasis upon the gradual rise
of David (13-31). While Saul is rejected for his disobedience,
David is anointed by Samuel. From the day that David
conquers Goliath he becomes an object of hatred to Saul, who
makes attempts against his life and pursues him in the deserts
to the South. Because of this David is forced to take refuge
in the land of the Philistines until the tragic death of his
persecutor on Mount Gelboe. The third part is the history of
David's reign (2 Sam. 1-20) : his rule first at Hebron, then
at Jerusalem; his piety and the divine promises, his victories,
his sin, and the revolts of Absalom and of Seba. An appendix
contains as supplements the Canticle of David and his last
words (21-24).

Literary Characteristics [2].

The Books of Samuel lack the theological framework and
the systematic chronology of Judges. The narrative contains
in itself a marked unity. It is progressive, and events converge,
as though spontaneously, towards David, and the culminating
point is the prophecy of Nathan (2 Sam. 7). In this way the
author shows clearly the position that royalty holds in the
Yahwist theocracy, and stresses especially the legitimacy of
the line of David, whose throne is for this reason forever secured.

---

[1] *Prologus galeatus*, or " Preface to the Books of Kings ", PL, XXVIII, col. 553.
    Translator's note. — [2 See R. DRIVER, *Notes on the Hebrew Text and Topo-
graphy of Samuel* (Oxford, 1913). M. H. SEGAL, " Studies in the Books of
Samuel ", *Jewish Quarterly Review,* New series (1914-1920), pp. 5-10].

The difference which exists between Judges and Samuel does not prevent Sam. 1–7 and 12 from being the continuation and conclusion of the history of the Judges. Certain indications (e.g., in 4 : 18ᵇ; 7 : 6, 15, 17; and 7 : 3, 4; 12) show that the relationship is not only logical but also literary, and that the documents employed in Judges continue to be employed in Samuel. In a general way, 1 and 2 Sam. have all the characteristics of a compilation : repetitions, abrupt changes, differences in style and point of view. This is a normal phenomenon, if one takes into consideration the superabundant material which the sacred writer had as his disposal, the great development in literature which is manifest from the tenth century in various places, especially prophetic centers, and the profound sympathy that David, the outstanding hero of the Books of Samuel, aroused everywhere. It would have been astonishing indeed if the accounts, coming as they do from such diverse sources, had not given rise to parallel narratives. In fact, critics have discovered them, sometimes to an exaggerated degree, throughout Samuel, and especially in the passages which recount the choice of Saul and describe David's appearance on the scene. A comparison of Sam. 16 : 14-23, and 17 : 32-54, with 17 : 22-31, and 17 : 51–18 : 5, is particularly striking in this respect.

Origin.

A number of critics, particularly since K. Budde (1902), see in Samuel a continuation of the sources of the Pentateuch. Gressmann (1910) initiated a reaction which took the form of a hypothesis of fragments or additions [1]. In any case, the admission of one or several deuteronomist interventions necessitates the dating of the work after the discovery of " the Book of the Law " (622).

It is not right, on the other hand, to attribute the composition of Samuel to the prophets Samuel, Gad, and Nathan on the basis of 1 Chron. 29 : 29, which in no way affirms this, nor even to insist necessarily on a date before 722. It seems more reasonable to believe that accounts, emanating in the North

[1] K. A. LEIMBACH, *Die Bücher Samuel* (Bonn, 1936), pp. 4-11, gives in detail the opinions of the various authors, Catholic and Protestant. [See also C. KEELEY, " An Approach to the Books of Samuel ", *CBQ* (1948), pp. 254-270].

and South, and composed around the time of David and Solomon, were brought together at a date which presupposes a considerable lapse of time from the actual events (I Sam. 27 : 6). This date seems to be after 722. The fall of Samaria afforded, in fact, the occasion for extolling the stability of David's dynasty and the means for completing the traditions of the South by those of the North.

5. — The Books of Kings [1].

Content.

Books I and 2 Kgs. (3 and 4 in the Septuagint and the Vulgate) present the facts in the history of Israel, and the religious considerations which they suggest, from the accession of Solomon about 971 to the release of Joachim, during the Babylonian captivity, in 562. The narrative falls naturally into three parts. The first treats of Solomon's reign (I Kgs. 1 : 1–11 : 43). The author describes with obvious complacency everything which manifests the glory of the great monarch, dwelling especially upon the building of the Temple. The second part tells of the schism and relates the history of the Northern and Southern kingdoms (I Kgs. 12 : 1-2 Kgs. 17 : 41). At first, down to the reign of Achab, they are enemies; then allies until the accession of Joas; and finally, indifferent or hostile to each other to the fall of Samaria. A concluding section (2 Kgs. 17 : 7-41) sets forth the religious reasons for this fact and discusses the origin of the Samaritan cult. The third part recounts the history of Juda now left solitary (2 Kgs. 18 : 1–25 : 30). Its existence seems already quite precarious under Ezechias in the period of the great Assyrian expeditions into Western Asia. The kings who follow precipitate its ruin by their wickedness. The work terminates with the story of the catastrophe of 597

Translator's note. — [1 E. KAUFMAN, *Toldot ha-emunah ha-yisre'lit*, I, 25 ff.; II, pp. 293-298 and p. 355 ff.; VIII, p. 39 ff. L. L. HONOR, *The Book of Kings : A Commentary* (New York, 1955). O. EISSFELDT, *Der Gott Karmel* (Berlin, 1956; cf. *RB* [1956], pp. 116-118). On the Chronicles of the Kings of Judah and Israel referred to in the Book of Kings, cf. B. MEZER in *Entzyklop. Miqr.*, 2, pp. 607 ff. See also the articles : " Ahab ", *ibid.*, pp. 196-206; " Jehneyakin ", 3, pp. 522-526; " Yehoyaqīm ", 3, pp. 526-530. S. ZEMIRIN, *Josiah and His Times* (Jerusalem, 1951; in Hebrew). J. LAUER, " Josiah ", in *Entzklop. Miqr.*, 3 (1958), pp. 417-424. C. TADMOR, " Ezechias ", *ibid.*, pp. 95-99].

and 586. The release of Joachim by Evil-Merodach injects a gleam of hope into the sombre picture.

Literary characteristics and purpose.

The author makes use of two kinds of sources. He himself cites the three principal ones : the Acts of Solomon (1 Kgs. 11 : 41); the Annals of the Kings of Israel (1 Kgs. 14 : 29, and in seventeen other places), and the Annals of the Kings of Juda (14 : 29, and in fourteen other passages). These writings emanate more or less directly from the royal chanceries and constitute, as it were, the skeleton of the work. The interruptions, the choppiness in the narration, the differences in style and point of view, all suggest the existence of other sources. Some dozen of these can be identified [1]. They come from the literary circles of the North and of the South, from the disciples of the prophets and from the Temple archives, and are concerned especially with David, Jeroboam I, Elias and Eliseus, Achab, Jehu, Ezechias, and Josias. These sources are, in general, either contemporary with the events or were compiled twenty-five or thirty years later. Those which reflect a more considerable lapse of time utilize earlier sources.

The sources are so arranged as to present a synoptic history of the North and the South. A given reign is treated without interruption. Then the writer takes up one or several parallel reigns. The whole is set forth according to a fairly regular scheme, with stereotyped formulae of introduction and conclusion (cf. 1 Kgs. 15 : 9-11 and 15 : 23-24; 15 : 33-34 and 16 : 5-6; 16 : 29-31 and 22 : 39-40; 2 Kgs. 15 : 1-7; 22 : 1-2, and 23 : 28-30). The instances where the schematic procedure is not followed are rare, and there is generally a reason, as in the case of Jeroboam I, Athalia, and Jehu.

The author stresses the idea of covenant, the purity of monotheism which is intimately connected with the unity of sanctuary, and national responsibility. The conduct of the kings is judged in the light of these principles. Those of the North have all betrayed their trust (1 Kgs. 15 : 26, 29, 30, 34...; 16 : 13, 25, 30-33). In Juda, several are likewise judged guilty (2 Kgs. 8 : 18-19, 27; 16 : 2-4; 21 : 2-16). Only eight remained

[1] A. ŠANDA, *Die Bücher der Könige*, I (1911), pp. XXX, XXXI, lists sixteen.

faithful, and six of these permitted sacrifice in the high places (1 Kgs. 15 : 14; 2 Kgs. 14 : 4; 15 : 35). Ezechias and Josias alone are free from all reproach. It is clear that the ideas of the author come from Deuteronomy and, to a smaller degree, from Jeremias. This double dependence is made more striking by the mechanical use of formulae borrowed from both [1].

Origin.

Critics are generally agreed that the Books of Kings are the work of two redactors. One probably worked under Josias, the other during or after the Exile. But the influence of Jeremias on both content and form extends over the entire book and is especially marked in the passages which give supernatural explanations for the last events in the period of the monarchy. On the other hand, except for 1 Kgs. 11 : 39, which does not appear in the Septuagint and is out of place in the context, there is no sound reason for challenging the passages which concern the Exile. Finally, the expression " unto this day " (1 Kgs. 9 : 13, 21, etc.) belongs to earlier documents, and the authentic close of the book is represented by 2 Kgs. 25 : 21. It must therefore be admitted that a single author composed this great work shortly after the deportation of 586. In the light of the teachings of Deuteronomy and Jeremias, the author invites the deportees to confess their guilt as a nation and to take cognizance of the fact that the apparent breaking of the covenant is not, on the part of Yahweh, an act of infidelity to His promises. The writer is not Jeremias, but some one who came under his influence.

6. — The Books of Chronicles [2].

Content.

The Books of Chronicles have received that name as a result of a suggestion made by Saint Jerome [3]. The Septuagint and

---

[1] For a fuller treatment, see Ch. VI, THE GENRES, pp. 492-496.

Translator's note. — [2] F. ZIMMERMANN, " Chronicles as a Partially Translated Book ", *Jewish Quarterly Review*, 42 (1952), pp. 265-282, and 387-412. C. C. TORREY, *The Chronicler's History of Israel. Chronicles-Ezra-Nehemiah Restored to Its Original Form* (New Haven, 1954; cf. *RB* [1956], pp. 119-120). B. MEZER, s. v., " Dibrey hayamīm ", in *Entzyklop. Miqr.*, 2, pp. 596-606].

[3] χρονικόν totius divinae historicae possumus appellare (*Prol. gal., PL*, XXVIII, col. 554).

the Vulgate call them the First and Second Books of Paralipomenon, a circumstance which would seem to present them
merely as a supplement to the historical books which had
preceded them. These books set forth the course of sacred
history from its origins to the decree of Cyrus (538). The first
nine chapters contain only genealogies, interspersed with brief
historical data. The author passes rapidly from Adam to the
twelve sons of Jacob and their posterity. The genealogy of
Juda is given first (1 Chron. 2 : 3-55). It is followed immediately
by the line of David, which is traced to the fifth generation
after Zorobabel (3). These nine chapters serve merely as an
introduction to the history proper, which deals only with the
kingdom of Juda (1 Chron. 10-2 Chron. 36 : 23). The twenty-one
kings of David's line pass in procession before us. The author,
however, goes into detail only in the case of the reigns which
are significant from the point of view of religion and worship,
namely, those of David, Solomon, Ezechias, and Josias. The
work does not end with the account of the final catastrophe
and captivity, but rather with the mention of the edict of Cyrus
(2 Chron. 36 : 22-23), the incomplete text of which is continued
in Esdr. 1 : 3 ff.

Sources.

The canonical books from Genesis to the Books of Kings
serve the author as a basis for his redaction, especially after
1 Chron. 10, when he begins to insert lengthy extracts from
Samuel and Kings. But while the Chronicler gives no references
for his Biblical borrowings, he expressly cites some twenty
non-Biblical sources. For the most part these are either of
an historical or a prophetical nature. It is generally agreed
that the references of the first type point, under various names,
to a single work, and even a great work, which we may call
the Midrashic [1] History of the Kings of Israel and Juda
(1 Chron. 9 : 1...; 2 Chron. 16 : 11; 24 : 27; 27 : 7...; 38 : 18).
On the other hand, the references of a prophetic nature
seem to be almost entirely taken from independent writings [2]
attributed to Samuel, Nathan, or Gad (1 Chron. 29 : 29),

---

[1] For the definition of this term, see p. 505.
[2] Cf. E. PODECHARD, " Les références du Chroniqueur ", RB (1915),
pp. 241-246.

to Ahias, Addo and Semeias (2 Chron. **9** : 29; **12** : **15**; **13** : 22),
to Jehu (**20** : 34), to Isaias (**26** : 22; **32** : 32), and to Hozai
(**33** : 19).

What is the attitude of the Chronicler toward his sources?
Since the canonical sources of the Chronicler's work are
available, a comparison with these is easy and extremely
instructive [1]. In general, he cites his basic text literally, but
he often handles it with a great deal of freedom. Thus, he
enlivens or renovates expressions; he abbreviates, omits,
transposes, or adds; and he even changes words and recomposes
sentences (cf., e.g., 1 Chron. **17** : 1-14 with 2 Sam. **7** : 1-17).
With regard to non-canonical sources it may be supposed that
his attitude on the whole was the same. Possibly he treated
them with less liberty. Since they were not much earlier than
his own period nor foreign to his environment, he probably borrowed from them the attitude which he adopts in interpreting
the canonical sources. The work, therefore, can be regarded
henceforth as a compilation of historical documents intended
to establish a solid foundation for certain doctrinal positions.

The purpose and spirit of the Chronicler [2].

The ideas which dominate the work of the Chronicler and
indicate his reasons for writing are principally the following.
1º He reiterates the unity of the chosen people, in which the
twelve tribes have been called without exception to form one
physical and religious whole. In theory, that unity persists
in spite of the schism of the ten tribes and there is a desire to
restablish it. In fact, however, the Kingdom of the North in
separating from Juda has not only severed its political and
religious relations, but has even renounced participation in
the promises. Therefore there is no point in mentioning it in
the history of Israel. 2º The person of David has a Messianic
significance, as is convincingly shown by a comparison of

---

[1] See especially, *Libri synoptici veteris Testamenti seu librorum Regum et
Chronicorum loci paralleli, quos hebraice, graece, et latine edidit* PRIMUS
VANUTELLI (Rome, 1931 and 1935).

[2] Cf. Ch. VI, pp. 508-509. [See also W. F. ALBRIGHT, " The Date and
Personality of the Chronicler ", *Journal of Biblical Literature*, XL (1921),
pp. 104-124. — A. C. WELCH, *The Work of the Chronicler* (London, 1939). —
F. C. BURNEY, *Notes on the Hebrew Text... of Kings* (Oxford, 1903)].

1 Chron. **17** : 11, 13, 14, with 2 Sam. **7** : 12, 14, 16, and with those writings which influenced the thought of the postexilic period (Is. **55** : 3-4; Jer. **13** : 5-33 : 14-17; cf. Ps. **89** : 1). David is given also a liturgical significance. As a second Moses, he establishes a new law by taking the initiative in the construction of the Temple. In this way unity of worship is realized at Jerusalem (2 Chron. **21**) in spite of the lawful claim of Gabaon (2 Chron. **1** : 3-6; cf. Lev. **17** : 1-9). 3° The Levites, especially the chanters and the musicians, have a noteworthy role within and without the Temple. Although the Torah gives them a much more modest position, their right is incontestable, since it rests on a genealogical proof and, in the last analysis, on the authenticity of the law established by David. 4° One of the characteristic features of the theology of the Chronicler is his very strict conception of earthly retribution. In this regard it is instructive to compare 2 Chron. **16** : 2-3, 7-10, 12, with 1 Kgs. **15** : 23; 2 Chron. **19** : 2-3, and **20** : 35-37, with 1 Kgs. **22** : 49; 2 Chron. **24** : 17-26, with 2 Kgs. **12** : 18-19; 2 Chron. **26** : 16-21 with 2 Kgs. **15** : 5; 2 Chron. **35** : 21-22, with 2 Kgs. **23** : 29.

The most serious charges have been made against the objectivity of the Chronicler, some even going so far as to accuse him of employing phantom sources to mystify his readers [1]. Thorough analysis of his method of redaction gives no support to such ill-founded opinions. The Wellhausen School [2] thinks that the Chronicler, dominated by the ideas of the Priestly Code, and wishing to write a history of worship with the Temple as its center, more or less knowingly distorts actual history. Neither as regards vocabulary or theological position, however, are the resemblances with the Priestly Code particularly striking [3]. In so far as they do exist, they are sufficiently explained by the ideas current in the Levitical environment to which the author belonged.

---

[1] C. C. TORREY, " The Chronicler as Editor and as Independent Narrator ", *American Journal of Semitic Languages and Literature*, XXV (1909), p. 195.
[2] See J. WELLHAUSEN, *Prolegomena zur Geschichte Israels* (1881, 6th ed., 1905), ch. VI. — J. BENZIGER, *Die Bücher der Chronik* (1901), pp. VIII-X. — R. KITTEL, *Die Bücher der Chronik* (1902), pp. VIII-X. — E. L. CURTIS, *The Books of Chronicles* (1910), pp. 6-15.
[3] G. VON RAD, *Das Geschichtsbild des chronistischen Werkes* (1930), especially pp. 38-63.

Moreover he is far from being an irresponsible or ignorant man. That his work is so difficult for us to interpret is due rather to the fact that it is the production of a scholar. He knows history perfectly and, even if he had wished, he could not have forced the acceptance of a version different from that of the canonical writings, for these were held by everyone and by the author himself to be inspired, and therefore completely trustworthy. His purpose is entirely different : it is that of a scribe who works not from facts but from texts, and who uses these texts as a vehicle for his theological teachings. His ordinary method of procedure is — as is often the case with us — that of accommodation. But, instead of superimposing explanations and arguments on the Scriptures, he sees nothing improper in changing the tenor itself of the texts to make them thus bear direct testimony in favor of his thesis. It is our task to learn to understand his intentions and his methods [1] and not to persist in requiring of him what was not in accord with his purpose or meaning.

Origin.

It is commonly admitted that the Chronicler also wrote the Books of Esdras-Nehemias, and that this great work was composed rather late in the postexilic period. At first sight, the genealogies of 1 Chr. 3 : 19-21 and of Neh. 12 : 10-11, 22, might seem able to furnish the elements of an exact dating. Actually, this is by no means the case, and they do not lead us to accept 300 (the current opinion) any more than they limit us to 400 (Rothstein and others). More reliable data demand our attention : Neh. 12 : 26-27 speaks of the days of Nehemias and Esdras as of time long past; 1 Chr. 29 : 7, 2 Chr. 36 : 22-23, Esd. 1 : 8, and Esd. 3 : 7 contain anachronisms; but, especially, the language of Chr. is closely related to that of writings as late as Est. and Eccles., and the work bears witness, in relation to the age of Nehemias and Esdras, to a considerable development in worship. These arguments are far from suggesting dates as low as 250 (Pfeiffer) or 190 B.C.

---

[1] On the development of these same methods in the later Judaism, see the valuable study of J. BONSIRVEN, *Exégèse rabbinique et exégèse paulinienne* (1939).

(e.g. Lods). It would seem very reasonable to choose a date between 332 and 300. Numerous additions have been made.

7. — The Books of Esdras and Nehemias [1].

Title and content.

The books which the present Hebrew Bible designates Esdras and Nehemias are called 2 and 3 Esd. in our editions of the Septuagint, and 1 and 2 Esd. in the Vulgate. The First Book of Esdras in the Septuagint is the apocryphal book which we call 3 Esd. At first they formed a single book under the title, Esdras.

The author gives a number of facts relative to the postexilic restoration, the facts which he judges particularly significant. They are ᵢ the return of the first repatriates and the vicissitudes in the rebuilding of the Temple (Esd. 1-6); the arrival of Esdras and the marriage reform (7-10); the arrival of Nehemias, the reconstruction of the city walls, and various administrative measures (Neh. 1 :1-7 : 73ᵃ); the solemn promulgation of the Law by Esdras and the renewal of the Covenant (7 : 73ᵇ-10 : 40); some complementary pieces of information (11 and 12); and the reforms introduced by Nehemias in the course of a second mission (13).

Literary characteristics and problems of historical criticism.

It is immediately evident that the work is composed of various documents. 1° Several passages (Esd. 4, 8 : 24ᵃ-5 : 1-6, 18; 7 : 12-26) have been inserted in their original language — Aramaic. They contain an official correspondence emanating from the Persian court. Verses 18 to 23 of Chapter 4, which treat of the times of Artaxerxes, should certainly be placed

---

Translator's note. — [1 Ez. KAUFMAN, *Toldat ha-emunah...*, VIII (1956), pp. 272-362. M. PELAIA, *Esdra e Neemia* (in *Sacra Bibbia*, ed. S. Garofalo, Turin [1957]; cf. *CBQ* [1957], p. 532). Z. CARL, in Kitbey ha-Hebrah..., I (1955), pp. 187-192, and Levinger, *ibid.*, pp. 193-207. See also " Yeb " (Elephantine), in *Entzyklop. Miqr.*, 3 (1958), pp. 425-444. W. RUDOLPH, *Esra und Nehemia mit 3 Esra* in *Handbuch zum A. T.* (Tübingen, 1949; see the reviews in *Bibliotheca Orientalis* [1951], pp. 185-187, and *Biblica* [1953], pp. 99-104). H. L. ABRIK, " The Lists of Zerubbabel (Nehemiah 7 and Ezra 2) and the Hebrew Numerical Notation ", in *BASOR*, No. 136 (1954), pp. 21-27. P. CHURGIN, *Studies in the Times of the Second Temple* (New York, 1949; in Hebrew), especially pp. 36-62, on the Samaritan Schism)].

after **6** : 18. 2⁰ The memoirs of Esdras and Nehemias are of
first-rate importance. They are presented in the first person,
and, therefore, are cited literally in Esd. **7** : 27–**8** : 34; **9** : 1-15;
and Neh. **1** : 1–**7** : 5; **13** : 4-31; and they are used in Neh. **8**–10 [1],
and in Neh. **11**–**12** : 31-43. 3⁰ Lists are numerous and seem,
for the most part, to have formed a part of the memoirs. That
in Esd. **2**, repeated in Neh. a, poses a complex problem. It
may be that in its primitive state it belonged to the memoir
of Nehemias (cf. Neh. **7** : 5) [2]. 4⁰ If the rest of the work is not
from the pen of the redactor himself, it comes from Levitical
sources having the same spirit and style as he.

Because of the resemblance that exists between the apocryphal
Esdras (3 Esd.) and our canonical books of Esdras-Nehemias,
the question has been raised as to which is the earlier work.
Most exegetes agree in recognizing that 3 Esd. did not have
Esdras-Nehemias as its source, but that it is the translation
of an independent Semitic text [3]. It can therefore be of real
service, although limited in this respect by its obscurities and
inconsistencies.

Phantom sources cannot be posited for Esdras-Nehemias
any more than for 1 and 2 Chronicles. The objectivity of our
author is indeed unassailable from the point of view of literary
criticism alone. It is abundantly confirmed by the considerable
information we can draw from extra-Biblical sources (3 Esd.
and Fl. Josephus), from archeological finds, and especially
from the Elephantine papyri [4]. The interpretation of the text
is not, however, always easy. Among the problems of historical
criticism which confront us, the possible identity of Sassabasar

---

[1] J. TOUZARD, " Les Juifs au temps de la période persane ", *RB* (1915),
pp. 118-133.
[2] *Ibid.*, pp. 87-88, 105-107.
[3] See H. Saint J. THACKERAY, *Esdras (First Book of)*, *HDB*, I (1898),
pp. 758-763. — P. VOLZ, *Ezra (the Greek)*, *EB*, I (1901), cols. 1490-1492. —
J. TOUZARD, *op. cit.*, pp. 68-75. — J. B. FREY, *Apocryphes de l'Ancien Testament*,
Supplément au Dictionnaire de la Bible, I (1926), cols. 431-432. [See also
A. VAN HOONACKER, " Néhémie et Esdras ", *Le Museon*, IX (1890); *Néhémie
en l'an 20 d'Artaxerxes I, Esdras en l'an 7 d'Artaxerxes II* (Ghent, 1892);
cf. *RB* (1923), 491 ff., and (1924), 33 ff. — A. KAPELRUD, *The Question of
Authorship in the Eszra Narrative* (OSLO, 1944; cf. J. COPPENS, *EThL* (1949),
pp. 136-137].
[4] See L. HENNEQUIN, *Elephantine (La colonie militaire juive d')*, *DBV*,
Suppl., II (1933), cols. 977-978, 998-999, 1018-1019. Cf. A VINCENT, *La
Religion des Judéo-araméens d'Elephantinz* (Paris, 1937).

and Zorobabel, and the chronological succession of Nehemias-Esdras are especially to be noted. In Chapter XV, a partial reply to these two questions will be given.

8. — The Book of Tobias [1].

Content [2].

Tobias the elder is a holy Israelite who was deported to Nineveh in the time of Shalmaneser. His piety and his good works do not shield him from suffering great hardships, as he loses the royal favor and becomes blind. His patience and confidence, however, do not fail. During the same period, at Ecbatana, Sara, the daughter of Raguel, who has suffered the loss of seven husbands in succession, also gives a good example of patience and goodness (1 : 1–3 : 23 (15). The body of the book (3 : 24 (16)–12 : 22) shows how God comes to the aid of these two afflicted souls. The son of Tobias, who bears the same name, was asked by his father to go to Rages in Media and seek from a certain Gabelus ten talents of silver which he had previously lent him. The archangel Raphael, under the name of Azarias, serves as a guide to the traveler, delivers him from being devoured by a huge fish, persuades him to ask for the hand of Sara in marriage, frees her from the attacks of the devil, leads the young man to Rages, and finally takes him back to his father, who is cured of his blindness. Only then does the archangel make himself known. The conclusion (13 : 1–14 : 17 (15) comprises the canticle of thanksgiving, the father's last instructions, an account of his death, and a brief description of the happy life of the son.

Text.

Until very recently we did not have the original text of Tobias. There was good reason, however, to believe that it was composed in Hebrew or Aramaic, and a fragment of the

---

Translator's note. — [1 A. VACCARI, review of A. Miller and J. Schildenberger, *Die Bücher Tobias, Judith, and Esther* [in the *Bonner Bibel*], *Biblica* (1948), pp. 133-141. G. PRIERO, *Tobia* (in *La Sacra Bibbia*, ed. Garafalo, Turin [1953]). D. FLOSER, art. " Book of Tobias ", in *Entzyklop. Miqr.*, 3 (1958), pp. 367-375].
[2] The references are given according to the Vulgate. Those to the Greek text are in parentheses.

text in Hebrew found among the Dead Sea Mss has confirmed this conjecture. The versions differ considerably from each another. Preference is given either to the Sinaïticus (א), which has the longest text, or to the Vaticanus (B), of which the Alexandrinus (A) is a revision. The translation in the Vulgate was made very hastily by Saint Jerome [1] from a Chaldean text. It betrays the influence of the *Vetus latina,* which itself stems from א [2].

Doctrine and literary characteristics.

The thesis of the book is that the just man may have to endure great trials, but, if he remains faithful, God will give him an abundance of temporal goods (3 : 25 (17); 4 : 23 (21); 11 : 17–12 : 12-14). With this fundamental thesis — to which the Vulgate gives almost a Christian sense (2 : 18; 3 : 6, 21, 22; 6 : 16-22; 12 : 13) — are combined important instructions : the value of legal observances (1 : 4-9, 12; 4 : 6); the even greater value of prayer (3 : 1 ff., 11 ff., 24 (Vulg.), 12 : 8ª, 12), of chastity (3 : 16-18 (14); 4 : 13 (12); 6 : 16-22 (Vulg.); 8 : 9), and of the works of mercy (1 : 15 (Vulg.); 2 : 1-2); the excellence of almsgiving (4 : 7-12 (11), 17 (16); 12 : 8ᵇ-9, 19-20ª (16-17ª), and of reverence for the dead (1 : 20ᵇ (17ᵇ), 21-22 (18-19; 2 : 1-9 (8); 4 : 18 (17); 12 : 12). Finally the book presupposes a well developed angelology (3 : 8; 5 : 21 (17); 8 : 3; 12 : 12, 15, 18-21). A nationalistic emphasis is equally manifest (3 : 1-6; 13 : 3-23; 14 : 6-9). One might say that the author presents the individual case of Tobias as the symbol and pledge of realization of the promises made to the nation.

Since the end of the nineteenth century, the question has been raised regarding the literary genre to which Tobias belongs, and, consequently, regarding its historicity [3]. Catholics generally regard the narrative as being strictly objective. However, א, B, the *Vetus latina* (1 : 21-22; 2 : 10; 11 : 17-18; 14 :

---

[1] " Unius diei laborem arripui ", he says in his Preface to the Book of Tobias, *PL,* XXIX, p. 26.

[2] The question of the text of Tobias is treated at length in Meinrad M. SCHUMPP, O. P., *Das Buch Tobias* (Münster i. W., 1933), pp. XIII-XLVII. [On the Hebraisms of the Codex Sinaïticus in Tobias, cf. JOÜON, *Biblica* (1923), pp. 168-174].

[3] For the history of the exegesis of Tobias, see Meinrad M. SCHUMPP, *op. cit.,* pp. LI-LIV.

10, 15), which are our best texts, and even the Vulgate (**11** : 20), allude to the Assyrian story of Ahikar (Achior in the Vulgate) [1]. There exist also, both in respect to the general theme and the linking of episodes, resemblances between Tobias and the story of " the grateful dead man " [2]. Moreover the very skill with which the progress of the story is presented gives it something of the artificial. The paraenetic element is elaborately developed, and several passages seem difficult to reconcile with known facts of history and topography. Finally, since Tobias was commented upon in Christian antiquity only by Saint Ambrose, and then only in a moral and allegorical sense, it cannot be said that any definite tradition exists regarding the nature of this book. Father Meinrad M. Schumpp, O. P., notes that many Catholic authors have been impressed by these consider-ations [3]. They are of the opinion that Tobias is an historical account, the basic facts of which were developed and embellished by a long oral tradition. The whole story reduces itself to this. During the Exile, a pious Israelite was rewarded in an extraordinary way for his fidelity to the Law and for his good works. It is beyond our powers to distinguish in detail what belongs to the primitive core and what is due to elaboration or embellishment [4].

Origin.

In the Greek text the account from **1** : 3 to **3** : 15 takes the form of a memoir written in the first person. This fact, combined with the indications of **12** : 20 and **13** : 1 (in the Greek), has often given rise to the belief that the book as a whole, or at least in its essential elements, goes back to the two Tobiases

---

[1] See Cosquin, *RB* (1899), 50 ff. See also Pirot, *DBV*, *Suppl.*, I, col. 198-207 (with bibliography).

[2] Cosquin, *l. c.*, pp. 513-520. [See also R. H. Charles, *The Apocrypha and Pseudepigrapha of the Old Testament in English* (Oxford, 1913), pp. 715-784. — A. Salhani, S. J., in *Contes Arabes* (Beyrouth, 1921) (Introduction, pp. 9-15; Arabic text, pp. 2-22). — A. Cowley, *Aramaic Papyri of the 5th Century B. C.* (Oxford, 1923), pp. 204-248].

[3] Schumpp, *op. cit.*, p. LVII.

[4] Father Schumpp observes that it is necessary to refer to the decree of the Biblical Commission on narratives which have only the appearance of being historical, if this interpretation is adopted (See below, p. 757). He himself believes that the question of the literary genre of Tobias is still open (*ibid.*, p. LIX). — [See also J. Prado, " La indole literaria del libro de Tobit ", *Sefarad* (1947), 373-394. He defends the substantial historicity of the narrative; *Sefarad, 9* (1949), 27-51].

themselves, or to one or the other of them. This view is now abandoned [1]. The entirely opposite opinion, according to which the work would date from the first years of the Christian era, has enjoyed only a limited success [2]. The majority of authors hold a middle position. In fact, everything points to the late postexilic period. Jerusalem has been destroyed (**13** : **11** (9) f.), the nation is completely dispersed, and eschatological aspirations are strongly accentuated (**13** : 12^b-23 (10^b-18); **14** : 7-9 (6-7). The regard for legal observances, almsgiving, and care of the dead are traits of Jewish psychology which will receive an ever increasing emphasis. On the other hand, it is wrong to date the book too late. It reveals no trace of the Machabean crisis, of the agitations of the Hasmonean period, of Hellenism, or of the exaggerations of the Pharisees. It was probably written about the year 200 B. C. Whether the author was a native of Palestine or a Jew of the Diaspora, cannot be determined.

9. — The Book of Judith [3].

Content.

Holofernes, charged with punishing the rebel vassals of Nabuchodonosor, gathers a large army, subdues Cilicia, Mesopotamia, and the region of Damascus, and, devastating everything along his way, appears in northern Palestine. The Jews prepare to resist, and humble themselves before God in fasting and prayer. Despite the counsels of Achior, Holofernes besieges Bethulia and at the end of thirty-four days the inhabitants are considering surrender (**1–7**). A rich and

[1] See the discussion in SCHUMPP, *op. cit.*, pp. XLVII-XLVIII.

[2] For an exposition and refutation of the arguments, see M. A. SIMPSON's article in R. H. CHARLES, *The Apocrypha and Pseudepigrapha of the Old Testament* (Oxford, 1913), pp. 183-184.

Translator's note. — [3 J. E. BRUNS, " Judith or Jael ", CBQ (1954), pp. 12-14; id., " The Genealogy of Judith ", *ibid.* (1956), pp. 19-22. F. STUMMER, *Geographie des Buches Judith* (Stuttgart, 1947; cf. *Theologische Revue* [1948], pp. 80-81). R. P. BARUCQ, *Judith, Esther* (in *Bible de Jérusalem*, Paris [1952]); cf. CBQ [1954], pp. 88-89). J. M. GRINTZ, *Sefer Yehudit* (Jerusalem, 1957, a comprehensive and important work in Hebrew. The author places the composition of Judith in the middle of the 4th cent. B. C. See also his art., " The Book of Judith ", in *Entzyklop. Miqr.*, 3 [1958], pp. 510-517). P. CHURGIN, *Studies in the Times of the Second Temple* (New York, 1949; in Hebrew), pp. 123-147].

beautiful widow named Judith is indignant at this thought, as showing a lack of confidence in God. Adorned with her most precious ornaments, she goes forth from the city and is led to Holofernes, to whom she promises victory. Three days later, being alone with him, she cuts off his head and returns with her trophy to Bethulia. The next day the besieged put the enemy to flight (**8** : **1**–**15** : 8). An epilogue relates the triumph of Judith and gives her canticle of thanksgiving (**15** : 9–**16** : 30). The Vulgate adds that a festival was instituted in memory of the victory (**16** : 31).

Text.

The original text of Judith is lost. The peculiarities of the Greek version would seem to indicate that the book was first written in Hebrew. The Greek version, which we possess in three recensions, is apparently trustworthy, especially in BA‭ℵ‬. The Vulgate translation which was made in one night by Saint Jerome [1], gives the sense of his Aramaic exemplar and takes into account the readings of the *Vetus latina*.

Teaching and literary characteristics [2].

The conflict which arose between Holofernes and Bethulia was the conflict between paganism versus monotheism. The material resources of Holofernes were formidable, but God reduced them to nothing by the hand of a woman. Thus, faith and patriotism, which are for the author one and the same, triumphed in a desperate situation. The book contains additional teachings : on strict legalism (**8** : 6; **11** : 11-13 (12-13, 16); **12** : 1-9, 19); on proselytism (**8** : 20-21; **11** : 21 (19); **13** : 31 (**14** : 7); **14** : 6 (10); on the excellence of strength of soul which comes from prayer (**4**; **6** : 15 (19); **8** : 10-34 (35); **9**; **13** : 7-11 (4f-9ᵇ), 22 (17).

Exegetes have long (Scholz as early as 1889) used the word apocalypse in respect to this book, and several features in form and content argue in favor of this view. But in the late period, genres tend to exchange their characteristics, and

---

[1] " Huic unam lucubratiunculam dedi ", *PL*, xxix, col. 39.
[2] References are given according to the Vulgate. Numbers in parentheses refer to the Greek text.

through all the same fundamental state of soul is revealed. In the case of Judith, two marks essential to the fully developed apocalyptic genre are missing, namely, emphasis on the marvelous and, especially, the grand historical perspective which introduces a real prophecy [1]. We get rather the impression that the author, on the basis of a historical tradition that perhaps was pretty thin, and with constant recourse to Scripture, constructs in the past a scene which gives the key to a present situation and ordains for his contemporaries a practical judgment and attitude that are supernatural in form. This kind of parallelism is utilized in Chr., and even more in Bar. 1 : 1-3 : 8. There is nothing of the historical novel in this procedure; we should see in it only the reflective and imaginative employment of history to serve a religious purpose.

Traditional exegesis always refused to consider the story of Judith fictitious. However, in modern times, the most varied hypotheses have been proposed, even among Catholics (cf. A. MILLER and A. METZINGER, *Introductio specialis in Vetus Testamentum* [Rome, 1946], nos. 263-265). It must be agreed that the author has composed his narrative with sovereign freedom. The historical data which he uses refer to situations and periods that are markedly different, without regard for the confusions which can be the result, and his geography, despite its apparent precision, is in part fictitious. Equally significant are the Biblical allusions, which often conceal things that are obvious, and the bent for archaism, even in matters of moral conduct. Finally, the art itself of the narrative reveals to us an author who is more preoccupied with psychology and doctrine than in avoiding improbabilities and inconsistencies. There is no reason either to condemn him or to excuse him; there is question merely of understanding him, recognizing that he is following a literary genre which may be disconcerting to our habits of mind but which was familiar to the Jews of the late postexilic period.

Origin.

The book of Judith was certainly written at the end of the Jewish era. This explains why it was not inscribed in the

[1] See Ch. VI, pp. 508 and 509 ff.

Palestinian Canon and why Josephus does not mention it. The majority of exegetes think of the age of the Machabees, but the arguments they bring forward are quite indirect, vague, or even questionable. If its dependence on Dan. and the Psalms of Solomon is established, it must be placed late in the Hasmonaean period. In that case, the narrative, written by a Pharisee, could present itself as a severe criticism of the monarchical pretensions and the pronounced secular policy of the Hasmonaean Dynasty.

10. — The Book of Esther [1].

Content.

After Assuerus has dismissed Queen Vasthi from favor, the Jewess Esther, niece of Mardochai, is chosen to succeed her. Mardochai reveals to the king a conspiracy of certain royal servants, but he also incurs the hatred of Aman, the first minister, for having refused to prostrate himself before him. Aman, to satisfy his resentment, petitions the king successfully to have all Jews in the Empire put to death on a single day (1–3). The monarch, however, has not forgotten the service rendered him by Mardochai, and, as a reward, he orders Aman to give him public honors. Now Esther, at her uncle's instigation, denounces the evil intentions of the first minister to the king. The minister is put to death. Mardochai inherits his office, and the Jews obtain permission to massacre their enemies (5 : 1–9 : 16). Thus, what was to have been a day of mourning becomes a day of rejoicing. This is the origin of the feast Purim or Feast of Lots. (9 : 17–10 : 3).

Text.

The Greek version, as compared with the Hebrew text, contains additions in eight places, and these additions make it a good third longer. Saint Jerome, who rendered the Hebrew *verbum e verbo, fideli testimonio simpliciter* [2], relegated to an

---

Translator's note. — [1 A. S. HARTOM, art., " The Book of Esther ", in *Entzyklop. Miqr.*, I (1950), pp. 486-492. LÖWENSTAMM, " Queen Esther ", *ibid.*, pp. 492-494. On the Feast of Purim, cf. E. KAUFMAN, *Toldot ha-emunah...*, VIII (1956), pp. 429-448].

² *Preface to the Book of Esther, PL,* XXVIII, cols. 1433-1435.

appendix (**10** : 4–**16** : 24) the fragments of the Greek, which he translated freely and marked with obelisks. Thus, he raised the question of authenticity in a way which implies a negative response. Contemporary Catholic exegetes are generally for the affirmative. In fact, the strongly Hebraic coloring of the fragments favors a Semitic origin, and the annotation contained in **11** : 1 shows that they were already a part of the work in 114 B. C. or, at the latest, in 48 B. C. Apart from all other considerations, however, the problem remains that the fragments in several places are not in agreement with the Hebrew text. Thus, Aman's hatred for Mardochai has not the same motive in **12** : 6 and **3** : 1-5; according to **11** : 3, Mardochai was already in the palace before the exaltation of Esther, while the contrary appears to be the case from **2** : 19; in contradiction to **6** : 3, we are told in **12** : 5 that his services were rewarded; the feast of Purim, which, according to **9** : 20-28, is for the Jews only, is for the Persians also according to **16** : 22. Finally, it has often been noted that God is not mentioned in the Hebrew, except perhaps indirectly in **4** : 14, while He is frequently mentioned in the fragments. It is difficult to believe that there was ever any thought of secularizing a story known and loved by all, and one destined to take its place in the Canon of the Scriptures. It seems, therefore, that the fragments, inspired though they are, were not a part of the original book. They very probably represent an independent tradition, or are simply a later addition.

Purpose and literary characteristics.

The Book of Esther was written to glorify the Jewish people; one cannot fail to recognize the exclusive and harsh nationalism which permeates it, and which stands in such sharp contrast to the warmth and abandon of the traditional historiography of Israel. It differs especially from earlier Scriptural writings by its silence respecting the divine conduct of events, and by the absence of all religious fervor and prayer, even in the dramatic circumstances where one would expect to come upon their spontaneous manifestation. The attitude of mind revealed by the Greek fragments is strikingly different; they put in high relief the power of the God of Israel, who is always ready to help His people in the hour of peril (cf. especially **13** : 8–**14** : 9).

It would be wrong, however, to conclude that the sole purpose of the book is to glorify vengeance and national hates. Nuances in its thought are to be recognized. In the first place, it shares with all the Sapiential Books the conviction that man is punished in the way he has sinned, according to the law of a strict determinism. Yet it is God who sets the machinery of retribution in motion. There is no doubt on this score, and conviction on this point is so deep and pervasive that there are numerous elliptical expressions in which God's action is presupposed without His name being mentioned (cf. *Mémorial Lagrange*, p. 178). This is the case in the story of Esther : " God is never named, but He guides all the actions in the drama, and the authors know this... The additions found in the Greek text have not transformed a profane book into a religious one : they rather express formally what the Hebrew author had left to be supplied ". (R. P. BARUCQ, *Judith, Esther* [Paris, 1952], pp. 82-83).

In brief, even if the author has no intention of defending a thesis, his narrative tends to show that God always comes to help His people in distress and by so doing He is glorified before the pagans. This is a familiar theme which the postexilic literature, beginning with Ezechiel and Isaias **40–55**, presupposes or develops in various ways. Among others, it is that of Judith, and it is worked out on the grand scale in the Book of Daniel. In Esther we are far removed from the spiritual loftiness of Daniel, and the bitterness of racial feeling does not make for the broadening of perspective. However, the theme mentioned underlies the Book of Esther, and its role and scope are not lessened by the fact that the events narrated are connected with the institution of a feast.

But what is to be thought of the historicity of these events? Many exegetes and Orientalists, faced with the difficulties presented by the Book of Esther, think that the author invented all parts of the drama which he narrates in order to introduce among the Jews a feast of Babylonian, Persian, or Greek origin. The historical difficulties are undeniable, and the feast of Purim is undoubtedly of Oriental origin. But the essential point is to understand the literary genre employed by the author. All are in agreement on his precise and extensive erudition : names of persons, chronological data, the topography of Susa and of the royal palace, the administration of the Persian Empire, requirements of protocol, the character of the sovereign and the intrigues going on around him, and the situation of the Jews in the Empire — all these details are familiar to him and give an objective character to his narrative. But it is equally certain that imagination plays an important role; the narrative is written with consummate art and with an astounding mastery of contrast. He has his own way of presenting characters, of having them speak, and of linking episodes. In such a composition, where does fiction stop? The actual evidence at our disposal does not permit us to give a definite answer, and the problem cannot be resolved a priori.

Origin.

The exegetes who consider Esther as strictly historical place its composition at Susa at the end of the 5th century; Mardochai would be its author, or it would be based on his memoirs (9 : 20). Others believe that it was written, whether in Palestine or in the Diaspora, at the end of the Persian period or in the course of the Greek period. It is placed by preference in the period following the revolt of the Machabees. The author in relating the persecution planned by Aman would be referring to that of Antiochus Epiphanes (168), and he would be trying to revive the national pride of the recent outlaws.

The problem is a difficult one to settle. Actually, the situation depicted in Esther is without any real analogy with that in the age of Antiochus, and the writer places himself in a completely Persian center and atmosphere. But this is undoubtedly an artifice, for the reign of Assuerus, i.e., of Xerxes I (485-465) is envisaged in marked perspective. Chapter 1 : 1-2, and the numerous details concerning Persian customs have an undeniable archaeological flavor. Furthermore, it is necessary to consider the connections of the book with the literature of the late period and the peculiarities of a language that is obviously very late. At all events, it cannot possibly be dated earlier than the second century, as 2 Mach. 15 : 36 suggests, and Est. 11 : 1 (Vulg.) requires, if this fragment points to a date 114 rather than a date 48.

II. — The Books of Machabees [1].

1 Machabees.

Content.

This book tells of the heroic struggle which the Machabees maintained against Syrian oppression. The events cover a period of forty years, from the accession of Antiochus Epiphanes in 175, to the death of Simon Machabeus in 135. The narrative follows a chronological order. Chapters 1 and 2 are introductory and deal with the following events : the death of Alexander the Great and the division of his Empire, the persecution of Antiochus Epiphanes, and the revolt of Mathathias. In Chapter 3, the history of the Machabean wars opens with the struggles of Judas against the Syrian generals (3 : 1–9 : 22). He defeats in order Apollonius, Seron, Gorgias, Lysias, and Nicanor. His victories permit him to purify the Temple, he concludes a treaty with the Romans, and he dies gloriously on the battlefield of Elasa. Jonathan (9 : 23–12 : 54) succeeds him. Although he is powerless against Bacchides for a long time, he finally prevails over him, and Judea enjoys peace. He puts the violent rivalry between Demetrius and Alexander Balas to good account, receiving from the latter the title of high priest and many other advantages. He is adroit in supporting now Demetrius II, and now Antiochus VI. Finally he perishes as a victim of Tryphon's ambition. His successor, Simon (13–16), makes an alliance with Demetrius II. The independence of Judea is recognized, and Simon is proclaimed high priest, general, and ethnarch. Under his rule the country enjoys peace and prosperity. Soon, however, Antiochus VII Sidetes renews hostilities through his general Cendebeus, who is defeated. Simon is assasinated, together

---

Translator's note. — [1 For general background, see F. M. ABEL, O. P., " Hellénisme et Orientalisme en Palestine au déclin de la période Séleucide ", *RB* (1946), 385-402. See also H. A. FISCHEL, *The First Book of Maccabees* (New York, 1948). M. GRANDCLAUDON, *Les livres des Maccabées* (*La Sainte Bible*, ed. Pirot and Clamer [Paris, 1951]; cf. review by F. M. ABEL, O. P., *RB* [1951], pp. 91-93). F. M. ABEL, O. P., *Les livres des Maccabées* (*Bible de Jérusalem* [1948]; cf. review by D. Schotz, *Theologische Revue* [1952], pp. 9-12). J. C. DANCY, *A Commentary on 1 Maccabees* (Oxford, 1954). P. CHURGIN, *op. cit. supra,* pp. 173-255].

with two of his sons, by his son-in-law, Ptolemy. His third son, John Hyrcanus, succeeds him.

Text and integrity.

The Greek text represented by ℵ, A, the Codex Venetus, and some Mss. written in minuscule, bears witness to a very poor Hebrew original now lost. The translation found in the Vulgate is the Old Latin unrevised. It was made from an older and better Greek text than that of our extant mss. Thus, from the critical point of view, it can be of great service [1].

The authenticity of **8**; **10** : 22-27; **12** : 1-23, and especially of the end of the book (**14** : 16-**16** : 24), has been doubted. But if we take into account the freedom with which the author handles his sources, the difficulties vanish. The fact that the historian Josephus in his *Ant. Iud.* does not refer to 1 Mach. from **14** : 16 on is not enough to cast suspicion on the authenticity of these chapters, especially since they are so similar to the others in ideas and in style [2]. However, the last two verses in the book may be challenged on this score.

Teaching and literary characteristics.

The book does not contain a doctrinal thesis nor moral exhortations, but it relates, and occasionally comments upon, the deeds of those who through their ardent faith, trust in Providence, and strength of soul, have freed their country, and won the right to practice their religion. The author is deeply convinced of the unique excellence of the privilege enjoyed by Israel, the Chosen Nation; the paganism of the Gentiles and the apostasy of his compatriots fill him with horror. This basic disposition and attitude explain his nationalism, his admiration for the Machabees, and his attachment to the Hasmonaean Dynasty. Furthermore, underlying the presentation of historical events, we find also the great basic dogmatic and moral characteristics of Judaism, namely :

---

[1] DOM DE BRUYNE, " Le texte grec des deux premiers livres des Macchabées ", *RB* (1922), pp. 31-54. On *Les anciennes traductions latines des Macchabées* ed. by Dom Donatien de Bruyne with the collaboration of Dom Bonaventure Sodar, O. S. B., (1932), see *RB* (1933), pp. 264-269.

[2] See on this subject WOODHOUSE, *Macchabees (Books of)*, in Cheyne, *EB*, III, cols. 2863-2865; and D. H. BÉVENOT, *Die beiden Makkabäerbücher* (1931), p. 8.

a profound consciousness of the divine transcendence (e.g., 3 : 18-22; 4 : 30-33), an inviolable attachment to the sanctuary of Sion and to the Holy City (e.g., 3 : 43, 45, 59; 4 : 36-60; 7 : 33-38, 41-42), and fidelity to the observances of the Torah (e.g., 1 : 11; 2 : 68; 3 : 47-51; 13 : 3-6).

The author has the deliberate intention of furnishing an exact narrative of events. The liveliness of his account and his precision in details would indicate that in many cases he is relying on personal recollections. He also refers to sources (cf. 9 : 22, and perhaps 16 : 23-24), and often he even transcribes diplomatic or private documents, which he has certainly not fabricated. He reports facts simply and clearly, and with a dignity which does not prevent him from registering his own preferences, but in a temperate manner.

These are guarantees of his objectivity. They do not exclude, however, the employment of certain conventions and certain deficiencies which the modern reader ought to know how to evaluate. As a man steeped in Scripture, the author wishes to be, and to be regarded as being, a continuator of the traditional historiography, and he borrows its formulae and devices. As a literary artist, he abandons himself here and there to poetry, and he has no scruples about hyperbole. As a man of his time and milieu, he does not try to free himself of deficiencies in knowledge, confused ideas, or of prejudicial judgments which were common to Palestine as regards foreign countries and peoples. Commentators are agreed that these imperfections in detail do not affect appreciably the historical value of his work.

Origin.

The feelings and outlook of the author and his knowledge of history and topography indicate that the work was produced in Palestine. The final redaction is not later than 63, the date of the capture of Jerusalem by Pompey (cf. 8). It is not earlier than 136, the year of the death of Simon Machabeus (cf. 16 : 11-12). If the authenticity of 16 : 23-24 is accepted, it could well be assigned to the years following the death of John Hyrcanus, i.e., after 104 [1].

---

[1] For problems of chronology, see V. COUCKE, *Chronologie biblique*, *DBV*, *Suppl.*, I, 1273-1279.

2 Machabees.

Content.

At the beginning of the book are inserted two letters sent from Jerusalem to the Jews of Egypt, urging them to celebrate the Feast of the Dedication (**1** : 1–**2** : 19) [1]. The author then announces that his narrative is simply an abridgement of the work of Jason of Cyrene (**2** : 20-33). This narrative is divided into two parts. The first deals with events which took place under Antiochus Epiphanes (**3** : 1–**10** : 8) : the struggles for the office of high priest and attempts at Hellenization, the profanation of the Temple and the persecution, the defeat of the Syrians, the death of Antiochus Epiphanes, and the purification of the Temple, followed by a feast which was to be celebrated annually. The second part (**10** : 9–**15** : 37) relates events connected with the reigns of Antiochus V Eupator and Demetrius I : the struggles against the neighboring peoples, against the Syrians, and especially against Nicanor. The defeat of the last mentioned occasioned the institution of a feast called the Day of Nicanor. The few words of conclusion (**15** : 38-40), on the nature of the work, recall those of the preamble (**2** : 20-33).

As is evident, 2 Mach. is in great part parallel to 1 Mach., but covers a period of only seventeen years.

Text.

From the style [2], which is that of the best writers of the last century B. C., it is evident that 2 Machabees was written in Greek. The two letters, likewise composed, according to all indications, in Greek, bear, however, the stamp of Hebrew genius. The text contained in the Vulgate is that of the Old Latin Version unrevised.

Purpose and literary characteristics.

The book seems to have been composed to reawaken among the Alexandrian Jews a consciousness of their community

---

[1] *Translator's note.* — [See F. M. ABEL, O. P., " Les lettres préliminaires du 2e livre des Macchabées ", *RB* (1946), 513-533].
[2] Cf. Saint Jérôme, *PL*, xxviii, col. 557.

of race and religion with their brethren in Palestine. It seeks also to comfort them by showing, through the example of the martyrs and heroes of their faith, that trial inevitably receives its recompense. Within this framework and perspective it is quite natural to find affirmations of very important theological beliefs, which, in certain circles, were still matters of controversy, namely : the resurrection of the dead (7 : 9, 11, 14, 36; 12 : 43, 44; 14 : 46), rewards and punishments after death (6 : 26; 7 : 36; 12 : 45), prayer for the dead (12 : 43, 44, 46), and intercession of the saints (15 : 12-16). It is noteworthy that the Temple forms the center of perspective in these pages of history. They recount its profanations, its liberation, and its purifications, and they explain the origin of the two feasts which concern it : the Feast of Dedication and that commemorating the victory over Nicanor.

The book belongs to the literary genre called " pathetic historiography " [1], a type in keeping with the taste of the period. This genre postulates the intention, not of relating facts exactly, but of presenting them in such a vivid and moving manner as to make them convey their lesson in themselves. This is the explanation of the special features in a narrative which, in comparison with that of 1 Mach., appears to us, when it is considered as a whole, as very artificial. The author has no scruples about stressing the accessory in place of the essential, about mixing perspectives, or about turning events to suit the advantage of his hero. He forgets to take the factor of human causes into account and has the supernatural intervene in a quite unaccustomed manner. These peculiarities do not prevent the work from possessing vivid and precise features, in which a firsthand knowledge must be recognized.

Origin.

Jason of Cyrene probably wrote his great work at Alexandria. He did not undertake its composition, however, until after he had collected in Judea all kinds of written and oral information. His literary activity is necessarily later than the defeat of Nicanor in 161 (2 Mac. 15). On the other hand, one of the two letters sent to the Alexandrian Jews is dated 188 of the Seleucid Era (1 : 10), i.e., 124 B. C. There are no

---

[1] F. M. ABEL, *Les livres des Maccabées* (Paris, 1949), p. XXXIII.

sound grounds for questioning the correctness of this information
nor the authenticity of the letters and their employment as
a part of the original book [1]. These dates give a *terminus
a quo* for the origin of 2 Machabees, but it is more difficult to
determine a *terminus ante quem*. The best evidence which we
have is the allusion to this book to be found in Philo († 40
A. D.) [2], and in the Epistle to the Hebrews [3] (composed about 66
A. D.). It is probable that 2 Machabees was written around
100 B. C.

<h3>3. — THE PROPHETICAL BOOKS [4].</h3>

[A Gelin]

<h2>I. — The Book of Isaias [5].</h2>

The Book of Isaias surpasses all the other prophetical books.
It is the locus classicus of messianic and eschatological prophecy,
expressed, moreover, from different points of view. In their
reading of the book, students have been more aware of its
constant than of its divergent elements. The theme of the

[1] See C. C. TORREY, *EB*, III, cols. 2875-2878.
[2] *Quod omnis probus liber*, 13.
[3] Cf. Heb. 11 : 35[b] and 2 Mach. 6 : 19, 28; 7 : 9.
Translator's note. — [4] ENGNELL, " Profeter ", in *Svenskt Bibl. Uppslagsverk*,
2, 727-774; P. VAN IMSCHOOT, in Haag, *Bibellexikon*, 1367-1383. O. EISSFELDT,
" The Prophetical Literature ", in H. H. Rowley, ed., *The Old Testament and
Modern Study* (Oxford, 1951), pp. 115-161. H. E. W. FASBROOKE, " The
Prophetical Literature ", in *Interpreter's Bible*, I (1952), 201-211. P. BÉGUERIE,
J. LECLERCQ, and J. STEINMANN, *Études sur les prophètes d'Israël* (*Lectio
Divina* 14, Paris, 1954). J. RIDDERBOS, *Profetie en Ekstase* (Aalten, 1941).
W. ZIMMERLI, *Le prophète dans l'A. T. et dans l'Islam* (Lausanne, 1945).
H. H. ROWLEY, ed., *Studies in O. T. Prophecy* (Edunburgh, 1950). J. CHAINE,
Introduction à la lecture des prophètes (Paris, 1956). J. COPPENS, *Les harmonies
des deux Testaments...* (Tournai, 1948). J. KLAUSNER, *ha-Nebi'im* (Jeru-
salem, 1954). E. KAUFMAN, *Toldot ha-emunah...*, VI (1947), 1-289 on Amos,
Osee, Isaias, Micheas); VII (1948; on Zach., Joel, Soph., Nahum, Hab.,
Jeremias, Ezechiel). Th. C. VRIEZEN, " Prophecy and Eschatology ", *Vetus
Testamentum, Suppl.* (Leiden, 1953), 199-229. S. MOWINCKEL, *Han som
Kommer* (Copenhagen, 1951; English trans. by G. W. Anderson, *He That Comes*
[Abington Press]; cf. *CBQ* [1957], 274-278; J. COPPENS, *EThL* [1957], 93;
R. DE VAUX, *RB* [1958], 101-106). J. SCHILDENBERGER, " Messiaserwartung ",
in Haag, *Bibellexikon*, 1117-1136. R. E. MURPHY, O. CARM., " Notes on
O. T. Messianism and Apologetics ", *CBQ* (1957), 5-15. A. BENSON,
" Messianism in Amos ", *ibid.*, 199-212. E. H. MALY, " Messianism in Osee ",
ibid., 213-225. H. RINGGREN, *The Messiah in the O. T.* (Chicago, 1956;
cf. *CBQ* [1957], 279-280). J. COPPENS, *De messiaanse verwachting in het Psalm-
boek* (Brussels, 1955, with excellent bibliography, pp. 30-34). R. T. SIEBENECK,
" Messianism of Aggeus and Proto-Zacharias ", *CBQ* (1957), 312-328.
N. FLANAGAN, " Messianic Fulfillment in St. Paul ", *ibid.*, 474-484. A. DE GU-
GLIELMO, " Fertility of the Land in the Messianic Promises ", *ibid.*, 306-311.

God of Majesty whose name is the Holy One of Israel, and the themes of faith, of the " Remnant ", and of the " poor ", connect the several parts of this great work with one another. It is a composition in which a school, it seems, finds expression, namely, the Isaian School. Saint Thomas distinguished two main parts in the Book of Isaias : the book of divine judgments and the book of consolations. The analysis of modern criticism has emphasized the impression of complexity which the Book of Isaias presents. The work of Catholic scholars during the past fifty years has increased the probability of the " reading " hypothesis which divides the book into three sections.

R. A. F. MACKENZIE, S. J., " The Messianism of Deuteronomy ", *ibid.* (1947), 299-305. R. E. BROWN, " The Messianism of Qumrān ", *ibid.* (1957), 53-82. I. ENGNELL, " Messias ", *Svenskt Bibl. Uppslagverk*, 2, 245 ff].

Translator's note. — [5 See H. HÖPFL, *Introductio specialis in Vetus Testamentum* (5th ed., Rome, 1946), pp. 418 and 423. J. COPPENS, *The Old Testament and the Critics*, Engl. translation (Paterson, N. J., 1942), p. 153 ff. A. FEUILLET, art. " Isaie ", *DBV, Suppl.*, IV, 698; R. T. MURPHY, O. P., " Second Isaïas : Literary Problems ", *CBQ* (1947), 170-178. A. G. HERBERT, *The Throne of David. A Study of the Fulfillment of the Old Testament in Jesus Christ and his Church* (London, 1942; cf. *Nouvelle Revue Théolog.* [1949], 651). R. CRIADO, S. J., *La Sagrada Pasion en los Profetas* (Madrid, 1944; cf. *Bibliotheca Orientalis* [1948], 58). R. T. MURPHY, O. P., " Second Isaias : the Servant of the Lord ", *CBQ* (1947), 262-274. C. LATTEY, " The Term Almah ", *ibid.* (1947), 89-95; " Various Interpretations of Isa, 7 : 14 ", *ibid.* (1947), 147-154. J. E. STEINMVELLER, " The Etymology and Biblical Usage of Almach ", *CBQ* (1940), 28-48. R. MARGOLIOUTH, *Ehad hu Yesha 'yahu* (Jerusalem, 1954; on the unity of Isa.). S. TALMON, " Variant Readings in the Scroll of Isa. I ", *Kitbey ha-Hebra...*, I (1955), 146-147. F. L. MORIARTY, " The Emmanuel Prophecies ", *CBQ* (1957), 213-225. I. P. SEIERSTAD, *Die Offenbarungsergebnisse der Propheten Amos, Jesaja u.Jeremia* (Oslo, 1946; cf. *Bibliotheca Orientalis* [1948], 58-59). On the Emmanuel prophecy, see C. C. LATTEY, S. J., in *CBQ* (1946), 369-376; *ibid.* (1947), 89-95 and 147-154. On the rendering of *ha-'almah*, Isa. 7 : 14, see E. P. ARBEZ, *CBQ* (1955), 469-474. On the " Servant of Yahweh ", see : R. TOURNAY, O. P., " Les chants du Serviteur dans la seconde partie d'Isaïe ", *RB* (1952), 355-384. J. LINDBLOM, *The Servant Songs in Deutero-Isa.* (Lund, 1951; cf. *RB* [1952], 428-430; cf. also J. COPPENS, *EThL* [1952], 694). C. C. LATTEY, S. J., " The Book of the Prophet Isaias ", *Scripture* (1952), 2-7. W. ZIMMERLI and J. JEREMIAS, *The Servant of God* (English trans., Naperville, Ill., 1956; cf. *CBQ* [1957], 535-538). H. H. ROWLEY, *The Servant of God and Other Essays* (London, 1952; cf. *Theologische Revue* [1952], 213-215). N. J. McELENEY, " The Translation of Isa. 41 : 27 ", *CBQ* (1957), 441-443. E. KAUFMAN, *Toldot ha-emunah...*, VIII (1956), 51-156, and 499-501. V. DE LEUUW, *De Ebed Yahweh-Profetieën* (Louvain, 1956; cf. A. M. DUBARLE, *Revue de Sci. Phil. et Rel.* [1958]; 135; also, J. COPPENS, *JTS* [1958], 114-117). H. CAZELLES, " Les poèmes du Serviteur ", *RSR* (1955), 15-51. J. FISCHER, " Gottesknecht ", in Haag, *Bibellexikon*, 609-619. R. BLOCH, in *Moïse l'homme de l'Alliance* (Paris, 1955), 183 ff. (on the Messianic doctrine of Second Isa.). The art. " Isaiah " in *Entzyklop. Miqr.*, 3 (1958), 908-936. J. STEINMANN, *Le Prophète Isaïe* (Paris, 1950)].

The author and his times.

Isaias heard the call of God in the year of King Ozias' death (738) [740] and he exercised his ministry down to the reign of Ezechias (718-689) [716-687] [1]. He was an outstanding personality, who in Rabbinic tradition has become a nobleman of royal blood. He was a man of imperious will and resolution and of keen intelligence, as is evident from his interventions in state policy. He had a gift for observation in which the ironic finds a place, and his feelings are never superficial. He is a patriotic aristocrat who is conservative in his outlook. Vividness of imagination, great evocative power, and splendid diction characterize his literary genius.

He lived in the period of the advance of the Sargonids westwards, and the events connected with it have left their mark on his oracles. They are : the Syro-Ephraimite war (734-732) which ended in the fall of Damascus and Assyria's annexation of the northeastern part of the Kingdom of Israel; the rebellion of Israel and the fall of Samaria (724-722); the revolt of the small States of the West in 711, which ended in the capture of Ashdod [Azotus]; Ezechias' adoption of an anti-Assyrian policy probably under the influence of that revolt, but also connected with the program of religious reform in which he was engaged; from 705, endemic revolts in the West, in part inspired by the intrigues of the Babylonian patriot, Merodach-Baladan [Marduk-Apal-iddina]. Sennacherib's Palestinian campaign against Ezechias, now in open rebellion, is described in greatest detail. It ended in Juda becoming a vassal and remaining under Assyrian domination for nearly a century. But Jerusalem was saved from destruction, and the high point of Isaias' ministry is reached in this crisis, at which the prophet affirmed the inviolability of Sion.

A. Isaias 1-39.

Main points of his teaching.

Isaias' God in " the Holy One ". This title keeps recurring as a motif in the Code of Holiness (H), i.e., in Lev. **19–26**, which perhaps belongs to the time of the prophet. It is the designation

---

Translator's note. — [1 The dates in square brackets are taken from the *Bible de Jérusalem].*

of Him who is " Altogether Different ", mighty and majestic, terrifying, yet attractive. This name expresses His moral perfection, but especially His absolute unapproachableness. Isaias' inaugural vision (6) echoes the experiences of fear and trembling of Abraham, Moses, Elias, and Job when they approached the divine mystery. But the God of Isaias is also the " Holy One of Israel ", an expression which conveys a sense of the infinite character of the divine condescension. God has made His people the focal point of history. God's plan is being fulfilled (10 : 12; 14 : 24), and Israel is the witness.

Faith must welcome God's actions. It is the practical conviction of the exclusive importance of Yahweh. The believer, accordingly, must avoid human covenants and turn aside from the terror caused by foreign armies : " If you do not believe, you will not stand " (7 : 9) [1]. Faith in Isaias is very close to humility (2 : 6-22).

The structure of Israel as a nation is one of the essential features of this theology. Sion is the palladium of the Chosen People and Isaias, unlike Jeremias, believed that it could not perish (28 : 16). Its dynasty is celebrated in song, as in the oracle of Nathan (2 Sam. 7) and in the old royal Psalms; Isaias' messianism stresses the idea of an ideal king who will succeed in promoting the interests of the Covenant and in establishing peace and justice. Isaias looked for his coming somehow in connection with the crisis of his times (7 : 14; 9 : 1-6). He describes his reign in terms of the golden age in order to make men realize its exceptional character, quite outside the range of human experience. " The knowledge of Yahweh ", finally disseminated over the earth (11 : 1-9), occupies the center of his vision.

Isaias is a witness of an important stage in the history of religion. Into the midst of a people that was becoming more obdurate (6 : 10) he cast his idea of a " Remnant ". Chapter 8 : 16 even attests the emergence of a spiritual society consisting of his disciples and distinct from the rest of the nation.

Translator's note. — [1 There is a play on words in the Hebrew which it is practically impossible to reproduce in English : *im lō' ta' amīnū Ki lō, te' amēnū.* Cf. Moffatt's rendering : " If your faith does not hold, you will never hold out "].

Content and formation of the book.

The book is an aggregate of collections of texts written by the prophet (6 : 15; 30 : 8) or by his disciples, to which, in the course of time, later additions were made. It contains oracles and autobiographical and biographical narratives.

At first sight, the division of its contents seems quite clear. According to Duhm there are : *a)* 1–12, oracles on Juda and Jerusalem; *b)* 13–23, oracles concerning the Nations, collected separately as in Jeremias and Ezechiel; *c)* 24–27, eschatological oracles or the great Apocalypse of Isaias; *d)* 28–33, a collection of " Woes "; *e)* 34–35, eschatological oracles or the minor Apocalypse of Isaias; *f)* 36–39, an historical appendix.

This division may be kept as a first approximation, but with the reservation that it cannot explain the complex character of Isaias' writings. Thus, to consider only the first so-called collection mentioned, 1–12, it does not account for the presence of certain titles (1 : 1 and 2 : 1), or the existence of narratives among the oracles, or the obvious break in connections between 5 and 10. We might distinguish with greater justification within 1–12 : *a)* 6–9 : 6, the book of Emmanuel, into which has been gathered autobiographical and biographical narratives and messianic oracles connected chiefly with the crisis of 734-732 — the whole prefaced by the narrative of the prophet's call. This is probably the oldest collection of Isaias. — *b)* 1, a booklet of oracles undoubtedly dating from Sennacherib's destructive invasion, and compiled by a disciple of Isaias; *c)* 2–5, and 9 : 7–11 : 9, oracles of various dates, some of which may go back to the time of Joatham and Achaz, before the Syrian war of 734, while others, e.g., 11 : 1-9, represent one of the prophet's last interventions. This composite collection continues throughout the entire book, in which its elements have been scattered; *d)* 11 : 10–12, a messianic and liturgical appendix later than Isaias.

This example is sufficient to indicate that the formation of the book has had a complicated history. Substantial additions can be detected in the oracles against the Nations introduced by the word *massa* (" burden ", " oracle ") : 13–14 : 23; 15–16; 19; 21; 23. But it should be remembered that writings often went through a process of reworking and reinterpretation in

Israel : they were the object of meditation and reapplied to new situations. Thus **14** : 4ᵇ-21 seems to represent an Isaian satire on Sargon, king of Assyria, written on the occasion of his death (705), but it is inserted within the framework of an oracle against Babylon (**13–14**, 4ᵃ, 22-23) dating from the Exile. Thus read again in a new light, it became a satire against the king of Babylon.

The minor Apocalypse, **34–35**, reflects the same atmosphere as the Second Part of Isaias. The great Apocalypse, **24–27**, consists of descriptive poems and lyrical interludes which fit very well into the postexilic period. It announces cosmic catastrophes connected with the Day of Yahweh which will terminate history; a messianic feast is prepared in Sion for the just of Israel, from which the pagan nations are excluded. Other examples of this literary genre are found in Zacharias **9–14** and in Daniel.

Editors brought the First Part of Isaias to a close with an historical appendix (**36-39**), which certainly has an apologetic value : it emphasizes that events have confirmed Isaias. Chapters **36–39** are parallel to 2 Kgs. **18** : 13-**20** : 19. Both texts may go back to a common source. An inversion in the order of this group of chapters has been noted : **38–39**, which relate the sickness of Ezechias and the embassy of the Babylonian Merodach-Baladan, are chronologically earlier than **36–37**, which give an account of Sennacherib's invasion. The editors of Isaias mentioned this invasion first in that it supplied a conclusion to the poems of the First Part, where there are so many references to the Assyrians, and they then recorded the sickness of Ezechias and the embassy of the Babylonian king because the announcement of the captivity, which closes these two episodes, furnished a good introduction to the poems of the Second Part.

B. Isaias 40-55.

Content of the Second Part of Isaias.

The general theme is the consolation of Israel. A solemn introduction (**40** : 1-11) furnishes the basic theme, and this is orchestrated in a series of poems which give the impression of a mighty unity, of a grand symphony. The Exile is going to end, Yahweh is going to free His people by the hand of Cyrus, who is presented at first mysteriously and then declared to be invested with the function of a pagan messias (**44** : 24–**45** : 13). Babylon, the great center of magic and divination, is about to fall (**47**). Then, through the Syrian desert Israel will relive a more wonderful Exodus than the one of old (**41** : 17-19; **43** : 19-20). Israel will again occupy Jerusalem, where God will reign. God's action and the glory of His people will be so great that the Nations will be converted and will be incorporated in Israel (**44** : 5; **45** : 14-17; **55** : 4-5). The Israel in question is a " qualitative " people, heir to the privileges granted long ago to Abraham, Moses, and David. It is called by God, His Servant [1].

Intermingled with this first current of thought which looks to the glorious restoration of the kingdom of Yahweh is another which is represented by the Songs of the Servant : the kingdom of God will be assured in the future through the preaching and martyrdom of a mysterious personage. Duhm distinguished four poems, the precise limits of which are difficult to fix and which are now presented thus : *a)* **42** : 1-4, an investiture oracle of the Servant; *b)* **49** : 1-6, an autobiographical account of his call; *c)* **50** : 4-9, a confidence, after the manner of Jeremias, in which the Servant relates his sufferings; *d)* **52** : 13–**53** : 12, the lament of the kings of the earth over the death of the Servant. This lament is placed within the framework of two divine oracles.

The problems of the Second Part of the Book of Isaias.

Roughly, there are two basic problems. The first is the question of the relation of the two parts of the book. Do they belong to the same author, namely, the contemporary of Ezechias? This is the solution found in Ben Sira (Ecclus. **48** : 24-25) : " He looked into the future and consoled the mourners of Sion; he foretold what should be..., hidden things yet to be fulfilled ", i.e., he prophesied for the generation which would live towards the end of the Exile in Babylonia. But this solution runs into a number of difficulties. In the first place, the analogy of the other prophets is against it : they address

---

Translator's note. — [1 " Qualitative "; so the French original. The meaning is an Israel membership which depends on moral-religious qualities].

themselves directly to their contemporaries. What interest would the mention of Babylon and Cyrus have for the people of the 8th century who were threatened by Assyria? It must be noted, too, that the destruction of Jerusalem and the captivity are regarded as accomplished facts, and Cyrus is looked upon as a contemporary who has already achieved great victories. Again, if Isaias 40 ff. was written in the 8th century, it must be supposed that these chapters remained secret, for neither Jeremias nor Ezechiel, who lived in the 7th and 6th centuries, are acquainted with them, and yet they would have found in them good arguments to confirm their teachings on the coming judgment of Jerusalem.

In the second place, the theology of the Second Part is more developed. Monotheism is defined here in the clearest terms and finds a natural place in an elaborate polemic against idolatry, universalism is definitely taught, and the messianic expectation is presented in a form which differs from that in the First Part, where it revolves about a Davidic king. Lastly, the style is much fuller and shows marked lyrical coloring.

These various difficulties, however, do not swing the balance definitely in favor of the critical thesis. The tutioristic decree of the Biblical Commission (June, 1908) invited exegetes to make a deeper study of the problem. They must take into account especially the resemblances in thought and expression which we mentioned at the beginning of our exposition and also the tradition attested in Ben Sira and continued in the New Testament, which quotes, under the name of Isaias, several texts taken from 40–66 (Mt. 3 : 3; Mk. 1 : 2-3; Lk. 3 : 4; 4 : 17; Jn. 1 : 23; Acts 8 : 26-33; Rom. 10 : 16, 20, 21). All this has led to the development of " reading " hypotheses which embrace the whole complexity of the problem. According to the Catholic exegete Kissane (1943), an anonymous prophet, living at the end of the Exile and thoroughly imbued with the teaching of Isaias, edited his master's book, and then extended the latter's preaching by adapting it to meet the needs of his own contemporaries in Babylonia. Bentzen (1948) thinks that a definite continuity between the three parts of Isaias was assured through the circles of his disciples. This is the idea of an Isaian School proposed at the beginning of the present exposition.

The second basic problem is the question of the relation
between the Second Part of Isaias and the Songs of the Servant.
Duhm's solution has been accepted by some Catholic exegetes
who regard these Songs as the work of a disciple of the Second
Isaias (so Auvray-Steinmann). Other critics consider them
to be the spiritual testament of that author (so North). The
latter, more impressed by the unquestionable unity of Isaias
40-66, are closer to the truth. Still others, finally, emphasize
this unity even more, and regard the figure of the Servant
as representing now the " qualitative " Israel, and now a
Personage in whom the full significance of that Israel is
concentrated (so Tournay).

C. Isaias 56-66.

These chapters constitute the so-called Trito-Isaias of the
critics. They are concerned with the return from the Exile
and seem to have been written to guide the community of the
Sionists in their work of restoration in Palestine. The latter
are eager to convert the indigenous population (Judaico-
Benjaminites), who have sunk into a semi-paganism; they
are filled with zeal for purity of religion and long to rebuild
the Temple (**66** : 1-2). Some exegetes (so Auvray-Steinmann)
see here a collection of anonymous texts in which the Isaian
School finds expression. But within the last few years, some
progress has been made in that the unity of authorship has
been recognized (Elliger), and, according to Glahn, the author
should be identified as the Second Isaias himself, after his
return with the exiles to the Promised Land.

2. — The Book of Jeremias [1].

Jeremias and his age.

Jeremias, a native of the village of Anathoth, situated
about four miles N.E. of Jerusalem, probably was a descendant

Translator's note. — [1 J. BRIGHT, " The Date of the Prose-Sermons of
Jeremias ", *Journal of Biblical Literature* (1951), 15-35.   J. ZUCKERBRAM,
" Editorial Changes : 2 Kgs. **24-25** and Jer. **39** and **42** ", *Melilah* (University
of Manchester, 1950), 1-54. M. S. SEGAL, " Jeremias ", in *Entzyklop. Miqr.*, 3,
866-885.   Dom R. AUGÉ, *Jeremias* (Vol. XIV of *La Biblia* of Montserrat, 1950).   A. C. WELSH, *Jeremiah : His Time and His Work* (Oxford, 1951).
J. STEINMANN, *Le Prophète Jérémie* (Paris, 1952)].

of the priest Abiatar who was exiled to this place by Solomon. His call to the prophetic ministry occurred in 626. He was a witness of : the rapid decline and fall of Assyria; the religious Reform of Josias, connected with the discovery of Deuteronomy (621); the territorial extension towards the North, which for some years gave the Kingdom of Juda a power that recalled that of David; the death of Josias at Megiddo (609); the vassalage of the new king, Joakim (608-605), to Egypt; finally, the supremacy of Babylon, which was complete after the battle of Karkemish (605) and culminated for Juda in the two sieges of Jerusalem (598 and 587). The prophet passed through an enthusiastic phase at the time of the Reform of Josias, in which he undoubtedly participated (11 : 6, 8, 9-12), and he then spoke of the approaching return of the exiles of the Northern Kingdom (30-31 : 22). But this was only a happy accident in a painful career during which he repeatedly issued warnings to a stubborn people. He was not listened to, and he went through a real Gethsemani, knowing failure and being the victim of persecution and general prejudice. His " Confessions " preserve for us an echo of his discouragement and struggles. Chapter 15 : 1-18 marks a renewal of his call. It was at the time of the collapse of the State of Juda that he had his most profound and consolatory visions of the future and that he announced a new form of the Covenant (31 : 31-34). He had counted upon the Israel that continued to exist in the Exile, and it is there that he had the most real influence. After his death, he appeared as the father of Jewish piety as it is expressed in the psalms " of the poor ".

Content and formation of the book.

The two chief witnesses of the text differ both in respect to the extent and the order of the materials. The Greek text is about an eighth shorter than the Hebrew. Often there is question of single verses or parallel verses, but sometimes of short sections, some of which were not in the original (33 : 14-26), while others are lacking in the Septuagint as a result of accidents connected with textual criticism (39 : 4-13). The position of the oracles against the Nations is not the same in the Greek translation and in the Masoretic Text; the Septuagint puts them after 25 : 13, while the Hebrew groups them at the end of the book (**46-51**). This is all the more astonishing since **25** : 13⁹ is the title of these oracles and, in the Hebrew, it does not introduce anything. The form of the book attested by the Greek, then, is certainly the earlier one. On the other hand, the order in which these oracles are arranged is the original one in the Hebrew recension, for it corresponds to the data in **25** : 19-24. The order in the Greek text is logical and political, as it begins with the great powers.

Other literary facts accentuate further the impression of complexity : the abundance of doublets; the absence of sequence in the chronological data scattered through the book; the alternation of the classical types of literary forms — oracular material, biographical pieces, and autobiographical pieces; finally, interpolations, additions, and " rewrites ". The list of interpolated passages is not very extensive. The principal ones are : **10** : 1-16; **17** : 19-27; **30** : 10-11, 23-24; **31** : 10-11, 26, 38-40; **32** : 17-23 (in part); **33** : 14-26; **39** : 1-2, 4-13; **50-51**; **52**. Furthermore, the oracles against the Nations are the favorite place for reworkings or " rewrites ", as is evident from **48** : 1-47, and **49** : 7-22. Finally, attention has been drawn to certain pieces which are markedly deuteronomic in tone and could well represent reworkings and amplifications of Jeremias' preaching to serve the needs of synagogue reading in the period of the Exile (**7** : 1-**8** : 3; **11** : 1-14; **16** : 1-13; **18** : 1-12; **21** : 1-10; **22** : 1-5; **25** : 1-14; **34** : 8-22; 35), but this is only an hypothesis. A revision by Baruch of the discourses of his Master, after the latter's death, would furnish a sufficient explanation for these sections, which are in an excellent rhetorical prose, more or less common to this period. For that matter, there is no reason for not thinking that Jeremias himself employed it.

Chapter 36 gives us an important point of reference for the history of the book. In 605, Jeremias dictated a roll which contained all the oracles made from 626 against Jerusalem, Juda, and against all the Nations (**36** : 2, 29, 32). Roughly, it could contain **1** : 4-**6** : 30 (his preaching under Josias), **7-20** (his preaching under Joakim), **25**, and **46-49** : 33. According to **36** : 32, many utterances of the same kind were added to his basic roll. Warning oracles which had been given after 605 were now introduced (**10** : 17-22; **12** : 7-14; **13** : 12-19;

15 : 5-9; **16** : 16 18; **18** : 1 12; **46** : 13 26; **49** : 34-39), narratives emanating from Jeremias containing threats (**24, 27, 35**, and, finally, the precious leaves on which the prophet transcribed his " confessions ": **11** : 18–**12** : 6; **15** : 10-21; **17** : 12-18; **18** : 18-23; **20** : 7-18. It is only natural that we should connect Baruch, a professional scribe and the confidant of Jeremias, with the making of these additions or supplements.

Along with his work as a compiler, Baruch wrote a biography of Jeremias with an apologetic nuance in the presentation of facts. The chronological sequence is as follows : **19** : 2–**20** : 6; **26**; **36**; **45**; **28–29**; **51** : 59-64; **34** : 8-22; **37–44**.

Booklets containing passages from Jeremias were compiled and disseminated in Exile circles : **27–29** (message to the exiles); **30–31** and **32–33** (a book of consolation); **21** : 11–**23** : 8 (a collection against the kings); **23** : 9-40 (collection against the false prophets).

Towards the end of the Exile, an editor, beginning with all this complex material and employing the order which already existed in part, gave the Book of Jeremias its present form. We can distinguish the following divisions : *a)* **1** : 4– **25** : 13[b], oracles against Juda and Jerusalem; *b)* **25** : 13[c]-38; **46–51**, oracles against the Nations; *c)* **26–35**, prophecies of success and happiness; *d)* **36–45**, the sufferings of Jeremias; *e)* **52**, an historical appendix confirming his prophecies.

The teaching of Jeremias.

The theology of Jeremias is not as well constructed as that of Ezechiel. As among all the prophets, it reveals clearly a traditional accent. Hence, he only repeats the teaching of his predecessors on God the Creator, Master of empires, and merciful. The theme of the Covenant as a marriage (**3** : 19) is found in Osee, the superiority of moral conduct over cult (**7** : 21-23) is in Amos, and the denunciation of sin is an idea common to all the preceding prophets. But meditation on sin is developed more deeply by Jeremias, and he arrives at the conception of a sinful state (**22** : 21) which turns aside or destroys the spiritual reflections of the Covenant. The situation of Israel appears to him to be entirely and utterly de-pendent on the mercy of God for its solution. His criticism of the traditional institutions of salvation (the Temple, circumcision, the State, Royalty, the Law) shows that they have become incapable of performing their religious role. God is going to make for Himself a new people, with law and worship in their hearts, and ready to receive his mercy (**31** : 31-33). This text is of major importance. As Nötscher has said, " Nowhere has Jeremias expressed so happily and so strongly the thought that religion is an interior relationship which unites the individual with God. God grants this as a gift, and man must make use of it as a personal good ". One gets the feeling that this formulation transposes and concludes a life of mystic experiences. Jeremias has furnished some details on the Messianic era : a new king (**23** : 5-6), perhaps a series of good kings (**23** : 24), will be at the head of Israel, but the emphasis is on the quality of this new Israel.

Lamentations.

Lamentations are five short elegies describing the destruction of Jerusalem and the misery of its inhabitants. The accent on suffering is so strong and deep, that it still moves us today.

The first four lamentations are alphabetical. The first, second, and fourth have twenty-two strophes, each beginning with a different letter, in alphabetical order. The third has a more complicated structure; it is composed of twenty-two groups of three verses each, the verses within each group beginning with the same letter, but the groups themselves following an alphabetical arrangement. In Lamentations 2–4 the letter *Pe* comes before the letter *·Ain*, contrary to what is found in the first lamentation, where *Pe* comes after *·Ain*, as in the alphabet. Perhaps the order of the letters was not yet definitely fixed, or perhaps there were two different forms of the alphabet. The last lamentation, called in the Vulgate, " The Prayer of Jeremias ", does not follow this erudite form. Nevertheless, it has twenty-two groups of two verses each, corresponding to the number of the Hebrew letters. These five poems are written with a great deal of artistry, but the emotion remains genuine even though it is less spontaneous than in works composed without such affectation of form and style.

In the Greek and Latin Bibles, Lamentations form a first appendix to the Book of Jeremias and have a prologue which attributes them to the prophet. In the Hebrew Bible, however, they form a separate book, classed with the Hagiographa between Ruth and Ecclesiastes, and without either prologue or attribution to Jeremias. Today critics put less emphasis on the question of authorship than upon the literary genre and purpose of these poems. They appear to have been composed for liturgical use. According to Jer. **41 : 5** and Zach. **7 : 3**, it was apparently customary, after 587, to hold at Jerusalem itself a commemoration of the siege and fall of the city. Such a liturgical service was certainly conducted with appropriate chants which could well be our Lamentations. They are written in the style of the genre and in that of the period, for we find in them reminiscences of Jeremias and Ezechiel. The third poem, unlike the other four, presents itself as an individual lamentation, but the national lamentation included in it caused it to be inserted in the collection, in which the number of five pieces is perhaps intentional. This poem clearly makes full use of the figure of Jeremias. Through being inserted in the middle of the little book, it gave occasion to the rise and spread of a tradition which made Jerome himself the author of Lamentations.

Baruch and the Letter of Jeremias [1]

This Deuterocanonical book, attributed to Baruch, the scribe or secretary of Jeremias, affords us an intimate view of the Jewish communities of the Diaspora and gives us some of the reasons which explain their remarkable adherence to Judaism. Thus, we hear of their bond with Jerusalem through their contributions, their letters, and communion of prayers; of prayers in their synagogues; of the repeated reading of the Scriptures; of devotion to the Law; of fidelity to their authorities; and, finally, of their resentments and their hopes, which bear witness to an eschatological tension.

The unity of the book is entirely artificial. The following divisions can be made : *a)* **1 : 1-14**, a narrative introduction

---

Translator's note. — [1 P. CHURGIN, *Studies in the Times of the Second Temple* (New York, 1949), especially 105-122].

transporting us to Babylon, where a gathering of exiles, grouped around Baruch, sends to Jerusalem money, sacred vessels, a letter, and a prayer to be read in the Temple as a sign of communion — the episode is situated in 582; *b)* 1 : 15–3 : 8, a prayer of confession and hope in the style of Nehemias 1 and Daniel 9; *c)* 3 : 9–4 : 4, an exhortation and a prophecy in which the personified Jerusalem expresses her hatred of Babylon and her Messianic hopes in the tenor of Deutero-Isaias.

The Vulgate has joined to the preceding work a little treatise, called the Letter of Jeremias. It appears as a separate piece in the Septuagint. The Letter is an apologetic attack on pagan idols, the pagan gods being completely identified with their statues. The theme is the same as that found in Isa. 44 : 9-20 and Jer. 10 : 1-16. The idolatry in question is that of Babylon at a late period.

3. — The Book of Ezechiel [1].

The life and personality of Ezechiel.

Ezechiel belonged to a sacerdotal family (1 : 3), which was probably a Sadocite one, i.e., responsible for performing services in the Temple of Jerusalem. As the Deuteronomist, and the

---

Translator's note. — [1 J. STEINMANN, *Le Prophète Ezéchiel* (Paris, 1953; cf. *RB* [1954], 428-432). W. A. IRWIN, " Ezechiel Research since 1943 ", *Vetus Testamentum* (1952), 54-66; *id.*, *The Problem of Ezechiel* (Chicago, 1943; cf. *JTS* [1944], 211-213). W. ZIMMERLI, " Das Gotteswort des Ezechiel ", *Zeitschrift für katholische Theologie* (1951), 249-262. G. FOHRER, *Die Hauptprobleme des Buches Ez.* (Berlin, 1953; cf. *CBQ* [1954], 92-95). Dom R. AUGÉ, *Ezequiel* (*La Biblia* of Montserrat, 1955; cf. *Sefarad* [1956], 407-411). CASSUTO, " Ezechiel ", in *Entzyklop. Miqr.* 3 (1958), 634-655. H. M. ORLINSKY, " Where Did Ezekiel Receive the Call to Prophecy? ", *BASOR*, No. 122 (1951), 34-36. R. BLOCH, " Ez. XVI : exemple parfait du procédé midrashique dans la Bible ", *Cahiers Sioniens* (1955), 193-223. W. R. FARMER, " Ezekiel's River of Life ", *BA* (1956), 17-22. J. FINEGAN, " The Chronology of Ez. ", *Journal of Biblical Literature* (1950), 61-66; cf. *Sefarad* [1950], 469). P. AUVRAY, *Ezéchiel* (*Témoins de Dieu*, No. 10, Paris, 1947; cf. *RB* [1937], 432 ff.; *ibid.* [1938], 599; *ibid.* [1948], 302 ff.). C. G. HOWIE, *The Date and Composition of Ezekiel* (*JBL* Monograph Series, IV, Philadelphia, 1950; cf. the review by J. Reider, *JQR*, 41 [1951], 329-331). H. RIESENFELD, *The Resurrection in Ezekiel XXXVII and in the Dura-Europos Paintings* (Uppsala, 1948; cf. J. COPPENS, *EThL* [1949], 139-144). M. GOTSTEIN, in *Kitbey ha-Hebrah...* I (1955), 175-178 (on the connection between chapters 1–39 and 40–48).

Prof. A. VAN DEN BORN published, in 1947, " De historische situatie van Ezechiel's prophetie " (*Analecta Lovan. = EThL* [1947], 150-172, in which he argued very persuasively in favor of a Judean ministry of Ezechiel before his Babylonian work. The thesis, which agreed substantially with the views

Code of Holiness (Lev. **19–26**) on which he depends, he represents a synthesis of the priestly and prophetic offices. His religious temperament has a harshness about it that foreshadows Esdras. He does not allow his feelings or sensibilities to intrude upon his ministry (see, however, **9** : 7-8; **11** : 13). The deep emotion exhibited apparently at the death of his wife (**24** : 16) disappears before his sense of responsibility (**3** : 18 ff.; **33** : 1-9). No

defended so ably by Bertholet's Commentary and adopted by P. Auvray in his edition of Ezechiel *(Bible de Jérusalem)* and by Dom R. Augé in his Ezequiel *(La Biblia* de Montserrat), supposed only the displacement of some texts and the admission of some glosses and of some corrections. This enabled him to maintain the substance of the traditional view of Ezechiel — " acknowledged by almost all critics ". Yet, the traditional view has been challenged by a number of critics : Smith, Torrey, Messel, Herntrich, to mention only a few. The fact was that there was a problem of Ezechiel. It was the merit of A. Van den Born to continue his study of the prophet. The result — as he advised the present writer in notes written in 1955 (Apr. 8 and May 17) and again recently (June 29, 1958), and as revealed also in his study, " Ezechiel : Pseudo-Epigraaf? ", published in the *Studia Catholica*, 28 (1953-54), 94-104, and more fully in his volume *Ezechiel* (1954) in the excellent Dutch series, *De Boeken van het Oude Testament* (Roermond and Maaseik) — was a completely different view of the origin of the book. He holds that the book is a " pseudo-epigraphical work, a perfect unity, dating from the time of Esdras-Nehemias, written to be a ' prophetic ' accompaniment of the already published Priestly Code " (Letter of Apr. 8, 1955). For apologetic reasons Catholic writers defended the thesis that Ez. was later than P and H (Holiness Code). The arguments used so long to maintain the dependence of Ez. still hold good. Of the texts mentioned by Van den Born (Letter of June 29, 1958) as pointing to the dependence of Ez. on H., cf. Ez. **4** : 9-17 with Lev. **26** : 22 ff. Yahweh will " break the staff of bread " (Lev. **26** : 26 = Ez. **4** : 16 — the same expression in Hebrew, but not apparent in the new Confraternity Version — so that " ten women will bake your bread in one oven ", i.e., there will be so little to bake that they will need but one oven (Lev. **26** : 26). In Ez. **4** : 9, it is possible to scrape up only bits of six different kinds of meal which go into one vessel to make some kind of bread : hence, the bread can only be doled out in rations which cannot satisfy hunger (Lev. **26** : 26 = Ez. **4** : 10); the wretched bread (**4** : 9) has to be measured strictly. Lev. **26** : 29 (parents are driven to eat the flesh of their own sons and daughters) = Ez. **5** : 10. Why is Ez. **4** : 1–**5** : 17 followed by an address to the mountains of Israel, **6** : 1-7? We find the answer in Lev. **26** : 30-33, which is practically a parallel to Ezechiel. Ezechiel goes on immediately to the theme of the survivors of the catastrophe (**6** : 8 ff.) — described in such terms that survivors are hardly expected. The explanation is in Lev. **26** : 36-39, which deals with the same theme. Cf. Van den Born's *Commentary on Ez.* (p. 9b) : " The relationship between Ez. and Lev. **17–26**, the so-called Code of Holiness, is so striking that one saw here a criterium for the date of Lev. **17-26** and therefore of the Pentateuch. Most exegetes held that Ezechiel was more ancient, and thus the Pentateuch more recent, than Ezechiel. On the Catholic side, the priority of Lev. **17-26** was maintained... If the Book of Ezechiel should be regarded as a pseudepigraph, on the ground that it depends on Biblical texts which were composed *omnium consensu* after the Exile, a date in the time of Esdras-Nehemias would seem to be preferable ". Add to this, considerations of language (Aramaic influence), the presence in the first part of the book, which announces the judgment as coming, of texts which suppose the judgment

prophet shows such a vivid sense of his own nothingness before the divine power and majesty; the appellation, " son of Man " (= " mortal "), occurs as a refrain 87 times when God speaks to him. Ecstasy plays an important role in his life, as in the case of Saint Paul. Seized by the hand of God, or by His spirit, falling upon his face, in the silence and in the dazed state that follows a mystical experience, he seems also to have known the rapture which is such an important phase of ecstasy (3 : 22-24; 37 : 1 ff.). He is not to be treated as a sick or deranged person; he is in the direct line of his predecessors, but exhibits a more pronounced intensity. His symbolic actions are more astounding than theirs. His visual genius expresses itself in supercharged allegories and in scenes as vivid as they are terrifying. On hearing his preaching, men compared him to a sweet and pleasing singer (33 : 32).

His career as a prophet falls between 593 (1 : 3) and 571 (29 : 1-7). He has dated the events of his ministry more carefully than his predecessors. Whether this was the result of priestly custom or was based on the desire to mark what presented itself to his soul as sudden and unexpected, we do not know. A recent hypothesis (Bertholet and Auvray-Steinmann) posits a double ministry for Ezechiel, the first at Jerusalem and the second in the Exile. During the last few years, however, a strong reaction has set against this view, as it runs contrary to the text. Ezechiel is a prophet of the Exile. From Tell-Abib [near Babylon] he addresses Jerusalem in the manner of Isa. 52 : 1, 7-9, and 54 : 1 ff. He makes a sufficiently clear distinction between the exiles, whom he apostrophizes in the second person, from the people of Jerusalem, whom he threatens in the third : 5 : 1-17; 11 : 14-21; 12 : 17-20; 14 : 12-23. If he had been at Jerusalem, he would have preached repentance,

---

already accomplished (*op. cit.*, p. 9ᵃ). Pseudepigraphy — contrary indeed to our modern feeling — is a literary form accepted in the Bible. Thus, Ecclesiastes and Wisdom, not to speak of various laws in the Pentateuch attributed to Moses, but which are accepted by Catholics as well as by other critics as being of a later date (*op. cit.*, cf. p. 9).

Some thirty years ago, the Book of Ezechiel was taken for granted as being the work of a prophet of the Babylonian Captivity. This is no longer the case. There is at the present time a problem of Ezechiel — a problem of the unity of the book, cf the unity of the ministry of the prophet, even on the view of Ezechiel as a prophet of the 6th century, a problem of the literary relations of Ezechiel which will affect the question of the date.

as Jeremias did, who, psychologically, had no further hope.
Finally, his generally schematic portrayal of what concerns
the Holy City is not that of an eyewitness.

Kittel, in respect to Ezechiel, has spoken of two souls in
one breast, and it is certainly easy to stress the contrasts in
his career and character : priest and prophet; preacher and
scrupulously careful writer; herald of destruction and herald
of salvation; ecstatic and logician; a man of deep emotion
and a man of deep reflection; a dreamer and a realist; a man
of harshness and a man of mercy. These contrasts resolve
themselves in a unity : that of his call. He is conscious of
having a mission from God at a critical moment, namely,
that in which Israel is reflecting on her fate. Israel herself
is also " divided "; diverse cries rise from her midst : cries
of pride and nostalgia; of faith and hope; of discouragement
and remorse; of lassitude and energy. Ezechiel, as the prophet
of the Exile, is truly the embodiment of Israel. He is a little after
the likeness of his people. He is disconcerting, and he is hard
to read. Located at the end of a world that has fallen and
at the beginning of one in process of being made, he is filled
with memories and filled with points of departure. He cannot
be defined easily or briefly. At a crossroad in the history of
Israel, God raised up a complex personality in keeping with
the epoch : Ezechiel is a man belonging to an age of transition.

Content and formation of the book.

The literary unity of the book, so strongly affirmed by the
ancient critics, and also by some extremists among modern
exegetes who would like to consider the work a pseudoepigra-
phical product of the postexilic period, is really not supported by any foundation in fact. Actually, the book exhibits
artificial groupings, evident displacements (it is necessary
especially to reestablish in immediate succession : 3 : 22-27;
4 : 4-8; 24 : 25-27; 33 : 21-22 — as the events occur in this
order in 587), some secondary developments, and a number
of unauthentic passages.

Three stages can be distinguished in the progressive formation
of the book. The first stage is that of separate or detached
pieces. Ezechiel was not a professional scribe; he had a mission
to warn and to counsel. But he has committed to writing

his (eight) ecstatic experiences, his (twelve) symbolic actions, the words of Yahweh which comprise threats, lamentations, exhortations, and promises, answers occasioned by discussions, legislative programs, and instructions concerning the prophet personally. He has indicated the dates of these experiences or communications in 1 : 1-4; 8 : 1; 20 : 1; 24 : 1; 26 : 1; 29 : 1, 17; 30 : 20; 31 : 1; 32 : 1, 17; 33 : 21; 40 : 1. He sometimes reworked and rewrote these different pieces — a fact which suggests that for a time they had an independent existence.

The second stage is marked by the formation of collections. The materials were grouped either according to their origin (ecstatic experiences and symbolic visions), or around " key words " (" idols " in 6, " sword " in 21), or more often, according to their related content. Sequences were broken, pieces of different dates brought together, oracles announcing blessings juxtaposed to oracles containing threats (11 : 14-21; 17 : 22-24). Let us take two examples. Chapters 3 : 16ª–5 are a narrative devoted to symbolic visions. Chapter 3 : 16ᵇ-21 is an intercalation which transforms the whole ministry of Ezechiel into a pastoral one, and likewise 3 : 22-27, and undoubtedly 4 : 4-8 also, two passages which are to be placed around 587. The other symbolic actions are left, the first of which (4 : 1-3) dates from 593 (3 : 16ª). Another complex is found in 8–11 : 21. Here are grouped the accounts of ecstatic visits to Jerusalem; a promise softened their harshness (11 : 14-21).

The book itself is the third stage. Its arrangement was made on both a chronological and logical basis, which corresponded to the actual course of Ezechiel's activity. The four divisions adopted are as follows : a) 1–24 : After the narrative of the inaugural vision, Ezechiel threatens, announces chastisements, and dissipates illusions. All this is before 587 — at least ordinarily — and the public addressed comprises the deportees of 598 and those left in Jerusalem. b) 25–32 : oracles against the Nations; c) 33–34 : oracles on the restoration to come. This division, beginning with 33, in which the fall of Jerusalem is known, attests a change in the manner of Ezechiel. He gives us a glimpse of the Messianic age : the Messias (34), the defeat of Edom (35), the New Covenant (36), the resurrection of the people (37 and 39 : 21-29). The overthrow of Gog (38–39 : 20) is an awkward insertion, and is perhaps an unauthentic passage. *d)* **40–48** : the Torah of Ezechiel, or the chart containing the liturgical regulations for the new community (description of the temple to be built, promotion of the Sadocite clergy, details on ritual, ordinances for the prince, and the division of Palestine among the Twelve Tribes). It is possible that Ezechiel himself sketched this plan, but it seems preferable to see in it the hand of a redactor. Part b) which breaks the sequence between a) and c), i.e. between **24** and **33**, was introduced artificially. The book was certainly completed before the return from the Exile. The temple erected by Zorababel between 520 and 515 did not correspond to that described in Ezechiel's plan.

The theology of Ezechiel.

The theocentric note is especially in evidence. The transcendence of Yahweh is stressed in the inaugural vision (omnipresence, omniscience, and omnipotence of the All-Different), in the habitual appellation of " son of man ", in the denunciation of sin and pride (**28**), in the numerous expressions referring to the honor of God's name, in the fact that the Temple is first of all His dwelling, and, as it were, the introduction to His " holiness ", in the conception of catastrophic history which He carries out through His " days ", in the fact of His " world *parousia* ", and in that of His creative grace, which heralds Saint Paul.

Through his chapters **14** and **18**, Ezechiel proclaimed the principle of individual reward and punishment and prepared the ground for the discussions of Job and Ecclesiastes. His vision of the future Israel has been particularly fruitful. He spread and developed the views of Jeremias on the " qualitative " Israel. Henceforth the members of the Chosen People will have a " new heart ". Jewish voluntarism is at home in **18** : **31**, where " to make one's self a new heart " does not exceed the capacity of man. But **36** : 23-28, the center of Ezechiel's prophecy, asks for an initial pardon, and then the gift of " a spirit ", ordered to bring moral action to full realization. This people of the future resembles a Church, and the perspective of Ezechiel, unlike that of Second Isaias, remains particularistic.

4. — The Book of Daniel [1].

The personality of the prophet.

Ezechiel mentions a certain Daniel twice. In **14** : 16, 18, 20, he places him between Noe and Job, thus choosing three just men outside of Israel and introducing them because they were saviors of their children. In **28** : 3, he contrasts the wisdom of Daniel and the inordinate pride of the King of Tyre. The reference is to King Danel who is described in a poem discovered at Ras Shamra, called today " The Legend of Aqhat, Son of Danel ". This wise and just king of the Phoenician legend apparently restored his son to life by his prayer. He has nothing in common, save his name and reputation for wisdom, with the hero of our book. The Hebrew Daniel, at the court of Babylon, remains faithful to the Law. By his knowledge of dreams and visions, he acquires the position of a new Joseph, and God rescues him from unjust attacks. It is with this prophet of the Exile that the Book of Daniel connects a number of episodes and visions — the latter presented in autobiographic form (**7–12**). Only after a series of preliminary discussions will it be possible to consider the question of the respective roles of historical tradition and pseudonymous fiction in the book.

Translator's note. — [1 See C. LATTEY, S. J., *The Book of Daniel* (Dublin, 1948. H. L. GINSBERG, *Studies in Daniel* (New York, 1948). J. LINDER, S. J., *Com. in Librum Daniel* (2nd ed., Paris, 1939; cf. F. M. Abel, O. P., *RB* [1947], 443-445). See also the study of J. PRADO in *Sefarad* (1943), 167-194, and 393-427). C. VIROLLEAUD, *La légende phénicienne de Daniel* (Paris, 1936). Cf. H. H. ROWLEY, *Darius the Mede and the Four World Empires in the Book of Daniel* (Cardiff, 1935; cf. GALLING, in *ZDMG* [1941], 148-150. M. J. GRUEN-THANER, S. J., " The Four Empires of Daniel ", *CBQ* (1946), 78-82, and 201-212. E. F. SIEGMAN, " The Stone Hewn from the Mountain : Daniel **2** ", *CBQ* (1956), 364-379. Ez. KAUFMAN, in : *Toldot ha-emunah ha-yisre'elit* VIII (1956), 418-439 (on the narratives in Dan.). Dom R. AUGÉ, *Daniel* (with *Lament., Baruch, Epist. of Jer.*, in *La Biblia* of Montserrat (cf. *Sefarad* [1956], 177-180). H. L. JANSEN, *Die Politik des Antiochus IV (Epiphanes)* (Oslo, 1943; cf. *Biblioth. Orientalis* VIII [1951], 235-238). A. BRUNET, S. J., " La date de Daniel ", *Sciences Ecclés.* (1955), 239-255. On the prayer of Nabonidus (Dan. **3-4**), see D. N. FREEDMAN, " The Prayer of Nabonidus ", *BASOR*, No. 145 (1957), 31-32. J. T. MILIK, *RB* [1956], 407-411 and 415. On Dan. **4** : 33, cf. I. EITAN, *Hebrew Union College Annual*, 14 (1941), 16-17. On Dan. **5** : 1, see M. J. GRUENTHANER, S. J., " The Last King of Babylon ", *CBQ* (1949), 406-422. H. H. ROWLEY, " The Bilingual Problem of Daniel ", *ZATW* (1932), 256-268. H. GINSBERG, " Daniel ", in *Entzyklop. Miqr.*, 2, 686-697. J. STEIN-MANN, *Daniel* (Paris, 1950). P. CHURGIN, " The Daniel-Tales ", in *Studies in the Times of the Second Temple* (New York, 1949), 94-104 (in Hebrew)].

Structure and division of the book.

The book is made up of two parts and two appendices.

Part I : the episodes (**1–6**). Daniel and his friends are depicted as exemplary Jews living at the court of Nabuchodonosor (**1**). Then we see him interpreting the king's dream about the statue, the heterogeneous elements of which symbolize four empires, to be succeeded by the kingdom of God (**2**). The following episodes, the children delivered from the fiery furnace into which they had been thrown because of their refusal to adore a statue (**3**), the dream of the great tree and the madness of Nabuchodonosor (**4**), Baltazar's banquet (**5**), Daniel in the lions' den (**6**), all lead to the glorification of the one true God. God does not forsake His people, and His miraculous protection of them finds its counter-proof in the madness and disasters of their enemies.

Part II : the visions (**7–12**). This part is entirely concerned with the future. It describes prophetically, under several forms, the history of the Near East down to the establishment of the kingdom of God. We have in succession : *a)* the four beasts (**1**); *b)* the ram and the he-goat (**8**); *c)* the interpretation of Jeremias' prophecy respecting the 70 years of the Exile (**9**); *d)* the destinies of Greek domination and the persecution of Antiochus IV Epiphanes (**10–12**). In these chapters, Antiochus appears as the archenemy of God and the great adversary of Israel. His fall will inaugurate the Messianic kingdom. As in the other prophets, there is an absence of perspective, and the Day of Yahweh appears just beyond the horizon of the troubles one sees and experiences. Part II, which takes up again the ideas contained in Chapter 2, is apocalyptic. Daniel speaks here in the first person.

The appendices (**13–14**) contain the story of the chaste Susanna, with its double theme of the woman falsely accused and the wise young judge — in this case, Daniel, and also the stories of Bel and the Dragon. In the Bel story the deceitfulness of the Babylonian priests is exposed. The Dragon story takes up again the subject of Chapter **6** and incorporates some material from the Habacuc legend.

The problem of the structure of the Book of Daniel is made more complicated by the employment of three languages which do not correspond exactly to its organic divisions. Chapters 1–2 : 4ᵃ are in Hebrew, and likewise 8–12; 2 : 46–3 : 23 and 3 : 91–7 are in Aramaic; 3 : 24-90 (two psalms, the second of which in its literary form resembles Psalm 136) and 13–14 are in Greek. The Greek sections, which are called deuterocanonical, are to be compared with the additions made to Esther. They do not present a very difficult problem. The transition from Hebrew to Aramaic, however, and vice versa, is one of the enigmas of the Old Testament. The simplest solution is to think that in 1–2 : 4ᵃ the author wished to introduce his hero by using the sacred tongue, perhaps as a means of getting his book more easily into the canon. In that case, he translated into Hebrew what already existed in Aramaic. Chapters 8–12 were written in Hebrew from the first, as the national revival of the second sanctuary gave a new life to that language (2 Mach. 7 : 8). But this brings us to the problem of the date and literary genre of Daniel.

Literary genre and date.

Chapters 1–6 [of the Hebrew Bible — 1–2 : 4ᵃ in Hebrew, 2 : 4ᵇ–6 : 29 in Aramaic], and 7, written in Aramaic, contain pre-Machabean material and represent elements of a collection earlier than the second century. It is even possible that the Greek editor of Daniel took the episodes of Susanna and the Dragon from this collection [13–14 in the Greek and Latin Bibles; in A. Rahlfs' edition of the LXX, Susanna is presented separately before Daniel]. The collection belongs to the hagiographical genre; according to Nötscher, a *midrash*, with an historical foundation. This kind of writing aims at edification rather than at factual accuracy. It would be quite inappropriate, then, to dwell on the flagrant historical inaccuracies, since strict history is not involved. We may cite as examples : the deportation in the third year of Joachim (1 : 1); Baltasar [Belshazzar; Babylonian Bel-shar-usur, " Bel protects the king "] described as a king and the son of Nabuchodonosor, although he was neither (5 : 2, 11); the madness of Nabuchodonosor, of which history tells us nothing, but which might apply to Nabonidus (4); Darius the Mede, who is presented as reigning immediately after the fall of Babylon, is unknown (5 : 30–6 : 1).

The general background of this whole picture is the religious climate of the Diaspora where the Jews preserve their faith and religious practices intact in spite of the temptations and dangers of their surroundings. The kings are not persecutors in the strict sense. The Aramaic employed, in the opinion of specialists, is best placed in the third century. The words of Greek origin which occur (3 : 5, the names of musical instruments) suggest a redaction later than the Persian period. This date can be fixed more closely by the evidence contained in 2, where verses 42-43 reflect a revision of the text made *ca.* 245 (the allusion to the marriage, in 252, of Antiochus II and Berenice, the daughter of Ptolemy II); verse 41, which is original, supposes that Alexander is dead (321). Accordingly, the redaction of 2 cannot be put much later than that date. Chapter 7 in its first redaction may be slightly earlier. In the Machabean period it was adapted to new situations by the addition of verses 7b, 8, 11a, 20-22, 24-27, which refer to Antiochus IV Epiphanes. Originally, it only expressed the Messianic hope in the face of Greek expansion and conquest.

The central point in 8-12 is the reign of the persecutor, King Antiochus IV. The closer we come to his reign, the greater the definiteness with which events are reported. The Hellenizing attempts of Antiochus reached their high point when he dedicated an altar to Olympian Zeus in the Temple of Jerusalem. This was the " abomination of desolation " related in 1 Mach. 1 : 57 which took place in December 167. The Machabean guerilla warfare was organized and it succeeded in restoring worship in the Temple in December 164. Chapters 8-12 were written within these dates, but before the actual restoration of worship, which was not yet known to the author. It is the latter who worked over earlier materials and interpreted them in keeping with his own time. The result is a work of imposing unity, a vision of the end of time and the coming of the Messianic era, in which we find the characteristic features of apocalyptic : grandiose images, symbols difficult to represent, pseudonymity, calculation of ages, and especially that eschatalogical tension which is the Biblical form of hope.

This dating is confirmed by the place assigned to the Book of Daniel in the Canon. In the Hebrew Canon, it is put among the Hagiographa, i.e., the most recent books. Ecclesiasticus,

which praises Isaias, Jeremias, and Ezechiel, and which mentions
the twelve prophets — our Minor Prophets — (48 : 23-49 : 10),
does not speak of Daniel.   This silence of Ecclesiasticus, together
with the present place of Daniel in the Hebrew Canon, could
suggest that Daniel is not an old work.   Finally, the fact that
Ecclesiastes and Ecclesiasticus show no knowledge of the
magnificent teaching of Daniel on reward and punishment
points to the same conclusion.

Teaching.

A theology of history on the grand scale shows the rise,
succession, and destruction of empires while God is establishing
His kingdom.   This mastery in conception and this contrast
give the Book of Daniel its great interest.   Its thought underlies
Bossuet's *Discours sur l'histoire universelle*.   The Book of
Daniel looks forward to the Messianic Age and outlines its
characteristic features.

One should recall 9 : 24, which describes the inner character
of the Kingdom of God, and, especially, the prophecy on the
Son of Man (7), a new and strictly heavenly representation
of the Messias.   The *Book of Henoch* will take up this title
again, and Jesus will employ it actually as a title for Himself.
Finally it should be noted that it is stated in 12 : 1-3 that the
dead will rise again.

5. — The Twelve Minor Prophets [1].

The Twelve Minor Prophets, Osee, Joel, Amos, Abdias, Jonas,
Micheas, Nahum, Habacuc, Sophonias, Aggeus, Zacharias, and
Malachias already formed a collection by the time Ecclesiasticus
was written, i.e., between 200 and 180 B. C.   After having
mentioned Isaias, Jeremias, and Ezechiel, the author speaks
of the " Twelve Prophets " without naming them.   This generic
title, combined with the order of its occurence, indicates that
he was following the Hebrew canon as it is still constituted.
Just how early the collection was formed, is unknown.   Malachias

Translator's note. — [1 S. BULLOUGH, O. P., *Obadiah, Micah, Zephaniah,
Haggai,* and *Zechariah,* in Westminster Version of the Sacred Scriptures,
ed. C. C. Lattey, S. J. (London, 1953).   S. MOWINCKEL, *Tolv profetboken,* in
Det Gamle Testamente, III (Oslo, 1944), 567-783 and 813-827 (Bibliography)].

The synoptic table below will help the reader to grasp the unity of the Book of Daniel when viewed in a Machabean perspective.

The succession of Empires	The statue made of various materials (2)	The four beasts from the sea (7)	The ram and the he-goat (8)	The 70 weeks (9)	The non-mystical tableau (10-12)
1. The Second Babylonian Empire	= the head of gold	= the lion with clipped wings and the heart of a man		the first 7 weeks (587-539)	
2. The Medo-Persian Empire (539-332)	= the breast of silver	= the bear	= the ram with two horns	62 weeks	Summary of history (11:2)
3. Alexander (336-323)	= the belly of brass	= the leopard (or panther)	= the he-goat with one horn		Summary of history (11:3)
4. The Hellenistic dynasties	= the legs and feet of iron and clay	= with four heads (Macedonia, Thrace, Syria, and Egypt)	then with four horns		History in some detail
Especially the line of the Seleucids, above all, Antichus IV (raised almost to the stature of Anti-Christ)		= the fourth beast with 10 horns = the horn which speaks great things, and persecutes the saints of the Most High for 3½ years	= then a little horn ravaging the people of the saints and defiling the Sanctuary for 1150 days	= the 70th week	= 11:21-45 and 12:5 ff.
			The destruction of the enemy by a supernatural agency ("without hand". 8:25)	The end of sin and the establishment of eternal justice (9:24)	1290 days
5. The Kingdom of God	A stone which strikes the statue becomes a mountain and fills the earth	The destruction of the last beast and of the others. The investiture of the Son of Man and the reign of the saints of the Most High			Michael as God's champion in battle and the resurrection of the dead

wrote about 430. The Books of Joel and Jonas may be more recent, and the second part of Zacharias seems to allude to the conquests of Alexander. Accordingly, these books might be assigned to the fourth or third century B. C.

The enumeration given above follows the order of the Hebrew Bible, which would seem to be a chronological arrangement. The Septuagint generally has the order : Osee, Amos, Micheas, Joel, Abdias, Jonas. This order may possibly be based on the decreasing length of the writings. Furthermore, in both the Hebrew and the Greek, the book " of the Twelve " precedes Isaias.

It is obvious that the designation, " Minor Prophets ", concerns merely the extent of their writings which have come down to us and does not imply a judgment on their worth. Saint Augustine already commented on this point in his *De civitate Dei* (**18** : 29). Minor prophets like Osee, Sophonias, or Zacharias have marked the itinerary of Israel in outstanding fashion.

Osee [1].

A native of the Northern Kingdom, Osee began his ministry in the prosperous reign of Jeroboam II (**1** : 1). He saw the fall of Jehu (*ca.* 745) and the anarchy which engulfed Israel (**7** : 3-7, a palace revolution). According to **11** : 11, he was a witness also of the fall of Samaria (721), and was therefore a contemporary of Isaias.

The book comprises two collections. The first (**1–3**) contains oracular material (**2**) inserted between two narratives. One is biographical (**1**) and the other (**3**) is autobiographical, and they seem to be parallel. They tell of the marriage of the prophet to a sacred prostitute with whom he was in love. As in the case of the celibacy of Jeremias (**16** : 2-4) or the widowhood of Ezechiel (**24** : 15-24), Osee's marriage is a symbolic state intended to explain and emphasize the religious reality of the Covenant. The latter is a marriage, and this idea, which is taken up by Biblical tradition (Ez. **16**; Isa. **50** : 1-3;

Translator's note. — [1 J. COPPENS, " L'histoire matrimoniale d'Osée ", in *Alttestamentliche Studien Nötscher* (Bonn, 1950), pp. 38-45. A. BIRAM, " Osee **2** : 16-25 ", *Kitbey ha Hebrah...* 1 (1955), pp. 116-139. H. H. ROWLEY, " The Meaning of Osee ", *Bulletin of the John Rylands Library* (1956), pp. 200-233. CASSUTO, art. " Osee ", in *Entzyklop. Miqr.* 2, pp. 802-806].

59 : 1, 6), indicates a participation in a common work and gives an emotional shade to the relations between Yahweh and His people. The God of Osee is the God of love. His book presents a distant sketch, as it were, of the treatise on grace. The second collection (**4–14**) is later than the first. It comprises : *a)* a series of invectives and threats — assembled without any specific order — which deal with worship and politics (**4** 1–**9** : 9). Osee is a witness of the contamination of Yahwism by the cult of Baals. He attacks the representation of divinity under the form of bulls (**8** : 4-6; **10** : 5-6), and licentious (**4** : 14) or formalistic ceremonies (**8** : 13; **10** : 1); *b)* then come poems in which the prophet meditates on the past of Israel (**9** : 10–**14** : 9). This appeal to history characterizes the Deuteronomist also, to whom Osee is already related through his central theme : the kindness of God. The history of Israel is the break in a tradition. Osee goes back to the glorious point in the past where it was established, namely, the desert, the witness " of the days of her youth " (**13** : 5; **2** : 16-17). It is necessary to become reestablished in this spiritual climate. Chapter **11** is one of the most moving and beautiful passages in the Bible; Yahweh appears here as a father who will never abandon His children.

The two collections must have been composed very early, as is indicated by the fact that they show little evidence of being reworked. The sapiential epilogue (**14** : 10) is undoubtedly a note added by the editor.

Joel [1].

We have no information on the person or life of this prophet. His horizon, throughout his book, is limited to Juda and Jerusalem. The book is divided into two parts. Part I describes a scourge of locusts (**1–2**). A liturgy of mourning and supplication will avert it, and we are made witnesses of its performance. It closes with an oracle promising a restoration of well-being for men, for the earth, and for animals (**2** : 18-27). This evocation is very valuable to us, for it gives us the framework of collective lamentations like Ps. **74**; even here (**1** : 15-20;

Translator's note. — [1 CASSUTO, art., " Joel ", *Entzykl. Miqr.* 3 (1958), 575-577. Haag, *Bibellexikon,* 828-830. R. PAUTREL, *DBV, Suppl.* IV, 1098-1104].

2 : 7) psalms are outlined. Part II is an eschatological view
of the Day of Yahweh (3-4). Its preamble is the pouring
out of the spirit (3 : 1-2), which is described in terms taken
from Ezechiel (36 : 26-28 and 39 : 29). This gift is reserved
for Israel. The wondrous astronomical phenomena constitute
the second preamble; they will be terrifying to all except the
Jews (3 : 3-5). Then comes the drama of Josaphat (4 : 1-17);
in that valley — the same as in Ez. 38-39 and Zach. 14 —
the whole pagan world is brought face to face with the people
of God. The myth of the eschatological conflict corresponds
to that of the primordial conflict as it is described in Ps. 74 :
13 ff. A new order will spring up after the judgment and
destruction of the Nations, and the sorrow and resentment
of Israel will be over (4 : 2-8). The new order is outlined in
4 : 18-24 in terms which recall Ez. 47 : 1.

The Book of Joel raises two chief questions. The first is
that of the relation between its two parts. Since Part II
is clearly eschatological, it has been thought since Duhm that
Part I was connected with it by a series of editorial retouches,
especially by the introduction of the mention of the Day of
Yahweh (1 : 15; 2 : 1, 2, 11). Thus eschatologized, 1 and 2
would become a preamble for 3-4. But this theory of inter-
polation is not necessary. In fact, in the context of 1-2, the
invasion of locusts is a prelude to a manifestation of God,
the beginning of a greater chastisement that threatens the
Jewish people alone. Part I has its own proper atmosphere.
The one who added Part II — and, according to Trinquet,
he was a different author — considered the scourge of locusts
as the preface to the eschatological Day of Judgment.

The second question concerns the date. The place occupied
by the book in the Canon suggested an early date, but that
once proposed (8th-7th cent. B. C.) was abandoned more than
a hundred years ago. Sections 1 : 13-14, and 2 : 15-17, give
the impression that the priests are the heads of the community,
which is a mark of the period after the Exile. The dependence
on Ezechiel already noted, the precise definition of monotheism
in 2 : 27, the mention of the Greeks in 4 : 6, and especially
the manner of speaking of " all nations " (4 : 2, 11), point in the
same direction. The two parts of Joel were probably composed
between 400 and 350.

Amos [1].

Born in Thecua in the Desert of Juda, some five miles south of Bethlehem, this shepherd of flocks came down to the plains in springtime to incise sycamore figs (**7** : 14-15). He was a prophet who received His call from God (**3** : 3-8); he did not belong to the groups of official *nabis*, established around sanctuaries and kings, and he had not learned from them the oracular technique. His manner is concrete, picturesque, direct, and sharp. As a popular preacher, he reminds us of Bernardine of Sienna. He spoke in Israel, where Bethel is mentioned as the center of his intervention (**7** : 10-17), but undoubtedly he also visited Samaria (**3** : 9-11; **4** : 1-3; **6** : 1-7). His activity is placed *ca.* 760-750, hence before that of Osee; the Assyrian danger does not yet seem imminent (**5** : 27; **6** : 14). Jeroboam II was at the height of his glory and Israel was at peace. Below the surface of this order and peace, however, Amos perceived a deep moral disorder. Social oppression in all its forms — the venality of magistrates and cruelty of creditors (**2** : 6-8), avarice of merchants (**8** : 4-6), and luxury of the rich (**5** : 11; **3** : 15; **6** : 4-6) — is denounced by the uncouth prophet who comes from his country district like a " Danubian peasant " urged on by God. In the sanctuaries, he feels that he is out of his element, and reacts against their sumptious and formalistic worship (**5** : 21-26). He refers specifically to Gilgul, near Jericho (**4** : 4; **5** : 5), and Bersabee, because these old sanctuaries must have attracted pilgrims from the North.

The God of Amos is characterized by His justice, i.e., by His power to give the moral order realization on earth. This order is violated whenever the poor are not respected. This is why the " Day of Yahweh " will be terrible (**5** : 18 ff.) and why Yahweh will use Ashur as his instrument. Because of the privileges bestowed on Israel, the severity of God's judgment

---

Translator's note. — [1 A. NEHER, *Amos, Contribution à l'étude du prophétisme* (Paris, 1950). V. MAAG, *Text, Wortschatz und Begriffswelt des Buches Amos* (Leiden, 1951). LURIA, " Thecua, The City of Amos ", *Kitbey ha Hebrah*... I (1955), 104-115. M. A. BEEK, " The Religious Background of Am. 2 : 6-38 ", *Oudtest. Studiën*, V (1948). A. BENTZEN, " The Ritual Background of Am. 1 : 2–2 : 16 ", *ibid.*, VIII (1950). A. S. KAPELRUD, " God as Destroyer in the Preaching of Amos and in the Ancient Near East ", *JBL* (1952), 33-38. H. H. KRAUSE, " Der Gesichtsprophet Amos : ein Vorläufer des Deuteronomisten ", *ZATW* (1932), 221-229. I. ENGNELL, in *Svenskt Bibliskt Uppslagsverk* I, 59-63].

will be intensified.   God, after all, has not necessarily restricted His interest to that of a single people.   Amos knows, however, that God's plan will continue and his book ends with words of hope.

The book, undoubtedly, was compiled in Juda (hence the mention of Ozias, king of Juda, in **1** : **1**).   It combines oracular material with autobiographical sections (the cycle of five visions : **7** : 1-9; **8** : 1-3; **9** : 1-4) which one would rather expect to find at the beginning of the work, and with a biographical piece (**7** : 10-17).   After a " motif " which seems out of series (**1** : 2), we have oracles grouped by stereotyped formulas.   The denunciation of the sins of the Near East is followed by a denunciation of the faults of Israel, introduced by mnemonic phrases : " Hear this word " (**3** : 1; **4** : 1; **5** : 1), or " Woe " (**5** : 7, 18; **6** : 1).   The cycle of Amos' visions in **7** : 1–9 : 4 is broken by the account of the altercation between the prophet and the priest of the royal sanctuary at Bethel, and this insertion is made by the use of a key word " sword ", which is repeated in **7** : 9 and 17.   Following the insertion of oracular material in **8** : 4-14 (" Hear this "), there is a doxology (**9** : 5-6), which was probably added, as in the case of the two preceding ones (**4** : 13; **5** : 8-9), to serve the purposes of liturgical reading. The book comes to an end with the most harsh of the prophecies of Amos (**9** : 7), but this oracle is followed immediately by three promises : the first, on the small Remnant (**9** : 8-10); the second, on the restoration of the house of David which has fallen (**9** : 11-12); and the third, on a prosperity that will be like paradise (**9** : 13-15).   The authenticity of these verses has been much disputed, but it is more and more defended and acknowledged.   In particular, the fall of the house of David may not be a reference at all to 587, but rather to the schism of 935 which weakened the position of Yahweh's chosen dynasty.

Abdias [1].

The shortest book in the Old Testament is attributed to Abdias, whose name means " Servant of Yahweh ".   We know nothing about him except that he is very nationalistic in his

---

Translator's note. — [1 Ez. KAUFMAN, *Toldot ha-emunah ha-yisre'elit*, VII (1950), 363-365].

thought, and in this respect he differs completely from the other " Servant of Yahweh " whose lyrical biography is found in Isa. 53.

The unity itself of the book is disputed. Instead of thinking of two authors, however, it is better to think of two sections, each having its own proper atmosphere, and of an amalgamation of these sections by a redaction *ca.* 450. The first section (1-7, 10-14, 15^{cd}) is concerned with Edom and could be classified among " the oracles against the Nations ". We know that Edom profited from the destruction of Jerusalem in 587, and we observe in verse 11 the same note of resentment that is found in Ez. 25 : 12-14; Lam. 4 : 21-22; Ps. 137 : 7). But the threat against Edom has now been realized (5-7). But when and by whom was it dispossessed of its ancestral home? Diodorus Siculus (19 : 94) tells us that the Arabs were masters of Petra in 312; and in the time of Malachias, *ca.* 430, the land of Esau was in ruins. The affinity of the first section of Abdias with Jer. 49 : 9, 14-16, furnishes no precise information for dating it, because Abdias is probably the later piece. The second section (8-9, 15^{ab}, 16-21) describes the eschatological Day of Yahweh in its postexilic tenor : the destruction of the pagans and the restoration of Jerusalem. Edom now has a purely secondary role in this picture.

Jonas [1].

The story of Jonas in the belly of the great fish is so well known that it need not be summarized here. At a time when the reform of Esdras was erecting ever higher barriers between Judaism and the pagan peoples, a voice, perhaps from the Diaspora, was raised to proclaim views that were more liberal and more worthy of God. The isolation of the Jews was necessary to preserve the integrity of the people that was the witness of Yahweh, but the protective hedge of the Law should not prevent the diffusion of God's message. It was to teach this lesson that the Book of Jonas was written. It is a new call to the universalism which we find registered in the first

---

Translator's note. — [1 Haag, *Bibellexikon*, 847-850 (cf. also *ibid.*, " Jonas-zeichen ", 850-851). I. ENGNELL, in *Svenskt Bibliskt Uppslagsverk* I, 1105-1107. A. FEUILLET, " Le sens du livre de Jonas ", *RB* (1947), 340-361; *id.*, in *DBV*, *Suppl.* IV, 1104-1131. J. S. LICHT, s.v., in *Entzyklop. Miqr.* 3 (1958), 608-613].

chapters of Genesis and in the story of Abraham's mission. Yahweh orders His recalcitrant prophet to preach at Ninive. He gets him there after long detours — in which a humorous element is not lacking — and Ninive is converted.

History, clearly, knows nothing about a conversion of Ninive, and archaeology is equally ignorant respecting the enormous dimensions assigned to the great city (fifty some miles in breadth ! 3 : 3). The theme of the fish that swallows a man and preserves him is familiar to folklore, as we know e.g., from Lucian. Again, the theme of the prophet who resists Yahweh and is vanquished by Him occurs elsewhere in prophetic literature (1 Kgs. 19 : 4; Jer. 15). Finally, the Bible knows of a prophet named Jonas (2 Kgs. 15 : 25) who lived under Jeroboam II. This prophet, whom we know only by his name, which means " pigeon ", i.e., " home-abiding ", furnished the basis for a *midrash*. This literary genre, which was very much cultivated after the Exile and which we find later in Saint Paul (his treatment of the veil of Moses in 2 Cor. 3–4; and also his account of the two wives of Abraham in Gal. 5), is a narrative which is developed out of a Scriptural fact or event for the purpose of inculcating an edifying lesson.

Here the lesson is one of the most sublime in the Old Testament : we are reminded that all men — even the fiercest enemies of Israel — are called to salvation.

But the objection may be raised that the interpretation of the Book of Jonas as a parable, and not as a true story, does not give sufficient weight to the words of Our Lord, who cites Jonas' stay in the whale's belly and his preaching at Ninive as signs applying to Himself (Mt. 12 : 40-41). It is necessary rather to consider that Jesus makes use of the narrative as a citation or allusion. We ourselves speak thus of the Prodigal Son. We should not set up Our Savior as a literary or historical critic.

The psalm cited in Chapter 2 is the only extrinsic element in the book. In the Bible it is customary to give expression to feelings of personages by putting on their lips a psalm that is appropriate to the occasion (1 Sam. 2, the Canticle of Anna; Isa. 38, the Psalm of Ezechias). Here one would expect a psalm of lamentation rather than a canticle of thanksgiving.

Micheas [1].

A native from the vicinity of Gath near the Philistine country, Micheas whose name means, Who is like Yahweh? ", is a man of strong personality (3 : 8). He resembles Amos in some respects, exhibiting the same harshness (3 : 2, 10) and the same preoccupation with social evils. In his message of justice he adds nothing essentially new to Amos, or to Isaias, his contemporary (cf. 2 : 1-5 and Isa. 5 : 8-10). The splendid passage, 6 : 8, gives his whole conception of religion, and it is one of the high points of the Bible. Micheas left a strong impression, as Jeremias (26 : 18) attests a century later; at that time he seems to have been labelled as a prophet of calamity. His book, however, at least in the form that it has come down to us, contains oracles of prosperity as well as oracles of calamity.

The book comprises four parts, showing alternating contrasts in their arrangement. a) Threats against and condemnation of Israel (1–3). All in this section, with the exception of 2 : 12-13 (exilic), is authentic and represents an amalgamation of oracles of various dates. The chastisement of Samaria is announced in 1 : 2-7, which, accordingly, was uttered before 722. But the sins of the Southern Kingdom are soon denounced. Chapter 1 : 8-16 contains a description of Sennacherib's raid against Philistia and Juda in 701. In 2 and 3 he indicates the social sins that are being committed and those responsible for them (2 : 2, 9; 3 : 2-3). The section ends with the terrible oracle in which the destruction of Jerusalem is foretold (3 : 9-12). Jeremias informs us (26 : 18) that this threat was not realized; hence it was conditional. b) Promises to Sion (4–5). It has been said that 1–3 excluded all hope, but we have no right here, any more than in the case of Amos, to draw a conclusion that, on the basis of analogy, is so contrary to the practice of the prophets. It must be said at least that the majority of the passages breathe an anti-Assyrian hatred, and this fact places them very well in the age of Micheas or in the period immediately following. Only 4 : 6-7 and 5 : 6-7 (as 2 : 12-13, already mentioned) seem to be of exilic origin. One should note the famous oracle, " And thou Bethlehem " (5 : 1-5),

---

Translator's note. — [1 On the Hebrew text of 5 : 1 (2), cf. J. A. FITZ-MYER, S. J., *CBQ* (1956), 10-13].

which announces a descendant of David as the king of salvation.
c) Dialogue between Yahweh and Israel. God's complaints
(**6** : **1–7** : 7) are of the pre-exilic type; the sacrifices of children
(**6** : 7) may refer to the time of Achaz (2 Kgs. **16** : 3), and **6** : **16**
supposes that Samaria is still standing. *d)* Prayer for
deliverance (**7** : 8-20), which imitates a liturgy. All its elements place it definitely in the period of the Exile.

In short, the Book of Micheas has been reworked. The
prophetic books were in the hands of a living community.
It should be observed also that the designation " Israel "
is not confined to the Northern Kingdom; in **3** : 10, Juda is
given this name which has an eminently religious flavor.

Nahum [1].

Since 1923, we possess the record of the campaign waged
by the Scytho-Babylonian armies against Assyria in its death
agony. Ninive, the capital of the Sargonids, was taken and
burned in 612. Jeremias was a contemporary of the disaster,
but it was incumbent on an official or " cult prophet " to
predict it. This connection with public worship is evident
from his use of psalm forms. Nahum, whose Judean birthplace
is not identified and who is quite familiar with the topography
and customs of Ninive (**2** : 7; **3** : 17), has left us oracles charged
with savage irony, in which the descriptive tone of the Song
of Deborah lives again (Jdgs. **5**). It has been said that his
vigorous and turbulent style has no parallel elsewhere in the
Old Testament and very few parallels in other literatures.
The oracles on Ninive exhibit a marked homogeneity of style.
They were pronounced between 662, the date of the fall of
Thebes (**3** : 8), and 612, the date of the fall of Ninive.
Van Hoonacker would place them *ca.* 625. The book is a
nationalistic prophecy of the type opposed by Jeremias (**28**).
Nahum could serve as a commentary on Isa. **10** : 5-15. The
oracles are prefaced by a fragment of an acrostic hymn (**1** : 1-9).
Its fragmentary character is due either to mechanical causes
or to the fact that only that portion of the hymn was kept
which was in harmony with the general tenor of the book.

Translator's note. — [1 A. HALDAR, in *Svenskt Bibl. Uppslagsverk* 2, 416-419.
Haag, *Bibellexikon,* 1193-1194].

Although the book takes the form of a prophetic curse against an enemy, it ought not be regarded as devoid of a religious sense, especially since the enemy in question had been so identified with evil. In the perspective of temporal retribution, the cry of joy which accompanies the enemy's fall is equivalent to an expression of gratitude for God's justice.

Habacuc [1].

We have no information on the person of the prophet. A *midrash*, which is utilized by Daniel **14** : 32 ff., brings Habacuc into relation with Daniel in the lions' den, and the Septuagint in reference to the incident states that he is " the son of Jesus of the Tribe of Levi ". As in the case of Nahum, and for the same reason, it could be that he was a " cult-prophet ", i.e., that he belonged to the official prophets of the Temple.

His book is one of the most difficult in the Bible, and a critic of the calibre of Sellin made radical changes as often as three times in his exegesis. His pericopes have been inverted (Van Hoonacker). His key words have been changed; thus, in **1** : 6, Duhm proposed to read *Kittim*, Greeks, in place of *Kashdim*, Chaldaeans, and, relying on such a correction, to place the book in the period of Alexander the Great. The allegorical commentary on Habacuc found at Qumran attests precisely in the Essene sect a text twisting of this kind, and thus reads in filigree the events of the first century B. C. through the oracles of the sixth century B. C. Humbert has considered the book to be a libretto for a liturgy of mourning, composed by an official prophet against the royal authority of Joiakim. However, for a functionary of the Temple to take a stand against a king, would not be lacking in foolhardiness, and probability is not in its favor.

The book may be analysed as follows : *a)* A first complaint (**1** : 2-4) seems to be uttered in the name of Juda and more precisely in place of her oppressed. *b)* A first oracle of Yahweh (**1** : 5-11) replies by announcing the arrival of the Chaldaeans, the instruments of His justice. We know that the Babylonian

Translator's note. — [1 P. HUMBERT, *Problèmes du livre d'Habacuc* (Neuchâtel, 1944; cf. *Theologische Revue* [1948], 81-82). I. ENGNELL, *Svenskt Bibl. Uppslagsverk* 1, 769-771. Haag, *Bibellexikon,* 633-634. J. S. LICHT, in *Entzyklop. Miqr.* 3 (1958), 6-10].

expansion towards the West, clearly in evidence from 605, reached Juda *ca.* 600 (2 Kgs. 24 : 1-2) and that Jerusalem was invested and taken in 598. *c)* But a second complaint (1 : 12-17) is occasioned by the actual presence of the conquerors. This is a scandal and raises the problem of evil : why does God permit the oppression of His people by " the wicked who devour the man that is more just than himself? " (1 : 13). *d)* A second oracle (2 : 1-4) is the high point of the book. The intervention of God's justice will not fail; but it is necessary to wait and trust in Him. In 2 : 4, we have the famous theme of Gal. 3 : 11, where Saint Paul has enriched and " theologized " the old oracle. *e)* There follow five curses against the tyrant (2 : 5-20). *f)* The book closes with a psalm (3) which prays for God's intervention and describes His destruction of the oppressor.

Habacuc represents a meditation on the Plan of God, a meditation which will continue in the Exile : Why, having chosen Israel, does God permit her to be trampled upon and even to be effaced from history? The problem of evil in this same period is put also on an individual plane (Jer. 12 : 1-6). It is, in fact, a period of profound reflection on the call of Israel, on human happiness, and on the problem of Providence. The purely temporal perspective of religion does not exclude the response of faith.

Sophonias [1].

Sophonias is furnished with a genealogy (1 : 1). " This enumeration of ancestors, perhaps, is intended solely to show that, despite the name of his father (" the Ethiopian? "), Sophonias is of pure Judean blood " (George). He prophesied during the minority of Josias, and therefore before the reform of 621. Hence the condemnation of the ministers but not of the king (1 : 8-9; 3 : 3) ', the protest against the influence of Ashur (1 : 8; 2 : 13-15) and against the cult of Baal and the astral gods (1 : 4-5). The reform of Josias was to clean out idolatry — at least temporarily — and to coincide with an Assyrian retreat. We have noted in Jeremias this short period

---

of national hope and happiness. Sophonias exercised his prophetic ministry a little earlier than Jeremias.

His book is divided into four parts : *a)* The Day of Yahweh in Juda (**1** : 2–**2** : 3). A mysterious enemy coming from the North will be the scourge of God. This text has inspired the *Dies iræ*. *b)* Oracles against the Nations (**2** : 4-15). *c)* Oracles against Jerusalem (**3** : 1-8). *d)* Promises (**3** . 9-20). This last section contains some unauthentic passages, because they assume the Exile of 587, namely, **3** : 9-10, 18[b]-19, 20. But it is here also that we perceive the originality of Sophonias. He is the first to announce that the " Remnant " of Israel will be composed of " poor ". The vocabulary of poverty through him entered into a theology of grace. " The poor man " is the client of God as opposed to the proud man, and he attracts God's attention by his spiritual conduct (**3** : 11-13; cf. **2** : 3). Though the number of his oracles is small, Sophonias appears to us as a religious genius whose synthesis has had a marked influence on subsequent religious history.

Aggeus [1].

The joint activity of Aggeus and Zacharias is mentioned in Esdras **5** : 1 and **6** : 14, in connection with the construction of the Second Temple, that of Zorobabel (520-515). The Book of Aggeus places the intervention of the prophet in the second half of the year 520. Aggeus' attention seems to be wholly concentrated on the Temple, and it is possible that he was a " cult-prophet ", or official prophet. But there is nothing to prove that he has revealed himself completely in his book.

The work contains three popular " fervorini " against the apathy of the Judeans. Aggeus foments enthusiasm, restores in the people the sense of their destiny, and promises agricultural prosperity when they will truly devote themselves to building a house for Yahweh (**1** : 1-15 ; **1** : 15[b]–**2** : 9; **2** : 10-19). A final allocution is a homage to Zorobabel, who is saluted as the elect of Yahweh and the depositary of the Messianic hopes. The same thought is found again in Zacharias.

Zacharias [1].

The Book of Zacharias is difficult, and this is true of both parts of the collection : 1–8, in which he registers his inter-ventions between 520 and 518, and 9–14, where he looks into the future. When he was explaining these chapters, Saint Jerome spoke of passing " from the obscure to the more obscure ".

Part I (1–8). As regards its structure, critics regard it as a kind of dated record or " journal " in which Zacharias tells us of eight visions, often in the manner of Ezechiel. He speaks of the rebuilding of the Temple, but he also sketches the main lines of the theocracy. Among the visions which initiate the theocratic organization, we should note in particular that dealing with the investiture of the High Priest (3 : 1-10), and that devoted to the lampstand which is concerned with the two powers, the lay and the sacerdotal (4 : 1-14). The vision of the flying scroll (5 : 1-4) and that of the woman in the *epha* (5 : 5-11) attest the ideal of holiness which the prophet envisions for the community of Israel. The " journal " com-prises : 1 : 1–2 : 9 + 3 : 1-7, 9 + 4 : 1-6ᵃ, 10ᵈ-14 + 5–6 : 8, 15 + 7 : 1-3 + 8 : 18-19. Undated pieces have been intro-duced into this journal, but they are always autobiographical.: 4 : 6ᵃ-10ᶜ; 6 : 9-14; 7 : 4-14. The most important of these is the second, in which we see the coronation of Zorobabel, who is saluted with the Messianic title of " Bud ". Zorobabel, in fact, realizes the prophet's hope insofar as he is the stock from which is to come the ideal Messias of the future. A final element entering into the structure of the book is embodied in the " words " [of the Lord] which are introduced in objective fashion : 2 : 10-17; 3 : 8, 9ᶜ-10; 8 : 1-17, 20-23.

All critics accept the authenticity of Part I. Zacharias is a disciple of Ezechiel, and perhaps his sacerdotal connections (Neh. 12 : 16) reinforce this kinship in spirit. The latter is revealed by the place given to the Temple, to the priesthood,

Translator's note. — [1 M. DELCOR, " Les sources du Deutero-Zacharie et ses procédés d'emprunt ", *RB* (1952), 385-411. Ez. KAUFMAN, *Toldot ha-emunah...* VIII, (1956), 226-275. ZER-KEBOD, in *Kitbey ha-Hebrah...* I (1955), 179-186 (on the relationship between Zach., Jer., and Ez.). H. RIESENFELD, *Svenskt Bibl. Uppslagsverk* 2, 1009-1011. CASSUTO, *Entzyklop. Miqr.* 2, 923-929. Haag, *Bibellexikon*, 1733-1735].

to concern for purity, to the theology of the divine transcendence, and to angelology.

Part II (9-14). It is divided into two sections, each introduced by the word *massa* (oracle): 9 : 1-12 : 1. It is an anthology of Messianic scenes in which visions of a most varied character are found side by side : the expectation of a royal and humble Messias (9 : 9-10); a reevaluation of the house of David (12 : 7 ff.; 13 : 1); the reference to the Pierced One (13 : 3); the warlike theocracy (10 : 3-11 : 3); the theocracy in worship or cult (14). As regards date, Part II probably fits best into the last decades of the fourth century. When the Persian Empire was overthrown by Alexander (9 : 1-8), hope revived in a great surge — the last of importance before the Book of Daniel. It is from this angle that Zach. 9-14 has a special interest in us, because these chapters are a *locus classicus* in which Christianity as a historical phenomenon found support and justification.

Malachias [1].

It is generally agreed that the last book of the Old Testament is an anonymous work. The name Malachias means " my messenger " and is probably derived from 3 : 1. An editor perhaps employed it as a title for the work. The book is introduced by *massa*, as the two parts of Zach. 9-14. Originally, perhaps, it was not separated from Zacharias; their separation might have been made in order to obtain twelve Minor Prophets. If so, the separation was a happy one, because the thought of Malachias has its own well defined character.

The prophet who speaks is to be placed about the time of Nehemias and Esdras — we would say around 430. The Temple has been rebuilt and regular services are apparently being held in it. However, tithes are given unwillingly (2 : 17; 3 : 7, 10-14; cf. Neh. 10 : 32-39; 13 : 10-13); the priesthood lacks vitality (1 : 6-8, 12-13); mixed marriages are common (2 : 10-16; cf. Neh. 10 : 28-30; 13 : 23-30); social oppression is not unknown (3 : 5; cf. Neh. 5 : 1-13). Malachias denounces

Translator's note. — [1] Ez. KAUFMAN, *Toldot ha-emunah...* VIII (1956), 366-377. H. RIESENFELD, in *Svenskt Bibl. Uppslagsverk* 2, 185-187. Haag, *Bibellexikon*, 1065-1066].

the evils which will be attacked by the reformers, particularly by
Esdras. The characteristic trait of the book is the employment
of dialog, which must be an echo of actual controversies.

After an introduction in which Yahweh's " hate " against
Edom is recalled, we find a series of denunciations (1 : 6 to
2 : 16). The criticisms are directed against the priests in their
capacity as offerers of sacrifices (they are offering blemished
victims to Yahweh!) and against the doctors of the Law.
In contrast to their miserable offerings, Malachias, in a prophetic
present, celebrates the pure offering of the Messianic era (1 : 11).
This ritual sacrifice will be substituted for the sacrifices of the
Jews (1 : 10), and will be universal and unbloody *(minḥah)*.
After the priests, the whole Jewish community is reproved
(2 : 10-16) on the score of mixed marriages and divorce. Mixed
marriages are regarded as weakening the national religious
bond (2 : 11).

A second section (2 : 17 to 3 : 21) contains predictions of
blessings for the faithful elements of the nation : first for the
sons of Levi (3 : 3) and then for the Israelites (3 : 6). All the
just will gambol like calves in the barnyard and they will
trample upon the wicked.

Two appendices close the book. The first (3 : 22) recalls
the Law of Sinai, while the second (3 : 23) identifies the precursor
mentioned in 3 : 1 — it is Elias who is to return. This second
text represents a later commentary and is the only unauthentic
passage in the book. Through it the Old Testament ends with
the prophecy of the Precursor whose voice is heard in the first
pages of the New. The continuity of the two Covenants is
thus made manifest.

4. — *THE SAPIENTIAL BOOKS*[1].
[J. Chaine and A. Robert]
1. — **The Book of Job**[2].

Division and text.

The book opens with a prologue in prose which explains
Job's situation and opens the discussion (1-2). Then come

Translator's note. — [1 W. BAUMGARTNER, " The Wisdom Literature ",
in H. H. Rowley, ed., *The O. T. and Modern Study* (Oxford, 1951), 210-237.
W. A. IRWIN, " The Wisdom Literature ", *Interpreter's Bible* I (1952), 212-219.

three parts in verse, of very unequal length. The first (3-31) comprises three cycles of discourses. In the first cycle, after the pathetic plaint of Job, his three friends, Eliphaz, Baldad, and Sophar, take up the discussion in turn. Job replies to each questioner as soon as each has finished speaking, so that this first cycle includes seven speeches (3-14). The second cycle has six, the discourses of the three friends who speak in the same order, and the three replies of Job (15-21). In the last cycle (22-31) the text has visibly suffered in transmission. After the discourses of Eliphaz and Baldad, Sophar unexpectedly says nothing and does not appear. It is noteworthy also that the speech of Baldad is very short (25 : 1-6), and that the passages 24 : 18-24 and 27 : 13-23 are not appropriate to Job, for they contain ideas contrary to his own but in keeping with those of his friends. We observe, furthermore, that on two occasions (27 : 1; 29 : 1) Job is said to be resuming his discourse, although he has not stopped speaking from 26 : 1. The following corrections and transpositions may, therefore, be proposed. Ch. 26 : 5-14 seems to be part of the speech of Baldad and should be read after 25 : 1-6. Job replies to Baldad in

E. KAUFMAN, *Toldot ha-emunah...* V (1952), 631-727. S. N. KRAMER, " Sumerian Wisdom Literature : A Preliminary Study ", *BASOR*, No. 112 (1951), 28-31. J. J. VAN DIJK, *La sagesse suméro-accadienne* (Leiden, 1953). M. Noth and D. W. Thomas, edd., *Wisdom in Israel and in the Ancient Near East.* Essays Presented to H. H. Rowley (Leiden, 1955; *Vetus Testamentum,* Suppl. III)].

Translator's note. — [² Cf. P. WECHTER, " The Book of Job " *Jewish Quarterly Review* (1944), pp. 121-132. W. B. STEVENSON, *The Poem of Job* (The Schweich Lectures, Oxford, 1947; cf. *Bibliotheca Orientalis,* 1948, pp. 55-56, and *Journal of Theological Studies,* 1948, pp. 312-315). J. J. WEBER, *Le livre de Job et l'Ecclésiaste* (Paris, — Tournai, 1947). E. G. KRAELING, *The Book of the Ways of God* (New-York, 1939; with full bibliography). A. M. DUBARLE, O. P., *Les Sages d'Israël* (Paris, 1946), pp. 65-94. G. HÖLSCHER, *Das Buch Hiob* (2nd ed. Tübingen, 1952; cf. *CBQ* [1952], 393-396). W. B. STEVENSON, *Critical Notes on the Hebrew Text of the Poem of Job* (Aberdeen, 1951). N. H. TUR-SINAI, *Sefer Ijjob 'im perush hadash* (Tel Aviv, 1954). F. STIER, *Das Buch Ijjob : Hebräisch und Deutsch* (Munich, 1954; cf. *RB* [1956], 133-135). J. STEINMANN, *Le livre de Job* (Paris, 1955). A. LEFÈVRE, " Job ", *DBV,* Suppl. IV (1949), 1073-1098. N. H. TUR-SINAI, art. " Ijjob ", *Entzyklop. Miqr.* I, 241-257. J. NOUGAYROL, " Une version ancienne du ' juste souffrant ' ", *RB* (1952), 239-250. J. H. KROEZE, " Die Elihu-Reden im Buch Hiob ", *Oudtest. Studien* II (1943), 156-170. A. WEISER, *Das Buch Hiob* (2nd ed., Göttingen, 1956). L. DENNEFELD, *RB* (1939), 163-180 (on Elihu). On the view held by a few scholars that Job is an ancient work translated or edited from Arabic, cf. GOETTSBERGER, *Einleitung im das A. T.,* p. 228, n. 7; D. S. MARGOLIOUTH, in *Expositor* I (1900), 431 ff.; II, 25 ff.; L. CHEIKHO, S. J., *Le Christianisme et la littérature chrétienne arabe avant l'Islam* II (Beyrouth, 1923; in Arabic), p. 409].

26 : 1-4; **27** : 2-12.   Verse **27** : 1 is probably a gloss aiming to
correct the confusion which had been introduced into Chapter **26**.
Sophar ought to take up the conversation in **27** : 13, and after
this verse should come **24** : 18-24, and then **27** : 14-23.   Job
takes up the discussion again in **29** : 1 ff.   As will be noted
subsequently, Chapter **28**, which interrupts the discussion,
was doubtless inserted later by the author of the poem.   The
second part of the book contains the discourses of Elihu (32-37),
who delivers a long monologue.   Finally, the third part comprises
the intervention of God, who closes the debate, and two short
replies of Job (**38-42** : 6).   A prose epilogue completes the
work and is thus symmetrical with the prologue (**42** : 7-17).

Literary genre.

Job is not a Hebrew, but an Oriental of the land of Hus,
which is probably to be localized in Idumea.   He is a rich
patriarch.   The great age to which he is said to have lived
recalls the period of Thare, the father of Abraham (Gen. **11** :
24, 25), but the mention of Themam and of Suhe (Job **2** : 11)
forces us to come down one or two centuries after Abraham
(Gen. **25** : 2; **36** : 10, 11, 15), to about 1600.

Did Job really exist or is he only a legendary figure?   It is
quite possible that the memory of a famous personage was
passed on through many generations and that our author
has derived his account from this tradition.   But it was not
his intention, really, to write the history of Job.   It is significant
that in both the Hebrew Canon and in the LXX the book was
not listed among the historical writings, but, along with Psalms
and Proverbs, among the Sapiential Books.   The Babylonian
Talmud (*Baba bathra*, 15[a]) regards the story of Job as an
invention [1].

The testimony of the author himself, though only implicit,
is more convincing than external criticism.   His presentation
of his hero actually exhibits all the characteristics of an artificial
construction.   Job is idealized to the highest degree, the numbers

---

Translator's note. — [[1] In the discussion reported in the Talmud, there was
a difference of opinion as to whether Job was an historical character or not.
The Talmud reports the view of one who said that Job was not nor was he
created; he was a *mashal* (= " parable ", etc.).   Cf. Tor-Sinai's, *Commentary*,
pp. 391-394].

in the introduction are conventional, the dialogue unfolds in strictly schematic fashion, and the marvelous or supernatural element itself has all the appearance of a literary device. For these reasons, Job may be called a didactic story (A. Lefèvre, *DBV, Suppl.* IV, 1082). The whole effort and art of the author, certainly, can be explained on the basis of his desire to communicate teaching on an obscure and controversial subject. Hence he employs the many varieties and devices of the *mashal* (cf. Ch. VI, *infra*), but his work differs in many respects from other writings of the same genre and the rest of the Old Testament. His use of the dialogue deserves special attention, although this literary form was long and familiarly known in the Near East. Instead of expressing his thought in short sentences and with authority, or in short tableaux, the author sets up a long debate. In this way, he can criticize the traditional teaching and, at the same time, emphasize the various aspects of the mystery, and suggest that its solution is beyond the capacity of the human mind.

But, in addition, the problem of suffering is examined in a concrete case. The suffering just man is presented to us; we hear him; from his heart come cries of anguish which are at once profoundly human and inspired by the loftiest religious feeling. God Himself intervenes to close the debate. Thus, there is action with a plot which develops and is resolved according to a well-ordered plan. The Book of Job belongs in part to the dramatic and in part to the lyric genre. It is poetical in the highest degree. We admire the animation and liveliness of its style, its brilliant images, the boldness of its hyperboles, and its splendid descriptions. These qualities are especially prominent in the praise of Wisdom (**28**) and in the discourses assigned to God (38 ff.). In form and content, these chapters are among the most beautiful in Biblical literature, and even in world literature.

Purpose and teaching.

The Book of Job does not attempt to develop a thesis according to our Western manner of thinking, but it relates a dramatic story and thus presents a concrete case which invites reflection. It is the case of an innocent man who is suffering, and this poses the problem of the suffering of the just. But from what

point of view, it may be asked, is the problem envisaged?
Does the author intend merely to discuss the teaching on
temporal rewards and punishments current in his time? He
presents this teaching, it is true, through the three speakers,
who address the patriarch, and they set it forth at length and
in more rigid form than anywhere else in the Bible. Job opposes
them, for he finds their reasons insufficient and contrary to
experience. And yet he does not reject the principle : his
bitter complaints and his vehement protests show this. The
celebrated passage, 19 : 25-27, has an unquestionable eschatological significance, but it does not prove that the author
is acquainted with the doctrine of the resurrection; in that
case, he would speak differently of sheol, and the problem which
he is trying to solve would have had its solution.

Actually, the mystery which, under the spur of suffering,
Job is trying to penetrate, is the mystery of God's ways with
him. Against the accusations of his friends, Job strongly
defends his innocence (6 : 9, 10, 24, 27-30; 10 : 2-7; 23 : 2-12;
29; 31). But then, why does God allow the wicked to be as
happy as the just, and sometimes even more so (21 : 7-34)?
Why is He not concerned, apparently, with the crimes that are
committed (24 : 1-12)? And yet He is just (9 : 2-3) !

In trying to fathom the abyss of divine justice, Job goes
beyond the excessively narrow conception of God's justice
held by his opponents. Under the merciless God who crushes
him, he wishes to find again the just and kind God who is
faithful in helping His friends. He exhausts himself in vain,
but in the night in which he is struggling with himself, his
faith is made stronger and his trust in God remains unshakable
(16 : 18-22). Finally, God Himself intervenes (38–41) : man
does not comprehend the wonders of nature; with all the
more reason, then, he cannot penetrate the ways of God.
He must simply submit and adore the Divine Wisdom.

Such is the great lesson — and it is not a negative one —
of this profound book. It gives us, besides, a magnificent
exposition of God's grandeur, of the wonders of His creation,
of the practice of good works, of purity, detachment (cf. 31),
and wisdom. These lofty thoughts are expressed in a language
of incomparable beauty, the poetry of which unceasingly
charms and fascinates us.

Authenticity and date.

The author is unknown. He was a Palestinian Jew who, as the book bears witness, was well educated and had travelled much, for he knew Idumea, Arabia, and Egypt. He had seen the ostrich, the crocodile, and the mines of Sinai. He had admired the marvels of nature and was a poet of genius.

According to several critics the poetic portion does not come from the hand that composed the prologue and the epilogue. There was first a popular prose tale, already old, from which the author of the present book received his inspiration, and of which he retained only the beginning and the end, replacing the whole central portion with his own poem. The chief argument for this very questionable hypothesis is the difference of attitude in Job as presented in the prose parts, where he is patient and praised by God, and in the poetical parts, where he complains vehemently and criticizes Providence. Job's mounting, pathetic tone develops out of the discussion itself. The poem on wisdom (28) has likewise been the object of controversy, because it breaks the dialogue. It appears, however, to be from the same hand as the speeches in verse, although it may be conceded that it was added afterwards by the author of the work in order to show, at the end of the discussion, that wisdom escapes the effort of man and that it is possessed and granted by God alone.

The speeches of Elihu (32–37) are often considered an addition made by an inspired author who probably did not wish to leave without comment certain expressions of Job which the author of the poem had not refrained from using in order to describe the anguish of his hero (cf. 33 : 11 and 13 : 27; 35 : 9, 14-16, and 24 : 12; 21 : 14-21, etc.). Elihu is prolix in his language, and he employs a large number of Aramaic terms. Unlike the other personages, he is not named in the prologue, the epilogue, or in the discourse of Yahweh; he delivers a monologue to which there is no response. The participation of Elihu, therefore, can be regarded as a supplement which was added to the work later [1].

Translator's note. — [1 J. H. KROEZE, *Die Elihu-reden im Buche Hiob*, in *Oudtestamentische Studiën, II* (Leiden, 1943), pp. 156-170].

The presence of Aramaic words in the dialogue points to a postexilic composition for the book. The mention of the name of Job in Ez. 14 : 14, 20, indicates only that there existed a traditional story of Job, and one probably still oral, which a poet drew upon and made the subject of his work. The lamentation of the hero (Job 3) seems clearly to depend on Jeremias (20 : 14-18). The work probably appeared between 500 and 450, and the discourses of Elihu were added some time later.

2. — The Book of Psalms [1].

Name and Place in the Canon.

The Hebrew Bible calls the Book of Psalms, " Hymns ". As these hymns were sung for the most part to the accompaniment of stringed instruments, the Septuagint gave the collection

---

Translators's note. — [1 Cf. B. D. EERDMANS, *The Hebrew Book of Psalms* (Leiden, 1947); *id.,* various essays on the Psalms, in *Oudtestamentische Studiën,* I (Leiden. 1942), pp. 1-16, and 105-300. P. A. H. DE BOER, *ibid.,* II (1943), pp. 171-193 (on Ps. 8). J. PRADO, *Nuevo Salterio latin-espanol* (Madrid, 1948; cf. *Estudios Biblicos,* 1948, pp. 504-506); *id., Sefarad* (1945), pp. 457-461; *id.,* "La aportación historica... de los Salmos", *Sefarad* (1946), pp. 219-236. A Colunga, O. P., "El sentimiento de la naturaleza en los Salmos", *Ciencia Tomista* (1944), pp. 297-322. On the new Roman Translation of the Psalter, see A. BEA, S. J., *Le Nouveau Psautier Latin* (Paris, 1947), or *id., Die neue lateinische Psalmenübersetzung* (Freiburg i. Br., 1948); J. M. T. BARTON, *Clergy Review,* 30 (1948), pp. 10-22; J. BLOCH, *The New Latin Version...,* JQR, 38 (1948), pp. 267-288. For relations with the Ras-Shamra (Ugarit) literature, see J. COPPENS, *Le Muséon,* 64 (1946), pp. 113-142, and *id., Ephemerides Theol. Lovan.,* 23 (1947), pp. 173-177, and the references given. A. R. JOHNSON, "The Psalms", in H. H. Rowley, ed., *The O. T. and Modern Study* (Oxford, 1951), 162-209. J. ZIEGLER, "Das neue lateinische Psalterium in deutscher Übersetzung", *Theologische Revue* (1950), 181-190. I. ENGNELL, "Psaltaren", in *Svenkt Bibl. Uppslagsverk,* 2, 787-832 (an important article). J. COPPENS, *Het Onsterfelijkheidsgeloof in het Psalmboek* (Brussels, 1957), especially pp. 45-52 and 54-57. J. RIDDERBOS, *De Psalmen* 1-44 (Kampen, 1955; cf. RB [1955], 127-129). A. WEISER, *Die Psalmen,* (*Das A. T. Deutsch,* 14-15, Göttingen, 1955; cf. CBQ [1956], 203-205). J. M. GONZALEZ RUIZ, "Las teofanias en los Salmos", *Estudios Biblicos* (1954; cf. *Sefarad* [1955], 223). A. FEUILLET, "Les psaumes eschatologiques du règne de Yahweh", *Nouvelle Rev. Théologique* (1951), 244-260, 352-363 (Pss. 47, 95, 96-98). S. DEL PARAMO, S. J., "El genero literario de los Salmos", *Estudios Biblicos* (1947), 241-264. A. BENTZEN, *Fortolkning til de gammeltestamentlige Salmer* (Copenhagen, 1940). G. CASTELLINO, *Libro dei Salmi (La Sacra Bibbia,* ed. S. Garofalo, Turin, 1955). On the new Roman Psalter, see : E. P. ARBEZ, *American Eccl. Review* (July, 1945); H. RENCKENS, *Bijdragen Phil. Theol. Fac. Jezuieten* (1948), 187-208. M. J. GRUENTHANER, S. J., "The Future Life in the Psalms", CBQ, 2 (1940), 57-63; *id.,* "The Old Testament and Retribution in This Life", *ibid.* 4 (1942), 101-110. E. PODECHARD, S. S., *Le Psautier,* I-II (Pss. 1-110) (Lyon, 1949-1954; cf. R. A. F. MacKenzie, S. J., *Theological*

the name *Psalterion* (stringed instrument), and to designate a number of poems, called in Hebrew " chants ", it employed the word *psalmos* — hence the terms *Psalter* and *Psalm*.

The Psalter is the first of the Hagiographa in the Hebrew Bible. In the Greek Bible it has occupied various positions, but ordinarily it keeps the same place of honor as in the Hebrew. The Latin Bible puts it in second place, that is, after Job, among the Sapiential Books.

Division and text.

At first the Psalms existed as separate pieces, and then small collections of them were made for liturgical use. The present five books of the Psalter were at first five distinct collections (Ps. 1–41; 42–72; 73–89; 90–106; 107–150), which were made by authors who used still earlier collections. Each of the five collections ends in a doxology. It is difficult to determine the nature of the primitive collections which preceded our present five books, but the existence of these cannot be denied. In the third book, there is one group in which God is called Yahweh (Ps. 84–89) and another in which He is generally called Elohim (Ps. 73–83). In the fifth book, the Alleluia Psalms (113–118) and the Gradual Canticles (120–134) correspond to small ancient collections. It may happen that certain Psalm or parts of Psalms are repeated in different groups, as Ps. 14 = Ps. 53; Ps. 40 : 14-18 = Ps. 70. Sometimes the name Elohim has been substituted for Yahweh as in almost all the Psalms of the second book, and, as has been said, in a group in the third.

In early manuscripts the separation of the Psalms was not indicated, and this fact explains differences in division in the Septuagint — which the Vulgate follows — and in the present Hebrew Bible. Psalms 9 and 10, and 114 and 115 of the Hebrew Bible, form in the Septuagint and the Latin Bible Psalms 9 and 113 respectively. On the other hand, Psalms 116 and 147 of the Hebrew are each divided into two parts in the Septuagint

Studies [1950], 425-428). On Ps. 82, see R. O'CALLAGHAN, S. J., " Note on the Canaanite Background ", *CBQ* (1953), 311-314. J. LICHT, " Pss. 95-100 in Honor of Yahweh's Kingship ", *Kitbey ha Hebrah...* I (1955), 157-166. S. MOWINCKEL, *Det Gamle Testament IV. Skriftene I. Del* (Oslo, 1955; it contains Psalms, Job, and Proverbs)].

and the Latin Bible, and correspond in these texts to Psalms **114** and **115**, **146** and **147**. As a consequence of these different divisions the numbering varies in the Hebrew and in the Greek and Latin versions from Psalm **9** to Psalm **148**.

Through frequent recopying, the Hebrew text of the Psalms suffered very much, with the result that there are difficult and obscure passages in the translations. The text of the Psalms in the Vulgate is an Old Latin version based on the Septuagint and revised by Saint Jerome (see p. 649).

Desirous of facilitating the understanding of the Psalms and of making their liturgical use more fruitful, His Holiness Pius XII ordered a new critical Latin translation to be made. It was published on October 29, 1944.

Titles and superscriptions.

Most of Psalms are provided with titles. Among these indications, there are some that go back to the authors themselves, while there are others which, although very old, were added later. They are often very enigmatic, and many of them were no longer understood by the translators of the LXX.

The purpose of the titles is often to characterize briefly the literary nature of the psalm : canticle, hymn, prayer, didactic poem, lament... Or they are concerned with the musical execution. Thus, the word *sela*, the precise meaning of which is obscure [see, e.g., Koehler, *Lex. in V. T. Libros*, p. 659, and *Suppl.*, 1958, p. 174], is found repeatedly. David Kimchi thinks it means a raising of the voice, a *forte;* others — among them St. Augustine — think it means a pause, a rest; still others understand it as referring to a change of voices, a musical interlude. Sometimes a known air is indicated (Ps. **22**; **56**). The expression, " to the choirmaster ", undoubtedly indicates that the psalm was borrowed from the book of the one who directed the choirs in the Temple. Often the title has a liturgical reference : e.g., " for the Sabbath ", " Alleluia " (especially in the Hallel-Psalms). Psalms of " Ascents " or " Gradual " Psalms were doubtless sung by pilgrims when in the time of feasts they were ascending the mountainous slopes to reach Jerusalem.

Finally, there are numerous titles which state the origin of the Psalm. In such cases they mention the name of an individual or of a group; sometimes also, the event which was the occasion of the poem's composition. The personages listed are Moses, David, Solomon, Asaph, the sons of Core, Ethan, and Herman. The list is longer in the LXX.

Teachings.

The question of literary genres occupies a central place in the study of the Psalms and will be given a separate treatment later (Ch. VI). The genre is primarily concerned with the form, and does not affect the content to any appreciable degree. Hence it is not inappropriate to present the general teachings of the Psalter in one comprehensive synthesis. The Psalms are simply the echo of what the Bible tells us of God and of moral life and conduct.

There is only one God, and idols are nothing (**115**); He is the Creator (**8**; **33**; **89**; **90**; **102** : 25-28); He is all-just (**8** : 9–11 : 5, 7), all-good (**36**), all-merciful (**103**; **130**), and present everywhere (**139**). The world, which is His work, demonstrates at the same time His existence, His power, and His grandeur (**8**; **19**; **29**; **89**). One must be insane not to believe in Him (**14**). The psalmists devote their thoughts unceasingly to God, communing with Him, praising Him, thanking Him, calling upon Him for help. God is not an abstraction for them, but a living person who participates in all the events of their lives. The psalms of praise are very numerous (cf. **8**; **29**; **30**; **33**; **34**; **35**; **48**; **63**; **65**; **68**; **75**; **81**; **92**; **93**; **95–101**; **103–108**; **111**; **113**; **115**; **117**; **118**; **134–136**; **138**; **145–150**). Whether the source of his inspiration may be the marvels of nature, or public or private events, the psalmist sings of the grandeur, the power, the goodness of God; he praises the Lord and invites all to praise Him. At the same time, or on other occasions, he tells Him of his trust (**3**; **4**; **5**; **11**; **16**; **17**; **20**; **28**; **31**; **40**; **46**; **56**; **57**; **62**; **63**, etc.), and pours forth his gratitude (**18**; **30**; **40**; **66**; **116**). He speaks of the joy and happiness experienced in serving God (**1** : 1; **4** : 8; **5** : 12; **16** : 63; **84** : 6; **112**). In his need he calls upon God's help; his prayer is urgent and unrestrained. In other circumstances it is a cry of anguish, now prompted by despair, now showing trust in God (**6**; **13**; **22**; **44**, etc.).

His yearning for God is a thirst (42), and he would like to abide in the Temple forever (27 : 4). The Psalms adhere in general to the theology of temporal retribution maintained by the friends of Job. Psalm 1 summarizes well this conception of Providence, and it is perhaps for this reason that it is placed at the beginning of the Psalter. But some psalmists love God so much and know that they are so loved by Him that death seems powerless to separate them from Him : God will take them with Him into glory (16 : 10; 49 : 16; 73 : 23, 24). These sentiments of praise, adoration, trust, love, and the faith which inspires them, give the Psalms a permanent religious value. Praise occupied a very important place in Jewish prayer, which in this respect, attains a height not reached by the large number of Christians who regard prayer as petition only. Charity towards one's enemies, however, is absent from the Psalms, but these enemies are wicked and are persecutors, with respect to whom all attempts at conversion have failed. Nothing is left but to separate from them and curse them (cf. 59; 69; 109). In justification of this attitude, the psalmists can appeal to the whole Yahwist tradition, and especially to the spirit that permeates the Law Codes.

God wills justice, He loves the poor and the humble and comes to their aid (10 : 14; 69 : 34; 37; 70; 94). The worship which pleases Him is prayer and a moral life (50). Before Him, who is eternal, mortal man is nothing (39; 90; 144 : 3-4). Consciousness of sin and repentance are expressed with deep sorrow (31; 32; 38; 41; 51; 130). The whole Psalter speaks of God and leads to God; it is truly *the* religious book.

Origin of the Psalms.

Several Fathers, following the Rabbinic tradition without further examination, thought that David was the author of all the Psalms. This was the opinion, e.g., of Philastrius of Brescia (*Haer.* 130), St. Ambrose *(In Ps. 6)*, St. Augustine *(De civ. Dei* 17, 14), and St. John Chrysostom *(In Ps. 55)*. But St. Hilary *(In Ps. 2)* and St. Jerome *(Ep.* 140, 2) opposed this view and based their own position on the titles. While several ancient writers went too far in attributing psalms to David, several modern exegetes have gone too far in the opposite direction in leaving almost nothing to David. In reaction against the latter, the representatives of the *Formgeschichte* School, following especially S. Mowinckel, assign the composition of a large number of psalms to a remote past, but they see in them the expression of a religion that does not rise above the level of that of the Assyro-Babylonians.

The earliest psalm compositions may possibly antedate the institution of the monarchy. At that time there already existed religious poems, songs for special occasions, prayers, thanksgivings. The music and the dance of the nabis (1 Sam. 10 : 5-8) was undoubtedly accompanied by singing, and some ancient psalms may have preserved bits of such old poems. Tradition emphasizes David's part in the development of psalm composition, and it is with good reason that he has left in the Bible a reputation as a poet and musician (2 Sam. 1 : 17-27; 3 : 33; Am. 6 : 3; Ecclus. 47 : 8-9). In his reign the Ark was brought to Jerusalem and the Chronicler regards him as the organizer of worship in the Holy City. Under Solomon, following the building of the Temple, the Psalter, quite naturally, must have received increments, and new compositions of an historical, liturgical, or prophetic character continued to enrich it down to the day of catastrophe. During the Babylonian Exile, inspired singers express the sorrow and repentance of the captives (cf. Ps. 137); after the Exile, they tell of the sufferings of the return, celebrate the Law, develop themes on Wisdom, and make known the complaints of the lowly. The persecution of Antiochus Epiphanes and the revolt of the Machabees may have furnished a stimulation to the production of new religious lyrics. The " Psalms of Solomon " and those discovered at Qumran show that the genre continued to develop after the close of the Canonical Psalter.

3. — The Book of Proverbs [1].

Name and structure.

The word " proverb " has a wide variety of meanings in Scripture; it may mean a saying, a maxim, a biting remark,

Translator's note. — [1 Cf. J. M. McGlinchey, *The Teaching of Amen-em-ope and the Book of Proverbs* (Washington, 1938). P. W. Skehan, " Proverbs 5 : 15-19 and 6 : 20-24 ", *CBQ*, 8 (1946), 290-297; id., " The Seven Columns of Wisdom's House in Proverbs 1-9 ", *ibid.*, 9 (1947), 190-198; id., " A Single

a riddle, a parable, or an allegory (see the explanation of the *mashal* as a genre in Ch. VI, *infra*). The Book of Proverbs is a very composite one. Apart from its long title (1 : 1-7), which covers the work as a whole, we may distinguish the following collections : I (1 : 8–9 : 18); II (10 : 1–22 : 16); III (22 : 17–24 : 22); IV (24 : 23-34); V (25–29); VI (30 : 1-10); VII (30 : 11-33); VIII (31 : 1-9), and IX (31 : 10-31).

Collection I is composed of a series of brief sketches. The style is ordinarily direct, the tone hortatory and persuasive, the religious note prominent, and the notion of wisdom markedly developed. Collection II is composed of two sections : A (10–15) and B (16–22 : 16). In both we have maxims in distinct form, generally antithetic in A and synthetic in B. Collection III in its first part (22 : 17–23 : 11) is characterized by a special feature, namely, that it coincides in content, if not in form, with the Egyptian *Wisdom of Amenemope*. It is commonly held that the Biblical writer made considerable use of the Egyptian work but maintained his own independence. Collection V was compiled by the men of Ezechias (25 : 1) and, like Collection II, is presented as Solomonic. It is also composed of two parts : 25–27 and 28–29, both consisting of sayings arranged according to antithetic or synthetic parallelism.

Teaching of the book.

The collections of Proverbs suppose a world divided into two distinct categories : the wise and the foolish. An intermediate, but provisional, category is that of the simple or inexperienced, who are open to all influences, good or bad. The foolish are regarded as beyond conversion; accordingly, the teaching of our authors is addressed to the simple and the wise.

The ideal proposed is that of a religious humanism. Wisdom is really a kind of savoir-faire through which one expects to

Editor for the Book of Proverbs ", *ibid.*, 10 (1948), 115-130. A. M. Du-BARLE, O. P., *Les Sages d'Israël* (Paris, 1946), 25-63. G. R. DRIVER, " Problems in the Hebrew Text of Proverbs ", *Biblica* (1951), 173-197. N. H. TUR-SINAI, " Prov. 3 : 9 ", *Kitbey ha Hebrah...* I (1955), 167-168. S. MOWINCKEL (see Bibliography on Psalms, *supra*). The art. " Sprüche ", in Haag, *Bibellexikon*, 1545-1547. J. VAN DER PLOEG, *Spreuken*, in *De Boeken van het Oude Testament :* VIII, 1 (Roermond en Maaseik, 1952].

succeed in all things, and, accordingly, gain happiness here below. Although this last end of human activity lacks all transcendence, to attain it one must accept a law of stern discipline and live strictly according to the moral code. The maxims of Proverbs insist especially on sobriety in food and drink, control of the tongue, honesty in business, almsgiving, fidelity to marriage vows, and impartiality in judgment. There is hardly any allusion to worship.

However, all the collections make frequent mention of God and they look to Him to mete out, with sovereign justice, rewards and punishments. They identify the wise and the foolish with the religious and the godless respectively. The precepts in the Code of wisdom find their parallels in the Torah, and particularly in Deuteronomy. Several times, there is question of the Word, of the Commandment, of the Law: **6** : 23; **13** : 13; **28** : 4, 9; **29** : 18, and a definite equivalence is recognized between wisdom and the fear of God, or, let us say, between Wisdom and Religion : **1** : 7; **9** : 10; **15** : 33ª. Finally, Collection I introduces personified Divine Wisdom (**1** : 20-33; **8** : 1 ff.; **9** : 1-6), and tells of Its internal generation in God's bosom (**8** : 22 ff.).

The Book of Proverbs and the Wisdom of the Ancient Near East.

The Book of Proverbs resembles in some ways the Assyrian tale famous in antiquity which is called the *Story and Wisdom of Ahikar* (about 550). It bears more definite and striking resemblances to the Egyptian "Instructions" of the third and second millenia and to the inscriptions on scarabs at the end of the second millenium and during the first. To be noted especially is the dependence of Prov. **22** : 17–23 : 14) on the *Wisdom of Amenemope* (about 850 B. C.).

Generally speaking, the moral level of Israelite wisdom and of Egyptian wisdom is pretty much the same. There does not seem to be any doubt that the former borrowed from the latter its individualist concept, its division of mankind into the wise and the foolish, and, especially, the characteristic psychological attitude which consists in meeting the problems of life with reflection, prudence, and self-mastery with a view to success. The classic form of the Egyptian instructions in wisdom also passed into Biblical literature. A father or teacher is represented as addressing his son or his disciples in an insinuating manner; he endeavors to emphasize the advantages of a good life as compared with the drawbacks of an evil one.

And yet the teaching of Proverbs has its own special characteristics, which it would be seriously wrong to ignore. Its chief moral purpose is not, as in Egypt, to train public servants, but is more directly human. Under a secular appearance, it is deeply religious and carefully maintains its connection with the Torah. Finally, its ideal is " humility ", or, in other words, the fear of God, which is the most genuine expression of Yahwist holiness (cf. *supra*). On the general question of the origin and development of the sapiential genre in the Bible, the reader is referred to Ch. VI, *infra*.

The date of the collections and of the book.

A Solomonic origin of the whole book cannot be maintained. It would seem to be affirmed in 1 : 1-6, but it is commonly agreed that these verses are the later addition of a scribe who generalized the data of 10 : 1 and 25 : 1. These verses concern Collections II and V, which are the most ancient, but even within these restricted limits their testimony must be interpreted carefully. In view of the statement of 1 Kgs. 5 : 12, and from all we know of the king's relations with Egypt, we cannot doubt that Solomon and the learned men around him originated the sapiential genre, but it is impossible to determine the precise contributions made in their time. There are many indications that would suggest that Collections II and III existed first as oral teaching. The essential features of their literary aspect appeared gradually and their evolution was completed at the beginning of the 5th century. Collection III is probably postexilic. Collection I was composed as an introduction to the earlier compilations. It antedates Malachias and Job, and is to be assigned to the first decades of the 5th century. At what date the smaller collections were added to the preceding, we do not know, but there is good reason for holding that Proverbs existed in its present form before the end of the Persian period.

4. — Ecclesiastes [1].

The personality of Ecclesiastes.

In the epilogue the author is called in Hebrew " Qoheleth " (**12** : 9). The word means " president of the assembly ", and there is probably question of a body of sages of which he was the head. The term " Ecclesiastes " translates Qoheleth approximately, and from the Greek of the Septuagint it passed into the Vulgate. It is used to designate either the book or its author. The way in which " the holy place " and " the city " are spoken of makes it clear that the author lived in Jerusalem (**8** : 10). He was a sage of experience who had observed much. He often says, " I have seen ", as if he were a man of ripe age. We do not know whether he had suffered much, for pessimism comes from character as often as it does from misfortune. He is a more profound philosopher than the author of the Book of Job, but he is not a poet and he does not know how to arouse emotion. The style is often as sombre as the thought. Most of the book is written in prose.

Composition of the work.

A disciple added the epilogue (**12** : 9-14) to eulogize Ecclesiastes. This disciple was also a wise man; he says, " my son ", like the sages, and he handles maxims as an expert. Ecclesiastes ordinarily speaks of himself in the first person : " I have seen, I recognized, I said ", but in **1** : 2, **7** : 27-29, and **12** : 8, he is spoken of in the third person. Perhaps these three texts were added by the same disciple; **1** : 2 and **12** : 8 express a thought that the master must have been fond of repeating. This maxim placed at the beginning and at the

Translator's note. — [1 Cf. A. M. DUBARLE, O. P., *Les Sages d'Israël* (Paris, 1946), 95-128. S. ANSEJO, O. F. M. Cap., " El genero literario de Ecclesiastes ", *Estudios Biblicos* (1948), 369-406. F. ZIMMERMANN, " The Aramaic Provenance of Qohelet ", *JQR*, 36 (1945), 17-46. R. GORDIS, " The Original Language of Qohelet ", *ibid.* 37 (1946), 67-84; *id., Koheleth : The Man and His World* (New York, 1951; cf. *CBQ* (1952). N. ALLONY, " An Unknown Ms of Ben Qoheleth ", *JQR,* 38 (1947), 167-188. J. MUILENBERG, " A Qohelet Scroll from Qumran ", *BASOR*, No. 134 (1954), 20-28. H. L. GINSBERG, *Studies in Koheleth* (New York, 1950; cf. *CBQ* [1952], 400-401). A. BEA, S. J., *Liber Ecclesiastae* (Rome, 1950; cf. *Theologische Revue* [1951], 100-101). J. BLAU, in *Kitbey ha-Hebrah...*, I (1955), 208-209].

end of the book sums up its teaching very well. Chapter **7** :
27-29 might be a recollection recorded by the disciple, or else
one of the dicta composed by Ecclesiastes himself, but which
he had not included in his book. Even after we set aside
the texts just mentioned, the book still seems to be a collection
of complex, if not disparate elements. Autobiographic confidences, thoughts inspired by personal experience, exhortations,
reflections, maxims of wisdom, all occur without any definite
order. A certain number of clashing statements are also in
evidence : thus, e.g., among the texts concerning reward and
punishment, and the evaluation of wisdom.

In several places Qoheleth says that there is no earthly
retribution (**7** : 15; **8** : 10, 14; **9** : 1-6). He knows that God
is just, but says that he does not understand anything about
Divine Providence (**3** : 11; **8** : 16, 17; **11** : 5). But a series
of texts speaks of earthly retribution in the same manner
as the friends of Job (**2** : 26, except for the last line; **3** : 17;
7 : 26ᵇ; **8** : 5-8, 11-13). A comparison of **8** : 10, 14, with **8** :
11-13, is suggestive. Qoheleth proclaims that wisdom itself
is a vanity (**1** : 17; **2** : 15), and that it increases sorrow (**1** : 18).
Yet a series of texts praises wisdom in the usual manner of the
sages (**7** : 11; **8** : 1; **10** : 2, 3, 12, 13).

Several hypotheses have been advanced in ancient and
modern times to account for these incoherences. The ancients
assumed that Qoheleth was carrying on a dialogue with himself
or with opponents. Modern exegetes have thought rather
of contributions made by different authors at different times.
According to this view, besides the additions made by the
disciple who wrote the epilogue, a scribe inserted reflections
supporting temporal retribution and wisdom to temper the
animadversions that were regarded as excessively bold. Furthermore, a pious Jew probably added here and there some sayings
to remind us of God. (This is the opinion of Podechard).

At the present time, there is a return to less rigid explanations,
which also safeguard more satisfactorily the unity of the book.
Thus it is noted that, on the testimony of the writer of the
epilogue, Qoheleth, in the commonly accepted meaning of the
term, was a wise man who was quite familiar with classic doctrine
and was the interpreter of it in religious gatherings of the

people; yet he also had his personal views, which he could develop in his esoteric teaching. A disciple — most probably the writer of the epilogue - - recorded pell mell the maxims or developments of each of these currents of thought. In accordance with such a view, our book may be regarded as a kind of notebook (Dom Duesberg, *Les scribes inspirés*, II, 175-185).

Teaching.

Ecclesiastes examines the value of life. He draws up an inventory of the goods which man pursues, and proclaims their vanity. Wisdom is good (9 : 13-16), but does not yield happiness; it is difficult to acquire, and brings suffering (1 : 12, 13, 18); all its advantages cease at the hour of death (9 : 10). Ecclesiastes knows nothing of retribution beyond the grave (6 : 6; 9 : 4-5, 10). Upright life likewise does not yield happiness (7 : 15; 8 : 14; 9 : 1-3). Riches fail in the same way. They are acquired with difficulty (2 : 4-11, 22, 23; 4 : 8); they bring with them disagreeable elements; they are often lost even before they are enjoyed (5 : 9-16); and at death they are left to people who have not toiled to acquire them (2 : 18-21). Pleasures likewise do not satisfy the heart of man (2 : 1-11). Ecclesiastes declares the emptiness of pleasures, of riches, of wisdom, and of any human effort. All is a vain pursuit (1 : 14; 2 : 11, 17). There is no equivalence between the desires of the understanding and the heart and the realities of life. No progress is to be expected which will give in return for man's activity the true satisfaction of his deepest desires (1 : 3-11). Life does not suffice for man.

This whole negative side of Ecclesiastes is very strong. On the constructive side, he is weaker, and this is easy to understand, because he did not have the answer to the problem he posed. Life does not satisfy man; he thinks nevertheless that one should take from it whatever good there is in it (2 : 24; 3 : 12; 5 : 17-19; 9 : 7-9). God grants man some consolations (2 : 25; 3 : 13; 5 : 19). To isolate 2 : 24 and 9 : 7-10 would be badly to misread the thought of the author. Saint Jerome put 9 : 7-10 into the mouth of an Epicurean, and believed that he had a dialogue before him. But from the context it is very clear that there is question of innocent enjoyments. Even though they are vain, man can and ought to enjoy them, as a kind of providential compensation. Ecclesiastes is neither an unqualified pessimist nor a hedonist (cf. **10** : 17).

Job would not have complained if earthly reward and punishment had appeared to him to be realized. Qoheleth is much more profound. He finds life unsatisfying and would like goods which do not pass away (**2** : 16-21; **5** : 14; **6** : 6; **9** : 9, 10). His thought exercised a great influence upon Judaism. In making men's minds more anxious regarding reward and punishment, in proclaiming the vanity of the things of this world, he prepared souls for receiving the revelations of God upon the hereafter.

Origin.

In the title the author speaks of himself as a son of David and as if he were king (**1** : 1, 12). The Jewish tradition as represented in the Talmud has taken these texts literally, and has attributed the composition of the book to Solomon in his old age. The Fathers of the Church adopted the Jewish tradition. But there are many arguments against Solomonic authorship. The language with its Aramaisms is postexilic. Several observations regarding administration and power do not fit a king (**4** : 13-16; **5** : 7; **10** : 5-7, 20, etc.). The epilogue classes the author among the sages and does not consider him to be King Solomon (**12** : 9-14). It is recognized that the author of Ecclesiastes, by a fiction, speaks as if he were Salomon. In any event, we can see through his artifice easily, for he fails to put himself in the period of Solomon when he declares that he is wiser than all those who were before him in Jerusalem (**1** : 16). Solomon, who was the second king after David's conquest of the city, could hardly have compared himself with a line of princes or sages dwelling in Jerusalem before him. The work must have been composed between 300 and 200. In this period Palestine was under the domination of the Ptolemies. What is said of kings (**4** : 13-16; **8** : 2-4; **10** : 4, 20) fits better into the time of the Lagids than into that of the Persians, for the king of Persia was too far away and a satrap governed in his name.

5. — The Canticle of Canticles [1].

The title, " Canticle of Canticles ", signifies in Hebrew the canticle par excellence. Rabbi Aqiba excluded from the resurrection of the blessed those who sang it at banquets *(Tosefta Sanh.* **12** : 10). The Canticle seemed to him so beautiful that in his eyes it was equal in value to creation (*Yadaim* 3 : 5). Some rabbis raised doubts about its canonicity because certain images offended them, and especially perhaps because apparently this enigmatic book makes no mention of God, the Temple, the Law, or Israel. But tradition prevailed over all difficulties. The Christian Church, which found the book in the Jewish Canon, has always held it to be both inspired and canonical [2].

Unity and structure of the book.

Af first sight the Canticle looks like a composite collection, the unity of which is hard to discern. Hence several exegetes have seen in it an assemblage of originally independent fragments. The work has unity, however, and this unity can be perceived better when the question is examined from the psychological point of view.

Translator's note. — [1 Cf. S. KRAUS, " The Archaeological Background of Some Passages in the Song of Songs ", *JQR*, 33 (1942), 17-28, and *ibid.*, 35 (1944), 59-78. P. De AMBROGGI, " Il Cantico dei Cantici; struttura e genere litterario ", *Scuola Cattolica*, 76 (1948), 113-130. R. E. MURPHY, " The Structure of the Canticle of Canticles ", *CBQ*, 11 (1949), 381-391. L. WATERMAN, *The Song of Songs* (Ann Arbor, Mich., 1948). POUGET-GUITTON, *The Canticle of Canticles*, translated from the French by J. Lilly (New York, 1948). A. FEUILLET, *Le Cantique des Cantiques* (Paris, 1953; cf. *RB* [1953], 437). R. GORDIS, *The Song of Songs* (New York, 1954; cf. *RB* [1956], 284). A. CHOURAQUI, *Le Cantique des Cantiques* (Bruges, 1953). J. P. AUDET, " Le sens du Cantique des Cantiques ", *RB* (1955), 197-221. D. BUZY, *Le Cantique des Cantiques* (Paris, 1950; cf. review by R. Murphy, *CBQ* [1952], 200-202). N. H. TUR-SINAI, *The Song of Songs* (Tel Aviv, 1943, in Hebrew; cf. H. DANBY, *JTS* [1944], 227). A. ROBERT, " La description de l'Epoux et de l'Epouse du Cant. (**5** : 11-15 and **7** : 2-6) ", *Mélanges Podechard* (Lyon, 1945), 211-223. A. BEA, S. J., *Canticum Canticorum* (Rome, 1953; an excellent edition of the Hebrew text with Latin translation and notes)].

Translator's note. — [2 It is often said that Theodore of Mopsuestia was condemned for his views on C. C. by the Second Council of Constantinople (553). Actually, the council heard an accusation against him because of his interpretation, but did not pass sentence on this point. Theodore did not deny the inspiration of C. C., but only its prophetic significance — a view which was not isolated nor unique. See : A. M. DUBARLE, O. P., *Revue des Sciences phil. et théol.*(1958), 142. A. M. BRUNET, " Théodore de Mopsuestia et le Cantique des Cantiques ", *Etudes et Recherches* (Ottawa, 1955), 155-170].

After the title and an abrupt introduction (1 : 1-4), there is a succession of poems which can be reduced to five in number : 1 : 5–2 : 7; 2 : 8–3 : 5; 3 : 6–5 : 1; 5 : 2–6 : 3; 6 : 4–8 : 3. Each of them exhibits a rhythm of tension and repose. By tension we mean the different manifestations which indicate the mutual love of the bridegroom and bride and the mutual search which they make for each other. Their efforts end in a mutual possession — which is repose. This, however, will only become final at the end of the fifth poem. The crescendo of feeling which is manifest throughout the whole work is the bond uniting the poems and makes clear that the action, in spite of appearances, moves forward. In 8 : 4-7[a] it reaches its term. The verses which follow are later additions.

Literary genre.

The Canticle is very difficult to interpret, and no other Biblical book, except the Psalter, has given rise to so many hypotheses. Jewish tradition has always understood it as an allegory of the love of God and Israel, and Christian authors have not interpreted it otherwise, except that in place of Israel they have thought of it as referring to the Church, to the Blessed Virgin, or to the soul having arrived at perfection. In the 18th century some authors saw in the Canticle a drama with conjugal fidelity as its theme, an hypothesis which has met with new approval in our own days. The young woman, on having been taken to Solomon's harem, rejects the king's love and prefers a lowly shepherd. The author's purpose would be to show that conjugal love is exclusive, that it is incompatible with divorce, that the consent of the man and woman must be free, and their condition well matched.

In Protestant circles, the current view is that popularized by Budde in 1898 : the Canticle is a collection of secular songs employed at marriage feasts. A number of features are pointed out which recall marriage feasts in the region of Hauran, and parallels in Egyptian and Arab love poems are also cited. Finally, on the basis of some archaeological data, it has been supposed that the Canticle was originally a ritual which regulated in Palestine the cult of the vegetation divinities.

The study of the text itself of this controversial book shows in fact that, while it bears some resemblances to the Egyptian and Arabic love poems, it is essentially, both in content and form, a Biblical composition. There is no need to analyse each of the author's expressions; a glance at the central images, which give all its meaning to the work, reveals that they are traditional and have an eschatological significance : so the king, the shepherd, the flock, the vine, and even the garden, Lebanon, flowering springtime, night, and dawn. A realization of this fact should suffice to reject at once any naturalistic, mythological, purely moral, even merely parabolic interpretation. It brings us back to the ancient interpretation, but furnishes the latter with the exegetical justification which it lacked. It obliges us to introduce a change in perspective of great consequence. When we analyse the text of the Canticle, we are constantly led back to certain key or source passages, derived from the prophets, namely, Os. 2; Jer. 31 : 17 ff.; Isa. 51 : 17 ff.; 52 : 1, 2, 7, 8, 12; and, particularly, 54 : 4-8; 61 : 10-11; 62 : 4-5. Now these texts describe the unfaithful wife's return to favor, as if there were only question of a first and true marriage.

This seems to be the true situation in the Canticle, and the discreet warning with which the last poem closes (8 : 6-7) conveys it in veiled terms. The journey of the bride, accordingly, is that of the return to God after sin. It is made through a succession of incidents in which the divine bridegroom gives himself, but soon withdraws in order to increase the love and desire of her who has abandoned him. These seesaw movements, mutual advances, unforeseen incidents, and disappointments, which hasten to their denouement, connect the Canticle with the dramatic genre.

Finally, it must be noted, this beautiful poem, which is so capricious in appearance, is filled with veiled allusions to the disappointments of the postexilic period. The many disillusions of the time only make men more anxious in their expectation for the definite coming of Our Savior. The glowing expressions of love which rush from the lips of husband and wife, the classic character of the images which they employ, the direct Messianic allusions, and the theme itself which is the object of the book, all characterize it as an essentially eschatological work.

Origin of the book.

The attribution to Solomon appears only in the title. Even if the title is genuine, the attribution is fictitious. The evidence furnished by a study of the language shows definitely that it falls in the postexilic age. There are a number of Aramaisms, Late Hebrew forms of expression, and even two Persian words — *pardes*, " garden " or " paradise " (4 : 13), and *egoz*, " walnut tree " (6 : 11), but there is no trace of Greek influence. The historical allusions suggest a date soon after the rebuilding of the walls of Jerusalem by Nehemias (444).

6. — The Book of Wisdom [1].

Canonicity and division.

The Book of Wisdom, which is written in Greek, is not included in the Hebrew Bible. Hence, Protestants do not receive it as an inspired book. Following the Fathers and tradition, the Council of Trent defined its canonicity [2].

The work is divided into two parts : one didactic (1–9), and the other historical (10–19). The didactic portion sets forth the terrible error and punishment of the sinner (1–2), the hope of the just and the confusion of the wicked, with the lots reserved for both (3–5). The author then explains how, by prayer, he has obtained wisdom, and he describes its properties and its fruits (6–9). The historical part demonstrates from sacred history the consequences of wisdom, and how, because of it, God saves the good and punishes the wicked (10–12). In his further historical application, he deals specifically with idolatry (13–15), and with the deliverance of Israel and the punishment of the Egyptians (16–19).

Translator's note. — [1 Cf. P. W. SKEHAN, " Notes on the Latin Text of the Book of Wisdom ", *CBQ*, 4 (1942), 230-243. A. M. DUBARLE, *Les Sages d'Israël* (Paris, 1946), 187-235. J. REIDER, *The Book of Wisdom : An English Translation with Introduction and Commentary* (New York, 1957; cf. P. W. SKEHAN, *CBQ* [1958], 114-116). Dom H. DUESBERG, *Les Scribes inspirés*, II (Paris, 1939), 441-592].

Translator's note. — [2 For the history of the question of the language, see GOETTSBERGER, *Einleitung in das A. T.*, pp. 268-269].

Teaching [1].

The teaching of Wisdom serves as a prelude to that of grace in the New Testament. Wisdom dwells in holy souls (**1** : 4; **7** : 27), and it is put on a plane with the Spirit of God or the Holy Spirit (**1** : 4-7; **9** : 17). It is a treasure which procures the friendship of God (**7** : 14, 28). Furthermore, since it is God who grants it, one must ask it of Him (**7** : 7; **9**). Even if a man has all other good qualities, without wisdom he is as nothing before God (**9** : 6). Wisdom implies the observance of God's laws and leads to blessed immortality (**6** : 17-20; **8** : 17). Sinners do not possess it. It is noteworthy, too, that this wisdom appears in God as an hypostasis (**7** : 25-28).

At the moment of death sinners lose all and depart into darkness, and judgment for them is terrible (**5**; **7** : 21). For the just, death is only an appearance (**3** : 1-3). They preserve the immortality which wisdom gives (**8** : 17), and which God had in view in creation (**2** : 23, 24). The just are with God (**3** : 1-3, 5-9; **5** : 15-16; **6** : 19). In such a perspective the values of things change : the value of life is no longer to be judged by its length but by its employment (**4** : 7-19), and virtue is worth more than a numerous posterity (**3** : 13-15; **4** : 1). The weighty problem which had filled Ecclesiastes with gloom was resolved.

The author reiterates the thought of the Prophets in his announcement of the conversion of the pagans (**14** : 11-14; **18** : 4). Thus, humanity will resume its pristine destiny, for in the beginning there was no idolatry (**14** : 13).

Its teaching on reward and punishment makes the Book of Wisdom one of the most beautiful and most important works of the Old Testament.

Origin and readers.

The author claims to be addressing an audience of kings (**6** : 1, 9, 21); he speaks of himself as if he were a king (**7** : 1-6;

Translator's note. — [1 Cf. J. P. WEISENGOFF, " Death and Immortality in the Book of Wisdom ", *CBQ* 3 (1941), 104-133; *id.*, " The Impious of Wisdom 2 ", *ibid.*, 11 (1949), 40-65; P. W. SKEHAN, " Isaias and the Teaching of the Book of Wisdom ", *ibid.*, 2 (1940), 289-299; *id.*, " Borrowings from the Psalms in the Book of Wisdom ", *ibid.*, 10 (1948), 384-397].

9 : 7); his wisdom, riches, and knowledge are those of Solomon (**7** : 7-22; cf. 1 Kgs. **5** : 1-14).   His identification of himself as the glorious successor of David is, as in the case of Ecclesiastes, a fiction (**9**, and 1 Kgs. **3** : 4-15).   In actual fact, he was a Hellenistic Jew of the Diaspora who wrote in Greek.   Several Fathers, unaware of the fiction, thought that the Hebrew original had been lost, and attributed the work to Solomon. But Saint Jerome *(Praef. in lib. Salomonis)* and Saint Augustine *(De civ. Dei* **17** : 20) rejected this attribution.   As Saint Jerome had clearly perceived, the book was written in Greek.   The author uses a number of philosophical terms borrowed from the Stoics and the Platonists, like *intelligible* and *subtle spirit* (**7** : 22, 23), and *matter without form* (**11** : 17).   He calls manna *ambrosial nourishment* (**19** : 21).   Like Euhemerus, he explains the pagan divinities as being deified men (**14** : 12-20), or, following the Stoics, as originating through the divinization of the forces of nature (**13** : 1-9).   He has a high regard for the sciences, and perhaps knew the treatises of Aristotle (**7** : 17-20). He is well informed in respect to the various philosophies but is an adherent of none, and he does not attempt to syncretize Jewish and Greek thought, as was subsequently done by Philo. He remains completely loyal to the faith of Israel, but he borrows from Greek thought whatever can serve his own faith and aid him in the expression of his ideas.   He is always very orthodox.   His remarks on the cult of animals (**15** : 18, 19) shows that he lived in Egypt.   He wrote perhaps at Alexandria, the great capital of Hellenistic culture and the principal Jewish center of the Dispersion.

The book must have been composed about the end of the second century or the beginning of the first, roughly between 150 and 50 B. C.   The persecutions mentioned in **2** : 10-20, and the oppression referred to in **15** : 14, allude perhaps to the measures which Ptolemy Physcon took against the Jews who had opposed his government.

Some critics have denied that the book is a unit, and have attributed its two parts to two different authors.   But there is no solid support for this view.

The author writes to instruct the Hellenistic Jews and to sustain them in their faith.   Perhaps he also addresses himself to pagans in order to attract them to Judaism. In that case the veiled and often mysterious manner in which he speaks of the events of sacred history would be intended to pique their curiosity and hold their attention (**10-12**; **16-19**). This technique, which is used by the Sibylline Books, belongs to the midrashic genre (See Ch. VI, *infra*).

7. — Ecclesiasticus [1].

Name, text, and canonicity.

The Hebrews called the book " Ben Sira " (son of Sira) from the name of its author. The Greek version designates it, more explicitly, " The Wisdom of Jesus, Son of Sirach " [2]. Among the Latins the title commonly used is " Ecclesiasticus ", for in the early days of Christianity the book was used extensively in the Christian communities for catechumenal instruction. It was the book of the Church.

The Hebrew text was lost in ancient times, but between 1896 and 1900 a considerable portion of the book in its original language was rediscovered in the course of the investigations which were made in the *Genizah* (room used for storage of discarded texts) of the Synagogue of Ezra in Cairo [3]. The Greek version is the work of the grandson of Ben Sirach who translated the book for the Jews who no longer knew Hebrew.

Ecclesiasticus, which is not included in the Hebrew Bible, is not recognized as inspired by Protestants. But it was received by the Greek-speaking Jews, and from them the Fathers of the Church obtained it. The Council of Trent declared it to be canonical.

Translator's note. — [1 Cf. A. M. DUBARLE, *Les Sages d'Israël* (Paris, 1946), pp. 147-185. Dom H. DUESBERG, *Les scribes inspirés*, II (Paris, 1939), 232-440. M. S. Segal, *Sefer hokmat Ben Sira* (Jerusalem, 1933); *id.*, *Sefer Ben Sira hashalem* (*ibid.*, 1953; with full introduction and commentary); *id.*, art. " Ben Sira ", in *Entzyklop. Miqra'it* 2, 162-169].

Translator's note. — [2 The Greek transcription adds *ch.*, as, *e.g.*, in Ἀκελδαμάχ (Acts **1** : 19), possibly to make the word indeclinable].

Translator's note. — [3 For another portion discovered since, see J. MARCUS, *The Newly Discovered Original Hebrew of Ben Sira* (Eccles. **32** : 16-**34** : 1), *the Fifth Ms., and a Prosodic Version of Ben Sira* (Eccles. **22** : 22-**23** : 9) (Philadelphia, 1931; reprinted from an article in *JQR*, 21 [1931], 223-240)].

Structure and division.

The book opens with a prologue which is not considered part of Scripture. It is a short introduction which the translator added by way of preface to the work in order to explain the aim of his labor, and it contains some interesting details on the translation of the Bible into Greek.

The work is divided into two parts. The first (**1–43**) offers counsels of wisdom on sins to be avoided and virtues to be practiced. This whole first part is directly concerned with moral instruction, recalling in this connection the Book of Proverbs, and especially its first section (**1** : 8-9). The second part (**44–50** : 24) eulogizes the fathers and the great men of Israel, even including, in addition, a few of the patriarchs before the Flood. All these are presented as living examples of virtue. Two short epilogues, one against the Samaritans, and the other on the purpose of the book, and two appendices containing respectively a beautiful prayer composed by the author and an appeal to wisdom, complete the work (**50** : 25–**51**).

Teaching.

The son of Sirach does not examine the problems which were of such concern to the author of Job and to Ecclesiastes. He raises no doubt regarding temporal reward and punishment but expounds this doctrine in calm and concrete fashion (**1** : 12-13; **9** : 11-12; **11** : 14-26, etc.). He has the practical aim of teaching piety and morality.

What he says of wisdom recalls the Book of Proverbs. Wisdom comes from God as a gift (**1** : 2-10), and it renders man pleasing to God. It communicates fear of the Lord and confers numerous advantages (**1** : 14-20; **4** : 11-19; **6** : 18-37; **14** : 20; **15** : 10; **25** : 7-11). It leads to the Law (**24** : 23), and it has a hypostatic character (**24** : 3-17).

God is the creator of the world, and His works reveal His greatness (**16** : 22-28; **42** : 15; **43** : 33). He is just (**15** : 11; **16** : 21), good, and merciful (**17–18** : 13). He is a Father (**51** : 10 Hebr.). Man must fear Him (**1** : 11-30; **2** : 15-18; **10** : 19; **34** : 13-17), love Him (**7** : 30), and put his trust in Him (**2** : 7-11).

Sirach exhorts men to humility (**3** : 17-27), to kindness towards the poor (**7** : 32 ff.; **4** : 7-10; **29** : 1-13), and to almsgiving (**3** : 28; **4** : 6; **7** : 10). But he desires that generosity be shown to the virtuous only (**12** : 1-7). He denounces pride (**6** : 2-4; **10** : 6-18), sins of the tongue (**5** : 9; **6** : 1; **20** : 17-19; **23** : 7-15; **28** : 13-36), lying (**7** : 12, 13; **20** : 23-25), covetousness (**18** : 29; **19** : 3), adultery (**23** : 16-27), and sloth (**22** : 1-2). Man must flee sin (**21** : 1-3; **23** : 1-6), and must not regard himself as secure in sin (**5** : 4-7; **7** : 8, 9, 16). He must not be proud of his riches (**5** : 1-3, 8; **11** : 16-18), but must know how to make good use of them (**13** : 23; **14** : 19). The rich man is egotistical, and therefore prudence is necessary in all relations with him (**13**). Prudence is also highly recommended in relations with women (**9** : 1-9; **42** : 12-14), in various social connections (**8** : 1-16; **9** : 10-18), and in the practice of hospitality (**11** : 27-32). Likewise, sobriety and discretion are to be maintained at festivals (**31** : 12–**32** : 13).

Ecclesiasticus gives advice on family duties : the choice of a wife (**26** : 1-18; **36** : 20-28) and the proper attitude towards her (**7** : 19, 26; **9** : 2; **25** : 12-25), the training of children (**7** : 23, 24; **22** : 3-6; **30** : 1-13), the love of parents (**3** : 12-16; **7** : 27-28), conduct in time of mourning (**38** : 16-23; cf. **22** : 10), and treatment of slaves (**7** : 20-21; **33** : 24-31; **42** : 5-7).

All his moral instruction is inspired by religion, the service of God. The beautiful thought on forgiveness is especially noteworthy (**28** : 1-7). The book abounds in useful and religious counsels which are entirely practicable. With Ben Sirach the national spirit, which had been excluded from Job, Proverbs, and Ecclesiastes, is emphasized in the more specifically Hebrew treatment of wisdom (**35**: 21; **36**: 19; **44**–**50**: 24; cf. **24**: 23; **35**: 1).

Author and date.

The author was from Jerusalem, and he tells us that his name was Jesus, son of Sirach (**50** : 27; cf. the prologue). Hence, he is often called the Siracid. He had travelled much (**34** : 11, 12), had filled high positions, and had undoubtedly served as an ambassador (**51** : 3-7). The lofty idea which he has of his role as sage leads him, as it does certain Egyptian scribes, to scorn manual labor (**38** : 24; **39** : 11). According to the prologue, his grandson went to Egypt in the thirty-eighth year of the reign of Euergetes. There are two Ptolemies who took the name of Euergetes, or Benefactor (cf. Lk. **22** : 25). The reference here is not to Ptolemy III Euergetes I, for he ruled only 25 years (247-222), but Ptolemy VII Euergetes II must therefore be meant. He bore the nickname Physcon (the Fat) or Kakergetes (Evildoer). He ruled from 170 to 154 and again from 145 to 116. The thirty-eighth year would be calculated from 170. The translator, accordingly, went to Egypt in 132. If we take this date as a fixed point of reference, the literary activity of his grandfather can be placed between 175 and 200. Moreover, the high priest Simon, whom the author praises (50), served in his high office from 219 to 199. The book must have been written shortly after that time.

II. — THE BOOKS OF THE NEW TESTAMENT.
[J. HUBY.]

1. — *THE GOSPELS AND THE ACTS OF THE APOSTLES.*

I. — From the Oral Gospel to the Written Gospels.

The beginning of the Gospel. The oral Gospel [1].

The word, " Gospel ", arouses immediately in our minds the image of a book, the Greek text, the Latin Vulgate, or an

---

Translator's note. — [1 Cf. L. CERFAUX, *La voix vivante de l'Evangile au début de l'Eglise* (Tournai and Paris, 1946. B. S. EASTON, *The Gospel before the Gospels* (London, 1928). V. H. STANTON, *The Gospels as Historical Documents* (2 vols., Cambridge, 1901-1910). B. H. STREETER, *The Four Gospels* (London, 1924). X. LÉON-DUFOUR, " Exégèse du Nouveau Testament : Formgeschichte et Redaktionsgeschichte des Evangiles ", *RSR* (1958), 237-269 (an excellent critical survey of recent works). D. E. NINEHAM, " Eye-Witness Testimony and the Gospel-Tradition, I ", *JTS* (1958), 13-25. W. GROUSSOUW, art. " Evangelium ", in Haag, *Bibellexikon*, 449-455. N. A. DAHL, s.v. " Evangelium ", in *Svenskt Bibl. Uppslagsverk*, I, 487-496. R. H. STRAHAN, " The Gospel in the New Testament ", *The Interpreter's Bible*, VII (1951), 3-31. A. M. PERRY, " The Growth of the Gospels ", *ibid.*, 60-74. M. J. LAGRANGE and C. LAVERGNE, *L'Evangile de Jésus-Christ avec la Synopse évangélique* (Paris, 1954; cf. *CBQ* [1955], 639-640). J. JEREMIAS, *The Parables of Jesus* (New York, 1955; cf. *CBQ* [1955], 643-647. On the original German work, *Die Gleichnisse Jesu* [Zurich, 1947], cf. M. MEINERTZ, *Theologische Revue* [1950], 88-93]. L. PIROT, *Paraboles* (Paris, 1949; cf. *Theol. Revue* [1951], 208-209. M. MEINERTZ, *Die Gleichnisse Jesu* (Münster i. W., 1948; cf. *Theol. Revue* [1948], 82 f.). G. VERMÈS, " La littérature rabbinique et le Nouveau Testament ", *Cahiers Sioniens* (1955), 97-123. M. SMITH, *Tannaite Parallels to the Gospels* (Philadelphia, 1951; cf. E. P. ARBEZ, *CBQ* [1952], 191-194). D. DAUBE, *The New Testament and Rabbinic Judaism* (London, 1956; cf. *RB* [1957], 299-300). B. W. HELFGOTT, *The Doctrine of Election in Tannaitic Literature* (New York, 1954; cf. E. P. ARBEZ, *Theological Studies* [1955], 619-621].

English translation. In the first days of Christianity, however, this was not so. Before being a book, the Gospel was a Word; before being written, it was preached; before being read, it was heard. " Faith then depends on hearing, and hearing on the word of Christ " (Rom, 10 : 17). In its beginnings and in its first stage of development, the Gospel was the preaching of Christ, the *spoken* content of the divine message which He announced to men, the Good News (εὐαγγέλιον) of salvation which He offered them.

During His earthly life Christ was the Sower of the Word. He cast it into the hearts of His hearers, and, according to the dispositions which it found there, with different results. It withered through the shallowness of some, it was choked by the passions of others, but it grew and became fruitful in the souls of men of good will. After Pentecost, the Apostles, who even during the life of Christ had made some missionary attempts (Mk. 6 : 7-13), continued this ministry of preaching. Together with prayer and presiding over Christian meetings it was their essential task (Acts 6 : 4). They were the ministers of the Word (Lk. 1 : 2).

In one sense it can be said that this preaching of the Apostles was of wider scope than the *oral* message of Christ. He had announced to men the coming of the Kingdom of God, the conditions necessary for entering and living in this kingdom, the precepts which were to govern the relations of the Apostles with one another, with their Lord and Master, and with the Heavenly Father, the essential institutions and rites for grouping them into a society, the Church as distinct from the Synagogue. But Christ had not told His own earthly history, for this history was in process of being made, and one narrates only what is past. He went about from place to place doing good (Act. 10 : 38), healing sick bodies and sinful souls, engraving, in indelible lines, on the memory of his disciples the image of His goodness, of His mercy, of His purity, and of His ineffable union with His Heavenly Father. Furthermore, the attitudes and actions of Christ in working miracles, passing nights in prayer, practicing absolute poverty, suffering and dying for men, his brothers, belonged, in equal measure with his spoken message, to the revelation of the Incarnate Word. " Because Christ is the Word of God ", says Saint Augustine, " his action itself is a word for us " [1], i.e., it contains some teaching or instruction.

Charged with transmitting to men the revelation of the Son of God, what they had heard with their ears, seen with their eyes, and touched with their hands, relative to the Word of life (cf. 1 Jn. 1 : 1), the Apostles could not confine themselves to the preaching of the precepts laid down by Jesus and to public announcement of the statements He had made concerning His mission and His person, but they had also to bear witness to His actions, to describe the outstanding features of His life, especially of His public ministry, " what He had done ", as well as " what He had taught " (Acts 1 : 1). All this constituted " the things about the Lord Jesus ", τὰ περὶ τοῦ Ἰησοῦ (Acts 18 : 25–28 : 31).

Contrary to what the adherents of the *Formgeschichte* School [2] maintain, the primitive oral tradition, the influence of which on the formation of the written Gospels they acknowledge along with us, should not be identified with some popular tradition nor should it be considered the spontaneous and undivided product of the creative community, i.e., of everybody and of no one in particular. The tradition upon which our Gospels is based, and that part of it especially which is most contested by radical critics because of its supernatural element, namely, the accounts of miracles, stems from definite individuals, the first preachers of the Word, and among these individuals, more especially from an outstanding personality, Simon Peter, the head of the Twelve. As we shall see later, the Gospel of Saint Mark has kept the imprint of this characteristic influence. This tradition was not simply the mirror of the faith of the

---

[1] *In Joannis evang.*, tract. 24, 2.

[2] A term which we may translate with F. M. BRAUN as " History of the Gospel tradition through the examination of literary forms ". On this method, see F. M. BRAUN, *Où en est le problème de Jésus?* (Brussels and Paris, 1932), pp. 215-265; and *Formgeschichte (école de la)* in *DBV, Suppl.* (1936), II, 312-317, with bibliography. [See also : V. TAYLOR, *The Formation of the Gospel Tradition* (London and New York, 1933); S. E. DONLON, S. J., " The Form-critics, the Gospels and Saint Paul ", *CBQ*, 6 (1944), 306-325; P. BENOIT, O. P., " Réflexions sur la *Formgeschichtliche Methode* ", *RB* (1946), 481-521; R. M. LIGHTFOOT, *History and Interpretations in the Gospels* (London, 1935); E. B. REDLICH, *Form Criticism : its Value and Limitations* (London, 1939); C. H. DODD, *History and the Gospel* (London, 1938); M. DIBELIUS, *From Tradition to Gospel* (London, 1934). See also the artide of Léon-Dufour cited *supra*].

first community and of the worship it rendered to Christ, but it contained the facts of the life of Christ which had motivated this faith and this worship. It is purely gratuitous to insist that the first disciples of Christ were so completely absorbed in the adoration of His person, that they took no interest in His earthly history.

The apostolic Catechesis.

Since the Apostles could not relate everything in full, especially in their public preaching, — a form of presentation which is poorly suited to exhaustive treatments, they were naturally led to choose, among the actions and words of Christ, those which appeared to them most fitting to make Him known. Thus, there arose among the ministers of the Word a type of teaching which is uniform in its broad lines, a common manner of preaching the doctrine and the life of Jesus. This instruction has been given the name catechesis (a noun derived from the verb κατηχέω, used in Lk. **1** : 4; Acts **18** : 25; Gal. **6** : 6).

As we have already noted, there seems to be no question that in determining the general content of this catechesis, the members of the apostolic college, and especially Saint Peter, played a predominant role. Acts gives us a résumé of the first discourse of the head of the Apostles, and presents him as the principal preacher of the early Church. One of Peter's discourses, namely, that which he delivered before the centurion Cornelius, and his relatives and friends, is particularly significant, for it contains a sketch, as it were, of what must have been the earliest catechesis : " You know what took place throughout Judea; for he began in Galilee after the baptism preached by John : how God anointed Jesus of Nazareth with the Holy Spirit and with power, and he went about doing good and healing all who were in the power of the devil : for God was with him. And we are witnesses of all that he did in the country of the Jews and in Jerusalem; and yet they killed him, hanging him on a tree. But God raised him on the third day and caused him to be plainly seen, not by all the people, but by witnesses designated beforehand by God, that is by us, who ate and drank with him after he had risen from the dead " (Acts **10** : 37-41).

This résumé of the catechesis outlines also the plan which Saint Mark's Gospel will follow, with its division into four parts : 1° the preaching of John the Baptist and the baptism of Jesus; 2° the ministry of Jesus in Galilee; 3° the passage from Galilee into Judea and to Jerusalem; 4° the passion, death, resurrection of Christ, and His appearances after He had risen.

The two other Gospels, namely, of Saint Matthew and Saint Luke — the Gospel of Saint John is considered apart because of its peculiar character — will give more space to the discourses of Christ, but will retain, however, this same framework. It is possible to arrange a large part of their content in three parallel columns and to include it under one comprehensive glance *(synopsis)*. Hence the term, Synoptic Gospels, which has been given to them and has become current in New Testament criticism since the *Synopsis Evangeliorum* of Griesbach (1774; 2nd ed., 1796-1806; 4th ed., 1822).

The written Gospels.

Though we can affirm that the preaching of the Gospel preceded and effectively prepared for its commitment to writing, it is not possible, however, because of the lack of documents, to follow in detail the passage from preaching to transcription. According to ancient tradition, Matthew composed a first draft of the catechesis in Aramaic for the use of the Palestinian Jews who spoke that language. Then, in the Hellenistic circles of Jerusalem, and especially when the Gospel passed beyond Palestine to reach the Jews of the Dispersion in the Greco-Roman world and their " God fearing " followers among the pagans (Acts **10** : 22; **13** : 16, 26, 43, 50; **16** : 14 etc.), the need of *Greek* translations of the Gospel and of *written* translations quickly made itself felt [1]. Saint Luke tells us

---

Translator's note. — [1 The question of the Semitic substratum of the Gospels has been studied extensively in the last few years especially. Cf. e.g., P. JOÜON, S. J., *L'Evangile de Notre Seigneur Jésus Christ* (Paris, 1930); C. C. TORREY, *Our Translated Gospels* (New York, 1936); id., *The Four Gospels* (New York, 1933; 2nd ed., 1947); id., *Documents of the Primitive Church* (New York, 1941); C. F. BURNEY, *The Poetry of Our Lord* (Oxford, 1925); id., *The Aramaic Origin of the Fourth Gospel* (Oxford, 1922); M. BLACK, *An Aramaic Approach to the Gospels and Acts* (Oxford, 1946; cf. Dom H. CONNOLLY, *Downside Review*, 1947, 25-37; and P. BENOIT, O. P., *RB*, 1947, 440-443); E. C. COLWELL, *The Greek of the Fourth Gospel* (Chicago, 1931); A. T. OLMSTEAD, " Could an Aramaic Gospel be Written "? *Journal of Near Eastern Studies*, I (1942), 41-75, and II (1943), 1-34; E. J. GOODSPEED, " The Possible Aramaic Gospel ", *ibid.*, (1942), 315-340;

in the prologue of his Gospel that before him, " Many —
or several (πολλοί) — have undertaken to draw up a narrative
concerning the things that have been fulfilled among us, even as
they who from the beginning were eyewitnesses and ministers
of the word have handed them down to us " (Lk. 1 : 1-2).

Among those who preceded Saint Luke in narrating the
story of Christ we may cite Saint Matthew, who wrote in
Aramaic, and Saint Mark, who wrote in Greek the catechesis
of Saint Peter. But they were not the only ones to constitute
the " many " of which the Third Gospel speaks, especially
since Saint Luke must have been thinking in particular of persons
writing in Greek. Moreover, it is not established that these
writings had the same proportions as our present Gospels and
covered the whole history of Christ from His baptism by John
the Baptist to His passion and resurrection. As we have said
elsewhere [1], it may be conjectured that, before any attempt
was made to compose a continuous history of Christ's ministry,
incomplete or partial accounts of His words and actions were
written : groupings of sentences analogous to that which forms
the Sermon on the Mount in our First Gospel, or narratives
forming a definite unit, like the history of the Passion. The
question arises why, out of all these first productions of Christian
literature, our present Gospels have alone survived and have
been retained by the Church. They were probably the most
complete of the written narratives, and, as has been conjectured
with good probability, they had drawn upon earlier sources.
Thus, Matthew and Luke, for the discourses which they have
in common, suppose, if not an absolutely identical source (the
hypothetical document Q of the critics — so-called from
the German Quelle, " source "), at least documents closely
related to one another, whether they derive from the same
written source or from the same oral catechesis. Some have

S. J. FEIGIN, " The Original Language of the Gospels ", ibid., (1943), 187-197;
H. F. D. SPARKS, The Semitisms of Saint Luke's Gospel, Journal of Theological
Studies, 44 (1943), 129-138; J. BONSIRVEN, S. J., " Hoc est corpus meum ",
Biblica (1948), 205-219; id., " Les Aramaïsmes de S. Jean l'Evangéliste, ibid.,
(1949), 405-431. See the excellent survey by J. VERGOTE, " Grec Biblique ",
in DBV, Suppl., vol. III (1938), 1320-1369, especially 1338 ff., and also,
J. H. MOULTON, Grammar of New Testament Greek, vol. I (Edinburgh 1906;
1908; 1919), and vol. II, edited by W. F. HOWARD, (1919-1929). The Appendix
of vol. II contains a treatment of Semitisms].

[1] J. HUBY, L'Evangile et les Evangiles (Paris, 1940), p. 43.

conjectured in like manner that Luke had a special source for those portions of the Gospel teaching and narrative which are proper to him (Lk. 9 : 51-18 : 14, and some scenes of the Passion).

But the decisive reason for the choice of the Church has been based on the fact that our four Gospels presented themselves as vested with apostolic authority. Two of them were attributed to Apostles themselves, Matthew and John, and the two others to immediate disciples of the Apostles with whom they remained in close contact : Mark, who reported the catechesis of Peter, and Luke, who reflected the teachings of Paul. Written in the Church and for the Church, when it already existed as a society founded by Christ and governed by the Apostles, the Gospels could not take the place of its living magisterium. The Church, as faithful guardian of the deposit of revelation, whether committed to writing or not, remained its sole authorized interpreter in matters of faith and morals.

Even when the principal features of Christ's message were put into writing in various little books and by different authors, the Church retained very definitely the feeling that there was basically only *one* Gospel, as Christ Himself is also one. It knew only one good message of salvation, presented under four forms, *according to* Matthew, *according to* Mark, *according to* Luke, *according to* John. This fact explains the origin of the term " tetramorphic " as applied to the Gospel in Saint Irenaeus (*Adversus Hæreses* III, 11, 18).

Our Gospels arose under circumstances which stamp them with a strongly marked originality, and they constitute a new type in general literature. " None of the forms of classical literature or even of popular Greek literature served them as a model " [1]. While Saint Justin has called the Gospels the " Memoirs of the Apostles ", intending by this title to compare them to the *Memorabilia* of Xenophon on Socrates, this comparison must not be pushed too far [2]. The " Memoirs " of

---

[1] A. PUECH, *Histoire de la littérature grecque chrétienne* (Paris, 1928), vol. I, 60.
   Translator's note. — [2 Cf. J. A. KLEIST, S. J., *The Memoirs of Saint Peter* (Milwaukee, 1932; cf. the review-article on this book by J. DONOVAN, S. J., in *American Ecclesiastical Review*, 89 (1933), 126-138, and Father Kleist's reply, *ibid.*, 425-429); *id.*, " Rereading the Papias Fragment on Saint Mark ", *Saint Louis University Studies*, Ser. A : Humanities I (1945), 1-17; P. C. SANDS, *The Literary Genius of the New Testament* (London, 1932)].

Xenophon acquaint us with the thought of Socrates on different subjects, and the occasions for these teachings, but they do not present a biography of Socrates, even in outline. The Gospels, on the contrary, without giving a complete biography of Christ, sketch the principal features of His history.

The Gospels were not written directly to defend Christ against the attacks of enemies from without. They are the expositions of sincere witnesses who are convinced that the simple presentation of the life and doctrine of Christ will receive a warm welcome from souls of good will. " The Gospels ", says Father de Grandmaison, " are less apologies than epiphanies; they aim at nourishing the faith, at communicating it as a vital contagion, and at developing its pre-existing germ in those who are capable and worthy of receiving it " [1].

Along with these common traits which give them a family likeness, each of our Gospels has its own proper individuality, which we shall describe briefly.

2. — The Gospel according to Saint Matthew. [2]

Authenticity.

The Gospel according to Saint Matthew occupies first place in our editions of the New Testament, and it occupies this position also in the great majority of manuscripts. In giving

---

[1] *Jesus Christ*, Engl. trans. (New York, 1934), vol. I, 53.

Translator's note. — [2 Cf. A. SCHLATTER, *Der Evangelist Matthäus* (Stuttgart, 1929). A. H. Mc NEILE, *The Gospel according to Saint Matthew* (London, 1915). B. W. BACON, *Studies in Matthew* (New York, 1930). Th. SOIRON, *Die Logia Jesu* (Münster i. W., 1916). C. H. KRAELING, *John the Baptist* (New York, 1951). R. GUTZWILLER, *Jesus der Messias : Christus im Matthäusevangelium* (Einsiedeln, 1949; cf. *Theologische Revue* [1951], 103-104). B. C. BUTLER, O. S. B., *The Originality of St. Matthew* (Cambridge, 1951; cf. *Scripture* [1952], 72-76). E. FASCHER, *Jesus und der Satan* (Halle, 1949; cf. *CBQ* [1952], 387-389). Dom J. DUPONT, *Les Béatitudes : problème littéraire, message doctrinal* (Louvain, 1954; cf. *Cahiers Sioniens* [1955], 174-177). A. DESCAMPS, *Les justes et la justice dans les Evangiles et le Christianisme primitif hormis la doctrine proprement paulinienne* (Louvain, 1950; cf. *CBQ* [1954], 107-111). E. S. MAY, " Translation of Monetary Terms in St. Matthew's Gospel ", *CBQ* (1956), 140-143. M. MEINERTZ, " Das Vaterunser ", *Theologische Revue* (1949), 1-6. L. CERFAUX, " La mission de Galilée dans la tradition synoptique ", *EThL* (1951), 369-389; *ibid.* (1952), 629-647. K. H. SCHELKLE, *Die Passion Jesu in der Verkündigung des Neuen Testaments : Ein Beitrag zur Formgeschichte und zur Theologie des N. T.* (Heidelberg, 1949). A. PELLETIER, " La tradition synoptique du voile déchiré à la lumière des réalités archéologiques ", *RSR* (1958), 161-180].

it first place, Christian antiquity intended to indicate chronological priority. This does not mean that the early Christians regarded our actual *Greek* Gospel as earlier than Saint Mark's or Saint Luke's, but they were in agreement in looking upon Saint Matthew's Gospel as a translation of a Semitic original which was itself in date the earliest of our Gospels. They assigned its authorship to Matthew the publican, who had become one of the Twelve.

A number of convergent indications demonstrates the solid foundation of this tradition. The title κατὰ Ματθαῖον, which was inscribed as the title of the Gospel, at least from the middle of the second century, bears witness to the unanimous conviction of the Church at that date. Later, this attribution is confirmed by the testimony of the most important ecclesiastical writers at the end of the second century (Irenaeus in Gaul) and in the first half of the third (Tertullian, and then Saint Cyprian in Africa; Clement of Alexandria and Origen in Egypt; Saint Hippolytus at Rome).

But already before 150, the Gospel of Matthew was recognized in the Church as having apostolic authority, and it is by virtue of this fact that it was cited, without the express name of the author, by Clement of Rome, the Didache, Ignatius of Antioch, Polycarp, and the Epistle of Barnabas. One of these ancient ecclesiastical writers, Papias, Bishop of Hierapolis in Phrygia, has a particularly interesting text on the work of Saint Matthew. Papias had composed *ca.* 125-130 five books entitled *Explanation of the Oracles of the Lord*. The work is not extant, but Eusebius in his *Ecclesiastical History* (III, **39**) has preserved some fragments of it. After having transcribed Papias' remarks on the Gospel of Mark, Eusebius adds : " Concerning Matthew, here is what is said [in Papias] : ' So Matthew made a record of the Oracles of the Lord in the Hebrew tongue and others have translated them, each as well as he could ' " [1]. It is very probable that Papias received this information from the same

Translator's note. — [1 Cf. J. DONOVAN, S. J., *The Logia in Ancient and Recent Literature* (Cambridge, 1924); J. A. KLEIST, S. J., *The Didache, Epistle of Barnabas, Epistles and Martyrdom of Polycarp, Fragments of Papias, Epistle to Diognetus*, Westminster, Md., 1948 (Ancient Christian Writers, edited by J. Quasten and J. Plumpe, vol. 6), pp. 115 ff. and 204 ff.; E. MASSOUX, *Influence de l'Évangile de saint Matthieu sur la littérature chrétienne avant saint Irénée* (Louvain-Gembloux, 1950)].

source which he used for the Second Gospel, i.e., John the Presbyter, or the Elder. For Eusebius, who on this point differs from Saint Irenaeus, this John whose reminiscences were recorded by Papias, is not John the Apostle, but another John, perhaps an immediate disciple of the Lord, but certainly a man of the first Christian generation who had known the Apostles.

According to this testimony, which carries us back to the first century A. D., the work of Matthew had been composed in " the Hebrew tongue ". By this expression, as in several passages in the New Testament (Jn. 5 : 2; 19 : 13, 17, 20; 20 : 16; Acts 21 : 40; 22 : 6; 26 : 14), must be understood the language spoken at the time in Palestine, and which Jesus had used. This was not Hebrew proper, but Aramaic, which had gradually supplanted Hebrew after the Babylonian conquest. A more delicate problem is the meaning of the term Papias used to designate the work of Saint Matthew, " The Oracles " (τὰ λόγια). Does the passage mean that Matthew composed only a collection of the Lord's discourses, without a narrative section? Neither Eusebius, who had Papias' work before him, nor, any other witness of Christian antiquity considered such an interpretation. Many thought that Papias, when he spoke of " Oracles ", was referring only to that part of Saint Matthew's work which he had commented upon, and which constituted its most characteristic element and the best arranged, in contrast to Mark, " who wrote exactly, but without putting this material in order, all that he recalled of the words or actions of the Lord ".

But this first interpretation of *Logia* in the exclusive sense of " discourses " is not necessary. " According to the use of the word in the Septuagint, the New Testament, and the early Church, a broader signification of *Logia*, comprising things said or done by the Lord, is perfectly possible " [1]. The distinction made in Papias' text between Matthew and Mark does not mean that Matthew had collected only the discourses of the Lord while Mark had made a record of both discourses and deeds, but that Matthew, as distinct from Mark, had followed an orderly, didactic arrangement.

---

[1] G. KITTEL, *Theologisches Wörterbuch* (Stuttgart, 1938), vol. IV, p. 144, s. v. λόγιον, ll. 44 ff. It is to be noted that the Syriac version of Eusebius, *Hist. Eccl.*, III, 39, 16, translates τὰ λόγια by " Gospel ".

This Aramaic Gospel was translated into Greek during apostolic times, for Papias' text indicates that several tried their hands in this work of translation. One of these versions — Saint Jerome tells us that he did not know its author — prevailed, and, before the end of the first century, it acquired an official place in the Church. In retaining the title, " Gospel according to Saint Matthew ", for this Greek version, the Church affirmed its substantial identity with the Aramaic original. This does not eliminate the possibility of the translator's use of the Second Gospel to some extent, especially for the narrative sections. He may have borrowed from Mark, " along with certain episodic features, a number of expressions which could assist him in the difficult task of translating from Aramaic into Greek " [1].

Yet, whatever may be the nature of this dependance, which is difficult to determine precisely in detail, the translator knew how to preserve the proper character of the original, namely, the doctrinal and literary unity which was its distinctive mark.

Date of composition and for whom intended.

The Gospel of Saint Matthew, written in Aramaic, certainly before the destruction of Jerusalem in the year 70 — and probably a decade earlier, was composed for Palestinian readers. This fact can be deduced from the language of the work, and it is expressly affirmed by the testimonies of Irenaeus [2], Origen, Eusebius, and Saint Jerome.

Characteristic features.

The composition of the First Gospel corresponds to Papias' description. It follows an order which is much more didactic than chronological [3]. Saint Matthew, of course, does not ignore all chronology, but he confines himself to a few essential points of reference : the gospel of the infancy, the preparation for Jesus' ministry through the preaching of John the Baptist,

---

[1] L. DE GRANDMAISON, *Jesus Christ*, Engl. trans., vol. I, p. 117.

Translator's note. — [2] Cf. J. L. CURRAN, S. J., " Saint Irenaeus and the Dates of the Synoptics ", *CBQ*, (1943), 33-46; 160-178; 301-310; 445-457].

Translator's note. — [3] Cf. F. M. CATHERINET, " Y a-t-il un ordre chronologique dans l'évangile de saint Matthieu ", in *Mélanges E. Podechard* (Lyon, 1945), pp. 27-36].

the baptism of Jesus and His temptation in the desert, the ministry of Jesus in Galilee, the passage from Galilee into Judea and Jerusalem, the passion, death, and resurrection of Jesus, and His apparitions. But within these divisions, except in the case of the beginning (the gospel of the infancy, and the preparation for Jesus' ministry) and of the end (Jesus' going up to Jerusalem, His passion, and His resurrection), no strictly chronological order is observed in the facts related. This statement is valid for all that concerns the ministry of Jesus in Galilee, i.e., the largest portion of the First Gospel (4 : 12–19 : 1). We may note, it is true, and especially through the help furnished by a comparison with Saint Mark, some indications of a historical development : Jesus first preaches the Kingdom of God (4 : 17), He encounters an incredulous opposition (9 : 34–12 : 50), He withdraws from His people and manifests His design of founding His Church (16 : 13-20).

What is much more striking, however, is the didactic ordering of the words and miracles into distinct units. Five groupings of discourses are immediately evident : 5 : 1–7 : 28, the Sermon on the Mount; 10 : 5–11 : 1, instructions to the disciples sent out as missionaries; 13 : 1-51, parables on the Kingdom of God; 18 : 1–19 : 1, the practice of the Christian virtues, humility and charity; 24 : 1–26 : 1, an eschatological discourse. Each of these groups is introduced with a short setting, and closes with a kind of stereotyped formula (7 : 28; 11 : 1; 13 : 53; 19 : 1; 26 : 1). Chapter 23, in like manner, may be regarded as a short summary of the reproaches which Jesus addressed to the Scribes and Pharisees.

By an analogous procedure, after Jesus in the Sermon on the Mount has presented His teaching on the Kingdom of God, ten miracles are grouped in an order which does not reproduce their historical sequence as it appears in Saint Mark. They are gathered into a sheaf of arguments to accredit the person of Jesus. In contrast to Saint Mark, Saint Matthew drops the merely picturesque details and gives only the essential factual characteristics which are necessary for proof. The conjunction, *then* (τότε), so dear to Saint Matthew (90 examples), is therefore to be interpreted in these cases as a literary, editorial connective.

Within these groupings themselves, critics have noted the arrangement of sentences according to chosen numbers : three

or seven [1]. All these arrangements facilitated memorizing on
the part of both preachers and hearers. They were suggested
by a practice in use in rabbinical instruction, but not among
the Greeks.

Other characteristic features in Matthew's work also make
us think of the Jewish world, and especially that of Palestine.
They confirm the testimony of ancient tradition concerning
the people for whom the First Gospel was intended. Of the
three Synoptic Gospels, Saint Matthew's is the most Palestinian
in its local color, in the use of expressions traditional in Israel,
and in the allusions to Jewish manners and customs which
the Evangelist thinks it unnecessary to explain. Burkitt has
said that the author is " a Christian Rabbi, although doubtless
he would have refused this title ". He retains most carefully
the expressions which recalled the divine favors to the Jewish
people : Palestine is " the land of Israel " (**2** : 20, 21); its cities
are " the cities of Israel " (**10** : 23); its inhabitants, " Israel "
(**9** : 33) or " the house of Israel " (**10** : 6; **15** : 24); its God, " the
God of Israel " (**15** : 31); its capital, Jerusalem, is " the holy
city " (**4** : 5; **27** : 53); the Jewish people whom God wishes to
save through Christ is " his people " (**2** : 6); the Israelites are
" the children of the Kingdom " (**8** : 12), the first called; Jesus,
during His earthly life, normally limits His mission and that
of His Apostles " to the lost sheep of the house of Israel "
(**15** : 24), and it is only exceptionally that He enters into relations
with non-Israelites (**15** : 22-28).

To this vocabulary derived from Judaism belong likewise
expressions such as " kingdom of heaven " instead of " kingdom
of God ", in keeping with the Jewish usage of substituting the
term, heaven, for the all-holy name of Yahweh, " the
consummation of the world ", " the Father who is in heaven ",
" flesh and blood " in the sense of purely natural powers, the
metaphors of the " yoke " of doctrine, and of " binding " and
of " loosing " [2], " the gates of Hell " to designate the infernal
powers or the power of death, the description of hell by " the
exterior darkness, the weeping, and gnashing of teeth ". All
these locutions are found in Jewish writers.

---

[1] See the examples given in Chapter VI, GENRES, pp. 521-522.
Translator's note. — [[2] Cf. G. LAMBERT, S. J., " Lier-délier ", *Vivre et Penser* 3
(= *RB*, 1945), 91-103].

Addressing Jews, whether already converted to Christianity
or not, the Evangelist carefully collects the statements of Jesus
which stress the continuity of the Old and New Testaments.
When in the Sermon on the Mount Jesus proclaims the charter
of the Kingdom of God which He has come to establish, He
contrasts it with the Old Law, not so much for the purpose
of opposing precepts with precepts as of showing in the New
Law the fulfillment of the Old : " Do not think that I have
come to destroy the Law or the Prophets [i.e., the whole
dispensation of the Old Testament]; " I have not come to
destroy, but to fulfill " (5 : 17).   The commandments of the
Decalogue are not abolished, but they are made more penetrating
and internal in their meaning and application, becoming now
not only the norm of exterior action, but of the intimate thoughts
and desires of the mind and heart.   The justice of Jesus'
disciples should surpass that of the Scribes and Pharisees, but
this higher justice is reduced in the end to a more profound
understanding and a more perfect practice of the two fundamental precepts of the Old Law : the precept of the love of God
and the precept of the love of neighbor.

The end pursued by the Evangelist is likewise adapted to
readers of Jewish origin, namely, to show that Jesus of Nazareth,
although rejected by His people and especially by the heads
of the nation, is the Messias who has come to establish the
Kingdom of God.   As the Messias, He is the Son of David, the
heir of the promises, in whom the messianic prophecies are
fulfilled.   At the beginning of the Gospel the genealogy
emphasizes His relationship to David and His royal dignity.
The same apologetic intent is evident in the gospel of the
infancy : He whom the angel announces to Joseph, whom the
Magi have come from the East to seek and whom Herod pursues,
is the king of the Jews (2 : 2), the leader promised by God,
who is to free the people of Israel not from the Roman yoke,
but from the servitude of sin (1 : 21).   In the course of the
public career of Jesus, Saint Matthew likes to emphasize His
prerogatives as the Messias and Son of David (12 : 23; 20 : 30,
31; 21 : 5, 9).   To the proof from miracles, he adds another
argument which particularly impressed Jewish readers — that
based on the prophecies.   He insists on these much more than
the other Evangelists : out of twelve citations of prophetical

texts, only one is common to Mark and Luke, the others being exclusively his own.

Although rejected by His nation, Jesus will be, nevertheless, the founder of the Kingdom of God, which will extend beyond the borders of Israel over the entire world. The Church, founded by Christ on the Apostle Peter as its foundation (**16** : 18), will be the visible form of the kingdom here below. Like the other Gospels, that of Saint Matthew has a universal character. But as the work of an author who had to put Judaeo-Christian readers on guard against the attraction of Jewish worship and the objections of their former co-religionists, it is differentiated by its more pronounced opposition to Pharisaism and to the Synagogue, and by a more vivid presentation of the idea of the Church.

The Messianic Kingdom is not national and earthly, but spiritual and universal. So the Messias who founds it is not a mere descendant of David according to the flesh, or a victorious king in the manner of earthly conquerors. He is the Son of David, but also his Lord (**22** : 43-45). He is the Messias, the Son of the living God (**16** : 16). He is the Son to whom all things have been delivered by the Father, who alone knows the Father in His innermost being, as He Himself is known only by the Father (**11** : 27). He is the only Son, superior to all the prophets (**21** : 34-38). He is the Son of Man, exalted by His resurrection and sitting at the right hand of God the Father, and He will come again upon the clouds of heaven to judge the world (**26** : 63-64). In the bosom of the Trinity He is the Son equal to the Father and the Holy Ghost, ruling heaven and earth, and watching over the growth of His Church until the end of the world (**28** : 18-20). Thus, in a Palestinian framework, this Gospel contains a divine mystery which transcends the limits of space and time.

3. — The Gospel according to Saint Mark [1].

Authenticity.

Ancient tradition is unanimous in attributing the Second Gospel to a disciple of the Apostles, Mark, and, except for some eccentrics who in the accounts of Christian origins see only fiction and myth, modern critics, even those of radical views, no longer contest this attribution.

There is hardly any doubt that the Second Evangelist is the same person as the Mark, or, more exactly, John Mark, to give him his double Semitic and Graeco-Roman name, who is mentioned in several passages of the New Testament (Acts 12 : 12, 25; 13 : 5, 13; 15 : 37, 39; Col. 4 : 10; Phil. 24; 2 Tim. 4 : 11; 1 Pet. 5 : 13). He was the son of a woman of Jerusalem, named Mary, whose home served as a meeting place for the first Christians. When Saint Peter, who had been imprisoned by order of the Jewish King Herod Agrippa I in the year 44, was miraculously freed from his chains, he went straight from his prison " to the house of Mary, the mother of John who was surnamed Mark, where many had gathered together and were praying " (Acts 12 : 12). Mark was a cousin of Barnabas, one of the most prominent missionaries in the primitive Church, and was brought by him to Antioch. Thence, about the year 45, he went as a helper of Barnabas and Paul on their first great apostolic journey. He accompanied them across the island of Cyprus and to the shore of Asia Minor. At Perga in Pamphylia, Mark, for reasons unknown to us, left his companions and went back to Jerusalem. This departure offended Saint Paul and was later the cause of his passing disagreement with Barnabas. When, about the year 50, the two apostles were preparing to undertake a new journey, Barnabas wished to take Mark along. Paul refused with the result that, finally, each went his own way. Later Mark returned to Paul's good graces, for he is mentioned among his co-workers

Pontif. Inst. Bibl., 1937; cf. L. CERFAUX, Ephem. Theol. Lov. (1938), 120 ff.); A. MENZIES, The Earliest Gospel (London, 1910); W. C. ALLEN, The Gospel according to Saint Mark (London, 1915); H. B. SWETE, The Gospel according to Saint Mark (3rd ed., London, 1920); E. KLOSTERMANN, in Lietzmann's Handbuch (3rd ed., Tübingen, 1936); E. LOHMEYER, in Meyer's Kommentar (10th ed., Tübingen, 1937); B. W. BACON, The Beginnings of the Gospel Story (New Haven, 1909); id., The Gospel of St. Mark (ibid., 1925); J. M. C. CRUM, Saint Mark's Gospel (Cambridge, 1936). See also the series of studies on Saint Mark's Gospel by C. H. TURNER, in Journal of Theol. Studies (1925-1928). J. M. ROBINSON, " The Problem of History in Mark " (London, 1957; cf. JThS [1958], 126-127; CBQ [1957], 548-550). L. VAGANAY, " L'absence du Sermon sur la Montagne chez saint Marc ", RB (1951), 5-46. G. R. BEASLEY-MURRAY, Jesus and the Future : An Examination of the Eschatological Discourse, Mark 13... (London, 1954). V. TAYLOR, The Gospel according to Saint Mark (London, 1952)].

in his Epistles to the Colossians (4 : 10) and to Philemon (24), and in the Second Epistle to Timothy (4 : 11).

Mark was also a co-worker of Saint Peter, who had known him at Jerusalem in the house of Mary his mother, and had perhaps baptized him. When he was writing his first epistle from Rome, Peter had with him Mark, whom he calls " his son " (1 Pet. 5 : 13).

It is to this collaboration of Mark with Peter that tradition has assigned the composition of the Second Gospel. The first, and most explicit, testimony is that of Papias of Hierapolis in reporting the words of John the Presbyter or the Elder :

" The Presbyter said also : ' When Mark became the interpreter of Peter, he wrote down, though by no means with full detail, as much as he accurately remembered of the words and works of the Lord; for [1] he had neither heard the Lord nor followed Him, but he subsequently joined Peter, as I said. Now, Peter did not intend to give a complete exposition of the Lord's ministry, but delivered his instructions to suit the varying needs of the people. It follows, then, that Mark was guilty of no blunder if he wrote, simply to the best of his recollections, an incomplete account. For, of one matter he took forethought — not to omit anything he had heard or to falsify anything ' " (in Eusebius, *Hist. Eccl.* III, **39**, 15; Kleist's translation).

About 155, Saint Justin in his *Dialogue with Trypho* (**106**) cites the Second Gospel as " the Memoirs " of Peter (or of Jesus) [2]. After him, Saint Irenaeus about 180, Tertullian and Clement of Alexandria at the beginning of the third century, and, a little later, Origen affirm as an unquestioned tradition that Mark wrote his Gospel as he heard it from Peter.

Date and place of composition. For whom intended.

There is, however, disagreement on a point of chronology. According to Clement of Alexandria, it was during the lifetime of Peter that the Christians of Rome asked Mark to commit to writing the catechesis of the Prince of the Apostles. Irenaeus,

---

[1] What follows is considered rather a personal reflection of Papias.
[2] Cf. LAGRANGE, *Histoire ancienne du Canon du Nouveau Testament* (Paris, 1932), pp. 31-32.

on the contrary, puts this composition after the martyrdom of Saint Peter and Saint Paul. Whatever opinion be adopted, it is certain that the Second Gospel was written before the year 70 [1].

Tradition has made Rome the scene of the composition of the Second Gospel. Nothing in the work contradicts this possibility, and several indications confirm it. The author, certainly, writes for people living outside Palestine and who are not all of Jewish origin, explaining for them not only Aramaic expressions (3 : 17; 5 : 41; 7 : 11; 15 : 22, 34), but also Jewish customs and practices (7 : 3-4; 14 : 12; 15 : 42). He supposes that the two sons of Simon of Cyrene, Alexander and Rufus, are known to his readers (15 : 21). Rufus may well be the same Rufus whom Saint Paul greets among the Christians at Rome (Rom. 16 : 13), but whom he has known elsewhere with his mother, probably in Judea. Significant also, though not decisive, are the Latin words in Mark's vocabulary, the two most notable cases being 12 : 42 and 15 : 16 where a Greek word is explained by a Latin equivalent. If these Latinisms " do not prove incontrovertibly that the Second Gospel was written at Rome, they suggest at least that the author was more familiar with the Latin world than a Palestinian Greek ordinarily was, and everything would be easily explained if he had written at Rome " [2].

Integrity.

The question of the integrity of the Second Gospel is raised only in respect to its close (16 : 9-21). In verse 8, the account of Christ's resurrection stops with this sentence : The women " said nothing to anyone, for they were afraid ". We get the impression of a story brusquely interrupted. What follows does not really continue it, being a résumé of several apparitions of the risen Christ which are recounted at greater length in John and Luke. This résumé is introduced without any connection with what precedes, and in its narrative form and style it departs from the rest of the Gospel. The manuscript tradition bears witness to uncertainties in the transmission

---

[1] *Translator's note.* — [¹ Cf. the article by J. L. CURRAN cited on p. 392 above].
[2] LAGRANGE, *Evangile selon saint Marc* (4th ed., Paris, 1929), Introduction, p. CVII.

of the text. Several manuscripts, among them two of the most important, the *Vaticanus* and the *Sinaiticus* (4th cent.) omit Mk. 16 : 9-21, while others replace it by a shorter conclusion. On the other hand, Tatian and Saint Irenaeus attest the antiquity of the longer close. In conformity with the decree of the Council of Trent on the canon of the Sacred Scriptures (Denzinger, no. 784), it must be considered a part of Scripture and, therefore, inspired. But it cannot be proven to be the personal work of Mark [1].

Characteristic features.

The Gospel of Mark is the shortest of the three Synoptic Gospels, having only 746 verses in contrast to the 1068 in Saint Matthew and the 1140 in Saint Luke. Among the Gospels, it was commented upon least in Antiquity. The reason for this lesser interest is easy to explain. The First and Third Gospels offered Christian preachers almost everything that Saint Mark contained, and important discourses and narratives in addition. Saint Mark has only fifty verses which contain material not found in Saint Matthew and Saint Luke : the accounts of two miracles, the healing of a deaf-mute (7 : 31-37) and of the blind man of Bethsaida (8 : 22-26); a parable, that of the seed growing of itself alone (4 : 26-29); and two special episodes, the attempt of the relatives of Jesus to lay hold of His person (3 : 20-21), and the flight of a young man naked at the time of Jesus' arrest at Gethsemane (14 : 51-52). There are lacking the gospel of the infancy, notable parts of the narratives relating to John the Baptist, the Sermon on the Mount, a large part of Jesus' discourse dealing with the first mission of the Apostles, and several — and some of the most beautiful — of the parables. Papias was already aware of these differences when he remarked that Mark had written only a few of the facts, but accurately, according as he recalled them. So far as a fairly complete introduction to Christianity is concerned, the Second Gospel offers fewer elements than the First and Third. It is rather a vade mecum [2], furnishing

Translator's note. — [1 Cf. P. E. KAHLE, " The End ef St. Mark's Gospel : The Witness of the Coptic Versions ", *JTS* (1951), 49-57].
[2] L. DE GRANDMAISON, *Jesus Christ* (New York, 1934), vol. I, p. 73.

a number of characteristic scenes of the earthly career of
Jesus Christ.

Somewhat neglected in the past, the Second Gospel has
found favor in modern times. The study of the Synoptic
Problem and the search for the sources of the Gospels have
drawn attention to the work of Mark. Instead of regarding
Mark as the abbreviator and follower of Matthew, as
Saint Augustine expressed it, many critics have seen in his
Gospel one of the sources used by Luke and the Greek Matthew
for their narratives, thus making the Gospel of Mark our first
Greek Gospel.

This renewal of interest has placed in sharper relief the
characteristic features of Mark. Authors who differ widely
in their views are in accord in crediting him with much life and
freshness. Differing from Matthew who, in his narration of
the miracles, retains only what has apologetic value, Mark
has a faculty for making a scene and its actors live again.
In the accounts common to the three Synoptics, far from being
" the most divine of all abbreviators " (Bossuet), he shows
himself to be the richest in details, the most picturesque, and
the most concrete.

This fulness and this picturesqueness, moreover, have nothing
of the studied and of the polished about them. Mark relates
in the manner of simple folk, of a man of the people, when
such have the gift of seeing things. He seizes upon the
picturesque details of a scene, but with no attempt at combining
these features into a well-arranged story. Instead of preparing
his narrative like a man who is in full control of his recollections,
Mark seems to deal with events as if they were unfolding
before his eyes. Parentheses give the necessary explanations
in succession as the progress of the narrative requires (5 : 32;
10 : 22; 15 : 25; 16 : 4).

The Evangelist has only very modest means at his disposal.
His rude and poor Greek is used as a cloak for Aramaic thought.
This does not mean, however, that the Second Gospel is the
translation of a Semitic original. His narratives, while presenting
diverse personnages in various circumstances, are cast in
uniform molds. Not only are similar miracles, like the two
multiplications of loaves, written according to the same pattern,
but this kind of parallelism is found also in the narration of

events which differ from one another in notable respects. We may compare in this connection the healings of the deaf-mute (7 : 23-24) and of the blind man of Bethsaida (8 : 22-23), the sending of the two disciples to seek the colt (11 : 1-6) and to prepare the Pasch (14 : 13-16), and even the account of an exorcism (14 : 13-16) and of the calming of a tempest (4 : 39, 41).

If, in spite of this lack of artistic techniques, Mark gives us a vivid impression of reality, the explanation is to be sought in the fact, attested by tradition, that Mark transmits to us the recollections of Peter such as he had received them from the very mouth of the chief of the Apostles. The possibility remains that Chapter 13 of the Synoptic Apocalypse had a written source, but, considered as a whole, the Second Gospel presents itself as the reflection of life in an accurate memory, the memory of Peter, who is also the disciple whose figure stands out in sharpest relief.

The end aimed at by the Evangelist is simple like his manner : to spread knowledge of Jesus, the Messias and Son of God, whose power is manifested by His works, His miracles, and especially by the expulsion of demons. There is no reason to ascribe theological after-thoughts to Mark, and to transform his frank and direct narrative into a " deliberately Pauline interpretation of the primitive tradition " (Loisy). The " Paulinism " of Mark is nothing else than the Christianity of the first disciples.

4. — The Gospel according to Saint Luke [1].

Authenticity.

The Third Gospel was attributed to Saint Luke, the companion of the Apostle Paul, who calls him " our most dear physician " (Col. 4 : 14) [2]. It is cited in the writings of the Apostolic Fathers, though without the author's name, and also in Saint Justin who lists it among the " Memoirs of the Apostles " which were

---

Translator's note. — [1 Cf. B. S. EASTON, *The Gospel according to St. Luke* (New York, 1926). J. M. CREED, *The Gospel according to Saint Luke* (London, 1930)].

Translator's note. — [2 Cf. W. K. HOBART, *The Medical Language of Saint Luke* (Dublin, 1882); W. M. RAMSAY, *Luke the Physician* (London, 1908); A. VON HARNACK, " *Luke the Physician* ", in *New Testament Studies* (Engl. transl., London, 1907-1912); J. H. CADBURY, " Recent Arguments for Medical Language ", *Journal of Biblical Literature*, 45 (1926), 190-204].

composed by them or by their disciples (*Dialogue*, 103). The heretic Marcion, who separated from the Church of Rome in 144, retained, of the Gospels, only that of Luke, but in an altered and mutilated form. Then we have the explicit testimonies of Irenaeus in Gaul, Tertullian in Africa, Clement and Origen in Egypt, and the Canon or Fragment of Muratori, a kind of catalogue of the inspired books which were received at Rome about 200. There is no trace in Antiquity of the slightest question on this point.

Luke " did not see the Lord in His flesh ", the Fragment of Muratori tells us. He was not an immediate disciple of Jesus, but was a disciple of the Apostle Paul and became his helper. A native of Antioch in Syria (according to Eusebius, *Hist Eccl.* III, 4, 6, and ancient prologues of the Gospel which may go back to the end of the second century), and belonging by birth and education to the Hellenic world, he must have been converted to Christianity at an early date. A reading of Codex D in Acts (**11** : 28) makes him a member of the community of Antioch about the year 42. It is during Paul's second great missionary journey, about the year 50, that we find him with the Apostle when he was about to depart from Troas for Macedonia, a discreet " we " introducing him into the narrative of Acts (**16** : 10). He followed Paul to Philippi (Acts **16** : 12), but seems to have remained there for a time, leaving the Apostle to continue his course. Some years later, we find him again in the company of Saint Paul when the latter, in returning from Greece to Palestine, passed through Macedonia. From Philippi Luke accompanied the Apostle to Jerusalem. When Paul was arrested in the Temple, and was then led captive to Caesarea where he remained two years (57-59), Luke did not leave him; and again, when Paul, after his appeal to the emperor's tribunal, left Caesarea to be brought to Rome, Luke embarked with him. He was Paul's companion during the very dangerous and eventful crossing from Caesarea to Italy, and continued to serve as a co-worker (Col. **4** : 14).

Composition, and for whom intended [1].

In conformity with a custom frequent in the Hellenic world and followed by Jews who wrote in Greek, Saint Luke puts

---

[1] For the date and place of composition, see pp. 414-415.

a prologue at the beginning of his Gospel and explains his purpose.

" Inasmuch as many have undertaken to draw up a narrative concerning the things that have been fulfilled among us, even as they who from the beginning were eyewitnesses and ministers of the word have handed them down to us, I also have determined, after following up all things carefully from the very first, to write for thee, most excellent Theophilus, an orderly account, that thou mayest understand the certainty of the words in which thou hast been instructed " (1 : 1-4).

It is evident from this text that out of the preaching of those who had been from the beginning eyewitnesses of what Jesus had done and taught, and who later became ministers of the Word, had come several attempts at preserving and propagating in written form a more or less complete narrative of the life and teaching of Christ. Saint Luke knew of these narratives. He seems indeed to have used as an authorized source the Gospel of Mark, his companion in Rome (Col. 4 : 10, 14). He collected also the echoes of the Palestinian catechesis which had been given definite form in the Aramaic Gospel of Saint Matthew and had inspired other more or less fragmentary documents. Of these writings, Saint Luke was in a position to be well acquainted with copious extracts which had already been translated into Greek. But the fact that he had predecessors, and even quite respectable ones among them, was no reason for him to forego writing himself.

He was able to control or complete his written sources by living witnesses. His contacts with Saint Paul and his assistants, his sojourns in Palestine, at Jerusalem and at Caesarea, where he questioned disciples of the earliest period, allowed him to become accurately informed on all matters from the beginning. Thus, he could go back even to the infancy of Jesus. He did not set out to make a simple collection of sayings, but an ordered history, a logical and continuous narrative. This intent presupposes a certain care for chronology. Luke gives indications which connect certain facts in the Gospel narrative with the chronology of profane history, both Jewish and Greco-Roman (1 : 5; 2 : 1-2; 3 : 1-2), or which mark their relative sequence (9 : 28; 9 : 37; 9 : 51; 22 : 66). But this chronological framework has nothing rigorous about it. It

does not exclude displacements of episodes as compared with
Mark's order, even in some cases where Mark's order appears
more satisfactory, e.g., Jesus' visit to Nazareth (Luke 4 : 16-30),
nor groupings of sayings on the basis of analogy in subject
matter.

The work is dedicated to Theophilus, a Christian of high rank,
as the epithet, " excellent ", testifies (cf. Acts 23 : 26; 24 : 3;
26 : 25), and a man of Hellenic stock and background, if we
may base our judgment in this matter on the characteristic
traits of the Third Gospel. This dedication to a particular
individual does not prevent us at all from believing that the
Evangelist desired a wide diffusion for his work, and that he
undoubtedly counted on the assistance of Theophilus in reaching
other converts who likewise had come from the Greek world,
and in proving to them the solidity of the faith they had
received.

The Prologue is followed by the Gospel of the Infancy
(1 : 5-2 : 52), which has few points of contact with Matthew's
narrative [1]. Then comes an account of John the Baptist's
ministry, and of the baptism and temptation of Jesus (3 : 1;
4 : 13), which is much more developed than in Mark and shows
many similarities to Matthew. Luke begins the history of
Jesus' ministry in Galilee with His visit to Nazareth (4 : 16-30).
From that point to 9 : 51 inclusive, he coincides frequently
with Mark not only in the choice of episodes but also in their
sequence, yet with some exceptions (Lk. 4 : 31-6 : 19 = Mk. 1 :
40-3 : 19; Lk. 8 : 4-9 : 17 = Mk. 4 : 1-6, 44; Lk. 9 : 18-50 = Mk. 8 :
27-9 : 41). Luke omits everything found in Mk. 6 : 45-8 : 26. On
the other hand, he has a whole bloc which is absent from Mark,
including some elements in common with Matthew, and others
peculiar to himself : the Sermon on the Mount (Mt.), the healing
of the centurion's servant (Mt.) and of the son of the widow
of Naim, the discourse on John the Baptist (Mt.), the sinful
woman at Jesus' feet. In 9 : 51, a section begins which is

Translator's note. — [1 Several important studies on the Gospel of the Infancy
have been published in the last few years. See, e.g., R. LAURENTIN, *Structure
et théologie de Luc I-II* (Paris, 1957). J. GUITTON, *La Vierge Marie* (Paris,
1954), especially pp. 29-46. J. P. AUDET, " L'Annonce à Marie ", *RB* (1956),
346-374. P. WINTER, in *Vox theologica* (1958), 117-122. On Winter's views,
cf. J. COPPENS, *EThL* (1958), 438-439. P. CEROKE, " Luke 1 : 34 and Mary's
Virginity ", *CBQ* (1957), 329-342. B. HOSPODAR, *ibid.* (1956), 14-18 (on
Luke 1 : 39). For further bibliography, see the work of Laurentin listed above].

peculiar to Luke, although the discourses reported there contain elements in common with Matthew (and with Mark — the parable of the grain of mustard seed, Lk. 13 : 18-21), but in different contexts. This section peculiar to Luke extends as far as 18 : 14. Jesus sets out towards Jerusalem (9 : 51), and this information is repeated in 13 : 22 and 17 : 11 without the Evangelist making it clear whether there is question of one or of several journeys. Here indications of time and place are particularly lacking, undoubtedly because the author did not find them in his source. But within this loose chronological framework Saint Luke has kept some of the most beautiful pages of the Gospel : the parables of the Good Samaritan, of the lost sheep, of the lost drachma, of the prodigal son, of Lazarus and the rich man, and of the Pharisee and the publican.

In 18 : 15 Luke rejoins Mark at 10 : 13, and there is the same sequence of facts in Luke and Mark up to the resurrection of Christ, except for a few displacements and Luke's insertion of discourses and episodes missing from Mark — the conversion of Zaccheus, the parable of the talents, Jesus' weeping over Jerusalem, the contention among the Apostles at the Last Supper on the question of precedence and during the Passion, the apparition of the angel in the course of the agony at Gethsemani, the appearance of Jesus before Herod, the lamentation of the daughters of Jerusalem, the prayer of Jesus for His executioners, and the repentance of the good thief. As regards the apparitions of the risen Christ, Saint Luke does not report those which occurred in Galilee, but only those which took place at Jerusalem or in the neighboring region (Emmaus). He does not wish, apparently, to draw his readers outside Jerusalem, for it is from there that, in the Acts of the Apostles which follows the Gospel, he will make the history of the Church begin.

Characteristic features.

Although Saint Luke depended on written sources, he knew how to give his work a personal stamp. The Third Gospel is the only one which, in the strict sense, has a literary character. Two features distinguish the writer's manner : knowledge of Greek as it was spoken in the cultured world of his time, and a Semitic tinge which recalls the Hebraizing language of the

Septuagint. The second trait, particularly noticeable in the Gospel of the Infancy (Chs. 1 and 2), is probably to be explained not so much through a premeditated design as through Luke's use of sources which had originated in Judaeo-Hellenic Christian circles [1]. The comparison with Mark in the parts which they have in common shows that Luke, without suppressing every construction imitative of the Hebrew or Aramaic, has nevertheless been at pains to use a more literary and polished vocabulary than Mark's.

This style, elegant in its simplicity, was used for precise ends. The Third Gospel has its own special character, because its author had in mind readers of a particular kind. Writing for the faithful who had come from the pagan Hellenistic world, Luke discarded numerous elements which had less interest for Greeks than for Jews or Judaeo-Christians, so, e.g., in the Sermon on the Mount, the parallel emphasized in Saint Matthew between the Old Law and the New. Faithful to the spirit of him whom Tertullian (*Against Marcion*, IV, 2) called his " Illuminator ", the Apostle Paul, Luke has made Christ's mission as universal Savior stand forth in splendor, the Light to enlighten the Gentiles (2 : 32), as well as His role as the Son of Man who came to seek and to save what was lost (19 : 10). He has put in striking relief His merciful goodness and His kindness which turns in sympathy to all miseries, cures all ills of body and soul, and which, in that ancient world where woman was so often scorned, raises her, ennobles her, and calls her to collaborate in the spread of the Kingdom of God. Most of the narratives and parables which are peculiar to Saint Luke bring out this universal and merciful aspect of the Gospel of Jesus [2]. We need only recall the parables of the good Samaritan, the lost sheep, the lost drachma, the prodigal son, the rich man and Lazarus, the Pharisee and the publican, the tears of the sinful woman at the feet of Jesus, the conversion of Zaccheus, Christ's pardon of His executioners, and the repentance of the good thief. Hence Dante, struck by these appeals for mercy and forgiveness, has justly called Saint Luke " the historian of the gentleness of Christ ".

Translator's note. — [1 See the references given above, p. 402].
[2 Cf. P. GÄCHTER, " The Parable of the Dishonest Steward after Oriental Conceptions ", *CBQ* (1950), 121-135].

5. — The Gospel according to Saint John [1].

Authenticity.

As in the case of the three other Evangelists, the author of the Fourth Gospel likewise did not sign his name to his work. But, unlike his predecessors, he makes his appearance under the discreet veil of anonymity. He presents himself not only as a direct witness of the facts which he relates, but as one of the immediate disciples of Jesus, and more than that, as " the disciple whom Jesus loved " (Jn. 13 : 23; 19 : 26; 20 : 2; 21 : 7, 20), who took part in the Last Supper, resting on the Lord's bosom (Jn. 13 : 23), and who received His secrets and His last confidences — surely one of the Twelve.

Translator's note. — [1 Cf. B. F. WESTCOTT, *The Gospel according to Saint John* (2 vols., London, 1908); A. SCHLATTER, *Der Evangelist Johannes* (Stuttgart, 1930); J. JEREMIAS, *Das Evangelium nach Johannes* (Chemnitz, 1931); E. C. HOSKYNS, *The Fourth Gospel* (2 vols., 2nd ed., London, 1947); V. H. STANTON, *The Gospels as Historical Documents*, vol. III (Cambridge, 1920); J. DRUMMOND, *An Inquiry into the Character and Authorship of the Fourth Gospel* (London, 1903); W. SANDAY, *The Criticism of the Fourth Gospel* (Oxford, 1905); W. F. HOWARD, *The Fourth Gospel in Recent Criticism and Interpretation* (London, 1931); B. W. BACON, *The Fourth Gospel in Research and Debate* (London, 1910); H. L. JACKSON, *The Problem of the Fourth Gospel* (Cambridge, 1918); J. A. ROBINSON, *The Historical Character of Saint John's Gospel* (London, 1908; new ed., 1928); F. R. HORE, *The Original Order and Chapters of Saint John's Gospel* (London, 1944); E. A. ABBOTT, *Johannine Vocabulary* (London, 1905); *id.*, *Johannine Grammar* (London, 1906). On two important recent works, E. SCHWEIGER, *Ego Eimi* (Göttingen, 1939), and K. KUNDZINS, *Charakter und Ursprung der johanneischen Reden* (Riga, 1939), see P. BENOIT, O. P., *RB* (1946), 576-582; see also, W. GROSSOUW, *Pour mieux comprendre saint Jean* (*Bibliotheca Mechliniensis*, 10, 1946); A. C. HEADLAM, *The Fourth Gospel as History* (Oxford and New York, 1948). E. RÜCKSTUHL, *Die literarische Einheit des Johannesevangeliums. Der gegenwärtige Stand der einschlägigen Forschungen* (Freiburg i. d. Schweiz, 1951; cf. A. WIKENHAUSER, *Theologische Revue* [1952], 147-150; M. E. BOISMARD, *RB* [1952], 425-427). J. BONSIRVEN, S. J., *Le Témoin du Verbe...* (Toulouse, 1956; cf. E. MASSAUX, *EThL* [1957], 749-750). L. MOWRY, " The Dead Sea Scrolls and the Gospel of St. John ", *ibid.* (1954), 78-97. On the person and Gospel of St. John, cf. A. FRIDRICKSEN, in *Svenskt Bibl. Uppslagsverk* I, 1085-1098. *L'Evangile de saint Jean* (= *Recherches Bibliques* III, Bruges, 1958; a collection of essays on various aspects of St. John [Gospel and Epistles]). C. K. BARRETT, *The Gospel according to St. John : an Introduction with Commentary on the Greek Text* (London, 1956; cf. *RB* [1956], 267-272). V. MARTIN, *Papyrus Bodmer II : Evangile de Jean* (Geneva, 1956; cf. J. COPPENS, *EThL* [1957], 745-746). F. V. FILSON, " A New Papyrus Ms of the Gospel of John ", *BA* (1957), 54-63 (on the Bodmer Papyrus also). M. E. BOISMARD, *Du baptême à Cana* (Paris, 1956; cf. *CBQ* [1957], 288-289); *id.*, *Le Prologue de saint Jean* (Paris, 1953). L. BOUYER, *Le quatrième Evangile* (Tournai, 1955). P. H. MENOUD, *L'Evangile de Jean d'après les recherches récentes* (Neuchâtel-Paris, 1947). C. H. DODD, *The Interpretation of the Fourth Gospel* (Cambridge, 1953; cf. *RSR* [1956], 422-442)].

If we connect this first characteristic, intimacy with Jesus, with another special feature of the anonymous disciple, his friendship with Simon Peter (Jn. **13** : 24-26; **18** : 16; **20** : 3-9; **21** : 7, 21-22), we are led by the study of these same traits in the Synoptic Gospels and in the Acts of the Apostles to identify the writer with one of the sons of Zebedee, James or John. Since the elder, James, was put to death in the year 44 by King Agrippa I — too early for the Fourth Gospel to be attributed to him, there remains only John.

Upon leaving the New Testament, we shall not be surprised to find that the testimonies of Christian Antiquity are fully in agreement with these first indications and affirm definitely the Johannine origin of the Fourth Gospel. Already in the first half of the second century, the Letters of Saint Ignatius of Antioch and the Epistle of Saint Polycarp to the Philippians attest the existence of the Johannine teaching in the Christian communities of Syria and Asia Minor, and there is every reason to believe that it was known in its written form. In the second half of the second century, " the citations, allusions, and repeated mentions, multiply rapidly and come from all points of the doctrinal and geographical horizon. Thus, they are found in early Gnostics like Valentinus and his principal disciples, Ptolemy and Heracleon, as well as in their great adversary, Irenaeus of Lyons (*ca.* 173-180); in instigators of heresy like Marcion (*ca.* 140), as well as in his refuters, Melito of Sardes (*ca.* 110-170) and Tertullian (*ca.* 200); in Montanists (*ca.* 156-172), and in their orthodox adversaries, Apolinaris of Hierapolis and Apollonius; in isolated witnesses like Athenagoras (*ca.* 177), Theophilus of Antioch (*ca.* 181), Polycrates of Ephesus (190-195), and Clement of Alexandria (*ca.* 200), Tatian (*ca.* 175), and the author of the so-called Muratorian Canon (200) " [1]. The apocryphal " Letter of the Apostles ", about the end of the second century, may also be added to his list.

From this accumulation of witnesses it is clearly apparent that the Church received the Fourth Gospel, from its first diffusion, as the work of an immediate disciple of Jesus, of the " disciple whom Jesus loved ". Many designate the author

---

[1] L. DE GRANDMAISON, *Jesus Christ*, vol. I, p. 132.

by name, John the Apostle, e.g., — without speaking of the Gnostics Ptolemy and Heracleon — Tertullian in Africa, the Canon of Muratori at Rome, Clement at Alexandria, and Irenaeus at Lyons. This last witness is particularly important, for Irenaeus in his early youth had gone to Asia Minor and had known Polycarp, the bishop of Smyrna, who " had conversed with John and others of those who had seen the Lord " [1]. According to Irenaeus, John was the last of all : " John, the disciple of the Lord, who had rested upon His bosom, also published a written Gospel when he was living at Ephesus in Asia Minor " [2].

A precious *confirmatur* was given to tradition by the publication of two Egyptian papyri in 1935. The first, which papyrologists date from before 150, is a small fragment bearing on the recto Jn. **18** : 31-33, and on the verso, Jn. **18** : 37-38 [3]. The second, which is assigned to the middle of the second century and is perhaps even earlier, comprises three fragments which contain borrowings not only from the Synoptic Gospels but also from the Fourth Gospel as well [4]. These two papyri bear witness to the diffusion of the Gospel of Saint John in the first half of the second century in Egypt, far from the place where it had been written. This fact clearly implies its existence in the first years of the second century.

Place and date of composition.

According to the testimony of Saint Irenaeus, the composition of the Fourth Gospel should be assigned to the end of the first century when John, who had been exiled on the island of Patmos under Domitian, returned to Ephesus after the death of that emperor (96).

---

[1] *Letter of Irenaeus to Florinus,* in EUSEBIUS, *Hist. Eccl.,* V, **20**, 4.

[2] *Adversus Haereses,* III, **1**, 1.

Translator's note. — [3 Rylands Papyrus 457. It was identified and published by C. H. ROBERTS, " An Unpublished Fragment of the Fourth Gospel in the John Rylands Library ". *Bulletin of the John Rylands Library,* 20 (1936), 43-53. Cf. F. KENYON, *Our Bible and the Ancient Manuscripts* (New York, 1958), p. 189-190].

Translator's note. — [4 Cf. H. I. BELL and T. C. SKEAT, *Fragments from an Unknown Gospel and Other Early Christian Papyri* (London, 1935). The Ms. in question is Papyrus Egerton 2 of the British Museum. See also, C. H. DODD, " A New Gospel ", *Bulletin of the John Rylands Library,* 20 (1936), 156-92].

Purpose, and for whom intended.

The testimony of Clement of Alexandria deserves especially to be mentioned, because it characterizes the Fourth Gospel so happily : " John, then, the last, seeing that the external characteristics [of the life of Christ] had been related in the other Gospels, at the request of his friends, and under the inspiration of the Holy Ghost, composed a *spiritual* Gospel " [1], i.e., a Gospel which should unveil the heavenly mysteries beneath the visible facts, and which should emphasize the divine aspect of Christ's life.   Such appears indeed to have been the aim that Saint John proposed to himself.   He begins his Gospel with a solemn prologue in which the Word (Logos) is proclaimed to be God and is identified with Jesus Christ, and he thus indicates specifically that a very clear dogmatic design dominates the composition of his work.   This design is clearly described in the conclusion of Chapter 20 : 30-31, which was, it seems, the original close of the whole Gospel [2].

" Many other signs also Jesus worked in the sight of his disciples, which are not written in this book.   But these are written that you may believe that Jesus is the Christ, the Son of God, and that believing you may have life in his name ". Saint John did not write for the sake of converting people outside to Christianity, but for the sake of converts whom he wished to confirm in their faith.

Characteristic features.

In conformity with this design, the Evangelist retained, of the discourses of Jesus, those which present especially the

---

[1] Cited by EUSEBIUS, *Hist. Eccl.*, VI, 14.

[2] Chapter 21, which relates the appearance of the risen Christ on the shore of Lake Tiberias, is certainly Johannine.   It was added before the publication of the Gospel, either by John himself or by a secretary, to whom could be attributed the last two verses, 24-25.   The question of integrity comes up seriously only in the case of the episode of the adulterous woman (Jn. 7 : 53–8 : 1).   Although this account may be very ancient and belong to the most solid historical tradition, it is doubtful that it originally formed a part of the Gospel of Saint John.   The reasons for doubt are its absence from the oldest uncial Mss. (except D, *Codex Bezae*, sixth century), from several Mss. of the Old Latin version, from the Syriac, Coptic, and Armenian versions (except for some recent Mss.), and from all the Greek commentators before the eleventh century. Furthermore, the Greek Mss. which have retained it do not all have it in the same place, for some insert it by way of supplement at the end of the Gospel, and others after Lk. 21 : 38.   We may add that Jn. 5 : 3c-4 (the moving of the waters in the pool of Bethsaida by an angel) is poorly attested by the Ms. tradition and is regarded by many authors as a gloss.

revelation which Jesus gives on His person, on His Messianic and divine prerogatives, on His mission as Savior, and as the light and life of men. In particular, in the last discourse (Ch. 14-17), he dwells on Jesus' relations with the Father and the Holy Spirit, and on the part of the Blessed Trinity in the life of the disciples and of the Church [1]. The discussions with the Jews are ordinarily placed at Jerusalem because it was precisely there, in the center of the official priesthood, that Jesus had been most often questioned and attacked on the subject of His mission. The statements concerning the Kingdom and the precepts of the Christian life, summed up in " the new commandment " of charity (13 : 34), are mentioned only insofar as they are linked with the teaching of Jesus on His person and follow from it. Hence, the discourses have a certain uniformity which habitual techniques of style and composition only reinforce. The stylistic differences between these discourses and those in the Synoptic Gospels, like the ressemblances to the First Epistle of John, point, in the manner of the reporting of the words of Jesus, to the existence of " a personal element contributed by the writer " [2], who at times even adds his own separate comment (3 : 17-21; 31-36). But if John does not always give us the literal form of Jesus' discourses, he assuredly transmits to us the thought of the Master. Ancient tradition never had any doubts on this matter.

The choice and relation of the miracles are inspired by the same design, namely, to show forth in Jesus, the Messias, the Son of God, the light and life of men. Thus the most striking miracles are accompanied by a dialogue or a discourse explaining their significance : the discourse on the bread of life (6 : 26 ff.) clarifies the symbolical meaning of the multiplication of the loaves, the healing of the man born blind (9 : 6-7) supports Jesus' affirmation that He is the light of the world (9 : 4), and the resurrection of Lazarus witnesses to the power over life which resides in the Son of God (11 : 25).

These dogmatic preoccupations of the Evangelist do not transform the Fourth Gospel into a mystical contemplation,

---

Translator's note. — [1 On the last discourse, see especially, H. B. SWETE, *The Last Discourse and Prayer of Our Lord* (London, 1913); P. W. VON KEPPLER, *Unseres Herrn Trost* (2nd and 3rd ed., by S. WEBER, 1914)].

[2] LAGRANGE, *Evangile selon saint Jean* (Paris, 1925), Introduction, p. CXLVII.

indifferent to history. Quite to the contrary, Saint John, in order to reply to the first Docetic heretics, for whom the body of Christ was merely an appearance, undertakes to maintain firmly the reality of Christ and His works. This concern for history, required by the aim itself pursued by the author, is confirmed by the solidity of the chronological framework, particularly by the precise indications of Jewish festivals within the cycle of which the life of Christ is inserted, as well as by the exact and exceptionally frequent geographical references, which modern discoveries have only served to substantiate. Like the other Gospels, that of Saint John remains above all a " testimony ", the testimony of the disciple loved by Jesus and His Mother, who with eyes of love has penetrated most deeply into the secrets of the Word made flesh [1].

6. — The Acts of the Apostles [2].

The author of Acts.

As their Prologue (1 : 1) indicates, the Acts of the Apostles form the second volume of a work, of which the first was our present Third Gospel. They are by the same author, Saint Luke, who dedicates them to the same person, Theophilus. The same testimonies which furnish valid evidence for attributing the Third Gospel to Saint Luke furnish valid evidence also for his authorship of Acts : Irenaeus, Tertullian, the Canon of Muratori, Clement of Alexandria, Origen and, summing up all Christian Antiquity, Eusebius of Caesarea and Saint Jerome.

A difference between the Gospel and Acts is that, whereas Saint Luke was not an eyewitness of the history of Christ, he

---

[1] *Translator's note.* — [Cf. J. QUASTEN, " Parables of the Good Shepherd (10 : 1-21) ", *CBQ*, 10 (1948), 1-12 and 151-169; P. J. TEMPLE, " The Eucharist in St. John 6 ", *CBQ*, 9 (1947), 442-452; A. POWER, S. J., " The Original Order of St. John's Gospel ", *CBQ*, 10 (1948), 399-405].

Translator's note. — [2 Cf. W. L. KNOX, *The Acts of the Apostles* (Cambridge, 1948; see also his *Saint Paul and the Church of Jerusalem, ibid.*, 1925, and *Saint Paul and the Church of the Gentiles, ibid.*, 1939); A. WIKENHAUSER, *Die Apostlegeschichte und ihr Geschichtwert* (Münster i. W., 1924); A. VON HARNACK's studies on Saint Luke contained in his *New Testament Studies* (Engl. trans., London, 1907-1912). E. HAENCHEN, *Die Apostelgeschichte* (10th ed. Göttingen, 1956; cf. *CBQ* [1957], 289-290). E. TROCMÉ, *Le Livre des Actes et l'histoire* (Paris, 1957; cf. F. X. MURPHY, *CBQ* [1958], 125-128; E. MASSAUX, *EThL* [1957], 750-755)].

was in part a participant in and spectator of the events and achievements which he records in Acts. A companion of Saint Paul, he introduces himself by a simple " we " into the account of his travels : first from Troas to Philippi (16 : 10); then, some years later, from Philippi to Jerusalem (20 : 5), and finally, from Caesarea to Rome (27 : 1) [1].

Some radical critics have claimed to see in this companion of Saint Paul a person distinct from the author of Acts. But this contradicts completely the testimony of ancient tradition and the formal affirmation of the author of Acts, who presents himself as identical with this companion of Saint Paul, and who enters upon the scene with perfect discretion and naturalness.

Minute studies of style and vocabulary [2] have served to confirm the identity of the author for the travel journal, the remainder of Acts, and the Third Gospel. We not only discover the same language and style throughout Acts, but also the same vibrant tones of joy produced by the conquering Faith because it fights with the arms of the Spirit.

Place and date of composition.

There is no firmly established tradition among the ancients on the place and date of composition of the Acts of the Apostles. The book ends in a rather abrupt manner with the mention of Saint Paul's two years of captivity, without telling us anything of his ultimate fate. Hence, Saint Jerome concluded that Acts was written soon after the first imprisonment of Saint Paul. The argument is not absolutely decisive, since it was perhaps sufficient for the author's purpose to show us that the Gospel had been carried even to imperial Rome. The probabilities, however, favor the view that Luke must have composed his narrative shortly after these events, in the years 63-64, and that the composition of the Third Gospel is probably to be placed in about this same period, though earlier than Acts.

---

[1] The " We " passages (the *Wirstücke* of the German critics) comprise Acts 16 : 10-17; 20 : 5-15; 21 : 1-8; 27 : 1–28 : 16.

[2] Notably the studies of A. von HARNACK (collected in the *Beiträge zur Einleitung in das Neue Testament*, Hefte 1-4 (Leipzig, 1911) [Engl. trans., *New Testament Studies*, 3 vols., London, 1907-1912]; of Sir JOHN HAWKINS, *Horae Synopticae* (2nd ed. Oxford, 1909), p. 174 ff.; of V. H. STANTON, *The Gospels as Historical Documents* (Cambridge, 1909), vol. II, 240-260, 276-322, completed by an article in *Journal of Theological Studies*, XXIV (1923), 361-382.

In any case, it can hardly be doubted that the book was written before the destruction of Jerusalem and of the Temple in the year 70, for in Acts there is not the slightest allusion to this catastrophe, not the least indication that it was foreseen or that it could be regarded as having taken place.

Text of Acts.

The text of Acts offers a particular problem, having been transmitted to us under two appreciably different forms : in one longer and rather loose in style, the other more abbreviated and more polished. The first tradition is represented especially by the Greco-Latin codex D (*Codex Bezae*, 6th century), and in addition, by two important fragments of Egyptian papyri and by Mss of the Old Latin Version (except *e*), which more or less faithfully reproduce this same type of text. The second tradition has as its principal witnesses the uncial Mss B (*Vaticanus*, 4th century), S (*Sinaiticus*, 4th century), C (*Codex Ephraemi*, 5th century), and A (*Alexandrinus*, 5th century). In 1894, the German philologist F. Blass advanced the hypothesis that these two forms of the text represented two successive editions of the Book of Acts, both brought out by Luke himself. Although this theory was supported in 1896 by Th. Zahn with a great display of erudition, it is now abandoned. Of the two forms of the text, modern editors agree in preferring the second (type B). The other tradition, which seems to go back to the middle of the second century, is regarded as resulting from a revision made by omissions, but especially by additions and glosses, in order to explain obscure points, and thus to satisfy curiosity and piety. The possibility is not excluded, however, that the text, even altered in this fashion, may have preserved some original readings which were omitted or retouched in the other tradition, especially in the case of " topographical, chronological, or simply historical details, which would not have been invented by a reviser far from the facts, but which, on the contrary, another reviser would probably have suppressed as no longer having any interest in a book intended to instruct Christian generations " [1].

---

[1] LAGRANGE, *Critique textuelle*, p. 412, who regards as authentic the following passages containing material in addition to that found in the B text of Acts : 12 : 10; 19 : 9; 19 : 28; 20 : 15; 27 : 5; 28 : 16.

Purpose and content of Acts.

Before leaving His disciples on Ascension Day, Jesus spoke these last words to them : " You shall receive power when the Holy Spirit comes upon you, and you shall be witnesses for me in Jerusalem and in all Judea and Samaria and even to the very ends of the earth " (Acts 1 : 8). The purpose of the author of Acts is to show us this spread of Christ's Gospel by the power of the Holy Spirit, first throughout the Palestinian world, and then across the Greco-Roman world to Rome, its capital. The author, as a converted pagan, was not directly interested in the personal history of Peter, Paul, and the other Apostles, but rather in the transmission of the Gospel as it was passing from the Jews to the Gentiles, in the missionary work among these latter, and in the establishment of a Church of the Gentiles. Of the Apostles, even of Peter and Paul, we learn only of that part of their activity which is strictly related to the spread of the Gospel. Hence there are many features in their history which Saint Luke ignores.

The first twelve chapters tell us first of the spread of the Gospel in Palestine and neighboring Syria. Peter, as head of the Apostolic college, appears as the principal personage, the one who directs, commands, and takes the initiative, whether it be a question of preaching or of other activities affecting the first Christian community.

After the dedication to Theophilus (1 : 1-2) and the account of the Lord's Ascension, which serves as an introduction, Acts shows us the first community of disciples which is grouped around Peter, its head, receiving the Holy Spirit on Pentecost, and then increasing in Jerusalem amidst the miracles and persecutions which end with the martyrdom of the deacon Stephen and the dispersion of the Hellenist Christians, Jewish by race but speaking Greek as members of the Diaspora (2 : 1–8 : 3).

Then we see the Church extending its conquests outside Jerusalem, into Samaria through the deacon Philip, along the sea coast of Palestine through Saint Peter, and to Antioch through the anonymous missionaries whose work Barnabas continues and develops (8 : 4–12 : 25). Philip's baptism of an Ethiopian eunuch, the conversion of Paul near Damascus,

Peter's vision at Joppa, and the entrance of Cornelius the pagan centurion and his people into the Church at Caesarea, are the striking episodes of this period. They form the prelude to the evangelization of the Gentile world and to the reception of the Gentiles into the Church.

This first section closes with the persecution of the Jewish king, Herod Agrippa I, who martyred the first of the twelve, James the son of Zebedee and brother of John. Peter was arrested, but was miraculously freed from prison.

With Chapter **13**, the author begins the history of the spread of the Gospel in the pagan world. Since Saint Paul was the principal instrument of this expansion, he receives from this point on almost exclusive attention. Peter reappears only in Chapter **15**, at the time of the assembly in Jerusalem. This history of the expansion of Christianity is necessarily incomplete. With the exception of Barnabas and Apollos, we know nothing at all about the other missionaries of the Gospel, nor do we know, for example, how Christianity was planted in Rome or in Egypt.

Three great journeys of Saint Paul are described. The first journey was to Cyprus, Pamphylia, Pisidia, and Lyconia, with a return by sea to Antioch (**13** : 1–**14** : 28). The Council of Jerusalem then followed (**15** : 1-35), which considered the controversy on the relations of converted pagans to the Mosaic Law.

The second journey carried him into Asia Minor (**15** : 36–**16** : 8), into Macedonia (**16** : 9–**17** : 15), to Athens (**17** : 16-34), and to Corinth (**18** : 1-17), with a return to Antioch by way of Ephesus and Caesarea (**18** : 18-22) [1].

The third journey included a crossing of Asia Minor, a sojourn at Ephesus (**18** : 23–**19** : 40), and a second visit to Macedonia and Greece (**20** : 1-3). The return to Jerusalem was made by way of Macedonia and a sea voyage along the coast of Asia (**20** . 4–**21** : 16).

Translator's note. — [1 Cf. B. GÄRTNER, *The Areopagus Speech and Natural Revelation* (Uppsala, 1955; cf. *RB* [1956], 462-464. The author as opposed to Norden, Dibelius and others, maintains that this is a genuine speech of Paul representing primitive Jewish-Christian propaganda in the Greco-Roman world). See also O. Broneer, " Athens : City of Idol Worship ", *BA* (1958), 1-28 (in the time of St. Paul)].

From this point to the end, Acts is concerned exclusively with the captivity of Saint Paul : at Jerusalem, where he was arrested (**21** : **1-23** : 35); then at Caesarea, where he appeared successively before the Roman procurators of Judea, Felix and Festus (**24** : **1-26** : 32); finally at Rome, whither he was transferred after having appealed to Caesar and where he remained for two years (**27** : **1-28** : 31).

The two parts of the Book of Acts (Chs. **1-12**, and Chs. **13-28**) although by the same author, exhibit some differences in redaction. The second part, which is based on the personal recollections of Luke as an eyewitness, or on what he heard from Paul and his companions in the apostolate, is more detailed, the chronological indications are numerous, and the narrative, without entirely satisfying our curiosity, does nevertheless give an impression of a logical and continuous history. For the first part, Luke must have had to depend on the testimonies of the earliest disciples with whom he became acquainted either in Paul's entourage (like Mark), or more especially in the course of his residence in Palestine, at Jerusalem, and at Caesarea during the two years that Paul was a captive there. Critics are generally agreed in recognizing that Luke used written sources for this first part, although we cannot identify or define them precisely. The chronological references are vague and the narrative appears less continuous than that devoted to Saint Paul's apostolic activity. We have, in Acts, a fragmentary history which remains very precious, because, together with some allusions in the Pauline Epistles, it constitutes the sole evidence available to us for forming some idea of the earliest beginnings of the Christian community of Jerusalem [1].

2. — THE EPISTLES.

The Epistles of the New Testament are divided into two groups : those of Saint Paul, which are genuine letters [2], and

---

[1] On the problem raised by the numerous discourses reported in the Acts of the Apostles, see Ch. VI, THE LITERARY GENRES, pp. 538-539.

Translator's note. — [2 Cf. J. A. ESCHLIMANN, " La rédaction des Epîtres Pauliniennes d'après une comparaison avec les lettres profanes de son temps ", *RB* (1946), 185-196, and O. ROLLER, *Das Formular der paulinischen Briefe* (Stuttgart, 1933)].

the so-called Catholic Epistles (Jas., 1 and 2 Pet., Jude, and 1, 2, and 3 Jn.), which, except for 2 and 3 Jn., resemble instructions rather than letters proper and are of a more universal character than the Pauline Epistles. The name " Catholic " was applied by Origen to 1 Pet., 1 Jn., and Jude. Eusebius applied it to the whole group without indicating any number, but by Saint Jerome's time it was customary to speak of " the seven Catholic Epistles ".

A. — THE EPISTLES OF SAINT PAUL[1].

The Pauline group of epistles comprises fourteen letters, including the Epistle to the Hebrews. There were doubts on the authenticity of Hebrews even in Antiquity, and for that reason it was generally placed at the end of the list[2]. In the case of the thirteen other letters the Vulgate, and, with it, our present Bibles, follow an order which seems to have been established at the beginning of the fourth century, and one based, not on the chronology of the letters, but on their importance and lengths. First, in order of decreasing length[3], are the letters addressed to churches : Rom., 1 and 2 Cor., Gal., Eph., Phil., Col., and 1 and 2 Thess., and then the letters to private individuals : 1 and 2 Tim., Tit., and Philem.

These epistles are occasional writings composed in response to definite needs, and to serve as a substitute for the presence of the Apostle. In combination with the data furnished by

---

Translator's note. — [1 Cf. F. J. BADCOCK, *The Pauline Epistles and the Epistle to the Hebrews in Their Historical Setting* (London, 1937); A. DEISSMANN, *Saint Paul* (Engl. trans. of the 2nd ed., London, 1926); A. SCHWEITZER, *Geschichte der paulinischen Forschung* (2nd ed., Tübingen, 1933); F. A. SPENCER, *Beyond Damascus : A Biography of Paul the Tarsian* (London, 1935); J. HOLZNER, *Paul of Tarsus* (Saint Louis, 1944); E. B. ALLO, O. P., *Paul Apôtre de Jésus Christ* (Paris, 1946); J. BONSIRVEN, S. J., *L'évangile de Paul* (Paris, 1948); L. CERFAUX, *La théologie de l'Eglise suivant saint Paul* (Paris, 1948). Dom J. DUPONT, *Gnosis, La connaissance religieuse dans les Epîtres de saint Paul* (Paris, 1949; cf. R. MACKENZIE, *Theological Studies* [1950], 418-422). E. BENZ, " Das Paulus-Verständnis in der morgenländischen und abendländischen Kirche : Vorbereitungen zu einer künftigen Geschichte des Paulinismus ". *Zeitschrift für Religions-und Geistesgeschichte* (1951), 289-309].

[2] The oldest Ms. P⁴⁶ (Chester Beatty Papyrus, IIIrd cent.) shows this peculiarity, namely, that the Epistle to the Hebrews is inserted between Rom. and 1 Cor.

[3] There is only one exception. The Epistle to the Ephesians follows Galatians, although it is a little longer than the latter.

Acts, they shed a great deal of light on the career of Saint Paul, and, better than any other document, they make us thoroughly familiar with his doctrine and his soul.   In order that their teachings may be known to the fullest degree, they must be rearranged within the framework of Paul's life according to their chronological order.   We shall try to restore this sequence, with certainty or probability as the case may be, for some points remain obscure and controversial.

I. — The Epistles to the Thessalonians [1].

The recipients.

The Church of Thessalonica (modern Salonica) in Macedonia had been founded by St. Paul during his second great missionary journey (50-52), when from Troas in Asia Minor he had gone for the first time into Europe. He had come there from Philippi, following the Egnatian Way through Amphipolis and Apollonia.   Thessalonica, an important harbor on the Thermaic Gulf, possessed a Jewish synagogue (Acts **17** : 1). Paul, who was accompanied by Silas and Timothy, began preaching first in the synagogue on the Sabbath.   After having preached Christ for three successive Sabbaths, he converted some Jews and a numerous crowd of " God-fearing " Gentiles, among whom was an important group of noble women (Acts **17** : 4).   The Church of Thessalonica was therefore for the most part composed of converts of pagan origin.

The success of this apostolate aroused the hatred of the unbelieving Jews.   They hired certain disreputable characters to arouse the populace against the preachers of the Gospel and their host, Jason.   To save them from mob violence, the Thessalonian Christians prevailed upon the missionaries to go to Beroea.   From there, after a fruitful apostolate, Paul went to Athens, where Silas and Timothy, who had remained behind at Beroea, soon joined him.   During his stay at Athens Paul twice planned to return to Thessalonica to sustain the young community in the face of persecution, but " Satan hindered us " (1 Thess. **2** : 18).   Giving up the attempt, he sent Timothy in his place, while he himself went to Corinth.

Translator's note. — [1 Cf. B. Rigaux, O. F. M., *Les Epîtres aux Thessaloniciens* (Paris, 1956; cf. *CBQ* [1957], 285-287].

There Timothy again sought him out (Acts **18** : 5), bringing him news of the Church of Thessalonica.

The First Epistle to the Thessalonians

Occasion, place, and date.

Upon this report of Timothy, Paul resolved to send his first letter to the Thessalonians. It was therefore written at Corinth. If, as seems likely according to Acts **18** : 5, the arrival of Timothy at Corinth occurred shortly after Saint Paul had begun his ministry there, the Epistle may very probably be assigned to the year 50 (or 51).

Content.

This Epistle is in no respect a didactic composition. There is discernible in it, however, a more important purpose, namely, to correct the error of the neophytes regarding the lot of the just who die before the return or *parousia* of the Lord. But Paul reaches this matter only in the second half of the letter (**4** : 13 ff.) [1].

Between the initial address and the final brief salutations two parts may be clearly distinguished. The first part (**1** : 2–**3** : 13) is an unrestrained, tender demonstration of affection on the part of the Apostle for a community which is dear to him and which has had to suffer persecution. Paul recalls under what conditions he founded the Church of Thessalonica, and how he conducted his apostolate; he praises the fortitude and progress of the young church under persecution; he confides to the Thessalonians the desire which he had of seeing them again and the joy he has experienced at the good news brought back by Timothy.

From these outpourings of his heart the Apostle passes, in a second section (**4** : 1–**5** : 24), to moral exhortation and the instruction of the neophytes. After recommendations on purity of life, charity, and application in their work, Saint Paul broaches the subject of the second coming under a special aspect. Those who have died in Christ will not be disadvantaged at his *parousia*, but having risen, they will rejoin Christ with those who are

---

Translator's note. — [1 Fr. GUNTERMANN, *Die Eschatologie des hl. Paulus* (Münster i. W., 1932)].

still living and they will all be together with Him for eternity. While they are waiting, since the day of the Lord is to come like a thief in the night, they must be vigilant. The conclusion contains some specific advice on various duties of Christians within the community, then greetings, and final good wishes.

The Second Epistle to the Thessalonians.

Occasion and purpose.

Through his first letter, Saint Paul had reassured the faithful of Thessalonica on the lot of their dead when the Lord should come again. But this question of Christ's return continued to trouble their minds. Some imagined that the *parousia* was imminent, and to support their opinion they made much of certain prophecies, whether oral or written, which they attributed to the Apostle (2 Thess. **2** : 2).

Besides the anxieties which they aroused, such thoughts had immediately practical consequences : Christians, believing that the second coming was imminent, were on the point of abandoning their work, since it was being judged henceforth as superfluous. To dissipate these illusions Paul wrote a second epistle to the Church of Thessalonica.

Place and date of composition.

Like the first, this second letter must have been written at Corinth. The opening salutation is the same as in the first, being made in the name of Paul, Silvanus (Silas) and Timothy. Moreover, Acts indicates that the three missionaries were reunited at Corinth. Relations were frequent between the two ports of Corinth and Thessalonica, and Paul could easily be informed of what was taking place in the Macedonian community.

Since the Second Epistle is, in subject matter, closely connected with the first, it must have followed the latter by an interval of a few weeks or months. Its date is, therefore, approximately the end of 50 or the beginning of 51 (or the end of 51 or the beginning of 52).

Content.

After the salutation and a prayer of thanksgiving for his correspondents, according to the current usage in the epistolary

literature of the time, Paul recalls the persecutions suffered
by the Church of Thessalonica. He sees in them an omen of
the just judgment of God who will reward the faithful and
punish their oppressors (Ch. 1). He then comes to the principal
object of his letter, namely, to admonish the Thessalonians
that the Lord's second coming is not imminent. It is necessary
that apostasy come first, and that " the man of sin, the son of
perdition ", the Adversary, manifest himself, and that " he
who restrains him " be gotten out of the way. Then the Lord
Jesus will appear and, with a breath of His mouth, will destroy
the Adversary (2 : 1-12). How are we to envisage this Adversary
and the obstacle which restrains him? Are we to see here
individuals or collective powers? And if so, who or what are
they? All these questions remain mysterious to us, and they
have received various answers.

The letter continues with an exhortation to perseverance,
a request for prayers, and with a reprimand for those who
have abandoned themselves to idleness. At the end of the
letter, Paul, who according to his custom had dictated it, added,
by way of a greeting and good wishes, a few lines in his own
hand, which are a conventional sign for indicating the
authenticity of his letters (3 : 17).

The question of authenticity.

Unlike the First Epistle, which is commonly accepted as
Pauline, the authenticity of the Second has been contested by
some critics, but without valid reasons. It has in its favor
the testimony of the ancients from the second century on
(reminiscences in Saint Polycarp, citations in Saint Justin, and
formal testimonies in Marcion, Saint Irenaeus, and Tertullian).
It seems well adapted to a definite historical milieu and situation.
Finally, the intermixture of resemblances and differences
established by a comparison with the First Epistle has nothing
artificial about it and excludes the hypothesis of an imitation
or forgery [1].

Translator's note. — [1 C. MASSON, in his recent book, *Les deux Epîtres
de saint Paul aux Thessaloniciens* (Neuchâtel-Paris, 1957), regards Second
Thessalonians as not authentic. He realizes that this view is contrary to that
of all commentators consulted, but has challenged Pauline authorship on the
ground that the eschatological section, 2 Thess. 2 : 1-12, cannot be reconciled
with what we know of Paul's teaching].

2. — The Epistle to the Galatians.

Recipients and place and date of composition.

The authenticity of the Epistle to the Galatians has never been seriously contested, but the circumstances of its composition are not clearly known and remain a matter of discussion.

Two opinions are current on the identity of the Galatians to whom the letter is addressed. Some hold that the recipients of the Epistle are the faithful of the churches which Paul had founded with Barnabas during his first missionary journey (Acts **13** : 13–**14** : 27) at Antioch in Pisidia, at Iconium, at Lystra, and at Derbe in Lycaonia. These cities formed a part, so far as administration was concerned, of the Roman province of Galatia, which had been established in 25 B. C. This is the so-called " southern Galatia " thesis, because Pisidia and Lycaonia were situated in the southern part of the province. This theory, after having been very much favored, seems now to be in decline.

The other opinion holds that the Galatians of the Epistle are the inhabitants of Galatia proper, or Asiatic Gaul, " the Galatian country " (Acts **16** : 6), a part of the Roman province of Galatia. These Galatians were descendants of Celtic tribes which had settled there in the third century B. C. around the cities of Ancyra, Pessinus, and Tavium. Saint Paul traversed at least a part of their territory during his second missionary journey (Acts **16** : 6) and again at the beginning of the third (Acts **18** : 23), " fortifying his disciples " before settling down to his long sojourn at Ephesus. This is the so-called " northern Galatia " thesis. It was maintained in Antiquity by Saint Jerome and appears to us to be the better established. The Epistle, in fact, represents the evangelization of the Galatians as resulting from an accident, namely, an illness of the Apostle (4 : 13-14) which obliged him to make a stay among them, while the foundation of the churches of southern Galatia corresponds to a plan formed in advance. Paul praises the eager welcome he received from the Galatians (4 : 14-15), without making any allusion to the persecutions such as he had suffered in Pisidia and in Lycaonia. In recalling his first preaching to the Galatians, he does not mention Barnabas who had been co-founder of the churches of southern Galatia.

There are again divergences of opinion in respect to the establishment of the approximate date of the Epistle's composition. The partisans of the " southern Galatia " hypothesis place it generally before the Council of Jerusalem, held in 49, which secured the freedom of the Gentiles as regards the Mosaic Law (Acts 15 : 1-35). According to this interpretation, the Epistle to the Galatians is chronologically the first of the Pauline Epistles, and Paul's conference at Jerusalem with " the pillars " of the Church, Peter, James, and John (Gal. 2 : 1-10) is not the same event — viewed from a different angle — as the Council of Jerusalem in 49 (Acts 15 : 1-35). The supporters of the " northern Galatia " theory put the composition after Paul's second visit to the Galatian country (Acts 18 : 23; Gal. 4 : 13). Some, because of its doctrinal affinity with the Epistle to the Romans, place it shortly before this latter at Corinth (the winter of 57-58). Others, who do not consider this relationship of the two letters a sufficient reason for maintaining any closeness in their dates of composition, prefer to date the Epistle to the Galatians from Paul's stay at Ephesus (55-57).

Purpose and content.

The purpose of the Epistle is clearly defined : to refute the error of the Judaizers who had come to trouble the faith of the Galatians by preaching to them the need of observing the Mosaic Law, especially as to circumcision, and to show that the Law was a provisory institution and that through the coming of Christ its role was ended. Since Christ is the unique mediator, the Mosaic observances are abrogated.

To attain his purpose, Saint Paul, in a first section (Chs. 1 and 2), presents his authority for his apostolate and his Gospel, which he holds immediately from God. This Gospel is in agreement with that preached by the Twelve, as the " pillars " of the Church, Peter, James, and John recognized at the conference in Jerusalem : he proclaims the freedom of the Gentiles in respect to the Mosaic Law. If Peter at Antioch yielded briefly to Judaizing pressure, Paul's intervention brought him to recognize this deviation in practice, for it is an incontestable fact that no one is saved by the works of the Law but by faith in Jesus Christ. " It follows from this first point,

that the gospel preached to the Gentiles, which does not impose
upon them any obligation of the Law, is the Gospel of Jesus
Christ, willed by God, approved by the Apostles, and its true
nature must not be obscured for any practical consideration "
(Lagrange).

From this first section, which consists in large part of a personal
apology, Saint Paul proceeds to refute directly the error of the
Judaizers (Chs. 3 and 4). After appealing to the experience
of the Galatians themselves, who received the outpouring of
the Holy Spirit without passing under the Law, he opposes
the promise of blessing made to Abraham in return for faith
to the curses associated with the observances of the Law,
considered apart from the promise. The blessing and the
promise of Messianic salvation are obtained by the neophytes
only in Christ and by faith in Him. The institution of the
Law, from which the Promise, being purely gratuitous, is
independent, is therefore transitory : it was the tutor which
led unto Christ. Since Christ has come, the Law no longer has
any justification for existence. Under the Law we were children
enslaved under the " elements of the world ", under imperfect
religious institutions [1]. Through Christ we have entered into
the heritage promised to sons, into the liberty of the children
of God. The allegory of Sara as the type of the New Covenant
and the Church as free, and of Agar as the type of the Old
Covenant and of the Synagogue in slavery, is used to illustrate
Paul's teaching.

The conclusion to be drawn is clear. The Galatians must
choose whether they wish to remain in the liberty of Christ,
or, by accepting circumcision, to submit themselves to the
yoke of the Law, and henceforth renounce Christ and His
grace and the way of faith, hope, and charity in Him. Confident
of the docility of the Galatians, the Apostle explains Christian
liberty to them : it is the triumph of the spirit over the flesh.
Then follow some specific counsels on the avoidance of vain
glory, on mutual aid, interior humility, and the support of
the catechists.

---

[1] The " elements of the world " may refer to these institutions themselves,
or, as many moderns think, to the cosmic powers — and especially the stars —
to which these institutions were in a dependent relation.

The letter concludes with a paragraph (**6** : 11-18) written in Paul's own hand, in which he sums up in a few nervous phrases the alternatives he sets before the Galatians. They must either follow the Judaizers, who are urging them to circumcision in order to satisfy their own self love and avoid persecution, or they must obey their Apostle who glories only in the cross of Jesus Christ and bears in his body the marks of his fidelity in serving Him.

3. — The Epistles to the Corinthians [1].

The recipients.

The Church of Corinth, like that of Thessalonica, had been founded by Saint Paul in the course of his second missionary journey (Acts **18** : 1-18). From Macedonia the Apostle had gone to Athens, and then to Corinth. He remained in this latter city about two years, from the autumn of 50 to the autumn of 52 (or 51-52). When Paul left Corinth to return to Antioch by way of Ephesus and Judea (Acts **18** : 19-22), the Church he had founded was developing rapidly. Some time later a third journey brought Paul to Ephesus (Acts **19** : 1). During this stay, which lasted more than two years, Paul was in frequent communication with the Church of Corinth, for he considered himself as its father.

First Epistle to the Corinthians.

Place and date.

From Ephesus Paul wrote to the Corinthian community a first letter which has not been preserved to us, but which is alluded to in 1 Cor. **5** : 9-12. Then he sent a second which we do possess, being our present First Epistle to the Corinthians. Some, relying on the similarity between the plans for his travels described in 1 Cor. **16** : 5-9 and Acts **19** : 21, place it at the beginning of the year 57, shortly before the end of Paul's residence at Ephesus and his departure for Macedonia. Others, judging that this date leaves too little time for the events which they put in the period between 1 Cor. and 2 Cor. (the middle of the year 57), assign an earlier date for 1 Cor. (56, or even 55).

Translator's note. — [1 L. CERFAUX, *L'Eglise des Corinthiens* (Paris, 1946). P. CLEARY, " The Epistles to the Corinthians ", *CBQ*, 12 (1950), 10-33].

Occasion and content.

The situation at Corinth which provoked the sending of this letter was as follows. The unity and good order of the community were being threatened in various ways. Cliques had formed regarding various preachers of the Gospel; scandal was being given by an incestuous Christian and by the lawsuits between Christians which were being brought before pagan courts. " The house of Chloe " among others (1 Cor. 1 : 11) had made known to Paul the spirit of dissension which prevailed at Corinth. Moreover, three delegates of the Church of Corinth, Stephanus, Fortunatus, and Achaicus (1 Cor. 16 : 17), had gone to Ephesus probably bearing the letter to which Saint Paul alludes (1 Cor. 7 : 1), and which submitted for the Apostle's decision several points concerning marriage and virginity, idol offerings, the manner of holding religious gatherings, spiritual gifts (charisms) and their use, and the resurrection of the dead.

The Epistle is inspired by a double concern on Paul's part, namely, the correction of abuses and the answering of the questions raised by the Corinthians. Therefore in the composition of the letter there are two clear cut sections within each of which the topics treated follow one another without logical connection.

After the customary salutation and thanksgiving, comes the first section, in which the Apostle censures disorders (1 : 10–6 : 20). He reproves in turn :

a) the cliques or factions formed among the Corinthians, with some claiming that they belong to Paul, others to Apollos, others to Cephas, and still others to Christ. This leads Paul to describe his preaching of the doctrine of the cross, to discuss the opposition between the wisdom of the world and the wisdom of God, and then to explain the precise nature of the ministry of the Apostles, who are God's helpers, stewards of His mysteries, and subject to His judgment alone. This instruction ends with an exhortation in which Saint Paul, while blaming the self-sufficiency of the Corinthians, recalls his paternal devotion, and announces Timothy's pending visit and his own (1 : 10–4 : 21).

b) the tolerance of the Corinthians for an incestuous Christian, whom he excommunicates (5 : 1-13).

c) the lawsuits between Christians and their prosecution before pagan courts (**6** : 1-11).

d) the sins of immorality (**6** : 12-20).

The second section (**7** : 1–**15** : 58) contains Paul's replies to the Corinthians concerning :

a) Christian marriage and celibacy (**7** : 1-40). Here are to be found the teachings of the Apostle on the lawfulness of marriage, the reciprocal rights of husband and wife, the indissolubility of the marriage bond and the Pauline privilege, the excellence of virginity, and the state of widowhood.

b) idol offerings (**8** : 1–**11** : 1). The Christian's conduct must be regulated by a wisdom inspired by charity. In itself, as the idol is nothing, the immolation to this nonentity would not contaminate anyone. But those whose knowledge is still imperfect must be considered, lest scandal be given them. Through charity for these weaker souls, the brother who has knowledge will not use his liberty to the full (**8** : 1-13). Saint Paul presents himself as an example of these renunciations freely practiced. For the honor and profit of his ministry, he deprives himself of advantages which his title of apostle gives him the right to claim; he preaches the Gospel gratuitously without requiring anything for his maintenance. Like the athletes in the racing contests, in the hope of recompense he mortifies himself in all things (**9** : 1-27).

The Corinthians must guard themselves against evil desires and idolatry. The sins of Israel in the desert and the chastisements they brought in their wake should teach them to be vigilant over themselves (**10** : 1-13).

The Apostle then gives a practical solution of the problem raised by idol offerings. He prohibits participation in an idolatrous banquet, as this would be to sit at the table of demons (**10** : 14-22). Beyond that, if there is question of buying meats at the market or of accepting invitations from unbelievers, it is permissible, so long as the need for giving edification is taken into account. If anyone indicates that a piece of food has been offered to idols, it is better not to taste it, in order not to scandalize those present. In all things, the glory of God and the spiritual good of one's neighbor must be sought, as the

Apostle himself, in imitation of Christ, sets the example
(**10** : 23–**11** : 1).

c) good order in religious gatherings. Women should have
their heads covered during liturgical gatherings (**11** : 2-16).
The celebration of the Eucharist should not lead to the
excesses of a profane banquet, but should reenact worthily the
Last Supper of the Lord (**11** : 17-34).

d) spiritual gifts (charisms) and their use. Saint Paul presents
first general ideas on spiritual gifts : their divine origin, their
purpose, their variety, and the interdependence of their
functions, which are comparable to those of the members of the
human body (**12** : 1-30). Above all charismatic manifestations
is placed charity, without which all else is nothing, and which
alone remains forever (**12** : 31–**13** : 13). Then the Apostle
compares " prophecy " and the " gift of tongues ", giving
preference to prophecy, and he indicates the rules to be
followed in the use of these two spiritual gifts in public gatherings
(**14** : 1-40).

e) the resurrection of believers. Saint Paul begins by
establishing the fact of Christ's resurrection, which is attested
by numerous eyewitnesses, among whom he ranks himself
(**15** : 1-11). With the resurrection of Christ, the foundation
of our faith and hope, our own resurrection is indissolubly
linked. As in the first Adam all men died, so in the new Adam
all believers will rise again, and will constitute the final triumph
of Christ over all his enemies and the consummation of the
Kingdom of God (**15** : 12-28) [1].

Using the *argumentum ad hominem* as a means of confirmation,
Saint Paul appeals to the practice of Baptism for the dead and
to his own courage in meeting danger, for all this has no purpose
if the dead do not rise again (**15** : 29-34) [2].

Translator's note. — [1 Cf. E. F. F. BISHOP, " The Risen Christ and the
Five Hundred Brethren ", *CBQ* (1956), 341-344. Dom Ralph Russell, " Modern
Exegesis and the Fact of the Resurrection ", *Downside Review* (1958), 251-264
(to be continued)].

Translator's note. — [2 Cf. B. M. FOSCHIN, O. F. M., *Those Who Are Baptized
for the Dead :* 1 Cor. **15** : 29 (Worcester, Mass., 1951). The author proposes
a change in punctuation to which no serious objection can be made — since
the original did not have any punctuation. He would read the passage as
follows : " Otherwise what shall they do who are baptized? for the dead?
Indeed, if the dead do not rise again at all, why are people baptized? for them "]?

After establishing the fact of the resurrection, Saint Paul passes to further explanation. Through a comparison of the seed which perishes to give birth to a new body, and of the variety of heavenly and earthly bodies, he shows that from our mortal body sown in corruption God can raise up a glorious, spiritual body. So it shall be. On the last day the " mystery " announced by the Apostle will be accomplished. The dead shall arise incorruptible and the believers then living shall be changed. Then death shall be finally overcome and with it its sting, sin, shall be broken (**15** : 35-38).

The epilogue (Ch. **16**) contains various pieces of information on the collection for the Church of Jerusalem, Paul's plans, and a few words on Timothy, Apollos, and the three envoys from the Church of Corinth. After the customary greetings, Paul adds in his own hand a last admonition and good wishes.

The Second Epistle to the Corinthians.

Place and date.

It is difficult to reconstruct exactly the events which took place between the First and Second Epistles to the Corinthians. Many modern scholars are of the opinion that after First Corinthians Paul visited Corinth (cf. 2 Cor. **12** : 14; **13** : 1) [1].

I.e., are people baptized to be numbered among the dead? And this is just what would be the case if there is no resurrection : baptism would mean remaining among the dead if there is no resurrection. This would be an absurd hypothesis from St. Paul's point of view. Hence, there is no *argumentum ad hominem* here. We do not have to imagine St. Paul appealing to a strange practice of some Christians at Corinth — for which he would not have the slightest word of blame, and from which he would draw a very lame argument for the resurrection. Needless to say, the text cannot support the vicarious baptism of the Mormons. Early misunderstanding of the text gave rise to the practice of baptism for the dead, which, according to St. Epiphanius, existed among the followers of Cerinthus, and, according to St. John Chrysostom, among the Marcionites (cf. J. KEULERS, *De Boeken van het Nieuwe Testament :* 5 [Roermond-Maaseik, 1953], p. 304). The practice was condemned by the Third Council of Carthage in 397. See the various Commentaries. It may be noted that J. HERING (*La première Epître de saint Paul aux Corinthiens* [Neuchâtel-Paris, 1959]) enumerates the different hypotheses (142-143) and, after accepting the common view of a baptism for the dead, observes that one cannot help feeling " that the text is not quite in order " (143). He would like to correct the text, but it is not clear how this should be done].

[1] In this passage Paul speaks of his plan to visit the Corinthians for the third time. The text is not, however, decisive in support of a second visit between I Cor. and II Cor. It cannot be proven with certainty that this second visit did not take place before I Cor., although this supposition appears less probable.

But this visit had not sufficed to comfort their minds. One of the Corinthians in particular had saddened Paul by his attitude (2 Cor. 2 : 5; 7 : 12), and some Judaizing preachers, enemies of the Apostle, were fostering turmoil. On his return to Ephesus, Paul had written the Corinthians a very severe letter which has not been preserved (cf. 2 Cor. 2 : 3 f., 7 : 8 f.), and — here we leave the domain of conjecture — he had sent Titus on a mission to Corinth. This mission is mentioned in 2 Cor. 7 : 13-15. The same source furnishes the information that the Epistle was written after Paul had come from Ephesus to Troas, and had then gone to Macedonia (2 Cor. 2 : 12-13). There in some place which we do not know definitely (but probably Philippi), the Apostle was rejoined by Titus and received news of the Church at Corinth which was in part consoling and in part a cause for sorrow. Planning, then, to return from Macedonia to Corinth in order to spend the winter there, Paul wrote the Second Epistle to the Corinthians to prepare for his coming. It may be assigned with reasonable probability to the middle of the year 57.

Content and composition.

After the salutation and thanksgiving (1 : 1-11), the letter falls into three parts which do not form an organically connected whole, as each treats a particular subject.

In the first section (1 : 12–7 : 16) Saint Paul reviews past events and certain difficulties with the Church of Corinth of which we have very little knowledge. He refutes the charge of inconstancy and insincerity on the score of a visit which he had announced but has not made. Instead of going to see them he has written them " to spare them ", to leave them time for returning to better dispositions. The Corinthians have shown themselves obedient, and they have made amends for the insult by which one of them had offended Paul. Titus was able to reassure the Apostle concerning their dispositions.

After comparing his sincerity with the conduct of many others who adulterate the Word of God, Paul goes on to praise the apostolic ministry. He has been for the Corinthians a minister " not of the letter, but of the spirit "; he has preached the Gospel with a boldness which is in contrast to the way in which Moses covered himself with a veil — a veil which still covers the eyes of the unbelieving Jews.

In spite of his natural frailty and in a life full of trials, nothing daunts him, for he knows that when he departs from this perishable house he will be reunited with Christ.

Impelled by the love of Christ who died for all, Paul applies himself to his mission of reconciliation. In all things he tries to show himself commendable, like a true servant of God. After he has outlined the ideal of the apostolic ministry, he strongly exhorts the Corinthians to sanctification, and, referring to past incidents, he attests that the return of Titus bringing him testimony of their love has filled him with joy.

The second section (Chs. 8 and 9) is devoted to the matter of the collection for the Church of Jerusalem. Paul recommends Titus and two other brethren whom he has charged with the collection of alms, and he discusses the motives which should incite the Corinthians to generosity : emulation, charity, and the blessings which will reward their kindness.

The third section (10 : 1–13 : 10) has no apparent connection with the second. Paul assumes in turn the tone of admonition and that of personal apology. He urges the Corinthians to live in such a manner that on the occasion of his next visit he will not have to exercise his power in humbling the proud and punishing the rebellious. This authority he acquired by his foundation of the Church of Corinth, whose well-being he desires with a jealous care. He recalls his own disinterestedness at the time of his Corinthian apostolate, and, while excusing himself for speaking in his own favor, he opposes the detractions of his adversaries, false apostles disguising themselves as apostles of Christ, with his own titles to glory : the labors and trials of his ministry, his visions and revelations from the Lord, his being caught up to the third heaven, and even his weakness and infirmities, because in them the Lord triumphs.

Paul has been forced to make this apology, one which should have been more fittingly made by the Corinthians themselves. He insists again upon his disinterestedness and that of his co-workers. He expresses fear that at his arrival he may not find the Corinthians such as they ought to be, and he renews his warnings to them so that he may not have to treat them severely.

A very brief conclusion (**13** : 11-18) includes advice, greetings, and good wishes.

The authenticity of this Epistle is not seriously questioned. There is no other work which reveals a more pronounced Pauline tone, which permits us to penetrate more deeply into the Apostle's soul, or which makes us more familiar with the anguish of his deeply sensitive nature, his anxious and vigilant tenderness for his neophytes, the ardor of his zeal, the labors and trials of his ministry, and the graces which the Lord showered upon him.

The composition of the Epistle, on the other hand, especially its unity, remains a matter of discussion. The question has been raised why the tone suddenly changes in the third section, with its sharp reproaches and warnings, while the first section expresses confidence and consolation. A number of modern scholars have advanced the hypothesis that Chapters **10–13** form a fragment of another Pauline letter, and more precisely, the severe letter to which allusion is made in 2 Cor. **2** : 4, 9; **7** : 7 ff. This opinion finds no support among ancient authors or in the manuscript tradition. The defenders of the Epistle's unity add that a subtle analysis of the first part can find indications and hints of the ideas which are developed in the third part. Moreover, it need not be granted that the letter was composed at one sitting. After having dictated the first nine chapters, Paul may have received new information which led him to adopt a sharper tone [1].

4. — The Epistle to the Romans [2].

Place and date of composition.

The Epistle to the Romans was written at Corinth. This is the inference to be drawn from Rom. **16** : 1, where Paul

---

[1 Cf. the article by Cleary cited on p. 427 above].

Translator's note. — [2 Cf. L. CERFAUX, *Une lecture de l'Epître aux Romains* (Paris and Tournai, 1947). K. BARTH, *Kurze Erklärung des Römerbriefs* (Münster i. W., 1956; cf. *CBQ* [1957], 284-285. S. LYONNET, S. J., *Quaestiones in Epistulam ad Romanos.* I (Rome, 1955); II (1956). H. SCHWARZMANN, *Zur Tauftheologie des hl. Paulus in Römer* **6** (Heidelberg, 1950, cf. *CBQ* [1952], 401-404). A. VIARD, O. P., " Expectatio creaturae (Rom. **8** : 19-22) ", *RB* (1952), 337-354. J. MUNCK, *Christus und Israel : Eine Auslegung von Römer* **9–11** (Copenhagen, 1956; cf. E. Massaux, *EThL* [1957], 751-753)].

recommends to his correspondents Phoebe, deaconess of the Church of Cenchreae, the port of Corinth on the Saronic Gulf, and from **16 : 23**, where he says that his host is a Christian named Gaius, who is mentioned in **1 Cor. 1 : 14** among the few neophytes whom Paul had personally baptized at Corinth.

Quite apart from these references, which have no value in the eyes of those critics who consider that Chapter **16** did not belong originally to the Epistle to the Romans, a comparison with the Acts of the Apostles suggests the same conclusion. The Epistle was written at a time when Paul was about to depart for Jerusalem to carry thither the collection which had been taken up by the Churches of Macedonia and Achaia for the poor of the Holy City (Rom. **15 : 26**). Now Acts (**20 : 3**) informs us that the Apostle, supplied with these alms, set out for Jerusalem from Corinth.

Corinth, again, is the place indicated by subscriptions of Mss. and by the Latin prologues to the Pauline Epistles which are found in a number of the Mss. of the Vulgate [1].

As regards the date of composition of the Epistle, all critics are agreed to within a year, namely, the winter of 56-57, or the winter of 57-58. According to the chronology which we have adopted up to this point, we shall accept as our date the winter of 57-58.

Occasion and purpose.

Unlike the other letters, the Epistle to the Romans is addressed to a church which was not founded by Saint Paul or by one of his immediate co-workers. The Apostle has decided to write to the Roman community to inform them of the plan he had formed of visiting them on his journey to Spain (Rom. **15 : 24**). The Epistle to the Romans is to prepare for his coming, to serve as his first contact.

Saint Paul's purpose in composing this letter, which is the most important and the richest of all his letters from the doctrinal point of view, has been variously explained. There is no tradition on the subject, and our judgment can be based

---

[1] DOM DE BRUYNE attributes a Marcionite origin to these prologues, but Father Lagrange, for better reasons, thinks that they depend on Ambrosiaster, an anonymous commentator at the end of the 4th century. Cf. LAGRANGE, *Critique textuelle du N. T.* (Paris, 1935), p. 514.

only on the text itself. Several among the ancients looked upon the Epistle as a polemic against errors or Judaizing tendencies which had been introduced at Rome by the first preachers of the Gospel, without the neophytes having any suspicions of these dangers. Such was the view of Ambrosiaster and the Latin prologues. Others thought that, since the Roman community was composed of two groups of Christians, one of Jewish, and the other of pagan origin, and since this circumstance caused divisions, Saint Paul had probably intervened in order to preach peace and concord. This is a suggestion of Origen, which was formally developed later by Pelagius. Modern commentators do not ordinarily advance these old theses again, at least in their absolute form. Without denying a warning on the part of Saint Paul against Judaizers (16 : 17-20), they look upon the Epistle primarily as a doctrinal exposition in which the Apostle develops his concept of salvation and the Christian life. Paul teaches the Romans that the Gospel, taken in the sense of Christianity considered in its totality, is a principle of life, and that it is the sole efficacious power of salvation, in accordance with the declaration of Rom. 1 : 16 : " The Gospel is the power of God unto salvation to everyone who believes, to Jew first and then to Greek ".

Content.

The Epistle to the Romans opens with a salutation which is longer than that of any of the other letters and is densely packed with doctrine. It contains a résumé of God's plan for the salvation of the world, of its preparation in the Old Testament, and of its fulfillment in Jesus Christ (1 : 1-7).

Paul gives thanks to God for the faith of the Christians at Rome, expresses his desire and hope of visiting them very soon, and then states the principal theme of the Epistle : Salvation in Jesus Christ is accessible to everyone through faith (1 : 16-17). This theme is developed in two parts : justification, i.e., remission of sins and participation in the divine life in Christ (1 : 18–5 : 21); sanctification, i.e., progress and growth in the Christian life (Chs. 6, 7, 8).

In the first part, which deals with justification, the Apostle presents two pictures of men outside the Gospel who turn their backs to salvation : on one side, the pagans, because of their failure to recognize the true God, their sinful idolatry, and the vices which come from it (1 : 18-32); on the other, the Jews, because of their violations of the Law which, in spite of their privileges as a chosen people, put them along with the pagans among sinners liable to divine punishment (2 : 1–3 : 20).

In contrast to these two groups, through faith in Jesus Christ who has been an instrument of propitiation for our sins by His death on the cross, a man, whether he be Jew or Gentile, becomes just in the eyes of God without the works of the Law (3 : 21-31).

Saint Paul always stresses the continuity between the Old and New Testament, and, therefore, he shows how the Christian faith was prefigured in Abraham. In the case of the patriarch also, it was the principle of his justification, independently of circumcision (Ch. 4).

Ch. 5 serves as a transition to the second part. Justification brings us, along with the love of God poured into our hearts by the Holy Spirit, the definite hope of salvation, especially since the sin of Adam, which has passed to all mankind, has been atoned for to a superabundant degree by the sacrifice of Christ.

Chapters 6, 7, and 8 are concerned with sanctification or the development of the Christian life. Being freed from sin by Baptism, the Christian ought to live unto God and serve Him actively (Ch. 6). Freed from the servitude of the Law, in the eyes of which man without the grace of Christ is powerless (Ch. 7), the Christian united with Jesus Christ leads a life according to the Spirit, which enables him to triumph over the flesh and attain to the glory which is reserved for him as a son of God and brother of Christ. We have the strongest possible reasons for expecting to enjoy this final glorification : the yearning of all creation, our own groanings and desires, the intercession of the Holy Spirit who prays in us and with us, and the will of God who has ordered all things unto the good of these who love Him (Ch. 8).

The demonstration in detail of Rom. 1 : 16-17 ends with Ch. 8. In the three following chapters, 9, 10, and 11, he turns his attention to his own people who have remained outside the blessings brought by Christ, and he examines the unbelief of Israel, considering it under the three following aspects : the sovereign independence of God in the distribution of His gifts, the guilt of Israel, and the prospect of a future conversion.

The moral instruction begins in Ch. 12. Saint Paul teaches here the duties of the members of the Church in their relations with one another, especially charity (12 : 9-21), then obedience to civil authority (13 : 1-7) and again charity (13 : 8-10), and finally mutual forbearance in a community in which there were divergences between the ascetical practices of the strong and the weak (14 : 1-15 : 13).

In the epilogue (15 : 14-16 : 27), the Apostle makes known his intention of going to Spain by way of Rome, after having first journeyed to Jerusalem to deliver the alms contributed by the Churches of Macedonia and Achaia (15 : 14-33). Ch. 16 contains the greetings of Paul and his companions, which are especially numerous in this case, and ends with a doxology.

This final chapter is the only one which has raised any difficulties in respect to textual criticism or authenticity. The heretic Marcion, in the second century, rejected it, and also Ch. 15. In our days, all doubts concern Ch. 16 only. Apart from the doxology, several authors, while accepting the Pauline authorship of Ch. 16 : 1-24, maintain that this section did not belong originally to the Epistle to the Romans. They regard this passage as a fragment of a lost letter which might have been addressed to the Ephesians. This hypothesis, however, can hardly displace the traditional view.

The doxology (16 : 25-27) is a much more controversial matter. Some look upon it as an addition of Marcionite origin, but this view does not seem tenable. Others regard it as of Catholic origin, while others still defend its Pauline authorship and maintain that it formed a part of the Epistle to the Romans from the beginning. It must be recognized that the variable position of the doxology in the manuscript tradition — either after 14 : 23, or after 15, or 15 : 33, or 16 : 20, or 16 : 24, or after both 14 : 23 and 16 : 24 — raises a complex problem which has not yet been clarified.

5. — The Epistles of the Captivity.

Place and date of composition.

The designation, " Epistles of the Captivity ", is given to four letters of Saint Paul : Colossians, Philemon, and Ephesians, which have a close connection through doctrine (Col., Eph.) or through the circumstances of their composition (Col., Philem.), and Philippians, which is independent of the three others. They have this feature in common, namely, that they were written while the Apostle was a prisoner. There is a problem as to which captivity is meant, for Saint Paul bore chains more than once. The ancients who dealt with this problem maintained that it was the first Roman captivity (61-63). In our own days a certain number of critics have maintained various opinions. Some have held that it was Paul's captivity at Caesarea (at least in the case of Col. and Philem., together with or without Eph.), according as they do or do not admit the authenticity of the latter. Others place the composition either of the four epistles, or of the epistle to the Philippians alone, during the captivity of the Apostle at Ephesus (between 53-56 or 55-57). The principal objection advanced against this last opinion is that Saint Luke in Acts does not mention this Ephesian captivity. Since, according to Col. 4 : 10, and Philem. 24, Luke was near Paul and Paul was in prison when he was writing these letters, it would be strange, if they were composed at Ephesus, that Luke should be silent on this captivity which he would have shared. The account of the apostolate of Paul at Ephesus ought to have formed a part of the *Wir-Stücke* (" We-passages "), but this is not the case.

The traditional opinion places the composition of the four epistles at Rome, but it is difficult to decide on the order of their writing, i.e., whether the group Col., Philem., Eph. was written first, and then Phil., or inversely. In Phil. 2 : 24, the Apostle foresees his approaching liberation, but Philem. 22 can be interpreted in the same sense. Hence, scholars are inclined to allow for only a small interval between Col., Philem., Eph., and Phil. If this last letter is assigned toward the end of Paul's captivity (spring, 63), the three others probably preceded it by several months.

Epistle to the Colossians [1].

Occasion, purpose, and content.

The Church of Colossae in the Roman Province of Asia, as likewise its neighbors in the valley of the Lycus, the Churches of Laodicea and Hierapolis, had not been founded by Saint Paul in person [2]. The converts of these churches had not seen his face (Col. 2 : 1), although during his sojourn at Ephesus (55-57) his influence had reached them through his disciples. Paul gives the glory of having preached the Gospel in these regions to his collaborator Epaphras (Col. 1 : 7; 4 : 12-13). It is very probable that it was the information brought by Epaphras on the state of these churches which led Paul to write his letter to the Colossians.

Its purpose is to put them on their guard against innovators who threaten the purity of the faith and Christian practice. Although we cannot determine exactly the origin of these errors nor describe them in detail, Saint Paul's refutation permits us to pick out two principal points. The false teachers were interposing between God and man hierarchies of angels as instruments of mediation and objects of cult, to the detriment of the unique mediation of Christ and of His sovereign primacy. With this speculative error, with this false " gnosis ", were combined practices in which we recognize the influence of Judaism, which was flourishing in these regions : restrictions in the use of foods, observation of Jewish feasts, new moons, and sabbaths.

In opposition to these deviations, Saint Paul exalts the absolute primacy of Christ as the beginning and end of creation, as the head of the Church which is His body, and His unique and universal mediation, which, through the blood poured out on the cross, reconciles and pacifies all things. This primacy and this mediation raise Christ above all created beings, the angels included. This is the teaching which the Colossians

---

Translator's note. — [1 Cf. E. LOHMEYER, *Die Briefe an die Philipper, an die Kolosser und an Philemon* (Göttingen, 1953). J. MICHL, " Die Versöhnung : Col. 1 : 20 ", *Theologische Quartalschrift* (1948), 442-452. M. DE LA TAILLE, " Chirographum decreti ", *RSR* (1916), 458-471. On Col. 2 : 15, cf. F. PRAT, *ibid.* (1912), 201-229].

Translator's note. — [2 Cf. S. E. JOHNSON, " Laodicea and its Neighbors ", *BA*, XIII (Febr., 1950), 1 ff.].

received, the *mystery* of which Saint Paul is the minister
I : 15–2 : 5).

After this doctrinal exposition, the Apostle expressly warns
the Colossians not to let themselves be seduced by vain speculations, but to remain firmly attached to Christ, in whom dwells
the fulness of the divinity, and not to submit to the practices
extolled by the innovators, nor to their exaggerated cult of
angels. Dead with Christ " to the elements of the world ",
withdrawn in their religious conduct from every power other
than Christ, they ought to live in Him and by Him the life of
those risen (2 : 6–3 : 4).

The Apostle draws from this some applications on vices to
be mortified, virtues to be acquired, and presents a certain
number of special precepts : duties of husband and wife, of
parents and children, of masters and slaves, assiduous prayer,
good example given to those outside (3 : 5–4 : 6). He ends
with some items of news and salutations (4 : 7-18).

Epistle to Philemon.

Occasion and purpose.

This short letter has a close connection with the Epistle
to the Colossians. At the end of the latter, Paul announced
that he was sending to Colossae his fellow-worker, Tychicus,
with a companion, Onesimus (Col. 4 : 7-9). This Onesimus
was the slave of an important personage in Colossae, Philemon, a friend of Paul and won over by him to Christ probably
during the sojourn at Ephesus. After having fled from the
house of his master, Onesimus had come—after what experiences
we do not know—to Paul in his imprisonment. Paul
converted him and trained him in the Christian life.

Taking advantage of Tychicus' journey to Colossae, the
Apostle sent back the fugitive slave to his master Philemon
with a letter of recommendation to procure for him a favorable
welcome. With an admirable delicacy, which makes this letter
a " genuine little masterpiece of the epistolary style " (Renan),
Paul emphasizes the motives which may be calculated to obtain
the desired effect : his situation as a prisoner, the well-known
charity of Philemon, the conversion of Onesimus, now become
the brother of his master, and the spiritual services rendered

by the Apostle to his correspondent. The tone is not one of authority which commands, but of trusting friendship and of fraternity in Christ which is confident of its being reciprocated.

Epistle to the Ephesians [1].

The recipients.

The title, " Epistle to the Ephesians ", which we read in our editions of the New Testament, is not Saint Paul's, but comes from those who made the collection of his letters, the *Corpus Paulinum*. This title raises difficulties, some arising out of the manuscript tradition, others from the contents of the letter.

In the salutation of 1 : 1, " Paul, an apostle of Christ Jesus... to the saints who are *at Ephesus* ", the words " *at Ephesus* " are missing in the most ancient witnesses of the text : in P[46] (a papyrus of the third century), in the two most reliable uncials, the *Vaticanus* and the *Sinaiticus* (4th century), and in Ms 1739 of Mount Athos (10th century), and they were erased in *Codex Vindobonensis* 424 (11th century). In the middle of the second century, Marcion ignored or rejected this reading, and commentaries of Origen and of Saint Basil show that these two authors read simply " from those who are ", without the name of a city.

An examination of the epistle indicates that its contents do not agree very well with the destination, " at Ephesus ". We find no personal recollections, no allusion to the long sojourn that Paul made at Ephesus, no special greeting addressed to the numerous friends he had in that city. Moreover, he speaks of the faith and charity of his correspondents as if he had not personally preached the Gospel to them, and knew their merits only by hearsay (1 : 15).

To meet these difficulties, two opinions are advanced by Biblical scholars. One group proposes to see in the epistle a circular letter to a group of churches of the Province of Asia,

---

Translator's note. — [1 Cf. J. KONN, *Die Idee der Kirche* (Einsiedeln, 1946; cf. *Theologische Revue* [1950], 27). H. SCHLIER and V. WARNACH, *Die Kirche im Epheserbrief* (Münster i. W., 1949; cf. *Theologische Revue* [1950], 29-33). P. COLLI, *La pericope paolina ad Ephesios* 5 : 32 *nella interpretazione dei S.S. Padri e del Concilio di Trento* (Diss. Pont. Univ. Greg., Parma, 1951].

of which Ephesus was the capital. Many of the adherents of this solution would regard the words " at Ephesus " in Verse 1 as authentic and as having been suppressed later to emphasize to a greater degree the circular character of the letter. Others regard the epistle, which is called " To the Ephesians ", as destined for a particular church, which was not Ephesus, but Laodicea. This would be the letter to which Saint Paul alludes in Col. 4 : 16. " When this letter has been read among you, see that it be read in the church of the Laodiceans also; and that you yourselves read the letter from Laodicea ". This opinion can claim the ancient testimony of Marcion (middle of the 2nd century). There remains, however, to account for the suppression of the words " at Laodicea " and for their replacement by " at Ephesus ". The reason has been given that, on account of its conduct, which is severely blamed in the Apocalypse (3 : 15), the Church of Laodicea would have been judged unworthy to figure at the head of a letter of Saint Paul. This explanation cannot pretend to certitude. It is the weak point in an opinion which appears to us, however, as preferable to the hypothesis—unknown to Antiquity—of a circular letter.

Authenticy.

The Pauline origin of the epistle is firmly attested by the witnesses of Antiquity, without a discordant note. It was first attacked in the nineteenth century on the basis of arguments drawn from vocabulary, style, doctrine, and comparison with the Epistle to the Colossians. To meet the objections of a philological and stylistic order, it is sufficient to maintain that we must grant to Saint Paul as a writer a legitimate variety and freedom in expression. The teaching of Ephesians, in its essential points, does not contradict that of former epistles, but extends and deepens it. The comparison with Col. reveals a complex mixture of resemblance and of originality which could not be the work of a plagiarist.

Object and content.

While the central idea in the Epistle to the Colossians was the absolute primacy of Christ over every creature, in the Epistle to the Ephesians it is the Church, the body of Christ, and its plenitude or *pleroma*.

The exposition is divided into two parts, one dogmatic (1 : 3–3 : 21), the other moral (4 : 1–6 : 20). In the dogmatic part, Saint Paul teaches that all, Jews and pagans, without distinction of race or religion, are called to be united in Christ and to form a single body, which is the Church. This union has been decreed by the Father, merited by the redemption of Christ, and accomplished efficaciously by the Holy Spirit. The incorporation in Christ of Jews and pagans, realized in the Church, is the *mystery* that Saint Paul has the mission to preach.

The moral part has as its end to promote this union in Christ by general precepts which relate especially to the unity and sanctity of the faithful in the Church, and by particular precepts which concern domestic life. Marriage is the object of a special section (5 : 22-23). The epistle ends with an exhortation to spiritual combat and with a description of the Christian's armor.

Epistle to the Philippians [1].

Occasion.

As the text itself shows (1 : 7, 13, 14), this epistle was written when Saint Paul was in prison. Informed of his captivity, the Philippians had come to the aid of the man who had been the founder of their church (Acts 16 : 12-40) and who had kept up the most affectionate relations with them (Phil. 4 : 1, 10, 15 ff.). They had sent to him one of their community, Epaphroditus, to take him their alms. When Epaphroditus, after having fulfilled his mission and recovered from a grave illness, was preparing to return to Philippi, Saint Paul seized the occasion to write to the Philippians and to give them news and counsels.

Content.

It is useless to look for a systematic plan in the Epistle to the Philippians. It is the free and unrestrained conversation of a father with very dear children. We can, however, discern in it a dominant note, that of spiritual joy (3 : 1; 4 : 4). It is emotional feeling, therefore, which gives unity in this case, and not a doctrinal idea.

Translator's note. — [1 J. FORESTELL, " Christian Perfection and Gnosis in Phil. 3 : 1-16 ", *CBQ* (1956), 123-136. N. FLANAGAN, " A Note on Phil. 3 : 20-21 ", *ibid.* (1956), 8-9. J. GEWIESS, " Zum altkirchlichen Verständnis der Kenosisstelle (Phil. 2 : 5-11) ", *Theologische Quartalschrift* (1948), 463-487].

After the prayer of thanksgiving and of petition for the Philippians (1 : 3-11) and the news on the condition and feelings of the Apostle in prison (1 : 12-26), come exhortations to union, to humility, and to vigilance (1 : 26-2 : 18). Here is found the famous passage on Christ, who, preexisting in a divine state, made himself obedient for our sake, even unto the death of the cross (2 : 5-11). Having made known to the Philippians his projects concerning a mission of Timothy to Philippi and the return of Epaphroditus (2 : 19-30), Saint Paul passes abruptly to a sharp warning against the Judaizers. This is followed by an exhortation to perfection (3 : 1–4 : 1). Then come recommendations relative to some Christians of Philippi and a new call to joy, to prayer, to the seeking of all that is true, just, good, and lovable (4 : 2-9). The letter ends with thanks to the Philippians for the alms received (4 : 10 20) and with greetings from Paul and his companions, with whom are joined " the saints of Caesar's household " (4 : 21-23). This last reference is, together with the *praetorium* of 1 : 11, one of the indications which fix Rome as the place of composition of the Epistle to the Philippians, although the argument is not absolutely decisive.

6. — The Pastoral Epistles [1].

The recipients.

The title, " Pastoral Epistles ", is given to three letters which Saint Paul wrote to his disciples and co-workers, Timothy and Titus. Two of these letters are addressed to Timothy and the third to Titus. The title, " pastoral ", comes from the fact that they were destined for pastors of churches and treat of the duties of their office. When Saint Paul was writing to these helpers, Timothy was at Ephesus, where the Apostle had entrusted to him for a time the direction of the Christian community, and Titus was in Crete, likewise on a temporary mission to the faithful of that island.

Translator's note. — [1 Cf. C. Spicq, O. P., *Saint Paul : Les Epîtres pastorales* (Paris, 1947; cf. *Theologische Revue* [1951], 93)].

Place and date of composition.

I Tim. does not give us any definite information about the place where it was written. We may conjecture that it was Macedonia according to **1** : 3, and the same region or a neighboring region for Tit., according to **3** : 12 which fixes Nicopolis in Epirus as the place of meeting. The information in 2 Tim. is more explicit. From **1** : 16-17 we can infer that the Apostle is at Rome, and this is confirmed by the final salutation of **4** : 21, where the four names are Latin [1]. Paul is a captive, almost without companions, and he requests Timothy to come to him (**4** : 20).

The three epistles have an evident relationship to one another and were written at the same period in the life of Saint Paul. On the other hand, the indications given by 1 Tim. about Paul's journeys during thus period cannot be fitted into his apostolic career as covered in Acts up to the first Roman captivity (61-63). We may add that the manner in which Saint Paul speaks in 2 Tim. of his situation as a prisoner, of his almost universal abandonment (**4** : 16), and of his condemnation being regarded as certain (**4** : 6, 7, 18), supposes conditions harder than those of the first Roman captivity. We are led, therefore, to place the writing of these epistles between the end of the first Roman captivity (63) and the second captivity which ended in martyrdom (67).

Content.

The three epistles do not constitute, even when combined, a complete exposition of the duties of pastors, but a series of practical recommendations concerning the direction and organization of Christian communities : preservation of sound doctrine and of moral life as inculcated by the Gospel, guarding of the deposit of faith against false teachers (1 Tim. **1** : 3-11; **4** : 1-7; **6** : 3-4, 20; 2 Tim. **1** : 13-14; **2** : 16; **3** : 1-9, 13-17; **4** : 1-5; Tit. **1** : 10-16; **3** : 9-11), universal prayer — and especially for those who hold civil authority (1 Tim. **2** : 1-8), obedience to this authority (Tit. **3** : 1), dress and behavior of women in public gatherings (1 Tim. **2** : 9-15), the choice of sacred ministers,

---

Translator's note. — [1 Only two of the names, Pudens and Claudia, are clearly Latin].

presbyters-bishops (the two terms are equivalent, 1 Tim. 3 : 1-7; Tit. 1 : 5-9) and deacons (1 Tim. 3 : 8-13), conduct to be observed with regard to different classes of the faithful — old people, young people, slaves (1 Tim. 5 : 1-2; 6 : 1-2; Tit. 2 : 1-10), widows (1 Tim. 5 : 3-16), and presbyters (1 Tim. 5 : 17-22). With these recommendations of a general order are combined confidential observations, bits of advice which refer more especially and sometimes solely to the personal conduct of Titus and Timothy, and even to the health of the latter (1 Tim. 5 : 23). The Second Epistle to Timothy is distinguished by the tone of confident frankness with which Saint Paul speaks of himself and of his correspondent. It is the last and touching farewell of the old champion of the faith to his favorite disciple.

The question of authenticity.

From the content of the Pastoral Epistles, especially from the sections concerning ecclesiastical organization, which appears firmly established, and also from the vocabulary and the style, a number of critics have derived arguments against the Pauline authenticity. Some reject it totally, while others do so partially in the sense that they would regard the Pastorals as amplifications of Pauline notes, retaining only some authentic fragments. To such denials of Pauline authenticity Catholic commentators and some Protestant conservatives and Anglicans oppose the strength of the tradition which from the formation of the *Corpus Paulinum* has included these pastoral epistles among the Pauline Epistles : the concordant evidence of the ecclesiastical authors around the end of the second century (the Canon of Muratori at Rome, Saint Irenaeus at Lyons, Tertullian in Africa, Clement of Alexandria in Egypt), and the absence of any doubts whatever in the subsequent period, for Eusebius of Caesarea (*Hist. Eccles.* III, 3) ranks the Pastorals among the unquestioned writings of the New Testament. As for the arguments brought forward by our adversaries, we must recognize that the difference in vocabulary from that of the other Pauline Epistles is appreciable, but it can be explained by the nature of the Pastorals and their subject matter. While ecclesiastical organization occupies a more considerable place here than in the other epistles, this is not to be regarded as something new, for the essential features are already visible before, the distinction between presbyters-bishops and deacons being clearly marked previously, as in Phil. 1 : 1. We may well suppose that the Apostle, at the end of his life, insisted more strongly on the constitution of the Church, which was to continue his work.

7. — The Epistle to the Hebrews [1].

The Pauline authenticity.

The Epistle to the Hebrews constitutes a unity apart in the *Corpus Paulinum.* Its composition and its intended recipients equally raise problems, the solution of which remains clouded in obscurity. Christian Antiquity is not unanimous in its testimony. Although this epistle was utilized as early as the end of the first century by Clement of Rome, a number of writers in the West between the end of the second and the middle of the fourth century did not receive it as inspired Scripture because they did not believe it was Saint Paul's. This is especially true of the African writers. The Eastern Churches, on the contrary, were always in agreement in affirming the Pauline origin of the epistle, and in P[46] (3rd cent.) it is placed between Rom. and 1 Cor. From the middle of the fourth century this tradition gains ground in the West, and from the fifth century the Epistle to the Hebrews is inscribed in the catalogs of Scripture as belonging to Saint Paul. Although the ancients often combined the two questions, namely, that of canonicity and that of Pauline origin, they should be kept separate. The canonicity of the Epistle to the Hebrews, which involves its inspired character, is a truth of Faith, but the Church has made no definition respecting Pauline authorship. A decree of the Biblical Commission (June 24, 1914) affirmed it, but permitted a distinction—which the ancients, especially Origen, already took into account—to be made between *the author* of the letter, Saint Paul, to whom belongs its conception and the doctrine taught, and *the redactor,* who assumed the chief responsibility for its composition and literary form (see

Translator's note. — [1 Cf. W. MANSON, *The Epistle to the Hebrews : An Historical and Theological Reconsideration* (London, 1951). C. SPICQ, O. P., " Alexandriniennes dans l'Epître aux Hébreux ", *RB* (1951), 481-502. O. MICHEL, *Der Brief an die Hebräer* (Göttingen, 1955). J. HERING, *L'Epître aux Hébreux* (Neuchâtel-Paris, 1954)].

pp. 769-770). A comparison of the Epistle to the Hebrews with the other Pauline Epistles reveals definitely notable differences in style, and in the manner of quoting Scripture and of interpreting it allegorically. Rationalistic critics generally reject this distinction between author and redactor and do not consider the Epistle to the Hebrews as a work of Saint Paul but of a later writer (between 80 and 100), without, however, being in agreement on its doctrinal role in relation to Paulinism.

The recipients.

This is a question which remains very much disputed even among Catholics. The title, " To the Hebrews ", given to the epistle from the middle of the second century, suggests that the recipients be sought among the Christians converted from Judaism, and the contents of the epistle fit into this situation very well. The frequent recourse to texts of the Old Testament, the recalling of facts from the history of Israel supposedly known by the readers, and the contrast between the priesthood of Christ and Levitical religious practices, including details on aspersions and purifications, all appear to be explained best if the epistle is regarded as being addressed to Jews by birth rather than to converted pagans.

There is still great uncertainty regarding the identity of the Church to which the recipients belonged. Rome, Alexandria, Jerusalem (or a community in Palestine), among others, have been proposed. Saint John Chrysostom suggested Jerusalem, but we can scarcely grant more than a strong probability to this view.

Place and date of composition.

The place of origin remains uncertain. The final salutation of 13 : 24 has suggested Italy, but the text is not decisive, for the phrase can mean " the brethren who came from Italy " and who accompany me. Taken in this sense, the text is used as a supporting argument by those who make the Church of Rome the recipient of the epistle.

Catholics, in defending the Pauline authenticity of the Epistle to the Hebrews, place its writing during the last years of the Apostle. The internal evidence favors a date anterior to 70. As Father Lagrange has remarked, " We all know that Heb. speaks of sacrifices in the present. It is true that its outline is derived from Scripture rather than drawn according to reality, and that the tabernacle rather than the Temple of Herod serves as a basis for its exposition. But would the epistle have passed over in silence the catastrophe of the year 70? For going beyond the fatal date of that year, very grave reasons would be necessary, and these are lacking " [1].

Purpose and content.

The author himself has characterized his work as a discourse of exhortation (**13** : 22). The tone is oratorical and recalls the homiletic style. This discourse, however, remains in the form of an epistle, without the initial address, it is true, as 1 Jn., but with final salutations. The author has in mind definite correspondents, a particular community whose situation he knows well.

The purpose in view is not directly dogmatic but practical : to exhort and cheer members of the faithful who have already undergone persecution and remain under its threat, in order to avert the danger of defection and of apostasy, to reawaken faith, hope, and vigilant courage which will assure perseverance. But these warnings and exhortations, which are first combined with dogmatic explanations and then presented by themselves in the last chapters (**10** : 19–**13** : 17), rest on a doctrinal foundation. The central dogmatic theme is the priesthood of Christ considered in its basic character (the union of the divine and human natures in Christ, as this is brought out by comparison with the angels, **1** : 4-14; **2** : 5-17), and in its accomplishment. This sacerdotal theology is developed under the form of a comparison with the Levitical priesthood, and through this comparison the absolute and definitive superiority of Christ, sovereign Priest according to the order of Melchisedech (**7** : 1–**10** : 18), is made evident. The faithful will find consolation and comfort in this contemplation of Jesus, Son of God, who by his unique sacrifice saves them and purifies them, and who, as sovereign Priest, has entered heaven, where he lives forever and is zealous in interceding for their sake.

[1] *RB* (1919), 265.

B. — THE CATHOLIC EPISTLES.

1. — The Epistle of Saint James.

Authenticity.

As Saint Jerome noted, the Epistle of Saint James came to be known and acquired authority in the Church only slowly and progressively. It is not referred to in any explicit way by ecclesiastical writers before the third century. At this time, Origen testifies that it was accepted by the Church of Alexandria, and eventually, with the exception of some doubts and hesitations in the Syrian churches, this became the case throughout the East. Toward the middle of the fouth century, the West became acquainted with the epistle through the Eastern Churches, and it took its place unchallenged in the official lists of inspired books.

The author, who merely calls himself James without any further qualification (1 : 1), is identified by the Fathers with James, called " the brother of the Lord ", first bishop of Jerusalem, who was martyred in the year 62. This James is certainly distinct from the Apostle James, son of Zebedee and brother of John, and also, in our opinion, from the Apostle James, son of Alpheus. Hence, he was not a member of the college of the Twelve Apostles.

The recipients. Place and date of composition.

The epistle is addressed " to the twelve tribes that are in the Dispersion " (1 : 1). This is ordinarily interpreted as meaning Christians of Jewish origin dispersed through the world, rather than Christians in general. It must have been sent from Jerusalem where James resided. It was written before 62 (martyrdom of James). As regards the determination of a more exact date, Catholic authors differ in their opinions. Those who maintain that James knew the Epistles to the Galatians and to the Romans, and that he is rectifying the false interpretation that certain individuals were giving to justification by faith in Saint Paul, place the composition of the epistle between 57-58 (the date of the Epistle to the Romans) and 62. Among those who do not admit this dependence, many go back much further and put it before the Council of Jerusalem held in the year 49. The Protestant critics who reject its authenticity assign the epistle to a later date, placing it at the end of the first century or during the second.

Purpose and content.

The purpose of the epistle, which by its moral preaching and its practical character recalls the sapiential literature of the Old Testament, is to instruct and exhort. Its teachings do not form a series in rigorous sequence. The author treats successively of behavior to be observed in trials (1 : 2-12), of temptation (1 : 13-18), of duties with regard to speaking the truth (1 : 19-27), of mercy to be shown to all without respect to persons (2 : 1-13), of the necessity of combining works with faith (2 : 14-26), of sins of the tongue (3 : 1-12), of true and false wisdom (3 : 13-18), of faults which cause discord (4 : 1-12), and of chastisements which threaten the unjust rich (4 : 13–5 : 6). The epistle ends with a series of individual admonitions on swearing, on prayer, and on fraternal correction (5 : 7-20). It is here that we find a celebrated text on Extreme Unction and the public confession of sins [1].

One thought dominates all these instructions : the necessity of putting into practice one's religion, of combining works with faith. Written in an alert and picturesque style, the epistle is animated by an ardent conviction in which the inspiration of the Prophets is combined with evangelical simplicity.

2. — The Epistles of Saint Peter and of Saint Jude.

The First Epistle of St. Peter [2].

The question of authenticity.

Ancient tradition held firmly to the Petrine origin of this epistle. Apart from the fact that it was used by writers of the

---

Translator's note. — [1 With Jas. 5 : 14 ff. cf. Mk. 6 : 13. Cf. T. SPACIL, S. J., *Doctrina theologica Orientis separati de Sacra Infirmorum Unctione* (*Orientalia Christiana* 24, 2, Rome, 1931). J. KEULERS, *De Boeken van het Nieuwe Testament.* VII (Roermond-Maaseik, 1956), 58 ff. J. MICHL, *Die Katholischen Briefe* (*Regensburger N. T.* 8, 1953), 171-174].

Translator's note. — [2 Cf. E. G. SELWYN, *The First Epistle of St. Peter* (2nd ed., London, 1947; cf. *Theologische Revue* [1951], 93-94). On 1 Pet. 3 : 17 ff., cf. B. REICKE, *The Disobedient Spirits and Christian Baptism* (Copenhagen, 1947; cf. *RB* [1947], 448-449; *Theologische Revue* [1951], 88)].

second century (Clement of Rome, Papias, Polycarp, the Didache, the Epistle of Barnabas, Justin, the Shepherd of Hermas), it is formally attributed to Peter at the end of the second century and in the first half of the third by Tertullian, Clement of Alexandria, and Origen. The epistle itself (5 : 12) gives an answer to the objection which is made that Peter could not write Greek readily : Peter employed Silvanus (*alias* Silas) as secretary.

The recipients.

The letter is addressed to the elect who reside in the Diaspora in Pontus, Galatia, Cappadocia, Asia (the Roman Province), and Bithynia. The term *Diaspora* (Dispersion) would suggest Jewish Christians, but the allusions to the pagan customs of former times (4 : 3-4) point to Christians of Gentile origin. It is probable, however, that converted Jews formed a considerable element in these churches. The epistle is represented as having been written from Babylon, where Saint Peter was with Mark, his spiritual son (5 : 13). The ancient authors agree in regarding " Babylon " as a designation for Rome. The same metaphor is found in the apocalyptic Jewish literature and in the Apocalypse of Saint John.

Purpose and content.

The epistle tells us (4 : 12 ff.) that the faithful to whom it is addressed have had to pass through the " fire " of trial, without mention being made, strictly speaking, of an actual persecution instituted by the civil authorities. It does not appear clearly that the letter was written because of these tribulations. It presents itself as an exhortation to Christians to confirm them in the faith which they have received (5 : 12).

The epistle proceeds without following a clearly marked plan. However, apart from the prologue with its initial greeting and prayer of thanksgiving for the benefits conferred by Christ (1 : 1-12), and the epilogue with its final salutations (5 : 12-14), various groups of instructions can be distinguished.

In the first place, the author draws attention to several essential characteristics of Christian life (1 : 13–2 : 10) : sanctity, in order to conform to God who is holy and to recognize the redemption accomplished by the blood of Christ; fraternal charity; union of the faithful with Christ, the corner stone, in order that they may be so many living stones in a spiritual house. This is their nobility and their greatness, for they are a chosen race, a royal priesthood, a holy nation.

Following this picture sketched in broad lines, comes an exposition on a certain number of special duties (2 : 11–4 : 6) : exemplary conduct to be maintained when among pagans, duties toward civil authorities, duties of servants, of married women and of their husbands, duties of the faithful among themselves, conduct to be observed in respect to the pagans who calumniate and persecute them. It is here we find the passage on the descent of Christ into hell after his resurrection (3 : 19–4 : 6).

The author returns to general counsels : practice of the Christian virtues (prayer, vigilance, fraternal charity) while awaiting the coming of Christ, for " the end of all things is at hand ", and the maintenance of joyous confidence in the midst of persecutions (4 : 7-19).

Again mention is made of special duties, namely those of presbyters and the faithful (5 : 1-5). In closing, Peter admonishes all to humility, vigilance, firmness in the faith, confidence in God in trials. One might well say of this First Epistle of Peter that it is a letter to be read in time of persecution.

The Second Epistle of St. Peter.

The question of authenticity.

Although this letter presents itself as the work of " Simon Peter, a servant and apostle of Jesus Christ " (1 : 1), witness of the Transfiguration of the Lord (1 : 16-18), its authenticity — as distinct from its canonicity, defined by the Church — is much more difficult to establish than that of the First Epistle. Before the third century we do not find any definite mention of 2 Pet. Then we learn that the epistle was accepted by some (Origen, in the first place), but ignored or rejected by others, in the East as well as in the West. In the fourth century Eusebius places it among the contested writings.

To these uncertainties of tradition, which do not permit a definite judgment, are added the difficulties which are raised by internal criticism and which furnish arguments for postulating another author than Saint Peter and a date of composition later than his martyrdom in the year 64 : differences of vocabulary with 1 Pet.; curious similarities to the Epistle of Jude and probable dependence of 2 Pet. with regard to Jude; the response to objections based on the delay of the Second Coming (3 : 4, 9), a response which supposes another attitude than that of Peter in his first epistle and which is more easily explained after the first apostolic generation; and also such expressions as " the fathers ", or people of the first Christian generation, of whom the author speaks as of the faithful who are dead (3 : 4), and the allusion to the epistles of Saint Paul as forming, in whole or in part, a collection, and the designation of these epistles as " Scriptures " (3 : 15-16).   While several of these difficulties are not decisive, they become formidable, however, when considered as a whole.   The great majority of non-Catholic critics reject the Petrine origin of the epistle. Among Catholics, many revive a suggestion of Saint Jerome that Peter made use of a different secretary than the one he had employed for the first epistle.   Some judge that this hypothesis may explain differences of vocabulary and of style between 1 and 2 Pet., but it does not solve the other difficulties in a satisfactory manner.   Hence they see in 2 Pet. a case of pseudonymity analogous to that occurring in Wisdom and Ecclesiastes in the Old Testament.   According to this view, the author, who wrote in the years 70-80, after the capture of Jerusalem, was a disciple of the Apostles and perhaps of their chief, was qualified to transmit apostolic teaching, and borrowed Peter's name in order to give full authority to this transmission [1]. Others, struck by the fact that Chapter 2, in which 2 Pet. follows the Epistle of Jude, interrupts the development of the exposition on the Second Coming begun in 1 : 16-21, advance the " hypothesis of an authentic Petrine writing, which was taken up again later by a disciple who probably completed it with the aid of Jude and recast its whole composition " [2].

The recipients and content.

The initial greeting is very general : " To those who have obtained an equal privilege of faith with ourselves through the

---

[1] JOSEPH CHAINE, Les Epîtres catholiques, (Paris, 1939), pp. 30-31.
[2] P. BENOIT, Vivre et penser, (Paris 1941), p. 136, n. 2.

justice of our God and Savior Jesus Christ ". On account of
the allusion to a first epistle (3 : 1) it is possible that the recipients
of 2 Pet. are the same as those of 1 Pet., but this is not certain.
" The attack on licentiousness and the recourse to the great
authority of Saint Paul indicate communities of pagan rather
than of Jewish origin " (Chaine).

The epistle begins with an exhortation to the practice of
Christian virtues, which the author, in anticipation of his
approaching death, recalls to his correspondents, insisting on
the veracity of his testimony as of one who had beheld the
Transfiguration of Christ. He cautions the faithful against
false teachers, deniers of Christ, given to debauchery, greedy,
and rebellious to authority in the Church; they will be chastised
like the guilty angels, the impious at the time of the Deluge,
the inhabitants of Sodom and Gomorrha. These false teachers
scoff at the Second Coming, because it is delayed. The author
explains the delay by the patience and mercy of God; but the
day of the Lord will come as a thief, and with it the heavens and
the earth will be renewed. It is for the faithful to hasten this
coming by the holiness of their lives.

The Epistle of St. Jude.

Ancient tradition is definitely surer about the authenticity
of this epistle than it is in the case of 2 Pet. From the end of
the second century this little document was accepted at
Alexandria, at Carthage, and at Rome. It met serious resistance
only in Syria, without doubt on account of its borrowings from
the Jewish Apocrypha, the *Book of Henoch* (vv. 14-15), and,
according to Clement of Alexandria and of Origen, from the
Assumption (or *Ascension*) *of Moses* (v. 9), although others see
in this second passage rather an allusion to an oral Jewish
tradition.

The author, Jude, " brother of James " (v. 1), is the same
person as the Jude named in Mk. **6** : 3, among the " brothers "
of our Lord. It is not proved that he is to be identified with
the Apostle Jude, who is also called Thaddeus.

There is great uncertainty regarding the identity of the
recipients. Were they Judeo-Christians or converted pagans?
There is similar uncertainty about their location. Scholars are

inclined to think of communities in Syria or Palestine, but that
is also a matter of conjecture.

The epistle is a strong diatribe against the same dissolute
teachers whom we have seen denounced in 2 Pet.

3. — The Epistles of Saint John [1].

Character of the Johannine Epistles.

The Johannine epistles are three in number. The second and
third, which are very short (13 and 15 verses respectively),
have clearly the form of letters with an initial greeting and
a final salutation. This form appears less clearly in the first,
where these customary formulas are not found. It is presented
as a doctrinal instruction, sent to a group of the faithful for
whom the author, who has authority over them, has directly
written it (he repeats this thirteen times), and with whom he
is on close and intimate terms. These two characteristics, a
composition written with definite readers in view, and a tone
of intimacy, justify the use of the designation " epistle " in the
broad sense of the word.

The First Epistle of St. John.

The recipients and author.

The absence in the first epistle of personal allusions to
individual persons or to a distinct Church can be explained
if this work was addressed to a group of Churches. Such, in
fact, appears to have been its destination, in accord with the
tradition which attributes it to Saint John the Apostle. This
attribution was unanimously accepted during the first half
of the third century (Clement of Alexandria, Tertullian, Origen).
If we go back farther, the evidence furnished by Saint Irenaeus
and the Canon of Muratori toward the end of the second century,
and the citations which, according to Eusebius, Papias (first
half of the second century) made from this epistle, permit us
" to conclude that from the middle of the second century it
was accepted as a writing of Saint John " (Bonsirven). It offers

Translator's note. — [1 Cf. C. H. Dodd, *The Johannine Epistles* (London,
1946). F. Büchsel, *Die Johannesbriefe* (Leipzig, 1933; in Theol. Hd-Kom.
zum N. T.). R. Schnackenburg, *Die Johannesbriefe* (in Herders Theol.
Kom. zum N. T.; Freiburg i. Br., 1953)].

many points of resemblance to the Fourth Gospel in style and doctrine, which cannot be explained reasonably except by unity of authorship. The epistle is regarded, in general, as later than the Gospel. It was composed in a milieu where the Apostle was active during his last years, when, after the death of Domitian (97), he had returned from his exile at Patmos. He resided at Ephesus, capital of the Roman Province of Asia, and as the last survivor of the Twelve, exercised over the Churches of the region a kind of primacy, visiting them, installing bishops, and watching over the purity of the faith. The Apocalypse mentions seven Churches of the Province of Asia to which John sends a message (Apoc. 1 : 4–3 : 22); Ephesus Smyrna, Pergamum, Thyatira, Sardis, Philadelphia, Laodicea [1]. They were not the only Churches of the province, for we know in addition from Saint Paul, Colossae and Hierapolis, and from Saint Ignatius of Antioch, Tralles and Magnesia. It is to a group of these Churches that the epistle was probably addressed.

Purpose and content.

Saint John proposes to strengthen his correspondents in the faith and in the moral life emphasized by the Gospel and to put them on their guard against the dangers which threaten them from Christian apostates, " antichrists ", who deny that Jesus is the Christ, the incarnate Son of God and Savior of the world. Many scholars believe that reference is made here to the heretical teaching of Cerinthus. These defections may have been the occasion which provoked the epistle. [2]

The author does not follow a well defined plan. Expositions of doctrine, moral exhortations, warnings and words of encouragement are woven around certain dominant concepts : the life of the Christian in union with God the Father and with His Son Jesus Christ, the light which is not separated from love of God and neighbor, knowledge of God and faith in Christ which ought to be the beginning of sanctification, flight from the world and horror of sin, the exemplary love of God who has given us His Son Jesus Christ. In the Christian, life, light, and

Translator's note. — [1 Cf. the article by S. E. JOHNSON listed on p. 440 above].

Translator's note. — [2 Cf. A. WURM, *Die Irrlehrer im ersten Johannesbriefe,* Leipzig, 1903, and *Theologische Revue* (1904), 163 ff.].

charity come, through Christ, from God as substantial life, light, and charity. These are not distinct realities, but aspects of one and the same fundamental reality which will later be called " the life of sanctifying grace " [1].

Second and Third Epistles of St. John.

Authenticity.

They profess to be written by " the Ancient " (ὁ πρεσβύτερος). Catholic tradition has commonly identified this " Ancient " with the Apostle John. There were, however, some doubts and hesitations in Christian Antiquity. When Saint Irenaeus and Clement of Alexandria cite the Second Epistle as being Saint John's, Origen, and then Eusebius and Saint Jerome bear witness to the fact that the authorship of both the Second and the Third Epistle was contested. Saint Jerome says that several attribute these to John the Presbyter, who was distinct from John the Apostle. The difficulties raised regarding the apostolic origin of the Apocalypse, which some attributed to this John the Presbyter, were without doubt responsible for attributing to him also the two epistles of the " Ancient " (or Presbyter).

If, in order to confirm tradition, we have recourse to internal criticism, the two epistles appear manifestly as the work of one and the same author. On the other hand, they present

---

[1] In textual criticism only one problem has been raised, namely that of the *Comma Johanneum* (1 Jo. 5 : 7-8). A declaration of the Holy Office, dated June 2, 1927, interpreting an earlier decree of January 13, 1897, allows Catholic exegetes to discuss freely the literary authenticity *(genuinitas)* of this passage. In fact the Johannine origin of the *comma*, which is absent from the Greek mss., from the ancient versions, and from the more ancient and better mss. of the Vulgate, is generally abandoned today. The first incontestable evidence for the existence of this passage is found in a treatise *(Liber apologeticus)*, written in 384, and attributed for a long time to the Spanish heretic Priscillian. According to good judges (Dom Germain Morin, A. d'Alès), however, it ought to be restored to another Priscillianist, the bishop Instantius. [*Translator's note.* — On the *Comma Johanneum*, in addition to the pertinent sections in the Commentaries and the works on N. T. textual criticism, see especially the bibliography by A. BLUDAU in *LTK*, III (1931), 16. — F. PRAT, S. J., in *Etudes*, March, 1912, 829 ff. — J. RIVIÈRE, in *Revue Apologétique*, March, 1928, 303-309. — A. LEMONNYER, O. P., art. " Comma Johannique ", in *DBV, Suppl.* vol. II (1930), 67-73. — F. STUMMER, *Einführung in die lateinische Bibel*, Paderborn, 1928, p. 152 ff. and 183. — M. del ALAMO, in *Estudios Biblicos*, 2 (1943), 75-105. — T. AYUSO MARAZUELA, in *Biblica* 28 (1947), 83-112, and 216-235, and 29 (1948), 52-76. R. SCHNACKENBURG, *op. cit.*, 37-39. J. KEULERS, *De Boeken van het Nieuwe Testament.* VII (Roermond-Maaseik, 1956), 208-210].

many resemblances of thought and style to the first epistle, as writings which derive from the same source. This apostolic origin has won for them, in spite of their brevity, a place in the Canon of the Scriptures.

The title, " Ancient ", is explicable at the end of the first century; Saint John, the sole survivor of the Twelve, eminently merited the appellation, " Ancient ", which Papias gave to the Apostles and direct witnesses of the life of Christ.

The recipients and purpose.

The Second Epistle is addressed to an " Elect Lady ". The body of the letter indicates that the author is writing not to a single person but to a group. The " Elect Lady ", then, designates a Church, a community of the faithful, probably in Asia Minor, without our being able to be more precise. The instruction given recalls in general that of the First Epistle : exhortations to live in true faith and charity, to be on guard against seducers, the antichrists who deny the Word Incarnate, and not to receive the preachers of this false doctrine.

The Third Epistle is addressed to a certain Gaius, who is an intimate friend of the Apostle. Saint John praises him for his fidelity in walking in the truth, for his charity, and for his generosity in receiving visiting Christians, the itinerant preachers of the Gospel. He has not written directly to the head of the community, Diotrephes, because the latter shows himself rebellious to his authority, does not give hospitality to the " brethren ", and casts both them and their hosts from the assembly of the faithful. Gaius is exhorted to follow an opposite course, and the " Ancient " recommends to him especially Demetrius, an excellent man, to whom all render homage.

3. — THE APOCALYPSE [1].

Authenticity.

The book is presented as " the Apocalypse " (i.e., the Revelation) of Jesus Christ, which God gave Him, to make known to His servants the things that must shortly come to pass,

___

Translator's note. — [1 M. E. BOISMARD, " Notes sur l'Apocalypse ", *RB* (1952), 161-181. P. GÄCHTER, " The Role of the Memory in the Making of the Apocalypse ", *Theological Studies* 9 (1948), 419-452; *id.*, " The Original Sequence

and which he has signified by sending an angel to His servant John (1 : 1). We learn subsequently that this John suffered for the faith and was exiled to the island of Patmos, and that he acts as having authority over the Churches of Asia (1 : 11).

This John, the author of the Apocalypse, is identified with John the Apostle by Saint Justin, who towards 135, some forty years after the publication of the book, was converted at Ephesus, i.e., in the very city where tradition places the last years and death of John the Apostle. In the last quarter of the second century, this testimony is confirmed and strengthened by that of Saint Irenaeus, Bishop of Lyons, who had come to Gaul from Asia Minor, where he had associated with some disciples of the Apostles, and especially with Polycarp, Bishop of Smyrna. Saint Irenaeus attributes the Apocalypse to John, " the disciple of the Lord ", who for him is identical with John the Apostle.

While this tradition continues to be attested at Alexandria by Clement and Origen, in Africa by Tertullian and Saint Cyprian, and at Rome by the Canon of Muratori and Saint Hippolytus, certain doubts arise in both quarters in the course of the third century. At Rome, the priest Caius, to cut short, and in a most radical manner, the abuses which the Montanists were making of the Johannine writings, denied their authenticity and even went so far as to attribute them to the heretic Cerinthus. At Alexandria, Saint Dionysius (265), arguing against the Millenarians who were appealing to the visions of the Apocalypse, drew attention to the differences of vocabulary and of style between this book and the Fourth Gospel, in order to attribute the Apocalypse to another John, and not to John the Apostle. Eusebius echoes these doubts

of Apocalypse **20-22** ", *ibid.* 10 (1949), 485-521. The writer examines, among other things, Semitic literary forms in the Apocalypse. See Wikenhauser's analysis of these articles in *Theologische Revue* (1952), 57-60. Gächter, according to Wikenhauser, deserves special recognition for having established the presence of discrepancies in the Apocalypse against the thesis of Lohmeyer and Allo who maintain that the book was composed in accordance with a rigorous plan. How are the discrepancies to be accounted for? This is not clear. Gächter holds the " secretary ", and not the author himself, responsible for the defects, but it is really difficult to explain the problem satisfactorily. Boismard may be closer to a real solution with his theory of two Apocalypses — one from Nero's time, the other from the period of Vespasian and Domitian — which have been combined into our present Apocalypse].

and places the Apocalypse among the writings of the New Testament which are not accepted by all. The mistrust regarding the authenticity of the Apocalypse and also its canonicity persisted rather long in some Eastern circles. Saint Cyril of Jerusalem and Saint Gregory Nazianzen exclude it from their canons of Scripture, and Saint John Chrysostom and Theodoret do not cite it. The Apocalypse does not figure in the Peshitto, the official version of the Syriac Church (5th century) nor in the Armenian version. But tradition finally prevailed in the East as well as in the West.

The difficulties raised by Dionysius of Alexandria have been taken up again by modern critics. The defenders of tradition meet these by stressing the marked resemblances between the Apocalypse and the Fourth Gospel, and by explaining the differences on the basis of the diversity of subjects treated. On the special point of grammatical irregularities, frequent in the Apocalypse and absent in the Fourth Gospel, several advance as a probable hypothesis the different circumstances of composition : John could not have been able, in the case of the Apocalypse, to make use of a secretary's help as he had done in writing the Fourth Gospel. Such secretarial help would have assured a correct style while preserving its Semitic character.

Place and date of composition.

According to Apocalypse 1 : 9, John received his revelation in the island of Patmos, where he was banished because of his Christian faith. Saint Irenaeus gives us the date : it was " almost in our generation, toward the end of the reign of Domitian " (assassinated Sept. 18, 96). Eusebius and Saint Jerome also date the exile at Patmos in the fourteenth year of Domitian (94-95).

Some of the ancients (Apocryphal Acts of John, Tertullian) place the exile at Patmos and the visions of John under Nero. Several among the moderns, without accepting this date for the composition of the Apocalypse, admit that the author, according to a procedure characteristic of the apocalyptic genre, went back in imagination to the age of Vespasian (69), as if he had his visions at that time.

The recipients.

The work is addressed under the form of a circular letter to seven Churches of the Roman Province of Asia (**1** : 4, 11). Through them it would reach all the Christian communities in Asia, and would ultimately become the property of the universal Church.

Content.

After the title and its explanation (**1** : 1-3), comes the greeting of the author to his readers, together with his prayer for divine blessings and his praise of Christ, whose coming for the judgment is announced (**1** : 4-8).

Then the account of the revelations begins. Two main parts can be distinguished. The first part (**1** : 9-**3** : 22) opens with a vision in which John receives from Christ the mission to write seven letters to seven Churches of Asia, symbolized by seven stars and seven chandeliers of gold. Each of the letters describes the moral situation of the Church to which it is addressed, praises or blames it according to circumstances, and warns it to conduct itself in a manner to merit eternal beatitude.

The second part, which is much larger (**4** : 1-**22** : 5) presents a more complicated ensemble in which it is not always easy to discern the connections and progressive developments.

In a vision, which is an introduction to what follows, John beholds God on his celestial throne and the adoration given to him by twenty-four elders and four symbolic animals (**4** : 1-4) [1]. Then he sees in the hand of God a scroll closed with seven seals, which no one can open nor read except the immolated Lamb, whose praise, along with God's praise, is sung by the twenty-four elders and the four living creatures (**5** : 1-14).

The Lamb opens the seals in succession. The opening of the first four is accompanied by an account of John's vision of four horses, symbols of four scourges : a white horse, symbolizing a conquering horseman; a red horse, war; a black horse, famine; a pale-green horse, death (**6** : 1-9).

When the fifth seal is opened, we see under the altar the martyrs who call for vengeance; they must wait a little while

Translator's note. — [[1] On the twenty-four elders, see J. MICHL, *Die 24 Ältesten in der Apokalypse des hl. Joh.*, Munich, 1938].

longer, until the number of their brethren in the service of the
Lord and in martyrdom is complete (**6** : 9-11).

At the opening of the sixth seal, disturbances are produced
in nature : an earthquake, a darkening of the sun and of the
moon, the falling of stars, and lamentation of men awaiting the
great day of wrath (**6** : 12-17).

Before the opening of the seventh seal there is a vision in
which John beholds, marked with the sign of God, the elect
of the Jewish people and of the other nations of the earth, who
have come out of great tribulation; they have been saved by
the blood of the Lamb and now enjoy eternal life (**7** : 1-17).

With the seventh seal, the series of seals ends and the series
of trumpets begins.   When the seventh seal is opened, there
is silence in heaven for about half an hour.   Then seven angels
sound seven trumpets (**8** : 1–**9** : 21).

The first four trumpets (**8** : 7-12) announce cataclysms which
destroy a third of the earth, of the sea, of the waters (rivers and
springs), and of the stars.   An eagle flying through midheaven
introduces the last three trumpets which predict three great
evils (the *Three Woes*).   At the fifth trumpet, there appears
a plague of fantastic locusts which have as king the angel of the
abyss from which they have emerged; at the sixth trumpet,
a plague of horsemen and of horses not less fantastic than the
locusts.   A third of mankind is killed, but the rest do not repent
(**9** : 13-21).

Before the seventh trumpet, as previously before the seventh
seal, a vision is inserted : an angel appears in order to deliver
to John a little open scroll, which he eats so that he may prophesy
again.   John measures the temple of the Holy City.   Two
witnesses prophesy therein, and they are put to death by the
Beast who comes up out of the abyss; but God restores them
to life and glorifies them.   Seven thousand persons perish, and
the others give glory to God (**10** : 1–**11** : 13) [1].   An angel sounds
the seventh trumpet to announce the judgment (**11** : 15-19).

The series of trumpets is succeeded by a vision in which John
beholds the struggle of Satan, the great Dragon, against Christ

---

Translator's note. — [1 On the two witnesses, see J. CONSIDINE, " The Two
Witnesses (Apoc. **11** : 3-13) ", *CBQ* (1946), 311-392].

and the Church, represented by a woman [1]. Satan has for auxiliaries two Beasts, one of which comes up out of the sea and the other out of the earth. They make war on the saints and strive to seduce them. The second Beast is characterized as having the number 666 (12 : 1–13 : 18).

The Lamb, standing on Mount Sion, will triumph with those who have been redeemed (14 : 1-5).

Many authors see in this section (4 : 1–14 : 5) a series of tableaux alluding to events which took place between the reign of Nero and that of Domitian : the plagues symbolized by the horsemen and the trumpets, the martyrs (6 : 9 ff.) who were victims of the persecution of Nero, the fate of the Temple and of the two witnesses who are brought into relation with the siege and destruction of Jerusalem (11 : 1-14). In Chapter 13, the Beast which comes up out of the sea is considered to be the Roman Empire, and its seven heads, seven emperors, the last of whom is Domitian, as is indicated by allusion to the legend of Nero dead and returned to life *(Nero redux)*, and by the number 666 (or 616). In the Beast which comes up out of the earth and presses the adoration of the Beast-Empire, several have seen the priesthood of the imperial cult in the provinces, and some, even more precisely, the priests of Cybele [2]. The persecution envisioned in Chapter 13 is regarded as that which was begun by Domitian.

The chapters which follow (14 : 6–22 : 5) contain further allusions to the Roman Empire. Babylon, the city of seven hills, symbol of the earthly powers hostile to Christ and to the Church, is Rome, capital of the persecuting Empire and metropolis of idolatry. The two Beasts of Chapter 13 reappear, the False Prophet of 16 : 14, 19 : 20 and 20 : 10 being identified with the Beast which comes up out of the earth (13 : 11). But in this section the perspectives seem more vast, as if embracing the supreme struggles of Christ and the Forces of evil, and they are also less sharp and precise.

Three angels announce in succession an everlasting gospel or message, the ruin of Babylon, and the chastisement reserved

---

[1] *Translator's note.* — [Cf. B. J. LE FROIS, S. V. D. *The Woman Clothed with the Sun* (Rome, 1954)].

[2] Cf. P. TOUILLEUX, *L'Apocalypse et les cultes de Domitien et de Cybèle* (Paris, 1935), and the commentary of A. GELIN in *La Sainte Bible*, edited by Pirot, vol. XII (Paris, 1938).

GUIDE TO THE BIBLE

for the adorers of the Beast. Then, after a vision describing the last judgment (**14** : 6-20), a new sevenfold group of symbols is introduced : seven bowls are given to seven angels, who are commanded to pour them out upon the earth as so many plagues. The first four, as those of the first four trumpets, strike the earth, the sea, the rivers and fountains, and the stars; the fifth, the throne of the Beast; the sixth, the river Euphrates. When the seventh bowl has been poured out upon the air, there follow a tempest and an earthquake, which precede, at a future time which is not precisely defined, the judgment of the great harlot Babylon, i.e., Rome (**15** : 1-**16** : 21).

Babylon and its chastisement are described, as well as the lamentations which its fall provokes among the inhabitants of the earth, while Heaven sings the victory of God and prepares to celebrate the marriage of the Lamb (**17** : 1-**19** : 10).

A new group of visions show us the victorious combat of the Word of God against the Beast and the kings of the earth. The Beast and the False Prophet who is with it are cast alive into the pool of fire; the infernal Dragon is chained for a thousand years, during which the just reign with Christ (**19** : 11-**20** : 5). This millennium or reign of Christ during a thousand years has been variously interpreted. Several ancient Fathers, influenced by Jewish ideas, saw in the text of the Apocalypse the announcement of a reign of Christ on earth during a thousand years, between the resurrection of the just (or first resurrection) and the end of the world. Beginning with Saint Augustine, a spiritual interpretation has commonly prevailed among Catholic authors. The Bishop of Hippo considers the *millennium* as representing the reign of Christ in His Church, the Church Militant united with the Church Triumphant, from the Incarnation to the consummation of the world. The first resurrection is understood as referring to birth into the life of grace. A thousand years is a conventional figure to signify a long duration, and was chosen perhaps to dispel the idea of an imminent Second Coming. Some authors, while interpreting the *millennium* as a spiritual reign of Christ in the Church, see in it a historic period in which the Church would enjoy a greater tranquillity; for example, from the end of the persecutions through the peace of Constantine up to the last days. Following Saint Augustine, we should regard the *millennium*, not as a distinct period, but rather as one of the aspects of the history of the Church, co-existing with other aspects, even with persecutions. " The millenary peace is only relative, as is also the impotence of the Adversary " (Allo).

Satan, unchained after a thousand years, makes a supreme effort in alliance with the earthly powers, Gog and Magog, but he is vanquished and is cast into the pool of fire, where are also the Beast and the False Prophet (**20** : **7-10**). The revelation ends with a description of the judgment of the good and the wicked according to the Book of Life and with a vision of the Heavenly Jerusalem (**20** : **11–22** : **5**).

In the epilogue (**22** : **6-21**), the truth of the prophecy is affirmed by the angel, by John, and by Christ, to whom the Church prays that He may come. Christ then announces that he is coming quickly. A blessing closes the book.

Purpose of the Apocalypse.

John wrote " the things that he has seen, and the things that are, and the things that are to come hereafter " (**1** : **19**), for the purpose of correcting certain weaknesses, as we see by the letters to the Churches, and especially to console and fortify the Christians of Asia Minor who were exposed to persecution.

The symbolism of the visions has provoked many interpretations, and uncertainty remains on a number of points. Some exegetes confine the application of the Apocalypse to the end of the world and to the events immediately preceding it, while others maintain that it applies to the whole history of the Church, which coincides with the end of time (**1** Cor. **10** : **11**). In this second group, there are some who seek in the Apocalypse the prediction of definite events at successive epochs. But others abandon this kind of investigation, which, although undertaken repeatedly, always proves vain — apart from the proved allusions to the history of the primitive Church and the Roman Empire from Nero to Domitian.

Whatever may be the divergences in interpretation, one lesson ever remains actual and living : as in the time when John wrote, the Church throughout its history will know struggles and persecutions. The enemy powers, symbolized by the two Beasts that Satan urges on, will never cease from fighting against the Church. But Christ will conquer and, in spite of the most desperate combats, the Church, the society of the saints, will not perish. This victory will shine forth in glory at the judgment which will gather together all mankind. But this judgment is already being exercised on individuals and generations. Henceforth Christ triumphs; henceforth the Heavenly Jerusalem is being peopled.

BIBLIOGRAPHY

I. — *The Old Testament.*

1. *General works.* — Catholic : The Introductions, especially those of F. E. GIGOT, J. GOETTSBERGER, H. HÖPFL (5th ed. by A. MILLER and A. METZINGER, Rome, 1946). The articles in the *DBV*, and its *Supplement* (edited by L. PIROT, A. ROBERT and H. CAZELLES); *DTC; DAFC; Catholicisme* (ed. G. Jacquemet); *Bibellexikon* (ed. H. Haag [Einsiedeln, 1955]. It is based on the excellent Dutch *Bijbelsch Woordenboek* (edd. Alfrink, Van den Born *et al.*, Roermond, 1941; new ed. in preparation. An English ed. is also in course of preparation). The Commentaries : [*A Catholic Commentary on Holy Scripture* (edd. Orchard, Sutcliffe, *et al.* [London, 1953]. See also the important review — article on it by E. P. Arbez, *Dublin Review* [1953], pp. 405-418); *Cursus Scripturae Sacrae* (Paris); *Bonner Bibel (Die Heilige Schrift des Alten Testaments). Exegetisches Handbuch zum Alten Testament* of J. NIKEL. *La Sainte Bible* (edd. L. Pirot and A. Clamer). *La Sacra Bibbia* (ed. S. Garafalo). *La Sainte Bible (La Bible de Jérusalem). Echter Bibel, Die Heilige Schrift in deutscher Uebersetzung* (ed. F. Nötscher). [*La Biblia* (published by the Monastery of Montserrat). P. HEINISCH, *Theology of the Old Testament* (English trans. by W. Heidt, 1949). *Id., History of the Old Testament* (English trans. by W. Heidt, 1952)].

Non-Catholic works : The Introductions, especially those of S. R. DRIVER, O. EISSFELDT, A. WEISER, A. LODS, R. H. PFEIFFER, and A. BENTZEN [see 2 *infra*], to which may be added H. H. ROWLEY, *The Old Testament and Modern Study* (Oxford, 1951). [M. NOTH, *Die Welt des Alten Testaments : Einführung in die Grenzgebiete der alttestamentlichen Wissenschaft* (2nd ed., Berlin, 1953). A. JIRKU, *Die Welt der Bibel* (Stuttgart, 1957)]. The articles in the *HDB, EB, Religion in Geschichte und Gegenwart* (new ed. by K. Galling, Tübingen, 1956 ff.). *Theologisches Wörterbuch zum Neuen Testament* (ed. G. Kittel. Each article contains a synthesis of corresponding data from the Old Testament). The large Protestant Commentaries : *The International Critical Commentary. Cambridge Bible for Schools and Colleges.* [The *Interpreter's Bible* (New York, 1952 ff.). *The Clarendon Bible* (edd. Binns, Wardle, Robinson *et al.*, Oxford)]. *Göttingen Hand-Kommentar zum Alten Testament* (ed. W. Nowack). *Kurzer*

Hand-kommentar zum Alten Testament (ed. K. Marti). *Die Schriften des Alten Testaments* (ed. H. Gunkel, etc.). *Kommentar zum Alten Testament* (ed. E. Sellin). *Handbuch zum Alten Testament* (ed. O. Eissfeldt). *Das Alte Testament Deutsch* (edd. V. Herntrich and A. Weisser). R. H. CHARLES, *The Apocrypha and Pseudepigrapha of the Old Testament* (Oxford, 1913). [*Vocabulaire Biblique* (ed. J. J. von Allmen, Neuchâtel-Paris, 1954, English trans. 1958), and *Dictionnaire d'Archéologie Biblique* (ed. W. Corswant, *ibid.*, 1956).

The Scandinavian countries are contributing important studies. The following may be mentioned : *Svenskt Bibliskt Uppslagsverk* (edd. I. Engnell, A. Fridrichsen, Bo Reicke, 2 vols., Gäule, Sweden, 1948-1952). A. BENTZEN, *Introduction to the Old Testament* (2 vols., Copenhagen and London, 1948-1949). I. ENGNELL, *Gamla Testamentet : en traditionshistorisk Inledning*, I (Uppsala-Stockholm, 1945; an important work). There is a valuable translation of the Bible into Norwegian by S. Michelet, S. Mowinckel, and N. Messel : I, *the Law* (Oslo, 1930); II, *The Earlier Prophets* (1936); III, *The Latter Prophets* (1944). There are good introductions and notes). In Dutch there are two valuable series in course of publication comparable to the *Cambridge Bible for Schools and Colleges : Tekst en Uitleg* (edd. Bohl and van Veldhuizen, Groningen), and *Korte Verklaring der heilige Schrift* (edd. Aalders, van Gelderen, *et al.*, Kampen).

Judaism, naturally, has produced an abundant literature in modern times — much of it in Hebrew — and therefore often overlooked by non-Jewish writers in accordance with the maxim, *Hebraicum est, non legitur*. Among the more important Jewish works may be mentioned the following : *Entzyklopedyah ha-Miqra'it* (*Encyclopedia Biblica;* published by the Bialk Foundation, Jerusalem) : I (1951); II (1954); III (1958 — from *Alef* to the end of *Yod*. This work, on which leading Jewish scholars are collaborating, is an outstanding contribution. Its bibliographical information is very full, and Catholic scholarship is not neglected. The numerous plates, maps, and diagrams are excellent). C. H. GORDON, *Introduction to Old Testament Times* (Ventnor, N. J., 1954). Ez. KAUFMAN, *History of the Religion of Israel* (in 7 parts, Tel Aviv, 1937-1948). M. S. SEGAL, *Introduction to Scripture.* I (Jerusalem, 1945); II (*ibid.*, 1946). U. CASSUTO, *The Documentary Hypothesis and the Composition of the Pentateuch* (Jerusalem, 1941); *id., From Adam to Noah* (*ibid.*, 1944); *id., From Noah to Abraham* (*ibid.*, 1949). S. L. GORDON, *Commentary on the Old Testament* (11 vols., Warsaw and Tell Aviv, 1925-1933). A. EHRLICH, *The Bible according to Its Literal Sense* (3 vols., Leipzig, 1899-1901); *id., Randglossen zur Hebräischen Bibel* (7 vols., Leipzig, 1908-1914). *The Soncino Books of the Bible* (ed. A. Cohen, 12 vols., London 1945-1951; the Hebrew text with an English translation). M. ZER-KABOD, *Esra and Nehemiah* (Jerusalem, 1948). *The Pentateuch and Haftorahs* (ed. by Chief Rabbi J. H. Hertz, with English trans. and commentary, 5 vols., London, 1929-1936; one vol. ed., 1938). *The Holy Scripture with Commentary* (Jewish Publication Society of America, Philadelphia, 1938 ff.; in English). N. B. Apart from the book of

C. H. GORDON, all the other works mentioned, unless reference is made specifically to English, are written in Hebrew.

On the "Apocrypha and Pseudepigrapha", see also the following : W. O. E. OESTERLEY, *Introduction to the Books of the Apocrypha* (New York, 1935). M. R. JAMES, *The Lost Apocrypha of the Old Testament* (London, 1920); *id.*, *The Biblical Antiquities of Philo* (London, 1917). R. T. HERFORD, *Talmud and Apocrypha* (London, 1933). H. J. WICKS, *The Doctrine of God in the Jewish Apocryphal and Apocalyptic Literature* (London, 1915). C. C. TORREY, *The Apocryphal Literature : A Brief Introduction* (New Haven, 1945). *Hassefarim hahisonim (The Books Outside* [the Canon], ed. A. Kahana, 2 vols. in 3 parts, Tell Aviv, 1936-1937; in Hebrew). S. S. TEDESCHE, *I (III) Esdras* (New Haven, 1928; a critical ed. of the Greek text); *id.* with S. Zeitlin, *The First Book of Maccabees : An English Translation, with Introduction and Commentary* (New York, 1950). A. KANIMKA, *IV Esdras (The Book of the Visions of Assir She'alti'el)* (Tell Aviv, 1936; in Hebrew). PINKHOS CHURGIN, *Studies in the Time of the Second Temple* (New York, 1949; in Hebrew).].

2. *The Law.* Catholic works : E. F. SUTCLIFFE, S. J., and R. J. DYSON, S. J., "Introduction to the Pentateuch ", *A Catholic Commentary on Holy Scripture*, pp. 164-176. See also *ibid.* the Commentaries on Genesis (by SUTCLIFFE), Exodus (by Power), Leviticus (by SAYDON), Numbers (by SAYDON), and Deuteronomy (by MACKENZIE), pp. 177-273. H. HÖPFL, "Pentateuque et Hexateuque ", *DAFC*, III, 1883 ff. E. MANGENOT, *L'authenticité Mosaïque du Pentateuque* (Paris, 1907). J. TOUZARD, "Moïse et Josué ", *DAFC*, III, 708 ff. A. VAN HOONACKER, *De compositione litteraria et de origine mosaica Hexateuchi disquisitio historico-critica* (Brussels, 1949). [J. COPPENS, *The Old Testament and the Critics* (English trans. by E. A. Ryan, S. J., and E. W. TRIBBE, S. J. (Paterson, N. J., 1942)]. P. HEINISCH, *Das Buch Genesis* (Bonn, 1930); [*id.*, *Das Buch Exodus* (*ibid.*, 1934); *id.*, *Das Buch Leviticus* (*ibid.*, 1935); *id.*, *Das Buch Numeri* (*ibid.*, 1936). H. JUNKER, *Das Buch Deuteronomium* (*ibid.*, 1941)]. J. CHAINE, *Le livre de la Genèse* (Paris, 1948). A. CLAMER, *Genèse* (*La Sainte Bible*, I, Paris, 1953); *id.*, *Lévitique, Nombres, Deutéronome* (*La Sainte Bible*, II, 1940). H. CAZELLES, *Études sur le Code d'alliance* (Paris, 1946); *id.*, "Loi israélite ", *DBV, Suppl.* V, 497 ff. C. HAURET, *Origines de l'univers et de l'homme (Gen.* **1-3)** (3rd ed. Paris, 1952).

Non-Catholic works : [D. C. SIMPSON, *Pentateuchal Criticism* (Oxford, 1924). J. B. HARFORD, *Since Wellhausen* (London, 1926)]. H. GUNKEL, *Genesis* (5th ed., Göttingen, 1922). O. PROCKSCH, *Die Genesis* (Leipzig, 1924). G. VON RAD, *Das erste Buch Mose* (Göttingen, 1950-1952). S. R. DRIVER, *The Book of Exodus* (Cambridge, 1911); *id.*, *Deuteronomy* (3rd ed., Cambridge, 1901). G. BEER, *Exodus* (Tübingen, 1939). M. NOTH, *Ueberlieferungsgeschichte des Pentateuch* (Stuttgart, 1948).

3. *The Historical Books.* Catholic works : [*A Catholic Commentary on Holy Scripture*, pp. 279-411 (on Josue, Judges, Ruth, Kings, Paralipomenon, Esdras-Nehemias, Tobias, Judith, and Esther)]. A. SCHULZ, *Das Buch*

Josue (Bonn, 1924). A. FERNANDEZ, *Commentarius in librum Josue* (Paris, 1938). P. AUVRAY, " Josué (Le livre de) ", *DBV, Suppl.* IV (1949), 1131-1141. A. GELIN, *Josue,* R. TAMISIER, *Le livre des Juges,* and *Le livre de Ruth,*A. MÉDEBIELLE, *Les livres des Rois (La Sainte Bible,* III, Paris, 1949). L. MARCHAL, *Les Paralipomènes,* A. MÉDEBIELLE, *Esdras-Néhémie,* A. CLAMER, *Tobie,* L. SOUBIGOU, *Judith* and *Esther,* E. ROBIN, *Job (La Sainte Bible,* IV, Paris, 1949). M. J. LAGRANGE, *Les livres des Juges* (Paris, 1903). H. CAZELLES, " Juges (Le livre des) ", *DBV, Suppl.* IV (1949), 1394-1414. [A. SCHULZ, *Das Buch der Richter und das Buch Ruth* (Bonn, 1926)]. P. JOÜON, *Ruth* (Rome, 1924). P. DHORME, *Les livres de Samuel* (Paris, 1910). A. SCHULZ, *Die Bücher Samuel* (Münster i. W., 1919-1920). S. LANDERSDORFER, *Die Bücher der Könige* (Bonn, 1936). A. SANDA, *Die Bücher der Könige* (Münster i. W., 1911-1912). S. GAROFALO, *Il libro dei Re* (Rome, 1951). J. GOETTSBERGER, *Die Bücher der Chronik oder Paralipomenon* (Bonn, 1939). A. NOORDZIJ, " Les intentions du Chroniste ", *RB* (1940), 161-168. A. FERNANDEZ, *Commentarios a los libros de Esdras y Nehemias* (Madrid, 1950). M. M. SCHUMPP, *Das Buch Tobias* (Münster i. W., 1933). A. LEFÈVRE, " Judith (Le livre de)", *DBV, Suppl.* IV (1949), 1315-1321. J. SCHILDENBERGER, *Die Bücher Tobias, Judith und Esther* (Bonn, 1940-1941). J. STEINMANN, *Lecture de Judith* (Paris, 1953). T. CORBISHLEY, S. J., " 1 and 2 Maccabees ", *A Catholic Commentary on Holy Scripture,* pp. 706-723. F. M. ABEL, *Les livres des Maccabées* (Paris, 1949). A. LEFÈVRE," Maccabées (Livres I et II des) ", *DBV, Suppl.* V (1957), 597-612. M. GRANDCLAUDON, *Les livres des Macchabées* (Paris, 1951).

Non-Catholic works : J. GARSTANG, *Joshua, Judges* (London, 1930). M. NOTH, *Das Buch Josua* (Tübingen, 1938). W. RUDOLPH, *Das Buch Ruth* (Leipzig, 1939). J. A. MONTGOMERY, *The Book of Kings* (Edinburgh, 1951). A. C. WELCH, *The Work of the Chronicler, Its Purpose and Its Date* (London, 1939). G. VON RAD, *Das Geschichtsbild des chronistischen Werkes* (Stuttgart, 1930). W. RUDOLPH, *Esra und Nehemia (mit 3 Esra)* (Tübingen, 1949). K. GALLING, *Die fünf Megilloth* (Tübingen, 1940).

4. *The Prophetical Books.* Catholic works : E. F. SUTCLIFFE, S. J., " Prophetical Literature ", in Orchard, Sutcliffe, *et al., A Catholic Commentary on Holy Scripture* (London, 1953), pp. 527-538. J. COPPENS, *Les prophètes d'Israël. Le prophétisme en Israël, les prophètes orateurs* (Malines, 1932). J. CHAINE, *Introduction à la lecture des prophètes* (Paris, 1946). P. SYNAVE and P. BENOIT, *La prophétie* (Paris, 1947). F. CEUPPENS, *De prophetiis messianicis Testamenti Veteris* (Rome, 1935). E. F. SIEGMAN, *The False Prophets of the Old Testament* (Washington, 1939). The pertinent Commentaries in the *Cursus Scripturae Sacrae,* and the articles on each of the Prophetical Books in *DBV,* especially in the *Supplément,* and in *DTC.* On *Isaias :* A. CONDAMIN, *Le livre d'Isaïe* (Paris, 1905); *id., Poèmes de la Bible* (Paris, 1933). L. DENNEFELD, *Les Grands Prophètes (La Sainte Bible,* edd. Pirot-Clamer, Paris, 1946). E. J. KISSANE, *The Book of Isaias* (2 vols, Dublin, 1941-1943). A. FEUILLET, " Isaïe ", *DBV, Suppl.* IV (1949), 647-727 (with copious bibliography). E. POWER, S. J.," Isaias ",

in *A Catholic Commentary on Holy Scripture*, pp. 539-573. J. STEINMANN, *Le prophète Isaïe : sa vie, son œuvre et son temps* (Paris, 1950). P. AUVRAY and J. STEINMANN, *Isaïe (Bible de Jérusalem*, Paris, 1951). On *Jeremias :* A. CONDAMIN, *Le livre de Jérémie* (Paris, 1920). G. RICCIOTTI, *Il libro de Geremia* (Turin, 1924). L. DENNEFELD *(op. cit. supra).* C. LATTEY, S. J., " Jeremias ", in *A Catholic Commentary on Holy Scripture*, pp. 574-591. A. GELIN, *Jérémie, Les Lamentations, Le Livre de Baruch (Bible de Jérusalem*, Paris, 1951). J. STEINMANN, *Le prophète Jérémie : sa vie, son œuvre et son temps* (Paris, 1952); *id.*, " Jérémie ", *DBV, Suppl.* IV (1949), 857-889, and " Lamentations ", *ibid.* V (1957), 237-251. On *Ezechiel :* P. AUVRAY, *Ezéchiel (Bible de Jérusalem*, Paris, 1949). L. DENNEFELD, *(op. cit. supra).* E. POWER, S. J., " Ezechiel ", in *A Catholic Commentary on Holy Scripture*, pp. 601-620. J. STEINMANN, *Le prophète Ezéchiel* (Paris, 1953). On *Daniel :* L. DENNEFELD *(op. cit. supra).* J. DE MENASCE, *Daniel (Bible de Jérusalem*, Paris, 1954). H. CAZELLES, " Daniel ", *Catholicisme* III (1952), 447-453. J. STEINMANN, *Daniel* (Paris, 1950); M. J. LAGRANGE, " Les prophéties messianiques de Daniel ", *RB* (1904), 494 ff.; *id.*, " Le prophète des soixante-dix semaines de Daniel ", *ibid.* (1930), 167-198; *id.*, *Le Judaïsme avant Jésus-Christ*, Chapters IV and V (3rd ed., Paris, 1931). On the *Minor Prophets :* A. VAN HOONACKER, *Les douze petits prophètes* (Paris, 1908). E. OSTY, *Amos, Osée (Bible de Jérusalem*, Paris, 1953). A. GEORGE, *Michée, Sophonie, Nahum (ibid.*, 1952). J. TRINQUET, *Habaquq, Abdias, Joël (ibid.*, 1953). A. FEUILLET, *Jonas (ibid.*, 1951). A. GELIN, *Aggée, Zacharie, Malachie (ibid.*, 1948). J. COPPENS, *Les Douze petits Prophètes ; bréviaire du Prophétisme* (Paris, 1950). See also P. SAYDON, *et al.*, in *A Catholic Commentary on Holy Scripture*, 644-705.

Non-Catholic works : S. DRIVER, *Introduction to the Literature of the Old Testament* (Edinburgh, 1913). A. BERTHOLET, *Hesekiel* (Tübingen, 1936). A. LODS, *Les prophètes d'Israël et les débuts du Judaïsme* (Paris, 1935). M. BUBER, *The Prophetic Faith* (New York, 1949). H. GUNKEL, *Die Propheten* (Göttingen, 1917). J. KLAUSNER, *The Messianic Idea in Israel* (2nd ed., Jerusalem, 1927; in Hebrew). J. SKINNER, *Prophecy and Religion : Studies in the Life of Jeremiah* (Cambridge, 1922). J. S. ZUCKERBRAM, *The Age of Jeremiah* (New York, 1944; in Hebrew). A. C. WELCH, *Jeremiah : His Time and His Work* (London, 1928). W. F. LOFTHOUSE, *The Prophet of Reconstruction : Ezechiel* (London, 1920). G. FOHRER, *Die Hauptprobleme des Buches Ezechiel* (Berlin, 1952). P. HUMBERT, *Problèmes du Libre d'Habacuc* (Neuchâtel-Paris, 1944).

5. *The Sapiential Books.* Catholic works : E. TOBAC, *Les cinq livres de Salomon* (Brussels, 1926). Dom H. DUESBERG, *Les scribes inspirés* (2 vols., Paris, 1938-1939). A. M. DUBARLE, *Les sages d'Israël* (Paris, 1946). H. RENARD, *Le livre des Proverbes*, D. BUZY, *L'Ecclésiaste* and *Le Cantique des Cantiques*, J. WEBER, *Le livre de Sagesse*, C. SPICQ, *L'Ecclésiastique (La Sainte Bible*, ed. Clamer, VI, Paris, 1946). P. DHORME, *Le livre de Job* (Paris, 1926). J. STEINMANN, *Job* (Paris, 1946). A. LEFÈVRE, " Job (Le livre de) ", *DBV, Suppl.* IV (1949), 1073-1098.

R. P. Larcher, *Le livre de Job* (*Bible de Jérusalem*, Paris, 1950). B. Hugueny, *Le Psautier du Bréviaire* (Paris, 1933). J. Weber, *Le Psautier du Bréviaire Romain* (3rd ed., Paris, 1941); id., *Le livre de Job*. *L'Ecclésiaste* (Paris, 1947). J. Calès, *Les Psaumes* (Paris, 1936). E. Paunier, *Les Psaumes* (2nd ed. by H. Renard, Paris, 1950). E. Podechard, *Le Psautier*, I, *Ps. 1-75* (Lyon, 1951; II, *Ps. 76-100 et 110* (1954). J. Steinmann, *Les Psaumes* (Paris, 1951). R. Tournay, *Les Psaumes* (Paris, 1950). E. Podechard, *L'Ecclésiaste* (Paris, 1912). R. Pautrel, *L'Ecclésiaste* (Paris, 1951). P. Joüon, *Le Cantique des Cantiques* (Paris, 1909). G. Pouget and J. Guitton, *Le Cantique des Cantiques* (Paris, 1934; English trans. by J. Lilly, 1948). A. Robert, *Le Cantique des Cantiques* (Paris, 1951). A. Feuillet, *Le Cantique des Cantiques* (Paris, 1953. P. Heinisch, *Das Buch Weisheit* (Münster i. W., 1912). E. Osty, *Le livre de la Sagesse* (Paris, 1950). N. Peters, *Das Buch Jesus Sirach oder Ecclesiasticus* (Münster i. W., 1913).
R. A. Dyson, S. J., " The Poetical and Wisdom Literature ", in *A Catholic Commentary on Holy Scripture*, pp. 412-416, and the Commentaries ibid. on Job (by Sutcliffe), Psalms (by Bird), Proverbs (by Dyson), Ecclesiastes (by Leahy), Canticle of Canticles (by Saydon), Wisdom (by Lattey), and Ecclesiasticus (by Kearns). P. Boyland, *The Psalms : the Vulgate Psalter in the Light of the Hebrew* (2 vols., Dublin, 1920; 4th reprint, 1936). G. Ricciotti, *Il libro di Giobbe* (Turin, 1924); id., *Il Cantico dei Cantici* (ibid., 1928). E. J. Kissane, *The Book of Job* (Dublin, 1939); id., *The Book of Psalms* (2 vols., Dublin, 1953-1954). J. M. McGlinchy, *The Teaching of Amen-em-Ope and the Book of Proverbs* (Washington, 1939)].

Non-Catholic works : A. F. Kirkpatrick, *The Book of Psalms* (Cambridge, 1913). H. Gunkel, *Die Psalmen* (Göttingen, 1926). R. Kittel, *Die Psalmen* (Leipzig, 1929). A. Weiser, *Die Psalmen* (Göttingen, 1950). J. Lévy, *L'Ecclésiastique ou la Sagesse de Jésus, fils de Sira* (Paris, 1898-1901). R. Smend, *Die Weisheit des Jesus Sirach* (Berlin, 1906). [E. König, *Die Psalmen* (Güttersloh, 1927). W. O. E. Oesterley, *The Psalms* (2 vols., London, 1939); id., *The Book of Proverbs* (London and New York, 1929). M. Buttenwieser, *The Psalms : Chronologically Arranged* (Chicago, 1938)].

II. *The New Testament :* Catholic works : The Commentaries in the large collections : *Cursus Scripturae Sacrae* (edited by the Jesuits, Paris, 1890 ff.). *Études Bibliques* (under the direction of the Dominicans of the École Biblique de Jérusalem, Paris, 1907 ff.). *Verbum Salutis* (edited by the Jesuits, Paris, 1924 ff.); *La Sainte Bible* (edd. Pirot and Clamer, Paris, 1935 ff.). *La Sainte Bible* (*Bible de Jérusalem*, Paris, 1948 ff.). See also the references to Catholic and non-Catholic Works given *supra* under Old Testament, I.

Among the manuals may be mentioned : E. Jaquier, *Histoire des livres du N. T.* (Paris, 1928-1935). A. Merk, S. J., *Introductionis in Sacrae Scripturae libros compendium* (12th ed., Paris, 1940). H. Höpfl, B. Gut, A. Metzinger, O. S. B., *Introductio specialis in N. T.* (5th ed., Rome,

1949; = *Compendium*, Vol. III). A. WIKENHAUSER, *Einleitung in das N. T.* (Freiburg i. Br., 1956²; English trans., *N. T. Introduction* [New York, 1958]. It has copious bibliography). See also the following non-Catholic works : M. GOGUEL, *Introduction au N. T.* (Paris, 1922-1926). J. MOFFATT, *An Introduction to the N. T.* (3rd ed., Edinburgh, 1918).

On the Gospels and other books of the N. T. : L. DE GRANDMAISON, S. J., *Jesus Christ.* I (New York, 1934). F. PRAT, S. J., *La théologie de Saint Paul* (11th ed., Paris, 1925; English trans., London, 1926). E. BOISMARD (articles cited *supra* under the section on the Apocalypse). See also the following non-Catholic works : K. LAKE and H. J. CADBURY, *The Beginnings of Christianity*, Vols. IV-V, London, 1933). H. D. SWETE, *The Apocalypse of St. John* (3rd ed., London, 1909). R. H. CHARLES, *The Revelation of St. John* (Edinburgh, 1920).

[Additional Catholic works on the New Testament : The articles on Introduction to the N. T. and the Commentaries on the individual Books in *A Catholic Commentary on Holy Scripture* (edd. Orchard, *et al.*, London, 1953), pp. 724-1208. *Commentary on the New Testament* (published by the Catholic Biblical Association, New York, 1942). *Die Heilige Schrift des Neuen Testaments* (Bonn). *Das Regensburger Neue Testament* (edd. A. WIKENHAUSER and O. KUSS, Regensburg, 1938 ff.). E. B. ALLO, *L'Apocalypse de Saint Jean* (3rd ed., Paris, 1933); *id.*, *Saint Paul : Première épître aux Corinthiens* (*ibid.*, 1935); *id.*, *Seconde épître aux Corinthiens* (*ibid.*, 1937). J. HUBY, *Saint Paul : Les épîtres de la captivité* (*ibid.*, 1940); *id.*, *La première épître aux Corinthiens* (*ibid.*, 1946). J. CHAINE, *L'épître de Saint Jacques* (*ibid.*, 1927); *id.*, *Les épîtres catholiques* (*ibid.*, 1937). U. HOLZMEISTER, *Epistola prima sancti Petri* (*ibid.*, 1937). J. BONSIRVEN, S. J., *L'épître de Saint Jean* (*ibid.*, 1936); *id.*, *L'épître aux Hébreux* (*ibid.*, 1943); *id.*, *Les enseignements de Jésus-Christ* (*ibid.*, 1946); *id.*, *Textes Rabbiniques des deux premiers siècles chrétiens pour servir à l'intelligence du Nouveau Testament* (Rome, 1955; of basic importance). J. SICKENBERGER, *Erklärung der Johannesapokalypse* (2nd ed., Bonn, 1942). R. J. LOENERTZ, O. P., *The Apocalypse of St. John* (English trans., New York, 1948).

Additional non-Catholic works on the New Testament : FEINE-BEHM, *Einleitung in das Neue Testament* (10th ed., Heidelberg, 1954). STRACK-BILLERBECK, *Kommentar zum Neuen Testament* (4 vols. in 5 parts, Munich, 1922-1929). See also the bibliography at the end of Chapter XX. K. and S. LAKE, *An Introduction to the New Testament* (New York, 1937). R. H. PFEIFFER, *History of New Testament Times* (New York, 1949). *The Clarendon Bible* (vols. on Matthew, Mark, Luke, Acts, Romans, Corinthians, Galatians, Hebrews). *Das Neue Testament Deutsch* (edd. P. Althaus and J. Behm, 5 vols., Göttingen, 1937-1938). E. STAUFFER, *Die Theologie des Neuen Testaments* (Stuttgart, 1947). J. G. HOFFMANN, *Les vies de Jésus et le Jésus de l'histoire* (Uppsala, 1947; a study of non-Catholic works in French on the life of Jesus from Renan to Guignebert). M. KIDDLE, *The Revelation of St. John* (New York, 1940; cf. *CBQ* [1942], 189-191]).

CHAPTER VI

THE LITERARY GENRES

by A. ROBERT and A. TRICOT

CHAPTER VI

THE LITERARY GENRES

INTRODUCTORY OBSERVATIONS.

[A. ROBERT]

1. *What is meant by literary genres.*

The visitor who endeavors to understand a cathedral does not confine himself to the consideration of each detail independently of the whole, nor even of the whole itself independently of the general data of history and art. The special features of the plan, of the construction, of the sculpture, etc., reveal a design or purpose, and this purpose is expressed necessarily in terms of the material, intellectual, artistic, and religious media of a given epoch. These various elements in combination determine what is called a style, that is, a form of thought, of feeling, and of realization, which reflects the civilization of a country and of a period and which develops, reaches its zenith, and then declines, dies, or gives birth to new forms.

In literature, we do not speak of styles [in the architectural sense], but of genres. By genres, says Abbé Cl. Vincent [1], we mean " certain general and artistic forms of thought, which have their own characteristics and laws. They constitute certain classes or categories, in which may be grouped the works of the spirit, works which are so complex and so diverse in character ". Like architectural styles, they have their structural features, their rules, and their expressive power. They have also their birth, their growth, their death, and their metamorphoses. More directly than architectural styles, they reflect the soul of a milieu and of a period, with its language, its literary accomplishments, its institutions, its beliefs, its trials, and its hopes.

---

[1] *Théorie des genres littéraires*, (Paris, 1934), p. 1. *Translator's note.* — [See also the chapter, " Literary Genres ", in R. WELLEK and A. WARREN, *Theory of Literature*, (New York, 1948), pp. 235-247].

2. How the problem of literary genres has arisen [1]

The problem of literary genres did not attract the attention of exegetes before the end of the nineteenth century. At that time, certain Catholics, in their concern for safeguarding the principle of inerrancy in the face of difficulties that were regarded as insoluble, formulated a hypothesis of a variety of historical forms in which the sacred writer, with more or less freedom, narrates the events of the past. This point of view doubtlessly implied a true feeling for and a sense of the complexity of literary forms and the extreme versatility of the Semitic genius, but is was wrong in concentrating attention on historical writings only and in considering the problem from the very special angle of the demands of inerrancy. It was soon to be perceived that the problem was quite different in scope and character.

Actually during these years the marked advances in archaeology were revealing the existence, in the Ancient Near East, of a certain unity of ideas as regards legislation, worship, and human aspirations and ideals. Increasing cognizance was being taken of the numerous ties that in both space and time connect the Bible with its milieu. Thus, there arose in Germany the hypothesis of literary forms which, in their early, basic state were, at a time more or less remote, in the closest relation with the ancient Near Eastern conception of Divinity, along with myths, legends, local folklore, sanctuaries, festivals, and monarchy as an institution.

A method of interpretation was then developed, with H. Gunkel as its chief promoter. It consists in determining the first unities of Biblical literature, in characterizing them

Translator's note. — [1] Cf. HAAG, Bibellexikon, s.v. " Formgeschichtliche Methode ", 492-494. " Los generos literarios de la Sagrada Escritura " (by various contributors, Congres de Ciencias Ecclesiasticos, Barcelona, 1957; cf. EThL [1957], 745). J. DE FRAINE, S. J., " Les implications du 'Patternism' ", Biblica (1956), 59-73 (on the Uppsala School). A. BENTZEN, Introduction to the Old Testament. I (2nd ed., Copenhagen and London, 1952), 102-264 (" The Forms of Literature "). I. ENGNELL, Gamla Testamentet : en traditionshistorisk Inledning (Uppsala, 1945), pp. 39-108. See also the following articles by the same scholar in Svenskt bibliskt Uppslagsverk : " Gamla Testamentet ", I, 657-661; " Formhistorisk Metod ", I, 557-560); " Traditionshistorisk Metod " I, 1429-1437; " Litterärkritik ", 2, 89-97; " Religionsvetenskap ", 2, 885-903. H. CAZELLES, s. v." Mythe et A. T. ", DBV, Suppl. V (1957), 240-252].

in terms of their content and especially of their literary physiognomy, in rediscovering their point of insertion into social life *(Sitz im Leben)*, and in arranging them in categories : narratives in prose of varied style, and poetic compositions of a profane or religious nature. Finally, an attempt is made to retrace the historical development of each of these forms *(Formgeschichte)* from their preliterary stage to the elaborate composite writings found in our Bible.

This method in itself is clearly legitimate and fruitful, but it offers dangers which it has not succeeded in avoiding : abuses in the comparative use of extra-Biblical material, the exaggerated importance given to form at the expense of content, the failure to recognize the specific characteristics of the Religion of Israel and the stability of its traditions, the accumulation of conjectures, and a simplified notion of the principle of evolution. Accordingly, the exegete who wishes to be objective and who, at the same time, has a proper understanding of the Bible, should exercise precaution in his use of the method of the *Formgeschichte* School and of the data which it has accumulated. He should not be a victim of certain slogans which are often accepted without further examination. He should understand that the comparative method within the Bible — and applied vertically, if one may presume to say so — is still more important than the horizontal method of extra-Biblical comparison, and that, finally, everything should be thought out in an atmosphere that is philosophically and theologically wholesome. In brief, this is precisely the task that Pope Pius XII proposed to Catholics, when he emphasized the importance of the literary genres and described the spirit in which the study of Sacred Scripture ought to be now understood (Encyclical *Divino afflante Spiritu, ASS* XXXV [1943] 314-316) [1].

I. — THE LITERARY GENRES OF THE OLD TESTAMENT.

In Western classical literature it is often difficult to distinguish genres. How much more is this the case in Biblical literature, which belongs to a distant past, and is animated by a spirit so markedly different from ours ! It would be awkward and

---

Translator's note. — [1 See the English translation published by the NCWC, pp. 18-23].

imprudent to wish, at all costs, to make it fit into the frames of our classical thought. Here, more than anywhere else, the scientific spirit demands that one know how to submit himself to his subject matter and to be prepared for some surprises.

To grasp more surely the character, the complexity, and the mutual relations of the Biblical genres, it seems proper to begin with the threefold division of the Hebrew canon, which distinguishes the Law, the Prophets, and the other books. This division is unusually flexible and penetrating; no other, furthermore, is more authentic. We shall follow it, then, as our guide.

1. — THE PRIMITIVE HISTORY.

Primitive History, or the History of Creation, is narrated in the eleven first chapters of Genesis. It is composed of fragments borrowed now from the Yahwist Source and now from the Priestly Source. The redactor who compiled them presents them to us as a preface to the history of the Patriarchs and of the Twelve Tribes. The modern reader, who is usually too much concerned with material details, does not give enough attention to the fact that these chapters are intented primarily to furnish doctrinal instruction of the greatest importance. Creation, the original happiness of man, the fall and its consequences, the increasing degradation of mankind despite the first achievements of civilization, the great punishment of the Flood and that of the confusion of tongues, all these are truths which manifest the power, wisdom, holiness, and mercy of God, and, at the same time, explain the present condition of man. These truths are facts, or they are essentially connected with facts. Our sources relate them with the same gravity and the same authority as the whole subsequent history, and, consequently, they certainly intend to make them a matter of our belief.

Accordingly, we cannot follow the views of the Liberal School of Criticism, which reduces these narratives to the rank of myths, sagas, and legends. Does this mean that we must regard them as historical in the Western and modern sense of the term? " These literary forms ", declares the Pontifical Biblical Commission, " correspond to none of our classical categories and cannot be judged in the light of Greco-Latin or modern literary styles. One can, therefore, neither deny or affirm their historicity, taken as a whole, without unduly attributing to them the canons of a literary style within which it is impossible to classify them ". (Letter to Cardinal Suhard, *Guide to the Bible* I, 775).

Actually, the events in question fall in a domain which is beyond the farthest horizon of historic time. Therefore they cannot be the object of any human testimony. The epoch to which they belong is, according to the geologists (see *Guide to the Bible* II, 41-53), so remote from us, that it is impossible to imagine a tradition which could have preserved any detailed recollections. The few facts, the little anecdotes, the short genealogical successions which are furnished by the Biblical narrative are but feeble lights lost in an endless night.

On the other hand, if the composition of the chapters in question is examined, one cannot fail to note the important role played therein by literary artifice. The Sacerdotal texts are marked by their schematic character and their concern for logical arrangement. Thus, Chapter 1 is made up of a succession of bold and peremptory sentences. In indicating God's activity, it employs only the indispensable anthropomorphisms : " God says ", " God rested ". The arrangement of the narrative follows the law of a strict progression. The eight works of creation follow each other in two periods of time : the separation of the elements, which proceeds from the general to the particular; and the adornment of the cosmos, which proceeds from the imperfect to the most perfect. The seven days are superimposed on the works simply for the purpose of comparing the Divine week to toiling activity followed by rest. This is a literary fiction intended to make us understand the nobility of human toil and the sacred character of the Sabbath rest.

The technique of the Yahwist texts is quite different. In Chapters 2 and 3, e.g., we also find an ordered and progressive presentation of facts, but it is literary and psychological in character and bears witness to an astonishing artistic sense. It is a series of tittle tableaux centered around the principal event, the fall. Each of these is sketched with a few concrete strokes. Images are employed in profusion, along with naive anthropomorphisms. Yahweh appears on the scene and fills

various roles. E.g., He is a potter (2 : 17 and 19), a gardener
(2 : 8), a surgeon (2 : 21), a peaceful landowner (3 : 8), an examining magistrate (3 : 9-13), and a judge who passes final sentence
and sees that it is carried out (3 : 14-19, 23-24).

Literary convention is found, too, in the genealogical lists.
Their schematic character is unmistakeable : the recurrence of
the same names in different series, the correspondence of name
with function, and of the activities or existence itself with the
personage who bears it. Thus, Adam is man (made of earth,
2 : 7); Eve is (she who gives) life (3 : 20); Cain means forger
(4 : 22); Henoch evokes the idea of foundation (4 : 17); Jubal,
that of the horn and trumpet (4 : 21); Cain, condemned to
ceaseless wandering, goes to the land of Nod — a name derived
from the verb meaning " to wander " (4 : 14, 16).

In the interpretation of the first eleven chapters of Genesis,
another very important literary phenomenon must also be
taken into account, namely, the numerous and undeniable
resemblances between the Biblical narratives and the ancient
traditions of Babylonia. In both mention is made of the
primordial ocean (tiamtu in Babylonian, tehom in Hebrew) from
which the world came forth. At Babylon, the material out of
which man is made is mixed with divine blood; this is equivalent
to saying that man is created in the image of divinity. The
great poem, Enuma Elish, presents the formation of the cosmos
in the two periods of time indicated by Genesis : separation
of the elements, and their adornment. In both cases, the stars
are regarded as having been made to mark day and night and
the seasons.

The second narrative of the Creation (Gen. 2) begins like
Enuma Elish. What follows shows more or less precise contacts
with isolated data derived from various documentary sources :
thus, the mention of Eden, the existence of wonderful gardens,
of sacred trees, of a tree of life or truth, of a plant of life guarded
by the gods and then stolen by a serpent, and, finally, of genii
serving as guardians, and of three-forked lightning — the sign
of anathema.

The genealogical list in Gen. 5 also has its parallel at Babylon.
It gives the same number of patriarchs, they enjoy an extraordinary longevity, and the last name mentioned is that of the
hero of the Flood. The Babylonian account of the Flood

exhibits particularly striking resemblances to that found
in the Bible. The cataclysm is willed by the gods and is
announced by revelation. It is caused by rain, and all men are
destroyed with the exception of one chosen individual. The
ark which carries him also shelters animals. It is finally grounded
on the top of a mountain, most probably in Armenia. The
Babylonian Noe releases birds on three different occasions,
and on leaving the ark he offers a sacrifice, of which the gods
smell the sweet odor. Finally, in Chapter 11, the Tower of
Babel recalls the *ziggurat*, a characteristic element in Babylonian
cult, of which traces are found here and there in Lower Mesopotamia.

This list of resemblances, however, ought not cause any
illusions. Even if they are considered in their material tenor
alone, they often show an intermixture of differences. Above
all, they are found integrated in religious contexts which are
in absolute contrast. On the one hand, despite a real philosophical effort, we have the strange inventions of a polytheism
without horizon and without moral principle; on the other,
the tranquil possession of a monotheism that is sure of itself
and of a full realization of its demands. The Creator whom
Gen. 1 introduces into its narrative does not have to fight
against rival divinities. He says a word, the elements appear,
and then arrange themselves into an harmonious whole. His
work is beautiful and good, and evil arises only as a result
of man's sin. This is what the Yahwist shows so forcefully.
His God is essentially the living God. We see Him mixing with
men, who by their evil will continually oppose His plans of
salvation. And yet He never ceases affirming that He is the
absolute Master of the universe, and especially of history.
According to a preconceived plan, He conducts history to its
term, and in doing so He makes known, along with His wisdom
and His holiness, the depths of His mercy. Here in brief form,
we already have the teaching of the whole Bible.

How then, finally, ought we understand the composition
of Gen. 1-11? The religious teaching of these chapters, together
with the essential facts with which it is indissolubly connected,
can come only from a revelation that was made at a time and
to recipients that we do not know. This teaching finds expression in images and symbols which are related to the Ancient

Babylonian narratives. Here and there, perhaps, the Biblical narrative could have been influenced directly by a written source, but in its totality it gives rather the impression of a diffuse influence, or, as has been very well said, of an atmosphere. The general background of composition seems to be something like this : at some period in their history, perhaps at the time when they established themselves in Canaan, a land impregnated with Babylonian culture for some centuries, the Israelites became acquainted with the Babylonian traditions and shaped them according to their own genius and beliefs. This is the source of the history found in Gen. 1-11, which, while having a great charm and attraction in itself, teaches us with such great authority the most fundamental truths of our Faith.

2. — THE LAW [1]

Is it proper to speak of a legal genre? May one demand of laws anything more than that they be clear and practical? Would one take seriously a legislator who would try to be eloquent? Nevertheless, the laws of the Old Testament, in addition to their internal peculiarities, are indissolubly linked to a context which gives them an undeniable literary character. Their principal characteristics are the following :

The juridical texts are found only in the Pentateuch. They are represented there by entire books (Lev., Deut.,) or by some more or less extended sections. This ensemble is far from constituting a literary unity; it is essentially multiple and composite, both as to matter and to form. The laws are not methodically arranged according to their content, and a good many are repeated. Some, moreover, are brought into relation with a new historical context and have a more or less modified tenor. These details show that the legislation of Israel adheres very closely to the life of the nation and of the Semitic world in general, and that as a consequence it has undergone an

Translator's note. — [1 Cf. O. LINTON, " Lag ", Svenskt bibl. Uppslagverk, 2, 3-16. B. GEMSER, " The Importance of the Motive Clause in O. T. Law ", Vetus Testamentum, Suppl. I (Leiden, 1953), 50-66. G. E. MENDENHALI, " Ancient Oriental and Biblical Law ", BA (1954), 26-46 (cf. Sefarad [1955], 217); id., " Covenant Forms in Israelite Tradition ", ibid., 50-76 (cf. Sefarad [1955], l. c.). I. ENGNELL, " Mose " and " Moseböckerna " in Sv. bibl. Uppslagsverk, 2, 311-342. H. CAZELLES, " Pentateuch ", in Haag, Bibellexikon, 1296.]

evolution, the extent of which it is difficult to set within precise limits.

The differences in style emphasize the composite character of the texts. E.g., in Ex. **22** : 15-21 (16-22), i.e., in seven verses, we find no less than four kinds of style : conditional (15, 16), direct, in the second person singular or plural (17, 20, 21), declaratory (18), and participial (19).

We should note especially the conditional style, also called the casuistic style, which is found to a marked extent in Ex. **21-22**; Deut. **19, 22, 24, 25**, and which makes these passages seem like the older codes of the Orient : Sumerian, Babylonian, primitive Assyrian, and Hittite. The direct style, in the singular and with the verb in the future, indicates a particular solemnity, as in the Decalogue.

Elementary groupings are sometimes included in the formulas of introduction and conclusion : Lev. **6** : 2, 7, 18; **7** : 37; **11** : 46, 47. Most frequently, they show that the law goes back to God as its source, and therefore that it is the direct expression of the Divine Will : Ex. **19** : 3; Lev. **1** : 1, 2; Ex. **24** : 1, 12; **25** : 1, Lev. **4** : 1; **5** : 14; cf. Deut. **5** : 24 (27); Ex. **20** : 2; Deut. **5** : 6; Lev. **18** : 3, 5, 21, 30.

By reason of their content or external circumstances, certain larger groupings take the from of codes. Such are the Decalogue (Ex. **20** : 2-17; Deut. **5** : 6-18, 21); the code of the covenant (Ex. **20** : 22–23 : 19); the code of the renewal of the covenant (Ex. **34** : 10-28); the law of holiness (Lev. **17-26**); the Deuteronomic Code (Deut. **12-26**).

The most characteristic trait of this legislation is that it is directly linked to history, not only through the reality of fact, but in its literary presentation. Certain incidents are considered as typical cases, which give rise to permanent prescriptions : Num. **9** : 6-14; **17** : 1-15; **27**, **36**. Events which concern the nation give their meanings to certain ordinances, especially ritual ones : Ex. **12** : 27; Deut. **5** : 14, 15 (cf. Ex. **20** : 10, 11); Deut. **16** : 11, 12; **23** : 2-9; **26** : 1-10, etc. It is especially significant that the legislative sections alternate with the narrative, and that they are inserted in a closely woven web which leads us from creation to the departure from Egypt. The culminating point of this crescendo is represented by the events of Sinai. It is at Sinai that the people of Israel, led by Moses, meet their God. Detached from this frame, the Biblical legislation, even that concerning secular life, would be a body without a soul. This legislation is essentially religious, because it comes from God, who communicates his wishes himself or through Moses, revealing new dispensations or endowing the old Semitic law with his authority. It is indissolubly religious and national, because it rests on the idea of covenant. For the covenant expresses the choice which God makes in respect to a people, but in return he imposes his conditions. These are summed up in fidelity in the observance of laws. Without question, the whole Biblical tradition gives this meaning to the Torah, even if the Torah contains additions made after Moses. Such additions cannot really be anything more than an accommodation and practical commentary on the Mosaic ordinances, following the same type and in the same spirit.

If we adopt the point of view of the theology of the covenant, it is impossible not to give first place to two groupings of laws, each of which, in its own way, expresses this with the utmost clearness.

It is easiest to distinguish the ensemble of discourses ang laws which constituet the Book of Deuteronomy. Speakind of itself, it says : " This covenant, the book or the word of the covenant ". Speaking of the ark and the tables, it does not fail to designate them as " the ark and the tables of the covenant ". It relates the events of the Exodus and of Sinai as a fundamental explanation of the Mosaic legislation. It insists upon the unexpected character and the singular excellence of the divine choice. The precept of gratitude and love towards Yahweh, Father of Israel, is written into this context as if spontaneously, and likewise the sweet hope of the divine blessings. Yet, at the same time, in the case of infidelity, the prospect of terrible chastisements is also emphasized. Hence, because of the very theological idea itself which is, as it were, the center of crystallization in Deuteronomic thought, the legislator seems more preoccupied with making the articles of his code desired than with imposing them by authority. His language is at once ingratiating and vehement, solemn and eloquent. This style, which is so close to that of the prophets, is to be explained precisely through the fact that in Deuteronomy the legal idea and the prophetic idea are united in a harmonious synthesis. According to 5 : 5, 20-24; 18 : 15-17; 34 : 10-12, Moses is at once legislator and prophet; the divine word, while it binds wills, yet, at the same time, it stimulates and draws them. But Deuteronomy as a whole, and as much in legislation as in exhortation, is purely and simply the Word (4 : 2; 30 : 14; 32 : 47), i.e., Revelation.

In the sections of the Pentateuch which are assigned to the Sacerdotal tradition, and especially in the Code of Holiness (Lev. 18-26), we find a series of ritual ordinances which, although centered likewise upon the idea of covenant, sound a different note. God is here represented as the Holy One, i.e., the *One Apart*, whose transcendence and majesty are overwhelming. Nevertheless, it presents history in the light of the calling of Israel. Through the use of a genealogical approach, the realization of the divine plan is described in a concise and dynamic manner, four great stages being distinguished : Adam and the reign of man over creation; Noah, a new point of departure for humanity and the first covenant; Abraham, father of the chosen people and the second covenant; finally, the full realization of the divine arrangements in the call of Moses and the legislation of Sinai. Dating from this moment, Yahweh dwells in the portable tabernacle, around which the tribes camp in good order. He frequently manifests his glory to them and communicates his will. Revelation is the principal idea which these texts wish to place in relief. But ritual prescriptions occupy a considerable place here too. Beside Moses, the mediator of Revelation, stand Aaron and his brethren, charged with performing the priestly functions. Priests and faithful are subject to minute prescriptions which are motivated by a concern for honoring the divine presence and majesty. These deal with moral conduct and worship, and they proclaim that the holiness of Israel ought to be an imitation of and a participation in that of God. Naturally, the tone is grave, austere, and peremptory. The statement of the laws is not accompanied by exhortations destined to convince and to touch, but rather by mention of the chastisements reserved for prevaricators. This motive, however, is not ordinarily employed, for the thing, and the only unquestionable one which ought to guarantee compliance, is the simple use of the name of Yahweh. Hence the formulas so frequently repeated : " Yahweh spoke, saying;

This is what Yahweh has commanded; I am Yahweh; I am Yahweh Who sanctifies you ".

In short, the first elements of the Mosaic law, whether they deal with secular matters, or even if they are borrowed from foreign sources, enter the literature of Israel through the instrumentality of the historico-theological idea of covenant. This idea engenders a special style and mode of presentation in Deuteronomy and in the ritual passages considered above. Accordingly, at least in these two last cases, we may speak of a legal literary genre.

3. — THE PROPHETS.

The Jewish canon comprises under this heading two quite different groups : the Former Prophets (Jos., Jdgs., 1 and 2 Sam., 1 and 2 Kgs.) and the Latter Prophets (Isa., Jer., Ez., and the Twelve Minor Prophets).

This second group must be examined first, in order to grasp the prophetic genre in its purest form.

1. — The Latter Prophets. [1]

The characteristics of the prophetic genre are explained chiefly through the psychology of the prophet and the nature of his mission. His role is essentially to speak, not of his own accord nor in his own name, but because God has inspired him. God reveals to him his will and makes him his herald for the purpose of recalling, developing, and insisting upon the observance of the great principles of the Mosaic covenant. The prophet judges events under the divine light : alliances, wars, public calamities. He censures idolatry, debauchery, the excesses of luxury and of power, and various forms of injustice. He announces chastisements, exhorts to repentance, comforts in time of trial, promises salvation, and opens up vistas of the Messianic era. It is a heart, even more than a mind, that thrills, that is constantly and intensely occupied with the interest of Yahweh and his people, and that is passionately for good and against evil.

Translator's note. — [1 I. ENGNELL, " Profeter ", *Sv. bibl. Uppslagsverk* 2, 727-774. P. VAN IMSCHOOT, " Prophet " and " Prophetismus " in Haag, *Bibellexikon*, 1367-1376, 1378-1383].

Under these conditions, the prophet — in the golden age at any rate — has nothing of the scholar, the bookman, or the theorizer about him. He is a man of action. If he writes or permits his utterances to be written down, he does so only in order to extend and perpetuate his activity. The prophetic books, accordingly, are, in the highest degree, writings of circumstance, and even polemical in nature, and they will present all the characteristics of such works both in form as well as in subject matter.

The prophetical books are in general very composite. The facts which they contain, in addition to their not being arranged according to a rigorous chronological or logical order, are diverse in their nature and origin. Broadly speaking, they fall into one or other of the three folowing categories : historical facts, giving the outline of the prophet's activity and written by men of his own time and milieu, doubtless his disciples; biographical details coming from the prophet himself or from his disciples; finally and chiefly, collections of prophecies and exhortations. It goes whitout saying that these last elements are, in every respect, the principal ones. Even if in their actual redaction they are sometimes by another hand than that of the man who uttered them, even if they are a simple résumé of authentic discourse, even if, in their ensemble, they represent only samples of a preaching that was delivered over a long period of years, they afford us, nevertheless, the opportunity of detecting, in its spontaneous outbursts, the prophetic spirit in its purest form. It is in these prophecies and exhortations that we should seek the characteristics of the genre.

In respect to content, a prophecy or oracle is a solemn declaration made in the name of God with respect to a future event, happy or unhappy. It is at once an exhortation, a notice of warning, a threat, and a promise. According to circumstances one or other of these elements assumes a greater importance, and, in the course of time, this or that element among them, e.g., promise, will be paramount. Yet we have no justification for isolating them, nor for supposing that they succeed one another according to a law of unilateral development. Taken together, they really characterize complex states of soul, which express themselves spontaneously in an eloquence worthy of the name and in each period (Os. 11 ff.; Isa. 8-9; Jer. 11 and 12).

Quite naturally also, but especially at a later period, the prophetic genre borrows from time to time the color of related forms : the exhortation of the Deuteronomic style, with its base in history (Jer. 7 : 1-8 : 3); the didactic explanation, beginning with a proverb (Ez. 18); the allegory (Isa. 5 : 1-7; Ez. 17, 21 : 1-4; 24 : 3-14; Zach. 11-13 : 7-9); the lament (Am. 5 : 1, 2; Mich. 2 : 4); satire (Isa. 14 : 3-21; 37 : 22-29).

In respect to form, a prophecy exhibits the following characteristics. Since the prophet is the organ of God, it is natural that the divine origin of the declaration should be affirmed with various formulas (Jer. 13). It is done chiefly with these expressions, " Thus saith Yahweh ", " the word ", " the oracle of Yahweh ", which are found, sometimes at the beginning, sometimes at the end, and at other times in the interior of a passage (Am. 1 : 3-2 : 16). It is not always easy to determine whether the author is transmitting as exactly as possible the divine message or whether he is glossing freely, whether he is reporting immediately what he has just learned or whether he is going back to an earlier revelation. Sometimes the divine will (Jer. 24) and, first of all, the call to the apostolate (Isa. 6; Jer. 1; Ez. 1 : 1-3 : 21), has been communicated in a vision. Accounts of visions take a more and more important place in the latest development of the genre (cf. Ez., Zach.).

The moral preoccupation which animates the prophets is put in strong relief by the fact that their predictions are always motivated. The outline of a prophecy really reduces itself to the announcement of a future happening and its moral cause. Sometimes the cause is mentioned first (Isa. 28 : 7-13; Os. 4 : 7-10; Am. 3 : 2, 10-11), and sometimes the prediction is given first and the reason is then introduced by means of a causal particle (Isa. 3 : 13-15; Jer. 35 : 17; Am. 1 : 3b-5). Occasionally the motive, twice repeated, encloses the prediction (Isa. 5 : 7-11) or reciprocally (Soph. 1 : 12-13). In every way there exists a necessary bond between the future event and the actual moral state of the people. God, then, is not arbitrary in his decisions, but he governs his attitude by that of men. This apologetic finds its raison d'être in the fact that, especially before the Exile, the prophets ordinarily announce misfortune (Jer. 28 : 8-9). They do not question the divine fidelity in regard to the chosen people, but they see themselves obliged to stress

the disheartening persistence of prevarications. Hence, while
their pessimism is sombre, it is only relative, and occasionally
it gives brilliant flashes of light on final salvation (so Os. 3;
Jer. 30, 31).

The prophetic exhortation is by its nature quite different
from the prophecy. It often opens with the word " hear ",
and the verbs are ordinarily in the imperative. It announces
promises under hypothetical form, and it sometimes mentions
also possible misfortune in order to urge the hearer to avoid it
(cf. the frequency of the expression " lest "). The tone of the
prophecy is vehement, but the tone of the exhortation is softened
and winning; it is that of the friend who wishes to persuade,
of the master who is instructing, of the educator who is seeking
to gain acceptance. The exhortation is already definitely found,
or is present at least in embryonic form, in Am. (3 : 1-8; 5 : 1,
4-11; 14-15); it crops up in Os. and readily assumes in him an
historical aspect (2 : 16-17; 9 : 3, 10...); it is a marked
characteristic of Jer. (e.g., 3 : 11-15; 4 : 1-4; 15, 6 : 8; 7 : 1-12);
it becomes didactic or allegorical in Ez. (e.g., 16, 17, 19, 22, 23)
and consolatory in Isa. (41 : 8-10; 43 : 1-7...); finally, it urges
reflection in Ag. (1 : 5-7; 2 : 15-19).

However different may be the characteristics proper to
prophecy and exhortation, they harmonize to produce a total
effect which is singularly impressive. The affirmation of divine
origin communicates to the prophetic argumentation as a whole
a character of incomparable solemnity, nobility, and authority.
But, in contrast to the legal and liturgical texts studied
previously, in which God commands as master in a peremptory
fashion, here He explains, He discusses, He invokes His love and
the proofs of His kindness, and He pursues tirelessly the nation
which He wishes to consider as an unfaithful spouse. Or even
more, as if He were powerless in the face of the wills which
He covets and which remain obstinately intractable, He becomes
angry, He urges His rights, He threatens, even though He may
allow a glimpse of His acts of mercy in the future. Thus, by
an admirable contrast, the affirmation of authority opens the
way to the most vehement, the most pathetic, and the most
touching human sentiments. The resources of such a rich
oratorical theme are inexhaustible, as is shown especially by
Osee, Isaias, and Jeremias.

Moreover, the sublimity of the truths taught, the nature of the language, and the psychology of the listeners, demand that the orator address himself to the imagination. He does this at first by combining a symbolic action with his discourse, an action which sometimes is purposely strange. Inherited from ancient times (1 Kgs. **20** : 35-43; **22** : 11; 2 Kgs. **13** : 14-19), this procedure continues to be employed by the great prophets of the classical age (Isa. **20** : Jer. **27** : 1 ff.; Ez. **4** : 1 ff.). The question arises whether all the symbolic actions recorded in the Bible actually took place [1]. Whatever the fact may be regarding its objective reality, the symbolic action becomes a literary device insofar as it is described in our books and is explained and developed in narrative fashion.

The imagination likewise has its part in the announcement of coming events. Enlightened by God as to the fact, the seer is not always equally informed in respect to the time and the manner; hence there arises an element of personal conjecture and of idealization. Thus are explained the scenes relating to the invasion of Sennacherib (Isa. **10** : 28 ff.), to the ruin of Babylon (Isa. **13**, **47**; Jer. **50**, **51**) and of Jerusalem (Ez. **9** : 1-**10** : 8), etc. It is necessary to interpret in similar fashion more than one description dealing with the Messianic Age and with the moral, political, and material advantages which it will procure for the chosen people (Isa. **7** : 14 ff.; **8** : 8 ff.; **11**, etc.). For us who live after the accomplishment of these great events, it is easy to discern the role of the literary cloak or covering in the most authentic prophecies, and the predominance of the spirit over the letter.

Such are the principal characteristics of the prophetic genre. They gradually lose some of their sharpness and force. From the beginning of the Exile, the prophet writes more than he speaks, and he refers, implicitly or explicitly, to the prophecies of his predecessors. At the same time, contacts with the wisdom literature multiply, perspectives of the future assume a more and more pronounced eschatological form, images become fixed, and thus little by little prophecy gives place to apocalyptic [2].

Translator's note. — [1 A. VAN DEN BORN, *Profetie metterdaad* (Roermond, 1947 (on the symbolic actions of the Prophets; cf. *Theologische Revue* [1950], 137-138)].

Translator's note. — [2 G. E. KAUFMAN, *Toldot ha-emunah...* VIII (1956), 378-408 (on the end of prophecy).]

2. — The Former Prophets [1].

The Jewish canon so designates the Books of Jos., Jdgs., Sam., and Kgs., all of which are called historical writings in the classification of the Christian canon. Whatever may be the identity of the presumed authors, it is certain that the Jewish tradition has perceived exactly the true sense of these writings and the source from which they are derived. The literary form of the Former Prophets is characterized by the materials used, by the way in which they are assembled, and by the theological meaning which is given them.

The author who undertakes to recount the events of the past is dependent on his sources to the maximum. It is not his intention to create history, but simply to repeat what oral or written tradition reports. He is essentially, therefore, a compiler. The sources which he incorporates have their own individual character and come from different milieux : popular narratives, annals concerning origins, the priesthood, the cult of sanctuaries, prophetic cycles, writings composed in a royal environment — books of functionaries, inventories, tax reports, chronicles, diplomatic documents. The knowledge that we have of the ancient Orient indicates that writing was known there from an early date and men were concerned with some kind of training in composition. Such sources used by the " Former Prophets " are quite extensive and they present the qualities of great history. Thus, 2 Sam. 9-20, and 1 Kgs. 1-2, which relate the episodes of the succession of David, are remarkable for the precision, the finesse of observation, and the consummate art with which the narrative is unfolded, and, finally, for a strict impartiality which does not prevent the sympathies of the author from being discreetly revealed.

The sources are handled in the simplest possible manner. No attempt whatever is made to assimilate them, to weigh them, or to fuse them into a personal synthesis. The originality of the writer consists solely in making a choice among his documents of those which suit his purpose. Moreover, he feels

Translator's note. — [1 Cf. I. ENGNELL, s.v. " Historiaskrivning ", *Sv. bibl. Uppslagsverk* 2, 866-867. R. E. DENTAN, ed., *The Idea of History in the Ancient Near East* (New Haven, 1955; cf. *CBQ* [1956], 193-197). The art. " Geschichtsschreibung " in Haag, *Bibellexikon,* 557-559.E. KAUFMAN, *Toldot ha-emunah...* VIII (1956), 451-481 (on historiography and history in the Persian Period)].

free to summarize or gloss them, and to introduce minor or casual modifications. This done, he arranges them in order, or combines the fragments [1]. There is, then, a total absence of composition in the modern sense of the word, and the result is most strikingly evident in cases where two pieces of evidence, of different provenance and representing different points of view, are recorded side by side. This is a disconcerting procedure for the litterateur but providential for the critic, if it is true that two witnesses are better than one. In any case, it gives proof of a most scrupulous loyalty and of a religious respect for tradition.

Materially speaking, the work lacks unity. It is incontestable, however, that a certain unity exists, although it is more or less loose. Let us consider its source and character. In Jos. it is as slight as possible, for it is secured only by the logical sequence of events. In Sam. it results from a crescendo, which, rising through Samuel and Saul, attains its peak in David. The preeminence of David is to be explained by the fact that by virtue of his piety he has received for his dynasty, through the instrumentality of Nathan the prophet, the promises of perpetuity (2 Sam. 7). This affirmation brings into play the theology of the covenant, according to the spirit of Deut. and the Prophets. We find the same general fact underlying the narrative of Jdgs. by virtue of the fundamental explanation of the events which took place in the course of the unsettled period which followed the installation in Palestine. The misfortunes of the nation are a punishment for its faults; its relief is the recompense for its repentance. The idea of covenant takes here, accordingly, the form of what has been called pragmatism in four terms : prevarication, punishment, repentance, deliverance. Hence we have a frame, the compartments of which hold the materials and impose upon them an accidental, external, unity. And hence, especially, we have a philosophico-theological view of history, which ,in the interests of believers, transforms history into a higher School of Religion. Did the Prophets ever look at history from any other angle?

---

[1] See the studies of I. Guidi, " L'historiographie chez les Sémites ", *RB* (1906), 509-519, and of Cardinal TISSERANT, " Fragments syriaques du livre des Jubilés ", *RB* (1921), 55-86; 206-232. [*Translator's note. —* E. P. ARBEZ, " Some Parallels from Arabic Literature to Problems of the Old Textament ", *CBQ*, 7 (1946), 58-71, especially, 66-68, and the references there given; *id.*, " *Genesis*, I-XI ", *Am. Eccl. Review* (Sept., 1950)].

Nowhere does this method achieve a greater perfection and fullness of meaning than in the Books of Kings. The three major sources which the author cites explicitly, and the dozen others which in an examination of his work the eye discerns without too much effort, exhibit an initial unification which is entirely material; they are, in fact, juxtaposed in order to present alternately the course of events in the Northern and Southern Kingdoms. This synoptic process is set in relief for each kingdom by the stereotyped formulas of introduction and conclusion : e.g., 1 Kgs. 15 : 9-11, and 15 : 23-24; 2 Kgs. 15 : 1-7. Upon this first bond there is superimposed another, which is entirely spiritual and theological. To understand its significance it must be recalled that the author wrote in exile, just after the ruin of Jerusalem, and that he addresses himself to readers profoundly disturbed by an event which seems to contradict the most indubitable divine promises. He undertakes, then, to examine the conscience of the nation. The nation, considered as a moral person who has been living for centuries, is invited to think back upon its conduct, in order to judge it in the light of present calamities. Perhaps in this way it will be able to disavow its faults and by its repentance prepare for the coming of better times. The general idea which serves as the criterion in the distinction between good and evil is that of the covenant of Yahweh with His people through the medium of the Davidic monarchy (cf. 2 Sam. 7). The kings of the North and of the South are judged on the basis of this principle, and their moral attitude is considered only in relation to their response to two practical exigencies, which, moreover, are closely linked to each other, namely, opposition to idolatry and fidelity to the temple at Jerusalem. Around these two chief ideas, other considerations come to be centered, e.g., the legitimacy of the Levitic priesthood alone, and the authority of the Prophets, who, in the name of God, do not cease to intervene in history, especially in critical periods.

But these thoughts represent the most fundamental features of the Deuteronomic doctrine. Deut. is, in fact, essentially the book of the covenant; it promulgates the exclusive rights of the Temple of Jerusalem and the Levite priesthood, and it envisages prophecy as a permanent national institution. 1 and 2 Kgs., as regards subject matter, depend, then, on Deut., but they depend on it also in respect to form. In the testament of David (1 Kgs. 2 : 2 ff.), in the prayer of Solomon (8), in the judgments which concern the conduct of the kings, in the sentences of condemnation pronounced by the Prophets (e.g., 11 : 29-39; 13 : 1-32; 14 : 1-18), and in the words which are spoken by God Himself (3 : 14; 6 : 12; 9 : 5-9; 2 Kgs. 10 : 30), we find an accumulation of formulas borrowed from the vocabulary which is so characteristic of Deut [1].

Yet our author does not intend to follow Deuteronomic thought solely. He interprets it under the influence of the ideas of Jeremias. The seer of Anathoth, who was prophesying on the eve of the ruin of Juda, emphasized unceasingly that this calamity should be recognized as a punishment for national faults, above all for idolatry. But nowhere does he raise the question of the unity of sanctuary. This reserve on the part of Jeremias enables us to understand an important nuance in the teaching of Kgs. However closely linked may be the two precepts of monotheism and the unity of sanctuary, they are not put on the same plane by the writer. In his eyes, the ruin of the Northern Kingdom is due to the worship of calves and to formal idolatry, but it does not result from the fact alone of the multiplication of the sanctuaries of Yahweh. The kings of the South who have fallen into this fault are blamed without doubt, but discreetly. No prophet ever rises up to call down the vengeance of heaven upon their persons or their dynasty; if they have suffered misfortunes, no connection is ever established between these reverses and their shortcomings. There is, then, a distinction between the faults against dogmatic and ritual orthodoxy, and those committed solely against the unity of sanctuary. We might easily say that the second are venial. In any case, they are not of consequence from the point of view of the religious philosophy of history. Kgs. occupies then, on the doctrinal side, a position midway between Deut. 12 and Jer.

The dependence of Kgs. in respect to Jer. is further indicated by the identity of a certain number of formulas. These are taken especially from the prophecies delivered under Joachim and Sedecias, which predict in a most vehement fashion the

---

[1] See the list in Burney, *Hasting's Dictionary of the Bible*, II, 859-860, and also, the same author's *Notes on the Hebrew Text of the Books of Kings* (1903).

ruin of the Temple. In Kgs., they stand in close relation to the formulas of Deut. and to those of the redactor in certain doctrinal passages of an incontestable unity. Hence, they were inserted intentionally by him.

Such is the literary genre of the " Former Prophets ". It is a documentary history, yet one that does not seek to be erudite; it is a history which is adressed to the people, but this does not mean that it is popular in character. It is even rather learned, because of its deliberately planned attachment to the spirit and the letter of Deut. and the Prophets, and of the application which it makes of their teaching to past events. Nothing, in any case, exhibits to a higher degree the realization of the notion of sacred history.

4. — DIDACTIC AND LYRIC POETRY. [1]

1. The prophetic writings are not poetic except in a limited sense. The majority of the sapiential books, and above all the Psalter, are par excellence the representatives of Hebrew poetry.

The poetic impulse rises spontaneously among the Hebrews from certain deep sources which no other people has had the privilege of possessing to the same degree. Their language is concise, colorful, and, by a charming gaucherie, cannot express abstractions and higher realities except by means of images which are often naive. Their psychology has an extraordinary power of intuition; it sees immediately the central, familiar, and realistic trait, and it has an almost invincible propensity for emphasis. Finally, their religion is that of the invisible God. It is necessary then, in order to reach Him, to have recourse to anthropomorphisms, the boldness of which is sometimes disconcerting. He is the God of nature and of history, and His free will, which may be detected everywhere, replaces our narrow deterministic conceptions and gives life and development to beings and events. Finally, His moral demands are very exacting. What aspirations, what agonies, what struggles,

---

Translator's note. — [[1] Cf. J. MUILENBERG, " The Poetry of the O. T. ", in Introduction to the *R.S.V.* (1952), 62-70; *id.*, " A Study on Hebrew Rhetoric : Repetition and Style ", *Vetus Testamentum, Suppl.* I (1953), 97-111. T. H. ROBINSON, " Hebrew Poetic Form : The English Tradition ", *ibid.*, 128-149; G. R. DRIVER, *ibid.*, 20-39. S. N. KRAMER, " Sumerian Wisdom Literature ", *BASOR*, No. 122 (Apr., 1951), 28-39].

what triumphs there are in individual souls and in society! Such thoughts and feelings open the way to the most affecting lyrical expression.

We do not know very much about the use made by the Israelites of the means by which all poetry seeks to express rhythm, namely, meter, verse, and stanza [1]. Their meter is doubtless determined by the succession of accents, and in conformance with the nature of the language it seems to be of the iambic or anapaestic type. The form of the verse depends upon the number of accents, and the most characteristic is that of the " quiah " [i.e., " lament "], in which the place of the caesura produces a halting rhythm. Series of verses can be grouped in stanzas, which are delimited by the meaning, refrains, alphabetic arrangement, and sometimes by the repetitions of words and sounds. It does not seem, however, that there was a Hebrew strophic system as such, i.e., one intentionally developed and almost always employed, and exhibitng definitely established procedures. In fine, the material means of rhythmic expression seem never to have been very precise in Israel. The situation is quite different regarding an original element which is hardly known elsewhere, and which is essential to Hebrew poetry, namely parallelism. This term is used to describe the process which consists in presenting the came thought in two or sometimes several balanced and symmetrical phrases. This produces a balancing of ideas which doubles the sonorous rhythm of the verses.

The most celebrated student of parallelism, the English writer Lowth (1753), distinguished three kinds : the synonymous, which repeats in equivalent terms a thought already stated (Ps. 114 : 1-6); the antithetic, which opposes the second member to the first (Prov. 10); and, finally, the synthetic, in which the second member continues the first without resemblance or contrast. It may be questioned whether this last variety should really be called parallelism.

Translator's note. — [[1] On Hebrew poetry, see the valuable articles in *Sefarad :* J. M. MILLÁS VALLICROSA, " La tradición del estrofismo biblico en las poesias medievales " (1941), 45-87. — D. G. MAESO, " Contribución al estudio de la métrica biblica " (1943), 3-47. — A. DÍEZ MACHO, " Estudio de la hazarda en la 'Poesia hebraica' de Mose ibn Ezra y en el texto masorético ", (1947), 3-29, and 209-230; *id.*, " La homonimia o paranomasia " (1948), 293-321, and (1949), 269-309].

2. The resources of poetry, and especially of parallelism, serve most effectively the special ends of the didactic genre. Into this category fall the writings which make up the literature of the *Hokmah*, that is, the literature of wisdom. These writings are : Prov., Job, Eccles., Ecclus., Wis., Bar. (3 : 9–4 : 4), and in some respects the Psalms. Furthermore, throughout the Bible we encounter a number of allusions, sayings, and even passages of some length which in varying degrees exhibit the characteristics proper to sapiential literature.

Biblical wisdom literature finds its expression in the genre called the *mashal*. This device, which is quite oriental, presents itself to us under the most diverse forms : the popular saying, the sententious phrase or the gnomic discourse, the mordant witticism more or less mixed with irony which can approach satire, the parable, the allegory, and, finally, the riddle, which sometimes assumes the proportions of a mysterious problem. These different forms of the *mashal*, it seems, all posit a case or situation from real life which draws the attention and demands reflection. The mind and the imagination seize upon this objective reality to turn it into a typical case or to raise a problem. All this is done, not through mere curiosity or as a literary pastime, but with a view to the conduct of life, and with reference, at least implicit, to Religion.

The procedures of the *mashal* in the concrete are inspired by this state of mind. In the first place, the genre has a clear pedagogical purpose. The master seeks to arouse the curiosity of the pupil, to make him reflect, and to impress the maxims of wisdom on his memory. Hence we have the careful and elaborate use of parallelism, the expressions full of imagery, which are often picturesque and even sly, the assonances and alliterations, and the employment of acrostic arrangements. Hence, too, we have the numerical *mashal* (Prov. 30 : 15-33) : the first *stichos* presents the theme, and the following ones apply it to a series of cases in preparation for the statement of a borderline example.

It is important to note that the tone of the wisemen, far from being peremptory and vehement as in the Law and the Prophets, is ingratiating and mild. On their lips, the imperative does not express commands strictly speaking, but only recommendations which appeal to common sense. They do not have recourse to faith, but to experience and to reason insofar as the latter emphasize the criterion of personal interest. The sages thus stimulate interior deliberation which should lead an individual to make the most advantageous choice.

The wisdom literature has such a special and different character that one is led to ask himself how it could have had birth and development in Israel, in the very bosom of the Yahwist tradition, the spirit of which is so different, if not even contradictory to it.

The reply to this question requires a preliminary, if rapid glance at the literatures of Egypt and Babylonia. In addition to the gnomic maxims inscribed on " scarabs ", Egypt possessed a learned wisdom literature which is embodied in the so-called " Instructions ". From the Old Kingdom to the Greco-Roman period, these compositions represent an unbroken traditional teaching which formed the souls of pupils in the schools for scribes and of an incalculable number of other readers. We hear in them a sage speaking from the distant past; he addresses his son and gives him a series of practical counsels, from which religion is not absent. They are the fruit of experience, and tradition confers on them an authority that puts them above all discussion. Their purpose is primarily to train functionaries, but also men, so that they may become masters of themselves, gracious, cultivated, upright, and worthy. In Babylonia, wisdom is not distinguished from magic and divination. It finds expression, however, in the gnomic maxim and in the fable or story, which is very popular. It produced also more extensive compositions of a philosophic nature. These deal especially with the problem of suffering and, ordinarily, they exhibit a spirit of deep pessimism.

The exegetes of the *Formgeschichte* School do not hesitate to seek the origins of Biblical wisdom literature in Egypt and Babylon. According to them, it was imported from without and at first maintained a lay character, if it did not actually enter into rivalry with Yahwism. On some points, perhaps, it exercised an influence on the prophets, but, above all, it came to be dominated by the latter. From that time, it became permeated more and more with traditional ideas. Thus, at the end of its development, i.e. in Ecclus., Wis., and Bar., we see it clearly striving to achieve a synthesis of its own teaching and that of the Torah.

The foreign origin of the Biblical sapiential genre is undeniable. The geographical position of Palestine, the contacts of Israel with the great neighboring empires during almost all periods of its history, the international character of the scribes as an institution, the high antiquity of the extra-Biblical literatures in relation to the Biblical *Hokmah* which appears with a fully developed and fixed character from the first, the presence, in the foreign productions, of the various forms of the genre in the *Hokmah*, as already mentioned above all these facts support the hypothesis of a borrowed literay type. The foreign influence, in fact, may be recognized in several specific cases, e.g. : Prov. 22 : 17–23 : 11, which is to be compared with the *Wisdom of Amenemope;* Ecclus. 38 : 24 and 39 : 11, to be compared with the classical Egyptian theme of the satire on professions; Tob., which makes allusion to the story of the Assyrian Ahikar, etc.

If the foreign origin of Hebrew wisdom literature is once admitted, it is easy enough to explain its presence as a special and well-defined bloc within the national, Yahwist literature. We have no right, however, to speak of a lay code of morality. As indicated earlier (p. 368), even in the oldest collections in Proverbs, the maxims, although neutral in appearance, are actually deeply religious and from time to time show, however unobtrusively, connections with the Torah.

The relations between the wisemen and the prophets were what one might expect. Here and there we can detect friction between the men of the Spirit and scribes of the politician variety, as, e.g., Isa. 5 : 21; 29 : 14, Jer. 8 : 8-9; 9 : 12-13, without doctrine necessarily being a cause of conflict. As regards this last point, it was inevitable that prophets and scribes would reach a mutual understanding, since both were engaged in isolating and defining the moral element contained in the Law. May we speak of a reciprocal influence? It is possible that the wisemen facilitated the development of teaching on individual responsibility as we find it in Ezechiel. But, generally speaking, their influence on prophetic teaching could not be very deep, since the doctrine of the prophets is original and depends on divine revelations. On the other hand, it is clear that the wisemen drew much from the prophets; they borrowed from the latter vocabulary and themes which were in keeping with the laws of their genre. But they showed this receptivity precisely because from the very beginning, while introducing the points of view and procedures of the international wisdom literature, they remained in their hearts disciples of Moses. Their impassiveness, accordingly, was simply an attitude, pure conformity with the laws of their genre. This is why progressively, and without clash or break, the identification of wisdom literature and the Torah became manifest in the course of centuries, reaching its full and clear climax in Ecclesiasticus, Wisdom, and Baruch.

Thus, Revealed Religion never lost the consciousness of its unique excellence, even when it opened its doors to receive foreign elements. It took over the forms of the sapiential genre with marked facility because in the moral doctrine which they contained it recognized its own property.

3. The Psalter, dear to the piety of all ages, is an incomparable monument of religious lyric. From the point of view of literary form, however, it does not constitute a homogeneous whole, but is made up of various elements, the character of which is notably different. Since Gunkel, recent criticism has been trying to identify them by postulating as a point of departure for its analyses the two following axioms : Israelitic Psalmic falls into the more general field of Oriental religious poetry, especially Assyro-Babylonian; among other Oriental peoples, as well as in Israel, psalmic is intimately bound up with national liturgical institutions.

Taken in a general sense, these principles are true. But when we undertake to go into detail, we can draw from them only a small number of sure conclusions. Doubtless, the Psalter needs to be explained by something besides itself, but before seeking light from the Assyro-Babylonians and pretending the existence, during the period of the monarchy, of certain liturgical ceremonies of which we find no mention whatever, it will be proper to question the Bible itself. The psalmists, whatever their quality or their epoch, did not work in a vacuum. Now, generally speaking, three great currents constitute the literary and doctrinal history of Israel : the legal writings, the prophetic writings, and the sapiential writings. While each developed along its own line, it is clear that they all have some connections with one another until they finally become inter-mingled. According to their date, their author, and their purpose, the Psalms fall into a given category of writings or undergo a multiplicity of blended influences. As compared with these Biblical contacts, the Akkadian analogies appear very remote and pale. There is no reason, however, for excluding the thought that the Exile, by bringing the Israelites into direct relations with Assyro-Babylonian cult, gave an increase in vitality to certain already existing genres.

We can accept, moreover, as highly probable the hypothesis of a psalmic tradition linked with worship from the very beginnings of settled life. We do not know what place sacred chant occupied in ceremonies; a fortiori, we simply cannot say whether there was any definite relation between a given poem and a given rite. In general, we may suppose that the most ancient psalms were rather the expression of a collective and national piety, and that the individual point of view becomes more assertive from the time of Jer., Ez., and the authors of the wisdom literature. But, since there is no antagonism between worship and piety, since some individuals have always been able to imitate on their own account the official canticles, and since, finally, the intensity of religious sentiment, of suffering, etc., has been capable, at all periods, of making the heart overflow in rhythmic prayers, the question of the liturgical destination or non-destination of a psalm, or of that of collective or individual piety, cannot be introduced a priori, with any certainty at least, for the classification of genres and the history of their evolution.

With these reservations, we can distinguish in the Psalter several different types, but between them the boundaries are often indistinct.

The hymns comprise the most clear-out category; they celebrate the attributes of God, which manifest themselves in nature or in the history of the chosen people : thus, Ps. **8, 104, 113, 114, 136**. They are to be brought into close relation with Gen. **1**, with the narratives of the Exodus, and with Isa. **40**. The canticles of Sion are hymns inspired by the classical theme of the Temple of Jerusalem, the dwelling of Yahweh and the palladium of Israel. This thought animates Ps. 46, 48, 76, 84, 87, 122, as well as such passages as Isa. 25 : 6 ff.; 33 : 20-21; 56 : 5, 7; 57 : 15; 64 : 11, 66 : 20-23.

Besides the hymns, the most remarkable group is that of the Psalms of petition. It contains the largest number of Psalms and comprises several types : the Psalms of collective lamentation, such as 44, 74, 79, 80, 83 (cf. Jer. 4 : 19 ff.; 8 : 18 ff.; 9 : 17-22; 10 : 29-25; 14 : 22 : 10-23; Lam.), or of individual lamentation motivated by illness, false accusations, and vexations of every sort. Such pieces as 71, 88, 102, 120 make one think of Job, Isa. 56 : 9–57 : 2; 59, Jer. 15 : 10-21; 20 : 7-18, etc. The Psalms of lamentation are also psalms of hope and trust, and sometimes this sentiment predominates (130, 131). Finally, the petition granted blossoms out into the thanksgiving. There are thanksgivings of Israel (67, 107, 124, 129, etc.) and private thanksgivings (92, 100, 116, etc.). Here or there allusion is made to the events of the Exodus, and certain expressions recall the universalist views of the end of Isa., etc.

The Psalms which manifest an intention of giving instruction can all be placed in the same class and called didactic, provided that this word be allowed a certain indefiniteness. The instruction concerns the Torah, i.e., the Law, a term which is here rather prophetic than Mosaic (1, 82, etc.); it concerns also the teaching of Wisdom (49, 73, 112, 127, 128, etc.).

Some eschatological traits are manifest in a great number of Psalms, belonging, moreover, to different categories. But some are more characteristic in this respect, as 50, 75, 82, 149, and in that way approach the prophetic genre. They show a fondness for envisaging the new era under the form of an enthronement of Yahweh, ushering in the definite reign of justice and happiness, e.g., 47. Eschatology reunites the hymnal genre (149), the genre of the canticles of Sion (46, 48, 76; cf. Isa. 25 : 6 ff.), and the genre of prophetic moral instruction (82, etc.).

The era of universal renovation envisaged by the eschatological Psalms is nothing else but the Messianic era itself. They are, then, in this sense already Messianic (cf. 85). The same idea is found, in a different way however, underlying 45 and 132.

Ps. **2**, **72**, **110** allude without any doubt to the person of the Messias Himself. On the basis of the testimony of the New Testament and Christian tradition, the same is true of **16**, **22**, and of a certain number of passages found in **8**, **19**, **35**, **40**, **41**, **68**, **69**, **78**, **97**, **102**, **109**, **118**. The most direct justification of the Messianic character of a Psalm is contained in the parallelism used by the author : 2 Sam. 7 : 14-16 (the prophecy of Nathan); Isa. 9 : 5-6; 11 (the Messias, son of David, instituting a reign of peace and prosperity); 1 Kgs. 4, 20; 5 : 1 (he is a second Solomon); Pr. 8 : 22 ff. (he is begotten by God before the beginning of the world) [1].

The different types which have just been enumerated are not rigorously opposed to one another. The Psalter manifests constantly the phenomenon of a mixture of genres. Hence, it cannot be said that there is a mixed genre as opposed to certain pure types. Certain Psalms, however, are particularly representative of the mingling of genres. Such is Ps. **119**, which celebrates the excellence of the Law, understood, moreover, in the broad sense of the Prophets, but which, at the same time, exhibits the characteristics of the individual lamentation and the wisdom literature.

Finally, the Psalter offers us under the form of prayers the best that the other books, especially the prophetical books, contain. At the same time, and for that very reason, it adapts itself marvellously to all the states of our soul. Of it, as of the Holy Eucharist, one can say : " Omne delectamentum in se habentem ".

Translator's note. — [1 Cf. J. COPPENS, *De Messiaanse Verwachting in het Psalmboek* (Brussels, 1955; with excellent bibliography on the Messianic Psalms). H. RIESENFELD, " Messias ", *Sv. bibl. Uppslagsverk* 2, 245-268. S. MOWINCKEL, *Han som kommer (He Who Comes)* (Copenhagen, 1951; available also in English trans.); *id., Offersang og Sangoffer* (Oslo, 1951; pp. 664. The author treats in great detail questions he had already dealt with in earlier publications, but his views have changed on a number of points. He takes up here, e.g., psalm and religious life, types of psalms, royal psalms, hymns, psalms for the feast of Yahweh's kingship (a favorite topic of his), prophetic psalms, dates, verse forms, the Psalms and the Christian Church. In short the book covers literary, historical, and religious problems connected with the Psalms, on which he had been working in preparing an edition of the Psalms — with Job and Proverbs — for the Norwegian Bible, which was published in 1955)].

5. — *SPECULATION OF A DOCTRINAL AND EDIFYING NATURE BASED ON THE ANCIENT TEXTS AND TRADITIONS.*

The " Former Prophets " (Jdgs., Sam., Kgs.) recounted the events of the past by lining up a series of documents and interpreting their data according to the theology of the covenant. After the Exile, men were preoccupied more than ever in their search for light and encouragement from the past.

We hear mention being made at this time of *midrashim* (2 Chron. 13 : 22 ; 24 : 27), and the author of Ecclesiasticus makes allusion to his " house of *midrash* " (51 : 23). The verbal root of this word signifies " seek ", " investigate ". There is question of an attentive study relating to the ancient texts of Scripture or to traditions that are authoritative. It is a genuine form of exegesis which occupies not only the faculties of analysis and reflection, but also the imagination. It absorbs the whole attention of the soul and fills it with a desire for a life more in conformity with the will of God. In this work the pious Israelite is stimulated by his personal trials or those of his nation, by the religious problems which, according to his milieu, he poses for himself, and also by an eschatological anxiety that is ever on the alert [1].

The midrashic genre was destined to experience an extensive development in Rabbinic literature. In the juridical sphere, but above all in the historical and moral, it will give birth to strange forms in which the religious sense will too often give way to a thousand subtleties and to all the aberrations of an unbridled imagination. The Biblical passages which by anticipation, as it were, may be called midrashic do not fall into these excesses. However, the freedom with which they interpret and reemploy earlier texts could disconcert the modern reader and produce serious misapprehensions in his mind.

While the midrashic genre is found especially in the last part of the Jewish Canon, we find samples of it — or at least tendencies toward it — nearly everywhere in the Bible. This will be clear from the following examples, which are presented purely on a sampling basis. The Book of Ezechiel, which repre-

---

Translator's note. — [[1] Cf. I. L. SEELIGMANN, " Voraussetzungen der Midrasch Exegese ", *Vetus Testamentum, Suppl.* I (1953), 150-181].

sents, in a sense, a converging point for various literary and
theological currents, contains several elaborate historical
allegories, namely 16, 19, 23. At first glance, they betray a
deliberate mixture of reality and fiction, dominated by a concern
for instruction and edification. A deeper analysis shows that
all the constructions are based on old narratives in Scripture
and are employed by the prophet, even down to small details,
to serve his purpose. The Book of Jonas, with respect to which
exegesis was so long on the wrong track and was at an impasse,
must be understood simply as a didactic work. Its purpose
is to show that, even in the case of pagans, prophecies of doom
are conditional and that the way is left open for repentance
and pardon. A truth which seems so clear to us was, in the
middle of the fifth century B.C., a daring affirmation that
scandalized the pure. But what objection could they raise
against a thesis which, in veiled terms, referred constantly
to the declarations of Jeremias, presented very subtly in relief
by contrast with Ezechiel?   A. Feuillet, who has defined
excellently the purposes and devices of this curious book,
concludes very justly that there is no question here of a popular
tale. The Book of Jonas is a learned book, a herald of midrashic
literature, for its author, who had an amazing knowledge of
earlier books of Scripture, employed them constantly to serve
a carefully thought out doctrinal purpose (cf. FEUILLET, *Le
livre de Jonas*, p. 18).

The first collection in Proverbs (1–9), while belonging to a
different genre, follows the same tendency when it transposes
systematically classic material from Deuteronomy, Isaias, and
Jeremias and employs it to formulate a well-knit teaching
on wisdom that has all the appearance of being new.   And
Ecclesiasticus 24, in its turn, takes over the most beautiful
section in this collection (8 : 22 ff.) and presents it in a new
form.   The author of the first collection in Proverbs, while
avoiding any allusion to the history and religion of Israel,
declared implicity the identity of Wisdom and the Law. Ben
Sirach states clearly the same thesis when he shows wisdom
descending from heaven, establishing herself in Israel, and
performing the sacred functions in the Temple.   The reference
to the history of the Chosen People is even more explicit in the
Book of Wisdom. One of the most curious sections is that in

which the author treats in his own way the earlier narrative of the plagues in Egypt (**16-19**). In accordance with his own ideas, he expands or abbreviates the traditional data. He puts greater emphasis poetically on the supernatural element, contrasts artificially in seven antitheses the respective lots of the Egyptians and the Hebrews, and gives to the account a new sense. " This part of his work — that perhaps most pleasing to his contemporaries — is the part that for us become the most antiquated; but it presents a fully developed form of midrashic exegesis and brings out strongly and vividly certain favorite ideas and preoccupations of the author " (E. OSTY, *Le livre de la Sagesse*, p. 19).

The Psalms also furnish examples of midrashic exegesis. Ps. **132** may be taken as typical. The author's point of departure is the historical fact that David planned to build a temple to Yahweh (2 Sam. **7** : 2 ff.), but he gives this pious thought the form of a solemn oath, which is cast in hyperbolic language. The Israelites are represented as responding to David's oath by going in search of the Ark in its exile. This is a dramatization of 2 Sam. **6** : 1-2. The Ark is asked to come and establish itself in its place of rest, as if the Temple were immediately and directly concerned. Verse 10 is a rapid transition, introducing an oath by Yahweh that is symmetrical to David's; but while the king spoke of the Temple, Yahweh promises the restoration of his dynasty. The connection of the two points of view is justified by 2 Sam. **7** : 2, 5, 11. We understand, accordingly, that, in the eyes of the author, the intention which God had shown of dwelling in Sion is a guarantee of His other intention of maintaining the Davidic dynasty there. This reasoning, based on Scripture, is strictly midrashic. It is especially appropriate after 515, the date of the dedication of the Second Temple; the author can then encourage his compatriots by furnishing proof that the reconstruction of the Holy Place is the pledge of a future restoration of the monarchy.

Although the midrashic genre is a kind of parasitic growth on the multiple and varied forms of Biblical literature, it always has some connection with history — as is evident from the examples cited *supra*. Thus, it is not strange that it appears, especially in the direct line of the Historical Books, as the last stage in the development of that genre. If the interpretation of Tobias, Judith, and Esther presented earlier (pp. 299-308) is correct, these writings are certainly to be regarded as *midrashim*. They may have their origin not only in Biblical facts, but also in traditions foreign to Scripture and to Palestine. The presentation can attain a high degree of literary perfection that is much closer to our modern conception than the usages of Yahwist historiography. This is true, e.g., of the Book of Esther.

The Books of Chronicles are quite different, and yet they furnish us an example of a well-defined midrash which we see taking shape, so to speak, under our eyes. Actually, the juxtaposition in this work of long canonical citations which the author borrows and presents in altered form, and of his non-canonical sources or of his personal contributions, permits us, by contrast to grasp his own intentions and his own ideas. May we say that he is performing the work of an historian when he aspires to complete or correct the perspective of Samuel and Kings? Without doubt, he has at hand a certain amount of new information; but what are we to think of his desire to retouch or alter narratives, the divine authority of which is accepted by himself as well as by his readers? Let us say rather that he is not solely and absolutely concerned with such sacred texts as history, but with such sacred texts in his role as theologian and canonist. In the light of the traditions of his age, he reflects upon their meaning and upon the conclusions that can be drawn from them. As a theologian, he sees the figure of David in the divine plan and recognizes in it a typological meaning in relation to the Messias. As a canonist, he sees the same David completing the liturgical work of Moses, and having a mandate from God to establish by law a levitical organization much more complex than that of the desert.

These conclusions are the product of an exegesis of a scholastic character. A modern scholar, while giving his references carefully, would have presented his conclusions under a speculative form and would have made them the subject of a separate volume. Furthermore, he would have presented them as a commentary quite distinct from the canonical texts. The Chronicler presents them quite naively under the concrete form of narratives intermingled with those of his sources. This procedure was no cause of scandal either for him or for his readers. When we have once decided to adopt this perspective, we shall see that many imaginary difficulties disappear. Throughout this curious work, we shall hear the soul of an age, with its aspirations and its anxieties, and in the answer that is given to it we shall recognize the development of fundamental themes of Revealed Religion.

6. — APOCALYPTIC [1].

The midrashim look towards the past and the apocalypses towards the future. On the part of both, there is the same spirit of synthesis, the same fondness for systematic views, the same outburst of imagination, and, fundamentally, the same indestructible faith in the authority of the inspired Book. For these reasons, apocalyptic develops beside the midrash in the apocryphal literature, and between the two a distinction will sometimes be difficult to make.

It is necessary first of all to indicate what were the distant antecedents of the genre in Biblical literature, and what definitive form it takes in the apocrypha. After describing and contrasting two extremes, it will be easy later on to make clear the characteristic features of the Book of Daniel.

In its first manifestations, the apocalyptic genre dates from very early times. Assuredly it has its chief source in certain prophetic writings (Isa. 11 : 11-16; 24–27; 34–35; Ez., Joel, Zach., Mal.), but it appears quite unexpectedly also in the most varied writings. It occurs, e.g., in Deut. 28 : 60-68, which contains a series of maledictions inspired by the remembrance of the plagues of Egypt, and especially in the Psalms, where we often observe the emphasis placed on eschatological expectation, e.g., 11, 48, 50, 73, 83, 97, 98. It is plainly evident in prayers, as Ps. 46 and 75. The same tendency is manifest in the wisdom literature : Pr. 1 : 20-33; Job 18 : 5-21; 20 : 22-29; 27 : 19-23; 38 : 1; Wis. 5 : 20-23; 11 : 15-19; 17–19; Ecclus. 36 : 1 ff.

These texts disclose a state of suffering and, at the same time, an invincible confidence in the glorious intervention of God, who will reestablish order to the profit of the just. It is

Translator's note. — [1 Cf. N. A. DAHL, " Apockalyptik ", _Sv. bibl. Uppslags-verk_ 1, 86-90. J. BLOCH, _Apocalyptic in Judaism_ (Philadelphia, 1953; cf. _CBQ_ [1954], 98-100].

natural that this genre should reveal more sharply the principal
traits of its character in the postexilic period. There is, in fact,
in this age a general and continual uneasiness. Discouragement
takes possession of souls so often deceived. Further, prophecy
is in its decline, and men, more and more, are accustomed to
scrutinize the ancient inspired texts in order to find in them
the answer to the difficulties of the present and the mysteries
of the future.

For these same reasons, the genre will have its last flowering
in the apocryphal literature from the second century B. C. to
the second century A. D. To the souls who are weary of
suffering and waiting, these writings undertake to show that the
promises of the Holy Books continue to be worthy of faith.
To this end, they introduce a personage of ancient times, who
is supposed to receive, under the form of visions, communication
of the divine intentions regarding the conduct of the world.
Expressed by certain symbols, history unrolls by successive
stages, taking as its last horizon the epoch in which the author
and those to whom he addresses himself are living. It is a
tableau of general history in which are blended features at once
precise and arbitrarily vague. This attitude is a consequence
of the fiction that is at the base of the genre, and in virtue of
which the true author yields place to the supposed author, who
can speak only in prophecy. The reader is evidently forced to
concede that the unfolding of the facts, however long and
involved it may be, has been foretold correctly. It remains for
him then to await in confidence the early realization of the last
stage in the perspective, namely, the last judgment and the
advent of happiness without end.

To sum up, the apocalyptic genre is conditioned by the
following elements : pseudonymity; esoteric character of its
teaching, of which the secret must not be revealed before the
end of time, i.e., before the epoch of the true author; a motion-
picture and, to some extent, a deterministic idea of history, the
concatenation of facts having been fixed once and for all by the
all-powerful will of God; frequent intervention of angels,
whose action replaces that of secondary causes which are
themselves rendered unnecessary; finally, a universalism more
apparent then real, inasmuch as the authors of this genre think
of the pagans rather in terms of confounding them and of

centering them around Israel than of converting them and of procuring their welfare. From the point of view of literary form, the apocalyptic genre is artificial, cold, pedantic, dependent upon traditional clichés, and forced to employ subtlety and hyperbole as a consequence of its pretense that it is translating into human language the deepest and most obscure realities.

The Book of Daniel occupies a place intermediary between prophecy and apocalyptic. It has all the features of apocalyptic, excepting the cosmogonal and eschatological fantasies that the apocryphal authors welcome so gladly. It presents itself as a sealed book (**8** : 26; **12** : 9), communicating revelationes received in the period of the Exile and destined to be divulged at the time of the consummation of the world. Half of the book is devoted to the narration of different visions. These are explained by angels and announce the future destiny of empires. They are : the dream of Nabuchodonosor (**2**); the visions of the four animals (**7**), of the ram and the goat (**8**), and of the 70 weeks of years (**9** : 20-27); finally, the vision which describes the history of the Seleucids and the Lagids (**10–12**). There is more and more agreement, even among conservative exegetes, in thinking that the last horizon of all the visions is the era of Antiochus Epiphanes, considered as the mediate or immediate prelude to the coming of the kingdom of God. The purpose of the book, therefore, would be to assuage the anguish of souls distracted by persecution, and to promise them the imminent end of trial and the glorious fulfillment of the ancient prophecies. For all these reasons, we may say, with Father Lagrange, that Dan. is " the first and most perfect of the Jewish apocalypses " [1].

But it is necessary to observe with him that the author, despite what has just been said, does not leave the terrain of ancient prophecy. Even if it be admitted that the redaction of the book in its present form was not made before the time of Antiochus Epiphanes, the fact remains that the announcement of the miserable end of the tyrant (**7** : 26; **8** : 25; **9** : 26-27) is a true prediction verified by the event (1 Mach. **6** : 16; 2 Mach. **9** : 28). It is to be noted especially that the first object of the message brought by Dan. to the persecuted is to announce

[1] *RB* (1904), p. 494.

GUIDE TO THE BIBLE

the coming of the kingdom of God.   The ancient empires, and on the same terrestrial plan, are to be succeeded by a universal and eternal kingdom governed by a visible king, the Messias, the Son of Man and heir of the promises made of old to David. If the Book of Daniel thus has connections with traditional prophecy, it develops its most spiritual aspects to a marked degree.   It is very far from any dream of a political hegemony of Israel, even were this destined to serve the cause of the true religion.   In conformity with the doctrinal and literary train of thought begun by Isa. **9** : 5^b, and developed, each in its own way, by such texts as Isa. **45** : 8; **55** : 10-11; Ps. **72** : 6; **85** : 12-13; Prov. **8** : 22 ff., Eccles. **24** : 3 ff., the Messias-King of Dan. has all the transcendence of a divine being; he comes down from heaven (**7** : 13-14) and his kingdom will be purely and simply that of the saints.   Doubtless the elect are first — as is just — the saints of Judea, but no barrier is raised against the accession of the Gentiles.   It must be said likewise that the announcement of the resurrection of the dead (**12** : 1-3), the immediate preliminary of eternal rewards and punishments, presupposes a doctrine emphasizing the individual and proclaims the universality of salvation.   The Jews, accordingly, are not received simply in virtue of their title of sons of Abraham, but because they are saints.   They are still to have, moreover, a keen realization of the faults of their nation.

" To sum up. Dan. announces an act of the mercy of God, drawing men to justice.   It is an anticipation of the preaching of Jesus : Do penance, for the kingdom of God is at hand. It is a sketch of the whole view of Saint Paul on the justice bestowed by God.   From this time on, prophecy is at an end, the reality which is its accomplishment is in view, and this reality is the anointing of a very holy thing (**9** : 24).   In this we cannot refuse to recognize the Church of Jesus Christ " [1].

Such is the loftiness of the doctrine of Dan.   Obviously, it is drawn from the most authentic sources of the prophetic spirit; but in keeping with the taste of the time, it is presented by means of the ordinary procedures of the apocalyptic genre.

---

[1] M. J. LAGRANGE, *Le Judaïsme avant Jésus-Christ*, p. 68.

CONCLUSION.

This study of the literary forms of the Old Testament suggests some useful reflections. They can be comprised under three principal heads.

1. Between doctrine and literary presentation there exists a close bond. Like soul and body, the two elements are distinct but are intimately united. The expression of revealed ideas translates itself through words and through processes that are classical, if not even entirely technical, which we meet repeatedly to a greater or lesser degree in the various sections of the Canon and in the various epochs of the history of Israel. The literary study of the Sacred Scriptures, if it is well understood, is not, therefore, simply the study of the vocabulary and the external forms of thought, but also a study of doctrine. And, conversely, we may say that a theological synthesis erected without consideration of the literary factor runs the risk of being artificial and inexact.

2. The comparison that can be made of the different stages of any one genre and of different genres reveals an admirable continuity of subject matter and form. The Jewish soul looks persistently towards the past, not only to draw inspiration therefrom but also to find therein a material base, a firm terrain on which to stand, before making a new leap forward. This feature of religious psychology reveals itself everywhere. We recognize it particularly in the following sequences : Chr. leans upon Kgs., Kgs. upon Jer. and Deut., Jer. upon Osee, Deut. upon the Code of the Covenant. Again, in the domain of the Sapiential Books, Ecclus. depends upon all the preceding books, especially upon Prov., and Prov. itself depends upon Deut., Isa., and Jer. We could develop this point even further. Thus, definite converging lines would be found, ending in certain source-writings whose loftier teaching and more attractive form impressed forever the soul of Israel. In brief, the ultimate explanation of this process of close interlocking is the belief in the divine origin of the texts. And this belief goes back very far, even as far as the belief in the charism of prophecy.

We see through the above examples that the Biblical tradition is not only continuous, but progressive. A link in a chain is only welded to preceding links in order to lengthen them. The authority of ancient books is only invoked in order to go beyond them. Ancient ideas are only examined for the sake of finding in them values in terms of the present. This march forward cannot take place without an extented employment of the procedure which we call accommodation. Hence Scripture is not a dead text; it is an organic whole which lives, which draws from the surrounding milieu, and which has an unlimited capacity of adaptation in developing along its own line. Recent authors are not fettered by the ancient, but interpret them with a freedom which is disconcerting to us. Who gives them this right? First of all, the Holy Spirit, Who directs them towards the summits of the Gospel. But we may not forget that Scripture is only the partial and accidental expression of the religious life of Israel. Scripture was born in tradition and, in a certain way, of tradition. It developed along with tradition, and it never ceased to reflect the successive stages of tradition.

An equally fundamental conclusion based on this study is that the cold and static individualistic concept of Scripture which Protestants have made for themselves is to be rejected. For us Catholics, on the other hand, it recalls the necessity of accepting the fact of a literary evolution, since we accept that of an evolution in dogma and in the religious life of Israel. This attitude is the only one which permits us to understand the Old Testament both in itself and as a preparation for the teachings and for the literary forms of the New.

II. — THE LITERARY GENRES OF THE NEW TESTAMENT.

As regards literay genres, the New Testament does not offer the same variety as the Old. This is due to several causes. First of all, the history of the composition of the books of the Old Testament corresponds to the different stages in the religious and national life of the Israelites during a dozen centuries, whereas the writings of the New Testament were produced in the course of a relatively short period time — about sixty years. Accordingly, New Testament literature, unlike that of the Old Testament, does not reflect a process of development based on the recasting and rewriting — under new forms — of much earlier documents which serve as a point of departure for a more explicit teaching or one better adapted to the needs of the moment. Moreover, the infant Church, which had received from the Synagogue its prophecies and its books of prayer and wisdom, was content to utilize that heritage without giving it any complement of the same kind. The prophecies were being fulfilled, the traditional formulas of prayer and of praise were adapting themselves to the new faith, and the rules and counsels touching the religious and moral attitude of man retained all their force. Finally, it should not be forgotten that the first task of the Apostles and their immediate disciples was to devote themselves entirely to propagation of the Faith; therefore, to teaching. Among the workers in the Christian mission, those who wrote did so only in order to cooperate actively in the task of conquest, wishing by this means to consolidate, extend, and amplify the effects of the oral message (cf. Luke 1 : 3-4). Thus, in contrast to the Books of the Old Testament, composed to protect a deposit, to maintain traditions, to preserve the remembrance of the past and to revive the national hopes, the New Testament collection represents above all a literature of propaganda.

Strictly speaking, the writings of the New Testament can be brought only with difficulty or in a superficial way under the common types of literature. However, in accordance with customary usage, they can be distributed into three groups : the historic or documentary type (Gospels and Acts), the epistolary type (Epistles of Saint Paul and the so-called " Catholic " Epistles), and the apocalyptic type (Apocalypse of Saint John). This division, established on the basis of literary form, has no relation to the chronological classification of the same documents. The first Epistle to the Thessalonians, in fact, must be dated in the year 51 or 52, whereas the Johannine Epistles belong to the end of the first century. Furthermore, we shall see later how within the first group the Fourth Gospel, as compared with the Synoptics, represents a particular form of the historical genre, and how, in the epistolary group, some are true letters, as the Epistles to the Corinthians, while others are instructions of a doctrinal or moral character which have been given something of an epistolary form to assure them the benefit of a more extensive and more rapid diffusion, as the Epistle of Saint James and the Second Epistle of Saint Peter.

1. — THE HISTORICAL NARRATIVE OF THE GOSPELS AND OF ACTS.

The history of Jesus and the résumé of his teaching have been preserved for us in four little booklets known under the name of the Gospels according to Matthew, according to Mark, according to Luke, and according to John. The Acts of the Apostles, which give a summary view of the propagation of Christianity, first in Palestine and subsequently in the Greco-Roman world, i.e., in the Jewish milieu and among the Gentiles, serve to complete the Gospel history. The Gospel according to Luke and the Book of Acts, written by the same author and both bearing a dedication to the same personage in imitation of the dedications which were customary at that time, are related in such a way that the second work is the natural sequel of the first. These writings together, Gospels and Acts, contain the history of the beginnings of Christianity, and the five belong to the historical genre. Among the Gospels, there are three which resemble one another in numerous points and which have received the name Synoptic, because it is often possible to arrange their texts in parallel columns so as to embrace them, as it were, under a single glance (synopsis). Since, so far as literary form is concerned, this triad resolves itself into a single type, there is every advantage in examining together these three documents, the close relationship of which is denied by no one. It will then be in order to compare with them the Gospel according to John, which is so markedly different in character. Finally, we shall examine the Book of Acts.

1. — The Gospels [1].

A — The Synoptics, at first sight, appear to be biographies of the Master; they sketch his ministry in broad outlines and they summarize his teaching. And yet none of these little books is

---

Translator's note. — [1 Cf. J. M. BOVER, " Tipo literario de los Evangelios ", *Sefarad* (1946), 237-252]; H. RIESENFELD, s.v. " Logia ", *Sv. bibli. Uppslagsverk* 2, 119-120, and " Talkällan ", *ibid.*, 1937. A. FRIDRICHSEN, s.v. " Liknelser " (Parables), *ibid.*, 83-88. D. M. STANLEY, S. J. " Didache as a Constitutive Element of the Gospel-Form ", *CBQ* (1955), 336-348.]

a biography of Jesus in the true sense of the word, not only because they furnish such very meager information on the words and deeds of our Lord, but especially because it was not the purpose of the authors to compose a narrative of this type. The term " gospel " of itself indicates that it is concerned with a joyous announcement, with good news, and in the New Testament the word never means a book, but always the message of salvation realized by Christ. Moreover, when certain writings received the title of gospel, in order to distinguish them and to indicate their authors, they were called the Gospel according to Matthew, the Gospel according to Mark, etc. The most ancient witness for the use of the word in the plural is found in the *First Apology* of Saint Justin (ch. 66) where there is mention " of the Memoirs of the Apostles which are called Gospels " [1]. It must be remembered, then, that the written gospel presents itself above all as the announcement of good news given to the Apostles and transmitted by them.

By its nature and content the gospel message under its first form, which was oral, was bound to furnish testimony on the person, the doctrine, and the work of Jesus, since the end in view was to convert Jews and Gentiles to the new faith. Besides, the Apostles, as we see from the Book of Acts, announced themselves as witnesses (1 : 8, 21-22; 2 : 32; 3 :1 5; 4 : 20; 5 : 32; 1 : 39), and their preaching possessed its authoriyt from the fact that they could claim " to have seen and heard ". The choice of the elements which constituted their testimony was necessarily determined by the desire to win the adherence of their hearers. Of the deeds and teachings of Christ, only those were retained in their catechesis which seemed suited to instruct and convince. Thus, the testimony was limited, and it included only a restricted number of facts, sayings, and discourses, as the résumé of the instruction of Saint Peter to the centurion Cornelius and to the people about him shows (Acts 10 : 36-41).

The arrangement of these elements was a matter of secondary importance to the missionaries, who were not any more concerned than their hearers about precise chronological

---

[1] There is every reason for believing that this designation (" Memoirs of the Apostles "), which occurs frequently in Saint Justin, was suggested to him by the title of Xenophon's work on Socrates rather than furnished by tradition.

sequence. They contented themselves with indicating some
points of reference to facilitate their catechetical exposition :
after the preparation of Christ for His ministry, the preaching
in Galilee; then, the journey from Galilee to Jerusalem; finally,
the last days marked by His passion, death, and resurrection.
The main lines in the life of Jesus were thus indicated. In this
general framework, as simple as it was flexible and easy to
remember, the action was revealed in a progressive manner.
Doubtless there were repetitions, restatements, and even
regressions, but progress remained no less assured, and that
was the essential for a message preached *ad probandum*.

The repetition of this witness-message and its faithful
transmission under a quasi-stereotyped form or under very
similar forms are easily explained in their environment and at
a time when the spoken word, not the written, played the
same role as the printed text among us. Renan and many
others after him have remarked that the memory of man was
then like a book. In the Jewish world, maxims, sententious
expressions, and explanations of the sacred text were transmitted
orally for generations before being committed to writing — the
Mishna is a proof of this. The Qoran in some of its parts was
preserved at first in the same way. Even today, certain ethnic
groups preserve their religious or national traditions, without
writing them, under the form of faithfully reproduced recitations.
In the beginning, the Christian preachers did the same, availing
themselves of mnemonic devices familiar to anyone who makes
habitual and exclusive use of the oral style : rhythm, refrains,
responses, guide words, catchwords, numerical groupings, etc. [1].
This would not exclude, even in the period of the first Christian
generation itself, the use of collections of the type of florilegia
or notebooks, or of those catechetical efforts to which Saint Luke
makes allusion in the prologue of his Gospel (1 : 1).

The general remarks upon the apostolic catechesis take on
their full significance when it comes to defining or specifying
the literary genre represented by the Synoptics, for no one

---

[1] On all this, see M. Jousse, *Le style oral et mnémotechnique chez les Verbo-moteurs. Etudes de psychologie linguistique*, (Paris, 1925), and C. F. Burney, *The Poetry of Our Lord* (Oxford, 1925). [Also L. de Grandmaison, *Jésus Christ*, vol. I (New York, 1934), " Note C. The Rhythms of the Oral Style in the New Testament ", pp. 203-213. — Dom John Chapman, " Jousse on the Oral Style ", *The Dublin Review* (July, 1929), 12-25].

denies the close dependence of these texts in relation to the oral gospel, i.e., to the witness-message of which we have just spoken. As the point of departure or at the base of the narratives of Saint Matthew, of Saint Mark, and of Saint Luke, we find the catechesis. Each author knew it under the form of oral tradition or of a written document and utilized it as a source, directly or indirectly, and to a degree which is revealed by a detailed comparison of the three documents.

The Gospel according to Mark, which has not more than 50 verses peculiar to itself, is found again almost entirely in the First and Third Gospels. The little book shows very well what must have been the type of popular instruction given in order to introduce men to Christianity. The manner is simple and direct, the form concise and a little crude, the narrative progressive and without well marked articulations.

It would be useless to look here for biographical details in the strict sense : the name of Joseph, the (legal) father of Jesus, is not mentioned, although the surname of the sons of Zebedee is indicated (3 : 17), and likewise the name of the blind man of Jericho (10 : 46); nothing is said of the life of Jesus before His baptism by John; very frequently, when the author recalls the teaching of Jesus presented before audiences, however precisely defined these may be, he furnishes no information on the subject treated; chronological points of reference are completely lacking, and geographical data are reduced to the absolute minimum.

The opening sentence indicates specifically in its way the purpose of the author: " the beginning of the Gospel (i.e., of the Good News) of Jesus Christ, Son of God " (1 : 1). This designation or this title given to Jesus is revealing, for it underlines implicitly the writer's purpose. The episodes related in the course of the narrative are intended to support and confirm this basic declaration respecting the person of Jesus, even if they are not bound together and interlinked as in a systematic or merely didactic demonstration. It is clearly apparent that words and facts are reported as sufficient in themselves, *prout sonant*, for what they are and for what they signify. But the reflection of the centurion takes up again directly the affirmation made at the beginning : " Truly this man was the Son of God ", (15 : 39). It is no exaggeration to say that, from the beginning

to the end of the book, the thesis discretely indicated at the
outset is established progressively, and, as it were, course by
course, without argument or demonstration. Furthermore,
in this Gospel there is no trace of theological preoccupations
or symbolic language, and no concern for literary composition.
The author has simply reported what he knew in an honest and
almost brusque fashion. His work is not a biography of Jesus,
but neither is it what we moderns call a " historical work ".
It belongs to the unique genre assumed by the current apostolic
preaching on Jesus, His acts and words. It is a narrative
without literary pretension, popular in tone, and a bit rough
and sharp; it consists of pieces that are juxtaposed rather than
united with each other and it is presented as an invitation to
hope and faith.

The most ancient tradition, attested by Papias of Hierapolis
(c. 125), saw in this Gospel the faithful echo of the catechesis
of Saint Peter, such as the Apostle preached it to the Gentiles
(Eusebius, *H.E.*, III, 39 : 15) [1]. But this close and direct
dependence does not exclude the possible use by Saint Mark
of some written account for the redaction of the last chapters of
his book.

The Gospel according to Saint Matthew is not a biography of
Christ in the modern sense of the term any more than is the
Gospel of Saint Mark. However, on the other hand, it is not
a simple collection of sayings on moral instructions, edifying
anecdotes, or miraculous deeds. It would be more exact to
describe it as a kind of manual containing the essential elements
for initiation into the Christian faith. Based in large part on
the common foundation of the primitive catechesis, this work
serves a twofold purpose of its author, and this purpose
determines to some extent its genre. Matthew intended to
give as complete a sketch as possible of the teaching of Jesus
(his didactic purpose), and, in addition, he wished to prove
that Jesus was indeed the Messias promised by God to the
Jewish people, announced by the Prophets and expected by
Israel (his major thesis, which is both doctrinal and historical).
His book presents itself as a manual and as a proof.

Translator's note. — [1 On the texts of Papias quoted in Eusebius, see especially J. A. KLEIST, S. J., in *Ancient Christian Writers*, 6 (Westminster, Md.,
1948), p. 118 and pp. 207 ff.)].

Since Matthew wrote to instruct after the manner of a teacher or a catechist, rather than to narrate in the fashion of an historian, he was concerned about the arrangement and presentation of the elements he employed, and he organized them into a systematic exposition. This is what Papias called the " oracles of the Lord in Aramaic " collected by the Evangelist Matthew (as cited by Eusebius, *H.E.* III, 39 : 16). Matthew shows a liking for good arrangement, the effects of mass, and vivid synthesis. He has grouped carefully into six great discourse-programs the sayings which Jesus uttered and the teachings which He gave on especially important subjects, under different circumstances and before different audiences. This is a pedagogical procedure which enabled him to produce a stronger impression and to present a more complete and more gripping view of Christ's doctrine. These discourses are distributed throughout the book, which is " erected ", as it were, and in a very skillful fashion : **5-7, 10, 13, 18, 23, 24-25**. These deliberate groupings of maxims, parables, and instructions give the First Gospel its special physiognomy and coloring. Without doubt, the procedure adopted by the author is only a device of composition, but — and this is the essential thing — the words of Jesus were accurately reported. The situation was quite different in the " Lives " of famous men composed by numerous Classical authors, which we put under the heading of " oratorical history " because of the imaginary character of the speeches. Matthew, while giving his own arrangement to the materials furnished by the catechesis, has scrupulously reproduced the sayings and discourses of Jesus according to their original tenor, as is shown by a comparison of the parallel passages in the Synoptic Gospels.

There are other indications which enable us to discern the influence of the apostolic catechesis on the redaction of the First Gospel. In addition to the frequency of stereotyped formulas and rhythmic sequences, we find to some extent throughout the book numerical arrangements of maxims, parables, and miracles grouped in threes, sevens, or nines. Thus, there are three temptations (**4** : 1-11), three examples of Christian " justice " (**6** : 1-18), three prohibitions (**6** : 19–**7** : 6), three announcements of the Passion (**16** : 21; **17** : 21; **20** : 18-19), three invitations in respect to prayer (**7** : 7), three

prayers of Jesus at Gethsemani (26 : 39-44), three denials by
Peter (26 : 69-75); seven petitions in the Our Father (6 : 9-13),
seven parables of the Kingdom (13 : 3-50), seven curses against
the Pharisees (23 : 13-36), and nine miracles in series of threes
(8 and 9). All these definite references to recitals, the verbal
rhythm, and the groupings were designed to aid the memory
of the narrators [1].

There is universal agreement that Matthew wrote for the sake
of readers of Jewish origin and more particularly for Judeo-
Christians. It was natural under these circumstances that his
book should be a demonstration of the Messianic character
of Jesus, that Jesus the Messias should be his major thesis.
In order to establish and prove his thesis, the author appealed
to facts known by those who had been auditors and witnesses.
He emphasized the unique authority of the Doctor and the
absolute power of the Thaumaturge. In addition, he employed
the argument best suited to convince Jews, namely, the realization in the person of Christ of the Messianic oracles. His recourse
to Scripture, to the witness of the Prophets, now in the form of
explicit citation, now by simple allusion, is constant from the
beginning to the end of the First Gospel, and it is much more
marked there than in the other Synoptics. From the genealogy
given at the beginning to the narrative of the Passion at the end,
Jesus appears as the Messias announced and sent by God, as the
son of David, and as the Anointed of the Most High.

All these observations lead to the conclusion that the Gospel
according to Saint Matthew presents itself as a manual of
instruction or as a catechetical manual, and as a work of propa-

---

[1] In the Talmudic treatise, *Pirke Aboth*, we find the same procedures employed
to facilitate and assure the accurate transmission of the statements or maxims
of the Ancients.

[Pirke Aboth, called in English " Sayings of the Fathers ", is a tractate
from the Mishnah where it stands as the second last tractate in the 4th order
(Nezikin). It consists of 5 chapters plus an additional 6th chapter " on the
acquisition of the Torah " from the Baraitha. Containing the favorite maxims
of some sixty early Rabbis, it is a sort of epitome of moral and religious teaching
and enjoys great popularity. It is the best known of the Mishnah tractates,
and has been edited and commented upon more frequently than the other
Rabbinical writings. It has found a place in the Jewish Prayer Book. See,
for instance, Dr. Joseph H. HERTZ (late chief Rabbi of the British Empire),
the *Authorized Daily Prayer Book* (revised edit., New York, 1948, pp. 610-721
(Hebrew text, translation and commentary), Published also separately
under the title : *Sayings of the Fathers* (New York, 1945). Cp. also R. T.
HERFORD, *Pirke Aboth* (New York, 1945 : Introd., text, transl., and comm.].

ganda possessing a doctrinal character. Its genre is thus defined as precisely as possible.

In the Gospel of Saint Luke we have a work which is more personal in nature and which, with good right, can be regarded as a literary production. The author, in a prologue composed according to classical rules (1 : 1-4), justifies his undertaking, speaks of the inquiries made by him on the subject, and sets forth his purpose. He declares in particular that he plans to write καθεξῆς, i.e., in sequence or order, a procedure in harmony with the precepts of the ancient rhetors concerning the arrangement (τάξις) of the different parts of an historical narrative. In his prologue, Luke indicates clearly that he intended to compose a history of Jesus, and, accordingly, of the beginnings of Christianity, on the basis of information which he has gathered and checked. He proposes to give a more exact and complete narrative of events than those of his predecessors. This preliminary declaration, which is without parallel in the New Testament, has a very great interest from the viewpoint of literary history, for it not only clarifies for us the intentions of the writer, but it also indicates the genre and character of his book; the writer, manifestly, meant to write an historical work.

We know that Luke took care to connect the Gospel history with profane history. Hence, he mentions the census of Quirinus when he relates the birth of Jesus, and he establishes a sixfold synchronism to mark precisely the time of John the Baptist's entry upon the scene. But, apart from these references, he is not any more exact in his chronology than the other two Synoptics. His narrative progresses within the same framework and presents the same arrangement of episodes. Usually, the disposition of data is identical with that adopted by Mark, and there are no significant points of reference in geography or chronological order. On the other hand, the personal contribution of Saint Luke is important, for it amounts to a good third of the book (especially, 9 : 51–18 : 14, the journey to Jerusalem).

Those who might be expecting something more and better of an " informed " writer and of an author intending to compose a genuine historical work, may feel that they have been somewhat deceived, although the narrative is admirably written. But such critics ought to remember that Saint Luke, like his predecessors, composed a " gospel ", and not a biography of Jesus. He wrote the history of the Good Tidings with the preoccupation of reproducing faithfully what, for a believer, constituted its essential and permanent value. To do this, he had, necessarily, to remain in the line of and in dependence upon the apostolic catechesis, which pressed with all its authority, and also with all its weight, on anyone who undertook to write of Christ and about Christ. No one at this period and in these centers in which the Church was growing had any idea or need of a gospel conceived under the form of annals of the Classical Greek genre or under that of chronicles of the biographical type. In order to pass a fair judgment on the historical value of the Third Gospel, it is necessary to examine the style and characteristic features of " Book II ", i.e., of the Acts of the Apostles, the continuation and completion of " Book I ". In Acts, the author shows that he is a true historian.

The foregoing remarks concerning the composition of the Synoptic Gospels bring us back repeatedly to the same point : the apostolic catechesis, the nature and characteristics of which have been pointed out above. As a result, the literary genre of these writings can be determined precisely, at first by elimination, and then by approximation. The three first Gospels were written to serve the purposes of instruction and edification, and with the interests of the propagation of the Faith in mind, by authors not one of whom, not even Saint Luke, was a historian by profession. Hence, they are neither biographies nor chronicles in the modern sense of these terms. They are not, however, mere collections of anecdotes or more or less legendary recollections, grouped and crystallized around a name or a figure. They differ greatly from the half-whimsical, half-historical works which we call romanticized biographies, and equally likewise from the marvelous stories drawn from popular folklore. They are not related to that form of ancient classical literature which is known as oratorical history. By taking into consideration only the style, which is frequently oracular, and the form, which is rhythmic or marked by a certain hieratic quality, we cannot define them purely and simply as books of worship, for, on the one hand, the catechesis preceded the ritual or liturgical use of these writings, and, on the other, these texts show plainly the influence of the style of the Septuagint. The Synoptic Gospels, as the Books of Samuel and of Kings in the Old Testament, represent a particular form of the historical genre or of documentary history, with this added qualification that they were not written according to the procedures of modern historiography. They may be qualified as *popular writings*, if it is intended by this designation to emphasize the impersonal manner of the narration, the absence of scholarly composition, the lack of chronological and topographical references, the naive simplicity of the narrative, and the ignorance of all rhetorical devices. The literary genre to which the Synoptic Gospels belong can only be determined by examining their prehistory and the purpose which determined their redaction. It is necessary to see in them, as in the oral catechesis, an instrument of instruction. These writings were not composed, any more than the catechesis, in the interests of history; but, in the manner of the catechesis and its extension, they made their appearance and were used as a witness and as a proof. This circumstance guarantees their value from the point of view of the reality of the facts and of the discourses recorded, and justifies the traditional title of historical works which has been applied to them.

B. — The Method Called " Form Criticism ".

Beginning nearly forty years ago, the representatives of a new school of exegetical and historical criticism have applied themselves to clarifying and explaining the origin and formation of the Synoptic tradition through the study of literary forms. Convinced of the inadequacy and weakness of the methods employed for more than a century to find a satisfactory solution for the problems posed by the Gospel texts, a number of German scholars — philologists, exegetes, and historians — have considered that it is possible to go beyond the results obtained previously by the analysis of the sources or documents employed by the Evangelists. To this end, they have applied themselves to the study of the " prehistory of the Gospels ", taking as their point of departure the various literary forms which they believe it is possible to discern in the Synoptics. Their method is quite different from that extolled by the adherents of the documentary theory, for research is no longer concentrated on the tradition fixed by writing, but rather upon the genesis and history of this tradition, upon its formation and its evolution within the first Christian communities of Syria and Greece in the period before the redaction of the Gospels.

The name adopted to designate this system of Gospel criticism (*Form Criticism, Formgeschichtliche Methode, Methode de l'histoire des formes*) comes from Martin Dibelius who, in 1919, published a book entitled *Die Formgeschichte des Evangeliums*. In rapid succession, in less than four years, K.L. Schmidt, R. Bultmann, M. Albertz, and G. Bertram followed the road opened up by M. Dibelius [1]. Basically, it was the method adopted by Hermann Gunkel in his studies on Genesis (1901), and later on the Psalms (1931).

It will be useful to indicate the chief principles and characteristic features of this system because of its actuality, importance, and vogue in many non-Catholic circles. M. Dibelius and R. Bultmann have presented them clearly in their various works.

1. The Synoptic Gospels are mosaics or collections of an impersonal character made up of more or less developed pericopes, and arranged in some fashion or other, not by authors, but by redactors who could not fuse these *membra disiecta*, these isolated and disparate elements, and make literary works out of them. The Evangelists performed the role of compilers only, for they did nothing more than group haphazardly in a framework furnished by tradition the little narratives transmitted orally or under a written form. The majority of the episodes

---

[1] The numerous works dealing with or referring to the *Formgeschichtliche Methode* are indicated in E. FLORIT, " La storia delle forme nei Vangeli ", *Biblica*, 14 (1933) 212-248. Cf. also : F. M. BRAUN, " Formgeschichte (Ecole de la) ", *DBV, Suppl.* III (1938), 312-317. P. BENOIT, " Réflexions sur la Formgeschichtliche Methode ", *RB* 53 (1946), 481-512. A. WIKENHAUSER, *Einleitung in das N. T.* (Freiburg i. Br., 1953; English trans., New York [1958]), 182-199. For the more important works, see the Bibliography at the end of this chapter. On H. GUNKEL, cf. L. HENNEQUIN, " Hermann Gunkel ", *DBV, Suppl.* III (1938), 1374-1377. [Cf. also : R. BLOCH, " Midrash. Origines Bibliques ", *DBV, Suppl.* V (1957), especially 1278-1279. I. ENGNELL, S.V., " Formhistorisk Metod ", *Sv. bibl. Uppslagsverk* I, 557-560. A. FRIDRICHSEN, s.v. " Litterärkritik " 2, 97-99. Bo Reicke, s.v. " Traditionshistorisk Metod ", *ibid.* 2, 1437-1440. H. J. SCHÜTZ, *Beiträge zur Formgeschichte synoptischer Wundererzählungen, dargestellt an der Vita Apollonii des Philostratus* (Jena, 1953). A. LEGAULT, C. S. C., " An Application of the Form Critique Method to the Anointings in Galilee and Bethany ", *CBQ* (1954), 131-145. *La formation des Evangiles : Le problème synoptique et Formgeschichte* (Recherches Bibliques 2, Bruges, 1957)].

are presented without precise chronological or geographical references and appear to have been juxtaposed at random. Only a single piece, namely, the account of the Passion, shows coherence and is organized in a literary way. None of the Synoptic narratives exhibits the organic unity which is the first mark of a literary work in the proper sense of the word. The first three Gospels belong to the class of writings which can be put under the heading of " minor literature " or " popular literature ", and which belong to a genre that is rightly called " infra-literary ".

2. None of the Gospels gives us a consistent and historical picture of the life of Jesus. They furnish no precise and certain information on his early training, on his personality, on the progressive development of his thought or of his conscience, on the manifestations of his inner life, or on the forms of his religious activity. The lack of historical and psychological data is equally marked as regards the personages around him, whose names we hardly know, whether there is question of the members of his family, of his disciples, of his opponents, or of the masses. Personalities, with the exception of Peter, appear without delineation or relief; they lack the illumination which can only be furnished by impressions based on direct and personal contacts.

3. The Gospel narratives are the product of a tradition which had its origin and received its form in the Christian communities of the first generation and which, under the influence of the creative action of the collectivity, developed along the lines of their faith in the course of the thirty years that followed the death of Jesus. The Gospel message was lived by its believers before becoming fixed in writing, and the various elements of this message were inevitably adapted to the Christological teaching of which they were both the support and the expression. The comparison of parallel texts reveals this adaptation, and shows that it was an evolutionary development. Furthermore, modern studies on the effect of sociological factors within human groups in process of organization project some light on the quasi-spontaneous formation of collective and anonymous works that present striking analogies with the Gospels. In the primitive community, the requirements of preaching, apologetics,

liturgy, and worship exercised a powerful influence on the genesis, growth, and flowering of more or less developed narratives dealing with an utterance of Christ or with one of his deeds. The religious literatures of the same epoch, both among the Greeks as well as among the Jews, exhibit an identical process of formation and development : a tradition is born, organized, and amplified through the action and power of a creative faith, which is always effervescent in its beginnings. The Gospel tradition took shape and embellished itself in the same manner as the others.

4. It is the function of critics to determine, from the literary point of view, the type or genre of each of the elements or fragments incorporated into the redaction of the Gospel history. M. Dibelius and R. Bultmann, in particular, have applied themselves to this work of dissection and analysis; they take into account for each piece or pericope what Gunkel called its *Sitz im Leben*, i.e., its place, its nature, and its signification in the life of the Christian communities, and likewise its connections with the needs or functions of these same groups (instruction, moral discipline, apologetics, polemics, prayer, and liturgy).

A schematic sketch of the results of these studies will be helpful to the reader.

The Gospel material is divided into two parts : what may be comprised under *Logia* (words, sayings, discourses) of Jesus, and what may he classified as history or a fragment of narrative about Jesus. Some references to texts will enable the reader to get a better idea of the reasons for the classifications proposed, and regarded as solidly established by the two protagonists of the method.

According to R. Bultmann, the *Logia* fall into 6 groups : sapiential statements and proverbial maxims (Mt. **6** : 19-24); prophetic and eschatological utterances (Mt. **5** : 3-9); legal precepts and rules of discipline (Mt. **6** : 2-18; **18** : 15-22); declarations of Jesus on his coming and on his mission (Mt. **10** : 34-36; Mk. **2** : 17), or on his person (Mt. **11** : 25-30); comparisons and parables (Mt. **13**); apothegms of various kinds : some, polemic (Mk. **2** : 1-12, 23-28); others, didactic (Mk. **10** : 17-22); still others, biographical (Mk. **6** : 1-6) — all these apothegms exhibit this characteristic, that an utterance is presented or encased in a context.

The classification of the *Logia* given by M. Dibelius under the general heading of Paraenesis (moral and disciplinary teaching) is quite close to that of R. Bultmann. However, it differs on one important point : the apothegms — called paradigms by Dibelius — do not appear in the section of *Logia* or utterances, but under that of stories or narratives.

The narrative elements are classified by Dibelius under five heads : paradigms, little stories, legends, narrative of the Passion, and cycle of myths. The paradigms (the apothegms of R. Bultmann) are short anecdotes emphasizing a statement of Jesus (Mk. **2** : 1-12; **10** : 17-27). The little stories –– more detailled narratives than the paradigms — relate miracles and emphasize the thaumaturgic power of Jesus (Mk. **4** : 35-41; **6** : 35-44). The legends — the word is used in the etymological sense of " text to be read ", as in the expression, " Legends of the Saints " — represent a more elaborate genre; they relate episodes in the life of Christ (Lk. **2** : 41-50; **19** : 1-10) or of his disciples (Lk. **5** : 1-11; Mt. **14** : 28-31). The narrative of the Passion is the oldest piece in the catechesis, the foundation stone of the apostolic preaching. The cycle of myths, which had its origin and developed under the influence of Pauline Christology, comprises the narratives of Christ's baptism, of the temptation in the desert, and of the transfiguration : three scenes conceived in terms of Saint Paul's thesis of the Son of God incarnate in the person of Jesus, Messias and Savior of mankind.

The genres or forms which R. Bultmann distinguishes in the mass of narratives reduce themselves to three types : 1) apothegms, incisive in tone and short in form, each based on a noteworthy utterance of Jesus; 2) narratives of miracles (called " little stories " by M. Dibelius); 3) biographical anecdotes or edifying legends created to serve the purposes of instruction. The history of the Passion stands apart from the rest as a distinct unit established from the very beginning.

After these minute analyses, in which there are constant interferences between literary criticism and material or historical criticism, the two authors take pains to declare that the literary forms which they have thus defined and catalogued rarely appear in a pure state in the Synoptics. Contaminations took place : first during the period when the themes of preaching were being elaborated, and then during the years when the catechesis was being transmitted solely under an oral form. Furthermore, they observe, the redactors of the Gospels, in their work of compilation, often modified the original physiognomy of what tradition had transmitted to them.

Although this exposition of the theory of literary forms as conceived and applied by M. Dibelius and R. Bultmann is too short and incomplete, it will suffice to give some idea of the originality and interest of the new method. As stated *supra*, the purpose of the critics mentioned — identical, for that matter, with that of all historians of the beginnings of Christianity — is to reach the primitive substratum in its historical reality, to push below the Gospel texts and a tradition that, during thirty or forty years, had been built up within the communities founded in the Hellenized centers of Syria and Asia Minor. The natural and normal result of these investigations is a reconstruction of the history of Jesus on the basis of conclusions which are regarded as solid or at least as possessing probability.

What is the value of this method, if we envisage and judge it under the aspect of genres or literary forms, and exclusively from this point of view, which is that of the present study?

1. That the Gospels are not biographies of Jesus; that they have as a substratum the oral tradition or catechesis, of which they represent a form already elaborated; that they are essentially collections of sayings and deeds; that they belong to a literary genre which moderns refuse to call historical composition [in the strict sense] — these observations or assertions are not open to discussion, reservation being made, however, for explanations. That these narratives are composed in the manner and under the form of what is called " popular history ", i.e., history without artifice and without affectation, in which oral traditions and written documents are amalgamated without concern for chronological order and geographical localization, and are most frequently presented without connections or organic linking — all this, too, is made evident by a methodical and objective analysis of the Synoptic texts. But the absolute

value of the theory of Form Criticism is not thereby established, neither as regards its principles nor in respect to its conclusions.

2. The principles are for the most part unproven postulates : the creative power of the collectivity; the relation of cause and effect between the offices or functions of the primitive community and the literary or " infra-literary forms " uncovered by the analysis of the Gospel pericopes; the genesis and development of the ancient tradition on Jesus owing to the same religious and sociological factors that occasioned the origin and composition of certain popular Jewish and Hellenistic writings; the priority of certain forms (the apothegms and paradigms) in relation to others (the little stories and legends). The list of these postulates would have to be lengthened if we wished to make it complete. There is no question here of indisputable axioms, but rather of presuppositions that are open to challenge. Almost all of them, moreover, belong to historical, and not to literary criticism, a fact that has been observed by excellent judges, free from any preoccupations of a doctrinal, philosophical, or dogmatic nature.

3. The proposed classification of literary forms is, from many sides and for many reasons, arbitrary and artificial. Lists are drawn up which correspond perhaps to theoretical views and ideal canons, but which do not correspond to reality. The representatives of the method in question, it seems, having become fascinated by details, have not been able to see and grasp *in concreto* the indications which reveal the spirit and personal activity of the redactors. The Evangelists, actually, were not compilers, but redactors in the proper sense of the term. Each of them has organized and arranged in his own way the materials furnished by oral tradition or coming from written sources. Their three narratives are personal works, each having its own unity and its special characteristics, and they are not to be identified with mosaics made of recollections and pieces assembled at random. On the literary side, it is impossible to distinguish in them — except in rare instances — forms corresponding to those which M. Dibelius and R. Bultmann have defined so precisely. To label with different names the " little units " through which the Gospels are formed, and to specify in the case of each of these units its origin, age, type, purpose, *Sitz im Leben*, etc., is and will remain a mark of a most rash and

presumptuous procedure in exegesis. The arbitrary plays inevitably too great a role in an exercise that is so delicate and hazardous. In short, if the method is ingenious in construction, its solidity is, at the very least, doubtful.

Nevertheless, Form Criticism, as applied to the study of the Gospel tradition in its foundation, its evolution, and its fixation in writing, has opened up new horizons and has brought to light certain literary facts which exegetes must take into account. While it is established that the theory is disappointing when applied to works which exhibit only remote analogies with the productions of profane literature, it can, however, furnish orientation to specialists in their search for the historical nucleus which is at the base or at the point of departure of the Christian movement and the religion of Jesus. As the Arab proverb puts it, the texts do not have a father to defend them. It is easy to subject them to treatments which they cannot resist; accordingly, it is necessary to study them with the help and support of history written in the facts, in institutions, and in the hearts of men. This is the situation, it seems, as regards the Gospel narratives.

C. — The Gospel according to John, in spite of the marked, and even disconcerting, differences which distinguish it and separate it from the others, is also a form of the Good News of salvation, and hence a gospel in the primary meaning of the word. Must we or can we bring it under the literary genre represented by the Synoptics? To the question so put the most ancient interpreters would have given a negative reply. In fact, in a work which has been preserved to us, the *Hypotyposeis*, Clement of Alexandria, referring to a tradition received from the Ancients, makes this observation : " John, the last, seeing that the material facts (τὰ σωματικά) had been stated clearly in the [other] Gospels, urged on by his friends and inspired by the Spirit, composed a spiritual (πνευματικόν) Gospel " (quoted by Eusebius, *H. E.*, VI, 14 : 7). No other qualifying term could indicate more precisely the character of the Fourth Gospel. The intention of its author continually manifests itself as doctrinal; the views and principles which summarize and govern the theology of the Incarnation are already presented in the prologue; Christ gives here a definition of His Person and His mission, the full understanding of which presupposes faith; the ideas of Life, Light, and Truth, are given a primary place; the work of Jesus is regarded as a manifestation of the eternal light and leads to a communication of the divine life; the material facts, and they are few in number, almost always have a symbolic significance; the institution of the sacraments (Baptism and the Eucharist) is placed in a new light; mystical feeling asserts itself and experiences a full development; finally, the witness is concerned above all with supernatural realities. The antithesis of the " material " or " corporeal " Gospels and the " spiritual " Gospel, emphasized by Clement of Alexandria on the authority of the old presbyters, explains why John was surnamed " the Theologian " by ancient tradition [1].

The author has clearly stated his intention at the end of his own exposition. " These signs have been written that you may believe that Jesus is the Christ, the Son of God, and that believing, you may have life in His Name " (20 : 31). He intended, therefore, to clarify and to perfect the faith of Christians. Since the book is not one of popular propaganda in the manner of the Synoptics, it is necessary to think of fully trained Christians, who were in possession of the common catechesis and had been initiated in the sacramental mysticism (cf. the expressions " to be born of water and the Spirit ", " water springing up unto life everlasting ", " to eat the flesh and drink the blood of the Son af man " (3 : 5; 4 : 14; 6 : 53-56). We may say of this Gospel that it was written ἐκ πίστεως εἰς πίστιν. To carry out his purpose, the author has chosen only a small number of particularly significant facts, which were not taken from traditional sources but were furnished by his personal recollections, and he has revealed the profound signification of these " signs " [2]. If the facts related in the Fourth Gospel are few in number, the discourses on the contrary hold a major place, and very often they serve to complete the " sign " in the

Translator's note. — [1 Cf. H. BECKER, *Die Reden des Johannes-Evangeliums und der gnostischen Offenbärungsrede*, with a Foreword by R. Bultmann (Forschungen zur Rel. u. Lit. des A. T. u. N. T., N. F. 50, Göttingen, 1956). B. VAWTER, C. M., " The Johannine Sacramentary ", *Theological Studies* (1956). O. CULLMANN, *Early Christian Worship* (London, 1953); *id.*, *Les sacrements dans l'Evangile Johannique. La vie de Jésus et le culte de l'Eglise primitive* (Strasbourg and Paris, 1951)].

[2] The σημεῖον, miracle or not, material fact or discourse, is a sign or symbol which is always connected with the person or work of Christ, and it is also a proof or argument.

manner of an explanation or of a doctrinal commentary. Thus there exists a close relation, and in a certain way an organic one, between the cure of the paralytic at the pool of Bethsaida and the exposition on the relationship of the Son with the Father (5 : 1-47), and between the multiplication of the loaves and the discourse on the bread of life (6 : 1-59). In similar fashion, the cure of the man born blind (9 : 1-7) and the resurrection of Lazarus (11 : 38-44) clarify, by throwing light upon them, the statements of Jesus in presenting Himself as " the light of the world " (8 : 12) and as " the resurrection and the life " (11 : 25). In the narrative parts as in the discourses, the same dogmatic purpose makes itself evident, i. e., to set forth the mystery of the Word Incarnate and to reveal in Jesus the Son of God the Life and Light of men. The Johannine narrative presents a new picture of Christ. He is no longer viewed from the angle of the Synoptics. Throughout the book Jesus explains Himself on the basis of His origin and His nature, and of His mission and role. In Part I (1 : 19–12 : 50), He manifests Himself to the world as the Son of God; in Part II (13 : 1-17 : 26), He completes for His disciples His revelations on His person and on the connections which unite Him with His Father. The doctrinal and didactic purpose of the author gives his work its special character. His exposition is basically history, but for Saint John the meaning of the facts reported goes far beyond their interest and value as concrete historical data. The work as a whole constitues less a demonstration than an instruction, in which the material facts become an integral part of the theological doctrine and are habitually interpreted as the symbols of a spiritual or mystical truth.

If we bring the Fourth Gospel into close relation with the three others in order to make a comparison between them, notable differences are evident at first glance, not only as regards content but also as regards form. Doubtless, there are contacts in certain places, and a minute comparison leads even to the further conclusion that in some passages there is a literary dependence of Saint John upon the texts of Saint Mark and Saint Luke [1]. But the elements are not the same on both sides, whether the narrative parts or the discourses are concerned.

---

[1] For the details, see B. H. STREETER, *The Four Gospels* (London, 1924), pp. 392 ff.

The main outline of the public ministry of Jesus in the Johannine Gospel differs from that of the Synoptics in chronology [1] as well as in the scene of the apostolate [2]. The Savior's manner of instruction, moreover, is not the same in the Fourth Gospel as it is in the first three. In these, e.g., we do not find language with a double sense, which causes misunderstanding in the hearer (Jn. 2 : 20; 3 : 4; 4 : 33; 6 : 34; 8 : 32, 33; 11 : 12, 24; 14 : 5, 8), nor the combination of the highest spirituality with the most pronounced realism (3 : 3-8; 4 : 8-15; 6 : 47-59; 20 : 19-23), nor the systematic use of certain words such as life, light, darkness, truth, flesh, spirit, judgment, etc., which taken together constitute a special vocabulary.

The Gospel of Saint John, the literay unity of which cannot be seriously disputed, was conceived and composed independently of the primitive catechesis by an author, and not by a compiler. In his redaction the author followed a plan, with divisions and connections carefully marked. While each episode constitutes a complete or independent sketch, the catenation of events is patent and the action exhibits a regular progression in the development of the narrative. A drama is prepared, progresses, and reaches its final climax. Literary unity is even accentuated by the constant utilization of two devices indicated *supra* : recourse to the use of language in a double sense, which provokes misunderstandings, and the employment of abstract but suggestive terms which produce vividness. The Fourth Gospel is a work of marked and powerful originality; it continues and crowns the other three Gospels as the capital completes the column and emphasizes its equilibrium.

The preceding remarks lead to this double conclusion that Saint John, adopting a highly personal approach, has written

---

[1] The chronological indications are not any more numerous in the Fourth Gospel than in the Synoptics. Some points of reference are furnished by chance through the mention of certain Jewish feasts, especially three successive Passovers (2 : 13, 23; 6 : 4; 11 : 55; 12 : 1; 13 : 1; 18 : 28), a circumstance which requires a minimum of two years and some months fot the duration of the public ministry. An important special feature is the deliberate correction of the date which the Synoptic tradition could appear to assign to the death of Jesus. According to Saint John, the Savior died on 14 Nisan, the eve of the Passover, and not on 15 Nisan, the first day of the paschal week (13 : 1, 29; 18 : 28; 19 : 14, 31).

[2] In the Synoptics the ministry in Galilee is in the foreground through its importance and duration. In the Fourth Gospel, Jesus exercises his apostolate especially at Jerusalem.

of Jesus as if making marginal annotations on the Synoptics, and that his Gospel is not a biography of Christ. Does that mean that this work, for which we know of no parallels either in Biblical or in ancient classical literature, should be regarded as a collection of meditations on the mystery of Christ, or as a sequence of fictitious symbols designed to serve as the vehicle of a spiritual instruction, or a series of theological themes built on given articles of faith, or even as an " essay " inspired by personal religious experiences over a long period? To accept one or other of these definitions would be to mistake completely one of the chief characteristics of the book and to misunderstand the author's intention. The Evangelist really represents himself as a witness of what he relates, of the discourses as well as the facts, and he intends that the reader should accept his testimony as authoritative. In his presentation he has made use of a language and a style that are peculiar to him, he has made certain groupings or arrangements, he has emphasized this or that point of doctrine, he has noted and explained the deep meaning of certain facts or of certain words, he has introduced expressions or formulas consecrated by liturgical or religious life, and he has added his own interpretation and sometimes his commentary (examples in 1 : 1-18; 3 : 16-21, 31-36; 12 : 44-50); but all this does not detract in any way from his qualifications as a faithful witness. The exegete and the historian ought, however, to take into account this personal contribution of the Evangelist when they wish to sketch an outline of the ministry of Jesus and to reconstruct his teaching in its original form.

The Gospel material had a certain plasticity, as is evident from a comparison of parallel or merely related texts. Just as Saint Matthew has grouped around five principal themes the instructions given by the Savior before different auditors and at different moments, Saint John has been able to include in the discourse after the Last Supper words of instruction and counsel which had been given previously on other occasions. The same remark holds for most of the great discourses addressed to the Jews of Jerusalem (see especially chs. 5, 7, and 8).

Furthermore, no one has ever claimed that these discourses were reproduced word for word. The essential thing in the mind of the Evangelist was to present faithfully the thought of

Jesus, and to do this, it was not enough to be content with the likely or probable, but it was necessary rather to stick to what had actually been taught. The Greek and Roman historians never had any scruples about using fiction in speeches; but this literay artifice deceived no one, since no one was concerned about it. The same was not true in the case of Saint John, who appeared as a witness, and one whose testimony — given orally hundreds of times before being committed to writing — had been presented by him as a faithful echo of the words of the Master.

As regards the question of literary genre, the Fourth Gospel cannot be assimilated purely and simply into the category of the first three. That is more than clear from what has just been said above. In certain aspects it falls under the historical genre, and in others it has close affiliations with theological and mystical writings. It is a unique example of a mixed or composite genre and it ought to be treated as such. Our examination of the book leads us to share on this point the feeling of numerous interpreters of the " spiritual " Gospel and invites us to practice their method, both in respect to the understanding of the text and the use of the work for the history of Jesus and for that of the Christology of the apostolic age.

2. — The Acts of the Apostles.

Indisputably the Acts of the Apostles forms a sequel to the Third Gospel. Together they constitute one work in two parts, as the two dedications addressed to the same person prove, and as Saint Luke himself indicates in speaking of his Gospel narrative as a " first book " (Luke 1 : 1-4; Acts 1 : 1-3). He is concerned in both with the origins of Christianity. After having written a " gospel " to confirm " the certainty of the instructions received " by Theophilus, i.e., of the apostolic catechesis, the author relates in Acts the spread of the Christian faith through the ministry of the Apostles after the death of Jesus. The two books treat of the same subject, and there is every reason to believe that Saint Luke from the beginning had the idea and the intention of completing his Gospel with a sequel, namely, Acts.

The " second book " of Saint Luke is a literary work, composed with art and method, carefully written and well balanced in its various parts.   The artistic manner of the author is evident in the narrative parts as well as in the discourses.   The presentation of events and the language of the speakers give the impression of real life (see especially **10** : 1-48; **13** : 52; **17** : 15-34; **19** : 23-40; **21** : 27–**22** : 29), and this for every writer and for an historian in particular is a mark of success.   The style, which is simple and transparent, supple and varied, and the steady progression in the relation of facts indicate an excellent education and a genuine talent for exposition.

This literary work belongs to the historical genre and can be compared with various works of Classical Antiquity.   We actually find employed in it certain usages of Greek historiography.   It is well known that the ancient historians, following the example of Thucydides, took pleasure in inserting speeches in the course of their narrative.   This was for them a means of delineating the character of a person, of describing the aspect of a situation, of emphasizing some teaching, or of rendering some historical truth more intelligible.   Actually, it mattered little to them whether the speeches had been delivered or not, so long as they remained within the bounds of probability.   Invention in these circumstances was not considered to be an artifice unworthy of history.   Polybius was the only one among the Greeks to condemn the use of such a procedure, one which Saint Luke would have surely judged incompatible with his purpose and his task.

In the Book of Acts we count eighteen discourses or speeches, which taken together make up a fourth of the work.   Like Thucydides in his *History of the Peloponnesian War*, Saint Luke has placed one at each stage of his narrative : the discourses of Saint Peter after the Ascension (**1** : 15 ff.), after Pentecost (**2** : 14 ff.), after the cure of the lame man in the Temple (**3** : 12 ff.), before the Sanhedrin (**4** : 8 ff.); the discourse of Gamaliel before the same assembly (**5** : 34 ff.); the discourse of Stephen following the conflict between the disciples of Jesus and the Jews of strict observance (**7** : 2 ff.); the discourses of Paul before the Jews of the Diaspora (**14** : 16 ff.); the discourse of Peter and of James at the conference at Jerusalem (**17** : 7 ff., 13 ff.); the discourse of Paul at Lystra before an uneducated pagan crowd (**14** : 13 ff.); the discourse of Paul at Athens before a cultivated audience (**17** : 22 ff.), and the speech of the town clerk of Ephesus (**19** : 35 ff.); the discourse of Paul before the presbyters of the Church of Ephesus (**20** : 18 ff.), and before the Jews of Jerusalem after his arrest (**22** : 1 ff.); the speeches of the lawyer Tertullus and of Paul before the procurator Felix (**24** : 2 ff., 10 ff.); the discourse of Paul at his interview with the Jews of Rome (**28** : 17 ff.).

There is another point in which a resemblance exists between the Book of Acts and the works of profane historians, namely, in the incorporation of an official report, a relation, a travel diary, into an historical work, with combination of the first and third persons in the narrative parts. E. Norden has studied at length this literary peculiarity in the ancient writers, a peculiarity which is all the more singular, since one of the rules of ancient historiography demanded objectivity in exposition, i.e., the impersonal from of presentation [1]. In the second part of the Book of Acts, which contains the account of the missions of Saint Paul, the narrative appears sometimes under an impersonal form, and sometimes under a personal form in the first person plural. The " we " is employed in the following passages : **16** : 10-17; **20** : 5-15; **21** : 1-18; **27** : 1-**28** : 16, or in about one-tenth of the work, and without any injury to the connection of these passages with the immediate context.

Must it be concluded from these two sets of facts that Saint Luke was acquainted with profane literature? It is quite possible, for among the writers of the New Testament the author of Acts shows definitely that he has had a rather thorough Greek education. Yet the answer should not necessarily be affirmative. As a matter of fact, Saint Luke could have drawn his inspiration for the use of speeches and for his mixing of the impersonal and personal styles from examples furnished by certain books of the Greek Bible, especially those of Esdras, Nehemias, Tobias, Judith, and Machabees.

Now that these analogies have been noted and precisely defined, we must show why the Book of Acts ought to be placed in the class of historical books.

---

[1] See the examples in E. NORDEN, *Agnostos Theos. Untersuchungen zur Formengeschichte religioser Rede* (Leipzig and Berlin, 1913), pp. 318 ff.

Manifestly, the purpose of the author was to give religious instruction based on history and through the medium of an historical narrative. It matters little that he wished at the same time to serve the interests of the faith, to be an apologist for the Christian religion before the pagan world and more especially before the Roman power, to show the continuity which made Christianity the consummation, as it were, of Judaism, and to attest the unity of views and principles which made the apostolate of Saint Paul a prolongation of the ministry of the Twelve. The fact remains, nevertheless, that he intended to write a history of the early years of the Church. The title shows clearly the nature of the work. If it is not Saint Luke's own, it comes from the first readers of the book, who chose it with a sure instinct. The word πράξεις, in the strict sense of history, was employed among the Greeks to designate writings recounting the exploits, prodigies, great deeds *(Acta, Facta, Res Gestæ)* performed by such heroes as Hercules or by famous men like Alexander. The author, in fact, has related the achievements of several of the Apostles, and in particular those of Saint Peter and Saint Paul. His work is a peculiar historical genre, clearly distinct from chronicles and annals, in which events are presented in their chronological sequence; distinct also from memoirs, in which personal recollections are especially utilized, and from biographies, in which the abundance and precision of details combine to give a faithful picture of a man's life.

Since Saint Luke intended to write a history, it was necessary for him to become thoroughly informed on the events of which he had not been an eyewitness. He had done this before writing his first book (Luke 1 : 1-4), and a literary analysis of the second proves that he had recourse to various sources in preparing for its composition. During the past sixty years, numerous historians and exegetes have applied themselves to the problem of determining the sources used by Saint Luke. The researches of Ramsay, Harnack, Stanton, Cadbury, Zahn, Loisy, Wikenhauser, Jacquier, and J. Jeremias [1] — and the list

---

[1] For bibliography, see E. JACQUIER, *Le livre des Actes* (Paris, 1926). L. PIROT, art. " Actes des apôtres ", *DBV, Suppl.* I (1926), 85-86. A. WIKEN-HAUSER, *Einleitung in das N. T.* (1956), 227.

is not exhaustive — bear witness in various ways to the efforts
accomplished in this respect. It can hardly be said that the
written documents exploited by the author for the composition
of the first part of Acts (1-12 : the history of the Christian
community of Jerusalem) have been precisely delimited, and
still less reconstituted. For the writing of the second part
(13-28 : the history of the missions of Saint Paul), Saint Luke,
besides his personal recollections and his diary, used the oral
information which he could easily obtain from Saint Paul
himself and from the Apostle's companions. In the second
part chronological and geographical data are more frequent and
precise than in the first. In many instances, the eyewitness
reveals himself through the concrete details given and observations of a quite personal character.

Saint Luke's method of composition can be established
through a comparison of parallel texts in the Second and Third
Gospels. While he exercises a certain amount of freedom in
handling the text of his source, Saint Mark, he reproduces it
faithfully as to substance. We are right in thinking that he
applied the same method in the Book of Acts in dealing with the
events and the speeches with which he had become acquainted
through the testimony of others. There is every reason to
believe that he informed himself as carefully as he could and
that he reproduced conscientiously whatever was furnished him
by tradition, whether written or oral. This is not a prejudiced
judgment in his favor, but is is a judgment based on fact;
furthermore, it is reinforced by a proof, the importance of which
could hardly be exaggerated : numerous epigraphical discoveries
confirm the perfect exactness of Saint Luke on all points on
which control has been possible. Furthermore, the Letters of
Saint Paul — and they certainly were not used as a source by the
author of Acts — enable us to verify in respect to various
points what is related about the missionary activity of the
Apostle. Comparisons and cross-checks prove that Saint Luke
composed his work as a conscientious and well-informed historian. Without doubt, he left in obscurity or passed over in
silence certain facts, but such preteritions or omissions ought
not to disqualify him in the eyes of impartial judges, for his
purpose was to collaborate through his book in the common
task of evangelical propaganda, not to highlight the disagree-

ments that might have arisen at times among the leaders of the Christian mission.

As regards the discourses or speeches, we would not be giving proper consideration to what we know with certainty respecting the author's method of composition, if we should look upon them purely as free and artificial compositions. Doubtless, there was in this matter the tradition of ancient historiography; doubtless also, no one among the Christians of the first or the second generation accorded the same authority to the words of the Apostles as to the sayings of Jesus; but we may believe that Saint Luke, so far as speeches are concerned, shared the opinion of Polybius rather than that of the other Greek historians. This supposition, moreover, is not gratuitous, for it follows from the habitual manner of the writer in his Gospel history and from his own declaration in the prologue of the same book. If Luke the historian has shown himself to be scrupulous regarding the truth of the facts related by him, why would he not have had the same concern for fidelity in the case of his speeches, considering the result which he was expecting from his testimony?

We may believe, then, that in these speeches composed by him, the author of the Book of Acts has preserved, under the form of outlines or succinct résumés, the leading ideas or the substance of what had actually been said by the personages of his narrative.

It would be an exaggeration, if we should put this work of modest proportions beside the great histories of Thucydides and Tacitus. There is no common measure of comparison between them. It is the merit of Saint Luke that he took care to become informed, and was able to report " honestly " as a historian what he had learned or what he had seen with his own eyes of the accomplishments of the *epigoni* in implanting the religion of Jesus in the Greco-Roman world.

2. — *EPISTOLARY LITERATURE.*

Introduction.

The canonical collection of the New Testament contains twenty-one epistles which are subdivided into two groups: the fourteen Pauline Epistles and the seven so-called Catholic

Epistles attributed to various Apostles. All these writings present themselves under the epistolary form, and, at first sight, it would seem that they ought to be placed under one and the same literary label, as falling within the same genre. But actually, some of them are quite different in character from pieces of correspondence. Beside genuine letters, in which the personal or occasional aspect is clearly marked, there are compositions of a pastoral or theological nature, in which only the external form belongs to the epistolary genre. Hence, the epistles taken as a whole do not constitute a homogeneous group and do not fall as such under a common category of literature [1].

Customarily, we distinguish between letter and epistle, the former word being applied to a written communication of a private character, and the latter designating a composition destined for the public or for a particular public, and we keep this distinction whatever may be the subject treated, the development, the style, or the occasion. Under these conditions the letter is a kind of conversation from a distance, of a free turn in its style, familiar in manner, and not connected with a literary genre with its fixed rules, while the epistle habitually assumes a more careful form, namely, that of a treatise or essay, and it constitutes a literary work in the strict sense, being composed in accordance with a rather clear and definite canon. The letter, which a visit would render useless, takes the place of living speech, it conveys to the one for whom it is destined something of the intimate life of the author, and, ordinarily, it is not fully intelligible except to one who knows the situation of writer and recipient. The epistle, on the contrary, is not intended to be a substitute for a personal interview, for it is addressed to a public which is not limited as to time or space, it is employed to treat a question in itself and not in terms of individual situations or particular circumstances, and to be understood it does not require knowledge of a whole ensemble of concrete details. There have come down to us from pagan Antiquity a great number of letters and epistles : e.g., the Letters of Epicurus and of Cicero, and the

Translator's note. — [1 N. A. DAHL, " Bref ", *Sv. bibl. Uppslagsverk* 1, 209-301. A. SALLES, " La diatribe paulinienne ", *RB* (1957), 516-537].

Epistles of Aristotle and of Seneca. From the Hellenistic period we have, thanks to the papyri unearthed from the sands of Egypt, a rich collection of little notes and private letters in all styles and of extremely varied content. The Jewish literature of Alexandrian origin includes a work which had the widest diffusion in the synagogues of the Diaspora and in the ancient Christian communities, namely, the Epistle of Aristeas, which relates a legend on the translation of the Pentateuch by the Seventy.

Making this distinction between the letter and the epistle his starting point, Deissmann [1], in a series of penetrating and well documented studies, has determined the character of the different writings represented by the epistolary literature of the New Testament. According to him, the Pauline writings — with the exception of the Epistle to the Hebrews — and 1 and 2 John are true letters, for each of these documents corresponds to a particular circumstance, meets a need of the moment, furnishes instruction on a strictly determined point, refers directly to some incident or to some fact of current life which has occasioned its writing, takes the place of a personal visit, and shows the traits characteristic of an oral conversation. It matters little that most of these writings are addressed to churches or even to groups of churches, for the recipients are none the less individuals who, in one way or another, were in relation with the Apostle and to whom he is sending instructions, counsels, and information, whether in answer to questions which have been asked, or as a result of news brought to him by travelers or messengers, or simply through apostolic solicitude. It matters little also that these writings of circumstance, often composed in haste and to meet some necessity of the moment, were later grouped in a collection, employed for public reading in religious gatherings, and finally treated as " Scripture ". Their original character ought not be lost sight of on that account. Before circulating from church to church like encyclicals, and before being used for catechesis as standard texts in matters of faith and morals, these documents were not treatises under the form of letters, but simply letters. For

[1] See especially his *Licht vom Osten*, (4th ed., Tübingen, 1923), pp. 116-213, and *Paulus* (2nd ed., Tübingen, 1925), pp. 5-20. [There is an Engl. trans. of the first work under the title, *Light from the Ancient East*, (New York, 1927)].

exegetes to treat them otherwise would be to misunderstand their true nature and to incur the risk of giving them a false interpretation. As to the other writings in epistolary form (the Epistle to the Hebrews, 1 John, 1 and 2 Peter, and the Epistles of James and of Jude), these, according to Deissmann, are not letters, but epistles in the sense defined above. They are not, however, uniform in type from the literary standpoint.

Without pronouncing for the moment on this reclassification, let us note only that, if the views of Deissmann are right as to the distinction established between the epistle and the letter, the line of demarcation between the two genres remains, in many cases, quite indefinite. For if a public letter or a pretended letter is in reality an epistle, and if the same is true of a philosophical dissertation or a dogmatic treatise dressed up as a letter, it can happen that a letter destined for only one reader or for a definite group of readers may, at the same time, be addressed to a merely possible group of people. In this case it is difficult to distinguish the letter from the epistle, for it loses inevitably its intimate and personal character to the extent to which the image of the unknown recipients occupies the writer's mind. There exists, then, an intermediate zone, as it were, in which the two genres are so close that in the end they compenetrate and merge with each other.

This observation holds true especially for the correspondance of Saint Paul, for the letter was surely for him the means of extending, of completing, and of diffusing his instruction without limit of any sort either in time or in space. He uses it like a conversation at a distance, but also as a way of preaching. On this point, the quasi-liturgical structure and character which result from the use of the formulas of thanksgiving or of the blessings which figure at the beginning and at the end of his letters leave room for no doubt. Moreover, in these occasional writings, in which the dictated phrase often assumes an oratorical turn, the missionary has inserted, beside his improvised sections, passages, which by their harmonious balance, rhythm of form, the methodical progression of reasoning or argumentation, and doctrinal richness, bear witness to studied care in their elaboration (thus, 1 Th. 4 : 13–5 : 11, on the glorious coming of the Lord; 1 Cor. 1 : 17-31, on the wisdom of the world and the wisdom of God; 12 and 14, on charisms; 13, on charity; 15, on the Resurrection of Christ and of the dead; Rom. **5-8**, on justification and its effects). Hence, as regards the Pauline writings, the definition and the principle of classification formulated by Deissmann are not to be applied in a mechanical way or too absolutely. To do otherwise would be to sin by excess, and the excess would quickly become damaging to the interpretation of these documents.

1. — The Corpus Paulinum.

Of the fourteen letters in the collection, there are thirteen which in structural plan and development resemble one another closely. The Epistle to the Hebrews represents a particular type. These writings begin with an address or superscription, which is ordinarily followed by a kind of doxology. The body of the letters is made up of sections which succeed one another sometimes methodically, as in the Epistles to the Galatians and the Romans, and sometimes without apparent connection, as in the Epistles to the Corinthians. Occasionally also, the part dealing with moral life, is sharply separated from that which is strictly dogmatic (Gal. **5-6**; Rom. **12-15**; Eph. **4-6**; Col. **3-4**). In his conclusions the author adds advice, news of a more personal character, and salutations, and he ends with good wishes. To obtain a concrete idea of the structure of the Pauline Epistles, it is sufficient to examine cursorily the Epistle to the Galatians or that to the Philippians.

The Epistle to the Romans possesses at the same time the characteristics of the letter and the epistle, and for two chief reasons : on the one hand, Paul did not have any direct or personal connection with the Christian community of Rome, and on the other, he desired to prepare for the visit which he was planning to make to that Church. He wished to treat of the relations between Christianity and the Mosaic Law, but he could do so only under the form of a systematic exposition giving a dogmatic instruction of universal import, as in an epistle. Yet in addressing himself to a body of the faithful whom he knew only by hearsay, and whose sympathy he was trying to win, it was necessary that he should also express to them some particular sentiments as in a letter. Consequently, here and there the form is that of a letter, but the more habitual manner is that of an epistle. Thus, the composition can justly be qualified as literary, although at the time the author did not have the intention of producing a literary work.

This epistle, in which many passages certainly represent fragments of the oral catechesis of the Apostle, permits us to know directly some of the devices utilized by him in argumentation : the illustrative proof from Scripture presented as an irrefutable witness (3 : 10-18; 9 : 25-29; 10 : 15-21; 11 : 8-10; 15 : 9-12) ; reasoning by induction *de minori ad maius* (5 : 15, 17; 11 : 12, 15) or by deduction *de maiori ad minus* (5 : 9; 8 : 32; 11 : 24); analogy between two beings or two works (5 : 12-21; the parallel between Adam and Christ; cf. 1 Cor., 15 : 22 ff., 45 ff.); finally, and especially, the diatribe. The diatribe (διατριβή) was a very vivid kind of exposition in which the dialogue is transformed into a monologue, but with this special feature, that a fictitious interlocutor interposes questions, remarks, or objections generally introduced by φησίν *(inquit)* or some analogous formula. The *Diatribes* of Epictetus are the classical type of the genre. In the first century of our era, the Cynic and Stoic preachers who went about the Greek world made use of the diatribe as a means particularly suited to awaken conviction in the minds of their hearers. Saint Paul could not be ignorant of this form of presentation in current use among popular orators, and he himself employs it liberally in the Epistle to the Romans, where the fictitious interlocutor is introduced frequently either to challenge or to be challenged (2 : 1 ff.; 3 : 1 ff.; 4 : 1; 6 : 1, 15; 7 : 7; 9 : 19; 11 : 19; 14 : 4; 15 : 20. 22). In addition to the formula characteristic of the diatribe, ἐρεῖς οὖν (9 : 19; 11 : 19), the Apostle uses the expression μὴ γένοιτο (3 : 4, 6, 31; 6 : 2, 15; 7 : 7; 9 : 14; 11 : 1, 11) in the same way as Epictetus. In all this Saint Paul did not imitate intentionally a procedure employed by profane writers and speakers; he simply turned as if by instinct to a type of demonstration with which he was familiar through his ordinary contacts and experience [1].

---

[1] On the diatribe, see especially R. BULTMANN, *Der Stil der Paulinischen Predigt und die kynisch-stoische Diatribe* (Göttingen, 1910). [See also W. CAPELLE and H. I. MARROU, " Diatribe ", in Klauser, *Reallex. f. Ant. u. Christ.,* III (1951), 990-1009.]

The two Epistles to the Corinthians are, properly, speaking, occasional writings. In the first, in which the most varied subjects are treated, so that it is impossible ot discern the motives which determined the arrangement in the treatment of material, the author makes allusion to the reports which have reached him from various sources upon the internal condition of the Church of Corinth (**1** : 11; **5** : 1; **11** : 18) and refers to a letter which his correspondents have sent him (**7** : 1). This epistle gives us an idea of the variety of means at the disposal of Saint Paul for expressing his thought and transmitting his sentiments. It shows us also how, without ever becoming a slave to school practices, the Apostle knew how to use rhythmical style. In this respect, two passages (**4** : 7-13, and **13** : 1-13), of markedly different tone, are particularly instructive, for they are composed of short phrases of appreciably equal length, sometimes parallel and sometimes antithetic, and exhibiting repetition of words and deliberate striving for assonance. Greek rhetoric taught all these devices for embellishing style, and Saint Paul had been able to observe the advantage which the popular orators derived from them; but his own manner of style always remains so free and so natural that a conscious and deliberate imitation is not to be thought of.

As regards the Second Epistle to the Corinthians, a problem of literary criticism arises which is not concerned with the nature of the work, for it is a genuine letter and perhaps the most typically " Pauline ", but rather with its unity of composition. Between the first part (**1-9**) and the second (**10-13**), the contrasts with respect to tone, sentiments, and manner are manifest : on the one hand, a letter of reconciliation and of consolation, in which the dominant note is confidence; on the other, a severe letter, full of reproaches and threats, in which the bitterness beneath an ironical phrasing is discernible. Further, in the first part, the section **6** : 14–**7** : 1 (an exhortation to shun the pagans) appears to be an insertion without connection with the context, while **9** appears to be a restatement of the subject treated in Chapter **8** (the collection for the Church of Jerusalem). Various hypotheses [1] have been advanced to

---

[1] There is a summarized account of these hypotheses in E. B. ALLO, *Seconde épître aux Corinthiens* (Paris, 1937), " Excursus XII and XIV ", pp. L-LVI.

explain the juxtaposition in the same letter of sections which seem so difficult to harmonize. The most satisfactory explanation is to regard the epistle as we read it today as an amalgam of passages from various letters [1], As a matter of fact, however, this explanation itself presents as many difficulties as advantages. In any case, the lack of coherence does not affect at all the literary genre of this document, whether one accepts the hypothesis just mentioned or decides in favor of unity of composition [2].

In the Epistle to the Galatians we have an answer of Saint Paul to the intrigues of the Judaizers who had tried to ruin both his reputation and his work in a Christian community founded by him. This letter, which has been compared to a torrent of burning lava, was written under the stress of highest emotion and indignation. Pathetic entreaties and effusions of the heart are mingled with cries of protestation and scathing remarks on the machinations of those who have abused the good faith of the Galatians. It is necessary to take into consideration the apologetic and polemic intention of the author in the interpretation and use of the pages in which he affirms his independence with respect to the Apostles and gives a rapid sketch of his relations with them (1 : 11–2 : 14). The material facts related are surely exact, but Saint Paul has only mentioned some of them, i.e., those which furnished an argument in an apology for his ministry. We really have before us a letter written in the heat of the combat, and not a methodical exposition conceived and composed in complete serenity of mind and soul. Another observation is called for from the literary point of view, namely, the close kinship which exists in places between the Epistle to the Galatians and the Epistle to the Romans : thus, in the statement of the principle of justification (Gal. 2 : 16; Rom. 3 : 28), in the use of the same Scripture texts (Gal. 3 : 6, 11, 12; Rom. 4 : 3-9; 1 : 17; 10 : 5), and in the argument drawn from the story of Abraham (Gal. 3 : 6-18; 4 : 21-24; Rom. 4 : 1-25; 9 : 7-9). The Apostle did not have at hand the text of the first of the two letters when he

---

[1] Saint Paul alludes to one or several letters which he addressed to the Corinthians, and which have not been preserved (2 Cor., 2 : 3, 9; 7 : 8-12).

Translator's note. — [2 Cf. P. CLEARY, " The Epistles to the Corinthians ", *CBQ*, 12 (1950), 10-33, for a reconstruction of four Epistles to the Corinthians].

wrote the second, but his thought remained fixed on the same ideas, and so much so that the Epistle to the Romans presents itself in a certain fashion as a commentary on the Epistle to the Galatians in respect to the doctrine of justification by faith.

The Epistles to the Ephesians, the Philippians, and the Colossians, to which may be added the short Letter to Philemon, form a group apart in the *Corpus Paulinum* and are often called " the Epistles of the Captivity ", because Saint Paul makes allusion in them to the chains which he bears or he speaks of his liberation, which he envisions as near [1].

The Epistle to the Philippians, who were so tenderly loved by the Apostle, is a testimony of affection and remembrance and, at the same time, a free outpouring of the heart, a true letter under the form of unaffected conversation, in which there is no indication of the order or connection in the sequence of subjects treated.

Saint Paul had not personally founded the Church of Colossae and he had not visited it (Col. 2 : 1), but he had been able to become acquainted with some members of that Church during his prolonged sojourn at Ephesus (Acts 20 : 31), and he had gained some precise information upon the state of that young Christian community from a person named Epaphras (Col. 4 : 12; Phil. 23). He wrote to the Colossians to put them on their guard against some innovators whose teaching was menacing Christian faith and morals. The fact that the Apostle did not have direct and personal contact with the Christians of Colossae explains why the letter assumes a slightly formal tone and contains few details of an intimate character, but, in spite of this, it is really a letter. The bearer, Tychicus from Asia, was to make the journey with a certain Onesimus, a slave originally from Colossae, who had run away. Saint Paul had converted Onesimus and was sending him back to his master Philemon. Onesimus was carrying a letter of recommendation from his father in the faith. It is interesting to compare this Letter to Philemon with two letters sent by Pliny the younger to his friend Sabinianus, the one to obtain pardon in favor of a

---

Translator's note. — [1 Cf. A. C. COTTER, S. J., " The Epistles of the Captivity ", *CBQ*, II (1949), 370-380].

fugitive freedman and the other to thank him for the favor granted [1].

The Epistle to the Ephesians reproduces about a half of the Epistle to the Colossians either word for word or with simple recasting in detail. The impersonal character is particularly pronounced, as if the author had written for an indefinite public, and the reader is thus given the impression that he has a treatise or a kind of encyclical before him, an epistle, let us say, rather than a true letter. It seems unlikely that Saint Paul, in writing to the Church of Ephesus which he had founded, would have used this impersonal genre [2]. On the other hand, the matter is easily explained if the epistle was addressed to the Church of Laodicea, as was thought, according to Marcion, about the middle of the second century.

The two Epistles to the Thessalonians are filled with expressions of affection and with instructions on particular points. They would not have been written if the author had been able to visit the faithful of Thessalonica (cf. 1 Thess. 2 : 17-18; 3 : 6) and this remark of itself alone characterizes the genre of these writings. The news brought to the Apostle by Timothy was the occasion of the first letter. The purpose of the second was to put an end to the agitation and trouble which the feverish expectation of the Second Coming had engendered and fostered in the community.

The three epistles, commonly called the " Pastoral Epistles " (1 and 2 Timothy and the Epistle to Titus), form a unit. They deal with the same subject — the establishment of bishops and ecclesiastical discipline; they combat the same errors — Gnostic teachings of Jewish origin; and they reflect the same milieu, namely, Asia Minor. One of them (2 Timothy) exhibits in places, especially in 4 : 9-22, a very personal note, but this is not their general tone. These three writings are basically instructions presented under epistolary form, and not letters of a private character. The moral recommendations, and the regulations concerning the organization of the hierarchy and

---

[1] PLINY THE YOUNGER, *Letters*, IX, 21 and 24. Text and Melmoth's translation in *Pliny : Letters*, vol. II (London and New York, 1927; Loeb Classical Library). See also J. HUBY, *Saint Paul. Les épîtres de la captivité* (Paris, 1935), pp. 116-117.
[2] The most ancient witnesses for the text do not carry the name of Ephesus in the address or title.

actions to be taken against the machinations of heretics, are addressed to all pastors in charge of the Christian churches at this time. Through Timothy and Titus the author had in view all who " were tending the flock of God " (cf. Acts **20** : 28).

To the collection of Pauline letters is added the Epistle to the Hebrews. It is not sure that the superscription, " To the Hebrews ", is the author's, and, to judge by the content of the document, it does not seem that the addressees were necessarily the Judeo-Christians in Palestine. We do not find at the beginning of this work either an address or a preamble furnishing information on the mutual situation or on the connection between the author and those to whom it is addressed. On the other hand, certain allusions and details may be noted here and there which suppose particular or personal relations between the author and the addressees (see especially **5** : 11–**6** : 12; **10** : 32-34; **13** : 18-25).

The work has the general character of a doctrinal treatise, composed to edify, encourage, and instruct a community which has suffered persecution, which remains exposed to new trials of the same kind, and which is threatened by a propaganda with a Judaizing flavor (**10** : 32-34; **12** : 1-4; **13** : 9). The oratorical character is pronounced and it is maintained unabated to such a degree that the reader at times has the impression that he is listening to a homily. The author himself qualifies his composition as a " discourse of exhortation " (**13** : 22). Whatever may have been his origin, he had the advantage of a careful literary education; he was thoroughly familiar with rhetoric and he knew how to use it skilfully. The richness of the vocabulary, the elegance of form, and the balance in the development of his topics reveal an expert hand in the art of composition and win for the author the honor of being classed together with Saint Luke, i.e., in the very first rank of the writers of the New Testament.

In both content and form this document is, properly speaking, an epistle and not a letter.

What has just been said about the Pauline literature gives some idea of the special way in which one ought to look at these writings when he attempts to interpret them as witnesses of historical facts or as the expression of a body of theological thought. The letters of the Apostle are like so many pieces of his life, and his life was that of a man of action. Before being the theologian of Christ, Saint Paul was His missionary, the messenger of the Good News of salvation, one who preached to convince and convert; he became a writer only by necessity and wrote rarely. His letters are occasional compositions, independent of one another, due to chance causes, and written in haste in connection with particular facts or needs of the moment. To consider them as collections of dogmatic statements or as theological treatises would be to mistake their true nature. We should not seek in them systematic and complete doctrinal expositions, for usually the subjects begun are abandoned before being fully treated.

This observation is particularly valid in respect to eschatology, the relations between the Law and the Gospel, the concept of the Mystical Body of Christ, the role of works from the point of view of justification, the institution of the sacraments, the plan of redemption, predestination, etc. On all these points a work of synthesis has to be carried out, which consists in grouping the elements furnished by different letters upon the same subject for the purpose of establishing order among them and for reconstituting teachings given in a fragmentary manner, i.e., by simple references or brief allusions, into an harmonious and organic whole. This reconstitution is possible, but on condition that we do not lose sight of the special character of the documents used. They are letters in the sense defined *supra* (pp. 543-546), and letters always suppose that more is known of things than they explicitly mention, and their interpretation cannot be made in the abstract.

2. — The " Catholic " Epistles.

The name " Catholic " Epistles is given to seven works in epistolary form attributed to James, Peter, John, and Jude, The qualification of " catholic ", employed originally by Origen, seems to have designated epistles addressed to all Christendom, like papal encyclicals. We shall see that the epithet is badly suited to two of these documents.

The Epistle of James is a moral instruction of very general character, good for Christians of all times and places. According to the superscription, it is addressed to " the twelve tribes of

the Dispersion ", a symbolic expression designating the faithful
living outside of Palestine.   We do not find in it any personal
note or any circumstantial detail of a nature to enlighten us
as to the author or the addressees.   This epistle presents itself
as a collection of moral statements, continuing and extending
in the light of Christ's doctrine the teaching of the ancient
Sages of Israel.   When compared closely with the wisdom
books of the Old Testament (Pr., Ecclus., Wis.), it offers many
points of contact with them, and it seems especially to proceed
from the same spirit.   The author was well acquainted with
gnomic literature and was inspired by it.

The First Epistle of Peter is an epistle more than a letter.
Basically, it is an exhortation and, at the same time, a moral
instruction on some of the duties that are incumbent on every
Christian, particularly in time of persecution.   The tone is that
of a pastoral homily, inspired by paternal affection.   The author
did not know personally the addressees indicated in the
superscription, and consequently he could not communicate
with them in a personal or special manner.

The Second Epistle of Peter begins as a true encyclical
addressed to all believers (1 : 1-2).   Its primary purpose is to
combat the doctrines of false teachers, but the description
of these purveyors of error is so vague that they cannot be
identified with certainty.   This Second Epistle of Peter is
even less to be classed as a letter than the First.

The same must be said of the Epistle of Jude, which closely
resembles the preceding in subject matter as well as in form.
It is not known for whom this brief encyclical, in which the
author has inserted two quotations taken from Jewish
apocrypha — the *Assumption of Moses* and the *Book of Henoch*
(9-10; 14-15), was intended.

The First Epistle of John does not even affect the form of an
epistle.   There is no address at the beginning, no salutations,
and no expression of good wishes at the close.   It is a message
to Christendom as a whole or at least to the Churches known
to the author.   As there is an allusion in the first lines to the
beginning and to the end of the Fourth Gospel (1 John 1 : 1-2;
cf. John 1 : 1-4, and 20 : 25-27). it may be asked whether this
Epistle might not be a kind of introduction to this same Gospel,
and written for the purpose of calling attention to it as a

revelation of the mystery of Christ and as an antidote against the dangers of nascent Gnosticism.

The Second Epistle of John is addressed to a particular church, adorned with the title of " Elect Lady ", and the Third to a personage named Caius or Gaius. Here and there, the author designates himself as " the Presbyter " [" the Ancient "] and he writes to confirm in the faith those who are exposed to danger from false teachers. These two documents should be regarded as letters.

In short, most of the Catholic Epistles are homilies or pastorals in the guise of epistles. Hence we see why and how much they differ from the Pauline Letters, inasmuch as they are coordinated with the Christian catechesis of the most general type and treat of questions of interest not only to particular groups, but to all believers collectively. They represent a form of instruction given in the early days of Christianity which follows the impersonal manner employed previously in the Jewish world by the Rabbis and also in the pagan world by certain Stoic philosophers.

3. — APOCALYPTIC.

Something was said of the origins of the apocalyptic genre apropos of the literary genres of the Old Testament [1], and it was stated in that connection that among the books of the Synagogue the prophecy of Daniel was the first of the apocalypses in date. When the voice of the prophets ceased to be heard in Israel, apocalyptic immediately began to flourish under the form of apocryphal writings and soon became the most popular literary genre, its vogue embracing the last two centuries B. C. and the first two centuries of our era. Christians borrowed this genre from the Jews in order to express under this form, which was already old, their great hope in a complete and final victory of God and of Christ over Satan and the powers of evil. The continuity between the Jewish and the Christian apocalyptic is manifest from the Book of Daniel to the Apocalypse of John, from the Book of Henoch to the Apocalypse of Peter. The Christian writers merely followed a tradition when they made use of this special literary genre. But apocalyptic never had in Christian circles the same success as in

---

[1] See pp. 509-512 above.

the Jewish world. Even in the latter, the taste for this lite-
rature had declined to a marked degree before the middle
of the second century, and, apart from the Gnostic productions,
Christian apocalypses are very few in number. In the New
Testament the genre is represented omly by the Apocalypse of
Saint John.

The Greek word " apocalypse " (ἀποκάλυψις, *revelatio* in Latin)
signifies *manifestation* or *revelation* of things kept secret, things
which can be happenings of the past equally as well as events
of the future. In apocalyptic, revelation takes place ordinarily
by means of visions which the seer describes or transcribes in
conventional language. The author of an apocalypse has his
eyes turned towards the future, even when he is making use of
ancient or comtemporary history, and it is likewise toward
the future that the reader is invited to look. Under such
circumstances, confusion can and often does occur, the true
perspective not always coinciding with that of the author,
and that of the reader not necessarily being that of the seer.
As a result, the reader is instinctively led to take as predictions
in the strict sense what for the author is often no more than
a conventional tableau, the elements of which have been
borrowed in whole or in part from the domain of already
accomplished facts.

Usually the future events which God reveals or is represented
as revealing to the seer refer to the end of the present world,
to the vengeance of God upon His enemies, and to the judgment
of humanity. Hence the very pronounced *eschatological*
character of most of the apocalypses.

Moreover, since apocalyptic is very closely related to prophecy,
which it claims to continue, there exists between the two a
certain number of common elements or characteristics. Thus,
in both God intervenes personally or through heavenly spirits
in the revelation of secret things, of which He guarantees the
reality or the execution; a preestablished and infallible design
rigorously governs the action or presides over the development
of the different parts of the drama seen by way of vision ; the
descriptions habitually present themselves under the form of
juxtaposed tableaux, the chronological connection of which is
rarely marked; and the communication of things seen or heard
is made in a figurative and mysterious language which is deliber-

ately employed to serve as a veil, to stimulate curiosity, and to provoke attention.

We see from this that the apocalyptic genre is a true literary type, having its own laws, characteristics, and methods. History indicates that it developped especially in moments of crisis as a reaction of faith threatened or oppressed, and in the form of a counterstroke to triumphant impiety and persecution. The authors of apocalypses clearly gave rein to their imaginations in these compositions, in which their problem was to describe what they had seen in spirit. For relating visions of this nature, an appropriate language was necessary : vehement expressions, grandiose formulas, brilliantly colored images, strange personifications, and all this without concern for proportion or probability to such an extent, that upon minds formed in the Greek and Latin cultural tradition the first contact with this literature leaves a disconcerting and rather painful impression.

The Apocalypse of Saint John is a message of Christian faith and hope and, at the same time, a manifesto against official and imperial paganism. The author is a *witness* of Christ eternally living, and he speaks with the authority of the ancient prophets commissioned by God, borrowing from them many images and symbols. To his brethren in the faith he brings the testimony of Christ on Himself and on His Church, and his book is, as it were, an illustrated commentary on the statement of Jesus to His Apostles : " In the world you will have affliction; but have courage : I have overcome the world " (John **16** : 33). Just as the prophecy of Daniel — another witness — had as its purpose the reanimation of the spiritual energies of the Jewish nation at a time when monotheism was menaced by pagan Hellenism (Dan. **7-12**), so the Johannine Apocalypse was composed to console and fortify in the faith certain Christians who were exposed to persecution (**2** : 8-10, 12-13; **6** : 9-11; **7** : 14; **13** : 11-17; **17** : 6; **20** : 4). Upon this point no doubt is possible. In both instances, the intention is the same, and likewise the devices or artifices employed for the setting or representation. Since in the age of Saint John the persecutor was the Roman Empire, and since the most immediate danger for the faithful of the Province of Asia was the worship of Rome and Augustus (the tableau in ch. **13**), the book took the form

of an *anti-Roman* and anti-imperial manifesto, directed against
the central power and against the religion of the State. The
contemporary reader of John knew perfectly how to understand
the veiled allusions to this situation which are made repeatedly
throughout the work.

The author of the Apocalypse declares solemnly in an editorial
prologue that he has received a mandate from Christ " to make
known to His servants the things that must shortly come to
pass ", all things which he himself " has seen " (1 : 1-3). The
address follows : " John, to the seven Churches that are in
Asia " (1 : 4). Although the Churches are designated by their
names in Chapters 2 and 3, the prophetic exhortation is
addressed to all the communities in the Province of Asia and
also to Christendom as a whole, for seven is a symbolic number
which denotes universality. The inaugural vision (1 : 9-20),
which may be compared with those of Isaias (6), of Jeremias (1),
and of Ezechiel (1), commands that letters be sent to the sevep
Churches, one of the features of the vision which is repeaten
in the case of each of them (2 : 1, 8, 12, etc.).

In these letters, addressed to the " angels " of the Churches,
may be noted a curious mixture of symbols and concrete
observations, of fiction and reality, for if at first sight they
seem to be only moral exhortations of a general character under
allegorical form, they contain allusions to precise facts, a
circumstance which proves that the author was well acquainted
with the communities designated by name (see in particular
the letters to the Churches of Pergamum and of Laodicea,
2, 12-17, and 3 : 14-22).

The prophetic revelation (4 : 1–22 : 5) unfolds in a series of
tableaux. Their plan as a whole cannot be determined with
certainty, but the features of their composition are constantly
the same — an indication of the perfect literary unity of the
work. Among these features, the following may be mentioned.

The series of seven letters is only the first of the series of
sevens, being followed by the seven seals of the book of the
divine decrees (5 : 1–8 : 1), the seven trumpets (8 : 2–11 : 19),
and the seven bowls (15 : 1–16 : 21). These three series of
sevens, in the interest of describing the effects produced, are
separated into two groups of four and three elements respectively (5 : 1–6 : 8, and 6 : 9–8 : 1; 8 : 2-13, and 8 :14–11 : 19;

15 : 5-**16** : 9, and **16** : 10-21). Before the last phase of each series there is a rest or interlude : before the seventh seal is opened (**7** : 1-17), before the sounding of the seventh trumpet (**10** : 1-**11** : 13), before the seventh bowl is poured out (**16** : 13-16). The opening of the seventh seal serves as an introduction to the seven trumpets (**8** : 1-2); the seventh trumpet, to the seven bowls (**11** : 15-18); the seventh bowl, to the events of the end (**16** : 17), which will usher in the kingdom of God and the triumph of Christ. Thus, the denouement of the drama expected by the reader is found regularly postponed at the end of each group of seven.

The reader becomes a spectator at a scenic representation in the grand style. A drama is enacted before him, and on the issue of this drama will depend the future lot of humanity. The scene changes constantly, with the action developing simultaneously on two planes, the one heavenly and the other terrestrial. Nevertheless, unity is maintained, for the tableau of Chapter 4 (the throne of God and the celestial court) constitutes a permanent stage setting. Furthermore, earth is connected with heaven by the comings and goings of angels who transmit or execute the divine decrees. The members of the cast move outside the common limits of space and time, but this does nor detract from the interest. Emotion increases steadily up to the final denouement which assures, in a glorious apotheosis (**19** : 11-**22** : 5), the triumph of Good over Evil, of God over His enemies.

Symbolism appears in all the tableaux : the Lamb always figures Christ; the Woman represents the Jewish community and the Christian Church; the Dragon, the powers hostile to the kingdom of God; the two Beasts of Chapter **13**, the Roman Empire and the imperial cult; the Beast of Chapter **17**, *Nero redivivus;* Babylon, pagan Rome, etc. The white garments are for those who wear them the sign of victory and especially of immortality.

The numbers employed also have a symbolic value : [1] seven corresponds to fulness or to universality, while three and a

Translator's note. — [1 On the number seven and derived numbers, cf, B. CELADA, " Numeros sagrados derivados del siete ", *Sefarad* (1948), 48-77. 333-356; (1950), 3-23. Cf. the articles " Zahlensymbolik " and " Apokalyptische Zahl ", in HAAG, *Bibellexikon*, 1736, and 80-81. Cf. also *Sv. bibl. Uppslagsverk* 2, 1098-1099].

half gives the idea of something precarious or disturbing; 666,
in virtue of a process known to the Jews as well as to the Greeks
and the Romans, namely, *gematria*, represents *Cæsar Nero* by
the numerical equivalent of the Hebrew letters used to
transcribe this name.

These various established facts, to which others could be
added, are convergent, and they indicate that the composition
of the book in question is quite learned in character. This
impression is confirmed when we see how and to what degree
the author, for his images, symbols, and allegories, has drawn
from written texts or oral traditions of quite diverse origin and
character. He has made use of the Old Testament, and
especially of the prophetic books, Isaias, Jeremias, Ezechiel
and Daniel, constantly, and Zacharias, Joel, Amos, and Osee,
to a lesser degree. Among the Jewish apocalyptic works which
influenced him, must be mentioned the *Books of Henoch*, the
Testament of Levi, the *Assumption of Moses*, and also the *Psalms
of Solomon*. He certainly knew the Synoptic apocalypse as it
is presented in Saint Matthew (**24-25**) and Saint Luke (**21** : 5-36),
as well as the First Epistle to the Thessalonians and the First
and Second to the Corinthians, for the literary connections are
manifest. Finally he drew upon the folklore of oriental and
Hellenic imagery, many elements of which came from
astronomy, astrology, and ancient myths [1].

It must be recognized that the author of the Apocalypse was
endowed with an uncommon power of assimilation, for the
borrowings are constant from one end of his book to the other,
and yet he has put his personal mark on all the symbols
employed. Furthermore, while this work is a *Summa*, as it
were, of the earlier apocalyptic literature, it would be a chimer-
ical enterprise if one should attempt to determine precisely
the written sources which entered into its composition in order
to reconstruct them in detail.

If one wishes to have a concrete and exact idea of the way in
which the prophet-writer works, it will suffice to compare
9 : 3-11 (the Locusts) with Ex. **10** : 12-15, and Joel **1** : 4 ff.;

---

[1] For details, see R. H. CHARLES, *A Critical and Exegetical Commentary on
the Revelation of Saint John* (Edinburgh, 1920), pp. LXII-LXXXVI, and E. B. ALLO,
L'Apocalypse de Saint Jean (3rd., Paris, 1933); check through the *Index* of
this book).

13 ff. (the Beast) with Dan. 7-8; 18 : 9-20 (lamentation on the fall of Babylon) with Isa. 23 and Ez. 26 : 16–27 : 31. As regards the images and symbols borrowed from astral mythology, immediate parallels or influences are difficult to establish. But it is to be remembered that the author lived and composed his book in an age and in a milieu in which astronomy and astrology enjoyed the highest credit in educated circles as well as among the masses. We may add that, in the descriptions of the celestial court and of the ceremonies performed before the throne of God, the writer was inspired by what he had seen himself at the Temple of Jerusalem before the catastrophe of the year 70.

It is evident that the genre of the work governs its interpretation. The Apocalypse of John, like all other apocalypses, is closely related to prophecy. But its literary antecedents furnish us with information on the nature of the prophecies thus presented under the conventional veil of apocalyptic. These predictions are not to be taken as history written in the future tense, nor to be understood as the translation into plain language of realities or events to come. It is because of their total ignorance of the laws and devices of this special literary genre that some interpreters, such as Joachim of Flore (at the end of the 12th century), Nicholas of Lyra (at the beginning of the 14th century) and a good many others after them, have gone astray.

It must be recognized that symbolism gave rise to these misinterpretations. Like the authors of the Jewish apocalypses, John has used fiction. On a foundation canvas which depicts in outline the end of time and the general judgment, he has depicted symbolically different episodes in the ceaseless combat which God wages against the forces of evil, and he has done so without indicating any of the successive stages of their historical realization. He placed himself, apparently, at the beginning of the reign of Vespasian (69) in order to contemplate and describe prophetically the events which had taken place up to the time at which he wrote. He thus employed a literary artifice which casts reflection neither on the inspiration of the book nor on its prophetic character, but which the reader should take into account. The author wrote for men who lived at the end of the first century and for Christians of the Province of

Asia, and this is a factual point which should never be forgotten. Before being a message universal " in time and space ", the Apocalypse of John was and remains a work deeply implanted in a given milieu and in a definite historical epoch.   The points of contact with the history of the time are numerous in the work. While many of these can be identified definitely, there are others which probably never will be.

CONCLUSION.

At the end of this exposition some conclusions at least appear as self-evident.

1.   The beginning, formation, and development of the New Testament literature were conditioned by the needs of Christian propaganda.   This is an historical fact which explains and justifies the pronounced " pragmatic " character of the various writings comprised in the New Testament collection.   All these writings present the Good News of salvation through Christ either under the form of apostolic catechesis, or as an extension or elaboration of this catechesis.

2.   This literature, as compared with ancient profane literature, is clearly distinguished from the latter in respect to the literary genres employed by the sacred writers.   The genres of the New Testament do not coincide with those of the classical canon, Greek or Latin.   Hence the profoundly original character of New Testament literature.

3.   Of all the books of the New Testament, not one was composed by a professional writer, i.e., by an author anxious to conform to the rules of a strictly defined literary genre.   The qualification, " popular literature ", understood in this sense, is perfectly suited to the ensemble of New Testament literature.

4.   With the exception of the Synoptic Gospels, whose kinship is close both in content and form, of the Epistles to the Ephesians and the Colossians, and also of two of the Catholic Epistles, those of Peter and Jude, which are alike in several points, the writings of the New Testament are independent of one another. They do not present themselves as an ensemble whose different parts are interrelated and mutually dependent.

5. In the New Testament, nevertheless, there is a unity, not a literary but an internal or organic unity, resulting from the fact that all these writings reflect the same faith and proceed with the same purpose : to make known the person and the work of Christ, the principle and author of salvation for every man who believes in Him.

APPENDIX.

THE SYNOPTIC QUESTION [1]

[A. Tricot]

1. — The Fact and the Problem.

Of the four canonical Gospels there are three which run parallel, while the fourth, that of John, goes its own particular way. The three narratives of Matthew, Mark, and Luke have common or corresponding parts which can be arranged and set side by side in parallel columns. Thus, a double or triple relation, as it were, of the same Gospel fact (event or discourse) can be obtained, and by a simple glance of the eye resemblances as well as differences in detail may be easily established. The text arranged in this fashion is called a *synopsis*, from the Greek σύνοψις (general view); hence the name of *Synoptics* [2], given since the end of the eighteenth century to the three Gospels whose relationship is manifest [3].

The *Synoptic Fact* is established by the multiple resemblances revealed by a comparison of the first three Gospels. In a general way, what can be called the Gospel theme is found to be the same in each. This in itself is not at all surprising, since the same history is involved.

With the exception of some twenty verses, Mk. is found entire in Mt. or in Lk., and thus corresponds to a little more than a

---

[1] The *Synoptic Question* constitutes in itself a chapter in the literary history of the New Testament, and it is independent of the problem of the literary genre of the Gospels. The exposition which follows has been placed here under the form of an *Appendix* for purely practical reasons.

[2] The *Synopsis Evangeliorum* of J. J. GRIESBACH (1774) played an important part in the adoption of the expression, " Synoptic Gospels ".

[3] What is called a *Harmony of the Gospels* is a connected account of the history of Jesus, in which all elements are taken from the Four Gospels, but without indication of parallel narratives. The *Diatessaron* of Tatian was a harmony and not a synopsis.

half of the First Gospel and to about two-fifths of the Third. Moreover — leaving out of consideration the Gospel of Mk. — about a fourth of Matthew's narrative has its parallel in Luke, and a fifth of Luke has its parallel in Mt. [1].

The main outlines of the Gospel history are the same in the three accounts, and, likewise the few geographical and chronological references : the ministry of John the Baptist and the entrance of Jesus on the scene; the preaching in Galilee and the regions situated to the east and to the north of the Sea of Tiberias; the journey to Jerusalem; the passion, death, and resurrection of Christ.

The resemblance of the three narratives is particularly pronounced in the relation of certain facts which mark stages in the career of Jesus : the baptism of Jesus, His controversies with opponents, the multiplication of the loaves, the confession of Peter, the last days at Jerusalem after the triumphal entry, the arrest, judgment, and death of Our Savior. Resemblances in these points furnish the first proof of relationship.

The second proof follows. In a general way, or " by and large ", the materials of the Gospel history are distributed in the same manner in the three Synoptics. Thus, in many instances the episodes of this history follow one another and are linked together in an identical manner in the three accounts : the paralytic of Capharnaum, the call of Levi, and the question of fasting in Mt. 9, 1-17, Mk. 2 : 1-22, Lk. 5 : 17-39; the stilling of the tempest, the demoniac of Gerasa, and the daughter of Jairus in Mt. 8, 19–9 : 34, Mk. 4 : 35–5 : 43, and Lk. 8 : 22-56; the confession of Peter, the first announcement of the passion, the transfiguration, the cure of the epileptic, and the second announcement of the passion in Mt. 16 : 13–17 : 32, Mk. 8 : 27–9 : 32, and Lk. 9 : 18-45; four questions on the tribute to Caesar, the resurrection, the greatest commandment, and the Son of David in Mt. 22 : 15–23 : 12, Mk. 12 : 13-40, Lk. 20 : 20-47; five points developed in the discourse on the end of the world : the destruction of the Temple, the great tribulation, the abomination of desolation, the coming of the Son of man, and the hour of judgment in Mt. 24 : 1-44, Mk. 13 : 1-37, and Lk. 21 : 5-33. " We might speak in all these cases of an arcade

---

[1] For statistics in detail, see M. GOGUEL, *Introduction au Nouveau Testament* (Paris, 1924), vol. I, *Les Evangiles Synoptiques*, pp. 181 ff.

of unified style, with its columns and its sculptured capitals, moved as a single unit and set among monuments in themselves differently orientated and arranged " [1].

It is plain that such an agreement in subject matter and its order of presentation could not be fortuitous, and it ought to be possible to furnish an explanation.

A third proof of relationship is based on a study of literary form. Even a rapid examination of the parallel texts reveals how frequently the form of expression is almost identical, the differences in style or vocabulary being as insignificant as if there had been originally only a single redaction. For examples, cf. the episode of the plucking of the ears of grain in Mt. **12** : 1-4, Mk. **2** : 23-26, and Lk. **6** : 1-4; the parable of the mustard seed in Mt. **13** : 31-32, Mk. **4** : 30-32, and Lk. **13** : 18-19; the necessity of renunciation in Mt. **16** : 24-28, Mk. **8** : 34–**9** : 1, and Lk. **9** : 23-27; the rich young man in Mt. **19** : 16-26, Mk. **10** : 17-27, and Lk. **18** : 18-27.

Agreement is equally striking in the following parallels : Mt. **3** : 7-10 and Lk. **3** : 7-9; Mt. **11** : 4-6 and Lk. **7** : 22-23; Mt. **11** : 25-27 and Lk. **10** : 21-22; Mt. **15** : 32-39 and Mk. **8** : 1-10; Mt **20** : 20-28 and Mk. **10** : 35-40; Mt. **23** : 37-39 and Lk. **13** : 34-35; Mt. **24** : 32-36, Mk. **13** : 28-32, and Lk. **21** : 29-33; Mk. **12** : 41-44 and Lk. **21** : 1-4.

Such a close literary relationship would appear to be natural enough when there is question of the especially significant words spoken by Jesus. It is at least unexpected in purely narrative parts, and, *a fortiori*, in connecting or transitional sentences (cf. Mt. **8** : 16, Mk. **1** : 32, and Lk. **4** : 40; Mt. **19** : 13, Mk. **10** : 13, and Lk. **18** : 15).

The last proof of relationship involves certain stylistic or grammatical peculiarities and quotations from the Old Testament. Here also, some examples are indispensable for giving a concrete idea of this literal verbal accord which is so characteristic : οἱ υἱοὶ τοῦ νυμφῶνος (a Semitism) in Mt. **9** : 15, Mk. **2** : 19, and Lk. **5** : 34; ἀπεκατεστάθη (a form with double augment peculiar to the *Koine*) in Mt. **12** : 13, Mk. **3** : 5, and Lk. **6** : 10; the anacoluthon in Mt. **9** : 6, Mk. **2** : 10, and Lk. **5** : 24; δυσκόλως

---

[1] See L. DE GRANDMAISON, *Jésus-Christ*, vol. I, pp. 94-95. [Engl. trans. (New York, 1934), vol. I, p. 94].

a rare word) in Mt. **19** : 23, Mk. **10** : 23, and Lk. **18** : 24; πτερύγιον (only examples) in Mt. **4** : 5, Lk. **4** : 9; ἐπίβλημα (a little used term) in Mt. **9** : 16, Mk. **2** : 21, and Lk. **5** : 36; οὐ μὴ γεύσωνται θανάτου (an expression from post-Biblical Hebrew) in Mt. **16** : 28, Mk. **9** : 1, and Lk. **9** : 27; καὶ ἐχορτάσθησαν (a realistic detail) in Mt. **14** : 20, Mk. **6** : 42, and Lk. **9** : 17; ἕως πότε ἀνέξομαι ὑμῶν (redundance) in Mt. **17** : 17, Mk. **9** : 19, and Lk. **9** : 41; εἷς τῶν δώδεκα (needless precision) in Mt. **26** : 47, and Lk. **22** : 47.

The quotations from the Old Testament agree sometimes *ad litteram* in the three Synoptics, even when they correspond neither with the Hebrew text nor with that of the Septuagint : cf. the prophecy of Isaias in Mt. **3** : 3, Mk. **1** : 3, and Lk. **13** : 4, and that of Malachias in Mt. **11** : 10, Mk. **1** : 2, and Lk. **7** : 27.

Such a collection of ressemblances, considered as a whole, cannot be the effect of chance; their number is too high, they are too particular in nature, and their sequences are too constant. The first impression left by the attentive reading of a triple or double account is that of a common underlying work.

Four examples are presented here, each representing one of the possible cases of relationship (Mt. + Mk. + Lk.; Mt. + Mk.; Mt. + Lk.; Mk. + Lk.). The translation follows the Greek text word for word and a typographical device indicates more sharply what is common in the parallel accounts.

1. — *THE CONFESSION OF PETER.* [1]

Mt., **16** : 13-21.	Mk., **8** : 27-32.	Lk., **9** : 18-22.
13. Now Jesus, having **come into** the district of **Caesarea Philippi, was asking his disciples, saying,** " **Who do men say** the Son of man is? ".	27. And **Jesus** and **his disciples went out into** the villages of **Caesarea Philippi;** and on the way he asked **his disciples, saying to** them, " **Who do men say that I am** "?	18. And it came to pass as he was praying in private that too the **disciples** were with him and **he asked them, saying,** " **Who do** the crowds **say that I am?** ".
14. **But they said,** " **Some say, John the Baptist : and others Elias,** and others, Jeremias **or one of** the **prophets** ".	28. **But they said to** him, saying, " **John the Baptist : and others, Elias : and others, one of the prophets** ".	19. And **they** answering said, " **John the Baptist : and others** Elias : and others, that one of the ancient **prophets** has risen again ".
15. He says **to them,** " **But you, who do you say that I am?** ".	29. Then he **asked** them, " **But you, who do you say that I am?** "	20. And **he said to them,** " **But you, Who do you say that I am?** "

16. Simon **Peter answered and said,** "Thou art the Christ the Son of the living **God**".

17. But Jesus answering said, "Blessed art thou, Simon Barjona, for flesh and blood has not revealed this to thee, but my Father in heaven.

18. I say to thee, thou art Peter, and upon this rock I will build my Church, and the gates of hell shall not prevail against it.

19. And I will give thee the keys of the kingdom of heaven; and whatever thou shalt bind on earth shall be bound in heaven, and whatever thou shalt loose on earth shall be loosed in heaven ".

20. Then **he ordered** the disciples **to tell no one** that he was the Christ.

21. From that time Jesus **began** to show his disciples **that he must** go to Jerusalem and **suffer many things from the elders, and chief priests, and scribes, and be put to death, and on the third day be raised again.**

Peter answering says to him, " **Thou art the** Christ ".

30. **And he strictly charged them to tell no one** about him.

31. And he **began to** teach them **that the Son of man must suffer many things, and be rejected by the elders and chief priests and scribes, and be put to death, and after three days rise again.**

Peter answering said, the Christ of God ".

21. But **he strictly** charging **them** commanded **them to tell this to no one,**

22. saying, " **the Son of man must suffer many things, and be rejected by the elders and chief priest and scribes, and be put to death, and on the third day be raised again** ".

---

2. — THE CANAANITE WOMAN.

Mt., **15** : 21-28.

21. And going forth **from there** Jesus retired to the district **of Tyre and Sidon.**

22. And behold, A Canaanite **woman** coming out of that territory cried, saying to him, " Have pity on me, O Lord, Son of David ! My daughter is sorely beset by a **devil** ".

23. But He answered her not a word. And his disciples coming up requested him, saying, " Send her away, for she is crying after us ".

24. But he answering said, " I was

Mk., **7** : 24-30.

24. And **from there** rising he departed for the territory **of Tyre and Sidon.** And entering a house he wanted no one to know, and he could not escape notice.

25. But immediately **a woman** whose little daughter had an unclean spirit, on hearing of him **coming in** fell down at His feet.

26. Now the woman was a Greek, a Syrophoenician by birth. And she requested him to cast the **devil** out of her daughter.

not sent except to the lost sheep of the house of Israel ".

25. But she coming worshipped him, saying, "Lord, help me! ".

26. He answering said, " It is not fair to take the children's bread and cast it to the dogs ".

27. But she said, "Yes, Lord; yea even the dogs eat of the crumbs that fall from their masters' table ".

28. Then Jesus answering said to her, " O woman, great is thy faith! Let it be done to thee as thou wilt ". And her daughter was healed from that moment.

27. And he said to her, " Let the children first have their fill, for it is not right to take the children's bread and cast it to the dogs ".

28. But she answered and said to him, " Ves, Lord, even the dogs under the table eat of the children's crumbs ".

29. And he said to her; " Because of this answer, go thy way; the devil has gone out of thy daughter",

30. And going to her house, she found the child lying upon the bed and the devil gone.

3. — THE MESSENGERS OF JOHN THE BAPTIST.

Mt., 11 : 2-6.

2. But John hearing in prison of the works of Christ, sending through his disciples said to him :

3. " Art thou he who is to come, or shall we look for another? ".

4. And Jesus answering said to them, " Going report to John what you hear and see :

5. the blind see, and the lame walk, the lepers are cleansed, and the deaf hear, and the dead rise, and the poor have the Gospel preached to them.

6. and blessed is he who is not scandalized in me ".

Lk., 7 : 18-23.

18. And John's disciples brought him word of all these things. And John summoning two of his disciples

19. sent them to the Lord, saying " Art thou he who is to come, or shall we look for another? "

20. The men presenting themselves to Him said : " John the Baptist has sent us to Thee saying : Art Thou He Who is to come, or shall we look for another? "

21. At that moment, He cured many people of diseases, and infirmities and evil spirits, and He restored sight to many blind.

22. And answering he said to them : "Go tell John what you have seen and heard : the blind see, the lame walk, the lepers are cleansed the deaf hear, the dead rise, the poor have the Gospel preached to them.

23. and blessed is he who is not scandalised in me ".

4. — THE DEMONIAC OF CAPHARNAUM.

Mk., 1 : 23-28.

23. And immediately in their synagogue there was a man with an unclean spirit, and he cried out.

24. saying, What have we to do with thee, Jesus of Nazareth? Hast thou come to destroy us? I know who thou art, the Holy one of God ".

Lk., 4 : 33-37.

33. And in the synagogue there was a man possessed by the spirit of an unclean devil, and he cried out with a loud voice.

34. " Let us be! What have we to do with thee, Jesus of Nazareth? Hast thou come to destroy us? I know thee who thou art, the holy one of God ".

25. And Jesus rebuked him, " Hold thy peace, and go out of him ".
26. And the unclean spirit, convulsing him and crying out with a loud voice, went out of him.
27. And they were all amazed, so that they inquired among themselves, saying, " What is this? A new doctrine with authority : he commands even the unclean spirits, and they obey him ".
28. And his fame went forth immediately everywhere into all the region round about Galilee.

35. And Jesus rebuked him, saying, " Hold thy peace, and go from him ". And the devil from throwing him down into the midst, went out from him, without harming him at all.
36. And amazement came upon all, and they kept speaking together with one another, saying, " What is this word? For with authority and power he commands the unclean spirits, and they come out ".
37. And rumor concerning him was going out into every place of the region round about.

As we see, the relationship between the parallel texts is plain. But there is another side, for the divergences are not less numerous nor less characteristic than the resemblances, and these affect, furthermore, the content as well as the form of the three Synoptic narratives.

It might well be imagined that, in the case of the words of Jesus, literalness was particularly or scrupulously respected, but the differences are sometimes disconcerting. It will suffice to cite two classic examples : the Our Father (Mt. **6** : 9-13, Lk. **11** : 2-4) and the institution of the Eucharist (Mt. **26** : 26-28, Mk. **14** : 22-24, Lk. **22** : 19-20).

As regards the subject matter of the Gospel history, a number of differences are to be noted. Only Mt. and Lk. give accounts of the birth and infancy of Jesus, and these two narratives are completely independent of each other [1]. Mk. alone relates the parable of the seed which grows of itself. The parables of the cockle, of the hidden treasure, of the pearl of great price, of the leaven, of the net, and of the unmerciful servant appear only in Mt. On the other hand, the parables of the prodigal son, of the good Samaritan, of the Pharisee and the Publican, and of the Rich Man and Lazarus are to be read only in Lk. Of twenty accounts of miracles, Lk. has six which are peculiar to him. The same Evangelist knows nothing or says nothing of some episodes related by Mt. (**14** : 22–**15** : 39) and by Mk. (6 : 45–8 : 10) following the multiplication of the loaves (the walking on the

---

[1] [Cf. L. RICHARD, " L'Evangile de l'Enfance et le décret impérial de recensement ", in *Mémorial J. Chaine* (Lyon, 1950), p. 297 ff.]

water, cures at Genesareth, the journey into Phoenicia, the Canaanite woman, the journey through Decapolis, the cure of the deaf-mute, the second multiplication of loaves). On the other hand, numerous elements in an important section of the Third Gospel (the journey to Jerusalem, 9 : 51-18 : 14) are found neither in Mt. nor in Mk.

The arrangement of facts and discourses presents differences which are quite equally pronounced. Thus the Sermon on the Mount constitutes in Mt. a whole or a unit clearly defined (5-7). Yet it is lacking in Mk., and, while it is found in Luke, its elements are scattered through nearly a dozen different passages (chs. 6, 11, 13, 14, and 16). The order is not the same in Mt. 3-14 as in Mk. 1-6 : 13, whereas in other parts of the first two Gospels the episodes are arranged in almost identical fashion (Mt. 14-18, and Mk. 6 : 14-9; Mt. 19-20 : 34, and Mk. 10; Mt. 26-27 and Mk. 14-15). The preaching of Jesus in Nazareth is read in Lk. before the calling of the Apostles (4 : 16-30), but it comes at a much later period in Mt. (13 : 53-58) and in Mk. (6 : 1-6). If we compare Lk. with Mt. and Mk., we find that the first is independent of the two others regarding the account of the journey to Jerusalem (9 : 51-18 : 14), whereas it is in perfect accord with Mk. from 4 : 31 to 6 : 19, from 8 : 4 to 9 : 50, and from 18 : 14 to 21 : 38. The accounts of the Passion present, in general, the same sequence in the three Synoptics. Nevertheless, quite noteworthy differences may be observed : Mt. (27 : 46) and Mk. (15 : 34) give only one word of Christ on the cross, and precisely this same word is lacking in Lk., who, on the other hand, gives three others (23 : 34, 43, 46). The risen Christ appeared to the disciples in Galilee according to Mt. 28 : 16-20 and Mk. 16 : 6-7 (not counting the last time), but at Jerusalem and its environs according to Lk. 24 : 13-53. Mt. alone mentions the guards who were placed before the tomb and bribed by the chief priests of the Jews (27 : 62-66; 28 : 11-20). The narrative of the disciples who went to Emmaus is to be read only in Lk. (24 : 13-35).

Such established examples, and the number given above is far from exhausting the list, justify the application of the term, *concordia discors*, to the *Synoptic Fact*. The comparative study of the three narratives reveals a blending of resemblances and differences as remarkable as it is constant. Sometimes minor and sometimes important, these are extremely diverse in nature, and it is very difficult, not to say impossible, to classify them. Such is the material fact with its essential data. By reason of its complexity, it is without parallel in the domain of literary works, ancient or modern, Classical or non-Classical. Every biographer of the life of Jesus is obliged to take this fact into account in his inquiry into the sources, for it governs the problem of their value or authority. Thus it is that the *Synoptic Fact* is of direct concern to *historical* criticism.

The explanation of this disconcerting intermixture of materials involves what is called the *Synoptic Problem*. A solution can be obtained only by applying the principles and methods which in their ensemble constitute the body of rules or laws of *literary* criticism, and, on this score, the investigation of the problem in question falls under the literary history of the New Testament.

The Synoptic Problem was not really perceived and envisaged in itself before the beginning of the nineteenth century. The Fathers of the Church and the Mediaeval theologians had noted the differences and divergencies presented by the Gospel texts, but their sole concern was to establish and demonstrate a satisfactory agreement among the narratives by " harmonizing " them. The explanations and judgment given by Saint Augustine on this question in *De consensu Evangelistarum* (c. 400) was generally adopted and followed.

We need not retrace here the history of this problem, since it is covered in the *Manuals* or *Introductions to the New Testament*. It will suffice to recall that, for more than a century and a half, researches and publications have multiplied on this question — certainly the most debated of all those which are concerned with the history of primitive Christianity. Actually, no completely satisfactory solution of this literary phenomenon has been furnished up to the present time, and this must be honestly recognized. Yet it must be emphasized that such great efforts on the part of the higher criticism have not been expended uselessly. Far from it ! For the Gospel texts, thanks to these patient and methodical studies, are better known in themselves, and in respect to their pre-history, their history, and their mutual relations.

2. — Hypotheses upon Hypotheses.

Some have thought that the Synoptic Gospels are derived from a common source and that this source was the primitive catechesis, determined and fixed in its essential elements by the Apostles, and transmitted orally and preserved under a quasi-stereotyped form, as it were, during the first Christian generation. Mt., Mk., and Lk. would have utilized, each in his own way and independently of each other, the narratives and didactic outlines which made up the catechesis, such as the missionaries presented it under slightly different forms in Palestine, in Syria, and at Rome.

The apostolic catechesis underwent changes in the course of its employment by various missionaries and in different centers. It eventually assumed two chief forms : that of the Galilean Apostles, and that of Saint Paul and the Hellenist preachers. The Gospels of Matthew and Mark reproduce the first of these forms, and that of Luke the second.

This hypothesis, which is called that of *Oral Tradition,* was advanced by J. G. HERDER in 1796 *(Vom Erlöser der Menschen nach den drei ersten Evangelien)* and in 1797 *(Von der Regel der Zusammenstimmung unserer Evangelien).* It was taken up again and presented under a systematic form by J. C. L. GIE-SELER *(Historisch-kritischer Versuch über die Entstehung und die frühesten Schicksale der schriftlichen Evangelien,* 1818). It has been held by a good number of Catholic and Protestant exegetes (among Catholics : Knabenbauer, Cornely, Kaulen, T. Soiron, J. M. Vosté, and P. Vannutelli). It has the merit of being simple. Furthermore, its basic principle is indisputable, for the recollections contained in the Gospels were transmitted orally over many years and in an almost stereotyped form. But, however great the influence of this oral transmission on the redaction of the Gospel texts, it explains neither the close literary connection of parallel passages, nor the succession of numerous episodes in the same order, nor the stylistic or linguistic peculiarities which are encountered in almost identical pericopes.

2.   The hypothesis of the *Primitive Gospel (Urevangelium),* proposed by G. E. LESSING *Neue Hypothese über die Evangelisten als bloss menschliche Scriftsteller betrachtet,* 1784), was given systematic form by J. G. EICHHORN *(Einleitung in das Neue*

Testament, 1804) : The Synoptics have their origin in a primitive gospel composed in Aramaic shortly after the death of Jesus; they are three translations of the same basic document; the translations were made independently and are both " different and similar " (Lessing). This primitive gospel was translated into Greek and was embellished and reworked before being utilized for the redaction of the Synoptics (Eichhorn). These views were not adopted by Biblical scholars and are mentioned here merely " as a matter of record ".

3. The hypothesis of *Utilization* or *Mutual Dependence*, whatever may be its variants, always comes back to the supposition that the first of the Gospels in date was followed by the two others as derivatives, but independently of each other, and that the third depends on the first and second — hence the resemblances. The differences arise from the fact that each Evangelist made use of oral or written sources with which he was personally familiar. Basically, this was the opinion of Saint Augustine, who believed that Mk. followed Mt. faithfully, although abridging it, while Lk. employed the two earlier redactions.

This explanation was proposed by J. J. Griesbach — with the sequence Mt. - Lk. - Mk. — in several studies published between 1783 and 1790. It was adopted, in more or less modified form, by a number of distinguished Catholic exegetes : P. Schanz, J. E. Belser, T. Calmes, and P. Dausch. It has been taken up again — at least partially — by M. J. Lagrange and P. Benoit. At the end of his exhaustive study of the Synoptics, M. J. Lagrange reached the following conclusions : the independent existence of a primitive Aramaic text of Mt.; the utilization of Mk. for the Greek translation (Canonical Mt.) of Aramaic Mt.; the independance of Greek Mt. in relation to Lk.; the indirect dependence (probable) of Lk. in relation to Mt. (LAGRANGE, *Ev. selon s. Matthieu*, p. 11). The literary genres of the Synoptics as sketched by P. Benoit (*Ev. selon s. Matthieu*, Paris, 1950) is more complex : first, Aramaic Mt. and Greek translations of this text; next, Mk. utilizing one of these translations; finally, Canonical Mt. and Lk., both depending on the Greek translation of Aramaic Mt., on Mk., and on various sources, among them a collection of *Logia*.

The objection is raised against this explanation, that the most ancient tradition, that of the second century represented by Papias, Saint Irenaeus, and Clement of Alexandria, knew nothing of this relation of mutual dependence. Furthermore, it is to be noted that this hypothesis does not explain the intermittent character of the resemblances in the narratives which are common, and still less the omissions. Why would Mk., if he knew Mt., have left out so many sayings and discourses of Jesus? And how would Lk., who aimed at giving an " orderly " history —hence, as complete as possible — have omitted important parts of Mt. (**14** : **22–16** : **12**) and of Mk. (**6** : **45–8** : **26**)?

4.   The hypothesis of the *Two Sources*, as it is called (the *Quellentheorie* of the German critics), has one point in common with the preceding.   The relationship of Mt., Mk., and Lk. is such that it implies either the utilization of the same written document by the three, or the dependence of two of them in relation to the third.   Since, on the one hand, the whole of Mk. may be found in Mt. and in Lk., and on the other, the Gospel of Mk. is surely not an abridgment of a pre-Synoptic document, nor of the account of Mt., nor of that of Lk., is it not probable that Mk. is the common source of Mt. and of Lk., at least for an important part of their content (more than a half in the case of Mt., and two-fifths in that of Lk.)?

This supposition, it is pointed out, is confirmed *in concreto* by three proofs : 1.   The order and the sequence of facts are more often the same in Mt. and in Lk. than in Mk.   When there is a divergence, this is only true of Mt. or of Lk., separately, and the reason for its is usually apparent.   2.   The vivid attractiveness and the popular bent of the narrative of Mk., the simple and somewhat unpolished manner of the author, the total absence of elegance in composition, the Semitic flavor, are all characteristic marks of an independent composition, " primary " as eruptive rock.   In instances where the comparison of parallel texts leads to the conclusion that some retouching has been done for one reason or another, it is always the reading of Mk. which appears to have been the original one.   Classic examples : the word χράβαττος (bad Hellenistic Greek) is used four times by Mk. **2** : **1-12**, but it does not appear in either Mt. or Lk. in the corresponding passage; Mt. **8** : **16** and Lk. **4** : **40** emphasize, more than Mk. **1** : **34**, the thaumaturgic power of Jesus; the formula of Mt. 13 : 58 softens that of Mk. 6 : 5.

So much on the first point. Let us now consider a second point.

Mt. and Lk. have a surplus of material in comparison with Mk., and this surplus comprises, apart from the subject matter peculiar to Mk. and that peculiar to Lk., a portion common to these two Evangelists. This portion in common corresponds to a third of the Gospel of Mt. and a little more than a fourth of that of Lk. What is peculiar to each is taken from information or sources utilized separately by the one or the other. It remains to examine what is common to them and what cannot be derived from Mk.

The comparative study of these selections reveals a related origin, less close, it is true, than that existing between the accounts of Mk. on the one hand and those of Mt. and Lk. on the other, but of the same type : the material is substantially the same and the expression is often identical. Whence comes this common possession which comprises especially the discourses of Jesus, His sayings, and parables? Lk. could have drawn upon Mt., or vice versa. But it appears that this supposition should be discarded, since the arrangement of the selections is not the same in both, and since now one of the two texts, and now the other, seems to ne the earlier. Besides, how explain why Lk., if he borrowed from Mt., did not respect the excellent arrangement of the Sermon on the Mount (Mt. 5-7)?

Under these circumstances, there is every reason to believe that Mt. and Lk. had recourse to an identical document, outside of and in addition to the Gospel of Mk., and that this document was a collection of discourses of Jesus enclosed within an historical frame of reference. The most ancient tradition, it may be added, confirms the existence of a collection of this kind (the collection of *Logia*), for " Matthew, as Papias says, arranged (reading συνετάξατο rather than συνεγράψατο) in the Hebrew language the sayings (Logia) and each translated them as best he could " (cited by Eusebius, *Ecclesiastical History*, III, 39 : 16). Greek translations of this Aramaic collection were made very early, already from the middle of the first century. Mt. and Mk. thus had at hand a second source which both employed, each in his own way.

This hypothesis was first advanced in a study of F. SCHLEIER-MACHER which was published in 1832 *(Ueber die Zeugnisse des Papias von unsern beiden ersten Evangelien)*, and it was enthusiastically received. According to Schleiermacher, the Synoptics have come from two writings, of which there are no existing remains : a Proto-Matthew, a collection of the discourses of Jesus in Aramaic, and a Proto-Mark, notes made by Mark based on the catechetical expositions of Peter. This is the foundation on which was erected the system of the *Two Sources* which has won the adherence of most non-Catholic critics. The learned expositions of H. J. Holtzmann, A. Reville, C. von Weizsäcker, B. Weiss, and P. Wernle mark its successive developments from 1862 to 1899. P. Wernle in 1899, Harnack in 1907, J. Hawkins in 1911, and others, presented a reconstruction of one of these sources : the collection of *Logia* mentionned by Papias (the document currently called Q, the first letter of *Quelle*, the German word for " source "). The results of these laborious investigations are disputable and they have been discussed; many good scholars hold that the real state of things was much more complex.

What judgment is to be passed on this brilliant hypothesis, which has been accepted and retained by the majority of non-Catholic exegetes and historians?

As regards the literary dependence of Mt. and Lk. on Mk., doubt is scarcely possible, for there are too many indications in favor of the priority of Mk. Still, it must be observed that this conclusion based on internal evidence seems to oppose the affirmation of tradition which must be recognized by the critic and the historian as a fact. The most ancient tradition is actually unanimous in recognizing a priority in content and a redaction (in Aramaic) for the Gospel of Mt. In this matter, Origen is a witness whose authority should not be impugned. Now, according to him, Mt. was the first to write, he wrote for Jewish Christians, and he wrote in Hebrew (in Eusebius, *Ecclesiastical History*, VI, 25 and 32). Since the Gospel of Mt. as we have it, does not seem to be a translation, but appears to have been composed in Greek upon the basis of an earlier text translated from Aramaic, there is notting in itself against the belief that the author also employed the Gospel of Mk. for his redaction and depends upon it in a literary way, although a dependence of this nature does not harmonize very easily with the personal note which characterizes Matthew's narrative.

Regarding the existence and utilization of this common source, called Q, by Mt. and Lk., however well-founded the supposition may be, several reasons invite prudence when it comes to determining its nature. Examination of the many attempts at reconstruction of this document indicates that it would have to embrace, in addition to discourses, quite extensive narrative elements. How could it be imagined, in fact, that a little book of missionary propaganda, composed during the first Christian generation, would contain nothing or almost nothing on essential episodes in the life of Jesus? Granted that it should be regarded only as a little manual, yet, even under this form, a skeleton or framework of facts would be needed for the discourses and sayings of Christ.

Moreover, of the collection of sayings arranged by Mt., we know only what Papias said of it around 125-130, referring to the remarks of a " presbyter " as his source. The old Phrygian bishop has not defined the content of the collection in any specific way, and it is precisely on this point that difficulty arises. He himself had composed a work entitled " Explanations of the Logia of the Lord ". It is quite tempting to see in this work a commentary on the Gospel of Mt., translated from the Aramaic into Greek. But such a view is purely conjectural, and the whole problem remains unsolved. In any case, Eusebius who had the work of Papias before him and recommended that it be read by those desiring information on the question, does not appear to have had a suspicion that the Gospel of Mt. consisted ,for Papias, of a simple collection of discourses or " oracles " of Jesus (see above, pp. 390-392).

To sum up, the theory of the *Two Sources* remains an hypothesis, and let us even say, an excellent *working hypothesis;* but is it only an hypothesis, and should not impose itself *de plano* in the name of literary criticism. This conclusion, which is justified by the observations made *supra*, shows the cogency of the directives given in respect to this matter by the Pontifical Biblical Commission (Decisions of June 19, 1911, and June 26, 1912) [1].

---

[1] For the text of these decisions, see pp. 763-768, *infra.*

As regards the *Synoptic Question*, these official documents require that the following position be taken in teaching : 1. The chronological order of composition of the Gospels is the following : Mt. in Aramaic, Mk., Lk. 2. There is " substantial identity " [1] between the Aramaic Gospel of Mt. and its Greek translation. 3. Catholic exegetes are free to accept one or other of the following hypotheses : oral tradition, written tradition, mutual dependence. 4. They may not adopt lightly nor defend *freely* the hypothesis known as that of the Two Sources.

Manifestly the Biblical Commission wished to remind Catholic exegetes that the traditional data must not be lost sight of or neglected in the search for a solution to the Synoptic Problem. These data really possess the character of historical facts, and, as such, they command the attention of the critic.

In keeping with these directives, several Catholic exegetes have applied themselves in recent years to the solution of the problem : in particular, J. SICKENBERGER *(Biblische Zeitschrift,* 1933; *Kurzgefasste Einleitung in das N.T.,* 2nd ed., 1939), A. WIKENHAUSER *(Römische Quartalschrift,* 1931; *Lexikon für Theologie und Kirche,* IX, 1937; *Einleitung in das N. T.,* 1953), L. CERFAUX (several articles in *Ephemerides theologicæ Lovanienses,* 12 [1935]; 15 [1938]; 27 [1951]; 28 [1952]), and L. VAGANAY *(ibid.,* 28 [1952]). All have tried to open a new way in their attack on the problem. No definitive results, however, have yet been attained through these learned and patient studies [2]. The comparison of texts, which has been made with increasing thoroughness and penetration, is helping to clarify numerous points of detail; but it does not seem that,

---

[1] The expression ought to be understood in the currently accepted sense, when there is question of comparing two texts or two documents. In the present case this *substantial identity* continues to exist even if the original work has been pretty thoroughly recast as regards form or presentation. What guarantees the substantial identity of two literary works is the preservation of basic elements, of essential and characteristic subject matter. Several books of the Old Testament furnish instructive examples in this respect. If the Hebrew text and the Greek text — substantially identical — of Jeremias, Job, Proverbs, and Esther are compared, a very concrete idea may be obtained of what is to be understood by " substantial identity ".

[2] The author of the present study did not learn of the new work by L. VAGANAY, *Le problème synopte* (Paris, 1954) in time to make use of it *supra.* See especially 443-449 of this book for pertinent views on the present and future of the Synoptic Problem.

up to the present, a really satisfactory explanation has yet been found for the Synoptic Fact as envisaged in its genesis, in its development, and in its literary aspects.

3. — Conclusions.

Let it suffice now to indicate in summary fashion what appears to be certain and to note what is merely probable.

1.   The Synoptics are not a material transcription of the oral tradition.   Without doubt, they reproduce the principal elements of the apostolic catechesis, but the redactors of the Gospels had recourse to other sources of information, some oral, and some written.

2.   The hypothesis of a single written source, of a Proto-Gospel from which the Synoptics might have come directly, does not account for the connections that exist among the three narratives.

3.   The hypothesis of mutual dependence does not suffice to explain all the problems which are raised by a comparison of the texts, whatever may be the sequence adopted for the order of composition of the Synoptics.

4.   The Gospel of Mt., under its Greek form, was very probably — with certainty, according to the majority of critics — composed in that language, and consequently, is not a direct translation of an Aramaic original.

5.   We cannot question the literary dependence of Mt. and Lk. in relation to Mk., and Mk. must be regarded as the oldest of our Gospels in the Greek language.

6.   It is hardly probable that Lk. is in direct literary dependence on Mt.; the differences are too marked both as regards facts (narratives of the infancy, ministry outside Galilee, apparitions of the Risen Christ) and as regards discourses (Sermon on the Mount, parables).

7.   It is probable that Mt. and Lk. employed, especially, for the discourses, documents very similar in content, namely, different recensions of a collection written in Aramaic but available for a long time in a Greek translation — this explains the relationship of the Third Gospel with the First in the case

of the discourses and sayings of Jesus. In composing his work, Mt. kept closer to the tenor and style of this source than Lk. Lk., on the other hand, has preserved better the general arrangement and order.

8. This collection of discourses can be identified with that mentioned by Papias when he refers to the statements of John the Presbyter and adds that it had been translated from Aramic into Greek to meet the needs of preaching. It is quite probable that one of these translations served as a basic document for Mt. when he wrote the first of our Gospels, with the account of Mk. serving him as a complementary source for his own narratives.

9. Luke certainly made use of personal information, which he drew either from oral tradition or from written sources.

10. The following diagram indicates connections and relationships.

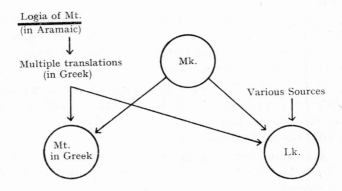

BIBLIOGRAPHY

I. *Literary Genres of the Old Testament.*

Catholic works : D. Buzy, *Les symboles de l'Ancien Testament* (Paris, 1923). — A. Durand, " Critique biblique ", *DAFC*, I (Paris, 1925), 760-804. — H. Höpfl, " Critique biblique ", *DBV*, *Suppl.* II (Paris, 1934), 202-212. — A. Bea, *De Scripturae sacrae inspiratione. Quaestiones historicae et dogmaticae* (3rd ed., Rome, 1935), Nos. 87-94; ID., *Questioni bibliche alla luce dell'Enciclica " Divino Afflante Spiritu "* (2 vols., *ibid.*, 1949-1950). — A. Robert, " Littéraires (Genres) ", *DBV*, *Suppl.* V (1957), 405-421. — C. Hauret, *Origines de l'univers et de l'homme* (Gen., *1-3*) (3rd ed., Paris, 1952). — A. Clamer, *Génèse* (*La Sainte Bible*, I, Paris, 1953).

H. CAZELLES, " Loi israélite ", *DBV*, *Suppl.* V (1957), 497-530. — E. TOBAC, *Les prophètes d'Israël*, I (Lierre, 1919), pp. 43-54, and 145-151 [first part of Vol. I published in a new ed. revised by J. Coppens, Malines, 1932]. — J. COPPENS, " Les particularités du style prophétique ", *Nouvelle Revue Théologique* (1932), 673-693. — A. ROBERT, " Historique (Genre) dans l'Ancien Testament ", *DBV*, *Suppl.* IV (1949), 7-23. — M. J. LAGRANGE, " La parabole en dehors de l'Evangile ", *RB* (1909), 198-212, and 342-367; ID., " Les prophéties messianiques de Daniel ", *ibid.* (1904), 494-520; ID., " Les prophéties des soixante-dix semaines de Daniel ", *ibid.* (1930), 179-198. — J. B. FREY, " Apocalyptique ", *DBV*, *Suppl.* I (1928), 326-354.

Non-Catholic works : O. EISSFELDT, *Der Maschal im A. T.* (Giessen, 1913). — H. GUNKEL, *Genesis* (*Götting. Handbuch zum A. T.*, I, 5th ed., Göttingen, 1922). — H. GUNKEL and J. BEGRICH, *Einleitung in die Psalmen* (Göttingen, 1933). — G. VON RAD, *Das Geschichtsbild des chronistischen Werkes* (Stuttgart, 1920). — A. BENTZEN, *Introduction to the Old Testament* (2nd ed., Copenhagen and London, 1952). — J. HEMPL, *Die althebräische Literatur und ihr hellenistisch-jüdisches Nachleben* (Wildpark-Postdam, 1930). — I. ENGNELL, *Gamla Testamentet : en traditions-historisk Inledning*, I (Stockholm, 1945), especially 39-108 (on the literary genres)].

II. *Literary Genres of the New Testament.*

The Gospels. — M. J. LAGRANGE's *Introductions* to his four great commentaries on the Gospels. — A. DURAND, *op. cit.*, *supra.* — M. JOUSSE, *Le style oral et mnémotechnique chez les Verbo-moteurs. Etude de psychologie linguistique* (Paris, 1925). — L. DE GRANDMAISON, *Jésus-Christ.* I (Paris, 1928), 38-56 [English trans., I, New York, 1934, 39-56]. — F. M. BRAUN, *Où en est le problème de Jésus* (Paris and Brussels, 1932), pp. 215-265; ID., " *Formgeschichte* (Ecole de la) ", *DBV*, *Suppl.* III (1938), 312-317 (with copious bibliography). — L. VENARD, " Historique (Genre) dans le Nouveau Testament ", *ibid.*. IV (1949), 23-32.

On the application of the Method of Form Criticism to the Synoptics see : M. DIBELIUS, *Die Formgeschichte des Evangeliums* (1st ed., Tübingen, 1919; 2nd ed., 1933). — K. L. SCHMIDT, *Der Rahmen der Geschichte Jesu. Literarkritische Untersuchungen zur ältesten Jesusüberlieferung* (Berlin, 1919); ID., " Fondement, but et limites de la méthode de la Formgeschichte appliquée aux Evangiles ", *Revue d'histoire et de phil. rel.*, 18 (1938), 3-26. — R. BULTMANN, *Die Geschichte der synoptischen Tradition* (1st ed., Göttingen, 1921; 2nd ed., 1931). — M. ALBERTZ, *Die synoptischen Streitgespräche. Ein Beitrag zur Formengeschichte des Urchristentums* (Berlin, 1921); ID., *Die Botschaft des N. T.*, I, *Die Entstehung der Botschaft* (Zollikon-Zurich, 1947). — G. BERTRAM, *Die Leidensgeschichte Jesu und der Christuskult. Eine formgeschichtliche Untersuchung* (Göttingen, 1922). [— A. WIKENHAUSER, " Formgeschichte der synoptischen Evangelien ", in his *Einleitung in das N. T.* (Freiburg i. Br., 1956). — L. MC GLINCHY, S. J., *Form Criticism of the Synoptic Healing Narratives* (Woodstock, Md., 1944). S. E. DONLON, S. J., " The Form Critics, the Gospels and Saint Paul ", *CBQ* (1944),

306-325. — P. BENOIT, O. P., " Réflexions sur le Formgeschichtliche Methode ", *RB* (1945), 481-512. — V. TAYLOR, *The Formation of the Gospel Tradition* (London, 1933). — B. S. EASTON, *The Gospel Before the Gospels* (London, 1928). — F. V. FILSON, *Origins of the Gospels* (New York, 1938). — A. RICHARDSON, *The Gospels in the Mcking* (London, 1938); ID., *The Miracle Stories of the Gospels* (London, 1941). — E. B. REDLICH, *Form Criticism : Its Value and Its Limitations* (London, 1939). — H. D. MAYOR, T. W. MANSON, and C. J. WRIGHT, *The Mission and Message of Jesus : An Exposition of the Gospels in the Light of Modern Research* (New York, 1938)].

The Acts of the Apostles. — A. WIKENHAUSER, *Die Apostelgeschichte und ihr Geschichtswert* (Münster i. W., 1921). — F. J. F. JACKSON and K. LAKE, *The Beginnings of Christianity.* Part I, *The Acts of the Apostles : Prolegomena* II, *Criticism* (London, 1922). — L. PIROT, " Actes des apôtres ", *DBV, Suppl.* I (1928), 42-86. — E. JACQUIER, *Les Actes des apôtres* (Paris, 1926). — J. JEREMIAS, " Untersuchungen zum Quellenproblem der Apostelgeschichte ", *Zeitschrift für die Ntl. Wissenschaft* (1937), 205-221.

The Epistles. — P. WENDLAND, " Die urchristlichen Literaturformen ", in his *Die hellenistisch-römischen Kultur in ihren Beziehungen zu Judentum und Christentum* (2nd and 3rd ed., Tübingen, 1912), 342 ff. — A. DEISS-MANN, *Licht vom Osten* (4th ed., *ibid.*, 1923). — F. PRAT, *La théologie de saint Paul* (11th ed., Paris. 1925; English trans., 1926). — J. A. ESCHLI-MANN, " La rédaction des épîtres pauliniennes ", *RB* (1946), 185-196. — C. SPICQ, *Saint Paul. Les épîtres pastorales* (Paris, 1947); ID., *L'épître aux Hébreux*, I (*ibid.*, 1952). — J. CHAINE, *Les épîtres catholiques* (*ibid.*, 1939),

The Apocalypse. E. B. ALLO, *Saint Jean. L'Apocalypse* (3rd., Paris. 1933). — M. E. BOISMARD, *L'Apocalypse* (*ibid.*, 1950). — J. BONSIRVEN, *L'Apocalypse* (*ibid.*, 1951).

III. *The Synoptic Question.*

Synopses.   A. WRIGHT, *Synopsis of the Gospels in Greek* (London, 1903). — W. LARFELD, *Griechische Synopse der vier neutestamentlichen Evangelien* (Tübingen, 1911). — E. D. BURTON and E. J. GOODSPEED, *A Harmony of the Synoptic Gospels in Greek* (Chicago, 1920). — M. J. LAGRANGE, and C. LAVER-GNE, *Synopsis evangelica graeca* (Barcelona and Paris, 1926). — A. HUCK and H. LIETZMANN, *Synopse der drei ersten Evangelien* (9th ed., Tübingen, 1936). — [W. G. RUSHBROOKE, *Synopticon.   An Exposition of the Common Matter of the Synoptic Gospels* (London, 1880; in great detail). — A. WRIGHT, *The Gospel According to Saint Luke in Greek* (London, 1900. — A. CAMER-LYNCK, *Evangeliorum secundum Matthaeum, Marcum et Lucam Synopsis* (Bruges, 1921). — P. VANNUTELLI, *Evangelia synoptice secundum Graecum textum disposita* (Turin, 1935). — X. LÉON-DUFOUR, S. J., *Concordance of the Synoptic Gospels in Seven Colors* (English trans. by R. J. O'Connell, S. J., Tournai, 1957)].

Special Studies. — M. J. LAGRANGE'S, *Introductions to* his commentaries. (*Evangile selon Saint Matthieu*, 4th ed.; *Evangile selon Saint Marc*, 5th ed.;

Evangile selon Saint Luc, 4th ed.). — E. MANGENOT, *Les Evangiles Synoptiques* (Paris, 1911). — L. DE GRANDMAISON, *Jésus-Christ,* I (Paris, 1928), 91-118 [English trans. I New York, 1934), 91-124]. — P. WERNLE, *Die synoptische Frage* (Freiburg i. Br., 1899). — A. VON HARNACK, *Sprüche und Reden Jesu,* in *Beiträge zur Einleitung in das Neue Testament* (Leipzig, 1907). — J. HAWKINS, *Horae synopticae* (2nd ed., Oxford, 1909). — W. H. STANTON, *The Gospels as Historical Documents* (Cambridge, 1903-1909). — W. SANDAY, *Studies in the Synoptic Problem by Members of the University of Oxford* (Oxford, 1911). — J. MOFFATT, *An Introduction to the Literature of the New Testament* (3rd ed., Edinburgh, 1920), pp. 117-211. — B. H. STREETER, *The Four Gospels* (London, 1924). — P. BENOIT, *L'Evangile selon Saint Matthieu* (*Bible de Jérusalem,* Paris, 1950). — P. VANNUTELLI, *Quaestiones de synopticis Evangeliis* (Rome, 1933). — L. G. Da FONSECA, *Quaestio synoptica* (3rd ed., Rome, 1952). — L. VAGANAY, " L'absence du Sermon sur la montagne chez Marc " *RB* (1951), 5-46; ID., *Le problème synoptique* (Tournai and Paris, 1954; with copious, select bibliography; [cf. also the excellent review of this work by D. M. STANLEY, S. J., *CBQ* (1955), 647-655. — B. C. BUTLER, *The Originality of Saint Matthew* (Cambridge, 1951); ID., " The Synoptic Problem ", in DOM B. ORCHARD, *et al.,* *A Catholic Commentary on Holy Scripture* (London and New York, 1953), pp. 760-764. — A. WIKENHAUSER, *Einleitung in das N. T.* (Freiburg i. Br., 1956), pp. 162-182 (with good bibliography). — J. SCHMID, *Das Evangelium nach Matthäus* (3rd ed., Regensburg, 1950; cf. *RB* (1957), 434-436. — P. PARKER, *The Gospel before Mark* (Chicago, 1953). — J. LEVIE, S. J., " L'Evangile araméen de saint Matthieu est-il la source de l'Evangile de saint Marc? " *Nouvelle Revue Théologique,* 76 (1954), 689-715, and 812-843. — C. PERROT, " Chronique Synoptique ", *Cahiers Sioniens* (1955), 124-137. — D. E. NINEHAM, " Eye-Witness Testimony and the Gospel Tradition ", *JTS* (1958), 13-25. — J. SCHMID, *Synopse der drei ersten Evangelien* (2nd ed., Regensburg, 1956. Johannine parallels are included). — J. LEAL, S. J., *Synopsis de los cuatro Evangelios* (Madrid, 1954)].

PART III
THE SACRED DEPOSIT

CHAPTER VII.

THE TRANSMISSION OF THE TEXT

by His Eminence Cardinal E. TISSERANT
and M. J. LAGRANGE

CHAPTER VII.

THE TRANSMISSION OF THE TEXT

I. — HISTORY AND CRITICISM OF THE TEXT OF THE OLD TESTAMENT.

[Cardinal E. TISSERANT].

1. — *HISTORY OF THE HEBREW TEXT* [1].

The Hebrew Mss. of the Old Testament are very numerous. In 1780, Benjamin Kennicott examined personally about 261 and secured collations of selected passages in 349 others. But he was a long way from having made a complete inventory, for Giovanni Bernardo de Rossi boasted two years later that he himself possessed 310 Mss. in his own personal library which were unknown to the English scholar. Since that time, the number of Mss. of the Hebrew Bible has increased tremendously. The Firkovitch collection at Leningrad, made during the second half of the 19th century, alone contains 1582 volumes on parchment and 765 on paper. The opening of the Genizah or depository of discarded Mss. at the Synagogue in Old Cairo in 1896 has furnished us with more than 100 other ancient fragments, preserved today at Oxford, Cambridge, New York (Jewish Theological Seminary), and at Leningrad (the collection of the metropolitan Antoninos).

Actually, this large number of Mss. is of little value [for textual criticism]. The Jews have always tried to maintain

---

Translator's note. — [1 Cf. Sir F. KENYON, *Our Bible and the Ancient Manuscripts*. Revised by A. W. Adams, with an Introduction by G. R. Driver (New York, 1958). E. WÜRTHWEIN, *The Text of the Old Testament*. English trans. by P. R. Ackroyd (Oxford, 1957). B. J. ROBERTS, *The Old Testament Text and Versions* (Cardiff, 1951). D. W. THOMAS, " The Textual Criticism of the Old Testament, " in H. H. ROWLEY, Ed., *The Old Testament and Modern Study* (Oxford, 1951). A. DIEZ MACHO, " Importante hallazgo biblico, " *Estudios Biblicos* (1954), 207-210, and 247-265 (on a new family of Hebrew Mss.); *id.*, " Nuevos manuscritos importantes, biblicos o liturgicos, en hebreo o Arameo, " *Sefarad* (1956), 3-22; *id.*, " Manuscrito Yemeni de la Biblia Babilonica, " *ibid.* (1957), 239-279; *id.*, " Fragmento al Num. en el sistema babilonico, " *ibid.* (1957), 386-388].

their traditions as rigidly as possible and no tradition could be dearer to them than those pertaining to their sacred text. In proof of this may be cited the fact that they still cling to the inconvenient form of the primitive roll. For liturgical purposes, the Jews still use only leather scrolls on which the text has been written by hand without vowel points.

From an early date, however, the absence of vowel signs in the Semitic alphabets troubled readers, and Jewish schools from the early Middle Ages on had to devote themselves to the task of establishing the traditional pronunciation of a sacred text written in a language which had long been dead. To protect the text, generations of Rabbis, accordingly, shared in erecting a " fence or hedge " — the Masora — which comprises an important series of elements : vowel points, diacritical signs indicating precisely the pronunciation of certain consonants, a mark indicating doubling, conjunctive and disjunctive accents, marginal notes furnishing numerous observations concerning the use of rare words and doubtful spellings, innumerable statistics on words and verses, and, finally, treatises in which certain questions of grammar, punctuation, and writing are discussed *ex professo* [1].

Information on the Masoretes is not lacking in Hebrew literature, but it is only during the last forty years that the study of Mss. has made it possible to construct a documented history of their work. Thus the existence of two schools, an Eastern and Western, was discovered from the Masoretic notes, but it was only about 1860 that the study of the Codex Petropolitanus (written in 916), which contains the Prophets, drew attention to the evidence of the Oriental Masora. The examination of fragments belonging to more than 100 different Mss. helped P. Kahle to distinguish two systems of punctuation in usage in the Babylonian schools. The first, and the simpler,

---

Translator's note. — [1 Cf. the saying in *Pirke Abot* (I, 1) : " Moses received the Torah (Law) on Sinai, and handed it down *(mesārāh)* to Josue; Josue to the Elders; the Elders to the Prophets; the Prophets handed it down *(mesārūhā)* to the men of the Great Synagogue. These said three things : be careful in judgment; raise up many disciples; *make a fence* (or hedge : *seyāg) to the Torah* ". In this text, the reference is, of course, not to devices to safeguard the proper pronunciation and therefore the meaning of the text, but to additional rules destined to secure the better observance of the prescriptions of the Law. The expression could be extended naturally to the various means taken later to protect the Biblical text].

is based on an imitation of that employed by the Eastern Syrians, while the second, which is much more complex, was developed toward the end of the eighth century and during the course of the ninth. The system of punctuation is not, however, a guarantee of the nature of the text, since some Mss. copied in Yemen with the later Babylonian punctuation exhibit regularly the Western readings.

In Palestine there were also two systems. The older, with its signs written above the consonants, is quite similar to that found in the Samaritan Mss. Jewish authors have called it the Palestinian punctuation. But in trying to mark in a more precise manner all the shades of pronunciation, the Rabbis of Tiberias introduced a new system toward the end of the eighth century and the beginning of the ninth which has prevailed in the Mss. and has become enshrined through printing. While the earlier systems recorded the traditional pronunciation in an empirical manner, the Masoretes of Tiberias elaborated a complete system based on a grammatical theory. Their work reveals also the influence of the Arab grammarians who, in this same period, were defining the manner of reading the Qoran. The latter in turn were being encouraged by the trends among the Karaites [1], who were giving the Bible text a new import in their religious system.

One family played an important role in this fixation of the smallest details in the sacred text, namely, the family of

Translator's note. — [1 The name, which appears only in the 9th century, is interpreted as meaning " the people of Scripture " *(miqra)* or " Callers " (to a new faith) *(qārā*, to call). The origin of the movement is still obscure. An important early leader was Anan ben David (second half of the 8th century). In the first half of the 10th century Jacob al Kirkisani wrote in Arabic the *Kitāb al anwār wal marāqib* (Book of Lights and Watchtowers). A partial translation of this work was published in the *Hebrew Union College Annual* (Cincinnati, 1930, pp. 317 ff), and the text itself was published by L. NEMOY (New York, 1939). He also wrote the *Kitāb al riyād wal hada'iq* (Book of Gardens and Parks); cf. H. HIRSCHFELD, *Qirqisani Studies* (1918). See M. STEINSCHNEIDER, *Die arabische Literatur der Juden* (Frankfurt a. M., 1902), n. 43, pp. 79-81. In the second half of the 10th century, David ben Abraham al Fasi wrote his famous Hebrew dictionary *(Jāmi al alfāz)*, which has been published in masterly fashion by S. L. SKOSS (2 vols., New Haven, 1936 and 1945). Cf. also M. STEINSCHNEIDER, *op cit.*, n. 47, p. 86. To the same period belongs Yaphet ha-Levi ibn Ali, translator and commentator. Cf. M. STEINSCHNEIDER, *op cit.*, n. 44, pp. 1-84. In the 19th century, Abraham ben Samuel Firkovitch (1785-1874) — mentioned above — collected a large amount of archeological and literary material for which he deserves recognition, although he tampered with the dates in several cases].

Ben Asher, of which five successive generations are known from 800 to about 925. A Ms. of the Prophets, written in 895 by Moses ben Asher IV, is still extant in the Synagogue of the Sefardim of Aleppo, after having been preserved at Jerusalem and at Cairo where it served for a long time as a model for copyists.

Another famous Masorete, and probably of the same period, was Moses ben David ben Nephtali. His peculiarities are often noted in the margin or in special lists, and thus contrasted with the Ms. readings of Aaron ben Asher. It seems that the final success of Ben Asher should be attributed to Maimonides [1]. No known Ms. has preserved completely the work of Ben Nephtali.

Other Mss. also are mentioned in the Masoretic notes, some of which have a history : e.g., the one ascribed to *Hillel*, thought to have been written around 600 and long preserved in Spain, and the so-called Jerusalem Ms., which during the Middle Ages was at Saragosa. The Rabbis, moreover, never stopped adding to the annotations of the original Masoretes. One of the greatest authorities on Masoretic matters, Elias Levita [1468-1549], was the contemporary of Jacob ben Chayim, whose edition with Masoretic notes was published by Bomberg in Venice in 1524-1525, and became the *textus receptus* of the Hebrew Bible.

The text of Jacob ben Chayim served as a basis for all the editions published up to very recent years. The third edition of the Hebrew Bible by Kittel, the text of which has been established by P. Kahle, appeared in parts from 1930 to 1937. It is the first edition which has freed itself from Ben Chayim's influence [2].

Translator's note. — [1 Moses ben Maimon, also called Rambam, born at Cordoba, 1135, died in Egypt, 1204].

Translator's note. — [2 In addition to the general references at the end of this chapter, see the following. : P. Kahle's section on the Masoretic transmission of the Hebrew text of the Bible in BAUER and LEANDER, *Historische Grammatik der hebräischen Sprache des Alten Testaments*, I (Halle a. S., 1918), 71-162; id., *The Cairo Geniza* (London, 1947), 36-116 (on the Hebrew text of the Bible). — Sir FREDERIC KENYON, *Our Bible and Ancient Manuscripts* (New York, 1958), 61-88. — A. BENTZEN, " The Text, " in his *Introduction to the Old Testament*, I (2nd ed., Copenhagen and London, 1952), 42-72. — J. BALESTRI, *Biblicae Introductionis Generalis Elementa* (Rome, 1932), 70-95 and 107-111 (with bibliography). — C. GINSBURG, *Introduction to the Massoretico-Critical Edition of the Hebrew Bible* (London, 1897); id., *A Series of 15 Facsimiles from Manuscript Pages of the Hebrew Bible* (London, 1897). Fine plates of Mss. are also available in P. Kahle, *Masoreten des Ostens*, and *Masoreten des Westens* (Stuttgart, 1913, and 1927-1930)].

2. — *THE SAMARITAN PENTATEUCH* [1].

The Samaritans were a small ethnical group composed of Jews who had belonged to the Kingdom of Israel and of settlers who had moved from Babylonia to Samaria. Although now reduced to a few families, they were once spread over a considerable area with flourishing communities at Damascus and Cairo. The contemporary Samaritans still preserve and follow the Pentateuch in accordance with a tradition which is peculiar to them. Their Mss. are not earlier in date than those of the Masoretic text, as the most ancient seem to have been written in the twelfth century. They are extant under two forms, namely, liturgical rolls and books composed of folded leaves, but there are no completely vocalized texts and there is no Masora.

Since the opposition between the Samaritans and the Jews began, at the latest, in the time of Esdras, it was thought that the Mss. of the Hebrew Pentateuch written in Samaritan letters would be more important than the Mss. written in Hebrew characters. The arrival in Europe of the first Samaritan manuscript, which had been bought at Damascus by Pietro Della Valle in 1616, started a controversy, in which the Oratorian, Jean Morin, a warm supporter of the Samaritan text, was attacked mainly for dogmatic reasons by Protestant authors who did not wish to see the authority of the Hebrew text impaired.

It is generally admitted today that the Samaritan tradition is inferior to that of the Hebrew Masoretic text. The more frequent employment of the *matres lectionis* (the addition of the consonants ',h, y, w* as vocalic signs), the more exact observance of grammatical rules, the disappearance of archaic forms, the substitution of more recent words for older ones, and various syntactical peculiarities show that the Samaritan text — at least in its present form — is later than the text which had been preserved through the work of the Masoretes. Hence,

---

Translator's note. — [1 F. PEREZ CASTRO has announced (in *Sefarad* [1956]) the coming publication of *Sefer Abiša'*, an edition of the sacred Samaritan Scroll of Nablus. S. TALMAN, " The Samaritan Pentateuch, " *Journal of Jewish Studies* (1951), 144-150. Sir F. KENYON, *op. cit.*, 89-94].

there is little to be expected from the written Samaritan Pentateuch.

But we are interested in another matter among the Samaritans of Nablus rather than in their old rolls of the Law, namely, in the manner in which they read them. While their Mss. present little of value for the study of the consonantal text, we might expect that they have preserved better than the Jews certain traditional pronunciations which could suggest new interpretations of this or that group of consonants. At the time of the first Palestinian punctuation, the Samaritans made some feeble attempts at vocalization, but there is nothing more than passing traces of this in non-Biblical Mss. H. Petermann, accordingly, had the whole Book of Genesis read to him and in 1868 he published a transcription of what he had heard. Since the Masoretic punctuation is largely theoretical in character, being based on a tradition without doubt, but influenced also by the punctuation of the Aramaeans among whom the Jews were living, all documents which furnish evidence on punctuation previous to the Masora must be examined. The transcription of H. Petermann deserves to be considered, but no matter how persistent tradition may be, it must not be denied that at Nablus also it may well have suffered certain contaminations [1]

Translator's note. — [1 Cf. H. PETERMANN, Versuch einer hebräischen Formenlehre, in Abhandlungen f. d. Kunde des Morgenlandes, 1 (Leipzig, 1868); outline of grammar according to Samaritan pronunciation, pp. 1-160; text of Genesis in Latin characters according to Sam. pron., 161-218; list of variants between Samaritan and Masoretic texts, 219-326). Petermann published the Pentateuch in the Samaritan characters, Pentateuchus samaritanus ad fidem librorum manuscriptorum: Genesis (Berlin, 1872); Exodus (1882); Leviticus (1883); Numeri (1885); Deuteronomium (1891). — C. HELLER, The Samaritan Text of the Pentateuch (Berlin, 1923). — M. GASTER, Hebrew Illuminated Bibles of the IXth and Xth Centuries (London, 1901; contains a treatment of a Samaritan scroll of the Law of the XIth cent., pp. 23-52, plates VII and VIII. — A. VON GALL, Der hebräische Pentateuch der Samaritaner (Giessen, 1913-1918; in Hebrew characters, with elaborate critical apparatus, and prolegomena, pp. i-xciv). — On the language, cf. J. ROSENBERG, Lehrbuch der samaritanischen Sprache und Literatur (Vienna and Leipzig, 1901). — F. DIENING, Das Hebräische bei den Samaritanern, (Bonner Orientalistische Studien, 24, Stuttgart, 1938). — Sir FREDERIC KENYON, op cit., pp. 88-94. — P. KAHLE, The Cairo Geniza (London, 1947; in Index s. v. Samaritans). Cf. also Z. BEN HAYYIM, The Literary and Oral Tradition of Hebrew and Aramaic amongst the Samaritans (2 vol., Jerusalem, 1957 [in Hebrew]. The author, on the basis of a wealth of material systematically examined, holds that the Samaritan tradition is the remnant, we may say, of a tradition shared also by the Jews at an earlier date. The linguistic data of the Dead Sea Scrolls confirms this view)].

3. — *THE TARGUMS* [1].

The Hebrew language ceased to be the common spoken language of the Jews in the period of the Exile. Respect for tradition, however, preserved the original text of the Sacred Books. Although the gatherings in synagogues were designed for instruction in the Law rather than for the performance of ritual, the Hebrew text was employed for public reading at these meetings. But while the custom of chanting the Psalms in their original tongue was maintained, it soon became evident that, if sections of the Torah were read in Hebrew only, there was danger of failing in the purpose intended. What profit would the listeners derive from a text which they understood only in part? Thence arose the practice of translating verse by verse the lessons which had just been read. The translation was made into Greek in the synagogues of Egypt and into Aramaic in the synagogues of Palestine, Syria, and Mesopotamia. Two members of the community shared these duties : one read and the other translated (*Megilla*, **4**, 4) [2].

Translator's note. — [1 Cf. A. DIEZ MACHO, " Una copia completa del Targum Palestiniense al Pentateuco en la Biblioteca Vaticana, " *Sefarad* (1957), 119-121. — P. KAHLE, " The Targums ", in *Melilah*, University of Manchester, 1950), 70-76. — Sir F. KENYON, *op. cit.*, 94-97].

Translator's note. — [2 The Mishnah Tractate *Megillah* (Scroll, viz., of Esther) is found in the second order or division known as *Mo'ed* towards the end; in some editions, as the last tractate. It deals largely with the writing and public reading of the scroll of Esther, but some other matters such as the reading and the translating of other parts of Scripture have come to find a place in the text of the tractate. Thus, ch. 4 begins with some details regarding the reading of Esther, then takes up the question of Scripture lessons : the number of readers, which varies according to the dignity of the day; matters of public worship in the synagogue; then in nº 4 : " He who reads the Law may not read less than three verses. He may not read more than one verse to the interpreter (Torgman), and in the (case of the) Prophets, three (verses). If the three of them form three (separate) sections (as e. g. in Isa. 52, 3-5, which the Gemara, (commentary), refers to in this case : *Bab. Talmud; Meg.* 24 a), he reads them one by one. One may skip (a passage) in the (lesson from the) Prophets; but one may not skip (a passage) in the (lesson from the) Law. How much may one skip? Only so much that the Interpreter (Torgman) does not have to pause ". Further on in the same chapter, no. 6 notes that a minor may interpret *(methargēm)* the Law; a poorly clad person or a blind man may interpret the Shema prayer; no. 10 mentions some passages of Scripture which are read, but not translated, or are neither read nor translated. For this tractate, see J. RABBINOWITZ, *Mishnah Megillāh* (Oxford, 1931, text and English translation, introduction and commentary). — H. DANBY, *The Mishnah* (Oxford, 1933), pp. 201-207 (English translation with brief notes). This text is used also in the tractate *Soferim* (Scribes) : XI, 1. — See M. HIGGER, *Masseket Soferim* (New York, 1937), p. 217 f., a very elaborate critical edition and commentary (all in Hebrew) which traces the echoes of our text in other early Rabbinic works].

The translator was called *targman* or *torgman*, and the
the translation, *targum*. [1] These translations were at first
improvised, but undoubtedly it was not very long before they
were written out. The translation of the Pentateuch, prepared
for the use of the Alexandrian synagogues, was the nucleus
about which the Greek Bible developed.

[The Aramaic Targums were slower in taking form, and for
some few Books (Daniel, Esdras, Nehemias) they do not exist
at all. The Targum to Proverbs is essentially the Syriac
Peshitta rendering of the Book transposed into the Jewish
square-letter script, and hence it is of no independent value.

The earliest written Targum of which Jewish tradition preserves a specific memory is that for Job, which was repudiated
and immured in a wall by Rabban Gamaliel I, the teacher of
St. Paul. Parts of a first century scroll of what must be this
same Targum were found in 1956 in the region of the Dead Sea
cliffs south of Jericho (Khirbet Qumran area, Cave 11). The
Qumran discoveries have also yielded bits of a Targum of
Leviticus (from Cave 4 : before A.D. 68).

In general, Targums are of two sorts. There are fulsome,
paraphrastic Targums with instances of double renderings and
variant readings for their Hebrew original, with application
of the text to later conditions, with narrative and other expansions, with reworkings of the text in the light of parallel passages
in the same or other Biblical books; these are usually associated
with Palestine. Then there are Targums much more exactly
fitted to the Masoretic text as we know it, to the point of being
labored and stiff in their language, standardized, and in some
sense official; these derive, in their present form, from Babylonia.
The names of Onkelos and of Jonathan (ben Uzziel) which are
attached to the best known of these latter are a literary fiction,
based on the Hebraizing of the names of Aquila and Theodotion,
the well-known figures in the history of Bible translation
into Greek. These names do, however, serve rather aptly to
suggest special characteristics of the renderings to which they
are applied. The Palestinian Targums (which survive sometimes

---

Translator's note. — [1 From Aramaic *targēm*, to interpret. This word of
Assyrian origin has passed also into Arabic].

N. B. Msgr. P. W. Skehan has added the new material on the identity of
Onkelos and Jonathan with Aquila and Theodotion respectively].

only piecemeal in citations of their longer narrative expansions embedded in copies of the more literal Babylonian renderings) are clearly the older type, though the fluid state of their text at all periods left room for the introduction of later material. The *Targum of Onkelos* on the Pentateuch, and that of Jonathan on the Prophets (including Josue-Kings as well as the " writing Prophets ", Isaias, etc.), are documents of the fifth century and later, as we have them. Their standardized form is to be explained by a progressive desire for exactness in reflecting the texts read publicly in the synagogue. No definitive text of the Targum to the " Writings, " the third and last part of the Jewish canon, seems ever to have been established. One of the most surprising discoveries of recent years has been that of a complete copy of a Jerusalem (i.e., Palestinian) Targum to the Pentateuch, in the *Codex Neofiti 1*, now in the Vatican library; this is being prepared for publication by A. Diez Macho].

The Syriac version of the Old Testament originated from a very early Targum. Thus there was in the beginning a close relationship between the Biblical text of the Aramaic-speaking Christians at Edessa and Nisibis and the one which the Syrian and Mesopotamian Jews of the Diaspora heard at their meetings on the Sabbath [1]. For the Pentateuch, the Samaritans also have an Aramaic Targum in their own script, with a text that varies notably from one copy to the next.

Translator's note. — [1 For the Targums, cf. J. BALESTRI, *op. cit.*, pp. 163-166. — A. BENTZEN, *op. cit.*, I, 68-72. — A. MERX, *Chrestomathia Targumica* (Berlin, 1888). — P. KAHLE, *The Cairo Geniza*, pp. 117-132. — J. F. STENNING, *The Targum of Isaiah* (Oxford, 1949; with introduction, Engl. trans., and variants). The text of the Targums is contained in the following works. On the *Law* : Targum *Onkelos*, e.g. in " Rabbinic Bibles ", as Buxtorf, *Biblia Rabbinica* (Basle, 1619); *London Polyglott*, ed. B. Walton (1654-1657). — A. E. SILVERSTONE, *Aquila and Onkelos* (Manchester, 1931). Other Targums : *London Polyglott* (see above). — M. GINSBURGER, *Fragmenten-Targamim* (Berlin, 1899); *id.*, *Pseudo-Jonathan* (1903). — C. HELLER, *A Critical Essay on the Palestinian Targum to the Pentateuch* (New York, 1921). On the *Prophets* : Targum *Jonathan*, in the *Biblia Rabbinica* and *London Polyglott*. — P. DE LAGARDE, *Prophetae Chaldaice* (Leipzig, 1872). — F. PRAETORIUS, *Das Targam zu Josua in jementischer Überlieferung* (Berlin, 1899); *id.*, *Das Targam zum Buch der Richter in jementischen Überlieferung* (Berlin, 1900). On the *Writings* : P. DE LAGARDE, *Hagiographa Chaldaice* (Leipzig, 1873); PINKHOS CHURGIN, *The Targum to the Hagiographa*, (New York, 1945, in Hebrew). There are many editions also of the text of the Targums to different parts of the Bible, and also special lexicons and studies dealing with the Targums. See, e. g., H. FUCHS, " Targum ", in the *Universal Jewish Encyclopedia*, vol. 10 (New York, 1943), 173-175. A. SPERBER, *The Bible in Aramaic*. I (Leiden, 1959; to he completed in 4 vols). For English translations of certain Targums, see J. W. Etheridge, *Targum Onkelos and Jonathan... on the Pentateuch, etc.* (2 vols., London, 1862 and 1865).

4. — *CRITICISM OF THE TEXT OF THE OLD TESTAMENT.*

To reconstitute the original text of the Old Testament
critics have at their disposal not only Hebrew or Samaritan
Mss. and Targums, but also several ancient versions. Among
the versions, some are primary, as the Greek, Syriac, and Latin
Vulgate, while others are secondary, as the Old Latin, Coptic,
the Syriac Hexaplar, Ethiopic, Georgian, and Arabic.   The
Hebrew Mss. bear witness to the state of the texts at the
time at which they were written.   The versions, in so far as
their original form can be reconstituted, have a maximum
value, at most, for the respective Mss. from which they have
been made.

Three elements have contributed to change the texts : the
negligence or ignorance of copyists and the boldness of revisers.
The first two factors operate in all links in the transmission,
but the third in a restricted number only.   The Hebrew Mss.
were at first subject to the ordinary variations which occur in
the process of the transmission of texts.   Thus is to be explained
the divergences present in the text underlying the Septuagint
translation.   The large roll of Isaias found at Qumran, as P. Vaccari observed, bears witness to this progressive decline in the
accuracy of the texts.   Ir is to be placed in general between
the Septuagint and the Masoretic Text.   It exhibits a number
of readings proper to itself, some of which, while not in agreement
with the Greek, deserve to be considered as original.   Apparently between 70 and 130, perhaps owing to the loss of a
large number of Mss., an effort was made to fix the text.   The
fragments found in the caves of Murabba'at exhibit generally
the readings of the Masoretic text.

The Hebrew Mss. have varied extremely little from the
ninth century to the discovery of printing.   The fact may be
verified by a check of the variants in the edition with the
fullest apparatus, that of Christian D. Ginsburg, with its text
of the Pentateuch based on the collation of about 70 Mss.
It is often necessary to read several pages to find a reading
substantially different from that received in the text.   This is
because the collation of Aaron ben Ašer prevailed rapidly
in the Western rabbinical schools, and gradually in the Eastern
schools themselves.

The *textus receptus* of the Hebrew Old Testament, the Rabbinical Bible of Jacob ben Chayim, like that of the New Testament established by Robert Estienne (Stephanus) in 1550, is eclectic; i.e., Jacob ben Chayim selected his variants from the numerous Mss. which he had at his disposal, and, at the same time, he tried to bring his text into harmony with the data contained in the Masoretic notes furnished by these same. Mss. The preparation of this text demanded enormous labor, and the task was done well. But no historical work was then available which could furnish the editor a scientific basis for his choice of variants.

The collectors of variants, Kennicott, De Rossi, and Ginsburg, in spite of the extent of their collations did not dare attempt a classification of manuscripts. Although Ginsburg, in his two editions of 1894 and of 1908-1911, recognized the importance of several ancient Mss. (9th to 11th century), he limited his efforts to a meticulously exact reproduction of the text of 1525.

If Kahle has been able to attempt the introduction of a new text, he has done so on the basis of some thirty years of study which he devoted to the thorough historical investigation of the ancient Mss., even in the most minute details. The text which he has published in the third edition of Kittel's Bible is that of Aaron ben Asher, not according to the autograph, however, which is too jealously guarded by the authorities of the Sephardic Synagogue at Aleppo, but according to a copy made in 1008 and preserved in Leningrad under the shelfmark B 19 A. Now that this edition is complete, Biblical scholars have at their disposal the text, with its Masora, which the Masoretes of Tiberias read toward the end of the tenth century.

In the notes of this edition, we find the consonantal variants of the Mss. which Paul Kahle had studied in his works on the Eastern and Western Masoretes. The seventh edition, which appeared in 1951, contains in addition, the variants of two Mss. found at Qumran, the Isaias Scroll and the Commentary on Habacuc. The variants of these Mss. and those of the other fragments discovered at Qumran and Murabba'at will undoubtedly open up new horizons to Biblical scholars. But for the greater portion of the Sacred Text, it will still be necessary to be satisfied with the material furnished by the Mss. previously known. The question may be raised whether these fragmentary or complete Mss., coming as they do from the mediaeval period, will permit us to attain to a knowledge of the text at an earlier date.

What information can be drawn from the Masoretic notes for determining the state of the text in Mss. earlier than that in which they appear? When, for example, a note indicates for a word that there is a *qerē* and a *ketīb*, it is a sign that scribes continued to copy traditionally in the Mss. a word or *qerē* which has been corrected in another [1]. It is for critics to determine the value of the discarded reading. Certain variants put under the heading *Sevīrīn* belong, it seems, to the *qerē* type. They have gone out of use, but are attested for an earlier pesiod. The lists of divergences between the Easterners and Westerners, i.e., between the Schools of Babylonia and Palestine, give variants whose quality is not judged by the Masoretes, and the same is true of those given as preferred by Ben Asher and Ben Nephtali. Through these last variants, we arrive at the Ms. which Kahle proposes to us as the archetype. From the later Mss. there is probably something to be gleaned, but very little. Unfortunately, the majority of variants contained under all these rubrics are almost always concerned with vowel points, accents, and, at most, with the presence or absence of mute consonants or *matres lectionis*, which are used to indicate the presence of certain vowels.

Hence, for reconstituting the form of the text as it existed before the tenth century the study of Mss. furnishes very little. It is necessary to have recourse to the indirect testimony of the Targums and the versions. The differences between the Targums and the Hebrew of our Mss. are explained in part by the the differences which may have existed between the Mss. upon which the Targums were prepared and the much later Mss. which we now possess. But the authors of the Targums, even when there is a question of a Targum as literal as that of Onkelos, did not always try to make a perfect reproduction. They had religious scruples and modified certain

---

Translator's note. — [1 *Ketīb*, the word as *written* in the text itself; *qerē* the word which the Masoretic note directs *to be read* instead; *sebir* the word which is *conjectured* to represent the correct text instead of the actual reading which is regarded by the Masoretes as due to a mistake of the copyists. Cf. R. GORDIS, *The Biblical Text in the Making. A Study of Kethīb-Qerē* (Philadelphia, 1937)].

formulas. Furthermore, they permitted themselves to be influenced by the pronunciation of Aramaic which they habitually spoke, and, as a result, they mistook certain grammatical forms. Finally, it is important to remember that the archetype of the best Targum is a witness only for the text in general use in the place where it was made, and at a given time, namely, in Babylonia or Palestine in the first and second centuries of our era.

The study of the Greek Targum, i.e., of the Alexandrian version, or the Septuagint, carries us back to the last centuries B. C. The work of translation undoubtedly continued for some generations, beginning about 300 years before Christ, but we have not yet found a Ms. of the Greek Old Testament earlier than our era nor have we even yet been able to assign any piece among the numerous Biblical fragments on papyrus to a date before Origen. That great scholar had set out to compare and reconcile the Hebrew and Greek texts which were circulating in his time. In reducing their differences he lessened our possibilities of investigation.

On the other hand, he tried to preserve, in the first column of his Hexapla, a document of capital interest, namely, the transliteration of the Hebrew text in Greek characters. This transliteration must have been made in the heyday of the Alexandrian Jewry to enable those who were acquainted only with the Greek alphabet to read the sacred text, nevertheless, in its authentic form. The great work of Origen is almost completely lost, but the text of some Psalms found by Cardinal Giovanni Mercati in 1896 in a palimpsest in the Ambrosian Library has permitted F. Wutz and others in recent years to examine in a new light the manner in which the Hebrew text was transliterated. As the majority of the errors arise from confusions between letters which are similar, it is obvious how interesting it would be if we had two parallel lines in the transmission of the same text — one in Hebrew characters, and the other in Greek letters.

The study of the transliterations in the Greek Bible and in the Latin Vulgate show what confusions arose most easily, and furnishes certain principles which ought to reduce the role of the imagination in our attempts at reconstructing the original text. The consonantal Hebrew text in the period of Saint Jerome was already that which is contained in our Mss., but this text was far from being fixed when the Greek version was made. There is an interval of seven centuries between the beginnings of the Greek Targum under Ptolemy Philadelphus and the Latin translation made by the secretary of Pope Damasus. During this long period the Hebrew text was exposed to a twofold influence : on the one hand, to the deterioration common to all frequently copied texts which is caused by the continual introduction of new readings, and on the other, to the efforts of the Rabbis to restore unity among divergent texts, a process which was not kept within the limits of a return to the original readings.

The Septuagint Version is of capital importance, since [until recently] it has been our sole witness for the state of the text before the Christian era. But even if we were able to find it in its original form, would it give us the Hebrew text of the second and third centuries before the Christian era? Not perfectly, for the translators were not all of equal skill, and poor translators distort a text in their attempt to translate it. The various books of the Old Testament have been treated differently by different translators. We must recognize this clearly and not imagine a Hebrew text different from ours when we find some paraphrase from the pen of a translator who simply did not know how to translate a text closely. A concordance of the Septuagint makes it possible to see how many Hebrew words correspond to each Greek word, and it is an indispensable tool for the scholar who wishes to go back to the Hebrew through the Greek.

On the other hand, it appears that the Alexandrian Jews in making their translation employed Mss. in which the writing was in a transitional stage, the passage from the archaic alphabet to the square alphabet not having yet been completed. Moreover, these manuscripts exhibited the *scriptio continua*, i.e., words were not separated from one another either by regular spaces or by points or vertical lines, and the special final forms for *k, m, n, p, s*, did not yet exist. Hence the diversity between the Septuagint and the Masoretic Hebrew in the manner of grouping letters to form words.

Friedrich Delitzsch published a collection, with examples, of the errors which were responsible for producing new readings in the transmission of the Biblical text : wrong attachment of a letter to the end of the preceding word or to the beginning of the following word; wrong combining of words — two in one, three in two, or three in one; wrong divisions — one word divided into two, or two words into three; haplography, which causes the loss of the last letter or the first letter of a word; diverse interpretations resulting from the irregular spelling of the *matres lectionis;* repetitions; omissions through homoioteleuton; confusion of letters due to similarities in form or pronunciation; inclusion in the text of marginal notes.

Those who wish to work efficaciously in the field of Old Testament textual criticism must have a thorough and systematic knowledge of all these accidents, i.e., of paleography (the primitive alphabet and the square alphabet), and of the mechanism of the Greek and Latin transcriptions. The attempts to reconstruct the original text will have value only in so far as they are established on such positive foundations [1].

Translator's note. — [1 The Biblical texts found among the Dead Sea Mss. are proving to be of the greatest value for the history of the Hebrew text (see the special section on the Dead Sea Scrolls, *supra*, pp. 113-123). In general, the text of the books or fragments found in the caves agrees with the Masoretic text, which is thus shown to represent an ancient line of the transmission of the text, as had indeed been long maintained. But the new finds prove also that there was another line, namely the forms of the Hebrew text agreeing with the Septuagint, which thus appears to have followed a Hebrew tradition different from the Masoretic, e.g., in the Books of Samuel. We have, therefore, new evidence which must be taken into account in textual criticism. (Cf. W. F. ALBRIGHT, " New Light on the Early Recensions... ", *BASOR*, No. 139 [1955], 27-33; cf. *Sefarad* [1956], 447 ff.; P. W. SKEHAN, in *CBQ* [1957], 435-440). The new evidence, however, will not suffice to settle all textual problems. In the absence of much older evidence which could bring us closer to the original form, we must continue to rely upon the method outlined *supra* in the text. The comparison with the other Semitic languages may also help in a number of instances to restore to Hebrew words meanings which had become lost in the later period. We can thus retain the traditional text while giving it a new and more suitable meaning. Among the authors who have followed this method (it is not entirely new, for it was already applied by critics of the 18th and 19th centuries, but with more limited means at their disposal) may be mentioned : F. WUTZ, P. JOÜON, G. R. DRIVER, D. W. THOMAS, I. EITAN. An example of this method will be found, e.g., in the new Roman translation of the Psalms (Ps. **16 (17)** : 4 b). Cf. E. P. ARBEZ, in *American Eccl. Review*, July, 1945, 21 ff. Cf. also W. F. ALBRIGHT, " The Old Testament and the Canaanite Language and Literature ", *CBQ* (1945), 5-31. On the textual criticism of the Old Testament in general, see e.g., the following studies. — J. COPPENS, " La critique du texte Hébreu ", *Biblica* (1944), 9-49. — E. P. ARBEZ, " Translating the Old Testament out of the Original Languages ", *CBQ* (1945), 48-75. — J. KENNEDY, *An Aid to the Textual Amendment of the Old Testament*, (Edinburgh, 1928) ; F. PERLES, *Analekten zur Textkritik des Alten Testaments*, (Münster i. W., 1895); id., *Analekten...*

II. — THE TEXTUAL CRITICISM OF THE NEW TESTAMENT.

It is not the purpose of this simple sketch to furnish arguments, nor to reproduce the technical rules and procedures for preparing a list of Ms. [1]. We intend only to indicate here the results of a rather prolonged study, and applying specifically to the New Testament. The choice between different readings, which is the whole aim of textual criticism, will depend on the history of the witnesses.

1. — HISTORY OF THE TEXT AND OF THE VERSIONS.

The writings of the New Testament were composed in Greek. Although Saint Matthew wrote in Aramaic, the Church possesses his Gospel only in a Greek translation which has the authority of an original. It is the Greek text, then, which textual criticism must establish in as close conformity as possible to the redaction of its authors. The versions can, in certain cases, however, represent an older text than that of all the Greek Mss., and, therefore, must be studied also.

We shall first consider the Gospels, and then, more briefly, the other books.

Neue Folge, (Leipzig, 1922). — M. SCOTT, *Textual Discoveries in Proverbs, Psalms and Isaiah*, (SPCK, London), — S. R. DRIVER, *Notes on the Hebrew Text and the Topography of the Books of Samuel*, (Oxford, 1913; the Introduction contains excellent material from the point of view of textual criticism). — J. FISCHER, *Das Alphabet der LXX-Vorlage im Pentateuch*, (Altestament. Abhandlungen, X, 2, Münster i. W., 1924); *id.*, *In welcher Schrift lag das Buch Isaias den LXX vor?* (Giessen, 1930). — A. FERNANDEZ TRUYOLS, S. J., *Breve introducción a la crítica textual des A. T.* (Rome, 1917); *id.*, *I Sam.* 1-15 : *Critica textual*, (Rome, 1917). See also the Bibliography at the end af this chapter].

[1] On these two points, it is sufficient to refer to our work, *Introduction à l'étude du Nouveau Testament, Critique textuelle. II La critique rationnelle,* with the collaboration, for the Armenian, of Father Lyonnet, S. J., (Paris, 1935). Sir F. KENYON, *Our Bible and the Ancient Manuscripts* (New York, 1958), pp. 155-219. J. DUPLACY, " Où en est la critique textuelle du N. T.? I, Introduction générale : sources ", *RSR* (1957), 419-441; *id.*, " Problèmes de méthode; histoire de la tradition manuscrite ", *ibid.* (1958), 270-313. G. SACCO, *La Koiné del N. T. e la trasmissione del Sacro Testo* (Rome, 1928), 151-327. A. F. J. KLIJN, *A Survey of the Researches into the Western Text of the Gospels and Acts* (Diss. Utrecht, 1949). B. M. METZGER, *Annotated Bibliography of the Textual Criticism of the N. T.* (Copenhagen, 1955; cf. *CBQ* [1955], 660-661); *id.*, " Recently Published Greek Papyri of the N. T. ", *B A* (1947), 20-44].

I. — The Gospels.

1. *History of the text represented by the Greek manuscripts.*

From the earliest times we notice the simultaneous presence of two types. To choose between them is the principal object of criticism. One is represented especially by B *(Vaticanus)* of the 4th century, and we thus call it *B*. The other is represented by Ms. D *(Codex Bezae)* of the 6th century, and, in like manner, we call it *D*. Ms. D is the most recent (6th century) but Type *D* was in existence from the end of the second century, as is proved by the ancient Latin versions which are based on it. It is the easiest to characterize, precisely because of its very prominent faults. When the Gospels present some differences in the manner of recounting the same fact, it will freely make Mark agree with Matthew or Luke, or even John with one of the other three. It wishes to be understood by everybody, and this entails the addition either of explanatory glosses or, on the contrary, the suppression of difficult terms, or at least some modifications in them. Hence, a striking expression, too pregnant with meaning to be universally understood, is replaced by a commonplace phrase. Simple souls were apt to be amazed that Jesus' own people thought that He was beside Himself (Mk. **3** : 21), and therefore Type *D* introduces the scribes here by way of substitution. A few clever changes can take care of difficulties very well.

These traits and others indicate that more is involved than the negligence of a distracted or drowsy copyist. We can recognize an intention here, and, as several characteristics present themselves under the same aspect, we detect a general motivation and direction, the work of a reviser. This does not mean that we should impute to such a man the pretention of correcting the Holy Spirit. He perhaps considered rather that he was doing a useful and pious work in putting the sacred thought above all reproach and in restoring it, as he thought, to its primitive purity. This edition was produced, accordingly, in the interest of the Christian people, and in actual fact it spread throughout the whole ancient world.

Type *D* encountered a rival in Type *B*, which is almost free from such manipulations, especially under the form of Ms. B. The latter does not harmonize the Gospels, nor does it gloss their text. Consequently, it is more difficult to read, but its readings, once fully understood, are singularly expressive. The superiority of *B* over *D* appeared so evident to two great English editors, Westcott and Hort, that they have qualified *B* as " neutral ", i.e., free from those alterations which betray the hand of a revising editor.

We recognize today that this praise is exaggerated. B, in fact, is too brief in parts. It has omitted the account of the adulteress (Jn. **7** : 53–8 : 11), the end of Mark (**16** : 9-20), the angel of Gethsemani and the bloody sweat (Lk. **22** : 43-44), the pardon accorded to the Jews (Lk. **23** : 43), and other passages also. It is not then entirely free from systematic tendencies. These indications as well as some slight embellishments prove that it also has been revised. But we believe that, although the primitive type fell into the hands of scholars who exaggerated their rights as critics, yet the model which they had before them was excellent, and the one which was closest to the authentic original.

This is still the most widely accepted opinion. Some, however, reason otherwise. Type *D* with its fullness, or, let us say, with its redundancies, with its air of simplicity, and its popular style, appears, e.g., to Mr. and Mrs. Kirsopp Lake, as the spontaneous product of the first Christian writers who, even Luke included, were little concerned with studied and labored thoughts which could not be understood without difficulty, or with picturesque elements introduced for the sake of impressing men of education and culture. According to this opinion, Type *B* would be nothing more than a strict revision, carried out in a critical way by a man animated, e.g., with the spirit of Origen. But we cannot admit this reversal of relationships, and for quite obvious reasons.

1) The harmonization of the Evangelists, noted as a fact and condemned by Saint Jerome, is by definition a secondary procedure. Therefore the supreme rule for editors of the text is to give to each Gospel its own proper character. Type *D* then, is, from this point of view, a corrupt text, for it falls very often into the fault from which Type *B* is free.

Furthermore, the difficult readings of B are not elegant words or expressions for admirers of fine language, but readings with definite significance which are only fully comprehended through a clearer understanding of the general situation, of places, and of customs. This clarity, which is not immediately apparent, can not be ascribed to a reviser, already far removed in time and space.

Finally, Type *D*, after a rapid and widespread diffusion had almost disappeared in the sixth century. This means that it was judged inferior throughout the whole Church. The struggle with B was not favorable to *D*.

2) In truth, as in every struggle, a desire for conciliation arose in some quarters. It is to this tendency that we attribute the birth of a text first recognized by Mr. Lake and called Caesarean because he believed that it came from Caesarea. In reality, like *B* and *D*, it originated in Egypt through a sort of blending of their variants. It was recently discovered among the Chester Beatty Papyri of the 3rd century published by Sir Frederick Kenyon. This hybrid text, however, had so little success that its existence has only been tracked down in our own times.

3) The *D* Text, then, was vanquished, but *B*'s triumph was dearly bought. *B* itself disappeared almost entirely, having been supplanted by a new type which issued from it. This new transformation was much more conservative than that represented by *D*. We believe that we have succeeded in describing the process comparatively by saying that *D* worked with an axe, and *A* with a file. *A*, i.e., the fourth type of text, corresponds to the attitude of the Church when it had gained literary men for its ranks, or at least a cultivated public attached to a literary style of writing.

The Gospels were composed in Greek, but as the echo of the words of Jesus, who spoke Aramaic. Saint Luke was better trained in Greek than Saint Mark, but, in the last analysis, all this prose still retained the flavor of its Semitic origin. At a very early date, even as early as the third century, in the period of the Beatty Papyrus, it was felt necessary to revise this prose, not to the extent of giving it a pure Attic form, but rather to bring its syntax into closer conformity with standard grammar and, in any case, to give it more polish. The authors of this revision adopted the *B* Text as their base, but they could not free themselves entirely from the additions of *D*. The mixture of the two types of readings side by side in *A* betrays in itself alone the secondary character of *A*. This type of the text had its origin in Alexandria, but it is probably at Antioch at the beginning of the fourth century, and through the work of Lucian of Antioch, priest and martyr, that it received its definite form. Its success was complete. It contained in substance the better text, that of *B*, but it made it more pleasing, more fluent, and less shocking to Greek ears. From Antioch it passed into general use at Constantinople, the Greek Church par excellence which had set itself up as a rival of Rome. This is the Greek text which became familiar to the West in early modern times, and, when printing began, this polished text, which one might say was written to please Erasmus, became the received text *(textus receptus)* par excellence.

The Humanists were succeeded in the 18th century by critics who were determined to recover the original form of the authentic words by removing a flattering but deceiving veneer. They began with a surreptitious attack on the received text by filling its margins with hostile notes. Then a new text was printed by Lachmann. Tischendorf made further revisions with the aid of his *Sinaiticus* (4th century), and Westcott and Hort obtained general acceptance for the variants of B. It is in this spirit that the recent Catholic editions of H. J. Vogels, and especially of A. Merk, S.J., have been conceived. We have not spoken at all of the edition of von Soden, for the building was hardly erected before it cracked and fell to pieces. The materials, i.e., certain gigantic preparatory works retain some interest [1].

2. The Versions.

Translations of the New Testament were destined to arise, sooner or later, and in imitation of those of the Old Bible. How much more useful was it for the Christians to understand

---

Translator's note. — [1 Practical critical editions : Eberhard Nestle, *Novum Testamentum*, 18th ed., by Erwin Nestle (Stuttgart, 1948), and also editions by the same authors of the Greek and Latin texts with critical apparatus. — A. MERK, S. J., *Novum Testamentum Graece et Latine* (7 th ed. by S. Lyonnet, S. J., (Rome, 1958). — J. M. BOVER, S. J., *Novi Testamenti Biblia Graeca et Latina* (Madrid, 1943). On textual criticism of the Gospels, cf. T. AYUSA MARAZUELA, " Texto arrecensional, recensional o prerrecensional? ", *Estudios Biblicos* (1947), 35-90].

what was read at the Eucharistic gatherings, and above all else the words of the Savior whom they were preparing to receive! These readings were the theme of the sermon, and what had just been read to them in Greek had therefore to be translated aloud into the vernacular. A trained cleric was wont to do this without difficulty, and such was still the practice of the Church of Jerusalem in the time of the pilgrim Etheria, near the end of the fourth century. But Greek was not known in the country parishes, and even a cleric might have been embarrassed in translating extemporaneously. It is very probable, therefore, that the clergy in the large cities wrote their translations for their confreres in the country districts. At the same time, these versions spread among the faithful.

The Syriac Versions.

In Syria the vernacular was almost the same as that which Jesus had spoken. A translation into Aramaic seemed to render more exactly the very sound of his words. Such a translation must have been desired in the region of Edessa, where there were very few who spoke Greek.

The Church of Edessa offered a unique phenomenon, the *Diatessaron* of Tatian. We have seen in Type *D* a tendency to harmonize texts, by enriching, e.g., the *Pater* of Saint Luke with the petitions proper to Saint Matthew. Why not go the whole way, and, in place of introducing combinations in each Gospel, was it not simpler to group into a single work whatever each Gospel had as peculiar to itself? This was the objective of Tatian, a Syrian well-trained in Greek philosophy, who thought he could thus condense all ideas into one formula, avoid repetitions, emphasize the harmony of the Evangelists in a single Gospel, and, in the interests of the faithful, remove their difficulty of having to bring different aspects into agreement.

This was done about 172 A. D. The four canonical Gospels had a place apart. The work of Tatian, composed out of all four Gospels, was given the significant title of *Diatessaron* (" through four "). The Syrian Church adopted this ingenious work, which was incomparable in its own way, and for a long time it knew the Gospel only under this form. The *Diatessaron* still served as the basis of the explanations of Saint Ephraem, the greatest doctor in the region of Edessa († after 373) [1].

Catholic sentiment, however, did not permit such a peculiar attitude to continue on a point as important as this. Everywhere in the universal Church four Gospels were read. The Syrians, accordingly, wished to have an exact translation of the individual Gospels, and, as Type *D* was then most widespread, it was adopted as the basis for the Syriac version. This version is contained in the Cureton Ms. and the Lewis Ms. *(Syriacus Sinaiticus)*, both incomplete, and in our opinion it is to be dated from the beginning of the fourth century. Some scholars, however, suggest the end of the second [2].

Edessa, however, belonged to the Patriarchate of Antioch, which had adopted the recension of the priest Lucian. When the bishop of Edessa, Rabbula († 435), wished to introduce an official edition of the individual Gospels among his clergy, he had translated—or rather translated himself—the text of his metropolis, Antioch, which became the received text at Constantinople, but one still showing some mixture. This version was called "The Simple" (Peshitto). As the official text of the Syrians, it imposed itself on the Nestorians and the Monophysites as well as on those who remained true to the Catholic Church [3].

The Monophysites, meanwhile, undertook a new translation on the basis of a Greek text which showed a marked admixture in its readings. This version was called the *Philoxenian* [4], after

---

Translator's note. — [1] On a Greek Fragment of the Diatessaron, cf. C. H. KRAELING, *A Greek Fragment of Tatian's Diatessaron* (London, 1935). — M. J. LAGRANGE, *RB* (1935), 321-343; and for the Greek text itself, *Zeitschr. N. T. Wiss.* (1935), 292, and *RB* (1936), 236. An Arabic Version of the Diatessaron was published by A. Ciasca, *Tatiani Evangeliorum harmoniae Arabice* (Rome, 1888), and more recently, by A. S. MARMADJII, O.P., *Diatessaron de Tatieh* (Beyrouth, 1935), with French translation, full introduction, and notes. See also A. PLOOIJ, *A Primitive Text of the Diatessaron* (Leiden, 1923; on this medieval Dutch translation found in a Liège Ms., see also H. J. VOGELS, *Theologische Revue*) 1923, 81-84)].

Translator's note. — [2] For editions of this Syriac Version, see F. C. BURKITT, *Evangelion da-Mepharreshe* (Cambridge, 1904; the Cureton Ms. with variants of *Syriacus Sinaiticus*), and S. S. LEWIS, The *Old Syriac Gospels or Evangelion da-Mepharreshē* (London, 1910; *Syriacus Sinaiticus* with variants of the Cureton Ms.)].

Translator's note. — [3] For a handy edition of the N. T. in Syriac, see *The New Testament in Syriac*, published by the British and Foreign Bible Society (London, 1905 and 1920). The text of the Gospels is that of the critical edition of Pusey-Gwilliam, but without the variants].

Translator's note. — [4] Edited by J. GWYNN : *Remnants of the Later Syriac Versions* (Oxford, 1909)].

Philoxenus of Mabbug, an ardent sectary, who had it prepared by the chorepiscopus Polycarp, or the *Heraclean* [1], after Thomas of Heraclea, who enriched it with marginal material borrowed from Type *D*.

Finally in Palestine, where for centuries a dialect quite different from that of Edessa was spoken in the rural districts, there was a desire to have the whole Bible in the language of the country. This version, which is called the *Hierosolymitan* or *Palestinian*, was made, apparently, in the fifth century [2].

The Latin Versions.

The history of the Latin translations is less complicated. Rome spoke Greek down to the end of the third century, and it was not there that need of a Latin translation made itself felt most strongly. Gaul had become enamored of Roman culture, but Africa, especially Carthage, had advanced much farther than Gaul in this respect. All evidence points to the fact that the Gospels received their first Latin form in Africa. This version existed very probably before the end of the second century, although Tertullian by no means recognized its authority. He could translate Greek with trifling ease whenever the occasion demanded. These first African texts followed Type *D*. Saint Cyprian adheres to a Latin version already received, which is consequently regarded as of African origin. In the third century, the time had already arrived when neither Gaul nor Rome could dispense with a Latin text, even for the liturgy. The translator who provided for this

---

Translator's note. — [[1] Edited — wrongly as Philoxenian — by I. WHITE Oxford, 1778, 1799 and 1803)].

Translator's note. — [[2] Editions : P. DE LAGARDE, *Bibliothecae Syriacae...* (Göttingen, 1892; *Evangeliarium Hierosolymitanum*, pp. 257-403). — A. S. LEWIS and M. D. GIBSON, *The Palestinian Syriac Lectionary of the Gospels* (London, 1899; based on two Sinai Mss. and Lagarde's edition). — A. S. LEWIS, E. NESTLE and M. D. GIBSON, *A Palestinian Syriac Lectionary* (Studia Sinaitica VI, London, 1897; contains lessons from the Pentateuch, Job, Proverbs, Prophets, Acts, and Epistles). — H. DUENSING, *Christlich-palästinisch-aramäische Fragmente* (Göttingen, 1906; contains, besides fragments of early Christian literature, a number of New Testament texts). For a dictionary to most of the texts, see F. SCHULTHESS, *Lexicon Syropalaestinum* (Berlin, 1903). — See also F. SCHWALLY, *Idioticon des christlich-palästinischen Aramäisch* (Giesen, 1893), and F. SCHULTHESS, *Grammatik des christlich-palästinischen Aramaisch*, ed. E. LITTMANN (Tübingen, 1924; contains also a good bibliography, chrestomathy, and lexicon)].

need intended, indeed, to produce a new work, but he had doubtlessly heard of the version in use in Africa and he saw no reason against employing it as required. The European texts came into existence in this manner, and were as closely connected with Type *D* as their African counterparts.

At the court of the highly cultured Pope Damasus (366-384), there was increasing concern at finding so many differences in the Latin texts and such a general departure from the more sober texts which were beginning to supplant Type *D*. It was necessary to obtain a Latin unity solidly established upon a good Greek text.

Precisely the man was found who appeared predestined for this work, Jerome from Stridon in Dalmatia. He possessed all the secrets of Latin elegance; he knew Greek perfectly; he had studied exegesis under the great doctors of the Orient, and he knew how to distinguish a pure text from a harmonized text. At the invitation of Pope Damasus he undertook the revision of the Old Latin Version. His liking for Cicero did not lead him to make a travesty of the simplicity of the Gospels by presenting their thought in harmonious periods, terminating in rhythmical endings. He took as his basis the unpretentious Latin of the first translators, but always with due regard for correct Latin expression. He aimed above all else at approaching closely the authentic Greek original, which he thought was contained in Type *B*, although sometimes corrected in the interests of elegance by Type *A*.

This work performed by a master hand imposed itself on the Christian clergy rather through its own intrinsic value than through the patronage of the pope. Augustine adopted it so far as the Gospels are concerned, although he felt free to correct it.

Gradually the old editions disappeared, at least in the case of the Gospels, but not without leaving some troublessome traces in the new. Finally, the revision of Jerome, as is thoroughly understandable, became the Vulgate, i.e., the text recognized by everyone, the text which carried authority. Until the Renaissance, the invention of printing, and the Protestant Revolt, no one ventured to undertake a similar work.

This success had its dangers. An edition which everyone bought, and which had to be sold cheap for students who were little concerned with accuracy of reproduction, was soon worth only what its manuscripts had cost. This disorder irritated scholars like Roger Bacon in the 13th century. The invention of printing finally permitted men to aim at a practically perfect unity.

After various individual and unfruitful attempts, which only resulted in increasing the confusion, the Council of Trent understood that it was necessary to maintain the principle of tradition. One version used in the liturgy, and cited in the councils, was already in fact the official or authentic version of the Church. This prerogative was solemnly accorded to it, but where was an authentic copy to be found, however, among so many manuscripts? Unity can be assured only by the supreme authority. The Council, therefore, begged Pope Pius IV to prepare a corrected edition of the Vulgate. This edition, which was finally completed only under Clement VIII, was made official. The supreme editor did not issue it as a perfect work. But it suffices that it contains no error in Faith by virtue of the Providence of God watching over His Church.

The edition of Clement VIII could not be presented as imperfect and as definitive at the same time. Pope Pius X judged that the time had come to correct certain faults of copyists, and, so far as at all possible, to establish the text exactly as it was issued by Saint Jerome himself. The Benedictines charged with preparing this better edition have not yet published the New Testament (see p. 664 below) [1].

The Coptic Versions.

The other versions have a simpler history. The Coptic or Egyptian translations are the most important. We possess versions of the Gospels in the Sahidic dialect of Upper Egypt and in the Bohairic dialect of the Delta. The Sahidic version is the older and has kept some traces of the domination of Type *D*, while the Bohairic is a more faithful reproduction of Type *B*.

Translator's note. — [1 There is a very convenient edition by J. WORDSWORTH and H. J. White, *Novum Testamentum Latine Secundum Editionem Sancti Hieronymi...* (Editio minor by H. J. WHITE, Oxford, 1911). — See also C. H. TURNER, *The Oldest Mss. of the Vulgate Gospels* (edited by A. Souter, Oxford, 1931; the text is that of the Saint Gall Ms.)].

We would place them respectively in the third and fourth centuries [1].

The Gothic Version.

The Gothic version originated in the Orient at the end of the fourth century among the Goths, who were alternately threatening the Roman Empire or putting themselves at its service. Through this contact they became Christians, but Arian Christians. Since they were living in the environs of Constantinople, they took its text as their basis. When the Ostrogoths became installed in Italy, however, their version probably came under the influence of the Old Latin texts, and hence of Type *D*. [2].

The Armenian Version [3].

The Armenian version is the first to raise the question of a translation from an intermediary version. It thas long been maintained, in fact, that the Armenian version was translated from the Syriac, and this is perhaps still the dominant opinion among Armenian scholars. But the work of F. Macler and S. Lyonnet, S. J., seems to have proved that it was based on the Greek, and especially, according to Father Lyonnet, on a Greek text of the Caesarean type. Father Lyonnet concludes as follows : " Gradually, from a patient study of the text, critics have perceived clearly through the work of the translators itself that they were grappling with a Greek model. They have caught them, as it were, in their difficulties as inexperienced

---

Translator's note. — [1 Editions : G. HORNER, *The Coptic Version of the New Testament in the Southern Dialect, Otherwise Called Sahidic and Thebaic* (7 vols., Oxford, 1911-1924); id., *The Coptic Version of the N. T. in the Northern Dialect, Otherwise Called Memphitic and Bohairic* (4 vols., Oxford, 1898-1905). Both editions contain full critical apparatus and are accompanied by a literal English translation. — See also : I. BALESTRI, *Sacrorum Bibliorum Fragmenta Copto-Sahidica... Novum Testamentum* (Rome, 1904). — Sir HERBERT THOMPSON, *The Gospel of Saint John According to the Earliest Coptic Mss.* (London, 1924; the text with plates facing it, Engl. trans., and collation with the Greek. See also p. 633, *infra*].

Translator's note. — [2 Editions : G. W. S. FRIDRICHSEN, *The Gothic Version of the Gospels* (Oxford, 1926). — W. STREITBERG, *Die gotische Bibel* (2nd ed., Heidelberg, 1919; text and lexicon). — See also A. WILMART, *RB* (1927), 47 ff. (on the Gothic Gospels)].

Translator's note. — [3 Cf. F. MACLER, *Le texte arménien de l'Evangile d'après Matthieu et Marc* (Paris, 1919; a thorough study of the text considered in itself and in its relations to the Greek and Syriac texts)].

Hellenists who sometimes derive inspiration from a Syriac version and are even guilty of gross confusions, and they have discovered incontestable traces of numerous successive revisions " [1].

The first attempts date from the beginning of the fifth century.

The Georgian Version.

The Georgian version is the theme of even more thorny discussions, which do not enter into the scope of the present work. It is enough to state that this version also, which has two distinct forms, furnishes evidence for the so-called Caesarean type of Greek text, which the Lazi communities found probably in the Patriarchate of Jerusalem.

The history of the other versions, Arabic, Ethiopic, Persian, etc., is not without interest for the history of the Church, but these versions cannot furnish any appreciable help for the establishment of the text [2].

2. — The Other Books of the New Testament.

What we have said of the Gospels applies to the other books of the New Testament, but with some differences in individual cases. The more important of these will be indicated.

The Acts of the Apostles. — There is the same opposition between Ms. B and Ms. D. The latter is characterized by special historical details, some of which may well be based on reality, but the Beatty Papyrus clearly belongs with Type *B*. This is equivalent to saying that Acts did not give rise to the so-called Caesarean type. There is the same distribution of the Syriac and the Latin versions into old texts reflecting Type *D* and texts revised on the basis of *B* and *A*.

The Epistles of Saint Paul [3]. — Ms. D of the Gospels *(Codex Bezae)* does not contain the Epistles of Saint Paul. Some

---

[1] *Recherches de Science religieuse,* 25 (1935), 186-187.

Translator's note. — [2 See, however, the more favorable view expressed by Father Boismard on the value of these versions for textual criticism, p. 617, *infra*].

Translator's note. — [3 Cf. G. D. KILPATRICK, " Western Text and Original Text in the Epistles, " *J. Th. Studies,* 45 (1944), 60-65.   G. ZUNTZ, " Réflexions sur l'histoire du texte Paulinien ", *RB* (1952), 5-22].

Greco-Latin Mss., the chief of which is another D *(Claromontanus)* represent Type *D*, but in a very attenuated form, being between *B* and the Antiochene type, parent of the received text. The types, moreover, are less accentuated. There are always two strata in the Syriac and Latin versions. A special Latin revision served as a basis for Saint Augustine, but there is no proof that he was its author, as Dom de Bruyne has maintained.

The Catholic Epistles. — Type *D* is scarcely represented. The Antiochene text is only a substitute for *B*.

The Apocalypse. — Ms. B, owing to the vicissitudes of time, lacks the Apocalypse. The best representative of Type *B* is, in this case, Ms. A *(Alexandrinus)*, of the fifth century, which appears to have preserved best the rough style of the original. The Latin versions, which on account of the high esteem of the West for the Apocalypse, underwent much recasting, furnish testimony in favor of the old uncial Mss. of Type *B*. Saint Jerome's work was even more discreet. Since the Syrian Church did not possess the Apocalypse in its earlier canon, nor, likewise, the four shorter Catholic Epistles, its translation of the earlier type did not contain them. Two revisions are represented, one of the *Peshitto* type, and the other of the *Philoxenian*.

2. — THE EMPLOYMENT OF WITNESSES FOR THE ESTABLISHMENT OF THE TEXT.

According to their history, these witnesses are types or families, both among the Greek manuscripts and among the versions, which have been differentiated or identified through the efforts of textual critics.

While the work of classification was proceeding, scholars were induced to arrange the types or families in order of worth on the simple basis of a systematic evaluation of their peculiarities. Since Type *A*, or the Antiochene, is only an elegant finish on Type *B*, with some traces of *D*, its own readings have little chance of being original. C. H. Turner, a distinguished English critic, declared that it was as dead as Queen Anne. H. von Soden made some moves in its favor, and has been supported by H. Vogels, but A. Merk, S. J., has remained in the Tischendorf-Westcott-Hort-Nestle line, excluding the readings peculiar to the received text or vulgate of Constantinople.

The so-called Cæsarean type is in the same condition of inferiority, since it is eclectic, attempting a conciliation between *B* and *D*. It was given prominence, moreover, only for the Gospels, especially for that of Saint Mark, and its translation was disseminated in very few copies.

The two rivals of early days, *B* and *D*, still retain the same relative positions. Type *B* is unquestionably superior, and to a marked degree. But since it itself has suffered from excessive critical retouching, it should be given preference only after applying, in each doubtful case, criteria which assure superiority to the whole family, Such are expressive readings in place of hackneyed ones, i.e., those which are in accord with the genius of the author, unpolished readings in place of elegant, simple or unsophisticated expressions in place of circumspect or studied language, and, above all else, the rejection of harmonizing readings or tendencies.

In a case where none of these criteria may permit a decision, one's doubt ought to be stated. But since a text must actually be edited, an editor will probably not run serious danger of being wrong if he gives preference to witnesses whose testimony is usually irreproachable.

Type *B*, therefore, will ordinarily be followed, except in the instance of readings contrary to the criteria which are responsible for its being given preference in general. It is obvious that each text ought to be cleansed first from all the scribal errors which violate the universal laws of textual criticism.

As regards the versions, they can only lend their support to the type which they present. With the support of the early Syriac Version, Blass attemped to reconstruct Type *D*, which he regarded as an edition issued by Saint Luke himself. This system has fallen into discredit on account of the subjective element involved in the necessity of making a decision among so many variants. The Peshitto version is scarcely more than one more witness, and a poor one, in favor of the Antiochene or received text, which no one would now venture to defend. The other Syriac versions are very faithful to their Greek source, especially the Philoxenian, but this source is of a mixed type without authority. The Heraclean margins are an excellent contribution, but only for Type *D*,

The Old Latin versions are excellent witnesses for Type *D*, sometimes being even superior to Ms. D, in so far as they fill its lacunae. But this is a very modest asset. On the other hand, the Vulgate of Saint Jerome, long held in contempt by Protestants, has been restored to honor among them by von Harnack. Jerome's decision to eliminate the redundancies of *D*, and to employ some good Mss. of Type *B*, makes his text an excellent example of this type toward the end of the fourth century. Since it was free also from the polishimg characteristic of the Antiochene text, it permitted Catholics to reject the received text, which had a very coherent ecclesiastical tradition in its favor.

The Coptic versions are scarcely cited, since their adherence to Type *B* is so constant. The peculiarities of the Sahidic version attract attention but do not require acceptance.

The Gothic version, on the basis of its origin, belongs among the witnesses of the Antiochene type. Its revisions did not bring it any closer to the good Type *B*.

The Armenian and Georgian versions have become the object of a more attentive curiosity since their dependence upon the so-called Caesarean type has been recognized, a type, which, however, can hardly be regarded as authentic.

Scriptural quotations in the Fathers ought also to be taken into account, but we cannot deal with this difficult subject here.

The recent discoveries of manuscripts and papyri have been numerous and unusually valuable. Never has textual criticism been practiced with such ardor. In our opinion, however, it is difficult to imagine that a more informed criticism will depart very far from the text of Westcott-Hort. For the present, it would perhaps be best to re-edit it, furnishing it with an apparatus of variants as complete and clear as possible. This is what has been done recently in an edition of Saint Mark, the title of which indicates a long program for the future [1].

---

[1] Novum Testamentum graece secundum textum Wescotto-Hortianum, *Evangelium secundum Marcum cum apparatu critico novo plenissimo, lectionibus codicum nuper repertorum additis, editionibus versionum antiquarum et patrum ecclesiasticorum denuo investigatis edidit S. C. E. LEGG, A. M.* — Oxonii, e typographo Clarendoniano, MCMXXXV.

3. — *PRESENT TENDENCIES IN TEXTUAL CRITICISM* [1]

Twenty years ago, one could have thought that textual criticism had reached its full term and that the results obtained could be considered, in their main lines at least, as definitive. The several witnesses of the Sacred Text were divided into four categories or principal " Texts " : the Alexandrian, Western, Caesarean, and Antiochene. The Alexandrian Text had long been recognized as the best. Hence, it was deemed sufficient to edit it, with a certain number of corrections being made, to obtain the text which had the best chance of representing the original Biblical text. In fact, the critical editions, considered in their ensemble, reproduced substantially a text that was more or less closely related to the Alexandrian.

This reliance on the Alexandrian Text, however, did not prevent some scholars from feeling a certain uneasiness, which became marked in the publications of the last fifteen years. Today, the positions held twenty years ago are questioned or challenged. The current tendencies in textual criticism may be schematized as follows :

I.   In the first place, scholars have become increasingly aware that the working base employed up to the present is too narrow. Are we justified in wishing to reconstitute the primitive Biblical text almost exclusively on the basis of the great uncial Mss? New studies have been made which show the importance of the minuscules. Some of these, although relatively late in date, still reflect a very old text. We have also begun to take cognizance of the value of other witnesses hitherto neglected, as, e.g., the lectionaries. Similarly, many investigators are attempting to obtain a better knowledge of the ancient versions and, consequently, to put them to better use. The most significant studies have been concerned with the Old Syriac and Old Armenian versions. But it will be necessary also to explore domains that are still almost untouched, e.g., the Ethiopian, Arabic, and Persian versions. Finally, more importance is now being given to Biblical citations made by the Fathers of the Church, which are often earlier witnesses of the text than our most ancient Mss. There is good reason to believe

---

[1] Supplementary section by M. E. BOISMARD, O. P.

that all these studies will probably attach increasing significance to the versions and to Patristic citations in their investigation of the primitive text and, consequently, will dethrone
the great uncial Mss. from the absolute supremacy which they
have enjoyed for more than a century.

2. Specialists in textual criticism have become quite sceptical
on the objectivity, and even on the utility, of the division of
the various witnesses into rigidly established families. At times,
the justification itself of this division into families is questioned.
But, without going as far as that, many critics now consider
that this division, as employed in the past, is much too systematic and ignores or eliminates important variations. In the
case of the Western text, we now recognize that D is a bad
representative of it. Hence, for determining the value of the
Alexandrian and Western texts, it is necessary, not to compare B
and D, but rather B and the primitive Syro-Latin text, insofar
as it is possible to reestablish it. Moreover, is it really so easy
to determine just what is the Western text? Numerous influences operated upon the Old Latin, for example. Are all these
to be connected with the Western text? To put the matter
more precisely, even the groupings, Old Latin-Old Syriac,
seem due to various influences. Is it right to characterize this
whole complex uniformly as " Western "? In respect to the
Cæsarean text, it is now doubted seriously that it can be
considered, without qualification, as a compromise between the
Alexandrian and Western texts. Would there not be rather
a pre-Alexandrian state of the text? Finally, the Alexandrian
text itself is not as precisely determined as is too often imagined.
One of its " best " representatives, the *Sinaiticus*, often appears
closer to the Syro-Latin text than B (e.g., in the seven first
chapters of Saint John). The problem then presents itself :
when one or several witnesses of the Alexandrian text offer
" Western " readings, is this the result of contamination coming
from that [the Western] text, or, on the contrary, may they not
have preserved early readings, common to the Syro-Latin and
Alexandrian texts, but abandoned by B and the rest? Accordingly, the principle itself of the division into " texts " duly
defined must be revised.

3. In the light of these uncertainties, a tendency is becoming
more and more manifest, which may be formulated as follows :

for recovering the primitive text, it is illusory to judge a variant in terms of its belonging to such and such a text; it may even be dangerous to depend exclusively on the number and " quality " of the witnesses which attest it. The value of a variant ought to be judged, above all, on the basis of internal criteria, and no variant may be rejected *a priori* because it belongs to a discredited text, or because it does not have the support of any of the great uncial Mss that used to exercise supreme authority, or even because it is attested only by versions or Patristic citations. We may even believe that the day will come when there will be no fear of admitting a reading for which all witnesses have disappeared, but which can be conjectured with sufficient probability on the basis of divergent readings actually known. It has long been recognized that the scribes recopied Mss. and were subject to certain constants in the process. These established data have long been applied when there is question of judging a variant attested by the great uncial Mss. Why should not these principles apply likewise in the case of such and such a variant attested solely by a small number of ancient witnesses?

An Anglo-American Committee has been formed for the purpose of preparing a new critical edition of the New Testament. The spirit animating the committee seems to encompass all the best tendencies noted *supra*. It has decided to take as the basis of its edition, not the text of Westcott-Hort, but the *Textus Receptus* (accordingly, making use exclusively of the support furnished by the variants). In doing this, it has recognized : 1) that the Alexandrian Text has forfeited its old prestige, and 2) that it is still premature to try to establish a New Testament text which would claim to represent the original best. Moreover, particular attention is being given to the collation of new Greek Mss. and lectionaries. A special section has been established for the study of versions and Patristic citations, the testimony of which will be given even if it is not supported by any Greek Ms. Thus, specialists in Biblical textual criticism will have a tool and apparatus which will give them a sufficiently broad base for obtaining objective results in their research.

620 GUIDE TO THE BIBLE

BIBLIOGRAPHY

I. *History and criticism of the text of the Old Testament :*

KENNICOTT, *Vetus Testamentum hebraicum cum variis lectionibus* (2 vols., Oxford, 1776 1780). — G. DE ROSSI, *Specimen variarum lectionum sacri textus...* (Romae, 1782). — D. GINSBURG, *Introduction to the Massoretico-Critical Edition of the Hebrew Bible* (London, 1897). — P. KAHLE, *Der massoretische Text des Alten Testaments nach der Ueberlieferung der babylonischen Juden* (Leipzig, 1902); ID., *Massoreten des Ostens (ibid.*, 1913); *Massoreten des Westens* (2 fascicles, *ibid.*, 1927 and 1930). — F. WUTZ, *Die Transkriptionen von der Septuaginta bis zu Hieronymus* (2 fascicles, Stuttgart, 1925 and 1933). — F. DELITZSCH, *Die Lese- und Schreibfehler im Alten Testament...* (Berlin and Leipzig, 1920). See also the articles in the Dictionaries of the Bible and the Biblical Introductions.

II. *The textual criticism of the New Testament :*

E. JACQUIER, *Le Nouveau Testament dans l'Eglise chrétienne.* II, *Le texte du Nouveau Testament* (Paris, 1913). — L. VAGANAY, *Initiation à la critique textuelle néotestamentaire* (Paris, 1934); English trans., *Introduction to the Textual Criticism of the New Testament* [London, 1937]). — H. J. VOGELS, *Handbuch der neutestamentlichen Textkritik* (Münster i. W., 1923).—C. R. GREGORY, *Textkritik des Neuen Testaments* (Leipzig, 1900-1909); ID., *Einleitung in das Neue Testament.* II, *Kritik des Textes (ibid.*, 1909). — F. G. KENYON, *Handbook to the Textual Criticism of the New Testament* (2nd ed., London, 1912); ID., *The Western Text in Gospels and Acts* (Oxford, 1939); ID., *Our Bible and the Ancient Manuscripts* (revised ed., New York, 1958), 155-178. — H. PERNOT, *Recherches sur le texte original des Evangiles* (Paris, 1938). — K. AND S. LAKE, *The Text of the New Testament* (9th ed., London, 1933; IDD., *The Text according to Mark, with a Collation of Codex 28 of the Gospels* (London, 1941). — A. F. J. KLIJN, *A Survey of the Researches into the Western Texts of the Gospels and Acts* (Utrecht, 1947). — M. M. PARVIS and A. P. WIKGREN, *New Testament Manuscript Studies* (Chicago, 1950). — S. LYONNET, *Les origines de la version arménienne des Evangiles et le Diatesseron* (Rome, 1950). — A. VÖÖBUS, *Studies in the History of the Gospel Text in Syriac* (Corp. Script. Christ. Orient., Vol. 128, Louvain, 1951). — E. MASSAUX, " État actuel de la critique textuelle du N. T.," *Nouvelle Revue Théologique* (1953), 703-726. — Dom B. BOTTE, " Manuscrits grecs du Nouveau Testament ", *DBV, Suppl.* V (1957), 819-835. — [R. V. G. TASKER, " An Introduction to the Mss. of the New Testament ", *Harvard Theological Review* (1948), 71-81. — A. WIKENHAUSER, *Einleitung in das N. T.* (revised ed., Freiburg i. Br., 1956), 46-109.]

CHAPTER VIII

THE VERSIONS
by G. Bardy and A. Tricot

CHAPTER VIII

THE VERSIONS [1]

I. — THE SEPTUAGINT AND THE OTHER GREEK VERSIONS
OF THE OLD TESTAMENT [2].

[G. BARDY]

From an early date, Jewish colonies of greater or less
importance had settled in Egypt, and the Aramaic papyri
found at Elephantine afford us valuable information on the life
of one of these colonies in the fifth century before our era.
The conquests of Alexander the Great opened the land of Egypt
to the Jews on a much larger scale. After the foundation of
Alexandria, Alexander attracted thither colonists of Jewish
origin and granted them the right of citizenship with important
privileges. Hence the city rapidly developed into a Jewish
metropolis.

Translator's note. — [1 For a good survey of the Ancient Versions, see
J. BALESTRI, *Biblicæ Introductionis Generalis Elementa* (Rome, 1932),
pp. 141-211 (with good bibliography). Sir F. KENYON, *Our Bible and the
Ancient Mss.* (revised ed., New York, 1958), 97-134. J. W. WEVERS, " Prin-
ciples of Interpretation regarding the Fourth Translator of the Book of the
Kingdoms, " *CBQ* (1952), 40-56. H. S. GEHMAN, " The Hebraic Character
of Septuagint Greek, " *Vetus Testamentum*, I (1951), 81-90. *The Septuagint
Bible.* English trans. by C. Thomson, revised by C. A. Muses (Indian Hills,
Colo., 1954; cf. *CBQ* [1955], 623-624; *RB* [1956], 115). I. SOISALON-SOININEN,
Die Textformen der Septuaginta-Uebersetzung des Richterbuches (Helsinki, 1951;
cf. *Theologische Revue* [1953], 17-18). J. ZIEGLER, " Der Text der Aldina im
Dodekapropheton, " *Biblica* (1945), 37-51. For a comprehensive survey of
versions ancient and modern, see especially the article, " Bibelübersetzungen, "
LTK, II (2nd ed., 1958), 375-411. H. SCHNEIDER, " Die biblischen Oden im
christlichen Altertum ", *Biblica* (1949), 28-65, 239-272, 433-452, 479-500;
cf. *Theol. Revue* [1951] 206-207). P. KATZ, *Philo's Bible* (Cambridge, 1950;
cf. *Theol. Revue* [1951], 201-203). On the revival of the idea of the inspiration
of the Septuagint Version, cf. P. BENOIT, O. P., " La Septante est-elle inspirée? "
in *Festschrift für M. Meinertz* (Münster i. W., 1951), 41-49. P. AUVRAY,
" Comment se pose le problème de l'inspiration des Septante? " *RB* (1952),
321-336. See also the valuable notes in F. Sagnard's ed. of Irenaeus, *Contra
Haereses* (*Sources Chrétiennes*, No. 34, Paris [1952], 351-355, and 432-433;
cf. *Theol. Revue* [1952], 146)].

Translator's note. — [2 P. E. KAHLE, *The Cairo Geniza* (London, 1941),
pp. 132-179].

Naturally, the Jews of Alexandria did not delay in acquiring Hellenic culture. They soon felt the need of possessing a Greek version of the Sacred Books. The Letter of Aristeas to Philocrates relates that, at the demand of King Ptolemy II Philadelphus (285-246), the High Priest Eleazar sent seventy-two old men from Jerusalem to Alexandria, six from each tribe, with a commission to translate the Law, a copy of which, written in gold letters, they carried with them. Their translation was intended to take its place in the Library which had just been established at Alexandria by an Athenian exile, Demetrius of Phaleron. The seventy-two translators were settled on the Ile of Pharos, and in seventy-two days they finished their work.

Aristeas' account, of course, is legendary, although it was accepted by Philo, Josephus, Saint Irenaeus, Clement of Alexandria, and many others, and was enriched along the way with fabulous details. We can retain from it that the Pentateuch was translated first and that this translation was most probably made in the reign of Ptolemy Philadelphus. Its author or authors were not Palestinian Jews, and the language which they employed justifies us in regarding them as Alexandrian Jews, long familiar with Greek as it was then spoken in Egypt.

The other Books of the Bible were translated gradually, but we have very incomplete information on the dates and order of these translations. The prologue of the Greek translation of Ecclesiasticus, which is to be dated, it seems, about 130 B.C., informs us that at this time the Law, the Prophets, and the rest of the books had been translated into Greek and were in current use among the Jews in Egypt. By the words, " rest of the books ", is meant the Hagiographa. Some further data — all too rare from our point of view — furnish grounds for believing that a complete version of the Old Testament existed toward the end of the second century before Christ. To the books translated from the Hebrew it added, apparently, some in Greek, like the Book of Wisdom.

Until very recently, these conclusions were generally accepted. It was believed that the activity of the first translators should not be extended at most beyond some hundred years and it was thought their work was completed between about 145 and 129. Recent studies force critics to reexamine *ab ovo* the pro-

blem of the Greek translations of the Bible. While it is admitted
as very probable that the first Greek translations of the Sacred
Books were not made to satisfy the curiosity of a royal biblio-
phile, but rather to meet the liturgical needs of a people who no
longer understood the ancient language in which their Sacred
Books were written, F. Wutz thinks that the first stage was
the transcription of the Hebrew text of the Bible into Greek
characters, and especially those parts of the text which were
employed for public reading in the service of the synagogue,
namely, the Law and the Prophets. He holds that the translation, in the strict sense, into Greek was made from the transcription. P. Kahle, for his part, regards such a transcription into
Greek characters as a useless or needless stage. According to
him, the work of translation began, without literay pretension,
with the passages of the Old Testament which were to be read
in the synagogue. Thus a series of partial translations came into
existence which were quite similar to the Aramaic *targums* in
Palestine (cf. pp. 593-595). These translations were finally amalgamated and corrected. Furthermore, the Bible was translated
also for private use, and no longer solely for liturgical use.

The verification of these hypotheses is all the more difficult
because the most ancient Mss. which we have at our disposal
up to the present are of Christian origin, and are not earlier than
the third century of our era. In default of Mss., the study of
Biblical citations in writers like Philo and Josephus is absolutely
necessary. The examination of Philo's works leads to results
that raise further problems. While the majority of the Mss.
containing his works reproduce a Biblical text which corresponds
to the Septuagint, two *codices*, a *Vaticanus* and a *Laurentianus*,
diverge from it and present Biblical citations much nearer the
Hebrew and closely related to the text of Aquila. It was
generally agreed that the translation of Aquila was not earlier
than the second century, and P. Katz, consequently, was led
to conclude that the Philonian citations found in the two
Mss. mentioned, had been revised and corrected according
to it. However, discoveries made in August, 1952, compel
us to believe that a Greek Bible was being used in Palestine
before the second century A.D. whose text is very close to
Aquila's. Thus, the problem of Biblical citations in Philo
must be approached on a new basis.

The case of the historian Josephus is less complex. Although of Palestinian origin and familiar with the Hebrew text of the Bible, Josephus spent a great part of his life in Roman circles and it is for those that he wrote his works in Greek. It is only natural, therefore, that he employed the Septuagint in its current text and that his Biblical citations present no special problems.

The Scriptural citations of the Old Testament found in the New in most cases follow the Septuagint (see pp. 679-684).

The Septuagint translation was made by Jews and for Jews. Accordingly, the Jews, and especially those of the Dispersion, were the first to use it. Philo tells us that the Jews in Egypt, to commemorate the work of the first translators, had even instituted a feast and a pilgrimage to the Island of Pharos where the translation had been made.

The Christian Church, as the heir of the Sacred Books of Judaism, from the beginning adopted the Septuagint as its own property. The Greek Fathers in succession used it exclusively, and it was the basis for the ancient Latin, Coptic, and other versions. The Christians regarded its authority to such a degree that the majority of the Fathers, if not all, accepted the inspiration of the Greek translators as practically an article of Faith. Apart from some doubts expressed by some exegetes in the Middle Ages, it is only from the Renaissance on especially, that the authority of the Septuagint and belief in its inspiration lost credit among Catholic theologians and critics. It is all the more remarkable that, at the present time, a movement favoring the inspiration of the Septuagint seems to be under way. It may be observed in this connection that certain difficulties would be resolved if this movement were to continue and reach its logical conclusion (See Chapter I, pp. 32-34).

The Christians placed a constantly increasing reliance on the Septuagint, even to the point of neglecting the original text. The Jews, however, carried through a contrary movement. From the second century, the Pharisees established the cultural isolation of Judaism in systematic fashion. They began to pay the Hebrew text of the Old Testament a respect that we regard as exaggerated, and to neglect the Biblical Books which, as in the case of Wisdom, were originally written in Greek. as accursed; and under the pretext that the Christians had

introduced deliberate falsifications into the Septuagint, they
desired to have, for those among their people who did not
understand Hebrew, new and literal Greek translations which
should be exclusively theirs.

It is hardly necessary to add that the value of the Septuagint
Version is very unequal and varies according to the translators.
The Pentateuch is very faithfully rendered, and witch greater
accuracy than all the other books. The translation of the
Historical Books is good also. On the other hand, the Poetical
and Prophetic Books leave much to be desired, for we find here
constantly mistranslations, omissions, and glosses, all being
witness to work done in a rather hasty manner and by translators
who were not sufficiently competent. Finally, in certain books
the work of two translators, who divided their labors, is
recognizable.

In spite of these remarks, we must not forget that the Septuagint is still our witness for an older text, and sometimes a better
one than that which is preserved in the Hebrew manuscripts.
In the Book of Proverbs, e.g., the Greek translation presents
numerous transpositions, a large number of additions, and
some omissions. The Greek text of the Book of Job, as Origen
read it, was noticeably shorter than that contained in our
extant manuscripts and in the Masoretic text. The Greek
Book of Esther is composed of 270 verses, 107 of which are
lacking in the Hebrew which we read today. In the Book of
Jeremias, the transpositions, omissions, and additions are very
numerous and important. The Book of Daniel possesses in
Greek the story of Susanna, the story of Bel and the Dragon,
and the story of the three children in the furnace, three narratives
which are not included in the Hebrew text. These are only
a few examples. Each case must be studied individually.
Only a careful examination of the text and of the conditions
of its transmission can give us a knowledge of its true value.

As in the case of all texts frequently recopied, the Septuagint
suffered so many alterations in the course of centuries that
the time came when it was felt that a revision was necessary.
So far as we know, the first scholar to undertake a vast critical
work on the text of Septuagint was Origen, at the beginning
of the third century. To emphasize the exact relationship
between the original Hebrew and the Greek translation, Origen

decided to publish a parallel edition of the two texts. He included also copies of the Greek translations made after the Septuagint, which we shall take up later. His work thus comprised six columns : the first reproduced the Hebrew text in Hebrew characters; the second, the same text transcribed in Greek characters; the third, the version of Aquila; the fourth, the version of Symmachus; the fifth, the Septuagint; the sixth, the version of Theodotion. An abridged edition, the Tetrapla, contained only the last four columns and omitted the Hebrew. For the Book of Psalms, Origen, having discovered two new Greek versions, added them to the preceding ones, so that the Hexapla, in this case, took the form of an Octapla.

While the other texts were reproduced just as they were, Origen applied himself to a careful revision of the Septuagint in order to restore it to its primitive purity and to bring out its relation to the original Hebrew. To accomplish this purpose, he adopted the critical signs which had long been employed by the Alexandrian scholars in their editions of secular authors. He indicated by an obelus the passages which were missing from the Hebrew but were added by the Greek, and by an asterisk, the passages which appeared in the Hebrew but were not contained in the Septuagint. At the end of the passages thus marked with the obelus or asterisks he placed a third sign, the metobelus, to indicate specifically the length of such passages.

The Hexapla was a very large work, for it has been estimated that it must have comprised around 3250 pages. Under these conditions, it was difficult to multiply copies, and it may even be questioned whether the work ever existed in completed form. The original manuscript was available for a long time at the library of Caesarea in Palestine. At the end of the fourth century Saint Jerome could still consult it, and it seems that it was there even as late as the sixth century. It disappeared, apparently, in the seventh century when the city was taken by the Saracens. Cardinal Mercati, in 1896, announced his discovery of a palimpsest fragment of the Hexapla at the Ambrosiana in Milan [1]. Ancient exegetes, furthermore, often cited readings from the various translations copied by

[1] Cf. H. B. SWETE, *An Introduction to the Old Testament in Greek* (Cambridge, 1902), pp. 61-65. [New edition by R. L. OTTLEY, 1914].

Origen, and through their works we thus possess important passages.

In the absence of the complete work, the fifth column at least, which contained the Septuagint, was copied, but the special critical symbols were allowed more or less to drop out, as they practically ceased to have any significance, once the Hebrew had disappeared. We call the text thus revised by Origen the Hexaplaric Recension, and a very considerable number of manuscripts have preserved it, at least in part.

Origen was not alone in desiring to publish a critical edition of the Septuagint. At the beginning of the fourth century, the Alexandrian Hesychius likewise revised the text of the venerable translation, and his work was transcribed often enough to become current in Egypt. About the same time an Antiochene priest, Lucian, carried out a similar undertaking and tried to bring the Greek closer to the Hebrew original. Lucian's recension was adopted at Antioch, in Syria, and even as far as Constantinople. It should be observed that our knowledge of these two recensions is very limited although they are represented by a certain number of Mss. It is difficult, especially, to get a precise idea of the text of Hesychius, and it is probable that Lucian and Hesychius utilized for their work texts already revised by unknown predecessors.

We still possess a large number of manuscripts which contain the Septuagint Version either in whole or in part. In 1827, Holmes and Parsons listed three hundred and eleven manuscripts which they had used for their edition. This figure has increased considerably since their time because the rich collections of libraries have been better explored and new discoveries have been made. The oldest and best known manuscripts of the Septuagint are : the *Alexandrinus* (A), 4th—5 th century, today in the British Museum at London; the *Vaticanus* (B), 4th century at the Vatican Library; the *Sinaiticus* (ℵ), discovered in the Monastery of Saint Catherine on Mount Sinai by Tischendorf between 1844 and 1859, and now divided between the libraries of Leipzig and the British Museum; the *Codex Ephraemi Rescriptus*, 5th century, very incomplete, its Biblical text badly effaced and hidden under sermons of Saint Ephraem written over it, now at the Bibliothèque Nationale in Paris; the *Codex Marchialanus* (Q) of the 6th century, a Ms of 416 leaves containing the Prophetical Books; the *Codex Basiliano-Vaticanus* (N) and the *Codex Venetus* (V), 8th-9th century, which are really two parts of the one manuscript, and hence ought to be considered together.

To the manuscripts in the strict sense, it is proper to add the papyri which the sands of Egypt are making available to scholars. Usually, these papyri are very fragmentary and of interest only for specialists concerned with the history of the text. Sometimes however they are of considerable importance. Thus the Rylands Papyrus 458, which contains some fragments of Deuteronomy, probably dates from about the middle of the second century before our era, and is therefore much earlier than any of our known manuscripts. The Chester Beatty Papyri 961 and 962 and Papyrus 911 of Berlin, the first dating from the first half of the 4th century, and the second and third from the second half of the 3rd century, have preserved a more complete text of Genesis than that of the great manuscripts of the 4th century [1]. The fragments of Proverbs, preserved in the papyri of Antinoopolis, are the first substantial contribution made to this book by the papyri [2]. Its text has a considerable interest, for it is characterized by a large number of readings which are either unique or are known solely through the Hebrew text or the translations other than the Septuagint. The fragments of Wisdom preserved in the same collection are very short but sufficient to reveal the text as being very eccentric. A parchment roll, discovered in August, 1952, in one of the caves near the Dead Sea and assigned to the last century B.C., contained originally the Greek text of the Minor Prophets and still exhibits parts of Micheas, Jonas, Nahum, Habacuc, Sophonias, and Zacharias. It owes its importance not only to its Palestinian origin, but also to the fact that its text is a recension characteristic of the Septuagint and that this recension is of Jewish origin [3].

The first printed edition of the Septuagint is that of Alcala (Complutum) in Spain. The printing was completed in 1517

---

[1] See *The Chester Beatty Biblical Papyri*. Edited by F. KENYON (London, 1933-1937), and *Two Biblical Papyri*. Edited by C. H. ROBERTS (Manchester, 1936).

[2] *The Papyrus of Antinoopolis*. Edited by C. H. ROBERTS (London, 1950).

[3] D. BARTHÉLEMY, " Redécouverte d'un chaînon manquant de l'histoire de la Septante ", *RB* (1953), 18-29.

under the direction of Cardinal Ximenez but the work was published only in 1520. The Alcala Bible is a polyglot, which, in addition to the Septuagint, presents the Hebrew text with the Targum of Onkelos and also the Latin Vulgate. The Aldine edition was published at Venice in February, 1518, and appeared thus before that of Ximenez, although its printing had been completed a little later. In 1587, the Vatican edition of the Septuagint appeared under the auspices of Sixtus V. It reproduces regularly the text of the *Vaticanus*, and is thus much better than the preceding editions.

In the eighteenth century, J. Grabe, and, after his death, Fr. Lee and W. Wigan published at Oxford (1707-1720) a new edition based on the *Codex Alexandrinus*. As is evident, each of these four editions reproduces only one type of the manuscripts, or even only one manuscript. The distinction of undertaking a truly critical edition was reserved for R. Holmes and, later, for J. Parsons. The volumes of this monumental edition appeared at Oxford from 1798 to 1827. The edition of Holmes-Parsons has been much discussed and it is certain that is is far from perfect. Such as it is, it represents a remarkable progress over those which had preceded it. A. Rahlfs, in 1914, published a list of the manuscripts of the Septuagint, in which the series of sigla used by Holmes-Parsons is continued as far as 2408 (some numbers, however, not being utilized) [1]. At present, the Universities of Cambridge and Göttingen are sponsoring the preparation of two new editions.

The Göttingen edition intends in principle to reconstitute, in the first place, as faithfully as possible the three or four great recensions of which traces are found in the Greek manuscripts : those of Lucian and Origen, a third of unknown origin (Hesychius?), and a fourth re-established especially on the basis of the fragments contained in the *Catenæ*. On the foundation of these recensions, a single text is then to be constituted which, in the opinion of the editors, would be as close as possible to the original translation. After the death of A. Rahlfs, who was the first editor, the work has been taken over by Kappler [2] and

---

[1] A. RAHLFS, *Verzeichnis der griechischen Handschriften des Alten Testaments* (Göttingen, 1914).

[2] Kappler died in 1944.

Ziegler. The Cambridge edition, prepared by A. E. Brooke and N. Mc Leane, and then by H. St. John Thackeray, is less ambitious, but is also more realistic. It always takes Ms B, wherever it is extant, as its point of departure, and it gives the variants of the great uncial Mss along with those of 32 other Mss selected for the Octoteuch from the Old Latin, the Coptic versions, the Syro-Hexapla, the Armenian version, Josephus, Philo, and the principal Fathers.

Workers have two manual editions at their disposal, that of H. B. Swete, which reproduces B with the variants from the great unical manuscripts (Cambridge, 1887), and that of A. Rahlfs, which gives an eclectic text based mainly on A, B, and ℵ (Göttingen, 1935).

II. — The Versions of Aquila, Theodotion, and Symmachus

The Septuagint, as we have already mentioned, is not the only Greek version which was made of the Old Testament. In spite of the value and authority of this translation, the need for new translations which would be more faithful in rendering the letter of the Hebrew text was felt very soon in Jewish circles.

The first is the work of Aquila, a Jewish proselyte and native of Sinope in Pontus, who lived in the time of the Emperor Hadrian (117-138). It was extremely literal and endeavored to render into Greek the least details of the original Hebrew. We possess only fragments transmitted by writers who quoted the Hexapla of Origen and some passages preserved in palimpsests found in Cairo. Since the discovery of the Greek fragments of the Minor Prophets made in August, 1952, it must be acknowledged that the work of Aquila was neither as complete or as original as we thought. Aquila's achievement, in fact, was apparently limited to this : he carried through for the whole Bible a recension which had already begun to see the light in Palestinian Judaism before the Second Jewish Revolt of 130, very probably in connection with the integralist and unifying reform which followed the year 70. This first recension probably even had time, before Aquila, to get a foothold in Egypt, at Ephesus, and in Greece.

The second is due, according to Saint Irenaeus, to a Jewish proselyte of Ephesus who lived at the end of the second century and bore the name of Theodotion. His knowledge of Hebrew was inadequate, so that he sometimes merely transcribed what he did not understand. In general, he follows pretty closely the Septuagint text, which he corrects with the aid of Aquila and the Hebrew. Rather than a new version in the strict sense, his work is a recension or revision of the Septuagint. Our knowledge of Theodotion's translation is very limited. We do know, however, that, in the case of the Book of Daniel, it replaced the Septuagint version in all but two manuscripts (*Codex Chusianus* and the *Codex Ambrosianus* of the Syro-Hexapla) [1]. It seems, moreover, that Theodotion had revised this book on the basis of a text different from that of the Septuagint.

Symmachus, the author of a third Greek version, was probably, according to Saint Epiphanius, a Samaritan convert to Judaism, who lived in the reign of Septimus Severus (193-211). His translation appears to have been elegant and clear, but it was too free and frequently became a mere paraphrase. We now have nothing more than fragments of this work.

Eusebius informs us that Origen had discovered two or three other Greek translations of the Bible which are known only under the names of *Quinta, Sexta,* and *Septima,* i.e., according to the places which they occupied in the Hexapla. Of the last, *Septima,* we know nothing at all, and even its very existence is open to doubt [2]. Of the two first we have a few fragments, but they scarcely permit us to form any concrete idea of their character.

. The *Quinta* was probably found at Nicopolis in Epirus; the *Sexta,* in the vicinity of Jericho.

Finally, a Jew of the fourteenth century is the author of a translation of the Pentateuch and of certain other books (Prov., Ruth, C. C., Eccles., Lam., Jer., Dan.). This translation is known only through a single Ms of the 14th—15th century, preserved at Venice.

---

[1] The Chester Beatty Papyri preserve the LXX text of Daniel 3 : 92-6 : 18 and 7 : 1-8 : 27.

Translator's note. — [2 See the discussion of Eusebius' text on the matter in J. BALESTRI, *op. cit.,* p. 139 and note].

II. — The Ancient Oriental Versions [1].

[G. Bardy]

Of the ancient Oriental versions of the Old Testament, some depend on the Hebrew and others on the Septuagint.

The New Testament was translated into various Oriental languages either from Greek or from some earlier version.

1º *The Egyptian versions* [2]. — While Greek was the language spoken at Alexandria and in the towns on the Mediterranean coast of the Empire, the inhabitants of the interior continued to employ their own native idioms. At a quite early date, it seems, the Christians of Egypt felt the need of reading the Bible in the Coptic dialects which they used in their daily life, and it is probable that, toward the end of the 2nd century of our era, the essential parts at least of the Old (according to the Septuagint) and New Testaments had already been translated into Coptic.

We possess the remnants of several Coptic versions, for in Egypt Christianity spread among the masses to such a degree that the Bible was translated into the vernacular, and each of the great dialects used in Upper, Lower, and Middle Egypt had its own more or less complete version or versions. We are familiar, e.g., with the existence of a Bohairic translation for Lower Egypt, a Sahidic translation for Upper Egypt, and Fayumic and Akhmimic versions for Middle Egypt.

2º *The Ethiopic versions* [3]. — Christianity was introduced into Ethiopia, according to tradition, in the 4th century. The work of translating the Septuagint into Ethiopic began almost at once, and this version was finished by the end of the 5th century.

Translator's note. — [1 See pp. 611-613 *supra*, and also the article " Bibelüber- setzungen ", *LTK* (2nd ed., 1958), 384 ff.]

Translator's note. — [2 For references to the works of J. Balestri, H. Hyvernat, etc., see J. Balestri, *op. cit.*, pp. 238-250. For a list of the texts published in the different dialects, see A. Vaschalde, " Ce qui a été publié des Versions Coptes de la Bible (premier groupe : Textes Sahidiques) ", *RB* (1919), 220-243, 513-531; (1920), 91-106, 241-258; (1921), 237-246; (1922), 81-88, 234-258; *id.*, " Deuxième groupe (Textes Bohairiques), *Le Muséon*, 23 (1930), 412-433; 45 (1932), 117-156; " Troisième groupe (Textes en moyen Egyptien) ", 46 (1933), 299-313].

Translator's note. — [3 Cf. J. M. Harden, *An Introduction to Ethiopic Chris- tian Literature*, SPCK (London, 1926); I. Guidi, *Storia della letteratura Etiopica*, (Rome, 1932). For editions of the text of the Bible, see M. Chaine, S. J., *Grammaire Ethiopienne* (Beyrouth, 1907; reprinted 1938), Appendix, p. 268].

We have no information on the translators, nor on the date of their work, and our manuscripts are too recent — the oldest being from the 13th century — to give us any useful indications. The first complete edition of the Ethiopic Bible was published in 1920-1926. It should be noted that this Bible contains a certain number of *pseudepigrapha* *(Henoch, Jubilees,* and *4 Esdras).*

3º *The Arabic versions.* [1] — A number of Arabic translations of the Bible were made; some according to the Greek of the Septuagint for the Old Testament and the original Greek for the New, others according to the Syriac text of the Peshitto, and still others according to the Hebrew. The oldest Arabic translation of the Gospels which we possess dates from the 8th century, and it is only at the end of the 13th century that a revision of the Gospels was imposed on the Arabic-speaking Christians of Egypt. It is recognized that the Arabic translation of the Old Testament from the Hebrew made by Rabbi Saadia Gaon († 942) possesses some value.

4º *The Syriac versions.* [2] — The Syriac versions are very important on account of their antiquity, but their history

---

Translator's note. — [1 The best and most complete account of Arabic versions of the Bible will be found in G. GRAF, *Geschichte der christlichen arabischen Literatur,* I (Rome, 1944), pp. 85-195, with a full treatment of the Apocrypha and Pseudepigraphica, pp. 196-297. The collection of Arabic Mss of St. Catherine's Convent in Sinai microfilmed by the joint labors of the Library of Congress and of the University of King Fuad I in Alexandria will make available abundant material for the study of the Arabic Versions. Cf. *al-Kitab* (Oct., 1950), 762-763. A. S. ATIYA, *The Arabic Manuscripts of Mount Sinai* (Baltimore, 1955; cf. *RB* [1955], 632-633). L. CHEIKO, S. J. (in his *Christianity and Christian Literature before Islam,* Part 2, No. 1, 254 ff. [Beyrouth, 1919; in Arabic]) holds that there was an ancient Arabic translation of the O. and N. T. that is now lost. (Cf. also *Theologische Revue* [1951], 91)].

Translator's note. — [2 For the Isaias Ms (British Museum, Add. 14512), see W. WRIGHT, *Catalogue of Syriac Mss. in the British Museum,* I. (1870), p. 251ª; for the Pentateuch Ms (British Museum, Add. 14425), *ibid.,* III (1872), Plate II (= Exodus 27, 1-14). Leviticus is not in the Pentateuch Ms. For both Mss, see also W. H. P. HATCH, *An Album of Dated Syriac Mss* (Boston, 1946), Plate II, and p. 53; Plate IV, and p. 55. On the Yonan Codex, represented by some of its advocates as most ancient, even as reproducing the original language of Christ, see the sober account of E. F. SIEGMAN in *CBQ* (1956), 151-157. On the work of Vööbus on the Syriac versions, see *Theologische Revue* (1951), 91 ff., and his own article in *LTK* (2nd ed., 1958), 386-392. On the *Diatessaron,* which had great influence on textual criticism, see Sir F. KENYON, *Our Bible and the Ancient Manuscripts* (revised ed., 1958), pp. 221 ff.; A. WIKENHAUSER, *Einleitung in das N. T.* (Freiburg, i. Br., 1956), pp. 81-84; S. LYONNET, S. J., *Les origines de la version arménienne et le Diatesseron* (Biblica

remains extremely obscure. According to Moses Bar-Cephas († 913) there were two Syriac translations of the Old Testament; the Peshitto, translated from the Hebrew in the time of King Abgar [† 50 A.D.], and the version of Paul of Tella, made from the Septuagint [in 616-657]. This is a simplified view of the facts, but it has the advantage of giving prominence to the Peshitto or simple version.

The Old Testament which is found in the Peshitto was translated very early and according to the Hebrew. We possess a Ms of it dated 460 (Isaias, fragmentary) and another dated 464 (the Pentateuch), and we know through Saint Ephrem that this translation was already old in the 4th century. It is the work of several authors, probably Jews, and for its oldest parts it must go back to the 1st or 2nd century. The translation of the New Testament in the Peshitto seems more recent. It existed, certainly, in the 5th century, since it is quoted by Isaac of Antioch, but we have nothing definite on its earlier history.

We are sure, however, that the Gospels at least had been translated into Syriac at a much earlier date. We owe to Tatian a harmony of the Gospels, the *Diatessaron*, which was originally composed in Greek, but, on being translated into Syriac, was officially received in the Churches of the Euphrates region, and appears indeed to have been the oldest version of the Gospels. The so-called Cureton and Sinaitic translations which are perhaps, however, only recensions of one and the same work, not independent versions, seem to be a little later.

The version made by Paul of Tella, which dates from 616-617, includes the Old Testament only. It is a literal translation of the Septuagint, as it was found in Origen's Hexapla, and it scrupulously retained the critical symbols employed in the latter. Hence the name Syro-Hexaplar, which it likewise bears. We possess extensive fragments of this version, which are very important for completing our direct knowledge of the Septuagint in Origen's recension. The version of the New Testament made at Alexandria by Thomas of Heraclea, who was then in

et Orientalia, No 13, Rome, 1950; cf. on this, M. A. VAN DEN OUDENRIJN, O. P., in *Bibliotheca Orientalis* [1951], 243-244). G. MASSINA, S. J. *Diatesseron persiano* (Rome, 1951; cf. B. M. METZGER, in *Journal of Biblical Literature* [1952], 45-48). W. J. FISCHEL, " The Bible in Persian Translation ", *Harvard Theol. Rev.* (1952), 3-45. L. MARIÈS, " Le Diatesseron à l'origine de la Version arménienne ", *RSR* (1952), 247-256].

exile, comes from this same period. It is a very literal translation which endeavors to reproduce all the details of the Greek text.

Another Syriac version, likewise from the Septuagint, was made by the chorepiscopus Polycarp. The latter prepared it about 508 at the demand of his bishop, Philoxenus of Mabbug. Hence the name Philoxenian Version under which we know it.

Other Syriac translations also were made from the Greek, e.g., the Syro-Palestinian, the version of James of Edessa, etc [1].

5° *The Armenian version.* — The Armenian writers of the 5th century attribute the translation of the Bible in their language, or at least the initiation of the work, to Bishop Mersop or Machtots and his associates. The translators perhaps began their work with the Book of Proverbs. It was long thought that the Armenian version was made from the Syriac, but it is now admitted rather that this translation was made from the Greek of the Septuagint for the Old Testament and from the original Greek for the New. But this does not exclude the possibility that, for the Gospels, there was first a *Diatesseron*, translated from the Syriac and employed at least to the end of the 5th century [2].

6° *The Georgian version.* — The beginnings of the Georgian version are obscure. It seems that the translation of the Gospels goes back to the 5th century and that as early as the 6th century the Georgians possessed the entire Bible in their language. This version, derived from the Armenian, was subsequently collated with and influenced by the Syriac translation. Later, it was revised according to the Greek text [3].

7° *The Slavic version.* — This version goes back in part to the two apostles of the Slavs, Saints Cyril († 869) and Methodius († 885), who translated the most important books of the Old Testament, and in particular, the Psalter, for liturgical use. But the Slavic Bible long remained incomplete. The translation of the whole Bible into Slavic was only completed towards the

---

Translator's note. — [1 On the Syriac versions cf. J. BALESTRI, *op. cit.*, pp. 251-269; P. KAHLE, *The Cairo Geniza* (London, 1947), pp. 179-197 pp].

Translator's note. — [2 Cf. A. BAUMSTARK, *LTK*, II (1932), pp. 320-321].

Translator's note. — [3 Cf. J. MOLITOR, in *LTK*, II (2nd ed., 1958), p. 398. M. TARCHNIŠVILI, *Geschichte der kirchlichen georgischen Literatur* (Rome, 1955), pp. 313-328].

end of the 15th century through the care of Gennadius, Archbishop of Novgorod.

8º *The Gothic version*. — Socrates and other Greek historians of the 5th century relate that the Gothic bishop Ulfilas († 381) invented a system of writing for his fellow countrymen and translated the Bible into Gothic, following the Greek text. It is added, however, that he omitted the Books of Kings because he did not wish to stimulate further their bellicose instincts. A 6th century Ms has preserved Ulfilas' version of a large part of the Gospels. For the Old Testament, we have only fragments extant, but they are sufficient to indicate the value of this translation, which was as elegant as it was faithful.

III. — THE LATIN VERSIONS. THE VULGATE.

[A. TRICOT]. [1]

Greek was the original language of the Church [2] : Missionaries of the first and second Christian generations preached in Greek, the Books of the New Testament were written in Greek, the liturgical language at first was Greek, and Greek was employed in the reading of the sacred texts in the religious assemblies. For the Old Testament, the Septuagint Version was used, and for the New Testament, the texts in the original. Christianity passed from the East to the West through the medium of the Greek language, with which the peoples living on the shores of the Mediterranean, even in southern Gaul and on the east coast of Spain, were sufficiently familiar. The Church of Rome used Greek to the middle of the 3rd century (liturgical books, funeral inscriptions of the Catacombs, names of the Popes, etc.). It is necessary to keep this fact in mind in order to understand the genesis and character of the earliest Latin translations.

---

[1] The author of this study has put to good use the remarks and suggestions of Dom Charlier of the Abbey of Maredsous.

Translator's note. — [2 On the use of Greek in the Early Church and, in particular at Rome, cf. : G. BARDY, *La question des langues dans l'Eglise ancienne*, I (Paris, 1948), 1-121, and 155-164. J. A. JUNGMANN, S. J., *Missarum Sollemnia. Eine genetische Erklärung der römischen Messe* (2 vols., 2nd ed., Vienna, 1949), I, 65 ff. C. MOHRMANN, *Liturgical Latin : Its Origins and Character* (Washington, 1957); *id.*, " Les origines de la latinité chrétienne à Rome ", *Vigiliae Christianae* (1949), 67-106, and 163-183].

The need of a version of Holy Scripture in the Latin language made itself felt as soon as large groups in the Roman world who did not understand Greek had been converted to Christianity. In the Churches where the Latin speakers predominated, a Latin text of the Bible became absolutely necessary for teaching purposes. The same need was felt also in the work of spreading the Faith among the pagans in certain western provinces of the Roman Empire, in which Greek was known only by the educated and where the masses had some familiarity with Latin. This was the case in North Africa, especially in Proconsular Africa and in Numidia, where Latin was obligatory for the municipal assemblies, for the courts, and for the army, in which so many natives were serving. The same condition prevailed in the southern region of Gaul. In the persecution of 177, the Church of Lyons already comprised, besides its Asiatic elements, members of the faithful who preferred to answer in Latin the questions put to them by the magistrates.

These facts indicate that the cradle of the first Latin versions of the Bible ought to be sought in environments of this kind. The oldest evidence for a Latin translation of a part of the New Testament is furnished us in Africa by the *Acta* of the Scillitan martyrs. Twelve members of the faithful at Scillium, a little town in Proconsular Numidia, were arraigned before the tribunal of the proconsul Saturninus at Carthage on July 17, 180. These people of lowly condition, who certainly did not know Greek, declared to the magistrate that they had with them *libri et epistulæ Pauli, viri iusti*. Some years later Tertullian had at hand at least two versions of the New Testament in Latin, one of which was a Marcionite text. In the time of Saint Cyprian (died in 258) all the books of the Bible, or nearly all, had been translated into Latin. In the same period the Church of Rome was in possession of a Latin version of the Scriptures, as is proved by the writtings of Novatian.

What do we know of and what remains to us of these first attempts at translation of the Bible into Latin? The answer is to be found in the history of the Latin versions before Saint Jerome, i.e., before the revision of the Latin text of Holy Scripture undertaken and completed by the great Doctor at the demand of Pope Damasus. The exposition of the origin and development of the translation by Saint Jerome, which became the Vulgate, will permit us to pursue the history of the Latin versions in its successive stages.

1. — THE LATIN VERSIONS BEFORE SAINT JEROME [1].

The Latin translations before Saint Jerome (the *Old Latin*, according to our current usage) have awakened the curiosity of critics and retained their attention only since the end of the seventeenth century. After Richard Simon, J. Martianay, P. Sabatier, and J. Bianchini all recognized the importance of these texts in the eighteenth century, and they edited whatever of these materials they could find. Although the work has been continued, it is far from being finished, and we do not yet have a critical edition of the Old Latin versions. This situation is not due to the fact that the text or manuscript tradition is rich in itself. We have hardly more than some fifty Mss, or fragments of Mss, and the more important of these have been published. But, generally speaking, the majority of the problems which arise in respect to each of these texts (author, place of origin, date, transmission, influences and their effects, etc.) are not yet completely solved. In the case of the New Testament, the studies of H. J. Vogels, and especially the work of A. Jülicher, of which three volumes have appeared to date, represent a valuable contribution [2].

The importance of the Old Latin versions as witnesses for the text depends, first of all, on their age, for some of them date from the second half of the 2nd century. Tertullian had at hand a Latin version of the New Testament ,and the Marcionite text which he possessed was apparently a text in the Latin language. Next, it depends on the character of the translation.

Translator's note. — [[1] Cf. M. STENGEL, " Zur Frühgeschichte der lateinischen Bibel ", *Theologische Revue* (1953), 97-103 (a survey-article). K. T. SCHÄFER, *LTK*, II (2nd ed., 1958), 380-384. A. WIKENHAUSER, *Einleitung in das N. T.* (Freiburg i. Br., 1958), 68-79, and 410. For further bibliography on the Old Latin, see the Bibliography at the end of this chapter.]

[2] See the Bibliography at the end of this chapter. Two collections of Old Latin texts have been published, and the publication of a third — and more important one — has commenced : *Old Latin Biblical Texts*, I-VII (Oxford, 1883-1923); *Collectanea Biblica Latina*, edited by the Benedictines of St. Jerome's Abbey in Rome (Rome, 1912 ff.; 11 vols. to date, the majority of which are devoted to the Old Latin); *Vetus Latina. Die Reste der altlateinischen Bibel nach P. Sabatier neu gesammelt und herausgegeben von der Erzabtei Beuron* (Freiburg i. Br., 1948 ff.; *Genesis* [1951-1954]; *Epistolae Cath. et Apoc.* [1956 ff.)].

Usually, the desire to be faithful to the original degenerates into servility, and this very literalness is in itself of great help for the reconstruction of the underlying text. Finally, it depends on the fact that these versions represent the so-called " Western " text, which in the 2nd and 3rd centuries had become disseminated a little everywhere, both in the East as well as in the West.

We may consider the distinction of the two principal types as settled, one called the *African*, and the other the *European*, their characteristic features being sufficient to prevent them from being confused [1]. In both we find the same popular Latin with its peculiarities of vocabulary, of spelling, and of syntax, that incorrect and even vulgar and trivial form of speech, which shocked Saint Augustine as much as irreverence toward the word of God. In both, the translation is strictly literal, even slavishly literal, the Latin words rendering the Greek absolutely word for word almost like a stamp or pattern, at the expense of the shades of meaning intended in the original text. What may be called the specific differences between the two groups consists in some lexicographical peculiarities, constantly attested, or in readings peculiar to each, the origin of which must be sought in the Greek text used for the revisions, when they are not to be assigned to the copyists.

As regards the Old Testament, there can be no doubt that a number of translators worked on it, and its translation must be regarded as a collective work. A second point, equally certain, is that the translation was made, not from the Hebrew text, but from the Septuagint such as it was before the Hexaplar recension of Origen. The Pre-Hieronymian text of the Book of Wisdom, of Ecclesiasticus, of Baruch, of 1 and 2 Machabees, of Esther (**10** : 4–**16** : 24), and of Daniel (**3** : 24-100, **13-14**), has been preserved more or less pure in the Vulgate, since,

---

[1] It is better not to employ the term *Itala* to designate either the Old Latin versions in their totality, or the European group, or one of the texts of this group. The epithet is used by Saint Augustine with reference to a Latin version which he judged was more literal and more clear than others (*verborum tenacior cum perspicuitate sententiæ*. Cf. *De Doctrina Christiana*, II, **15**, 22). What was this version? Certainly it was not a version of the African type. Was it perhaps an Italian text in use in the Church of Milan? *Translator's note.* — [For a discussion of this text of Saint Augustine, see J. BALESTRI, *op. cit.*, pp. 169-179, and especially Dom B. BOTTE, " Itala ", in *DBV, Suppl.*, IV, 777-782].

in the case of the Deuterocanonical Books and Fragments of the Old Testament, Saint Jerome made a new translation only of Judith and Tobias [1]. Among the Mss, we must mention for the Heptateuch : the *Codex Lugdunensis*, 6th century; the *Codex Monacensis*, 5th-6th century : the *Codex Wirceburgensis*, 6th century; the fragments of *Codex Ottobonianus*, 7th century; for the Historical Books (Samuel and Kings) : *Codex Vindobonensis*, 5th century, and *Codex Quedlinburgensis*, 7th century, both very incomplete; for the Prophetical Books : *Codex Wirceburgensis* and *Codex Constantiensis*, 6th century; for the Psalms : *Codex Sangermanensis I*, 6th century, and *Codex Coislinianus*, 7th century. The *Speculum* or *Liber de divinis Scripturis*, a collection of texts from the Old Testament falsely attributed to Saint Augustine, is a witness of great interest for the Old Latin Version.

The study of the witnesses (Mss and patristic quotations) of the Latin text before Saint Jerome is much more advanced for the New Testament than for the Old. Among the Mss which, basically, represent the African text, it is necessary to cite for the Gospels : the *Codex Bobbiensis (k)*, 4th or 5th century, and *Codex Palatinus (e)*, 5th century; for the Acts of the Apostles : the *Palimpsest Floriacensis (k)*, the 6th or 7th century, incomplete; for the Catholic Epistles and the Apocalypse : the *Palimpsest Floriacensis*. Besides the Mss in the strict sense, we have also, as a witness of the African text, the *Speculum* or *Liber de divinis Scripturis (m)*, a collection of extracts from almost all the books of the New Testament, preserved in several copies, one of which dates from the 8th or 9th century. Finally, the Scriptural quotations of Saint Cyprian, Priscillian, Tyconius, and Primasius correspond to this same African text.

As regards the European text, there are several famous Mss among the witnesses. For the Gospels, there are two distinct types; on the one hand, a text which is only a European recension of the African text, as in the case of the *Codex Veronensis (b)*, and the *Codex Corbeiensis II (ff²)*, both of the 5th century; on the other, a less homogeneous text represented by *Codex Vercellensis (a)*, 4th century, and *Codex*

---

[1] On the work of Saint Jerome, see pp. 645 ff. below.

Bezæ (d), 5th century. For the Acts of the Apostles, we have this same Ms *(d)*; the *Codex Gigas (g)*, 13th century; the *Palimpsest Bobbiensis (s)*, 5th or 6th century, and the quotations of Lucifer of Cagliari; for the Epistles of Saint Paul : the *Codex Claromontanus (d* — the Latin side of this bilingual Ms.), 6th century, and the *Codex Boergerianus (g* — the Latin side of this bilingual Ms), 9th century; for the Apocalypse : the *Codex Gigas* and the commentary of Saint Victorinus of Pettau [1].

It will suffice to compare two parallel passages (Mt., 2 : 10-20), one from the *Codex Bobbiensis* and the other from the *Codex Vercellensis*, in order to show that the style is not the same in both, and that, therefore, the separation of the Old Latin witnesses into two groups is fully justified.

Codex Bobbiensis (k)

Mt. **2,** 10. cum vidissent autem stellam gavisi sunt gaudium magnum nimis 11. et cum introissent domum viderent infantem cum mariam matre eius et prostrati adoraverunt illum, et aperunt thensauros suos. et optulerunt et dona. aurum et thus et murram. 12. et responso moniti in somnis non reverti ad heroden per aliam quam reversi sunt in regionem suam. 13. et cum illi discessissent. ecce angelus dōm apparuit in somnis iosef dicens. ei sure et gadiume puerum et matrem eius et fugit in aegyptum et esto illic quodadusque. tibi dicam quaesiturus est enim erodes puerum ut eum perdat 14. ille autem exsurrexit et adsumpsit puerum et matrem eius nocte et secessit in aegyptum. 15. et fuit illic donec moreretur herodes. ut adimpleretur quod dictum est a domino profetam dicentem ab aegypto vocavit filium meum. 16. tunc herodes. cum vidisset quoniam inlusus est magis

Codex Vercellensis (a)

Mt. **2,** 10. Videntes autem stellam gavisi sunt gaudio magno valde. 11. et intrantes in domum viderunt puerum cum mariam matre eius et procedentes adoraverunt eum et apertis thensauris suis obtulerunt ei munera aurum thus et murra 12. et admoniti in somnis ne redirent ad herodem per aliam viam regressi sunt in suam regionem 13. Qui cum recessissent ecce angelus dm̄i apparuit in somnis iosef dicens surge et accipe puerum et matrem eius et fuge in aegyptum et esto ibi usque dum dicam tibi futurum est enim ut herodes quaerat puerum istum perdere. 14. Surgens autem iosef a somno accepit puerum et matrem eius et abiit in aegyptum 15. et erat ibi usque ad mortem herodis ut adimpleretur quod dictum est a dm̄o per prophetam dicentem Ex aegypto vocavi filium meum 16. tunc herodes ut vidit quoniam delusus est a magis iratus est valde et misit et occidit omnes pueros qui

---

Translator's note. — [1 For a more complete list and description of the Mss, including their contents and a bibliography for each of the texts, see J. BALESTRI, *op. cit.*, pp. 79-185; *ibid.*, pp. 187-189].

indignatus est nimis et misit inter-
fecit omnes pueros qui fuerunt
bethlem. et in omnibus finibus eius
a bimatum et infra secundum tempus quot exquisierat a magis.
17. tunc adimpletum est quod
dictum est per hieremiam profetam.
dicentem 18. vox in rama audita est
ploratio et fletus. rachel plorantis
filios suos. et noluit consolari quia
non sunt 19. cum autem mortuus
est herodes ecce angelus dōm apparuit in somnis iosef. 20. dicens ei.
exsurge et adsume puerum. et
matrem eius. et vade in terram
isdrael. mortui sunt enim. qui
quaerebant animam pueri.

erant in bethlem et in omnibus
regionibus eius a bimatu et infra
secundum tempus quod exquisierat
a magis 17. Tunc adimpletum est
quod dictum est per hieremiam
prophetam dicentem 18. vox in
rhama audita est fletus et ululatus
multus rachel plorans filios suos
et noluit consolari quia non sunt
19. Defuncto autem herode ecce
angelus dmī apparuit in somnis
iosef in aegypto 20. dicens surge et
accipe puerum et matrem eius et
vade in terram istrahel defunctus
est enim qui quaerebat animam
pueri.

A more extensive and more thorough investigation of the differences which justify the distinction between the two types of texts, namely, the African and the European, might lead perhaps to the conclusion that they do not stem from one same original version. Certain scholars, and among them Father Lagrange, have pronounced definitely in favor of a plurality of versions. According to these critics, the African text, which is older than the European text, represents an original translation made in Africa and the work of several authors, while the European text comes from another translation, made independently of the African. These views are not accepted by all scholars who have devoted themselves to the study of the Old Latin translations. There are some who favor one basic version of African origin. The work of revisors with their corrections and alterations would have resulted in the formation of a new text, the European text; the two texts would then have reacted on each other, compenetrating and contaminating each other by mutual interference and influence, following a process which can be traced historically in the Mss.

The problem is extremely complex and is still *sub iudice*. It is best to examine it concretely, with each book being taken separately, before formulating a judgment. It is thus that A. Jülicher has concluded that there was a single basic text, of African origin, for the Book of Acts. In like manner, Billen reached the same conclusion for the Heptateuch, and

Dom de Bruyne for Machabees, Wisdom, and the Canticle of Canticles. Thielmann distinguishes, in the unique version of Ecclesiasticus, the work of three translators, one an African, and the other two, Europeans. On the other hand, Vogels has declared himself in favor of three translators for the Apocalypse, and Dom R. Weber gives the same number for 2 Chronicles. As regards the Gospels, it is very difficult to decide between a revision or recension of an ancient text and a new translation made on the basis of an earlier version.

Whatever may be the solutions given to this literary problem, one point remains constant and firmly established, namely, that the African texts stand out as the more homogeneous and have the advantage of being earlier. After Africa — and we should think primarily of Carthage — it is in Northern Italy and Southern Gaul that it is most fitting to locate the centers of translation, of revision, and of diffusion of the Old Latin Versions.

In the case of the African text of the New Testament, the question has arisen whether, in its first form, it did not stem from the Latin translation of Marcion's *Evangelion* and *Apostolicon*. For two reasons, it seems that the answer should be in the negative. In the first place, the priority of the Marcionite version is not proven. In the second place, the diffusion of Marcion's Bible was scarcely beginning in the Churches of North Africa at a time when we already have our first definite testimony on the existence of the African text. There is little doubt that, subsequently, the Marcionite edition may have exercised some influence on the Latin text. The Latin translation of the anti-Marcionite prologues of the Gospels and the employment of the expurgated Marcionite prologues as headings or prefaces for the Pauline Epistles point in the same direction. But there can be question of an indirect influence only, occasioned by the reaction provoked by Marcionite propaganda.

The hypothesis of a direct and preponderant influence of the Latin *Diatessaron* of Tatian on the African version of the Gospels can no longer be retained as firmly established. That some retouching of a harmonizing nature was carried out, and at a very early date, even as early as the last quarter of the second century, is an undeniable fact, for its is clearly shown through a comparison of our earliest witnesses. But contamination resulting from harmonization of the Gospel text in the African version ought not to be attribued exclusively to the influence of the Latin Diatessaron, and in substantiation of this observation it should be noted that our oldest African Ms of the Gospels, the *Codex Bobbiensis (k)*, presents a short text.

With copies of both texts multiplying constantly to meet the needs of the liturgy and the apostolate, differences could not fail to increase, not only between the two fundamental types but also among the copies of each of these texts. Under such conditions, whoever, in the fourth century, desired to have at his disposal a Latin translation of guaranteed quality, had, first of all, to assume the role of revisor himself. Today, when we compare the witnesses of the Old Latin text with one another, we notice immediately the large number both of different readings, due to deliberate retouches and corrections, and of mixed readings, due to the reciprocal interferences or influences of the Mss.

Parallel with this work of revision, which was pursued constantly in order to obtain a closer agreement with the Greek — a process which multiplied the differences in translation — there developed a progressive contamination of the witnesses through borrowings and harmonizing adjustments, and all this tended to take away or destroy their original individual characteristics. Hence, under the circumstances, no real improvement of the Latin versions was brought about, and the embarrassment of workers in all fields — catechists, theologians, apologists, and exegetes — was only increased by the multiplicity of these texts, none of which enjoyed universal credit or unquestioned authority.

2. — *THE VULGATE OF SAINT JEROME.* [1]

I. — The Work of Saint Jerome.

The number of the Latin versions of the Bible toward the end of the fourth century was equalled only by their variety. This situation caused great inconvenience in the public reading

---

Translator's note. — [1 For bibliography, see the Bibliography at the end of this chapter].

of Scripture, in liturgical usage, in catechetical instruction, and in controversies with Jews or heretics. The authorities in the Church, as guardians of the Faith, became much concerned, and rightly, over a state of affairs which hampered seriously their apostolic action, based primarily as it was on the Word of God, and therefore on the Scriptures. The revision of the sacred text used in the Latin Churches imposed itself as an urgent necessity.

Two men at this period had a clear vision of the task to be accomplished and they applied themselves to it, each in his own manner, with equal ardor and tenacity. One was a monk of austere and imperious character, Eusebius Hieronymus (Jerome); the other bore the name of Augustine and governed the Church of Hippo with an authority that was only equalled by his gentleness.

Jerome was born about 347-349 at Stridon, a little town on the coast of Dalmatia. When he had completed his studies at Rome under the famous grammarian Donatus, he set out for the Orient. He lived as an ascetic in the desert of Chalcis, attended at Antioch the lectures on exegesis given by Apollinaris of Laodicea, then, at Constantinople, those delivered by Gregory Nazianzen, and, in the meantime, learned Hebrew. Pope Damasus noticed the theological and scriptural learning of Jerome at the council held at Rome in 382. He encouraged him, therefore, to continue his work, gave him proof of his most intimate friendship, turned to him for information and counsel, and, finally, entrusted to him the task of revising the Latin translation of Holy Scripture. From that day the erudite and diligent monk entered upon a career which he was to follow throughout his life. Before examining the nature of his work, however, it will be only fitting to note the place of Saint Augustine in the history of the Latin Bible.

Augustine had for Holy Scripture the same devotion and the same interest as Jerome, and his critical work merits more than a simple mention : cuique suum. Since he was rightly concerned with the need of having available a satisfactory text of the Scriptures, he did not cease to improve the Latin version which he used. As proof, we have the innumerable citations — P. de Lagarde has counted 42,816 — with which his writings are adorned. On the basis of Greek manuscripts of the

Alexandrian type, regarded as the best by modern critics, he revised carefully not only the books of the New Testament but also several of those in the Old.   His work was not as extensive as that of his contemporary.   He sought to meet his own needs, checking critically the text of the books which he used daily (the Psalms, Gospels, Epistles of Saint Paul) or that of the books upon which he was writing a commentary (e.g., the Heptateuch).   Augustine's work, moreover, is of inferior quality so far as the Old Testament is concerned, because he believed in the inspiration of the Septuagint and held the Greek translation in equal authority at least with the original Hebrew. In spite of this, the merit of the great bishop must not be underestimated.   The text, as revised and amended by him, had a real value from a critical point of view, as can be seen from what has been preserved of the Verona Psalter (R), the Toulouse Fragments of Ecclesiasticus and Wisdom, and the Freising Fragments or *Fragmenta Frisingensia (r)*.   All in all, there remains of this text a complete Psalter, the Fourth Gospel almost complete, and three-fourths of the Epistles of Saint Paul. In the judgment of Dom D. de Bruyne, an outstanding specialist in this matter, the Augustinian Psalter " is not perhaps the best of the Latin Psalters translated from the Greek, but it is the most personal, the most original ".   Augustine's text of Saint Paul's Epistles is the fruit of a revision made on the Old Latin, and it is superior to the text of the Clementine Vulgate [1].

Jerome, encouraged by Pope Damasus and with his full support, entered upon his task in 383.   He began with the Gospels, the constantly multiplying copies of which exhibited marked differences, due especially to the great number of translators and to the vogue for harmonizing Gospel narratives by means of additions.   In Saint Jerome's mind, there was not so much a question of making a new translation as of carrying out a careful revision of the version used at Rome.   This was a particularly delicate task, since he had to preserve the current Latin text as much as possible in order not do make undue changes in habitual readings, and, at the same time, to correct

---

[1] On the work of Augustine on the Biblical text, see Dom D. DE BRUYNE, *Saint Augustin réviseur de la Bible*, in *Miscellanea Agostiniana*, II (*Studi Agostiniani*, Rome, 1931), 521-606.

all the manifestly faulty passages in order to reproduce faithfully the true sense of the Greek : " A pious exercise, the scholar will say, but how perilously presumptuous " !

With a remarkable critical sense Jerome chose as a basic Latin text the European recension which had been altered least, namely that which has been preserved for us in the *Codex Veronensis (b)* and the *Corbeiensis II (ff²)* [1]. The Greek manuscripts used as a norm for this work of revision were from Type *A*, a derivative of Type *B* (see pp. 603 ff.). The preference thus accorded the Lucianic or Syro-Byzantine recension was due without doubt to the literary qualities of this text, habitually more elegant and more fluent than that of the Alexandrian recension. Among other advantages, it assured the rejection of most of the faulty readings from the " Western " text.

The work was finished in 384. In his prefatory letter *(Novum opus)* to Pope Damasus, Jerome stated that he had restrained his pen in making corrections and minor alterations in order that the new text might not differ too much from that in common use. It is still repeatedly said, on the authority of Wordsworth and White, that this revision of the Gospels was very cursory. But Vogels has estimated an average of twenty-five to thirty corrections per chapter, which gives an impressive total. This first work of revision was a success. The new Latin text was much better than the old. It is found without change in the Clementine Vulgate.

Did Jerome revise next the text of the other books of the New Testament? This may well be doubted, for he himself makes only two or there very vague allusions to a work of this kind. Moreover, we have no preface for these books such as Jerome was wont to place at the beginning of his works. Finally, Jerome never quotes the other books of the New Testament according to the text of the Vulgate. Very often, he even gives a different text, especially in his commentaries on Galatians, Ephesians, and Philippians, in which may be found severe criticisms of the typical readings of that version.

But now the question very naturally arises : what is the source of the Vulgate text of the New Testament apart from

---

[1] On this point, see the exhaustive and definitive study of H. J. VOGELS, *Vulgatastudien. Die Evangelien der Vulgata untersucht auf ihre lateinische und griechische Vorlage*, (Münster, i. W., 1928).

the Gospels? Strictly speaking, we can give an answer only in the case of the Epistles of Saint Paul. About 406, the Irishman Pelagius composed a very brief commentary on these Epistles, annotating in the margins the version which he had at hand. The text of this version, the fruit of an unknown revision, is found to be very close to that of the Vulgate. This commentary of Pelagius spread very rapidly, especially after it had been enlarged and placed under the name of Saint Jerome about 450. Cassiodorus, the great scholar who played such a decisive role in the diffusion of the Vulgate, possessed the work in its two stages. He carefully expurgated it from all heretical doctrine and used it as the basis of a new commentary. Our text of the Vulgate appears for the first time in this work of Cassiodorus, definitely established with its characteristic readings.

About the same time in which he was busy with the Gospels, Jerome revised the Latin Psalter according to the Greek of the Septuagint, but rapidly *(cursim)* and with a light hand. It was long believed that this first revision was preserved for us in the Roman Psalter which remained in use to the time of Saint Pius V and which is still kept in certain parts of the Missal and Breviary. But this is actually not so at all. The Roman Psalter is an Old Latin Psalter. As Dom de Bruyne has proved, the text of Jerome's first revision of the Psalter is found in his *Commentarioli* on the Psalms [1].

A second revision of the Psalter was made at Bethlehem between 387 and 388, and this time according to the Hexapla of Origen. The name, *Gallican*, was given already in the 9th century to this new Latin text of the Psalms, because it was thought to have been in very wide use in Gaul. It would have been more exact and more in keeping with the truth to call it " the Hexaplaric ". It was, in origin, a scholarly edition, equipped with critical signs, and not intented for liturgical use. It is regrettable that it found a place, after Sixtus V and Clement VIII, in the official edition of the Vulgate. A better Hieronymian text was available, namely, the translation made by Jerome from the Hebrew about a dozen years later.

---

[1] See Dom D. DE BRUYNE, " Le problème du psautier romain ", *Revue Bénédictine*, 42 (1930), 101-126. The *Commentarioli* were edited for the first time by Dom G. MORIN in *Anecdota Maredsolana*, III, *pars I*ᵃ (1895).

After the Psalms, the Latin versions of Job, Chronicles, Proverbs, Ecclesiasticus, and the Canticle of Canticles were retouched according to the Hexapla. From this revision only the text of Job has come down to us.

This work of revision, which, in fact, was at second hand in respect to the Biblical Books written in Hebrew, was not continued. Jerome decided to undertake a bolder task, of greater scope and of a more scientific and personal character, namely, the translation of the Books of the Old Testament from the original text, i.e., from the Hebrew. Jerome's love for the Scriptures had grown constantly, and he was filled with the thought of placing in the hands of Christian apologists a Biblical text of quality which they could use as a sure weapon in their controversies with the Jews. To guarantee the ultimate success of his enterprise, he began the study of Hebrew with ardor and even with passion. He visited Palestine in order to become better acquainted with the sites, traditions, and customs; he conversed as much as he could with the rabbis who were most qualified through their knowledge; he made a copy of the sacred roll in the synagogue at Bethlehem; in short, he neglected no means which could serve his purpose. Actually, there was no question — and there could not be any question — of an absolutely new translation, since a Latin version of the Bible already existed. But this Latin text had to be reworked fundamentally as well as in form in order that the true and complete sense of the original text, what Jerome called the *veritas Hebraica*, might be faithfully rendered. It is obvious that he was aided in this arduous task by the Septuagint Version, which he recognized, moreover, as an official authority, and also by the other Greek versions made by the Jews Aquila, Symmachus, and Theodotion whose work was available to him in the Hexapla of Origen.

From 391 to 405, he translated successively the Major and Minor Prophets, the two Books of Kings, the two Books of Samuel, the Psalms *(Psalterium ex Hebræo)*, Job, Esdras and Nehemias, the two Books of Chronicles, Proverbs, Canticle of Canticles, Ecclesiastes, the Pentateuch, Josue, Judges, Ruth, Esther, Tobias, and Judith. His version, with the exception of the Psalms, is found in the Latin Vulgate.

During these same years, in an atmosphere of feverish activity and battle — for it was the period of conflicts with John of Jerusalem, and then of the quarrel with Rufinus, to mention only Palestinian adversaries — the master composed his *De viris illustribus* and *Adversus Jovinianum*, wrote numerous works of a polemical or a personal apologetic character and exegetical commentaries, carried on a heavy correspondence with the West, and governed two monasteries founded by him at Bethlehem !

Jerome's translation of the Bible is in our possession and we can evaluate it. It is not surprising that the various parts of his work, although all are good, differ in value. Pressed hard by tasks as multiple as they were diverse, he sometimes worked too fast, and he himself admits it. Thus the Books of Solomon (Proverbs, Canticle of Canticles, and Ecclesiastes) were translated in three days, Tobias in one day, and Judith in one night ! Assuredly, the " dictation " of these translations had been preceded by long and minute study of the text. The principles and method employed by the translator are expounded either in the prefaces or prologues to certain books (among others, the Preface *Novum opus*, the Prologue to his commentary on *Ecclesiastes*, the *Præfatio in Isaiam, in Job, in Paralipomenon, in Pentateuchum, in Judith*), or in some of his letters (notably, *Epist.* 27, 31, 32, 57, 106, 112). The preliminary work consisted of correcting carefully the Latin text of the Bible, and this could only be done by a " return to the sources ", to use Jerome's own expression, i.e., to the originals, through an examination of the Mss regarded as the best.

In textual criticism, Jerome adhered to the lines established by his master Origen. He is to be reproached on one point only, namely, his failure to give full value to the Septuagint as an ancient witness of the Hebrew text. He habitually preferred to it, when there was any disagreement, the reading of a Hebrew Ms in use in his own time, the text of which did not differ much from our Masoretic text. This attitude of Jerome toward the Septuagint Version, for which, however, he professed esteem and respect, reflected his deliberate reaction against the belief in the inspiration of the Septuagint which was then so common. He rightly saw in this view a false and injurious prejudice. It was false, because no decision of the

Church authorized it, and it was injurious, because it actually put an obstacle in the way of the return to the sources and, therefore, interfered with scientific work.

Every translation is an interpretation, and the best interpretation presupposes a judicious choice of words and expressions of such a kind that the version is at once agreeable to read, accessible to all by its simplicity, and yet scrupulously faithful. Jerome knew this better than anyone. Without doubt he overstressed the Messianic sense in some passages of the Old Testament (thus in Isa. **11** : **10**; **12** : 3, **16** : **1**; **45** : 8; **51** : 5) and dogmatic preoccupation influenced him in the choice of variants or in translation, but it must be recognized that this sort of thing is relatively rare.

The literary value of Jerome's text is high. A lover of beautiful language, the translator, while striving to render as exactly as possible the sense of the original texts, had a care for literary correctness and aimed at elegance in the handling of a language with whose possibilities he was thoroughly acquainted. While respecting — indeed sometimes while preserving the expressions and turns proper to Hebrew — Jerome sought, for the translation of such idiomatic material. terms and locutions in accordance with the genius of the Latin language. We can only admire the suppleness and versatility of Jerome's talent as a writer and the high quality of his exegetical scholarship when we compare the text of the Old Latin versions with his translation. In his version of the Bible, a work as thankless as it was difficult, Jerome reveals himself a master of Latin prose in the Early Christian period. The faults and errors which may be detected here and there are hardly perceptible blemishes; they cannot diminish sensibly the beauty or soundness of the whole.

Through the genius and labor of Jerome, the Western Church was endowed with an edition of the Bible which was a worthy companion to the Septuagint Version.

2. — History of the Hieronymian Text. The Vulgate.

The novelty of this version provoked criticism. Some contemporaries, like Rufinus, called Jerome a forger and a heretic, while others long refused to admit the timeliness or even the utility of a work of this kind. Priests and faithful raised difficulties about changing their habits, i.e., about reading or chanting Scripture according to a translation which differed appreciably from those used up to that time in the Western Churches. But, especially, cultivated circles accused the translator of having unjustly and offensively slighted and diminished the authority of the Septuagint Version, which many regarded as inspired. Jerome responded to these criticisms, justified himself, defended his work, protested his respect for the Septuagint, and multiplied and spread copies of his translation, all the while invoking as his supreme argument the rights of truth. Saint Augustine's reserve was especially painful to him. Actually, in the case of the Bishop of Hippo, there was no insurmountable prejudice in the matter, since he sometimes used the new version of the Gospels, if not for public reading or pastoral instruction, at least in his writings. But customary routine and attachment for the old texts retarded the success of Saint Jerome's Bible for a long time. It should be added that Jerome's work had never received the official recognition of the *magisterium* of the Church. The intervention of Pope Damasus was an entirely personal matter. We know that even at Rome, toward the middle of the fifth century, Saint Leo the Great used the new translation only as a complement to the old, and that, at the end of the following century, Saint Gregory the Great, in his *Moralia*, gave the same authority to both.

The diffusion of Saint Jerome's version took place very gradually, and separately for each book or group of books. The history of this diffusion is very obscure, especially in its first phase. In Africa Saint Augustine was only partially acquainted with the work of his contemporary, In the 6th century, Cassiodorus was the prime mover in the diffusion which we observe in this period both in Italy and in southern Gaul. The famous *Codex Amiatinus*, as we know, was copied directly from one of his manuscripts. The same influence made itself felt in Northumbria, where Jerome's version became authoritative in the 7th century. At this date it had penetrated into Spain and into Ireland. But its full triumph was not assured before the end of the 8th century, and was due especially to the energetic measures of Charlemagne. Some were already

employing the term *Vulgate* (common or popular text) to
designate Saint Jerome's translation, It is only in the
13th century, however, that this title, under the influence of
Roger Bacon, was to become general, and it was not to receive
official sanction before the Council of Trent.

During this long period the text suffered a great deal : it was
the price of success. As the copies increased, alterations became
more numerous. The Old Latin versions which had been
evicted were, as Dom Quentin has said in his *Essais de critique
textuelle*, in a sense revenged. Copyists and revisers deformed
Jerome's translation by introducing readings borrowed from the
Old Latin versions. Jerome, even in his own lifetime, had
protested against revisions and interpolations which were
disfiguring his work. Three centuries after his death, he would
not have recognized his text under the form in which it was
presented in certain manuscripts.

As early as the 6th century, Cassiodorus had carried out
the first attempt at purifying the text. Toward the end of the
8th century, at the request of Charlemagne, Alcuin, Abbot of
Saint Martin of Tours, undertook a revision which was
primarily concerned with the correct literary and grammatical
form, while Theodulf Bishop of Orleans on the other hand
— and on his own initiative — endeavored to restore Jerome's
text to its original purity. Theodulf's recension, as a private
enterprise, did not enjoy the circulation which was given to
Alcuin's revision through the emperor's support and authority.
Alcuin's text was reproduced almost everywhere during the
following centuries and experienced the same fate as Jerome's;
i.e., repeated transcription modified it profoundly. In the
first half of the 12th century, Saint Stephen Harding, the
third abbot of Citeaux, also wished to correct the Latin text,
but his work was scarcely known beyond the Cistercian
monasteries and had practically no effect on the copyists of
his time.

The 13th century was the century of the *correctories*.
Confronted by an ever increasing number of variants, masters
and students became more and more confused, especially in the
Universities, where there was constant recourse to the Bible.
Before the end of the 12th century, the University of Paris,
perhaps under the influence of and with the help of Peter

Lombard, selected a text from among those in use at the time and ordered that this text alone should be recopied, the so-called Parisian text. Unfortunately, the model chosen was rather defective, and this explains the criticism of Roger Bacon against the *exemplar vulgatum quod est Parisiense*. The sole merit of the Bible of the University of Paris was the division of the different books into chapters, an innovation of a practical nature made by Stephen Langton, Archbishop of Canterbury. The Dominicans and Friars Minor, in order to improve the recension used in teaching, compiled *correctoria biblica*. The sacred text remained the same, without modifications or revisions, but the corrections were listed either in the margin of the manuscript copies or in separate books. In the end, the correctories, naturally, exercised an influence on the Parisian text. But this type of the text held its place pretty well until the 15th century, i.e., to the invention of printing.

The first Bible printed was that of Gutenberg — or the Mazarin Bible, after the name of the library in which it is found — which appeared at Mainz, *ca.* 1450-1452. The text reproduced was of the University of Paris type, and so by a stroke of fortune this type gained a foothold for half a century, since all the printed editions before 1500, except that of Vienna, which appeared in 1476, were derived from the Gutenberg Bible. As the volumes came from the presses in ever increasing tempo — there were about one hundred and twenty editions between the years 1450 and 1520 —, the text continued to be as defective as ever. No one was concerned about going back to manuscripts prior to Alcuin, nor even to a good exemplar of Alcuin's recension. And yet Roger Bacon, two centuries earlier, had declared that it was necessary to rely on the oldest and most accurate manuscripts. Some attempts in this direction were made by the Dominican Albert de Castello, Cardinal Ximenez, and the Protestant theologian Andreas Osiander, but the first to work in this field with a penetrating and sound intuition was Robert Estienne, who published nine editions of the Latin Bible between 1528 and 1557. The progress made was considerable, for Estienne produced a text which was appreciably improved through his use of old manuscripts, the variants of which, after careful collation, were placed in the margins of the printed sheets. Furthermore, the chapters were divided into verses. Unfortunately, Estienne was less concerned with restoring Jerome's version to its original form than with producing a Latin text in conformity with the Hebrew for the Old Testament and with the Greek for the New. From a strictly critical point of view, his work suffered very much from the effects of this tendency. He could not, or he did not dare, free himself completely from the University of Paris recension. During his lifetime, however, one scholar did shake off the yoke, namely, the Carthusian Gobelinus Laridius. In his *Biblia iuxta divi Hieronymi Stridonensis tralationem (sic)*, an edition published at Cologne in 1530, Jerome's text was reproduced from excellent manuscripts. But no editor of the time followed the example of Gobelinus Laridius, not even the celebrated masters of Louvain, John Hentenius and Lucas Brugensis, who adopted the text of Robert Estienne as the basis of the editions published under their direction between 1547 and 1583

The work of these scholars of Louvain indicated a reaction against the spirit and methods of certain Protestant editor who, in attempting to make a more accurate Latin translation, did not hesitate to correct it according to the Hebrew and the Greek. The attitude of the *Lovanienses* had been inspired by a decree of the Council of Trent, promulgated April 8, 1546, after long deliberations which had begun on March 1 of the same year. The Fathers of the Council, recognizing the major place given to the argument from Scripture by the Protestant theologians, and believing that in discussions with heretics it was most important to be solidly based on a good edition of the Scripture, decreed that " the ancient and Vulgate edition, approved through long use by the Church itself during so many centuries " should " be considered as authentic ", and that its text should be printed " as correctly as possible " *(Decretum de editione et usu sacrorum Librorum)*. It follows clearly from the minutes of the deliberations of the Council that the Fathers had fixed their choice on the Latin version which for centuries had enjoyed the approval of the Church, the text which was ordinarily called the Vulgate and which was regarded as the work of Saint Jerome. It will be noted later in what sense the Council intended that the Vulgate mentioned was " authentic ".

When the decree became known at Rome, it provoked deep agitation among theologians. Many of them actually thought that the Fathers had granted too much authority to the Vulgate and that it would be very difficult to select from among the current editions the one that was best. The papal legates were urged to indicate the reasons for and to state precisely the meaning of the decree. Through the papal legates as its intermediaries, the Council said in reply to the Roman Court that the Fathers considered it necessary to adopt a single version as the authentic text, that no other translation offered the same qualifications or guarantees as the ancient Vulgate, that without doubt the text of the Vulgate was faulty in the current editions, but that it was relying on the Pope to see that as perfect an edition as possible should be printed, and, finally, that the assistance of the theologians of the Council was assured. Thereupon preparatory work was undertaken at Trent and at Rome. It proceeded so slowly that in various quarters other attempts were made to attain the desired objective. We saw above the outcome of the work done by the doctors of Louvain. At Monte Cassino, the Benedictines accomplished, between the years 1550 and 1569, a considerable amount of work, for they collated the variants of twenty-four Mss, covering all the books of the Bible in the process.

Nothing was ready for the printing of the text when the Council of Trent closed in 1563, although a Papal Commission had been appointed for the purpose by Pius IV. A new commission was named by Saint Pius V. In spite of the persistent labors of Cardinal Sirleto and the good will of Cardinal Carafa, no serious result had been attained to the death of the pontiff (1572) because of lack of harmony in the views of the correctors. During the pontificate of Gregory XIII, all efforts were centered on the edition of the Septuagint. The prime mover in this task was Cardinal Perretti. When the latter became Pope Sixtus V in 1585, he decided to bring to a successful conclusion the work which the Council of Trent, forty years earlier, had pointed out to the Holy See as being particulary urgent. Cardinal Carafa was made head of the Commission, which was composed of qualified scholars. They had at hand excellent Latin Mss, among them the *Codex Amiatinus*, which the monks of Monte Amiata, after repeated refusals, finally placed at their disposal. They had the collations made by the Benedictines of Monte Cassino and by Cardinal Sirleto, and also a collation of the *Codex Legionensis*, which had been made at Leon in Spain. Finally, they could refer to the *Codex Vaticanus* (Greek). The basic text upon which the corrections were made was that of John Hentenius (Louvain Bible, edition of 1583) which, through the medium of Robert Estienne's text, was ultimately related to the University of Paris text of the 13th century. This disadvantage, however, was compensated for in part by the constant use of the *Codex Amiatinus* dating from the early 8th century, one of the best witnesses of Jerome's text.

As soon as the work of revision was completed, Cardinal Carafa, at the beginning of 1589, sent to Sixtus V a copy of the Bible, in which the corrections proposed by the Commission were placed in the margins. On the whole, the result was good and marked definite progress. Unfortunately, the pope claimed for himself, and for himself alone, the right to pass judgment and to choose. He began, accordingly, to prepare the text for printing. In eight cases out of ten he discarded the corrections indicated, keeping the current reading, i.e., Hentenius' or Robert Estienne's, without taking into account the testimony of the ancient Mss. He deleted doublets, or certain passages which he regarded as doublets, he changed the division of verses as introduced by Robert Estienne, and he made numerous alterations in spelling. During more than a year, the old pontiff, with the help of a few secretaries, did over again in his own way the work of the Commission. Sections were printed as he proceeded, because of his great haste to see " his " edition published. On May 2, 1590, the first copies were distributed to the cardinals; on May 31, twenty-five were sent to the princes, and the work was to be put on sale very soon. The sale had hardly begun when Sixtus V died, Aug. 27, 1590. Nine days later, the Congregation of Cardinals stopped the sale of the Sixtine Bible, and also the promulgation of the bull *Æternus ille* which presented the new edition as the text in conformity with the desires of the Council of Trent. Such a measure could only mean the suppression of the criticized edition. On the advice, however of Saint Robert Bellarmine, Gregory XIV refused to pass a sentence of condemnation on the work of his predecessor, and he decided that, after correction, the Bible should be printed with and under the name of Sixtus V [1].

The recasting was accomplished quickly by men who had already worked on the Sixtine edition, and who had available materials which had been worked up previously. Moreover, it had been agreed that fundamentally the new edition would conform to the old. The revision involved primarily the removal of all changes introduced by the deceased pope on his own initiative; hence the restoration of the discarded passages, a return to the division into verses adopted from Robert Estienne, and, finally, the elimination of additions not supported by any manuscript authority. In the course of the revision a certain number of corrections proposed previously by the Commission of Cardinal Carafa were examined and adopted and the text was improved considerably thereby. The final details and the printing were entrusted to two former collaborators of Sixtus V, both very competent, Francisco Toledo, a Jesuit, and Angelo Rocca, an Augustinian. Gregory XIV died in October 1591. Innocent IX reigned but a few weeks, so that the new edition appeared only during the pontificate of Clement VIII, toward the end of the year 1592. In the official preface written by Cardinal Bellarmine, it was mentioned, in incidental fashion, that this publication was in accord with a plan of Sixtus V himself, who had declared that the numerous mistakes in printing had disfigured the text prepared under his care. But what is more important, it was specified in this preface and in the bull of promulgation that the use of the new text of the Vulgate was obligatory for the whole Church, and that this official text could be reproduced by publishers, but without change of any sort, and without the addition of variants in the margins [2]. Thus, the text of the Vulgate was fixed in definitive

---

Translator's note. — [1] Cf. F. Amann, *Die Vulgata Sixtina von* 1590, (Freiburg i. B., 1912), and on this study, P. M. Baumgarten, *Theologische Revue* (1912), 608-611; P. M. Baumgarten, *Die Vulgata Sixtina und ihre Einführungsbulle* (Münster i. W., 1911); F. Stummer, *Einführung in die lateinische Bibel* (Paderborn, 1928), p. 181 ff.; id., " Vulgata ", *LTK*, vol. X (1938), cols. 703-706].

[2] The Biblical Commission (Decree of November 17, 1921) has authorized editions of the Vulgate with " critical apparatus " added *ad calcem textus*. On the other hand, " It is not forbidden by the decree of the Council of Trent to make translations into the vulgar tongue, even directly from the original texts themselves, for the use and benefit of the faithful... " (Encyclical, *Divino afflante*, par. 21).

fashion. Jerome's version, after a long evolution, still remained
the best of the ancient translations of the Bible [1].

Since that time, the Sixto-Clementine, or simply Clementine,
editions of the Bible — the name of Clement VIII was added
to that of Sixtus V from 1604 — have multiplied without
alteration of the text. Among the most carefully published
editions may be mentioned in particular those of Father
Vercellone, Rome, 1861, of Father Hetzenauer, Innsbruck,
1906, and of Monsignor Gramatica, Milan, 1914 (2nd ed., 1922,
new ed., 1941) [2].

3. — The Vulgate as the " Authentic " Version.

The Fathers of the Council of Trent declared that " the
ancient and vulgate edition, approved through long use by the
Church itself during so many centuries, is, among all the Latin
editions of the Sacred Books, the authentic one ". They knew
perfectly well that the text of the version selected, Saint Jerome's
translation, was defective, and they even insisted in the same
Decree *Insuper* that this text be corrected and amended.
Nevertheless, from a doctrinal point of view, they conferred
on it exceptional authority by declaring it " authentic ".

There is no possible doubt as to the meaning of the word.
The theologians of the Council understood "authentic " primarily
in a juridical sense : [3] an authentic text is one which deserves
credence, is an authority, and whose testimony cannot be
challenged in a discussion or trial. The original document is

---

Translator's note. — [1 Cf. H. Höpfl, O. S. B., *Beiträge zur Geschichte der
Sixto-klementinischen Vulgata* (Freiburg i. Br., 1913); on this study, *RB* (1914),
146 ff., and P. M. Baumgarten, *Theologische Revue* (1914), 172-175.
X. M. Le Bachelet, *Bellarmin et la Bible Clémentine* (Paris, 1911); on this
work, *RB* (1912), 310 ff.].

Translator's note. — [2 To these editions may be added the following : *Biblia
Sacra juxta Vulgatam Clementinam* (Tournai, 1927; with good analysis of
chapters and cross references). *Biblia Sacra*, edd. A. Colunga, O. P., and
L. Turrado (Madrid, 1953; with a number of special features, including the
printing of the new Latin translation of the Psalms and the traditional Latin
text in parallel columns). *Biblia Sacra Latina Veteris Testamenti Hieronymo
interprete ...in stichos descripta*, edd. Heyse and Tischendorf (Leipzig, 1873;
based in part on Vercellone, but especially on the *Codex Amiatinus*. The
Prolegomena contain St. Jerome's *Praefationes* and the *Capitula* of the books
according to the *Codex Amiatinus*)].

[3] " And so its authenticity is not specified primarily as *critical*, but rather as
juridical " (Encyclical *Divino afflante*, par. 21).

preeminently the authentic one, but the copy, and even the translation of this document, can be declared authentic texts when they are in conformity with the original. In calling the *vetus et vulgata editio* authentic, the Fathers of the Council of Trent clearly intended and desired to indicate in this way the text whose authority would be indisputable, as in the case of an official and regulative document.

It goes without saying, however, that the Council intended to sanction this authenticity only because it considered the Vulgate free of all error in matters of faith and morals. In this respect the Decree *Insuper* has a certain doctrinal import, but it does not cover the question of the conformity of the Vulgate with the original texts. Nor could the matter be otherwise, since the same document proclaimed that it was necessary to correct this version. The Fathers declared the Vulgate authentic because of its antiquity, and because it enjoyed the time-honored approval of the Church. The decree itself is perfectly plain on this point, as are also the official proceedings or *Acta genuina* of the Council of Trent (ed. Theiner and Merkle-Ehses). The Council could have added that the universal use of the Vulgate and the approval given by the Church for centuries to this text were a sufficient guarantee of the fidelity of this version to the originals, but it did not do so, because this particular point had not been the object of examination or discussion.

It is to be noted, too, that the Council expressed itself on the choice of a Latin text among other Latin texts, that it referred neither to the Septuagint Version, nor to the Hebrew and Greek originals, that it rejected neither the other Latin versions nor the ancient Oriental versions, and that it said nothing of editions of the Bible by heretics. This observation is important especially in so far as the originals are concerned. The Hebrew text for the Old Testament, and the Greek for the New, retained all their value, and, therefore, their rank, which could only be regarded as first.

What were the consequences of this declaration on the authenticity of the Vulgate? In the first place, the use of the Vulgate became obligatory in all public acts of the *magisterium* of the Church, and in particular, for pastoral and theological instruction. Furthermore, the substantial identity of the

Vulgate with the original texts was implicitly guaranteed from the time that this version was presented by the Church herself as an official witness of the traditional Faith [1]. Did it follow that every dogmatic text of the Vulgate had necessarily to be found in the original, or that every dogma presented in the original had to be found in the translation also? Since the Council had not expressed itself on this point, one could hesitate to say. But it does seem that the Fathers answered negatively, since they refused to declare authentic, along with the Vulgate, an edition of the Hebrew text of the Old Testament and another of the Greek Bible [2]. Finally, it was evident from the decree that the Vulgate was free from error in matters of Faith and that nothing in it was contrary to dogmatic truth as taught by the Church [3].

4. — Manuscripts and Critical Editions of the Vulgate.

The manuscripts which reproduce Jerome's text in whole or in part, and in varying degrees of accuracy, can be counted by the thousands. About 700 of them are prior to the 11th century. Among the oldest should be mentioned the *Turonensis* or *Pentateuch of Tours*, 6th century, in the Bibliothèque Nationale at Paris; the *Codex Sangallensis* (Gospels), 6th century, at Saint Gall; the *Codex Fuldensis* (New Testament), 6th century, at Fulda; the *Ottobonianus* (Heptateuch), 7th century, in the Vatican Library; the *Codex Foroiuliensis* (Gospels), 7th century, at Cividale; the *Codex Oxoniensis* (Gospels), 7th century, in the Bodleian Library at Oxford; the *Codex Dunelmensis* (Gospels), 7th or 8th century, at Durham; the *Codex Lindisfarnensis* (Gospels), 7th or 8th century, in the British Museum; the *Codex Amiatinus* (the complete Bible), 8th century, in the Laurentian Library at Florence; the *Bible of Mordramnus*, 8th century, at Amiens;

---

[1] The dogmatic decree *De canonicis Scripturis*, in which the Council declared the books contained in the Vulgate sacred and canonical, gave the same guarantee.

[2] Theologians explain that if the Vulgate contains any dogmatic assertion that is not found in the original texts, it is authoritative in this case, not as the authentic version, but as an official witness of Tradition.

Translator's note. — [3] On the authority of the Vulgate, see J. BALESTRI, *op. cit.*, pp. 215-237, and the references there given; J. M. VOSTÉ, O. P., " The Vulgate at the Council of Trent ", *CBQ*, (1947), 9-25].

the *Codex Toletanus* (the complete Bible), 8th century at Madrid; the *Codex Cavensis* (the complete Bible), 9th century, in the abbey of La Cava, Italy; the *Codex Vallicellianus* (the complete Bible), 9th century, in the Vallicelliana Library at Rome; the *Codex Laudianus* (Deuteronomy-Ruth), 9th century, in the Bodleian Library at Oxford; the *Codex Complutensis* (the complete Bible), 9th century, at Madrid; the *Codex Legionensis* (the complete Bible), 10th century, at Leon, and others.

For a description and classification of the Mss of the Vulgate by groups or families, one should consult the admirable studies of Wordsworth-White (*Novum Testamentum Domini Nostri Jesu Christi latine*, vol. I, " Epilogus "), Samuel Berger *(Histoire de la Vulgate pendant les premiers siècles du Moyen-Age)*, and Dom H. Quentin *(Mémoire sur l'établissement du texte de la Vulgate)*.

We have seen above how and why the text of the Sixto-Clementine Vulgate was only an imperfect reproduction of Jerome's version. But Rome, in editing an official Bible, had not intended to forbid scholarly labors which could improve the chosen recension. Actually, however, nothing was undertaken in this direction before the middle of the last century.

The first to embark on such an enterprise was a Roman Barnabite, Father Charles Vercellone. Encouraged by Pius IX, he collected methodically the variants which might help in restoring Jerome's text to its original form, and published in 1860 and 1864 two large volumes, covering from Genesis to the Fourth Book of Kings, entitled : *Variæ lectiones Vulgatæ latinæ Bibliorum editionis*. The work was interrupted by the death of the author.

Two English scholars, John Wordsworth, Bishop of Salisbury, and Henry Julian White, who later became Dean of Christ Church at Oxford, began, in 1889, the publication of the *Novum Testamentum latine secundum editionem sancti Hieronymi* (Gospels from 1889 to 1898, Acts in 1905, Romans in 1913, etc.). Wordsworth died in 1911, and White assumed the task alone until his death in 1934. The work was continued under the direction of H. F. D. Sparks, with the collaboration of C. Jenkins, and the third and final volume was completed and published in

1954. The objective was the restoration of Jerome's text in so far as this can be done. The realization of this objective does honor to the scholars whose names are inscribed on the title page of this work of textual criticism in the grand style [1].

A similar undertaking was entrusted in 1907 by Pius X to a Pontifical Commission, appointed " for the revision of the Vulgate " and composed of Benedictines, among whom were Dom John Chapman, Dom de Bruyne, and Dom Quentin. The last scholar mentioned, who was the leading spirit in the group thus constituted, advocated in his *Mémoire sur l'établissement du texte de la Vulgate* (1922) the use of a new and more exact method of classifying Mss. He claimed that through this new method he could reduce to three the basic Mss from which the others are derived and which ought to make possible the reconstitution of the archetype. He would place this archetype about one hundred or one hundred fifty years after Saint Jerome. For the Octateuch, Dom Quentin chose the *Turonensis* of the Spanish group, the *Ottobonianus* of the Theodulfian group, and the *Amiatinus* of the pre-Alcuinian group. This method was the object of very heated controversy and criticism. A reorganization of the Benedictine collaborators followed, and, in 1933, the Abbey of Saint Jerome was founded at Rome, with Dom Quentin as director of the work. Genesis was published in 1926, Exodus and Leviticus in 1929, Numbers and Deuteronomy in 1936, Josue, Judges, and Ruth in 1939, 1 and 2 Samuel in 1944, 1 and 2 Kings in 1945, Malachias in 1945, Paralipomenon in 1948, Esdras, Tobias, and Judith in 1950, Esther and Job in 1951, Psalms in 1953, and Proverbs, Ecclesiastes, and Canticle of Canticles in 1957. The edition bears the title : *Biblia sacra iuxta latinam vulgatam editionem.* Dom Quentin died in 1935, but in that beehive of scholarly Benedictine labors, Saint Jerome's Monastery in Rome, the work continues for the benefit of science and for the glory of the Church [2].

---

[1] H. J. WHITE published in 1911 an *editio minor* of the entire New Testament, with a critical apparatus containing only the variants of the nine Mss which he considered the most important.

Translator's note. — [2 See J. O. SMIT, *De Vulgaat* (Roermond, Holland, 1948), which deals especially with the Benedictine undertaking].

IV. — The translations into the vernacular [1].

[P. W. Skehan]

During the early Middle Ages, the rendering of the Biblical text into the vernacular took the same course in England as in several other parts of western Europe. There were at the beginnings poetic paraphrases, then interlinear glosses on the Latin Psalter and on the Gospels, and, only later, connected prose renderings of various parts of the New Testament and of the Old (the latter usually in an abridged form). For the Saxon period, the names of Caedmon (c. 670), Saint Bede (673-735), and King Alfred (849-99) are among those cited in this connection. What remains to us in extant manuscripts, however, is for the most part anonymous work. A version of the Four Gospels produced in Wessex in the tenth century is the first extensive translation, properly so-called, to which we can point. Aelfric, abbot of Eynsham in Oxfordshire (c. 955-1020), wrote prose adaptations of a number of Old Testament historical books and of Job. The Norman invasion brought a new orientation for all such activity. A poetic paraphrase of Proverbs in Anglo-Norman was followed by versions of the Psalms and of the Apocalypse, and eventually a complete Bible was produced in that tongue.

With the resurgence of English as the language of all classes of the population, the fourteenth century saw new attempts at an English Bible. A metrical and two prose versions of the Psalter were produced; and the popular Norman commentary on the Apocalypse was done into English. From toward the close of the century, when the Wycliffite controversy had already broken out, a small number of extant manuscripts furnishes us with all parts of the New Testament, except Saint John's Gospel, in versions distinct from the " Wycliffe Bible", and mainly in a dialect traceable to the north midlands. In a southern or Kentish dialect, both the Pauline and the Catholic Epistles are extant from the same period. Collected

Translator's note. — [1 This section, replacing a corresponding one in the French original, was specially written for the *Guide to the Bible* by Monsignor Patrick W. Skehan, S. T. D., Professor of Semitic Languages and Literatures at the Catholic University of America].

homilies on the Sunday Gospels, including independent translations of their text, as well as lives of Christ and Gospel harmonies in prose or verse were in more general circulation.

Beginning before 1180 in southern France, however, and spreading through many parts of Europe up to the time of the invention of printing, there was a connection between the circulation of vernacular Scriptures among the laity and the propaganda activities of various heretical groups : the Waldensians, the Cathari, the " Friends of God ", and, in England, the Lollards. The danger from these sources varied from place to place, and the local Church authorities were always less sympathetic to the spread of vernacular translations in direct proportion to the danger of heretical abuse of them. Papal policy during this period is represented by a correspondence of Innocent III with the archbishop and the people of Metz in 1199 (PL 214, 695-99); even in the face of a present danger, Innocent keeps in view the salutary possibilities of a rendering done from worthy motives and employed in accord with the spirit of the Church. This was also the official attitude in England, where a provincial council at Oxford in 1408, under Archbishop Arundel, issued the constitution : " ...we decree and ordain that no man hereafter by his own authority translate any text of Sacred Scripture into English or any other tongue, by way of a book, booklet or tract, nor read any such book, booklet or tract now lately composed in the time of John Wyclif aforesaid, or since, either in part or in whole, publicly or privately, under pain of major excommunication, until that translation be approved by the Ordinary of the place, or, if the case demand it, by a Provincial Council. He that does contrary to this shall likewise be punished as a fosterer of heresy and error ". Nevertheless, the period of manuscript transmission of the English Bible begins its last stage, apparently, with the complete translation of both the Old and the New Testaments from the Latin Vulgate by followers of John Wycliffe. This undertaking was largely completed, in its earliest form, by 1382. The name of Nicholas of Hereford is the only one that can with certainty be connected with the work. While some thirty Mss survive as partial witnesses to its text, this recension of the Wycliffe Bible was rapidly supplanted in popularity by a thoroughgoing revision completed about 1395-6 and commonly attributed to John Purvey. Of some 140 Mss that still attest this revision, about ten contain also a " general prologue " which was justly characterized by Saint Thomas More as heretical. The text itself, however, is a reasonably adequate rendering of the Vulgate, not distorted or tendentious. It seems altogether probable that this was the vernacular Bible of fifteenth and early sixteenth century England, even in the most orthodox circles, and that in view of the integrity of its text its origins were partially forgotten and obscured. Though Saint Thomas More was himself convinced otherwise, it would, then, have been primarily with copies of this Bible in mind that he wrote, " myself have seen and can shew you bybles fayre and old writen in Englyshe, which have been knowen and seen by the bishop of the dyoces, and left in laymen's handes, and women's, too, suche as he knewe for good and catholike folke that used it with devocion and sobrenes " (*Dial. conc. Tyndale*, III, xiv). A text of the Penitential Psalms, based on the Vulgate, from the hand of Saint John Fisher, was the first portion of an English Bible to appear in print : and this as late as 1505. Meanwhile, the attacks upon the integrity of the Christian faith which had been associated with the movement for widespread dissemination of the Bible in English at the end of the fourteenth century instilled grave doubts in the leaders of both Church and State as to the prudence of encouraging any similar project. England, where printing was in general slow to spread, was in a rather different case from Germany and the Low Countries, where some eighteen printed editions of complete vernacular Bibles were produced before Luther's translation was begun. French, Italian, Catalan and Czech versions were also printed and circulated before the " Reformation ", though orthodox Catholic opinion was far from generally upholding the prudence of this activity. In actual fact, the first undertaking to render the New Testament from Greek into English, by William Tyndale, was made by the translator the occasion for a full-scale and vicious attack upon both the teachings and the practice of the Church. Already suspect of heresy in 1520, Tyndale became an open partisan of Luther on the Continent in 1524. His first printing of an English New Testament was interrupted in Cologne in 1525, and he left with the printed sheets of a part of the work for Worms, whence two separate editions were shipped into England surreptitiously in the beginning of 1526. As Saint Thomas More at once pointed out, Tyndale's choice of terms in this rendering was the deliberate foundation for heretical misrepresentations of the constitution of the Church and the efficacy of the sacrament of Penance; an extreme from which the King James version later withdrew.

England was cast into the flood tide of the Reformation by events which had nothing to do with the vernacular Bible; and the successive versions between Tyndale's first efforts and the King James Bible of 1611 were in great part produced, and sometimes printed, on the Continent, subject to a very pronounced influence from diverse Protestant groups. Myles Coverdale brought from the presses at Zurich in 1535 the first complete Bible printed in English; it included Tyndale's previously published translation of the Pentateuch (1530) as well as of the New Testament, and a makeshift rendering by Coverdale, from secondary sources, of the rest of the Old Testament. A reprint of this in England in 1537 was the first Bible " set foorth with the Kynges moost gracious licence ". Under the pseudonym of Thomas Matthew, the literary executor of Tyndale produced in Antwerp in 1537, for a London firm, an edition in which the Old Testament was Tyndale's from Genesis through 2 Chronicles (2 Para.), while the rest of the Old Testament was that of Coverdale. The final product of Henry VIII's reign was the " Great Bible " of 1539, printed at Paris and later in England (with imported types and craftsmen), a revision of the Matthew Bible supervised by Coverdale. Its Psalter has survived to our own day in the *Book of Common Prayer.* The Great Bible was still the official text for public use in England, despite widespread opposition to it within the Anglican Church, when in 1568 a haphazard revision known as the "Bishops' Bible " succeeded to its unpopularity. During the reign of Mary Tudor a group of Protestant exiles produced a new translation at Geneva under the influence of Theodore Beza. The actual printing of the complete " Geneva Bible " occurred in 1560, when Elizabeth had already come to the English throne. It was in some ways more satisfactory than the Great Bible, and it continued to be better received than the Bishops' Bible until both were supplanted. The Geneva Bible imitated Tyndale's Pentateuch by including controversial (and, of course, anti-Catholic) notes.

A Catholic translation of the New Testament was issued at the temporary English College at Rheims, in 1582, under the sponsorship of William (later Cardinal) Allen. This rendering from the Vulgate was part of a complete Bible (the Doway-Rheims version), of which the Old Testament could not be printed, chiefly for lack of funds, until 1609-10, when its two volumes were issued at Douai, the accustomed place of English Catholic training for the priesthood in that period. The bulk of the work was done by Gregory Martin. His competence and that of his associates is generally acknowledged. The familiar reproach of excessive Latinity in the English diction of this translation is justified by the canons of literary taste of a later age; what is ignored is the fact that this feature of style was far from uncommon in English writing of that day. The Rheims New Testament exercised a distinct influence on the later King James Bible among Protestants. The makers of the latter version used the Rheims text in a parallel edition of it with that of the Bishops' Bible, prepared in 1589 by W. Fulke, for the purpose of showing faults in the Catholic edition and replying to its notes. The Doway Old Testament was too late in publication to have any influence of a similar kind.

The King James Bible itself was a revision undertaken in 1604, at the royal behest, by some fifty-four translators grouped into six 'companies'. Its principal sources apart from the original texts were, in English, the Bishops' and Geneva Bibles and the Rheims New Testament; along with these, the various Latin versions of the sixteenth century, as well as earlier commentaries and patristic works in a lesser degree. It was completed in 1611, and has become known as the 'Authorized' Version by falling heir to the privileged position of earlier Bibles " appointed to be read in Churches ". Its influence on literary English down to the present day has often been described, and can scarcely be overestimated. Despite the fact that it has many inadequacies from the standpoint of present day Scriptural knowledge, it continues to enjoy an overwhelming preference in Protestant religious circles. Modern critical study and changing language patterns have called forth among non-

Catholics a variety of later renderings, beginning with a " Revised Version " of 1881-1885 which took slightly different forms in England and America. One of its main objectives was to secure a sounder critical base for the New Testament than the Greek *textus receptus* reflected in the " Authorized Version ". Most recently a *Revised Standard Version* (N. T., 1946; O. T., 1952; " Apocrypha " — the Deuterocanonical Books — 1957) has been produced in the United States; a committee is at work in England to produce an independent text. Other non-Catholic versions now current include James MOFFATT'S *The Bible: a New Translation* (revised ed., 1935); *The Complete Bible: an American Translation* (1939), edited by J. M. P. Smith and E. J. Goodspeed; and *The Holy Scriptures according to the Masoretic Text*, a revision, by a Jewish group under the editorship of M. L. Margolis, of the Hebrew Old Testament in the King James version. New editions intended to supplant the last two are currently being prepared. [1]

In Catholic circles, the Rheims New Testament had four early printings, and the Old Testament was reprinted once, in 1635. Both then lapsed for a hundred years, as far as new printings are concerned, and they finally were subjected to a rather drastic revision and modernization by Bishop Richard Challoner, coadjutor to the Vicar Apostolic of the London District. Challoner's New Testament of 1749, after many vicissitudes, became standard, and was the text in almost universal use by English-speaking Catholics as late as 1940. In 1750, Dr. Challoner published the entire Bible; and his Old Testament (which he revised in 1763) has persevered down to our own day without a serious rival. A yet more extensive reworking of the New Testament, by the same editor, in 1752, provided the basic text of most Catholic editions till about 1815, and of a decreasing number till 1853. There have been other New Testament translations or revisions from the Latin by Drs. Nary (1718). and Witham (1730); from the Greek, by

---

[1] Recent curiosities of no scientific standing are a translation from the Peshitta Syriac by G. Lamsa (1957), a rendering from the Septuagint of 150 years ago " revised and enlarged " in 1954, and the Bible of the Jehovah's Witnesses (N. T., 1950; O. T., 1953-   ); this last reflects preconceptions that can no longer be called Christian.

Fr. F. A. Spencer, O. P., (1901-1937), and (Gospels only) by the historian, Dr. Lingard, anonymously, in 1836. The entire Bible was revised from the Latin by Archbishop F. P. Kenrick, between 1849 and 1861; and an entirely fresh translation, also based on the Vulgate, has been published by Msgr. R. A. Knox (1944-50). The *Westminster Version*, edited by C. A. Lattey, S. J., offers a complete New Testament from the Greek (1913-1935), and presents a translation of a number of Old Testament books (Psalms, Ruth, Jonas, Nahum, Habacuc, Malachias, Daniel) based on the original Hebrew text. The *Confraternity of Christian Doctrine* New Testament (1941) is based on the Latin, and is a sweeping revision of Challoner's text. The Episcopal Committee for this same *Confraternity* is now sponsoring a complete Bible prepared on critical principles from the original texts; of this, *Genesis-Ruth* (1952) and *Job-Sirach* (1955) have appeared, and the Prophets are in press (1959). Meanwhile, the equivocal and dubious advertising of greedy publishers for second-rate patchwork editions of the Sacred Text continues unabated.

The comparative uniformity of English Biblical texts in common use among Catholics has for a long time been in marked contrast to the variety available in French, German, or Italian. One effect of the modern progress of Biblical studies has been a movement in various countries to secure fresh Catholic versions of the Bible reflecting the originals as fully and directly as possible. Such undertakings have borne fruit in complete translations in French, German, Italian, Spanish, Catalan, Dutch, and Maltese; and new efforts of the sort continue to be made in these and in other languages. The position of the Holy See in this matter was set forth by Pope Pius XII in the Encyclical *Divino afflante* (1943), in which he declared that the endorsement of the Latin Vulgate by the Council of Trent was not intended to be a barrier against " translations into the vulgar tongue, even directly from the original texts themselves, for the use and benefit of the faithful and for the better understanding of the divine word, as we know to have been already done in a laudable manner in many countries, with the approval of Ecclesiastical authority " (par. 22). Perhaps the most unexpected development is, that following upon the new Latin Psalter from the Hebrew issued for liturgical use (1945), there has been a decided interest shown in critically prepared, annotated translations into Latin itself, of other Biblical books (v.g., *Liber Ecclesiastæ qui ab Hebraeis appellatur Qohelet*, ed. A. Bea, S. J., Rome, 1950).

The current canon law with respect to the use of Biblical texts by Catholics is as follows : 1) Editions of the Holy Scriptures in the vernacular are not to be printed unless they either have the approbation of the Holy See or are edited under episcopal supervision with notes drawn chiefly from the Fathers of the Church and from competent Catholic writers (Canon 1391). 2) The use of editions, whether of the original texts or of the ancient versions, or of Scriptural translations into any language, produced or published under non-Catholic auspices, is forbidden (Canon 1399, 1°). An exception is made for the use of these (and of such other editions as may violate Canon 1391) by serious students of Theology or Sacred Scripture; with the proviso that the editions so used must be faithful and complete, and without preliminary matter, notes, or appendices attacking the dogmas of Catholic faith (Canon 1400). The prudential necessity of this legislation should be clear from even the foregoing brief sketch of the development of vernacular Bibles; and the Church must act as the lawful custodian of the written word of God by virtue of her divine teaching mission.

BIBLIOGRAPHY

I. On the Septuagint, the best work for many years was H. B. SWETE, *An Introduction to the Old Testament in Greek* (revised by R. R. Ottley, Cambridge, 1914). It must now be supplemented. B. J. ROBERTS, *The Old Testament Text and Versions* (Cardiff, 1951). — H. St. J. THACKERAY, *The Letter of Aristeas* (London, 1918. [M. Hadas, ed., *Aristeas to Philocrates (Letter of Aristeas)*, with an English trans. (New York, 1951)]. — M. J. LAGRANGE, *Le Judaïsme avant Jésus-Christ* (Paris, 1932), 524-532. — F. G. KENYON, *The Text of the Greek Bible* (2nd ed., London, 1949); ID., *Our Bible and the Ancient Manuscripts* (revised ed., New York, 1958), 97-134. — F. X. WUTZ, *Systematische Wege von der Septuaginta zum hebräischen Urtext* (Stuttgart, 1937). — A. BARROIS, " Une nouvelle théorie de l'origine des Septante ", *RB* (1930), 332-361. — P. E. KAHLE, *The Cairo Genizah* (London, 1947); *id., Die Massoreten des Westens*, II. (Giessen, 1930). — P. KATZ, *Philo's Bible. The Aberrant Text of the Bible Quotations in Some Philonic Writings and Its Place in the Textual History of the Greek Bible* (Cambridge, 1950); ID., several articles in *Theologische*

Literaturzeitung, from 1951 to date. On the inspiration of the Septuagint : P. BENOIT, " La Septante est-elle inspirée? ", in *Vom Wert des Lebens*, *Festschrift für Max Meinertz* (Münster i. W.), pp. 41-49; — P. AUVRAY, " Comment se pose le problème de l'inspiration des Septante, " *RB* (1952), 321-336. On Aquila : D. BARTHÉLEMY, " Redécouverte d'un chaînon manquant de l'histoire de la Septante, " *RB* (1953), 14-29. On Symmachus : — H. J. SCHOEPS, *Theologie und Geschichte des Judenchristentums* (Tübingen, 1929); ID., *Aus frühchristlicher Zeit. Religionsgeschichtliche Untersuchungen* (*ibid.*, 1950), pp. 82-129. On Saint Lucian of Antioch : A. RAHLFS, *Septuaginta Studien III : Lucians Recension der Königsbücher* (Göttingen, 1911); — G. BARDY, *Recherches sur saint Lucien d'Antioche et son école* (Paris, 1936), pp. 164-182. On the history of the text of the Septuagint, there is an excellent summary (in Latin, English, and German) in the Introduction to A. Rahlfs' *Handausgabe* of the Septuagint (2 vols., Stuttgart, 1935) I, XXII-XXXI. [C]f. also : H. St. J. THACKERAY, *The Septuagint and Jewish Worship* (2nd ed., London, 1923). — G. BERTRAM's survey of publications, in *Theologische Rundschau* (1931), 238 ff.; (1933), 172 ff.; (1938), 69 ff., and 133 ff. — J. W. WEVERS, " Septuaginta-Forschungen ", *ibid.* (1954), 85-1138; 171-190. — I. L. SEELIGMANN " Problemen en Perpektiven in het moderne Septuaginta-onderzoek ", *Ex Oriente Lux* (1939-1942); ID., " The Septuagint Version of Isaiah : A Discussion of Its Problems " (*ibid.*, 1948). — L. PRIJS, *Jüdische Tradition in der Septuaginta* (Leiden, 1948). — H. M. ORLINSKY, " The Septuagint : Its Use in Textual Criticism ", *BA*, No. 2 (1946); ID., " On the Present State of Proto-Septuagint Studies ", *American Oriental Society Offprint Series*, XIII (1941; 11 pages). — J. ZIEGLER, " Bibelübersetzungen, I. Griechische B., " *LTK*, II (revised ed., 1958), 375-380 (with bibliography). In the *L'Année Philologique, Bibliographie critique et analytique de l'Antiquité gréco-latine*, edd. J. Marouzeau and J. Ernst (Paris, 1924 ff.), there is an excellent coverage of studies dealing with the Septuagint, especially on the philological side, under the heading " Vetus Testamentum " in the section " Auteurs et Textes ".].

II. The ancient Oriental versions : S. LYONNET, *Les origines de la version arménienne et le Diatessaron* (Rome, 1950). — L. MARIÈS, " Le Diatessaron à l'origine de la version arménienne ", *RSR* (1952), 247-256. — A. VÖÖBUS, " La première traduction arménienne des Evangiles, " *ibid.* (1950), 581-586. — A. BAUMSTARK, *Geschichte der syrischen Literatur* (Bonn, 1922), pp. 18-25, and 73-73. — L. HAEFELI, *Die Peschitta des Alten Testaments mit Rücksicht auf ihre textkritische Bearbeitung und Herausgabe* (Münster i. W., 1929). The only edition of the Peschitto actually available is that wich was republished by the Imprimerie catholique at Beyrouth in 1951 : *Biblia Sacra iuxta Versionem Simplicem quae dicitur Peschitto* (It is edited carefully, but it does not pretend to be a critical text). — J. KARST, *La littérature géorgienne chrétienne* (Paris, 1934), 40-43. — A. VASCHALDE, *Ce qui a été publié des versions coptes de la Bible* (see the references given *supra*, p. 633). — F. H. HALLOCK, " The Coptic Old Testament "

American Journal of Semitic Languages (1933), 325 ff. — G. GRAF,
Geschichte der christlichen arabischen Literatur, I (Rome, 1944), 138-185.
A. VÖÖBUS, A. BÖHLIG, J. ASSFALK, J. MOLITOR, and G. PATTI, in the
article, "Bibelübersetzungen", *LTK*, II (1958), 386-399 (with most
recent bibliography).].

III. The Latin Versions. 1. The Old Latin versions : L. MÉCHINEAU,
"Latines (versions)," *DBV* IV, 97-123. — H. A. A. KENNEDY, "Latin
Versions (the Old)," *HDB*. — DOM H. LECLERCQ, "Itala", *DACL*,
VII², 1606-1611. — DOM B. BOTTE, "Itala", *DBV*, *Suppl.*, IV (1949),
777-782; ID., "Latines (versions antérieures à saint Jérôme)," *ibid.*, V
(1957), 334-347. — L. ZIEGLER, *Die lateinischen Bibelübersetzungen vor
Hieronymus* (Munich, 1879). — P. CORSSEN, "Bericht über die lateinischen Bibelübersetzungen," *Jahresbericht des classischen Altertumswissenschaft*, 101 (1899), 11-83. — E. NESTLE, *Urtext und Übersetzungen
der Bibel* (Leipzig, 1897), 86-95. — P. MONCEAUX, *Histoire littéraire de
l'Afrique chrétienne*, I (Paris, 1901; especially, Chapter III). — De
LABRIOLLE-BARDY, *Histoire de la littérature latine chrétienne* (3rd ed.,
Paris, 1947), 61-83. — HANS VON SODEN, *Das lateinische Neue Testament
in Africa zur Zeit Cyprians* (Leipzig, 1909). — HERMANN VON SODEN, *Die
Schriften des Neuen Testaments*, I (Berlin, 1902-1907), 1544-1572. — H. J.
VOGELS, *Handbuch der neutestamentlichen Textkritik* (Münster i. W., 1923;
2nd ed., 1955), 78-110, and 152-220. — M. J. LAGRANGE, *Critique textuelle
du Nouveau Testament*. II, *La critique rationnelle* (Paris, 1935). —
A. JÜLICHER, *Das Neue Testament in altlateinischer Überlieferung*, I,
Matthäus-Evangelium (Berlin, 1938); II, *Markus-Evangelium* (1940);
III, *Lukas-Evangelium* (1954. Vols. I and II were actually edited by
M. Matzkow, and Vol. III by W. Matzkow and G. Aland). — [B. FISCHER
et al., *Vetus Latina. Die Reste der altlateinischen Bibel nach P. Sabatier
neu gesammelt und herausgegeben von der Erzabtei Beuron*. I. *Verzeichnis
der Sigel* (Freiburg i. Br., 1949); II, *Genesis* (1951-1954); XXVI, *Epistolae
Catholicae et Apocalypsis* (1956 ff.). For an excellent critical evaluation
of the "New Sabatier", including a valuable comparison with the "Old
Sabatier", see the review-article by B. M. Peebles in *CBQ* (1954), 210-225.
—DOM R. WEBER,*Les anciennes versions latines du deuxième livre des Parali-
pomènes* (Rome, 1945; Collectanea Biblica Latina, VIII); ID., *Le Psautier
Romain et les autres Psautiers latins. Edition critique* (1953; same series, X.
It has a very valuable *Index verborum*, 359-410). — M. STENGEL, "Zur
Frühgeschichte der lateinischen Bibel", *Theologische Revue* (1953), 97-103
(a survey article). — A. WIKENHAUSER, *Einleitung in das N. T.* (2nd ed.,
Freiburg i. Br., 1956), 68-79, and 410. — T. AYUSO MAZARUELA, *La Vetus
Latina Hispana*. I, *Prolegomenos. Introducción general, estudio y analisis
de las fuentes* (Madrid, 1953; cf. *Sefarad* [1955], 171-179, and *RB* [1956],
454-455). — H. J. VOGELS, *Das Corpus Paulinum des Ambrosiaster* (Bonn,
1957; cf. *CBQ* [1957], 551-552)]. 2. The Vulgate. The articles by :
E. NESTLE, HERZOG-HAUCK, *Protestantische Realencyclopädie*, III (3rd ed.),
36-49; — H. J. WHITE, *HDB*. IV, 873-890; — E. MANGENOT, *DBV*, V,
2456 2500; — A. DURAND, *DAFC*, IV, 1943-1980. — F. CAVALLERA,

Saint Jérôme, sa vie et son œuvre (Louvain and Paris, 1922. — WORDS-WORTH-WHITE, *Novum Testamentum D. N. J. C. latine secundum editionem sancti Hieronymi*, I (Oxford, 1898), " Epilogus ", 651-779. — S. BERGER, *Histoire de la Vulgate pendant les premiers siècles du Moyen Age* (Paris, 1893). — H. GLUNZ, *History of the Vulgate in England from Alcuin to Roger Bacon* (Cambridge, 1933). — HERMANN VON SODEN, *Die Schriften der Neuen Testaments*. I, 1524 ff., 1797 ff., and 1007 ff. — F. G. KENYON, *Handbook to the Textual Criticism of the New Testament* (2nd ed,. London, 1912); [ID., *Our Bible and the Ancient Manuscripts* (revised ed., 1958), 139-144, and 238-264)]. — H. J. VOGELS, *Vulgatastudien* (Münster i. W., 1928). — A. CONDAMIN, " Les caractères de la traduction de la Bible par saint Jérôme ", *RSR* (1911), 425-440; *ibid*. (1912), 105-138. — Dom H. QUENTIN, *La revision de la Vulgate* (Rome, 1909 and 1912 (two studies); ID., *Mémoire sur l'établissement du texte de la Vulgate* (Rome and Paris, 1922); ID., *Essais de critique textuelle* (Paris, 1926). — M. J. LAGRANGE, *op. cit., supra*. — F. STUMMER, *Einführung in die lateinische Bibel* (Pader-born, 1928). — [Dom D. DE BRUYNE, " Saint Augustin réviseur de la Bible", *Miscellanea Agostiniana*. II (*Studi Agostiniani*, Rome 1931), 521-560. Dom H. DE SAINTE-MARIE, *S. Hieronymi Psalterium juxta Hebraeos*. *Edition critique* (Rome, 1953; Collectanea Biblica Latina, XI). — K. T. SCHÄFER, section on the Old Latin and the Vulgate in the article, " Bibelübersetzungen ", *LTK*, II (1958), 380-384 (with bibliography)].

[The Latin of the Old Latin versions and the Latin Vulgate : H. RÖNSCH, *Italia und Vulgata. Das Sprachidiom der urchristlichen Itala und der katholischen Vulgata erläutert* (2nd ed., Marburg, 1875; old, but still useful). W. E. PLATER and H. J. WHITE, *A Grammar of the Vulgate* (Oxford, 1926; brief, and weak on the historical side). — J. SCHRIJNEN, *Charakteristik des altchristlichen Lateins* (Nijmegen, 1932; Latinitas Christianorum Primaeva, I); ID., " Le latin chrétien devenu langue commune ", *Revue des Etudes Latines* (1934), 96-117 (primarily a reply to his critics). — C. MOHRMANN, " Le Latin commun et le latin des chrétiens ", *Vigiliae Christianae*, I (1947), 1-12; ID., " Quelques observations linguistiques à propos de la nouvelle version latine du Psautier ", *ibid*., 114-128, and 280-297; " Les éléments vulgaires du latin des chrétiens ", *ibid*., (1948), 89-101, and 163-184; ID., " Les origines de la latinité chrétienne à Rome ", *ibid*. (1949), 67-106, and 163-183; ID., " Les emprunts grecs dans la latinité chrétienne ", *ibid*. (1950), 193-211; ID., *Latin vulgaire. Latin des chrétiens. Latin médiéval* (Paris, 1955); ID., *Liturgical Latin : Its Origins and Character* (Washington, 1957); ID., *Etudes sur le latin des chrétiens* (Rome, 1958. This volume contains reprints of 28 articles or studies of the author on various aspects of Christian Latin, with valuable bibliography and indices). See also : E. LÖFSTEDT, " Zur Entstehung der christlichen Latinität ", in his *Syntactica. Studien und Beiträge zur historischen Syntax des Lateins*. II (Lund, 1933; reprinted, 1957), 458-473. — J. DE GHELLINCK, S. J., " Latin chrétien ou langue des chrétiens ", *Les Etudes Classiques* (1939), 449-478. — G. BARDY, *La question des langues dans l'Eglise ancienne*. I (Paris, 1948). — L. R. PALMER, *The Latin Language* (London, 1954),

especially, Chapter VII, " Special Languages — Christian Latin ", 181-205.
A. Blaise, *Manuel du latin chrétien* (Strasbourg, 1955; rather brief, but
very useful and furnished with a copious bibliography). — W. Matzkow,
*De vocabulis quibusdam Italae et Vulgatae Christianis quaestiones lexico-
graphicae* (Berlin, 1933). — M. Sainio, *Semasiologische Untersuchungen
über die Entstehung der christlichen Latinität* (Helzinki, 1940). — P. W.
Hoogterp, *Etude sur le latin du Codex Bobiensis (k.) des Evangiles* (Wage-
ningen, 1930). The great historical grammar of the Latin language by
Leumann-Hofmann, *Lateinische Grammatik* (Munich, 1928; a completely
revised edition is in press [1959]), includes Christian Latin within its scope
and furnishes copious bibliography. For the language and style of the
Latin Fathers of the Church, the pertinent monographs in the *Catholic
University of America Patristic Studies* and in the Nijmegen series, *Latinitas
Christianorum Primaeva*, will be found very useful. The following dictionaries are especially important : A. Souter, *A Glossary of the Later Latin
to 600 A. D.* (Oxford, 1949 (with a valuable list of authors and editions
of their works employed). — A. Blaise, *Dictionnaire latin-français des
auteurs chrétiens* (Strasbourg, 1954). *Thesaurus Linguae Latinae* (Leipzig,
1900 ff.); *A — H*, and more than half of *I* and of *M*, at the end of 1959.
This is indispensable as a practically exhaustive reference work.)

IV. Translations into the vernacular. Sir F. Kenyon, *Our Bible and
and the Ancient Manuscripts* (new and revised ed., London and New York,
1958), 265-342. — M. Deansley, *The Lollard Bible and Other Medieval
Biblical Versions* (Cambridge, 1920). — B. F. Westcott, *General View
of the History of the English Bible* (3rd ed. revised by W. A. Wright, London,
1905). — C. C. Butterworth, *Literary Lineage of the King James Bible,
1330-1611* (Philadelphia, 1941). — D. Daiches, *The King James Version
of the English Bible* (Chicago, 1941). — J. F. Tregear, " The First English
Bible ", *Clergy Review*, 27 (1947), 145-162 and 323-341. — H. Pope,
English Versions of the Bible. Revised by S. Bullough (St. Louis, 1952;
cf. also the review in *American Ecclesiastical Review* 127 [1957], 468-470).
An Introduction to the Revised Standard Version of the New Testament,
by Members of the Revision Committee (1946); *...of the Old Testament,*
by the same Committee (1952). — T. H. Darlow and H. F. Moule,
*Historical Catalogue of the Printed Editions of Holy Scripture in the Library
of the British and Foreign Bible Society* (2 vols., London, 1903-1908).
*La Sainte Bible, traduite en français sous la direction de l'Ecole Biblique
de Jérusalem* (one volume edition, Paris, 1956). For the history of translations of the Bible into French, see G. Bardy, " Les traductions en langue
vulgaire ", in Robert-Tricot, *Initiation Biblique* (3rd ed., Tournai, 1954),
440-444. *La sacra Bibbia tradotta dai testi originali con note a cura del
P. Instituto Biblico di Roma* (8 volumes, Firenze, 1943-1955). — G. Ricciotti, " Bibbia. VI. Versioni Moderne ", *Enciclopedia cattolica*, II (1949),
1556-1569. — J. Schmid, with the collaboration of J. Kürzinger (German
translations), P. Skehan (English), E. Beaucamp (French), and J. van
Dodewaard (Dutch and Flemish), " Bibelübersetzungen, Moderne ",

LTK (and ed., 1958), 401-411. See also the following important articles by E. P. Arbez : " The New Catholic Translation of the Old Testament ", *CBQ* (1952), 237-254); ID., " Scripture Translation ", *The Confraternity Comes of Age* (Paterson, N. J., 1956), 202-220; ID., " Modern Translations of the Old Testament : Dutch and Scandinavian ", *CBQ* (1954), 201-209); " German ", *ibid.*, 343-347; " Arabic, Maltese, Spanish, and Italian ", *ibid.*, 450-457); " French ", *ibid.* (1955), 76-87; " English ", *ibid.*, 456-485].

CHAPTER IX

INTERPRETATION

by G. Bardy, J. Bonsirven, L. Vaganay, L. Venard, and A. Vincent.

CHAPTER IX

INTERPRETATION

I. — HISTORY OF EXEGESIS [1].

1. — *EMPLOYMENT OF THE OLD TESTAMENT IN THE NEW.*

[L. VENARD]

The copious use of the Old Testament by the authors of the New can be ascertained through a cursory examination of any edition of the Greek New Testament in which special typographical characters indicate sentences or expressions taken from the Bible. It is immediately apparent that most of the New Testament Books are studded with quotations from the Old Testament, or at least with words or phrases borrowed from it. The quotations in the strict sense, whether introduced by special formulae or not (" it is written ", " as Isaias says ", " in order that what had been said might be fulfilled "), which emphasize reference to Scripture, exceed 200 in number, and more than half of these (118) occur in the Epistles of Saint Paul.

Translator's note. — [1 For a good survey, with bibliography, see : R. CORNELY, S. J., *Historica et Critica : Introductio I* (= *Introductio Generalis* ², Paris, 1925), 617-763 (covers Jewish, Catholic, and Protestant exegesis). There is a good sketch of the subject by F. X. SCHÜHLEIN and C. HOLZHEY in the article " Exegese ", *L T K*, III (1931), 901-907, with cross references to related articles and with good bibliography. See also especially R. SCHNACKENBURG, *et al.*, the article " Exegese ", *L T K*, III (2nd ed. 1959), 1273-1294. There is an old but still valuable work by L. DIESTEL, *Geschichte des A. T. in der christlichen Kirche* (Jena, 1869). H. J. KRAUS, *Geschichte der historisch-kritischen Erforschung des Alten Testaments von der Reformation bis zur Gegenwart* (Neukirchen, 1956; cf. the favorable reviews by A. M. DUBARLE, O. P., in *Revue des Sciences Phil.. et Theol.* [1958], 114-117, and R. DE VAUX, O. P., in *RB* 1958], 121-122. It is largely confined to Protestant research, but the reader will note especially a return to a more sound appreciation of the religious and theological value of the O. T.). E. G. KRAELING, *The Old Testament since the Reformation* (London, 1955; almost entirely confined to the O. T. in Protestantism). G. LINDESKOG, " Bibelvetenskap ", *Svenskt bibl. Uppslagsverk*, I, 270-276. On the use of the O. T. in the N. T., see also the section on the Dead Sea Scrolls, *supra*, pp. 113-123, and K. Stendahl, ed., *The Scrolls and the N. T.* (New York, 1957)].

Before we examine the spirit in which the writers of the New Testament used the Old, and attempt to determine precisely their methods of interpretation, two preliminary observations are in order. *a*) Biblical quotations in the New Testament are made most frequently according to the Greek of the Septuagint. Saint Matthew alone seems to have translated directly from the Hebrew text in some, at least, of his quotations. The other New Testament writers confined themselves to occasional slight modifications of the Greek version so as to bring it into closer conformity with the original, since the original doubtlessly seemed more appropriate to them in the passages in which they wished to make use of the text quoted. This preference for the Septuagint Version should not cause surprise, for the New Testament was written for Greek readers, to whom that version was familiar, and who granted to it, as an expression of divine revelation, an authority equal to that of the original text itself.   This unanimously recognized authority was sufficient to justify the use of the Septuagint, even in cases where the text gave a very different meaning from the original.   *b*) Furthermore, the quotations seem most frequently to be made from memory — some exception should be made perhaps for those contained in the Epistle to the Hebrews, since they are numerous and particularly long — and the sacred writers do not appear very much concerned about literal exactness in their quoting of texts.   Thus, a quotation may be modified in some words or phrases through reminiscences of other passages of the Old Testament (e.g., Rom. **11** : 9 = Ps. **69** : 23, 24, with a reminiscence of Ps. **35** : 18), or several scriptural passages offering a resemblance of ideas or of words may be blended into a single composite quotation (e.g., Rom. **3** : 10, 18 = Ps. **14** : 1-3 plus Ps. **5** : 10, plus Ps. **140** : 4, plus Ps. **10** : 7, plus Isa. **59** : 7,.8, plus Ps. **36** : 2).

If the writers of the New Testament have taken such great liberty in their quotation of scriptural passages, it will not be surprising to note a similar freedom in their manner of using these texts and of interpreting them.   Without doubt their interpretation, on the whole, may be called a *literal* interpretation in the sense that it is based on the literal meaning of the Biblical texts.   It is certainly not an *allegorical* interpretation in the manner of Philo the Jew, who, rejecting the literal meaning as inferior, substitutes for it, by a subtle interpretation of the words of the text, a meaning absolutely foreign to the thought of the Biblical writer. It must be recognized, however, that the interpretation given to the texts of the Old Testament quoted in the New is not always in conformity with the exact *historical* sense of these texts, and that there is often an enlarging, deepening, and spiritualization of that sense. Sometimes the divergence is so considerable that Rationalist Critics do not hesitate to speak of wrong interpretations. These, they add, can be explained by the use of methods of interpretation borrowed from Jewish exegesis of the time, of which the rabbinical books furnish characteristic examples. This severe evaluation seems scarcely justifiable, if care is taken to determine, first of all, in each case, precisely the meaning attributed by the writters of the New Testament to the quotations from the Bible, and if, secondly, there is a clear understanding of the concept of Scripture upon which their exegesis is founded.

Sometimes the quotations have only a purely *literary* value. The New Testament writers were so familiar with the Bible that reminiscences from the Old Testament came to their minds spontaneously, and they were led to make use of scriptural texts to express their own ideas without any thought of seeking in them actual proofs in support of what they wished to express. For Jewish listeners or readers, who admitted without question the absolute value of the Biblical texts, even independently of their original context, the employment of such texts must have furnished in itself a special force to the instruction which was being presented under a garb borrowed from the Old Testament. But in any event, we cannot accuse the Apostolic writers in such cases of making adaptations which give Biblical quotations meanings far removed from the original.

Sometimes the Biblical quotation seems to be introduced, not for the sake of a demonstration in the strict sense, based on the direct signification of the text, but only with the intention of illustrating, by a comparison which a passage from the Bible, the doctrine which the writer is explaining. Thus, when Saint Paul (Gal. 3 : 13) quotes the text from Deut. 21 : 23 : " Cursed is everyone who hangs on a gibbet ", it is not as a prophecy of the Passion of Christ, but as an illustration, by scriptural analogy, of the idea that Christ in dying on the cross became a curse for us.

In a great many cases, there is no doubt that the sacred writer's intention was to base a formal argument on the Biblical citation. The place held by the argument from the Prophets in early Christian apologetics is well known. Jesus Himself, in his discussions with the Doctors of the Law, relied on the texts of the Old Testament and on the prophetic significance that Jewish exegesis unhesitatingly attributed to them. Following His example, the Apostles and Apostolic writers were at pains, in their discussions with the Jews, to show in the life and work of Christ the accomplishment of the prophecies relative to the Messias and the Messianic era. This emphasis is particularly evident in the Gospel of Saint Matthew, where the frequent use of the expression, " that it might be fulfilled... ", stresses the accomplishment of a prophecy more strongly than the simple phrase, " it is written ". It is especially in respect to this category of texts that the question arises regarding the methods of interpretation used in the New Testament in applying the texts of the Old Testament to Christ and to Christianity.

In many instances, the Biblical passage upon which the New Testament writer bases his argument is clearly prophetic, and, even in its literal sense, points directly to the time, the person, and the work of the Messias, so that its application to the life of Jesus or to the history of the Apostles is in conformity with the *historical* meaning of the text. In this category we may place the quotations borrowed from the Prophet Isaias on the *Servant of Yahweh*, if, in fact, it is the Messias, and not, as some think, the people of Israel, who is designated under this name. Here also belong the quotations from Psalm 22, which describes the sufferings and the hopes of the Just Man in such terms that it seems really to have prophesied in a literal sense the sufferings of Christ in His Passion.

More frequently the argument is based, not on the historical sense of the text, but on the *spiritual* sense which the sacred writer discovers in it. The authors of the New Testament as all Jews of their time, believed that in the Bible there was a spiritual sense deeper than the literal sense, in consequence of which events and personages of Jewish history became, without, however, any doubt being cast on their reality and historical significance, the symbol or *figure* of spiritual realities to come. In this way, the Israelite nation was looked upon as a figure of Christ, to whom is applied what was written of Israel (e.g., Mt. 2 : 15, citing as prophetic the text of Os. 11 : 1, in which there is reference to Israel brought back from Egypt); the return from the Captivity becomes a figure of the Messianic period (Mt. 3 : 3; 11 : 10; Rom. 10 : 15); and the incredulity of the Jews toward the preaching of the Prophets is often alleged as a type of their incredulity in regard to the preaching of the Gospel (Mt. 13 : 14; Rom., 10 : 16).

In certain cases, this spiritual interpretation of the Bible is not the result of an immediately figurative exegesis, but of an adaptation, which, although arbitrary in appearance, is really based on reasoning by analogy. Convinced, on the one hand, that in the Bible the Spirit of God gives instruction which is useful not only for its first readers but for all time, and that, on the other, there is a harmonious connection between the works of God before Christ and the works of God in Christ, the sacred writer discovers, in the passage of the Old Testament which he quotes, a principle of divine government, and he applies this to present conditions. Thus, in Rom. 11 : 3-4, Saint Paul draws a lesson for his own time from the era of Elias, and affirms that, while the Jews as a whole have rebelled againts the Gospel, a small remnant of them will be saved.

Sometimes, especially in the Epistles of Saint Paul, the reasoning based on the spiritual sense of the texts offers some resemblance to certain rabbinical forms of exegesis, and it may be said that such reasoning was valid at least as an argument *ad hominem*. But it must be remembered also that even in the cases concerned, the exegesis of the New Testament writers is far removed from the fantasies of the Rabbis. We find in them a religious inspiration and a depth of spiritual vision which are absent from the contemporary Jewish exegesis. While based upon the existence of the spiritual sense, the exegesis of the New Testament writers is really a light of Faith, the value of which has compelling force obviously only if we acknowledge that they possessed a spiritual authority guaranteed by God. If we admit that they were supernaturally enlightened by the same Holy Spirit who inspired Scripture,

there is no difficulty in ignoring certain methods of interpretation
which may appear artificial, and in accepting their exegesis
as revealing the divine meaning of Biblical texts and the
providential significance of the facts contained in the Old
Testament.

JEWISH EXEGESIS [1].

[J. Bonsirven]

The religion of the Jewish people, " the people of the Book ",
necessarily played a primary role in exegesis. It is founded
actually on the Torah : the written Torah or sacred books,
and the oral Torah or ensemble of authoritative traditions.
Hence, the obligation of studying the sacred book and
of establishing the traditions of the ancients on the word of God.
And so all ancient Jewish literature takes an exegetical form :
commentaries on Scripture, or writings depending on Scripture.

We shall consider in some detail this ancient Jewish
or Talmudic literature, which presents all the types of exegesis
which will be put into practice later. We shall then give some
account of Jewish exegesis in the period following the Talmudic
age, i.e., after the 8th century. We shall not include the exegesis
of Philo [2], which is more Greek than Jewish and without
influence on Judaism, nor modern Jewish exegesis, which
is hardly to be distinguished from Christian or rationalistic
exegesis.

Translator's note. — [1 Cf. A. Geiger, *Urschrift und Uebersetzungen der Bible in ihrer Abhängigkeit von der inneren Entwicklung des Judentums* (ed. P. Kahle, Frankfurt a. M.,1928) ; *Jewish Encyclopedia*, III (New York,1907), 162-178; *Encyclopaedia Judaica*, IV (Berlin, 1929), 619-672; L. Prijs, *Jüdische Tradition in der Septuaginta* (Leiden, 1948). For the work of M. S. Segal, see the references given on p. 469. S. Rappaport, *Agada und Exegese des Flavius Josephus* (Frankfurt a. M., 1930)].

Translator's note. — [2 See P. Heinisch, *Der Einfluss Philos auf die älteste christliche Exegese*, in J. Nikel, *Altestamentliche Abhandlungen*, 1 and 2 (Münster i. W., 1908); E. Bréhier, *Les idées philosophiques et religieuses de Philon d'Alexandrie* (2nd ed., Paris, 1925); H. A. Wolfson, *Philo*, 2 vols. (Cambridge, Mass., 1948; especially, Vol. I, chap. I-III). On some peculiarities of Philo's Biblical Greek text, cf. P. Katz, *Philo's Bible* (Cambridge, England, 1950. See also, H. E. Ryle, *Philo and Holy Scripture, or the Quotations of Philo from the Books of the Old Testament, with Introduction and Notes* (London and New York, 1895); S. Belkin, *Philo and the Oral Law : The Philonic Interpretation of Biblical Law in Relation to the Palestinian Halakah* (Cambridge, Mass., 1940)].

1. — Talmudic Exegesis.

Esdras and the Scribes, " versed in the law of Moses " (Esd. 7 : 6), already practiced exegesis when they read the Book and explained it so that the text might be understood by the people (Neh. 8 : 8). Nevertheless, exegesis, as a discipline and method of juridical reasoning, developed only from the first century of the Christian era, through Hillel and his successors.

This type of exegesis pursues two ends and manifests two tendencies. It endeavors in the first place to single out and determine precisely the meaning of the sacred text, its juridical religious, historic, and moral sense. To achieve this objective, literal exegesis is required. We find it especially in the verbatim translations from the Hebrew, the Greek Septuagint Version, and the Aramaic translation of the Targums. Literal interpretation holds an important place also in the juridical commentaries (2nd cent. A.D.) on Exodus *(Mekhilta)*, on Leviticus *(Siphra)*, and on Numbers and Deuteronomy *(Siphre)* [1].

The Doctors used Scripture, furthermore, either as a foundation for traditions and juridical prescriptions *(halakha)*, which never ceased to flourish in abundance, or to support their preaching and non-juridical instruction *(haggada)*. These interpretations, having a demonstration or proof as their aim, in the course of time often became inaccurate on the literal side. We find them in two bodies of literature : (1) the *Mishnah* (less exegetical than its complement the *Tosephta)*, a juridical code drawn up by Rabbi Juda the Holy, toward the end of the second century [2], and its two commentaries, the *Talmud* (study)

Translator's note. — [1 On these Midrashim, see H. L. STRACK, *Introduction to the Talmud and Midrash* (Philadelphia, 1931), pp. 206-209; J. WINTER and A. WÜNSCHE, *Mechiltha. Ein Tannaitischer Midrash zu Exodus* (Leipzig, 1909); J. Z. LAUTERBACH, *Mekilta of Rabbi Ishmael* (3 vols. Philadelphia, 1933-1935. Schiff Library of Jewish Classics. A critical edition of the original text with English translation, introduction, and notes). I. FRANKEL, *Peshat in Talmudic and Midrashic Literature* (Toronto, 1956); I. HEINEMANN, *The Methods of the Agadah* (Jerusalem, 1949; in Hebrew); R. BLOCH, in *Moïse, homme de l'Alliance* (Paris, 1955), 90 ff.; *eadem*, " Midrash ", *DBV, Suppl.* V (1957), 1263-1281 (with valuable bibliography)].

Translator's note. [2 The *Mishnah* (= " teaching ") is a name given to the collection of legislative writings made *ca.* 200 A. D. by Rabbi Judah ha-Nasi [the prince] or the Saint. It was first handed down orally until circumstances endangering the faithful preservation of the traditions made it necessary to write them down. Preserving as it does the often divergent views of scholars of Jerusalem and the *Talmud* of Babylon (the redaction of which was completed about the seventh century) [1]; and (2) the *Midrashim*, the homiletic, historical, and haggadic commentaries on the Scriptures.

on matters of ritualistic, legal, or moral character, the *Mishnah* is a compilation made by an editor (Rabbi Judah), who only reproduces different views. The Mishnah is not a code in the proper sense of the word. The scholars whose views are reproduced in the Mishnah are known as the Tannaim (divided into " generations " -usually four). The Mishnah is divided into 6 *parts* (Seder, " order "), each of which has its name (e.g., I = *Zera'im*, " seeds "). Each Seder comprises a varying number of *treatises*. Thus, Seder III has 7 treatises, Seder IV has 10, Seder I and V have 11 each, Seder II and VI have 12 each, there being 63 treatises in all. Each treatise, *Masséket* (= " web ", cf. Latin *textus)* has its title and is divided into chapters, *Perek* (= " section "), and each chapter is subdivided into paragraphs (a paragraph is also sometimes called a Mishnah). To refer to the Mishnah, one mentions the name of the treatise, the chapter, and the paragraph, e.g. : *Shabbat* 3, 3 = the (first) treatise of that name in Seder II; *Baba qamma* 4, 2 = the (first) treatise in Seder IV, etc. There are numerous editions of the Mishnah, some in the original text (Hebrew) without annotations, and others in which the original text is accompanied by a translation and commentary. There is a good English translation, but without the Hebrew text, by H. Danby, *The Mishnah* (Oxford, 1935). For the language of the Mishnah, see K. ALBRECHT *Neuhebräische Grammatik* (Munich, 1913), and M. S. SEGAL, *A Grammar of Mishnaic Hebrew* (Oxford, 1927).

The *Tosefta* (an Aramaic word meaning " addition ", " complement ", " supplement ") is a collection of teachings of the Tannaim closely ressembling the Mishnah and for the most part parallel with it, but more extensive in its contents as implied by the name itself. It is divided into 6 *orders*, bearing identical names with those of the Mishnah. The individual *treatises* have, with few exceptions, the same names as those of the Mishnah. Four *treatises*, however, are not found in the Mishnah, namely, *Abot, Qinnim, Middot*, and *Tamid*. Each treatise is divised into chapters and each chapter into paragraphs, but generally the chapter division in the Tosefta, does not agree with that of the Mishnah. The precise relation of the Tosefta to the Mishnah is a difficult problem which has given rise to many theories. There are numerous editions of the Tosefta — in whole or in part — with translations and commentaries. The work of B. Ugolini (see the Bibliography at the end of this chapter) contains in vols. 17-20 a Latin translation of 31 treatises. Some Tosefta treatises — with Mishnah — have appeared in English translation : *Sanhedrin* (H. Danby, 1919), *Berakot* (A. L. Williams, 1921), *Sukkah* (A. W. Gollnup, 1925), all published in London by S. P. C. K.].

Translator's note. — [1 The *Talmud* exists in two forms : the Palestinian Talmud, generally known as *Yerushalmi* (of Jerusalem), and the Babylonian *(Babli)*. They are very large collections of encyclopedic character embodying the discussions of Jewish scholars of Palestine and Babylonia between *ca.* the 3rd and 6th centuries A.D. In the course of the discussions, all kinds of subjects are brought up, so that in the Talmud we have a mine of information about many different aspects of life : religious, moral, social, scientific, folklore, etc. For details on the contents of the Talmud presented according to topics treated, see especially A. Cohen, *Everyman's Talmud* (London, 1932).

The text of the Talmud, consists of two elements : a) a section of the *Mishnah* and, b) the *Gemara* (= " study ") on the Mishnah section. But instead of being merely a study of the Mishnah passage, the discussions of the Rabbis often wander off into treatments of topics which have little, if anything, to do with the passage in question. The Mishnah text is in fact only a starting point

What methods do these various types of exegesis follow? It is noteworthy that Judaism possessed rules of exegesis from an early date : the seven rules of Hillel, the thirteen of Rabbi Ismael († 135), the thirty-two attributed to Rabbi Eliezer ben Jose the Galilean (*ca.* 150), the principles of Rabbi Aqiba († 135). The formal statement of these rules does not give us by any

---

of discussion. Hence the Talmud is much more than a commentary on the Mishnah.

Of the *Yerushalmi* we know neither the date of its composition nor the name of its first editor. It may be surmised that it was completed in the first half of the 5th century, as after that date the state of Palestinian Judaism would hardly warrant the possibility of the compilation of such a work. The language is Palestinian Aramaic. See J. T. MARSHALL, *Manual of the Aramaic Language of the Palestinian Talmud* (Leiden, 1929). The *Yerushalmi* is incomplete, containing only the treatises of Seder I-IV plus a part of the Treatise *Niddah* in Seder VI, i.e., 39 treatises out of a total of 63. The first complete edition of the work as we have it was printed at Venice by Daniel Bomberg in 1523, and all references are made according to that edition. Each page has two columns (recto *a* and *b*, and verso *c* and *d*). Each Seder has its own pagination running right through. Thus, *Yerush.* Shabbat 7*d* will be found in Seder II (*Mo'ed*) where this treatise is found, p. 7, 4th col., i.e., p. 7 verso, col. 2 (left, as the text goes from right to left). There is a French translation of this Talmud : M. SCHWAB, *Le Talmud de Jérusalem* (Paris, 1878-1890).

The *Babli* is the better known and has exercised immense influence on Jewish life. It was practically completed by 500 A. D., but some few additions were made in the 6th-7th centuries. The scholars mentioned in the Gemara and in both Talmuds — thus between the Mishnah and the completion of the Gemara (6th and 7th cent. respectively) — are known as the *Amoraim* (plural of Amōrā, " speaker ", " interpreter " — of the law and bearer of the oral law), arranged into 5 " generations " in Palestine and 7 " generations " in Babylonia. The scholars of the 6th-7th centuries are the *Saboraim* (" the thinkers ", " those who reflect ") who completed the Talmud. The language of the Babli is an Eastern Aramaic dialect, closely related to Mandaic and to Syriac. See M. MARGOLIS, *A Manual of the Aramaic Language of the Babylonian Talmud* (Munich, 1910), and (more complete) C. LEVIAS, *A Grammar of Babylonian Aramaic* (New York, 1930, in Hebrew). The Babli covers 36 treatises of the 63 in the Mishnah. There is a facsimile edition by H. L. Strack of the one almost complete Ms, *Codex Monac. Hebr.* 95, copied in 1343 (Leiden, 1912). The first complete edition was printed in Venice by Daniel Bomberg, 1520-1523. There have been many editions of the work and translations of single treatises and selections. For details, it will suffice to refer to H. L. Strack's *Introduction* and similar works. A complete German translation was published by L. Goldschmidt in 12 vols. (Berlin 1929-1936). The same editor published *Der Babylonische Talmud*, with critical Hebrew text and German translation in 9 vols. (1897-1935; vols. 1-3, at Berlin, vols. 4-8 at Leipzig, and vol. 9, at The Hague). An English edition by the Soncino Press (London) is in course of publication under the direction of I. Epstein since 1935. The pagination of the first edition is preserved in all later editions, so that all references are made in the same manner. Each treatise has its own pagination, and each page its recto and verso. Thus, *Berakot* 39 *b* means Treatise *Berakot* — found in Seder I — p. 39 verso. The difficulty — in both Talmuds — is to find the particular passage referred to, which often can only be done by reading through the whole page or column, unless the reference is accompanied by some indication of the part of the page where the given text is to be found].

means the characteristic features of the Jewish commentaries, the hermeneutics of which is in other respects free and varied. A basic direction is often recalled, but more and more neglected, namely, that it is not right to go beyond the simple meaning of Scripture. In principle, likewise, juridical interpretation should have followed other methods than haggadic (edifying, historical), but, actually, the methods differ very little.

The first impression that one gets from the reading of these ancient Jewish juridical commentaries is that their authors wished to scrutinize every least particle of the Sacred Book. Why, it was asked, was there such a prescription or narrative? Why such a repetition? Why did these two sections succeed each other? How explain such apparent contradiction? What was the connection between analogous passages...? Could one not understand a law or a historical fact in such and such a way? And thus all possible meanings were envisaged. This profound study and meticulous examination led to a definition of the special literary features of the Bible and to the development of various kinds of topics for its interpretation.

The first endeavor of textual criticism is in evidence : to determine the true reading, the spelling and the pronunciation of the words, the division of sentences, the extent of sections. The knowledge of Biblical style and language makes it possible to affirm that certain words are equivalent, e.g., wine and a fermented drink (on Num. **6** : 3); determines the range of meaning of certain others, e.g., *cippor* (bird) designates a clean bird (on Deut. **14** : 11); makes possible the observation that the conjunction (on Lev. **23** : 29) introduces a new topic *(Talmud b. Pesaḥim 5a)*... Certain terms replace anthropomorphic or unsuitable expressions : thus " the pupil of his eye ", instead of " my eye " (Zach. **2** : 12); " we shall not die ", instead of " Thou (God) wilt not die " (Hab. **1** : 12)...; " Return to your tents " (Deut. **5** : 30) instead of " to your gods ". Ordinarily the mention of one fact after another indicates their chronological order (Num. **30** : 2). It is enlightening to arrange together matters of a similar nature, e.g., in what cases God calls the Israelites His sons or His slaves (Lev. **25** : 55). Finally, we meet two contradictory principles : a given passage can take many meanings; Scripture speaks the language of men, objects Rabbi Ismael to Rabbi Aqiba, who sees a reference to the two

worlds in the repetition of the verb meaning " to be destroyed "
(Num. **15** : 31).

We also find more precise philology : stabilization of
vocabulary, either through textual comparisons, which constitute
the prelude to concordances, or through etymologies, which
are sometimes exact but too frequently fantastic; grammatical
observations on the number and gender of words, and on certain
verbal forms... : " spoke " (sg.) in Num. **12** : 1 has a plural
subject " Mary and Aaron "...

The Doctors prefer to deduce the meaning by a process of
reasoning. This method of precedure is the primary concern
of the rules mentioned above. Some examples follow. The rule
of *a fortiori*, both from the greater to the less and from the less
to the greater : we can draw from Ex. **9** : 3 the principle that
" the hand of Yahweh " always designates the scourge of
pestilence. Included or excluded meaning : " man " excludes
" women and children "; " man-servant " excludes " maid-
servant "; on the other hand, " you will fear " (Lev. **19** : 3)
includes men and women. In general " a beast " is determined
by the particular qualification that follows : " large or small
cattle " (Lev. **1** : 2). The deductions that one might make
regarding the words " sin ignorantly " (Num. **15** : 27) are ruled
out by reference to the subject of the pericope or immediate
context. On the other hand, the context is used to support
interpretations which are often artificial. Thus, a widow cannot
be forced to marry a leprous brother-in-law, for before the law
of levirate it is stated (Deut. **25** : 4) : " Thou shalt not muzzle
the ox that treadeth out thy corn on the floor " *(Talmud
b. Yebamot* 4 a). The Doctors showed a fondness for analogies
and assimilations, which led to unexpected conclusions.

They make use of other procedures also, which carry them
much farther from the literal sense. E.g., allegory : " You shall
not eat anything with blood " signifies that a funeral meal
is not served for one condemned to death (on Lev. **19** : 26);
Sukkot designates the clouds of glory (on Ex. **12** : 37).
Symbolism discovers symbols of the Law in the water and in the
tree (Ex. **15** : 22, 25); or, in the vine shown to Pharaoh, images
of the Patriarchs, of the Law, or of Jerusalem... *(Talmud b.
Hullin* 92 a). To all this we may add the innumerable haggadic
embellishments which adorn Biblical history with all sorts on

legends : e.g., the story of the murmuring of Aaron and Mary against Moses is completed by a new piece of information, namely, that Moses no longer has relations with his wife (on Num. 12).

Among even more arbitrary methods it will suffice to mention the following. *Gematria* [1] : it can be deduced from Jer. 9 : 9 that no one passed into Juda for fifty-two years, because " cattle " has the numerical value of 52 *(Talmud b. Sabbat* 145b.) *Notariqon* [2] *:* Rabbi Joshua b. Levi (ca. 250) discovers that the letters of *ha-nehiloth* (with flutes, Ps. 5 : 1) indicate the five parts of the Torah, the fifty days between Easter and Pentecost, the Decalogue, the thirty just equal to Abraham, the six sections of the Mishnah, and the four hundred years of the sojourn of Israel in Egypt. Inversions, transpositions, and modifications of letters lead to still more extraordinary results. In short, a skillful and imaginative exegete discovers in every text the confirmation of his own thoughts.

2. — Jewish Exegesis in the Middle Ages. [3]

The Talmud was hardly completed, when several movements and developments turned men's minds to a more rational kind of exegesis : the contact with the Arabs and their philological methods; the development of Karaism [4], a Jewish heresy which, in opposition to the Rabbis, professed devotion to the letter; the active interest of the Jewish world in lexicographical and grammatical studies; the meticulous work of the Massoretes on

---

Translator's note. — [1 *Gematria*, Rabbinic Hebrew *Gematryā* or *Gimatryā*, from Greek γεωματρία, a cabbalistic method of interpreting the Hebrew Scriptures. It consists in the use of the numerical values of the lettres of a word for the purpose of comparing it with other words which give the same or similar combinations of numbers and of thus getting at the hidden meaning of the text].

Translator's note. — [2 Nōtārīqōn, from the Greek νοταρικόν, which is connected with Latin *notarius*, one writing in shorthand or cipher. It is a cabbalistic method of interpretation according to which every letter of a word is taken as the initial letter of some other word (an *acrostichon*). Thus, in the word for I ['anoky] the consonants are taken to stand for I ('ana) myself (nafshi) have written (ketabit) have given [the Law] (yehabit). Cf. JASTROW, *Dictionary of the Targumin*, etc., reprinted, 1926, p. 856. On *Gematria* and *Notarikon*, see also F. GIGOT, art. " Kabbala ", *Catholic Encyclopedia*, VII (1910), 590-591].

Translator's note. — [3. See S. BARON, *A Social and Religious History of the Jews. High Middle Ages, 500-1200.* Vol. VI, *Laws, Homilies and the Bible* [New York 1958.]

Translator's note. — [4 On Karaism, see p. 589, note 1].

the Sacred Text; and later, the spread of Aristotelian philosophy. We must mention the most conspicuous representatives of the main trends in Jewish exegesis as it then developed.

Saadiah Gaon (892-942) [1] returned in his commentaries and in his Arabic translation of the Bible to the literal sense. Among the commentators we may list : Abraham ibn Ezra of Toledo (1092-1167), whose interpretations are founded on grammar, on the natural meanings of words, and on the logical connection between the parts of discourse [2]; Rabbi Salomon b. Isaac (Rashi) of Troyes (1040-1105), who combined, with his literal exegesis, haggadic traditions and judicious personal views — a type pleasing to the Jewish mind, for his work is still classic [3]; David Kimchi (1160-1235) of Narbonne, who is still read, a famous grammarian and lexicographer, but an exegete lacking originality [4].

Maimonides (1135-1204) [5] did not write a Biblical commentary, but he often resorts in his writings, particularly in his

---

Translator's note. — [1 Saadiah ben Joseph, commonly known as Saadiah Gaon, born in Upper Egypt in 882 or 892 AD, died in Babylonia (Sura), the pioneer of Jewish-Arabic culture, and a vigorous opponent of Karaism. Gaon, — literally, " excellency " — was a title given to the heads of the Jewish academies (Sura and Pumbeditha) in Babylonia from the 7th to the 13-14thcent. Cf. S. L. Skoss, " A Study of Inflection in Hebrew from Saadiah Gaon's Grammatical Work Kutub al lughah ", *JQR*, 33 (1942-43), 171-212.]

Translator's note. — [2 Ibn Ezra was equally versed in Arabic and Hebrew. He lived in Spain until 1140, and then went to southern France, Italy, and England. It is in this second part of his life that he wrote his commentaries. They are printed in Buxtorf's *Biblia Rabbinica*].

Translator's note. — [3 He was famous as a Talmudic scholar also. His Talmud commentary is reproduced in the margin of editions of the Talmud. His commentaries are found also in Buxtorf. See further, Rosenbaum, Siilbermann, Blashki, and Joseph, *The Pentateuch with Targum Onkelos, Haphtarot and Prayers for Sabbath, with Rashi's Commentary*, translated into English and annotated (5 vols, London, 1929-1934)].

Translator's note. — [4 David Kimchi, also called Radak, wrote a Hebrew grammar *(Miklol;* cf. W. Chomsky, *David Kimchi's Hebrew Grammar (Miklol) Systematically Presented and Critically Annotated* [Philadelphia, 1933]) ; a Hebrew dictionary *(Sefer has shorashim,* or " Book of Roots "), which is really Part II of the *Miklol,* and in which he employs parallels from later Hebrew, Arabic, and Aramaic; commentaries on the Pentateuch (only Genesis is extant), the Prophets, the Psalms, and Chronicles. For the commentaires see Buxtorf *op. cit.*].

Translator's note. — [5 His full name was Moses ben Maimon, but he was also known as Rambam, an abbreviated form of his name. He was born in Spain (Cordoba), fled to Fez (Morocco) in 1160, and finally (1167) settled in Fostat (Old Cairo) in Egypt. A distinguished physican by profession, he wrote on medical subjects and natural sciences. But he also took a great interest in all problems of Jewish life — practical life, philosophy, theology, and exerted

" Guide for the Perplexed ", to a philosophical and rationalizing exegesis to explain the anthropomorphisms of Scripture (metaphorical or spiritual meanings) or certain of the more striking miracles. These rationalizing tendencies are found in others also, e.g., Moses Samuel ibn Gikatilla (11th century) [1] and and to a lesser degree in Levi ben Gerson of Bagnols (1288-1344)[2].

As opposed to this pronounced rationalistic approach, the mystic and cabalistic movement continued to grow steadily. On the mystic side, we find, e.g., Moses ben Nachman (1194-1270) [3] — still reprinted — who declared that each word conceals mysteries, and who searched after celestial wisdom. The Cabala combines with this mystic sense a theosophy, difficult to define, which approaches emanationistic pantheism. Its chief monument, the *Zohar* (Book of Splendor), which appeared toward the end of the 13th century, is in the form of a commentary. By its allegorical exegesis, by its mystico-alphabetical or mystico-numerical processes, and other means equally arbitrary, it attempted to explain the hidden sense of the Sacred Text, especially that of the Pentateuch and of the Canticle of Canticles. These lucubrations enjoyed a great success not only among the Jews, but also among Christians who believed that they could recognize in the cabalistic

---

an influence of the highest importance on Jewish thought. For references, see the article contribued by several scholars in *the Universal Jewish Encyclopedia*, VII (New York, 1942), 287-296a. See also Ueberweg-Geyer, *Geschichte der Philosophie : Die patristische und scholastische Zeit* (11th ed., Berlin 1928), 339-341, and 727 (bibliography). See also K. HRUBY, "Connaissance de l'œuvre de Maimonide ", *Cahiers Sioniens* (1955), 138-156].

Translator's note. — [1Spanish forms of his name are Chigitilla and Chiquitilla. He was born in Cordoba and became renowned as a Hebrew grammarian. As a Biblical scholar, his approach to the text was primarily historical. He suggested postexilic dates for several Psalms or additions of a later date to Davidic Psalms, and he assigned the second part of the Book of Isaias to a date after 587 B.C].

Translator's note. — [2 Levi ben Gershon, known as Gersonides and Ralbag, was a prolific and influential author. He wrote commentaries on most of the books of the Bible. After determining the literal sense, he sought for deeper meanings to apply to moral or philosophical questions].

Translator's note. — [3 Moses ben Nachman, known also as Nachmanides and Ramban, was born in Spain (Gerona) and died in Syria (Akka). His best known work is his commentary on the Pentateuch, which combines a rationalistic approach and a search for mysterious meanings. Ramban was not a Cabalist, but he was attracted to the Cabala and contributed to direct attention to it].

doctrines a preformation and, as it were, a confirmation of Christian dogma [1].

Conclusion.

This brief account should be sufficient to give an insight into the mixed character of Jewish exegesis. While certain aspects of it are totally obsolete and valueless, it has also sound and enduring elements which are still worth putting to use. Jewish exegesis exercised some influence on Christian scholars. We know what Origen and Saint Jerome owe to their Jewish masters. It is through the Jewish grammars and lexica, and through contact with rabbis, that Robert Grosseteste, Roger Bacon, Pico de la Mirandola, Reuchlin, and other Hebrew scholars enriched their knowledge. The authors of certain biblical correctories and some famous commentators, as Nicholas of Lyra, were likewise dependent on rabbinical exegesis. Through such channels Jewish learning made some contributions to the Christian tradition in exegesis [2].

Translator's note. — [1 On the Cabala, see S. KARPPE, *Etude sur les origines et la nature du Zohar, précédé d'une étude sur l'histoire de la Kabbale* (Paris, 1901), and J. DE PAULY, *Sefer ha-Zohar (le livre de Splendeur)* (6 vols.) Paris, 1906-1911; a French translation with explanatory notes.) For more rapid orientation, see the Jewish encyclopedias *(Jewish Encyclopedia, Universal Jewish Encyclopedia, Valentine's Jewish Encyclopedia)* s.v. Cabala and Zohar, the art. " Cabale " in *DTC*, II², cols. 1271-1291, and the art. " Kabbala ", in *LTK*, V, cols. 739-742)].

Translator's note. — [2 The following additional information on Jewish exegesis in the modern period will be of interest to our readers. Our exposition is based primarily on M. S. SEGAL's " *General Introduction to the Scripture,* " etc. (in Hebrew; see p. 469 *supra*). The modern period differs from the earlier ones in its independent attitude towards the Jewish tradition and in its increasing dependence on Christian scholarship. Moses Mendelssohn (born at Dessau, 1729, died at Berlin, 1786) may be regarded as its pioneer. He was a leader of " Enlightenment " (Haskalah) — the assimilation of western culture through the adoption of the language, dress, and ways of life of the Gentile environment, although he personally remained orthodox and advocated fidelity to the ceremonial laws. He undertook the translation of the Pentateuch and the Psalms into German, and he wrote a commentary *(Bi'ūr)* on Exodus and on a part of Genesis. The *Bi'ūr* on the rest of the Pentateuch was continued by several other scholars. In several places, Mendelssohn appeals to the authority of Gentile scholars, as did also his disciples. " Thus ", says Segal, " Jewish commentators began to depend on Gentiles, while formerly Christian commentators were wont to learn from the Jews ". Without denying the good points in Mendelssohn's translation, Segal notes that, while it helped to spread among Jews a taste for the German language and literature, it likewise contributed to the neglect of Hebrew and to the " blurring of Jewish education ". Jewish Biblical scholars began to publish their studies in foreign languages for Christian readers, they adopted the methods current among Christians, and they became more and more dependent on Christian scholarship. " It must

3. — *PATRISTIC EXEGESIS.*

[G. BARDY]

When the Christians began to write, they found it quite natural to use the Sacred Books either for proof or confirmation of their faith. They were content in so doing to imitate the examples given them by the Savior Himself and by the Apostles. But it was not long before they added the writings of the New Testament to those of the Old. This was done in such a spontaneous fashion that it is difficult to determine precisely the circumstances in which the first use was made of the Gospels and Epistles as sacred books.

1. — The Beginnings [1].

Among the Apostolic Fathers, Clement of Rome was especially familiar with the Sacred Books. The long prayer which occurs toward the end of his Letter to the Corinthians is, in some respects, almost a web of expressions borrowed from the Old Testament. But a system of exegesis, in the strict sense, cannot be discovered in his writings. Clement is content to cite texts. Most frequently, he wishes to encourage his readers to moral perfection, to show them the ugliness of sin and the benefits

be recognized ", says Segal, " that Christian Biblical Scholarship has widened and deepened our field of knowledge in many important details, thanks to the remarkable progress in our age of Semitic philology and Oriental archaeology. But it has also spread many distorted and injurious notions about Israel and its Law; the fountain spring of these is Christian theology which teaches that the Hebrew Scripture is only an antiquated, imperfect stage of revelation, destined to prepare for the perfect and final revelation in the Christian Messiah and his teachings ". The author regards this as most dangerous and ruinous from the Jewish point of view. It is to be hoped, he concludes, that in a not too distant future " Hebrew exegesis will learn to free itself from dependence on Christian scholars and will again draw its strength from its deep roots in the very soul of Israel. Then it will be again what it was formerly : a source of everlasting life for the people of Israel and a light enlightening the Gentiles ". The passages quoted from Segal are interesting, but also disquieting. By adopting such an attitude towards Christian exegesis and by employing Hebrew as the language of its scholarly publications is Jewish exegesis again going to cut itself off from intimate participation and cooperation in the international scholarship of the West? On Mendelssohn's work, see PEREZ SANDLER, *Mendelssohn's Edition of the Pentateuch*, with Introductory Note by J. Klausner (Jerusalem, 1940; in Hebrew)].

Translator's note. — [1 See H. SMITH, *Ante-Nicene Exegesis of the Gospel*, 6. vols. (London, 1925-1929, S. P. C. K. An Appendix in vol. 6 covers Ante-Nicene exegesis of Acts); J. DANIÉLOU, *Théologie du Judéo-Christianisme*, I (Tournai, 1958)].

of virtue. With this purpose in view, he had no need of interpreting the passages upon which he bases his exhortations.

The same cannot be said, however, of the unknown author of the Letter of Barnabas. This writer sets out to prove a thesis. He wishes to show that the role of Judaism is now ended and that the Christians have inherited the Sacred Books from the Jews as well as their prerogatives. To achieve his aim, he resorts to the allegorical method which had already been employed by Philo of Alexandria and the author of the Epistle to the Hebrews. But he uses it with an undeniable exaggeration and with a disconcerting prejudice, for he goes so far as to reproach the Jews for their obtuseness regarding even the clearest precepts. He maintains, e.g., that God has not demanded of them bloody sacrifices, but contrite hearts, not bodily fasts, but the practice of good works, not the circumcision of the flesh, but of the ears and of the heart, not abstinence from certain meats, but flight from the vices signified by impure animals, and he declares that it is because the Jews had not understood all these things that they were finally rejected.

The Apologists had little occasion to appeal to the testimony of the Sacred Books, at least when they were addressing the pagans. However, they insisted on maintaining that the writings of the Old Testament were older than those of the Greek poets and philosophers. They thus emphasized the antiquity of the Judeo-Christian religion and even offered this as evidence that the Greeks borrowed the best of their teachings from the Jews. This type of proof holds an important place in the writings of Saint Theophilus of Antioch, who, however, seems to make use of an allegorical explanation for the account of creation.

The Apologists do not give much emphasis to the argument based on prophecies, although almost all mention it. The only one who uses it in any detail, at least to our knowledge, is Saint Justin, whose literary activity falls between 150 and 160. Even the *First Apology* gives an important place to the testimony of the Prophets. The *Dialogue against Trypho*, as is natural, is concerned to a much greater degree with the discussion of this testimony. The anti-Jewish polemic in this work — the first of its kind which has been preserved — is based entirely on the examination of the texts which announced the coming of the Messias. Justin treats these texts with great simplicity and candor, and does not try to turn them in his favor by subtle or mystifying interpretations. His exegesis may be called a model of fidelity and sincerity.

While Catholics were using the Old Testament in this manner, the heretics of the second century, principally the Marcionites, did not hesitate to condemn it and to emphasize its seeming disagreement with the teachings of Jesus. Thus, Marcion wrote his *Antitheses,* in which he attempted to show the contradictions between the teachings of the Old Testament and those of the New. Not long after him, Apelles composed his *Syllogisms,* stressing the difficulties peculiar to the Old Testament. Tatian published a book of *Problems,* about which we have no other information, but it likewise appears to have dealt with certain seeming contradictions in the Sacred Books.

The opponents of heresy, on the other hand, became defenders of the Law and the Prophets. The *Adversus Hæreses* of Saint Irenaeus, and the *Contra Marcionem* and the other books of Tertullian, thus have an important place in the history of early Christian exegesis. In particular, we should not forget that Tertullian was the author of the argument of prescription, which denies to heretics the right of using and commenting upon the Sacred Books.

The interest in the study of Holy Scripture exhibited by the Gnostics deserves some mention. The oldest commentary on Saint John's Gospel is the work of one of them, a certain Heracleon. Another, Ptolemy, in a *Letter to Flora* [1], sets forth some curious principles of exegesis and declares, that in the Pentateuch, three divisions are to be distinguished : the first, which goes back to God and is good; the second, which is the work proper of Moses, and finally, the third, which comes from the Ancients of the people. Catholics made use of all these works, and their solicitude in presenting a methodical refutation

---

Translator's note. — [[1] See *Ptolémée : Lettre à Flora. Texte, traduction et introduction,* ed. G. Quispel (Paris, 1948; Sources Chrétiennes, no. 22). See also *Clément d'Alexandrie. Extraits de Théodote. Texte grec, introduction, traduction et notes,* ed. F. Sagnard, O. P. (Paris, 1948; Sources Chrétiennes, no. 23). The *Introduction* [pp. 7-40] contains an excellent study of the Gnostics' principles of exegesis.)]

of them was one of the important incentives for applying themselves to the study of the Sacred Books [1].

2. — Origen.

Clement [2] is the first known writer of the Catholic Church of Alexandria. His great works, the *Protrepticus*, the *Pedagogue*, and the *Stromateis*, are filled with Biblical erudition, a rather disordered erudition for that matter, but nonetheless remarkable. Clement preferred the allegorical sense and thus followed in the path traced by Philo Judaeus.

One name, that of Origen, dominates all others in the beginnings of scientific exegesis. Born at Alexandria *ca.* 185, Origen died at Tyre *ca.* 253. In the course of a troubled life, he never ceased studying and making comments on the Bible, with the result that all who came later depended more or less upon him, whether as imitators or as adversaries.

Mention has already been made (pp. 626-628) of the extensive critical work he undertook on the text itself of the Old Testament and which found expression in his Hexapla. His exegetical labors comprise three series of works : scholia, commentaries, and homilies [3]. The scholia are simple, unconnected notes which throw light upon obscure points in the Sacred Books. We know that Origen composed scholia on the first four books of the Pentateuch, on Isaias, on Ecclesiastes, on the Psalms, on the Gospels of Matthew and John, on the Epistle to the Galatians, and on the Apocalypse. Hardly any of this material

---

Translator's note. — [1 In 1946, a collection of Gnostic texts was discovered near Nag-Hammadi in Egypt. The collection, which totals more than 1000 pages of text in Coptic, comprises 37 complete works and 5 additional ones in fragments. This collection of papyri, one of the most important finds so far made, will give us a new and most welcome light on the history of Gnosticism in the first centuries of our era. See J. Doresse and Togo Mina, " Nouveaux textes gnostiques coptes découverts en Haute-Egypte. La bibliothèque de Chenoboskion ", *Vigiliæ Christianæ*, 3 (1949), 129-141. See also J. QUASTEN, *Patrology*, I (Utrecht and Brussels, 1950) 277)].

Translator's note. — [2 See TH. CAMELOT, O. P., " Clément d'Alexandrie et l'Ecriture ", *RB* 53 (1946), 242-248].

Translator's note. — [3 *Origène : Homélies sur la Genèse. Introduction de H. de Lubac, S. J. Traduction de L. Doutreleau, S. J.* (Paris, 1944; Sources Chrétiennes, no. 7), and *Origène : Homélies sur l'Exode. Traduction de P. Fortier, S. J. Introduction et notes de H. de Lubac, S. J.* (Paris, 1947; Sources Chrétiennes, no. 16)].

has been preserved. His commentaries are, as their name indicates, connected and detailed explanations on the various books of Scripture. Origen wrote commentaries on the first four chapters of Genesis, on several Psalms, on Proverbs, on the Canticle of Canticles (two different commentaries on this book), on most of the Prophets, on the Gospels (except Saint Mark), and on the Epistles of Saint Paul (except those to the Corinthians and those to Timothy). We still possess, besides numerous fragments of the rest, important parts of the commentaries on Matthew and on John, and a Latin adaptation of the commentary on the Epistle to the Romans. Fragments of the Greek original of Vols. V and VI of this commentary are contained in a papyrus found at Toura near Cairo in 1941.

The homilies were delivered at Caesarea in Palestine and deal with a large number of the books of the Old and New Testaments. Slightly more than two hundred homilies, some forty of them on the Gospel of Saint Luke, have been preserved for us, but in most cases only in the Latin translations of Rufinus or St. Jerome.

In spite of their diversity, all the exegetical works of Origen follow the same method and are inspired by the same principles. Origen believed that Scripture offers three different senses, which are not mutually exclusive, but are superposed upon one another : the corporeal or historical sense; the " psychic " or moral sense; the spiritual or allegorical sense. In practice, the moral sense is often difficult to distinguish from the spiritual sense, and, as a result, Origen habitually ignores it as such. Accordingly, there are left the corporeal, literal, or historical sense, and the spiritual sense. The first is sufficient for the simple faithful, who do not seek to penetrate the secrets of God; it is a sense truly willed by the Holy Spirit, except in some rather rare cases where it is manifestly to be rejected. But it cannot suffice for the perfect, who wish to see, beyond the letter, a deeper signification. All of Holy Writ, in the eyes of Origen, is a great allegory which has to be interpreted, explained, and clarified. As the physical world is the image of the spiritual world, so beneath the letter of the Scriptures there is hidden a deep meaning, the knowledge of which is reserved for the perfect. Numbers and proper names especially ought to receive the attention of the commentators. Philo of Alexandria had

already used the allegorical method in his treatises. Origen
expounds the theory of it in the fourth book of his *De principiis*,
and in all his writings he employed it with generous enthusiasm.
It need scarcely be added that too often he allowed himself
to be led into exaggerations. It is not surprising that after
his time, although the Alexandrians remained faithful in general
to allegorical exegesis, a whole school, namely that of Antioch,
opposed his theories and advocated the superiority, if not the
exclusive use, of the literal sense of Holy writ. It should
be added, that for Origen and his followers, allegory, far from
excluding the literal explanation, presupposes it as its point
of departure and as its solid foundation.

Origen is not only the most prominent representative of
allegorical exegesis in the sense in which we have just described
it; he is perhaps to be recognized even more as the authoritative
expounder of *typological* exegesis, who sees in the Old Testament
the prefiguration of the New. There is no longer merely
question of explaining — sometimes in a farfetched manner, as
Philo had done — the narratives of the Old Testament by
applying them to spiritual realities, but rather, of showing
through these writings that the personages who play significant
roles in them are prophets, images, and figures of the Messias
and the Church. Applied to the New Testament, this typology
became familiar to all the Fathers. For them, the New
Testament is hidden *(latet)* in history, while the Old Testament
is made manifest *(patet)* in the New. It is hardly necessary
to emphasize the importance given this kind of exegesis in the
works of Origen.

3. — The Exegetical School of Alexandria.

Among the exegetes who were connected with the School of
Alexandria, we must mention in the first place Saint Dionysius,
who was bishop of Alexandria from 248-249 to 264-265.
Saint Dionysius wrote commentaries on Ecclesiastes and
Saint Luke, and in a work entitled *On the Promises*, designed to
refute millenarianism, he gave a mystical interpretation of the
Apocalypse, although he rejected the authenticity of this work.

Eusebius of Caesarea [† *ca.*340] was the disciple of Pamphilus,
who had himself studied under Origen. His exegesis is largely

inspired by that of the Alexandrian master, although his temperament as an historian often led him to reject certain exaggerations of the allegorical method. Thus he is torn between two tendencies, so that his scriptural writings sometimes leave an impression of his embarrassment. He wrote commentaries on the Psalms, on the Gospel of Saint Luke, and on Isaias, and in his *Problems and Solutions* on the Gospels he examined the seeming contradictions in the Gospel accounts of the birth, passion, and resurrection of our Savior.

Of the exegetical writings of Saint Athanasius [† 373], there remains, apart from scattered fragments, only an exposition of the Psalms. This commentary emphasizes especially the moral and the spiritual sense of the Psalter. A little work addressed to Marcellinus on the *Interpretation of the Psalms* gives important counsels on the manner in which the Psalms should be read and studied, with insistence on their application to the different circumstances of life.

Didymus the Blind († 398) wrote commentaries on a large number of Biblical works, but these exegetical writings have completely disappeared,except for a certain number of fragments preserved in the Biblical *Catenae*, and which still remain to be examined critically. Like Origen, Didymus was a representative of the allegorical method, and it seems that in his explanation of the Old Testament, especially, he sought the spiritual sense of Holy Writ. His interpretation of the New Testament appears to have been more strictly literal. The papyri found at Toura near Cairo in 1941 have restored to us, it seems, the commentaries of Didymus on Genesis, Job, and Zacharias, but they have not yet been published.

The Cappadocians have connections with the School of Alexandria, but each of them interprets Scripture according to his own bent, giving a more or less prominent role to allegory. Saint Basil [† 379] was above all a practical man and an administrator. He did not write commentaries on Scripture for its own sake, but for the teaching contained in it which could be applied immediately to the needs of souls. He sought moral lessons in Scripture, and if in his *Homilies on the Hexameron* he opposed an allegorical treatment, he did so only to set in clearer relief the magnificence of God's work. The homilies

on the Psalms and the oratorical commentary on Isaias [1] bear
witness to the same moralistic tendency. To Saint Basil the
Sacred Books furnished scarcely more than the framework
for his spiritual counsels. Saint Gregory Nazianzen († ca. 390)
who comments on Scripture only incidentally in the course
of a letter or a sermon, handles Scripture in almost the same
manner as Basil. Saint Gregory of Nyssa († ca. 394), on the
other hand, was a true exegete, and he unhesitatingly adopted
the general principles of allegorical interpretation. We owe
to him, besides an *Hexameron* which completes and justifies
Saint Basil's, a book on the creation of man [2], a work on the life
of Moses [3], treatises on the titles of the Psalms, some homilies on
Ecclesiastes, on the Canticle of Canticles, on the Beatitudes, and
on the Lord's Prayer. In all these works the Sacred Books are
interpreted in terms of the demands of the mystical life, a field
in which the Bishop of Nyssa is an outstanding speculative
writer.

The last of the great representatives of the School of
Alexandria was Saint Cyril († 444). In his *De adoratione in
spiritu et veritate* and in his *Glaphyra*, he shows that the Old
Testament is a figure of the New. In the first of these works,
he deals primarily with Jewish worship, which foretold the
spiritual adoration rendered to God by the Christians; in the
second, he studies the figurative signs of the Savior. In his
commentaries on Isaias, on the Minor Prophets, and on
Saint John [4], the only ones which are extant of a very
considerable exegetical collection, he adheres constantly to the
allegorical method. His commentary on Saint John is
particularly noteworthy.

Translator's note. — [1 It is practically certain that Basil was not the author
of the commentary on Isaias mentioned. See O. BARDENHEWER, *Geschichte
der altkirchlichen Literatur,* III (2nd ed., Freiburg i. Br., 1923), 147-148.]

Translator's note. — [2 See *Grégoire de Nysse : La Création de l'homme.*
Introduction de J. Laplace, S. J., Notes de J. Daniélou, S. J. (Paris, 1944;
Sources Chrétiennes, no. 6).

Translator's note. — [3 See *Grégoire de Nysse; Vie de Moïse. Introduction
et traduction de J. Daniélou, S. J.* (Paris, 1942; Sources Chrétiennes, no. 1)].

Translator's note. — [4 (The Greek texts of both these works have been
edited and published by P. E. Pusey : *S. P. N. Cyrilli archiepisc. Alex. In XII
Prophetas,* (2 vols., Oxford, 1868), and *S. P. N. Cyrilli archiepisc. Alex. In
S. Ioannis Evangelium,* (4 vols., Oxford, 1872). See also J. REUSS, " Cyrill
von Alexandrien und sein Kommentar zum Johannes-Evangelium ", *Biblica,* 25
(1944), 207-209)].

4. — The Exegetical School of Antioch.

The foundation of the Exegetical School of Antioch is generally attributed to Saint Lucian, who died a martyr's death on January 7, 312. It must practically be admitted that we have no information on the exegesis of Lucian, and that he is really known only through his critical work on the Septuagint. We know that, from an early date, the Antiochenes and those connected with them opposed the allegorical theories of the Alexandrians and became ardent defenders of the literal sense. Thus, we can cite the names of Saint Methodius of Olympus [† 311], to whom we owe treatises on leprosy, on the leech, on the distinction of foods, on the red cow, and of Saint Eustathius of Antioch [† ca. 337], author of a homily on the witch of Endor.

The great theorist of the School of Antioch was Diodorus of Tarsus (ca. 330-392), whose exegetical work, unfortunately, has entirely disappeared with the exception of fragments preserved in the Biblical Catenae, and a commentary, still unpublished, on the Psalms[1]. Diodorus does not entirely reject the spiritual sense, theoria, as he calls it[2]. He insists, however, on the predominance of the literal and historical sense of Holy Writ, and demands that the spiritual sense be based on the letter of the text, instead of allowing himself to be carried away by pure supposition alone.

The best known disciples of Diodorus were Theodore of Mopsuestia [† 428] and Saint John Chrysostom [† 407]. Theodore is considered by the Nestorians to be the exegete par excellence. He explained his principles of exegesis in two lost works : De allegoria et historia and De perfectione operum contra allegoricos[3]. He wrote commentaries, furthermore,

Translator's note. — [1 See L. MARIÈS, Etudes préliminaires à l'édition de Diodore de Tarse Sur les Psaumes... Le caractère diodorien du Commentaire (Paris, 1933)].
Translator's note. — [2 See A. VACCARI, S. J., " La teoria esegetica antiochena ", Biblica, 15 (1934), 93-101].
Translator's note. — [3 The identification of the lost works of Theodore of Mopsuestia is a very difficult problem. Thus, it is very doubtful whether the title De perfectione operum contra allegoricos applies to a single work. There is rather question of two separate works, the De perfectione operum, and Contra allegoricos. The latter work may itself be identical with the De allegoria et historia, as Amann has suggested. See E. AMANN " Théodore de Mopsueste ", DTC, 15 (Paris, 1946), 238-240. [See also especially, R. DEVREESE, " La méthode exégétique de Théodore de Mopsueste ", RB 53 (1946), 207-241], and ID., Essai sur Théodore de Mopsueste (Rome, 1948; Studi e Testi, 141)].

on the whole Bible, but we have, apart from numerous fragments, only the ones on Saint Paul and Saint John. A certain number of his views were condemned by the Fifth Oecumenical Council : in particular his exclusion of the Books of Chronicles, Esdras, Job, and the Canticle of Canticles from the Canon of Scripture, his distinction between two kinds of inspiration in the Biblical authors, and his restrictions on the messianic character of the Psalms.

Saint John Chrysostom was above all else a preacher and a moralist. He has commented in his homilies on a considerable number of the Biblical books (Genesis, some passages in Kings, about sixty Psalms, some passages in Isaias, Saint Matthew, Saint John, the Acts of the Apostles, the Epistles of Saint Paul). He tried especially to emphasize the lessons for practical life which emerge from the texts.

Theodoret of Cyrus († 458) was the last great representative of the School of Antioch. In addition to didactic treatises in the form of *Questions and Answers* on the historical books of the Old Testament (the Octateuch, Kings, Paralipomenon), he wrote important commentaries on the Psalms, the Canticle of Canticles, the Prophets, and the Epistles of Saint Paul. His exegesis is perhaps not very personal and independent, but in general it is solid and of good quality. Theodoret is well informed and reasonable, and an exponent of moderation. He insists on the literal sense of the Scriptures, but, when occasion arises, he knows how to emphasize the moral and religious values of their teaching.

Among the exegetes connected with the School of Antioch, we must mention also : Saint Ephraem († 373), who wrote commentaries in Syriac on all the books of the Bible; Apollinaris of Laodicea († *ca.* 390), of whose writings we know only the too rare fragments in the Biblical *Catenae;* Severian of Gabala († after 408), who commented on the Epistle to the Galatians; Polychronius of Apamea († *ca.* 430), who was a prolific exegete; and Hadrian (first half of the 5th century) who has left an *Introduction to the Divine Scriptures.*

5. — Exegesis in the West.

Exegesis was cultivated at an early date in the West. The predominant tendencies among the Western theologians are usually an indifference to pure speculation and a marked interest in moral problems and lessons of a practical nature. Certain commentators, like Saint Ambrose and Saint Augustine, give more attention to allegorical interpretations; others, like Saint Jerome, show greater preference for the literal sense. But all this was a matter of temperament. There was no school of exegesis in the West during the Patristic Period.

Tertullian († *ca.* 220) did not write any Biblical commentaries as such. He must be mentioned here, however, because he made constant use of the Sacred Books, and he is our most ancient witness of the Latin Bible. In his five books *Against Marcion*, he cites a large part of the heresiarch's New Testament and gives proof of a very keen critical sense.

The first name to come to one's mind after Tertullian's is that of Hippolytus († 235),whose works were written in Greek. He has given us a treatise *On Antechrist*, a commentary on Daniel, and a commentary on the Canticle of Canticles. He composed other commentaries which are, for the most part lost, at least in the original text. Hippolytus adhered by preference to the allegorical sense of Scripture, but he generally avoids the excesses of subtlety.

Reticius of Autun († after 314) was the author of a lost commentary on the Canticle of Canticles, and Victorinus of Pettau (beginning of the 4th century), who explained many books of the Old and New Testaments, is known to us only through his commentary on the Apocalypse, which is clearly millenarian.

Saint Hilary of Poitiers († 376) has given us a commentary on Saint Matthew and a commentary on the Psalms (preserved in part only). In this second work the influence of Origen is again in evidence. The author showed his preference for allegorical interpretation, although this does not prevent him from displaying originality in a great many instances. A commentary on Job has been lost. His *Tractatus mysteriorum*, a part of which was discovered in 1887, are concerned with the study of the prophetic sections of the Old Testament.

The exegesis of Saint Ambrose († 397) is likewise influenced by Origen. Saint Ambrose was unexpectedly made bishop before he had time to complete his theological training, and, accordingly, he had to assimilate very quickly the writings of the great Eastern Doctors. But his common sense and his concern for the formation of souls easily guarded him against excess. Moreover, he never commented on the Bible as such. His exegesis is to be found rather in his numerous sermons on the Hexameron, paradise, Cain and Abel, Noah and the Ark, Abraham, Isaac, Jacob, Elias, Naboth, Tobias, Job, David, the Psalms, and the Gospel of Saint Luke. When these sermons were being prepared for publication, they sometimes lost their homiletic form, but it is not difficult to detect the preacher everywhere. His preferred masters were Philo of Alexandria, Origen, and the Cappadocians.

Saint Jerome († 419 or 420) is the great commentator of the West. It may be said that he dedicated his entire life to work on the Bible. He translated the Bible into Latin, and wrote commentaries on a large number of its books. His exegesis was inspired for the most part by that of the Alexandrian School. However, after the great storm raised by the Origenistic controversy, Jerome devoted himself more to the investigation of the literal sense, yet without abandoning allegorical interpretation. He has given us a number of translations of the homilies of Origen, and, in addition, commentaries on Ecclesiastes, on four of Saint Paul's Epistles (Gal., Eph., Tit., Phil.), on the Gospel of Saint Matthew, and on the Prophets. The commentaries on the Prophets, especially those on Isaias and Jeremias, are his masterpieces. The others were composed too quickly, and the author did not hesitate to draw inspiration for them from his predecessors — and to a greater extent than he himself admitted. But Saint Jerome's perfect knowledge of the Hebrew language, his long stay in Palestine, the countless observations that he amassed on the things and the people of the country assure for his exegetical works a place of distinction.

The name Ambrosiaster (Pseudo-Ambrose) has been used since the 16th century to designate the unknown author of a remarkable commentary on the Epistles of Saint Paul, apparently composed at Rome about 380. The allegorical method is not employed. The author adhered rather to the literal sense, and aims especially at the moral formation of his readers. He compiled also an important collection of *Questions and Answers* on the Old and New Testament.

The literary heritage of Gregory of Elvira († after 392) has been recovered piece by piece since the beginning of the present century, especially through the labors of Dom Wilmart. Thus, twenty *tractatus* on various books of Scripture formerly attributed to Origen, six homilies on the Canticle of Canticles, a homily on Noe's ark, and a commentary on Psalm 91 have been restored to him.

The Donatist Tyconius was the author of a *Liber Regularum*, (*ca.* 370), which was the first treatise on hermeneutics in the Latin language. He wrote also a commentary on the Apocalypse, which has been lost, but it is known through the compilation of Beatus of Libana (*ca.* 786). To Pelagius, we owe a commentary on the thirteen Epistles of Saint Paul (the Epistle to the Hebrews being omitted), which was used to some extent by later writers. Finally we must mention the *Opus imperfectum in Matthaeum*, apparently the work of an Arian bishop of the 6th century, which, under the name of Saint John, long enjoyed great popularity in the West.

Saint Augustine († 430), whose extraordinary activity embraced all domains, cannot be omitted in a survey of the great exegetes. He commented four times on the first chapters of Genesis : in the *De Genesi contra Manichaeos*, in the *De Genesi ad litteram liber imperfectus*, in the *De Genesi ad litteram*, and finally in the *Confessions*, XI-XII. He published several books of *Questions* on the Heptateuch, on the Gospels, and on the Epistle to the Romans. His *De consensu Evangeliorum* is a study of the problems raised by the comparison of the Gospel texts. Finally, in treatises or in popular sermons, he commented on the entire Psalter, the Sermon on the Mount, the Gospel of Saint John, the Epistle to the Galatians, and the beginning of the Epistle to the Romans. All these works bear the stamp of their author's genius. Saint Augustine shows a preference for the allegorical sense in his scriptural exegesis, but he is primarily concerned with deriving therefrom lessons for practical life. The *Enarrationes* on the Psalms, which, for the most part, were first presented as sermons, are perhaps the most perfect of his [exegetical] works.

Other names should also be mentioned, and in particular Cassiodorus († *ca.* 580), Saint Gregory the Great († 604), Isidore of Seville (636), and Saint Bede († 795). [1] Saint Gregory's *Moralia* on the Book of Job, his commentary on Ezechiel, and his homilies on the Gospels exercised considerable influence on Christian thought and life in the Middle Ages.

From the middle of the fifth century, however, Patristic exegesis, in the East as well as in the West, lost its originality. The commentators became more and more satisfied with copying their predecessors. They became compilers of *Catenae*, and the *Catenae*, assembled out of pieces and fragments, henceforth replaced the commentaries.

4. — EXEGESIS OF THE OLD TESTAMENT FROM THE END OF ANTIQUITY TO THE PRESENT TIME.

[A. VINCENT]

I. — The Medieval Period. [2]

In the face of dying paganism, the various beliefs of which were being synthesized in the neo-paganism of Plotinus, the Fathers of the Church emphasized the point that, if " true religion " is as old as the world, Christianity and the Mosaic Law, which was a preparation for it, show an indisputable superiority. Christians and pagans, at this time, admitted a kind of religious evolution in the world, a degeneration of the pagan religions, and a slow re-education willed by God, who, they thought, had caused humanity to pass from the intellectual and moral weakness of childhood to full maturity. To prove their thesis, ecclesiastical writers relied upon Scripture, advancing as evidence miracles and prophecies, while the last pagan philosophers, on the other hand, appealed to their most ancient historians. Thus, a first attempt was made to insert into the framework of the Bible the data of profane science, which were themselves so frequently open to serious criticism.

Translator's note. — [1 To this list should be added Junillus Africanus, *Instituta regularia divinae legis* (*ca.* 542), an introduction to the study of the Bible. It was adapted from Paul of Nisibis, who was influenced by the views of Theodore of Mopsuestia.]

Translator's note. — [2 Cf. B. SMALLEY, *The Study of the Bible in the Middle Ages* (2nd ed. revised, Oxford, 1952; cf. *CBQ* [1952], 381-383); P. C. SPICQ O. P., *Esquisse d'une histoire de l'exégèse latine au moyen âge* (Paris, 1944; from the 8th to the end of the 14th century)].

This kind of exegetical work could produce no results, for the critical treatment of sources remained either quite elementary or was completely absent.

Through the medium of the *Catenae*, the Middle Ages were acquainted to some extent with the thought of the Fathers. In the beginning, the Church was too busy with the task of evangelizing new peoples to investigate the problems raised in the preceding period. But soon the appearance of Islam and its subtle philosophic dogmatic speculation, controversies with the Jews, and the discovery of the East, compelled Western exegetes to abandon an interpretation of the Bible which was allegorical in tendency or too exclusively moral. Christian thinking reverted to the problems raised by the Fathers, and the necessity, in the face of the Jewish and Mohammedan philosophies, of affirming Christian dogma made exegesis predominantly theological. Confronted with the agnosticism or arbitrary symbolism of Averroes [1] and Maimonides [2], Saint Thomas established his theory of analogy. For that purpose, he had to have a reliable text, and it is for this reason that, after having declared that it was necessary above all to seek historical truth and to hold to the literal sense (*Sum. Theol.* I [a], CII, 1), the great Doctor carefully collected the variant readings in his commentaries, so that he could master the thought of the sacred writer with greater certainty. The *Studia Hebraica* of the Dominicans of the Middle Ages met in part the recognized necessity of having recourse to the original texts. They enabled Raymond Martini († 1270) to compose his *Pugio fidei contra Mauros et Judæos*, a masterpiece of rabbinical scholarship based on the Hebrew text, and other scholarly religious to attempt a first comparison between the Latin and original texts. [3]

Translator's note. — [¹ See M. ALONSO, S. J., *Teologia de Averroes* (Madrid-Granada, 1947); L. GAUTHIER, *Ibn Rochd (Averroès)* (Paris, 1948); M. DE WULF, *History of Mediaeval Philosophy*, translated by E. C. MESSENGER, I (3rd English edition, London and New York, 1935), 300-303; E. GILSON, *History of Christian Philosophy in the Middle Ages* (New York, 1955), 216-225, and 642-646].

Translator's note. — [² On Maimonides, in addition to the references given, on p. 692, see also de WULF-MESSENGER, *op. cit.*, pp. 303-306; E. GILSON, *op. cit.* 229-231, and 649-651].

Translator's note. — [³ On Franciscan exegesis, cf. P. DEMPSEY, O. F. M. Cap., *De principiis exegeticis S. Bonaventurae* (Rome, 1945; cf. *Theol. Revue* [1951], 99)].

A better knowledge of the Bible unquestionably resulted from these first attempts at textual criticism. As proof of this, it is sufficient to examine even cursorily the *Postillæ perpetuæ in Vetus et Novum Testamentum* of Nicolas of Lyra († 1349) [1]. This work shows definite progress over all preceding commentaries. The author, who was well acquainted with Hebrew, endeavored primarily to explain the literal sense, and his works contributed to the introduction of the historico-philological method in the Church. This scientific trend, unfortunately, was not destined to be continued without interruption, for in the following century Gerson († 1429), Tostat († 1455), and Denis the Carthusian († 1471) applied themselves particularly to stressing the spiritual senses, i.e., the allegorical and moral. Scholastic exegesis in its decline was not sufficiently concerned as to whether or not the text of the Scripture supplied an adequate basis for its theological deductions. Moreover, its tendency toward abstraction and its disdain for form could not fail to repel minds rejuvenated by contact with Antiquity or disturbed by the new principles of Protestantism.

2. — From the Renaissance to the End of the Eighteenth Century.

The acquaintance with Greek and Hebrew developed by Humanism, the curiosity provoked by numerous archaeological discoveries, and the exclusive appeal made by the Reformers to the authority of Holy Writ were destined to bring about a rapid transformation in Biblical studies.

A movement of broad scientific investigation applied itself to the task of producing as perfect a text as possible, although the principles of textual criticism were not yet fixed. Reuchlin († 1522) [2] composed the first Hebrew grammar and the first Hebrew dictionary to be published by a Christian. Erasmus († 1536), by a comparison of the manuscripts and the original texts, established the first principles of textual criticism and applied them in the successive editions of his *Novum*

Translator's note. — [1 On Nicolas of Lyra, see especially, J. SCHMID, "Nikolaus v. Lyra", in *LTK*, 7 (1935), 580-581, with good bibliography].

Translator's note. — [2 See B. WALDE, *Christliche Hebräisten Deutschlands am Ausgange des Mittelalters* (Münster i. W., 1916)].

Testamentum græce, which, in 1633, became the *Textus receptus*.

The Dominican Santes Pagnino († 1541) published under the title, *Veteris et Novi Testamenti nova translatio*, a literal Latin translation made from the Greek and Hebrew.

The Vulgate, however, was not neglected. Robert Estienne published an edition in 1540, and the editions of the University of Louvain (*Biblia Lovaniensia*, 1547-1588) represented a remarkable advance for their time. The Louvain Vulgate served as the basic text in the preparation of the " Sixtine " edition, published in 1590 by order of Sixtus V. The *Clementine Vulgate* appeared two years later, in 1592.

The need of comparing the different texts soon led to the publication of the first polygot Bibles : that of Alcala (1514-1517) under the direction of Ximenes; the Antwerp Polyglot (1569-1572) by A. Montano; the Paris Polyglot (1628-1645), which was chiefly the work of the Oratorian Morin; and the London Polyglot (1653-1657) edited by Walton. The Hebrew Bible of the Jew Athias (1661) served as a basis for the editions which followed it.

Adricomius († 1585), *Theatrum Terræ Sanctæ et Biblicarum Historiarum cum tabulis geographicis*, Quaresmius († 1660), *Terræ Sanctæ elucidatio*, and Reland († 1718), *Palestina ex monumentis veteribus illustrata*, are regarded as the fathers of sacred geography. In the same period, S. Bochart († 1667) made a study of natural history in the Bible in his *Hierozoicon*, which is still valuable, and Selden published, in 1617, his *De diis Syris syntagmata duo*, which constitutes one of the first studies made in the field of comparative religion in the Bible.

All Semitic scholars remain indebted to the two Johannes Buxtorfs, the father († 1629) and the son († 1664), for numerous grammars, dictionaries, and Hebrew and Aramaic concordances published by them. Their *Synagoga Judaica* (Basle, 1603) shows a remarkable acquaintance with the civil and religious institutions of Jewish antiquity. The *Critica Sacra* of the Protestant Jacques Cappel († 1628), published by his brother Louis Cappel († 1658), exerted considerable influence. The authors attacked the authority of the Massoretic text and laid down rules to be followed in restoring the Hebrew text to its original purity. In the *Horæ Hebraicæ et Talmudicae* of the Anglican John Lightfoot († 1675) may be found details of Talmudical learning borrowed from Rabbinical literature. In the history and criticism of the text, and in knowledge of the historical background, Protestant exegesis of this period was definitely more advanced than Catholic exegesis.

This enormous work, however, was not to produce immediately the results that might legitimately have been hoped for. Even Protestants themselves admit that the commentaries of the chief Reformers are weak. Without doubt, the translation of the Bible into German by Luther († 1546), *Biblia, d.i. die Gantze Heilige Schrifft, Deutsch, Mar. Luth. Wittenberg, MCXXXIV*, is a masterpiece from a literary point of view, but mistakes are not rare, and some have considerable dogmatic importance. As for the commentaries of Luther on the Old Testament, as likewise for those of Zwingli (1531), Melanchthon († 1560), and Calvin († 1564), it cannot be said that they show any progress whatever over similar works of the preceding period. While their authors claimed that they were adhering to the literal sense, actually the struggle which they had undertaken against Catholicism led them to develop especially dogmatic and polemical points of view. Only the exegesis of the Dutch Calvinist Drusius († 1616) marks any progress in the Protestant output as a whole.

All the Protestant commentators of this period recognize the inspiration of the Sacred Books. They acknowledge that the Bible is the source of faith and the foundation of religion, but they claim also that the meaning of the Bible is evident of itself and that, to understand it, it is sufficient to rely on one's own private judgment. Even before the beginning of the 17th century, Lælius Socinus (Lelio Sozzini, † 1562) and his nephew, Faustus Socinus († 1604), drew certain extreme conclusions from the principles of the Reformation. While they admit inspiration *de jure*, they profess *de facto* that reason is the medium through which we must unravel the true meaning of Scripture and that, consequently, all dogmas contrary to reason must be considered as non-scriptural (*De S. S. Script. Auctoritate*, Cracow, 1574; *Prælectiones theologicæ*, 1580). The Arminian H. Grotius († 1645) was to begin the application of these principles in his *Annotationes in Vetus Testamentum* (Paris, 1644), and J. Leclerc († 1736), in his *Moysis libri quinque*

(Amsterdam, 1698), was to emphasize even more the rationalistic character of his exegesis [1].

In the face of this copious Protestant production, Catholic learning made a good showing. The voluminous commentaries of Cornelius a Lapide († 1637) on all of Holy Writ furnished preachers with an inexhaustible mine, but they did nothing to advance science. On the other hand, the works of S. de Muis († 1644), especially his *Commentarius litteralis et historicus in omnes Psalmos et selecta Veteris Testamenti cantica cum versione nova ex Hebraico* (Paris,1630), are valuable contributions well in advance of their time. With him should be cited Maldonatus († 1583), whose commentaries on the great Prophets, however, did not enjoy an authority equal to that of his works on the Gospels, and especially Richard Simon (1638-1712), who is regarded today, and with good reason, as the father of modern criticism. In his *Histoire critique du Vieux Testament* (Paris, 1678), he perceived very keenly the problems raised by the Pentateuch, upon which modern scholars have labored since his time. In the article " Critique biblique " in the *Dictionnaire apologétique de la Foi catholique* (Vol. I, col. 764) Father Durand writes as follows : " It was the first comprehensive study claiming to date a Biblical book on the basis of a literary and historical analysis of its contents... Richard Simon was the founder of historical criticism of Holy Writ in the modern sense of the word ".

The eighteenth century marks a definite regression in the domain of exegesis. Calmet (1672-1757), although possessing great prudence and wisdom, was only a compiler. The Oratorian Houbigant († 1784), however, contributed to the formulation of more precise critical rules for establishing the Hebrew text (*Biblia Hebraïca cum notis criticis et versione Latina ad notas criticas facta*, Paris, 1753-1754). In 1753, another French Catholic, the physician Jean Astruc, published his *Conjectures sur les mémoires originaux dont il paraît que*

---

[1] It is not possible to speak here of the influence of Spinoza († 1677), who was neither an exegete nor an historian but a pantheistic philosopher who rejected as unauthentic all that he did not consider to be in conformity with the data available through reason. [However, Spinoza also offers arguments of a literary historical character. Cf., e.g., Ch. VIII of his *Tractatus theologico-politicus* (*Spinoza, Œuvres complètes* [Bibliothèque de la Pléiade, Paris, 1954], 790 ff. and 1440 ff.)].

Moïse s'est servi pour composer le livre de la Genèse (Brussels, 1753). He distinguished two principal documents on the basis of the names of God, Elohim and Yahweh, used by the sacred author. We know the success which this ingenious view was to enjoy. In the same year the Anglican Robert Lowth († 1787) discovered the rules of parallelism, one of the characteristics of Hebrew poetry (*De sacra poesi Hebraeorum*, Oxford, 1753).

3. — From the Beginning of the Nineteenth Century to the Present Time. [1]

The conflict over the truth of the Bible.

It is proper to distinguish in the history of the exegesis of the Old Testament two points of view which are unfortunately too often confused : the point of view of literary criticism, which is occupied with the manner in which the Sacred Books were composed and with the genre to which they belong, and that of historical criticism, which determines the literal sense and the value to be attached to it, and upon which, in the last analysis, the theological and philosophical interpretation of the Bible is based. Both can be the object of a Catholic, Protestant, or Rationalistic explanation.

The literary problem in the Old Testament [2].

The Protestants did not admit without dispute the conclusions of R. Simon and Astruc, and first Leclerc, and then Michaelis († 1791), attempted to refute them. But it was J. G. Eichhorn († 1827), *Einleitung in das Alte Testament*, 1780 (4th edition, 5 volumes, 1823-1826), who presented the various elements of the new hypothesis in a coordinated form. He did not consider that the divine names alone contributed to the distinction of sources, but he felt it was necessary also to take into account

---

Translator's note. — [1 Cf. M. GOGUEL, P. LESTRINGANT, O. CULLMANN, *et al.*, *Le problème biblique dans le Protestantisme* (Paris, 1955; cf. A. M. DUBARLE, O. P., in *Rev. des Sciences Phil. et Théol.* [1958], 123-124); H. J. KRAUS, *op. cit., supra*.]

Translator's note. — [2 See J. COPPENS, *The Old Testament and the Critics*. Translated from the French by E. A. RYAN, S. J., and E. W. TRIBBE, S. J. (Paterson, N. J., 1942). An excellent critical presentation with full bibliography.]

the ideas and style of each narrative, and he applied his system not only to Genesis but also to Exodus and Leviticus. He distinguished two principal documents, the Yahwist and the Elohist, in addition to which there were others of less importance. This is the *Documentary Hypothesis* in its first form.

The English Catholic, A. Geddes [1], in 1792, substituted for the hypothesis of continuous documents, that of fragments, only some of which would go back to Moses and which would have been put in order later by a redactor. He was followed by J. S. Vater (1805) and M. L. de Wette (1829). This is the *Fragment Hypothesis.*

Various critics objected to this dissection of the Pentateuch. H. Ewald (1803-1875) proposed the so-called *Supplement Hypothesis.* He took as his base a primitive nucleus or fundamental document *(Grundschrift)*, which constituted a complete history, and with this he would connect supplements of all sorts and lengths (*Die Composition der Genesis kritisch untersucht*, 1823). F. Bleek (1836), E. Tuch (1838), and de Wette (1840) supported this same theory. But Ewald himself did not remain satisfied with his hypothesis (*Geschichte des Volkes Israel bis Christus*, 1843).

H. Hupfeld returned to the *Documentary Hypothesis* and carried it further (*Die Quellen der Genesis und die Art ihrer Zusammensetzung*, 1853). He distinguished in the Pentateuch a basic document or first Elohist, a Yahwist, and then a second Elohist which was concerned more especially with the Patriarchs. The documents underwent corrections in the interests of harmonization.

In 1854, E. Riehm *(Die Gesetzgebung Mosis im Lande Moab)* made Deuteronomy a fourth source of the Pentateuch. Th. Nöldeke (*Untersuchungen zur Kritik des Alten Testaments*, 1869) applied the *Documentary Hypothesis*, which henceforth involves four sources, to the entire Hexateuch. He insisted on the question of dependence and of chronology. The first three documents (P, the First Elohist or Priestly Code; E, the

Translator's note. — [1 A. GEDDES, *The Holy Bible or the Books Accounted Sacred by Jews and Christians... Faithfully Translated from Corrected Texts of the Originals with Various Readings, Explanatory Notes and Critical Remarks.* I. *Pentateuch and Joshua* (London, 1792); ID., *Critical Remarks on the Hebrew Scriptures Corresponding with a New Translation of the Bible.* I. *Containing Remarks on the Pentateuch* (London, 1800)].

Second Elohist; J, the Yahwist) would date from the 10th or 9th centuries B.C. in the order : P, E, J. Deuteronomy would be a little earlier than the reform of Josias (621), and the Pentateuch would have taken its final form under Esdras, who would have promulgated it and brought about its acceptance by the people.

E. Reuss († 1891) had already remarked in his lectures et the University of Strasbourg in 1833 that the ritualistic regulations in Leviticus do not correspond to the social and religious condition of the Israelites in the time of the kings, and, *a fortiori*, to the period of the wanderings in the desert. He thought that he could affirm that the Major Prophets had ignored them. Accordingly, he put the Major Prophets before the Law, and in his chronological order assigned the last place to the Psalms (*La Bible, L'Ancien Testament*. Third Part : *L'Histoire Sainte et la Loi*, Vol. I, *Introduction*, Paris, 1879). H. K. Graf (1815-1869), in his *Die geschichtlichen Bücher des Alten Testaments* (1866), gave this theory the form that it was henceforth to retain, at least in its main outlines. The Levitical Code, which, incidentally, contains laws belonging to different periods, did not come into being before the capture of Jerusalem (586). The first source is the Elohist. The Yahwist, which comes from the time of Achab, is a revision of the Elohist. Deuteronomy, whose author was, perhaps, the Prophet Jeremias, is regarded as having been composed a little before 621. Ezechiel was the author of the Law of Holiness, and Esdras gave the Pentateuch its final form.

The ideas of Graf were not at first favorably received, but their acceptance by J. Wellhausen was to assure them a brilliant success (*Skizzen und Vorarbeiten*, 1884-1899 [1]; *Prolegomena zur Geschichte Israels*, 1882; Engl. trans., 1885 [2]; 6th Germ. ed., 1927; *Israelitische und jüdische Geschichte*, 1894 [3]; 8th ed., 1921). Wellhausen posits a Jahwist document *ca.* 850; an Elohist

---

Translator's note. — [1 To be mentioned also, his article, " Die Komposition des Hexateuchs " (1876), and his article, " Israel ", in the 9th ed. of the *Encyclopedia Britannica* (1879).]

Translator's note. — [2 *Prolegomena to the History of Israel*, with a Preface by W. R. SMITH (3rd ed., 1886)].

Translator's note. — [3 Engl. trans., *Sketch of the History of Israel and Judah* (1891)].

document, the religious tradition of the Northem Kingdom, *ca.* 750; a Jehovist document (J E,) of prophetic origin which effected the fusion of J and E; and finally, Deuteronomy and the Priestly Code. His method consists in comparing the first three strata with one another and in determining the relative place of each by comparison with the phases of the history of Israel.

This hypothesis of Wellhausen became classic among Biblical critics, and it was adopted particularly by Gunkel, C. H. Cornill, H. Holzinger, D. C. Steuernagel, Stade, etc. S. Driver popularized it in England *(Introduction to the Literature of the Old Testament)*. In French speaking countries, L. Gautier *(Introduction à l'Ancien Testament,* 1905) became its convinced champion. A. Loisy *(La Religion d'Israël,* 3rd ed., Paris, 1933, pp. 13-49) and A. Lods *(Israël. Des Origines au milieu du VIIIᵉ siécle,* Paris, 1930, pp. 10-18, and *Les Prophètes d'Israël et les débuts du Judaïsme,* Paris, 1935, pp. 6-15) [1] applied the ideas of Wellhausen to the whole of the Old Testament. It is maintained, in short, that each book contains legends and historical fragments, and that these were treated very freely by later redactors, who amalgamated, combined, and modified them according to their own historical or religious views. The prophetic literature has come to us only in a late redaction into which the old texts were admitted only in as far as they were in harmony with the main interests of the period and with current ideas, while the different law codes correspond to the different periods in the history of Israel and underwent a long labor of compilation and a rather clumsy revision during the course of the 4th century B.C.

After having adhered unreservedly to these views *(Hexateuch-Synopse,* 1922), O. Eissfeldt eventually gave the Wellhausen hypothesis a more varied and softened form *(Einleitung in das Alte Testament,* 1934). He admits " a lay source "

Translator's note. — [1 See also especially his *Histoire de la Littérature Hébraïque et Juive depuis les origines jusqu'à la ruine de l'Etat (135 après J. C.)* with a preface, an additional note on the Dead Sea Mss., and a bibliographical supplement by A. Parot (Paris, 1950). For his views on the Pentateuch, see *op. cit.,* 83-185, 198-219, 305-375, 491-496, and 529-536. See also the reviews of this work in *Bibliotheca Orientalis* (1950), 110-113, and *RB* 57 (1950), 443-447. On Loisy, see : J. BONSIRVEN, S. J., " Loisy (Alfred-Firmin) ", *DBV, Suppl.* V (1957), 530-544].

(*Laienquelle*, L), an account anterior to J and of a more archaic character, and also more indebted to priestly influences. It is thought to have been composed about 950 B.C. from older sources. Deuteronomy is regarded as presenting a basic document which was completed later. Eissfeldt has emphasized, too, how the study of literary genres and their evolution can furnish more help towards understanding the formation of the Sacred Books than the formal, critical study of the document alone. His thought is well summarized in the article " Pentateuch ", written for Pauly-Wissowa, *Real-Encyclopädie der class. Altertumswissenschaft* (XIX, 1 [1937], cols. 513-524).

For many years, however, a certain number of discordant voices have made themselves heard. The old masters of Protestant conservatism, Koenig and Kittel (" Die Zukunft der Alttestamentlichen Wissenschaft ", *ZATW* [1921], 81 ff.), did not refuse to admit the literary conclusions of Wellhausen — Koenig himself adhered to them in large measure — but they applied themselves especially to an energetic defence of the value of religious tradition. Sharper opposition came from Dahse (*Die gegenwärtige Krisis in der alttestamentlichen Kritik*, 1914), who attacked the literary theories of Wellhausen, yet without on that account admitting the Mosaic authorship of the Pentateuch. Löhr (1925) and Sternberg (1928) refused to admit the four documents, but recognized different strata in the narratives and laws, some of which they would regard as going back to the time of the Exodus. P. Volz and W. Rudolph resolutely reversed direction in their approach to the Pentateuch Problem (*Der Elohist als Erzähler. Ein Irrweg der Pentateuchkritik*, 1933) by taking the position that E and P are only recastings of or fragments borrowed from J.

A Jewish scholar, U. Cassuto, a professor in the University of Rome (*La questione della Genesi* ,1934) emphasized still more the unitarian character of the composition of Genesis [1].

Translator's note. — [1 Now at the Hebrew University in Jerusalem. See also his more recent works in Hebrew : *The Documentary Hypothesis and the Pentateuch* (Jerusalem, 1941); *Commentary on Genesis : I. From Adam to Noah (Gen.* 1-6, 8) (1944), and *II. From Noah to Abraham (Gen.*, 6. 9-11. 32) (1949). See also B. JACOB, *Das erste Buch der Tora : Genesis übersetzt und erklärt* (Berlin,

These attempts at the solution of the problem do not seem to have met with a favorable reception from the best qualified scholars.

Until the last quarter of the nineteenth century, Catholics did not become interested in the literary problem connected with the composition of the Sacred Books. All such questions had been considered until then as being incompatible *a priori* with Catholic doctrine. Cornely (*Introductio specialis in historicos Veteris Testamenti libros*, 1887), and especially F. Vigouroux (*Les Livres Saints et la Critique rationaliste*, 1884), made known in France the results of the Higher Criticism, but both held strictly to the traditional attitude. It was only at the International Congress of Catholics held at Fribourg (Switzerland) in August, 1897, that the problem was finally faced by Catholics, in particular by Baron von Hügel (*La méthode historique en son application à l'étude des documents de l'Hexateuque*) and Father M. J. Lagrange (" Les sources du Pentateuque ", *Revue Biblique*, 7 [1898], 10-32). Father Lagrange distinguished carefully between historical tradition and literary tradition. Moses, as the lawgiver of the Hebrews, and the Law of Moses, as the foundation of the whole history of Israel, constitute the historical tradition, while Moses as the author of the Pentateuch constitutes the literary tradition. Father Lagrange never expressed his views precisely on all points in the document theory, although he admitted this theory in principle. He believed that E was earlier than J. E is a very old document, which in part goes back to Moses and which cannot under any consideration be attributed to the Northern Kingdom. Deuteronomy is at the end of an evolution and was written a little before Josias. P dates from the Exile and nothing is later than Esdras.

Father Lagrange presented the final stage of his thought on this subject in his article, " L'Authenticité mosaïque de la Genèse et la théorie des documents ", *RB*, 47 (1938), 163-183.

1934), an exhaustive commentary with an Appendix on the " Analysis of the Sources " in which the author rejects the Documentary Hypothesis as not proven, pp. 949-1049. Many other scholars, both Jewish and Christian, question the correctness of the analysis of the sources advocated by the Wellhausen School without, however, rejecting the idea of sources in itself. Furthermore, many of the opponents of the Wellhausen School are far from the " Conservative " position in their literary and historical views].

He admits the existence of the documents E, J, and P. E is regarded as a document earlier than the revelation on Mount Sinai, and Moses made use of it. J is explained as a work suggested and outlined by Moses to one of his companions, or to someone else whom he approved. P is an epitome, containing only the essentials. E dates from *ca.* 1200 *B.C.* or even earlier. J and P are later and underwent some retouching.

Numerous Catholic scholars have admitted, at least in principle, the *Documentary Hypothesis*, from J. Brücker (*L'Eglise et la Critique Biblique*, 1908) to Heinisch (*Das Buch Genesis*, 1930; *Das Buch Exodus*, 1934). As Father A. Condamin has said : " The hypothesis of sources, which banishes so simply the incoherences in the narrative, seems to treat the inspired text more respectfully than an exegesis which stubbornly persists in inventing numberless subtleties in order to reconcile everything in the primitive account of a single author " [1].

The principal schools of rationalistic criticism.

All Protestant and Rationalistic Schools really reflect their connection with the principles laid down by the Reformers. From the moment that authority was not to intervene in the interpretation of the Scripture, reason was not slow to claim her independence and to erect her pretensions into systems.

In the eighteenth century, Germany entered the Age of Enlightenment (*Aufklärung*). Lessing (1729-1781), by the clever publication of certain writings of Reimarus under the title of *Fragments of an Unknown Writer* or *Wolfenbüttel Fragments*, separated religion from the Bible. The fundamental truths of religion have their roots and their foundation in the heart and mind of man. Semler (1721-1791) invented the accommodation theory. Scripture accommodates itself to the beliefs and prejudices of its time. We must free ourselves from these contingencies so as to keep only the speculative and practical truths which constitute genuine religion.

[1] See *Revue Apologétique*, 62 (1935), 216. See likewise the judgment passed on the Wellhausen theories by J. Coppens, professor at the University of Louvain, in his article, " Histoire critique de l'Ancien Testament. I, Les Origines ", *Nouvelle Revue Théologique*, 65 (1938), 550 ff. [See also ID., *The Old Testament and the Critics*, Engl. trans., by E. A. Ryan, S. J., and E. W. Tribbe, S. J. (Paterson, N. J., 1942), *passim*].

For Kant (1724-1804), exegesis consisted solely in drawing from the Bible moral values, the only ones that reason can know infallibly. Paulus († 1851), a disciple of Kant, maintained likewise that ethics alone, to the exclusion of dogma, constitutes religion, but, with Eichhorn, he eliminated all supernatural elements of a historical character. It is proper to distinguish in Scripture the objective element, the fact itself that history records, and the subjective element, the judgment that the witness or narrator made upon that fact. The fact can be true, but the interpretation is generally false, because the ancient witness or narrator was deluded or deceived when he was not more or less deliberately deceiving.

Hegel (1770-1831) taught that each religion marks a moment and a necessary moment in the evolution of the Idea (the Absolute), that, consequently, it is a transitory form under which God is conceived, and that a religious evolution must be admitted, advancing from the crudest forms of magic to the most perfect forms of Christianity. Each religion, then, is true in its own period and, for its understanding, it is sufficient to determine the precise stage to which it corresponds. The whole matter is very simple if the images, legends, and especially the myths which it employs, are properly understood. Vater († 1826), and particularly de Wette († 1849), applied these theories to the narratives in the Old Testament, which were regarded merely as myths, and Strauss († 1874) extended their application to the Gospels.

This mythical system is enjoying at present a renewed popularity in the *Formgeschichtliche Schule*. This "Morphological School", relying on the parallel texts furnished by the comparative history of religions, folklore, etc., endeavors to discern in a given religious text, if not the historical nucleus or objective remnant, at least the primitive faith which inspired the successive modifications. Its principal representatives, Dibelius, Bultmann, Wetter, Fiebig, lay down the principle that all religious faith creates its own object and its own proofs. There is thus a return to the exploitation of a myth fabricated in its entirety.

Baur († 1860), a disciple of Hegel, and to a greater extent of Schleiermacher († 1834), regarded religion as essentially an experience of God. He founded the historical criticism of the Tübingen School. Each of the books of the Bible is to be explained according to the religious tendency that inspired it. Hitzig, Nöldeke, and Ewald applied these principles to the chief books of the Old Testament.

Tylor (*Primitive Culture*, 1871) discovered animism, i.e., belief in the animation of all things by spirits. Thence, through a process of evolution are supposed to have come polytheism, henotheism, and finally monotheism. H. Spencer († 1903) reduced this cult of spirits to that of ancestors (manism). He thus gave religion a foundation which was much too narrow. Nevertheless, through his theory of evolution and his concept of the divine as an immanent and unknowable force, he exercised a tremendous influence over many exegetes. Lippert (*Der Seelenkult in seinen Beziehungen zur althebräischen Religion*, 1881) applied these principles to the religious evolution of the Jewish people. The idea was immediately accepted and used to advantage by two of the best known representatives of liberal Protestant theology in Germany, Stade (*Geschichte des Volkes Israel*, 1884) and Schwally (*Das Leben nach dem Tode*, 1892). Among the leading partisans of this school, we should mention Wellhausen, Marti, Nowack, Smend, Benzinger, A. Bertholet, Kuenen, Renan, Loisy, etc.

The religion of Israel, after having been originally a religion of nomads, without an elaborate mythology or complicated cult, reached under Moses the stage of monolatry. Yahweh was primitively only a tribal god, who became in Canaan a Baal, possessor of the land. The Prophets stressed the moral demands of Yahweh and attained monotheism. The codification by Esdras marks the beginning of the decline, which was caused by the encroachment of formalism.

The Pan-Babylonian School, represented by Winckler, Zimmern, Haupt, Hommel, Jeremias, Delitzsch, Jensen, and, to a modified degree, by Gunkel, Baudissin, and Langdon, does not attribute these superior elements of the Jewish religion to the Prophets, but to Assyro-Babylonia. A more or less hidden monotheism is assumed to have existed in Mesopotamia, and this region is regarded as the center from which radiated the religious ideas which transformed the ancient world. As regards later times, the Evolutionist School and the Pan-Babylonian School draw appreciably closer to each other and give an important place to Persian and Hellenistic influences.

Underlying all these exegetical schools is an undemonstrated and undemonstrable postulate, but admitted as a principle that is not even discussed, namely, the non-existence of the supernatural.

Christianity, on the contrary, and by that term can be understood not only Catholicism but also conservative Protestantism, posits, as the foundation for everything, the existence of the supernatural and, more particularly, of a personal God who can act in the world and who has no need of falsehood.

5. — *EXEGESIS OF THE NEW TESTAMENT FROM THE RENAISSANCE TO THE PRESENT TIME.*

[A. VAGANAY]

In order to keep this study within the limits agreed upon, it is necessary to make a choice. The writer must either confine himself to a tedious enumeration of authors and titles, or to an outline of the main movements and ideas in broad strokes, mentioning only the leaders. The second plan, though less simple, is preferable.

I. — Non-Catholic Authors.

The mysticism of the chief Reformers.

In the sixteenth century, non-Catholic exegesis is represented principally by the leaders of Protestantism : Luther (1482-1546), Calvin (1509-1564), and Melanchton (1497-1560). Their exegesis is permeated by a mysticism foreign to the historical sense. Man as a sinner is tortured by the uncertainty of his salvation. Faith in the grace of God and in the justice of Christ alone can justify him and give him complete assurance. It matters little whether the Church interprets the Sacred Books differently, for her authority is null in the matter. It is the Holy Ghost who, by means of an inward feeling, communicates to the faithful the savor and meaning of Scripture. The first result was that the contempt for facts was pushed so far that the scope of inspiration was exaggerated arbitrarily. Consequently, texts were harmonized in extreme fashion. These exegetes, e.g., go so far as to hold that the daughter of Jairus was raised to life several times, because the miracle was not placed at the same time in all the accounts. But there was a more serious consequence, namely, that the way was opened for "independent inquiry ", without any recourse to the traditional historical interpretation. Luther is the father of independent inquiry, as Voltaire is the father of " democracy ", which he detested (Lagrange).

The false glimmer of the philosophy of the Enlightenment

Under the term *Aufklärung* (enlightenment) is designated the vast intellectual movement which, in the 17th and 18th centuries, attempted to set itself free from the " darkness " of Christian Revelation. It had, as its basis, a philosophical principle, the denial of all that goes beyond human reason, *sola ratio*. This total emancipation, which philosophers such as Spinoza, Bayle, Lessing, and Hume advocated in Biblical Criticism, led the " rationalists ", the precursors of modern rationalistic exegesis, to different results according to country.

Thus, in England the deists stood, ordinarily, for natural religion : belief in God and in the immortality of the soul, without any formal worship. Revelation and the books which contain it were regarded as lies and impostures. In France, among the free-thinkers and philosophers, with Voltaire (1694-1778) at their head, there was the same hatred for Christianity and the same pamphleteer exegesis, but with more piquant scoffing and a more witty zest. In Germany, the " enlightened " rationalism finally made some contact with history. Reimarus (1694-1768), in the posthumous fragments of his *Apology for Rational Worshippers of God* [published by Lessing and others], continued to explain Christianity as a deliberate deception perpetrated by Jesus and his Apostles. He constructed a system, at any rate, which bore the appearance of history. Christ preached only a political Messianism and he failed; the Apostles idealized his life and his teaching in order to establish the new religion. Later, with Paulus (1761-1851), the thesis of rank fraud was completely abandoned. Far from being an impostor, Jesus was a wonderful preacher of morality. Far from being dishonest, the Evangelists were surprisingly naive. The rationalistic conception of the Gospel history did not lose its place on this account. In each miracle, it was sufficient to know how to distinguish, in the manner of Kant, between the objective fact, the purely natural act performed by Jesus, and the subjective fact, the account furnished by witnesses who were more or less victims of hallucination. It was thus that Lazarus, having fallen into a coma and thought to be dead, could be revived. Everything else was in keeping with this : puerile interpretations which exposed the older rationalism to ridicule and ruined it.

Under the storm-clouds of Hegelianism [1].

Hegel was wont to speak of the dull rationalism of the *Aufklärung* as *Ausklärung* (absence of light). Moreover, it was in terms of the new Hegelian dialectic that two famous systems of exegesis were then conceived. We shall summarize first the system of myths, introduced by D. F. Strauss (1808-1874) in his *Life of Jesus* (1835). On the one hand, numerous Gospel texts are contrary to reason, and on the other, the old rationalistie explanation is contrary to the texts. The facts recorded in these stories can have, then, only a mythical origin; either they werc invented in their entirety (pure myths), or merely embellished with details of a marvelous nature (historical myths) by popular imagination which succeeded in integrating into them the aspirations of the first communities. On this basis the author instituted a detailed criticism of the Gospels. But his exegesis always remains limited by certain philosophical presumptions. " There is no strictly historical thinking as long as one does not understand the indissolubility of the chain of finite causes and the impossibility of miracles " (*Life of Jesus*, translated by M. Evans, New York, 1860, Vol. I, p. 59). But the great principle, all that is rational is real, is not to be forgotten; thanks to this, the mythical stories of the Gospel cannot injure the " internal essence of Christian belief ", for religion rests, it seems, not on facts but on ideas. The supernatural itself is resolved in a myth, the unconscious act of Humanity, since " Humanity is the union of the two natures — the God become man... It is the child of the visible mother and invisible father, Nature and the Spirit " (*op cit.*, Vol. II, p. 895).

F. C. Baur (1792-1860), head of the Tübingen School, in order to complete and rectify the system of Strauss, endeavored to reconstruct the history of the early Church before the appearance of the Gospel myths. Here again, an Hegelian principle is the foundation : " The world and the Idea develop regularly, in nature and in history, according to the logic of thesis, antithesis, and synthesis ". Thesis, in the beginnings of Christianity, was supported by the Petrine party, the Judeo-Christians, who were devoted to the national hopes and legal practices of Judaism. Antithesis was defended by the Pauline party, the Christians of pagan origin, who fought for the abrogation of the Mosaic Law and for the holy liberty of the children of God. Synthesis was the fruit of mutual concessions, which, in the second century, gave birth to Catholicism. Now each book in the New Testament represents one or the other of these three doctrinal tendencies, and the latter thus make it possible to fix the date of each book's composition.

The systems of Strauss and of Baur were very soon pushed beyond all bounds by extremists. Thus, Bruno Baur (1809-1882) maintained that the very existence of Jesus Christ was a myth. This thesis has recently been taken up again by certain amateur exegetes (B. Smith, A. Drews, P. L. Couchoud). The Dutch radical school, for its part, asserted that the Pauline Epistles were apocryphal, and that almost nothing was known of the doctrine of Saint Paul, a thesis held later also by several misguided theorists in exegesis, e.g., J. Turmel.

The blurred picture of Jesus produced by the Liberal School.

Strauss and Baur, by their extreme views, provoked a reaction. It was already evident in their more or less faithful disciples, e.g., Renan (1823-1892). Without doubt the author of the *Vie de Jésus* (1863) always paraded the old rationalistic prejudice : " Its essence [criticism's] is the denial of the supernatural " (*Etudes d'histoire religieuse*, 6th ed., Paris, 1863, p. 137). " If miracle has any reality, my book is only a fabric of errors " (*Vie de Jésus*, 1883, Preface of the 13th edition, p. V). No doubt, too, he recognized his intellectual affiliations with

the theorists across the Rhine : " It is I, especially, who owe
to Germany what I prize most dearly, my philosophy, I may
almost say my religion " (*Pages françaises*, 5th edition, Paris,
1921, p. 101). Yet he felt the need of undertaking afresh the
literary criticism of the Gospel sources in order to establish
the *historical* personality of Jesus.

Such also, in spite of many differences, was the program
of the liberal Protestantism which was dominant during the
second half of the nineteenth century. While appealing solely
to history, it remained nonetheless under the dominion of
a subjectivist philosophy, of which Schleiermacher, whose
thought and influence were extended by Ritschl, was the
foster father. Religion is the personal feeling of contact with
God. Faith in Christ rests upon the long experience of the
Christian community and should not be made the slave of
a metaphysical construction. Therefore, without detriment
to faith, one can interpret freely the texts of history.
Unfortunately, this reputed historical interpretation was linked
to the different conceptions which liberal theologians formed
of Christianity. In the Gospel history they took only what
suited their personal religious philosophy. Hence the new
school reflected all the colors of the rainbow. It was more
traditional with B. Weiss, but more radical with T. Keim,
E. Reuss, and A. Reville. With H. J. Holtzmann (1832-1910)
and A. von Harnack (1851-1930) it followed a middle course.
For these scholars the essence of Christianity consisted in the
message of Jesus preaching the interior kingdom of God in souls
through the law of love. Christ was no more than the perfect
type of the modern religious man. All the Gospel texts which
go beyond this perspective were carefully shaded off. In short,
this is a misty kind of exegesis. It carries on an intermittent
flirtation with history, but eventually gives it the cold shoulder.

The learned vagaries of the sociological method.

The reaction against liberal theology began as early as the
end of the 19th century, with J. Weiss (1863-1914) and
W. Wrede (1859-1906). It was intended henceforth to escape
the influence of all " philosophism " by explaining Jesus and
Christianity through the social milieu which witnessed their

birth. An historical determinism, raised in more or less conscious fashion to the status of a law, was made the foundation of the new system. In the exegesis of texts which permit the use of the comparative method, arbitrary judgments and rough approximations reign supreme even where an acute sense of nuances would be required.

We shall mention first the confirmed eschatologists. In their interpretation of the books of the New Testament, they emphasize the influence of Jewish conceptions, and especially that of eschatological messianism. Jesus, as a man of his time, must have shared the illusions of his contemporaries. Accordingly, they make of Him, if not a political adventurer (R. Eisler), at least a fanatic, preaching the imminent and catastrophic advent of the kingdom of God — that new world ushered in by the Son of Man coming on the clouds of heaven. Paul, too, is regarded as haunted by the expectation of the return of Christ at short notice. His ethics, his conception of the sacraments, his theory of justification by faith, and all his thoughts are viewed as coming from this apocalyptical Judaism (A. Schweitzer).

Heading in an opposite direction, the rabid syncretists, such as R. Reitzenstein, are not content with putting the study of the New Testament " under the sign of the history of religions ", but claim to show that Jesus and early Christianity are a product of the religious evolution in the Hellenistic East. As regards the Pauline and Johannine doctrines, everything appears quite easy : They are to be closely connected with tendencies in the mystery religions, with Stoic morality, and with speculations held in high honor in the Greek world — without forgetting Mandaeism. The Gospel itself was submerged through heterogeneous elements, for late Judaism, which was its cradle, was dominated by Babylonian, Persian, Egyptian, and Hellenic syncretism. The success of Christian propaganda in its beginnings is thus to be explained (H. Gunkel, G. Vetter).

Somewhere between these extremes we should place the numerous critics (W. Bousset (1865-1920), Loisy (1857-1940), et al., who maintain that the New Testament is permeated both with the national hope of Jewish messianism and with

the spirit of pagan mysticism.   Their positions vary considerably
however, according to the greater or lesser part they attribute
to each of these different influences, and the importance they
attach to individuals or to groups in the elaboration of Christian
beliefs and practices, and according to the role that they assign
to Jesus and to Paul.   But in the last analysis they have in
common a systematic exegesis, in which the slightest analogy
of facts permits them to infer relationship or dependence.
Hence in their exegesis the history of Christian origins
is distorted from end to end.

The fruitless presumptions of the Formgeschichte School [1].

About 1920, a new school appeared (Dibelius, Bultmann,
Bertram, etc.).   Its point of departure is original.   It distinguishes in the Gospels, according to the form of the
pericopes, several literary types (stories, apothegms, discussions,
parables, accounts of miracles, anecdotes, etc.).   It then
analyzes these materials and compares them with similar
productions of Judaism and Hellenism.   Through this means
it attempts to retrace the history of the Gospel tradition.
Its program appears all the more pretentious since its method,
which is too often artificial, depends on old and outmoded
postulates, as any one may judge for himself.   Early Christianity,
created and transformed, according to its needs, the diverse
forms of the Gospel material.   In so doing, it remained under
the influence of Jewish conceptions and the mystery religions.
Hence, the Gospels merely reflect the beliefs and cult of the
first communities.   The figure itself of Jesus remains inaccessible
to the historian.   All that is left ot it is a mysterious element,
sufficient, it seems, as a foundation of the Christian faith
for religious souls who can distinguish the different stages
of knowledge.

Thus, it may be seen that the new structure rests on the
fragile foundation of a false conception of history.   Since the
personal action of individuals is thereby eliminated, everything
is explained by the creative power of the community, and
is resolved into an anonymous evolution which is deterministic
to the highest degree.

---

[1] For a fuller treatment of this school, see pp. 525-532, *supra.*

Conclusions.

In this sketch we have had to pass over the Conservative Protestant exegetes, both Anglican, such as Sanday, or Lutheran, as the heads of the School of Erlangen, Th. Zahn and recently K. Barth. They all follow the theology of the Reformers, as it has been more or less colored by liberal ideas. Likewise, we have spoken only of the principal systems of interest to historical criticism, and it must be acknowledged that, from the point of view of the literary criticism, the results are not always as disappointing. It should not be thought, moreover, that these theories destroy one another entirely; some elements here and there survive and deserve occasionally to remain. Yet this is very small profit for such enormous labor.

This futility of independent exegesis, as it calls itself, is explained by a fundamental vice, namely, a *philosophical* prejudice adopted before the examination of the facts, and not less tyrannical than other forms of bias. Whether independent exegesis admits the charge without evasion or protests against it, its works are always marked with the stamp of a contra-dogma, the *absolute* impossibility of the supernatural, a prejudiced judgment of the metaphysical order that can rightly be called " the scientific illusion ". Loisy himself (first stage) denounced it : Rationalistic science carries everywhere with it the error of its prejudice, namely, the strict denial of the supernatural " (*L'Enseignement biblique*, Nov.-Dec., 1893, p. 6). In actual fact, independent criticism is a myth. There are only critics who think that they are independent. Renan compared the orthodox theologian to a bird in a cage. We may grant that there is no cage for the rationalistic exegete, but his plight is much worse : he is caught in a snare.

2. — Catholic Authors.

The fundamental unity of Catholic exegesis stands out in contrast to the diverse positions of what is conventionally called " independent " criticism. From a purely human point of view, it possesses the double advantage of being objective in its method and coherent in its results. In order to interpret the books of the New Testament, it restores them to the milieu permeated with the supernatural in which they were conceived, and nothing is better for the understanding of the texts. It then explains them in the light of the living history of the Church. Thus, it has a precious source of information whereby it is enabled to get back to the primitive catechesis. In a word, it has the sense of Tradition, a primordial quality for understanding the past.

Moreover, the Catholic critic is, in principle, all the more at ease, since nothing obliges him to find in Scripture all the dogmas that he professes; for him, in direct contrast to the Protestant exegete, the Bible is not the sole rule of faith. Consequently, without putting aside, through prejudice, any document whatever, and without resorting to forced or far-fetched harmonizations, he is in a position to reconcile witnesses and to present the complex beginnings of Christianity in a truer light.

The history of Catholic exegesis can be summarized in a few lines. The first period (1550-1650), which is also called the golden age, is remarkable for its amplitude (Cornelius a Lapide, Menochius) and sometimes, too, for the intrinsic quality of its works (Sixtus of Sienna, Maldonatus). The second period (1650-1880) can boast of only one great name : Richard Simon (1638-1712) who, in spite of mistakes, is rightly regarded as the founder of the textual, literary, and historical criticism of the Bible. The works of Catholics in this period are too often marred by serious faults. In their Byzantine form of exegesis, they were content, at the cost of little effort, merely to compile patristic quotations. Again, they were exclusively defensive and absolved themselves from the obligation of solid and thorough work in order to develop a brilliant apologetic in a minimum of time. Finally, they had too little confidence in their own powers. They studied side issues and questions which were quite safe, but disliked to come to grips with the essential problems posed by the text.

During the last seventy years (1880-1950) there has been definite progress among Catholics in Biblical studies. To give a concrete idea of this progress, it will suffice to cite three names which will best represent different trends and environments. The first is that of P. Schanz (1841-1905), one of the most distinguished members of the Faculty of Catholic Theology at Tübingen. Although he held the professorship of sacred exegesis only seven years, and taught especially dogma and apologetics, he was able to employ a philological and historical method in all his work which combined respect for tradition and contempt for routine scholarship. The second name is J. Knabenbauer (1839-1911), one of the co-founders of the *Cursus Scripturæ sacræ*. His commentaries are a mine of exegetical material drawn primarily from the work of the Fathers. The third [and greatest] name is that of M. J. Lagrange (1855-1938), founder of the Ecole Biblique at Jerusalem, of the *Revue Biblique*, and of the *Etudes Bibliques*, a man of superior talent and learning. He combined in perfect harmony a solid theological formation and the broadest general culture, a painstaking care for details and a love of ideas, and a passion as ardent for safeguarding the principles of faith as for scientific research [1].

Delayed by the Modernist movement, this progress in Biblical studies became subsequently all the more rapid. The establishment of the Biblical Commission (1902), the creation of the Pontifical Biblical Institute (1909), and the reorganization of canonical faculties of theology (1931), were so many measures intended to promote the improved training which is demanded by the exigencies of our time in the scriptural field. The future, at any rate, looks all the more favorable, since the Catholic exegete will always have before his mind the Pontifical directives and, in particular, those which are contained in the recent Encyclical, *Divino afflante Spiritu*, of Pope Pius XII on Biblical studies (Sept. 30, 1943).

II. — CATHOLIC EXEGESIS.

[L. VAGANAY].

Etymologically, the word exegesis (ἐξήγησις, explanation) can be understood of the interpretation of any text whatsoever. As a matter of fact, it is used especially in speaking of the interpretation of the Sacred Books. When one speaks of Catholic

---

Translator's note. — [1 Cf. F. M. BRAUN, O. P., *L'œuvre du P. Lagrange* (Fribourg, Switzerland, 1943; cf. M. MEINERTZ, in *Theol. Revue* [1948], 89-90). Dom C. CHARLIER, O. S. B., *La lecture chrétienne de la Bible* (Maredsous, 1950)].

exegesis, he means Biblical exegesis as it should be practiced
by Catholics. But Catholics would not be able to do any real
exegetical work without the method of criticism (κρίσις, judgement, art of judging). For a long time this term offended
them, because criticism had become a weapon of combat against
their faith. Today, they have learned to handle this arm, which,
as applied to the Bible, is nothing else than a methodical
examination of the sacred texts for the purpose of discovering
their scope and meaning.

Four phases are to be distinguished in this examination :
textual criticism, literary criticism, historical criticism, and
interpretation or hermeneutics. Not that there are air-tight
partitions between these different disciplines, for, on the contrary, they continually overlap. Yet they are pursued according
to particular principles which must be carefully established.
Our exposition, which must be brief, will deal primarily with
the principles contained in the last papal Encyclical, *Divino
afflante*, " a breath of air, of pure air after the storm "
(Msgr. Charue) [1].

1. — *TEXTUAL CRITICISM* [2].

Textual criticism is concerned with the investigation of the
alterations which may have occurred in the text of a document
for the purpose of restoring it to its original form. As applied
to the books of the Bible, it has, then, a very specific object :
to classify the numerous variants recorded in the manuscript
tradition and *to choose* the one that most probably represents
the original reading. The task is a difficult one, but of primary
importance, because it is the basis of exegesis. One cannot
fail to be impressed at the insistence of the recent encyclical
on this point : " This art which is called textual criticism, and
which is used with great and praiseworthy results in the editions
of profane authors, is also quite rightly employed in the case

---

Translator's note. — [1 Cf. J. PRADO, " Orientaciones pontificias relativas
a la exegesis de la historia biblica ", *Sefarad* (1953), 131-158.]

Translator's note. — [2 See A. VACCARI, " Scrittura fenicia-Samaritana
nella Biblia ebraica ", *Biblica*, 19 (1938), 188-201; J. COPPENS, " La critique
du texte hébreu de l'Ancien Testament ", *ibid.*, 25 (1944), 9-49; E. P. ARBEZ,
" Translating the Old Testament out of the Original Languages ", *CBQ*, 7
(1945), 48-75].

of the Sacred Books, because of that very reverence which is due the Divine Oracles " (par. 17).

The *classification* of variants has been carried out in the great modern critical editions : for the Hebrew text (Kittel, 1937³), for the text of the Septuagint (Rahlfs, 1935), for the Greek text of the New Testament (Tischendorf, 1869-1872⁸, and von Soden, 1913). But we still lack an edition in which the positive and negative apparatus would be at once complete, exact, and well arranged. Hence the difficulty of making a *choice* among the different readings. Such a choice, however, is possible through the rules which have been established in this field. These rules are of two kinds : those covering involuntary textual changes (verbal criticism), and those covering voluntary or intentional changes (material criticism).

1. — Verbal criticism.

All the works of Antiquity that have come down to us through the copying of Mss have suffered thereby more or less serious alterations. The Sacred Books, which were copied and recopied more than all other texts — and too often by inexperienced scribes — have not escaped the common law.

Some of the accidental mistakes which occur both in the Hebrew and the Greek texts are : confusion of letters having nearly the same form (errors of sight) or the same sound (errors of hearing, in the case of dictated texts), especially in the transcription of proper names and numbers; addition, omission, transposition of letters, syllables, or words, and even of phrases or clauses; wrong combination or division of words in Mss written in continuous script without indication of word division; and also, special mistakes, due either to the copies of the Hebrew text (incorrect vocalization complicated by defective accentuation), or to those of the Greek text (iotacism or substitution of vowels which were pronounced in the same way).

To correct errors of this kind, which ordinarily escape attention, one must still rely on the *Manuel de critique verbale* of L. Havet (Paris, 1911) [and on F. W. Hall, *Companion to Classical Texts* (Oxford, 1913)] for Latin texts, on the similar works of Fr. Delitzsch and of Fr. Wutz (cf. p. 620) for the

Hebrew text, and on the collection of W. Milligan and A. Roberts, *The Words of the New Testament as Altered by Transmission and Ascertained by Modern Criticism* (London, 1873), for the Greek text [1]. In the near future, in place of this empirical process, we shall probably succeed in perfecting a scientific system which will permit us to track down, at leat in the case of the Latin Vulgate because of the richness of its manuscript tradition, the great majority of involuntary alterations (cf. Dom Quentin, *Mémoire pour l'établissement du texte de la Vulgate*, Paris, 1922, p. 445). Today verbal criticism is a science which is making good progress in its development.

2. — Material Criticism.

In the Sacred Books, as living and popular texts, the intentional variations are both numerous and diverse. The original was corrected to make it more elegant or more complete, less obscure or less offensive, in short, to bring it into closer harmony with the ideas then current in the Christian communities. Actually, none of these variants affects the substance of dogma. There is no mechanical system, furthermore, that can uncover these grammatical, literary, apologetic, and doctrinal retouchings, inasmuch as they are the reactions of free will. A more flexible method is needed for this purpose, namely, that of material criticism, based, on the one hand, upon the personal value of the witnesses for each variant (external criticism), and, on the other, upon the intrinsic quality of each reading (internal criticism).

1. External Criticism.

When one of the books of the Bible is being studied, it is necessary, above all, to acquire a thorough knowledge of its particular manuscript tradition, as this enables us to get some insight at least into the history of its text. This history is not the same for the books of the Old and New Testaments, respectively, and therefore external criticism must function

---

Translator's note. — [1 Cf. V. Coulon, *Essai sur la méthode de la critique conjecturale appliquée au texte d'Aristophane* (Paris, 1933); H. Pernot, *Recherches sur le texte original des Evangiles* (Paris, 1938)].

in a different way in each case. There is, however, a most
important similarity between the two situations that cannot
be neglected. During a long period, the Hebrew text and the
Greek text of the New Testament were in a state of more or less
restricted freedom before being reduced to more fixed forms
in the recensions.

1) *The traditional text of the Hebrew Bible* does not seem
to have been fixed in the same period for all the books. One
thing is certain, namely, that about the middle of the 2nd century of our era, the scribes succeeded in establishing a high degree
of uniformity in the text as a whole, a uniformity which was
to be carried even further by the Masoretes. But this fixation
was effected without benefit of critical method. Instead of a
comparative examination of the earliest witnesses being made,
one manuscript served as a type or model for each book, and
the greatest care was taken to reproduce it in a more or less
mechanical manner. Hence, the agreement among all the
extant manuscripts of the Hebrew text must not be considered
significant, for it furnishes no information on the ordinary
vicissitudes of the ancient books during the first period of their
circulation.

We must try to get back to the *text in its pre-recension form*
by employing either the rare fragments that still exist in the
Hebrew language [1] (the Samaritain Pentateuch, some examples
of *qere* and even certain *ketib*, but especially the parallel passages
in the Biblical text : Ps. **14** = Ps. **53**; Ps. **18** = 2 Sam. **22**;
Ps. **40**, 14-18 = Ps. **70**; Ps. **57** : 8-12 = Ps. **108**, 2-6; Ps. **60** :
7-14 = Ps. **108**, 7-14; 2 Rg. **18** : 13–20 : 19 = Isa. **36-39**, etc.),
or the versions made from the Hebrew text insofar as it was
not yet completely fixed (in particular, the Septuagint Version
and the Aramaic Targum of Onkelos, without forgetting the
other Greek, Syrian, and Latin versions). Not that the Masoretic text should be neglected, for it still remains the principal
witness for the primitive text of the Old Testament, but it
must always be checked against the pre-Masoretic text. Yet
it must be remembered at the same time that the pre-Masoretic
text itself may also represent the text in an already altered

---

Translator's note. — [1 See the section *supra*, pp. 113-123, on the Dead Sea
scrolls. The Biblical texts found among them must be taken into account].

form.   This means that, under the circumstances, the last word belongs to internal criticism (see pp. 592-602).

2) *The situation is the same as regards the Greek text of the New Testament* [1].   It was only towards the end of the 3rd century that the systematic recensions of the early current text were completed.   There are three of these : the Alexandrian recension, which aims at being ancient, brief, and noble; the Antiochene recension which aims at being elegant, fluent, and complete; and the Caesarean recension, for which, however, the evidence is too scanty and too controversial for any one to characterize its trends precisely.   For a long time, and even as late as the middle of the 19th century, the second recension was given preference because it had a copious manuscript tradition and seemed to be absolutely reliable.   It was called the " received " text.   Today, while the third recension, being so badly represented, is out of the running, the first recension, on the contrary, is regarded as offering on the whole a text of good quality and enjoys the preference of exegetes.   This does not mean, however, that certain tendencies in the Alexandrian recension are not open to criticism.   Its best Mss *(Sinaiticus and Vaticanus)* actually contain serious faults.

To get back to *the text anterior to these great recensions* is of first importance.   Unfortunately, this text is found only in rare and more or less defective witnesses, particularly for the Gospels. Furthermore, it offers a great variety of forms, showing alterations of all kinds (interpolations, suppressions, and especially harmonizations), the importance of which varies according to time and place.   Nevertheless, it is of the greatest interest for three reasons : first, for its antiquity — it certainly existed from the first half of the 2nd century, being the text of Marcion and of the Papyrus Egerton II; secondly, for its universality — it circulated almost everywhere, in the East (Egypt, Palestine, Edessa) as well as in the West (Rome and Carthage), and therefore has been incorrectly called " Western "; finally, for the quality of some of its variants, including

---

Translator's note. — [1 See G. D. KILPATRICK, " Western Test and Original Text in the Epistles ", *JTS*, 45 (1944), 60-65; T. AYUSO MARAZUELA, ¿" Texto arrecensional, recensional o prerrecensional? ", *Estudios Biblicos* (1947), 35-90 (on the Gospels); M. E. BOISMARD, O. P., " Critique textuelle et citations patristiques ", *RB*, 57 (1950), 388-408].

picturesque details and racy remarks which could not fail to shock sanctimonious editors.

Accordingly, even though the three great recensions may be in agreement with one another, it is always necessary to control them by a careful examination of the pre-recension texts, in which it may be possible to find original readings. Moreover, the variants, whether of the great recensions or of types of the text anterior to the great recensions, should be kept only insofar as they do not reflect the objectionable tendencies peculiar to each of these different forms of text. Finally, the greatest importance of all must be attached to the variants which occur simultaneously in several pre-recension types of the text, especially if they are found in the least contaminated types and in those most remote from one another, e.g., a, k, Sy^s, P^{45}, and *a fortiori*, if these variants are supported by some witnesses of the great recensions. Nevertheless, even under these conditions, internal criticism would still have something to say.

2. *Internal criticism.*

The ineffectiveness of external criticism, owing to the actual state of the documents, ordinarily obliges us to have recourse to internal criticism. What, then, are the qualities of the best variant? Numerous rules on this subject still occupy space in manuals and even in scholarly works. Basically, however, there are only two valid criteria, and these may be applied, moreover, to the books of the Old Testament as well as to those of the New.

1) *If we consider only the text,* we should choose the variant which best explains the origin of all the others, and which itself cannot be explained by the rival readings. This choice demands much patience when the number of readings is copious, because the variants must be compared one by one in detail, and each must be considered as an original in turn to discover, if possible, how this variant might have given birth to the others. It is rare that such an examination does not enable us to recognize the secondary character of certain readings which are manifestly dependent. In this way, a first grouping of related variants can be established. Then, on a second

examination, the heads of each group ought to be compared with one another, and that reading chosen as the original which explains all the textual data without the possibility of having been itself derived in any manner. It is not often possible to come to a definite conclusion on this "source variant ". Much experience is necessary and a certain distrust of self, two qualities which will encourage control of personal feeling by the earlier results obtained through external criticism and by the subsequent examination of the context.

2) *If we consider only the context*, we should choose the variant which agrees best with the particular tendencies of the author. Hence, we must understand not only the usage of the writer, i.e., his vocabulary, his grammar, his style, his manner of quoting and composing, etc., but also his individual character, his purpose, his ideas, his temperament, in a word, all the data of literary history which can throw any light on the best reading. Furthermore, when there is question of a text reproduced elsewhere under similar form, it is highly important to consider such parallel passages, and also — as is done too rarely — the variants of these parallel passages. If it is sometimes necessary, especially in the case of the Hebrew text, to propose conjectures, this should be done with the greatest reserve and always with the foregoing rules in mind.

Clearly, then, textual criticism is not a mere collection of forbidding symbols. It is the art of passing a well-founded judgment on the wording of a text by availing one's self of all the information furnished by the manuscript tradition and by combining with it, as the Encyclical, *Divino afflante*, says, " the greatest reverence for the sacred text with an exact observance of all the rules of criticism " (par. 19).

2. — *LITERARY CRITICISM.*

In order to interpret a book of the Bible properly, it is not sufficient to know how to establish the wording of its text, but its content must be studied as well. This activity is literary criticism. To carry it to a successful conclusion, each book has to be examined under the triple aspect of language, composition, and origin.

1. Language.

The importance of the philological study of the Sacred Text is emphasized in the encyclical just mentioned : " Let the exegete diligently apply himself so as to acquire daily a greater facility in Biblical as well as in other Oriental languages and to support his interpretation by the aids which all branches of philology supply " (par. 16).

Our Sacred Books were written in Hebrew, in Aramaic, or in Greek. In general, the exegete ought continually to improve his knowledge of these three languages. The second is too often neglected under the pretext that few of the books of the Old Testament were written in Aramaic. It is forgotten that Aramaic was the mother tongue of Jesus, whose *Logia* were even first written down in Aramaic. Furthermore, the authors of the New Testament, being Jews except Luke, thought in this language, and the Aramaic substratum crops out frequently in their works.

More particularly, before attempting to interpret a book of the Bible, one should become well acquainted with its vocabulary, grammar, and style. This holds especially for the writings of the Old Testament, in which it is necessary at times to make distinctions even between parts of the same book, as they may have been written by different authors. It holds equally also in respect to the books of the New Testament. Whether the book be composed in Hebrew or in Greek, it is possible to find certain peculiarities in the language and style, according to the period, the environment, and the personality of the writer. Unfortunately, there are few works in this field, apart from some studies dealing with the Johannine or Pauline corpus respectively. Accordingly, it is most usually necessary to make personal investigations on such matters. What has been said holds also for translation. Here one ought to try to emphasize, especially in passages from the Synoptic Gospels, the special characteristics of each author.

2. Composition.

1) The first work in this case consists in an *analysis* of the content, i.e., in a careful study of each detail which will make it possible to get out of a text all that is in it and nothing more.

One is naturally prone to find his own ideas in the work of another, and this tendency must be guarded against, especially in respect to the writings of Antiquity, and attention given simply and progressively to all points affecting events or teachings.   In doing this, one should note carefully how the connection is effected between episodes of a narrative or between the principal parts of the book.   In this way, the author's plan can sometimes be discovered, as also the progress of his thought, or at least the method adopted for the arrangement of his materials.   This is a difficult task, in which too often the judgement of others is reproduced blindly, but it is one which is of the highest importance for grasping the doctrinal import of a text.

2) After the analysis of the context comes the investigation of the sources.   It is generally admitted today that the sacred writers sometimes used written sources in the composition of their works.   The great problem is to discover them.   This is easy when there is question of formal quotations, but that is not often the case.   It is impossible when the ideas taken from the source have been elaborated upon to the extent of being completely fused in the account of the author.   This, however, is not the most common case.   The characteristic method of Semitic historiography, indeed of all Semitic composition, allows rather a gamut, extending from pure compilation, in which the materials are simply put side by side, to the most varied combinations, in which alterations of all kinds are made in the documents in order to adapt and harmonize them the better. It is important to find out, through the sources or in spite of the sources, how the book is rooted in the past and maintains, nevertheless, its own unity.

It sometimes happens, too, that, by a peculiar method of redaction, there is a juxtaposition of two or several accounts of the same event, but reported in different ways because they were taken from different sources.   Such narratives are called doublets.   In these cases, a prudent perspicacity is necessary : in the first place, for determining whether there is a doublet, and then for explaining the deviations recognized in the two or more accounts.   But the fact remains that a knowledge of these procedures helps greatly in the interpretation of certain books of the Bible, and, in particular, those of the Old Testament.

3) Another related and very important question is that of the *literary genre*. It has been given special prominence in the Encyclical, *Divino afflante*. " The interpreter must, as it were, go back wholly in spirit to those remote centuries of the East and with the aid of history, archaeology, ethnology and other sciences, accurately determine what modes of writing, so to speak, the authors of that ancient period would be likely and in fact did use... What those forms or kinds of speech exactly were, the commentator cannot determine as it were in advance, but only after a careful examination of the ancient literature of the East. The investigation, carried out on this point during the past forty or fifty years with greater care and diligence than ever before, has more clearly shown what forms of expression were used in those far off times, whether in poetic description or in the formulation of laws and the rules of life or in recording the facts and events of history " (par. 35-36).

All this research is necessary, because the sacred writer himself is dependent upon the literary genres in use in his milieu, and so much so, that a book of the Bible cannot be explained exactly without the help of the light furnished by the history of the Oriental literatures. Among the literary forms favored in the period in which the books of the Old and New Testaments were composed, there can be distinguished, e.g., those which belong to the poetic genre (fable, allegory, parable, lyric poetry, gnomic poetry, etc.), those which are related to the historical genre (popular traditions, moral or edifying history, the haggadic Midrash, history in the ancient manner, etc.), those which belong either to the epistolary genre (letters, epistles, notes), or to the didactic, prophetic, or apocalyptic genres — without mentioning less ambitious literary forms, such as the genealogy, discourse, apothegm, exhortation, maxim, etc. The basic difficulty is to prove that a given book of the Bible or a given passage in a Biblical book belongs to a specific literary genre. A keen feeling for nuances is needed here, for the literary genres are not to be thought of in terms of rigid compartments. But when once the proof has been furnished by a minute and penetrating comparison, there is no doubt that it becomes much easier to determine the original meaning.

3. Origin.

Whether a sacred or a profane book is concerned, its origin is established by an investigation of its authorship and of the circumstances under which it was composed. As regards the first point, authorship, it is important to know the writer's country, the principal facts of his life, the epoch and the environment in which he lived, his character, and his literary accomplishments. As to the second point, the publication of the work, it is very important to know the date, the place, the purpose, the occasion, and the recipients. It is easy to understand that all this information can be of great help in interpreting a text.

Now for acquiring this information, we have, ordinarily, two bodies of evidence. In the first place, we have formal attestations or simple quotations from the book, which enable us to know its author, or at least to know that he lived at a given time in history. Secondly, we have intrinsic evidence derived from the content and the character of the work. This kind of evidence strengthens or weakens the attribution furnished by tradition. Furthermore, it is necessary that these two bodies of evidence be subjected to the rules of literary criticism.

1) *The extrinsic evidence.* In principle, it is beyond dispute that this kind of evidence carries more weight, because it is habitually the most exact. In practice, each element in it should be examined separately and carefully. This examination should deal first with the source of the evidence. Is the testimony recorded formally in a work whose authenticity is unquestioned? If it has been transmitted to us only indirectly, what confidence should be placed in the agents of transmission? Next, it is important to determine the exact meaning of the testimony. Usually there is no reason to hesitate, yet there are some cases, e.g., the testimony of Papias on Matthew, where the matter is not so simple. Finally, the value of each piece of evidence remains to be established on the basis not only of the wording of the attestation but also on that of the qualifications or the defects of the witness.

When all this has been done, these different pieces of evidence are combined and thus form a tradition. But now new questions arise. To what extent does this tradition represent elements independent of each other? At what period did it make its appearance? Was it soon after the composition of the work or only ten centuries later? Is it always firm and constant in its historical development or does it leave room for curious variations? It is by answering questions of this kind that we can determine the value of the Jewish and Christian traditions on the origin of the books of the Old and of the New Testament.

2) *The intrinsic evidence.* Although this kind of evidence does not of itself suffice to establish the origin of the Biblical books, it sometimes furnishes arguments which cannot be neglected. First of all, there are pieces of information which are formally contained in the text. And yet a book may present itself under the name of a person famous in Biblical history, without this signifying anything more than the use of a literary artifice generally accepted at that time. This is true *a fortiori* if the title of a book is involved, which, in accordance with custom, refers to the book and not to the author. In any case, nothing should be decided lightly, and one always strengthens his position further by the examination of the other data which can be derived from the work in question.

If a person is willing, in fact, to make a thorough study of the language, style, historical and geographical data, and teachings contained in a given work, it will not be difficult for him to draw judicious conclusions in respect to its origin. Certain results, though negative, are nonetheless very appreciable. Thus, internal criteria are able to demonstrate that a Biblical book cannot be by a certain author or even from a certain period, even though great adroitness is required to bring this demonstration to a successful conclusion, being given the possible intervention of redactors, especially in the epistolary genre. Positive results are also obtained at times. The authenticity of a given work, e.g., may be solidly confirmed by the use of this method. In any case, the acquisition through internal criticism of a good knowledge of the literary habits, cast of mind, mood, and religious mentality of the author is of great assistance for explaining his text correctly.

3. — *HISTORICAL CRITICISM.*

To interpret a book of the Bible well, it is not sufficient to know merely its language, style, and content. It is necessary also to establish its value as an historical document, both as regards its facts and its teachings. This is historical criticism. Literary analysis has enabled us to note, in going through a work, all statements of importance in this respect. It remains now to form an opinion of their value. There are two means at our disposal. First, we have internal criticism, which seeks in the book itself arguments for or against the sincerity or the accuracy of the author; and secondly, external criticism, which is applied to the content of the work by means of the control furnished by other documents.

1. — Internal criticism.

As a starting point and as a basis for further investigation, it is necessary to use the conclusions of literary criticism on the personality of the sacred writer and on the character of his work.

1. The personality of the writer.

When we possess some information on a Biblical author, we are too often satisfied with knowing whether or not he is a contemporary or even an eye witness of the facts, and whether or not he is sincere and well informed, in short, whether he ought to be considered trustworthy. So far as this is possible, research must be pushed further, by examining very closely his purpose, his tendencies, and his sympathies, and at the same time without neglecting the circumstances under which his book was written. These are the general conditions which ought to help us to discover, by means of three very appropriate considerations, all the arguments which can be presented for or against the veracity of the author.

1) Is there any substantial reason for distrusting his *sincerity*, or, on the contrary, does his text supply serious arguments in favor of his good faith? This first examination is more difficult than it appears at first sight, because we are always tempted to seek how we would have acted in his place, while

it is the duty of the historian to efface himself in order to enter in some way into the soul of the personage who is the object of his study.

2) The second examination, which concerns the *accuracy* of the sacred writer, should be conducted in the same way. Considering the most common and habitual cases of error, have we any reason to mistrust his assertions, or, on the contrary, was he sufficiently well situated to be able to report exact facts? If he used documentary sources, was he likewise in a position to exercise sound control over them?

3) Finally, there is a third examination to be made, which considers simultaneously the author's *sincerity and accuracy*. Are there, in the Biblical story, any events in respect to which it was very difficult to deceive or to be deceived? This is a very important inquiry, for it permits us to reject many suspicions, and, when its results are combined with those of the two preceding inquiries, it contributes efficaciously towards the full comprehension of texts.

2. *The character of the book.*

As regards the Biblical writings, we sometimes have no definite information on the author as an individual. It is often difficult, even under the most favorable circumstances, to fathom his intentions. How, then, can an opinion be formed on the historical value of his work? In such a case, indeed in all cases, it will be of great advantage to remember the literary genre to which it belongs.

1) This method is not only permitted or tolerated by the Encyclical, *Divino afflante*, but it is recommended and even commanded : " The Catholic commentator... should also make a prudent use of this means, determine, i.e., to what extent the manner of expression or the literary mode adopted by the sacred writer may lead to a correct and genuine interpretation, and let him be convinced that this part of his office cannot be neglected without serious detriment to Catholic exegesis " (par. 38).

2) Moreover, this method is applicable not only to the poetic and didactic books alone, but is mentioned explicitly as applying

to the various modes of writing history : " Nevertheless no one...
will be surprised to find, even in the Sacred Writers, as in other
ancient authors, certain fixed ways of expounding and narrating,
certain definite idioms, especially of a kind peculiar to the
Semitic tongues, so-called approximations, and certain
hyperbolical modes of expression, nay, at times, even
paradoxical, which help to impress the ideas more deeply on the
mind " (par. 37).

3) The principal duty of the exegete in historical criticism
consists, then, in putting to use conclusions to which he has
come on this point in his literary criticism. For example, when
he has been obliged to classify a document as popular tradition
or as pious history, he will show that it would have been
wrong to seek therein a strictly faithful narrative of events
in accordance with our own conceptions of historical science.
And each of the Biblical writings should be investigated
in similar fashion. The task is a delicate one, but always
necessary.

2. — External criticism.

One should never be satisfied with the results of internal
criticism concerning the historical value of any book whatsoever.
In the case of our Sacred Books, the Catholic exegete ought
to verify content with the help of the documents of all kinds
placed at his disposal by the science of Biblical Antiquities
and by the general history of the ancient Near East. In this
connection, we can distinguish a twofold control.

1. *The control in the historical order for evaluating the accuracy of facts.*

1) *The positive argument.* History intervenes more or less
directly and distinctly in all our Sacred Books. Hence it is of
capital importance to know in what measure the documents
brought to light by modern excavation (inscriptions, pottery,
papyrus, coins, etc.) strengthen or contradict our construction
in the field of Biblical history. To attain this end, it is not
sufficient to be acquainted with the Palestinian milieu only,
but appeal must be made also to a whole complex of knowledge

embracing the Chaldaean, Assyrian, Hittite, Egyptian, and Greco-Roman areas. Archaeology has the role of making the Biblical past live again in its actual process of development. It is the duty of the exegete to utilize its accepted results to the best advantage in order to throw light upon the texts of the Old and of the New Testament. Consequently no reliance should be placed on the pretended discoveries of amateur archaeologists, but only upon work that has been pursued methodically and thoroughly. It is well to show the strength and the weakness of each piece of evidence. If necessary, one should wait to have the requisite control before taking a definite stand. Nevertheless, scientific research in this field should not be minimized, but, on the contrary, the precepts and recommendations of the encyclical should be followed : " Let those who cultivate Biblical studies... neglect none of those discoveries, whether in the domain of archaeology or in ancient history or literature, which serve to make better known the mentality of the ancient writers, as well as their manner and art of reasoning, narrating and writing " (par. 40).

2) *The negative argument.* It happens sometimes, however, that Biblical facts cannot be verified through the extra-Biblical evidence. Too often an argument against the veracity of the Bible has been drawn from this silence under the pretence that such and such a writer of Antiquity would have mentioned the matter if he had known it. The exegete must show the weakness of this argument. To this end, he should demonstrate that we are never in a position to prove in a peremptory manner that an ancient writer *should have spoken*, because, to do this, it would be necessary to penetrate his state of mind and his innermost thinking. It will be possible, then, to confirm this concretely by citing the numerous examples which recent discoveries have furnished to refute objections of this kind.

2. The control in the religious order for estimating the value of teachings.

1) *A new field of investigation.* The comparative history of religions has established many points of contact in beliefs, in morals, and in worship, between the religion of Israel and Christianity on the one hand, and, on the other, the ancient

Oriental religions (Babylonian, Assyrian, Egyptian, Iranian, Hellenic, Mandaean, etc.). On this basis, the Comparative School (*Religionsgeschichtliche Schule*) has claimed to explain the whole Old and New Testament in terms of a Judeo-pagan syncretism.

2) *The present task.* The Catholic exegete, in order to interpret the texts of the Bible properly, must also study this new discipline. The important thing in this instance is the employment of a sound method. In the first place, it is necessary to note meticulously the similarities as well as the differences between a given belief or custom described in the Bible and similar beliefs or customs found in other religions. Next the similarities and differences must be classified according to their characteristics : superficial (purely linguistic), material (based on the nature of things), fundamental (justified by the spirit animating the texts), without neglecting to observe the date of the documents in which they are found. Finally, the similarities and differences are to be explained judiciously, with all confusion between analogy, affinity, and dependence being avoided in the process. We should have no fear of this kind of comparison, but, on the contrary, we ought to regard it as a choice instrument for establishing the transcendency of a given doctrine. The exegesis of many Biblical passages will gain thereby in subtlety and in depth.

4. — CRITICAL INTERPRETATION OR HERMENEUTICS.

The exegete is now ready to begin his work proper. He is in possession of the elements furnished by textual, literary, and historical criticism on the Biblical book which is the object of his study. It is his business to use them to best advantage so as to penetrate deeper into the understanding of the text by fixing in detail the exact meaning of each pericope, of each sentence, of each clause, and of each word, but especially, by combining all these data in order to uncover thereby, through a profound understanding of all points, a moment, as it were, in the history of the Jewish or Christian conscience. This is critical interpretation, which is also called hermeneutics (ἑρμήνευσις, explanation). In this field, more than in any other, it is advisable to determine definitely the objective sought before justifying the method which will assure its attainment.

1. — The objective.

All the treatises on sacred hermeneutics contain a long chapter on the different senses of Scripture and their respective importance. It can be summarized in a few lines, in which the objective of critical interpretation will be precisely indicated.

1. *The different senses of Scripture.* [1]

We distinguish currently in the Sacred Books a twofold meaning : the literal sense and the spiritual sense.

1) All Biblical passages have and can have only one *literal sense*. This sense emerges from the terms themselves when correctly interpreted, and, consequently, it is the one which the author had directly in mind. The text of Osee, **11 : 1** : " I called my son out of Egypt ", refers, in the literal sense, to the return of the Hebrews from Egypt.

2) A number of events and words in the Old Testament may or ought, under certain conditions, to be interpreted as prefiguring what was to be accomplished under the New Covenant. This is the spiritual sense — also called the typical or mystical — which does not appear immediately from the words but from realities hidden beneath the words. Thus the passage from Osee, quoted above, is to be understood in the spiritual sense as referring to the return of the Holy Family from Egypt according to the interpretation of Saint Matthew (**2 : 15**), who saw in the Hebrew people the figure or type of the Messias.

3) Besides these two scriptural senses, there is sometimes attributed, more or less arbitrarily, to a given Biblical passage a meaning that has no connection with the literal or spiritual

Translator's note. — [1] See J. COPPENS, *Les harmonies des deux Testaments : Essai sur les divers sens des Ecritures et sur l'unité de la Révélation* (Tournai-Paris, 1940), with excellent bibliography. See the reviews by A. M. DUBARLE, O. P., *Bibliotheca Orientalis* (1950), 113-114, and R. DE VAUX, O. P., *RB*, 57 (1950), 280-281. On the *sensus plenior*, see Ch. I, Inspiration, pp. 34-37. See also : E. NÁCAR, " Sobre la unicidad o multiplicidad del sentido literal de las Sagradas Escrituras ", *Ciencia Tomista* (1943), 193-210; A. COLUNGA, O. P., " Dos palabras aun sobre los sentidos de la Sagrada Escritura ", *ibid.*, 327-346; G. W. LAMPE and K. J. WOOLCOMBE, *Essays on Typology* (Napierville, III., 1957; cf. *CBQ* [1957], 533-535)].

sense. This is the *accommodative sense,* by which, through simple analogy — sometimes purely verbal, the real or actual sense is accommodated to a situation totally foreign to the mind of the sacred writer. Let us suppose, for example, and this supposition is not without foundation, that a flattering preacher had applied the same text of Osee to Bonaparte on his return from Egypt before 18 Brumaire.

2. *The respective importance of the different senses of Scripture.*

1) The *accommodative sense* has nothing to do with scriptural exegesis, for it is purely adventitious and has no demonstrative force. Even in preaching ,it is necessary to confine oneself to the most widely accepted pious adaptations and to avoid in this field all " personal fancy " which would be " an abuse of the Divine Word ".

2) As regards the *spiritual sense* of the Old Testament, the exegete should endeavor to establish it with certainty in accordance with the sources of divine revelation, namely, the New Testament and the constant tradition of the Church (the unanimous agreement of the Fathers and liturgical practice — everything in matters of faith). He should apply himself in particular to showing that " the Scriptures ", not only in their individual parts, but especially in their entirety bear witness to Jesus (Jn. 5 : 39), the real and true end of ancient revelation. Besides this, he must give proof of the soundest discretion. Precisely on this point, the Encyclical, *Divino afflante,* reacts with vigor against " the rash pretentions " of those who, "affirming that they scarcely ever find anything in Biblical commentaries to raise their hearts to God, to nourish their souls, or to promote their interior life, repeatedly urge that we should have recourse to a certain spiritual and, as they say, mystical interpretation " (par. 25) [1].

3) With this in mind, the Sovereign Pontiff recommends especially the employment of the literal sense, and returns

Translator's note. — [1 As an attempt in this direction may be mentioned, W. VISCHER, *L'Ancien Testament témoin du Christ : Vol. I. La Loi ou les Cinq Livres de Moïse* (Neuchâtel-Paris, 1949). This work, a translation from the German, reveals a deep religious sense, but goes too far in its search for harmony between the Old and the New Testament (See the review in *RB,* 57 (1950), 284). For other Protestant works dealing with the same subject, see P. LESTRINGANT, *Essai sur l'unité de la Révélation biblique* (Paris, 1942);

repeatedly to this theme : " Let the Catholic exegete undertake
the task, of all those imposed on him the greatest, that, namely,
of discovering and expounding the genuine meaning of the
Sacred Books. In the performance of this task, let the
interpreters bear in mind that their foremost and greatest
endeavor should be to discern and define clearly that sense
of Biblical words which is called literal " (par. 23). Such is,
then, the objective of critical interpretation or hermeneutics.
Let is now consider how it is to be attained.

2. — The Method.

The investigation of the literal sense ought to be carried
out in two stages. The Catholic exegete should establish first
the original literal sense, and then the traditional literal sense.

1. *The original litteral sense.*

This is the sense that can be gotten from the text solely
by means of the common procedures proper to the philological,
literary, and historic orders.

1) In this regard the first duty of the exegete is to throw
light on *all the details* of the Biblical text. For each word
he should seek various meanings common at the time in which
the author used them, and he should choose the one which
harmonizes best with the grammatical context, the subject
treated, parallel passages, the logical development of the thought,
and the literary genre of the book in question. The expressions
of doctrinal import should be the object of special examination.
The poetical sections of the Bible also require particular
attention, study being given not only to the rhythm and
versification, but likewise to the spirit animating these pieces.
Moreover, whatever the literary genre may be, one must always
keep in mind the peculiar genius of Oriental languages, and,
in particular, their use of metaphor and hyperbole. Finally,

S. DE DIETRICH, *Le dessein de Dieu* [2] (Neuchâtel-Paris, 1948); O. CULLMANN,
Christ et le temps (*ibid.*, 1947); J. WOODS, *The Old Testament in the
Church* (London, 1949). The following Catholic work may be mentioned.
R. A. DYSON, S. J., and A. JONES, *The Kingdom of Promise : Its Preparation,
Foreshadowing, and Fulfillment* (London, 1947). These works go beyond the
question of the " spiritual sense ". They cover, in different ways, the argument
from prophecy and aim at showing in Christianity the fulfillment of the Old
Testament].

it is important never to neglect the particular circumstances under which the sacred book was written. The preoccupations of the sacred writer, the readers for whom he wrote, the environment in which he lived, in brief, the psychological and historical context, all this must be considered and will make it possible to interpret more correctly even the smallest details.

2) This first work ought to enable the exegete to acquire some general views of his problem, without which his interpretation will always be cramped in some respect. It is not only a matter of bringing into relief the artistic beauty of the narrative. It would not be sufficient, either, to revive, in the framework of a geography however concrete, the principal phases in the providential history of Israel and of early Christianity. The most important task is to record the progress of revealed religion. Besides and beyond the texts and anecdotal history, it is necessary to apply one's self to the investigation of doctrinal history. An endeavor should be made, e.g., to show how a certain book, fact, or personage in the Bible constitutes a stage in the historical evolution of God's revelations to the world. The exegete should not fail to make a synthesis of this progressive history — which is much more beautiful than the other type of history mentioned, after he has emphasized in the course of his systematic study all features that reflect a more personal intimacy with God, a more profound view of the dignity of man, and a more sharply defined perception of the grandeur of the spiritual life. And in all this, the original literal sense should be constantly regarded as basic.

2. The traditional literal sense.

This is the sense that ecclesiastical tradition obtains from the original sense of Scripture by means of a deeper investigation and understanding. This work of tradition operates in a twofold manner.

1) *Official dogmatic interpretation.* There are two authorities which the Catholic exegete must follow in his interpretation of the Bible in all matters of Faith and morals : the *magisterium* of the Church and the consent of the Fathers (Vatican Council, Sess. III, ch. 2). As regards the *magisterium of the Church,*

a distinction must be made, from the point of view of authority, between the extraordinary *magisterium* (definitions of the Pope or of general councils) and the ordinary *magisterium* (teachings of the Pope and of bishops apart from solemn definitions and doctrinal decisions of the Roman congregations — the Holy Office, and the Biblical Commission). Moreover, in each case, before establishing the import of an interpretation, it is important to determine its precise nature (whether direct and positive, direct and negative, or indirect). As regards *the consent of the Fathers*, it should be carefully remembered that their agreement ought to be morally unanimous, constant, and categorical, and deal with the same object concerning Faith or morals. Actually, the texts whose sense is thus officially fixed are very rare. In the interpretation of the other Biblical passages, the exegete ought, then, to respect *the rule of the analogy of Faith*, i.e., never to accept an explanation that would place the sacred writers in contradiction among themselves or in opposition to the teachings of the Church.

Such is the first form of traditional interpretation. Sometimes, certainly, it gives a deeper significance to the original literal sense. The role of the exegete should then be to show that it is none the less founded on reason. The Church, God's new Israel, goes back by a continuous tradition to the meeting point of the two Testaments, which she has, as it were, integrated in her Faith. She is therefore better situated than anyone to give a correct exegesis of the Biblical texts. In spite of the controversies and the differences that can be noted in the first Christian centuries, there was, nevertheless, a solid underlying basis on which everyone was in agreement. It is this inner core that the Church transmits in her official interpretation, in which she finds again the complete meaning of the Sacred Books. Sometimes, this is called a biased form of exegesis. It is useless to reopen this debate. The answer, which is seemingly paradoxical, may be expressed in a very short sentence : " One understands well what one loves ".

2) *Private theological interpretation*. The exegete ought not to confine himself to official dogmatic interpretation alone. He has the duty of promoting the theological teaching of Holy Scripture, drawing inspiration, in accordance with the strong

recommendation of the Encyclical, *Divino afflante*, from the works which have been left to us by the best ancient commentators. This private theological interpretation, which also rests on the original literal sense, belongs in some measure to the living tradition of the Church. But it has its own principles, and it would be wrong to ignore them.

Up to this point, the exegete, while tracing the history of Revelation in broad outline, has not done, strictly speaking, the work of the theologian. This outline, however elaborate, should not satisfy him. Biblical theology ought to be the final goal of his efforts. In this field the role of the exegete has too long been limited to preparing for theological speculation, i.e., to classifying the different kinds of revealed propositions contained in Scripture and determining precisely their revealed meaning. However useful this work of analysis may be, the theologian-exegete has something better to do, namely, to crown his studies with a doctrinal synthesis. He should begin with monographs devoted to a Biblical word or concept, either through a whole period, or simply in one book deliberately chosen. The essential point is to emphasize the theological import. He should pursue his task by composing more ample monographs, in which he should explore the doctrinal views of this or that Biblical author. It is only through making a systematic exposition of teachings according to the different phases of Revelation that he will be able to write a theology of the Old or New Testament. The great danger for the exegete is adding to the literal sense instead of going into it more deeply. He ought to cut through the surface layer, as it were, to extract the more substantial theological essence. If the danger mentioned is averted, he should be able to provide a complete and exact interpretation of the Sacred Text. As theology has nothing to fear from sound exegesis, so exegesis has nothing to fear from sound theology [1].

Translator's note. — [1 As an excellent introduction to the theological work described above may be recommended, A. GELIN, S. S., *Les idées maîtresses de l'Ancien Testament* (Lectio Divina, Paris, 1948), with good bibliography. See also Dom H. DUESBERG, *Les valeurs chrétiennes de l'Ancien Testament* (Maredsous, 1948). J. GUITTON, *Le développement des idées dans l'Ancien Testament* (Aix en Provence, 1947). A. DUBARLE, O. P., *Les Sages d'Israël* (Lectio Divina, Paris, 1946). P. HEINISCH, *Theologie des Alten Testamentes* (Bonn, 1940; Engl. trans. by W. G. HEIDT, O. S. B., based on a text revised by the author, Collegeville, Minn., 1950)].

We know of no better way to conclude this chapter than to quote one of the most beautiful passages in the Encyclical, *Divino afflante*, where His Holiness Pope Pius XII recommends charity in true liberty : " But this state of things is no reason why the Catholic commentator, inspired by an active and ardent love of his subject and sincerely devoted to Holy Mother Church, should in any way be deterred from grappling again and again with these difficult problems, hitherto unsolved... Let all the other sons of the Church bear in mind that the efforts of these resolute laborers in the vineyard of the Lord should be judged not only with equity and justice, but also with the greatest charity; all moreover should abhor that intemperate zeal which imagines that whatever is new should for that very reason be opposed and suspected... There remain therefore many things, and of the greatest importance, in the discussion and exposition of which the skill and genius of Catholic commentators may and ought to be freely exercised... This true liberty of the children of God which adheres faithfully to the teaching of the Church and accepts and uses gratefully the contributions of profane science, this liberty, upheld and sustained in every way by the confidence of all, is the condition and source of all lasting fruit and of all solid progress in Catholic science " (par. 46-47).

APPENDIX

DECISIONS OF THE PONTIFICAL BIBLICAL COMMISSION [1],

I. — ON THE TACIT QUOTATIONS CONTAINED IN HOLY SCRIPTURE (Feb. 13, 1905).

In order to establish a guide for students of Holy Scripture the following question has been proposed to the Biblical Commission :

Whether it is allowable for a Catholic commentator to solve difficulties occurring in certain texts of Holy Scripture, which apparently make

---

[1] Translation of the decisions published in the *Acta Sanctae Sedis*, XXXVII, (1905), ff., and in the *Acta Apostolicae Sedis*, I (1909), ff. [The English translation is taken from *Rome and the Study of Scripture. A Collections of Papal Enactments on the Study of Holy Scripture together with the Decisions of the Biblical Commission*, 4th edition (The Abbey Press, St. Meinrad, Indiana, 1946)]. On the Biblical Commission (institution, purpose, composition, procedure, duties, juridical value, and obligatory force of its decisions), see L. PIROT, " Commission Biblique ", in *DBV, Suppl.* II (1930), 103-113. [See also

historical statements, by asserting that we have in such texts tacit or implied quotations from documents written by a non-inspired author, and that the inspired author by no means intends to approve of these statements or make them his own, and that these statements cannot, in consequence, be regarded as free from error.

To this the Commission judged proper to reply : In the negative; except in the case when, subject to the mind and decision of the Church, it can be proved by solid arguments, first, that the sacred writer really does cite another's sayings or writings; and secondly, that he does not intend, in so doing, to approve them or make them his own.

E. F. SIEGMAN, " The Decrees of the Pontifical Biblical Commission : A Recent Clarification ", CBQ (1956), 23-29. This article presents the views of A. Miller and A. Kleinhans as expressed in their reviews of the revised edition of the Enchiridion Biblicum (Rome, 1954). Cf. also Father SIEGMAN's note, "On an Instruction of the Pontifical Biblical Commission ", CBQ (1956), 144-146, and A. KLEINHANS, " Bibelkommission ", LTK, II (2nd ed., 1958), 359-360. The observations of C. HAURET on the decrees of the Biblical Commission in his Origines de l'univers et de l'homme d'après la Bible (Genèse I-III) (Paris, 1953), 20 ff., are important and timely. They may be summarized as follows. It is agreed that the decrees of the Biblical Commission, important as they are, are not infallible or unchangeable. They were issued under circumstances quite different from present conditions. Their purpose was to meet special situations, for practical reasons; not properly to settle problems once and for all, but rather — as actually stated occasionally — to urge further consideration of the given question. In fact, as pointed out by numerous scholars, there are at times significant differences in several instances where the same problem has been considered after a period of some years. Thus, the first decision on the Pentateuch (June, 1906) maintained its Mosaic authenticity and spoke of " substantial integrity " in this connection. The term was susceptible of a narrow interpretation, but also of a broad interpretation as well. Actually, therefore, it left the door open for further investigation and did not impose a definite final solution for the problem. Father J. M. Vosté's letter to Cardinal Suhard (Jan., 1948) looks at the problem in a very different way. It urges a critical study of the data, and proper consideration of the results achieved by other sciences. It emphasizes the importance of the study of " literary forms " in Gen. I-II which are so different from modern literary genres. The student must collect and use the data furnished by paleontology, history, epigraphy, etc., which may help him to understand better the true character of some narratives. As regards the question of the composition of the Pentateuch, the letter takes for granted the existence of sources, both written and oral, a progressive development of the Mosaic laws owing to subsequent changes in the political and social life of the Hebrew People. There is, obviously, no contradiction between the directives contained in Father Vosté's letter and the earlier decision, but there is a marked difference in attitude. This difference is more noticeable if we compare the statements on the Mosaic authenticity or the substantial Mosaic authenticity and integrity of the Pentateuch contained in the earlier decree, with the declaration made in Father Vosté's letter, that unprejudiced study of the evidence " will doubtless establish the great part and deep influence of Moses as author and as lawgiver. " In the light of this declaration, later changes and additions may be regarded as Mosaic in a broader sense, i.e., as being in the line of the ancient principles laid down by Moses. Cf. J. COPPENS. Histoire critique des livres de l'Ancien Testament (3rd ed., Bruges, 1942. There is an English trans. of the 2nd ed. [1938] by Ryan and Tribbe, The Old Testament and the Critics [Paterson, N. J., 1942]; ID., A. VAN HOONACKER, De compositione litteraria et de origine Mosaica Hexateuchi (Brussels, 1949), 14].

II. — Concerning the Narratives in the Historical Books which have only the Appearance of being Historical (June 23, 1905).

The Biblical Commision answers the following question :

Whether we may admit as a principle of sound exegesis the opinion which holds that those books of Holy Scripture which are regarded as historical, either wholly or in part, sometimes narrate what is not really history properly so-called and objectively true, but only have the appearance of history and are intended to convey a meaning different from the strictly literal or historical sense of the words.

Answer : In the negative; excepting always the case — not to be easily or rashly admitted, and then only on the supposition that it is not opposed to the teaching of the Church and subject to her decision — that it can be proved by solid arguments that the sacred writer did not intend to give a true and strict history, but proposed rather to set forth, under the guise and form of history, a parable or an allegory or some meaning distinct from the literal or historical signification of the words.

III. — On the Mosaic Authorship of the Pentateuch (June 27, 1906).

The Biblical Commission answers the following questions :

1. *Authenticity.* — Whether the arguments amassed by critics to impugn the Mosaic authenticity of the sacred books designated by the name Pentateuch are of sufficient weight, notwithstanding the very many evidences to the contrary contained in both Testaments taken collectively, the persistent agreement of the Jewish people, and constant tradition of the Church, and internal arguments derived from the text itself, to justify the statement that these books have not Moses for their author but have been compiled from sources for the most part posterior to the time of Moses.

Answer : In the negative.

2. *Writer.* — Whether the Mosaic authenticity of the Pentateuch necessarily postulates such a redaction of the whole work as to render it absolutely imperative to maintain that Moses wrote with his own hand or dictated to amanuenses all and everything contained in it; or whether it is possible to admit the hypothesis of those who think that he entrusted the composition of the work itself, conceived by himself under the influence of divine inspiration, to some other person or persons, but in such a manner that they rendered faithfully his own thoughts, wrote nothing contrary to his will, and omitted nothing; and that the work thus produced, approved by Moses as the principal and inspired author, was made public under his name.

Answer : In the negative to the first part, in the affirmative to the second part.

3. *Sources.* — Whether it may be granted, without prejudice to the Mosaic authenticity of the Pentateuch, that Moses employed sources in

the production of his work, i.e., written documents or oral traditions, from which, to suit his special purpose and under the influence of divine inspiration, he selected some things and inserted them in his work, either literally or in substance, summarized or amplified.

Answer : In the affirmative.

4. *Changes and Textual Corruptions.* — Whether, granted the substantial Mosaic authenticity and the integrity of the Pentateuch, it may be admitted that in the long course of centuries some modifications have been introduced into the work, such as additions after the death of Moses, either appended by an inspired author or inserted into the text as glosses and explanations; certain words and forms translated from the ancient language to more recent language, and finally, faulty readings to be ascribed to the error of amanuenses, concerning which it is lawful to investigate and judge according to the laws of criticism.

Answer : In the affirmative, subject to the judgment of the Church.

IV. — ON THE AUTHOR AND HISTORICAL TRUTH OF THE FOURTH GOSPEL (May 29, 1907).

The Biblical Commission answers the following questions :

1. *External Evidence for Authenticity.* — Whether from the constant, universal, and solemn tradition of the Church coming down from the second century, as it is gathered chiefly : *a)* from the testimonies and allusions of the holy Fathers and ecclesiastical writers, nay even those of heretics, which since they must have been derived from the disciples or first successors of the Apostles, are joined by a necessary connection to the very origin of the book; *b)* from the fact that the name of the author of the Fourth Gospel was received always and everywhere in the canons and catalogues of the sacred books; *c)* from the most ancient manuscript codices of the same books and their versions in various languages; *d)* from the public liturgical use obtaining throughout the whole world from the very beginnings of the Church; leaving aside the theological argument, it is proved by such a solid historical argument that the Apostle John and no other must be acknowledged as the author of the Fourth Gospel, that the reasons to the contrary, brought forward by the critics, in no wise weaken this tradition.

Answer : In the affirmative.

2. *Internal Evidence for Authenticity.* — Whether also the internal reasons, which are drawn from the text of the Fourth Gospel considered separately from the testimony of the writer and the manifest kinship of the same Gospel with the First Epistle of the Apostle John, must be considered to confirm the tradition wihch unhesitatingly attributes the Fourth Gospel to the same Apostle. And whether the difficulties which are drawn from the comparison of the same Gospel with the other three, bearing in mind the diversity of time, of scope, and of the hearers for whom

or against whom the author wrote, can be reasonably solved, as the holy Fathers and Catholic commentators have done at all times.

Answer : In the affirmative to both parts.

3. *Historical Character.* — Whether, notwithstanding the practice which has constantly obtained in the whole Church from the first ages, of arguing from the Fourth Gospel as from a strictly historical document, and considering moreover the peculiar character of the same Gospel and the author's manifest intention of illustrating and vindicating the divinity of Christ from His own deeds and words, it can be said that the facts narrated in the Fourth Gospel are wholly or in part invented to serve as allegories or doctrinal symbols, and that discourses of our Lord are not properly and truly the discourses of our Lord Himself, but the theological compositions of the writer, albeit they are placed in the mouth of our Lord.

Answer : In the negative.

V. — ON THE CHARACTER OF THE BOOK OF ISAIAS AND ITS AUTHOR (June 28, 1908).

The Biblical Commission answers the following questions :

1. *Prophetical Character.* — Whether it may be taught that the prophecies which are read in the book of Isaias, and here and there in the Scriptures, are not real prophecies, but either narratives composed subsequent to the event, or, if it must be acknowledged that something was foretold before the event, that the prophet foretold the same, not from a supernatural revelation of God who foreknows the future, but by conjecturing through a happy sagacity and acuteness of natural intelligence from things that had already happened.

Answer : In the negative.

2. *Time of Fulfillment.* — Whether the opinion which holds that Isaias and the other prophets uttered prophecies concerning only those things which were to take place immediately or after a short space of time, can be reconciled with the prophecies, particularly the Messianic and eschatological, which were undoubtedly uttered by the same prophets as referring to the remote future, as well as with the common opinion of the Fathers who unanimously assert that the prophets foretold also those things which should be fulfilled after many ages.

Answer : In the negative.

3. *Character of the Prophetic Office.* — Whether it may be admitted that the prophets not only as correctors of human wickedness and heralds of the divine Word for the good of their hearers, but also as foretellers of future events, must always have addressed themselves to a present and contemporary and not to a future audience, so that they could be clearly understood by them; and that therefore, the second part of the book of Isaias (chapter **40-66**), in which the prophet addresses and consoles not the Jews contemporary with Isaias, but those mourning in the exile

of Babylon, cannot have for its author Isaias himself then long dead, but must be attributed to some unknown prophet living among the exiles.

Answer : In the negative.

4. *Unity of Authorship.* — Whether the philological argument, one derived from the language and the style, and employed to throw doubt upon the identity of the author of the book of Isaias, is to be considered weighty enough to compel a man of judgment, versed in the principles of criticism and well acquainted with Hebrew, to acknowledge in the same book a plurality of authors.

Answer : In the negative.

5. *Cumulative Arguments against Unity.* — Whether there are solid arguments, even when taken cumulatively, to prove that the book of Isaias is to be attributed not to Isaias alone, but to two or even more authors.

Answer : In the negative.

VI. — On the Historical Character of the First Three Chapters of Genesis (June 30, 1909).

The Biblical Commission answers the following questions :

1. *False Exegesis.* — Whether the various exegetical systems, which have been elaborated and defended by the aid of a science falsely so-called, for the purpose of excluding the literal historical sense from the first three chapters of Genesis, are based upon solid arguments.

Answer : In the negative.

2. *Historical Character of the Three Chapters.* — Whether we may, in spite of the character and historic mould of the book of Genesis, of the close connection between the first three chapters and those which follow, of the manifold testimony of the Scriptures both of the Old and the New Testament, of the practically unanimous opinion of the Fathers, and of the traditional view which — derived from the Jewish people — has always been held by the Church, teach that the three aforesaid chapters do not contain the narrative of things which actually happened, a narrative which corresponds to objective reality and historic truth; and whether we may teach that these chapters contain fables derived from mythologies and cosmologies belonging to older nations, but purified of all polytheistic error and accomodated to monotheistic teaching or that they contain allegories and symbols destitute of any foundation in objective reality but presented under the garb of history for the purpose of inculcating religious and philosophical truth; or, finally, that they contain legends partly historical and partly fictitious, freely handled for the instruction and edification of souls.

Answer : In the negative to each part.

3. *Historical Character of Certain Parts.* — Whether, in particular, we may call in question the literal and historical meaning where, in these

chapters, there is question of the narration of facts which touch the fundamental teachings of the Christian religion, as for example, the creation of all things by God in the beginning of time, the special creation of man, the formation of the first woman from man, the unity of the human race, the original happiness of our first parents in a state of justice, integrity, and immortality, the divine command laid upon man to prove his obedience, the transgression of that divine command at the instigation of the devil under the form of a serpent, the fall of our first parents from their primitive state of innocence, and the promise of a future Redeemer.

Answer : In the negative.

4. *Interpretation.* — Whether, in interpreting those passages of these chapters which the Fathers and Doctors have interpreted in divers ways without leaving us anything definite or certain, anyone may, subject to the decision of the Church and following the analogy of faith, follow and defend that opinion at which he has prudently arrived.

Answer : In the affirmative.

5. *Literal Sense.* — Whether all the constituent parts, namely, the single words and phrases, in these chapters must always and of necessity be interpreted in a literal sense, so that it is never lawful to deviate from it, even when expressions are manifestly not used in the strictly literal sense, but metaphorically or anthropomorphically, and when reason or necessity compel us to depart from the strictly literal sense.

Answer : In the negative.

6. *Allegory and Prophecy.* — Whether, granting always the literal and historical sense, the allegorical and prophetical interpretation of certain passages of these chapters — an interpretation justified by the example of the Fathers and the Church — may be prudently and usefully applied.

Answer : In the affirmative.

7. *Scientific Expression.* — Whether, since it was not the intention of the sacred author, when writing the first chapter of Genesis, to teach us the innermost nature of visible things, nor to present the complete order of creation in a scientific manner; but rather to furnish his people with a popular account, such as the common parlance of that age allowed, one, namely, adapted to the senses and to man's intelligence, we are always bound, when interpreting these chapters to seek for scientific exactitude of expression.

Answer : In the negative.

8. *Yom.* — Whether the word Yom (day), which is used in the first chapter of Genesis to describe and distinguish the six days, may be taken either in its strict sense as the natural day, or in a less strict sense as signifying a certain space of time; and whether free discussion of this question is permitted to interpreters.

Awerns : In the affirmative.

VII. — ON THE AUTHOR, TIME OF COMPOSITION, AND CHARACTER
OF THE PSALMS (May 1, 1910).

The Biblical Commission answers the following questions :

1. *Authorship.* — Whether the terms *Psalms of David. Hymns of David,*
the *Book of the Psalms of David,* the *Davidic Psalter,* which in the old
collections and even in the Councils are used to designate the Old Testament
Book of 150 psalms, as also the opinion of many Fathers and Doctors
who held that absolutely all the psalms of the Psalter were to be attributed
to David alone, are of such force that we have to consider David as the
sole author of the entire Psalter.

Answer : In the negative.

2. *Antiquity of the Titles.* — Whether, from the agreement of the Hebrew
text with the Alexandrian Greek text and with other old versions, we can
rightly conclude that the titles prefixed to the psalms in the Hebrew text
are of older date than the aforesaid LXX version, and that consequently
they are due, if not directly to the authors of the psalms, at least to very
ancient Jewish tradition.

Awerns : In the affirmative.

3. *Genuineness of the Titles.* — Whether the aforesaid titles, witnesses
to the Jewish tradition, can be reasonably called in question except where
there is solid reason for doubting their genuine character.

Answer : In the negative.

4. *Davidic Authorship.* — Whether, considering the not infrequent
testimonies in the Bible to David's natural skill, a skill further illumined
by the special gift of the Holy Spirit for the composition of religious odes;
whether, considering too, the arrangement drawn up by him for the liturgical
chanting of the psalms; the attributions also, both in the Old Testament
and the New, of psalms to him, as also in the actual inscriptions anciently
affixed to the psalms; whether, considering, moreover, the common opinion
of the Jews, and of the Fathers and Doctors of the Church, it can
be prudently denied that David was the principal author of the odes
contained in the Psalter. Whether, on the other hand, it can be maintained
that only a few of these odes are to be attributed to the Royal Psalmist.

Answer : In the negative to both questions.

5. *Davidic Authorship in Particular.* — Whether we can in particular
deny the Davidic origin of the psalms which, in both the Old and New
Testaments, are expressly cited as David's, especially such as, Ps. **2,** *Why
have the Gentiles raged;* Ps. **15,** *Preserve me, O Lord;* Ps. **17,** *I will love
Thee, O Lord, my strength;* Ps. **31,** *Blessed are they whose iniquities are
forgiven;* Ps. **68,** *Save me, O God;* Ps. **109,** *The Lord said to my Lord.*

Answer : In the negative.

6. *Changes and Additions.* — Whether we can admit the view held by some, namely, that certain psalms, whether by David or by other authors, have, for liturgical or musical reasons, or through the carelessness of copyists, or for other unexplained reasons, been divided or even welded together. Further, whether we can hold that some psalms, e.g., the *Miserere*, have for the sake of better adaptability to historical circumstances or Jewish festivals, been slightly remoulded or modified, either by the removal or addition of one or two verses, without detriment to the inspiration of the whole sacred text.

Answer : In the affirmative to both questions.

7. *Recent Psalms.* — Whether we can maintain with any real probability the opinion of those who, judging by internal grounds alone or basing their views upon an unsound interpretation of the sacred text, strive to demonstrate that not a few psalms were composed after the date of Esdras and Nehemias, nay, even in the Machabean age.

Answer : In the negative.

8. *Prophetic and Messianic Psalms.* — Whether, judging by the repeated testimonies of the Books of the New Testament, the unanimous consent of the Fathers, in agreement, too, with Jewish writers, we can hold that many psalms are to be recognized as prophetic and Messianic, i.e., as foretelling the coming of a future Redeemer, his kingdom, his priesthood, his Passion, death, and resurrection. And whether we must in consequence, reject the opinion of those who, perverting the prophetic and Messianic character of the psalms, limit these oracles, concerning Christ, to mere predictions of the future lot of the chosen people.

Answer : In the affirmative to both questions.

VIII. — On the Author, Date of Composition, and Historical Truth of the Gospel according to St. Matthew (June 19, 1911).

The Biblical Commission answers the following questions :

1. *Author.* — Whether, bearing in mind the universal and constant tradition of the Church dating from the first centuries, which explicit testimonies of the Fathers, the inscriptions of the codices of the Gospel, the oldest versions of the sacred books as well as their catalogues transmitted to us by the holy Fathers, ecclesiastical writers, Supreme Pontiffs and the Councils, and finally, the liturgical usages ot the Eastern and Western Church clearly record, it may and must be affirmed with certainty that Matthew, an Apostle of Christ, is in truth the author of the Gospel published under his name.

Answer : In the affirmative.

2. *Order of Composition and Language.* — Whether the opinion must be considered as sufficiently supported by the testimony of tradition, which holds that Matthew wrote before the other Evangelists and that

he wrote the first Gospel in the Hebrew dialect then in use by the Jews of Palestine, for whom this work was intended.

Answer : In the affirmative to both parts.

3. *Date of Composition.* — Whether the publication of this original text may be deferred beyond the time of the destruction of Jerusalem, so that the prophecies which are therein recorded concerning that event, were written after the destruction, and whether the frequently quoted testimony of St. Irenaeus [1], the interpretation of which is uncertain and controverted, must be considered of such authority as to necessitate the rejection of the opinion of those who consider it more in conformity with tradition that the first Gospel was completed even before the arrival of St. Paul at Rome.

Answer : In the negative to both parts.

4. *Compilation.* — Whether the opinion of certain moderns may be held as probable according to which Matthew is said to have composed the Gospel not exactly as it has been transmitted to us, but only a collection of the sayings and discourses of Christ, which an anonymous author, whom these modernists call the compiler of the Gospel, has used as sources.

Answer : In the negative.

5. *Identity of Hebrew and Greek.* — Whether, from the fact that the Fathers, all eclesiastical writers, and even the Church herself, from the very beginning, have used only the Greek text of the Gospel according to St. Matthew as canonical, not even excepting those who have explicitly testified that Matthew, the Apostle, wrote in the Hebrew dialect, it can be proved with certainty that the Greek Gospel is identical in substance with the Gospel written in the vernacular by the same Apostle.

Answer : In the affirmative.

6. *Historical Character.* — Whether, from the fact that the purpose of the author is principally dogmatic and apologetic, demonstrating that Jesus is the Messias foretold by the prophets and a descendant of the house of David, and that, moreover, the author does not always follow the chronological order in arranging the deeds and sayings which he narrates and records, it is consequently lawful to consider them as not true; and whether it may also be affirmed that the narration of the deeds and words of Christ, which is contained in the Gospels, has been subjected to changes and adaptions under the influence of the prophecies of the Old Testament and the more developed status of the Church, and that, consequently, this narration is not in conformity with historical truth.

Answer : In the negative to both parts.

Translator's note. — [1 The text of St. Irenaeus has come down to us in a Latin translation only : Ita Matthaeus in Hebraeis ipsorum lingua Scripturam edidit Evangelii, cum Petrus et Paulus Romae evangelizarent, et fundarent Ecclesiam. *Advers. Haeres.*, III, i, r, Migne, *P. G.* VII, 844.]

7. *Integrity.* — Whether in particular the opinion of those ought to be considered devoid of solid foundation, who call in question the historical authenticity of the first two chapters, in which the genealogy and the infancy of Christ are narrated, as also certain passages of great importance in dogma, such as those referring to the primacy of Peter (**16** : 17-19), the form of Baptism given to the Apostles together with the universal mission of teaching (**29** : 19-20), the Apostles' profession of faith in the divinity of Christ (**14** : 33), and others of this character, which are expressed in a manner peculiar to Matthew.

Answer : In the affirmative.

IX. — ON THE AUTHOR, TIME OF COMPOSITION, AND HISTORICAL TRUTH OF THE GOSPEL ACCORDING TO ST. MARK AND ST. LUKE (June 26, 1912).

The Biblical Commission answers the following questions :

1. *Authenticity.* — Whether the clear evidence of tradition, wonderfully harmonious from the earliest ages of the Church and supported by numerous arguments, viz., by the explicit testimonies of the Fathers and ecclesiastical writers, by the citations and allusions occurring in their writings, by the usage of the ancient heretics, by the versions of the books of the New Testament in the most ancient and almost universal manuscript codices, and also by intrinsic arguments from the text itself of the sacred books, certainly compels us to affirm that Mark, the disciple and interpreter of Peter, and Luke, a physician, the assistant and companion of Paul, are really the authors of the Gospels which are respectively attributed to them.

Answer : In the affirmative.

2. *Integrity of the Second Gospel.* — Whether the reasons, by which some critics endeavor to prove that the last twelve verses of the Gospel of Mark (**16** : 9-20) were not written by Mark himself but added by another hand, are of a kind to justify the statement that these verses are not to be received as inspired and canonical, or at least prove that Mark is not the author of said verses.

Answer : In the negative to both parts.

3. *Integrity of the Third Gospel.* — Whether likewise it is lawful to doubt of the inspiration and canonicity of the narration of Luke on the infancy of Christ (chapter **1–2**) or of the apparition of the Angel conforting Jesus and of the bloody sweat (**22** : 43-44); or whether at least it can be shown by solid reasons — as ancient heretics used to think and certain more recent critics hold — that these narrations do not belong to the genuine Gospel of Luke.

Answer : In the negative to both parts.

4. *The Magnificat.* — Whether those very rare and altogether singular documents in which the Canticle " Magnificat " is attributed not to the Blessed Virgin Mary, but to Elizabeth, can and should at all prevail against the harmonious testimony of nearly all the codices both of the original Greek text and of the versions, as well as against the interpretation clearly

required no less by the context than by the mind of the Virgin herself and constant tradition of the Church.

Answer : In the negative.

5. *Chronological Order.* — Whether, with regard to the chronological order of the Gospels, it is lawful to abandon the opinion, supported as it is by the most ancient as well as constant testimony of tradition, which testifies that, after Matthew, who first of all wrote his Gospel in his native language, Mark wrote second and Luke third; or is this opinion to be regarded as opposed to that which asserts that the second and third Gospels were composed before the Greek version of the first Gospel?

Answer : In the negative to both parts.

6. *Date of Composition.* — Whether it is lawful to set the date of the composition of the Gospels of Mark and Luke as late as the destruction of the city of Jerusalem; or whether, from the fact that in Luke the prophecy of our Lord concerning the overthrow of this city seems to be more definite, it can at least be held that his Gospel was written after the siege had been begun.

Answer : In the negative to both parts.

7. *Date of Composition of the Third Gospel.* — Whether it is to be affirmed that the Gospel of Luke preceded the book of the Acts of the Apostles (Acts I : 1-2); and since this book, of which the same Luke is author, was finished at the end of the Roman imprisonment of the Apostle (Acts 28 : 30-31), his Gospel was composed not after this date.

Answer : In the affirmative.

8. *Sources.* — Whether, in view both of the testimony of tradition and of internal arguments, with regard to the sources which both Evangelists used in writing their Gospels, the opinion can prudently be called in question which holds that Mark wrote according to the preaching of Peter and Luke according to the preaching of Paul, and which at the same time asserts that these Evangelists had at their disposal other trustworthy sources, either oral or already written.

Answer : In the negative.

9. *Historical Truth.* — Whether the sayings and doings which are accurately and, as it were, graphically narrated by Mark, according to the preaching of Peter, and by Luke, having diligently learned all things the from the beginning from eminently trustworthy witnesses, viz. " who from the beginning were eyewitnesses and ministers of the word " (Luke I : 2-3), are most faithfully set forth, have a just claim to the full and historical credence which the Church has ever given them; or whether, on the contrary, the same sayings and doings are to be regarded as devoid of historical truth at least in part, either because the writers were not eyewitnesses, or because in both Evangelists lack of order and discrepancy in the succession of facts are not infrequently found, or because, since they came and wrote later, they most necessarily have related conceptions

foreign to the mind of Christ and the Apostles, or facts more or less corrupted by popular imagination, or, finally because they indulged in preconceived dogmatic ideas, each according to the scope he had in view.

Answer : In the affirmative to the first part; in the negative to the second.

X. — On the Synoptic Question or the Mutual Relations between the First Three Gospels (June 26, 1912).

The Biblical Commission answers the following questions :

1. *Synoptic Question.* — Whether, observing absolutely all things that are to be observed according to what has been already laid down, especially as regards the authenticity and integrity of the three Gospels of Matthew, Mark, and Luke, the substantial identity of the Greek Gospel of Matthew with its primitive original, and the order of time in which they were written, it is lawful for exegetes, in order to explain the similitaries or dissimilarities between them, to dispute freely about all the varying and opposing opinions of authors and to appeal to hypotheses of oral or written tradition or even to the dependence of one on the one or both that precede.

Answer : In the affirmative.

2. *Two Source Theory.* — Whether what has been laid down above is to be considered as observed by those who, unsupported by any testimony of tradition or by any historical argument, lightly embrace the hypothesis commonly known as that of " the two sources ", which strives to explain the composition of the Greek Gospel of Matthew and the Gospel of Luke mainly by their dependence on the Gospel of Mark and on the so-called collection of " Sayings of the Lord "; and can they, therefore, freely advocate it?

Answer : In the negative to both parts.

XI. — On the Author, Time of Composition, and Historical Character of Acts (June 12, 1913).

The Biblical Commission answers the following questions :

1. *Author.* — Whether, in view especially of the tradition of the universal Church going back to the earliest ecclesiastical writers, considering the internal reasons furnished by the book of the Acts both in themselves and in their relation to the third Gospel, and particularly the mutual affinity and connection of the prologues of each (Luke I : 1-4; Acts I : 1-2), it is to be held as certain that the volume entitled, The Acts of the Apostles, or, Πράξεις 'Αποστόλων, has the Evangelist Luke for its author.

Answer : In the affirmative.

2. *Unity of Authorship.* — Whether it can be proved by critical reasons based on the language and style, on the method of narration, on the unity

of scope and doctrine, that the book of the Acts of the Apostles is to be attributed to one sole author; and that, therefore, the opinion of recent writers that Luke is not the sole author of the book, but that different authors of it must be admitted, is destitute of all foundation.

Answer : In the affirmative to both parts.

3. *We-Sections.* — Whether in particular, those well-known passages in the Acts in which the use of the third person is discarded and the first person plural (Wir-stuecke, we-sections) introduced, weaken the unity of composition and the authenticity; or whether these passages considered historically and philologically must rather be said to confirm the unity of composition and the authenticity.

Answer : In the negative to the first part, in the affirmative to the second.

4. *Integrity and Time of Composition.* — Whether from the fact that the book itself, after barely mentioning the two years of the first Roman captivity of Paul, abruptly closes, it is lawful to infer that the author either wrote another volume which has been lost, or intended to write one, and that the date of composition of the book can therefore be assigned to a time far later than this captivity; or whether rather it is rightly and properly to be held that Luke finished the book at the end of the first Roman captivity of the Apostle Paul.

Answer : In the negative to the first part, in the affirmative to the second.

5. *Historical Character.* — Whether, if we consider at once the frequent and easy relations which Luke undoubtedly had with the first and chief founders of the Church of Palestine as well as with Paul, Apostle of the Gentiles, to whom he was an assistant in his evangelical preaching and companion in his journeys; Luke's customary industry and diligence in examining withnesses and in seeing things for himself; and finally the evident and most remarkable agreement of the Acts of the Apostles with the Epistles of Paul and with the more genuine historical records; it is to be held for certain that Luke had in his hands most trustworthy sources and that he used them accurately, honestly, and faithfully, so that complete historical authority may be claimed for him.

Answer : In the affirmative.

6. *Objections to Historical Character.* — Whether the difficulties commonly alleged from the supernatural facts narrated by Luke; from his account of certain discourses which, being given summarily, are considered as made up and adapted to circumstances; from certain passages which are at least apparently in conflict with profane or biblical history; and, finally, from certain narrations which seem to be in opposition with the author of the Acts himself or with other sacred writers; are of a kind to render doubtful or at least in some way to diminish the historical authority of the Acts.

Answer : In the negative.

XII. — On the Authenticity, Integrity, and Time of Composition of the Pastoral Epistles (June 12, 1913).

The Biblical Commission answers the following questions :

1. *Authenticity.* — Whether, having in view the tradition of the Church universally and firmly persevering from the beginning, as ancient ecclesiastical records testify in various ways, it is to be held for certain that the Epistles known as Pastoral, viz., the two to Timothy and the one to Titus, notwithstanding the efforts of certain heretics who have without cause eliminated them from the number of Pauline Epistles as being contrary to their own teachings, were written by the Apostle Paul himself and ever counted as genuine and canonical.

Answer : In the affirmative.

2. *Compilation Theory.* — Whether the so-called " fragmentary hypothesis ", advanced and set forth in various ways by certain recent critics who, without indeed any probable ground and actually fighting among themselves, contend that the Pastoral Epistles were made up at a later period from fragments of Epistles or from lost Pauline Epistles, and greatly added to, can create the slightest prejudice against the clear and most firm testimony of tradition.

Answer : In the negative.

3. *Difficulties.* — Whether the difficulties commonly advanced in various ways from the style and language of the author, from the errors, especially of the Gnostics, which are described as already current at the time, from the state of the ecclesiastical hierarchy which is supposed to be already in an evolved condition, and other such reasons to the contrary, in any way weaken the opinion which holds as ratified and certain the genuineness of the Pastoral Epistles.

Answer : In the negative.

4. *Time of Composition.* — Whether, since not only from historical reasons and from ecclesiastical tradition in harmony with the testimony of the Eastern and Western Fathers, as well as from the very indications easily furnished both by the abrupt conclusion of the book of the Acts and by the Pauline Epistles written at Rome, especially the second to Timothy, the opinion as to the two Roman imprisonments of the Apostle Paul is to be held as certain, it can be safely affirmed that the Pastoral Epistles were written during the period between the liberation from the first imprisonment and the death of the Apostle.

Answer : In the affirmative.

XIII. — On the Author and the Manner and Circumstances of Composition of the Epistle to the Hebrews (June 24, 1914).

The Biblical Commission answers the following questions :

1. *Canonicity and Authenticity.* — Whether so much importance should be attached to the doubts concerning the inspiration and Pauline authorship

of the Epistle to the Hebrews — which, doubts entertained by some in the West, owing chiefly to its misuse by heretics, — that when we take into account the abiding, uncontradicted, and unbroken testimony of the Eastern Fathers, with which since the fourth century the whole Western Church has been in perfect accord; considering also the decrees of the Supreme Pontiffs and of the Sacred Councils, that of Trent especially, and finally the continuous practice of the universal Church, we may hesitate in reckoning the Epistle with certainty not only among the canonical Epistles (for that has been defined to be of faith), but among the genuine Epistles of the Apostle Paul as well.

Answer : In the negative.

2. *Objections.* — Whether the arguments generally advanced, drawn from the singular absence of St. Pauls' name and the omission of the regular introduction and greeting in the Epistle to the Hebrews; from the faultlessness of its Greek, its accuracy in phraseology and polish of style; from the way in which the Old Testament is quoted and argued from in it; or from some discrepancies which are alleged to exist between its teaching and that of the other Epistles of St. Paul, can in the least impair its Pauline authorship; or whether, on the other hand, the complete harmony of doctrine and principles; the similarity of the cautions and counsels; and the close correspondence in phrases and in the very words, proclaimed by some non-Catholics even, which are all discovered to exist between this and the other works of the Apostle of the Gentiles, do not rather go to prove beyond doubt this Pauline authorship.

Answer : In the negative to the first part, in the affirmative to the second.

3. *Writer.* — Whether the Apostle Paul must be accounted so to have been the author of this letter, that it must needs be asserted that he not only planned and composed it in its entirety under the inspiration of the Holy Ghost, but also that he put it in exactly the form in which it now stands.

Answer : In the negative, subject to further decision of the Church.

XIV. — On the Parousia or the Second Coming of our Lord Jesus Christ (June 18, 1915).

The Biblical Commission answers the following questions :

1. *Inerrancy.* — Whether to solve the difficulties which occur in the Epistles of St. Paul and of other Apostles, where the Parousia, as it is called, or the second coming of our Lord Jesus Christ is spoken of, it is permitted to the Catholic exegete to assert that the Apostles, although under the inspiration of the Holy Ghost they teach no error, nevertheless express their own human views, into which error or deception can enter.

Answer : In the negative.

2. *Harmony of the Apostle's Teaching.* — Whether, keeping before one's eyes the genuine idea of the Apostolic Office and of St. Paul's undoubted fidelity to the teaching of the Master; likewise, the Catholic dogma regarding the inspiration and inerrancy of the Scriptures, whereby all that the sacred writer asserts, enunciates, suggests, must be held to be asserted, enunciated, suggested by the Holy Ghost; also, weighing the texts of the Apostle's Epistles, considered in themselves, which are before all in harmony with the speech of the Lord Himself, it is meet to affirm that the Apostle Paul in his writings certainly said nothing which is not in perfect harmony with that ignorance of the time of the Parousia which Christ Himself proclaimed to be men's portion.

Answer : In the affirmative.

3. *Traditional Interpretation.* — Whether, attention being paid to the Greek phrase, ἡμεῖς οἱ ζῶντες οἱ περιλειπόμενοι, also the explanation of the Fathers being weighed, especially that of St. John Chrysostom [1], who was highly versed both in his country's language and in the Pauline Epistles, it is lawful to reject as far-fetched and destitute of solid foundation the interpretation traditional in the Catholic schools — also retained by the reformers of the sixteenth century themselves — which explains the words of St. Paul (1 Thess. **4** : 15-17) without in any wise implying the affirmation of a Parousia so imminent that the Apostle added himself and his readers to those of the faithful who should survive to meet Christ.

Answer : In the negative.

XV. — ON THE FALSE INTERPRETATION OF TWO TEXTS (July 1, 1933).

The Biblical Commission answers the following question :

1. *Ps.* **15** : 10-11. — Whether, especially considering the authentic interpretation of Sts.Peter and Paul, Princes of the Apostles (Acts **2**: 24-33; **13** : 35-37), a Catholic may interpret the words of Psalm **15** : 10-11, " Thou wilt not leave my soul in Sheol; nor wilt thou give thy holy one to see corruption. Thou hast made known to me the ways of life ", as if the sacred author had not spoken of the resurrection of our Lord Jesus Christ.

Answer : In the negative.

2. *Mt.* **16** : 26; *Lk.* **9** : 25. — Whether one may assert that the words of Jesus Christ — Mt. **16** : 26, " What doth it profit a man if he gain the whole world, but suffer the loss of his own soul? Or what will a man give in exchange for his soul "? and Lk. **9** : 25, " For what does it profit a man, if he gain the whole world, but ruin or lose himself "? — do not refer, in their literal sense, to the eternal salvation of the soul, but only to the temporal life of man, notwithstanding the meaning of the words themselves and their context, as also the unanimous interpretation of Catholics.

Answer : In the negative.

Translator's note. — [1 *In 1 Thess.*, hom. **7**, 2, Migne, *P. G.*, LXII, 436.]

XVI. — On the Use of Versions of Holy Scripture in Churches (April 30, 1934).

His Excellency, the Bishop of Hertogenbosch, in the name of all the bishops of the ecclesiastical province of Holland, proposed the following question :

Is is permitted, in the churches, to read to the people the liturgical selections from the Epistles and Gospels from a version which is not that of the Latin edition of the old Vulgate, but one made from the original Greek or Hebrew texts?

The Biblical Commission answers thus. *In the negative :* The translation of Holy Scripture to be read publicly to the Christian faithful must be one which has been made from the text approved by the Church for the sacred liturgy.

XVIa. On the Use of Versions of Sacred Scripture in the Vernacular. (August 22 1943). The Pontifical Biblical Commission deems it opportune to establish and commend the following norms as a solution to the question proposed to it concerning the use and the authority of Biblical versions in the vernacular, especially those translated from the ancient texts. These norms likewise explain more fully the Commission's decree : *De usu versionum Sacrae Scripturae in ecclesiis,* of April, 1934.

Since it was recommended by the Supreme Pontiff Leo XIII of happy memory, in the Encyclical Letter *Providentissimus Deus (Acta Leonis XIII,* Vol. 13, 342; *Enchiridion Biblicum,* n. 81) that the ancient texts of the Bible be used in order to gain a deeper knowledge and a richer expression of the divine word; and since by that recommendation, evidently not meant only for the help of exegetes and theologians, it was seen, and is seen to be almost necessary that the texts themselves be translated according to the approved rules for sacred, as well as profane science, into the commonly used or vernacular languages, always of course under the vigilant care of the competent ecclesiastical authority, and especially since for the most part the Biblical pericopes which must be used in the liturgical books for the most holy Sacrifice of the Mass and for the public recitation of the Divine Office are taken from the Vulgate edition, which the Sacred Oecumenical Council of Trent declared the one and only authentic version of all the Latin versions then in use (Conc. Trid., sess. IV, *decr. De editione et usu Ss. Librorum;* n. 46), all things considered :

I. Versions of Sacred Scripture translated into the vernacular either from the Vulgate or from the ancient texts may certainly be used and read by the faithful for their own private devotion, provided they have been edited with the permission of the competent ecclesiastical authority; moreover, if any version, after its text and notes have been seriously examined by men who excel in Biblical and theological knowledge, is found more faithful or better expressed, the Bishops, either singly or jointly in provincial or plenary councils, may commend it to the faithful entrusted to their special care, if they see fit.

2. Any vernacular version of the Biblical pericopes, which perhaps priests while celebrating Mass, according to custom or as opportunity presents itself, will read to the people after they have read the liturgical text, must conform to the Latin, the liturgical text, according to the response of the Pontifical Biblical Commission (*Acta Ap. Sedis*, 1934, 315), although they are permitted to explain properly this version, if need be, by using the original text or another more clear version.

The Holy Father, Pope Pius XII, in the audience of August 22, 1943, granted to the Most Reverend Secretary, approved this *Responsum* and commanded it to be published.

> Jacobus M. Vosté, O. P.
> Consultor ab actis.

XVII. — (Rome, January 16, 1948).

Letter of the Biblical Commission to His Eminence, Cardinal Suhard, Archbishop of Paris, concerning the time of the documents of the Pentateuch and concerning the literary form of the first eleven chapters of Genesis [1].

Your Eminence :

The Holy Father has been pleased to entrust to the examination of the Pontifical Commission for Biblical Studies two questions, which have been recently submitted to His Holiness concerning the sources of the Pentateuch and the historicity of the first eleven chapters of Genesis. These two questions with their considerations and propositions have been the object of the most careful study on the part of the Right Reverend Consultors and the Most Eminent Cardinals, Members of the above-mentioned Commission. As the result of their deliberations, His Holiness has deigned to approve the following reply in the audience granted to the undersigned on the 16th of January, 1948.

The Pontifical Biblical Commission is pleased to pay homage to the sense of filial confidence that has inspired this step, and wishes to correspond by a sincere effort to promote Biblical studies, while safeguarding for them the greatest freedom within the limits of the traditional teaching of the Church. This freedom has been explicitly affirmed by the encyclical of the Sovereign Pontiff gloriously reigning, *Divino afflante Spiritu,* in the following terms : " The Catholic commentator, inspired by an active and ardent love of his subject and sincerely devoted to Holy Mother church, should in no way be deterred from grappling again and again with these difficult problems, hitherto unsolved, not only that he may refute the objections of the adversaries, but also may attempt to find a satisfactory solution, which will be in full accord with the doctrine of the Church, in particular with the traditional teaching regarding the inerrancy of Sacred Scripture, and which will at the same time satisfy the indubitable conclusions of profane sciences. Let all the other sons of the Church bear in mind that the efforts of these resolute laborers in the vineyard of the Lord should

---

Translator's note. — [1 The French original and the English translation (adopted here) are available in *CBQ*, 10 (1948), 318-323].

be judged not only with equity and justice, but also with the greatest charity; all, moreover, should abhor that intemperate zeal which imagines that whatever is new should for that reason be opposed or suspected " (*A. A. S.*, 1943, page 319; English Edition [Vatican Press], page 22).

If one would rightly understand and interpret in the light of this recommendation of the Sovereign Pontiff the three official answers previously given by the Biblical Commission regarding the above-named questions, namely, that of 23rd June, 1905, on the narratives in the historical books of Holy Scripture which have only the appearance of being historical (*Ench. Bibl.*, 161), that of 27th June, 1906, on the Mosaic authenticity of the Pentateuch (*Ench. Bibl.*, 181-184), and that of 30th June, 1909, on the historical character of the first three chapters of Genesis (*Ench. Bibl.*, 336-343), one will readily grant that these answers are in no way opposed to further and truly scientific examination of these problems in accordance with the results obtained during these last forty years. Consequently, the Biblical Commission believes that there is no need, at least for the moment, to promulgate any new decrees regarding these questions.

I. In what concerns the composition of the Pentateuch, in the above-named decree of 27th June, 1906, the Biblical Commission already recognized that it may be affirmed that Moses " in order to compose his work, made use of written documents or oral traditions ", and also that modifications and additions have been made after the time of Moses (*Ench. Bibl.*, 183-184). There is no one today who doubts the existence of these sources or refuses to admit a progressive development of the Mosaic laws due to social and religious conditions of later times, a development which is also manifest in the historical narratives. Even, however, within the field of non-Catholic commentators, very divergent opinions are professed today concerning the nature and number of these documents, their denomination and date. There are, indeed, not a few authors in different countries who, for purely critical and historical reasons and with no apologetic intention, resolutely set aside the theories most in vogue until now, and who look for the elucidation of certain redactional peculiarities of the Pentateuch, not so much in the diversity of the supposed documents as in the special psychology, the peculiar processes of thought and expression, better known today, of the early Oriental peoples, or again in the different literary style demanded by the diversity of subject matter. Therefore, we invite Catholic scholars to study these problems, without prepossession, in the light of sound criticism and of the findings of other sciences connected with the subject matter. Such study will *doubtless* [1] establish the great part and deep influence exercised by Moses both as author and as lawgiver.

Translator's note. — [1 It should be noted that the French phrase, *établira sans doute*, is not as absolute as some have understood it. It does not mean " without doubt ", " certainly ", or the like, but rather : " doubtless " (as above), " no doubt ", " to be sure ", " probably ", etc. This nuance in meaning should not be overlooked].

II. The question of the literary forms of the first eleven Chapters of Genesis is far more obscure and complex. These literary forms correspond to none of our classical categories and cannot be judged in the light of Greco-Latin or modern literary styles. One can, therefore, neither deny or affirm their historicity, taken as a whole, without unduly attributing to them the canons of a literary style within which it is impossible to classify them. If one agrees not to recognize in these chapters history in the classical and modern sense, one must, however, admit that the actual scientific data do not allow of giving all the problems they set a *positive* solution. The first duty here incumbent upon scientific exegesis consists before all in the attentive study of all the literary, scientific, historical, cultural and religious problems connected with these chapters; one should then examine closely the literary processes of the early Oriental peoples, their psychology, their way of expressing themselves and their very notion of historical truth; in a word, one should collate without prejudice all the subject matter of the palaeontological and historical, epigraphic and literary sciences. Only thus can we hope to look more clearly into the true nature of certain narratives in the first chapters of Genesis. To declare *a priori* that their narratives contain no history in the modern sense of the term would easily convey the idea that they contain no history whatever, whereas they relate in simple and figurative language, adapted to the understanding of a less developed people, the fundamental truths presupposed for the economy of salvation, as well as the popular description of the origin of the human race and of the Chosen People. Meanwhile we must practise that patience which is living prudence and wisdom. This is what the Holy Father likewise inculcates in the encyclical already quoted : " No one ", he says, " will be surprised, if all difficulties are not yet solved and overcome... We should not lose courage on this account; nor should we forget that in the human sciences the same happens as in the natural world; that is to say, new beginnings grow little by little and fruits are gathered only after many labors... Hence there are grounds for hope that those (difficulties) also will by constant effort be at last made clear, which now seem most complicated and difficult " (*Ibid.*, p. 318; Engl. ed., pp. 21-22).

James M. Vosté, O. P.
Secretary of the Pontifical Biblical Commission.

BIBLIOGRAPHY

I. HISTORY OF EXEGESIS

1. W. DITTMAR, *Vetus Testamentum in Novo* (Göttingen, 1903). L. VENARD, " Citations de l'Ancien Testament dans le Nouveau Testament ", *DBV, Suppl.* II (1934), 23-51; ID.," L'utilisation des Psaumes dans l'épître aux Hébreux, " *Mélanges E. Podechard* (Lyons, 1945), 253-264. — J. BONSIRVEN, S. J., *Exégèse rabbinique et exégèse paulinienne* (Paris, 1938); ID., *Textes rabbiniques des deux premiers siècles chrétiens*

pour servir à l'intelligence du Nouveau Testament (Rome, 1955).—S. AMSLER, " Le typologie de l'Ancien Testament chez saint Paul ", *Revue de Théologie et de Philosophie* (1949), 113-128.

2. L. WOGUÉ, *Histoire de la Bible et de l'exégèse jusqu'à nos jours* (Paris, 1881). — R. KARPELÈS, *Histoire de la littérature juive*, adapted by I.Bloch and E. Levy (Paris, 1901). "Bibel" (VII, VIII, and IX), *Encyclopaedia Judaica*, IV (Berlin, 1929), 619-692. — M. MIELZINER, *Introduction to the Talmud* (New York, 1925), pp. 117-189. — H. L. STRACK, *Einleitung in Talmud und Midraš* (5th ed., Munich, 1921), pp. 95-109 (the various rules). [There is an English trans.: *Introduction to Talmud and Midrash* (Philadelphia, 1931)]. — J. BONSIRVEN, *opp. citt., supra.* — [R. BLOCH, " Midrash, " *DBV, Suppl.* V (1957), 1263-1281]. All the necessary information on the rabbinical commentaries will be found in Strack [and Bonsirven], and the text and translation of several in whole or part, will be found in [BONSIRVEN, *Textes rabbiniques...*] and in the *Thesaurus antiquitatum sacrarum* of UGOLINI. Some collections, such as the *Critici sacri*, quote mediaeval commentators extensively.

3. We do not yet have a real history of Patristic exegesis. The elements of such a history must be sought here and there in the works devoted to the history of Early Christian literature, e. g., in the well-known and easily available books of Bardenhewer, Tixeront, Puech, De Labriolle-Bardy, Altaner, [and Quasten]. The following articles and books, however, may be mentioned : G. BARDY, " Commentaires patristiques de la Bible ", *DBV, Suppl.* II (1934), 73-103; ID., " Interprétation chez les Pères ", *ibid.*, IV (1949), 569-591.— P. T. CAMELOT, " L'exégèse de l'Ancien Testament par les Pères ", in *L'Ancien Testament et les chrétiens* (Rencontres, 36, Paris, 1951). — J. DANIÉLOU, " Typologie et allégorisme ", *RSR* (1947), 180-226; ID., *Sacramentum futuri* (Paris, 1950); ID., *Bible et liturgie (ibid.,* 1951; [there is an English trans.]). — J. GUILLET, *Thèmes bibliques. Etudes sur l'expression et le développement de la Révélation* (Paris, 1950).— J. DANIÉLOU, *Origène* (Paris, 1948). — H. DE LUBAC, *Histoire et esprit. L'intelligence de l'Ecriture d'après Origène* (Paris, 1950). — C. MONDÉSERT, *Clément d'Alexandrie. Introduction à l'étude de sa pensée religieuse à partir de l'Ecriture* (Paris, 1948). — M. PONTET, *L'exégèse de Saint Augustin prédicateur* (Paris, 1946). — R. DEVREESSE, *Essai sur Théodore de Mopsueste* (Vatican City, 1948). — J. GUILLET, " Les exégèses d'Alexandrie et d'Antioche. Conflit ou malentendu ", *RSR* (1947), 257-302. — L. MARIÈS, *Etudes préliminaires à l'édition des commentaires de Diodore de Tarse sur les psaumes* (Paris, 1933). Several texts of special interest for the knowledge of Patristic exegesis have been published in the collection, *Sources chrétiennes* (Paris, 1941 ff) : *Origène. Homélies sur la Genèse*, by H. DE LUBAC; *Origène. Homélies sur l'Exode*, by H. DE LUBAC and P. FORTIER; *Origène. Homélies sur les Nombres*, by A. MEHAT; *Origène. Homélies sur le Cantique des Cantiques*, by DOM O. ROUSSEAU; *Saint Hippolyte. Commentaire sur Daniel*, by M. LEFÈVRE; *Saint Grégoire de Nysse. Vie de Moïse*, by J. DANIÉLOU, and *La création de l'homme*, by H. LAPORTE; *Saint Basile*

de Césarée. Homélies sur l'Hexaméron, by S. GIET; *Hilaire de Poitiers.*
Traité des mystères, by P. BRISSON; *Ptolémée. Lettre à Flora,* by G. QUISPEL,
etc. [See also : J. DE GHELLINCK, S. J., *Patristique et moyen âge* (3 vols.,
Brussels, 1946-1948). — B. SMALLEY, *The Study of the Bible in the Middle*
Ages (revised ed., Oxford, 1952)].

4. *Catholic commentaries :* [*A Catholic Commentary on Holy Scripture*
(edited by Dom B. Orchard, Edmund F. Sutcliffe, S. J., R. C. Fuller,
and Dom R. Russell, London and New York, 1953. Cf. the valuable
review-article by E. P. ARBEZ, *Dublin Review,* 1953, 405-418)]. *Cursus*
Scripturae Sacrae, auctoribus R. Cornely, J. Knabenbauer, F. de Hummelauer aliisque Societatis Jesu presbyteris (Paris, 1884 ff.; a valuable
work, but all volumes have not maintained the same high standard.
[The series is now in part antiquated]). *Etudes Bibliques,* published
under the direction of M. J. LAGRANGE, O. P. (Paris, 1903 ff.; some thirty
volumes to date, the scientific level of which leaves nothing to be desired).
La Sainte Bible, published under the direction of L. PIROT and A. CLAMER,
12 vols., Paris 1935-1957). *La Sainte Bible* (translated into French and
published under the direction of the Ecole Biblique de Jérusalem, Paris,
1948 ff.). *Kurzgefasster wissenschaftlicher Kommentar zu den Heiligen*
Schriften des Alten Testaments und des Neuen Testaments (edited by
B. Schäfer and E. Nagl, Vienna, 1901 ff.). *Exegetisches Handbuch zum*
Alten Testament (edited by J. Nikel and A. Schultz, Münster i. W., 1912 ff.).
Die heilige Schrift des Alten Testamentes übersetzt und erklärt (edited by
F. Feldmann and H. Herkenne, Bonn, 1923 ff.). *Die heilige Schrift in*
deutscher Uebersetzung (edited by F. Nötscher and K. Staab, Würzburg,
1947 ff.; the *Echter-Bibel*).

Non-Catholic commentaries : The *International Critical Commentary of*
the Holy Scriptures of the Old Testament (under the editorship of S. R. Driver,
A. Plummer, and C. H. Briggs, Edinburgh, 1885 ff. It has made known
the results of the higher criticism throughout the English-speaking world
and no other commentary is superior to it from the scientific point of
view.). *The Sacred Books of the Old Testament* (a critical polychrome
edition of the Old Testament, edited by P. Haupt, Leipzig, and London,
and Baltimore, 1893 ff. A collection of annotated translations under the
title, *New English Translation,* accompanies this edition.). *The West-*
minster Commentaries (edited by W. Lock and S. C. Simpson, London,
1904 ff. The first volume, on Genesis, was written by S. R. Driver.).
The Cambridge Bible for Schools and Colleges (edited by J. J. Stewart
Perowne, A. F. Kirkpatrick, and A. Nairne, 59 vols., Cambridge and
New York, 1880-1912; a very interesting series, which aims to " present
in lucid form the results of the best modern scholarship "). *The Inter-*
preter's Bible. The Holy Scriptures in the King James and Revised Standard
Versions (edited by G. A. Buttrick, 12 vols., New York and Nashville,
1951-1957; " the first major Bible commentary both exegetical and expos-
itory for many years in English "). The most significant non-Catholic
German commentaries are the following : W. NOWACK, *Handkommentar*

zu den Alten Testament (Tübingen, 1892 ff. Very scientific in tone, it popularizes the theories of Wellhausen in Germany.). — E. SELLIN, *Kommentar zum Alten Testament* (Leipzig, 1913 ff. It represents the critical Protestant point of view, but is more conservative). — K. MARTI, *Kurzer Handkommentar zum Alten Testament* (Tübingen, 1897 ff. This work gives more space and emphasis to the comparative history of religions). The French non-Catholic commentary, *La Bible du Centenaire* (Paris, 1916 ff.), is especially handy because of its critical data. [For a brief, but valuable up-to-date survey of Catholic and non-Catholic commentaries on the Bible, see the article by J. SCHMID, " Bibelkommentare ", *LTK*, II (2nd ed., 1958), 356-360. For further bibliography, including references to commentaries, translations, etc., by Dutch and Scandinavian scholars, see p. 469, *supra*.].

The British Society for Old Testament Study publishes an annual Book List of works on the Old Testament, and on the history and geography of the Near East. [See now, *Eleven Years of Bible Bibliography. The Book Lists of the Society for Old Testament Study* 1946-1956 (edited by H. H. Rowley, and published by the Falcon Press, Indian Hills, Colo., 1957)]. One will find the following works useful : MARTIN-ACHARD, *Etat présent des études vétero-testamentaires* (Montpellier, 1952). But there is no work which gives a really complete picture of contemporary exegesis. Apart from the articles, Biblical Criticism, Textual Criticism, Exegesis, etc., which are found in the various Biblical encyclopedias, the best way to become familiar with the main trends in exegesis is to run through the surveys, reviews, and abstracts, in the *Revue Biblique, Recherches de Science Religieuse, Biblica, Catholic Biblical Quarterly, [Internationale Zeitschriftenschau für Bibelwissenschaft und Grenzgebiete, New Testament Abstracts*, etc.].

5. So far as we know, the history of the New Testament exegesis from the Renaissance to the present remains to be written. There are numerous studies on this school or that, but comprehensive studies are rare and leave much to be desired. Among the most recent the following may be mentioned : F. M. BRAUN, *Où en est le problème de Jésus ?* (Paris, 1932). — L. C. FILLION, *Les étapes du rationalisme dans ses attaques contre les évangiles* (2nd ed., Paris, 1911). — P. HAZARD, *La crise de la conscience européenne* (1680-1715) (Paris, 1935; ID., *La pensée européenne au XVIIIe siècle* (1715-1780) (*ibid.*, 1946]. — M. JONES, *The New Testament in the Twentieth Century* (3rd ed., London, 1934). — M. J. LAGRANGE, *Le sens du christianisme d'après l'exégèse allemande* (Paris, 1918) [English trans. by W. S. REILLY, *The Meaning of Christianity according to Luther and His Followers in Germany* (New York, 1920)]. — W. SANDAY, *The Life of Christ in Recent Research* (Oxford, 1907). — A. SCHWEITZER, *Geschichte der Leben-Jesu-Forschung* (5th ed., Tübingen, 1933) [English trans. by W. MONTGOMERY, *The Quest of the Historical Jesus* (2nd ed., London, 1931)]. — H. WERNEL, *Jesus im 19. Jahrhundert* (3rd ed., *ibid.*, 1914; English ed., revised by A. G. Widgery [Edinburg, 1914]).

II. CATHOLIC EXEGESIS.

1. The chapters devoted to Hermeneutics in the General Introductions to Sacred Scripture in Latin (Balestri, Cornely, Fernandez, Janssens-Morandi, Prado, Höpfl-Leloir [1958]) or in French (Cornely-Merk, Lusseau-Collomb, Renié).

2. Numerous articles in the Dictionaries of the Bible, etc. In *DBV*, " Accommodatice (sens) " and " Herméneutique ", by E. MANGENOT; " Littéral (sens) ", by H. LESÊTRE. In *DBV, Suppl.* : " Critique Biblique", by H. HÖPFL; " Critique textuelle de l'Ancien et du Nouveau Testament ", by L. DENNEFELD, H. J. VOGELS, and L. PIROT; " Apparences historiques " and " Citations implicites ", by A. LEMONNYER; " Interprétation (Histoire de l') ", by J. BONSIRVEN, G. BARDY, M. JUGIE, C. SPICQ, A. ROBERT, and L. VAGANAY; " Littéraires (Genres) ", by A. ROBERT; " Lettres encycliques ", by G. COURTADE; [" Miracle, Valeur historique des récits ", by A. LEFÈVRE; " Moïse ", by H. CAZELLES; " Mystères ", by K. PRÜMM; " Mythe ", by J. HENNINGER and H. CAZELLES.] In *DAFC :* " Critique Biblique ", and " Exégèse ", by A. DURAND. In *DTC :* " Interprétation de l'Ecriture ", by E. MANGENOT and J. RIVIÈRE. [In *LTK* 2nd ed.) : " Bibelkritik ", by J. SCHMID; " Biblische Hermeneutik ", by A. BEA; " Exegese " by R. Schnackenburg, K. H. Schelkle, J. Schmid, H. I. Beck, J. Assfalk, A. Kleinhans, and H. Greeven. In *A Catholic Commentary on Holy Scripture :* " The Interpretation of Holy Scripture ", by R. C. FULLER; " Higher Criticism of the Bible ", by R. A. DYSON and R. A. F. MACKENZIE; " The Miraculous Element in the Bible ", by E. C. MESSENGER; " The Gospels and Non-Catholic Higher Criticism ", by E. GUTWENGER.].

3. The great Catholic treatises on Hermeneutics : H. HÖPFL, *Tractatus de inspiratione... et compendium hermeneuticae biblicae* (Rome, 1923). F. HILBER, *Biblische Hermeneutik* (Brixen, 1932). — F. X. KORTLEITNER, *Hermeneutica biblica* (Innsbrück, 1923). — J. SCHILDENBERGER, *Vom Geheimnis des Gotteswortes* (Heidelberg, 1950). — S. SZÉKEDY, *Hermeneutica biblica generalis* (Freiburg i. Br., 1902). — V. ZAPLETAL, *Hermeneutica biblica* (2nd ed., Fribourg, Switzerland, 1908); — S. ZARB, *De hermeneutica biblica* (Rome, 1929).

4. The two following works by Protestant scholars : E. KÖNIG, *Hermeneutik des Alten Testaments* (Gütersloh, 1916). — F. TORM, *Hermeneutik des Neuen Testaments* (Göttingen, 1930).

5. The multiplicity of the sense of Scripture has, in recent years, become a subject of controversy in numerous books and articles. Among the principal treatments the following may be cited : J. COPPENS, *Les Harmonies des deux Testaments. Esssai sur les divers sens de l'Ecriture et sur l'unité de la Révélation* (Paris, 1949; with copious bibliography); ID., *Un nouvel essai d'Herméneutique biblique (ibid.,* 1951); ID., *Nouvelles réflexions sur les divers sens des Saintes Ecritures (ibid.,* 1952). — L. CERFAUX

J. COPPENS, J. GRIBOMONT, *Problèmes et méthode d'exégèse théologique* (Paris, 1950). — J. DANIÉLOU, *Sacramentum futuri. Etudes sur les origines de la typologie biblique (ibid.*, 1950). — G. COURTADE, " Le sens de l'histoire dans l'Ecriture et la classification usuelle des sens scriptuaires ", *RSR* (1949), 136-141; ID., " Les Ecritures ont-elles un sens plénier? ", *(ibid.,* 1950), 481-499. — P. BENOIT, *Somme théologique de Saint Thomas d'Aquin. La Prophétie* (Paris, 1947), " Appendice II. Renseignements techniques ", 353-378. — Dom C. CHARLIER, *La lecture chrétienne de la Bible* (Maredsous, 1950), 284-324; ID., " Typologie et évolution. Problèmes d'exégèse spirituelle ", *Esprit et Vie* (1949), 578-597. — D. BUZY, " Un problème d'Herméneutique sacrée. Sens plural, plénier et mystique ", *L'Année Théologique* (1944), 385-408. — A. GELIN, " Le sens spirituel de l'Ecriture ", *L'Ami du Clergé* (1950), 641-646. — A. M. DUBARLE, " Le sens spirituel de l'Ecriture ", *Revue des Sciences Phil. et Théol.* (1947), 41-72. — J. LEVIE, " Exégèse critique et interprétation théologique ", *RSR* (1951), 237-252 *(Mélanges Lebreton).* — [R. E. BROWN, S. S., *The Sensus Plenior of Sacred Scripture* (Baltimore 1955; with valuable bibliography, 154-161). — J. COPPENS, " Le problème du sens plénier ", *EThL* (1958), 5-20.].

INDICES

Index I.   Ancient and Mediaeval Authors and Works

Index II. Modern Authors and Works

Index III. Index of Subjects

Abdias, Book of : place in the Jewish canon, 73, 77; the book, 344-345.

Acts of the Apostles, Book of : the author, 413-414, 418; purpose and content, 416-418; place and date of composition, 414-415; literary unity, 414; literary character of the work, 537-538; place and nature of the discourses, 538-539; the " We passages ", 414, 539; connections of with Greek historiography, 538-540; literary genre, 540-542; history of the text, 415; decision of the Biblical Commission on, 767-768.

Aggeus, Book of : place in the Jewish canon, 73, 77; the book, 351.

Amos, Book of : place in the Jewish canon, 73, 77; the man, 343; origin and content of the work, 343-344.

Apocalypse of Saint John : doubts concerning its canonicity among the Greek Fathers, 96-97, and among the Syrians, 102-103; authenticity, 460-462; purpose, 467-468, 557; place and date of composition, 462; recipients, 463; content, 463-467; procedures of composition, 558-559; symbolism, 559, 561; sources, 560; interpretation, 467-468, 561-562; history of the text, 614.

Apocalyptic : antecedents of the genre in certain prophetical writings, 509-511; its marked development in the Apocrypha, 105-106, 510, 555-557; general features of the genre, 510, 555-557; The Book of Daniel and apocalyptic, 337, 511-512.

Apocrypha of the Old and New Testament : history of the meaning of the term " apocrypha ", 70-71, 103-104; classification of the Apocrypha, 104-107; literary characteristics, 105; influence of in Jewish and Christian circles, 106-107; the chief Palestinian and Hellenic Apocrypha of the O. T., 107-112; the chief Apocrypha of the N. T., 123-126.

Aquila, Version of : 624, 631.

Aramaic : a conquering language, 136-137; adopted by the Jews after the Exile, 137-138; its characteristic features, 138; spoken by Jesus and the Apostles, 139.

Augustine, Saint : his exegetical work, 646-647, 706; his views on the inspiration of the Septuagint, and on Saint Jerome's translation from the Hebrew, 647, 653.

Baruch, Book of : listed among the Deuterocanonical Books, 70; content, 327-328.

Bible, The : names of, 3-4; Books of, 4-5; division into chapters made by Stephen Langton and into verses by Robert Estienne (Stephanus), 5, 655-656, 658; the Protocanonical and Deuterocanonical Books, 70; critical editions of the Hebrew Bible, 590, 596-597; of the Greek Bible (O. T.), 629-631; of the Greek New Testament, 606, 614-615, 616; of the Vulgate, 659-660, 663-664; English translations of the Bible, 665-672.

Biblical Commission : decisions of, 752-753; on implied quotations

375; literary genre and liturgical use (one of the *Megilloth*), 79.

Catechesis, The Apostolic: its content, 385-386; its division into four parts, 386, 517-518; stereotyped form of, 517-158.

Chronicles or **Paralipomenon, Books of :** place in the Jewish canon, 79; content, 292-293; sources, 293-294; purpose and spirit of the Chronicler, 294-296; origin of the work, 296-297; literary genre, 508-509.

Colossians, Epistle to : place and date of composition, 439; occasion, purpose, and content, 440-441; literary genre, 550-551.

Corinthians, First and Second Epistle to : the recipients, 427; place and date of composition, occasion, and content of the First Epistle, 427-431; place and date, content, and composition of the Second Epistle, 431-434; the literary genre of the two epistles, 548-549.

Covenant, the Old and the New : 3, 71; the Book of the Covenant, 485.

Criticism : textual criticism: verbal and material (witnesses of the text and internal criteria), 732-738; — textual criticism of the O. T., 596-601, 735-736; of the N. T., 602-619, 736-737 — literary criticism, 738-743; see also *Literary Genres* — historical criticism : internal and external, 744-748 — critical interpretation or hermeneutics, 748-755.

Daniel, Book of : place in the Jewish canon, 73; deuterocanonical sections, 70; the personality of the Prophet, 334; structure of the book, 335-336; literary genre and date of composition, 336-338, 511-512; its teachings, 338.

Dead Sea Scrolls : history of their discovery, 113-117; the documents and their classification, 117-120; the Qumran Community, 120-122; importance of the Qumran texts for the history of the Hebrew text of the O. T., 122-123; Hebrew writing in, 152.

Deuterocanonical Books, The : origin and meaning of the term, 70-71; list of, 70 — the Deuterocanonical Books of the O. T., : their place in the Hellenic Jewish canon, 81-83; their authority confirmed by the N. T., 83-84; their employment by the Fathers of the first centuries, 84; the unfavorable attitude respecting their canonicity in the Churches of the East in the third and fourth centuries, 84-85; the different attitude of the Western Churches in the same period, 85-86; the Fourth Council of Carthage, the Council in Trullo, the *Decretum pro Jacobitis,* the Council of Trent, and the Vatican Council, 86-87 — the Deuterocanonical Books of the N. T. : doubts and hesitations respecting their canonicity among the Greeks, Latins, and Syrians, 95-100, 102-103; " deuterocanonical " and " apocryphal ", 103-104.

Deuteronomy, Book of : name and place in the Pentateuch, 157; analysis of the book's contents, 241-281; literary characteristics, 243-244, 483-487; see also *Law.*

Diatesseron of Tatian: Greek the language of the original text, 91, 635; the Syriac translation adopted as an official text by the Syrian churches of Mesopotamia, 103, 607-608.

Diatribe, The : its employment by Cynic and Stoic preachers and in the Epistle to the Romans, 547.

and Prophetical inspiration, 12-16; the nature of the charism of inspiration — the theory of Cardinal Franzelin, 16-19; the sacred writer as an instrument of God, 19-22; inspiration distinct from revelation (Saint Thomas), 22-23; ideas and judgments in the inspired writers, 24-28; inspiration viewed in relation to the faculties of the writer, 28-29, to his work, 29-31, to tranlations and translators of this work, 32-34, and to all the senses of Scripture, 34-37; the criterion of inerrancy, 38-40; inerrancy envisaged as a consequence of inspiration, 40-52; Biblical inspiration in Protestantism : the Reformers, 52-54; from the XVIIth century to the present time, 54-58; inspiration in the Qoran and in the Bible, 59-64. See also *Inerrancy.*

Interpretation, Biblical : employment of the O. T. in the N. T., 679-684; Talmudic exegesis, 684-690; Jewish exegesis in the Middle Ages, 690-693; the exegesis of the Apostolic Fathers and the Apologists, 694-697; Origen, 697-699; the School of Alexandria, 699-701; the School of Antioch, 702-703; the Latin Fathers, 703-707; exegesis of the O. T. in the Middle Ages, 707-709; from the Renaissance to the end of the eighteenth century, 709-713; from the beginning of the nineteenth century to the present time — the literary problem of the O. T. among liberal and Protestant critics, and among Catholics, 713-719; the principal schools of rationalistic criticism, 719-722 — exegesis of the N. T. from the Renaissance to the present time : the leaders in Protestant and rationalistic exegesis, 722-729; Catholic exegetes, 729-731; the principles or rules of exegesis; textual criticism, 731-738; literary criticism, 738-743; historical criticism, 744-748; critical interpretation, or hermeneutics, viewed in terms of its purpose, 748-751, and its methods, 751-755; the decisions of the Biblical Commission, 755-775; see also *Biblical Commission,* and *Senses of Scripture.*

Isaias, Book of : Chs. 1-39 : the author and his age, 314-316; the leading ideas, 316-317; the content and formation of the collection, 318-139; Chs. 40-55 : (Deutero-Isaias), the content, 319-320; critical problems and the decree of the Biblical Commission, 320-322; Chs. 56-66 (Trito-Isaias), content and literary genre, 322.

James, Epistle of : doubts concerning its canonicity, 96, 97, 99-100, 102; author, 451; place and date of composition, and recipients, 451-452; purpose and content, 452; literary genre, 553-554.

Jeremias, Book of : Jeremias and his age, 322-323; place of the book in the Jewish canon, 78; content and formation of the collection, 323-325; doctrinal teaching, 325-326; the Hebrew text and the Greek text, 323-324; literary genre, 487-491; the Prayer of Jeremias, and the Letter of Jeremias, 226-328.

Jerome, Saint : his work as a translator, 645-652; his exegesis of Scripture, 705; see also *Vulgate.*

Job, Book of : division and text, 354-356; authenticity and date, 359-360; literary genre, 356-357; a sapiential book, 498; purpose and teaching, 357-358.

525-532; exegesis of the N. T. from the Renaissance to the present time, 722-731; see also *Form Criticism*.

Numbers, Book of : place in the Pentateuch, 157; analysis of the book's contents, 207-241. See also *Law*.

Old Testament : content, 4-5; general character of the Books of the O. T. from the literary point of view, 513-514; history of the Hebrew text, 80-83, 587-590; criticism of the Hebrew text, 596-599; history of the canon of the O. T., 72-74; the Books of the O. T., 157-382; the literary genres of the O. T., 164-166, 478-514; the versions of the O. T., 622-652, 665-672; history of the exegesis of the O. T., since the Renaissance, 709-722.

Oracle, The prophetic : its nature, 487-491; prophecy and Scriptural inspiration, 12-15, 22-24.

Origen : his work on the Septuagint, 599, 626-628; his exegetical method, 697-699.

Osee, Book of : place in the Jewish canon, 73, 77; the book, 340-341.

Papyrus, 154-155.

Paralipomenon, Books of : see *Chronicles*.

Parallelism : the different kinds of, 497.

Parchment, 154-155.

Pastoral Epistles : their name, 445; the recipients, Timothy and Titus, 445; place and date of composition, 446; content, 446-447; the question of authenticity, 447-448; literary genre, 551-552; decision of the Biblical Commission on, 769.

Pentateuch : see *Law* and *Torah ;* decision of the Biblical Commission on, 757-758; the Samaritan

Pentateuch and its origin, 76; its text, vocalization, and punctuation, 591-592.

Pesshitto : see *Versions, Syriac.*

Peter, First Epistle of : the question of authenticity, 452-453; the recipients, 453; purpose and content, 453-454; literary genre, 554.

Peter, Second Epistle of : doubts regarding its canonicity, 95-103; the question of authenticity, 454-455; recipients and content, 455-456; literary genre, 554.

Philemon, Epistle to : date, 439; occasion and purpose, 441-442; literary genre, 550-551.

Philippians, Epistle to the : place and date of composition, 439; occasion, 444; content, 444-445; literary genre, 550.

Poetry, Hebrew : 496-498; rhythm and strophic arrangement, 497-498; parallelism, 497-498.

Prophets, Books of the : list and place in the Jewish canon, 73, 76-77; divided into two groups — the collection of the Former Prophets and that of the Latter Prophets combined with the Books of the Law, 76-77, 487; the literary genre of the Former Prophets, 492-496; the literary genre of the Latter Prophets, 487-491; the collection of the Minor Prophets, 338-340.

Protestant Reformation. The, and the interpretation of the Bible; 709-712, 722-723.

Protocanonical Books : origin and meaning of the term, 70-71.

Proverbs, The Book of : the name of the book, 365-366; place in the Jewish canon *(Hagiographa),* 73, 79; teaching of the book, 366-367; connections with the wisdom literature of the Ancient East, 367-368, 498-501; the date of the different sections of the work, 368; literary genre, 498, 506-507.

Psalms, The Book of : the name of the book, 369-361; place in the Jewish canon *(Hagiographa)*, 73, 79, 361; divisions of the collection and the text, 361-362; titles and superscriptions, 362-363; teachings, 363-364; origin of the Psalms, 364-365; the different kinds of Psalms, 363-364, 501-504; decision of the Biblical Commission on the Psalms, 762-763.

Psalter : the Augustinian, 647; the Roman, 649; the Gallican, 649; that of Pius XII, 362.

Revelation : distinct from inspiration, 22-34.

Romans, Epistle to the : place and date of composition, 434-435; occasion and purpose, 435-436; content, 436-438; literary genre, 546-547.

Ruth, Book of : listed in the Jewish canon among the *Megilloth*, 79; content and authenticity, 286; character and purpose, 286; origin, 286-287.

Samuel, Books of : title and content, 287-288; literary characteristics, 288-289; origin, 289-290; literary genre, 492-493.

Senses of Scripture : existence and distinction of the different senses of Scripture (literal, spiritual, accomodative), 34-37; 680, 682, 749-755; the allegorical sense of Philo, 681-682; the corporeal, spiritual, and typological senses of Origen, 698-699; of the Alexandrians and the Cappadocians, 699-701; the literal sense of the Antiochenes, 702-703.

Septuagint Version : origin and value, 594, 599-601, 622-628; an inspired version (?), 32-34, 625-626; its usefulness in the textual criticism of the O. T.,

599-601, 626; the work of Origen *(Tetrapla, Hexapla, Octapla)*, 599, 626-628; the work of Hesychius and Lucian of Antioch, 628; Saint Jerome and the Septuagint, 651; the great Mss, 628-629; the papyri, 629; the Qumran roll, 629; the printed editions, 629-631.

Sophonias, Book of : place in the Jewish canon, 73, 77; the book, 350-351.

Symmachus, version of : 632.

Synopsis : origin and meaning of the term, 386, 563; the difference between " synopsis " and " harmony ", 563, n. 3.

Synoptic Question : the word " synoptic ", 386, 563; the *Synoptic Fact* established by a comparison of texts, 563-570; the *Synoptic Problem*, 570-571; the literary aspect of the problem, 516-525; hypotheses of the oral tradition, 572; of the Primitive Gospel, 572-573; of mutual dependence, 573-574; of the " Two Sources ", 574-577; decisions of the Biblical Commission, 577, 763-767; attempt at solution and conclusions, 578-580.

Talmud, The : composed of the *Mishnah* and the *Gemara*, 685; the two Talmuds, the Jerusalem and the Babylonian, 685-688; Talmudic exegesis, 685-690.

Targums, The : origin, 137, 593; the Targum of Onkelos, the Palestinian Targum, the Targum of the Prophets, 593-595; the origin of the names Onkelos and Jonathan, 594; the value of the Targums for the textual criticism of the O. T., 598-599.

Thessalonians, First and Second Epistles to the : recipients, 420-421; occasion, place of compo-

Printed in Belgium by Desclée & Cie, Éditeurs, S. A. Tournai. — 10.411